Principles and Practice

An Integrated Approach to Engineering Graphics and AutoCAD 2027

Randy H. Shih
Oregon Institute of Technology

SDC
PUBLICATIONS

SDC Publications
P.O. Box 1334
Mission, KS 66222
913-262-2664
www.SDCpublications.com
Publisher: Stephen Schroff

ISBN-13: 978-1-63057-828-2
ISBN-10: 1-63057-828-2

Printed and bound in the United States of America.

Preface

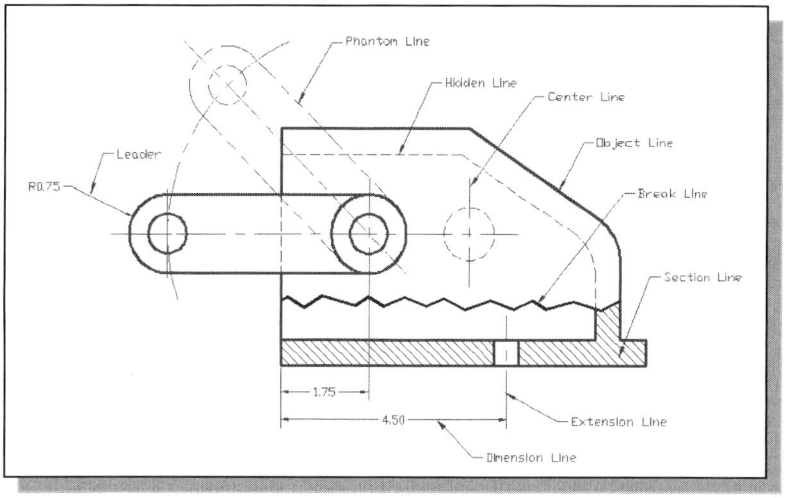

The primary goal of *Principles and Practice: An Integrated Approach to Engineering Graphics and AutoCAD 2027* is to introduce the aspects of Engineering Graphics with the use of a modern Computer Aided Design package – AutoCAD 2027. This text is intended to be used as a training guide for students and professionals. The chapters in this text proceed in a pedagogical fashion to guide you from constructing basic shapes to making complete sets of engineering drawings. This text takes a hands-on, exercise-intensive approach to all the important concepts of Engineering Graphics, as well as in-depth discussions of 2D CAD techniques. This textbook contains a series of twelve chapters, with detailed step-by-step tutorial style lessons, designed to introduce beginning CAD users to the graphic language used in all branches of technical industry. The CAD techniques and concepts discussed in this text are also designed to serve as the foundation to the more advanced parametric feature-based CAD packages such as Autodesk® Inventor. This book does not attempt to cover all of AutoCAD® 2027's features, only to provide an introduction to the software. It is intended to help you establish a good basis for exploring and growing in the exciting field of Computer Aided Engineering.

Acknowledgments

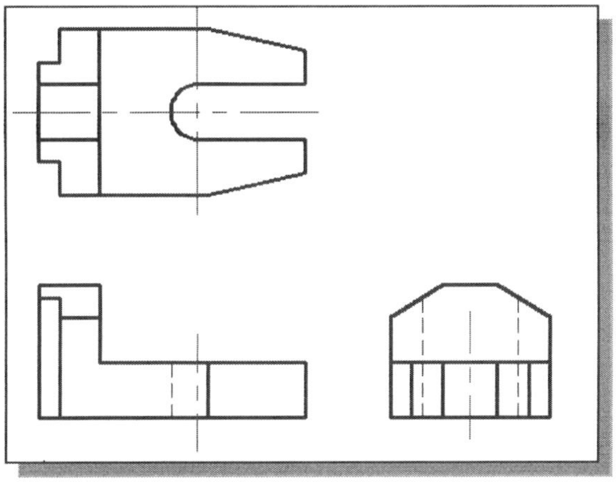

This book would not have been possible without a great deal of support. First, special thanks to two great teachers, Prof. George R. Schade of University of Nebraska-Lincoln and Mr. Denwu Lee from Taiwan, who taught me the fundamentals, the intrigue and the sheer fun of Computer Aided Engineering.

The effort and support of the editorial and production staff of SDC Publications is gratefully acknowledged. I would especially like to thank Stephen Schroff for his support of this project.

I am grateful that the Department of Mechanical Engineering and Manufacturing Engineering Technology at Oregon Institute of Technology has provided me with an excellent environment in which to pursue my interests in teaching and research. I would especially like to thank Emeritus Professor Charles Hermach for helpful comments and encouragement.

Finally, truly unbounded thanks are due to my wife Hsiu-Ling and our daughter Casandra for their understanding and encouragement throughout this project.

Randy H. Shih
Klamath Falls, Oregon
Spring, 2026

Table of Contents

Chapter 2
Geometric Constructions

Chapter 3
Object Properties and Organization

Chapter 4

Orthographic Projection and Multiview Constructions

Chapter 5
Pictorials and Sketching

Chapter 6
AutoCAD 2D Isometric Drawings

Chapter 7
Dimensioning and Notes

Chapter 9

Symmetrical Features in Designs

Chapter 10
Auxiliary Views

Chapter 11
Section Views

Appendix

Index

Notes on using this book to prepare for the AutoCAD Certified User Examination

This edition of the text can also be used as a preparation guide for the AutoCAD Certified User examination. The book's content has been expanded to include the majority of the topics covered in the examination. The reference tables beginning on the next page and located at the beginning of each chapter show the textbook's coverage of the Certified User Examination performance tasks. Students taking the certification exam can use the reference tables as both a check list for topics that they need to understand and as a way of finding particular topics. The tables are provided as a reference only. It is important for the user to work through the book chapters in sequential order, as each chapter builds on the skills learned in previous chapters.

PLEASE NOTE:
Every effort has been made to cover the exam objectives included in the AutoCAD Certified User Examination. However, the format and topics covered by the examination are constantly changing, so students planning to take the Certified User Examination are advised to visit the Autodesk website and obtain information regarding the format and details about the AutoCAD Certified User Examination.

AutoCAD Certified User Examination Overview

The AutoCAD Certified User examination includes 12 sections. The following tables show where the performance tasks for each section are covered in this book.

This Reference Guide is provided to give you a checklist of performance tasks covered on the Certified User examination and to show you on which page(s) specific tasks are covered.

Section 1: Draw with Accuracy

Objectives: Describe and set the workspace.

Certification Examination Performance Task	Covered in this book on Chapter – Page
Precision	1-21
Drawing Limits	1-21
Zoom All	1-22
Status Bar	1-25
GRID Display	1-29
PAN Realtime	1-35
Drafting Settings	2-35
Drawing Limits	2-36
UCS Icon	2-36
Use a Wizard	3-4
Zoom Realtime	3-22
Layer Visibility	3-27

Section 2: Draw Objects

Objectives: Create and edit geometry using the *Dynamic Input* interface.
Use running *Object Snaps* and object snap overrides to select *Snap* points in the drawing.
Use *Polar Tracking* and *PolarSnap* efficiently and effectively.
Use *Object Tracking* to position geometry.
Use the *Units* command to set drawing units.

Certification Examination Performance Task	Covered in this book on Chapter – Page
Format	1-20
Units Setup	1-20
LINE Command	1-24
Coordinates	1-24
Interactive Input Method	1-25
SNAP Option	1-27
World Space	1-30
User Coordinate System	1-30
World Coordinate System	1-31
UCS Icon Display	1-31
Coordinate Systems	1-32

Section 3: Modify Objects

Objectives: Use several different *Selecting Objects* methods to select objects.
Select Objects for grip editing and identify the type of editing that can be done using grips.
Move objects in the drawing using *Object Snaps*, *Coordinate* entry, and *Object Snap Tracking* for precise placement.
Use the *Copy* command to copy objects in the drawing.
Use the *Rotate* command to rotate objects in the drawing.
Use the *Mirror* command to mirror objects in the drawing.
Use the *Array* command to pattern objects in the drawing.

Section 4: Organize Objects

Objectives: Use *Layer tools.*
Describe the use and effect of the *ByLayer* property.
Use the Match Properties command to apply the *Properties* from a source object to destination objects.
Use the inquiry commands (Distance, Radius, Angle, Area, List, and ID) to obtain geometric information from the drawing.

Certification Examination Performance Task	Covered in this book on Chapter – Page
QuickCalc Command	2-49
Measure Distance and Angle	2-49
Layers	3-19
Layer Properties	3-20
Layer Control	3-22
Layer Properties	4-27
List Command	4-47
Properties Command	4-48
Layers Properties	7-17
Layers Properties	9-9
Viewport Properties	9-25
Layers Controls	10-13
Measure Area and Perimeter	10-35
Linetype Scale	11-22
IsoPlane and IsoDraft	6-6

Section 5: Altering Objects

Objectives: Use the *Offset* command to create parallel and offset geometry.
Use the *Fillet* command to create radius geometry connecting two objects.
Use the *Join* command to combine multiple objects into a single object.

Certification Examination Performance Task	Covered in this book on Chapter – Page
Chamfer Command	3-27
Offset Command	4-28
Break Command	9-38
Trim Command	10-26
Edit Polyline	10-37
Offset Command	11-14
Stretch	11-23
Rotate Command	13-23
Explode Command	13-23

Section 6: Working with Layouts

Objectives: Create a new layout.
Create and manipulate *Viewports*.

Certification Examination Performance Task	Covered in this book on Chapter – Page
Layout Mode	9-10
Viewports	9-24

Section 7: Annotating the Drawing

Objectives: Use the *Multiline Text* command to create and format paragraphs of text.
Create and use *Text Styles*.

Certification Examination Performance Task	Covered in this book on Chapter – Page
Single Line Text	7-42
Special Characters	7-43

Section 8: Dimensioning

Objectives: Create different types of *Dimensions* on linear objects.
Create and modify *Dimension Styles* to control the appearance of dimensions.
Create and edit *Multileaders*.

Certification Examination Performance Task	Covered in this book on Chapter – Page
Fractional Dimension	7-30
Overall Dimension Scale	7-30
Dimensions Toolbar	7-33
Dimension Style	7-33
Linear Dimension	7-33
Angular Dimension	7-34
Center Mark	7-36
Radius Dimension	7-40
Dimension Style	9-26
Scale Dimension to Layout	9-26
Dimension Update	9-27
MULTILEADER	11-25
Multileader Style	13-26
Multileader	13-27
Add Leader	13-28

Section 9: Hatching Objects

Objectives: Create *Hatch* patterns and fills.

Certification Examination Performance Task	Covered in this book on Chapter – Page
Hatch	11-29

Section 10: Working with Reusable Content

Objectives: Use the *Block* command to create a block definition.
Use the *Insert* command to insert a block reference in a drawing.

Certification Examination Performance Task	Covered in this book on Chapter – Page
Purge Blocks	7-43
Template File	9-13
Use a Template	11-12
Make Block	13-14
Insert Block	13-16
Paste as Block	13-22

Section 11: Creating Additional Drawing Objects

Objectives: Work with *polylines.*
Edit *polylines.*

Certification Examination Performance Task	Covered in this book on Chapter – Page
Polylines	2-44
Table Style	13-31
Table Command	13-32

Section 12: Plotting

Objectives: Create and modify page setup.

Certification Examination Performance Task	Covered in this book on Chapter – Page
Plot Style Table Settings	9-5
Plot Style	9-7
Plot Command	9-27
Plot Style Table Settings	10-32

The AutoCAD Certified User Examination is a performance-based exam. The examination is comprised of approximately 30 questions to be completed in 50 minutes. The test items will require you to use the AutoCAD software to perform specific tasks and then answer questions about the tasks. Performance-based testing is defined as ***testing by doing***. This means you actually perform the given task then answer the questions regarding the task. Performance-based testing is widely accepted as a better way of ensuring the users have the skills needed, rather than just recalling information.

For detailed information, visit **http://www.autodesk.com/certification**.

Tips on Taking the AutoCAD Certified User Examination

1. **Study**: The first step to maximize your potential on an exam is to sufficiently prepare for it. You need to be familiar with the AutoCAD package, and this can only be achieved by doing drawings and exploring the different commands available. The AutoCAD Certified User exam is designed to measure your familiarity with the AutoCAD software. You must be able to perform the given task and answer the exam questions correctly and quickly.
2. **Make Notes**: Take notes of what you learn either while attending classroom sessions or going through study material. Use these notes as a review guide before taking the actual test.
3. **Time Management**: Manage the time you spend on each question. Always remember you do not need to score 100% to pass the exam. Also keep in mind that some questions are weighed more heavily and may take more time to answer.
4. **Be Cautious**: Devote some time to ponder and think of the correct answer. Ensure that you interpret all the options correctly before selecting from available choices.
5. **Use Common Sense**: If you are unable to get the correct answer and unable to eliminate all distracters, then you need to select the best answer from the remaining selections. This may be a task of selecting the best answer from amongst several correct answers, or it may be selecting the least incorrect answer from amongst several poor answers.
6. **Take Your Time**: The examination has a time limit. If you encounter a question you cannot answer in a reasonable amount of time, use the Save As feature to save a copy of the data file, and mark the question for review. When you review the question, open your copy of the data file and complete the performance task. After you verify that you have entered the answer correctly, unmark the question so it no longer appears as marked for review.
7. **Don't Act in Haste**: Don't go into panic mode while taking a test. Always read the question carefully before you look out for choices in hand. Use the ***Review*** screen to ensure you have reviewed all the questions you may have marked for review. When you are confident that you have answered all questions, end the examination to submit your answers for scoring. You will receive a score report once you have submitted your answers.
8. **Relax before the exam**: In order to avoid last-minute stress, make sure that you arrive 10 to 15 minutes early and relax before taking the exam.

Every effort has been made to cover the exam objectives included in the *AutoCAD Certified User Examination*. However, the format and topics covered by the examination are constantly changing; students planning to take the *Certified User Examination* are advised to visit the Autodesk website and obtain information regarding the format and details about the examination.

Chapter 1
Introduction and AutoCAD Fundamentals

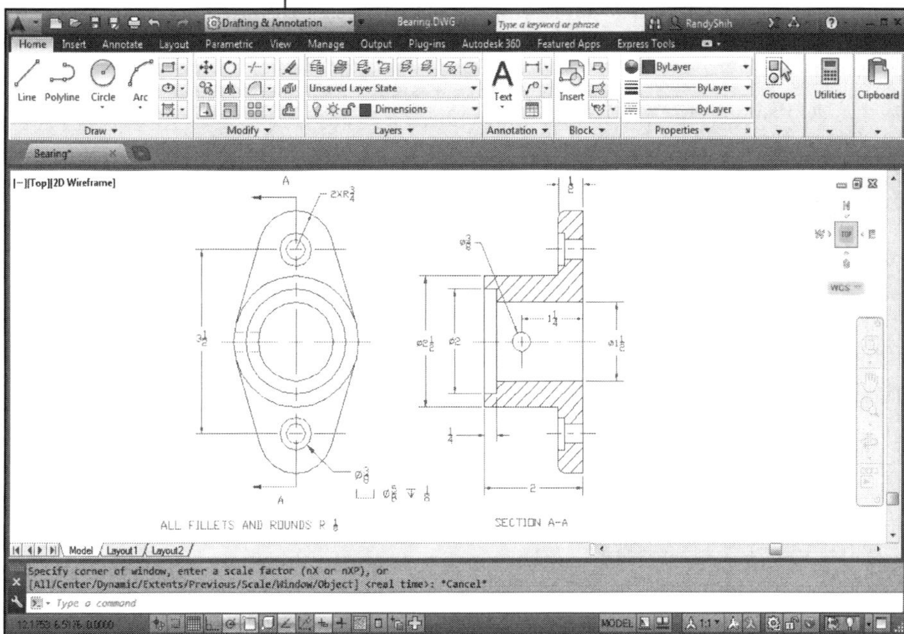

Learning Objectives

- The History and Importance of Engineering Graphics
- Be Familiar with the AutoCAD Toolbars
- Use the AutoCAD Visual Reference Commands
- Draw Using the Line and Circle Commands
- Use the Erase Command
- Define Positions Using the Basic Entry Methods
- Create and Save an AutoCAD Drawing

AutoCAD Certified User Examination Objectives Coverage

Section 1: Introduction to AutoCAD

Section 2: Creating Basic Drawings

Section 3: Manipulating Objects

Introduction

Engineering Graphics, also known as **Technical Drawing**, is the technique of creating accurate representations of designs, an *engineering drawing*, for construction and manufacturing. An **engineering drawing** is a type of drawing that is technical in nature, used to fully and clearly define requirements for engineered items, and is usually created in accordance with standardized conventions for layout, nomenclature, interpretation, appearance, size, etc. A skilled practitioner of the art of engineering drawing is known as a *draftsman* or *draftsperson*.

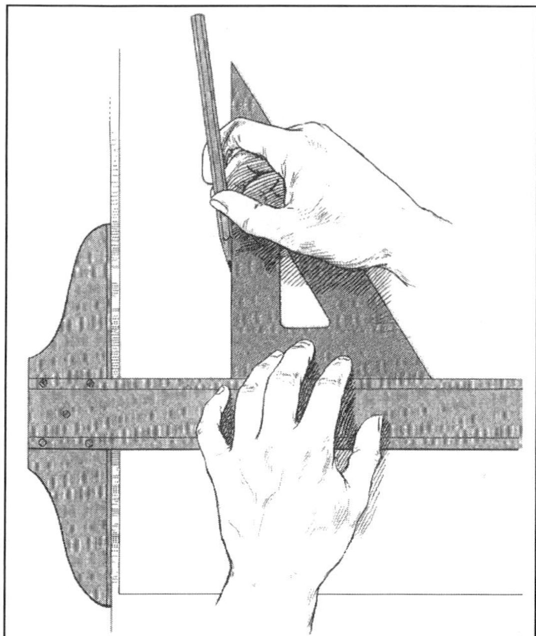

The basic mechanics of drafting is to use a pencil and draw on a piece of paper. For engineering drawings, papers are generally placed on a drafting table and additional tools are used. A T-square is one of the standard tools commonly used with a drafting table.

A T-square is also known as a *sliding straightedge*; parallel lines can be drawn simply by moving the T-square and running a pencil along the T-square's straightedge. The t-square is more typically used as a tool to hold other tools such as triangles. For example, one or more triangles can be placed on the T-square and lines can be drawn at the chosen angle on the paper.

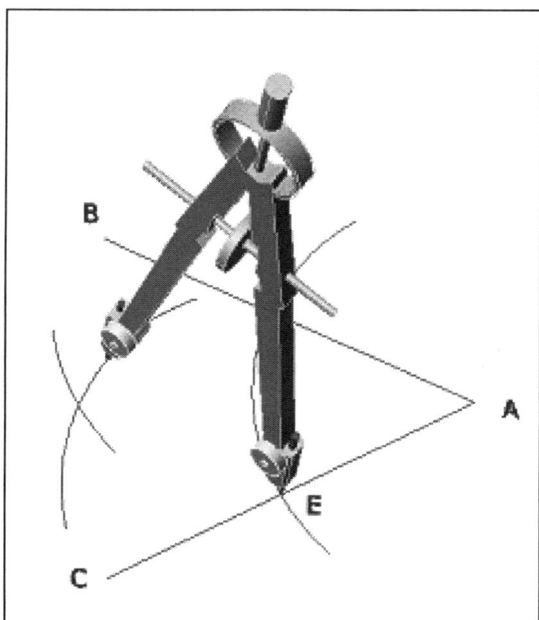

In addition to the triangles, other tools are used to draw curves and circles. Primary among these is the compass, used for drawing simple arcs and circles, and the French curve, typically a piece of plastic with a complex curve on it. A spline is a rubber coated articulated metal that can be manually bent to almost any curve.

This basic drafting system requires an accurate table and constant attention to the positioning of the tools. A common error was to allow the triangles to push the top of the t-square down slightly, thereby throwing off all angles. And in general drafting was a time-consuming process.

A solution to these problems was the introduction of the "**drafting machine**," which is a device that allowed the draftsperson to have an accurate right angle at any point on the page quite quickly. These machines often included the ability to change the angle, thereby removing the need for the triangles as well.

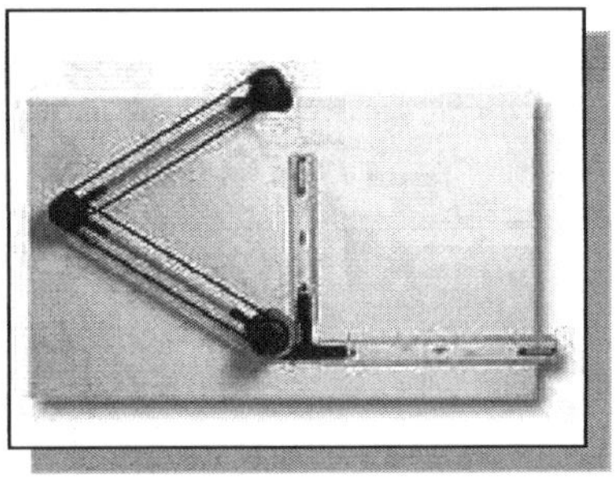

In addition to the mechanics of drawing the lines onto a piece of paper, drafting requires an understanding of geometry and the professional skills of the specific designer. At one time, drafting was a sought-after job, considered one of the more demanding and highly skilled of the trades. Today the mechanics of the drafting task have been largely automated, and greatly accelerated, through the use of **computer aided design** (CAD) systems. Proficiency in using CAD systems has also become one of the more important requirements for engineers and designers.

Drawing in CAD Systems

Computer Aided Design (CAD) is the process of doing designs with the aid of computers. This includes the generation of computer models, analysis of design data, and the creation of drawings. **AutoCAD 2027** is a computer-aided-design (CAD) software developed by *Autodesk Inc*. The **AutoCAD 2027** software is a tool that can be used for design and drafting activities. The two-dimensional and three-dimensional models created in **AutoCAD 2027** can be transferred to other computer programs for further analysis and testing. The computer models can also be used in manufacturing equipment such as machining centers, lathes, mills, or rapid prototyping machines to manufacture the product.

The rapid changes in the field of **computer aided engineering** (CAE) have brought exciting advances in industry. Recent advances have made the long-sought goal of reducing design time, producing prototypes faster, and achieving higher product quality closer to a reality.

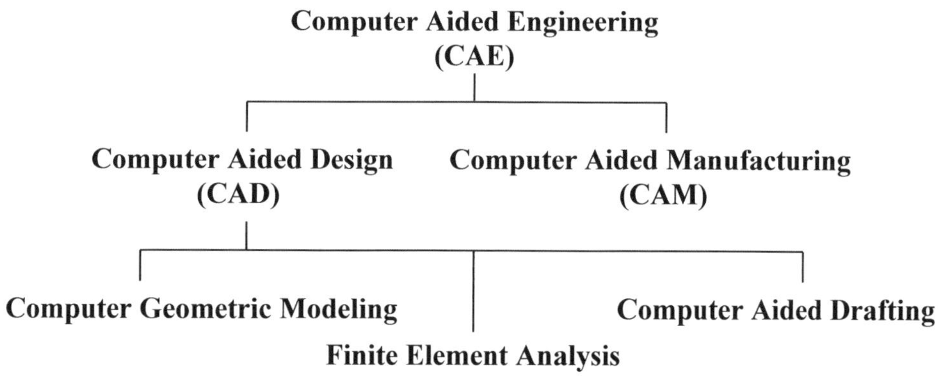

Development of Computer Geometric Modeling

Computer Aided Design is a relatively new technology, and its rapid expansion in the last fifty years is truly amazing. Computer modeling technology advanced along with the development of computer hardware. The first-generation CAD programs, developed in the 1950s, were mostly non-interactive; CAD users were required to create program codes to generate the desired two-dimensional (2D) geometric shapes. Initially, the development of CAD technology occurred mostly in academic research facilities. The Massachusetts Institute of Technology, Carnegie-Mellon University, and Cambridge University were the lead pioneers at that time. The interest in CAD technology spread quickly and several major industry companies, such as General Motors, Lockheed, McDonnell, IBM, and Ford Motor Co., participated in the development of interactive CAD programs in the 1960s. Usage of CAD systems was primarily in the automotive industry, aerospace industry, and government agencies that developed their own programs for their specific needs. The 1960s also marked the beginning of the development of finite element analysis methods for computer stress analysis and computer aided manufacturing for generating machine tool paths.

The 1970s are generally viewed as the years of the most significant progress in the development of computer hardware, namely the invention and development of **microprocessors**. With the improvement in computing power, new types of 3D CAD programs that were user-friendly and interactive became reality. CAD technology quickly expanded from very simple **computer aided drafting** to very complex **computer aided design**. The use of 2D and 3D wireframe modelers was accepted as the leading-edge technology that could increase productivity in industry. The developments of surface modeling and solid modeling technology were taking shape by the late 1970s, but the high cost of computer hardware and programming slowed the development of such technology. During this time period, the available CAD systems all required extremely expensive room-sized mainframe computers.

In the 1980s, improvements in computer hardware brought the power of mainframes to the desktop at less cost and with more accessibility to the general public. By the mid-1980s, CAD technology had become the main focus of a variety of manufacturing industries and was very competitive with traditional design/drafting methods. It was during this period of time that 3D solid modeling technology had major advancements, which boosted the usage of CAE technology in industry.

In the 1990s, CAD programs evolved into powerful design/manufacturing/management tools. CAD technology has come a long way, and during these years of development, modeling schemes progressed from two-dimensional (2D) wireframe to three-dimensional (3D) wireframe, to surface modeling, to solid modeling and, finally, to feature-based parametric solid modeling.

The first-generation CAD packages were simply 2D **computer aided drafting** programs, basically the electronic equivalents of the drafting board. For typical models, the use of this type of program would require that several to many views of the objects be created individually as they would be on the drafting board. The 3D designs remained in the designer's mind, not in the computer database. The mental translation of 3D objects to 2D views is required throughout the use of the packages. Although such systems have some advantages over traditional board drafting, they are still tedious and labor intensive. The need for the development of 3D modelers came quite naturally, given the limitations of the 2D drafting packages.

The development of the 3D wireframe modeler was a major leap in the area of computer modeling. The computer database in the 3D wireframe modeler contains the locations of all the points in space coordinates and it is sufficient to create just one model rather than multiple models. This single 3D model can then be viewed from any direction as needed. The 3D wireframe modelers require the least computer power and achieve reasonably good representation of 3D models. But because surface definition is not part of a wireframe model, all wireframe images have the inherent problem of ambiguity.

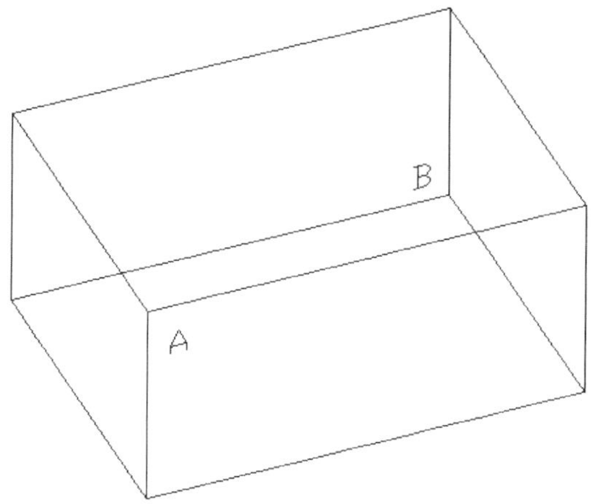

Wireframe Ambiguity: Which corner is in front, A or B?

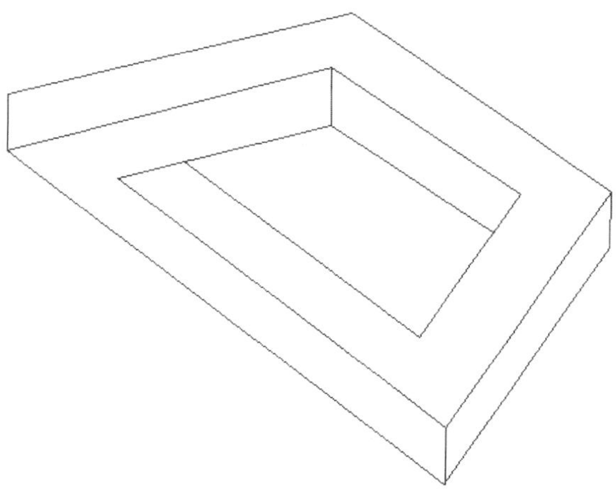

A non-realizable object: Wireframe models contain no surface definitions.

Surface modeling is the logical development in computer geometry modeling to follow the 3D wireframe modeling scheme by organizing and grouping edges that define polygonal surfaces. Surface modeling describes the part's surfaces but not its interiors. Designers are still required to interactively examine surface models to ensure that the various surfaces on a model are contiguous throughout. Many of the concepts used in 3D wireframe and surface modelers are incorporated in the solid modeling scheme, but it is solid modeling that offers the most advantages as a design tool.

In the solid modeling presentation scheme, the solid definitions include nodes, edges, and surfaces, and it is a complete and unambiguous mathematical representation of a precisely enclosed and filled volume. Unlike the surface modeling method, solid modelers start with a solid or use topology rules to guarantee that all of the surfaces are stitched together properly. Two predominant methods for representing solid models are **constructive solid geometry** (CSG) representation and **boundary representation** (B-rep).

The CSG representation method can be defined as the combination of 3D solid primitives. What constitutes a "primitive" varies somewhat with the software but typically includes a rectangular prism, a cylinder, a cone, a wedge, and a sphere. Most solid modelers allow the user to define additional primitives, which can be very complex.

In the B-rep representation method, objects are represented in terms of their spatial boundaries. This method defines the points, edges, and surfaces of a volume, and/or issues commands that sweep or rotate a defined face into a third dimension to form a solid. The object is then made up of the unions of these surfaces that completely and precisely enclose a volume.

By the 1990s, a new paradigm called *concurrent engineering* had emerged. With concurrent engineering, designers, design engineers, analysts, manufacturing engineers, and management engineers all work closely right from the initial stages of the design. In this way, all aspects of the design can be evaluated, and any potential problems can be identified right from the start and throughout the design process. Using the principles of concurrent engineering, a new type of computer modeling technique appeared. The technique is known as the *feature-based parametric modeling technique*. The key advantage of the *feature-based parametric modeling technique* is its capability to produce very flexible designs. Changes can be made easily, and design alternatives can be evaluated with minimum effort. Various software packages offer different approaches to feature-based parametric modeling, yet the end result is a flexible design defined by its design variables and parametric features.

In this text, we will concentrate on creating designs using two-dimensional geometric construction techniques. The fundamental concepts and use of different **AutoCAD 2027** commands are presented using step-by-step tutorials. We will begin with creating simple geometric entities and then move toward creating detailed working drawings and assembly drawings. The techniques presented in this text will also serve as the foundation for entering the world of three-dimensional solid modeling using packages such as **AutoCAD Mechanical Desktop, AutoCAD Architecture** and **Autodesk Inventor**.

Why use AutoCAD 2027?

AutoCAD was first introduced to the public in late 1982 and was one of the first CAD software products that were available for personal computers. Since 1984, **AutoCAD** has established a reputation for being the most widely used PC-based CAD software around the world. By 2019, it was estimated that there were over 6 million **AutoCAD** users in more than 150 countries worldwide. **AutoCAD 2027** is the forty-first release, with many added features and enhancements, of the original **AutoCAD** software produced by *Autodesk Inc.*

CAD provides us with a wide range of benefits; in most cases, the result of using CAD is increased accuracy and productivity. First of all, the computer offers much higher accuracy than the traditional methods of drafting and design. Traditionally, drafting and detailing are the most expensive cost elements in a project and the biggest bottleneck.

With CAD systems, such as **AutoCAD 2027,** the tedious drafting and detailing tasks are simplified through the use of many of the CAD geometric construction tools, such as *grids*, *snap*, *trim,* and *auto-dimensioning*. Dimensions and notes are always legible in CAD drawings, and in most cases, CAD systems can produce higher quality prints compared to traditional hand drawings.

CAD also offers much-needed flexibility in design and drafting. A CAD model generated on a computer consists of numeric data that describe the geometry of the object. This allows the designers and clients to see something tangible and to interpret the ramifications of the design. In many cases, it is also possible to simulate operating conditions on the computer and observe the results. Any kind of geometric shape stored in the database can be easily duplicated. For large and complex designs and drawings, particularly those involving similar shapes and repetitive operations, CAD approaches are very efficient and effective. Because computer designs and models can be altered easily, a multitude of design options can be examined and presented to a client before any construction or manufacturing actually takes place. Making changes to a CAD model is generally much faster than making changes to a traditional hand drawing. Only the affected components of the design need to be modified, and the drawings can be plotted again. In addition, the greatest benefit is that, once the CAD model is created, it can be used over and over again. The CAD models can also be transferred into manufacturing equipment such as machining centers, lathes, mills, or rapid prototyping machines to manufacture the product directly.

CAD, however, does not replace every design activity. CAD may help, but it does not replace the designer's experience with geometry and graphical conventions and standards for the specific field. CAD is a powerful tool, but the use of this tool does not guarantee correct results; the designer is still responsible for using good design practice and applying good judgment. CAD will supplement these skills to ensure that the best design is obtained.

CAD designs and drawings are stored in binary form, usually as CAD files, to magnetic devices such as diskettes and hard disks. The information stored in CAD files usually requires much less physical space in comparison to traditional hand drawings. However, the information stored inside the computer is not indestructible. On the contrary, the electronic format of information is very fragile and sensitive to the environment. Heat or cold can damage the information stored on magnetic storage devices. A power failure while you are creating a design could wipe out the many hours you spent working in front of the computer monitor. It is a good habit to save your work periodically, just in case something might go wrong while you are working on your design. In general, one should save one's work onto a storage device at an interval of every 15 to 20 minutes. You should also save your work before you make any major modifications to the design. It is also a good habit to periodically make backup copies of your work and put them in a safe place.

Getting Started with AutoCAD 2027

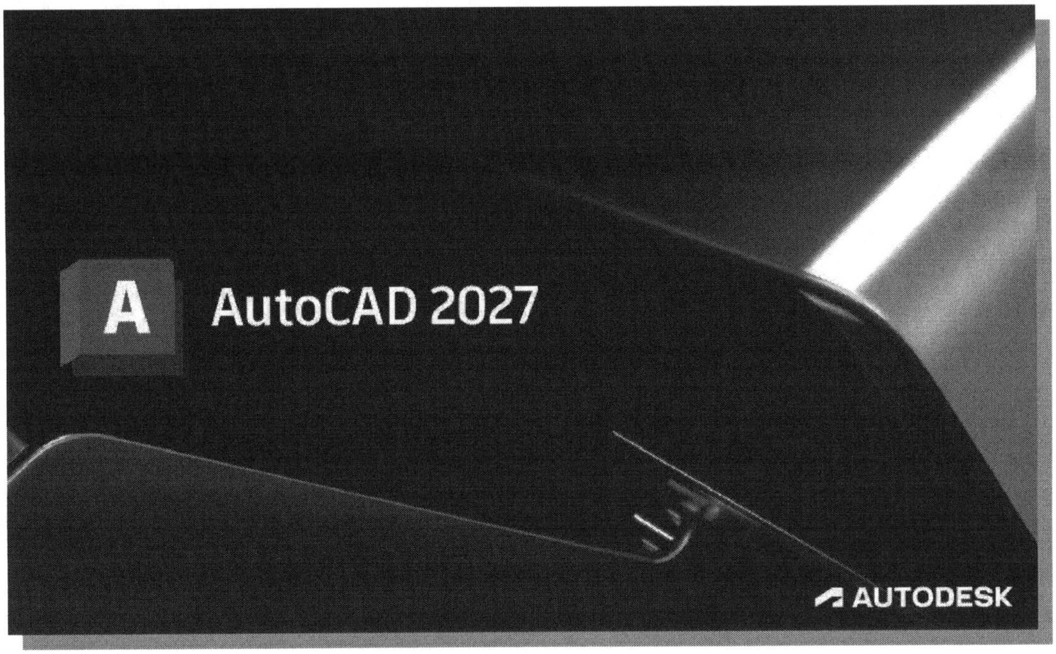

How to start **AutoCAD 2027** depends on the type of workstation and the particular software configuration you are using. With most *Windows* systems, you may select the **AutoCAD 2027** option on the *Start* menu or select the **AutoCAD 2027** icon on the *Desktop*. Consult with your instructor or technical support personnel if you have difficulty starting the software.

The program takes a while to load, so be patient. Eventually the **AutoCAD 2027** main *drawing screen* will appear on the screen. Click **New Drawing** as shown in the below figure. The tutorials in this text are based on the assumption that you are using **AutoCAD 2027**'s default settings. If your system has been customized, some of the settings may not work with the step-by-step instructions in the tutorials. Contact your instructor and technical support to restore the default software configuration.

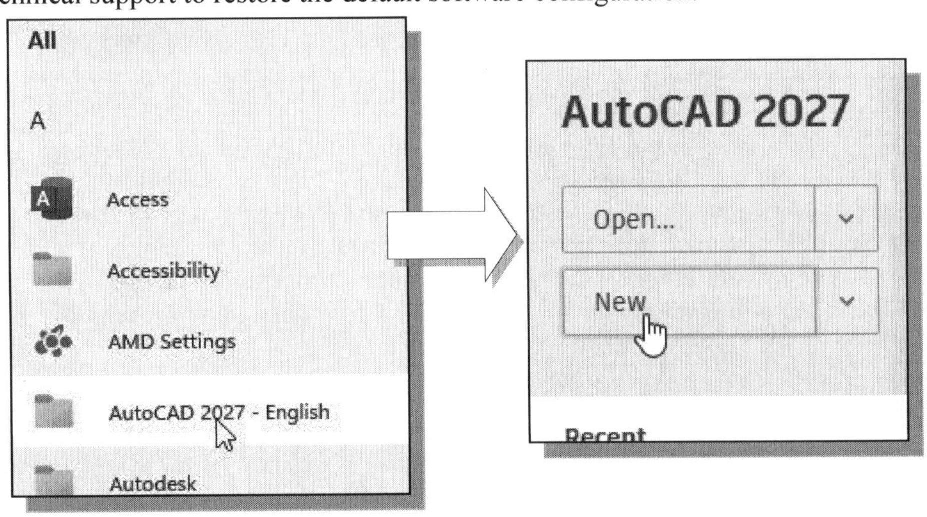

AutoCAD 2027 Screen Layout

The default **AutoCAD 2027** *drawing screen* contains the *pull-down* menus, the *Standard* toolbar, the *InfoCenter Help system,* the *scrollbars,* the *command prompt area*, the *Status Bar*, and the *Ribbon Tabs* and *Panels* that contain several *control panels* such as the *Draw and Modify* panel and the *Annotation* panel. You may resize the **AutoCAD 2027** drawing window by clicking and dragging at the edges of the window, or relocate the window by clicking and dragging at the window title area.

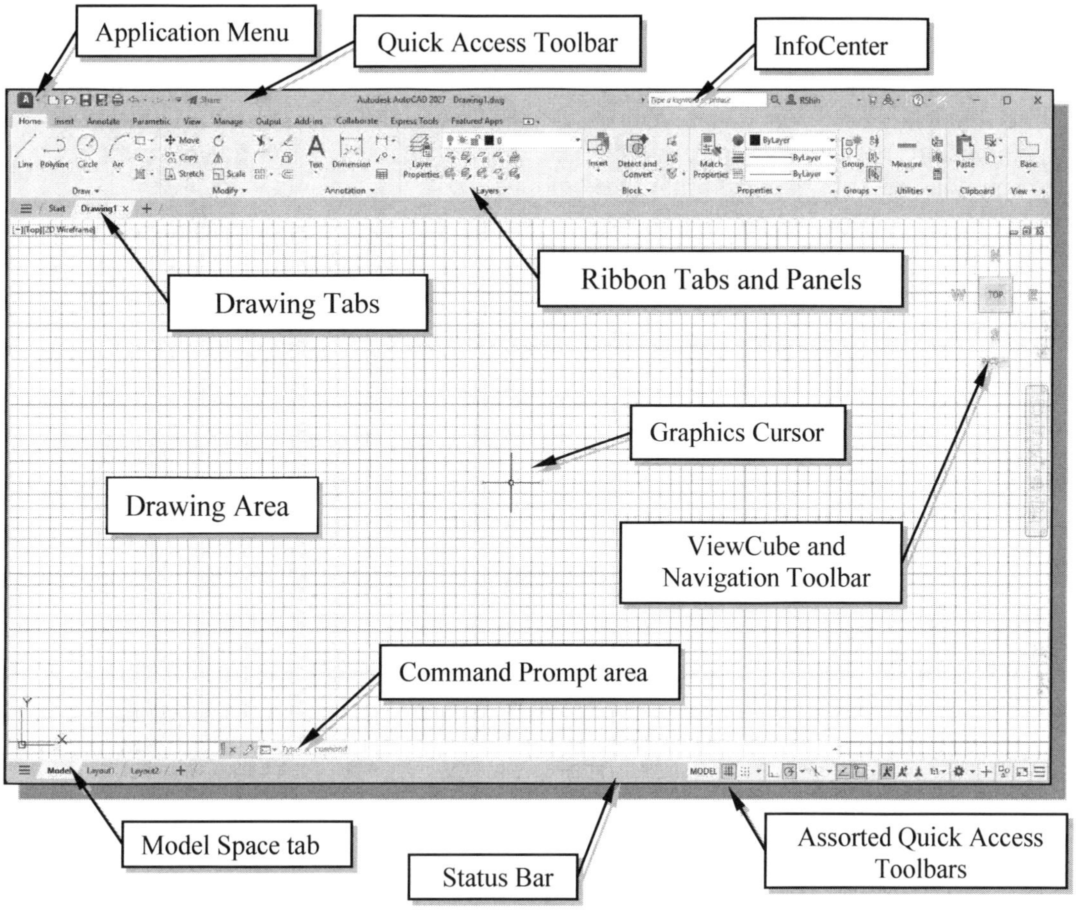

- Click on the down-arrow in the *Quick Access* bar and select **Show Menu Bar** to display the **AutoCAD *Menu*** bar. Note that the menu bar provides access to all of the AutoCAD commands.

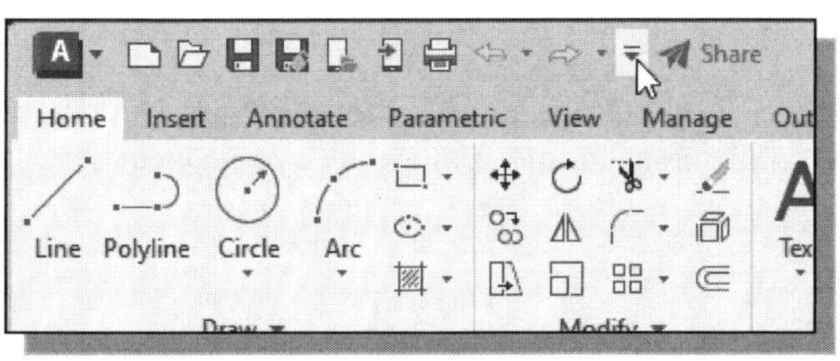

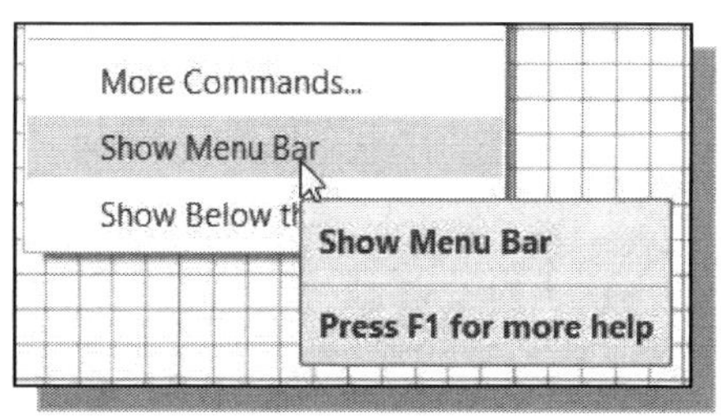

- **Application Menu**

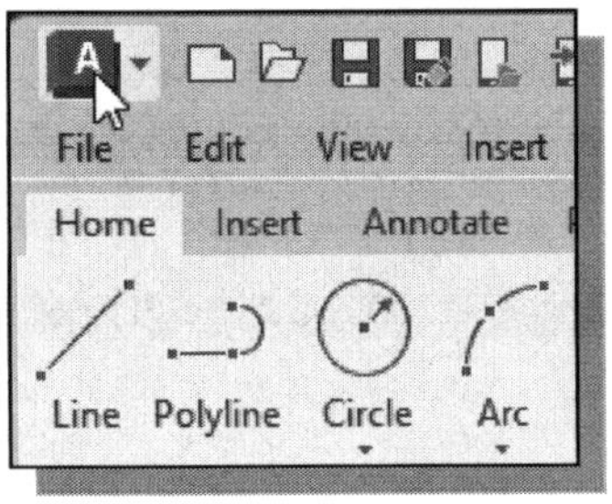

The *Application Menu* at the top of the main window contains commonly used file operations.

- **Quick Access Toolbar**

The *Quick Access* toolbar at the top of the *AutoCAD* window allows us quick access to frequently used commands, such as **Qnew**, **Open**, **Save** and also the **Undo** command. Note that we can customize the quick access toolbar by adding and removing sets of options or individual commands.

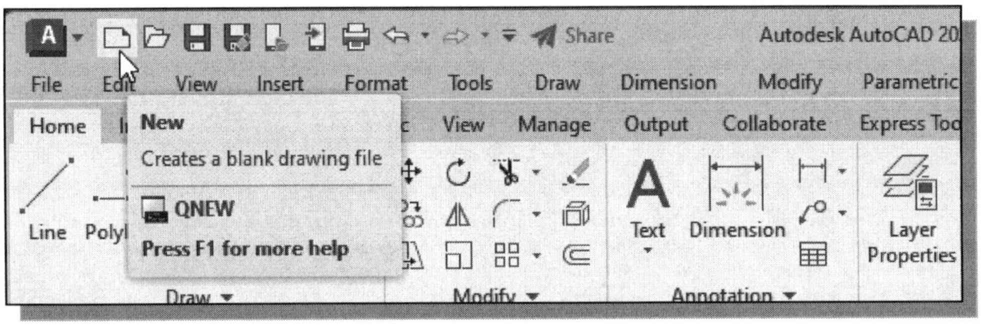

- **AutoCAD Menu Bar**

The *Menu* bar is the pull-down menu where all operations of AutoCAD can be accessed.

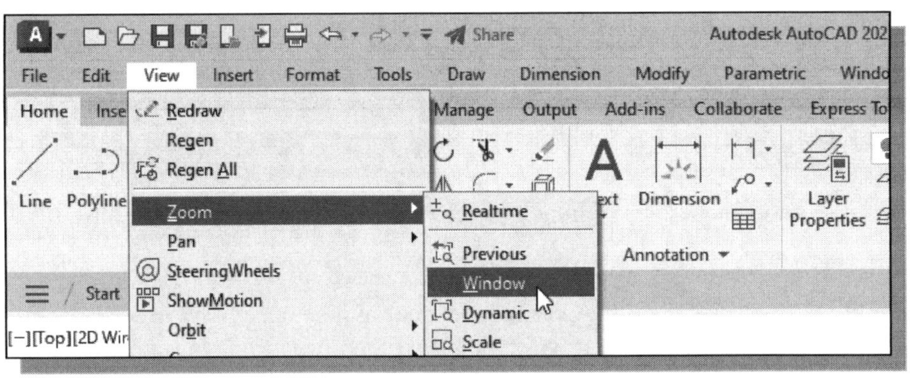

- **Layout tabs**

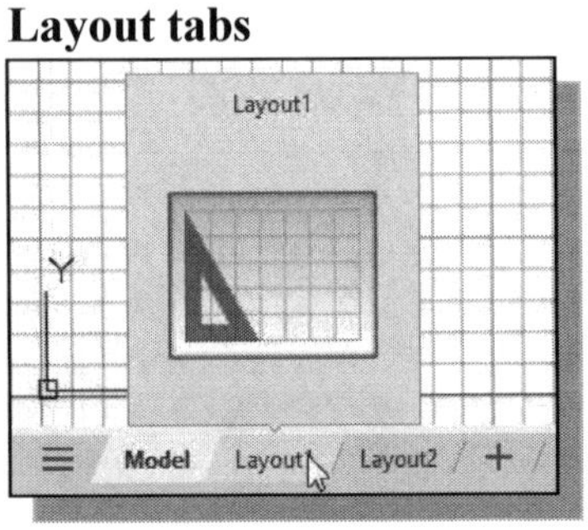

The Model/Layout tabs allow us to switch/create between different **model space** and **paper space**.

- **Drawing Area**
  The *Drawing Area* is the area where models and drawings are displayed.

- **Graphics Cursor or Crosshairs**

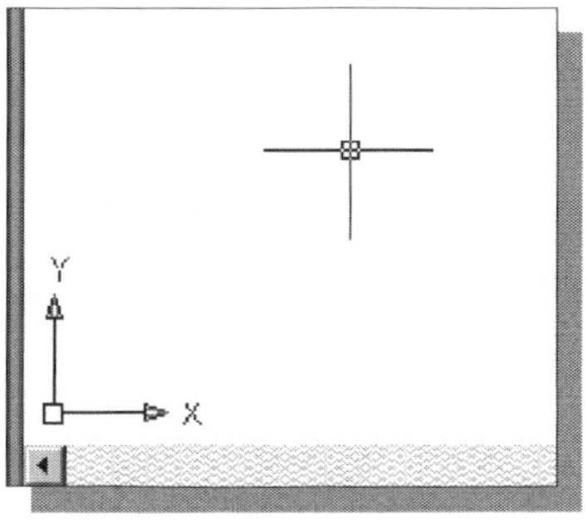

The *graphics cursor*, or *crosshairs*, shows the location of the pointing device in the Drawing Area. The coordinates of the cursor are displayed at the bottom of the screen layout. The cursor's appearance depends on the selected command or option.

- **Command Prompt Area**

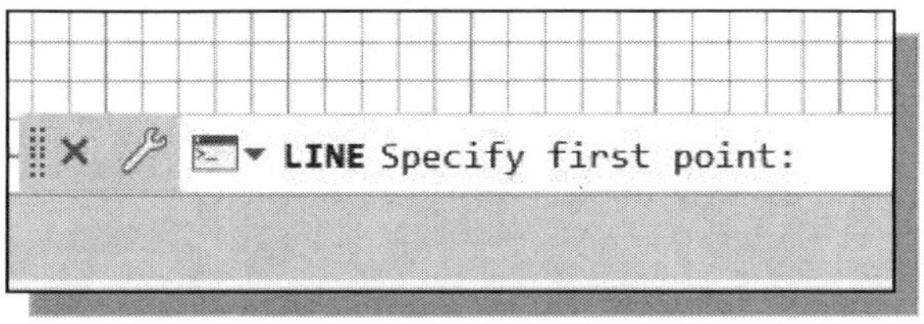

The *Command Prompt Area* provides status information for an operation and it is also the area for data input. Note that the *Command Prompt* can be docked below the drawing area as shown.

- **Cursor Coordinates**

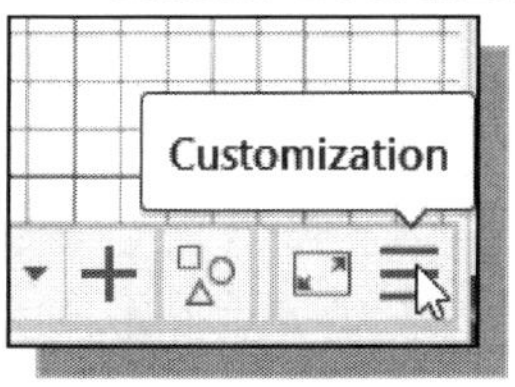

To switch on the **AutoCAD Coordinates Display**, use the *Customization option* at the bottom right corner.

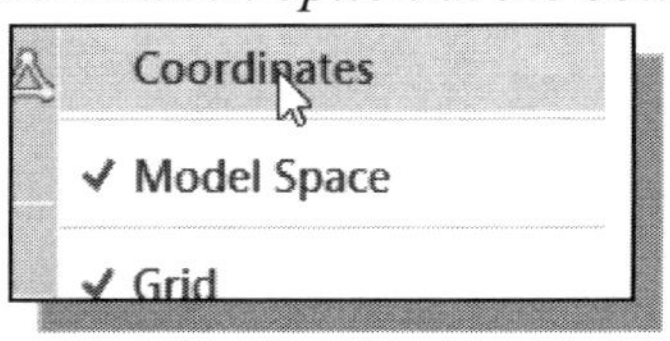

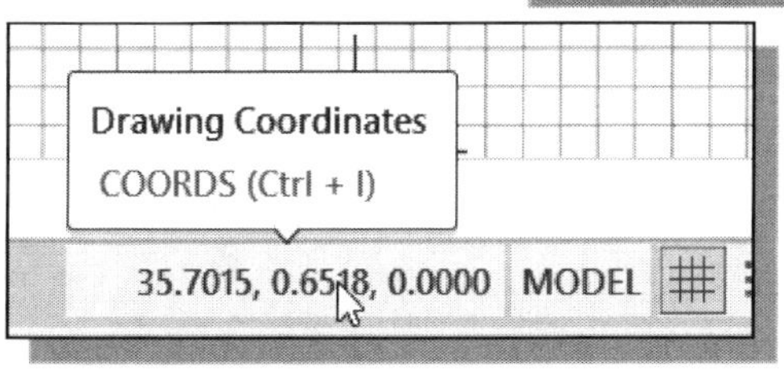

The bottom section of the screen layout displays the coordinate information of the cursor. Note that the quick-key option, [Ctrl+I], can be used to toggle the behavior of the displayed coordinates.

- **Status Toolbar**
  Next to the cursor coordinate display is the *Status* toolbar, showing the status of many commonly used display and construction options.

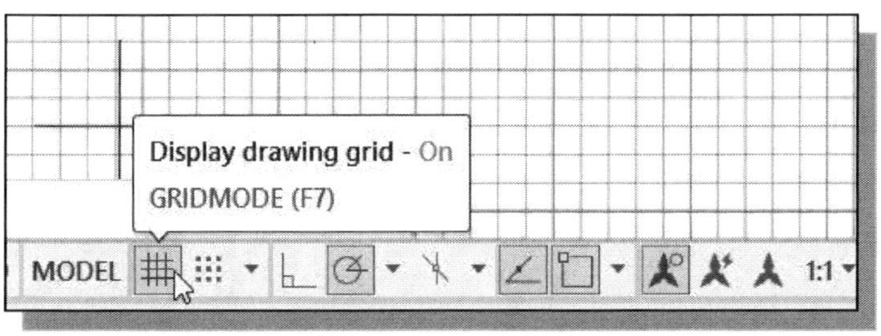

- **Ribbon Tabs and Panels**
  The top section of the screen layout contains customizable icon panels, which contain groups of buttons that allow us to pick commands quickly, without searching through a menu structure. These panels allow us to quickly access the commonly used commands available in AutoCAD.

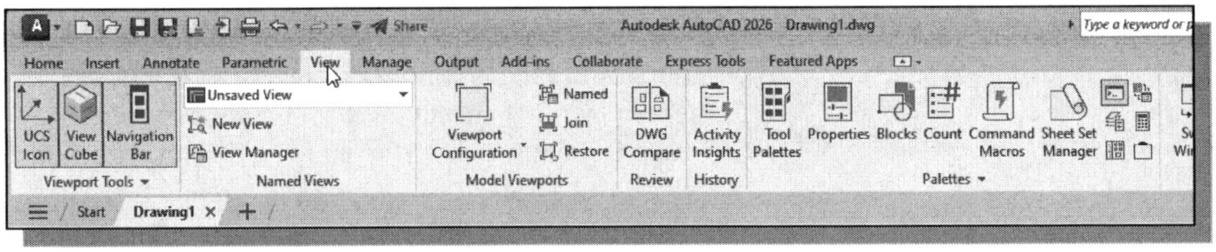

- **Draw and Modify Toolbar Panels**
  The *Draw* and *Modify* toolbar panels are the two main panels for creating drawings; the toolbars contain icons for basic draw and modify commands.

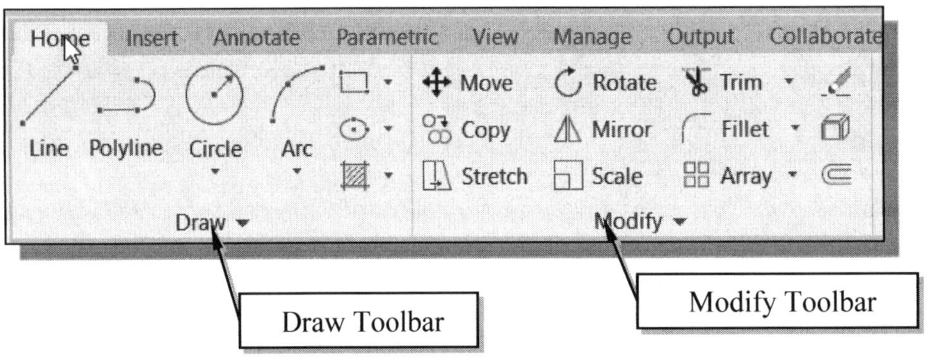

- **Layers Control Toolbar Panel**

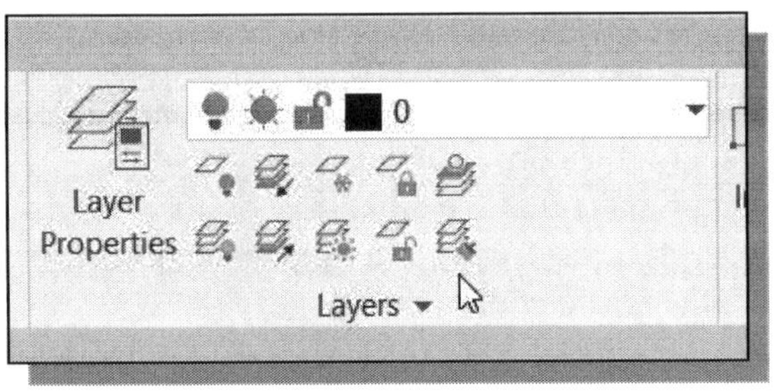

The *Layers Control* toolbar panel contains tools to help manipulate the properties of graphical objects.

- **Viewport/View/Display Controls**

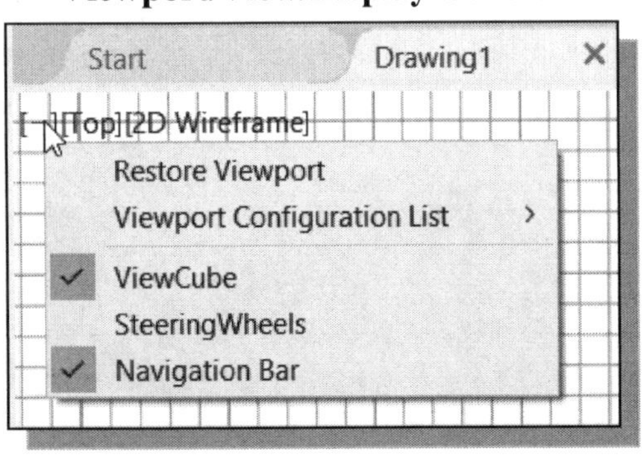

The *Viewport/View/Display controls panel* is located at the upper left corner of the graphics area and it can be used to quickly access viewing related commands, such as Viewport and Display style.

Mouse Buttons

AutoCAD 2027 utilizes the mouse buttons extensively. In learning **AutoCAD 2027**'s interactive environment, it is important to understand the basic functions of the mouse buttons. It is highly recommended that you use a mouse or a tablet with **AutoCAD 2027** since the package uses the buttons for various functions.

- **Left mouse button**
  The **left-mouse-button** is used for most operations, such as selecting menus and icons or picking graphic entities. One click of the button is used to select icons, menus and form entries and to pick graphic items.

- **Right mouse button**
  The **right-mouse-button** is used to bring up additional available options. The software also utilizes the **right-mouse-button** the same as the **ENTER** key and is often used to accept the default setting to a prompt or to end a process.

- **Middle mouse button/wheel**
  The middle mouse button/wheel can be used to Pan (hold down the wheel button and drag the mouse) or Zoom (rotate the wheel) real time.

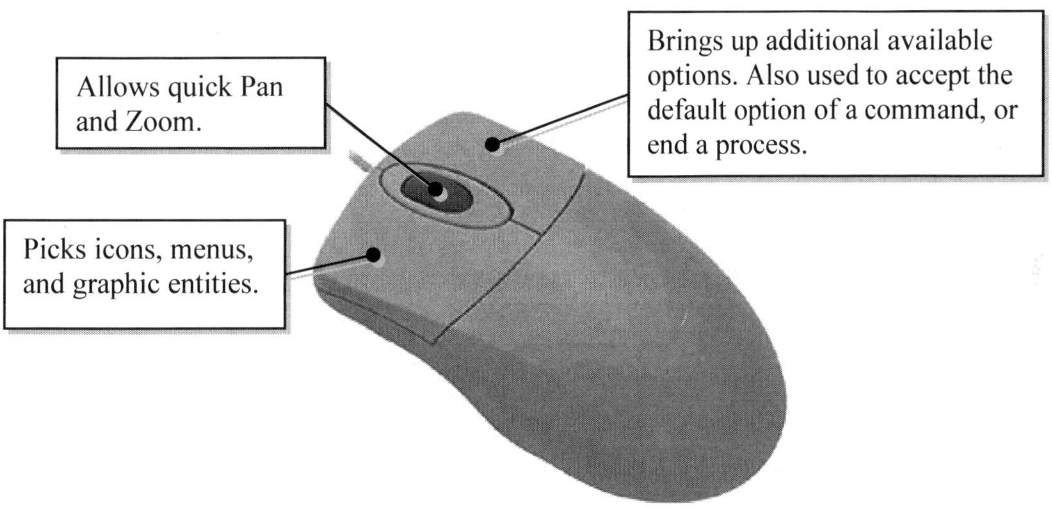

[Esc] – Canceling commands

The [**Esc**] key is used to cancel a command in **AutoCAD 2027**. The [**Esc**] key is located near the top-left corner of the keyboard. Sometimes, it may be necessary to press the [**Esc**] key twice to cancel a command; it depends on where we are in the command sequence. For some commands, the [**Esc**] key is used to exit the command.

Online Help

Several types of online help are available at any time during an **AutoCAD 2027** session. The **AutoCAD 2027** software provides many online help options:

- **Autodesk Exchange**:
  Autodesk Exchange is a central portal in AutoCAD 2027; AutoCAD Exchange provides a user interface for Help, learning aids, tips and tricks, videos, and downloadable apps. By default, *Autodesk Exchange* is displayed at **startup**. This allows access to a dynamic selection of tools from the *Autodesk community*; note that an internet connection is required to use this option.

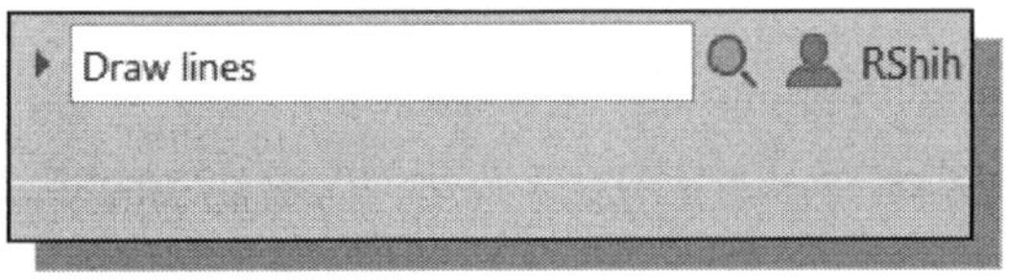

- To use *Autodesk Exchange*, simply type a question in the *input box* to search through the Autodesk's *Help* system as shown.

- A list of the search results appears in the *Autodesk Help* window, and we can also determine the level and type of searches of the associated information.

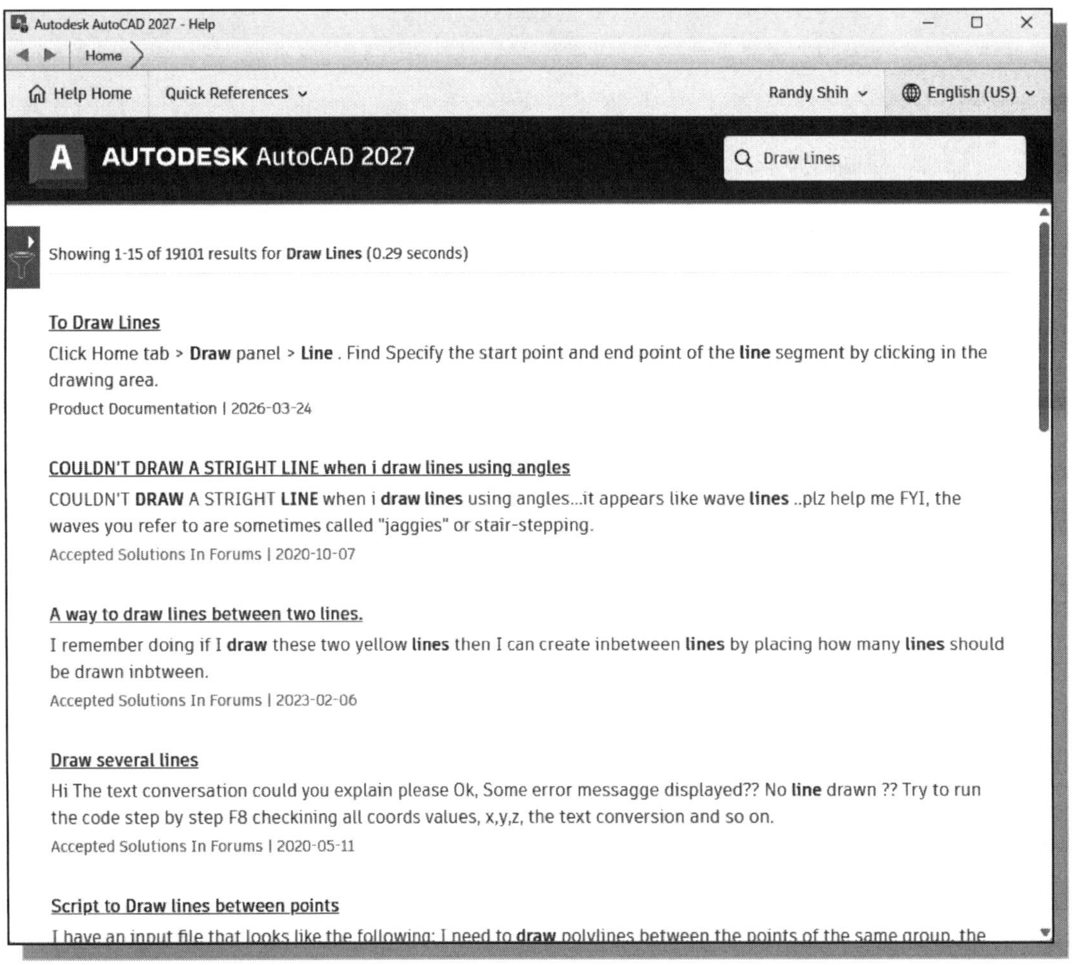

Leaving AutoCAD 2027

To leave **AutoCAD 2027**, use the left-mouse-button and click the **Application Menu** button at the top left corner of the **AutoCAD 2027** screen window, then choose **Exit AutoCAD** from the pull-down menu or type ***QUIT*** in the command prompt area.

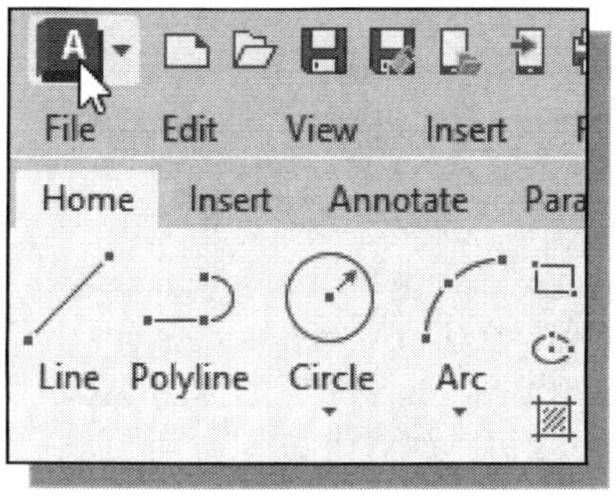

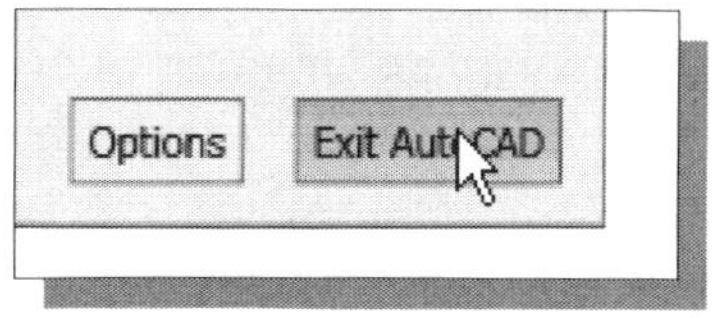

Creating a CAD File Folder

It is a good practice to create a separate folder to store your CAD files. You should not save your CAD files in the same folder where the **AutoCAD 2027** application is located. It is much easier to organize and back up your project files if they are in a separate folder. Making folders within this folder for different types of projects will help you organize your CAD files even further.

➢ To create a new folder in the *Microsoft Windows* environment:

1. On the *desktop* or under the *My Documents* folder in which you want to create a new folder.

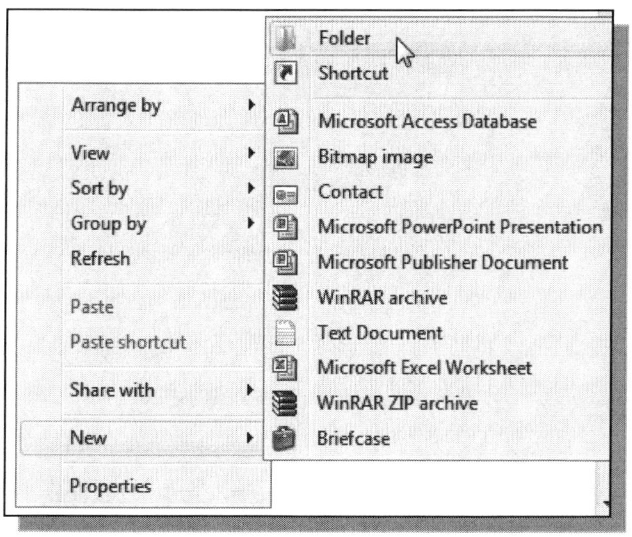

2. Right-mouse-click once to bring up the option menu, then select New→ Folder.

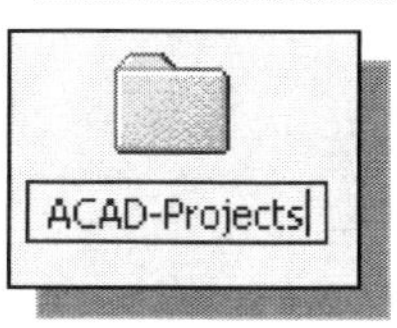

3. Type a name for the new folder, and then press **ENTER**.

Drawing in AutoCAD

Learning to use a CAD system is similar to learning a new language. It is necessary to begin with the basic alphabet and learn how to use it correctly and effectively through practice. This will require learning some new concepts and skills as well as learning a different vocabulary. All CAD systems create designs using basic geometric entities. Many of the constructions used in technical designs are based upon two-dimensional planar geometry. The method and number of operations that are required to accomplish the constructions are different from one system to another.

In order to become effective in using a CAD system, we must learn to create geometric entities quickly and accurately. In learning to use a CAD system, **lines** and **circles** are the first two, and perhaps the most important two, geometric entities that one should master the skills of creating and modifying. Straight lines and circles are used in almost all technical designs. In examining the different types of planar geometric entities, the importance of lines and circles becomes obvious. Triangles and polygons are planar figures bounded by straight lines. And Ellipses and Splines can be constructed by connecting arcs with different radii. As one gains some experience in creating lines and circles, similar procedures can be applied to create other geometric entities. In this chapter, the different ways of creating lines and circles in **AutoCAD 2027** are examined.

Starting Up AutoCAD 2027

1. Select the **AutoCAD 2027** option on the *Program* menu or select the **AutoCAD 2027** icon on the *Desktop*. Click **Start Drawing** to start a new drawing.

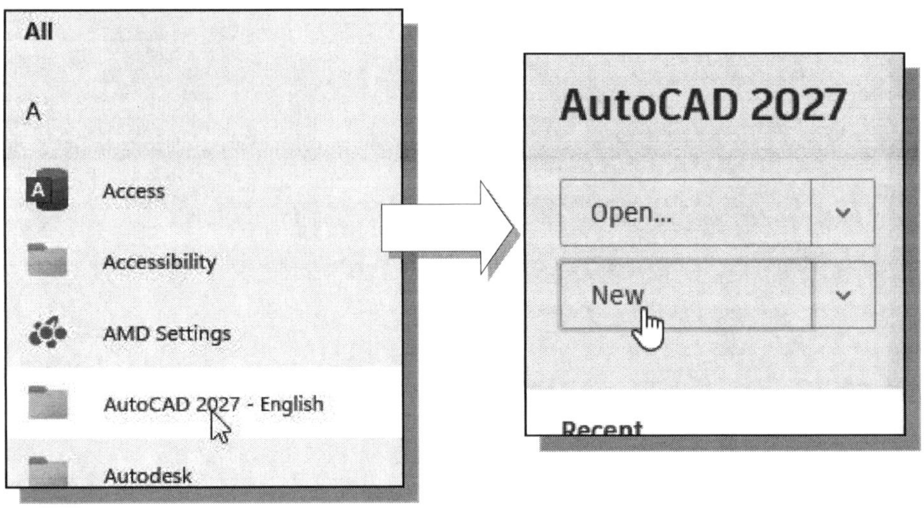

❖ Once the program is loaded into memory, the **AutoCAD 2027** main drawing screen will appear on the screen.

➢ Note that AutoCAD automatically assigns generic names, *Drawing 1*, as new drawings are created. In our example, AutoCAD opened the graphics window using the default system units and assigned the drawing name *Drawing1*.

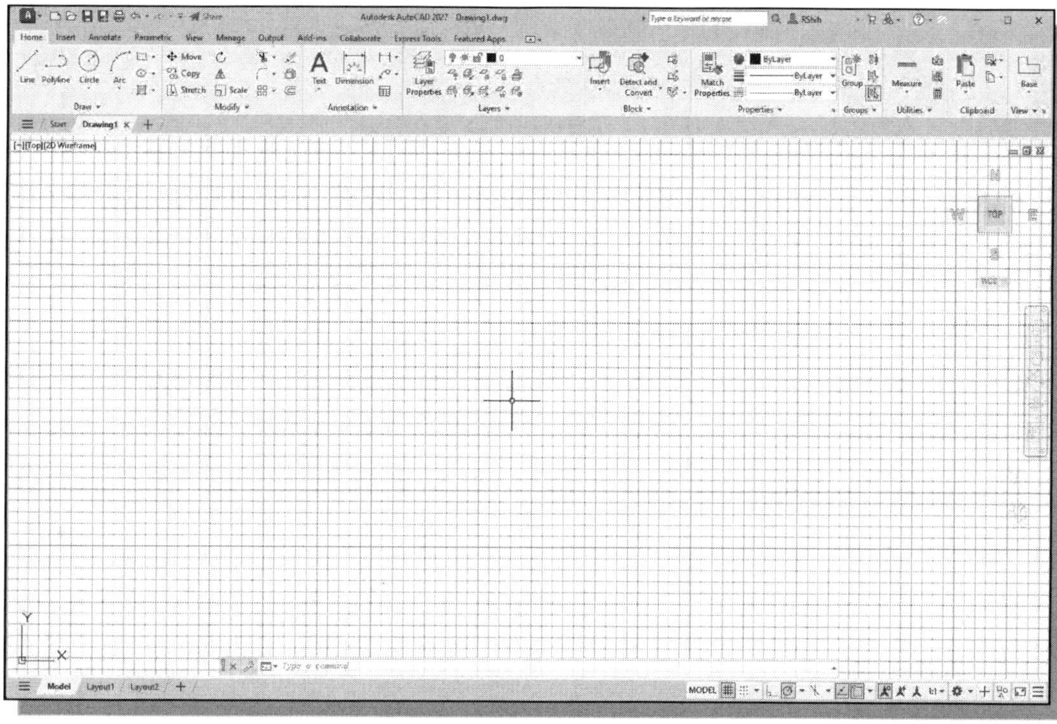

2. If necessary, click on the down-arrow in the *Quick Access* bar and select **Show Menu Bar** to display the **AutoCAD *Menu Bar***. The *Menu Bar* provides access to all AutoCAD commands.

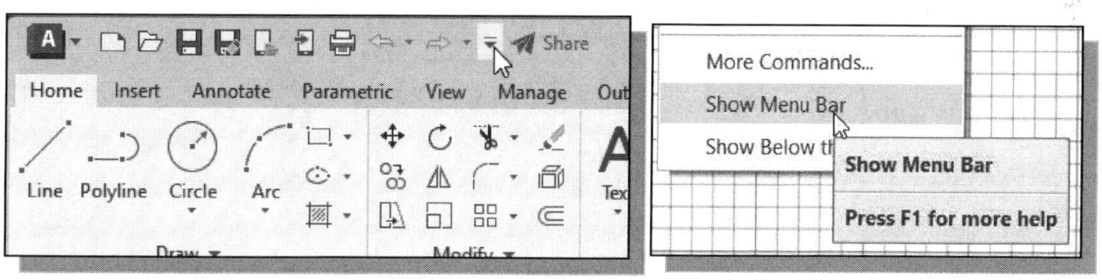

3. To switch on the **AutoCAD Coordinates Display**, use the *Customization option* at the bottom right corner.

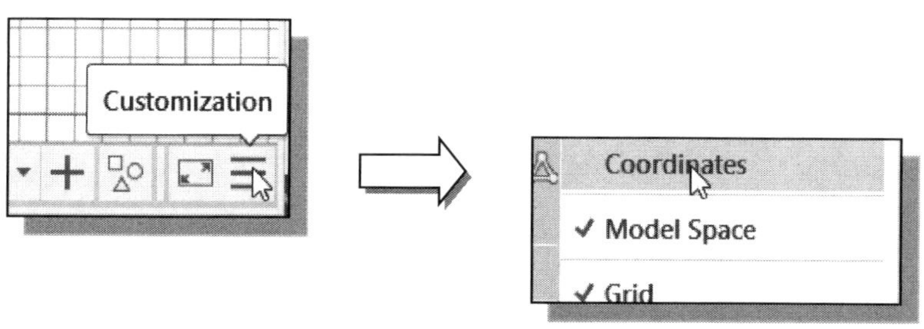

Drawing Units Setup

Every object we construct in a CAD system is measured in **units**. We should determine the system of units within the CAD system before creating the first geometric entities.

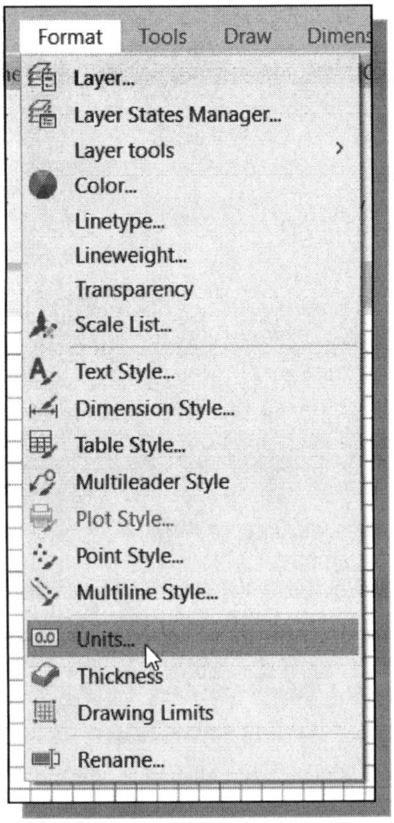

1. In the *Menu Bar* select:
   [Format] → [Units]

- The AutoCAD *Menu Bar* contains multiple pull-down menus where all of the AutoCAD commands can be accessed. Note that many of the menu items listed in the pull-down menus can also be accessed through the *Quick Access* toolbar and/or *Ribbon* panels.

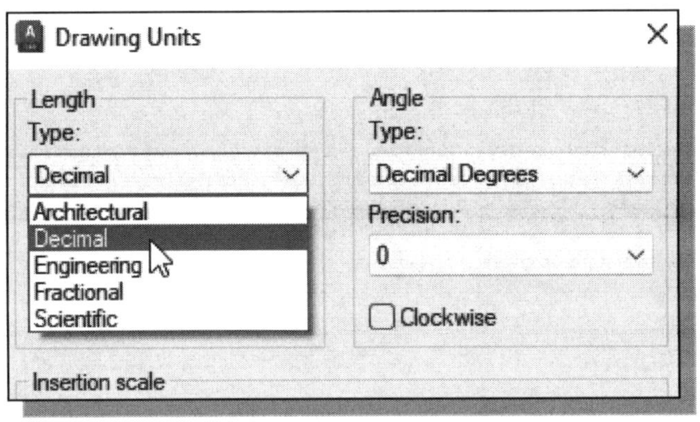

2. Click on the *Length Type* option to display the different types of length units available. Confirm the *Length Type* is set to **Decimal**.

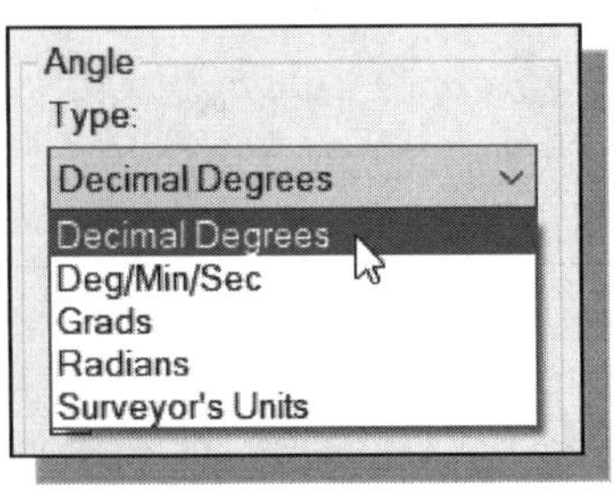

3. On your own, examine the other settings that are available.

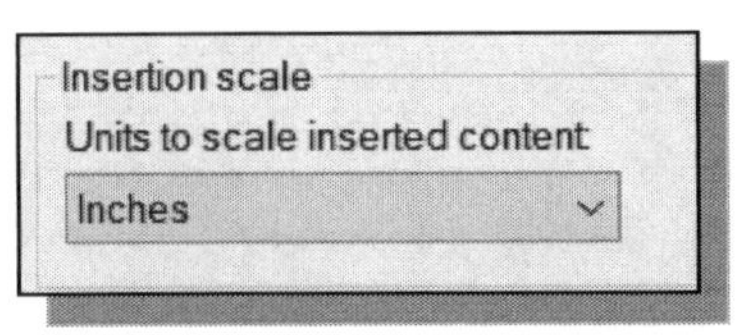

- Also note the Insertion Scale section will show the default measurement system, such as the *English* units, inches.

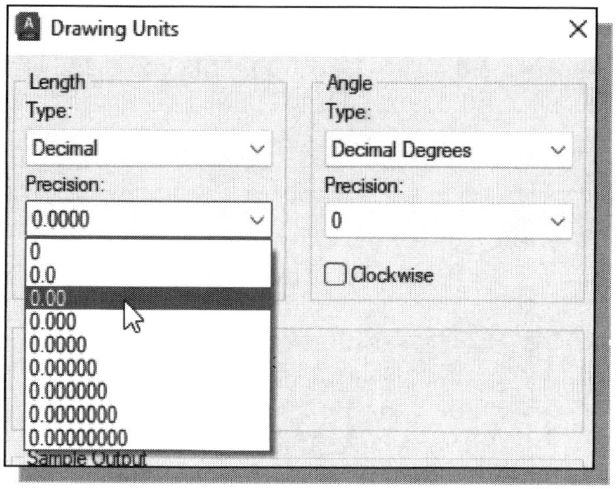

4. Set the *Precision* to **two digits** after the decimal point as shown in the above figure.

5. Pick **OK** to exit the *Drawing Units* dialog box.

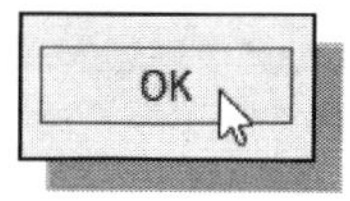

Drawing Area Setup

Next, we will set up the **Drawing Limits** by entering a command in the command prompt area. Setting the Drawing Limits controls the extents of the display of the *grid.* It also serves as a visual reference that marks the working area. It can also be used to prevent construction outside the grid limits and as a plot option that defines an area to be plotted and/or printed. Note that this setting does not limit the region for geometry construction.

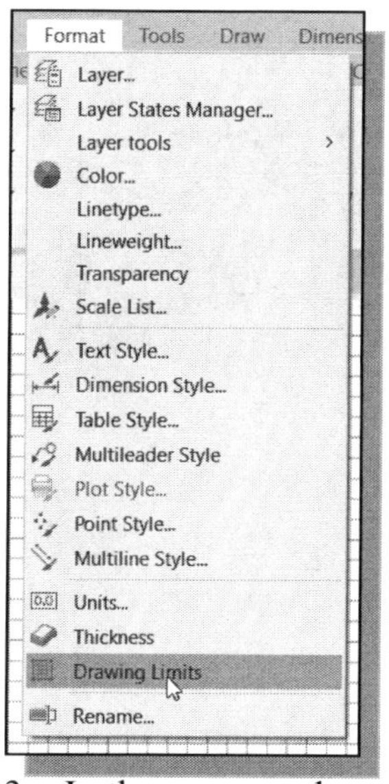

1. In the *Menu Bar* select:
   [Format] → [Drawing Limits]

2. In the command prompt area, the message "*Reset Model Space Limits: Specify lower left corner or [On/Off] <0.00,0.00>:*" is displayed. Press the **ENTER** key once to accept the default coordinates <**0.00,0.00**>.

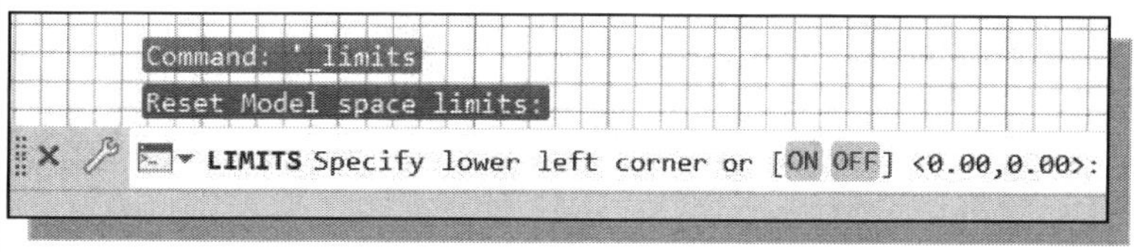

3. In the command prompt area, the message "*Specify upper right corner <12.00,9.00>:*" is displayed. Press the **ENTER** key again to accept the default coordinates <**12.00,9.00**>.

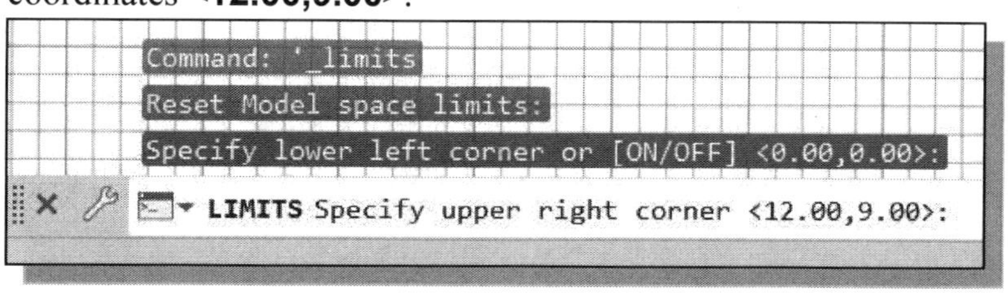

4. On your own, move the graphics cursor near the upper-right corner inside the drawing area and note that the drawing area is unchanged. (The **Drawing Limits** command is used to set the drawing area, but the display will not be adjusted until a display command is used.)

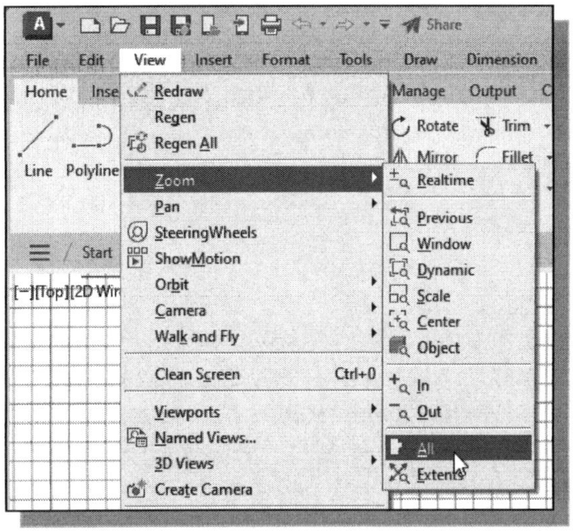

5. Inside the *Menu Bar* area select:
[View] → [Zoom] → [All]

❖ The **Zoom All** command will adjust the display so that all objects in the drawing are displayed to be as large as possible. If no objects are constructed, the **Drawing Limits** are used to adjust the current viewport.

6. Move the graphics cursor near the upper-right corner inside the drawing area and note that the display area is updated.

7. Hit the function key [**F7**] once to turn **off** the display of the *Grid* lines.

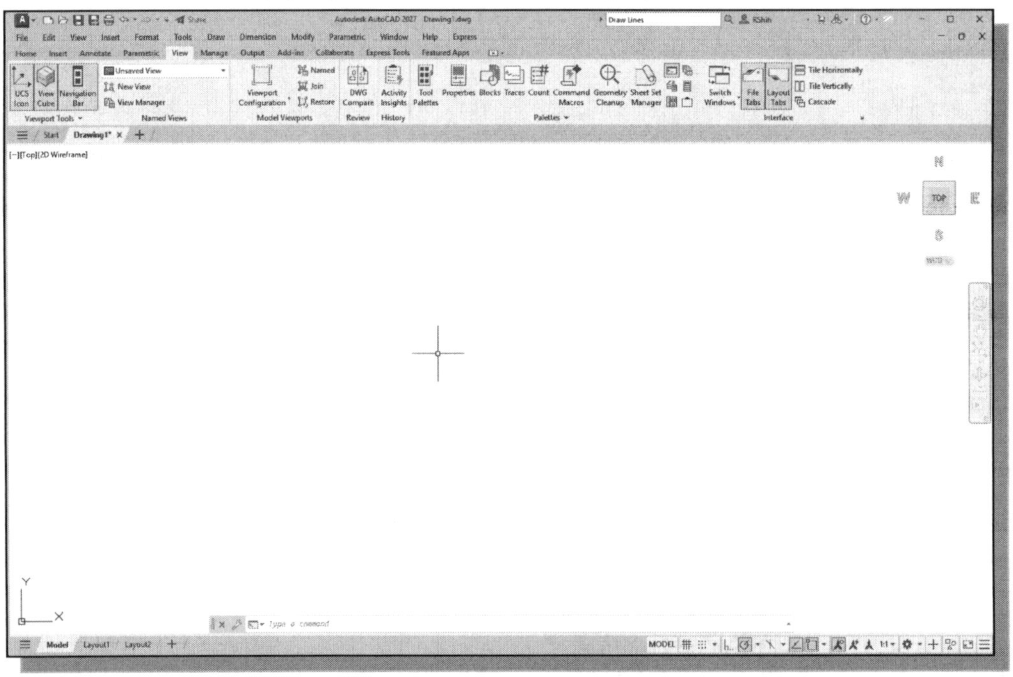

- Note that function key [**F7**] is a quick key, which can be used to quickly toggle on/off the grid display. Also, note the *command prompt area* can be positioned to dock below the drawing area or float inside the drawing area as shown.

Drawing Lines with the Line Command

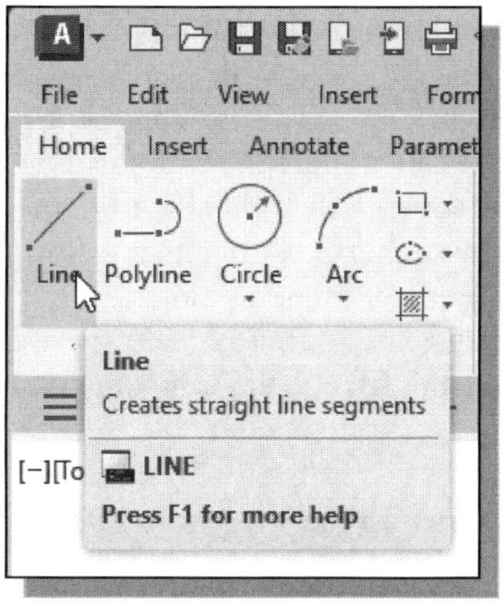

1. Move the graphics cursor to the first icon in the *Draw* panel. This icon is the **Line** icon. Note that a brief description of the Line command appears next to the cursor.

2. Select the icon by clicking once with the **left-mouse-button**, which will activate the Line command.

3. In the command prompt area, near the bottom of the AutoCAD drawing screen, the message "**Line** *Specify first point:*" is displayed. AutoCAD expects us to identify the starting location of a straight line. Move the graphics cursor inside the graphics window and watch the display of the coordinates of the graphics cursor at the bottom of the AutoCAD drawing screen. The three numbers represent the location of the cursor in the X, Y, and Z directions. We can treat the graphics window as if it was a piece of paper, and we are using the graphics cursor as if it was a pencil with which to draw.

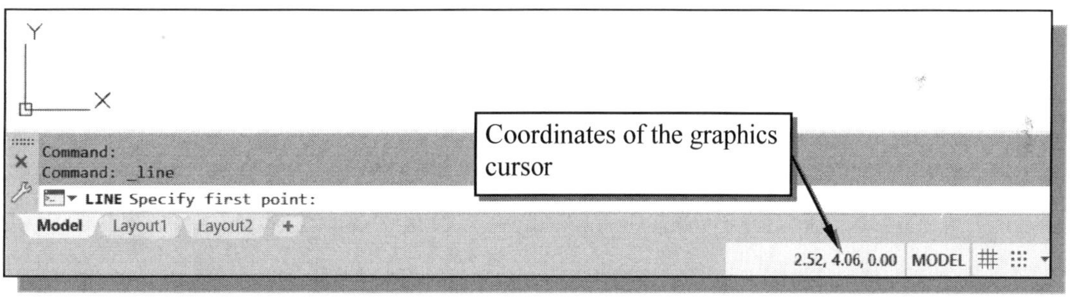

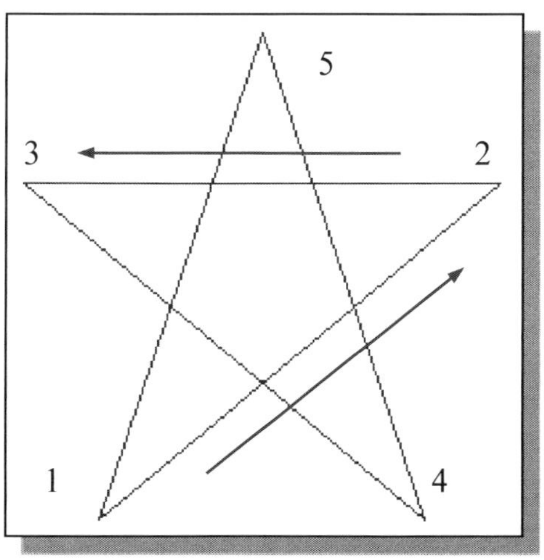

❖ We will create a freehand sketch of a five-point star using the Line command. Do not be overly concerned with the actual size or accuracy of your freehand sketch. This exercise is to give you a feel for the **AutoCAD 2027** user interface.

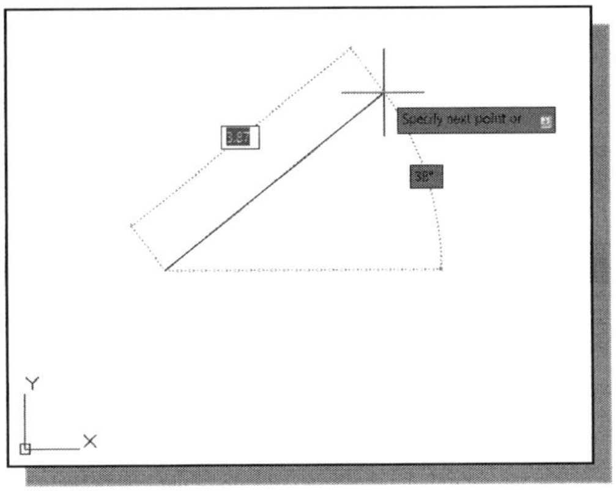

4. We will start at a location about one-third from the bottom of the graphics window. Left-click once to position the starting point of our first line. This will be *point 1* of our sketch. Next, move the cursor upward and toward the right side of *point 1*. Notice the rubber-band line that follows the graphics cursor in the graphics window. Left-click again (*point 2*) and we have created the first line of our sketch.

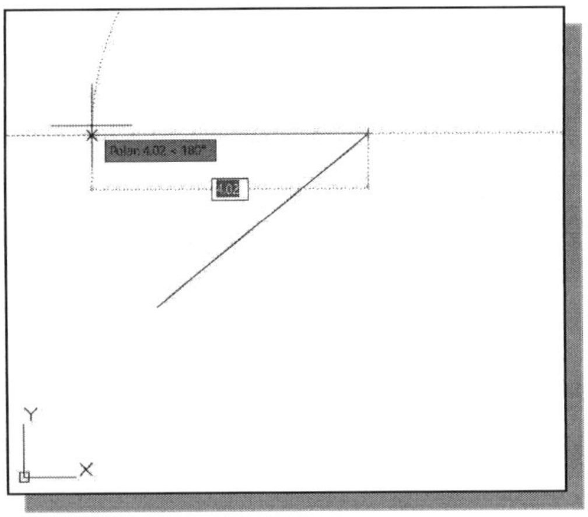

5. Move the cursor to the left of *point 2* and create a horizontal line about the same length as the first line on the screen.

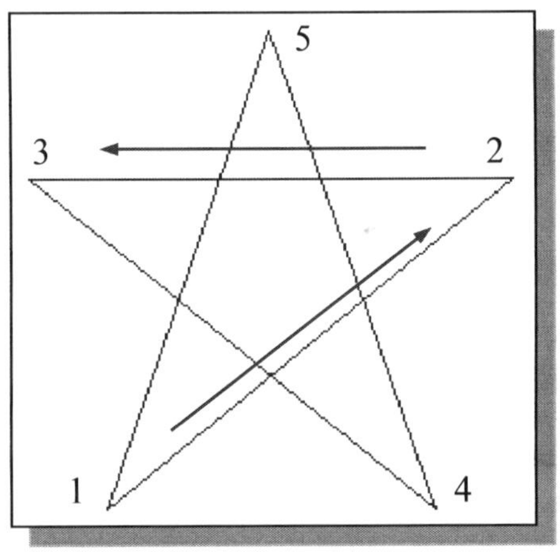

6. Repeat the above steps and complete the freehand sketch by adding three more lines (from *point 3* to *point 4*, *point 4* to *point 5*, and then connect to *point 5* back to *point 1*).

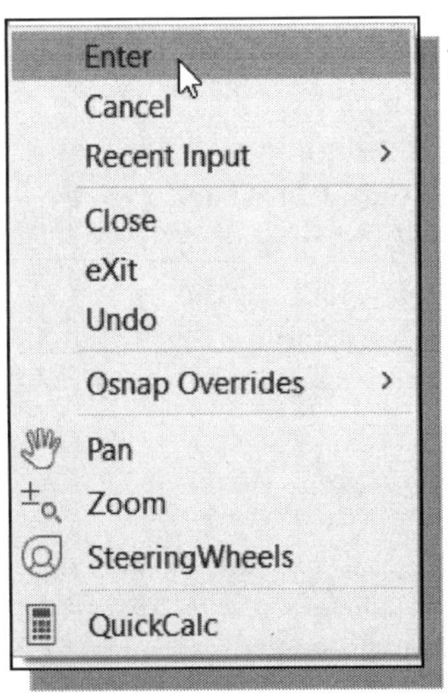

7. Notice that the **Line** command remains activated even after we connected the last segment of the line to the starting point *(point 1)* of our sketch. Inside the graphics window, **click once** with the **right-mouse-button** and a pop-up menu appears on the screen.

8. Select **Enter** with the left-mouse-button to end the **Line** command. (This is equivalent to hitting the [**ENTER**] key on the keyboard.)

9. Move the cursor near *point 2* and *point 3*, and estimate the length of the horizontal line by watching the displayed coordinates for each point.

Visual Reference

The method we just used to create the freehand sketch is known as the **interactive method**, where we use the cursor to specify locations on the screen. This method is perhaps the fastest way to specify locations on the screen. However, it is rather difficult to try to create a line of a specific length by watching the displayed coordinates. It would be helpful to know what one inch or one meter looks like on the screen while we are creating entities. **AutoCAD 2027** provides us with many tools to aid the construction of our designs. For example, the ***GRID*** and ***SNAP MODE*** options can be used to get a visual reference as to the size of objects and learn to restrict the movement of the cursor to a set increment on the screen.

The ***GRID*** and ***SNAP MODE*** options can be turned *ON* or *OFF* through the *Status Bar*. The *Status Bar* area is located at the bottom left of the AutoCAD drawing screen, next to the cursor coordinates.

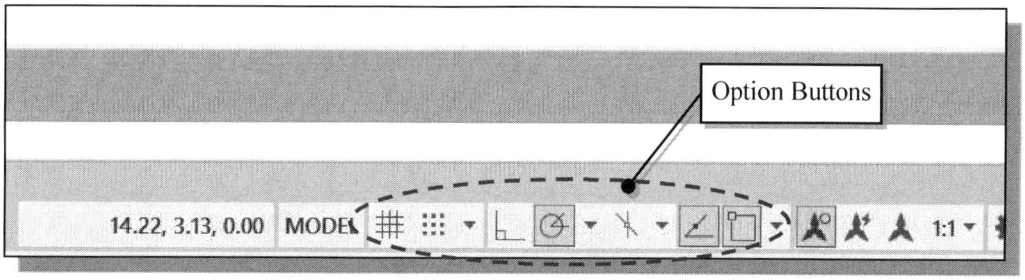

The second button in the *Status Bar* is the *SNAP MODE* option and the third button is the *GRID DISPLAY* option. Note that the buttons in the *Status Bar* area serve two functions: (1) the status of the specific option, and (2) as toggle switches that can be used to turn these special options *ON* and *OFF*. When the corresponding button is *highlighted*, the specific option is turned *ON*. Using the buttons is a quick and easy way to make changes to these *drawing aid* options. The buttons in the *Status Bar* can also be switched on and off in the middle of another command.

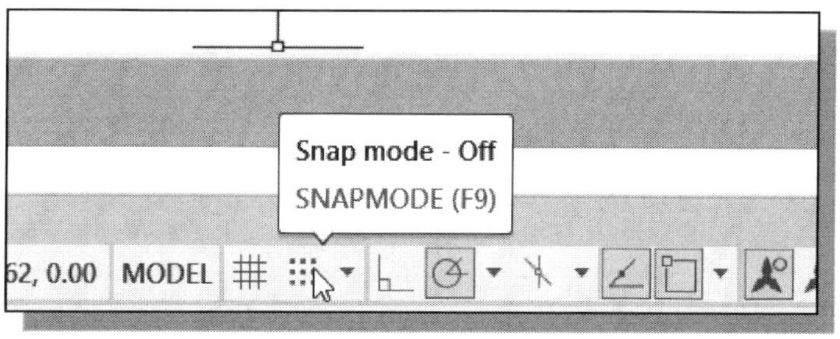

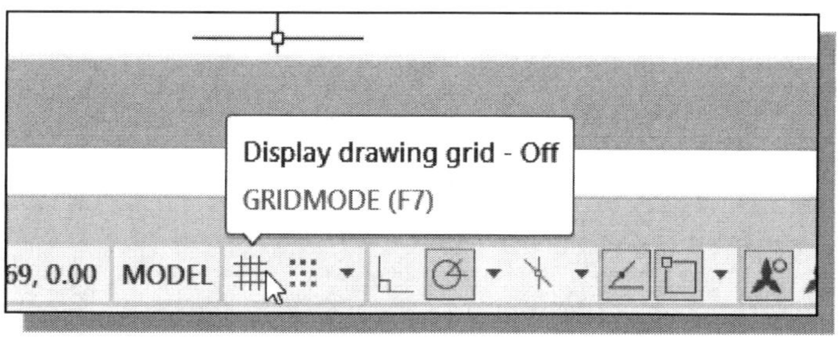

GRID ON

1. Left-click the ***GRID*** button in the *Status Bar* to turn ***ON*** the *GRID DISPLAY* option. (Notice in the command prompt area, the message *"<Grid on>"* is also displayed.)

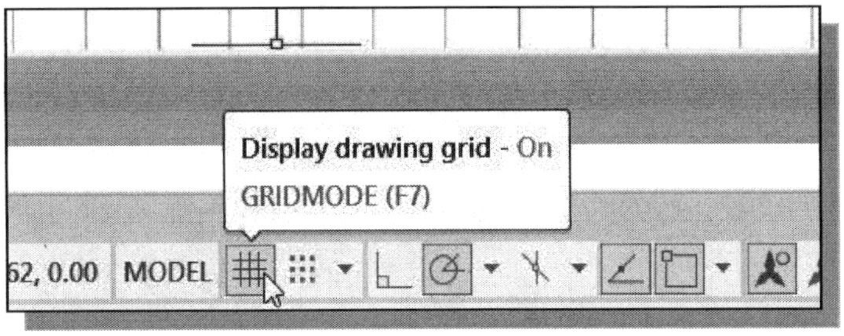

2. Move the cursor inside the graphics window, and estimate the distance in between the grid lines by watching the coordinates displayed at the bottom of the screen.

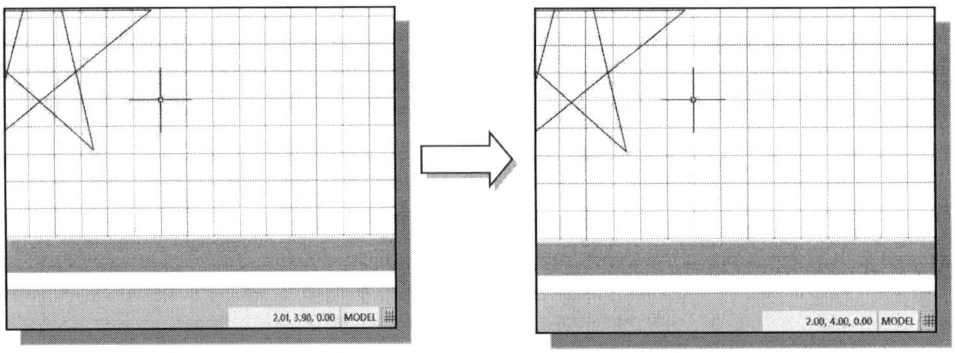

➢ The *GRID* option creates a pattern of lines that extends over an area on the screen. Using the grid is similar to placing a sheet of grid paper under a drawing. The grid helps you align objects and visualize the distance between them. The grid is not displayed in the plotted drawing. The default grid spacing, which means the distance in between two lines on the screen, is 0.5 inches. We can see that the sketched horizontal line in the sketch is about 4 inches long.

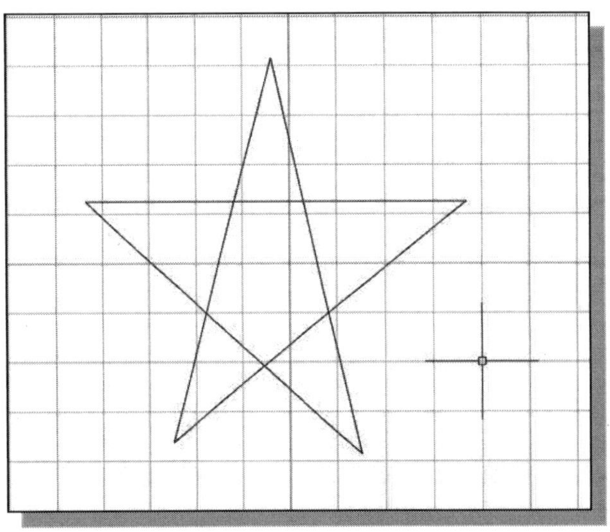

SNAP MODE ON

1. Left-click the ***SNAP MODE*** button in the *Status Bar* to turn ***ON*** the *SNAP* option.

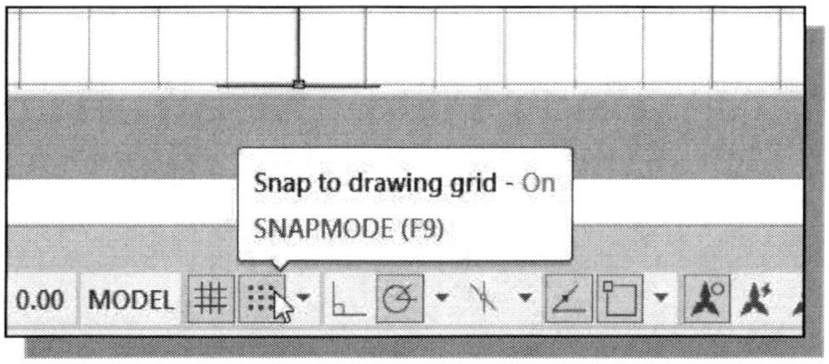

2. Move the cursor inside the graphics window, and move the cursor diagonally on the screen. Observe the movement of the cursor and watch the *coordinates display* at the bottom of the screen.

➢ The *SNAP* option controls an invisible rectangular grid that restricts cursor movement to specified intervals. When *SNAP* mode is on, the screen cursor and all input coordinates are snapped to the nearest point on the grid. The default snap interval is 0.5 inches and aligned to the grid points on the screen.

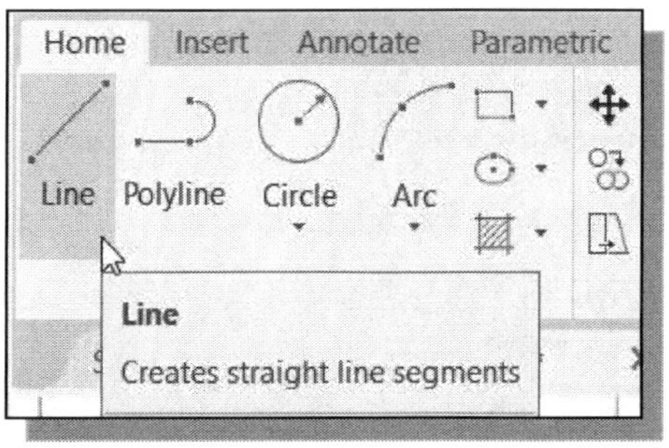

3. Click on the **Line** icon in the *Draw* toolbar. In the command prompt area, the message "*Line Specify first point:*" is displayed.

4. On your own, create another sketch of the five-point star with the *GRID* and *SNAP* options switched *ON*.

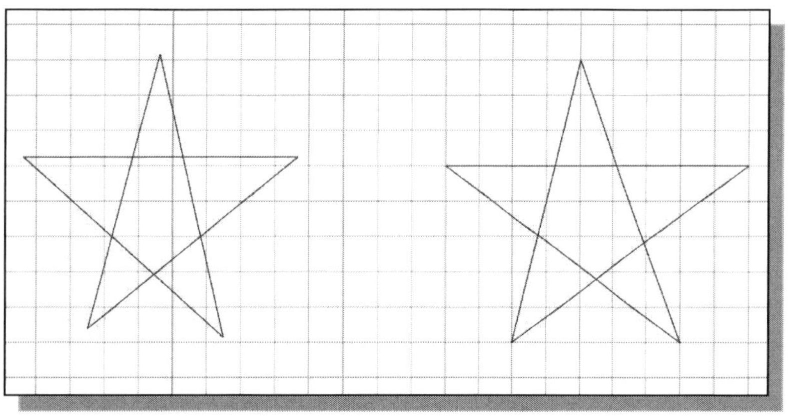

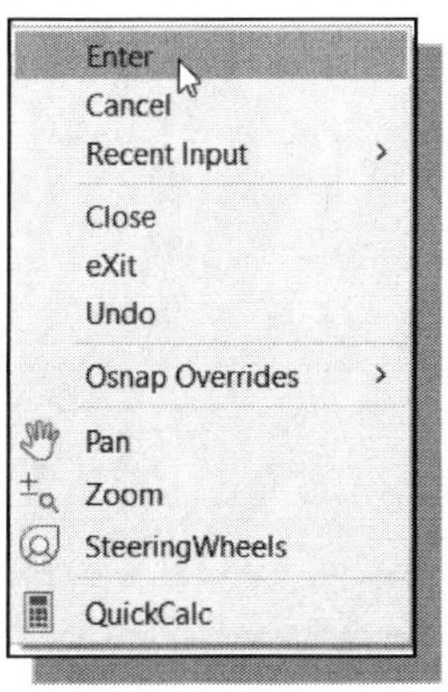

5. Use the **right-mouse-button** and select **Enter** in the pop-up menu to end the **Line** command if you have not done so.

Using the Erase Command

One of the advantages of using a CAD system is the ability to remove entities without leaving any marks. We will erase two of the lines using the **Erase** command.

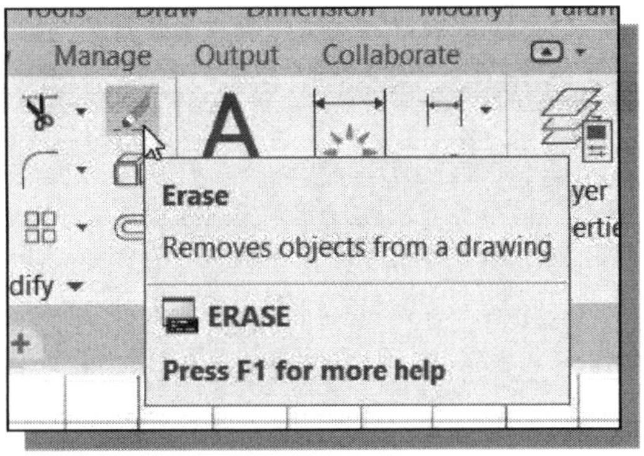

1. Pick **Erase** in the *Modify* toolbar. (The icon is a picture of an eraser at the end of a pencil.) The message "*Select objects*" is displayed in the command prompt area and AutoCAD awaits us to select the objects to erase.

2. Left-click the ***SNAP MODE*** button on the *Status Bar* to turn ***OFF*** the *SNAP MODE* option. We can toggle the *Status Bar* options *ON* or *OFF* in the middle of another command.

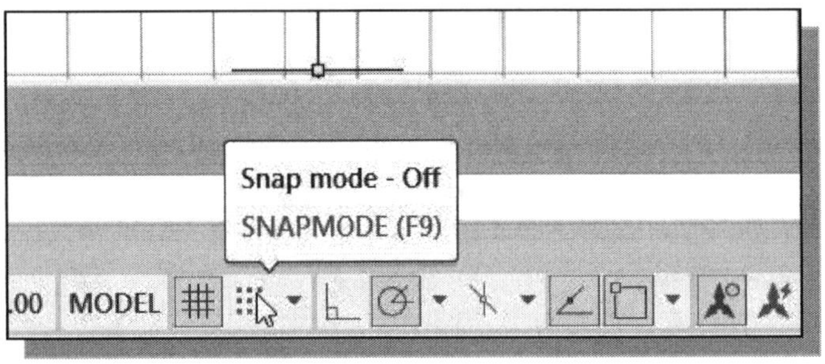

3. Select any two lines on the screen; the selected lines are highlighted as shown in the figure below.

➤ To **deselect** an object from the selection set, hold down the [**SHIFT**] key and select the object again.

4. **Right-mouse-click** once to accept the selections. The selected two lines are erased.

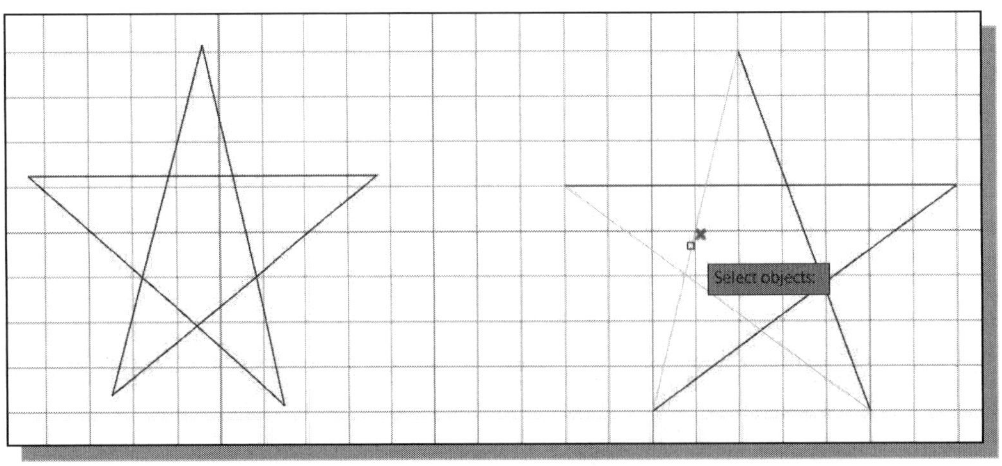

Repeat the Last Command

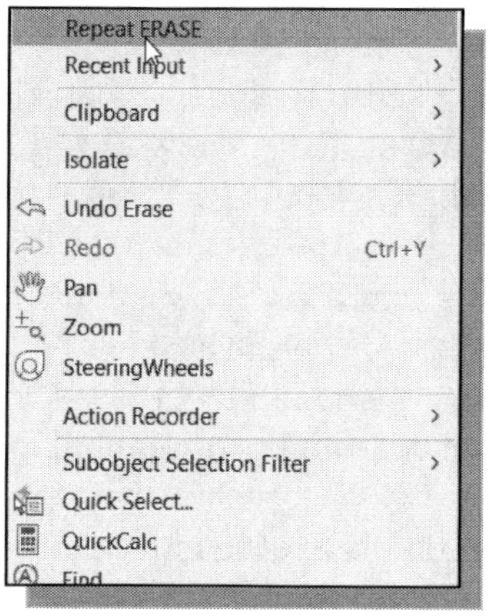

1. Inside the graphics window, click once with the **right-mouse-button** to bring up the pop-up option menu.

2. Pick **Repeat Erase**, with the left-mouse-button, in the pop-up menu to repeat the last command. Notice the other options available in the pop-up menu.

➢ **AutoCAD 2027** offers many options to accomplish the same task. Throughout this text, we will emphasize the use of the **AutoCAD Heads-up Design™** interface, which means we focus on the screen, not on the keyboard.

3. Move the cursor to a location that is above and toward the left side of the entities on the screen. Left-mouse-click **once** to start a corner of a rubber-band window.

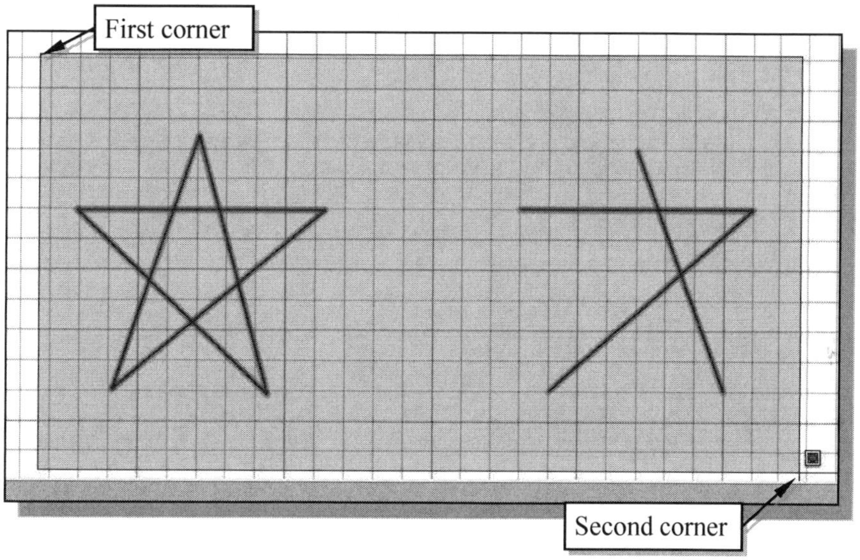

4. Move the cursor toward the right and below the entities, and then click once with the left-mouse-click to enclose all the entities inside the **selection window**. Notice all entities that are inside the window are selected. (Note the ***enclosed window selection*** direction is from **top left** to **bottom right**.)

5. Inside the graphics window, **right-mouse-click** once to proceed with erasing the selected entities.

➢ On your own, create a free-hand sketch of your choice using the **Line** command. Experiment with using the different commands we have discussed so far. Reset the status buttons so that **only** the ***GRID DISPLAY*** option is turned ***ON*** as shown.

The CAD Database and the User Coordinate System

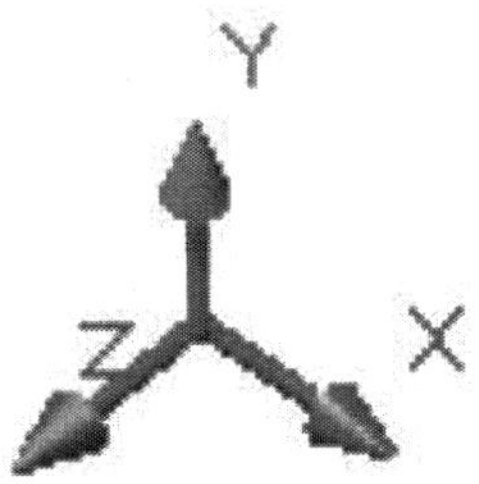

Designs and drawings created in a CAD system are usually defined and stored using sets of points in what is called **world space**. In most CAD systems, the world space is defined using a three-dimensional *Cartesian coordinate system*. Three mutually perpendicular axes, usually referred to as the X-, Y-, and Z-axes, define this system. The intersection of the three coordinate axes forms a point called the **origin**. Any point in world space can then be defined as the distance from the origin in the X-, Y- and Z- directions. In most CAD systems, the directions of the arrows shown on the axes identify the positive sides of the coordinates.

1. Click on the **[View]** pull-down menu and select **[Display] → [UCS Icon] → [On]**

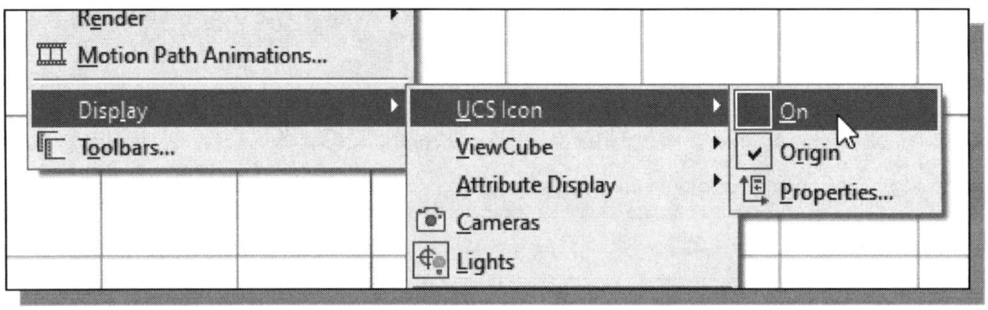

A CAD file, which is the electronic version of the design, contains data that describes the entities created in the CAD system. Information such as the coordinate values in world space for all endpoints, center points, etc., along with the descriptions of the types of entities, are all stored in the file. Knowing that AutoCAD stores designs by keeping coordinate data helps us understand the inputs required to create entities.

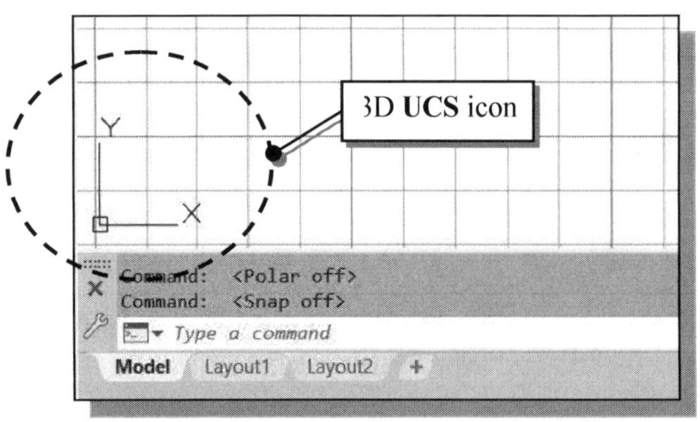

The icon near the bottom left corner of the default AutoCAD graphics window shows the positive X-direction and positive Y-direction of the coordinate system that is active. In AutoCAD, the coordinate system that is used to create entities is called the **user**

coordinate system (UCS). By default, the **user coordinate system** is aligned to the **world coordinate system (WCS)**. The **world coordinate system** is a coordinate system used by AutoCAD as the basis for defining all objects and other coordinate systems defined by the users. We can think of the **origin** of the **world coordinate system** as a fixed point being used as a reference for all measurements. The default orientation of the Z-axis can be considered as positive values in front of the monitor and negative values inside the monitor.

Changing to the 2D UCS Icon Display

In **AutoCAD 2027**, the **UCS** icon is displayed in various ways to help us visualize the orientation of the drawing plane.

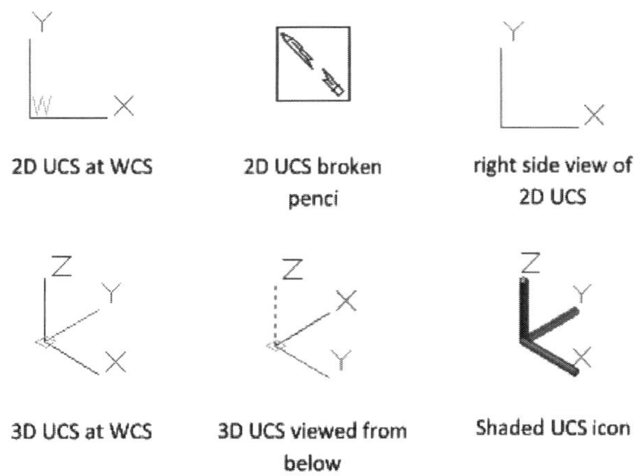

2. Click on the **[View]** pull-down menu and select **[Display] → [UCS Icon] → [Properties…]**

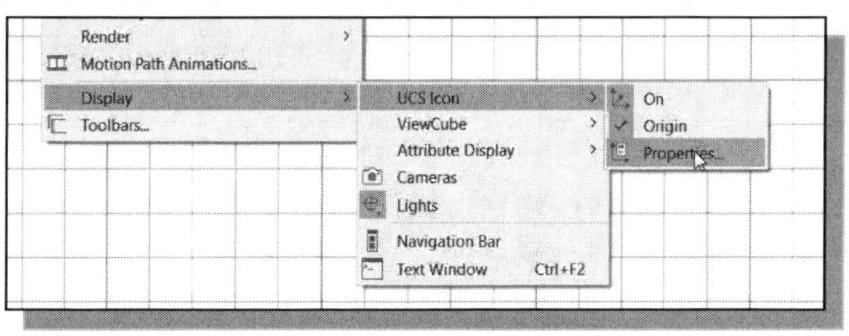

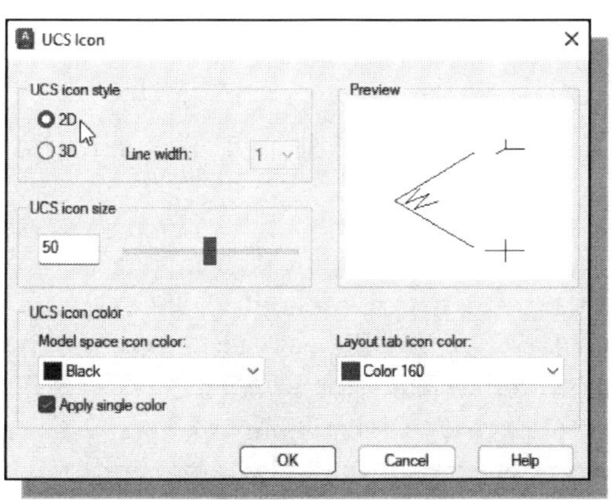

3. In the ***UCS icon style*** section, switch to the **2D** option as shown.

4. Click **OK** to accept the settings.

❖ Note the W symbol in the UCS icon indicates that the UCS is aligned to the **world coordinate system**.

Cartesian and Polar Coordinate Systems

In a two-dimensional space, a point can be represented using different coordinate systems. The point can be located, using a *Cartesian coordinate system*, as X and Y units away from the origin. The same point can also be located using the *polar coordinate system*, as r and θ units away from the origin.

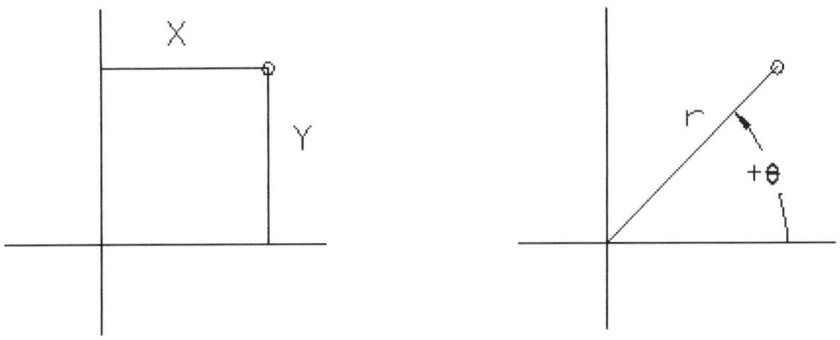

For planar geometry, the polar coordinate system is very useful for certain applications. In the polar coordinate system, points are defined in terms of a radial distance, r, from the origin and an angle θ between the direction of r and the positive X axis. The default system for measuring angles in **AutoCAD 2027** defines positive angular values as counterclockwise from the positive X-axis.

Absolute and Relative Coordinates

AutoCAD 2027 also allows us to use *absolute* and *relative coordinates* to quickly construct objects. **Absolute coordinate values** are measured from the current coordinate system's origin point. **Relative coordinate values** are specified in relation to previous coordinates.

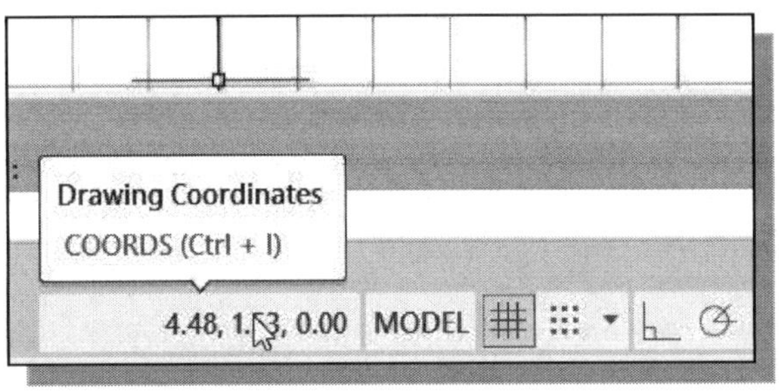

➢ Note that the *coordinate display area* can also be used as a toggle switch; each left-mouse-click will toggle the coordinate display *on* or *off*.

In **AutoCAD 2027**, the *absolute* coordinates and the *relative* coordinates can be used in conjunction with the *Cartesian* and *polar* coordinate systems. By default, AutoCAD expects us to enter values in *absolute Cartesian coordinates*, distances measured from the current coordinate system's origin point. We can switch to using the *relative coordinates* by using the @ symbol. The @ symbol is used as the *relative coordinates specifier*, which means that we can specify the position of a point in relation to the previous point.

Defining Positions

In AutoCAD, there are five methods for specifying the locations of points when we create planar geometric entities.

- **Interactive method**: Use the cursor to select on the screen.
- **Absolute coordinates (Format: X,Y)**: Type the X and Y coordinates to locate the point on the current coordinate system relative to the origin.
- **Relative rectangular coordinates (Format: @X,Y)**: Type the X and Y coordinates relative to the last point.
- **Relative polar coordinates (Format: @Distance<angle)**: Type a distance and angle relative to the last point.
- **Direct Distance entry technique**: Specify a second point by first moving the cursor to indicate direction and then entering a distance.

GRID Style Setup

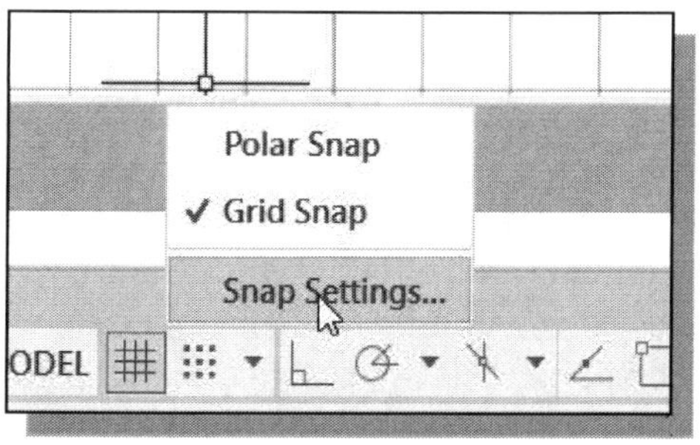

1. In the *Status Bar* area, **right-mouse-click** on ***Snap Mode*** and choose **[Snap settings]**.

2. In the *Drafting Settings* dialog box, select the **Snap and Grid** tab if it is not the page on top.

3. Change *Grid Style* to ***Display dotted grid in 2D model Space*** as shown in the below figure.

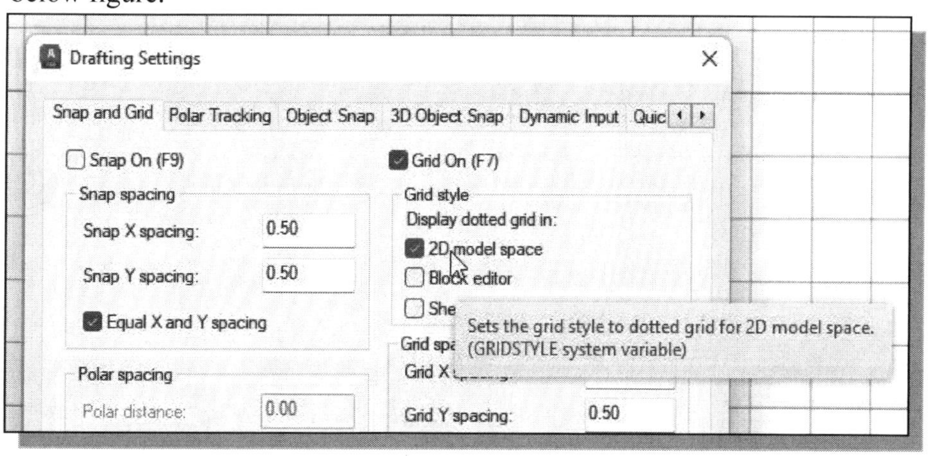

4. Pick **OK** to exit the *Drafting Settings* dialog box.

The Guide Plate

We will next create a mechanical design using the different coordinate entry methods.

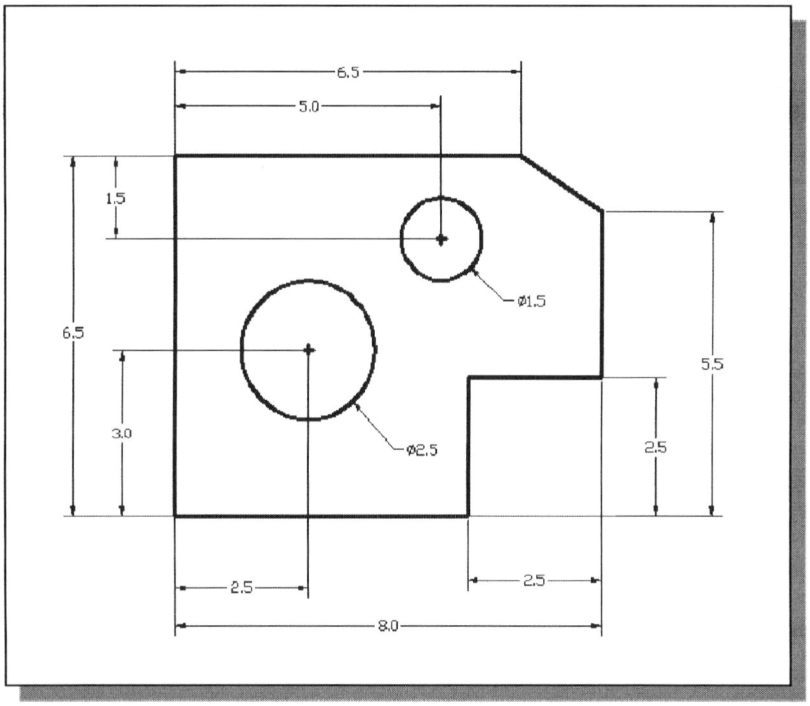

❖ The rule for creating CAD designs and drawings is that they should be created at **full size** using real-world units. The CAD database contains all the definitions of the geometric entities, and the design is considered as a virtual, full-sized object. Only when a printer or plotter transfers the CAD design to paper is the design scaled to fit on a sheet. The tedious task of determining a scale factor so that the design will fit on a sheet of paper is taken care of by the CAD system. This allows the designers and CAD operators to concentrate their attention on the more important issues – the design.

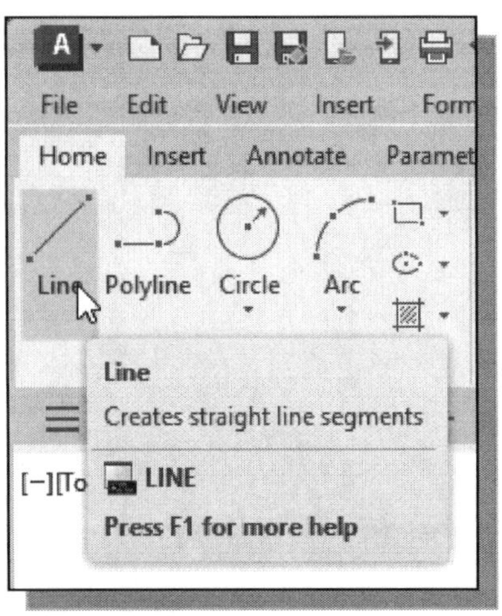

1. Select the **Line** command icon in the *Draw* toolbar. In the command prompt area, near the bottom of the AutoCAD graphics window, the message "*Line Specify first point:*" is displayed. AutoCAD expects us to identify the starting location of a straight line.

2. We will locate the starting point of our design at the origin of the *world coordinate system.*

   Command: Line Specify first point: **0,0**
   (Type ***0,0*** and press the [**ENTER**] key once.)

3. We will create a horizontal line by entering the absolute coordinates of the second point.
   Specify next point or [Undo]: **5.5,0 [ENTER]**

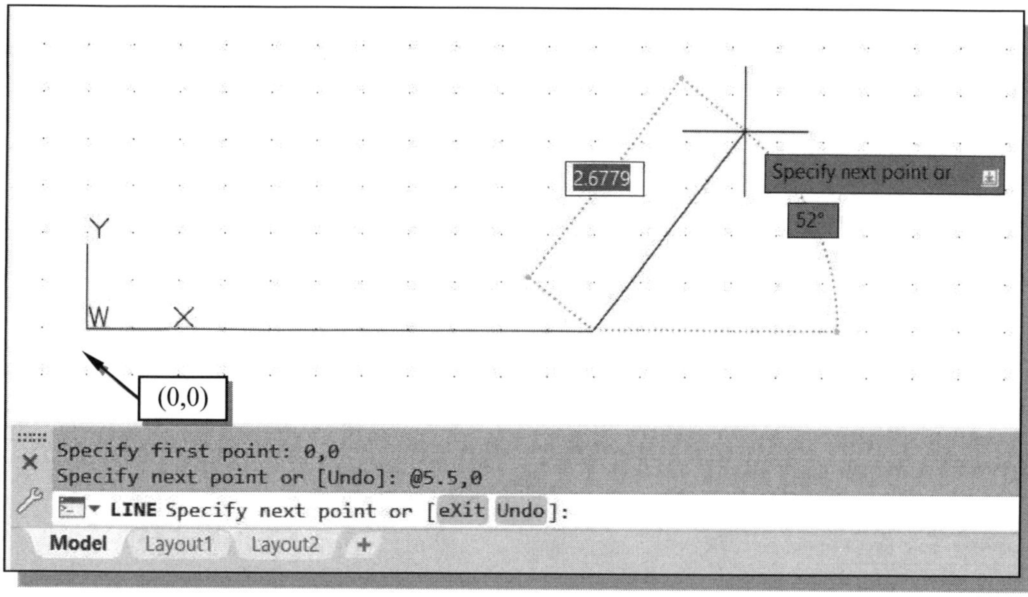

- Note that the line we created is aligned to the bottom edge of the drawing window. Let us adjust the view of the line by using the Pan Realtime command.

4. In the *Menu Bar* area select: **[View] → [Pan] → [Realtime]**

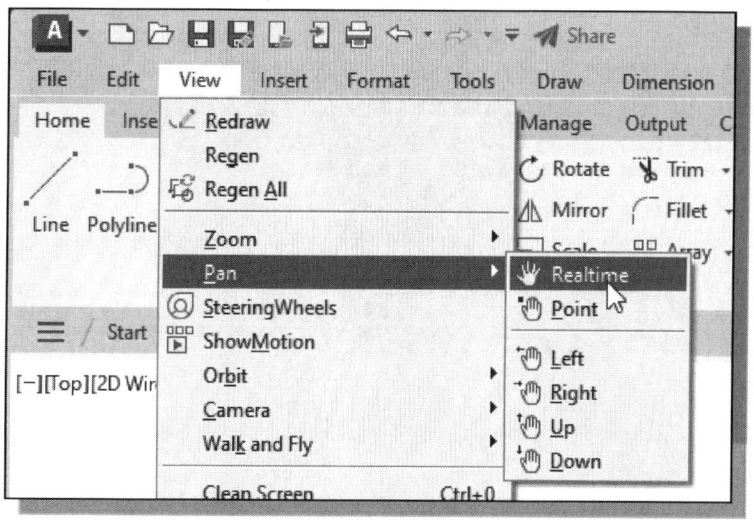

❖ The available **Pan** commands enable us to move the view to a different position. The *Pan-Realtime* function acts as if you are using a video camera.

5. Move the cursor, which appears as a hand inside the graphics window, near the center of the drawing window, then push down the **left-mouse-button** and drag the display toward the right and top side until we can see the sketched line. (Notice the scroll bars can also be used to adjust viewing of the display.)

6. Press the **[Esc]** key to exit the *Pan-Realtime* command. Notice that AutoCAD goes back to the Line command.

7. We will create a vertical line by using the *relative rectangular coordinates entry method*, relative to the last point we specified:
   Specify next point or [Close/Undo]: **@0,2.5 [ENTER]**

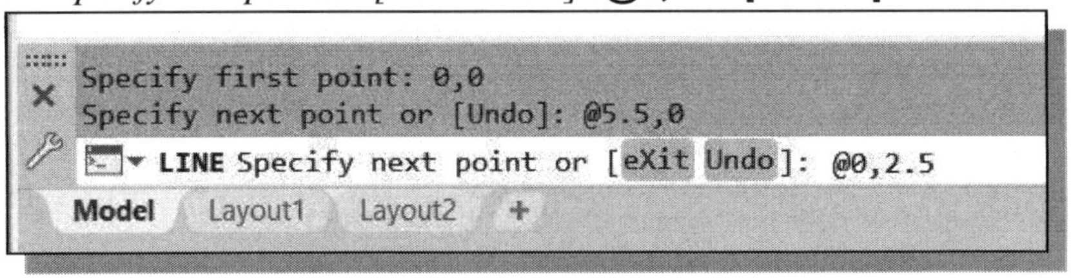

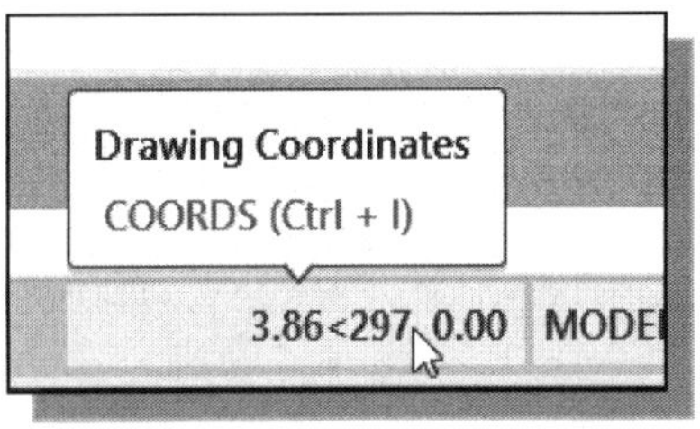

8. Left-click once on the *coordinates display area* to switch to a different coordinate display option. Click again to see the other option. Note the coordinates display has changed to show the length of the new line and its angle. Each click will change the display format of the cursor coordinates.

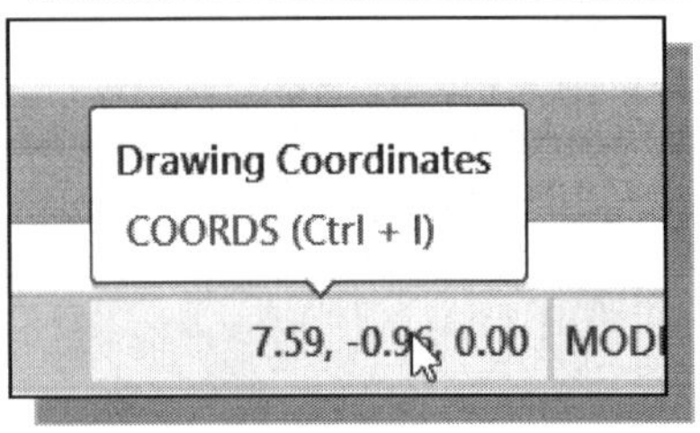

9. On your own, left-click on the coordinates display area to observe the switching of the coordinate display; set the display back to using the world coordinate system.

10. We can mix any of the entry methods in positioning the locations of the endpoints. Move the cursor to the *Status Bar* area, and turn ***ON*** the *SNAP MODE* option.

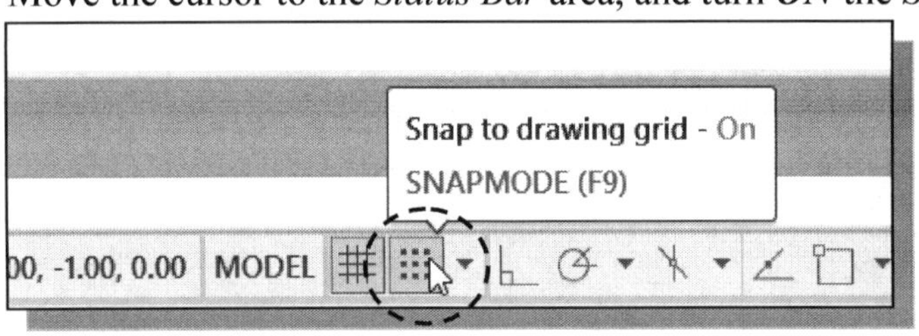

❖ Note that the Line command is resumed as the settings are adjusted.

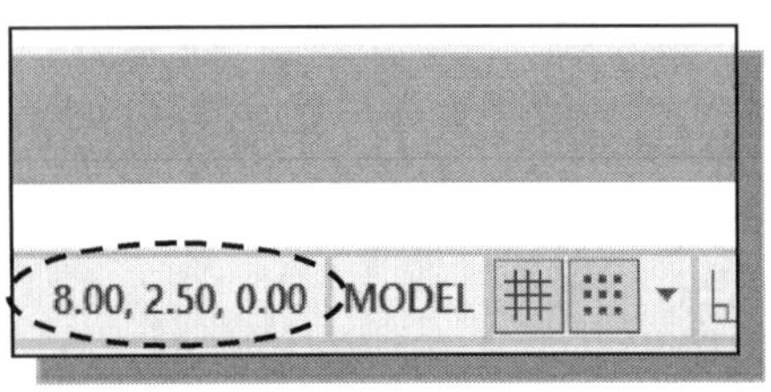

11. Create the next line by picking the location, world coordinates ***(8,2.5)***, on the screen.

12. We will next use the *relative polar coordinates entry method*; distance is ***3*** inches with an angle of ***90*** degrees, relative to the last point we specified:
    Specify next point or [Close/Undo]: **@3<90 [ENTER]**

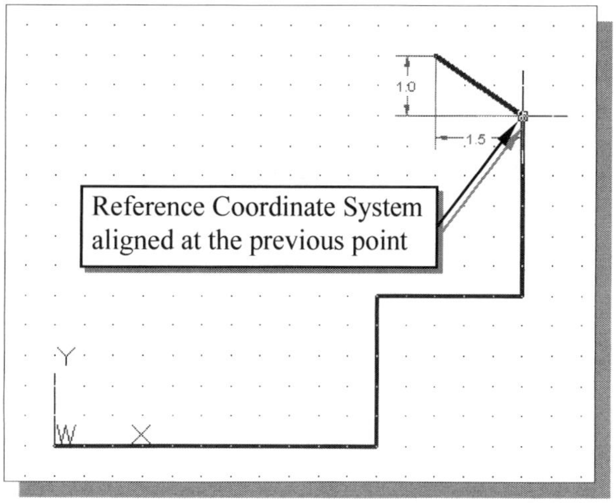

13. Using the *relative rectangular coordinates entry method* to create the next line, we can imagine a *reference coordinate system* aligned at the previous point. Coordinates are measured along the two reference axes.

Specify next point or [Close/Undo]:
@-1.5,1 **[ENTER]**

(***-1.5*** and ***1*** inches are measured relative to the reference point.)

14. Move the cursor directly to the left of the last point and use the *direct distance entry technique* by entering ***6.5*** **[ENTER]**.

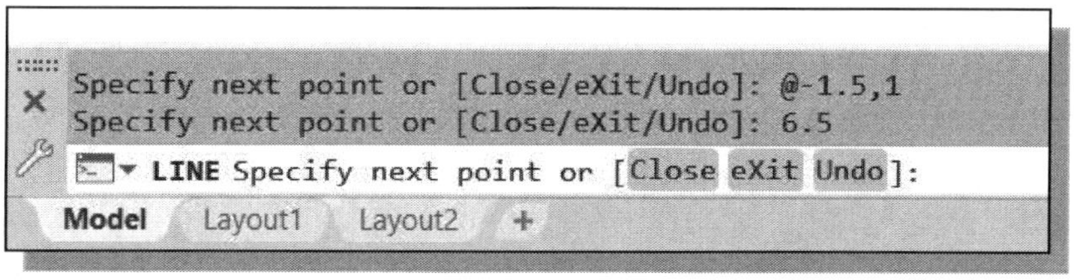

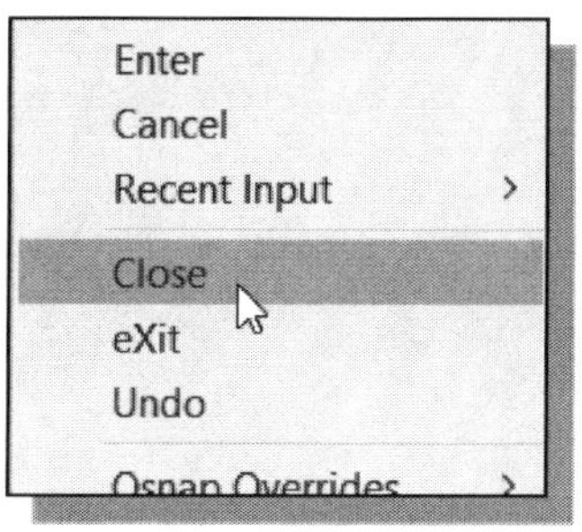

15. For the last segment of the sketch, we can use the **Close** option to connect back to the starting point. Inside the graphics window, **right-mouse-click** and a *pop-up menu* appears on the screen.

16. Select **Close** with the left-mouse-button to connect back to the starting point and end the Line command.

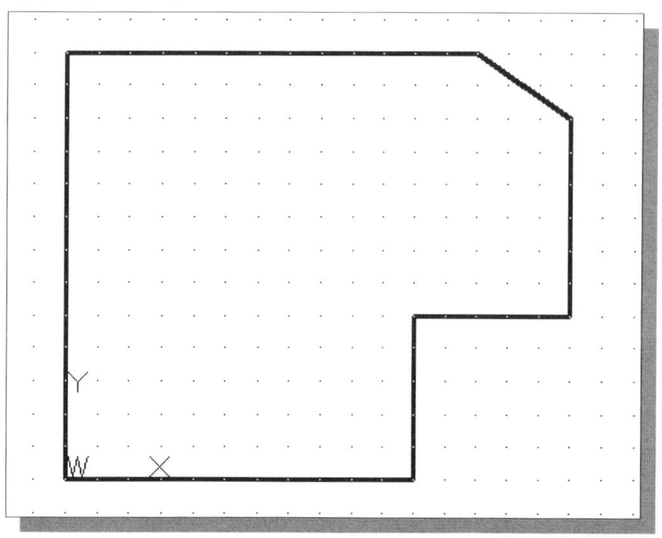

Creating Circles

The menus and toolbars in **AutoCAD 2027** are designed to allow the CAD operator to quickly activate the desired commands.

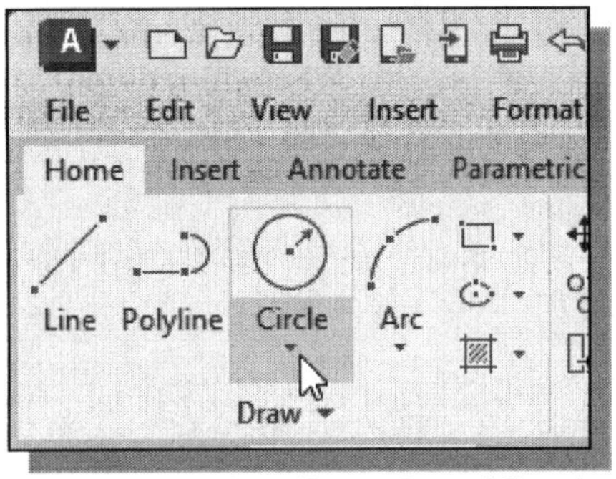

1. In the *Draw* toolbar, click on the little triangle below the circle icon. Note that the little triangle indicates additional options are available.

2. In the option list, select: **[Center, Diameter]**

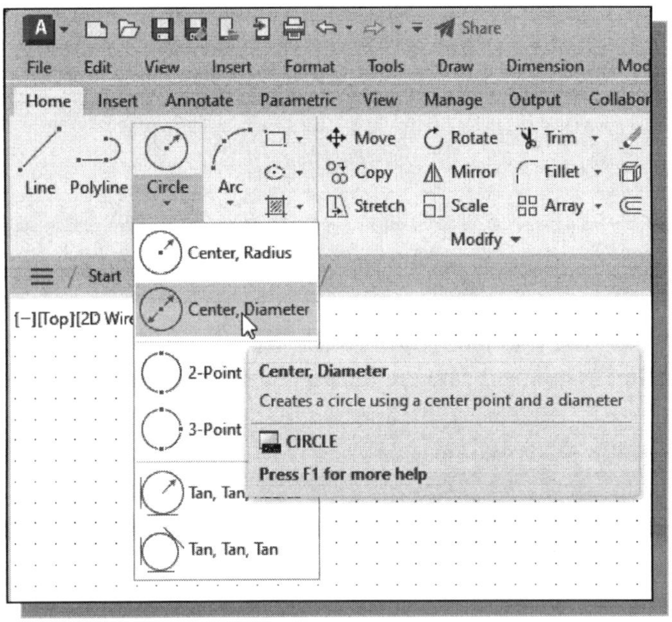

Notice the different options available under the circle submenu:

- **Center, Radius**: Draws a circle based on a center point and a radius.
- **Center, Diameter**: Draws a circle based on a center point and a diameter.
- **2 Points**: Draws a circle based on two endpoints of the diameter.
- **3 Points**: Draws a circle based on three points on the circumference.
- **TTR–Tangent, Tangent, Radius**: Draws a circle with a specified radius tangent to two objects.
- **TTT–Tangent, Tangent, Tangent**: Draws a circle tangent to three objects.

3. In the command prompt area, the message "*Specify center point for circle or [3P/2P/Ttr (tan tan radius)]:*" is displayed. AutoCAD expects us to identify the location of a point or enter an option. We can use any of the four coordinate entry methods to identify the desired location. We will enter the **world coordinates (*2.5,3*)** as the center point for the first circle.

   Specify center point for circle or [3P/2P/Ttr (tan tan radius)]: **2.5,3 [ENTER]**

4. In the command prompt area, the message "*Specify diameter of circle:*" is displayed.
   Specify diameter of circle: **2.5 [ENTER]**

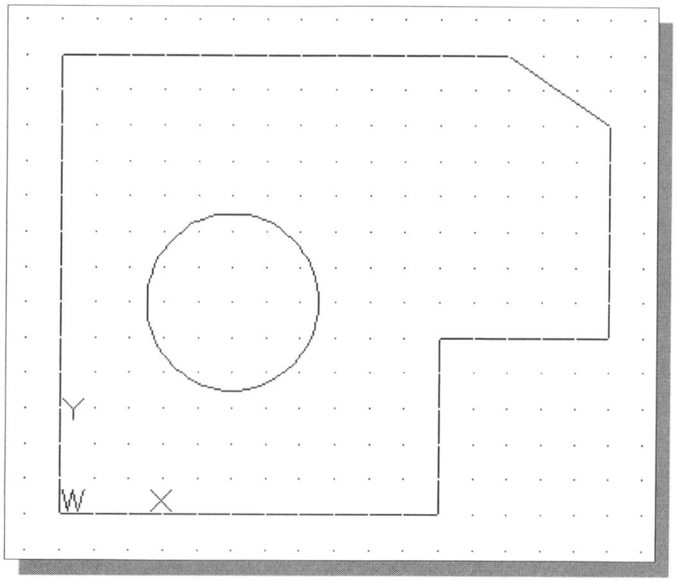

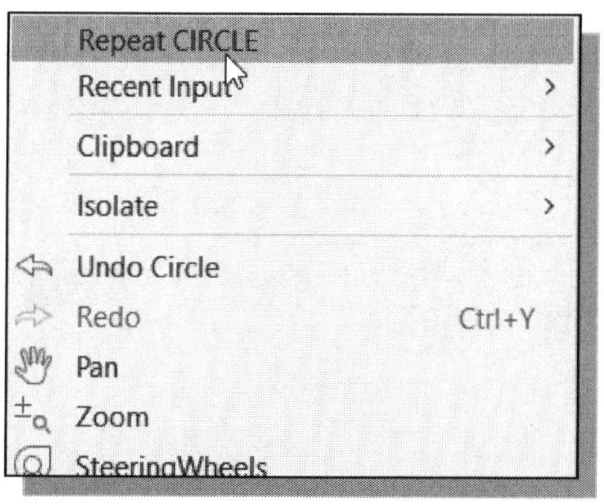

5. Inside the graphics window, right-mouse-click to bring up the pop-up option menu.

6. Pick **Repeat CIRCLE** with the left-mouse-button in the pop-up menu to repeat the last command.

7. Using the *relative rectangular coordinates entry method*, relative to the center-point coordinates of the first circle, we specify the relative location as **(@*2.5,2*)**.

Specify center point for circle or [3P/2P/Ttr (tan tan radius)]: **@2.5,2 [ENTER]**

8. In the command prompt area, the message "*Specify Radius of circle: <2.50>*" is displayed. The default option for the **Circle** command in AutoCAD is to specify the *radius* and the last radius used is also displayed in brackets.

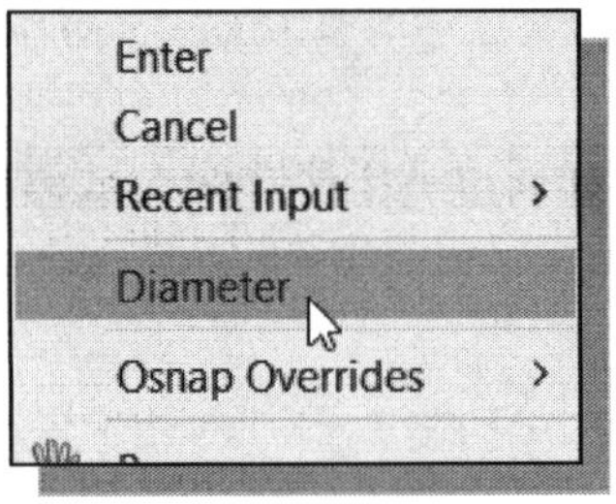

9. Inside the graphics window, **right-mouse-click** to bring up the pop-up option menu and select **Diameter** as shown.

10. In the command prompt area, enter ***1.5*** as the diameter.

Specify Diameter of circle<2.50>: **1.5 [ENTER]**

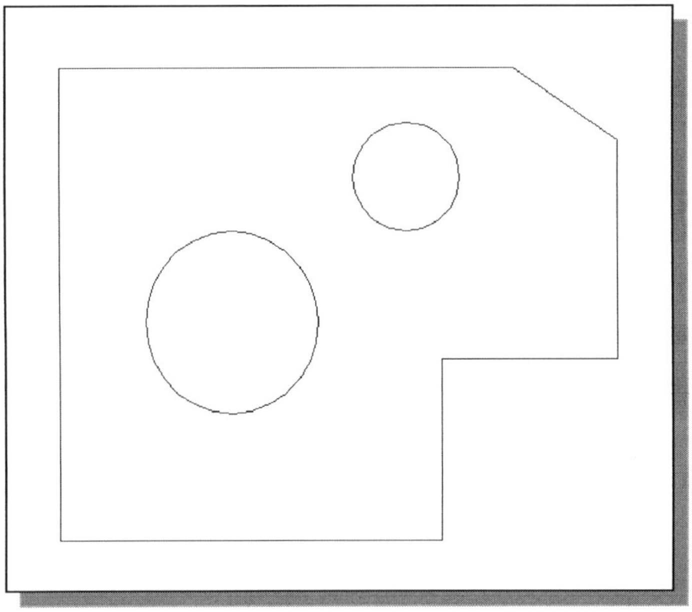

Save the CAD Design

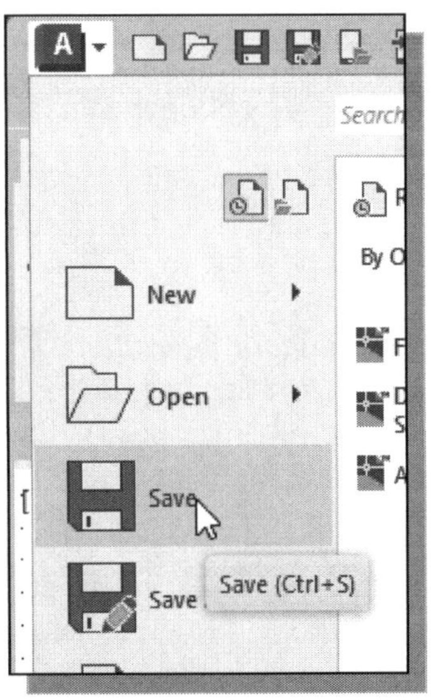

1. In the *Application Menu*, select:

[Application] → [Save]

❖ Note the command can also be activated with the quick-key combination of **[Ctrl]+[S]**.

2. In the *Save Drawing As* dialog box, select the folder in which you want to store the CAD file and enter ***GuidePlate*** in the *File name* box.

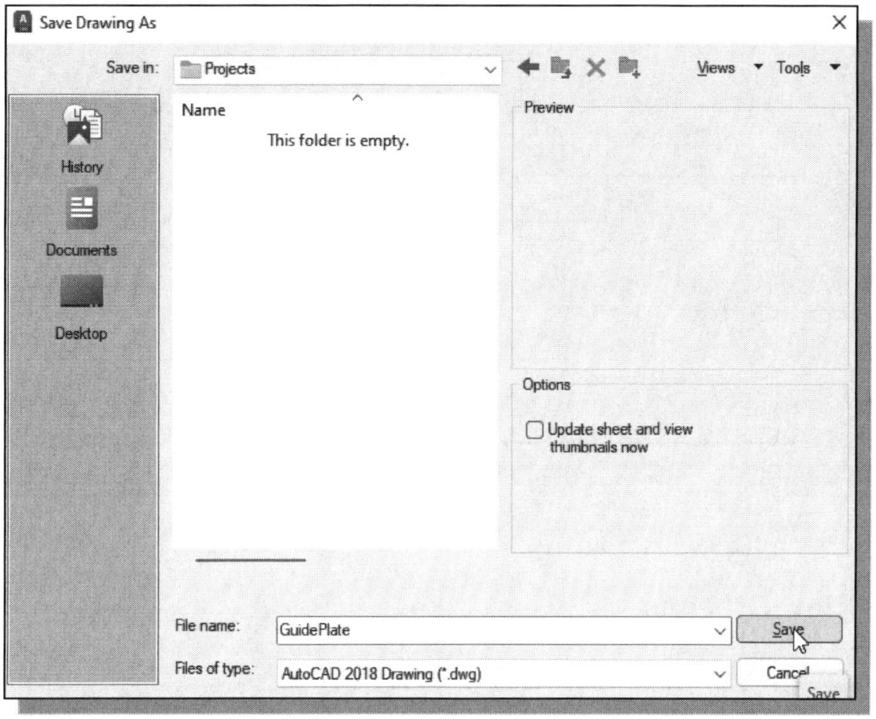

3. Click **Save** in the *Save Drawing As* dialog box to accept the selections and save the file. Note the default file type is DWG, which is the standard AutoCAD drawing format.

Close the Current Drawing

Several options are available to close the current drawing:

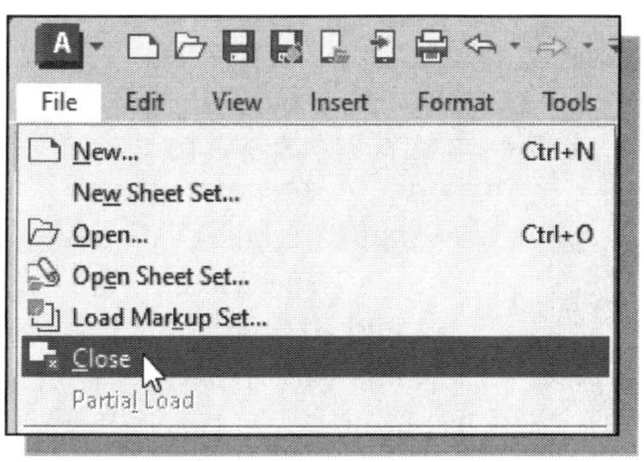

- Select **[File] → [Close]** in the *Pull-down Menu* as shown.

- Enter **Close** at the command prompt.

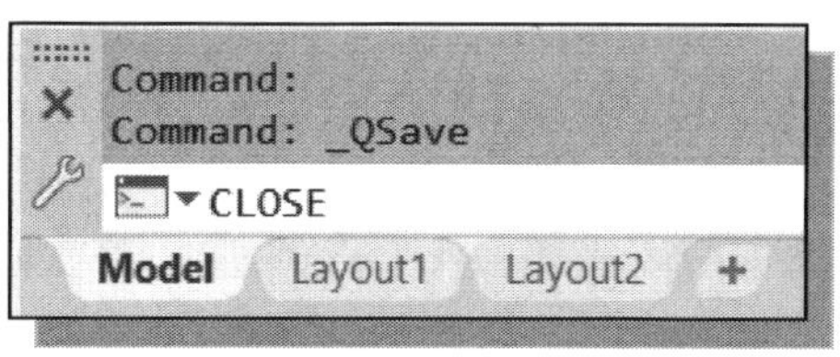

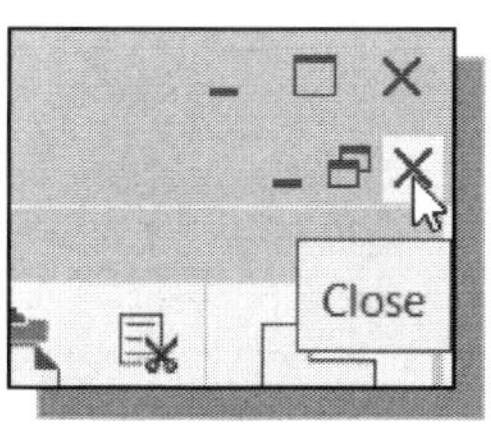

- Another option is to click on the **[Close]** icon located at the upper-right-hand corner of the drawing window.

The Spacer Design

We will next create the spacer design using more of AutoCAD's drawing tools.

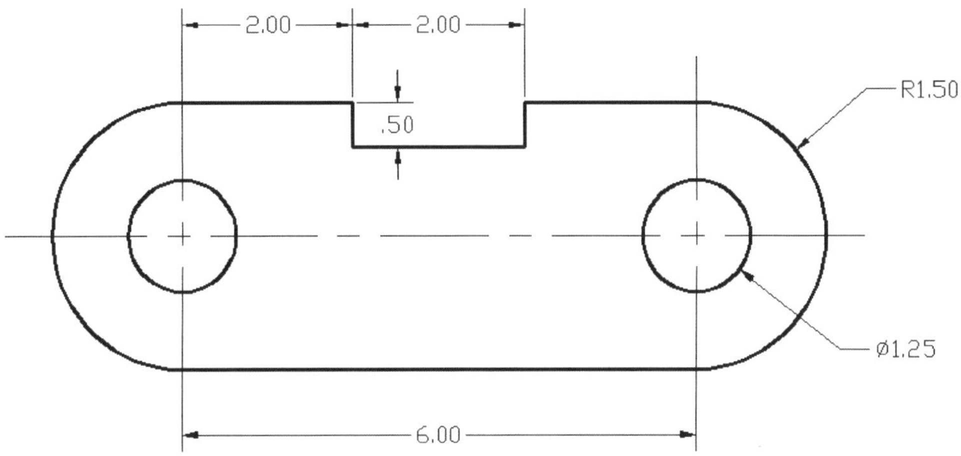

Start a New Drawing

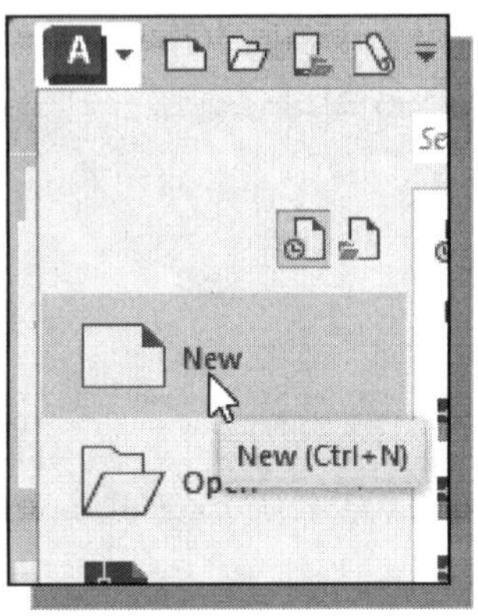

1. In the *Application Menu*, select **[New]** to start a new drawing.

2. The **Select Template** dialog box appears on the screen. Click **Open** to accept the default **acad.dwt** as the template to open.

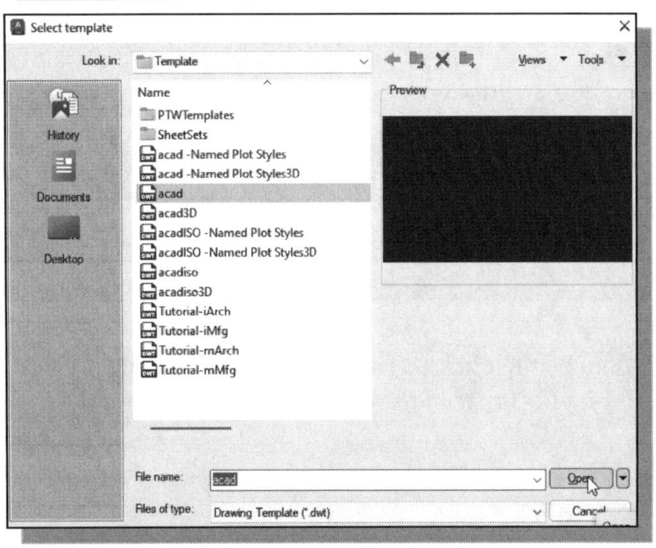

➢ The dwt file type is the AutoCAD template file format. An AutoCAD template file contains pre-defined settings to reduce the amount of tedious repetitions.

Drawing Units Setup

Every object we construct in a CAD system is measured in **units**. We should determine the system of units within the CAD system before creating the first geometric entities.

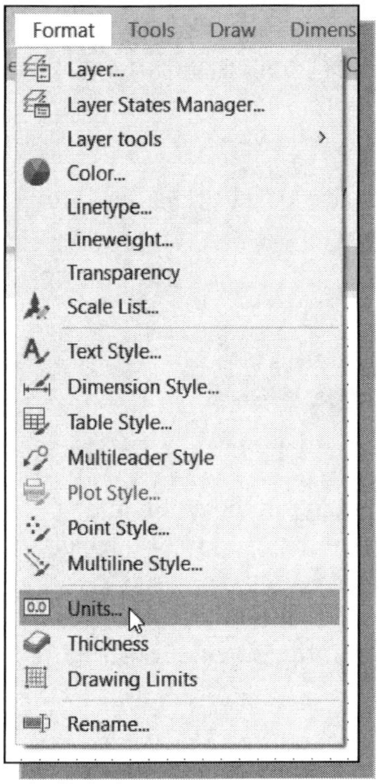

1. In the *Menu Bar* select:
   [Format] → [Units]

- The AutoCAD *Menu Bar* contains multiple pull-down menus where all of the AutoCAD commands can be accessed. Note that many of the menu items listed in the pull-down menus can also be accessed through the *Quick Access* toolbar and/or *Ribbon* panels.

2. Click on the *Length Type* option to display the different types of length units available. Confirm the *Length Type* is set to **Decimal**.

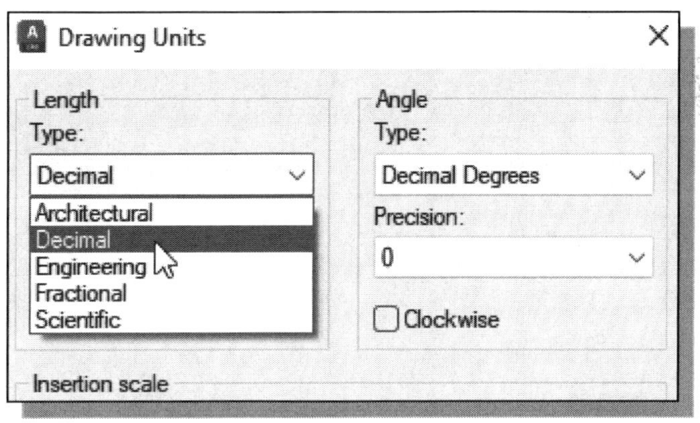

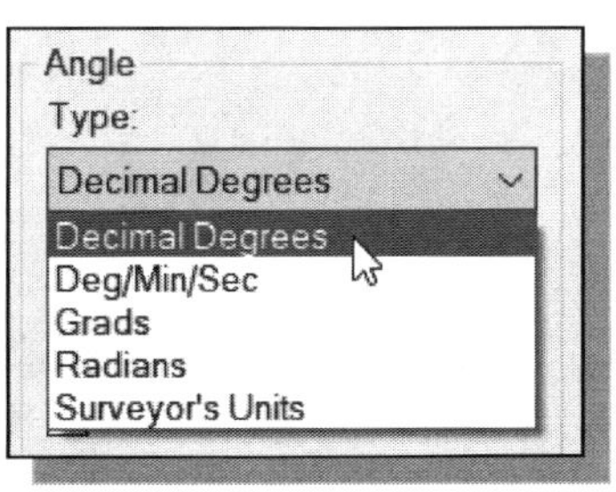

3. On your own, examine the other settings that are available.

4. In the *Drawing Units* dialog box, set the *Length Type* to **Decimal**. This will set the measurement to the default *English* units, inches.

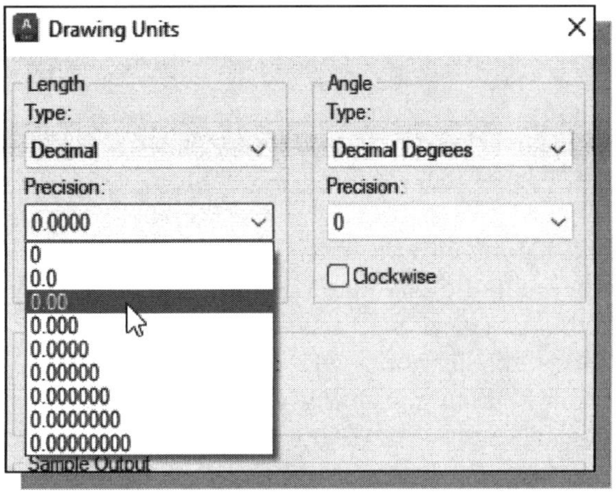

5. Set the *Precision* to **two digits** after the decimal point as shown in the above figure.

6. Pick **OK** to exit the *Drawing Units* dialog box.

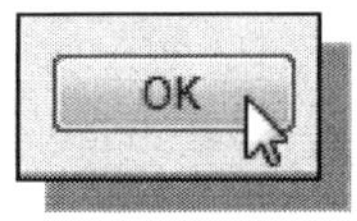

Drawing Area Setup

Next, we will set up the **Drawing Limits** by entering a command in the command prompt area. Setting the Drawing Limits controls the extents of the display of the *grid*. It also serves as a visual reference that marks the working area. It can also be used to prevent construction outside the grid limits and as a plot option that defines an area to be plotted/printed. Note that this setting does not limit the region for geometry construction.

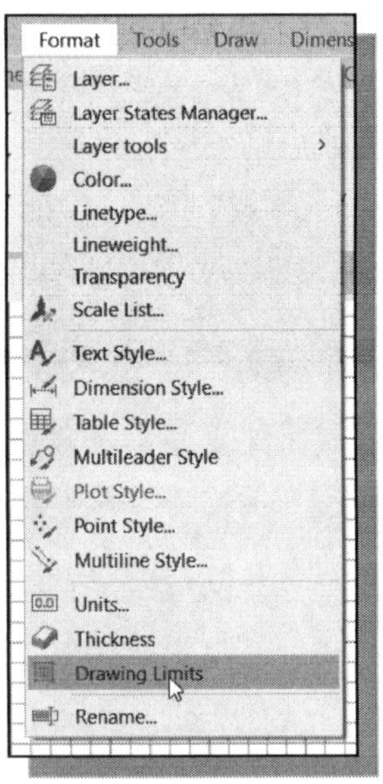

1. In the *Menu Bar* select:
   [Format] → [Drawing Limits]

2. In the command prompt area, the message "*Reset Model Space Limits: Specify lower left corner or [On/Off] <0.00,0.00>:*" is displayed. Press the **ENTER** key once to accept the default coordinates <**0.00,0.00**>.

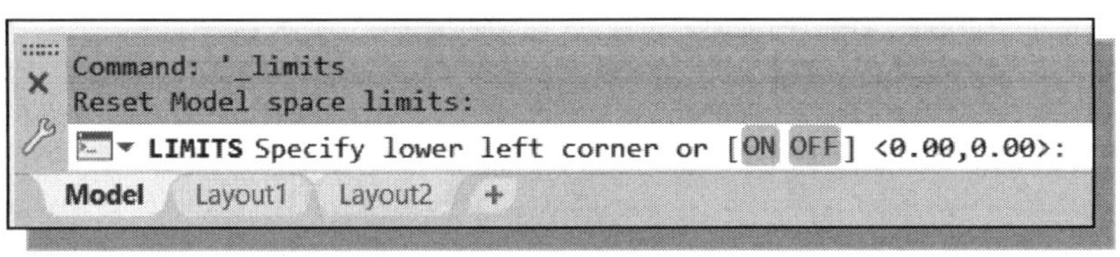

3. In the command prompt area, the message "*Specify upper right corner <12.00,9.00>:*" is displayed. Press the **ENTER** key again to accept the default coordinates <**12.00,9.00**>.

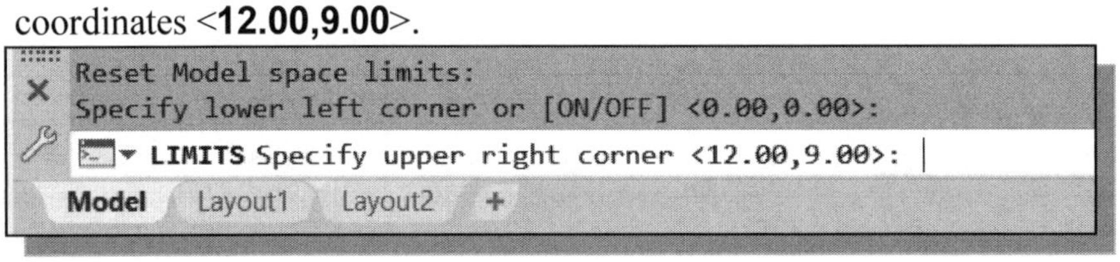

4. On your own, move the graphics cursor near the upper-right corner inside the drawing area and note that the drawing area is unchanged. (The Drawing Limits command is used to set the drawing area, but the display will not be adjusted until a display command is used.)

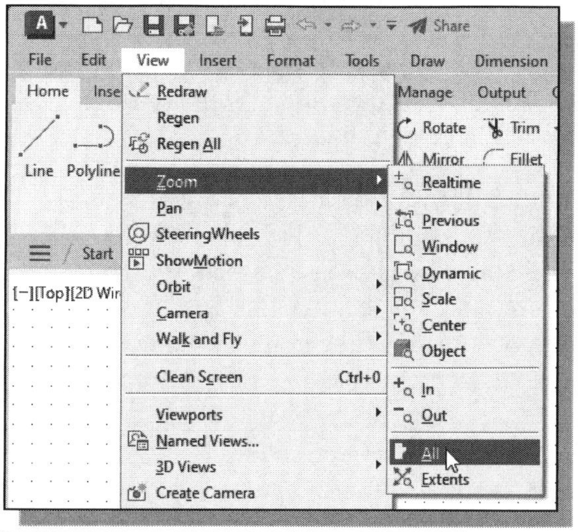

5. Inside the *Menu Bar* area select:
[View] → [Zoom] → [All]

❖ The **Zoom All** command will adjust the display so that all objects in the drawing are displayed to be as large as possible. If no objects are constructed, the Drawing Limits are used to adjust the current viewport.

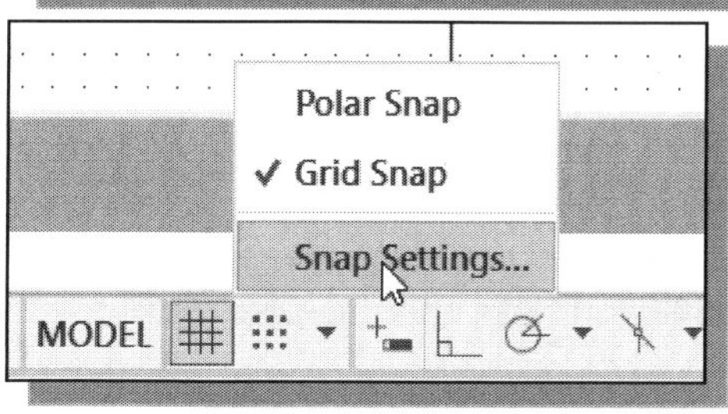

6. Move the graphics cursor near the upper-right corner inside the drawing area, and note that the display area is updated.

7. In the *Status Bar* area, **right-mouse-click** on ***SnapMode*** and choose **[Snap Settings]**.

8. In the *Drafting Settings dialog box*, switch **on** the **Snap** and **Grid** options as shown.

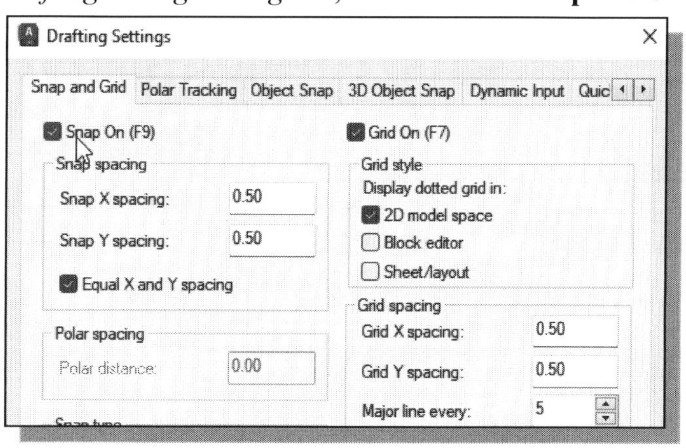

➢ On your own, exit the *Drafting Settings dialog box* and confirm that only ***GRID DISPLAY*** and ***SNAP MODE*** are turned ***ON*** as shown.

Use the Line Command

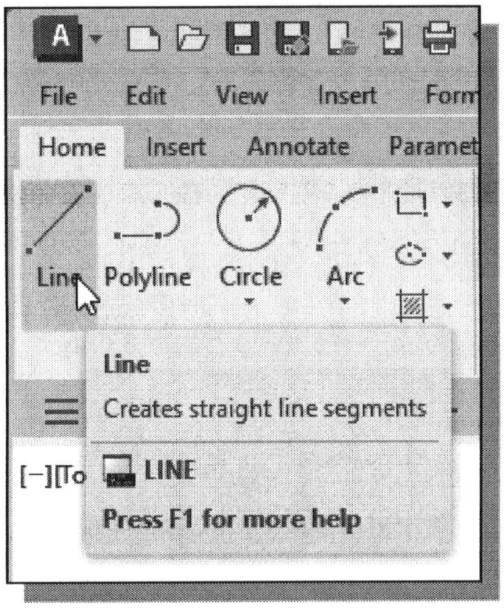

1. Select the **Line** command icon in the *Draw* toolbar. In the command prompt area, near the bottom of the AutoCAD graphics window, the message "*Line Specify first point:*" is displayed. AutoCAD expects us to identify the starting location of a straight line.

2. To further illustrate the usage of the different input methods and tools available in AutoCAD, we will **start the line segments at an arbitrary location**. Start at a location that is somewhere in the lower left side of the graphics window.

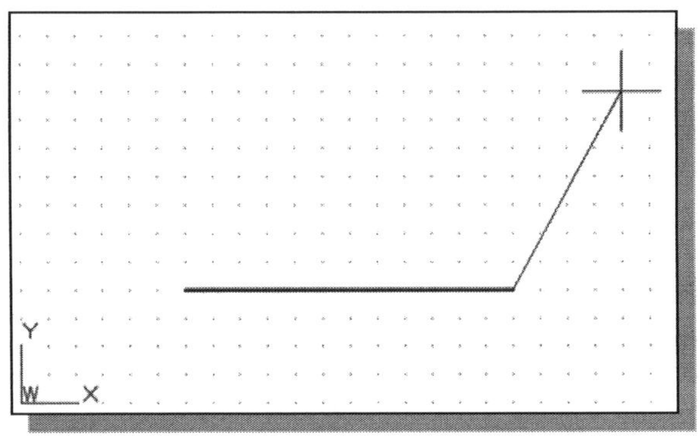

3. We will create a horizontal line by using the *relative rectangular coordinates entry method*, relative to the last point we specified:
   @6,0 [ENTER]

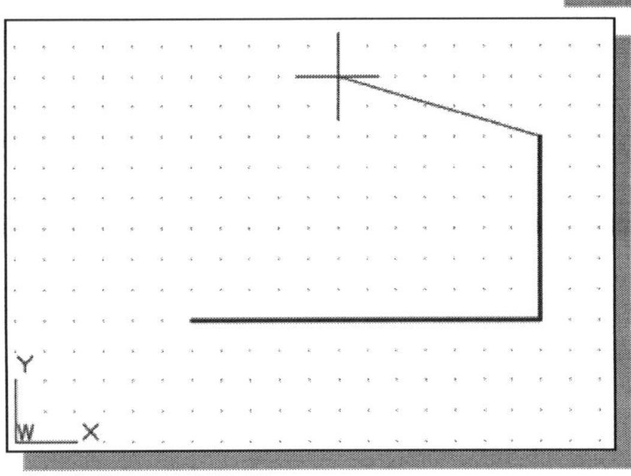

4. Next, create a vertical line by using the *relative polar coordinates entry method*, relative to the last point we specified: **@3<90 [ENTER]**

5. Next, we will use the direct input method. First, move the cursor directly to the left of the last endpoint of the line segments.

6. On your own, turn the mouse wheel to zoom in and drag with the middle mouse to reposition the display.

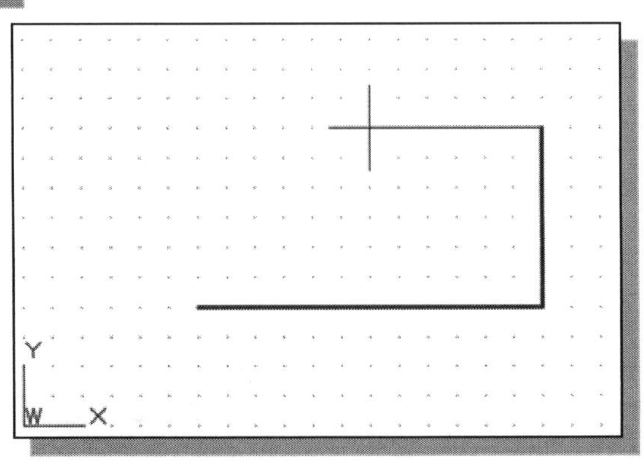

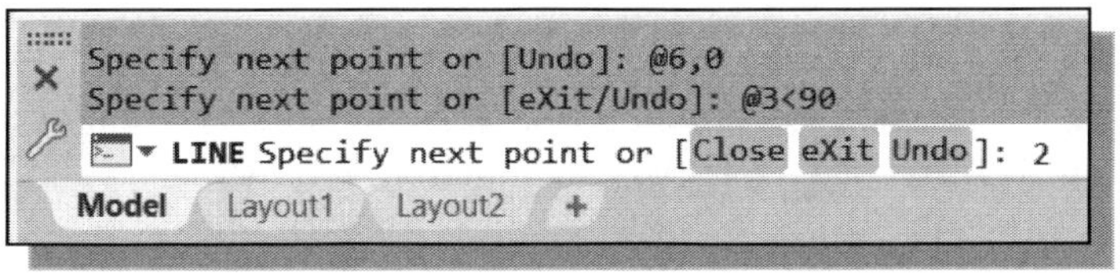

7. Use the *direct distance entry technique* by entering **2 [ENTER]**.

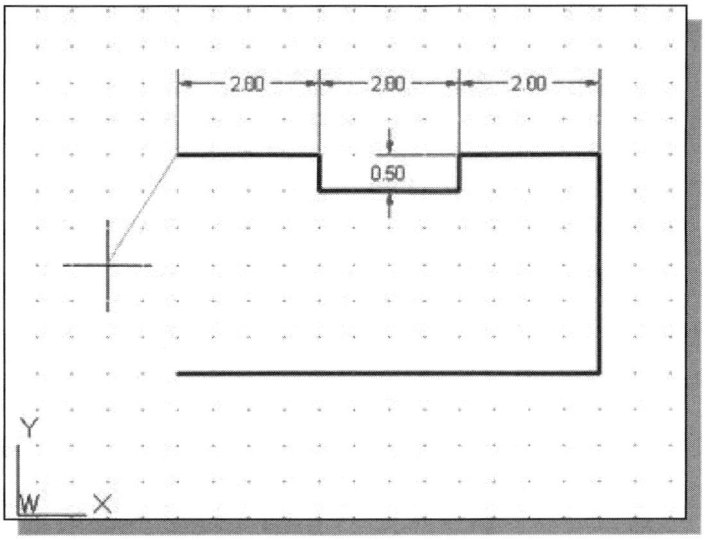

8. On your own, repeat the above steps and create the four additional line segments, using the dimensions as shown.

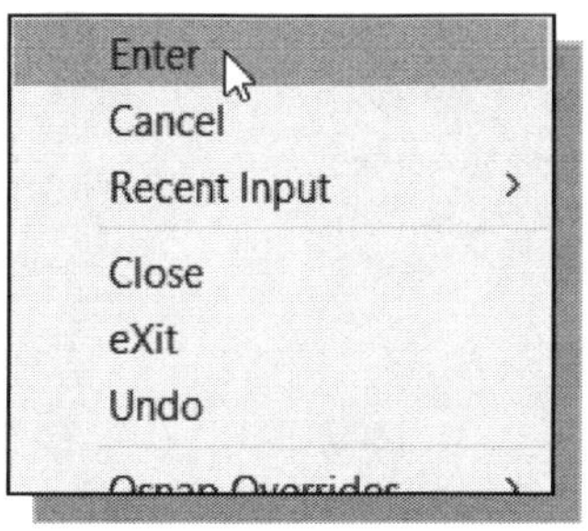

- To end the line command, we can either hit the [Enter] key on the keyboard or use the **Enter** option, **right-mouse-click** and a *pop-up menu* appears on the screen.

9. On your own, end the Line command.

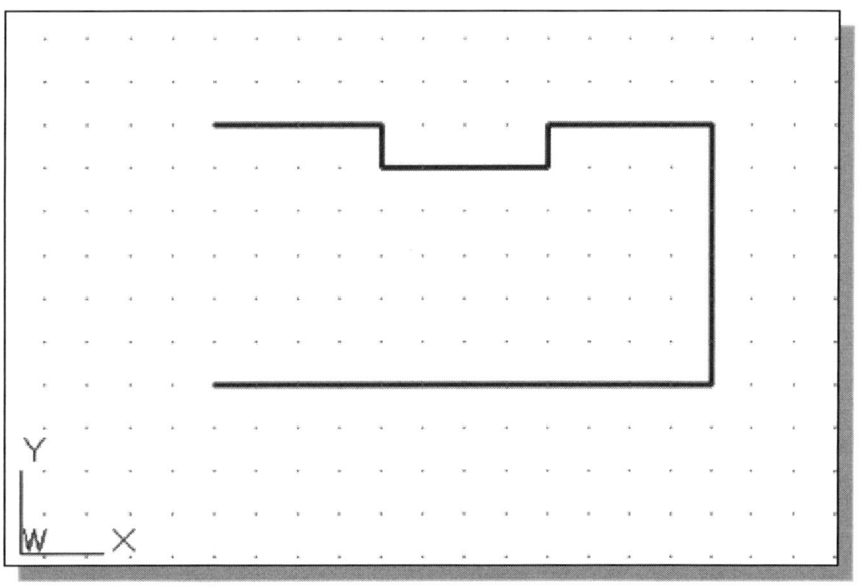

Use the Erase Command

The vertical line on the right was created as a construction line to aid the construction of the rest of the lines for the design. We will use the **Erase** command to remove it.

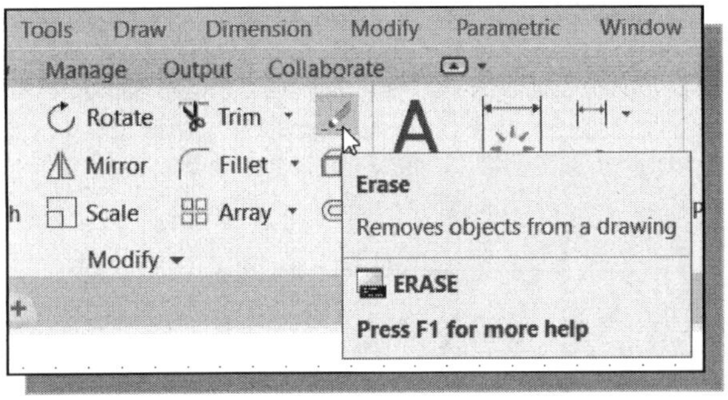

1. Pick **Erase** in the *Modify* toolbar. The message "*Select objects*" is displayed in the command prompt area and AutoCAD awaits us to select the objects to erase.

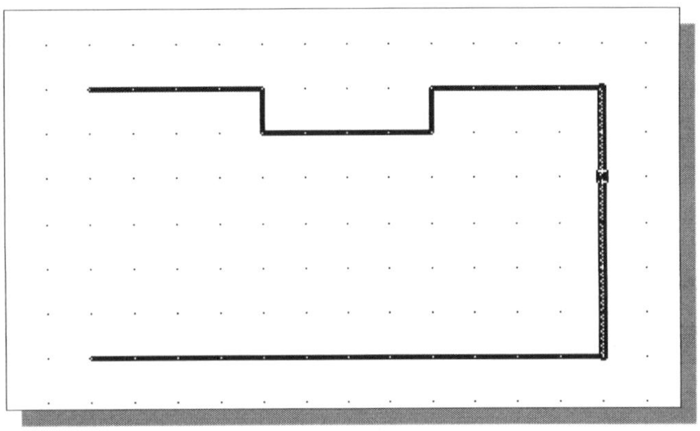

2. Select the vertical line as shown.

3. Click once with the **right-mouse-button** to accept the selection and delete the line.

Using the Arc Command

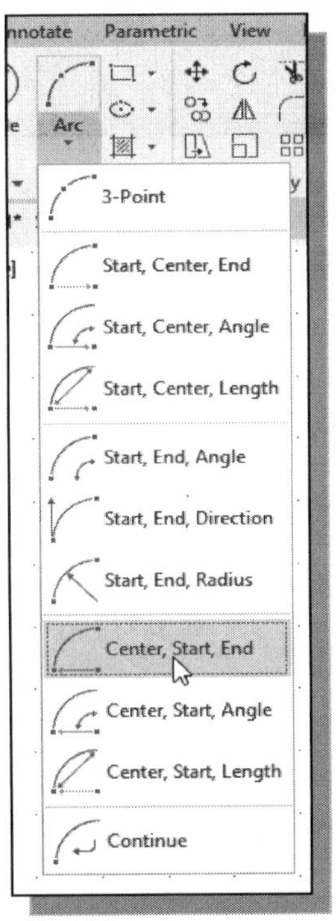

1. Click the down-arrow icon of the **Arc** command in the *Draw* toolbar to display the different Arc construction options.

➢ AutoCAD provides eleven different ways to create arcs. Note that the different options are used based on the geometry conditions of the design. The more commonly used options are the **3-Points** option and the **Center-Start-End** option.

2. Select the **Center-Start-End** option as shown. This option requires the selection of the center point, start point and end point location, in that order, of the arc.

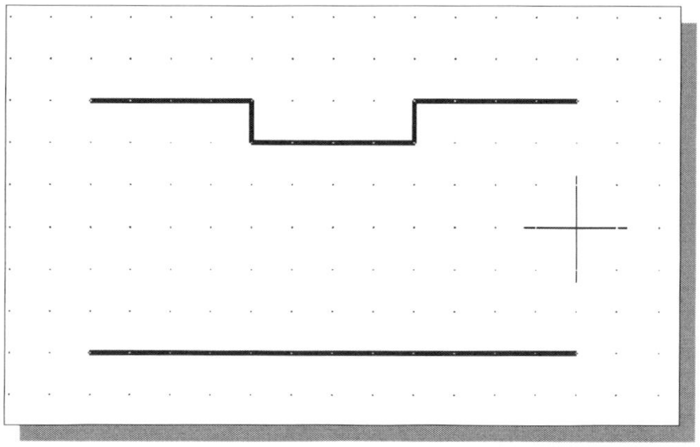

3. Move the cursor to the middle of the two horizontal lines and align the cursor to the two endpoints as shown. Click once with the **right-mouse-button** to select the location as the center point of the new arc.

4. Move the cursor downward and select the right endpoint of the bottom horizontal line as the start point of the arc.

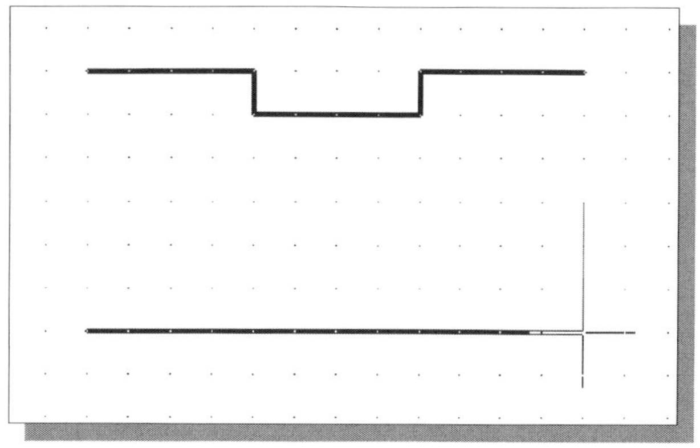

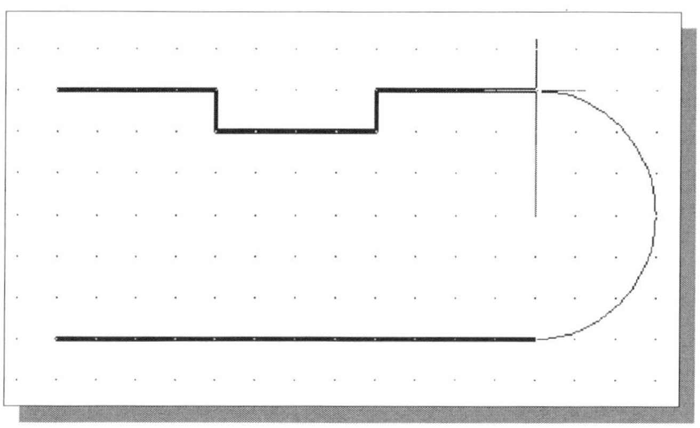

5. Move the cursor to the right endpoint of the top horizontal line as shown. Pick this point as the endpoint of the new arc.

6. On your own, repeat the above steps and create the other arc as shown. Note that in most CAD packages, positive angles are defined as going counterclockwise; therefore, the starting point of the second arc should be at the endpoint on top.

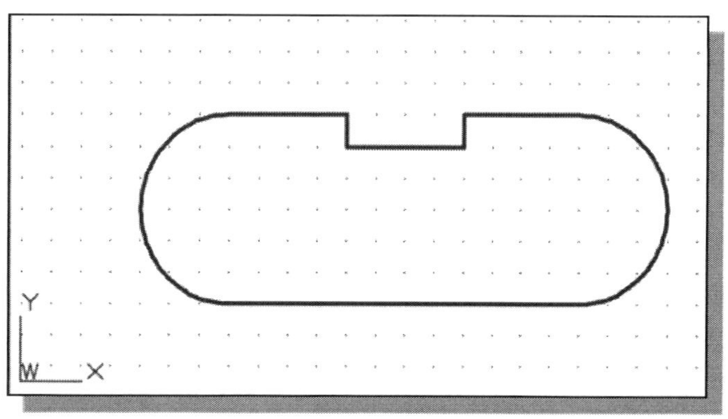

Using the Circle Command

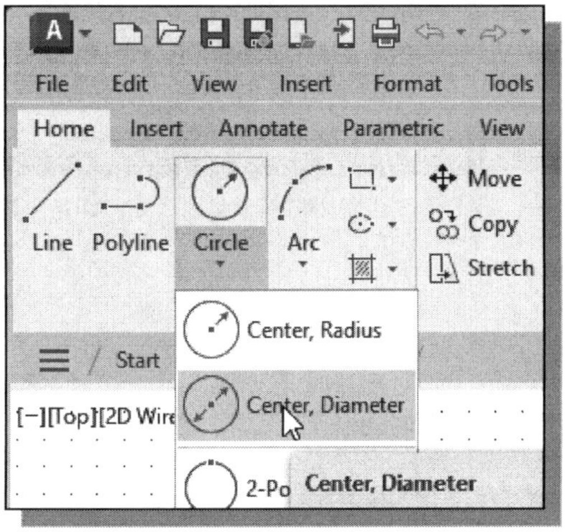

1. Select the **[Circle] → [Center, Diameter]** option as shown.

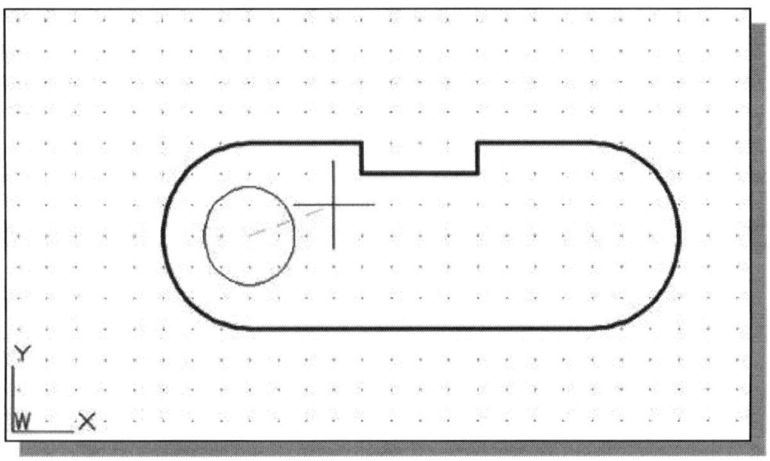

2. Select the same location for the arc center as the center point for the new circle.

3. In the command prompt area, the message "*Specify diameter of circle:*" is displayed. *Specify diameter of circle:* **1.25 [ENTER]**

4. On your own, create the other circle and complete the drawing as shown.

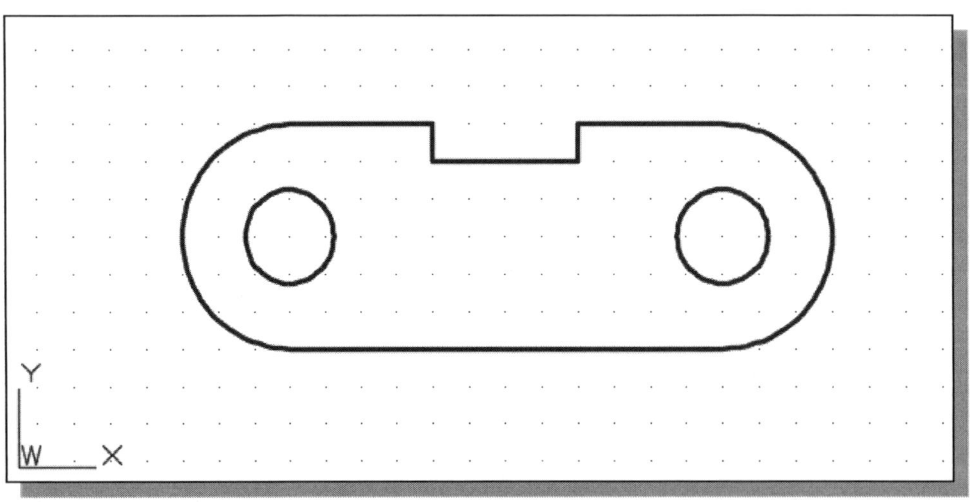

Saving the CAD Design

1. In the *Quick Access Toolbar*, select **[Save]**.

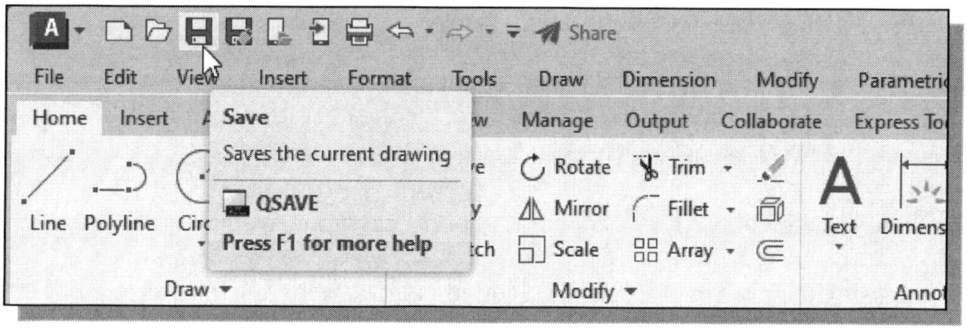

❖ Note the command can also be activated with the quick-key combination of **[Ctrl]+[S]**.

2. In the *Save Drawing As* dialog box, select the folder in which you want to store the CAD file and enter ***Spacer*** in the *File name* box.

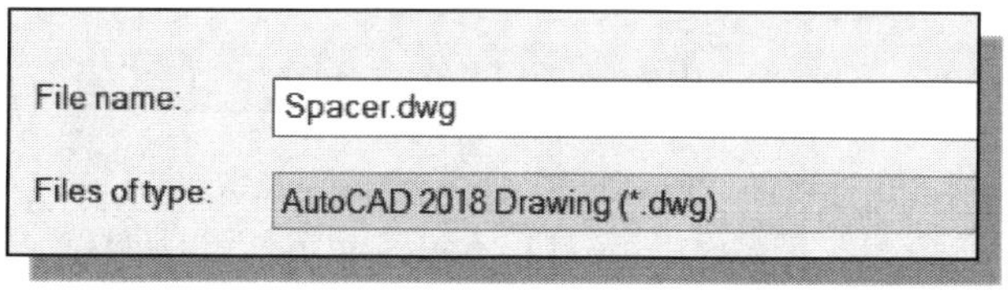

3. Click **Save** in the *Save Drawing As* dialog box to accept the selections and save the file. Note the default file type is DWG, which is the standard AutoCAD drawing format.

Exit AutoCAD 2027

❖ To exit **AutoCAD 2027**, select **Exit AutoCAD** in the *Menu Bar* or type ***QUIT*** at the command prompt. Note the command can also be activated with the quick-key combination of **[Ctrl]+[Q]**.

Review Questions: (Time: 20 minutes)

1. What are the advantages and disadvantages of using CAD systems to create engineering drawings?

2. What is the default AutoCAD filename extension?

3. How do the ***GRID*** and ***SNAP*** options assist us in sketching?

4. List and describe the different **coordinate entry methods** available in AutoCAD.

5. When using the Line command, which option allows us to quickly create a line-segment connecting back to the starting point?

6. List and describe the two types of coordinate systems commonly used for planar geometry.

7. Which key do you use to quickly cancel a command?

8. When you use the Pan command, do the coordinates of objects get changed?

9. Find information on how to draw ellipses in AutoCAD through the *Autodesk Exchange*, and create the following arc. If it is desired to position the center of the ellipse to a specific location, which ellipse command is more suitable?

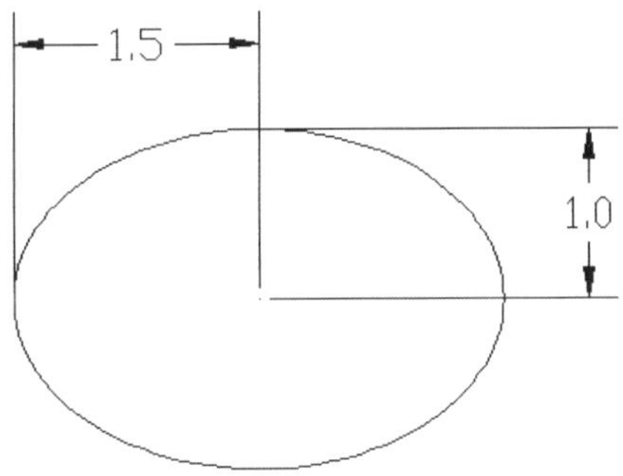

10. Find information on how to draw arcs in AutoCAD through the *Autodesk Exchange* and create the following arc. List and describe two methods to create arcs in AutoCAD.

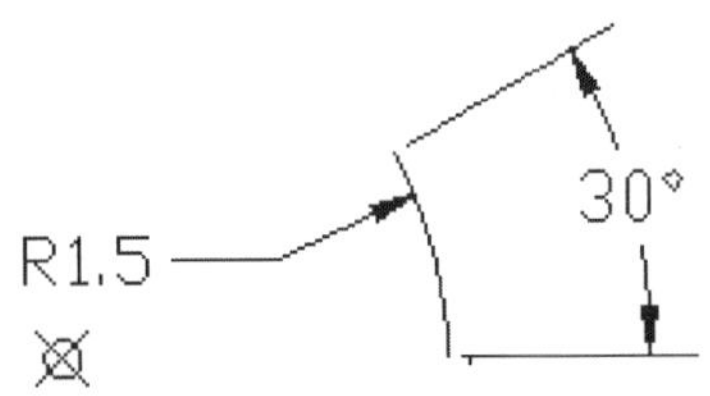

Exercises:

(All dimensions are in inches.) (Time: 90 minutes)

1. Angle Spacer

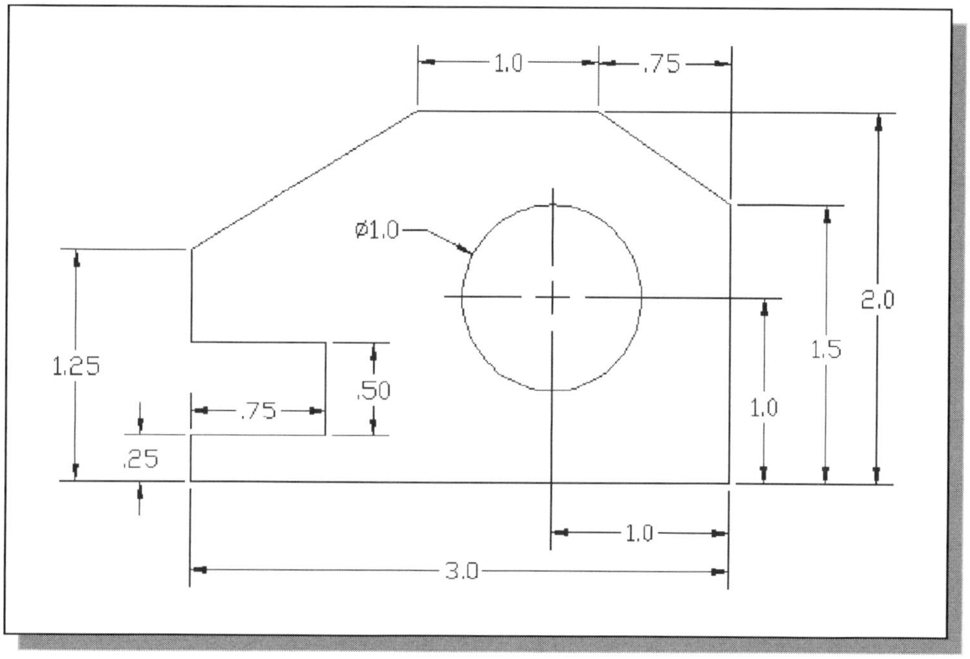

2. Base Plate

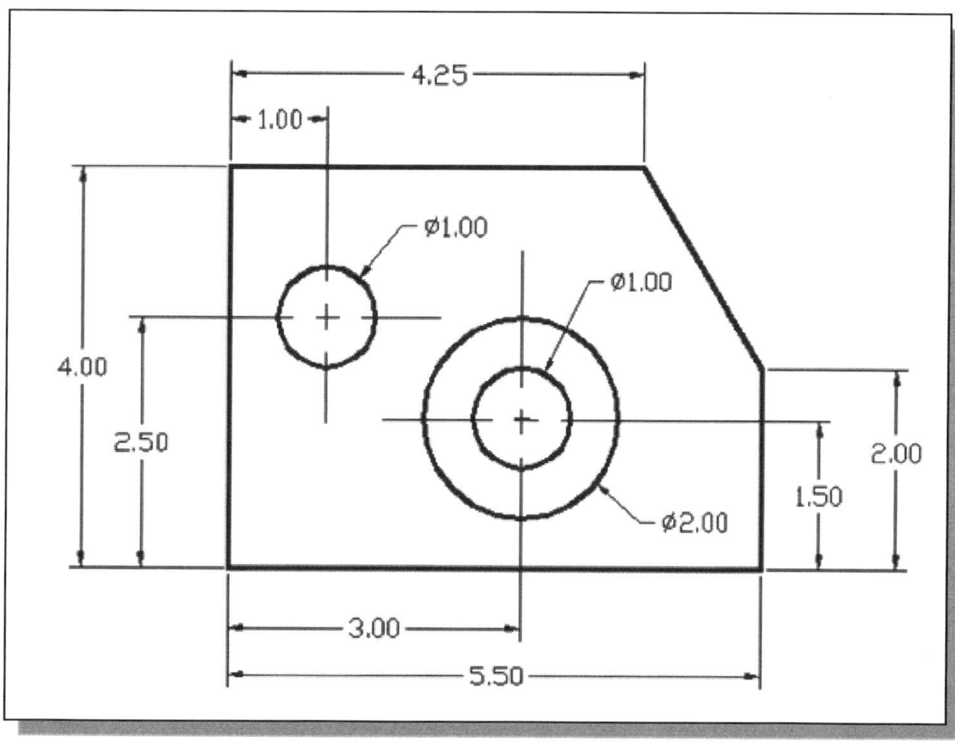

3. T-Clip

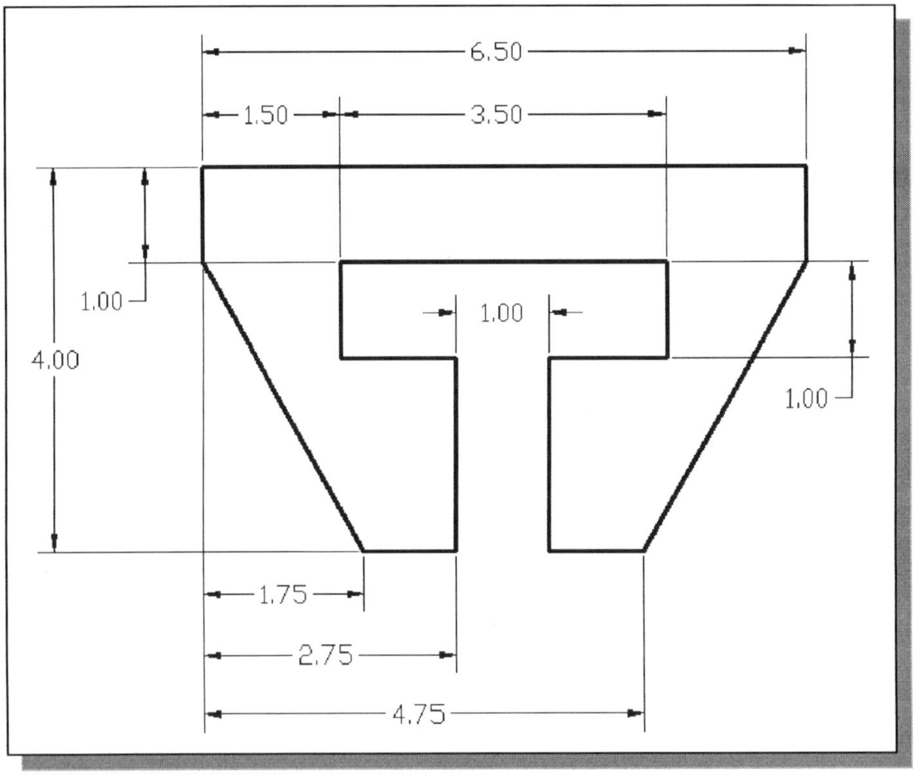

4. Channel Plate

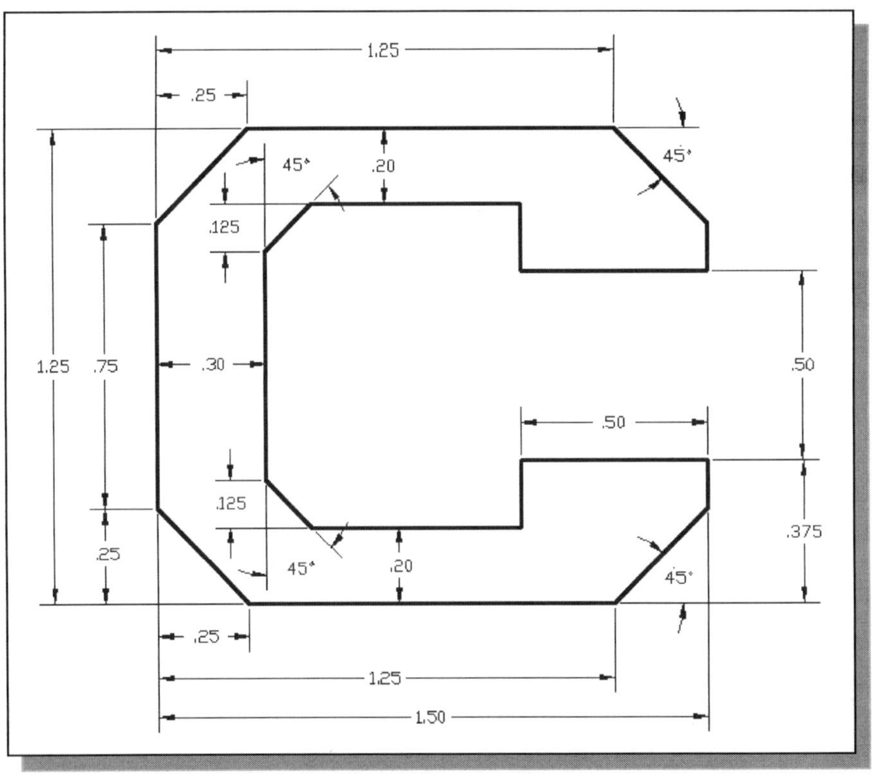

5. Slider Block

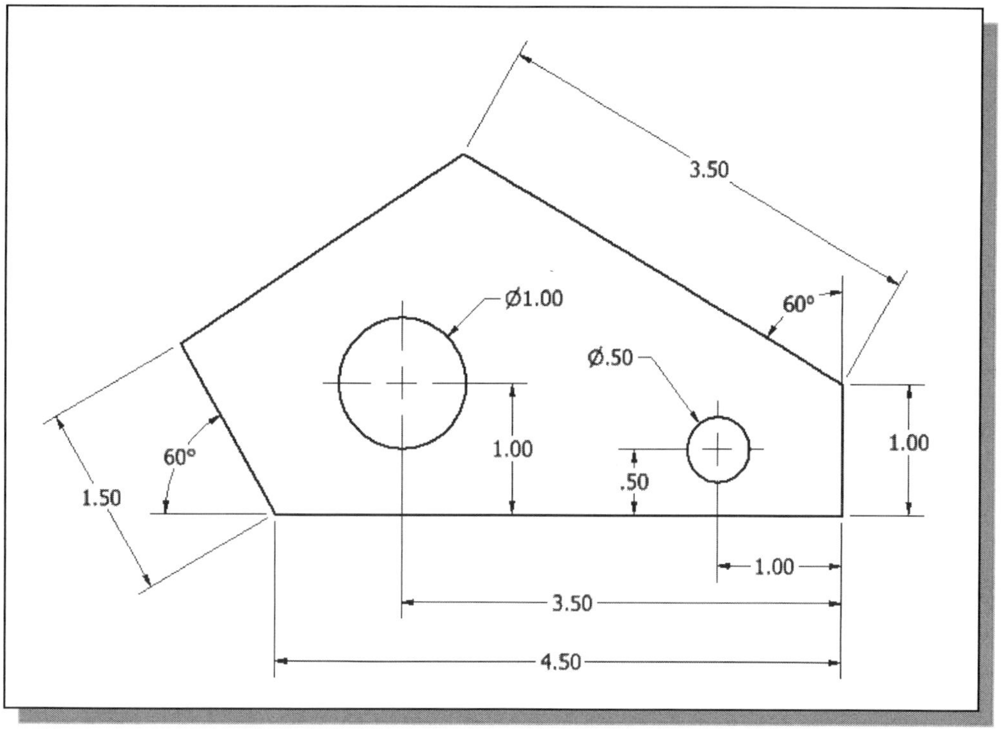

6. Circular Spacer

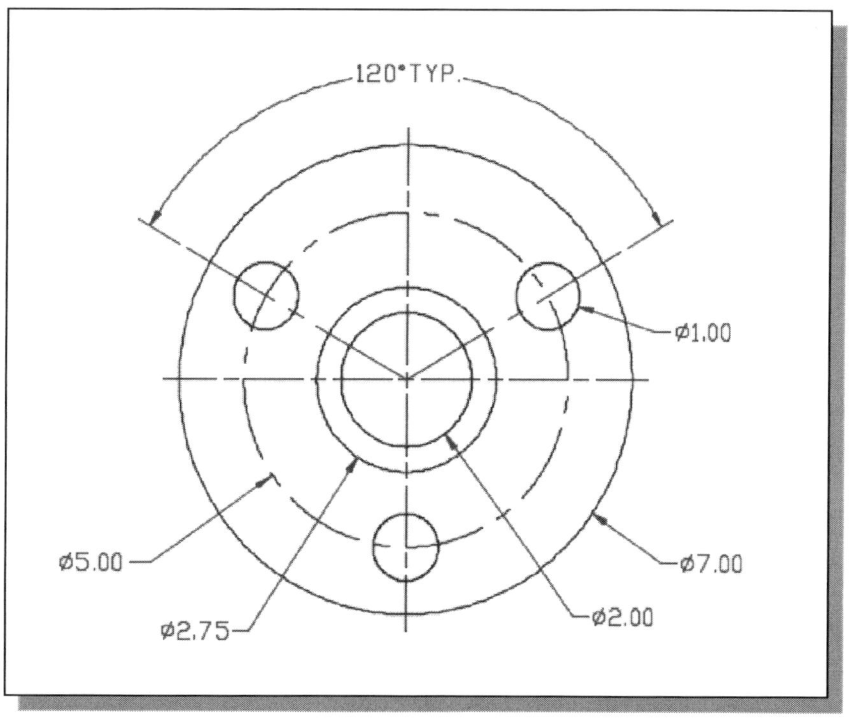

7. Angle Base

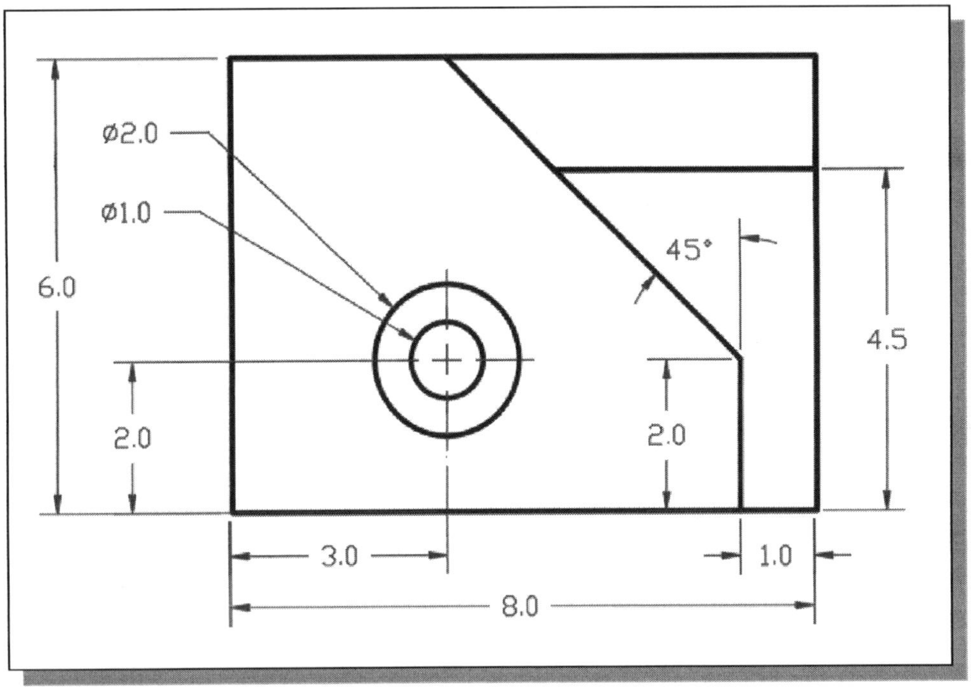

8. Index Key

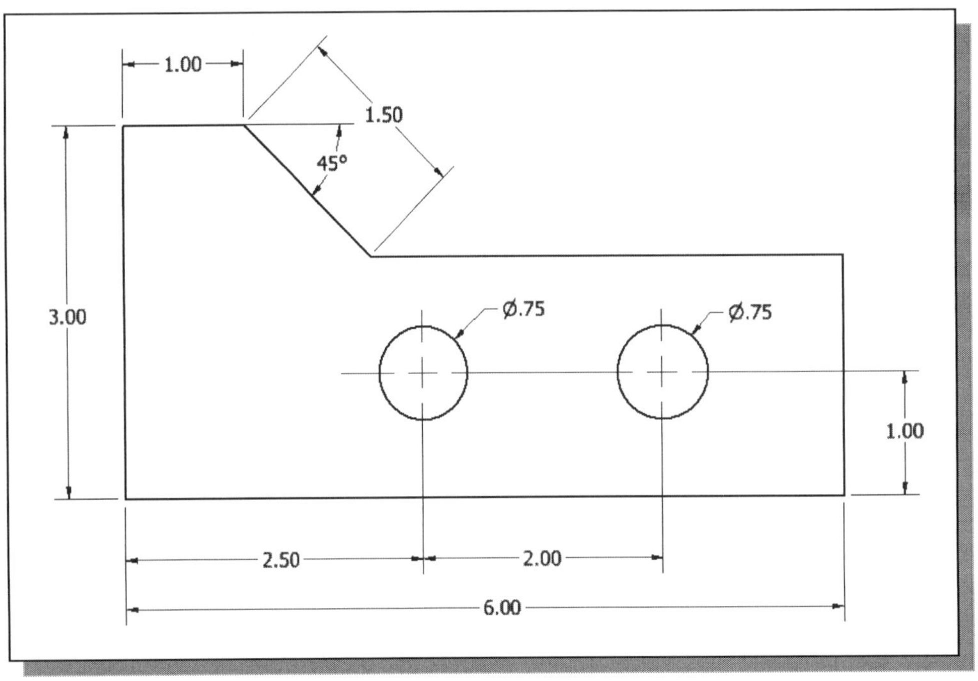

9. Guide Block

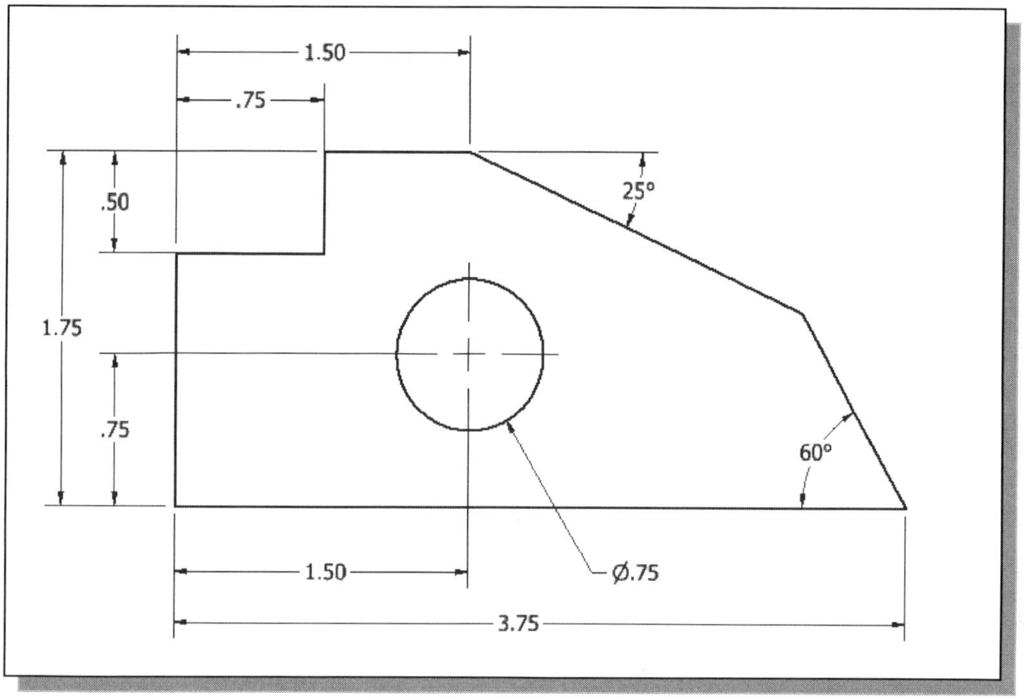

10. Positioning Key

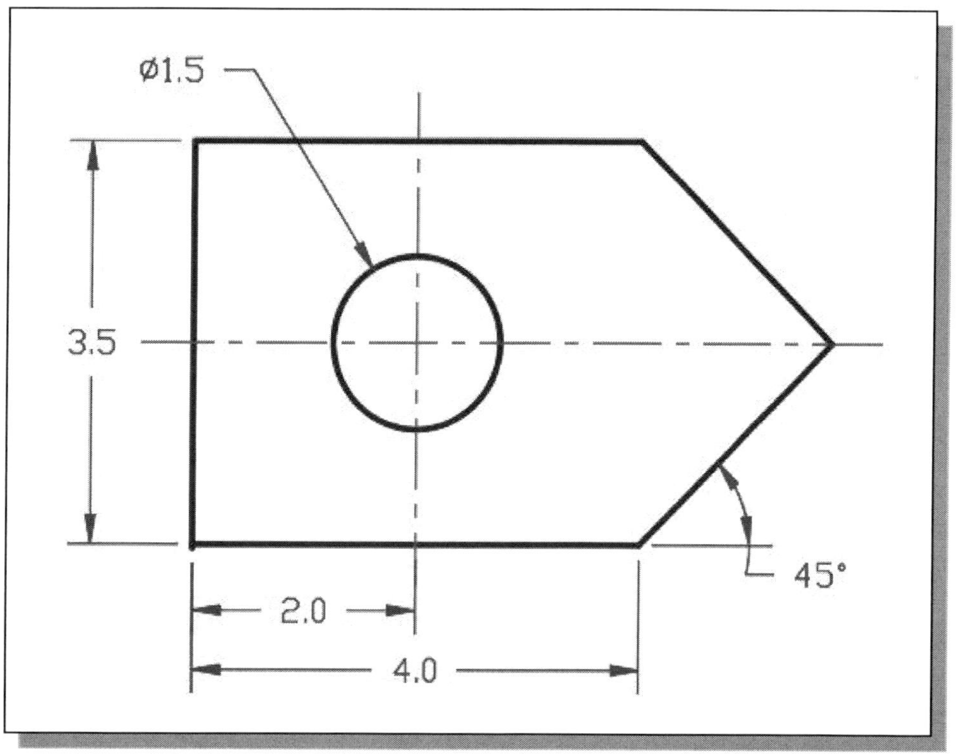

Notes:

Chapter 2
Geometric Constructions

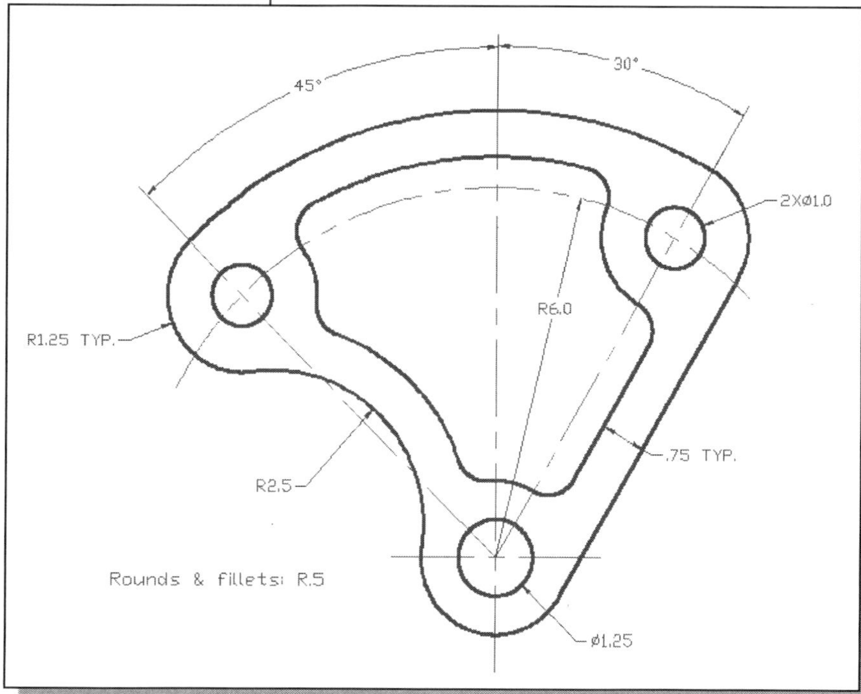

Learning Objectives

- Understand the Classic Geometric Construction Tools and Methods
- Reference the WCS
- Use the Startup Dialog Box
- Set Up Grid & Snap Intervals
- Display AutoCAD's Toolbars
- Set Up and Use Object Snaps
- Edit Using the Trim Command
- Use the Polygon Command
- Create Tangent Lines

AutoCAD Certified User Examination Objectives Coverage

Section 1: Introduction to AutoCAD

Section 2: Creating Basic Drawings

Section 3: Manipulating Objects

Section 4: Drawing Organization and Inquiry Commands

Geometric Constructions

The creation of designs usually involves the manipulation of geometric shapes. Traditionally, manual graphical construction used simple hand tools like a T-square, straightedge, scales, triangles, compass, dividers, pencils, and paper. The manual drafting tools are designed specifically to assist the construction of geometric shapes. For example, the T-square and drafting machine can be used to construct parallel and perpendicular lines very easily and quickly. Today, modern CAD systems provide designers much better control and accuracy in the construction of geometric shapes.

In technical drawings, many of the geometric shapes are constructed with specific geometric properties, such as perpendicularity, parallelism and tangency. For example, in the drawing below, quite a few **implied** geometric properties are present.

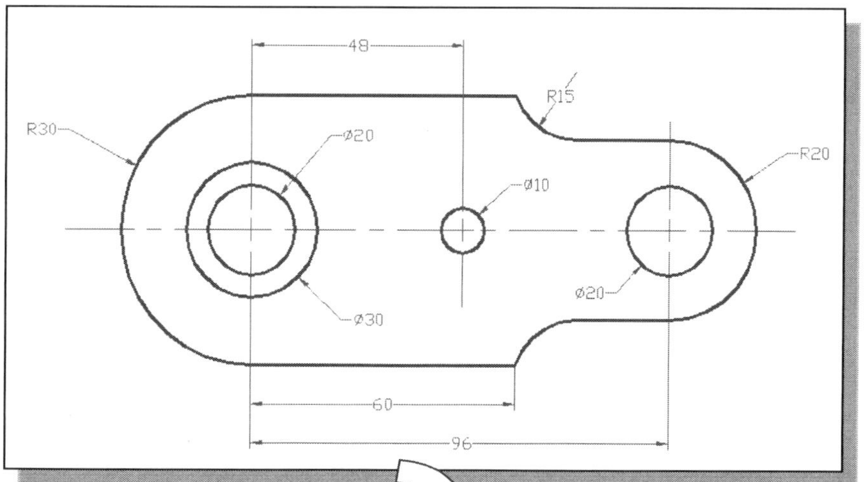

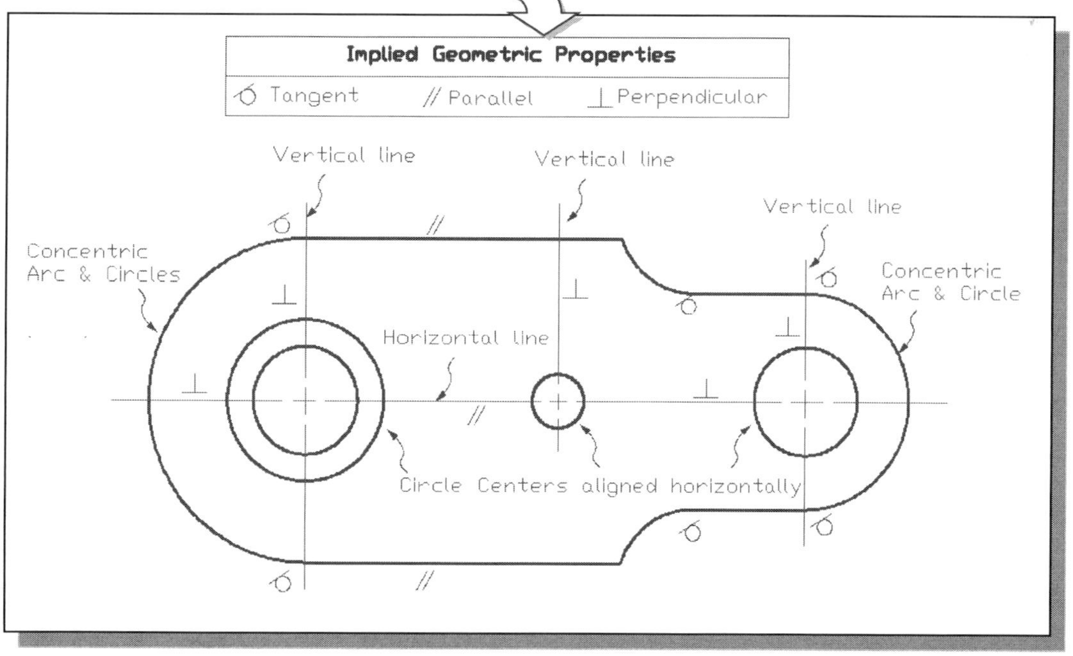

Geometric Constructions – Classical Methods

Geometric constructions are done by applying geometric rules to graphics entities. Knowledge of the principles of geometric construction and its applications are essential to Designers, Engineers and CAD users.

For 2D drawings, it is crucial to be able to construct geometric entities at specified angles to each other, various plane figures, and other graphic representations. In this section, we will examine both the traditional graphical methods and the CAD methods of the basic geometric constructions commonly used in engineering graphics. This chapter provides information that will aid you in drawing different types of geometric constructions.

- **Bisection of a Line or Arc**

1. Given a line or an arc AB.

2. From A and B draw two equal arcs with a radius that is greater than one half of line AB.

3. Construct a line by connecting the intersection points, D and E, with a straight line to locate the midpoint of line AB.

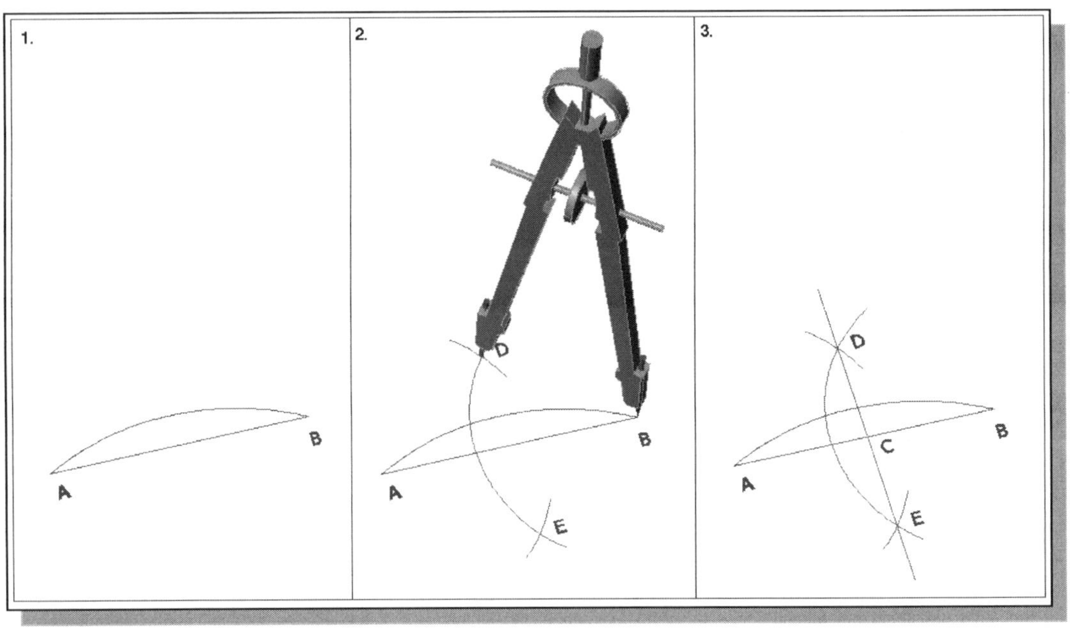

❖ Note that the constructed bisecting line DE is also perpendicular to the given line AB at the midpoint C.

• Bisection of an Angle

1. Given an angle ABC.

2. From A draw an arc with an arbitrary radius.

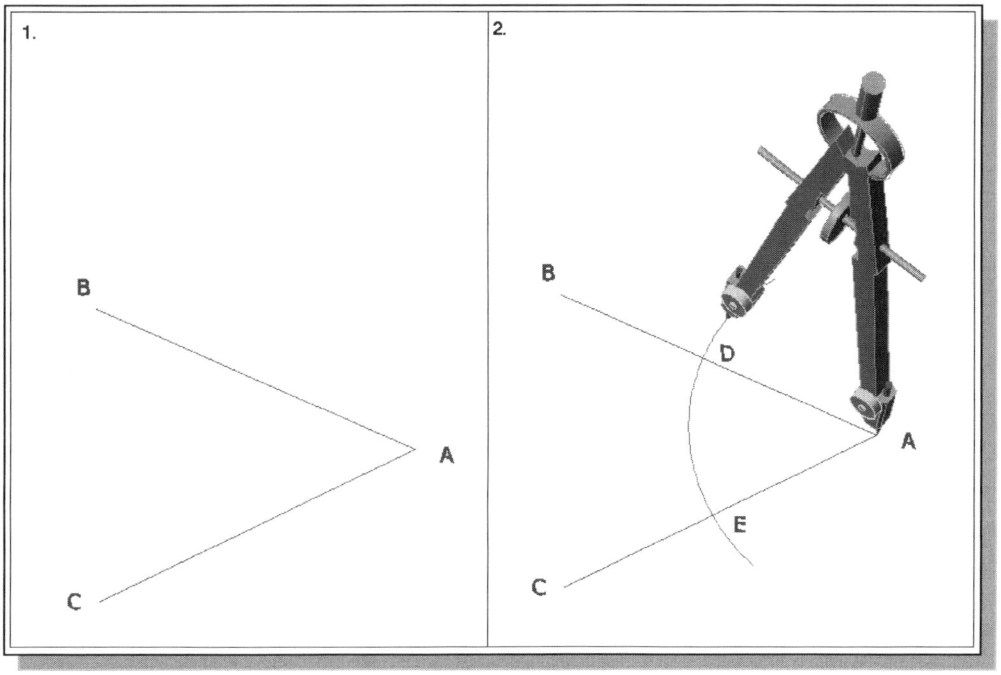

3. Construct two equal radius arcs at D and E.

4. Construct a straight line by connecting point A to the intersection of the two arcs.

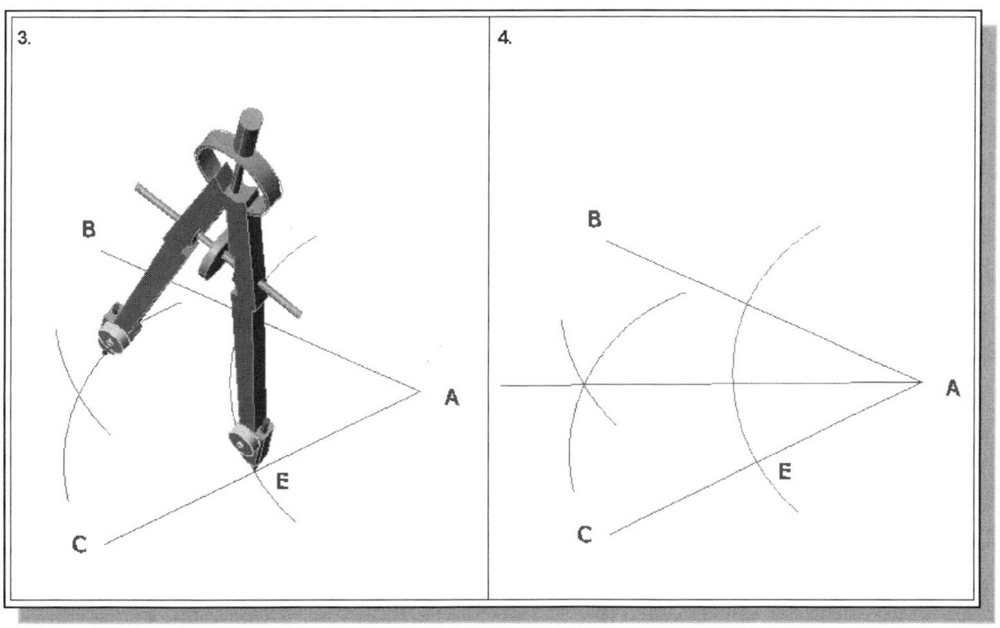

- ## Transfer of an Angle

1. Given an angle ABC, transfer the angle to line XY.

2. Create two arcs, at A and X, with an arbitrary radius R.

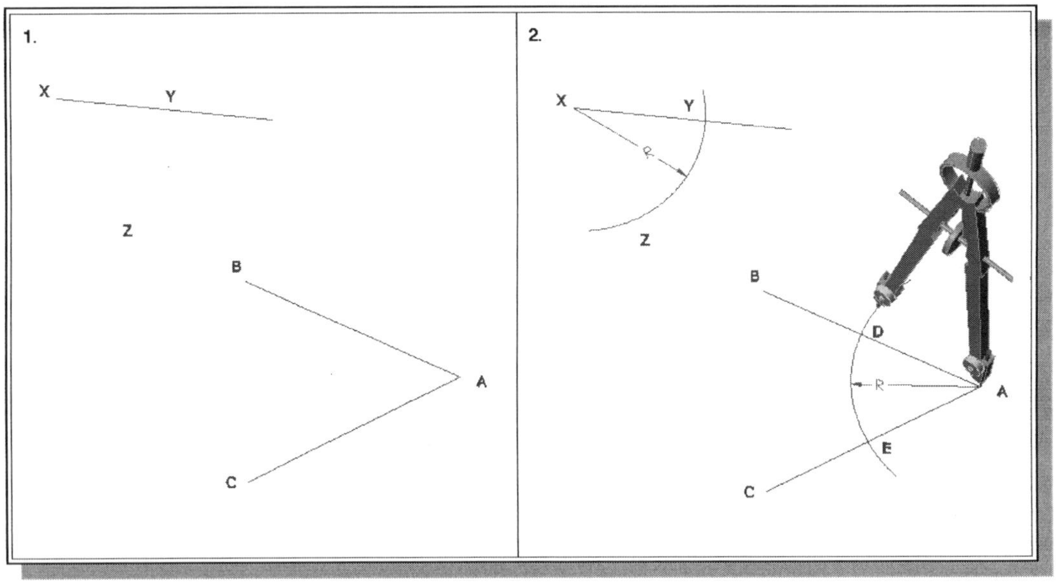

3. Measure the distance between point D and E using a compass.

4. Construct an arc at Y using the distance measured in the previous step.

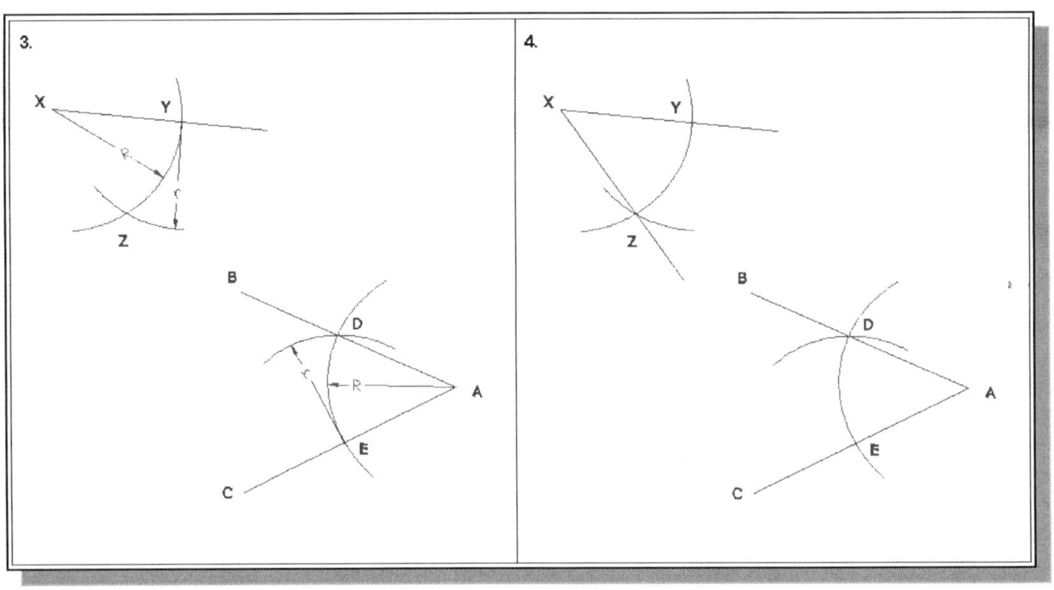

• Dividing a Given Line into a Number of Equal Parts

1. Given a line AB, the line is to be divided into five equal parts.

2. Construct another line at an arbitrary angle. Measure and mark five units along the line.

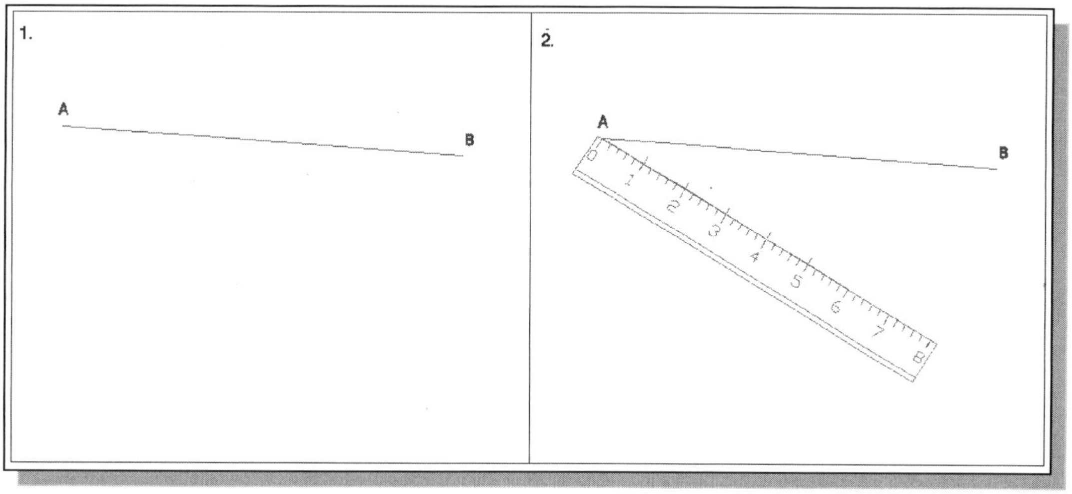

3. Construct a line connecting the fifth mark to point B.

4. Create four lines parallel to the constructed line through the marks.

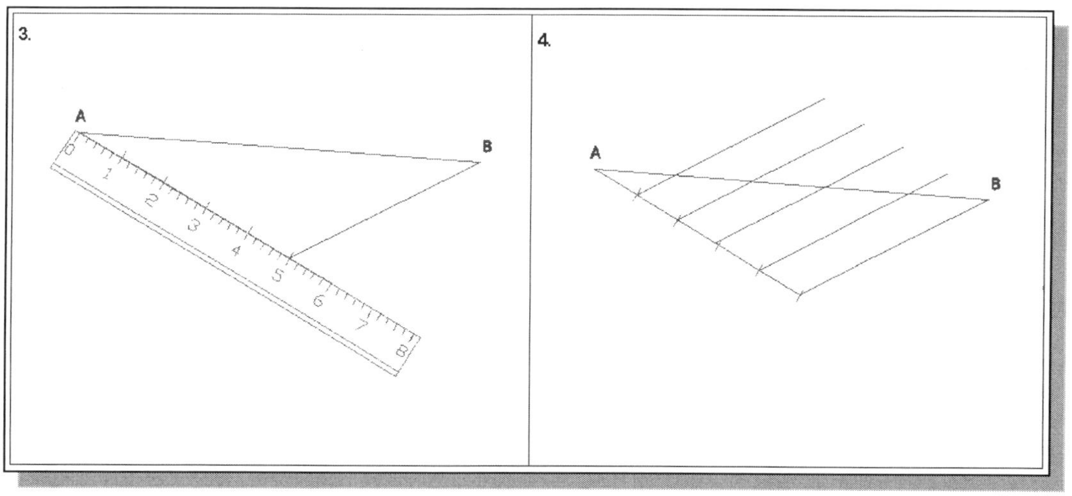

- **Circle through Three Points**

1. Given three points A, B and C.

2. Construct a bisecting line through line AB.

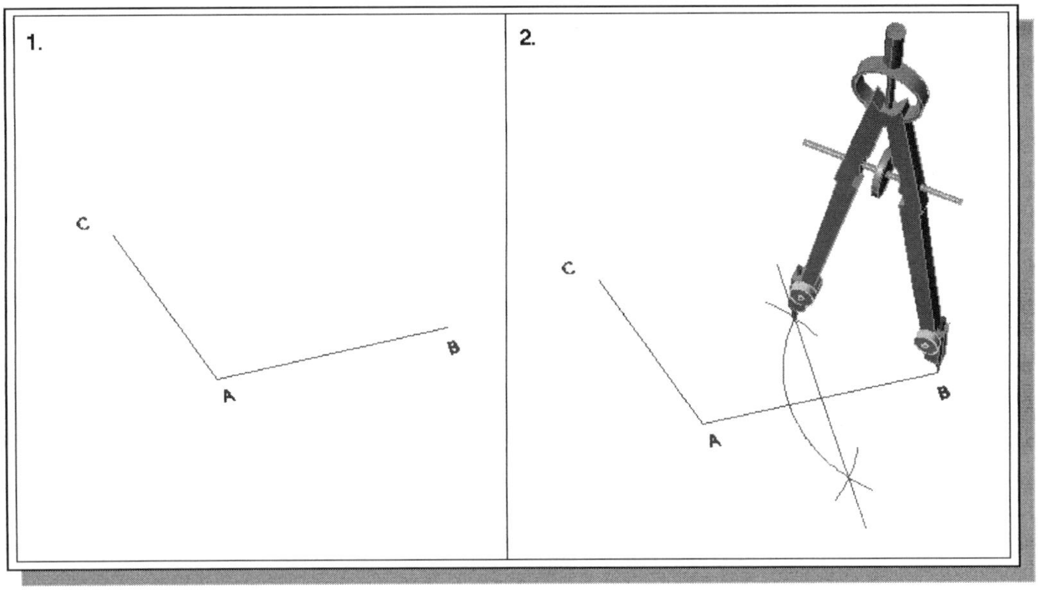

3. Construct a second bisecting line through line AC. The two bisecting lines intersect at point D.

4. Create the circle at point D using DA, DB or DC as radius.

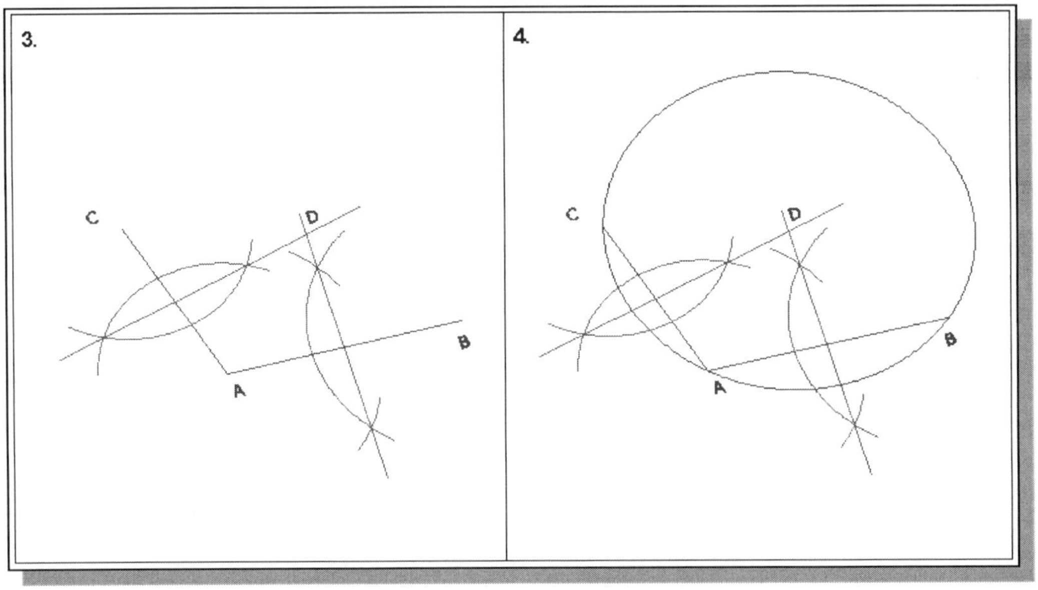

• Line Tangent to a Circle from a Given Point

1. Given a circle, center point C and a point A.

2. Create a bisecting line through line AC.

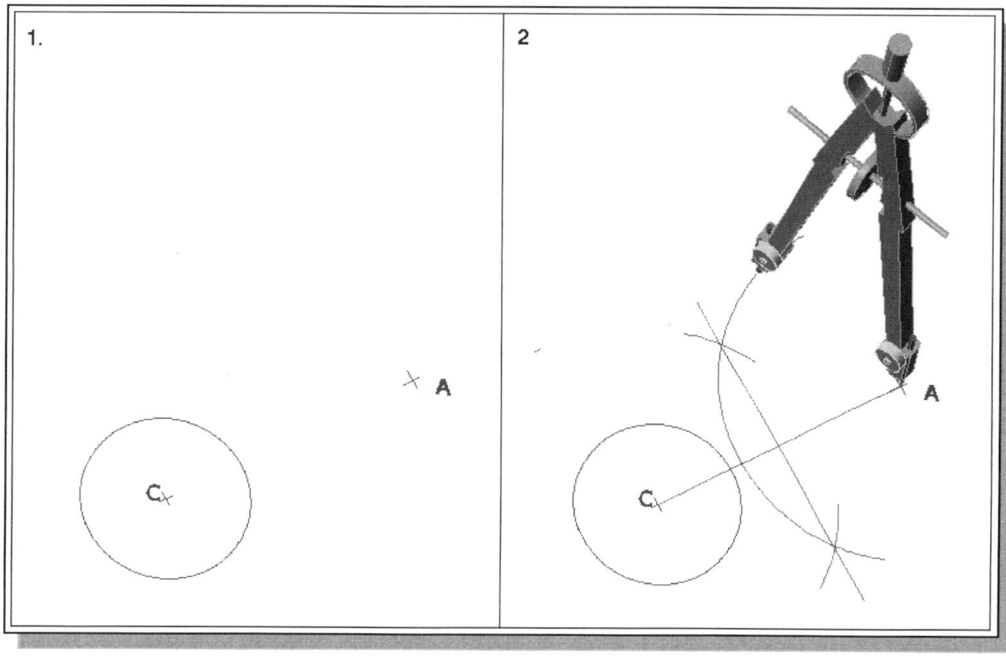

3. Create an arc at point B (midpoint on line AC), with AB or BC as the radius.

4. Construct the tangent line by connecting point A at the intersection of the arc and the circle.

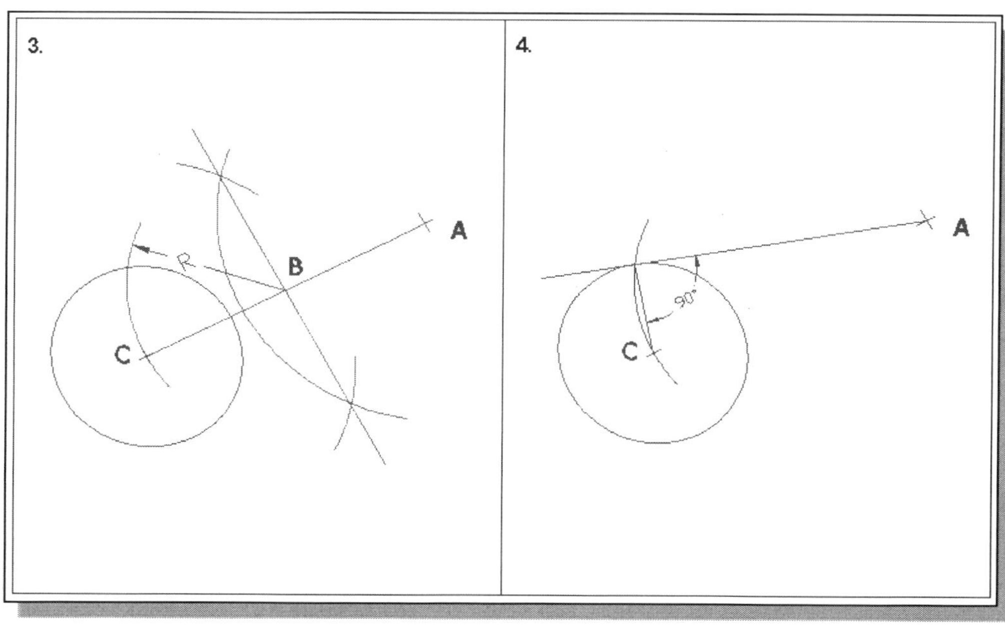

• Circle of a Given Radius Tangent to Two Given Lines

1. Given two lines and a given radius R.
2. Create a parallel line by creating two arcs of radius R, and draw a line tangent to the two arcs.

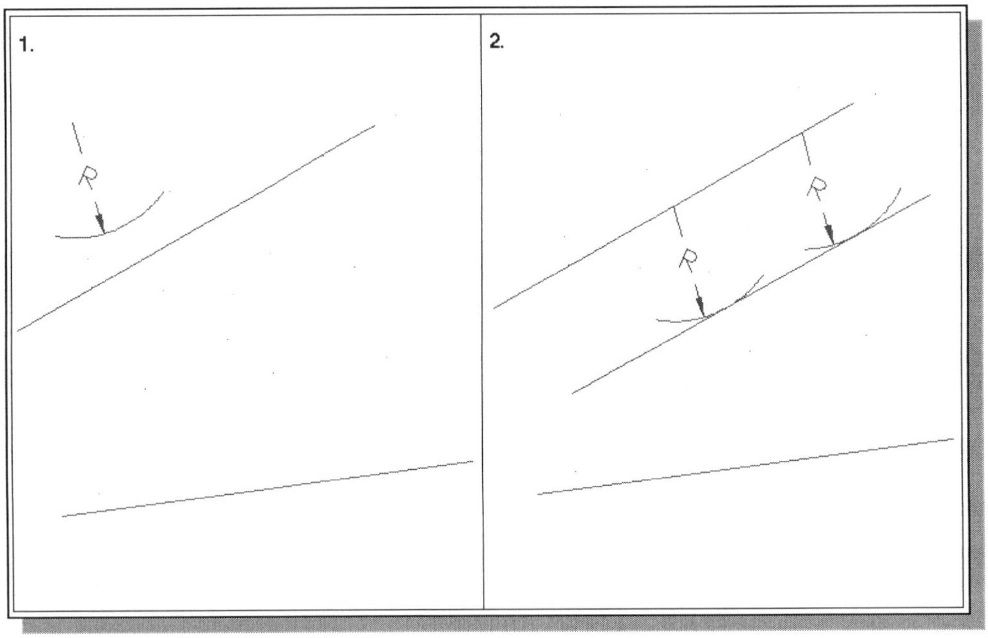

3. Create another line parallel to the bottom edge by first drawing two arcs.
4. Construct the required circle at the intersection of the two lines using the given radius R.

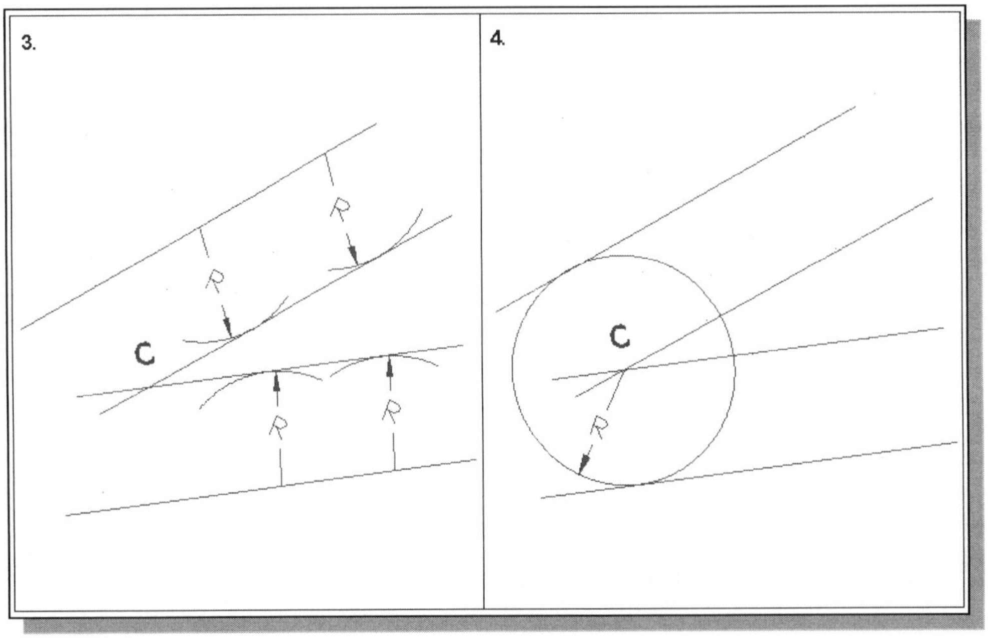

- **Circle of a Given Radius Tangent to an Arc and a Line**

1. Given a radius R, a line and an arc.

2. Create a parallel line by creating two arcs of radius R, and draw a line tangent to the two arcs.

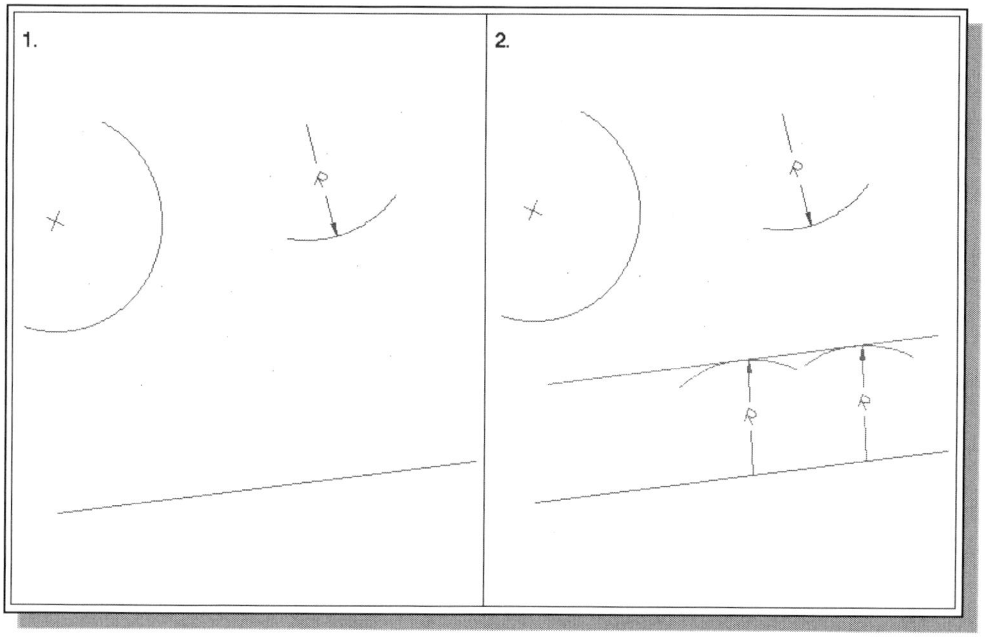

3. Create a concentric arc at the center of the given arc using a radius that is r+R.

4. Create the desired circle at the intersection using the given radius R.

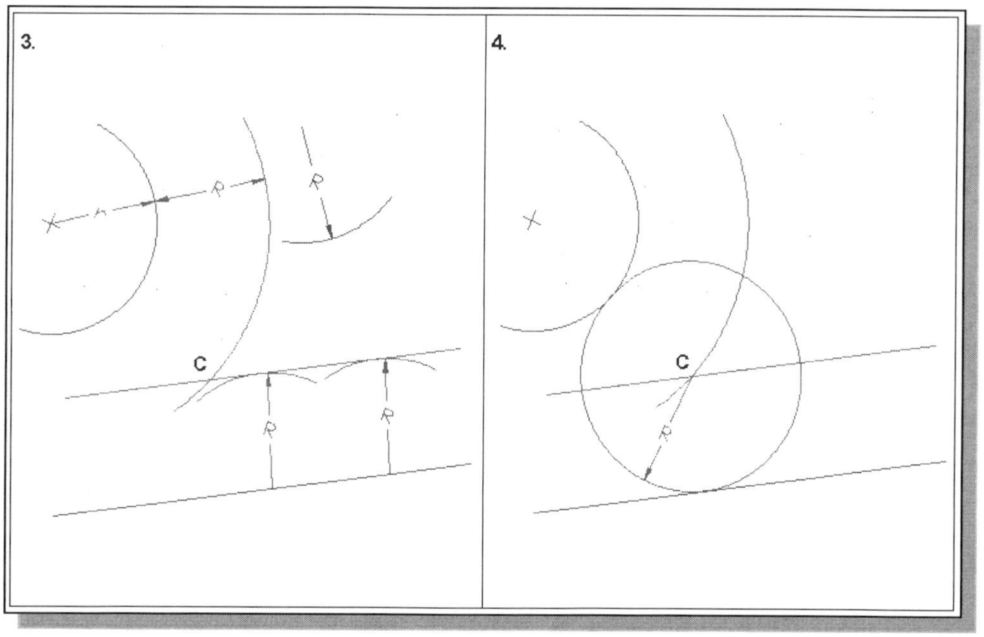

• Circle of a Given Radius Tangent to Two Arcs

1. Given a radius R and two arcs.

2. Create a concentric arc at the center of the small arc using a radius that is R distance more than the original radius.

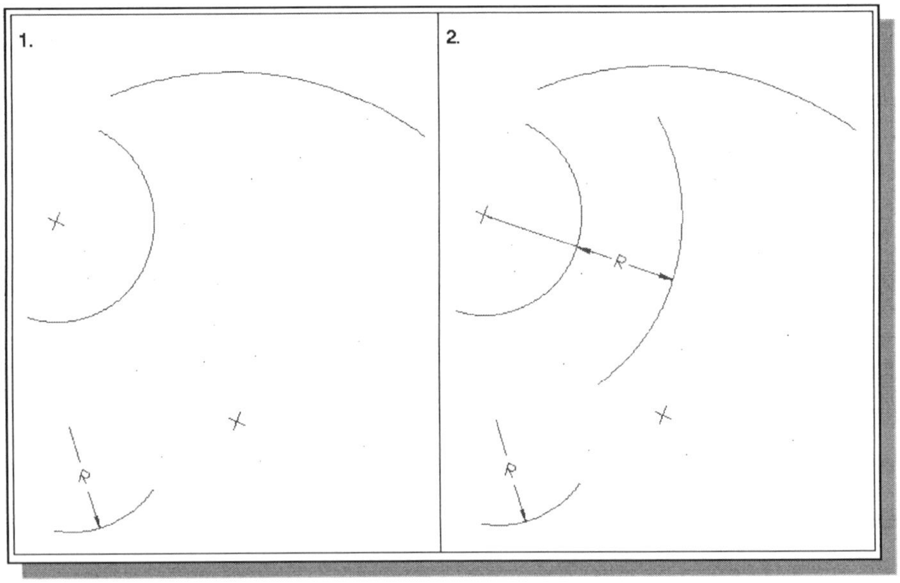

3. Create another concentric arc at the center of the large arc using a radius that is R distance smaller than the original radius.

4. Create the desired circle at the intersection using the given radius R.

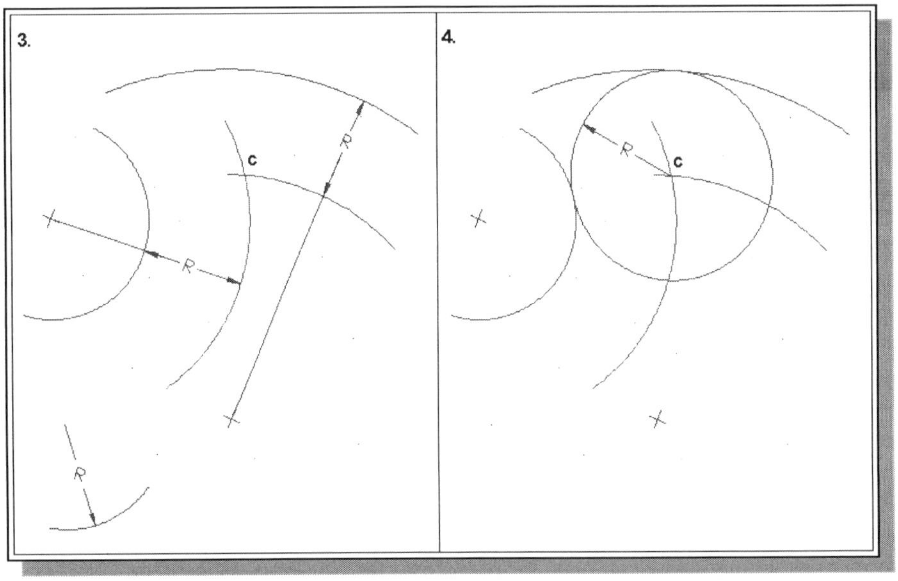

➢ Prior to demonstrating the computer method of geometric construction methods, the use of AutoCAD's ***Dynamic Input*** option is first illustrated.

Starting Up AutoCAD 2027

1. Start **AutoCAD 2027** by selecting the Autodesk folder in the **Start** menu as shown. Once the program is loaded into memory, the **AutoCAD 2027** drawing screen will appear on the screen.

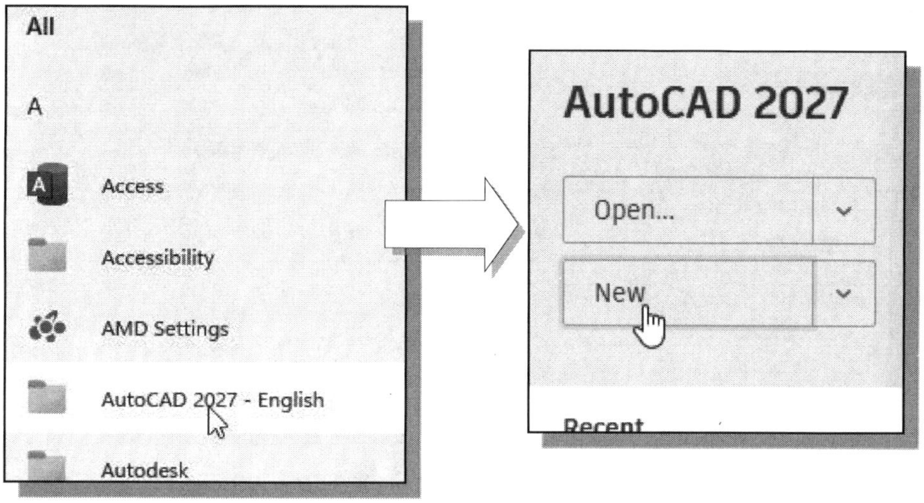

Dynamic Input

In AutoCAD 2027, the ***Dynamic Input*** feature provides the user with **visual tooltips** and **entry options** right on the screen.

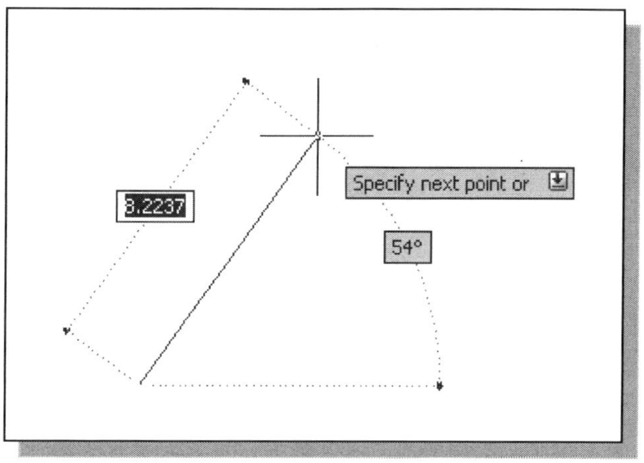

Dynamic Input provides a convenient command interface near the cursor to help the user focus in the graphics area. When *Dynamic Input* is *ON*, tooltips display information near the cursor that is dynamically updated as the cursor moves.

The tooltips also provide a place for user entry when a command is activated. The actions required to complete a command remain the same as those for the command line. Note that ***Dynamic Input*** is **not** designed to replace the command line. The main advantage of using the *Dynamic Input* options is to keep our attention near the cursor. The *Dynamic Input* features simply enhance the five methods for specifying the locations of points as described in Chapter 1.

1. To switch on the **AutoCAD Dynamic Input option**, use the *Customization option* at the bottom right corner.

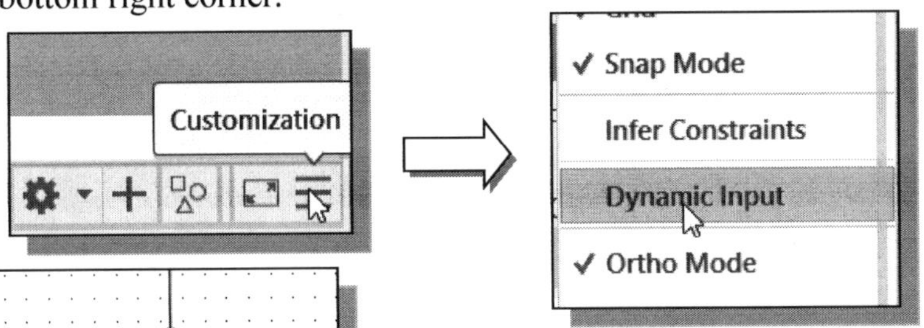

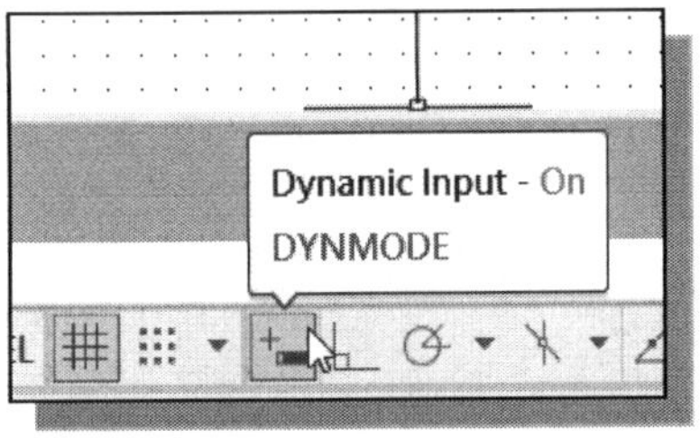

2. Switch ***ON*** the *Dynamic Input* option by clicking on the button in the *Status Bar* area as shown.

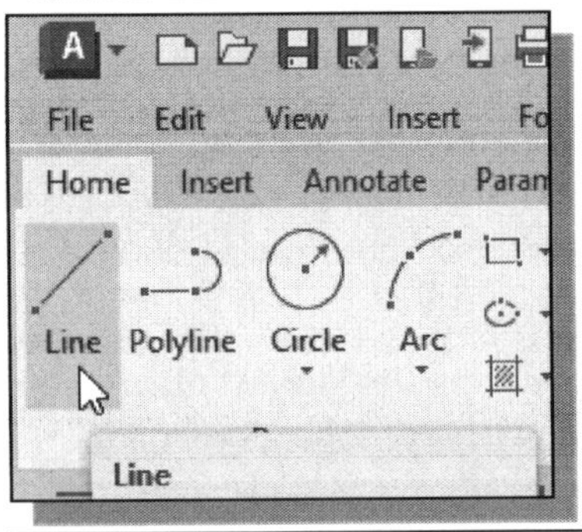

3. Click on the **Line** icon in the *Draw* toolbar. In the command prompt area, the message "*_line Specify first point:*" is displayed.

4. Move the cursor inside the *Drawing Area* and notice the displayed tooltip, which shows the coordinates of the cursor position.

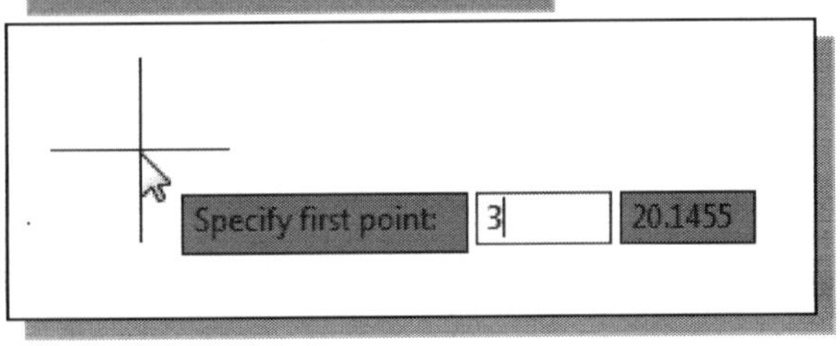

5. Type **3** and notice the input is entered in the first entry box.

6. Hit the **TAB** key once to move the input focus to the second entry box.

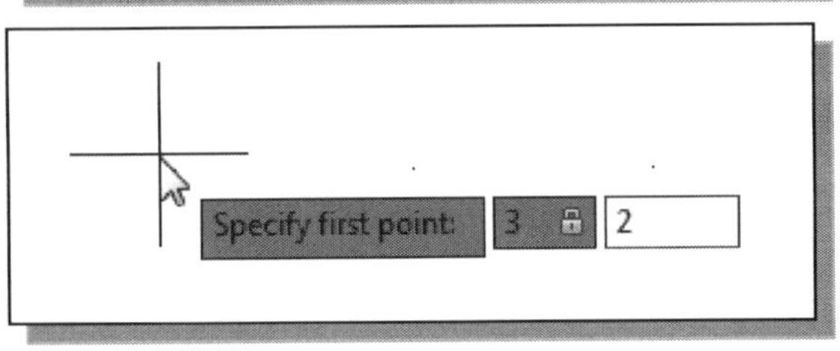

7. Type **2** and notice the input is displayed in the second entry box.

8. Hit the **ENTER** key once to accept the inputs.

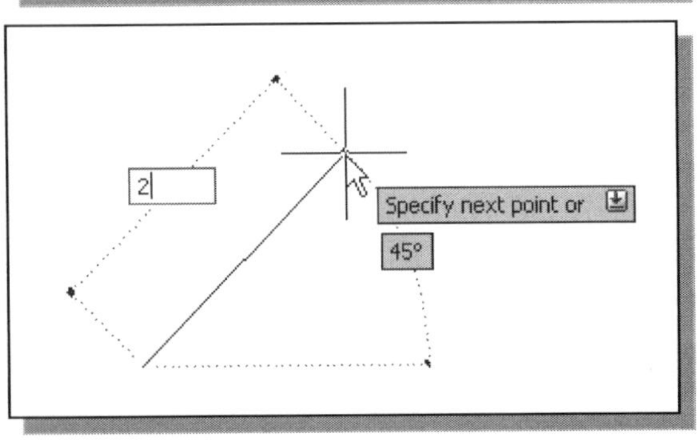

9. Move the cursor upward and toward the right side of the screen. Notice the tooltip is set to use polar coordinates by default.

10. Type **2** and notice the input is displayed in the entry box as shown.

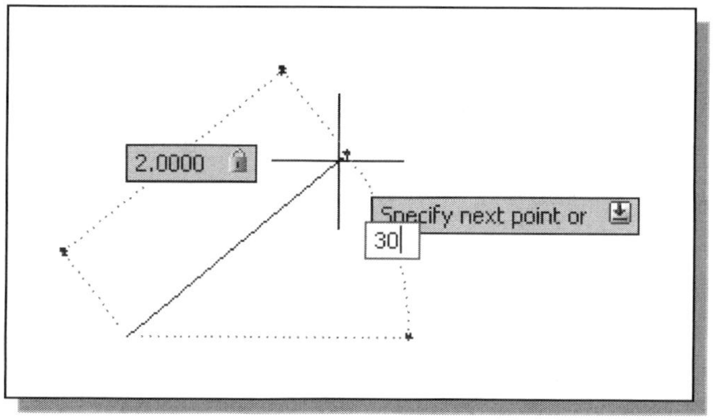

11. Hit the **TAB** key once to move the input focus to the second entry box.

12. Type **30** and notice the input is displayed in the angle entry box.

13. Hit the **ENTER** key once to create the line that is 2 units long and at an angle of 30 degrees.

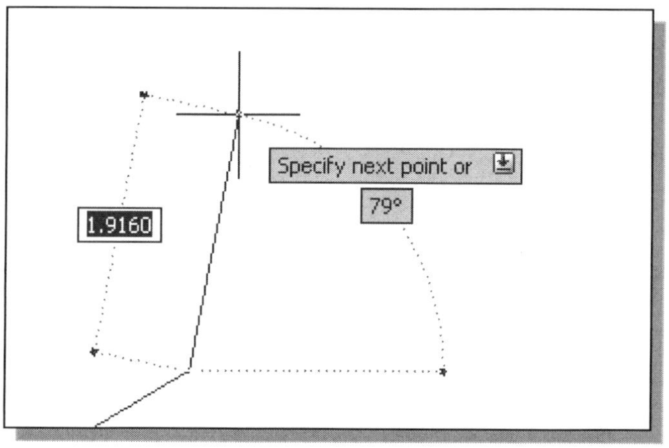

14. Move the cursor upward and toward the right side of the screen. Notice the tooltip is still set to using polar coordinates.

➢ To switch to using the relative Cartesian coordinates input method, use a **comma** as the **specifier** after entering the first number.

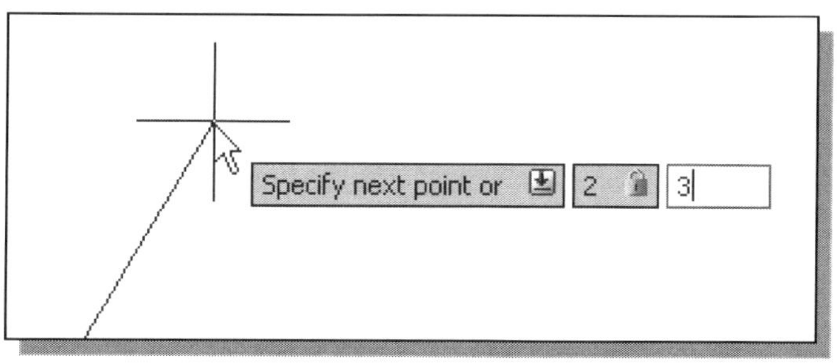

15. Type **2,3** and notice the input option is now set to using relative Cartesian coordinates as shown.

16. Hit the **ENTER** key once to accept the inputs.

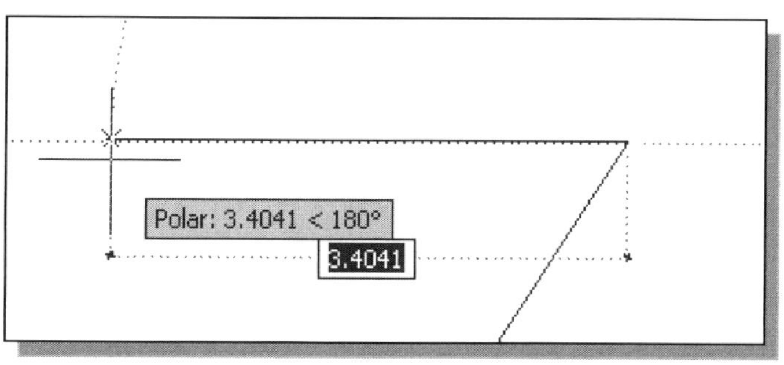

17. Move the cursor toward the right side of the last position until the angle is near 180 degrees as shown.

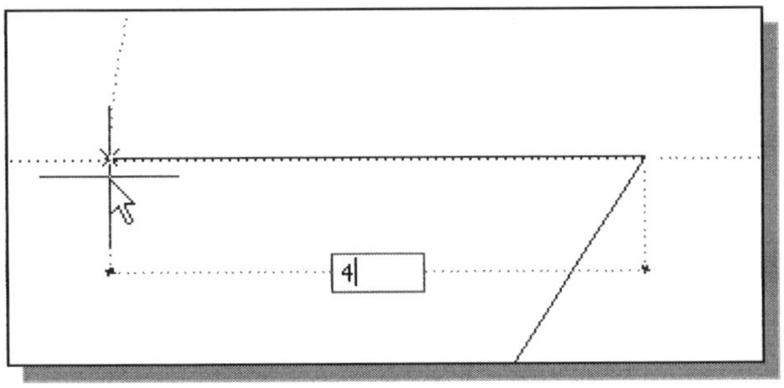

18. Type **4** and notice the input is displayed on the screen.

19. Hit the **ENTER** key once to accept the input and note a horizontal line is created.

➢ In effect, we just created a line using the ***Direct Distance*** option.

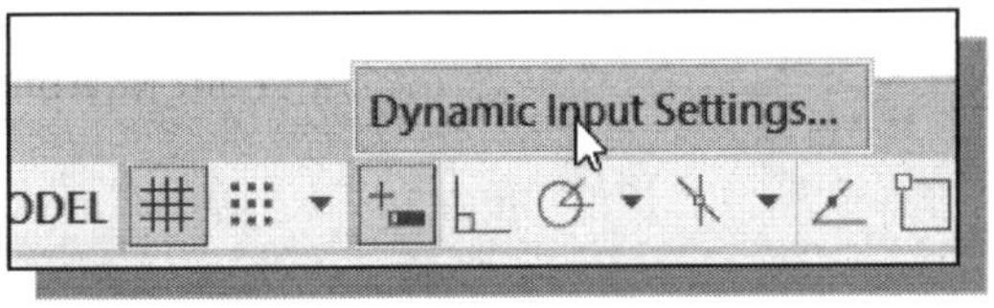

20. In the *Status Bar* area, **right-click** on ***Dynamic Input*** and choose the **Settings** option as shown.

❖ The *Settings* dialog allows us to control what is displayed when *Dynamic Input* is on.

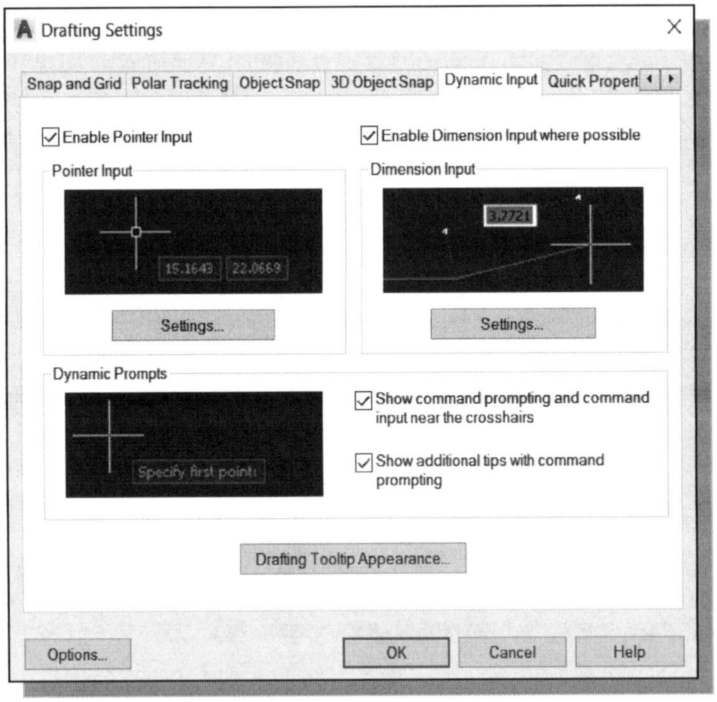

➢ Note that the *Dynamic Input* feature has three components: ***Pointer Input***, ***Dimension Input***, and ***Dynamic Prompts***.

21. On your own, toggle *ON/OFF* the three options and create additional line-segments to see the different effects of the settings.

Object Snap Toolbar

1. Move the cursor to the *Menu Bar* area and choose **[Tools] → [Toolbars] → [AutoCAD]**.

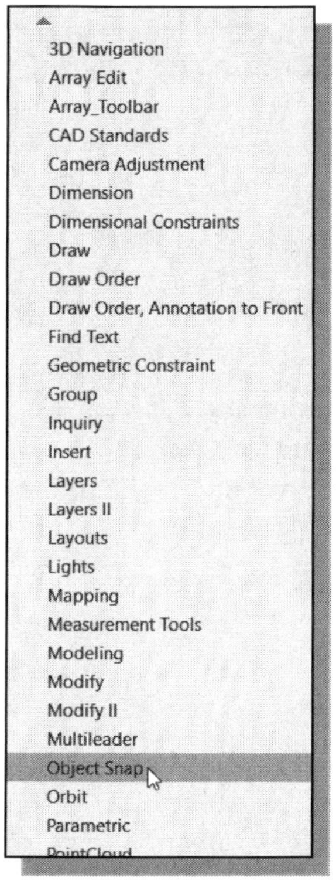

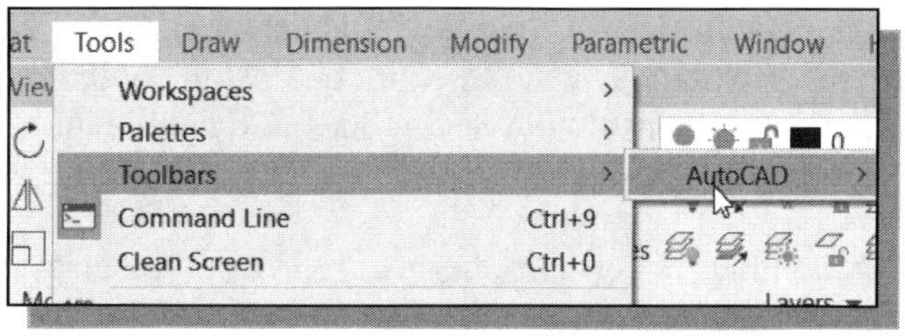

❖ AutoCAD provides 50+ predefined toolbars for access to frequently used commands, settings, and modes. A *checkmark* (next to the item) in the list identifies the toolbars that are currently displayed on the screen.

2. Select **Object Snap**, with the left-mouse-button, to display the *Object Snap* toolbar on the screen.

❖ **Object Snap** is an extremely powerful construction tool available on most CAD systems. During an entity's creation operations, we can snap the cursor to points on objects such as endpoints, midpoints, centers, and intersections. For example, we can turn on **Object Snap** and quickly draw a line to the center of a circle, the midpoint of a line segment, or the intersection of two lines.

3. Move the cursor over the icons in the *Object Snap* toolbar and read the description of each icon.

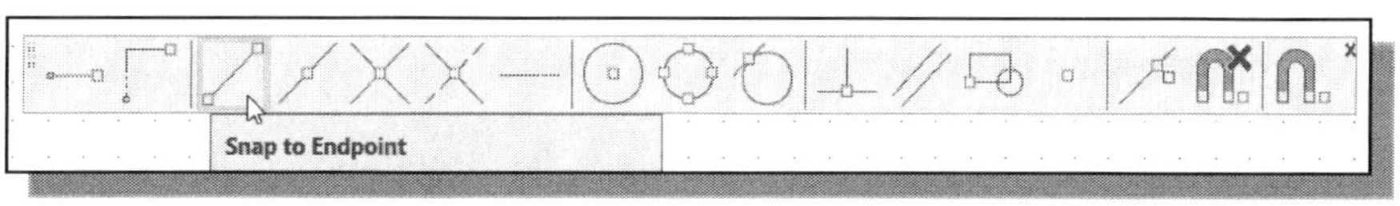

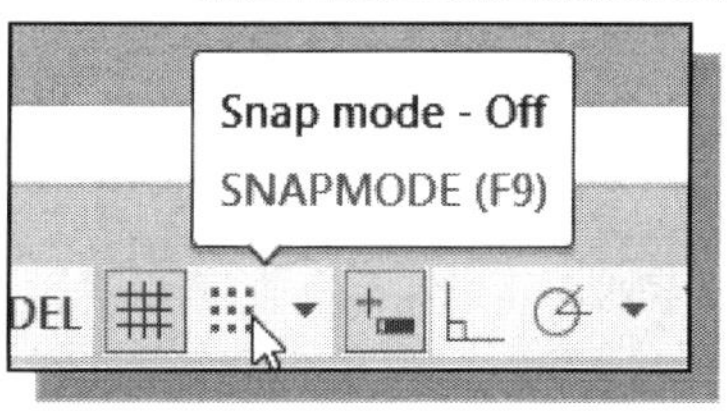

4. We will next turn ***OFF*** the *GRID SNAP* option by toggling off the ***SNAP Mode*** button in the *Status Bar* area.

5. On your own, reset the option buttons in the *Status Bar* area, so that only the *GRID DISPLAY* option is switched ***ON***.

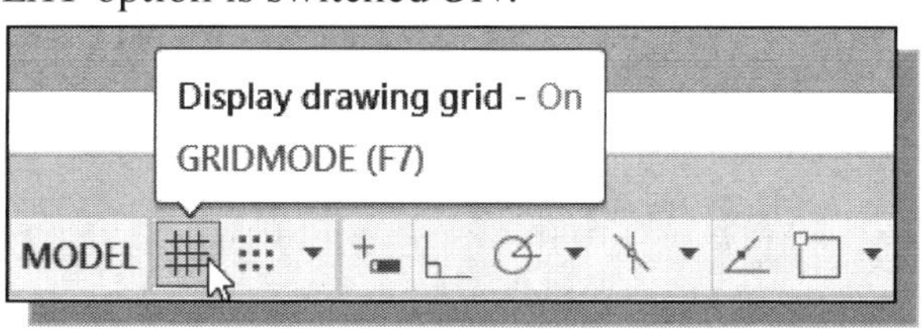

Geometric Construction – CAD Method

The main characteristic of any CAD system is its ability to create and modify 2D/3D geometric entities quickly and accurately. Most CAD systems provide a variety of object construction and editing tools to relieve the designer of the tedious drudgery of this task, so that the designer can concentrate more on design content. A good understanding of the computer geometric construction techniques will enable the CAD users to fully utilize the capability of the CAD systems.

➢ Note that with CAD systems, besides following the classic geometric construction methods, quite a few options are also feasible.

Bisection of a Line or Arc

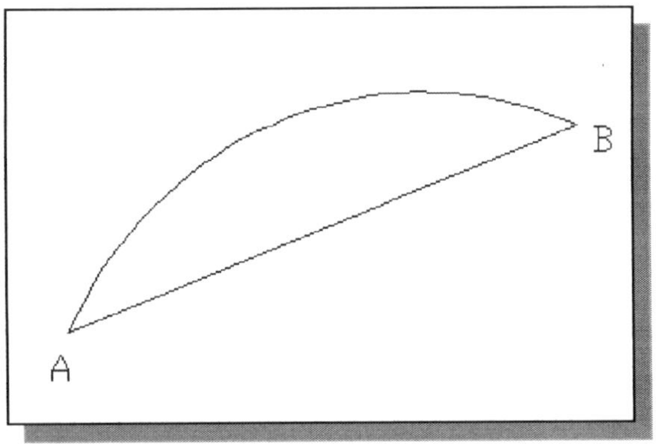

1. Create an arbitrary arc **AB** at any angle, and create line **AB** by connecting the two endpoints of the arc.

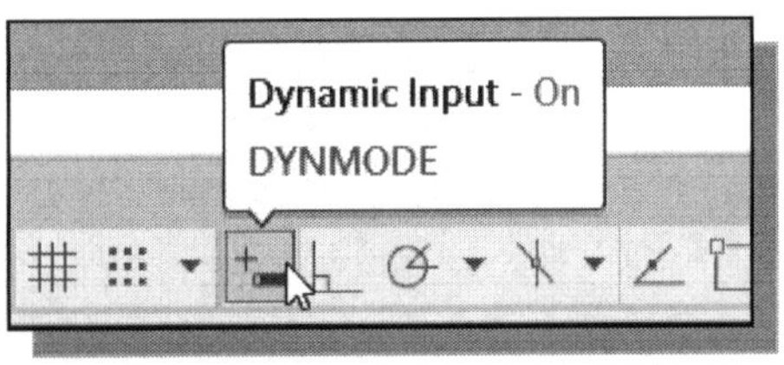

2. Switch *ON* only the *Dynamic Input* option by clicking on the buttons in the *Status Bar* area as shown.

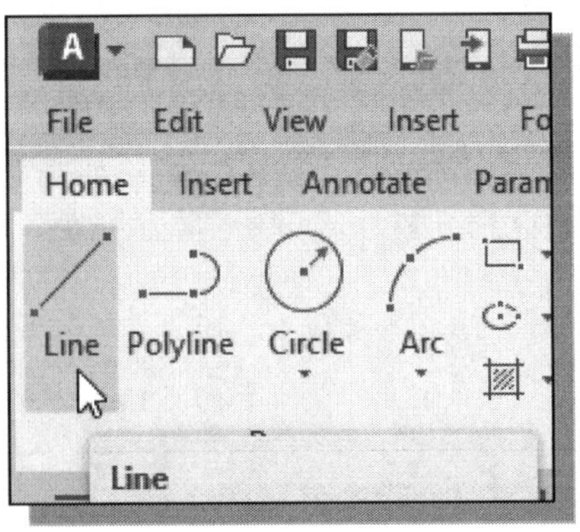

3. Select the **Line** command icon in the *Draw* toolbar. In the command prompt area, near the bottom of the AutoCAD drawing screen, the message "*Line Specify first point:*" is displayed. AutoCAD expects us to identify the starting location of a straight line.

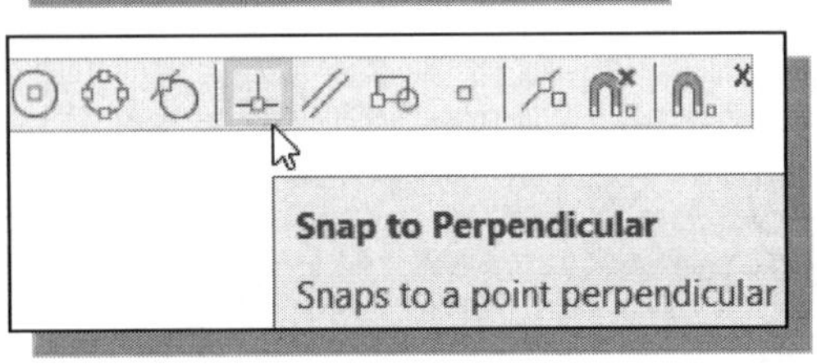

4. Pick **Snap to Perpendicular** in the *Object Snap* toolbar. In the command prompt area, the message "*_per to*" is displayed.

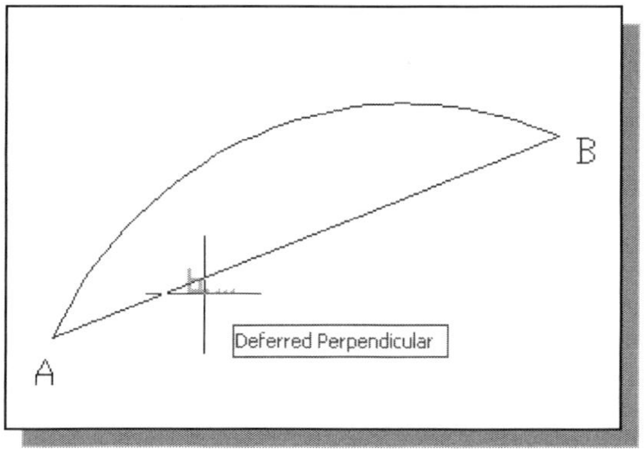

5. Select line **AB** at any position.

❖ Note the displayed tooltip ***Deferred Perpendicular*** indicates the construction is deferred until all inputs are completed.

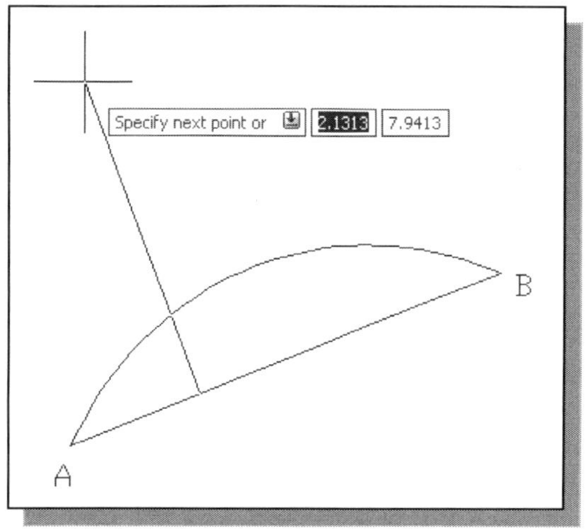

6. Select an arbitrary point above the line as shown.

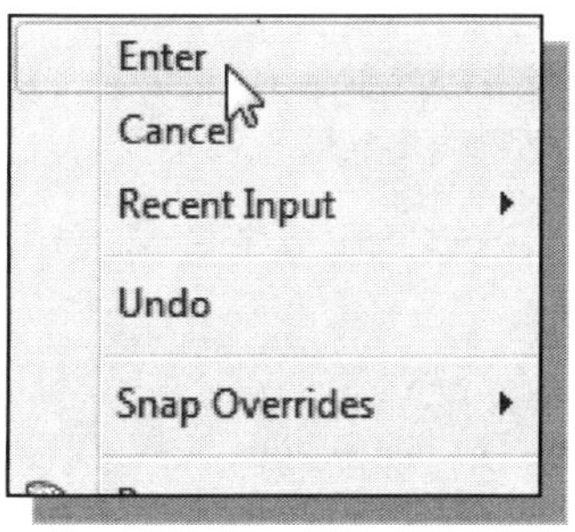

7. Inside the *Drawing Area*, **right-click** to activate the option menu and select **Enter** with the left-mouse-button to end the Line command.

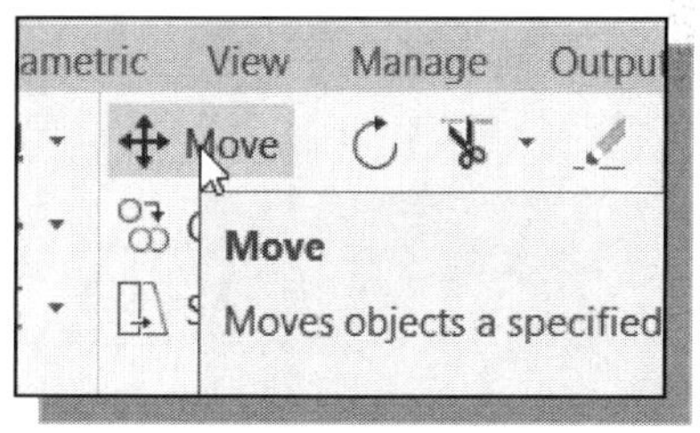

8. Select **Move** in the *Modify* toolbar as shown.

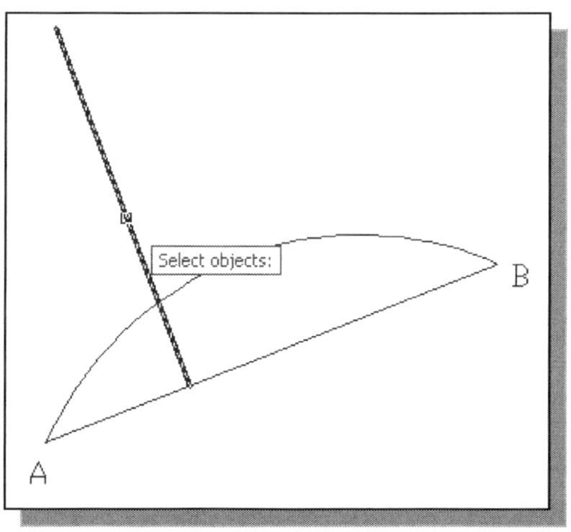

9. Select the **perpendicular line** we just created.

❖ In the *command prompt area*, the message "*Specify the base point or [Displacement]*" is displayed. AutoCAD expects us to select a reference point as the base point for moving the selected object.

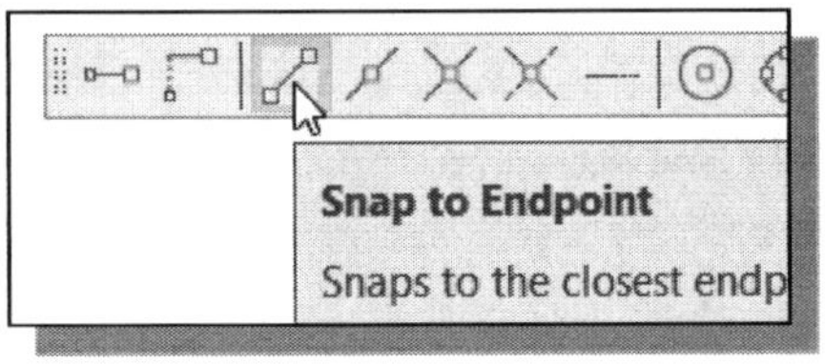

10. Pick **Snap to Endpoint** in the *Object Snap* toolbar.

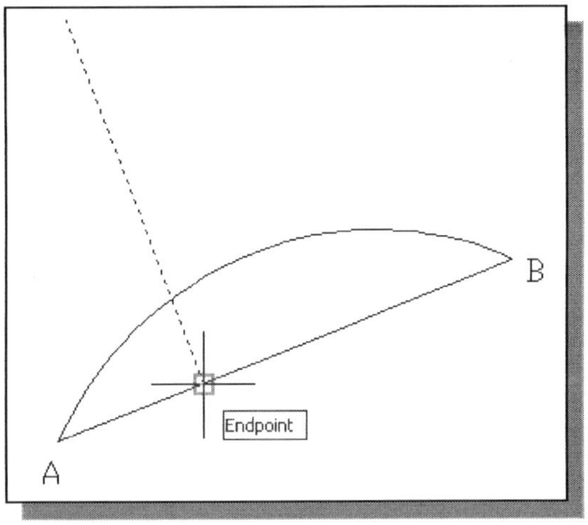

11. Select the lower **Endpoint** of the selected line as shown.

12. Move the cursor inside the Drawing Area, and notice the line is moved to the new cursor location on the screen.

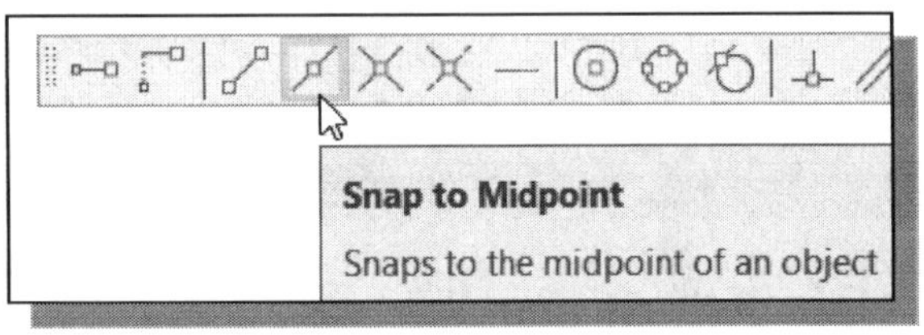

13. Pick **Snap to Midpoint** in the *Object Snap* toolbar.

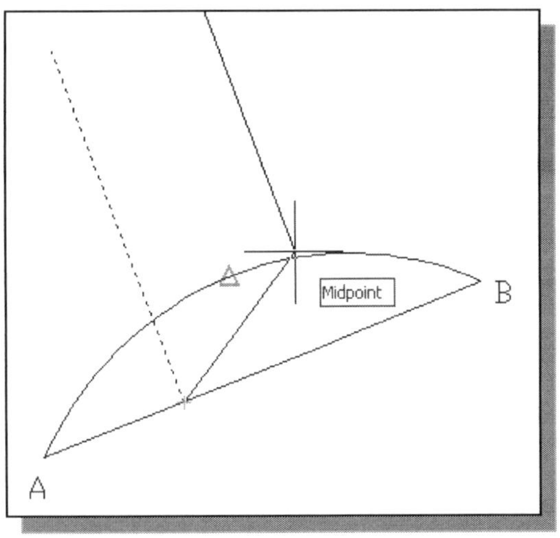

- ❖ In the command prompt area, the message "*_mid to*" is displayed. AutoCAD now expects us to select an existing arc or line on the screen.

14. Select the arc to move the line to the midpoint of the arc. Note that the midpoint of an arc or a line is displayed when the cursor is on top of the object.

15. On your own, repeat the above process and move the perpendicular line to the midpoint of line **AB**.

- The constructed bisecting line is perpendicular to line **AB** and passes through the midpoint of the line or arc **AB**.

• Bisection of an Angle

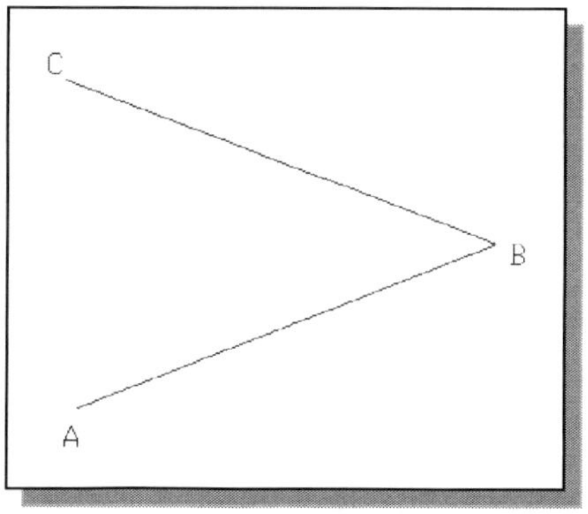

1. Create an arbitrary angle **ABC** as shown in the figure.

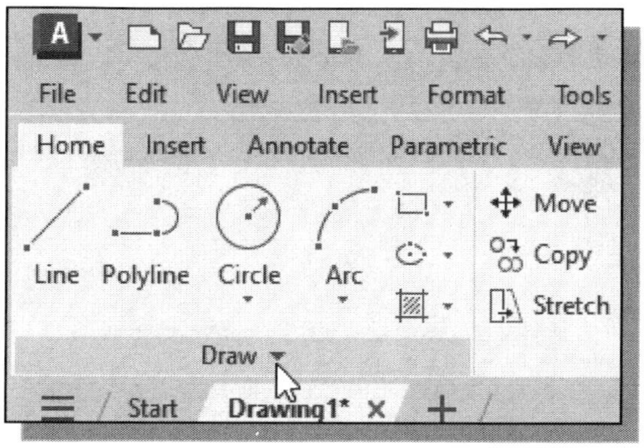

2. Click once with the left-mouse-button on the small triangle in the titlebar of the *Draw* toolbar as shown.

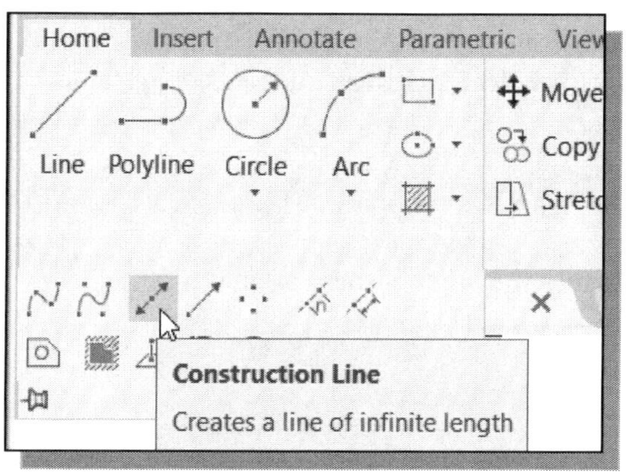

3. Select the **Construction Line** icon in the *Draw* toolbar. In the *command prompt area*, the message "*_xline Specify a point or [Hor/Ver/Ang/Bisect/Offset]:*" is displayed.

➢ *Construction lines* are lines that extend to infinity. Construction lines are usually used as references for creating other objects.

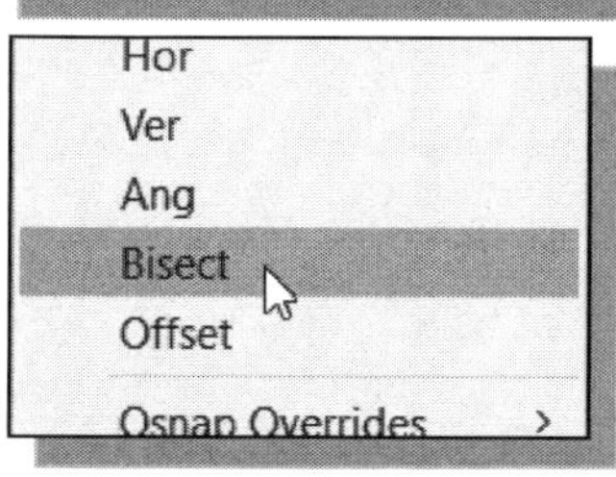

4. Inside the *Drawing Area*, **right-click** once to bring up the option menu.

5. Select **Bisect** from the option list as shown. In the command prompt area, the message "*Specify angle vertex point:*" is displayed.

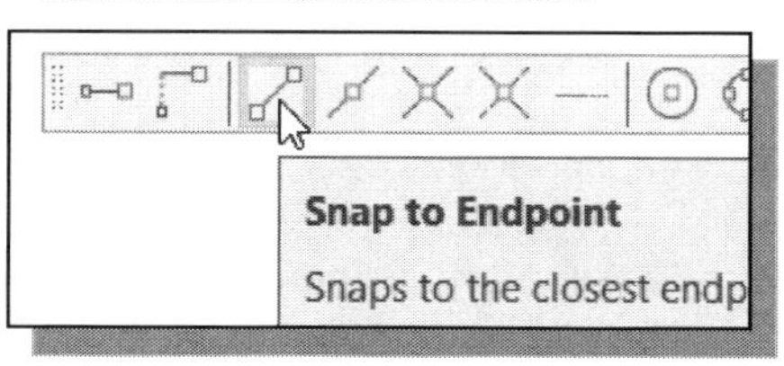

6. Pick **Snap to Endpoint** in the *Object Snap* toolbar.

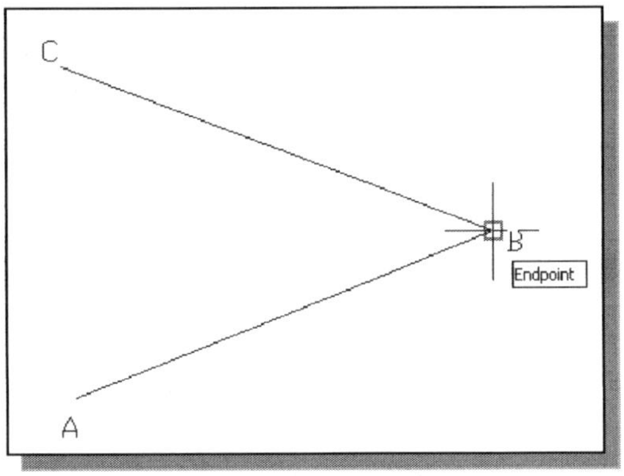

7. Select the vertex point of the angle as shown. In the command prompt area, the message "*Specify angle start point:*" is displayed.

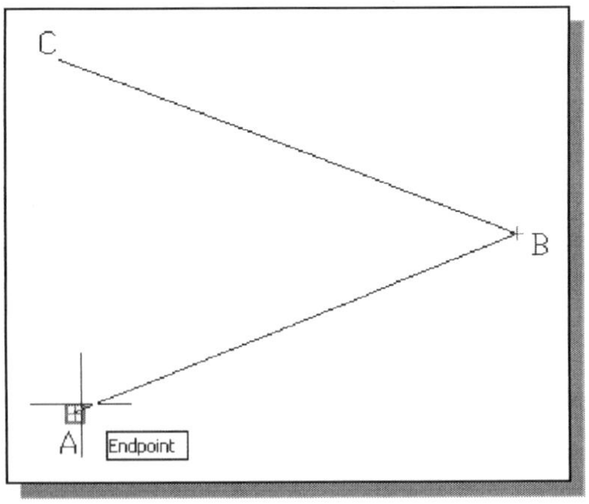

8. Pick **Snap to Endpoint** in the *Object Snap* toolbar.

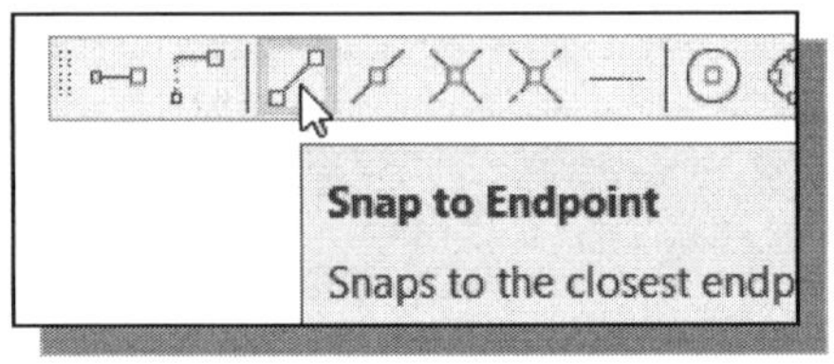

9. Select one of the endpoints, point A or C, of the angle.

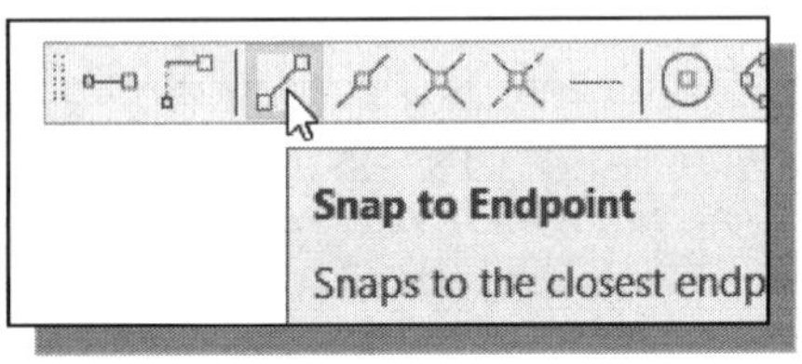

10. Pick **Snap to Endpoint** in the *Object Snap* toolbar.

11. Select the other endpoint of the angle.

➢ Note that the constructed bisection line divides the angle into two equal parts.

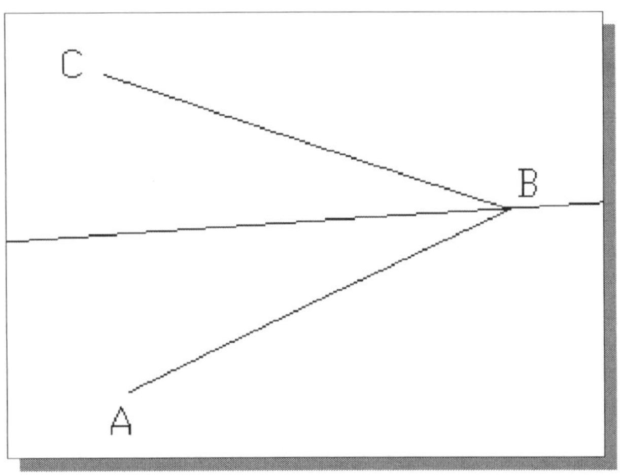

• Transfer of an Angle

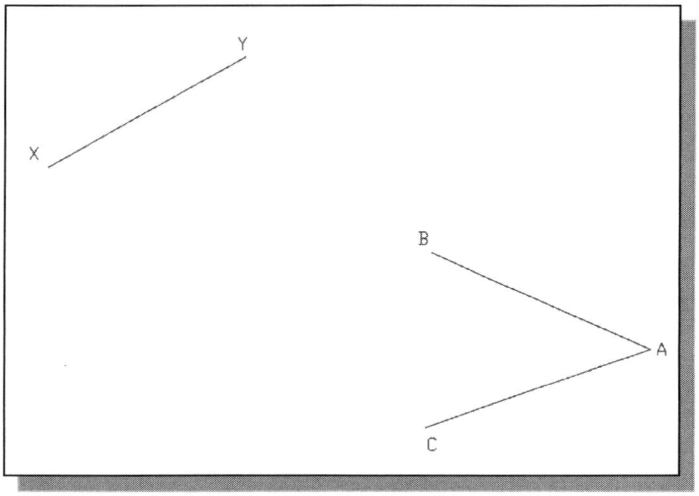

1. Create an arbitrary angle **ABC** and a separate line **XY** as shown in the figure.

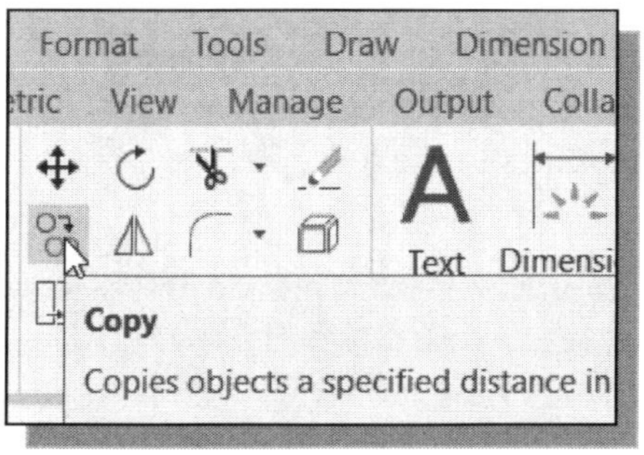

2. Select **Copy** in the *Modify* toolbar as shown.

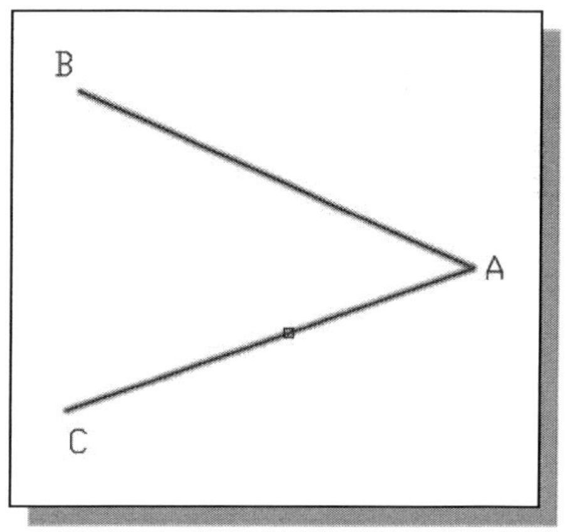

3. Select line AB and AC as the objects to be copied.

4. **Right-click** once to proceed with the Copy command.

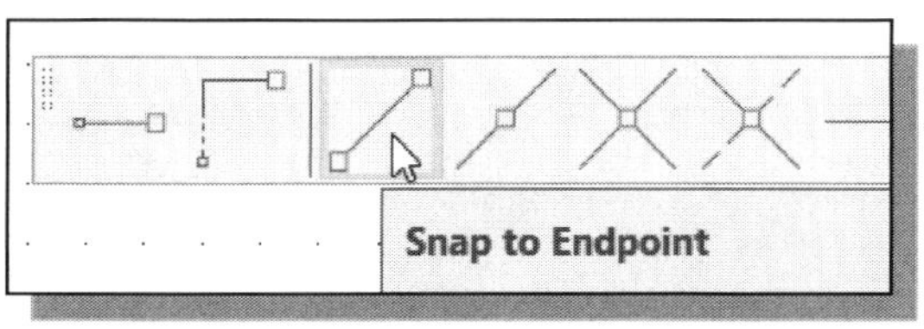

5. Pick **Snap to Endpoint** in the *Object Snap* toolbar.

6. Select point **A** as the base point.

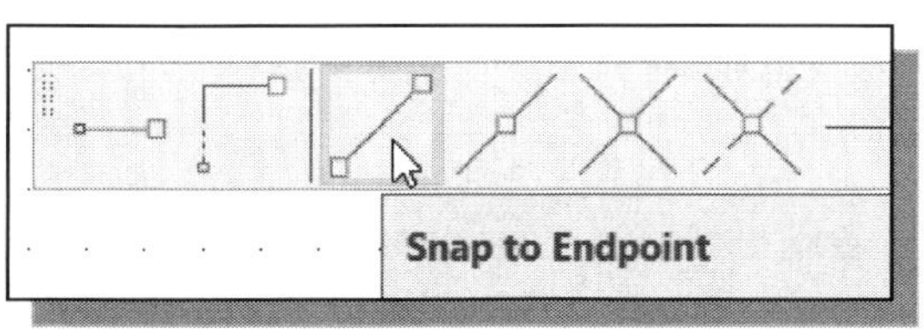

7. Pick **Snap to Endpoint** in the *Object Snap* toolbar.

8. Select point **X** to place the copied lines.

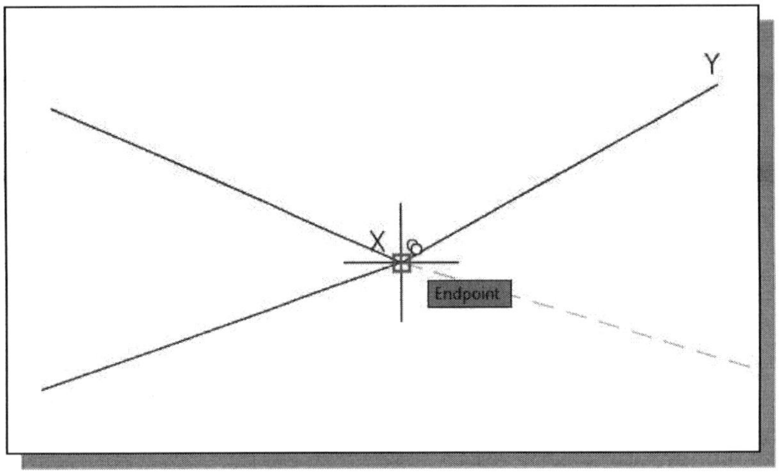

9. Hit the **ENTER** key once to end the Copy command.

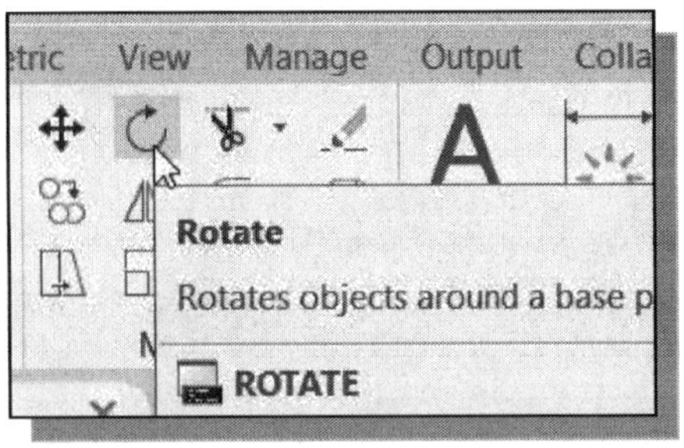

10. Select **Rotate** in the *Modify* toolbar as shown.

11. Select the two lines to the left of **X**.

12. **Right-click** once to proceed with the Rotate command.

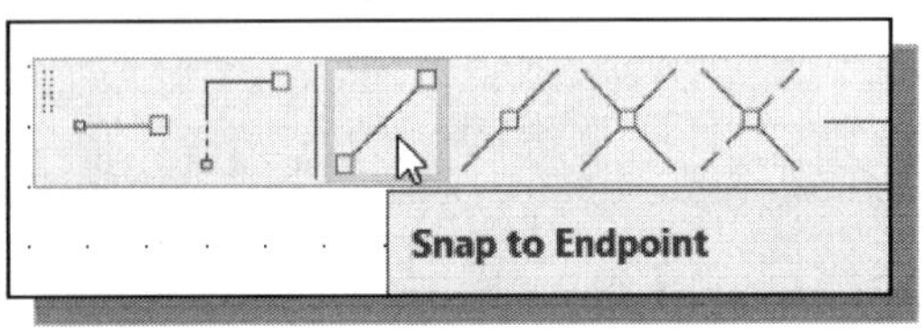

13. Pick **Snap to Endpoint** in the *Object Snap* toolbar.

14. Select point **X** as the base point for the rotation.

15. Inside the *Drawing Area*, **right-click** once to bring up the option menu.

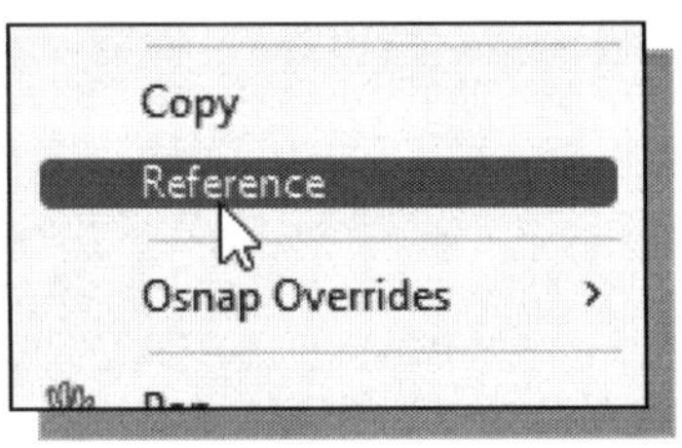

16. Select **Reference** in the option menu as shown.

17. Select point **X** as the first point.

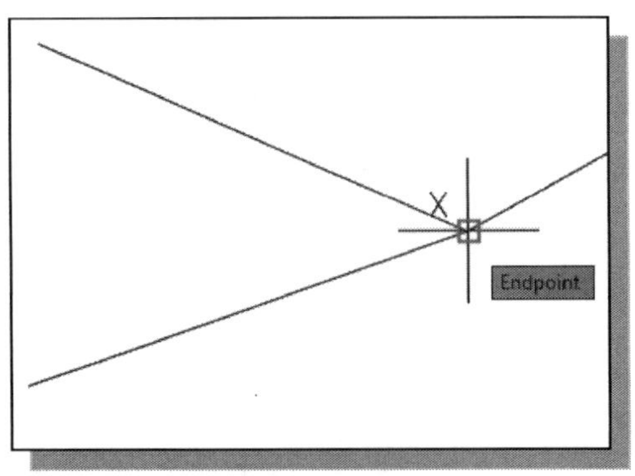

18. Select the left end point of the bottom line as shown.

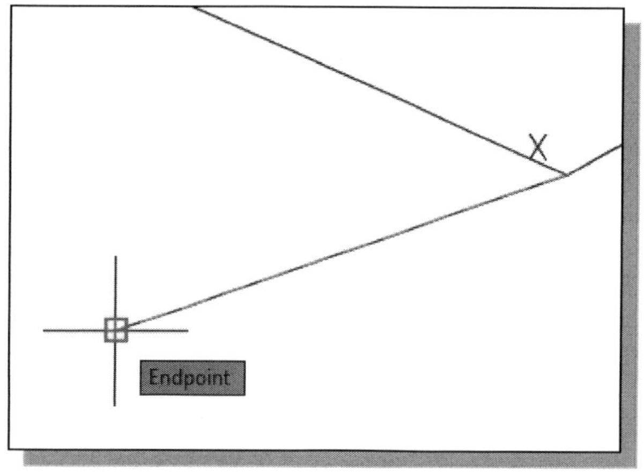

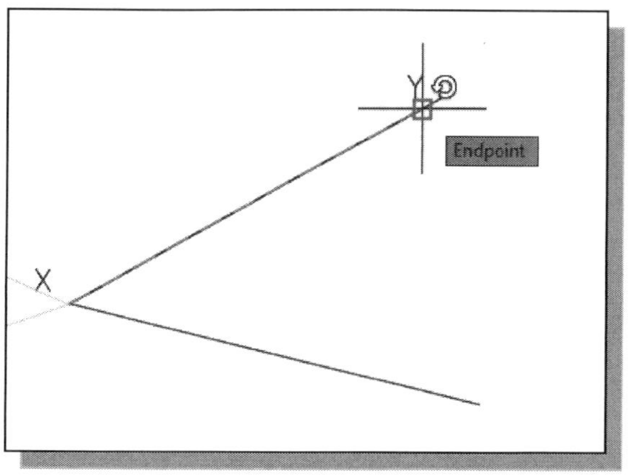

19. Select **Point Y** to align the lines as shown.

➢ Note the **angle** has been transferred to align to the XY line.

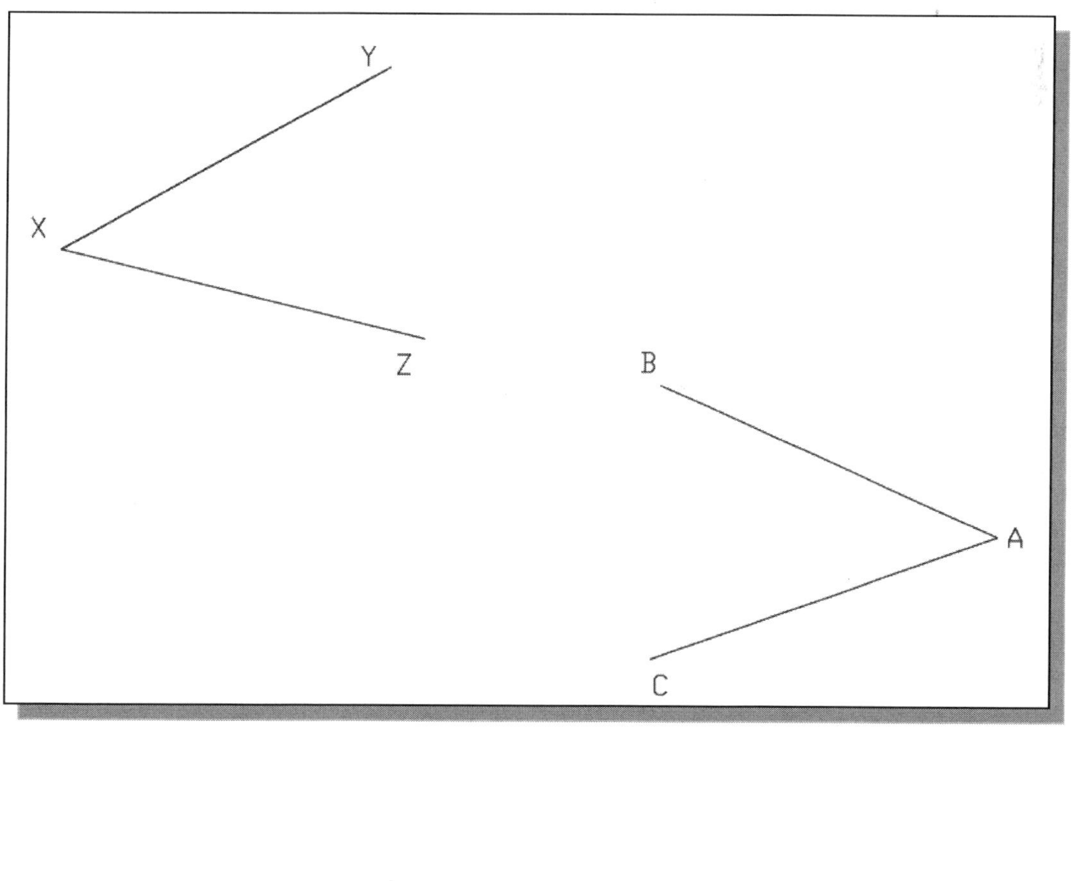

• Dividing a Given Line into a Number of Equal Parts

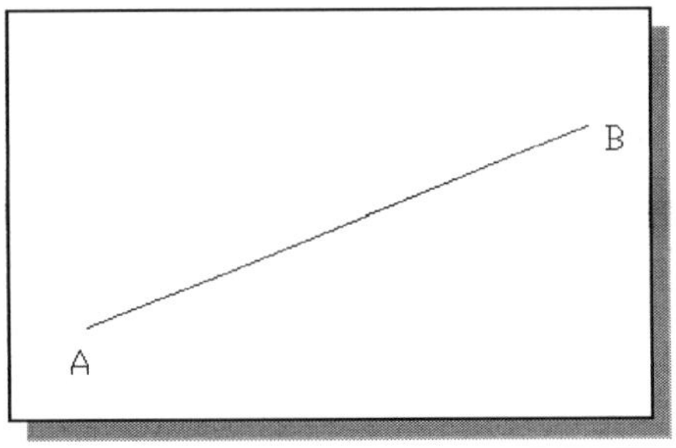

1. Create a line **AB** at an arbitrary angle; the line is to be divided into five equal parts.

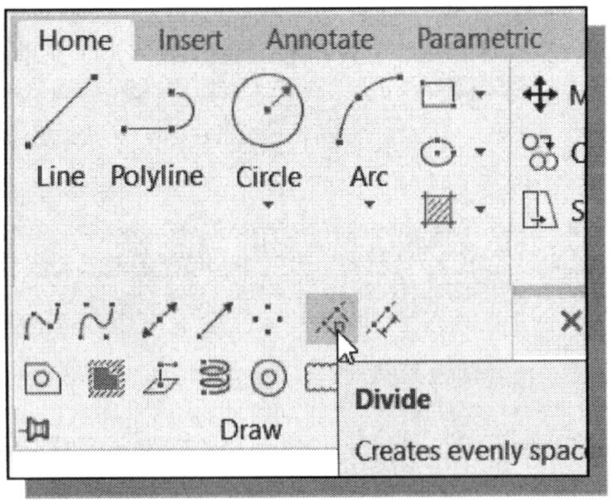

2. In the *Ribbon* toolbar, under *Draw*, select:

   [Divide]

3. Select line **AB**. In the message area, the message "*Enter the number of segments or [Block]:*" is displayed.

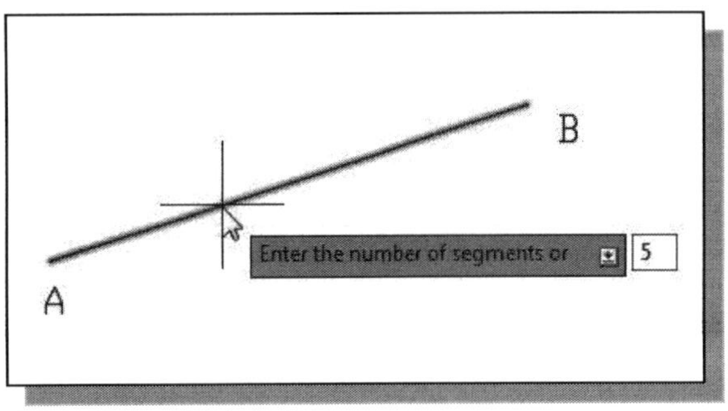

4. Enter **5** as the number of segments needed.

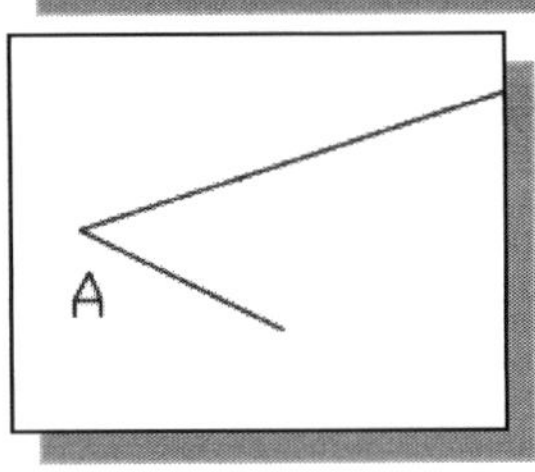

5. On your own, create an arbitrary short line segment at point **A**.

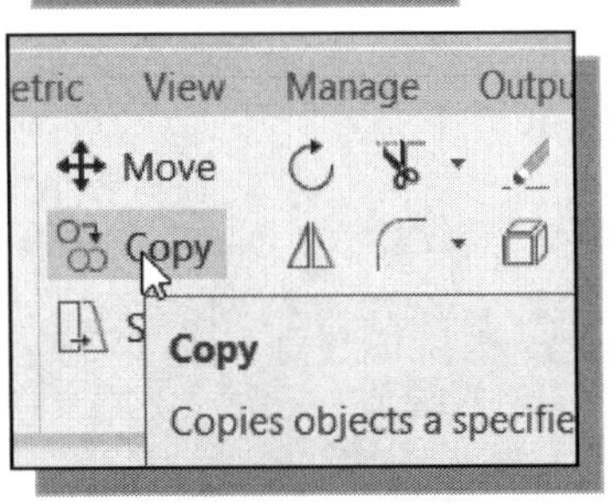

6. Select **Copy** in the *Modify* toolbar as shown.
7. Select the **short line** as the object to be copied.
8. **Right-click** once to proceed with the Copy command.

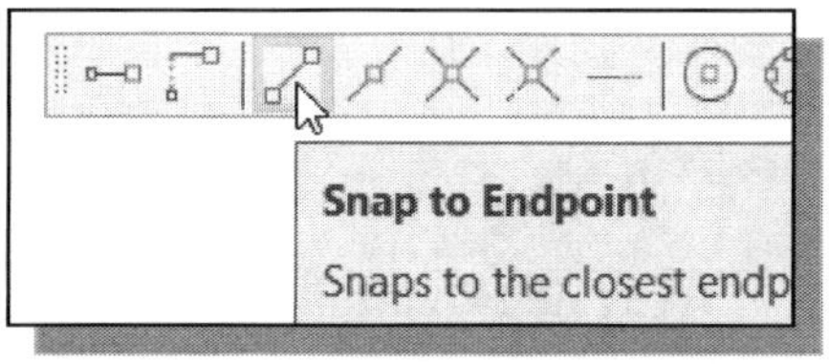

9. Pick **Snap to Endpoint** in the *Object Snap* toolbar.

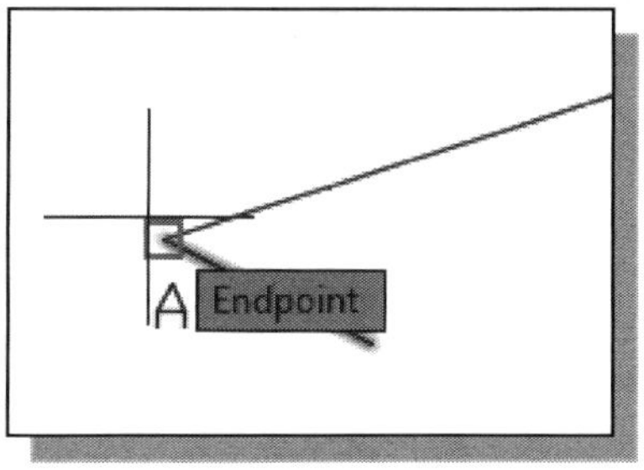

10. **Select** point **A** as the base reference point.

11. Pick **Snap to Node** in the *Object Snap* toolbar.

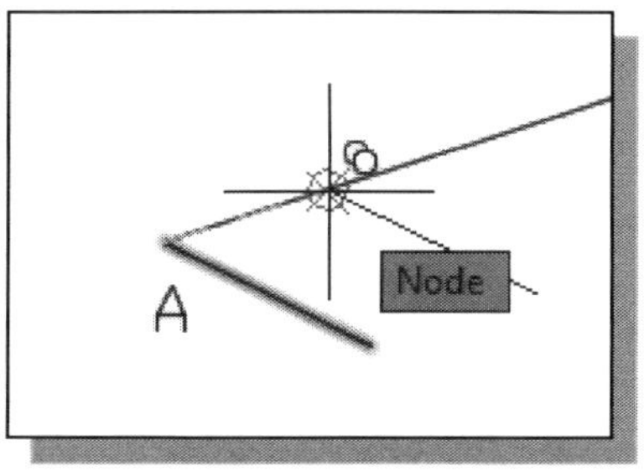

12. Move the cursor along line **AB**, and select the next node point as shown.

13. Repeat the above steps and create 3 additional lines at the nodes indicating the division of the line into five equal parts.

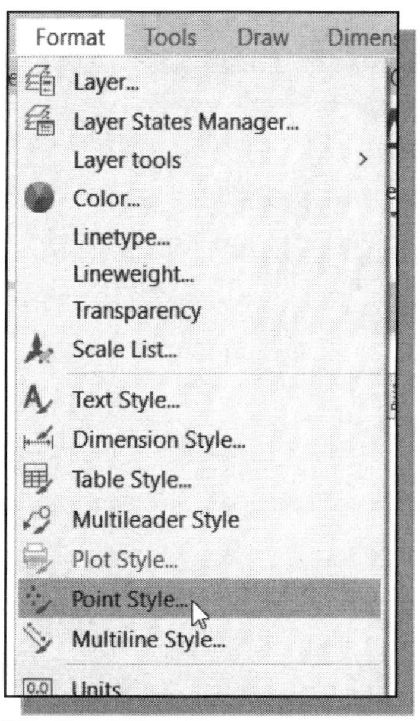

- We can also change the display of the created Points.

14. In the *Menu Bar*, select:

[Format] → [Point Style]

15. In the *Point Style* window, choose the 4th icon in the second row, as shown.

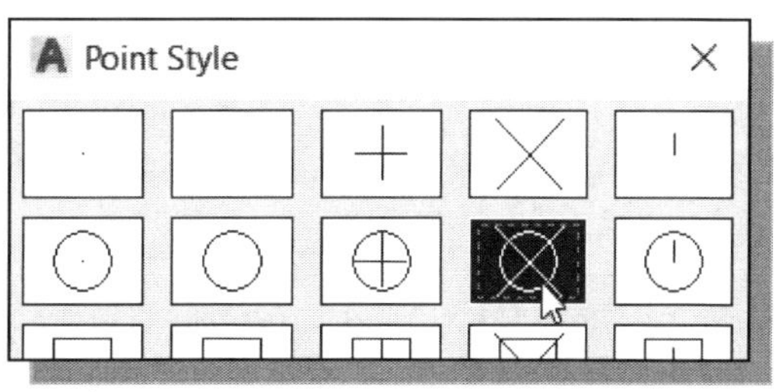

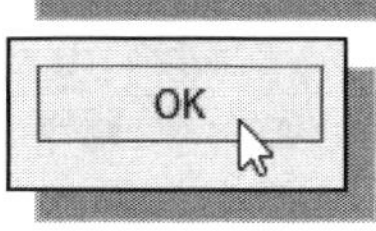

16. Click **OK** to accept the selection and adjust the point style.

- **Circle through Three Points**

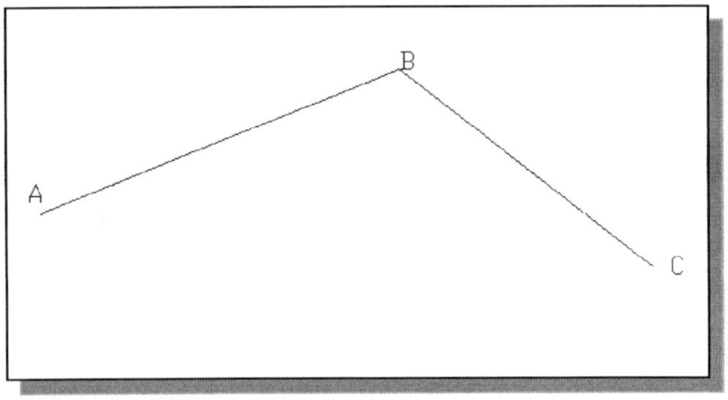

1. Create two arbitrary line segments, **AB** and **BC**, as shown.

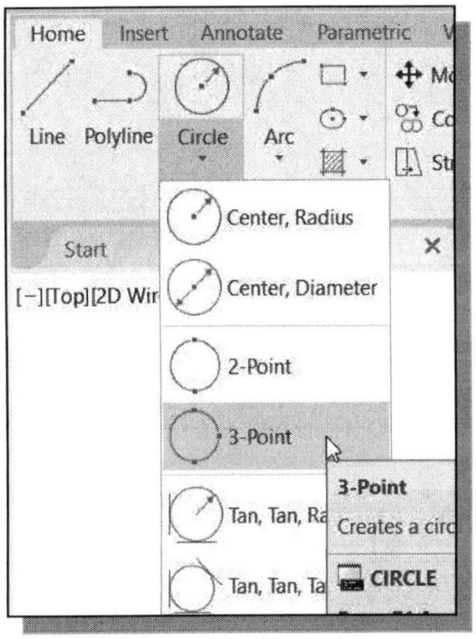

2. Select the **3-Point Circle** command in the *Draw* toolbar as shown.

3. Pick **Snap to Endpoint** in the *Object Snap* toolbar.

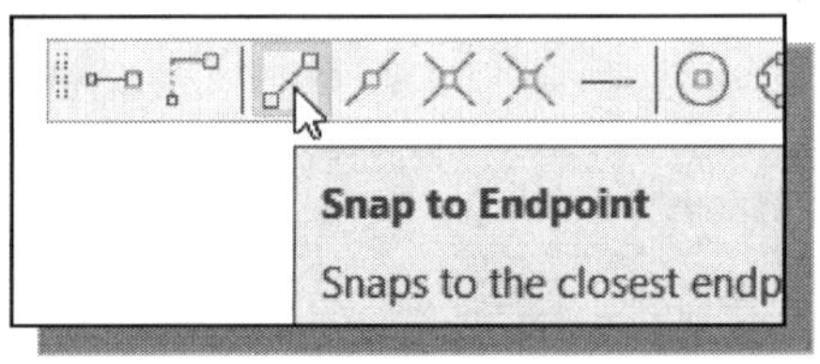

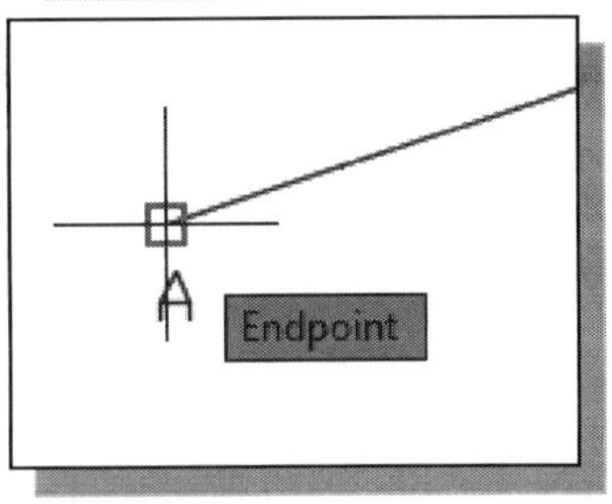

4. Select the first point, point **A**.

5. Repeat the above steps and select points **B** and **C** to create the circle that passes through all three points.

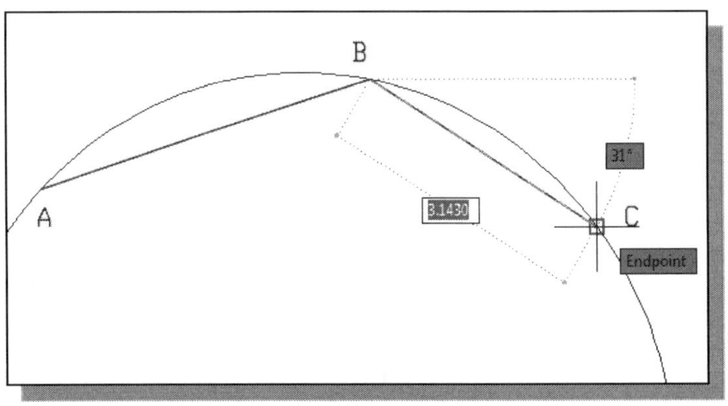

• Line Tangent to a Circle from a Given Point

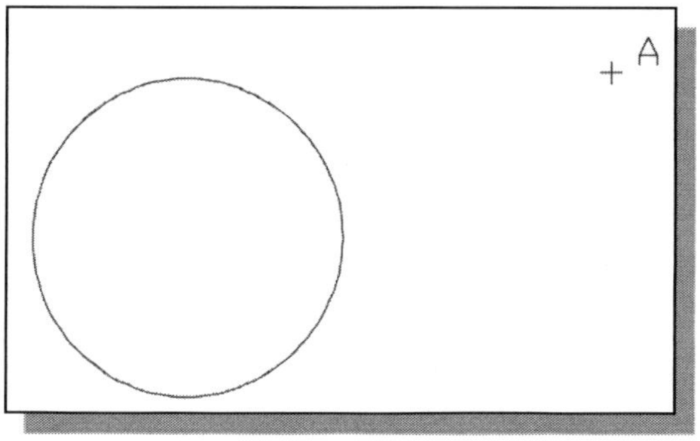

1. Create a circle and a point **A**. (Use the Point command to create point **A**.)

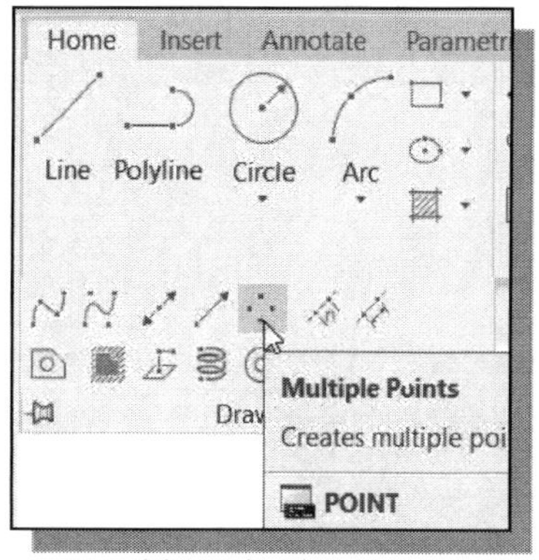

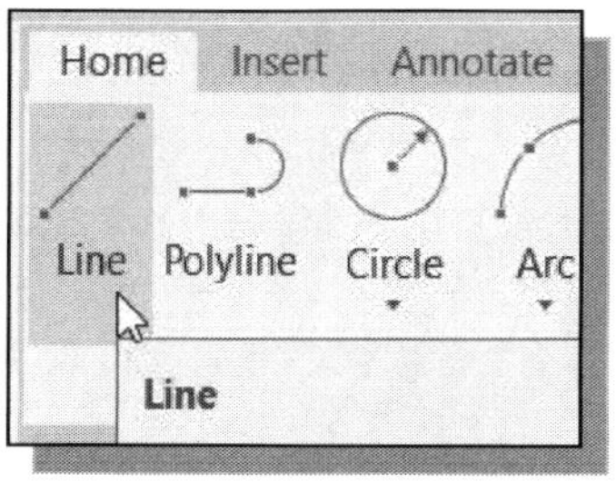

2. Select the **Line** command icon in the *Draw* toolbar. In the command prompt area, near the bottom of the AutoCAD drawing screen, the message "*Line Specify first point:*" is displayed. AutoCAD expects us to identify the starting location of a straight line.

3. Pick **Snap to Node** in the *Object Snap* toolbar.

4. Select point **A** as the starting point of the new line.

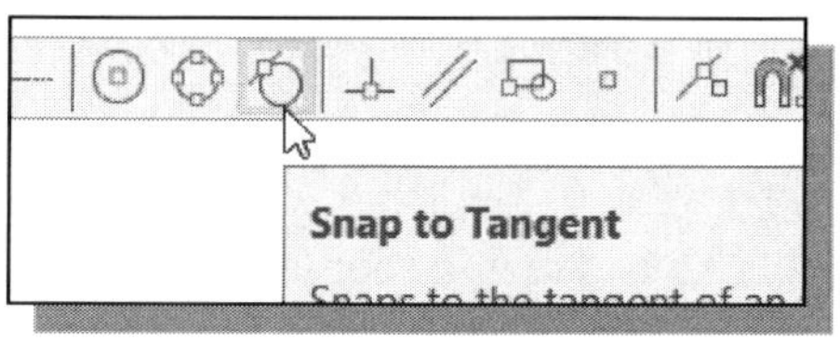

5. Pick **Snap to Tangent** in the *Object Snap* toolbar.

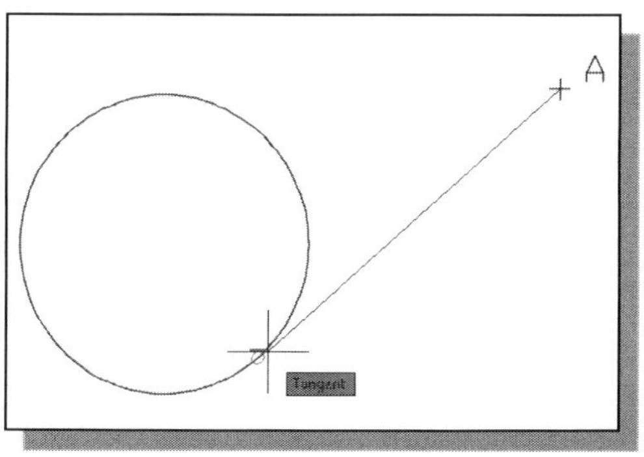

6. Move the cursor on top of the circle and notice the Tangent symbol is displayed.

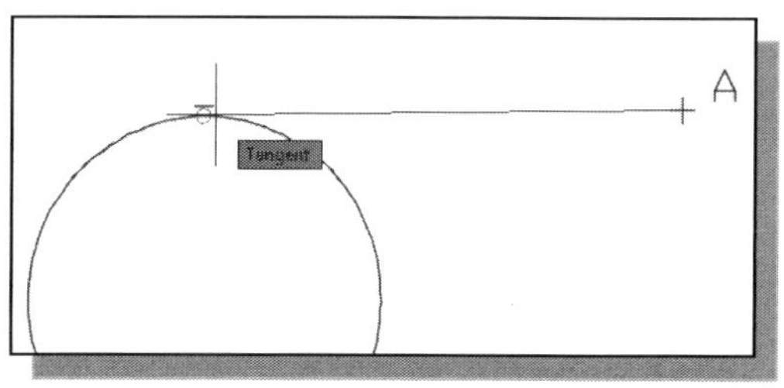

- Note that we can create two tangent lines, one to the top and one to the bottom of the circle, from point **A**.

- **Circle of a Given Radius Tangent to Two Given Lines**

Option I: TTR circle

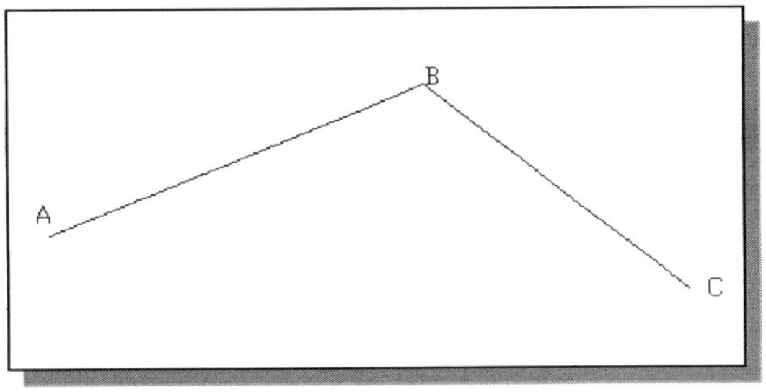

1. Create two arbitrary line segments as shown.

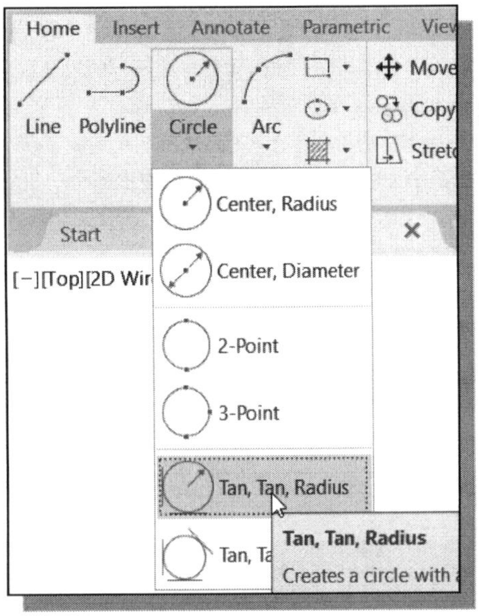

2. Select **TTR Circle** in the *Draw* toolbar as shown.

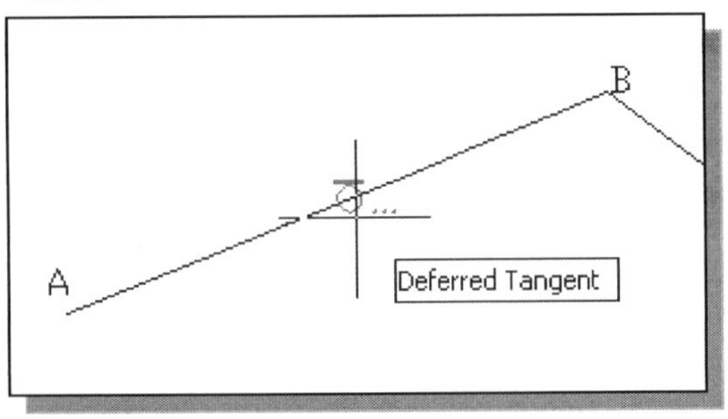

3. Select one of the line segments; note the tangency is deferred until all inputs are completed.

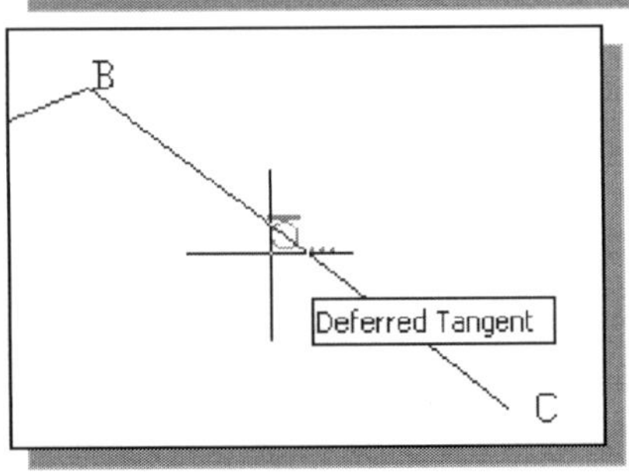

4. Select the other line segment; note the tangency is also deferred until all inputs are completed.

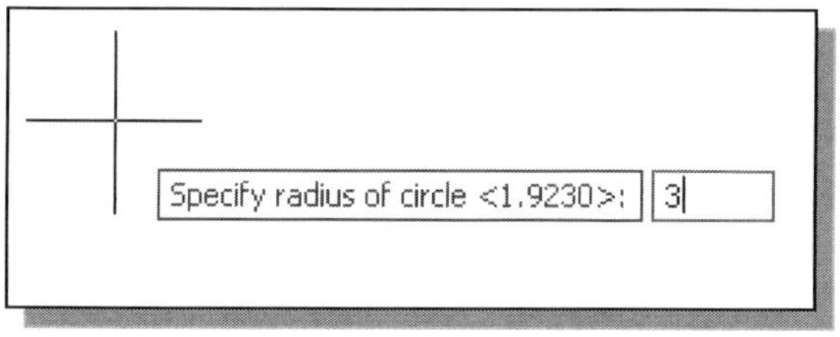

5. Enter ***3*** as the radius of the circle.

➢ The circle is constructed exactly tangent to both lines.

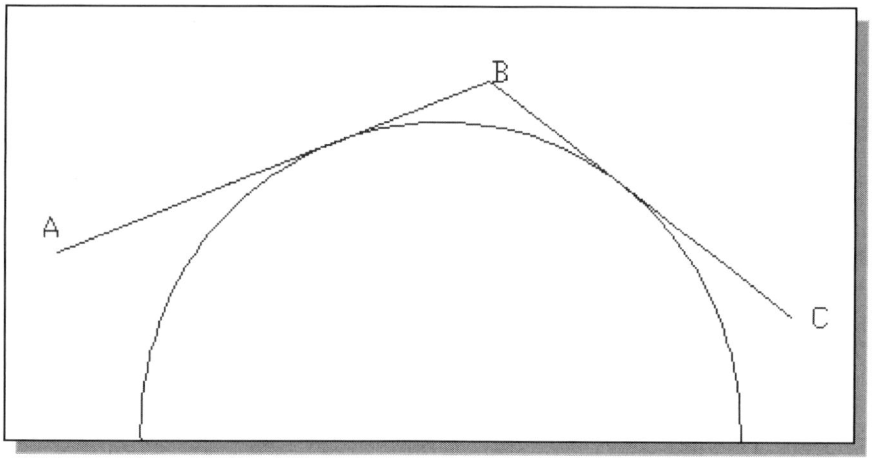

Option II: Fillet Command

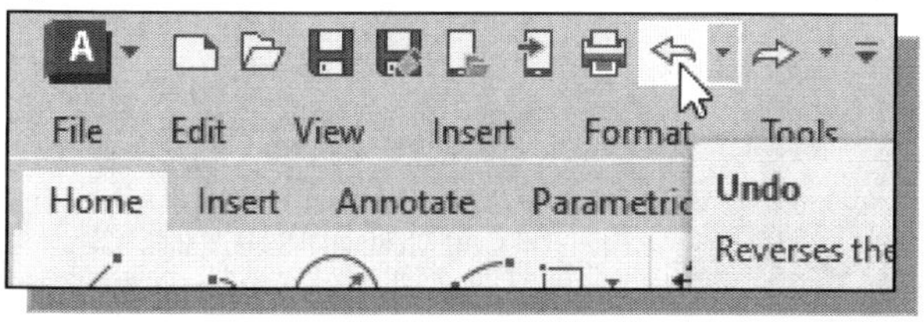

1. Select the **Undo** icon in the *Standard* toolbar as shown. This will undo the last step, the circle.

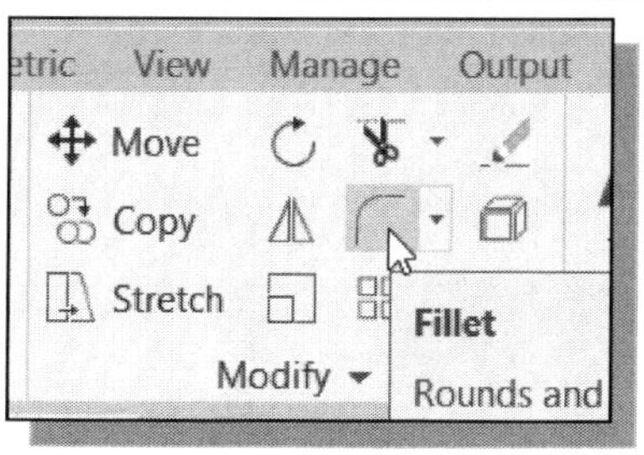

2. Select **Fillet** in the *Modify* toolbar as shown.

3. In the command prompt area, the message "*Select first object or [Undo/Polyline/Radius/Trim/Multiple]*" is displayed. By default, *Mode* is set to **Trim** and the current arc *Radius* is set to **0**.

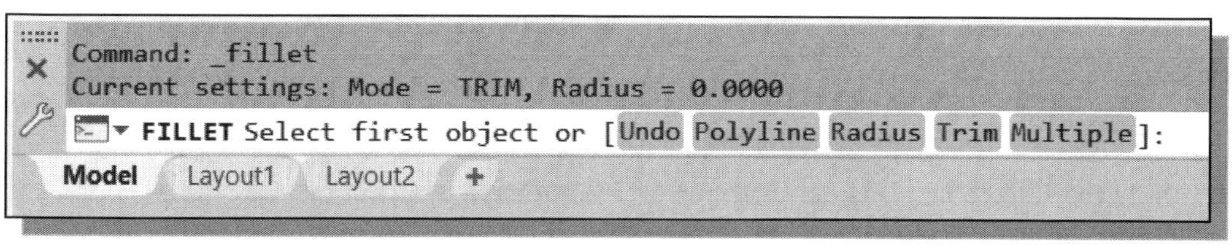

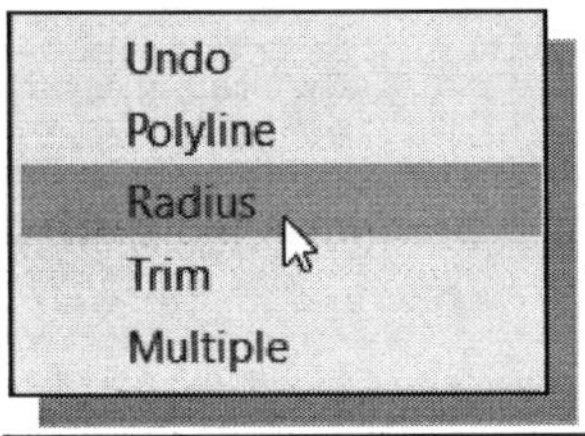

4. Inside the Drawing Area, **right-click** once to bring up the option menu.

5. Select **Radius** to adjust the radius of the fillet.

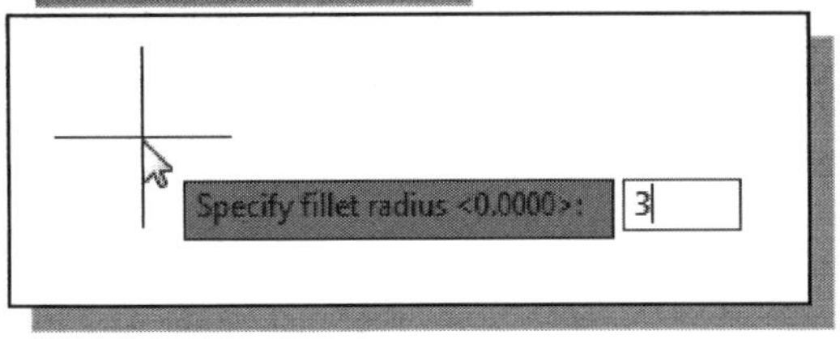

6. Enter ***3*** as the new radius of the Fillet command.

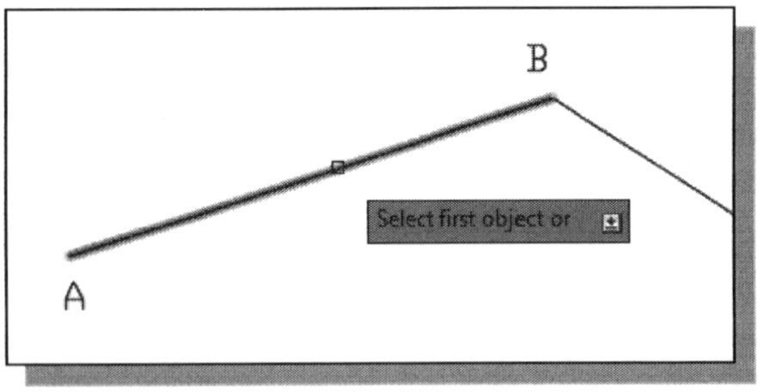

7. Select one of the lines as the first object.

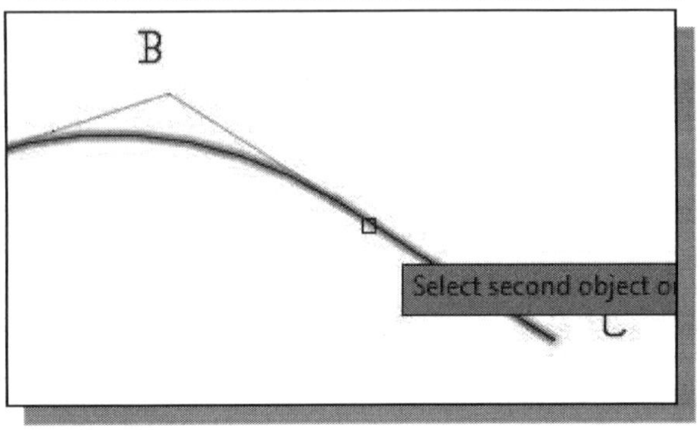

8. Select the other line as the second object.

➢ Note that the default setting of the Fillet command is to trim the edges as shown in the figure below.

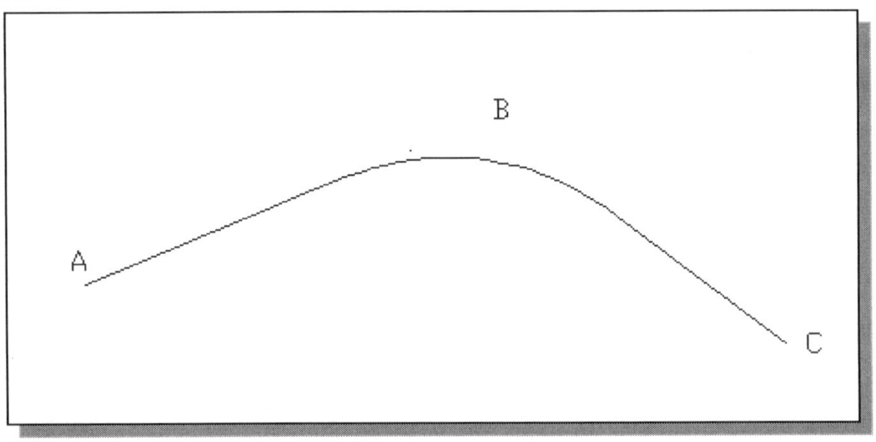

- Note that all of the classical methods for geometric construction, such as the one shown on page 2-8, can also be used in CAD systems.

The RockerArm Design

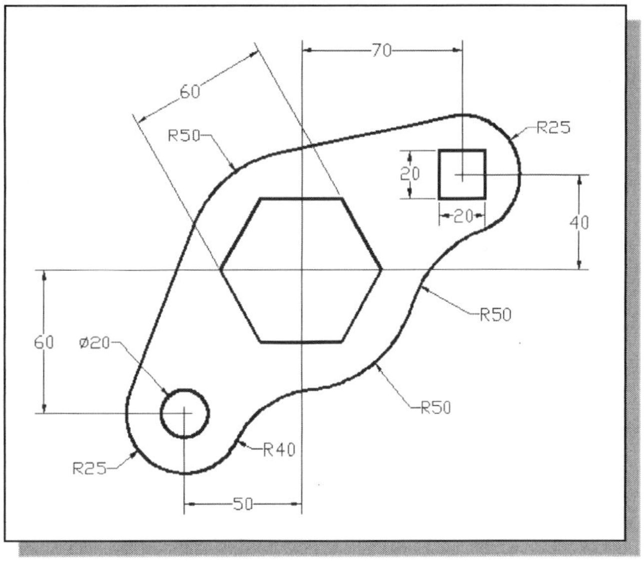

❖ Before continuing to the next page, on your own, make a rough sketch showing the steps that can be used to create the design. Be aware that there are many different approaches to accomplishing the same task.

Activate the Startup Option

In **AutoCAD 2027**, we can use the *Startup* dialog box to establish different types of drawing settings. The startup dialog box can be activated through the use of the **STARTUP** system variable.

The STARTUP system variable can be set to 0, 1, 2 or 3:

- 0: Starts a drawing without defined settings.
- 1: Displays the ***Create New Drawing*** dialog box.
- 2: Displays a ***Start Tab*** with options; a custom dialog box can be used.
- 3: Displays a ***Start Tab*** with the ribbon pre-loaded (default).

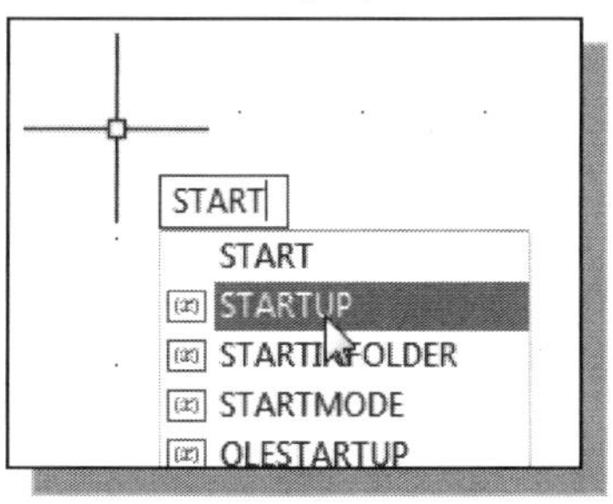

1. In the command prompt area, enter the system variable name:
   STARTUP [Enter]

2. Enter ***1*** as the new value for the startup system variable.

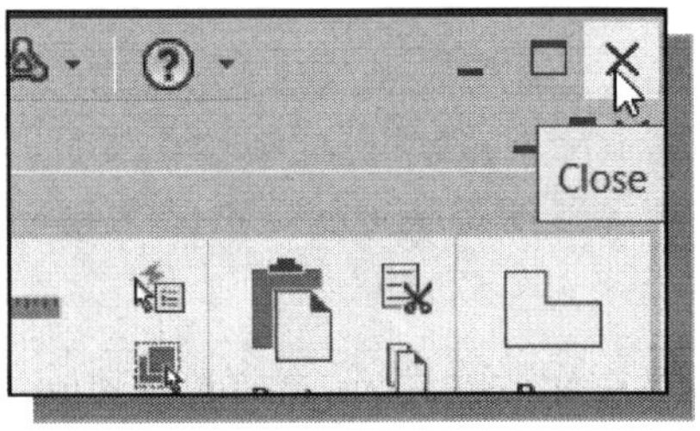

3. To show the effect of the *Startup* option, **exit** AutoCAD by clicking on the **Close** icon as shown.

4. Restart AutoCAD by selecting the **AutoCAD 2027** option through the *Start* menu.

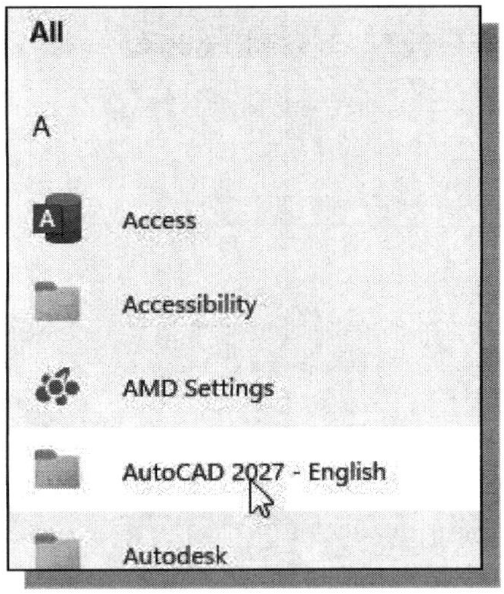

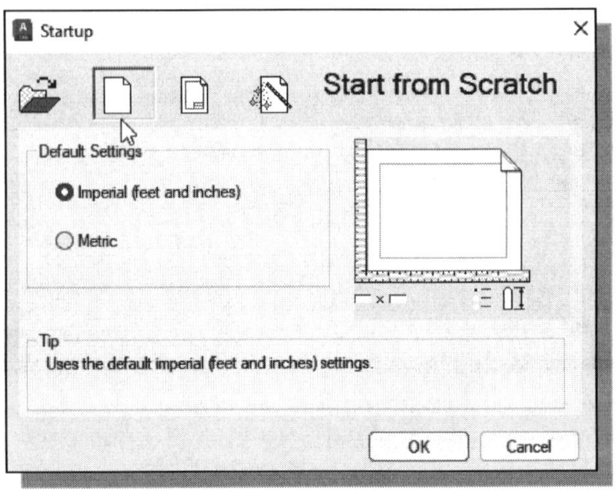

5. The *Startup* dialog box appears on the screen with different options to assist in the creation of drawings. Move the cursor on top of the four icons and notice the four options available:
(1) **Open a drawing**
(2) **Start from Scratch**
(3) **Use a Template**
(4) **Use a Setup Wizard**

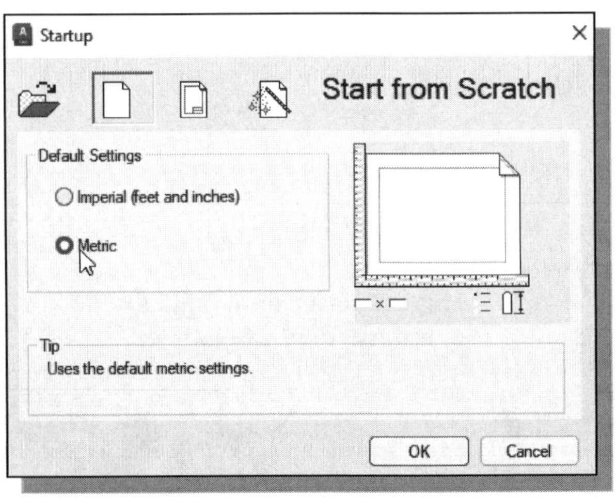

6. In the *Startup* dialog box, select the **Start from Scratch** option as shown in the figure.

7. Choose **Metric** to use the metric settings.

8. Click **OK** to accept the setting.

Drawing Units Display Setup

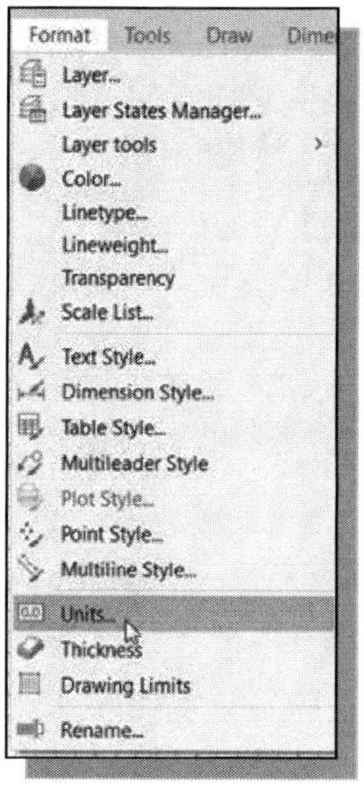

1. Click the *Menu Bar* area and select:
   [Format] → [Units]

2. Set the *Precision* to **no digits** after the decimal point.

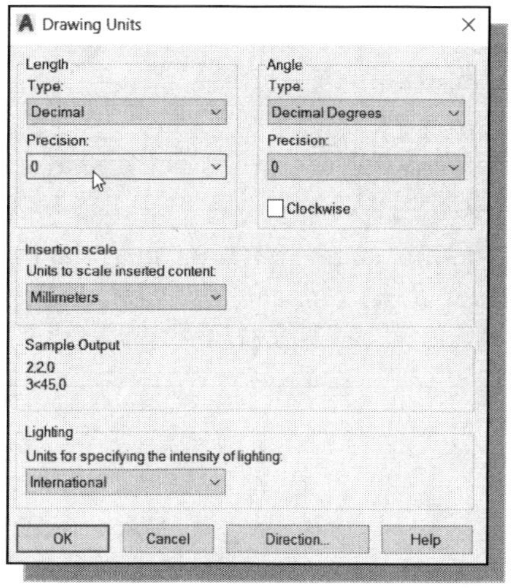

3. Click **OK** to exit the *Drawing Units* dialog box.

GRID and SNAP Intervals Setup

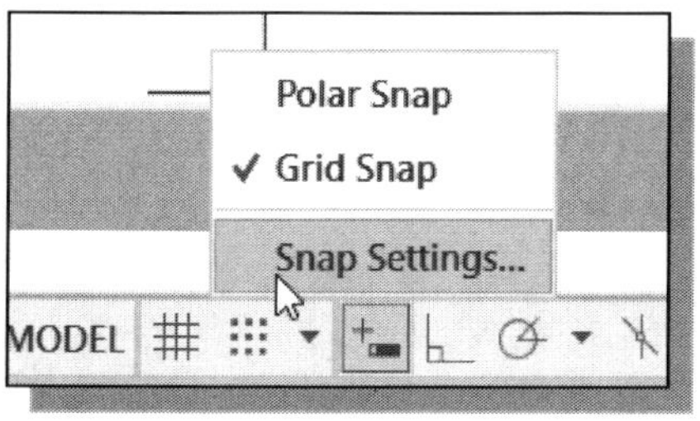

1. In the *Status Bar* area, **right-click** on ***Snap Mode*** and choose **[Snap Settings]**.

2. In the *Drafting Settings* dialog box, select the **Snap and Grid** tab if it is not the page on top.

3. Change *Grid Spacing* and *Snap Spacing* to ***10*** for both X and Y directions.

4. Switch ***ON*** the *Display dotted grid in 2D model Space* option as shown.

5. Switch ***ON*** the *Grid On* and *Snap On* options as shown.

6. Click **OK** to exit the *Drawing Units* dialog box.

Drawing Area Setup

Next, we will set up the **Drawing Limits**. Setting the **Drawing Limits** controls the extents of the display of the *grid*. It also serves as a visual reference that marks the working area. Note that this setting can also be adjusted through the use of the command prompt area.

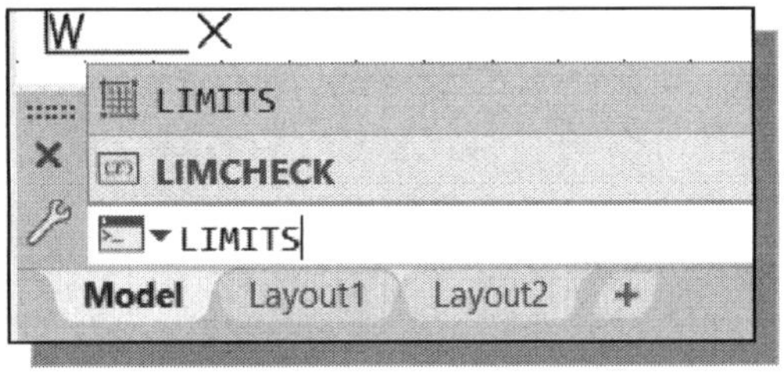

1. Click inside the *command prompt* area.

2. Inside the *command prompt area*, enter ***Limits*** and press the **[Enter]** key.

3. In the command prompt area, near the bottom of the AutoCAD drawing screen, the message "*Reset Model Space Limits: Specify lower left corner or [On/Off] <0,0>:*" is displayed. Enter ***-200,-150*** through the *Dynamic Input* entry boxes.

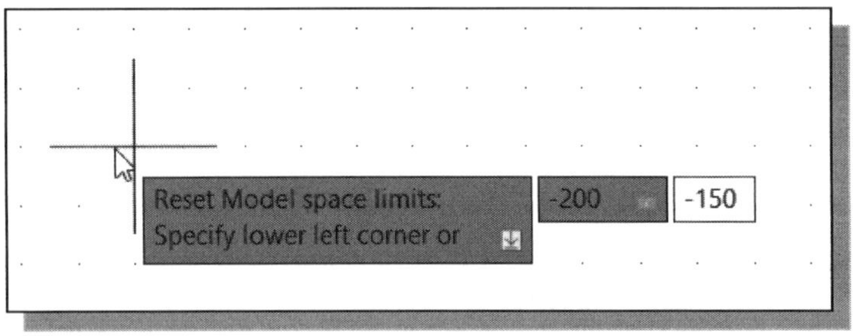

4. In the command prompt area, the message "*Specify upper right corner <420,297>:*" is displayed. Enter ***200,150*** as the new upper right coordinates as shown.

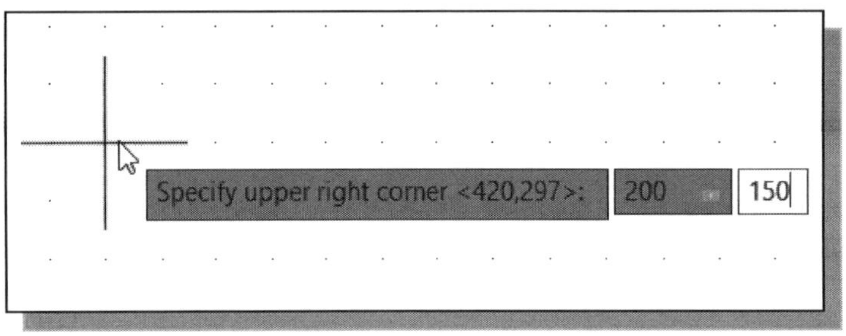

5. On your own, use the *Menu Bar* and confirm the **[View] → [Display] → [UCS Icon] → [Origin]** option is switched *ON* as shown. (The little checked icon next to the option indicates it is switched *ON*.)

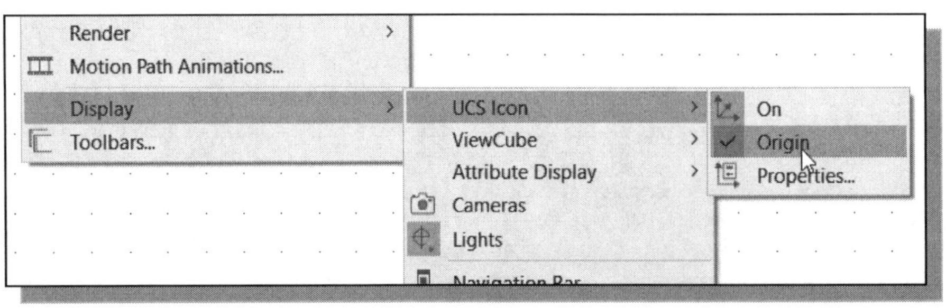

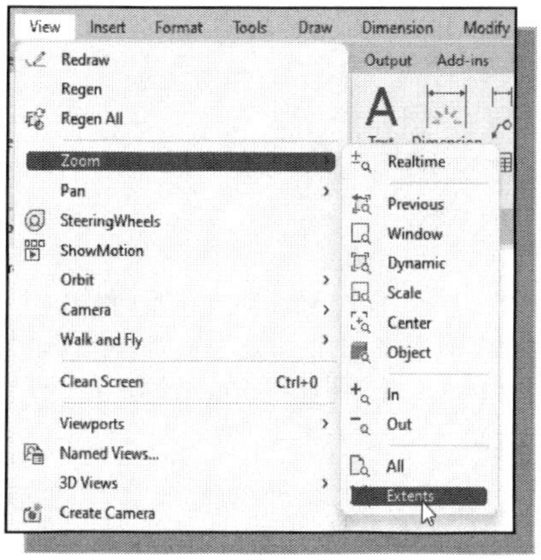

6. On your own, use the **Zoom Extents** command, under the **View** pull-down menu, to reset the display.

❖ Notice the *UCS Icon*, which is aligned to the origin, is displayed near the center of the Drawing Area.

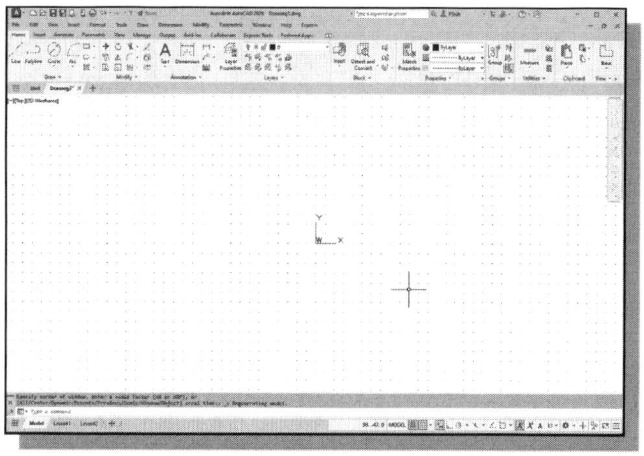

Referencing the World Coordinate System

Design modeling software is becoming more powerful and user friendly, yet the system still does only what the user tells it to do. When using a geometric modeler, we therefore need to have a good understanding of what the inherent limitations are. We should also have a good understanding of what we want to do and what to expect, as the results are based on what is available.

In most geometric modelers, objects are located and defined in what is usually called **world space** or **global space**. Although a number of different coordinate systems can be used to create and manipulate objects in a 3D modeling system, the objects are typically defined and stored using the *world space*. The *world space* is usually a **3D Cartesian coordinate system** that the user cannot change or manipulate.

In most engineering designs, models can be very complex, and it would be tedious and confusing if only one coordinate system were available in CAD systems. Practical CAD systems provide the user with definable **Local Coordinate Systems (LCS)** or **User Coordinate Systems (UCS)**, which are measured relative to the world coordinate system. Once a local coordinate system is defined, we can then create geometry in terms of this more convenient system. For most CAD systems, the default construction coordinate system is initially aligned to the world coordinate system.

In AutoCAD, the default **User Coordinate System (UCS)** is initially aligned to the XY plane of the **World Coordinate System (WCS)**. One simple approach to creating designs in CAD systems is to create geometry by referencing the **World Coordinate System**. The general procedure of this approach is illustrated in the following sections.

Creating Circles

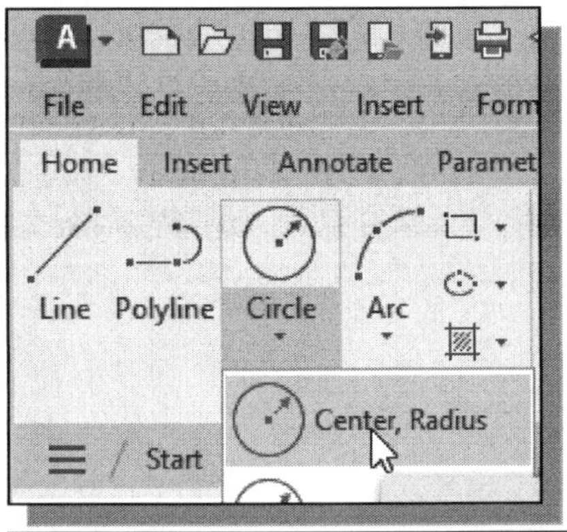

1. Select the **Circle – Center, Radius** command icon in the *Draw* toolbar.

2. On your own, dock the command prompt dialog box to the lower left of the graphics window. Note that you can adjust the size of the box by dragging the edge of the box.

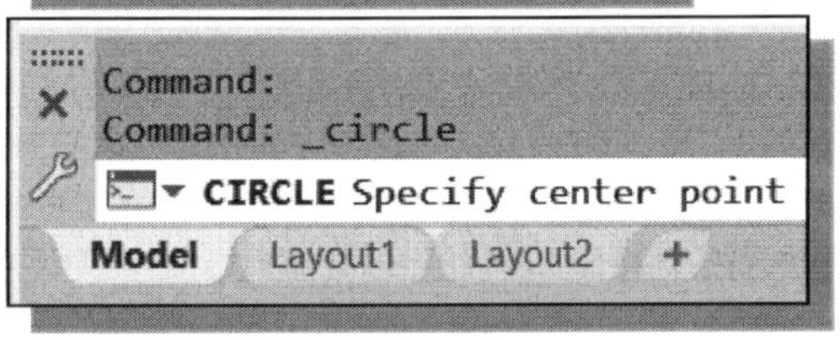

3. In the *command prompt area*, the message "*Circle Specify center point for the circle or [3P/2P/Ttr (tan tan radius)]:*" is displayed. Select the **origin** of the world coordinate system as the center point.

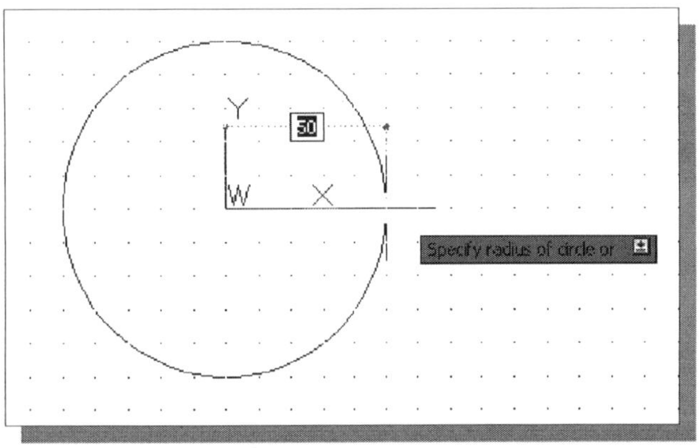

4. In the command prompt area, the message "*Specify radius of circle or [Diameter]:*" is displayed. AutoCAD expects us to identify the radius of the circle. Set the radius to ***50*** by observing the tooltips as shown.

5. Hit the **[SPACE BAR]** once to repeat the circle command.

6. On your own, select ***70,40*** as the absolute coordinate values of the center point coordinates of the second circle.

7. Set the value of the radius to ***25***.

8. On your own, repeat the above procedure and create another circle (radius ***25***) at absolute coordinates of ***-50,-60*** as shown in the figure.

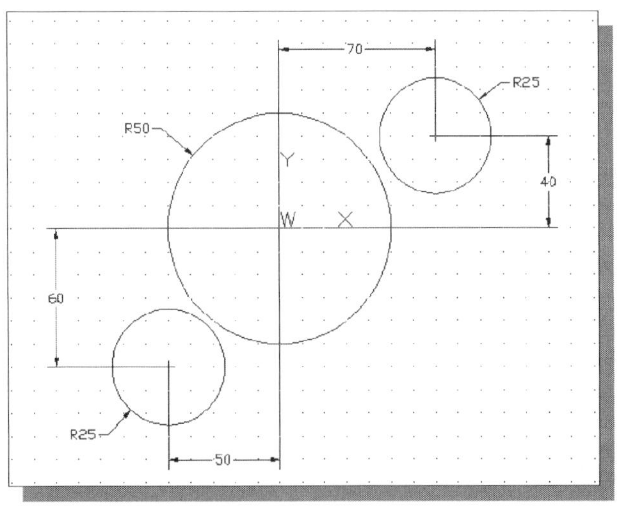

Object Snap Toolbar

1. Move the cursor to the *Menu Bar* area and choose **[Tools] → [Toolbars] → [AutoCAD]**.

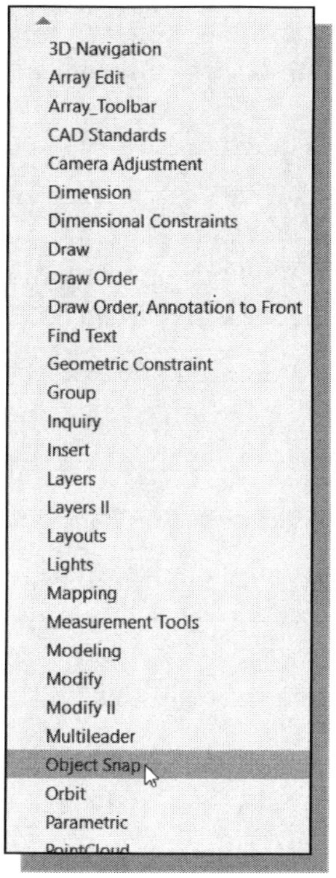

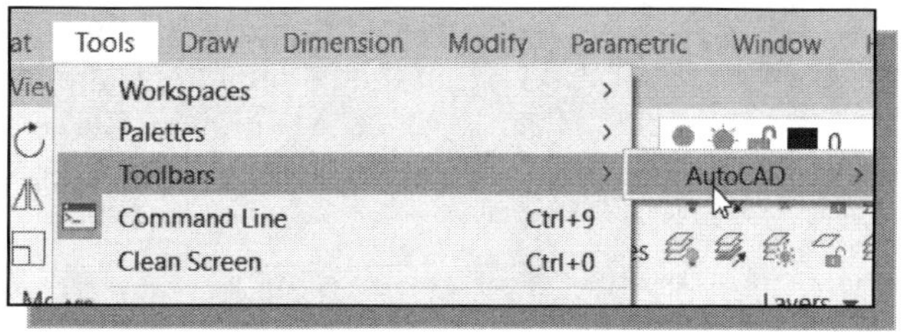

❖ AutoCAD provides 50+ predefined toolbars for access to frequently used commands, settings, and modes. A *checkmark* (next to the item) in the list identifies the toolbars that are currently displayed on the screen.

2. Select **Object Snap**, with the left-mouse-button, to display the *Object Snap* toolbar on the screen.

❖ **Object Snap** is an extremely powerful construction tool available on most CAD systems. During an entity's creation operations, we can snap the cursor to points on objects such as endpoints, midpoints, centers, and intersections. For example, we can turn on **Object Snap** and quickly draw a line to the center of a circle, the midpoint of a line segment, or the intersection of two lines.

3. Move the cursor over the icons in the *Object Snap* toolbar and read the description of each icon.

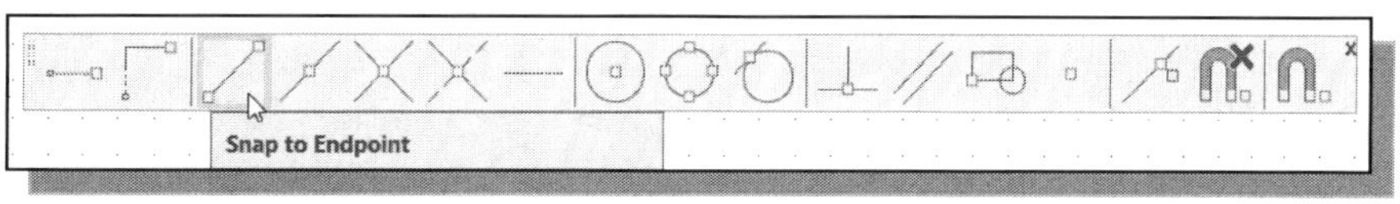

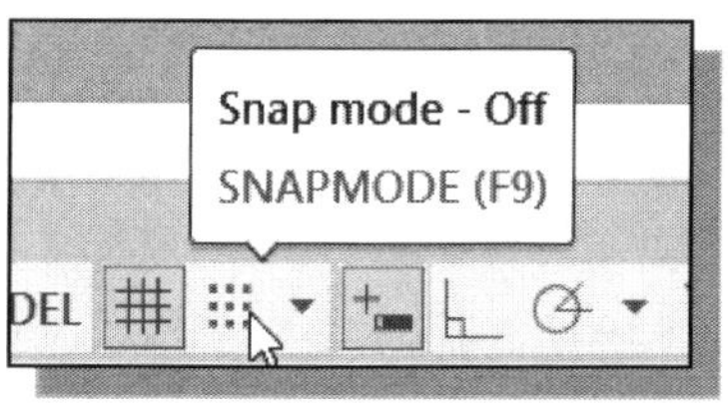

4. We will next turn ***OFF*** the *GRID SNAP* option by toggling off the ***SNAP Mode*** button in the *Status Bar* area.

5. On your own, reset the option buttons in the *Status Bar* area, so that only the *GRID DISPLAY* option is switched ***ON***.

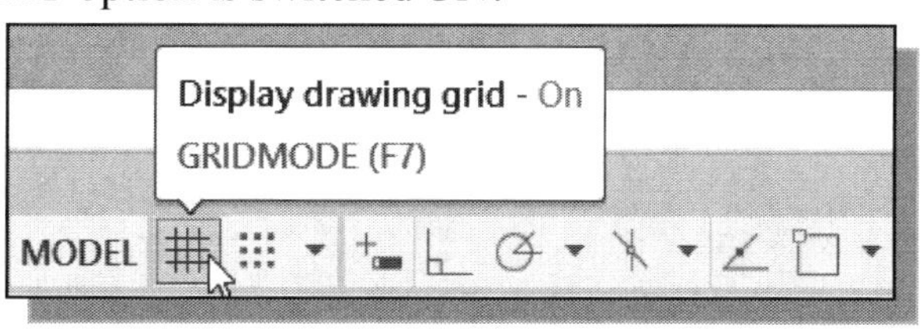

Using the Line Command

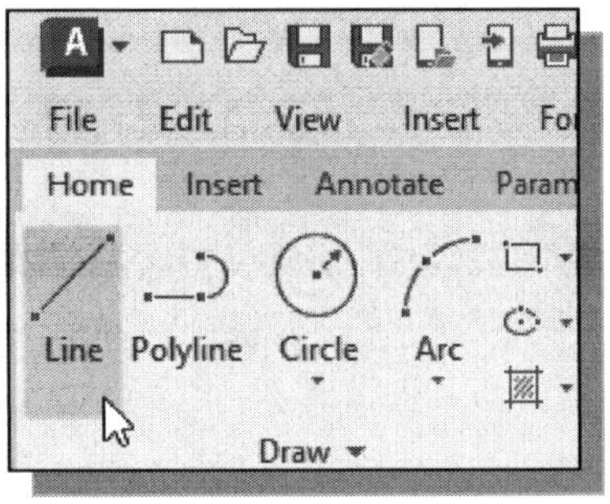

1. Select the **Line** command icon in the *Draw* toolbar. In the command prompt area, near the bottom of the AutoCAD drawing screen, the message "*_line Specify first point:*" is displayed.

2. Pick **Snap to Tangent** in the *Object Snap* toolbar. In the command prompt area, the message "*_tan to*" is displayed. AutoCAD now expects us to select a circle or an arc on the screen.

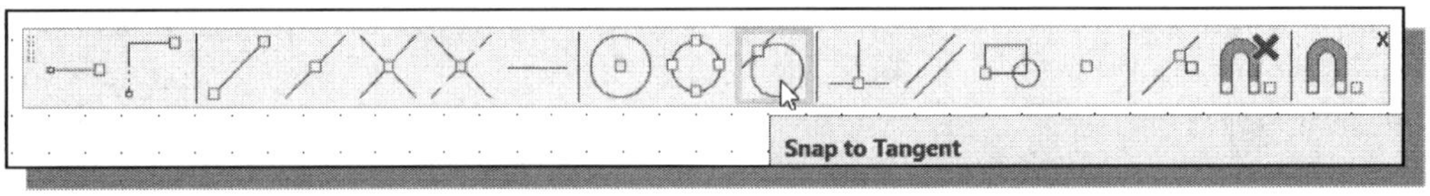

❖ The **Snap to Tangent** option allows us to snap to the point on a circle or arc that, when connected to the last point, forms a line tangent to that object.

3. Pick a location that is near the top left side of the smaller circle on the right; note the tangent symbol is displayed as shown.

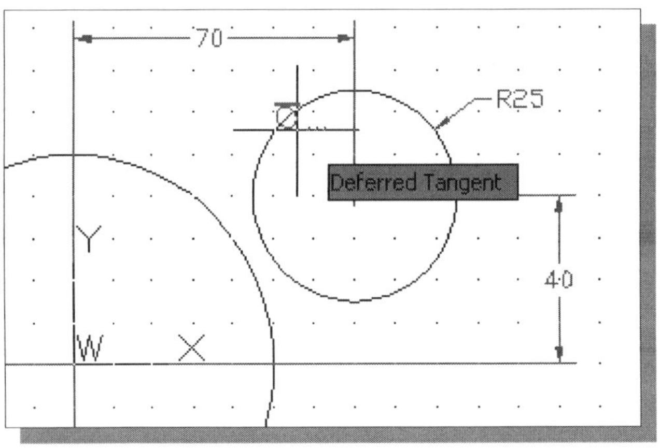

❖ Note that the note "Deferred Tangent" indicates that AutoCAD will calculate the tangent location when the other endpoint of the line is defined.

4. Pick **Snap to Tangent** in the *Object Snap* toolbar. In the command prompt area, the message "*_tan to*" is displayed. AutoCAD now expects us to select a circle or an arc on the screen.

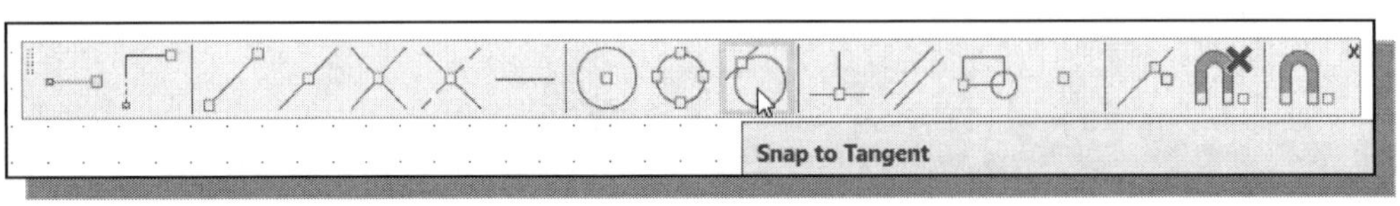

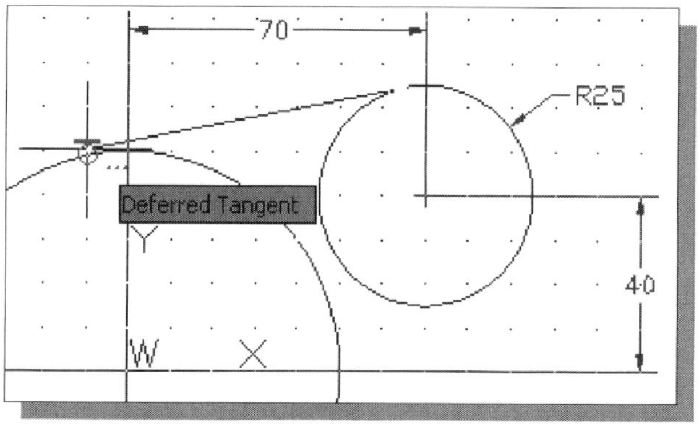

5. Pick a location that is near the top left side of the center circle; note the tangent symbol is displayed as shown.

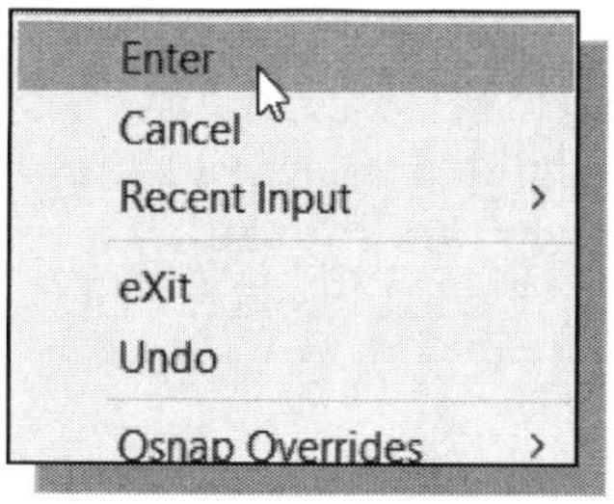

6. Inside the *Drawing Area*, **right-click** to activate the option menu and select **Enter** with the left-mouse-button to end the **Line** command.

❖ A line tangent to both circles is constructed as shown in the figure.

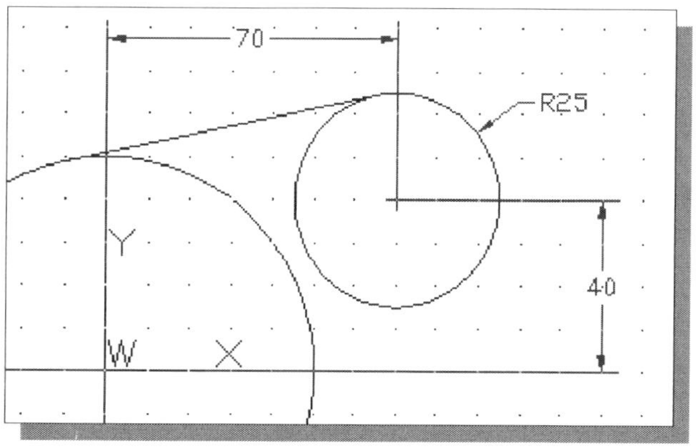

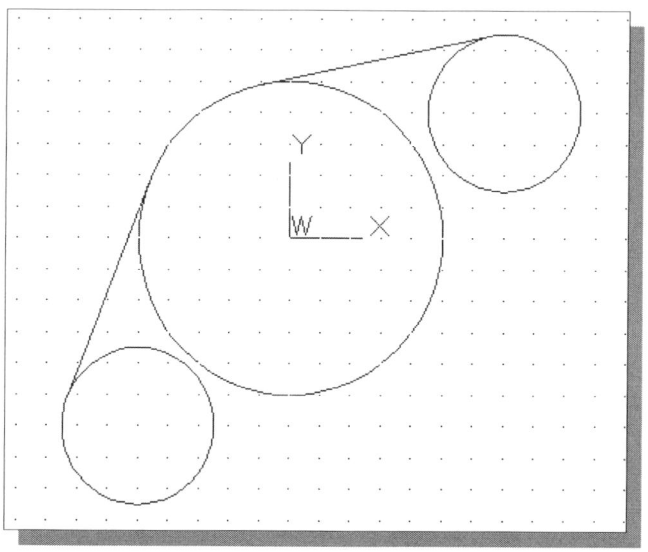

7. On your own, repeat the above steps and create the other tangent line between the center circle and the circle on the left. Your drawing should appear as the figure.

Creating TTR Circles

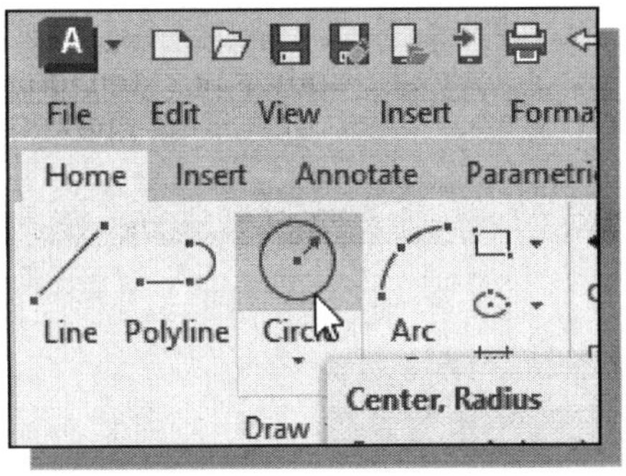

1. Select the **Circle** command icon in the *Draw* toolbar. In the command prompt area, the message "*Specify center point for circle or [3P/2P/Ttr (tan tan radius)]:*" is displayed.

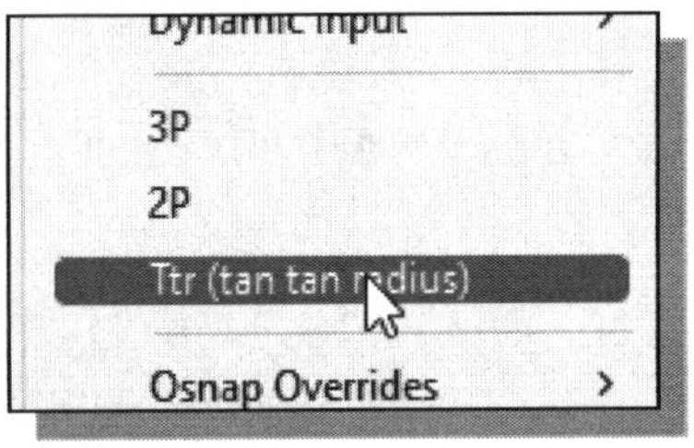

2. Inside the Drawing Area, right-click to activate the option menu and select the **Ttr (tan tan radius)** option. This option allows us to create a circle that is tangent to two objects.

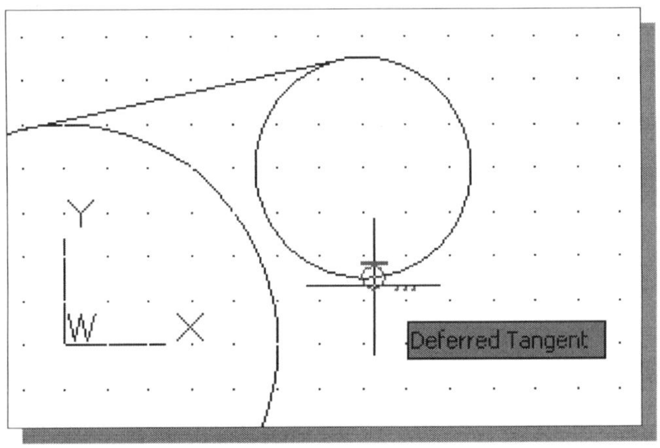

3. Pick a location near the **bottom of the smaller circle** on the right. We will create a circle that is tangent to this circle and the center circle.

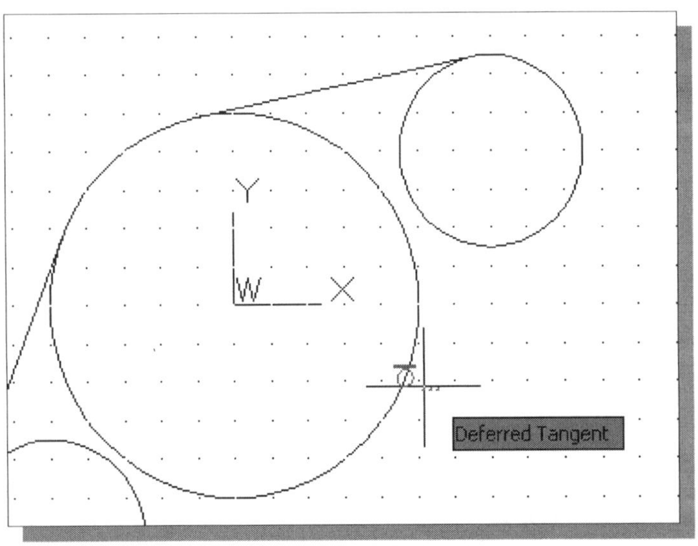

4. Pick the **center circle** by selecting a location that is near the right side of the circle. AutoCAD interprets the locations we selected as being near the tangency.

5. In the command prompt area, the message "*Specify radius of circle*" is displayed. Enter ***50*** as the radius of the circle.

   Specify radius of circle: **50 [ENTER]**

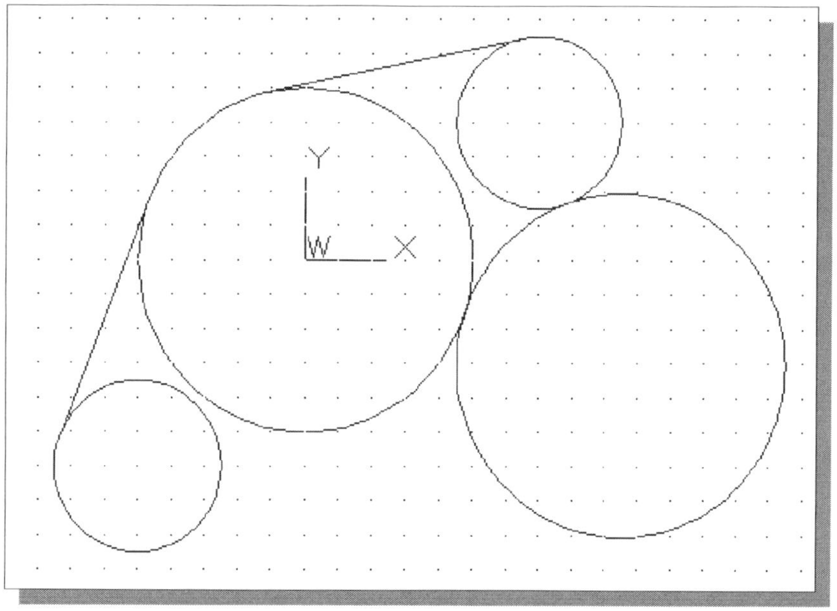

6. On your own, repeat the above steps and create the other TTR circle (radius ***40***). Your drawing should appear as the figure below.

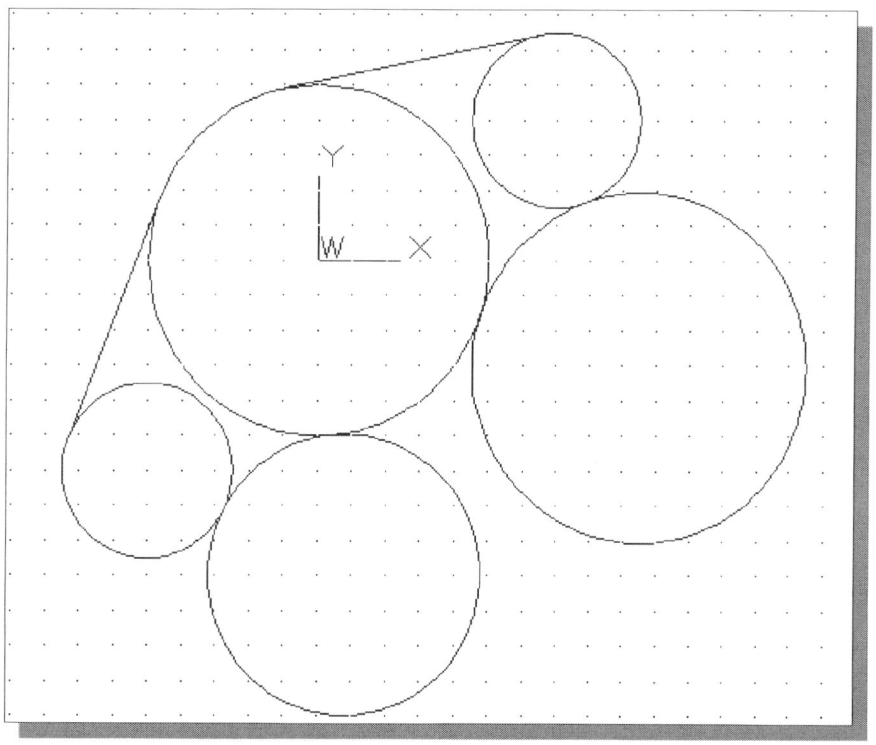

Using the Trim Command

The **Trim** command shortens an object so that it ends precisely at a selected boundary.

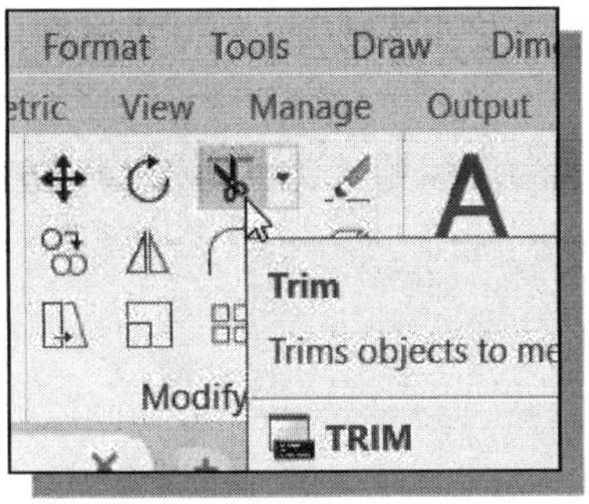

1. Select the **Trim** command icon in the *Modify* toolbar, and click on the down-triangle to display additional icons as shown.

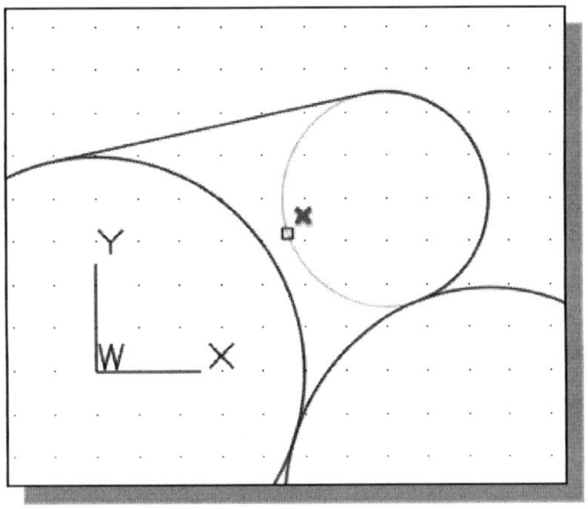

2. The message *"Select object to trim or shift-select object to extend or [Project/Edge/Undo]:"* is displayed in the command prompt area. Move the cursor on the **left** section of the upper right circle and note the selected portion is trimmed as shown.

❖ In AutoCAD, several options are available with the Trim command: (1) We can specify cutting edges at which an object is to stop. Valid cutting edge objects include most 2D geometry such as lines, arcs, circles, ellipses, polylines, splines, and text. For 3D objects, a 2D projection method can also be used, where objects are projected onto the XY plane of the current user coordinate system (UCS). (2) We can select objects to trim by defining a two-point rectangle. (3) We can erase an entire object while in the trim command.

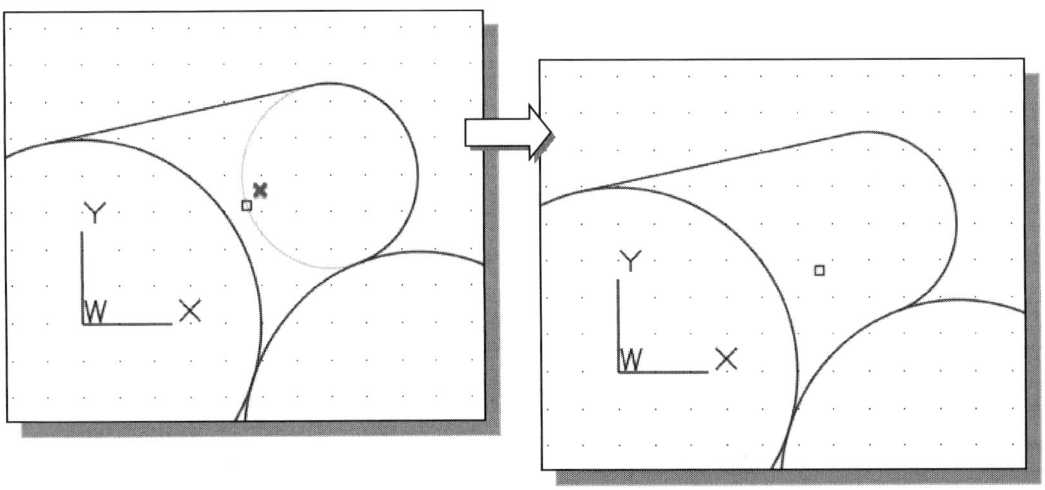

3. Select the upper right side of the center circle to remove the selected portion.

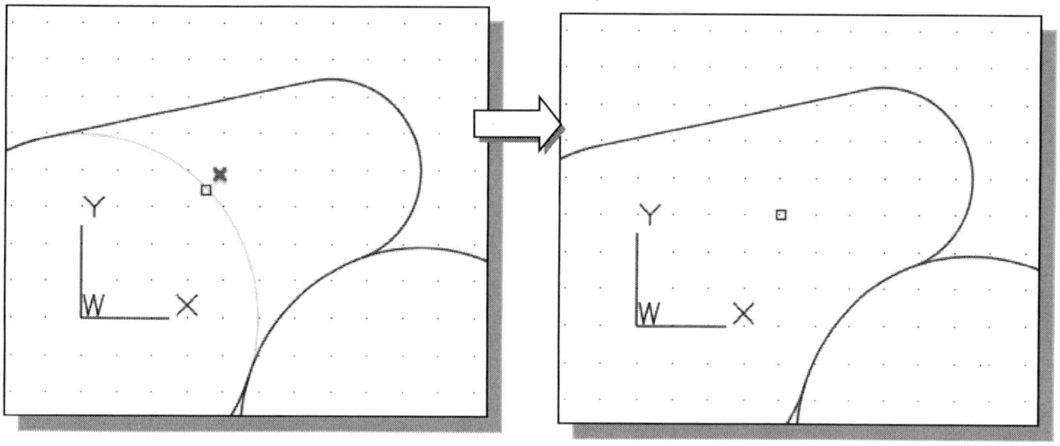

4. Select the upper right side of the circle on the lower right to remove the selected portion.

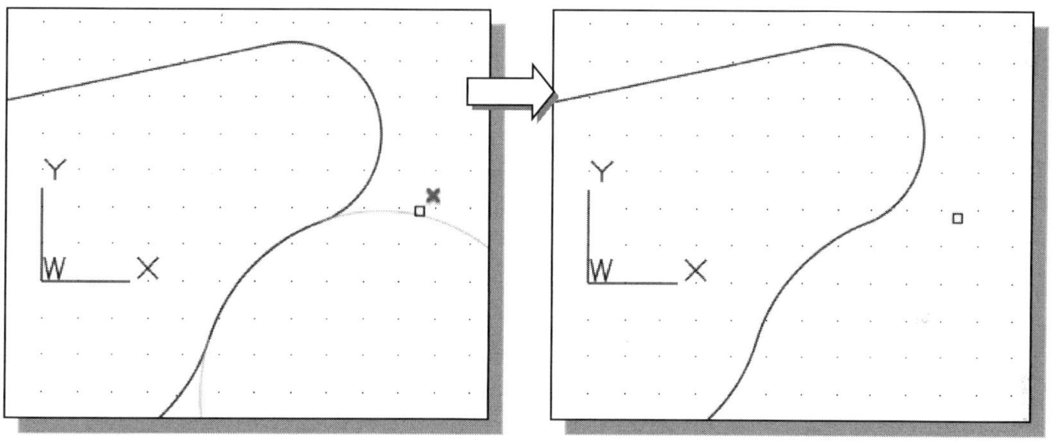

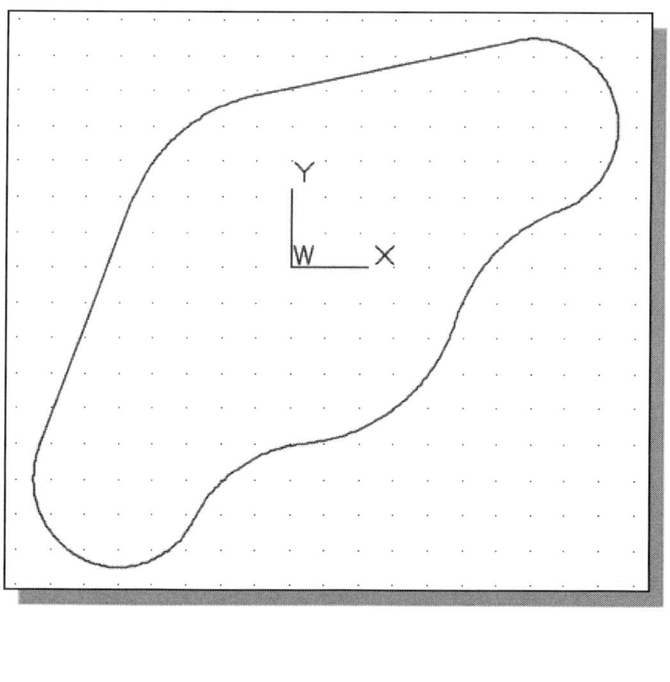

5. On your own, trim the other geometry so that the drawing appears as shown.

6. Inside the *Drawing Area*, **right-click** to activate the option menu and select **Enter** with the left-mouse-button to end the Trim command.

Using the Polygon Command

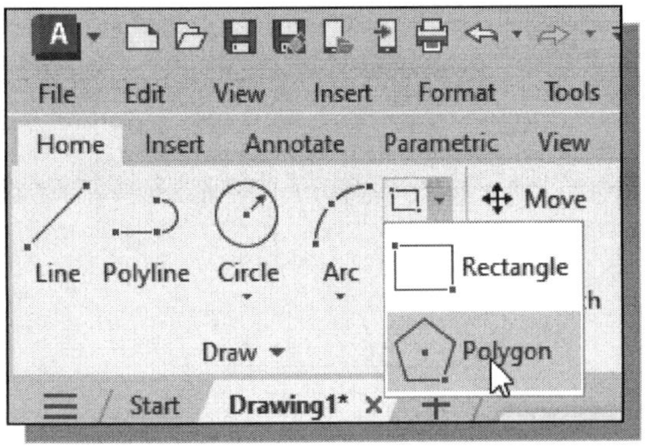

1. Select the **Polygon** command icon in the *Draw* toolbar. Click on the triangle icon next to the rectangle icon to display the additional icon list.

2. Enter ***6*** to create a six-sided hexagon.
polygon Enter number of sides <4>: **6** **[ENTER]**

3. The message "*Specify center of polygon or [Edge]:*" is displayed. Since the center of the large circle is aligned to the origin of the WCS, the center of the polygon can be positioned using several methods. Set the center point to the origin by entering the absolute coordinates. *Specify center of polygon or [Edge]:* **0,0 [ENTER]**

4. In the *command prompt area*, the message "*Enter an option [Inscribed in circle/ Circumscribed about circle] <I>:*" is displayed. Click **Circumscribed about circle** to select the *Circumscribed about circle* option.

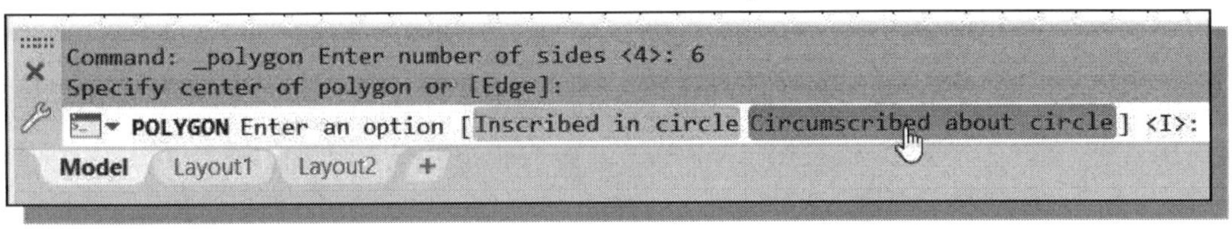

5. In the command prompt area, the message *Specify radius of circle:*" is displayed. Enter ***30*** as the radius.
Specify radius of circle: **30 [ENTER]**

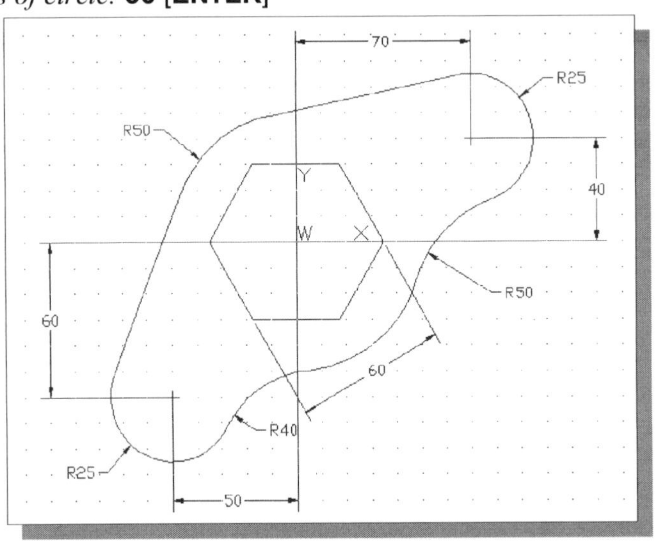

❖ Note that the polygon option **[Inscribed in circle/Circumscribed about circle]** allows us to create either **flat to flat** or **corner to corner** distance.

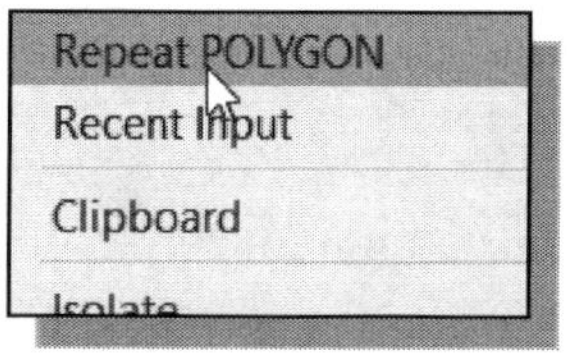

6. Inside the Drawing Area, **right-click** to activate the option menu and select **Repeat Polygon**. In the command prompt area, the message "*_polygon Enter number of sides <6>:*" is displayed.

7. Enter ***4*** to create a four-sided polygon.
   _polygon Enter number of sides <6>: **4 [ENTER]**

8. In the command prompt area, the message "*Specify center of polygon or [Edge]:*" is displayed. Let's use the *Object Snap* options to locate its center location. Pick **Snap to Center** in the *Object Snap* toolbar as shown.

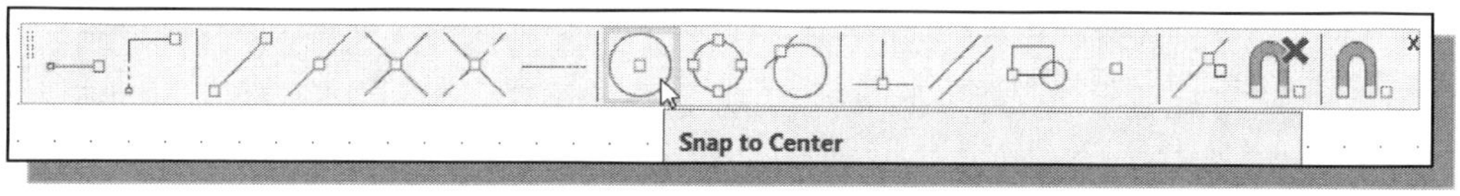

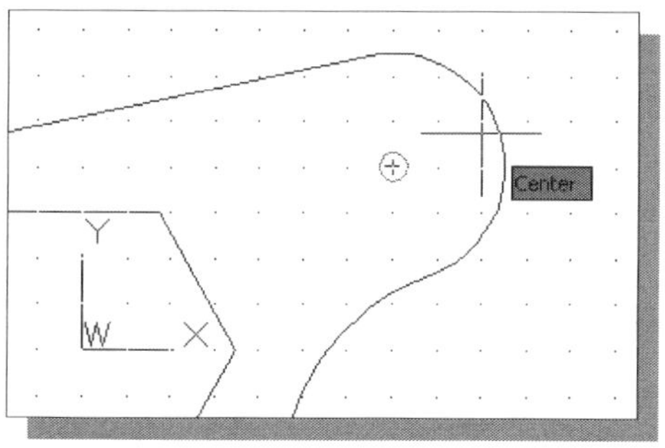

9. Move the cursor on top of the arc on the right and notice the center point is automatically highlighted. Select the arc to accept the highlighted location.

10. Inside the Drawing Area, **right-click** to activate the option menu and select **Circumscribed about circle**.

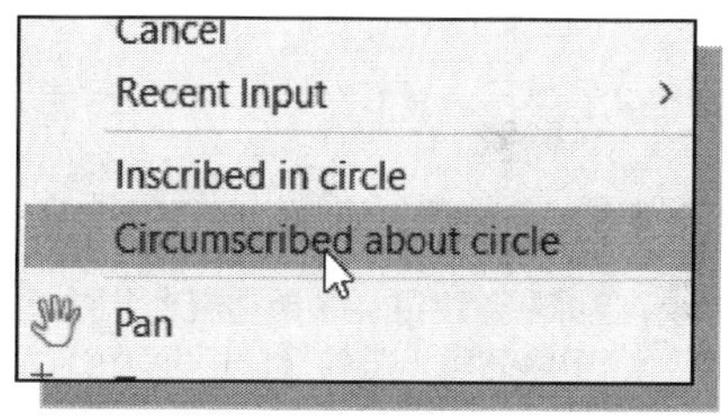

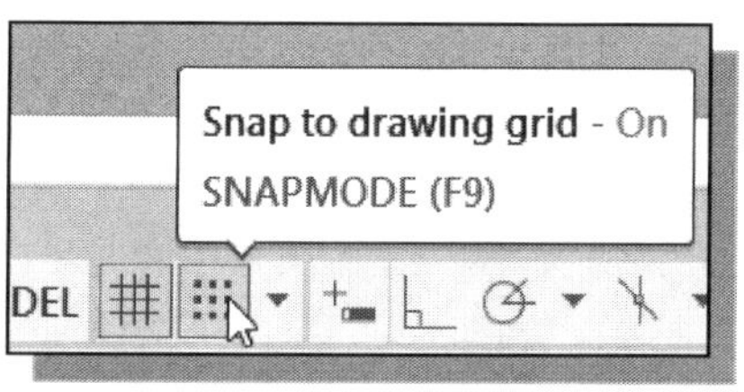

11. Switch ***ON*** the ***GRID SNAP*** option in the *Status Bar* as shown.

12. Create a square by selecting one of the adjacent grid points next to the center point as shown. Note that the orientation of the polygon can also be adjusted as the cursor is moved to other locations.

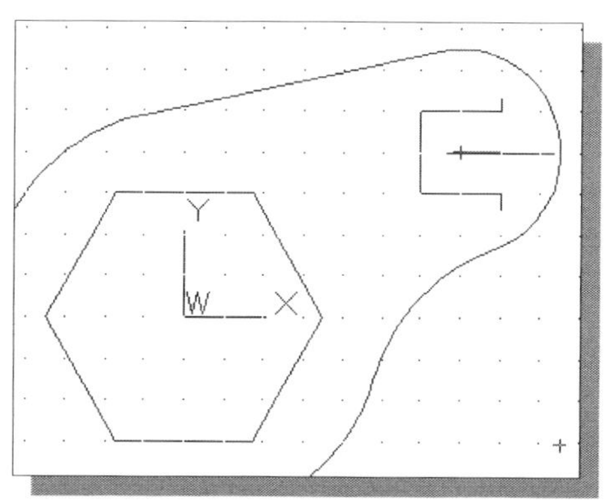

Creating a Concentric Circle

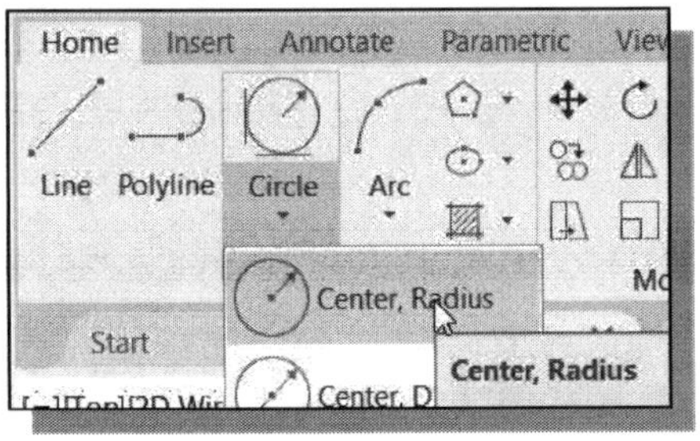

1. Select the **Circle, Radius** command icon in the *Draw* toolbar. In the command prompt area, the message "*Specify center point for circle or [3P/2P/Ttr (tan tan radius)]:*" is displayed.

2. Let's use the *Object Snap* options to assure the center location is aligned properly. Pick **Snap to Center** in the *Object Snap* toolbar as shown.

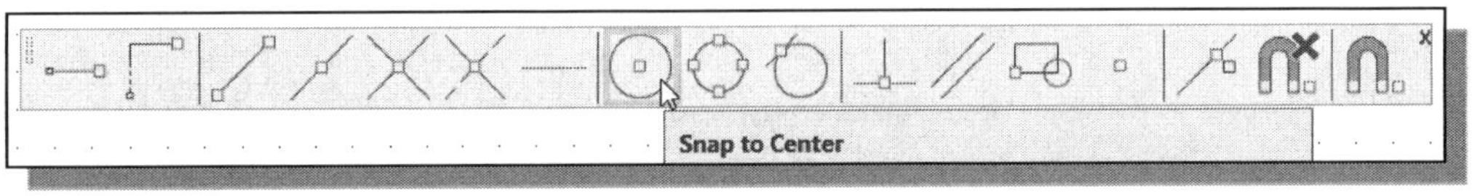

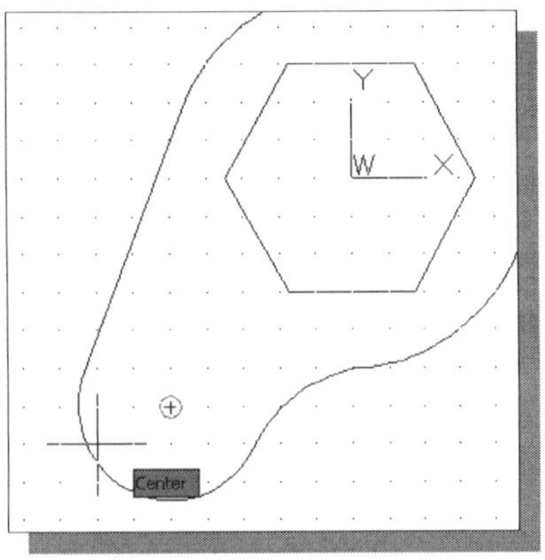

3. Move the cursor on top of the lower arc on the left and notice the center point is automatically highlighted. Select the arc to accept the highlighted location.

4. In the command prompt area, the message "*Specify radius of circle* <25>" is displayed. Enter ***10*** to complete the Circle command.
   Specify radius of circle <25>: **10 [ENTER]**

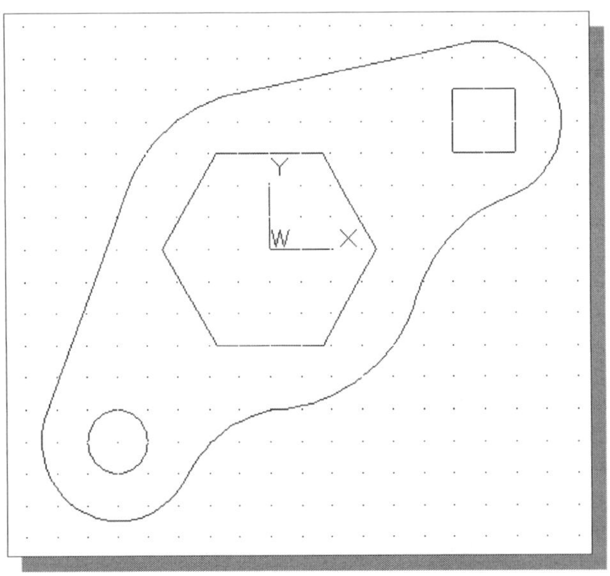

Using the QuickCalc Calculator to Measure Distance and Angle

AutoCAD also provides several tools that will allow us to measure distance, area, perimeter, and even mass properties. With the use of the *Object Snap* options, getting measurements of the completed design can be done very quickly.

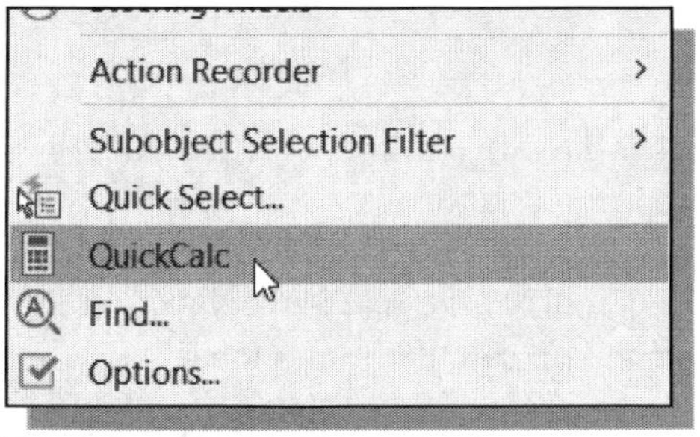

1. Inside the *Drawing Area*, **right-click** once to bring up the option menu.

2. Select **QuickCalc** in the *option menu* as shown.

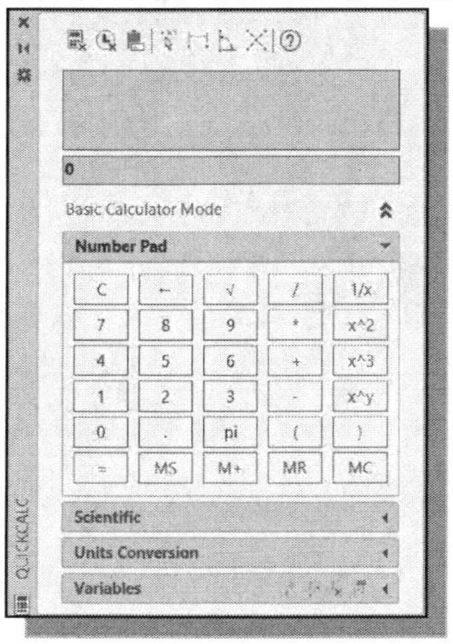

❖ Note that the QuickCalc option brings up the AutoCAD calculator, which can be used to perform a full range of mathematical, scientific, and geometric calculations. We can also use QuickCalc to create and use variables, as well as to convert units of measurement.

3. Click the **Measure Distance** icon, which is located on the top section of the *QuickCalc* calculator pad.

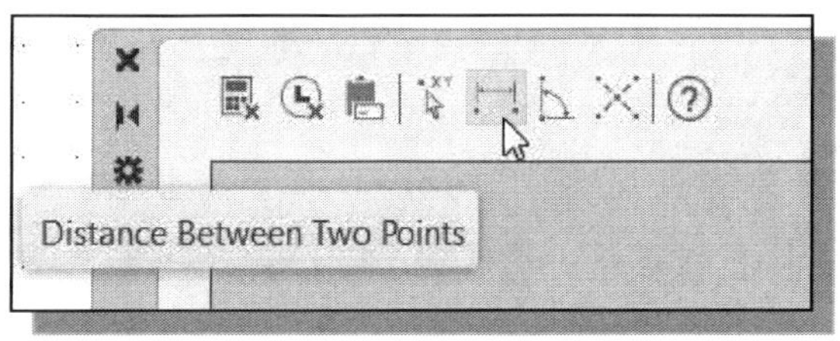

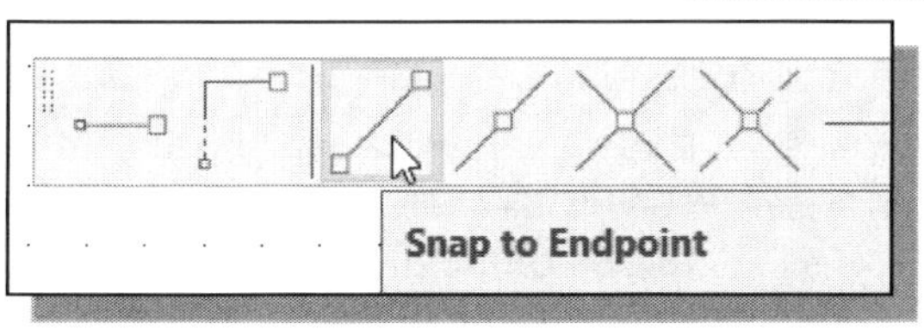

4. Pick **Snap to Endpoint** in the *Object Snap* toolbar.

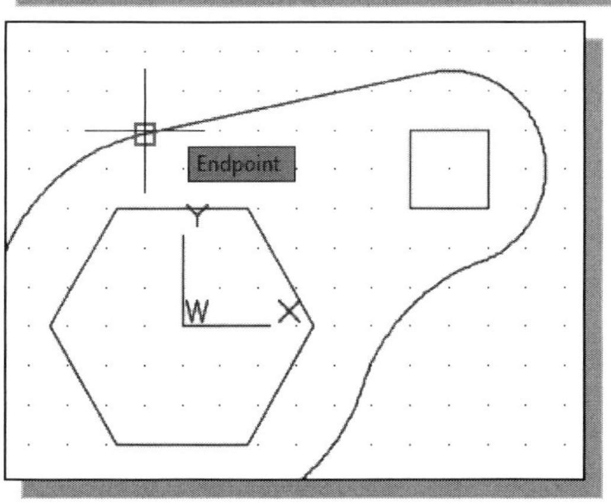

5. Select the **top tangent line**, near the lower endpoint, as shown.

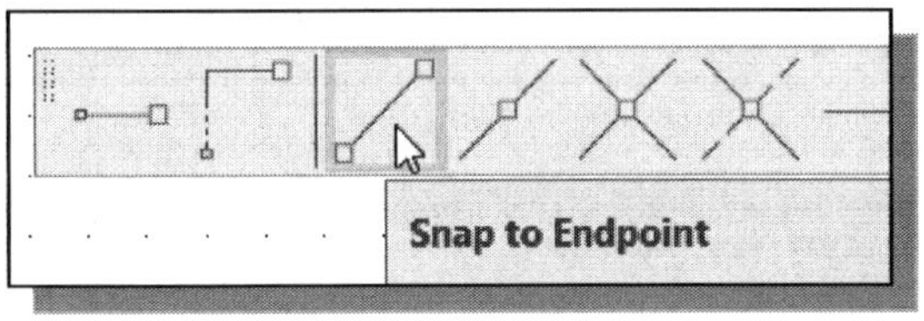

6. Pick **Snap to Endpoint** in the *Object Snap* toolbar.

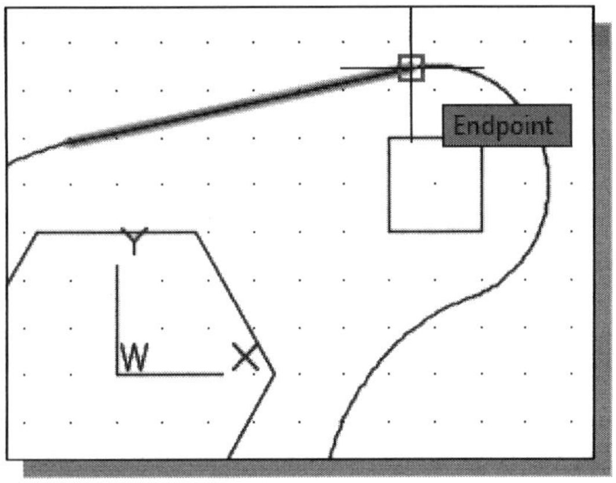

7. Select the tangent line, near the upper endpoint, as shown.

❖ The length of the line is displayed in the *QuickCalc* calculator as shown.

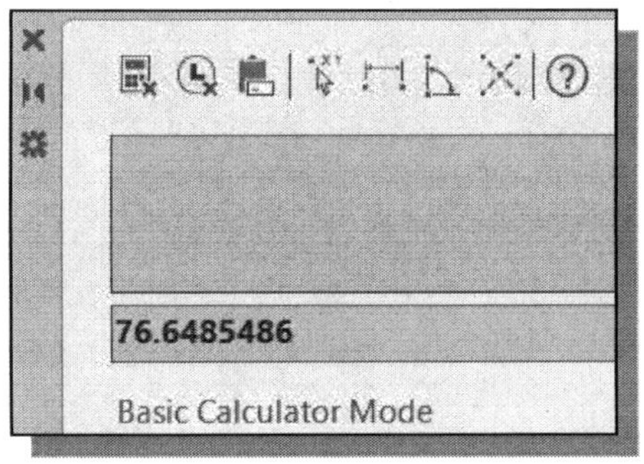

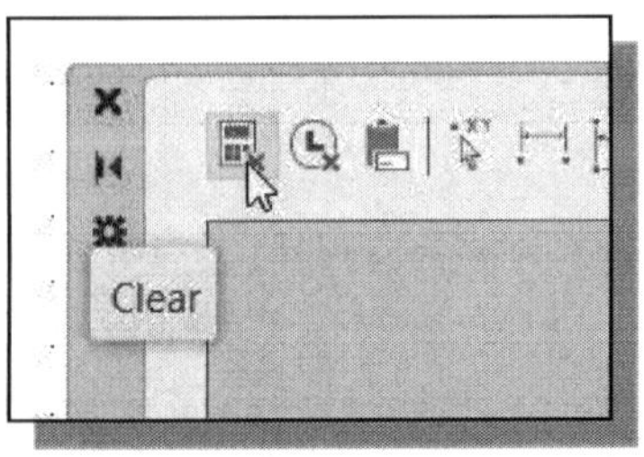

8. Click the **Clear** icon to remove the number displayed.

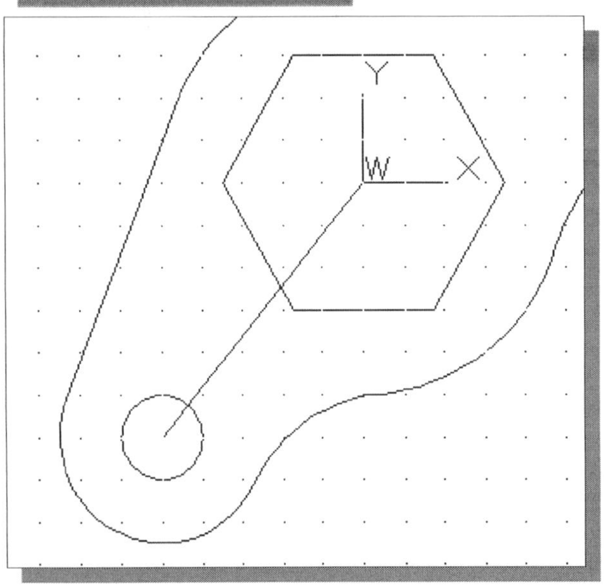

9. On your own, repeat the above steps and measure the center to center distance of the lower region of the design as shown. (Hint: use the Snap to Center option.)

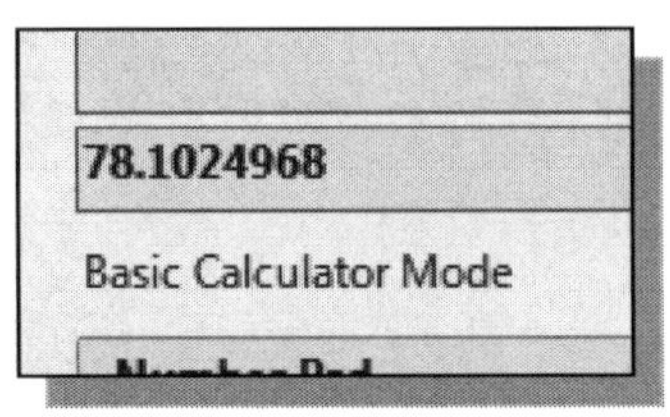

10. Click the **Measure Angle** icon, which is located on the top section of the *QuickCalc* calculator pad.

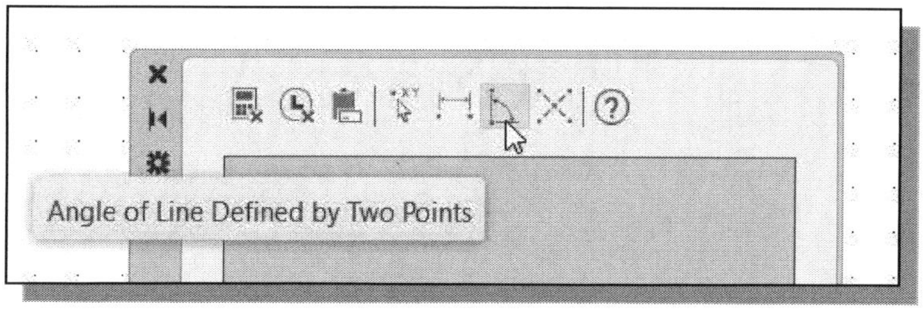

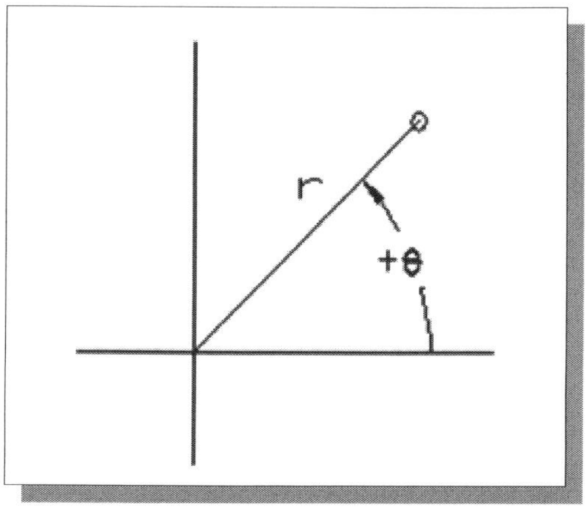

❖ Note that this option allows us to measure the angle between the horizontal axis and the line formed by the two selected points. A positive angle indicates a counterclockwise direction.

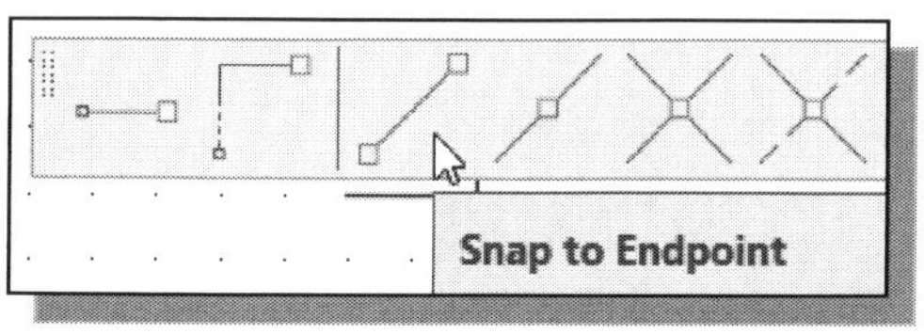

11. Pick **Snap to Endpoint** in the *Object Snap* toolbar.

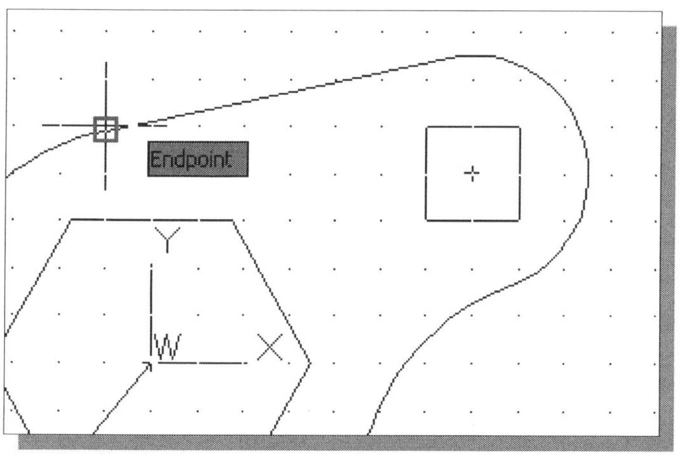

12. Select the tangent line, near the lower endpoint, as shown.

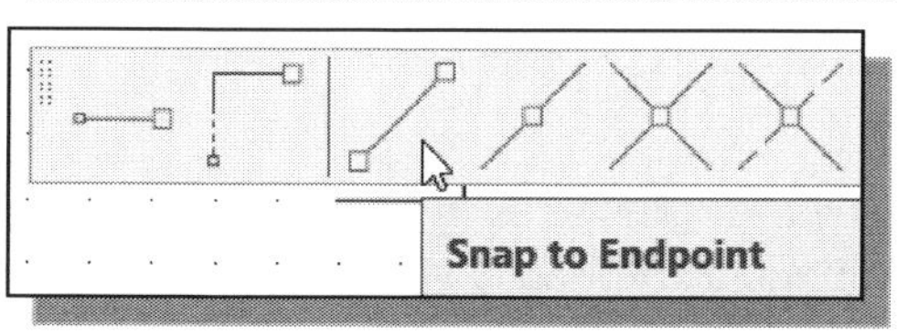

13. Pick **Snap to Endpoint** in the *Object Snap* toolbar.

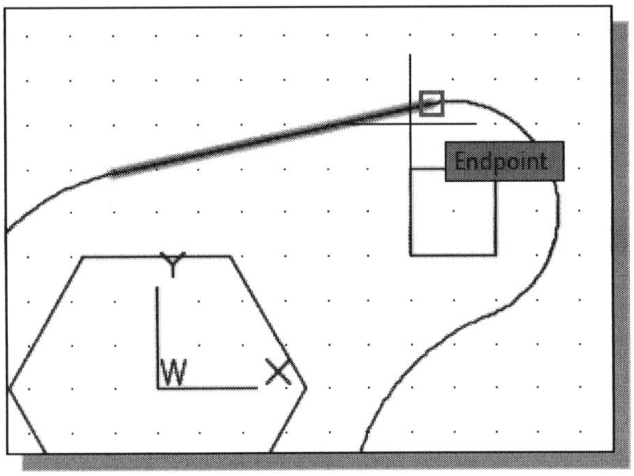

14. Select the tangent line, near the upper endpoint, as shown.

➢ The measured angle is displayed in the calculator pad as shown.

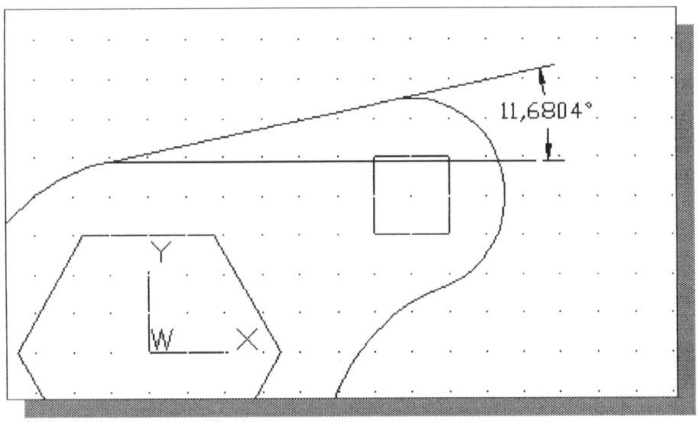

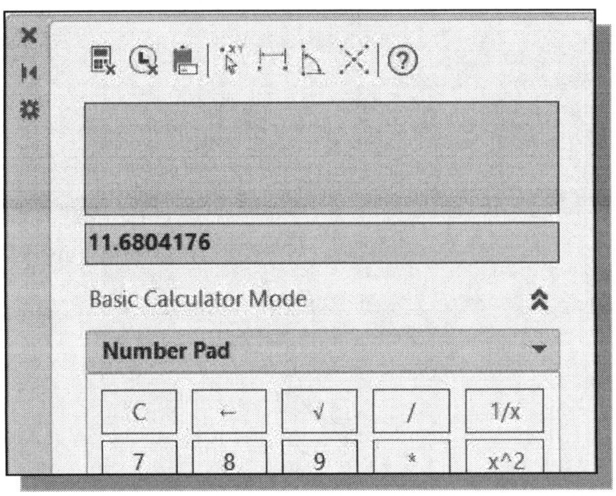

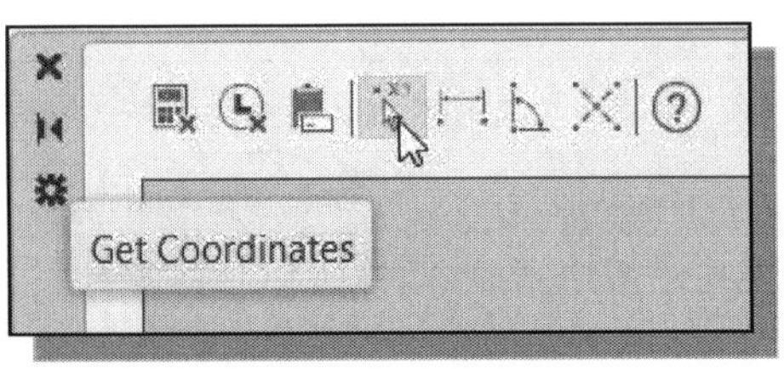

15. On your own, experiment with the available **Get Coordinates** options.

➢ Note also that the **QuickCalc** calculator can remain active while you are using other AutoCAD commands.

Saving the CAD File

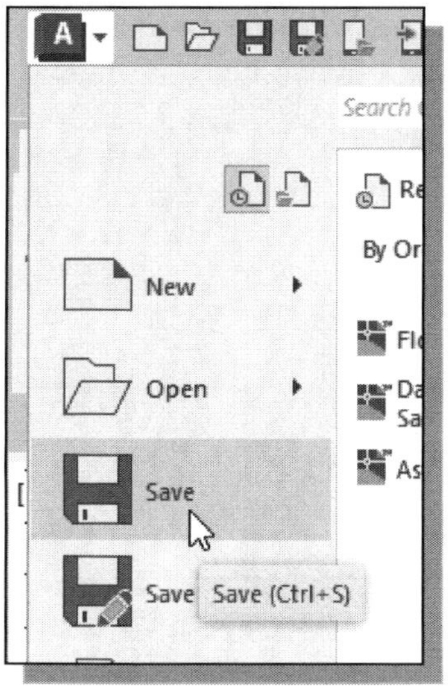

1. In the *Application Menu*, select:

   [Application] → [Save]

   ❖ Note the command can also be activated with quick-key combination of **[Ctrl]+[S]**.

2. In the *Save Drawing As* dialog box, select the folder in which you want to store the CAD file and enter ***RockerArm*** in the *File name* box.

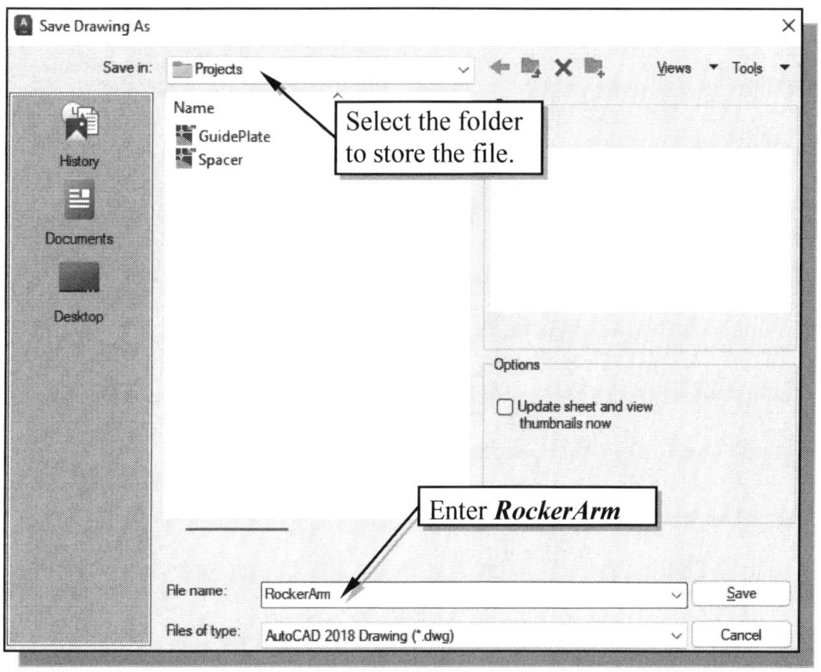

3. Pick **Save** in the *Save Drawing As* dialog box to accept the selections and save the file.

Exit AutoCAD

To exit **AutoCAD 2027**, select **Exit AutoCAD** from the *Application Menu* or type ***QUIT*** at the command prompt.

AutoCAD Quick Keys

Besides using the mouse and/or AutoCAD menu systems, AutoCAD also provides quick keys to access the more commonly used commands, with many of them being a single key stroke.

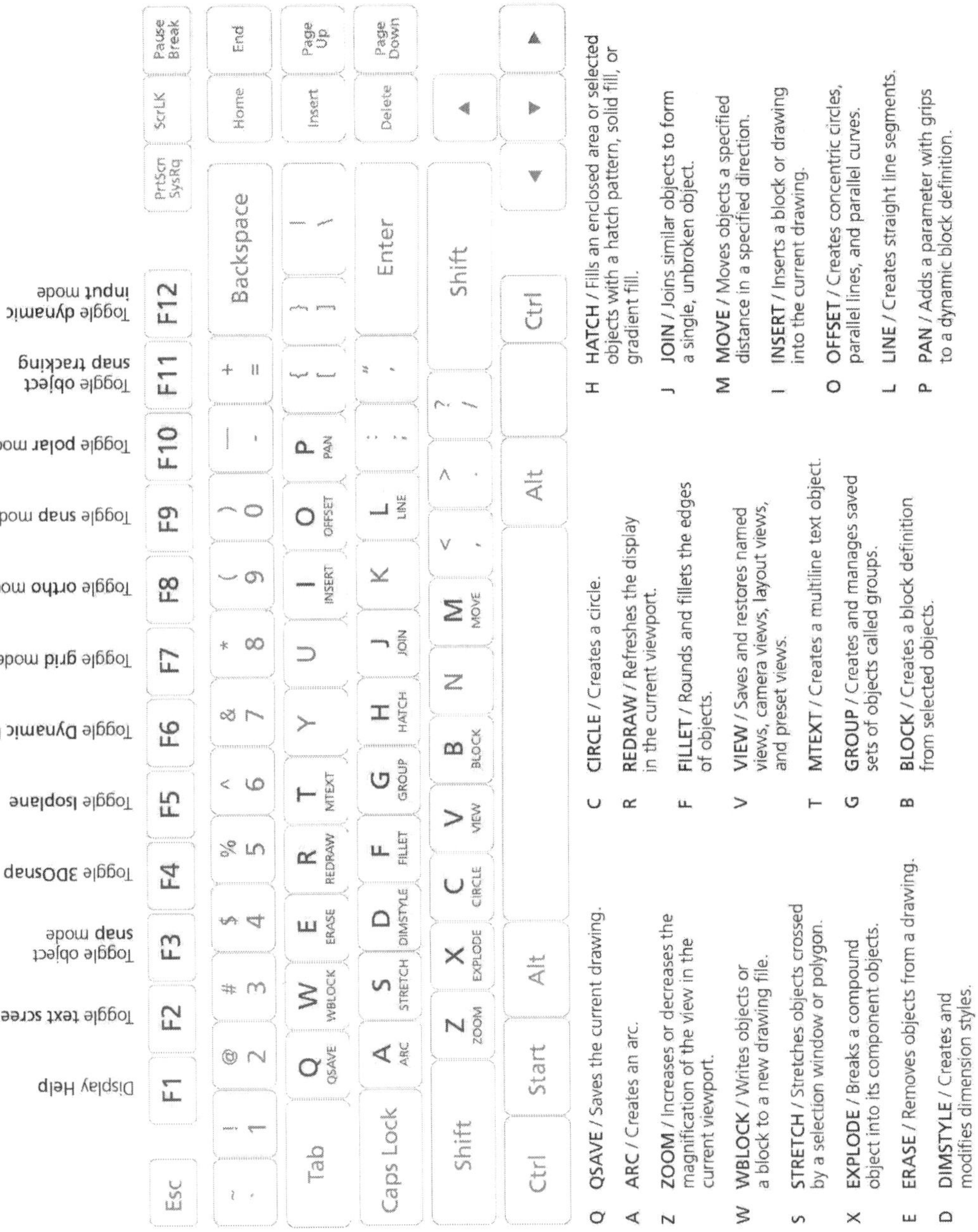

For a more detailed description on the quick keys, refer to the following Autodesk website:
http://www.autodesk.com/store/autocad-shortcuts

Review Questions: (Time: 20 minutes)

1. Describe the procedure to activate the AutoCAD **Startup** option.

2. List and describe three options in the AutoCAD *Object Snap* toolbar.

3. Which AutoCAD command can we use to remove a portion of an existing entity?

4. Describe the difference between the *circumscribed* and *inscribed* options when using the AutoCAD **Polygon** command.

5. Create the following triangle and fill in the blanks: Length = ____, Angle = ____. (Dimensions are in inches.)

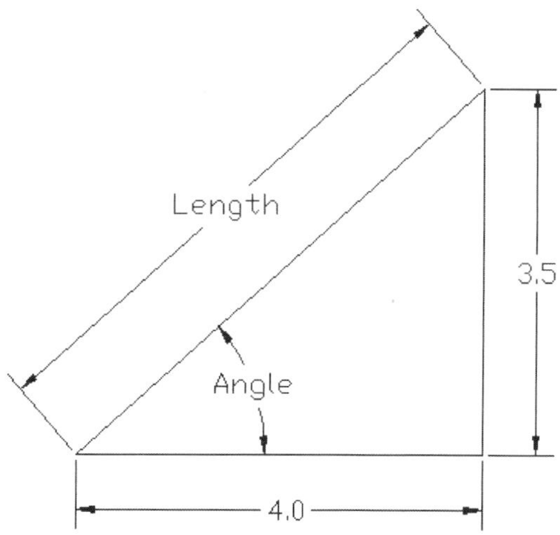

6. Create the following drawing; line *AB* is tangent to both circles. Fill in the blanks: Length = _____, Angle = _____. (Dimensions are in inches.)

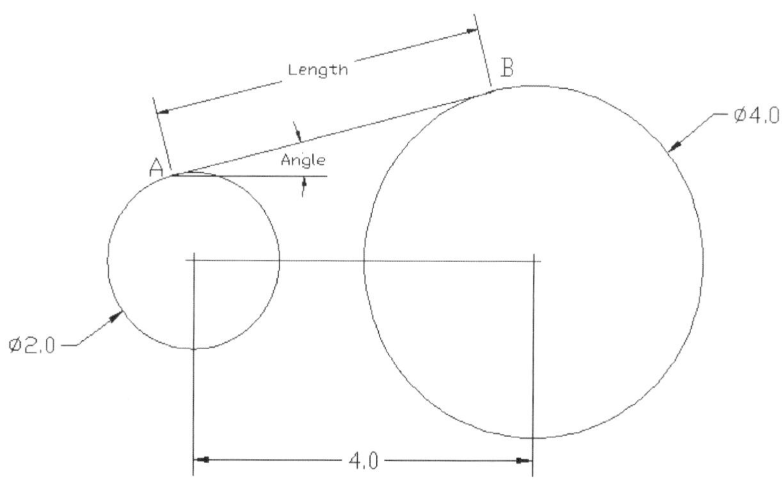

Exercises: (Time: 180 minutes.)

(Unless otherwise specified, dimensions are in inches.)

1. Adjustable Support

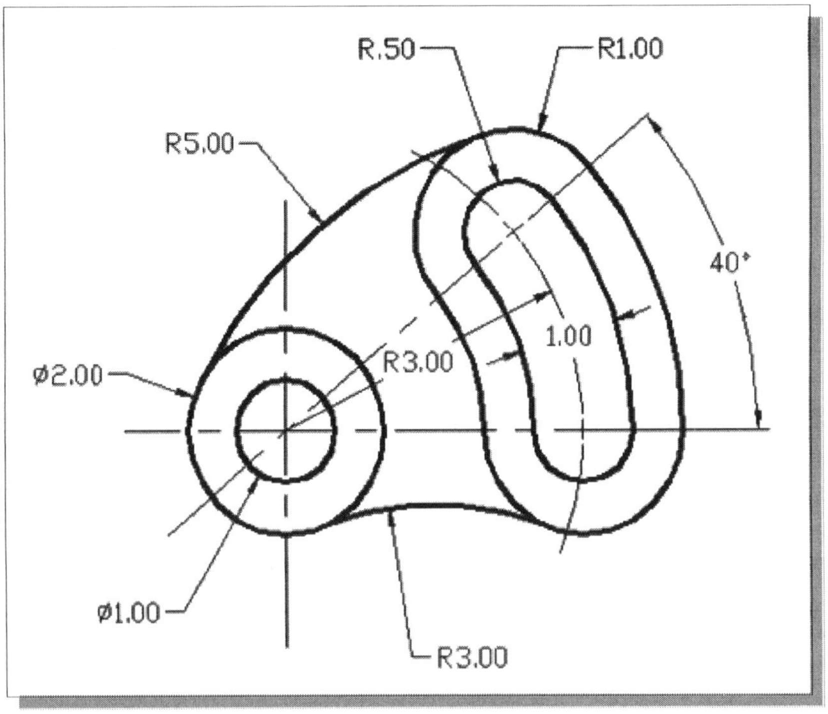

2. V-Slide Plate (The design has two sets of parallel lines with implied tangency.)

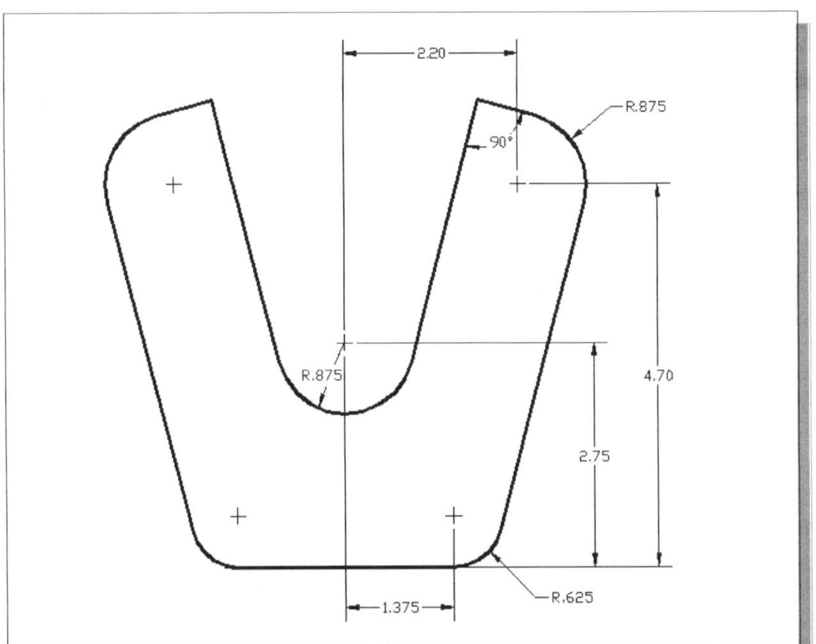

3. Swivel Base (Dimensions are in Millimeters.)

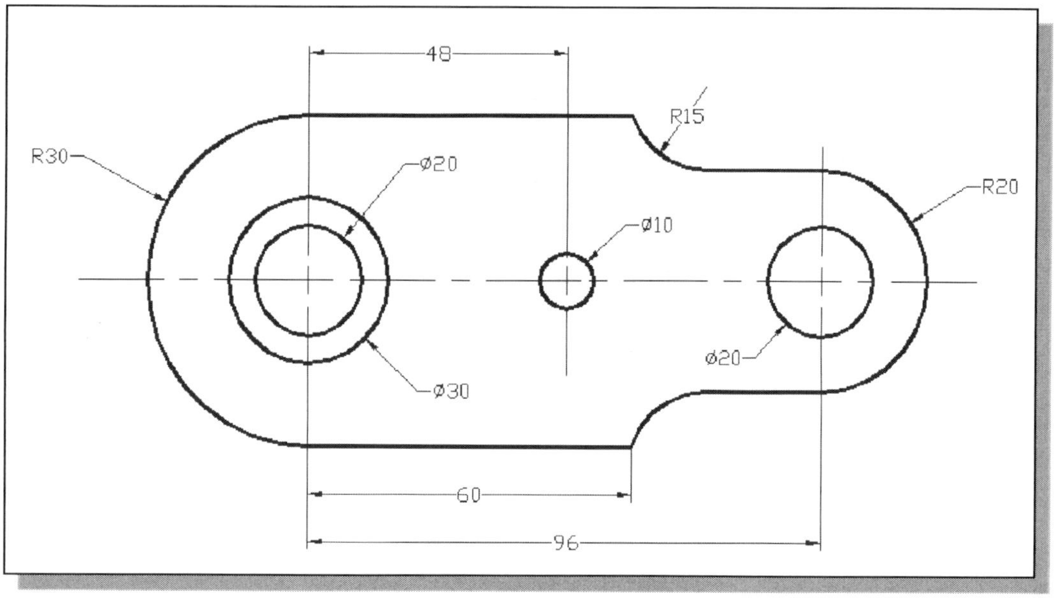

4. Sensor Mount

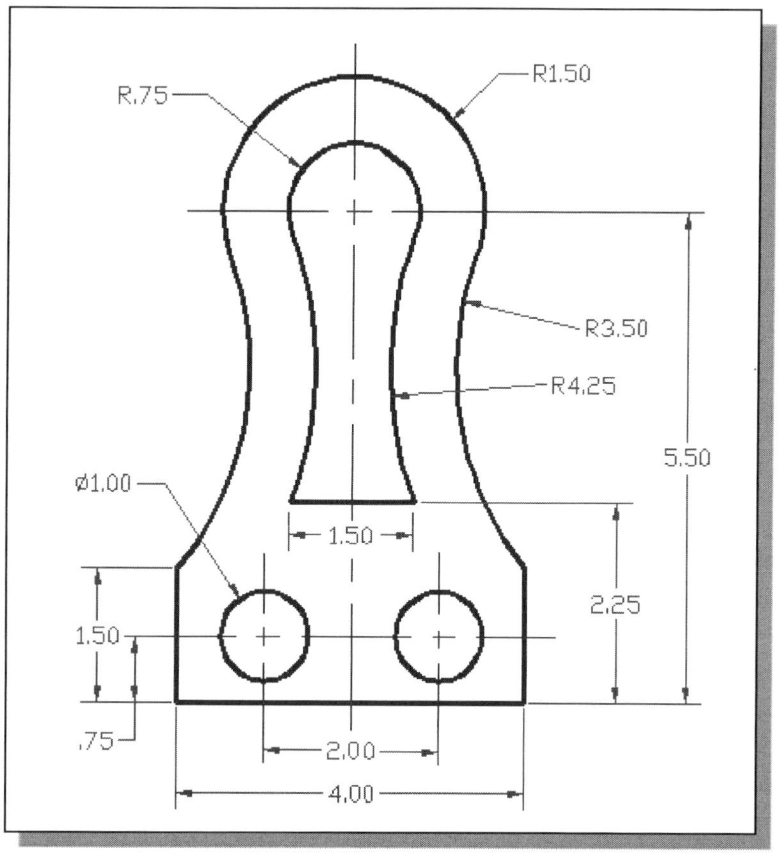

5. Flat Hook (Dimensions are in Millimeters. Thickness: 25 mm.)

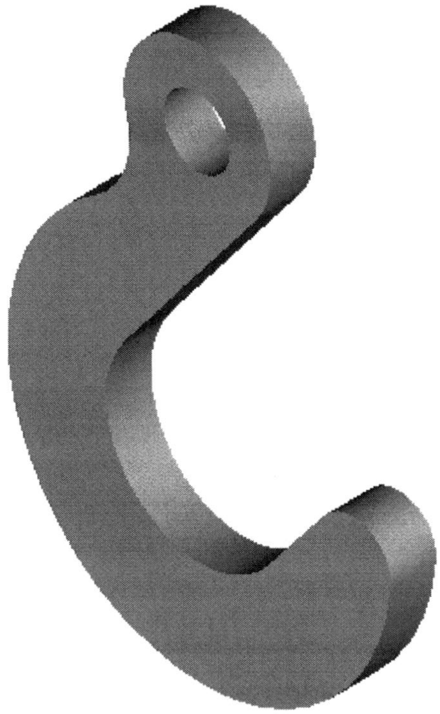

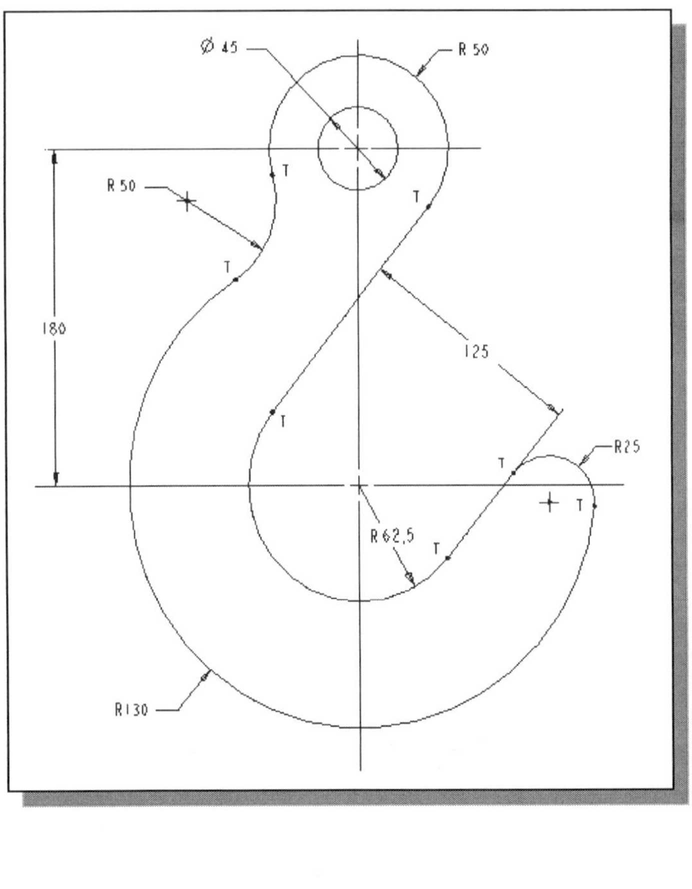

6. Journal Bracket

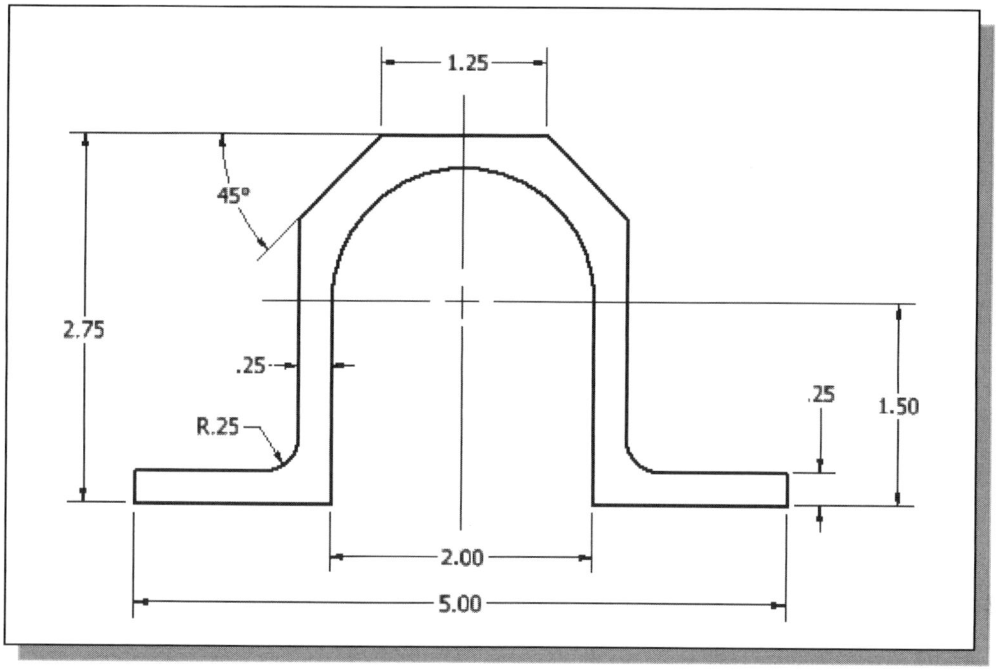

7. Support Base

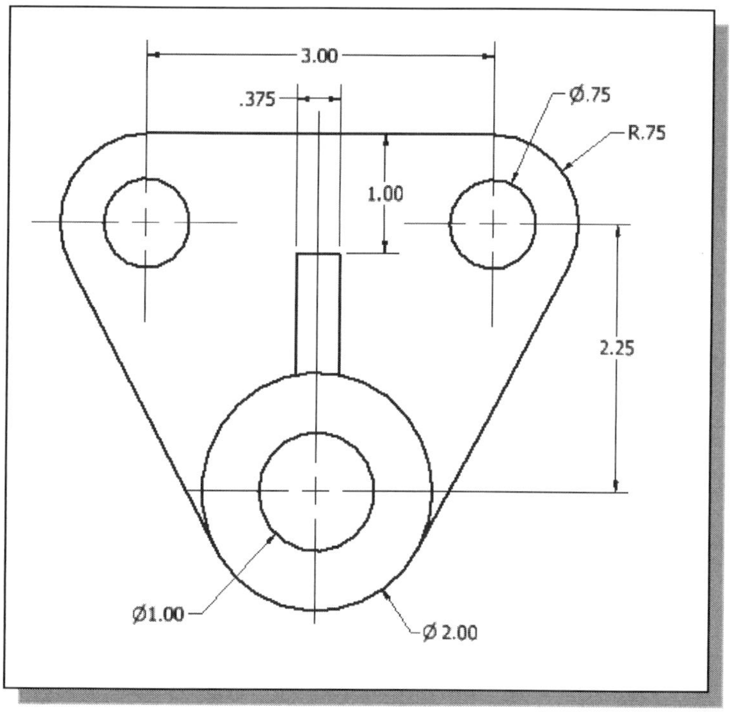

8. Pivot Arm

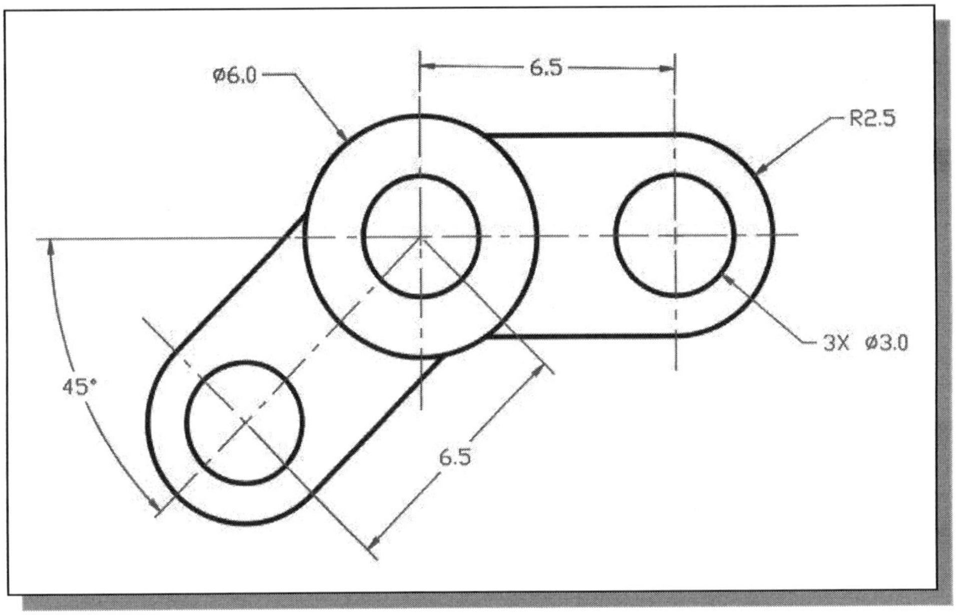

9. Polygons & Circles Pattern (Dimensions are in inches.)

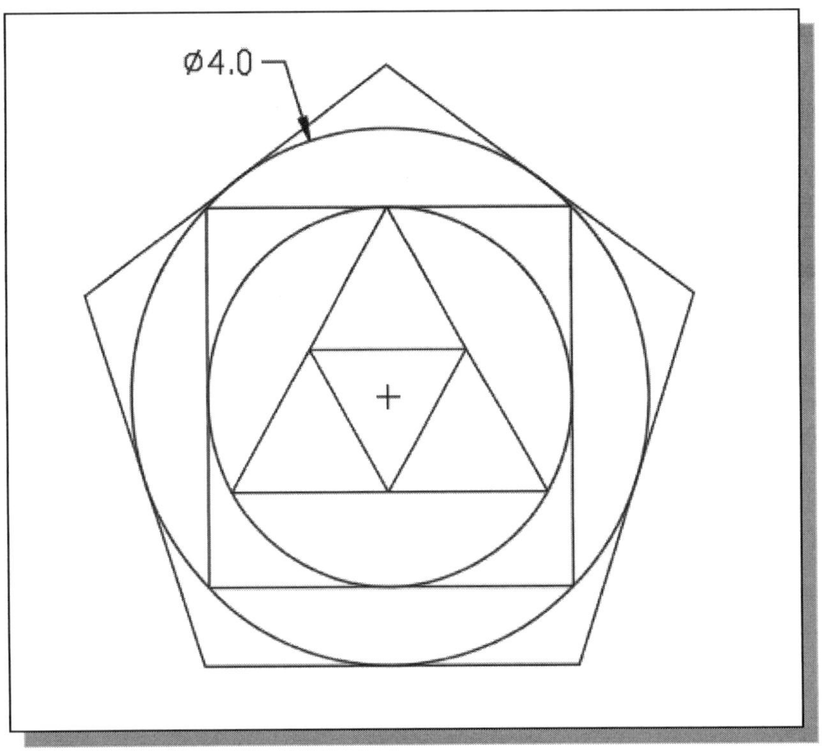

10. Extruder Cover (Dimensions are in Millimeters.)

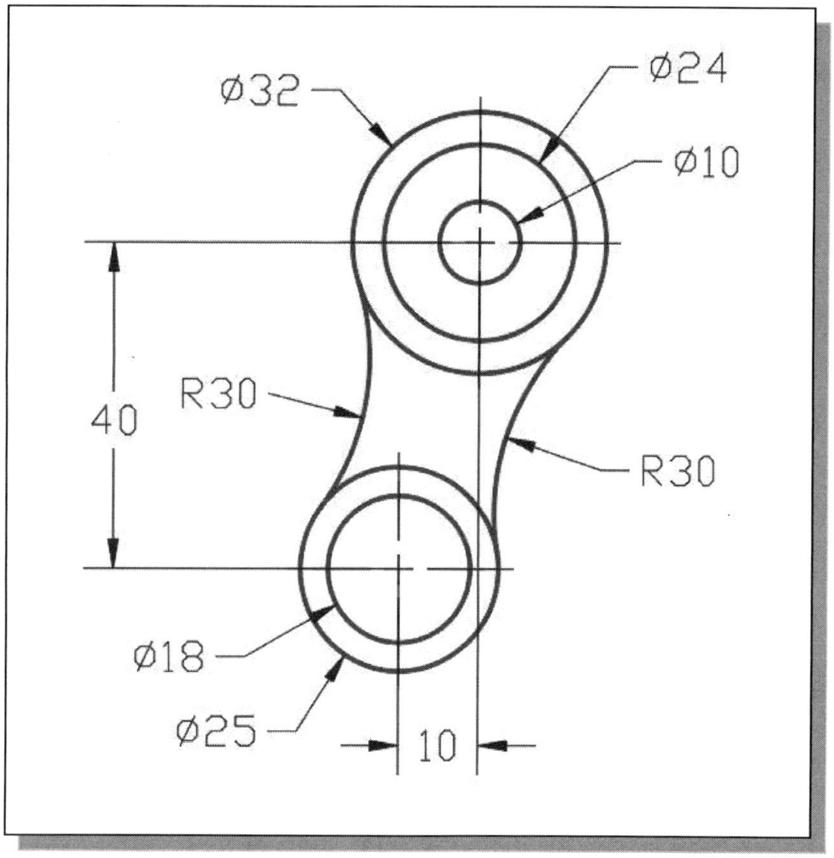

Notes:

Chapter 3
Object Properties and Organization

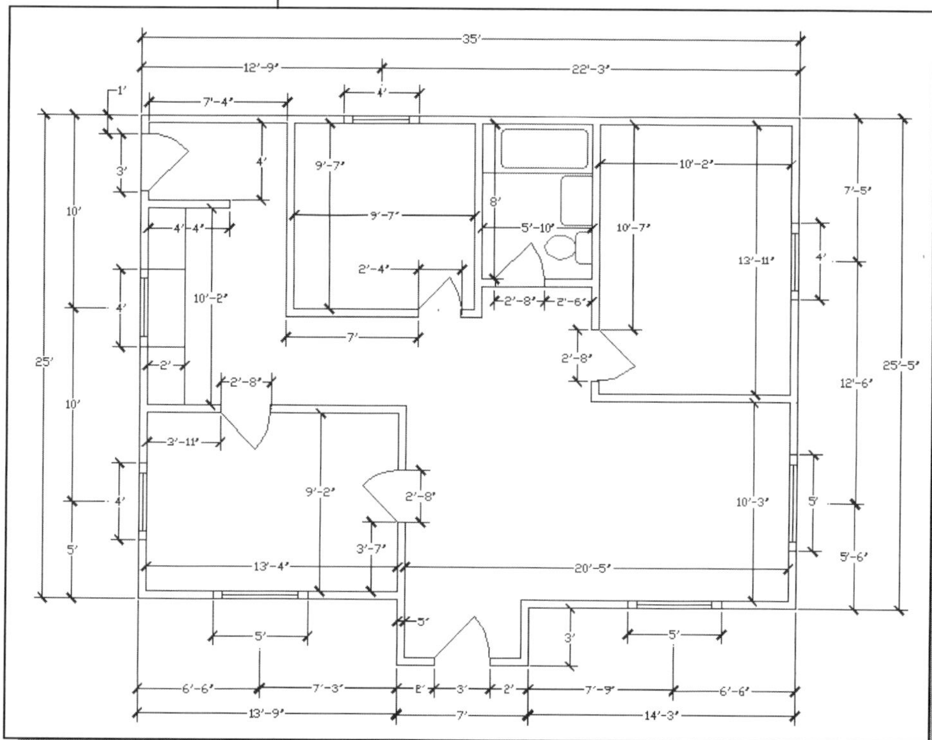

Learning Objectives

- Use the AutoCAD Quick Setup Wizard
- Create new Multiline Styles
- Draw using the Multiline command
- Use the Multiline Editing commands
- Create new layers
- Pre-selection of objects
- Control Layer Visibility
- Move objects to a different layer

AutoCAD Certified User Examination Objectives Coverage

Section 1: Introduction to AutoCAD

Section 2: Creating Basic Drawings

Section 3: Manipulating Objects

Section 4: Drawing Organization and Inquiry Commands

Introduction

The CAD database of a design may contain information regarding the hundreds of CAD entities that are used to create the CAD model. One of the advantages of using a CAD system is its ability to organize and manage the database so that the designer can access the information quickly and easily. Typically, CAD entities that are created to describe one feature, function, or process of a design are perceived as related information and therefore are organized into the same group. In AutoCAD, the Layer command is used extensively for this purpose. For example, an architectural drawing typically will show walls, doors, windows, and dimensions. Using layers, we can choose to display or hide sub-systems for clarity; we can also change object properties, such as colors and linetypes, quickly and easily.

In this chapter, we will continue to explore the different construction and editing tools that are available in **AutoCAD 2027**. We will demonstrate the use of the Limits, Mline, Medit, and Layer commands. As you become proficient with the CAD tools and understand the underlying CAD modeling concepts, you are encouraged to experiment with new ideas in using the CAD tools and develop your own style of using the system.

The Floor Plan Design

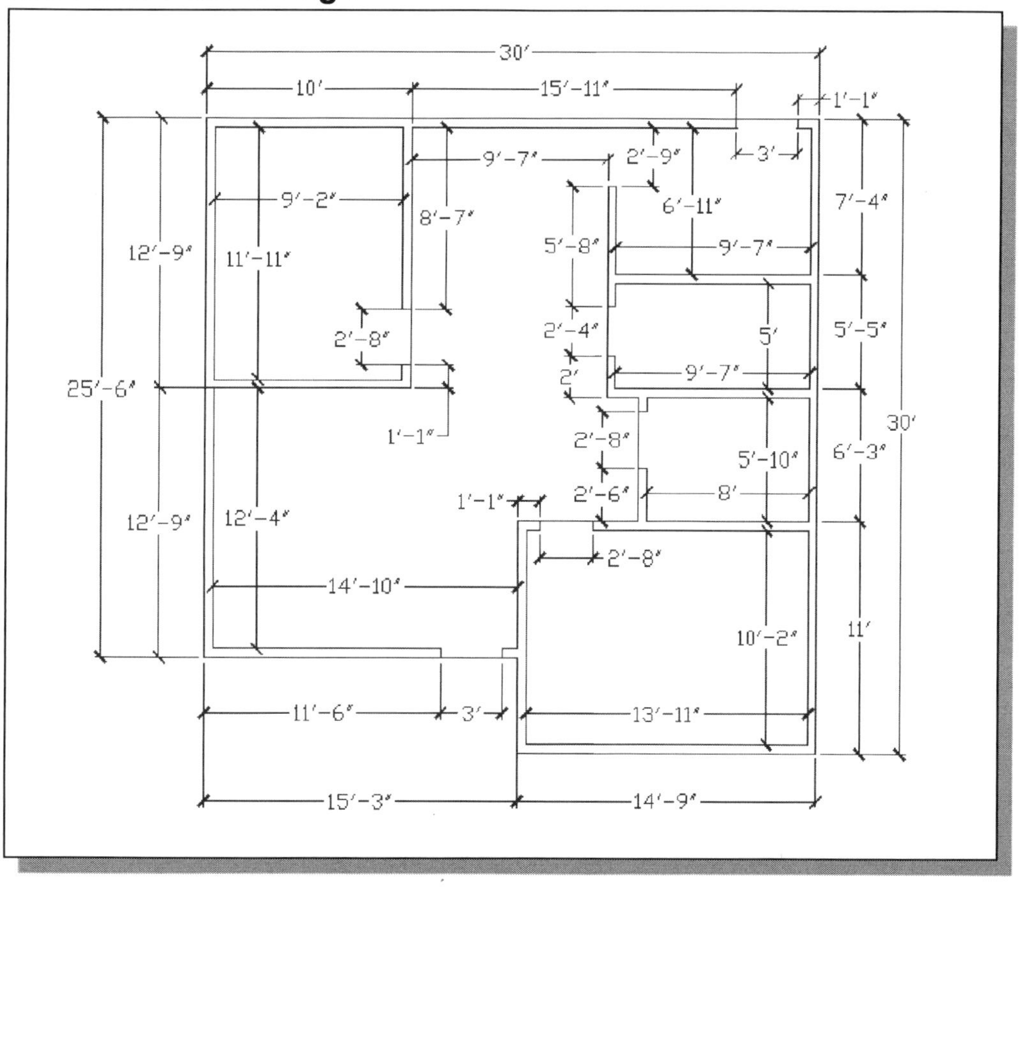

Starting Up AutoCAD 2027

1. Select the **AutoCAD 2027** option on the *Program* menu or select the **AutoCAD 2027** icon on the *Desktop*. Once the program is loaded into the memory, the **AutoCAD 2027** drawing screen will appear on the screen.

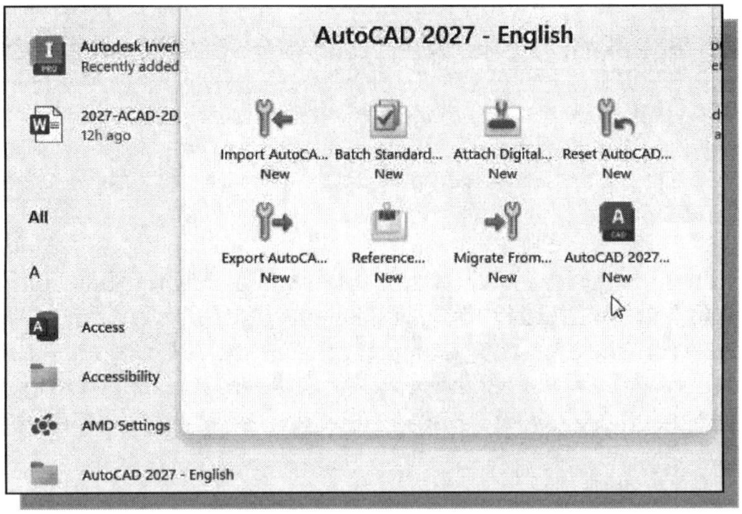

Using the Setup Wizard

1. In the *Startup* dialog box, select the **Use a Wizard** option as shown in the figure below.

2. In the *Select a Wizard* section, pick **Quick Setup**.

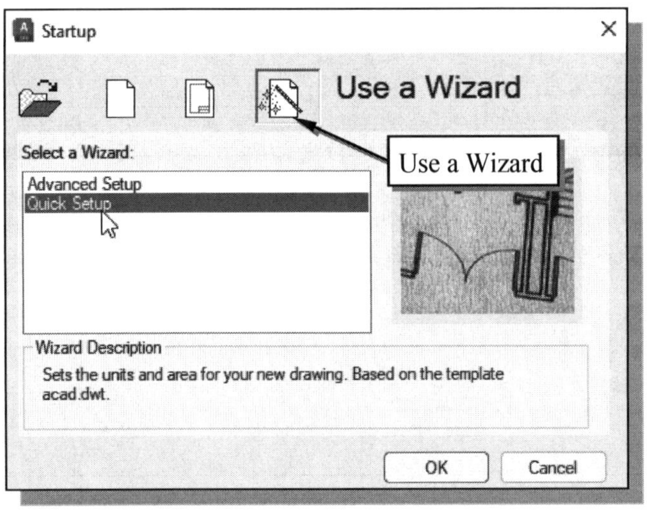

- AutoCAD setup wizards allow us to customize several of the AutoCAD settings depending on the wizard we choose. The *Quick Setup* wizard sets the units and grid display area. Choices for units include *Decimal, Engineering, Architectural, Fractional,* and *Scientific*. We can also specify the width and length of a two-dimensional area to establish the extents of the *grid* displayed, also known as the *limits* of the working area.

Drawing Units Setup

1. In the *Quick Setup Units* option, select **Architectural**.

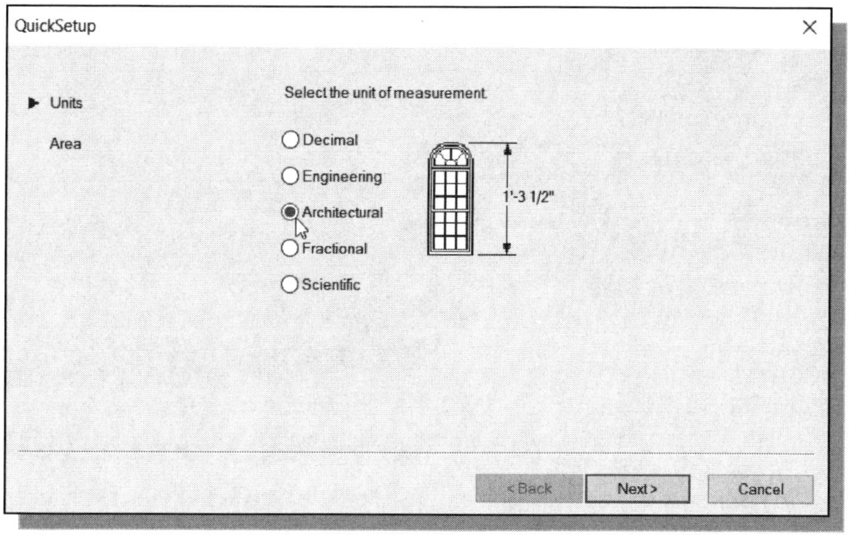

2. Pick **Next** to continue with the *Quick Setup* settings.

Reference Area Setup

1. In the *Quick Setup Area* option, enter ***60'*** and ***40'*** for the width and length.

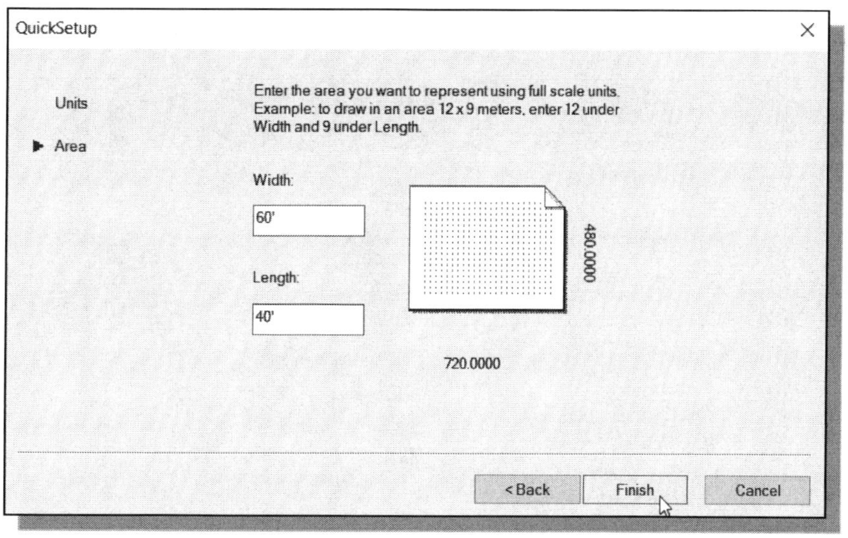

- The two-dimensional area we set up in the *Quick Setup* is the *drawing limits* in AutoCAD.

2. Pick **Finish** to accept the settings and end the *Quick Setup* wizard.

GRID and *SNAP* Intervals Setup

1. In the *Menu Bar*, select:
   [Tools] → [Drafting Settings]

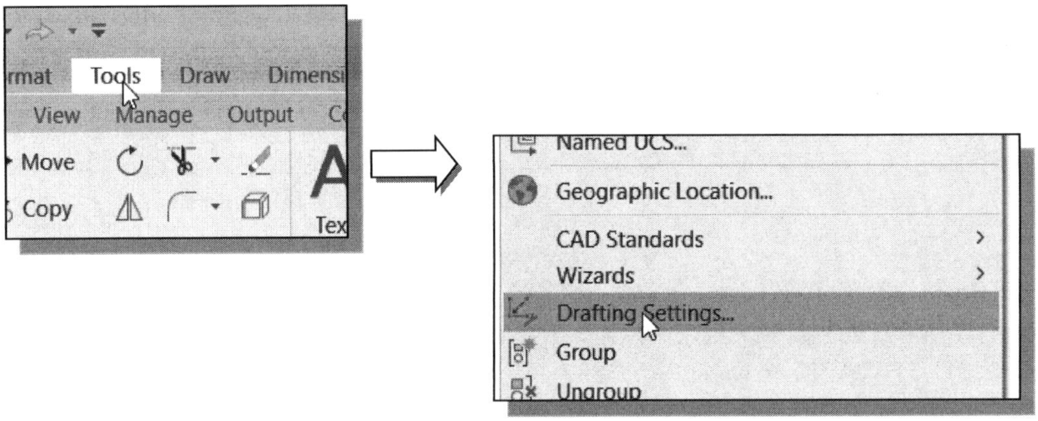

2. In the *Drafting Settings* dialog box, select the **SNAP and GRID** tab if it is not the page on top.

3. Change *Grid Spacing* to ***6″*** for both X and Y directions.

4. Also adjust the *Snap Spacing* to ***6″*** for both X and Y directions.

5. Turn ***OFF*** the **Adaptive Grid** option. (This switch is used to limit the grid display when zooming.)

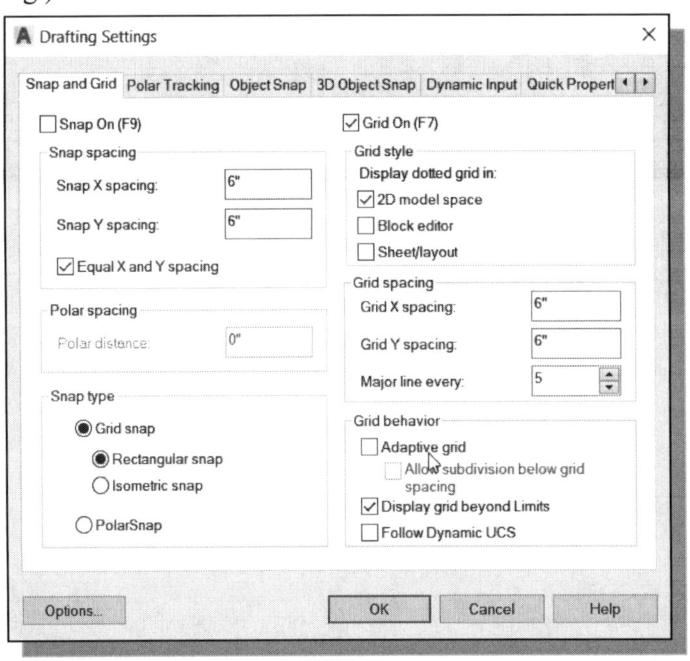

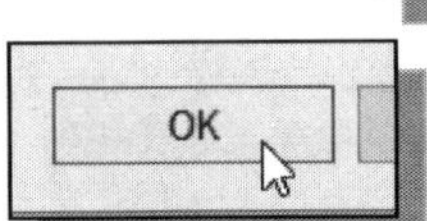

6. Pick **OK** to exit the *Drafting Settings* dialog box.

Using the Zoom Extents Command in the Navigation Bar

1. Move the cursor inside the *Drawing Area* and notice that, although we have set the *limits* to 40′ by 60′, the default display is still not adjusted to the new settings.

2. In the *Navigation* toolbar, select **Zoom Extents** by clicking the left-mouse-button on the icon as shown. We can also click on the triangle icon to select other *Zoom* options.

➢ The *navigation bar* is a user interface element that provides quick access to display related tools, such as **Zoom**, **Pan** and **3D rotation.**

The AutoCAD Multiline Command

The **Multiline** command in **AutoCAD 2027** is used to create multiple parallel lines. This command is very useful for creating designs that contain multiple parallel lines, such as walls for architectural designs and for highway designs in civil engineering. The Multiline command creates a set of parallel lines (up to 16 lines) and all line segments are grouped together to form a single *multiline object*, which can be modified using Multiline Edit and Explode commands. We will first create a new ***multiline style*** for our floor plan design.

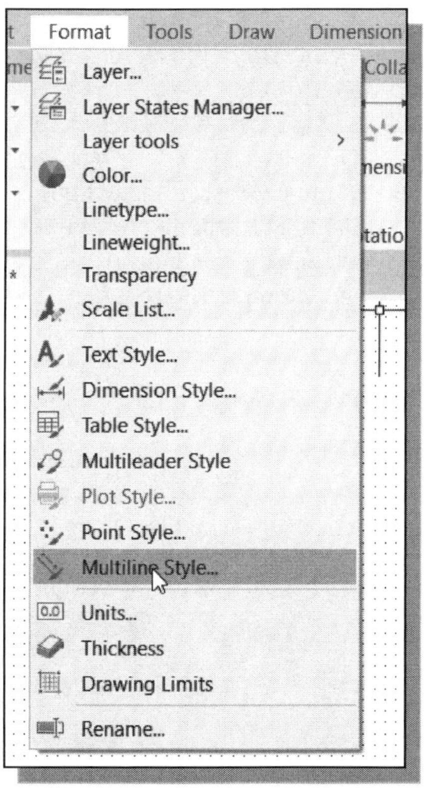

1. In the *Menu Bar*, select:

   [Format] → [Multiline Style]

❖ The default AutoCAD multiline style is called *STANDARD*, and it consists of two elements (two parallel lines) with an offset distance of 1.0 inch.

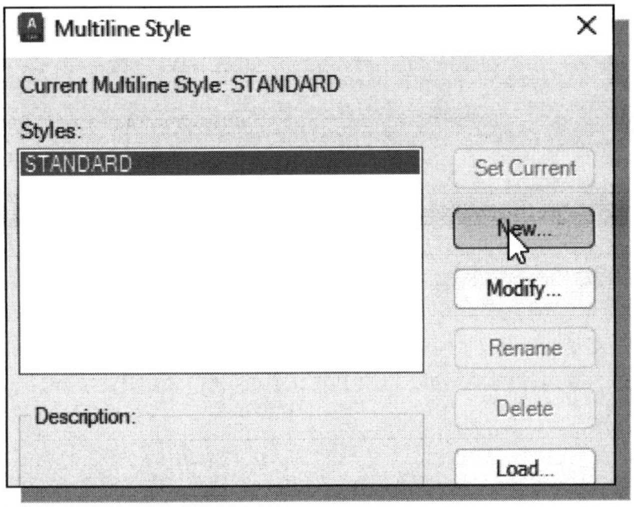

2. In the *Multiline Style* dialog box choose **New** to create a new multiline style.

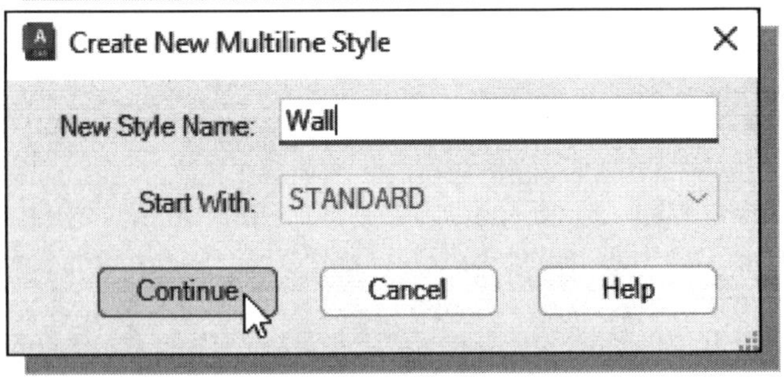

3. In the ***New Style Name*** box, enter ***Wall*** as the new *multiline style name.*

4. Click **Continue** to create the new style.

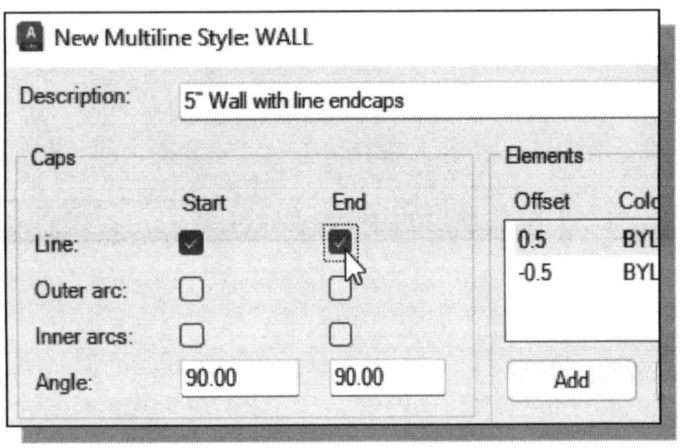

5. Enter ***5" Wall with line endcaps*** in the *Description* box.

6. In the *Caps* section, switch ***ON*** the **Start** and **End** boxes to enable ***Line*** endcaps as shown in the figure.

❖ All line elements in the multiline style are defined by an offset from a reference line, the *multiline origin.*

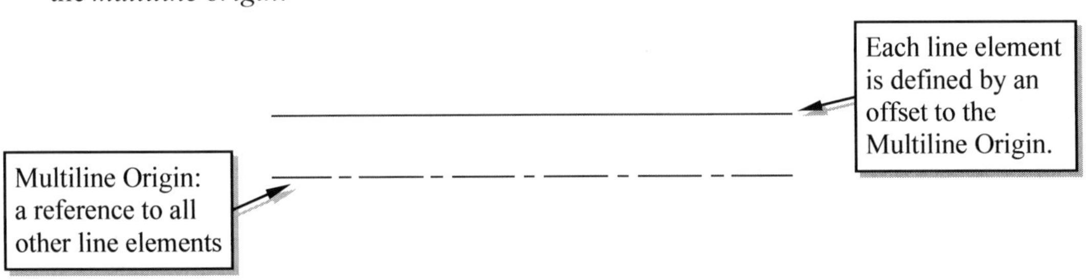

❖ Note that in the *Elements* section, all the line elements are listed in descending order with respect to their offsets. We will create two line elements representing a five-inch wall (offsetting on both sides of the reference location).

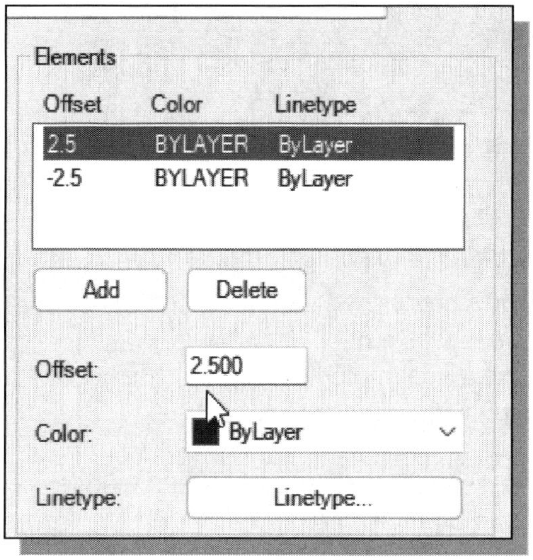

7. In the *Elements* section, highlight the first element in the list, and change the *Offset* to ***2.5***.

8. Pick the *second element* in the *Elements* section and change the *Offset* to **-2.5**.

9. Choose **OK** to exit the *Element Properties* dialog box.

❖ Notice the Add and Delete options are also available, which allow us to create or remove additional elements.

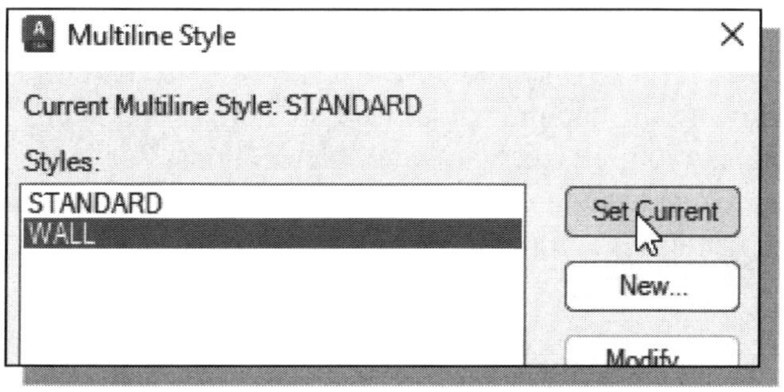

10. With the **Wall** style highlighted, click **Set Current** as shown.

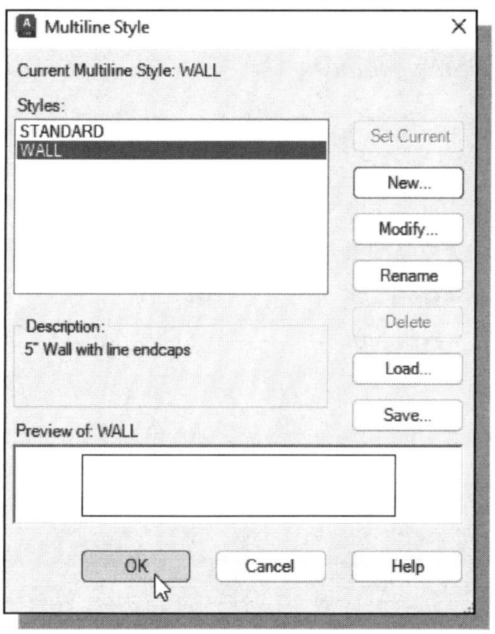

11. Click the **OK** button to end the Multiline Style command. (Note: The *Preview* section shows the current **WALL** style.)

❖ Note that the **Save** button will save a multiline style to the library of multiline styles. By default, AutoCAD saves the multiline styles information to a file called **acad.mln**. The **Load** button allows users to retrieve multiline styles from a library.

Object Snap Toolbar

1. Move the cursor to the *Menu Bar* area and choose **[Tools] → [Toolbars] → [AutoCAD]**.

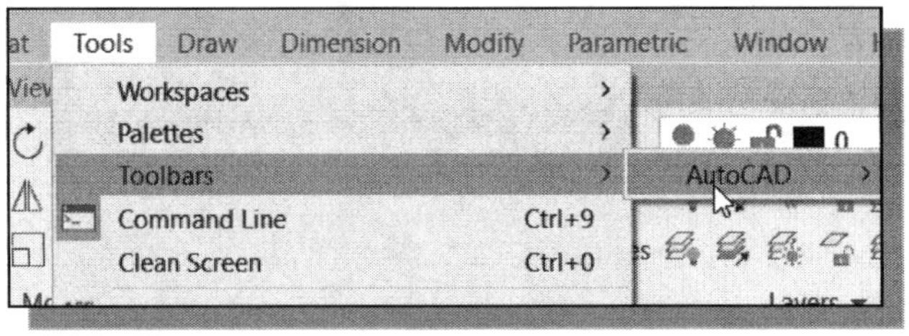

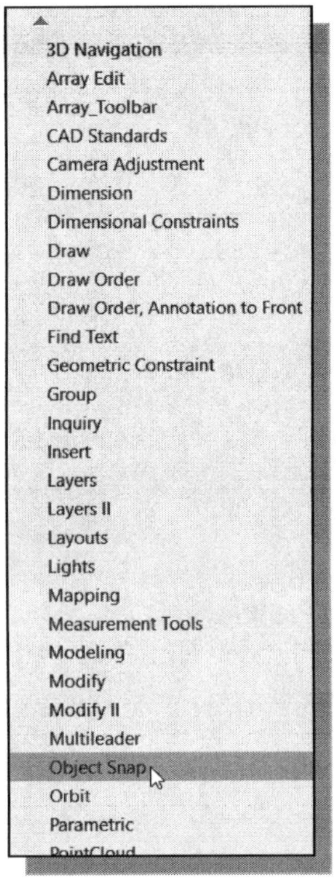

❖ AutoCAD provides 50+ predefined toolbars for access to frequently used commands, settings, and modes. A *checkmark* (next to the item) in the list identifies the toolbars that are currently displayed on the screen.

2. Select **Object Snap**, with the left-mouse-button, to display the *Object Snap* toolbar on the screen.

❖ **Object Snap** is an extremely powerful construction tool available on most CAD systems. During an entity's creation operations, we can snap the cursor to points on objects such as endpoints, midpoints, centers, and intersections. For example, we can turn on **Object Snap** and quickly draw a line to the center of a circle, the midpoint of a line segment, or the intersection of two lines.

3. In the previous chapter, we used several of the object snap options to quickly locate positions on existing geometry. In this chapter we will look at the **Snap From** option, which is the second icon in the *Object Snap toolbar*.

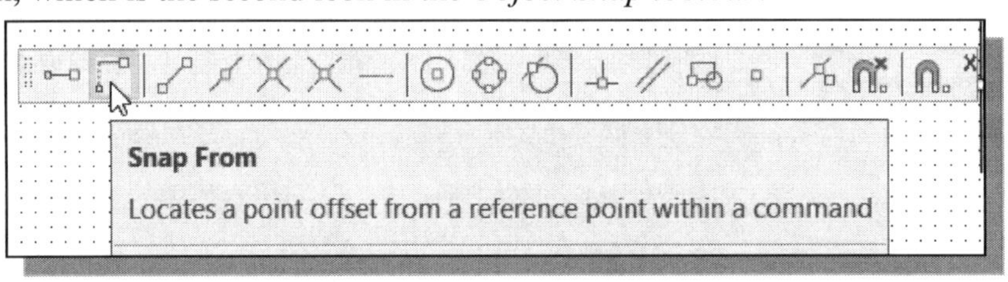

➢ The **Snap From** option allows us to locate a position using a relative coordinate system with respect to a selected position.

4. In the *Status Bar* area, reset the option buttons so that *GRID DISPLAY, SNAP MODE, DYNAMIC INPUT*, and *ORTHO* are switched ***ON***.

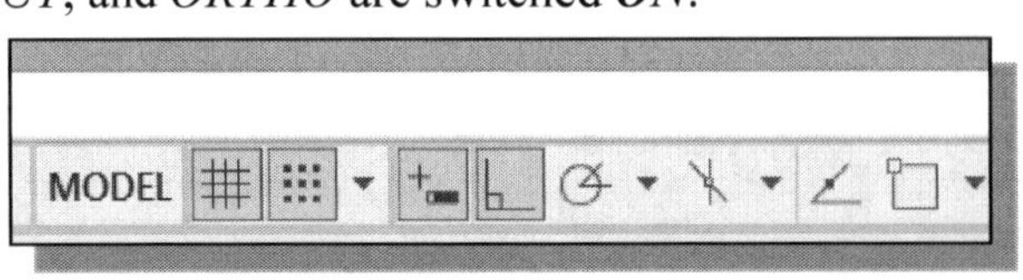

Drawing Multilines

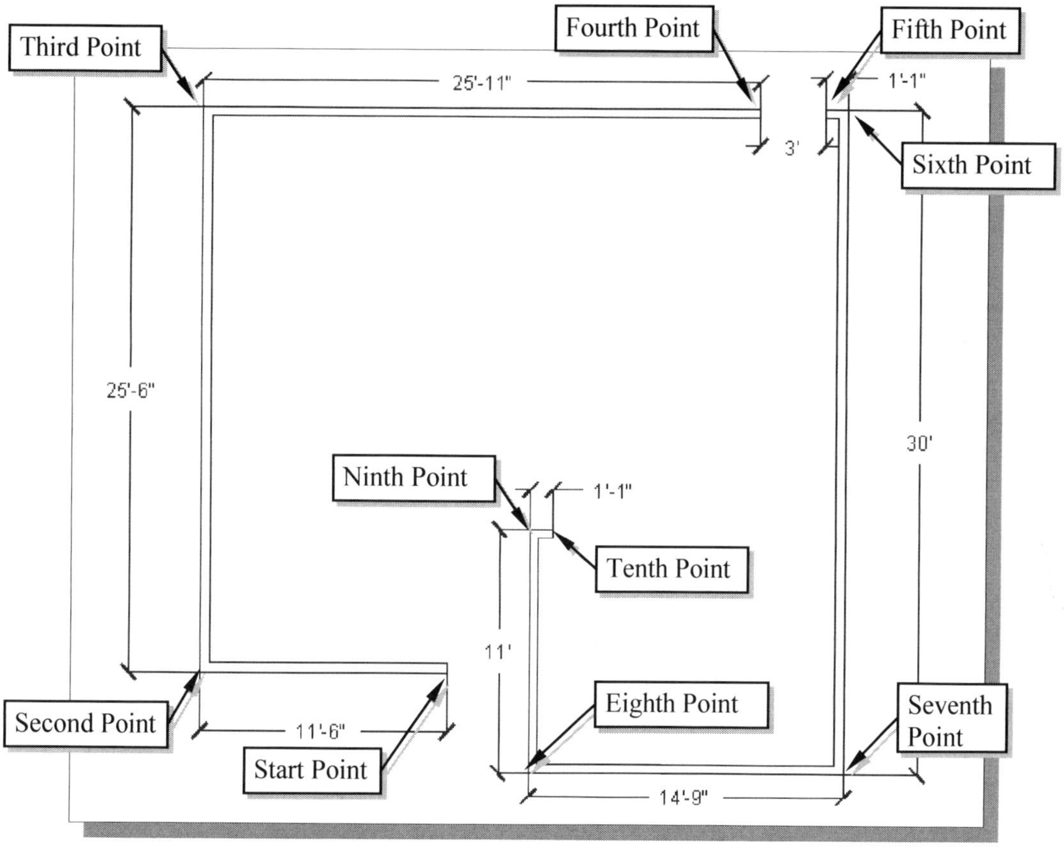

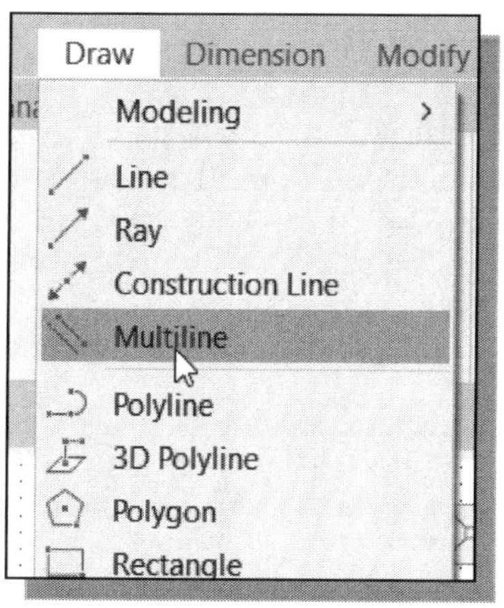

1. Select the **Multiline** command icon in the *Draw* pull-down menu, through the *Menu Bar,* as shown. In the command prompt area, the current settings, such as "*Justification* = ***Top****, Scale* = ***1.00****, Style* = ***Wall***" are displayed.

2. On your own, confirm the ***Scale*** is set to **1.00**, the ***Styles*** to **Wall** and the ***Justification*** to **Top**. You can use the **right-mouse-button** to bring up the option list and adjust the settings if needed.

3. In the command prompt area, the message "*Specify start point or [Justification/Scale/Style]:*" is displayed. Select a location **near** the bottom center of the *Drawing Area* as the **start point** of the multiline.

4. Create a horizontal line by using the *Dynamic Input* option or the *relative rectangular coordinates entry method* in the command prompt area:
   Specify next point: **@-11'6",0 [ENTER]**

5. Create a vertical line by using the *Dynamic Input* option or the *relative rectangular coordinates entry method* in the command prompt area:
Specify next point: **@25'6"<90 [ENTER]**

6. Create a horizontal line by using the *Direct Input* option; move the cursor to the right and enter the distance:
Specify next point: **25'11" [ENTER]**

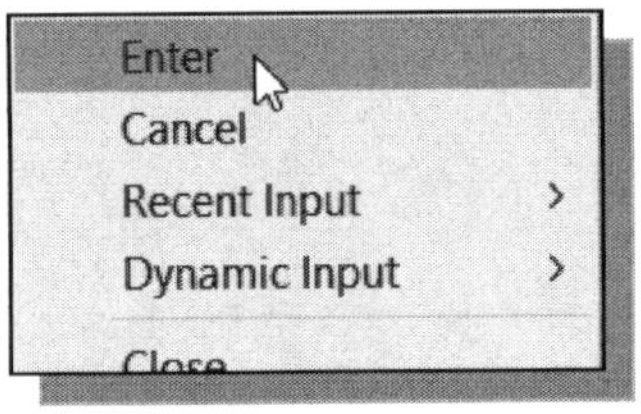

7. Inside the Drawing Area, **right-click** and select **Enter** to end the *Multiline* command.

8. Hit the **spacebar** once to repeat the last command, the **Multiline** command. In the command prompt area, the current settings "*Justification* = ***Top***, *Scale* = ***1.00***, *Style* = ***Wall***" are displayed.

9. We will use the **Snap From** option to continue creating the exterior walls. In the *Object Snap* toolbar, pick **Snap From**. In the command prompt area, the message "*_from Base point*" is displayed. AutoCAD now expects us to select a geometric entity on the screen.

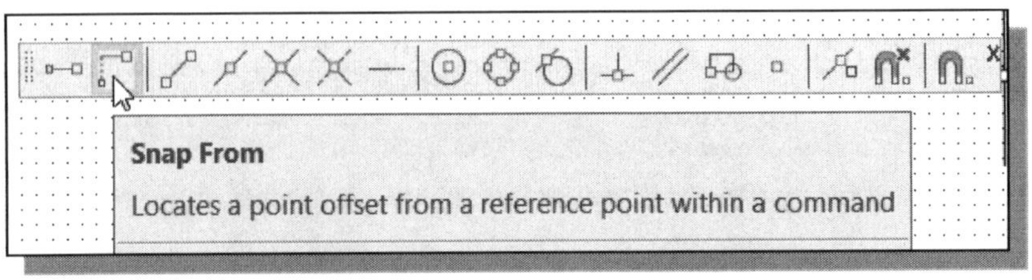

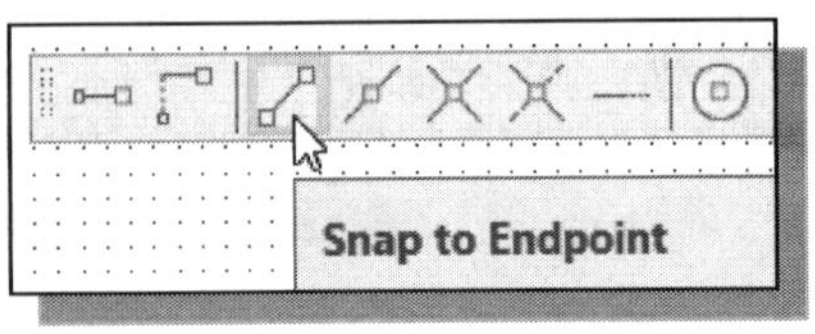

10. We will position the starting point relative to the last position of the previous *multiline*. To assure the selection of the endpoint, choose the **Snap to Endpoint** option as shown.

11. Pick the **upper corner** of the top horizontal multiline as shown.

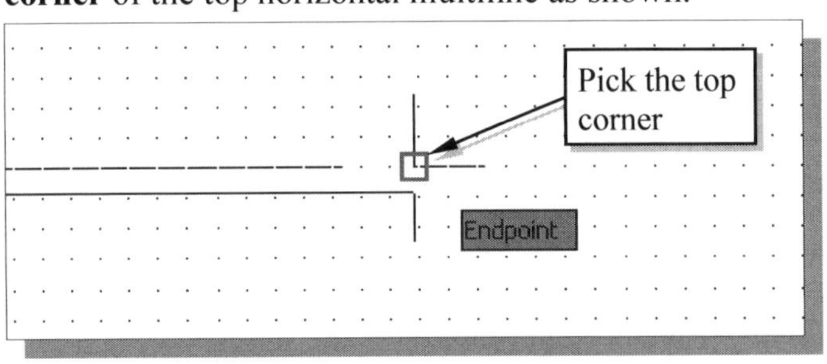

➢ Note that it is feasible to stack snap options for precise positioning of geometry.

12. The position of the starting point of the new *multiline* segments is 3′ to the right of the reference point we just picked. At the command prompt, enter @**3',0" [ENTER]**.

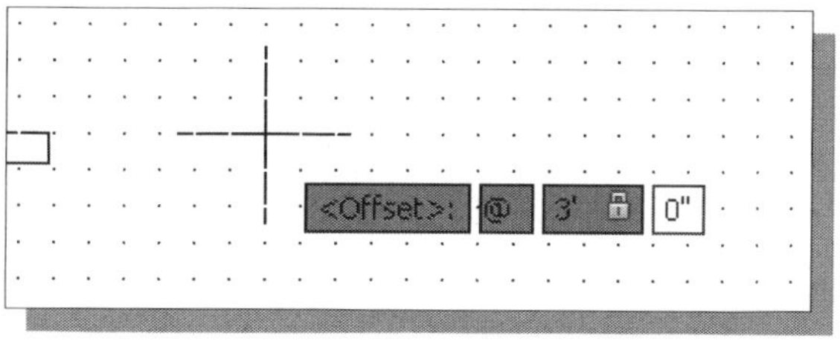

13. Now enter ***@1'1",0***, to define the top corner of the exterior wall.

14. On your own, complete the multiline segments by specifying the rest of the corners using the dimensions as shown in the figure below.

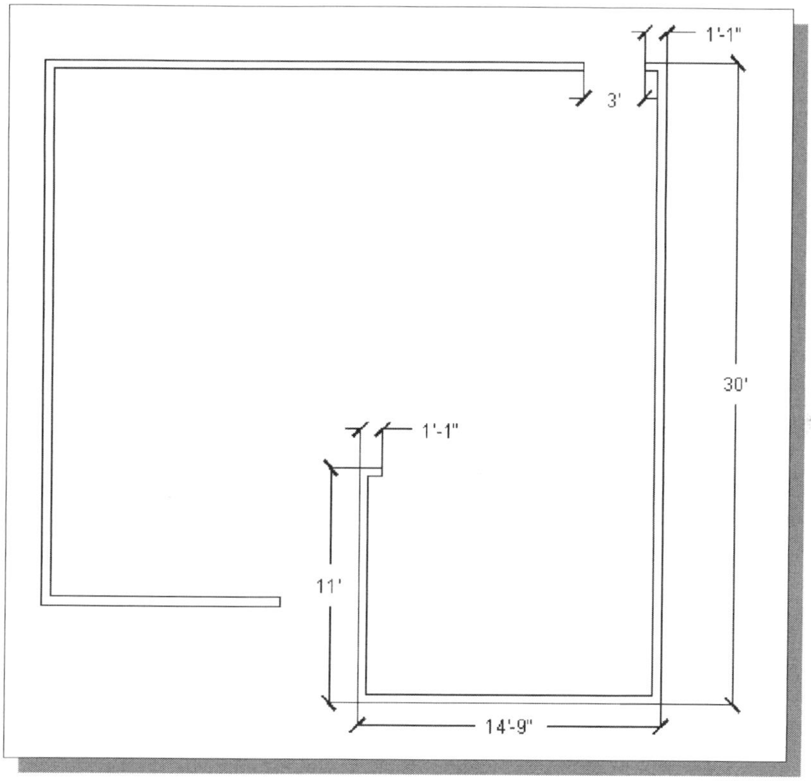

- Note that the points we specified are defining the outside corners of the floor plan design.

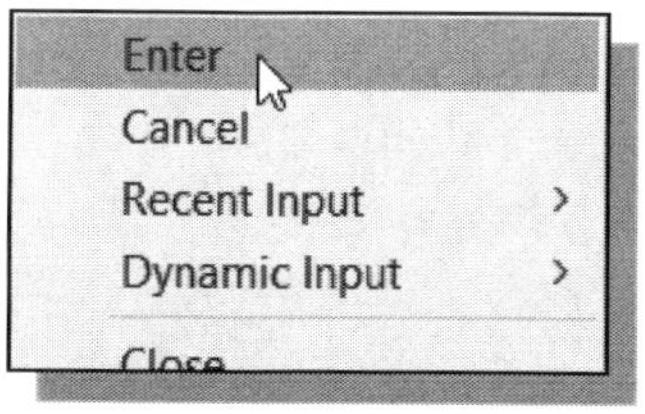

15. Inside the Drawing Area, right-click and select **Enter** to end the **Multiline** command.

Creating Interior Walls

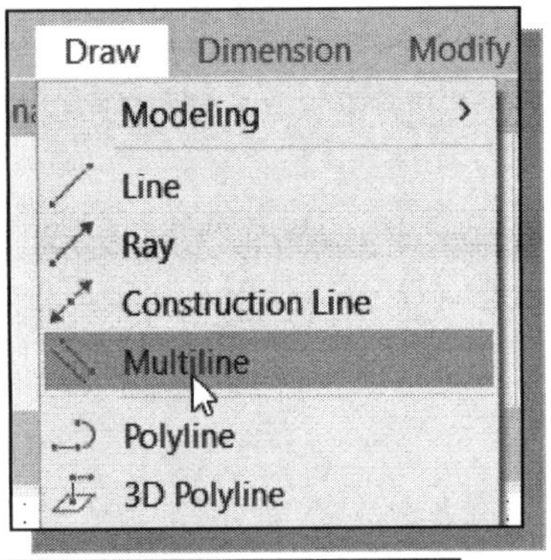

1. Select the **Multiline** command in the ***Draw*** *Menu Bar* as shown. In the command prompt area, the current settings *"Justification =* ***Top****, Scale =* ***1.00****, Style =* ***Wall****"* are displayed. In the command prompt area, the message *"Specify start point or [Justification/ Scale/Style]:"* is displayed.

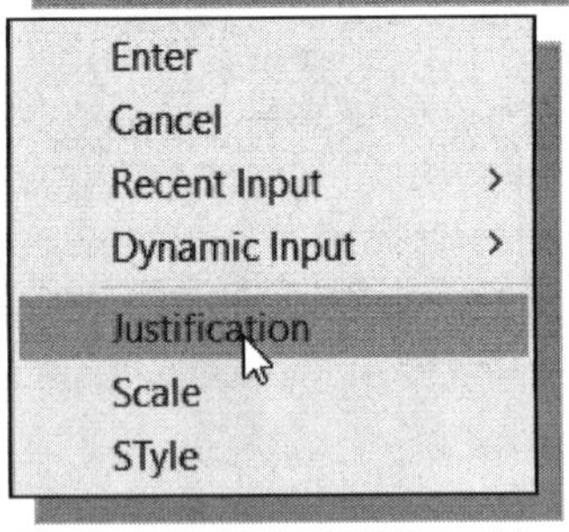

2. Inside the *Drawing Area*, **right-click** to display the option menu.

3. Pick **Justification** in the option menu. In the *command prompt area*, the message *"Enter justification type [Top/Zero/Bottom] <Top>:"* is displayed.

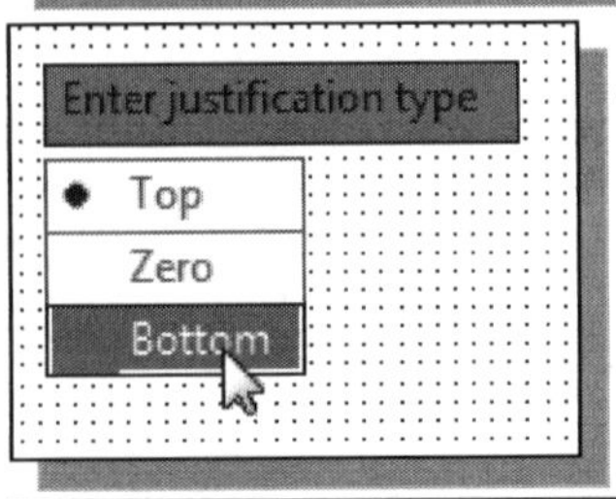

4. Inside the *Drawing Area*, right-click to display the option menu and select **Bottom** so that the points we select will be set as alignments for the bottom element.

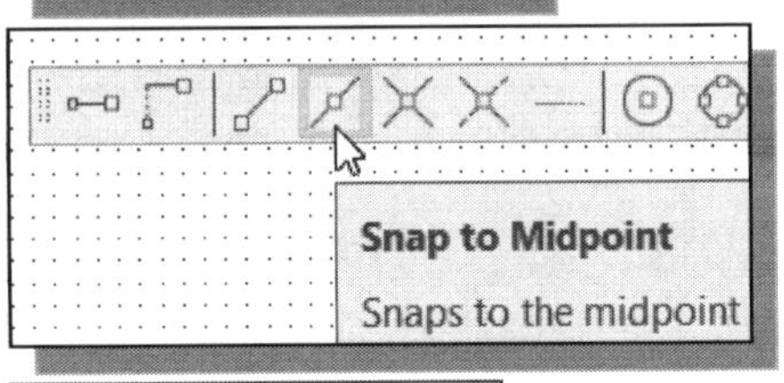

5. In the *Object Snap* toolbar, pick **Snap to Midpoint**. In the command prompt area, the message *"_mid of"* is displayed. AutoCAD now expects us to select a geometric entity on the screen.

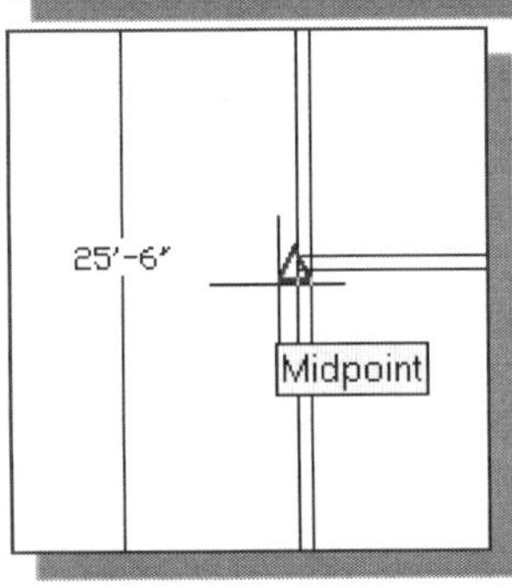

6. Select the outside **left vertical line** as shown.

7. Using the *Dynamic Input* option, create a ***10'*** inside wall toward the right.

8. Now enter ***@0,1'1"*** to define the vertical stub wall.

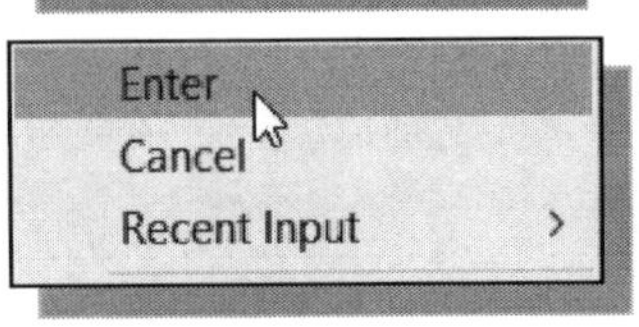

9. Inside the *Drawing Area*, right-click and select **Enter** to end the Multiline command.

- Next, we will create a vertical wall right above the last corner.

10. Hit the **spacebar** once to repeat the last command, the **Multiline** command. Since the last position used is directly below the new location, we will just enter the relative coordinates. At the command prompt, enter ***@0,2'8"*** **[ENTER]**.

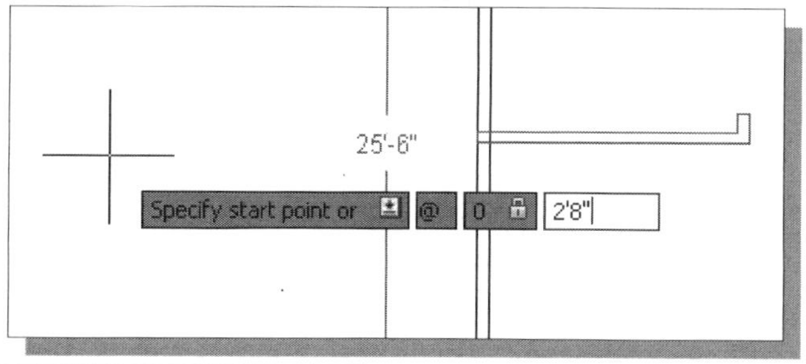

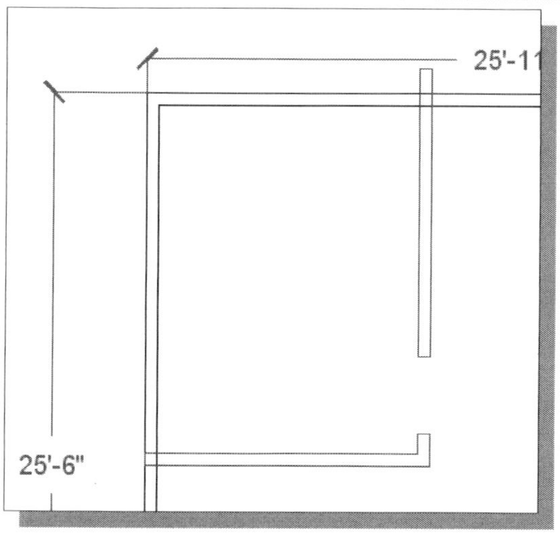

11. Place the other end above the top horizontal line as shown in the figure below. In the next section, we will use the **Multiline Edit** tools to adjust these constructions.

12. Inside the Drawing Area, right-click and select **Enter** to end the **Multiline** command.

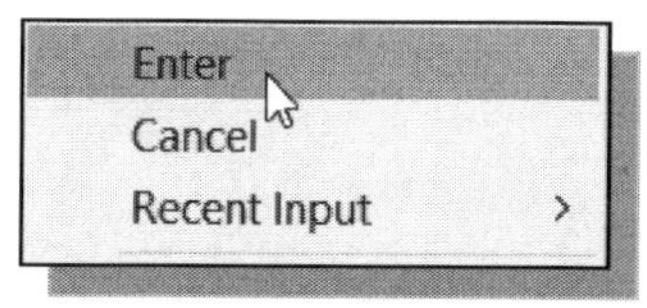

13. Hit the **spacebar** once to repeat the last command, the **Multiline** command. In the text window, the current settings "*Justification = Bottom, Scale = 1.00, Style = Wall*" are displayed. In the command prompt area, the message "*Specify start point or [Justification/Scale/Style]:*" is displayed.

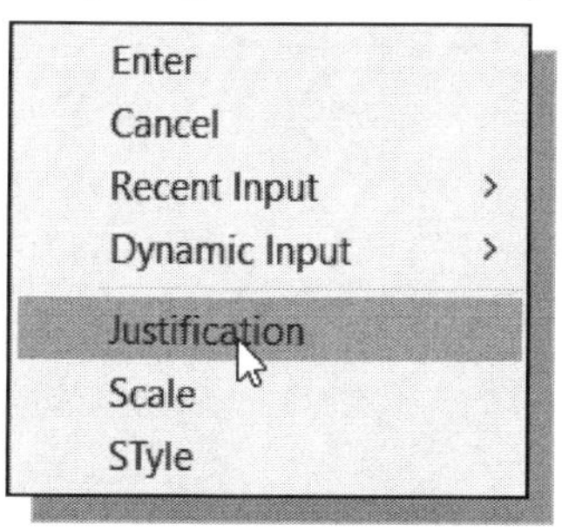

14. Inside the *Drawing Area*, **right-click** to display the option menu.

15. Pick **Justification** in the option menu. In the command prompt area, the message "*Enter justification type [Top/Zero/Bottom] <Bottom>:*" is displayed.

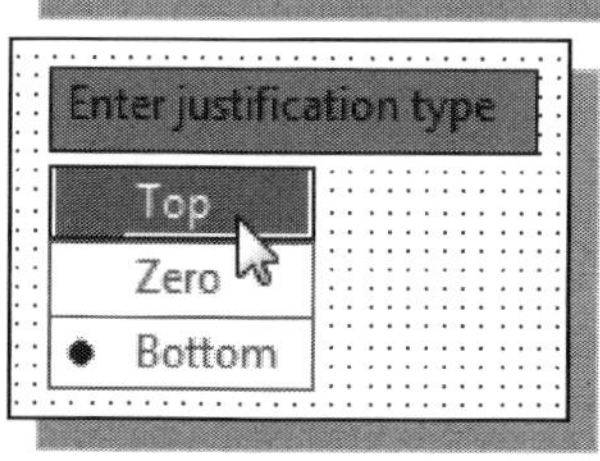

16. Inside the *Drawing Area*, right-click to display the *option menu* and select **Top** so that the points we select will align to the top element.

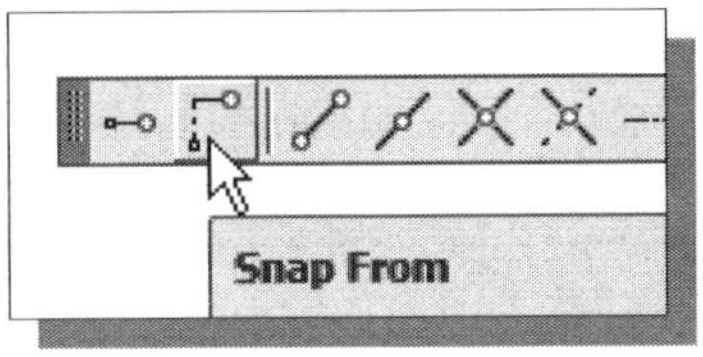

17. In the *Object Snap* toolbar, pick **Snap From**. In the command prompt area, the message "*_from Base point*" is displayed. AutoCAD now expects us to select a geometric entity on the screen.

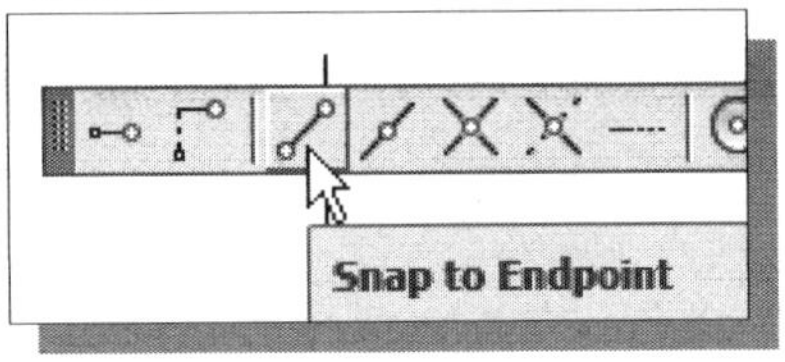

18. In the *Object Snap* toolbar, pick **Snap to Endpoint**. In the command prompt area, the message "*_endp of*" is displayed.

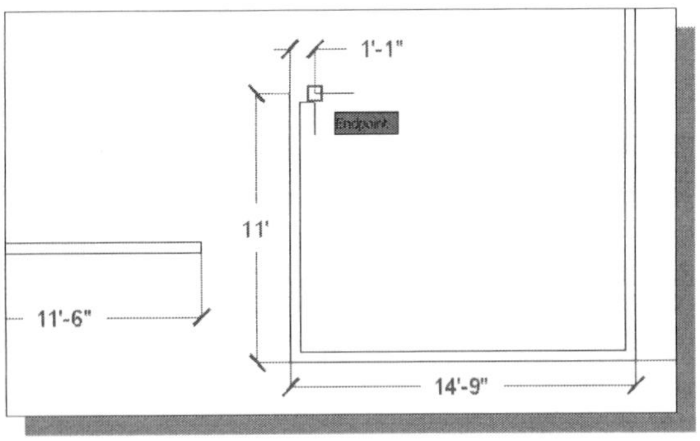

19. We will create another inside wall on the right side. Pick the corner as shown.

20. At the command prompt, enter ***@2'8",0*** **[ENTER]**.

21. Pick a location that is to the right of the right-vertical exterior wall. The drawing should appear as shown in the figure below.

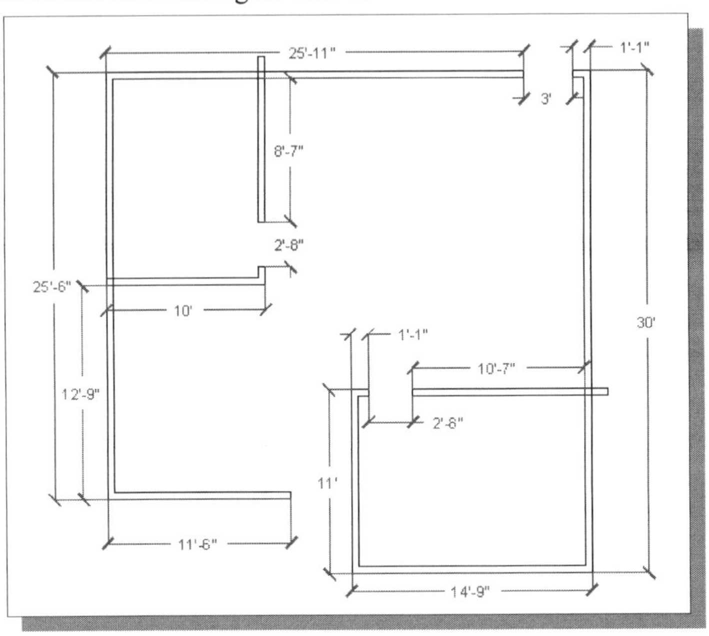

- ❖ One of the main advantages of using a CAD system to create drawings is the ability to create and/or modify geometric entities quickly, using many of the available tools. Unlike traditional board drafting, where typically only the necessary entities are created, CAD provides a much more flexible environment that requires a slightly different way of thinking, as well as taking a different view of the tasks at hand.

Joining the Walls Using Multiline Edit

1. In the *Menu Bar*, select **[Modify] → [Object]→ [Multiline]**.

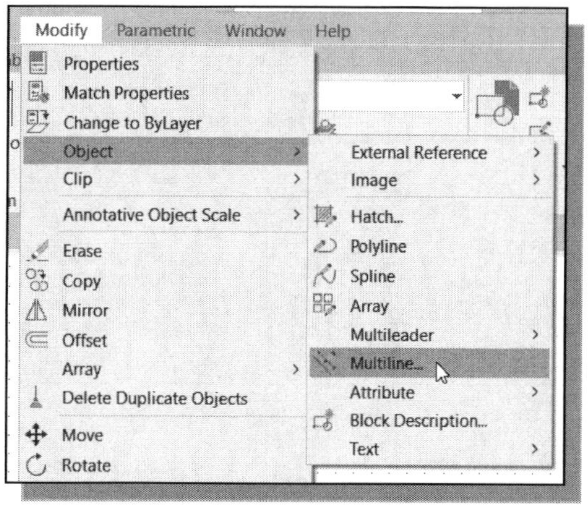

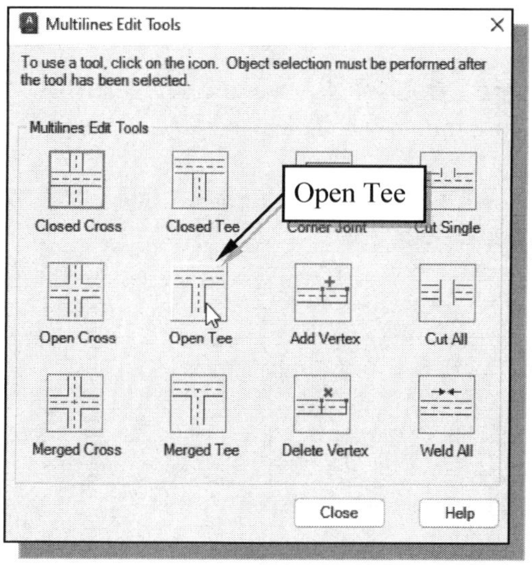

➢ The *Multiline Edit Tools* dialog box appears. Select the **Help** button to see the description of the available *Multiline Edit Tools*.

2. Pick the **Open Tee** option in the dialog box.

➢ We will need to select two multilines for this option: first, select the multiline to trim or extend; and second, select the intersecting multiline.

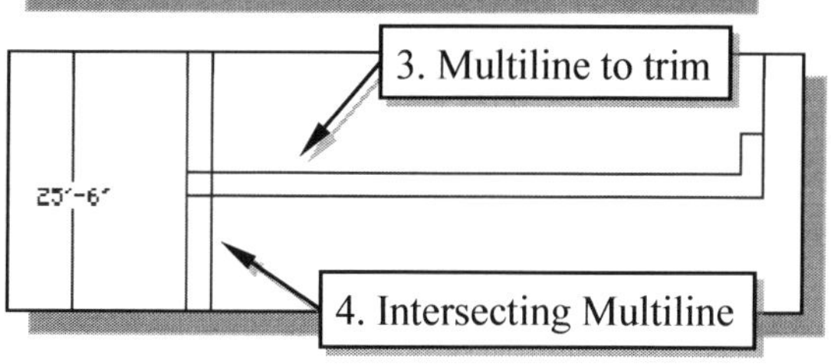

3. Pick the **horizontal multiline** as the first object, *multiline to trim,* as shown.

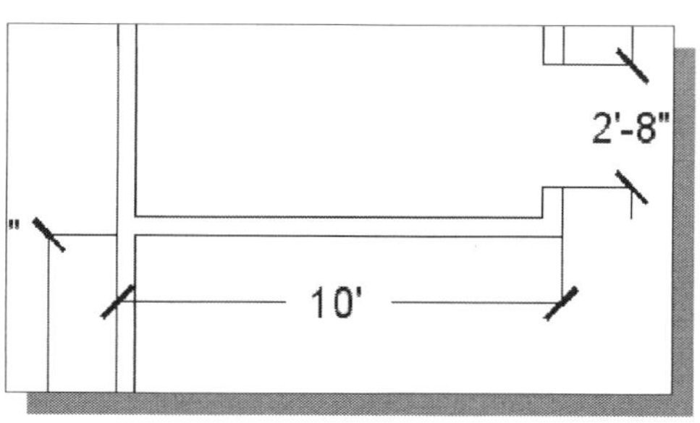

4. Pick the **vertical multiline** as the 2nd object, *intersecting multiline.*

➢ The **Open Tee** option automatically trims the lines to form the proper shapes.

5. Repeat the above steps and modify the connection of the other two inside walls.

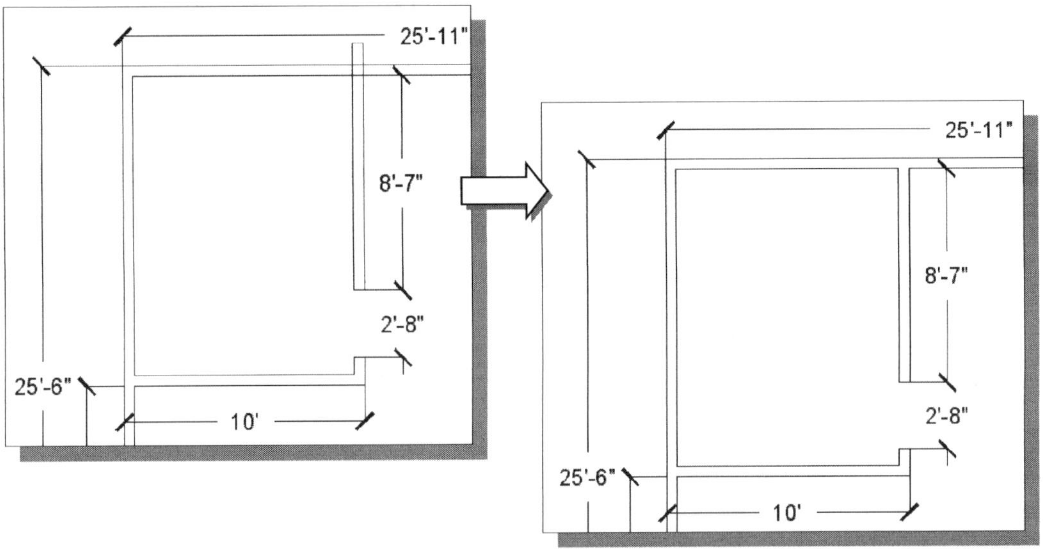

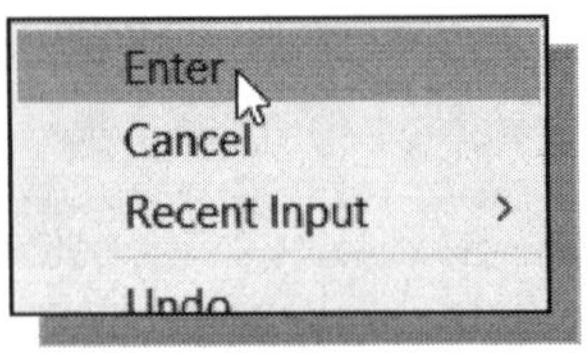

6. Inside the Drawing Area, right-click once and select **Enter** to end the **Mledit** command.

7. Using the *Multiline/MEdit* options, create the additional walls and doorways as shown.

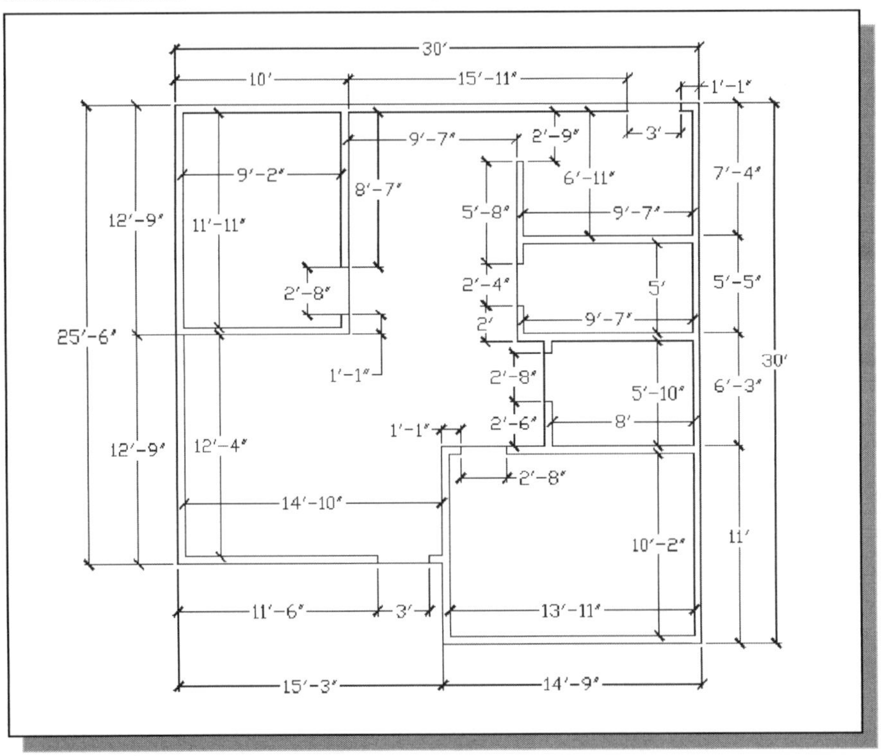

❖ Now is a good time to save the design. Select **[File] → [Save As]** in the *Menu Bar* and use ***FloorPlan*** as the *File name.*

Using Layers and Object Properties

In **AutoCAD 2027**, ***layers*** can be thought of as transparent overlays on which we organize different kinds of design information. Typically, CAD entities that are created to describe one feature or function of a design are considered as related information and therefore can be organized into the same group. The objects we organized into the same group will usually have common properties such as colors, linetypes, and lineweights. Color helps us visually distinguish similar elements in our designs. Linetype helps us identify easily the different drafting elements, such as centerlines or hidden lines. Lineweight increases the legibility of an object through width. Consider the floor plan we are currently working on. The floor plan can be placed on one layer, electrical layout on another, and plumbing on a third layer. Organizing layers and the objects on layers makes it easier to manage the information in our designs. Layers can be used as a method to control the visibility of objects. We can temporarily switch *ON* or *OFF* any layer to help construction and editing of our designs.

AutoCAD allows us to create an infinite number of layers. In general, twenty to thirty layers are sufficient for most designs. Most companies also require designers and CAD operators to follow the company standards in organizing objects in layers.

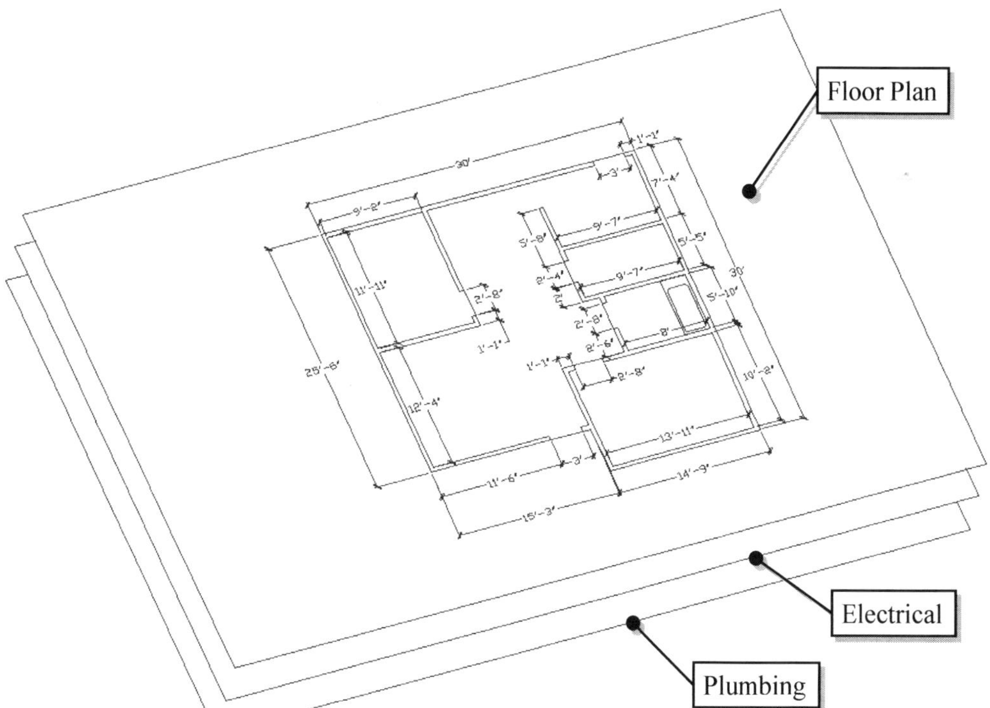

1. Pick **Layers Properties** in the *Layers* toolbar as shown.

❖ The *Layer Properties Manager* dialog box appears. AutoCAD creates a default layer, *layer 0*, which we cannot rename or delete. Note that *Layer 0* has special properties that are used by the system.

❖ In AutoCAD, we always construct entities on a layer. It may be the default layer or a layer that we create. Each layer has associated properties such as the visibility setting, color, linetype, lineweight, and plot style.

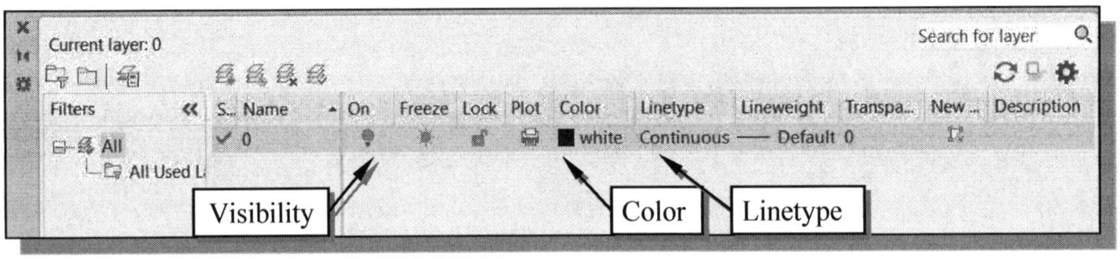

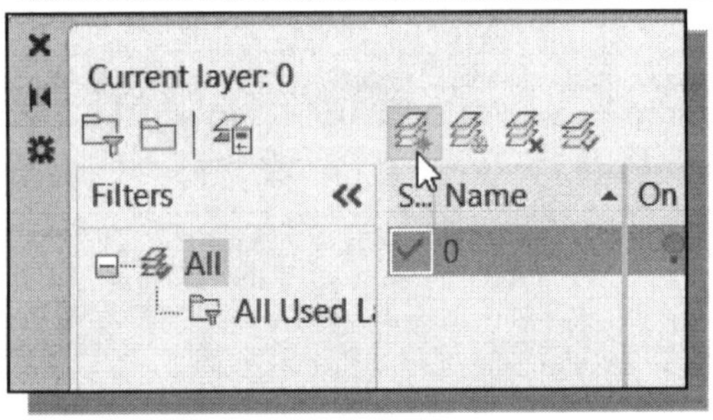

2. Click on the **New Layer** button. Notice a layer is automatically added to the list of layers.

➢ Note that we can create an unlimited number of layers in a drawing.

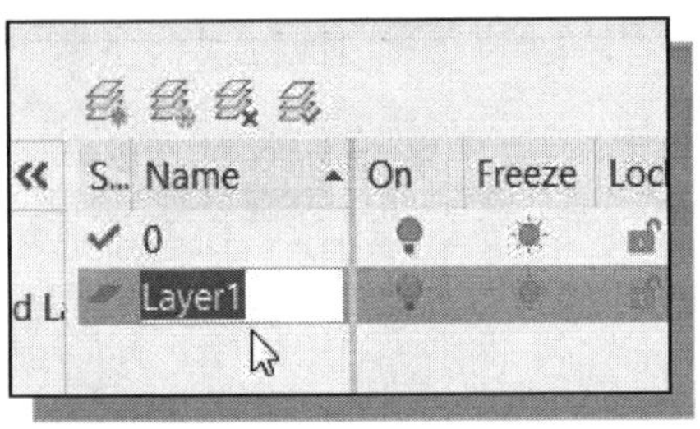

3. AutoCAD will assign a generic name to the new layer (*Layer1*). Enter ***BathRoom*** as the name of the new layer as shown in the figure below.

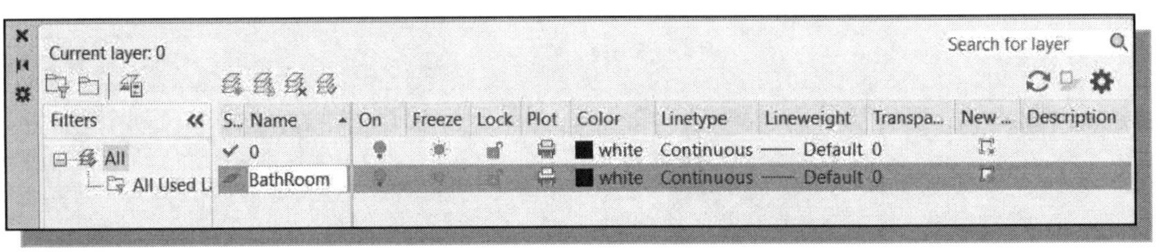

❖ Layer properties can be adjusted by clicking on the icon or name of a property. For example, clicking on the *light-bulb* icon toggles the visibility of the layer *ON* or *OFF*.

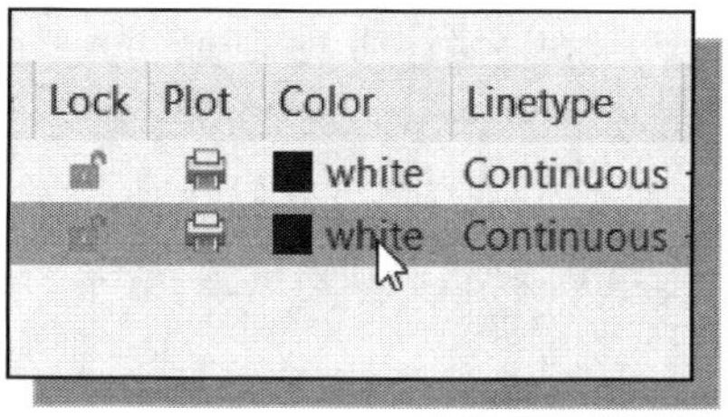

4. Pick the color swatch or the color name (**White**) of the *BathRoom* layer. The *Select Color* dialog box appears.

5. Pick **Cyan** *(Index color: 4)* in the *Standard Colors* section. Notice the current color setting is displayed at the bottom of the dialog box.

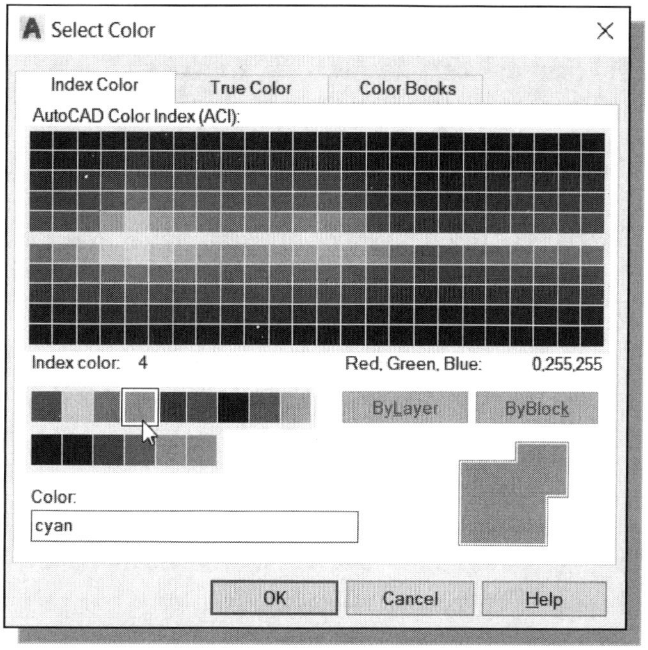

6. Click on the **OK** button to accept the color assignment.

7. Click on the **Set Current** button to make *BathRoom* the *Current Layer*. There can only be one *Current Layer*, and new entities are automatically placed on the layer that is set to be the *Current Layer*.

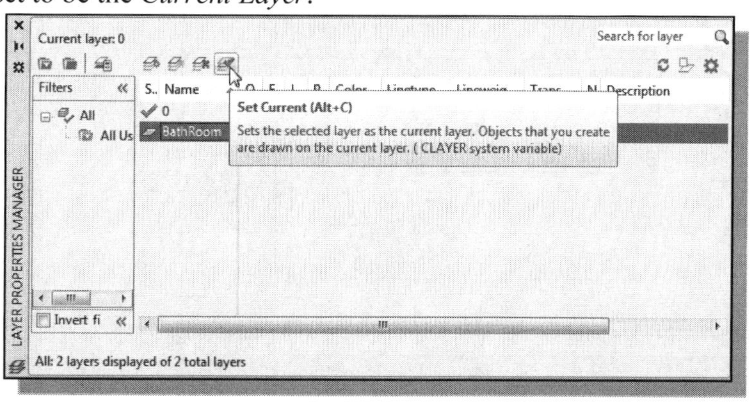

8. Click on the **Close** button, at the upper left corner of the dialog box, to accept the settings and exit the *Layer Properties Manager* dialog box.

❖ The *Layer Control* toolbar in the top of the AutoCAD toolbar panel shows the status of the active layer. The *BathRoom* layer is shown as the current active layer. Note that this *Layer* toolbar can also be used to control the settings of individual layers.

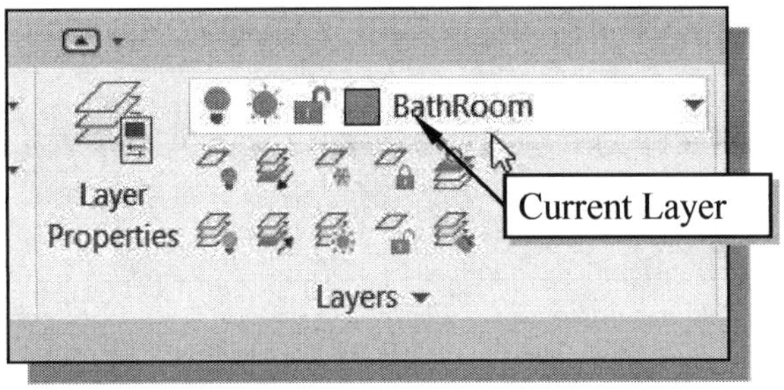

Use the Zoom Realtime option

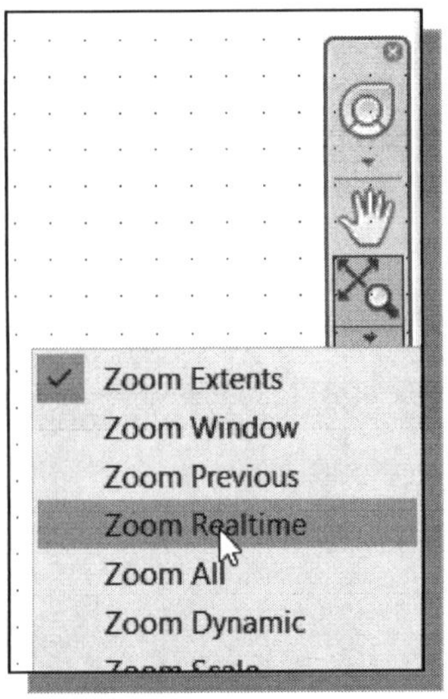

1. Click on the **Zoom Realtime** icon in the *Navigate* toolbar located to the right side of the Drawing Area.

2. Inside the *Drawing Area*, **push and hold down the left-mouse-button**, then move upward to enlarge the current display scale factor. (Press the **[Esc]** key to exit the Zoom command.)

3. Use the **Zoom Realtime** option to reposition the display so that we can work on the bathroom of the floor plan.

➢ Note that the mouse-wheel can also be used to Zoom Realtime; turning the wheel forward will enlarge the current display scale factor.

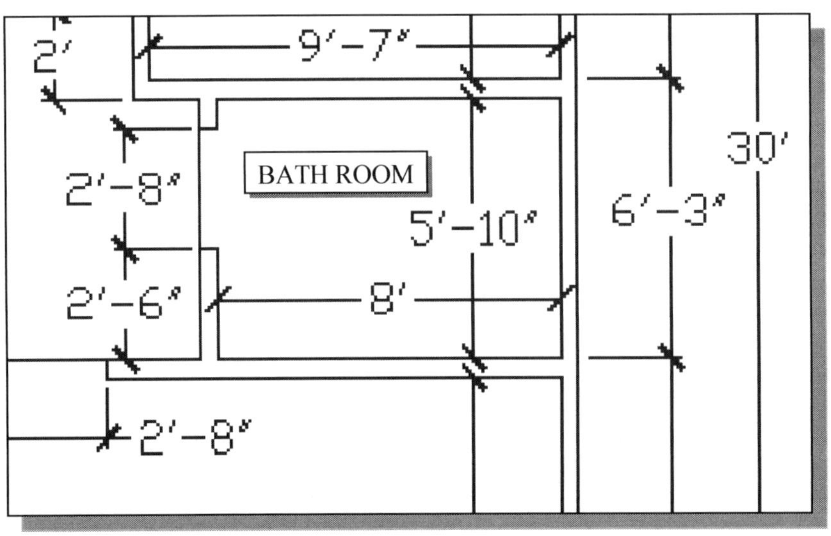

Modeling the Bathroom

1. In the *Status Bar* area, reset the option buttons so that all of the buttons are switched *OFF*.

2. Click on the **Rectangle** command icon in the *Draw* toolbar. In the *command prompt area*, the message "*Specify first corner point:*" is displayed.

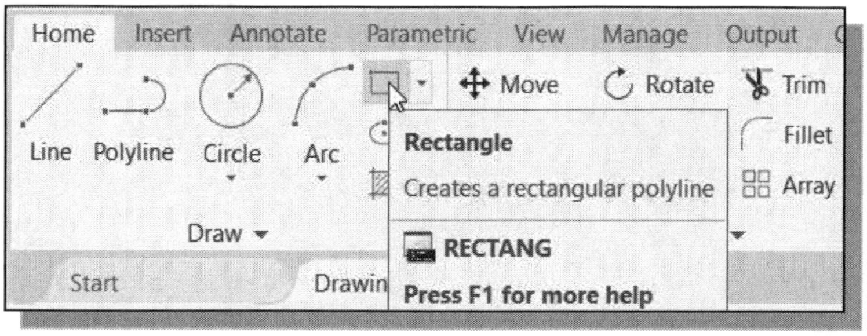

3. In the *Object Snap* toolbar, pick **Snap to Endpoint**. In the command prompt area, the message "*_endp of*" is displayed. AutoCAD now expects us to select a geometric entity on the screen.

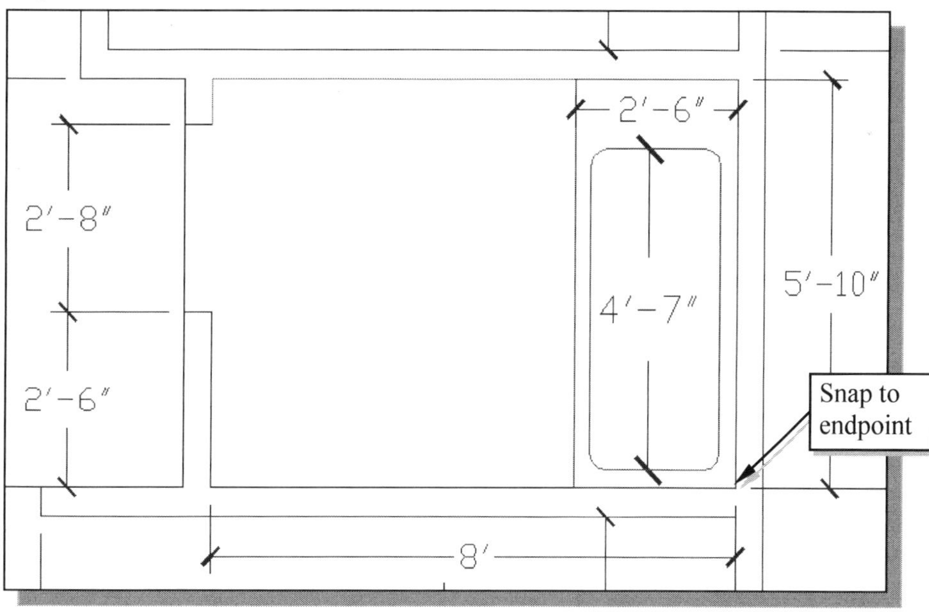

4. Use the *Dynamic Input* options and create the outer rectangle of the tub (***2'-6" x 5'-10"***).

5. Complete the inner shape by creating a rectangle with a distance of 3" from the outer rectangle and rounded corners of 3" radius.

6. Create two rectangles (*10″ × 20″* and *20″ × 30″*) with rounded corners (radius **3″**) and position them as shown.

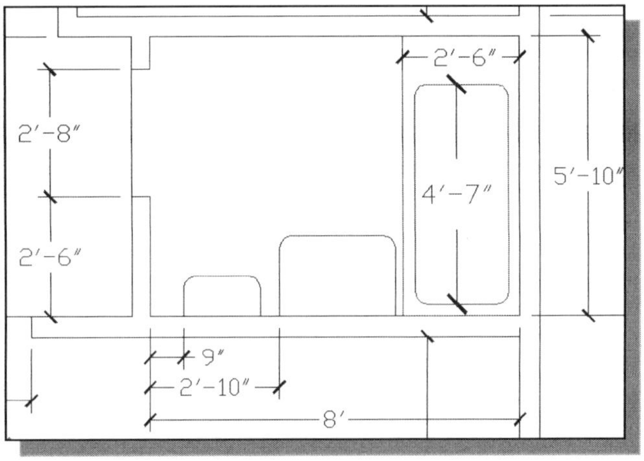

7. Select the **Ellipse → Axis, End** command icon in the *Draw* toolbar. In the command prompt area, the message "*Specify axis endpoint of ellipse or [Arc/Center]:*" is displayed.

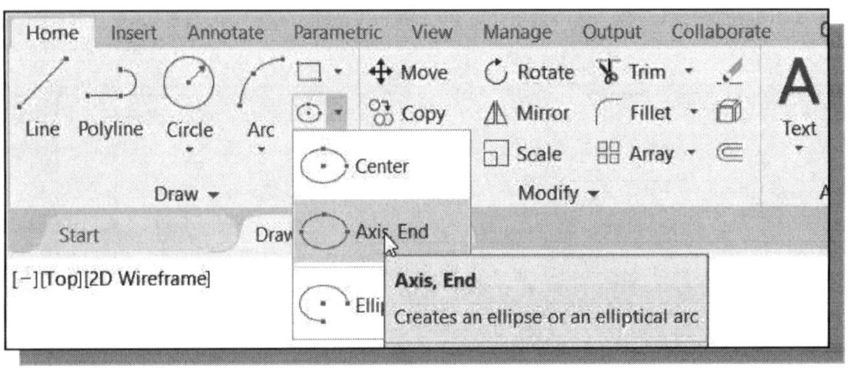

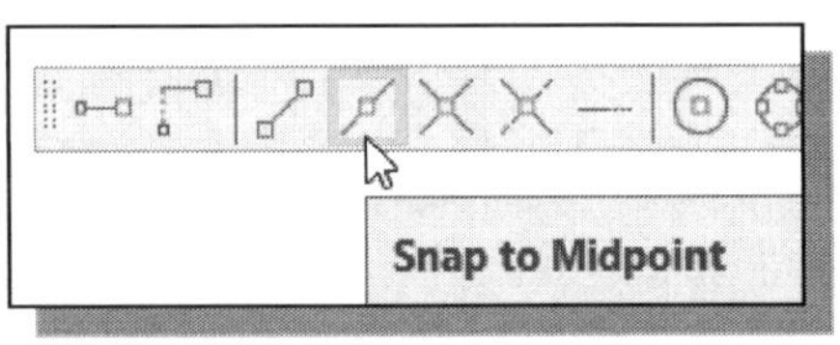

8. In the *Object Snap* toolbar, pick **Snap to Midpoint**. In the command prompt area, the message "*_mid of*" is displayed.

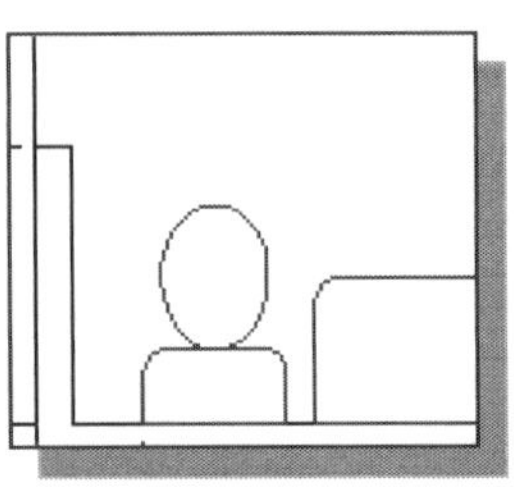

9. Pick the **top horizontal line** of the small rectangle we just created.

10. For the second point location, enter ***@0,20″* [ENTER]**.

11. For the third point, enter ***@7.5″,0* [ENTER]**.

❖ An ellipse has a major axis, the longest distance between two points on the ellipse, and a minor axis, the shorter distance across the ellipse. The three points we specified identify the two axes.

Using the Measure Tool to Measure Area and Perimeter

In AutoCAD 2027, the Measure tool is a tool that can be used to quickly measure distance, area, and/or perimeter.

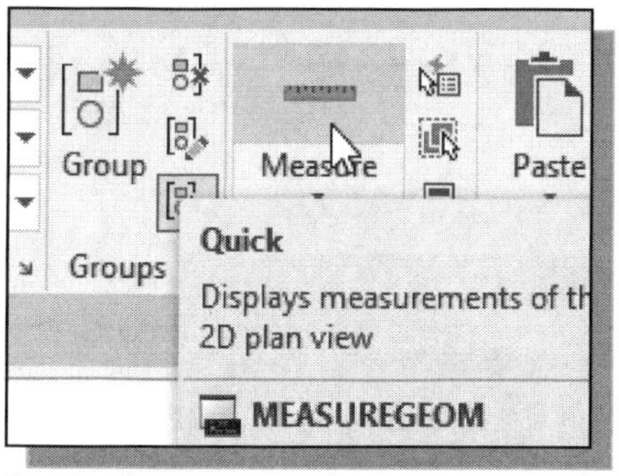

1. In the *Ribbon* tabs area, left-click once on the **Measure** title in the *Utilities* toolbar as shown.

➤ In AutoCAD 2027, the **Measure** command provides multiple options for calculating information related to the selected region.

3. In the command prompt area, the message "**MeasureGeom** Move cursor or *[Distance Radius Angle Area Volume Quick Mode eXit]:*" is displayed. By default, AutoCAD expects us to move the cursor inside a closed region and related information will be displayed and/or calculated. Move the cursor inside the bathtub and notice the related distances/dimensions are shown.

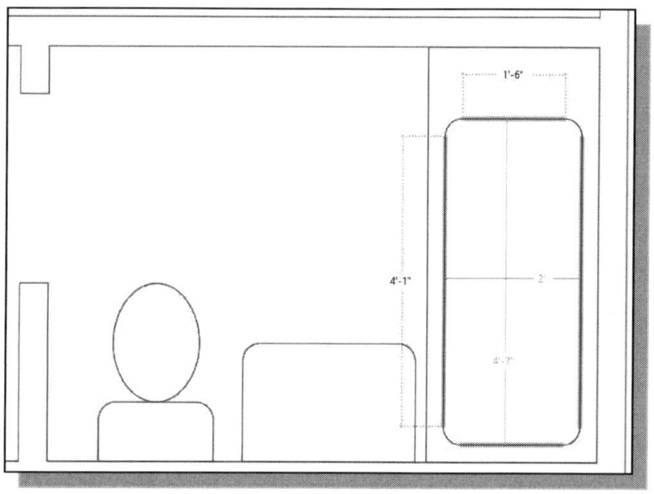

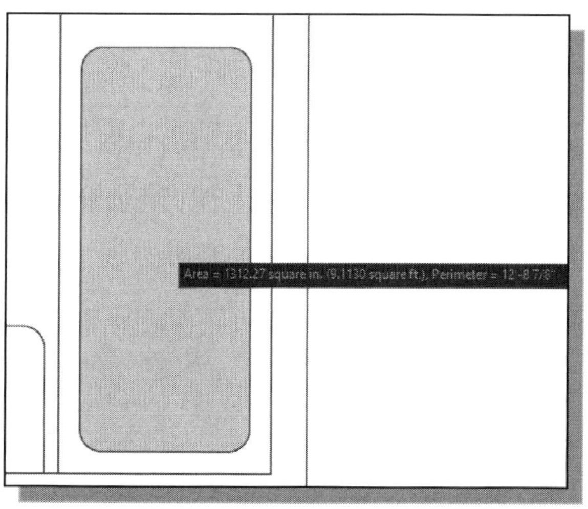

4. Click inside the bathtub and notice the area and perimeter of the highlighted region are calculated as shown:

   Area = 1312.27 square in. (9.1130 square ft.), perimeter = 12'-8 7/8"

- The area and perimeter of a closed region will be calculated by clicking on the inside of the region when using the **Measure** command.

➢ The area and perimeter of an **open region** can also be calculated by selecting points forming the region of interest as shown below.

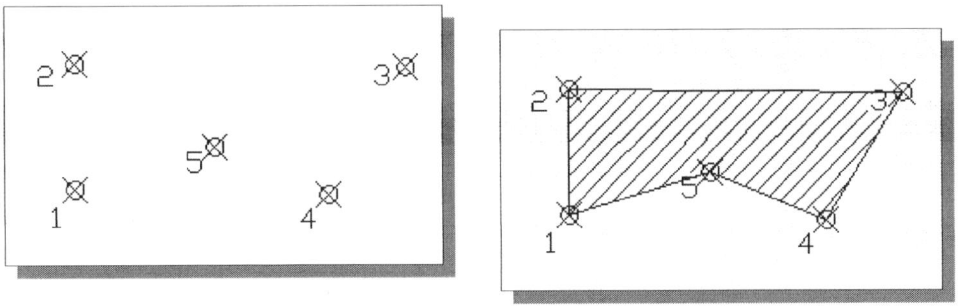

5. To activate this option, select **ARea** in the command prompt area as shown.

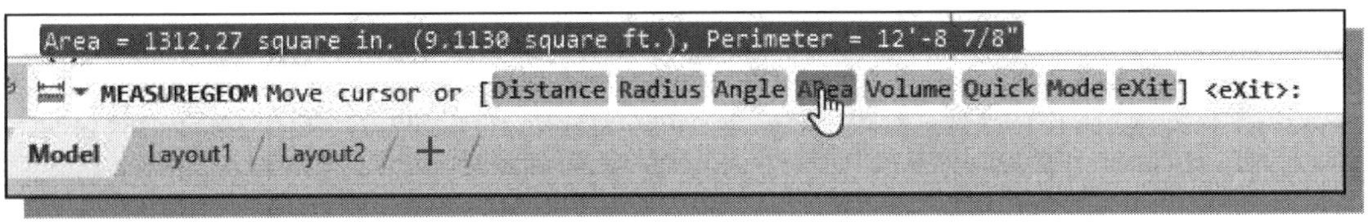

6. Pick the four inside corners of the bathroom, start at the upper left corner and go clockwise to select the other three corners as shown.

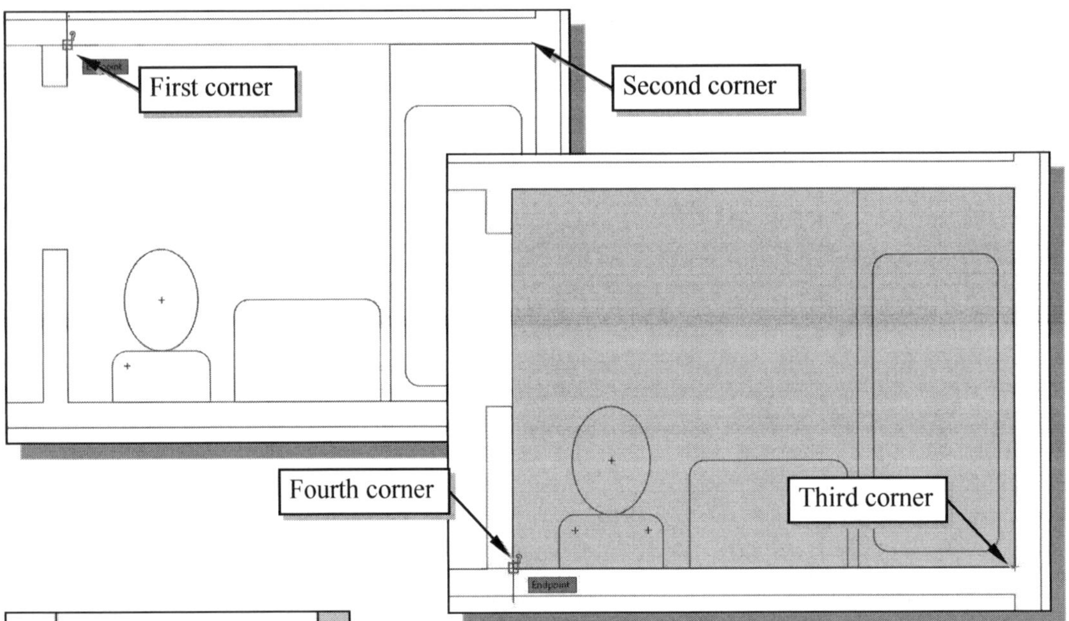

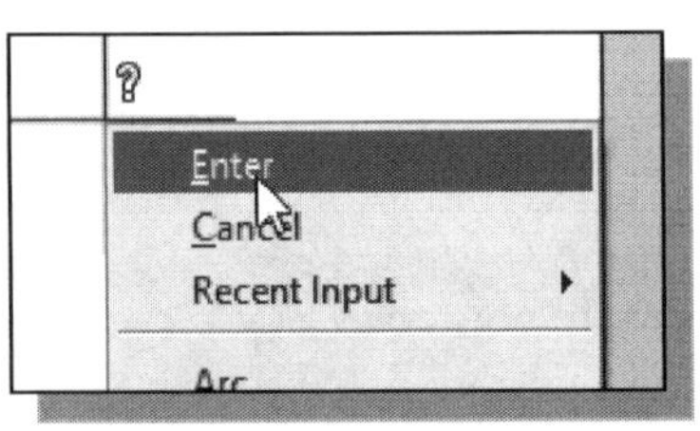

7. Inside the *Drawing Area*, right-click once to bring up the option menu and select **Enter** as shown. The area and perimeter of the bathroom is now calculated as: **Area = 6726.00 square in. (46.7083 square ft.), perimeter = 27'-8 1/8"**

8. Press the [**Esc**] key once to end the ***Measure*** command.

Controlling Layer Visibility

AutoCAD does not display or plot the objects that are on invisible layers. To make layers invisible, we can ***freeze*** or ***turn off*** those layers. Turning off layers only temporarily removes the objects from the screen; the objects remain active in the CAD database. Freezing layers will make the objects invisible and also disable the objects in the CAD database. Freezing layers will improve object selection performance and reduce regeneration time for complex designs. When we ***thaw*** a frozen layer, AutoCAD updates the CAD database with the screen coordinates for all objects in the design.

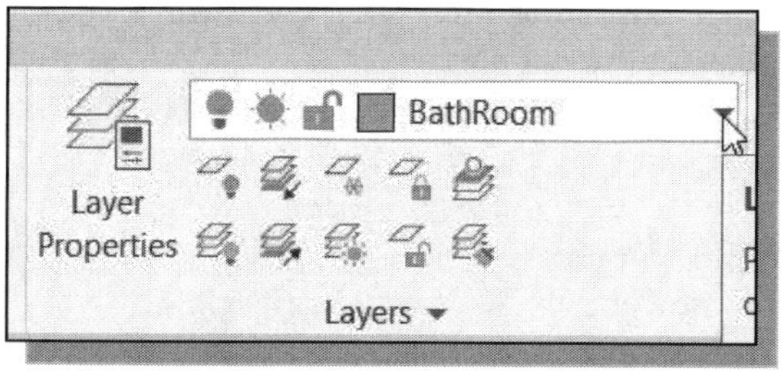

1. On the *Layers* toolbar panel, choose the triangle next to the ***Layer Control*** box with a click of the left-mouse-button.

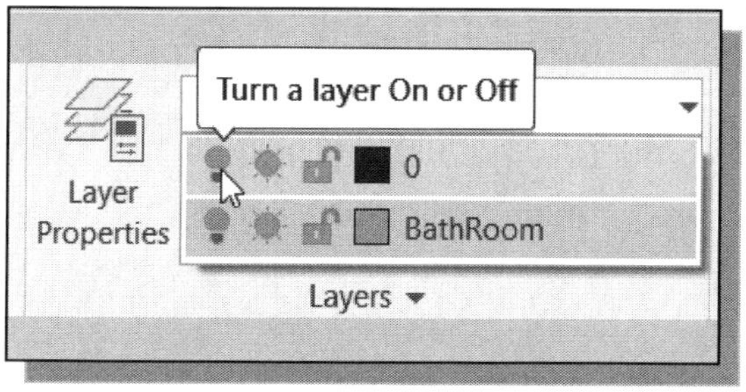

2. Move the cursor over the **lightbulb** icon for *layer 0*. The tool tip "*Turn a layer On or Off*" appears.
3. **Left-click once** and notice the icon color is changed to a dark color, representing the layer (*Layer 0*) is turned *OFF*.
4. Move the cursor into the Drawing Area and **left-click once** to accept the layer control settings.

➢ On your own, practice turning on *Layer 0* and freezing/thawing *Layer 0*. What would happen if we turn off all layers?

Adding a New Layer

1. Pick **Layer Properties Manager** in the *Layers* toolbar panel. The *Layer Properties Manager* dialog box appears.
2. Create a new layer (layer name: ***Walls***) and change the layer color to **Green**.
3. Turn ***ON*** the *0* layer, turn ***OFF*** the *BathRoom* layer, and set the ***Walls*** layer as the *Current Layer*. Click on the **Close** button to exit *Layer Properties*.

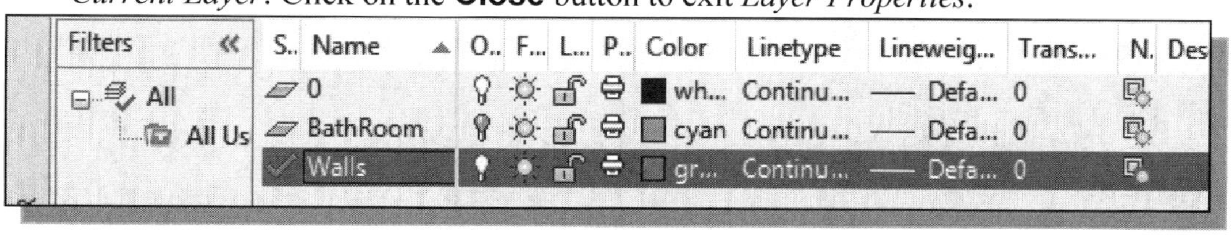

Moving Objects to a Different Layer

AutoCAD 2027 provides a flexible graphical user interface that allows users to select graphical entities BEFORE the command is selected (*pre-selection*), or AFTER the command is selected (*post-selection*). The procedure we have used so far is the *post-selection* option. We can pre-select one or more objects by clicking on the objects at the command prompt (**Command:**). To deselect the selected items, press the **[Esc]** key twice.

1. Inside the Drawing Area, pre-select all objects by enclosing all objects inside a **selection window** as shown.

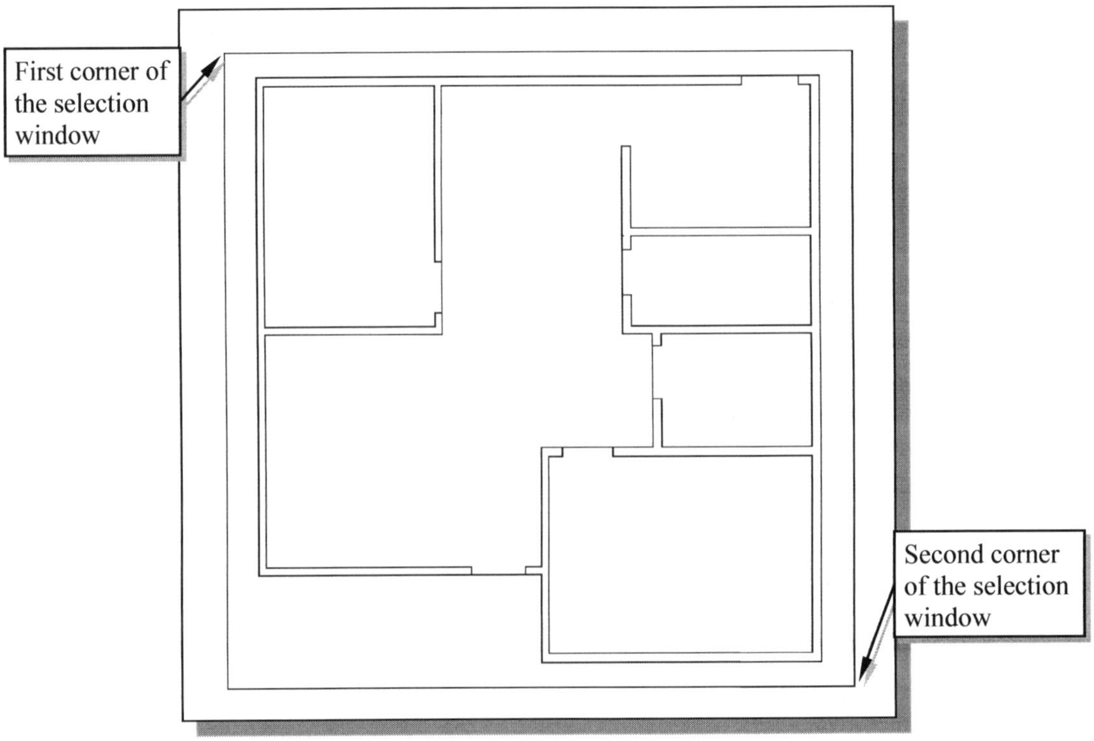

2. On the *Object Properties* toolbar, choose the ***Layer Control*** box with the left-mouse-button.

❖ Notice the layer name displayed in the *Layer Control* box is the selected object's assigned layer and layer properties.

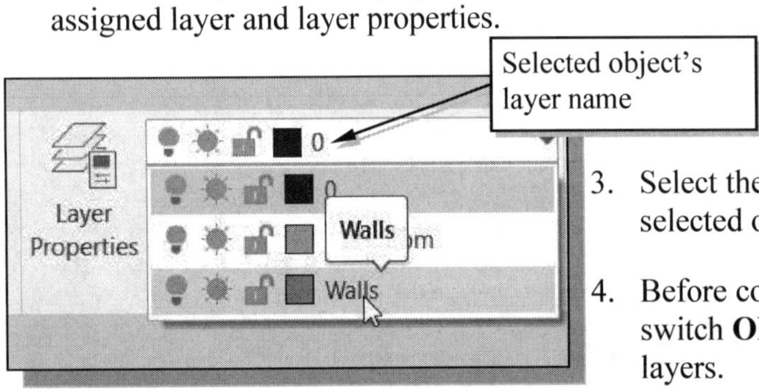

3. Select the ***Walls*** layer to move the selected objects to the new layer.

4. Before continuing to the next page, switch **ON** both *Walls* and *Bathroom* layers.

Matching Layer Properties

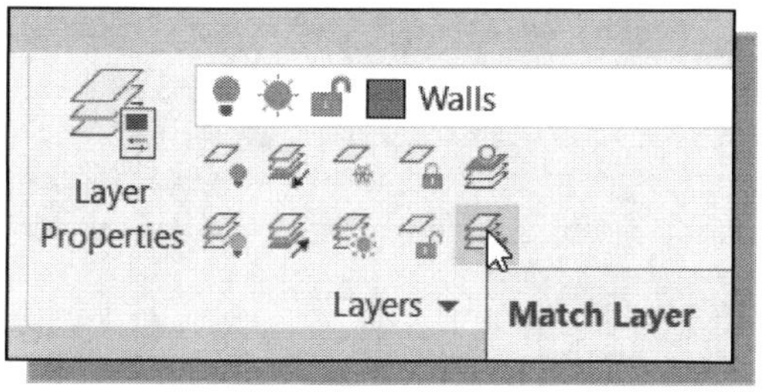

1. Pick **Match** in the *Layer control* toolbar panel. In the command prompt area, the message "*Select objects to be changed:*" is displayed.

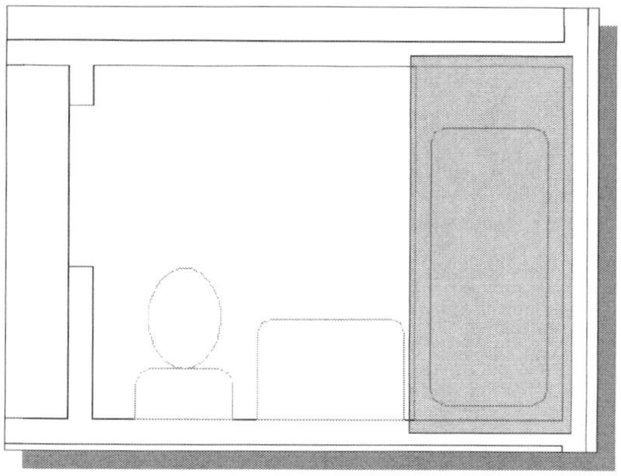

2. Select the **bathtub** using a selection window as shown.

3. Inside the Drawing Area, **right-click** once to accept the selection.

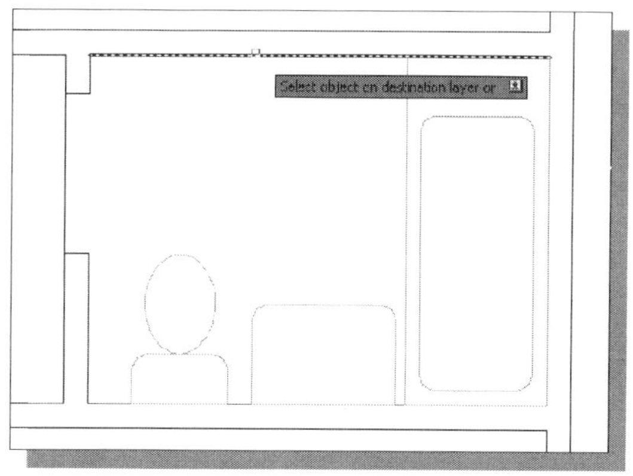

4. Select one of the **Walls** as the object properties to match.

➢ In the *command prompt area*, notice the selected objects have been moved to the Walls layer.

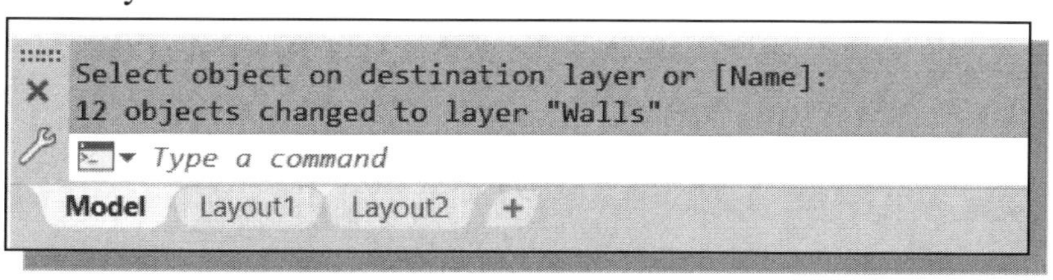

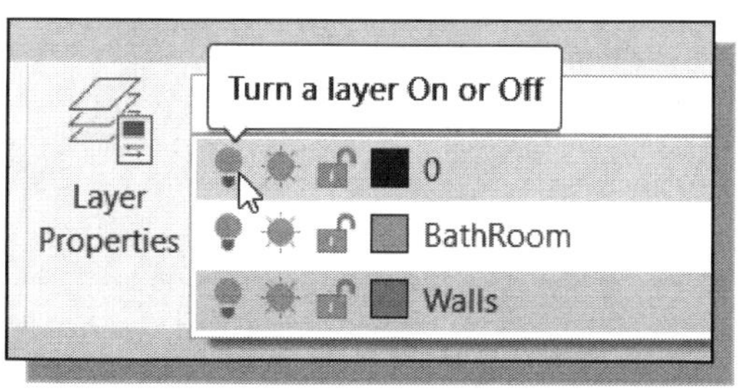

5. On your own, switch **on** and **off** of the ***Walls and bathroom*** layers to examine the results of the *Match Layer Properties* command.

➢ On your own, complete the floor plan by creating the 4′ and 5′ windows in a new layer *Windows*. The dimensions are as shown in the figure below.

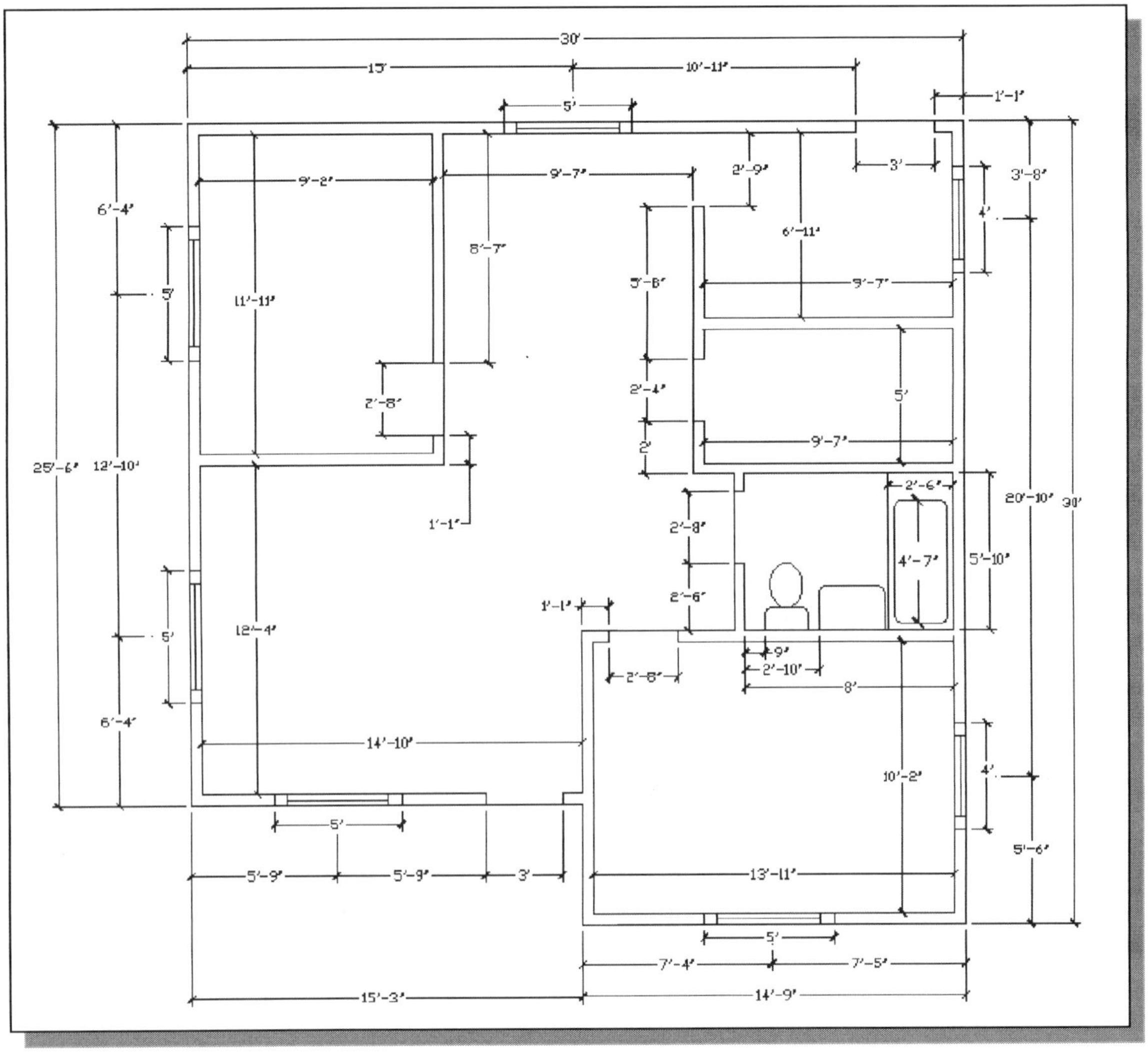

Review Questions: (Time: 25 minutes)

1. List some of the advantages of using *layers*.

2. List two methods to control the *layer visibility* in AutoCAD 2027.

3. Describe the procedure to move objects from one layer to another.

4. When and why should you use the **Multiline** command?

5. Is there a limitation to how many layers we can set up in AutoCAD?

6. List and describe the two options available in AutoCAD to create ellipses.

7. Is there a limitation to how many parallel lines we can set up when using AutoCAD Multiline objects?

8. What is the name of the layer that AutoCAD creates as the default layer (the layer that we cannot rename or delete)?

9. When and why would you use the Match Properties command?

10. A **chamfer** connects two objects with an angled line. A chamfer is usually used to represent a beveled edge on a corner. Construct the following corners by using the **Chamfer** command.

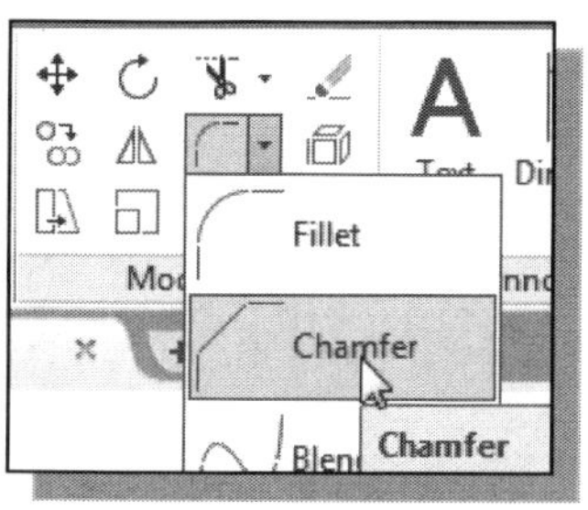

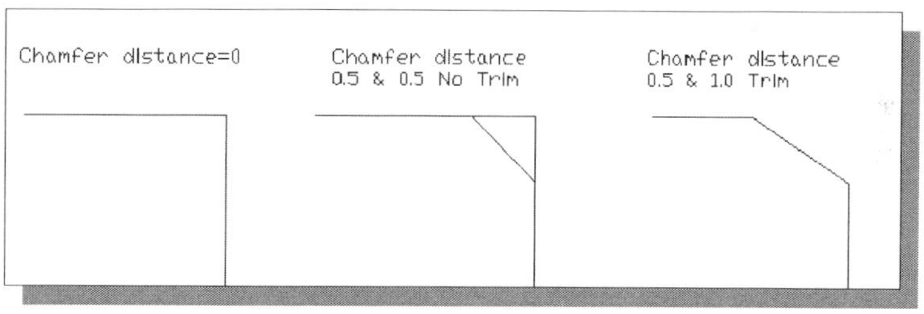

11. List the commands you would use to create the following multilines in a drawing.

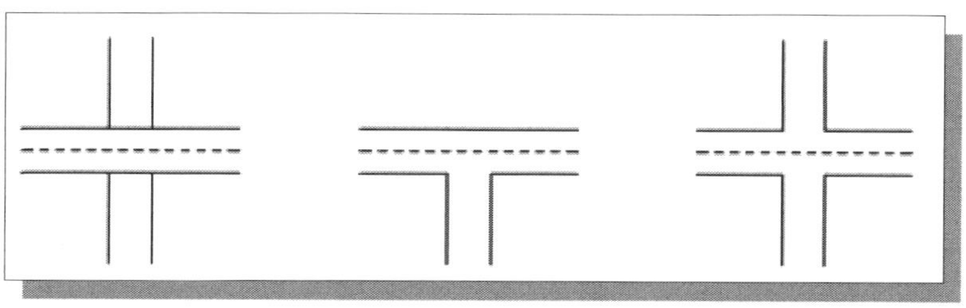

Exercises: (Time: 120 minutes)

1. Floor Plan A (Wall thickness: 5 inch)

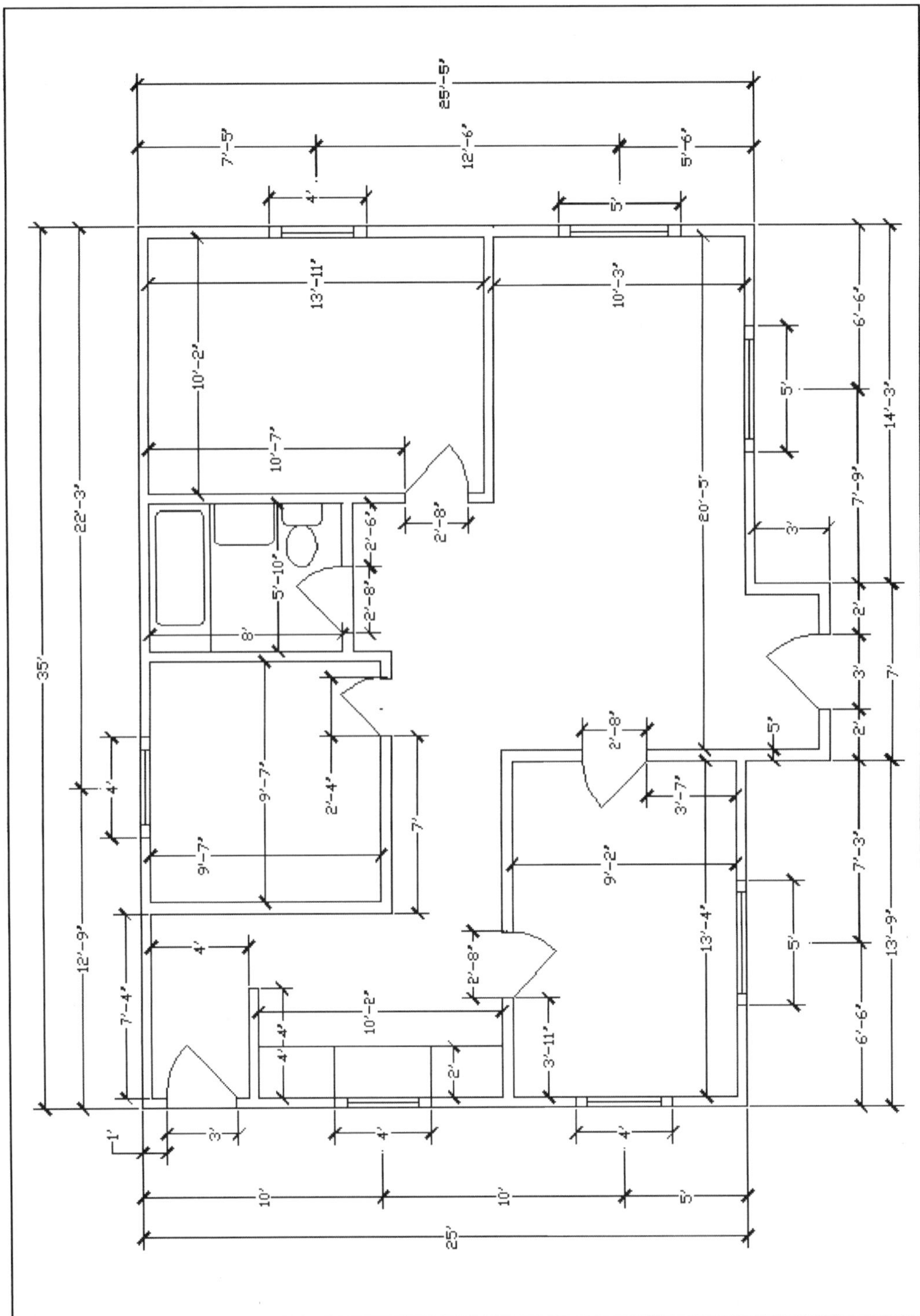

2. **Floor Plan B** (Wall thickness: 5 inch)

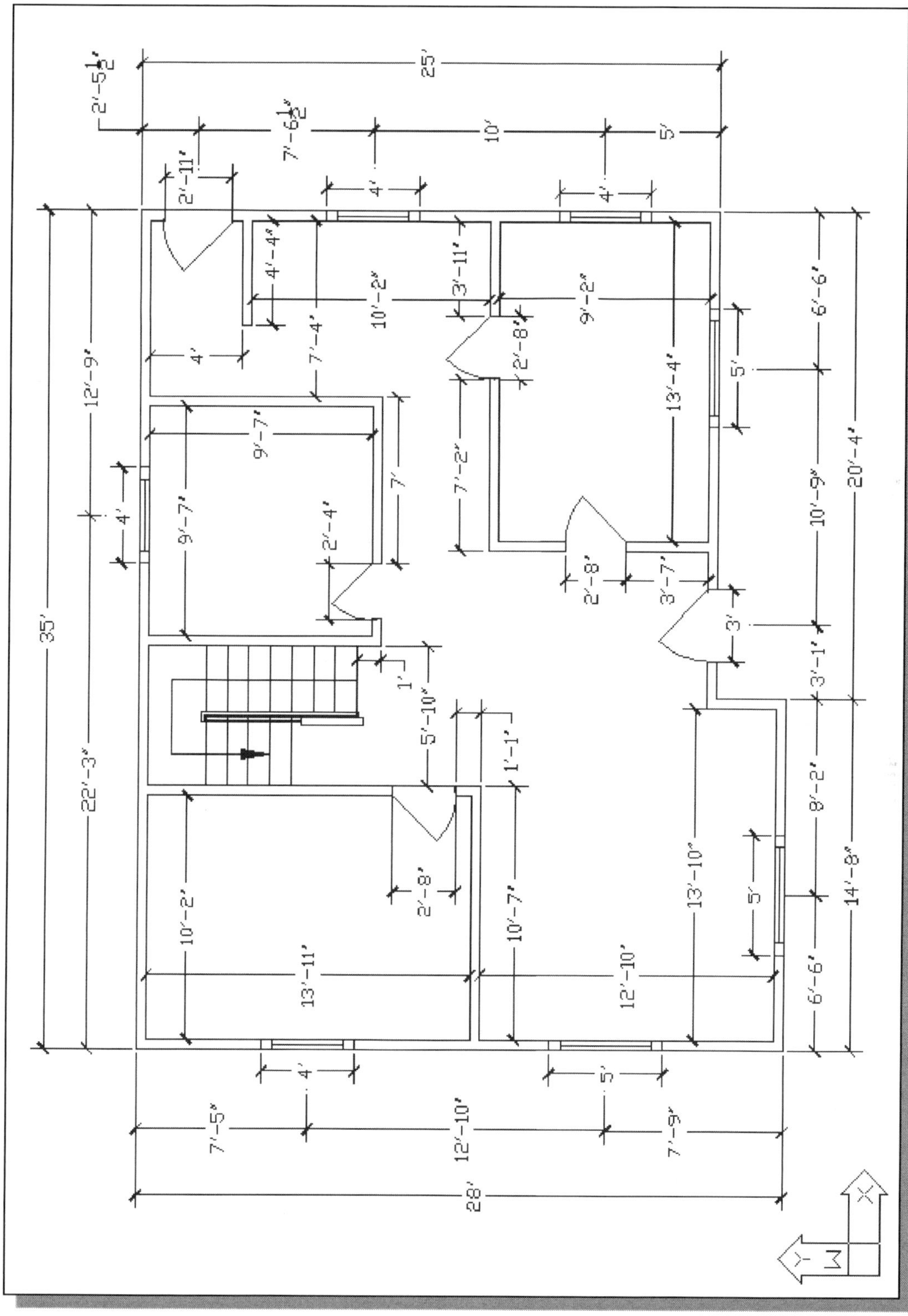

Notes:

Chapter 4
Orthographic Projection and Multiview Constructions

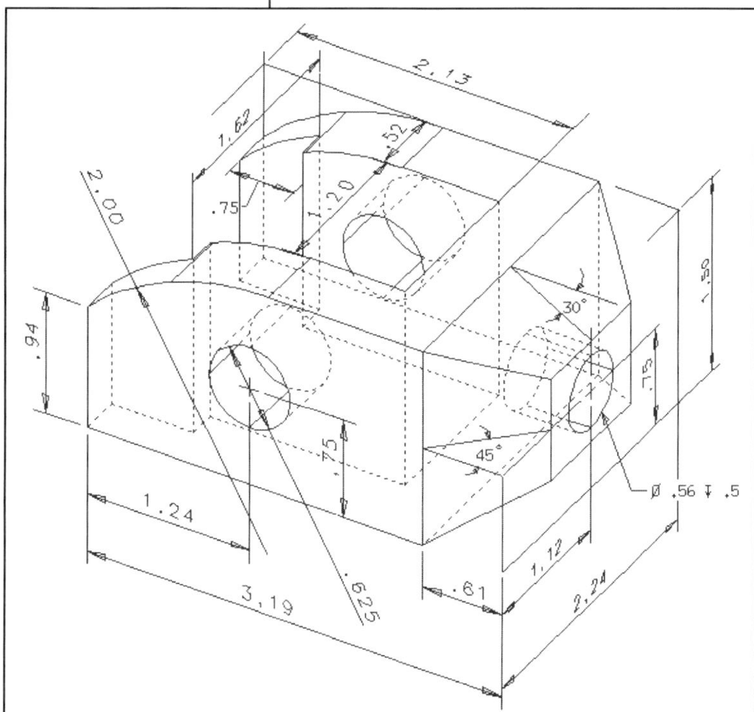

Learning Objectives

- **Understand the Basic Orthographic Projection Principles**
- **Be able to Perform 1st and 3rd Angle Projections**
- **Use the Construction Line Command in AutoCAD to Draw**
- **Use the AutoCAD Running Object Snaps Options**
- **Use AutoCAD's AutoSnap and AutoTrack Features**
- **Use the Miter Line Method**

AutoCAD Certified User Examination Objectives Coverage

Introduction

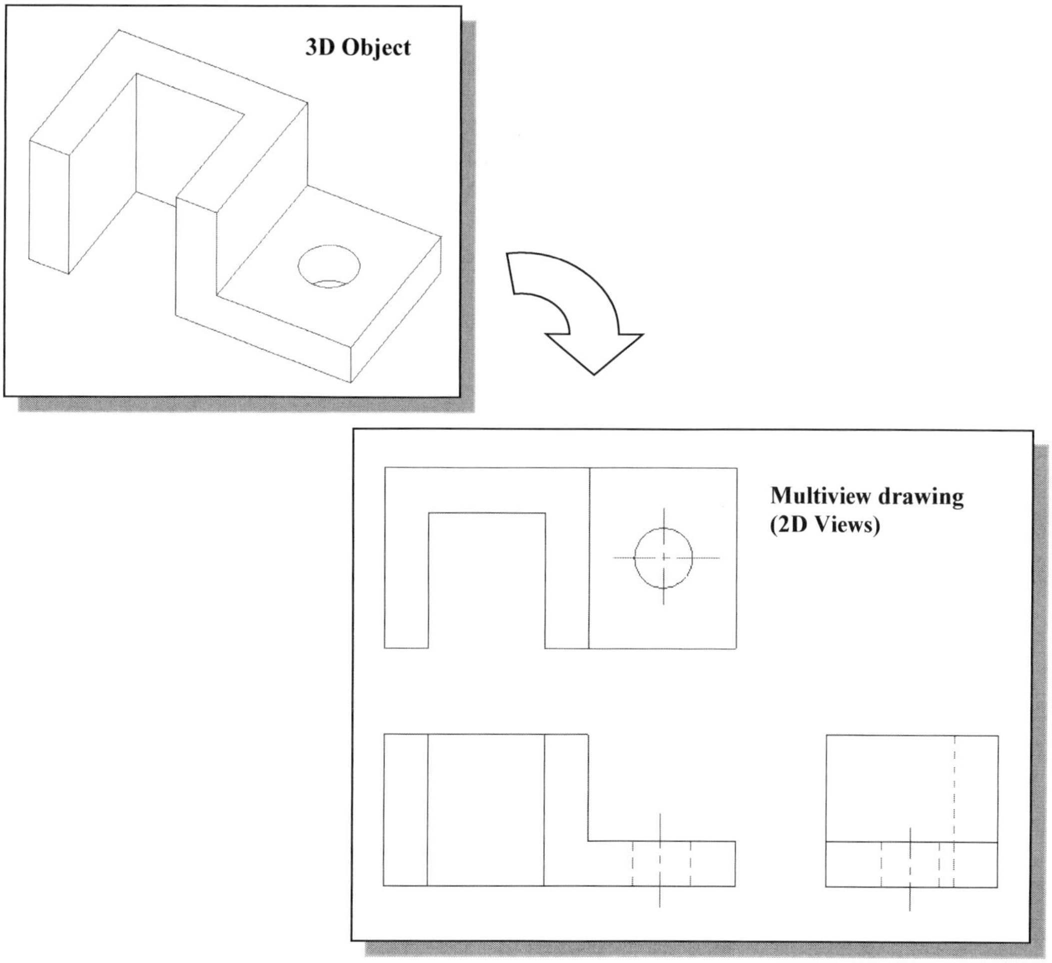

Most drawings produced and used in industry are ***multiview drawings***. Multiview drawings are used to provide accurate three-dimensional object information on two-dimensional media, a means of communicating all of the information necessary to transform an idea or concept into reality. The standards and conventions of multiview drawings have been developed over many years, which equip us with a universally understood method of communication.

Multiview drawings usually require several orthographic projections to define the shape of a three-dimensional object. Each orthographic view is a two-dimensional drawing showing only two of the three dimensions of the three-dimensional object. Consequently, no individual view contains sufficient information to completely define the shape of the three-dimensional object. All orthographic views must be looked at together to comprehend the shape of the three-dimensional object. The arrangement and relationship between the views are therefore very important in multiview drawings. Before taking a more in-depth look into the multiview drawings, we will first look at the concepts and principles of projections.

Basic Principles of Projection

To better understand the theory of projection, one must become familiar with the elements that are common to the principles of **projection**. First of all, the **POINT OF SIGHT** (a.k.a. **STATION POINT**) is the position of the observer in relation to the object and the plane of projection. It is from this point that the view of the object is taken. Secondly, the observer views the features of the object through an imaginary PLANE OF PROJECTION (or IMAGE PLANE). Imagine yourself standing in front of a glass window, IMAGE PLANE, looking outward; the image of a house at a distance is sketched onto the glass which is a 2D view of a 3D house.

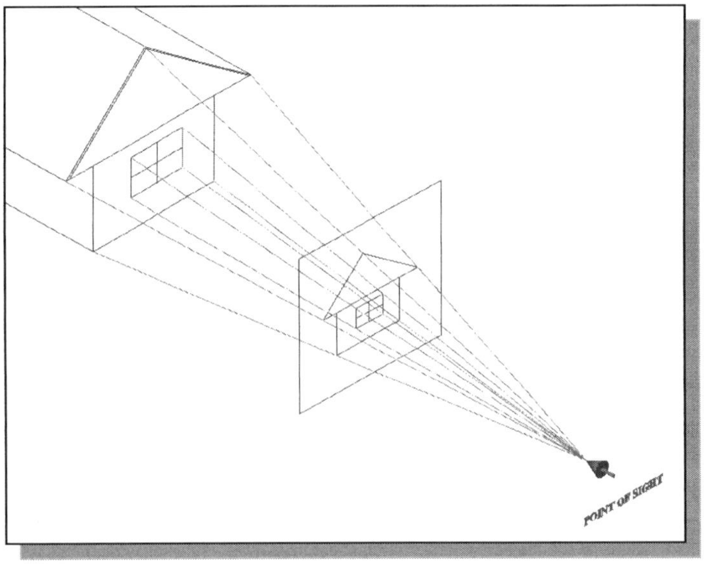

Orthographic Projection

The lines connecting from the ***Point of Sight*** to the 3D object are called the **Projection Lines** or **Lines of Sight**. Note that in the above figure, the projection lines are connected at the point of sight, and the projected 2D image is smaller than the actual size of the 3D object.

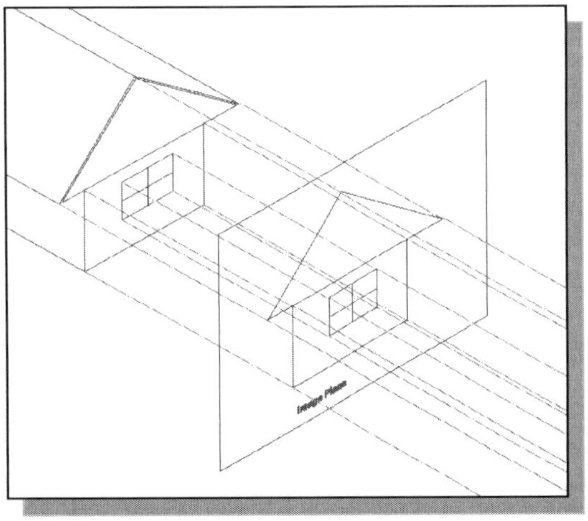

Now, if the *projection lines* are **parallel** to each other and the image plane is also **perpendicular** (*normal*) to the projection lines, the result is what is known as an **orthographic projection**. When the projection lines are parallel to each other, an accurate outline of the visible face of the object is obtained.

The term **orthographic** is derived from the word ***orthos*** meaning **perpendicular** or **90°**.

In *Engineering Graphics*, the projection of one face of an object usually will not provide an overall description of the object; other planes of projection must be used. To create the necessary 2D views, the *point of sight* is changed to project different views of the same object; hence, each view is from a different point of sight. If the point of sight is moved to the front of the object, this will result in the front view of the object. And then move the point of sight to the top of the object and looking down at the top, and then move to the right side of the object, as the case may be. Each additional view requires a new point of sight.

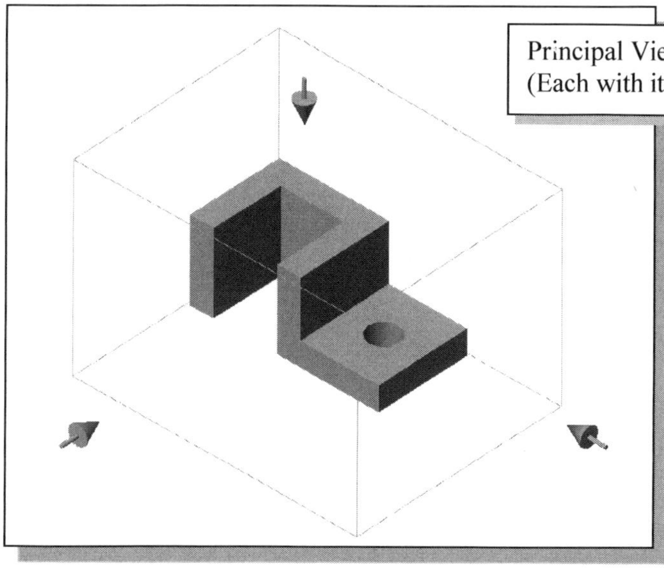

Multiview Orthographic Projection

In creating multiview orthographic projection, different systems of projection can be used to create the necessary views to fully describe the 3D object. In the figure below, two perpendicular planes are established to form the image planes for a multiview orthographic projection.

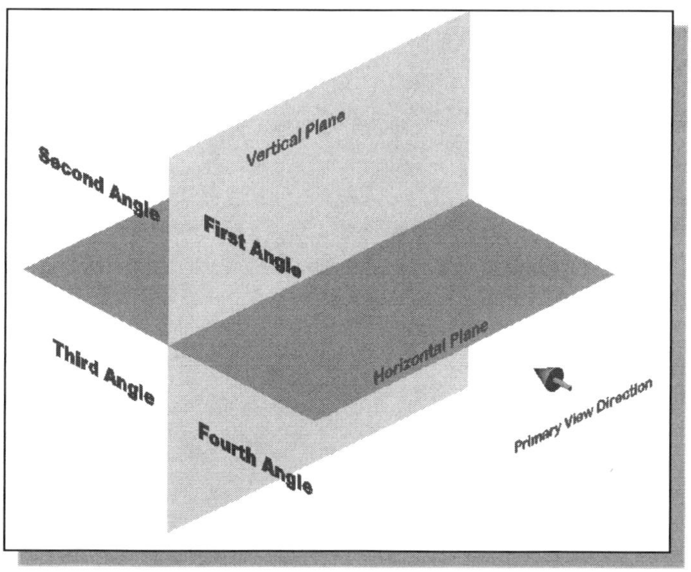

The angles formed between the horizontal and the vertical planes are called the **first**, **second**, **third** and **fourth angles**, as indicated in the figure. For engineering drawings, both **first angle projection** and **third angle projection** are commonly used.

First-Angle Projection

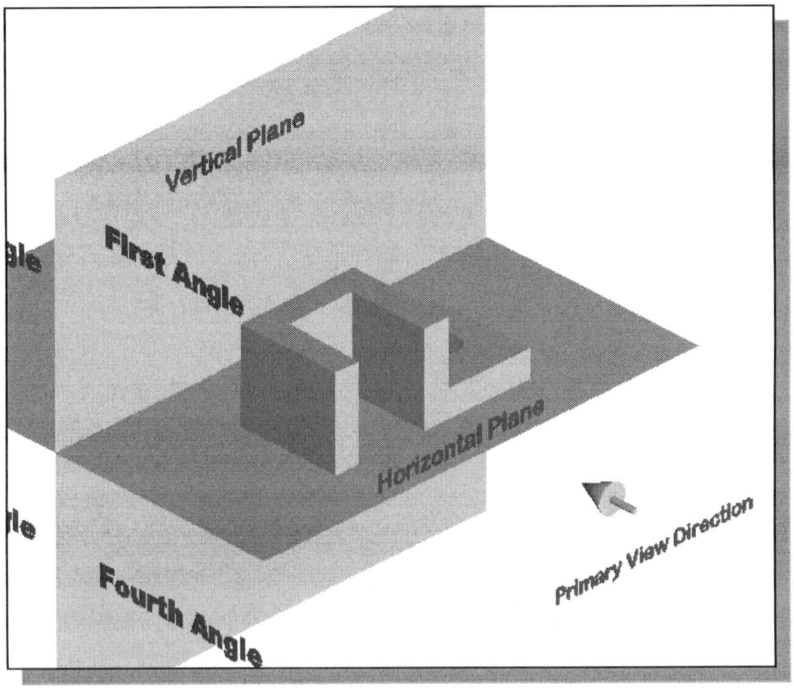

In first-angle projection, the object is placed in **front** of the image planes. And the views are formed by projecting to the image plane located at the back.

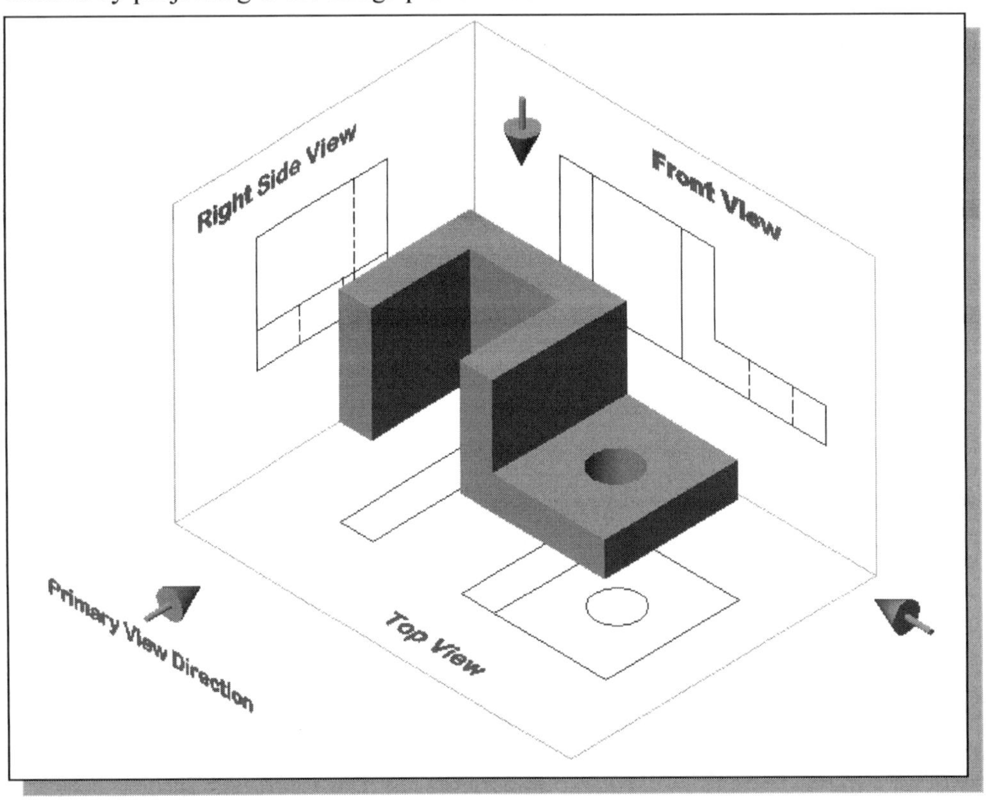

Rotation of the Horizontal and Profile Planes

In order to draw all three views of the object on the same plane, the horizontal (Top View) and profile (Right Side view) are rotated into the same plane as the primary image plane (Front View).

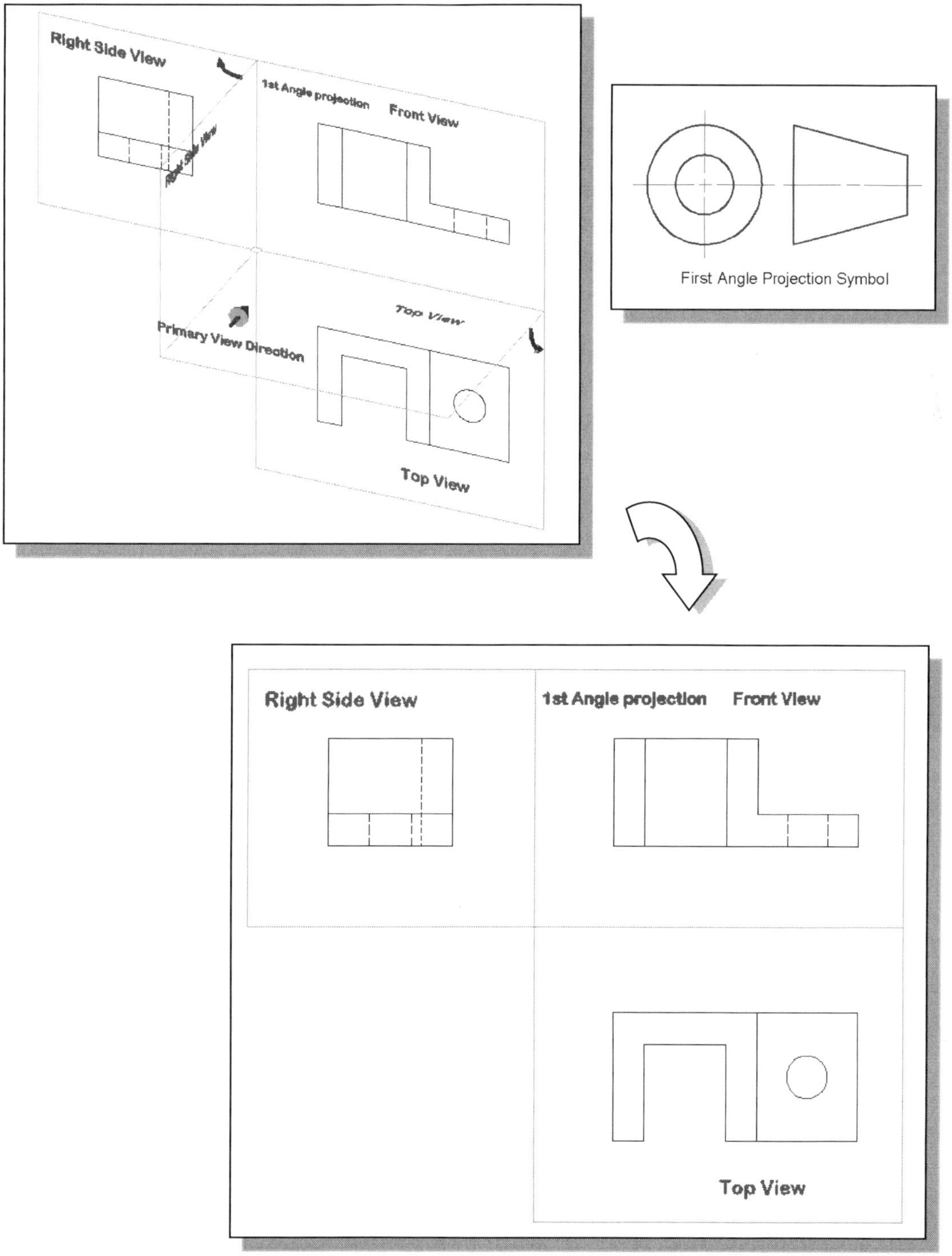

Getting the 3D Adjuster Model through the Internet

AutoCAD 2027 allows us to share files and resources through the Internet. Drawings can be placed and opened to an Internet location, blocks can be inserted by dragging drawings from a web site, and hyperlinks can be inserted in drawings so that others can access related documents. Note that to use the **AutoCAD 2027** Internet features an Internet connection is required.

We will illustrate the procedure to open an AutoCAD file from the Internet by *Uniform Resource Locator* (URL).

1. Select the **AutoCAD 2027** option on the *Program* menu or select the **AutoCAD 2027** icon on the *Desktop.*
2. In the AutoCAD *Startup* dialog box, select **Open a Drawing** with a single click of the left-mouse-button.

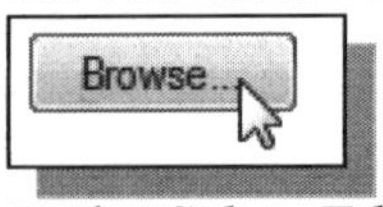

3. Click **Browse** to open the *Select File* dialog box.
4. In the *Select File* dialog box, enter ***http://www.sdcACAD.com/acad2027/Adjuster1stAngle.dwg*** as shown in the figure below.

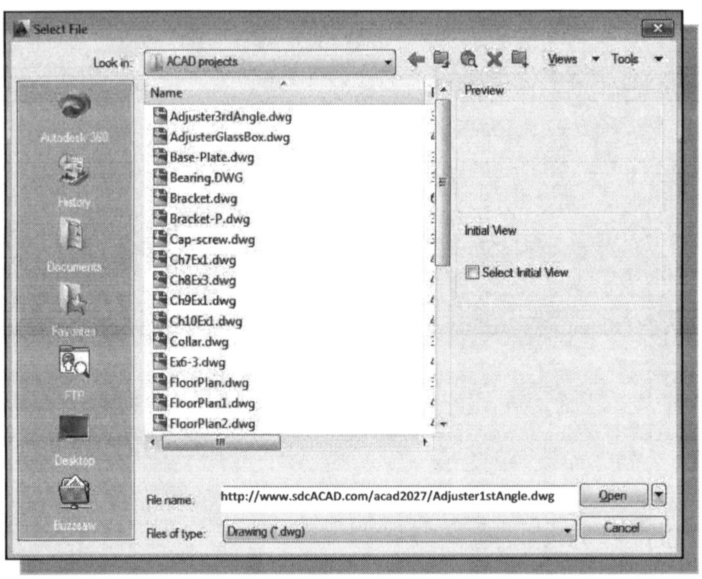

5. Click the **Open** icon and the file is downloaded from the www.sdcACAD.com website to the local computer.

➢ The URL entered must be of the *Hypertext Transfer Protocol* (http://) and the complete filename must be entered including the filename extension (such as .dwg or .dwt).

➢ As an alternative, the ***Adjuster1stAngle*** file can be downloaded using a web browser from the book's webpage at **www.SDCpublications.com**.

Dynamic Rotation – 3D Orbit

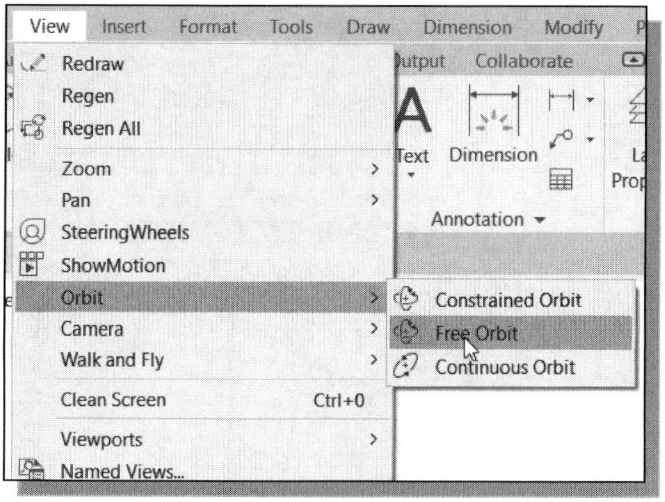

1. Select **3D Orbit** in the *Menu Bar*.
   [View] → [Orbit] → [Free Orbit]

❖ The Free-Orbit view displays an ***arcball***, which is a circle, divided into four quadrants by smaller circles. Free-Orbit enables us to manipulate the view of 3D objects by clicking and dragging with the left-mouse-button.

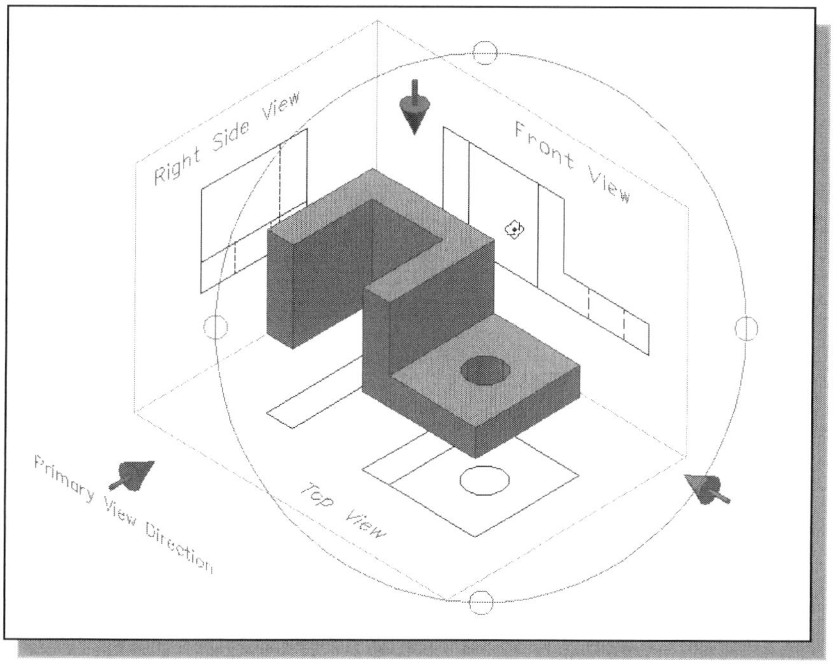

2. Inside the *arcball*, press down the left-mouse-button and drag it up and down to rotate about the screen X-axis. Dragging the mouse left and right will rotate about the screen Y-axis.

3. On your own, use the real-time dynamic rotation feature of the Free Orbit command and examine the relations of the 2D views, projection planes and the 3D object.

General Procedure: 1st Angle Orthographic Projection

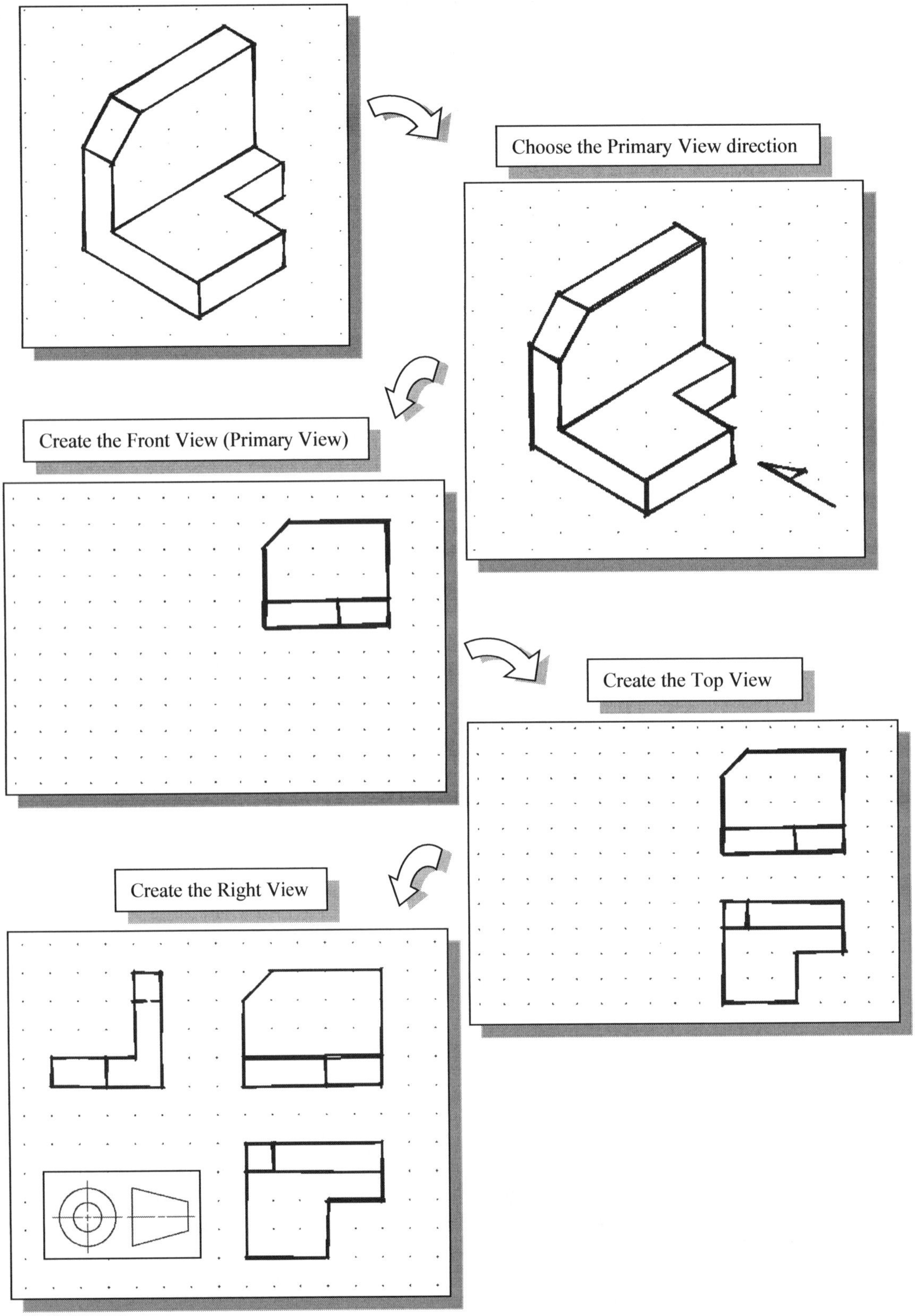

1st Angle Orthographic Sketching Exercises:

Use the grid to estimate the size of the parts, and create the standard three views by freehand rough sketching.

1.

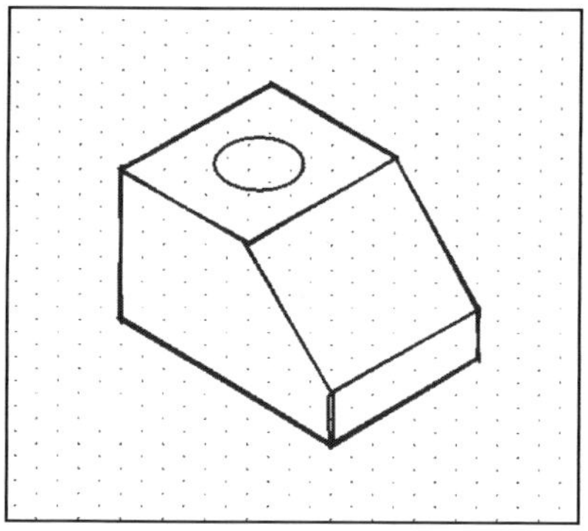

2.

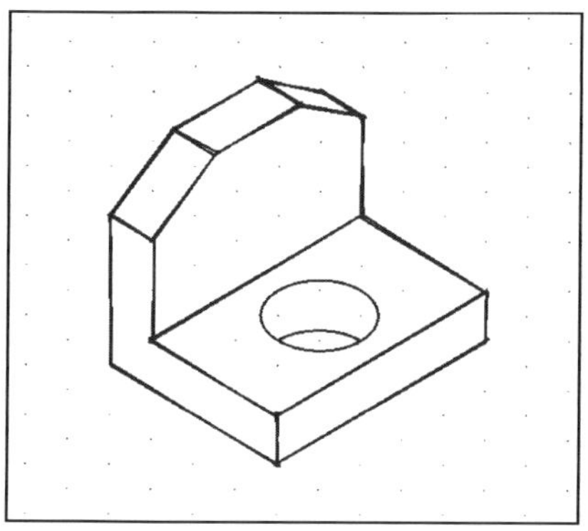

3.

4.

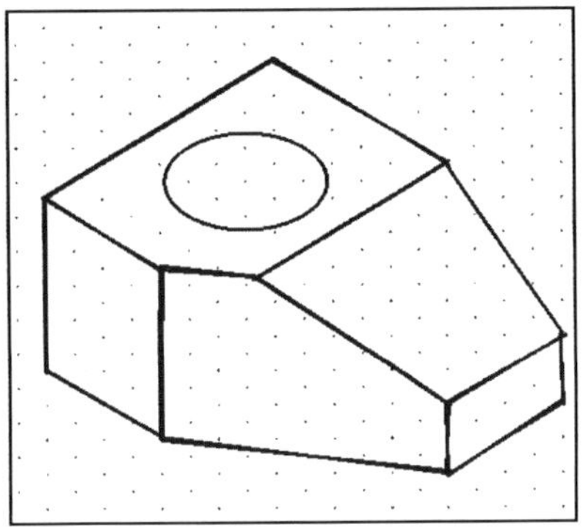

5.

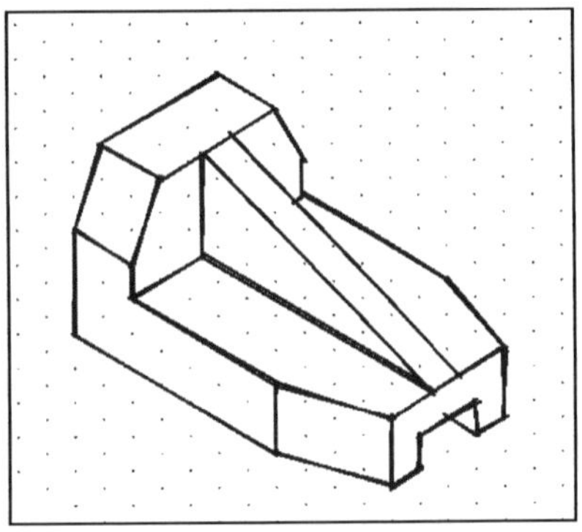

6.

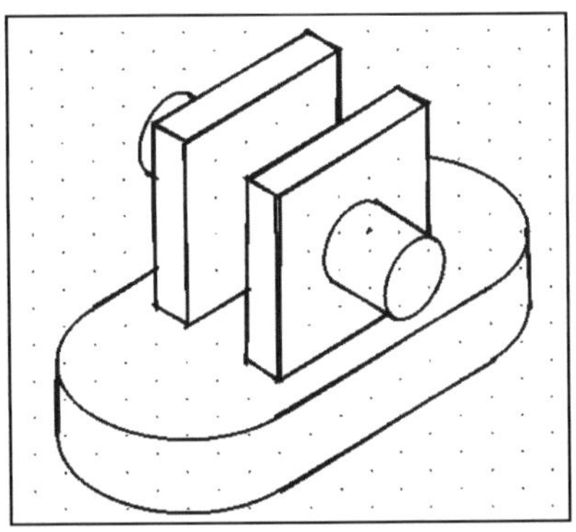

Third-Angle Projection

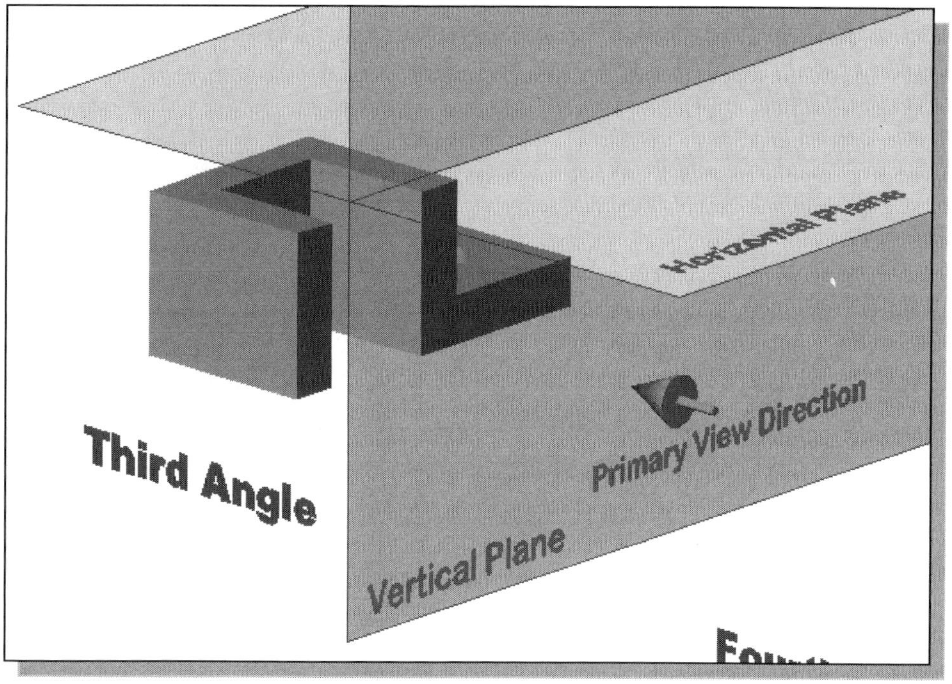

❖ In *third-angle projection*, the image planes are placed in between the object and the observer. And the views are formed by projecting to the image plane located in front of the object.

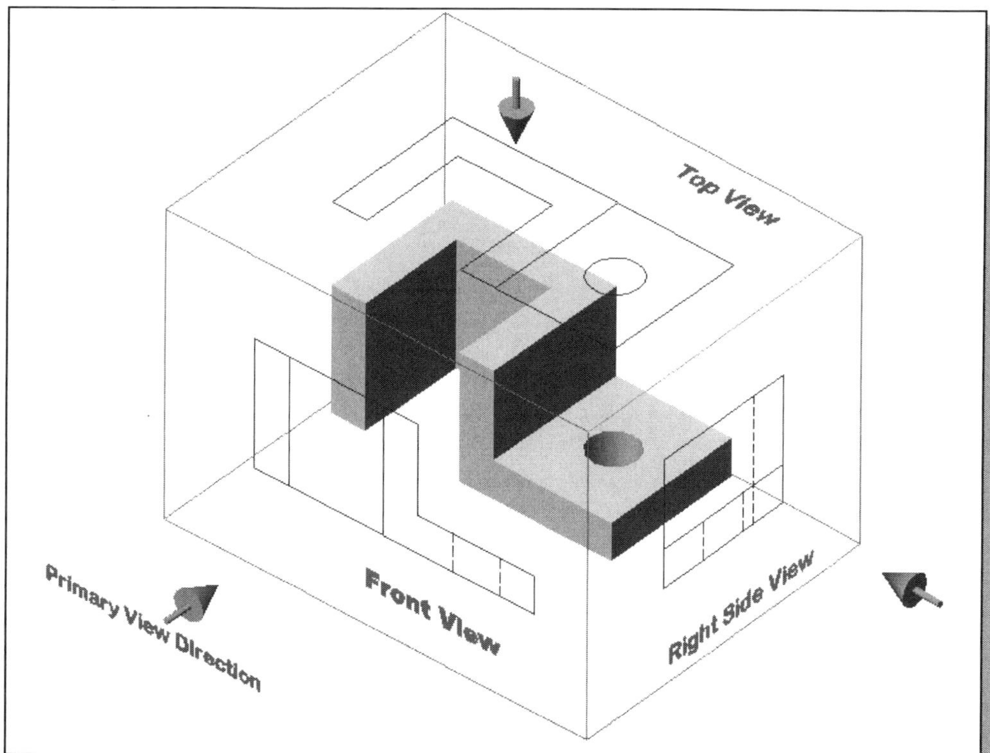

Rotation of the Horizontal and Profile Planes

In order to draw all three views of the object on the same plane, the horizontal (Top View) and profile (Right Side view) are rotated into the same plane as the primary image plane (Front View).

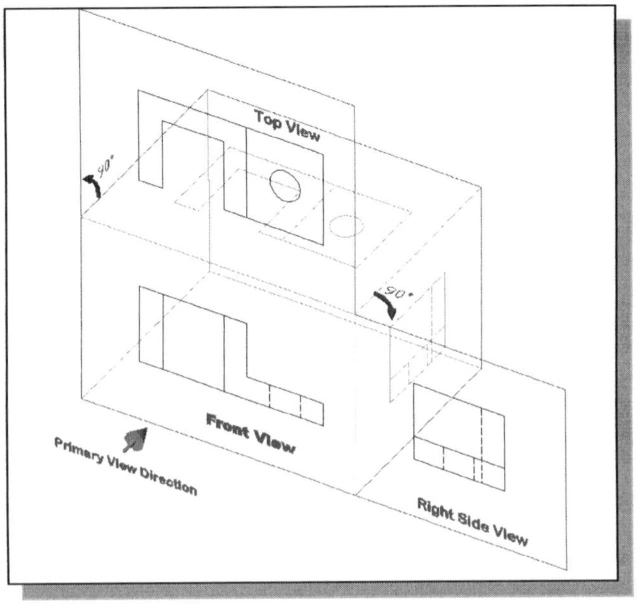

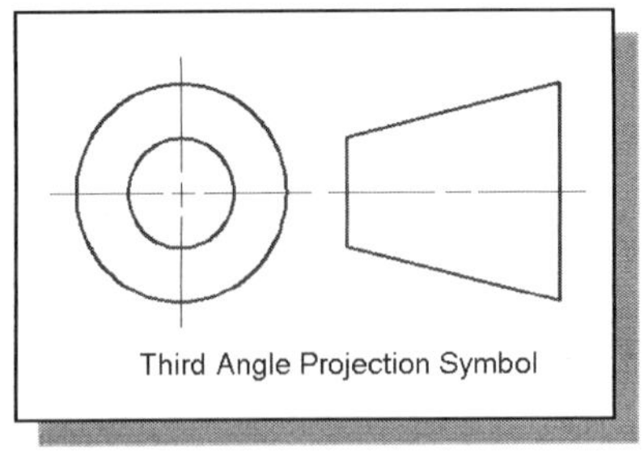

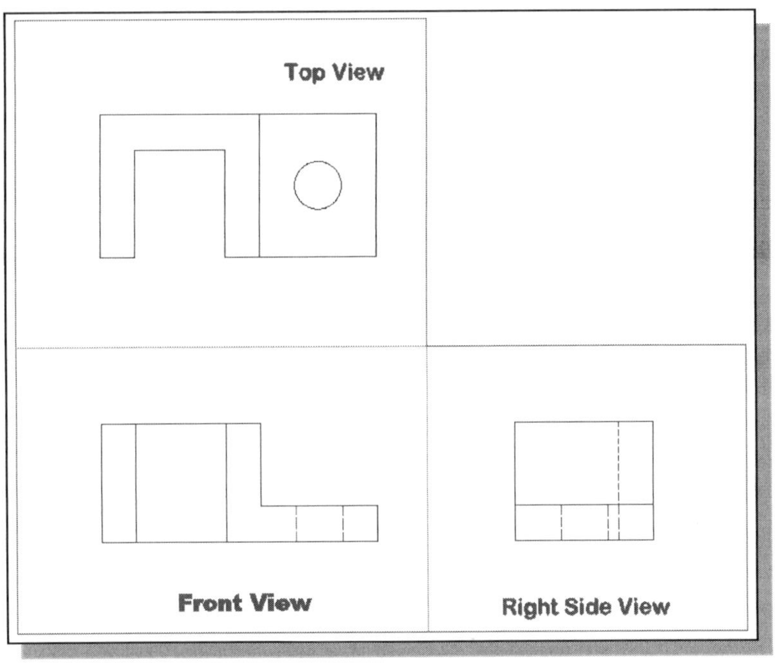

- Using an internet browser, open the Adjuster RTOP **avi** file to view the rotation of the projection planes:
  http://www.sdcpublications.com/downloads/978-1-63057-828-2

Examining the 3rd Angle Projection

1. Click the **Open** icon in the *Quick Access* toolbar area as shown.

2. In the *Select File* dialog box, enter the following file name:
   http://www.sdcACAD.com/acad2027/Adjuster3rdAngle.dwg

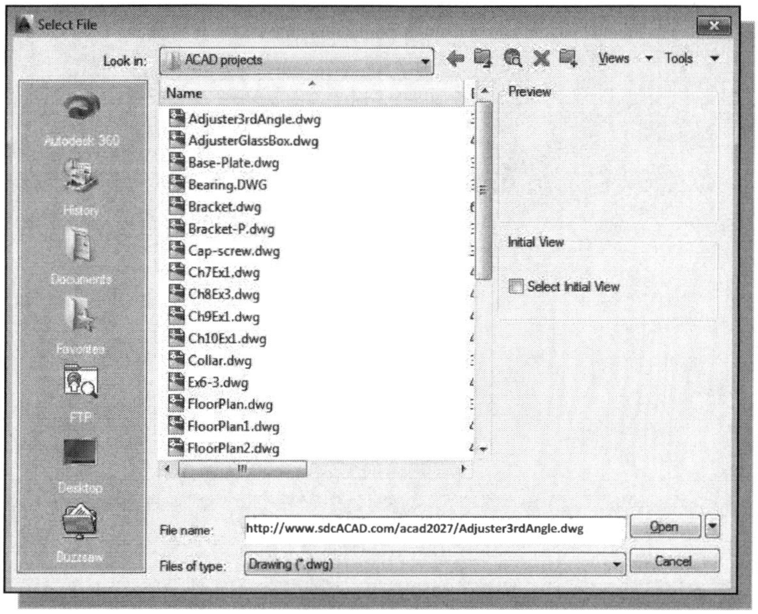

3. Click the **Open** icon and the ***Adjuster3rdAngle*** file is downloaded from the www.sdcACAD.com website to the local computer.

➢ As an alternative, the ***Adjuster3rdAngle*** file can be downloaded using a web browser from the book's webpage at **www.SDCpublications.com**.

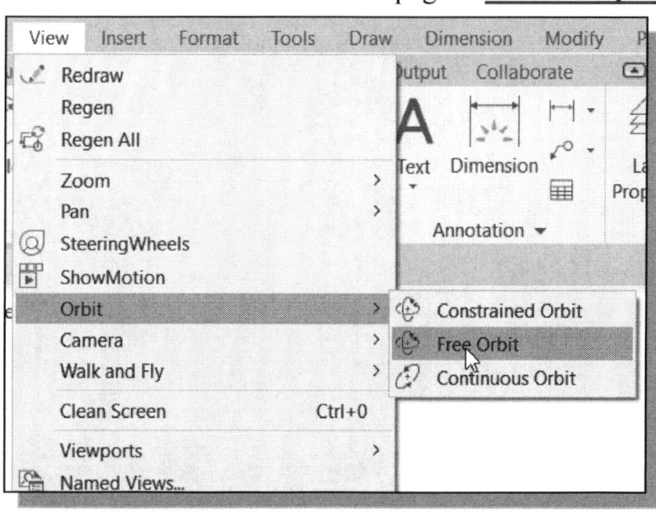

4. Select **3D Orbit** in the *Menu Bar*:
   [View] → [Orbit] → [Free Orbit].

5. On your own, examine the relations of the 2D views, projection planes and the 3D object.

The Glass Box and the Six Principal Views

Considering the third angle projection described in the previous section further, we find that the object can be entirely surrounded by a set of six planes, a Glass box. On these planes, views can be obtained of the object as it is seen from the top, front, right side, left side, bottom, and rear.

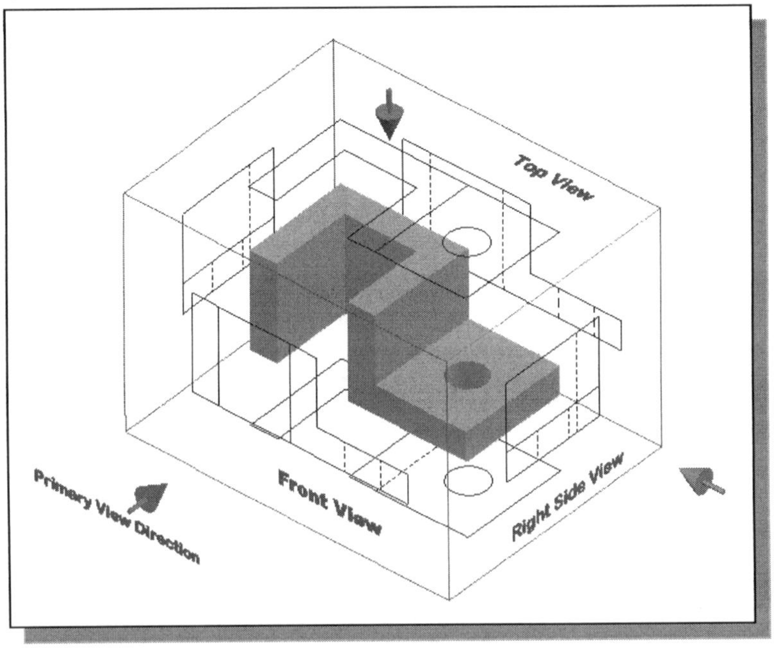

❖ Consider how the six sides of the glass box are being opened up into one plane. The front is the primary plane, and the other sides are hinged and rotated into position.

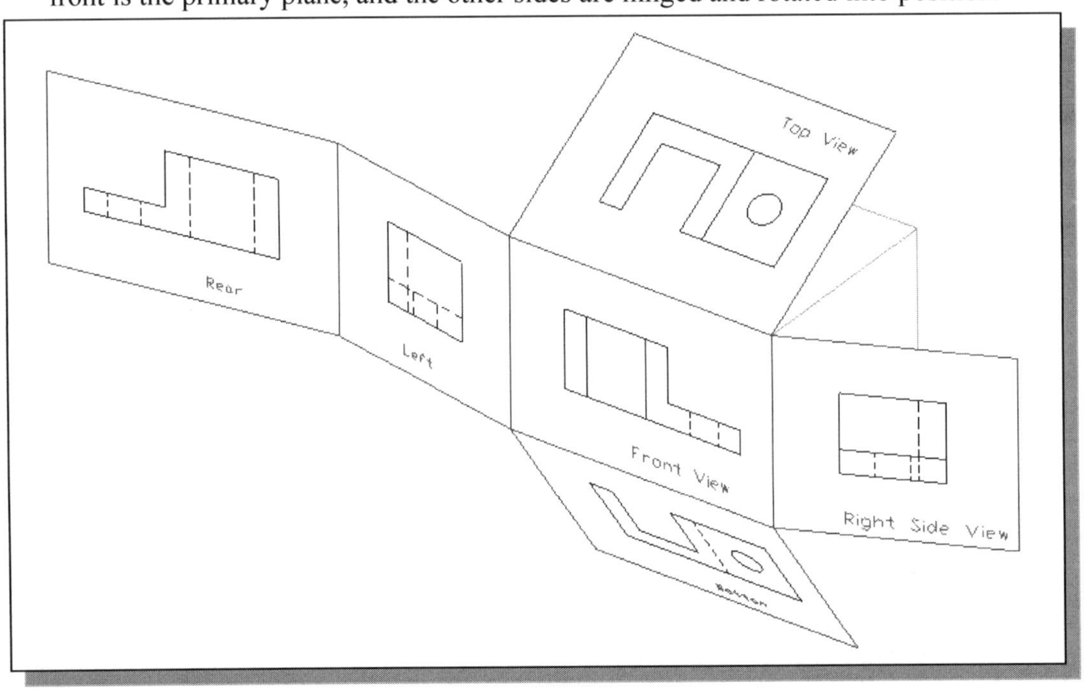

❖ In actual work, there is rarely an occasion when all six principal views are needed on one drawing, but no matter how many are required, their relative positions need to be maintained. These six views are known as the **six principal views**. In performing orthographic projection, each 2D view shows only two of the three dimensions (**height**, **width**, and **depth**) of the 3D object.

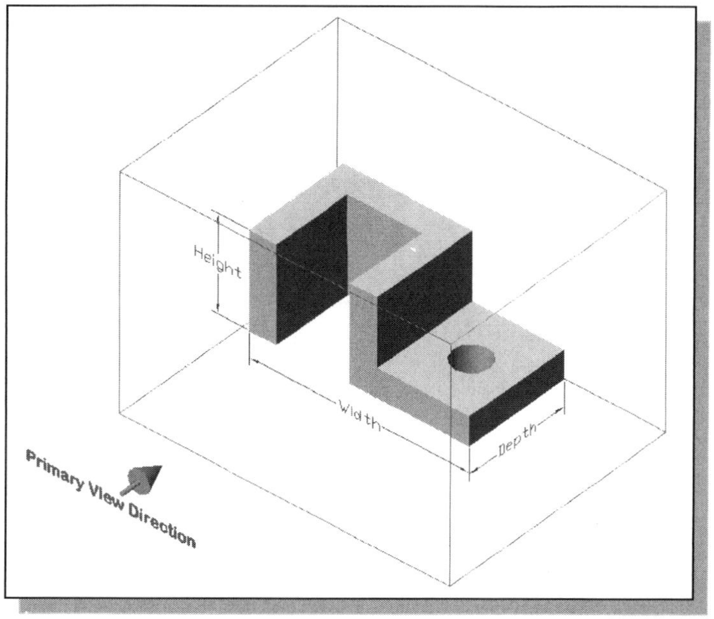

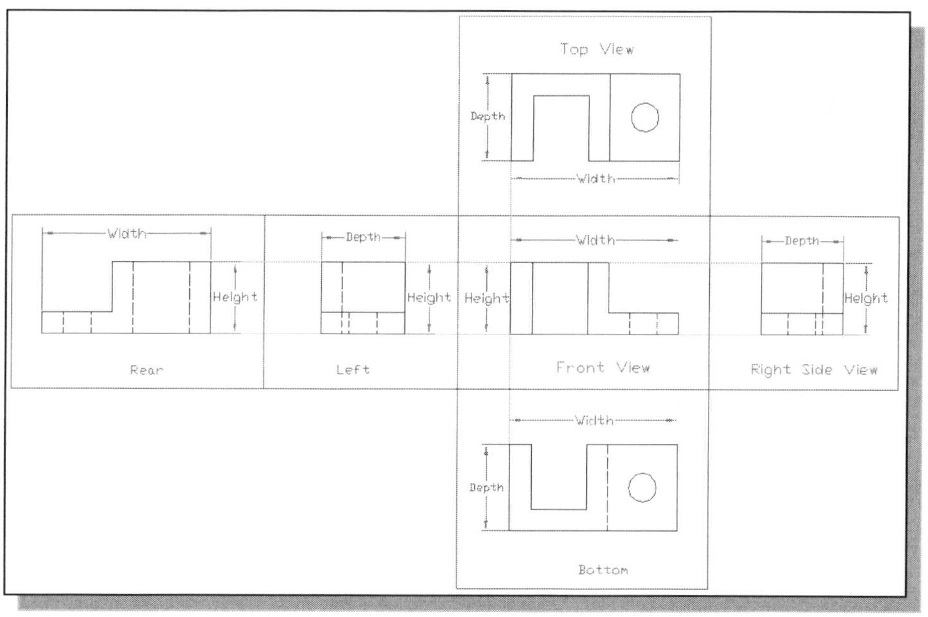

❖ The most usual combination selected from the six possible views consists of the *top*, *front* and *right-side* views. The selection of the *Primary View* is the first step in creating a *multi-view drawing*. The Primary View should typically be (1) the view which describes the main features of the design and (2) considerations of the layout of the other 2D views to properly describe the design.

Examining the Glass Box Model

1. Click the **Open** icon in the *Standard* toolbar area as shown.

2. In the *Select File* dialog box, enter the following file name:
   http://www.sdcACAD.com/acad2027/AdjusterGlassBox.dwg

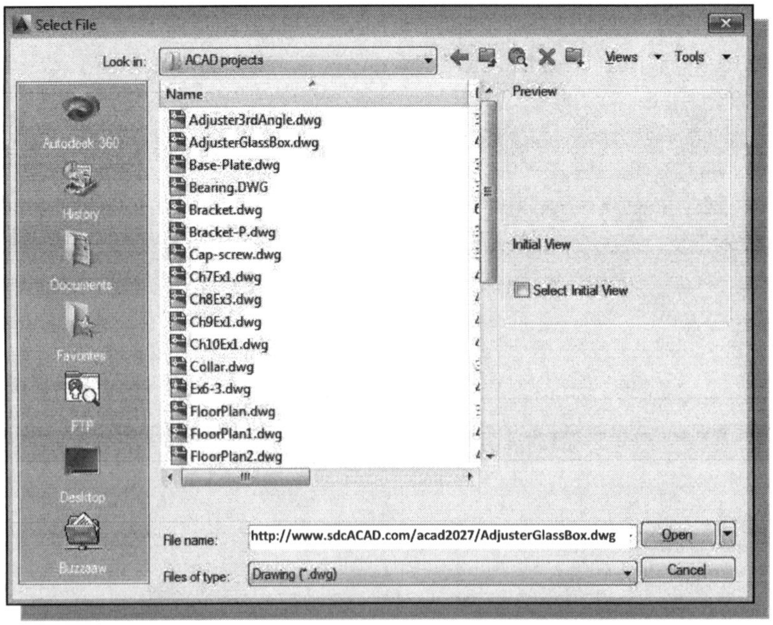

3. Click the **Open** icon and the ***AdjusterGlassBox*** file is downloaded from the www.sdcACAD.com website to the local computer.

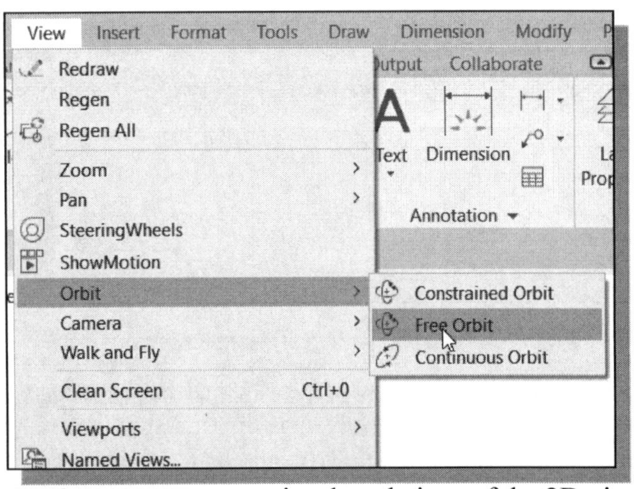

➢ As an alternative, the ***AdjusterGlassBox*** file can be downloaded using a web browser from the book's webpage at **www.SDCpublications.com**.

4. Select **3D Orbit** in the *Menu Bar*:
   [View] → [Orbit] → [Free Orbit].

5. On your own, examine the relations of the 2D views, projection planes and the 3D object.

General Procedure: 3rd Angle Orthographic Projection

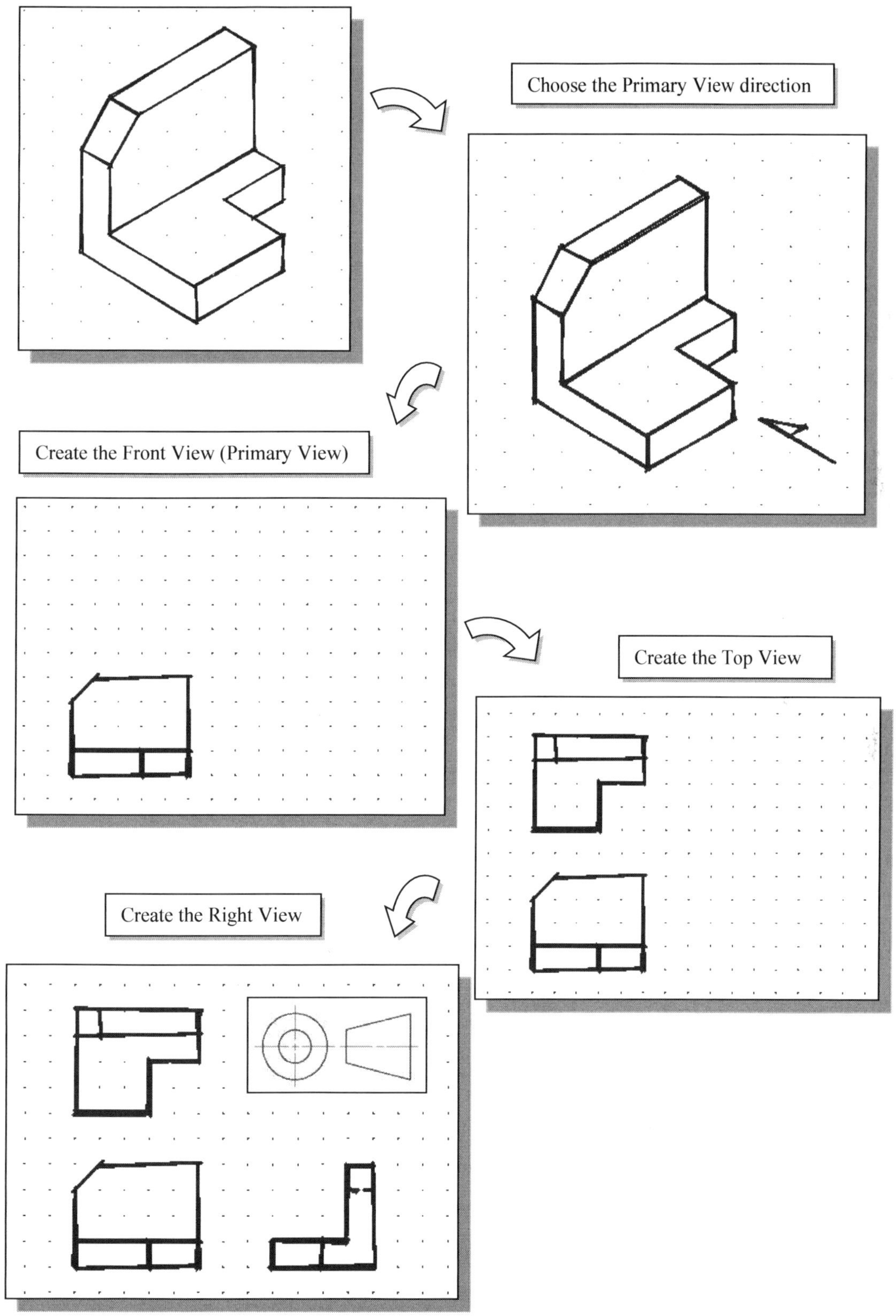

Example 2: 3rd Angle Orthographic Projection

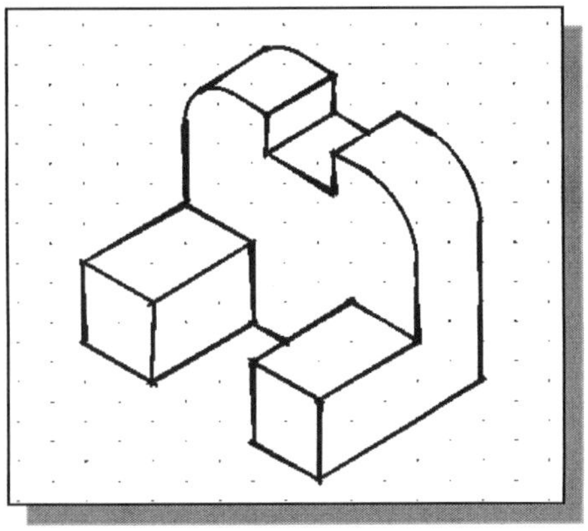

Choose the Primary View direction

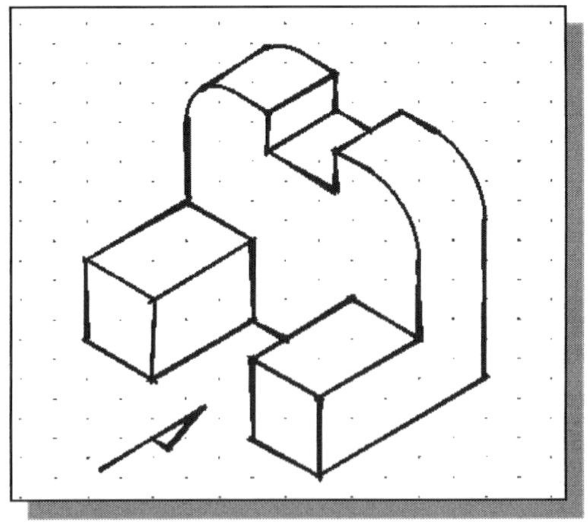

Create the Front View (Primary View)

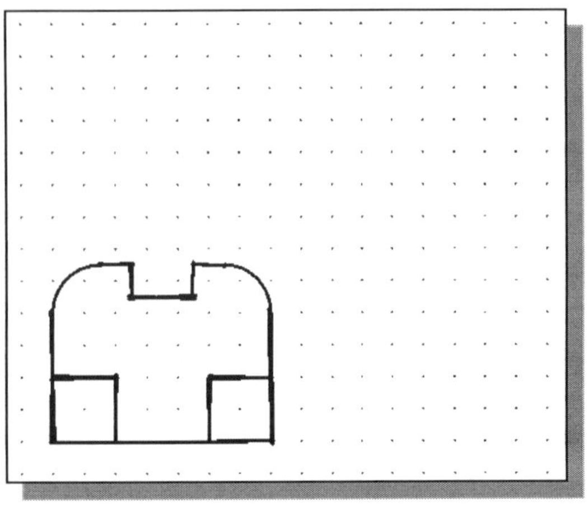

Create the Top View

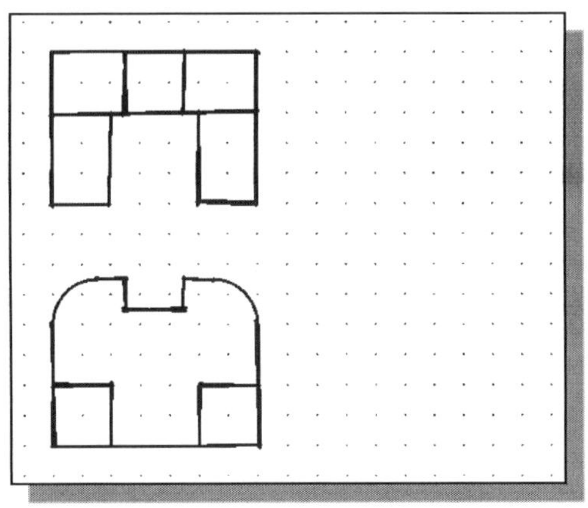

Create the Right View

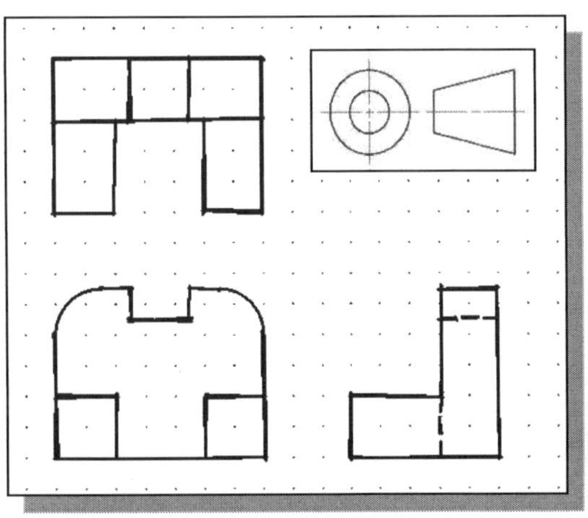

3rd Angle Orthographic Sketching Exercises:

Use the grid to estimate the size of the parts, and create the standard three views by freehand rough sketching.

1.

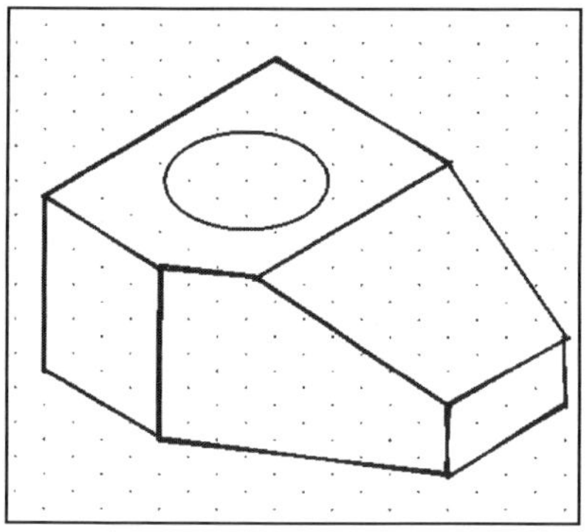

2.

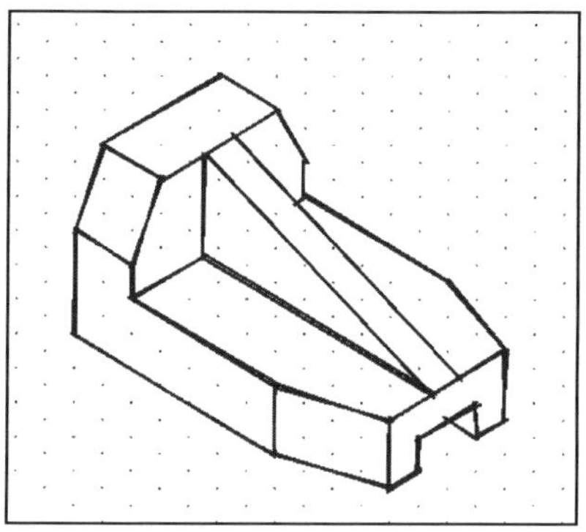

3.

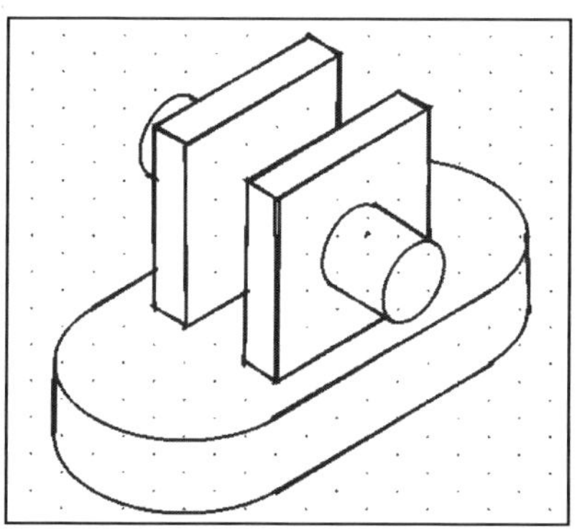

4.

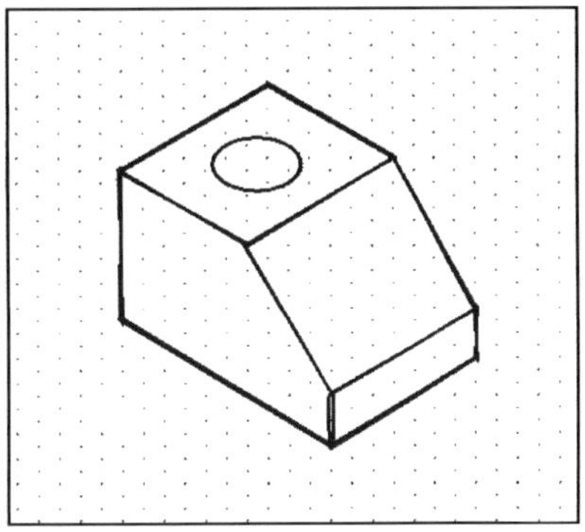

5.

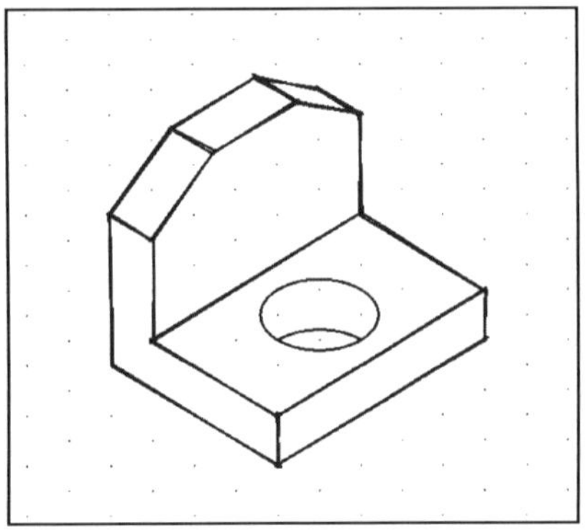

6.

Alphabet of Lines

In Technical Engineering Drawings, each line has a definite meaning and is drawn in accordance with the line conventions as illustrated in the figure below. Two widths of lines are typically used on drawings; thick line width should be 0.6 mm and the thin line width should be 0.3 mm.

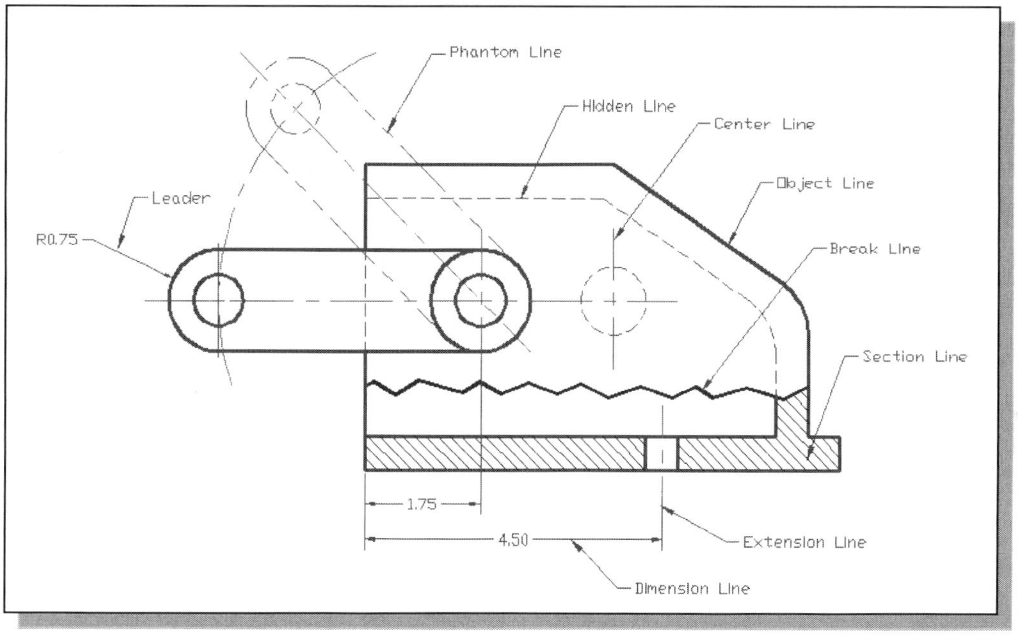

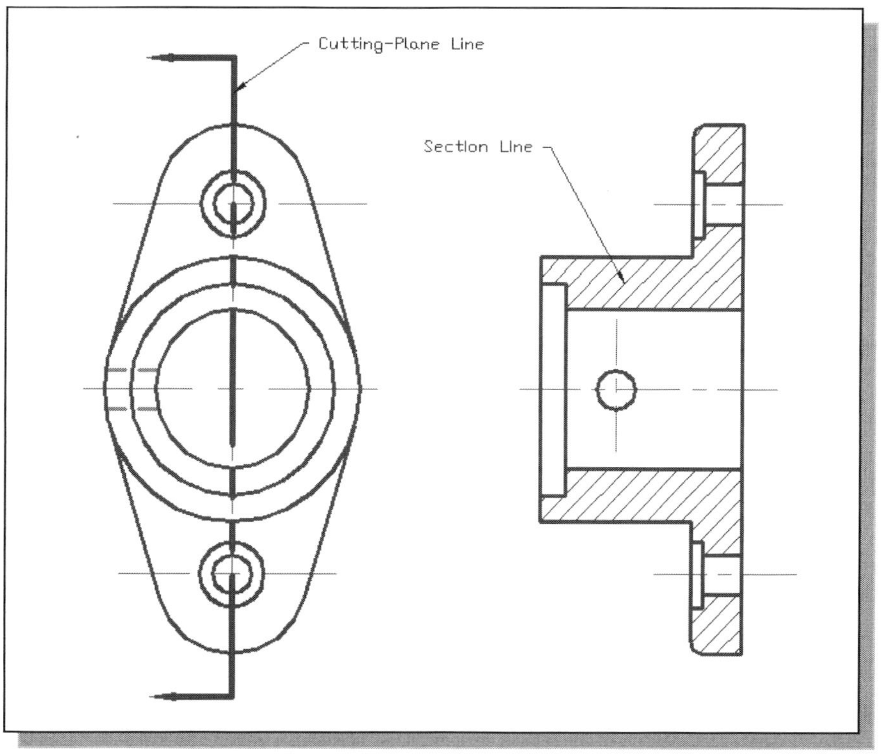

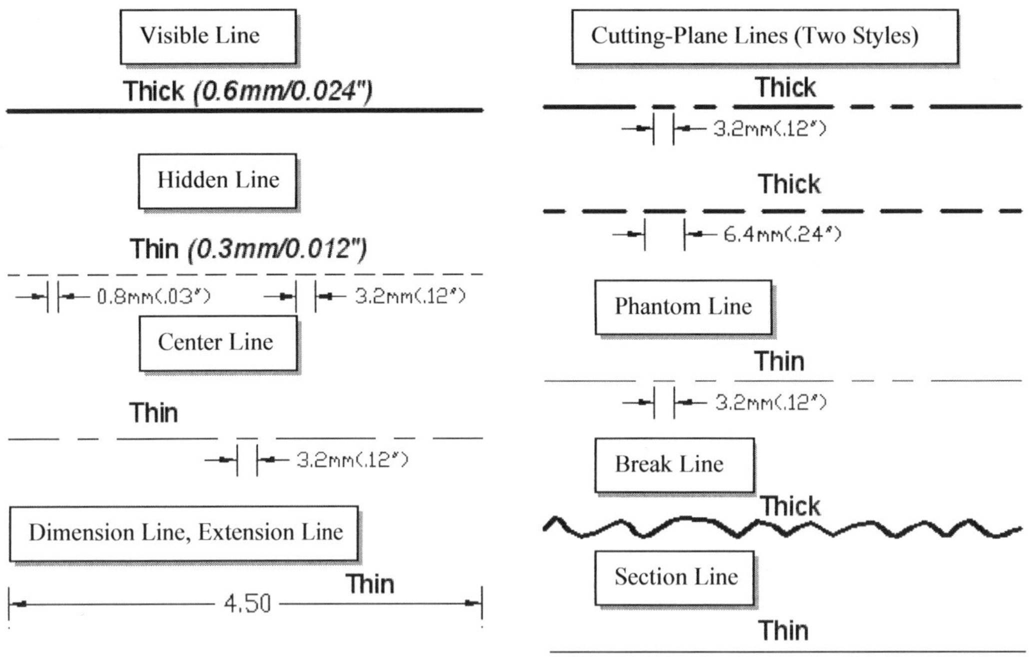

Visible Line Visible lines are used to represent visible edges and boundaries. The line weight is thick, 0.6mm/0.024".

Hidden Line Hidden lines are used to represent edges and boundaries that are not visible from the viewing direction. The line weight is thin, 0.3mm/0.012″.

Center Line Center lines are used to represent axes of symmetry. The line weight is thin, 0.3mm/0.012″.

Dimension Line, Extension Line and Leader Dimension lines are used to show the sizes and locations of objects. The line weight is thin, 0.3mm/0.012″.

Cutting Plane Lines Cutting Plane lines are used to represent where an imaginary cut has been made, so that the interior of the object can be viewed. The line weight is thick, 0.6mm/0.024″. (Note that two forms of line type can be used.)

Phantom Line Phantom lines are used to represent imaginary features or objects, such as a rotated position of a part. The line weight is thin, 0.3mm/0.012″.

Break Line Break lines are used to represent an imaginary cut, so that the interior of the object can be viewed. The line weight is thick, 0.6mm/0.024″.

Section Line Section lines are used to represent the regions that have been cut with the *break lines* or *cutting plane lines*. The line weight is thin, 0.3mm/0.012″.

Precedence of Lines

In multiview drawings, coincidence lines may exist within the same view. For example, hidden features may project lines to coincide with the visible object lines. And center lines may occur where there is a visible or hidden outline.

In creating a multiview drawing, the features of the design are to be represented; therefore, object and hidden lines take precedence over all other lines. And since the visible outline is more important than hidden features, the visible object lines take precedence over hidden lines, as shown in the below figure.

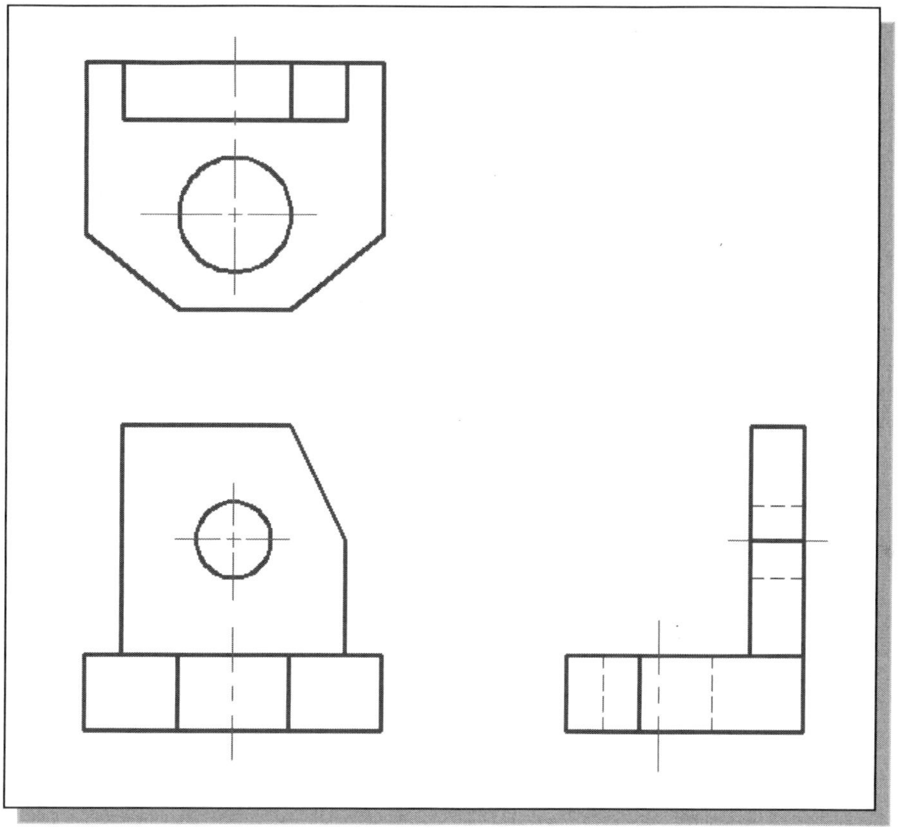

The following list gives the order of precedence of lines:

1. **Visible object lines**
2. **Hidden lines**
3. **Center line or cutting-plane line**
4. **Break lines**
5. **Dimension and extension lines**
6. **Crosshatch/section lines**

In the following sections, the general procedure of creating a 3rd angle three-view orthographic projection using AutoCAD is presented.

The Locator Part

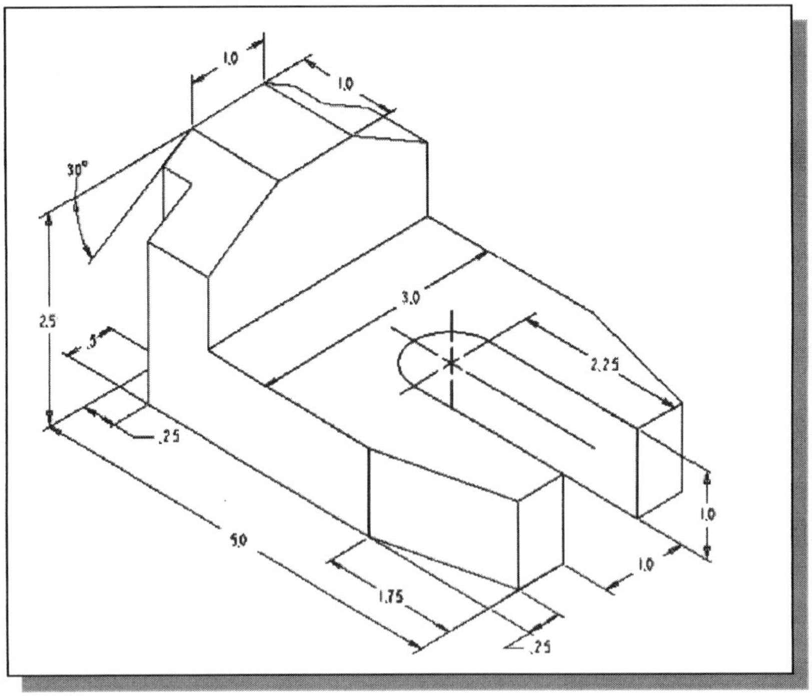

➢ Before going through the tutorial, make a rough sketch of a multiview drawing of the part. How many 2D views will be necessary to fully describe the part? Based on your knowledge of **AutoCAD 2027** so far, how would you arrange and construct these 2D views? Take a few minutes to consider these questions and do preliminary planning by sketching on a piece of paper. You are also encouraged to construct the orthographic views on your own prior to following through the tutorial.

Starting Up AutoCAD 2027

1. Select the **AutoCAD 2027** option on the *Program* menu or select the **AutoCAD 2027** icon on the *Desktop*.

2. In the *Startup* dialog box, select the **Start from Scratch** option with a single click of the left-mouse-button.

3. In the ***Default Settings*** section, pick **Imperial** as the drawing units.

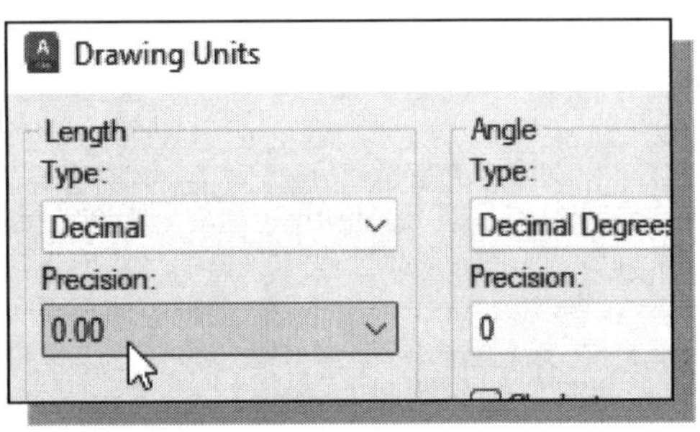

4. On your own, open up the *Drafting Settings* dialog box, and select the **SNAP and GRID** tab.

5. On your own, set the ***Grid Spacing*** and ***Snap Spacing*** to ***0.5*** for both X and Y directions.

Layers Setup

1. Pick **Layer Properties Manager** in the *Layers* toolbar.

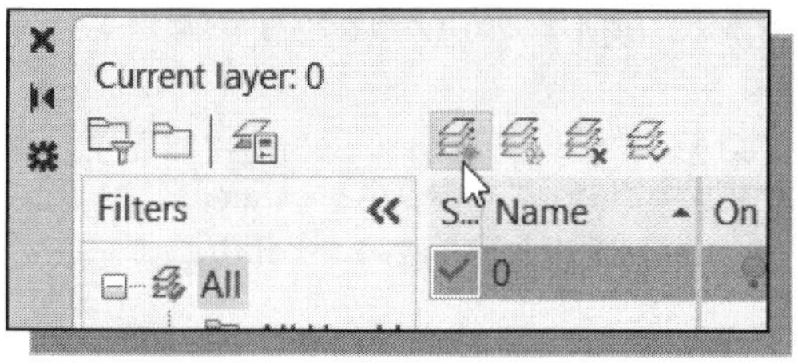

2. Click on the **New Layer** icon to create new layers.

3. Create two **new** layers with the following settings:

Layer	***Color***	***Linetype***
Construction	**White**	**Continuous**
Object	**Blue**	**Continuous**

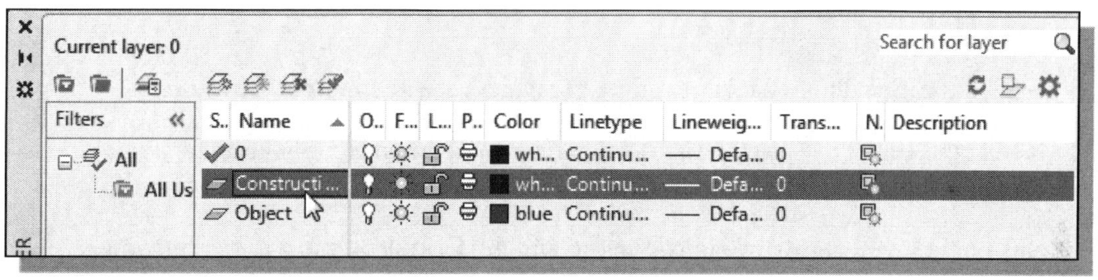

4. Highlight the layer ***Construction*** in the list of layers.

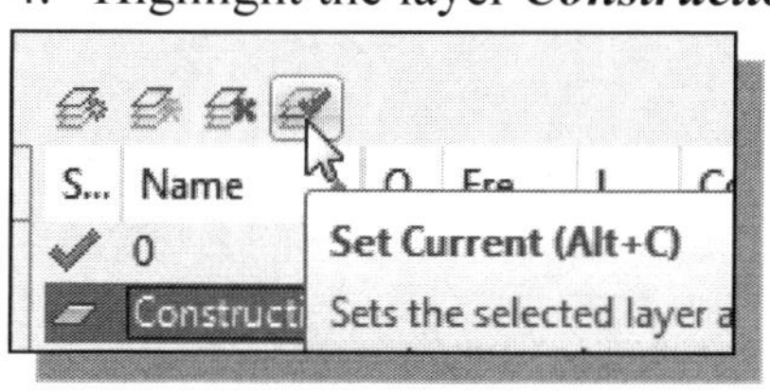

5. Click on the **Current** button to set layer ***Construction*** as the *Current Layer*.

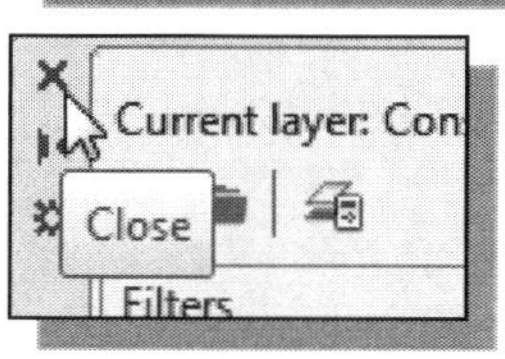

6. Click on the **Close** button to accept the settings and exit the *Layer Properties Manager* dialog box.

7. In the *Status Bar* area, reset the option buttons so that only *SNAP Mode* and *GRID Display* are switched ***ON***.

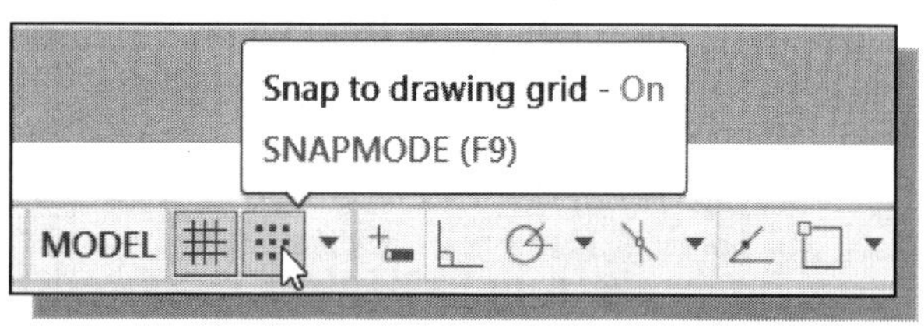

Drawing Construction Lines

Construction lines are lines that extend to infinity. Construction lines are usually used as references for creating other objects. We will also place the construction lines on the *Construction* layer so that the layer can later be frozen or turned off.

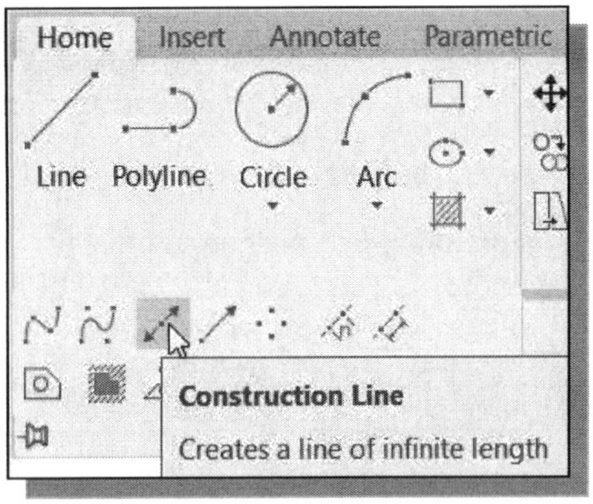

1. Select the **Construction Line** icon in the *Draw* toolbar. In the command prompt area, the message "*_xline Specify a point or [Hor/Ver/Ang/Bisect/ Offset]:*" is displayed.

- To orient construction lines, we generally specify two points. Note that other orientation options are also available.

2. Select a location near the **lower left corner** of the *Drawing Area*. It is not necessary to align objects to the origin of the world coordinate system. CAD systems provide us with many powerful tools to manipulate geometry. Our main goal is to use the CAD system as a flexible and powerful tool and to be very efficient and effective with the systems.

3. Pick a location above the last point to create a **vertical construction line**.

4. Move the cursor toward the right of the first point and pick a location to create a **horizontal construction line**.

5. Inside the *Drawing Area*, **right-click** to end the Construction Line command.

6. In the *Status Bar* area, turn ***OFF*** the *SNAP* option.

Using the Offset Command

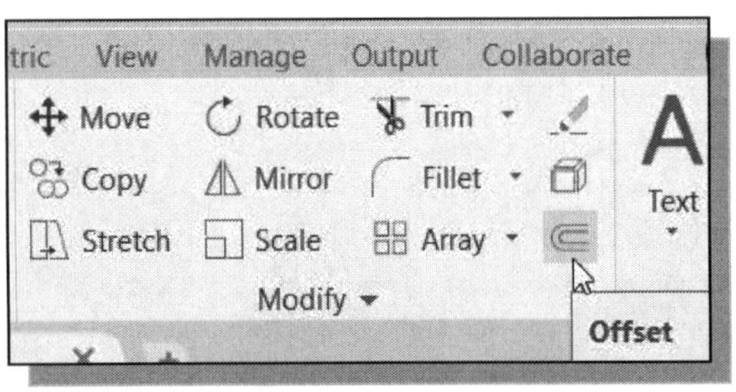

1. Select the **Offset** icon in the *Modify* toolbar. In the *command prompt area*, the message "*Specify offset distance or [Through/Erase/Layer]:*" is displayed.

2. In the *command prompt area*, enter ***5.0*** **[ENTER]**.

3. In the *command prompt area*, the message "*Select object to offset or <exit>:*" is displayed. Pick the **vertical line** on the screen.

4. AutoCAD next asks us to identify the direction of the offset. Pick a location that is to the **right** of the vertical line.

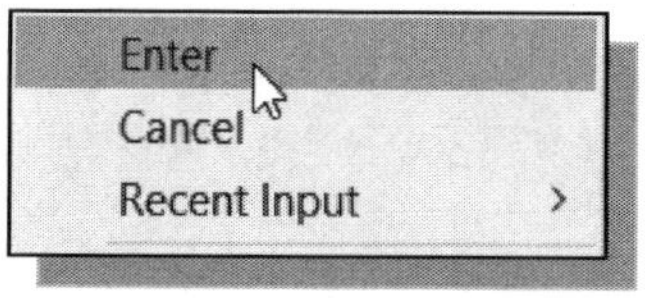

5. Inside the *Drawing Area*, **right-click** and choose **Enter** to end the Offset command.

6. In the command prompt area, click on the small **triangle icon** to access the list of recent commands.

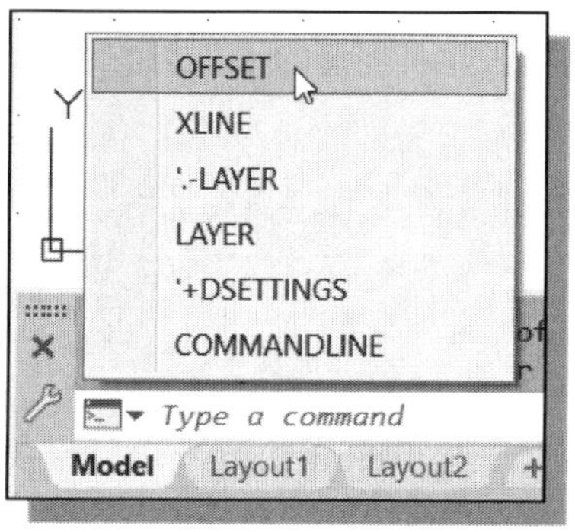

7. Select **Offset** in the pop-up list, to repeat the Offset command.

8. In the command prompt area, enter ***2.5*** **[ENTER]**.

9. In the command prompt area, the message "*Select object to offset or <exit>:*" is displayed. Pick the **horizontal line** on the screen.

10. AutoCAD next asks us to identify the direction of the offset. Pick a location that is **above** the horizontal line.

11. Inside the Drawing Area, **right-click** to end the Offset command.

12. Repeat the **Offset** command and create the offset lines as shown.

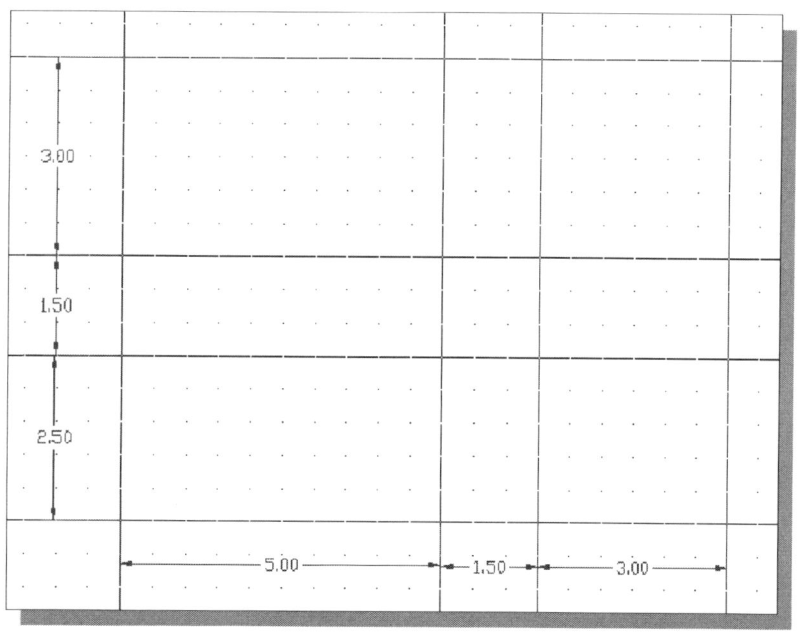

Set Layer Object as the Current Layer

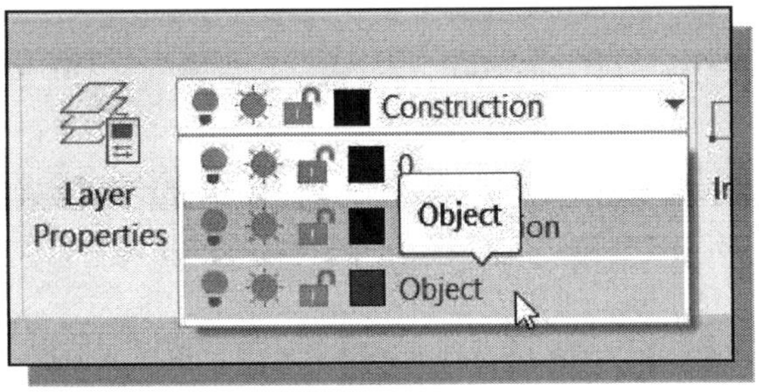

1. On the *Layers* toolbar panel, choose the ***Layer Control*** box with the left-mouse-button.

2. Move the cursor over the name of the layer ***Object***. The tool tip "*Object*" appears.

3. **Left-click once** on the layer *Object* to set it as the *Current Layer*.

Using the Running Object Snaps

In **AutoCAD 2027**, while using geometry construction commands, the cursor can be placed to points on objects such as endpoints, midpoints, centers, and intersections. In AutoCAD, this tool is called the ***Object Snap***.

Object snaps can be turned on in one of two ways:

- **Single Point (or override) Object Snaps**: Sets an object snap for one use.
- **Running Object Snaps**: Sets object snaps *active* until we turn them off.

The procedure we have used so far is the *Single Point Object Snaps* option, where we select the specific object snap from the *Object Snap* toolbar for one use only. The use of the *Running Object Snaps* option to assist the construction is illustrated next.

1. In the *Menu Bar*, select:

   [Tools] → [Drafting Settings]

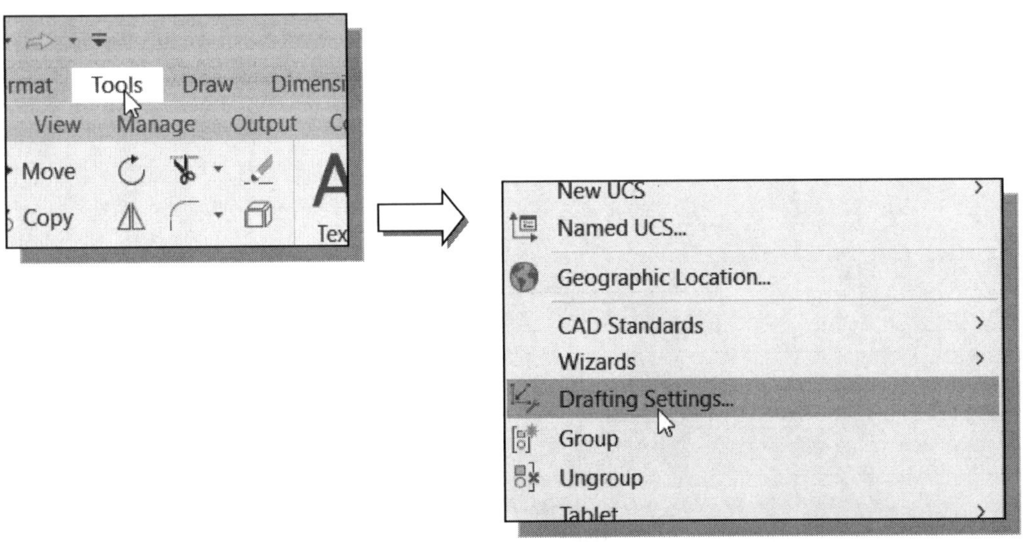

2. In the *Drafting Settings* dialog box select the **Object Snap** tab.

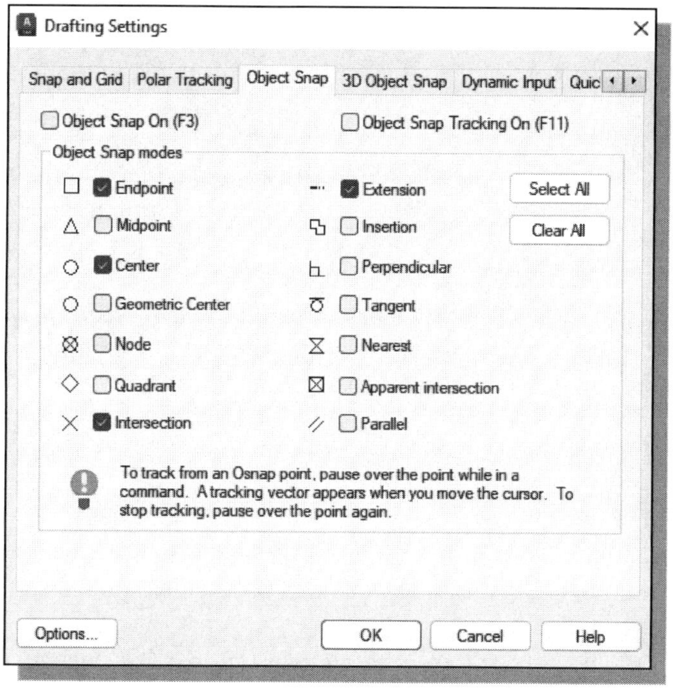

- The *Running Object Snap* options can be turned on or off by clicking the different options listed. Notice the different symbols associated with the different *Object Snap* options.

3. Turn ***ON*** the *Running Object Snap* by clicking the **Object Snap On** box, or hit the **[F3]** key once.

4. Confirm the ***Intersection***, ***Endpoint*** and ***Extension*** options are switched ***ON*** and click on the **OK** button to accept the settings and exit from the *Drafting Settings* dialog box.

❖ Notice in the *Status Bar* area the ***OSNAP*** button is switched ***ON***. We can toggle the *Running Object Snap* option on or off by clicking the *OSNAP* button.

5. Press the **[F3]** key once and notice the *OSNAP* button is switched ***OFF*** in the *Status Bar* area.

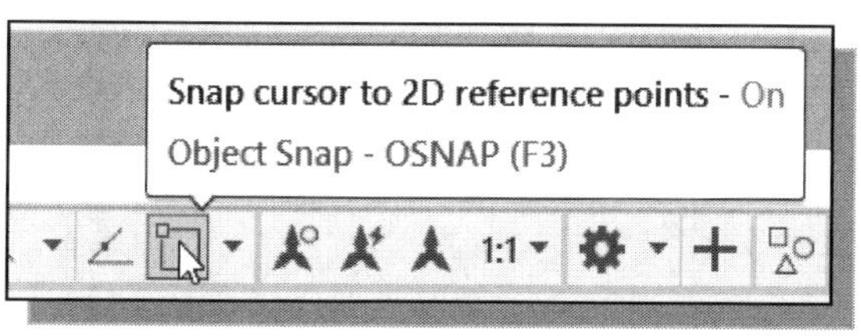

6. Press the **[F3]** key again and notice the *OSNAP* button is now switched ***ON*** in the *Status Bar* area.

➢ **AutoCAD 2027** provides many input methods and shortcuts; you are encouraged to examine the different options and choose the option that best fits your own style.

Creating Object Lines

We will define the areas for the front view, top view and side view by adding object lines using the *Running Object Snap* option.

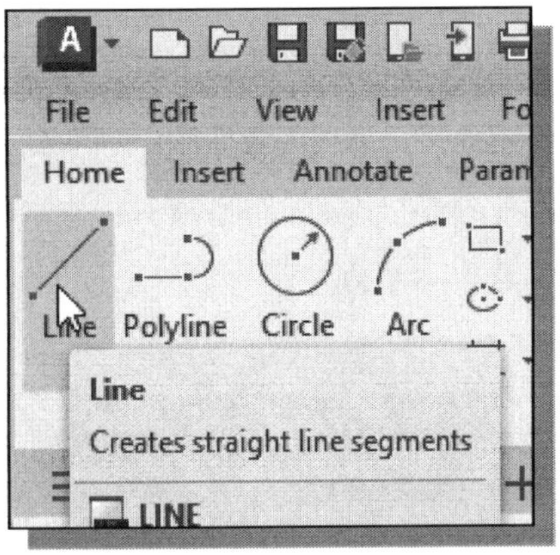

1. Select the **Line** command icon in the *Draw* toolbar. In the command prompt area, the message "*_line Specify first point:*" is displayed.

2. Move the cursor to the **intersection** of any two lines and notice the visual aid automatically displayed at the intersection.

3. Pick the four intersection points closest to the lower left corner to create the four sides of the area of the front view.

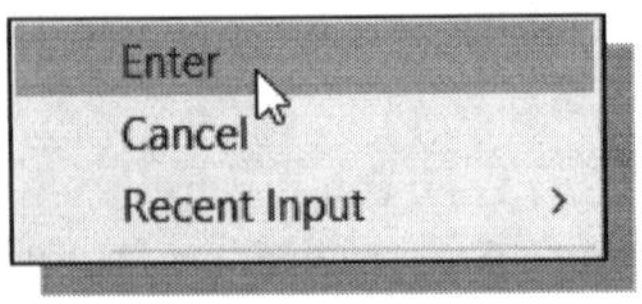

4. Inside the *Drawing Area*, **right-click** once to activate the option menu and select **Enter** with the left-mouse-button to end the Line command.

5. Repeat the **Line** command to define the top view and side view as shown.

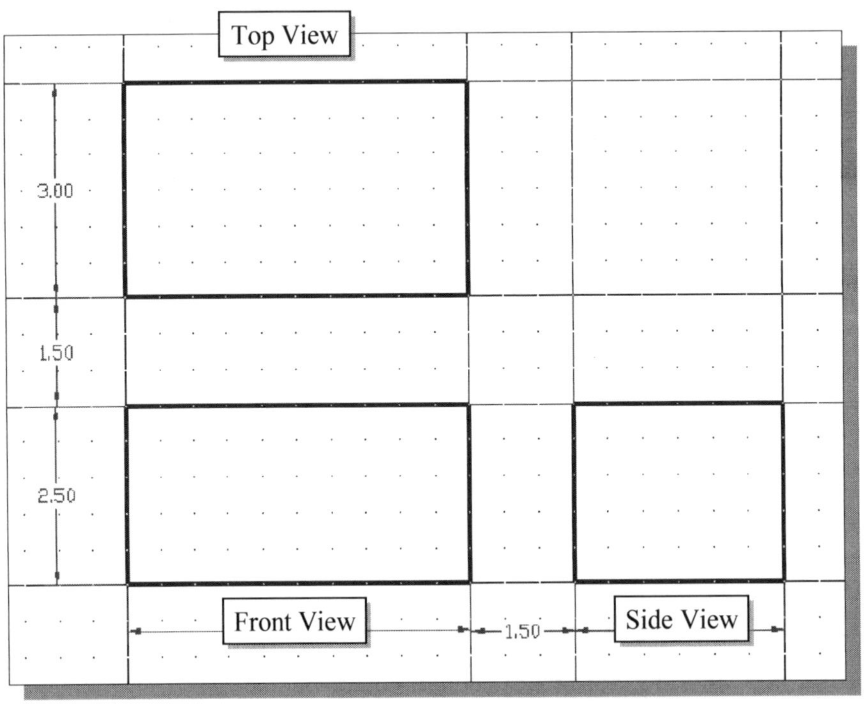

Turn Off the Construction Lines Layer

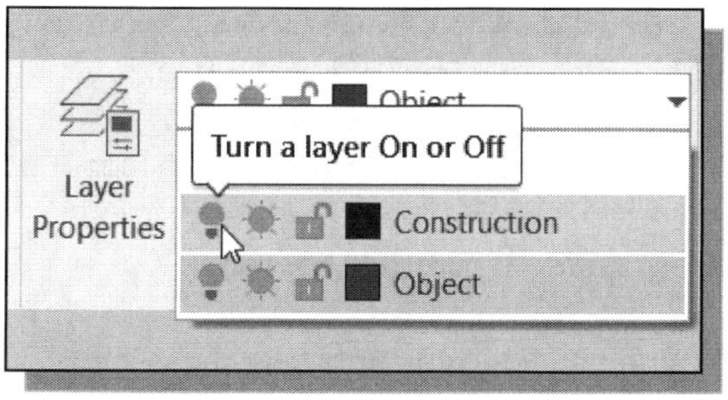

1. On the *Object Properties* toolbar, choose the ***Layer Control*** box with the left-mouse-button.

2. Move the cursor over the lightbulb icon for layer ***Construction***. The tool tip "*Turn a layer On or Off*" appears.

3. **Left-click once** on the *lightbulb* icon and notice the icon color is changed to gray color, representing the layer (layer *Construction*) is turned ***OFF***.

Adding More Objects in the Front View

1. Use the **Offset** command and create the two parallel lines in the front view as shown.

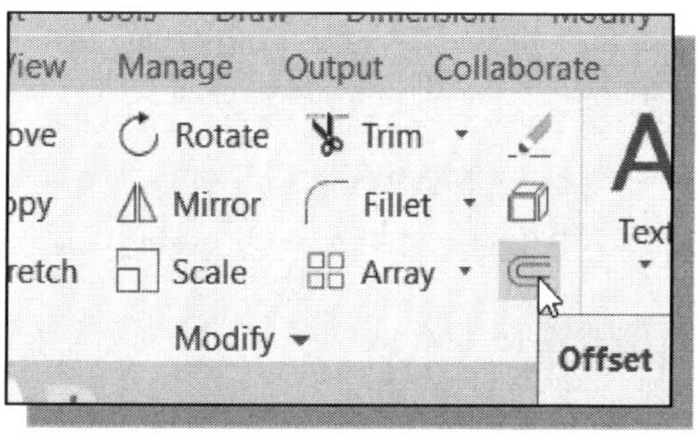

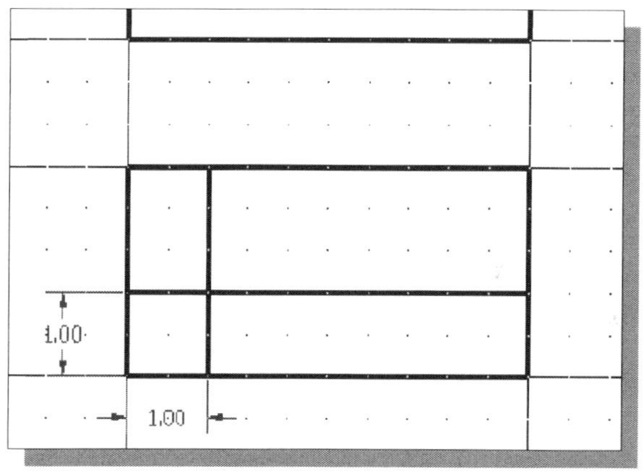

2. Use the **Trim** command and modify the front view as shown.

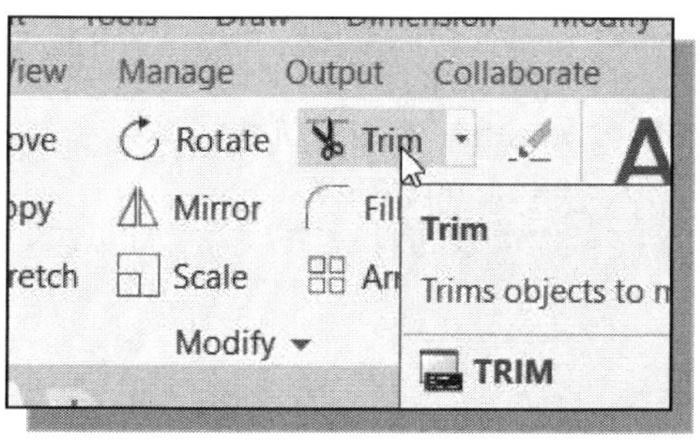

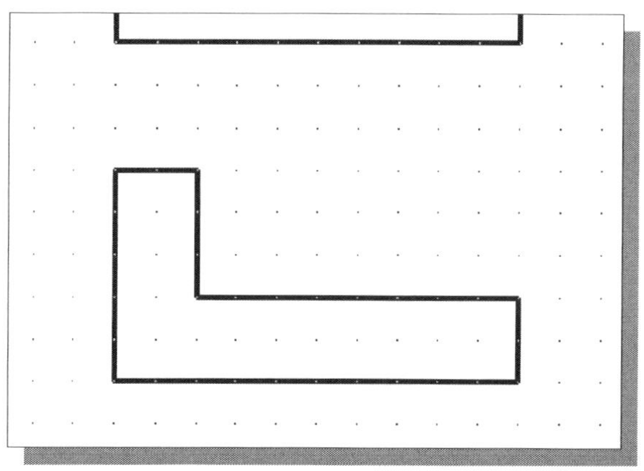

AutoCAD's AutoSnap™ and AutoTrack™ Features

AutoCAD's *AutoSnap* and *AutoTrack* provide visual aids when the *Object Snap* options are switched *on*. The main advantages of *AutoSnap* and *AutoTrack* are as follows:

- **Symbols**: Automatically displays the *Object Snap* type at the object snap location.
- **Tooltips**: Automatically displays the *Object Snap* type below the cursor.
- **Magnet**: Locks the cursor onto a snap point when the cursor is near the point.

With ***Object Snap Tracking***, the cursor can track along alignment paths based on other object snap points when specifying points in a command. To use *Object Snap Tracking*, one or more object snaps must be switched on. The basic rules of using the ***Object Snap Tracking*** option are as follows:

- To track from a *Running Object Snap* point, pause over the point while in a command.
- A tracking vector appears when we move the cursor.
- To stop tracking, pause over the point again.
- When multiple *Running Object Snaps* are on, press the **[TAB]** key to cycle through available snap points when the object snap aperture box is on an object.

1. In the *Status Bar* area, turn **ON** the *OTRACK/AUTOSNAP* option.

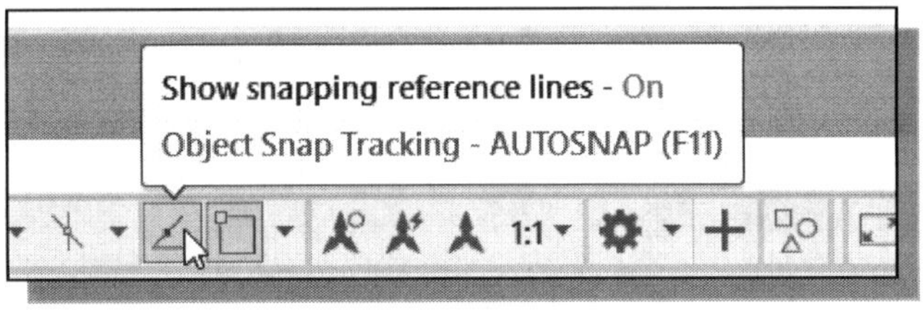

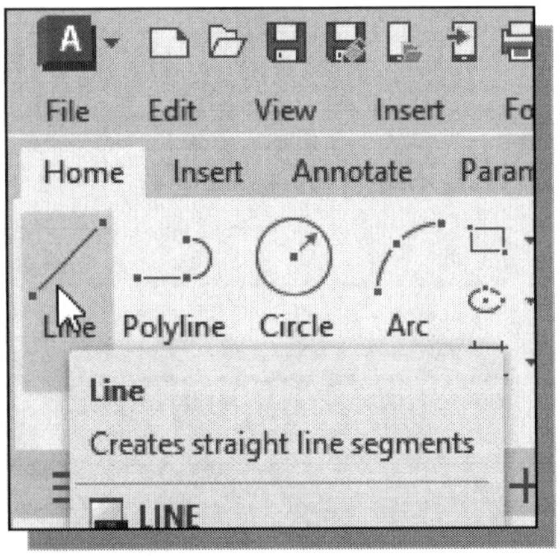

2. Select the **Line** command icon in the *Draw* toolbar. In the command prompt area, the message "*_line Specify first point:*" is displayed.

3. Move the cursor near the top right corner of the vertical protrusion in the front view. Notice that *AUTOSNAP* automatically locks the cursor to the corner and displays the ***Endpoint*** symbol.

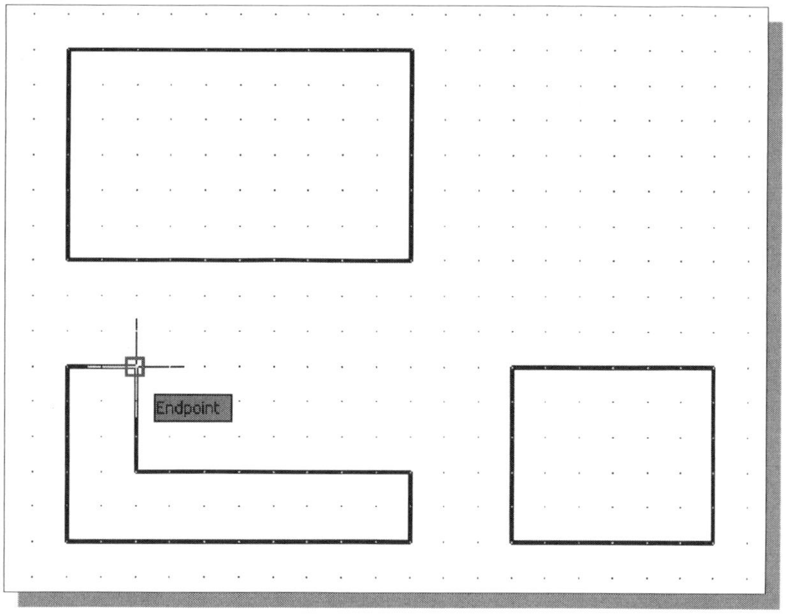

4. Move the cursor upward and notice that *Object Tracking* displays a dashed line, showing the alignment to the top right corner of the vertical protrusion in the front view. Move the cursor near the top horizontal line of the top view and notice that *AUTOSNAP* displays the intersection point.

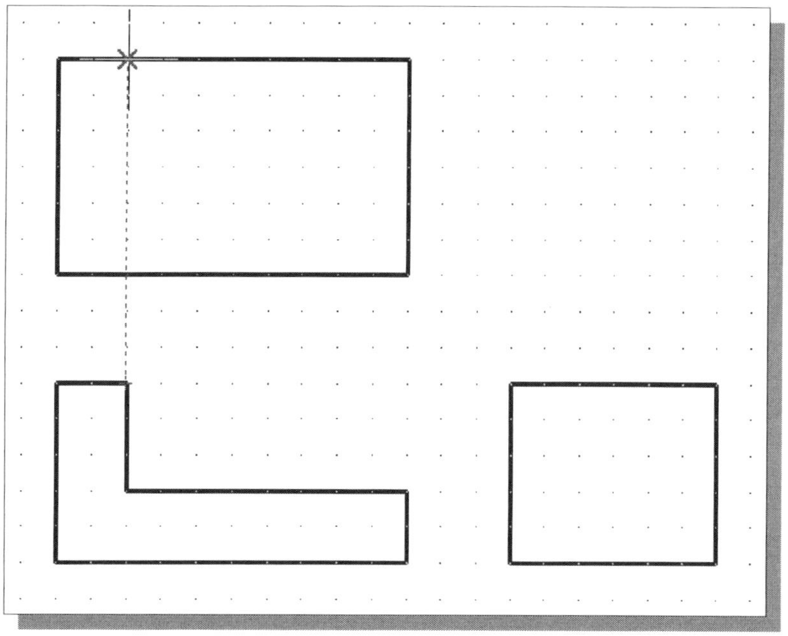

5. Left-click to place the starting point of a line at the intersection.

6. Move the cursor to the top left corner of the front view to activate the tracking feature.

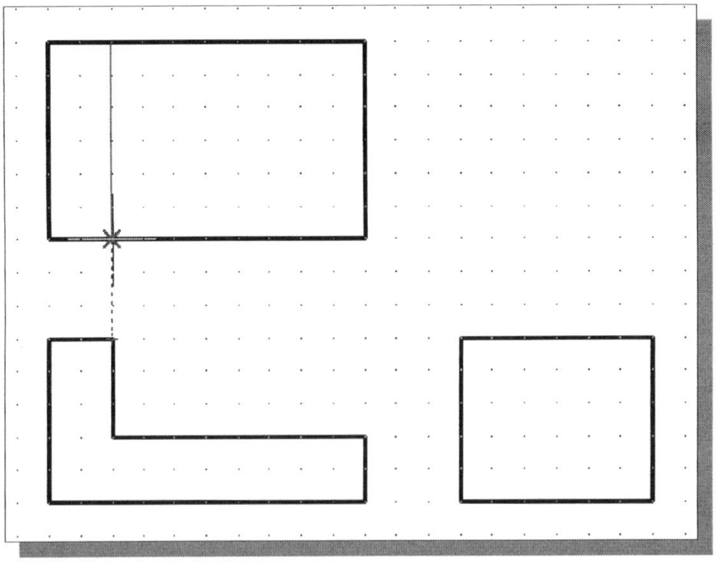

7. Create the line as shown in the above figure.

Adding More Objects in the Top View

1. Use the **Offset** command and create the two parallel lines in the top view as shown.

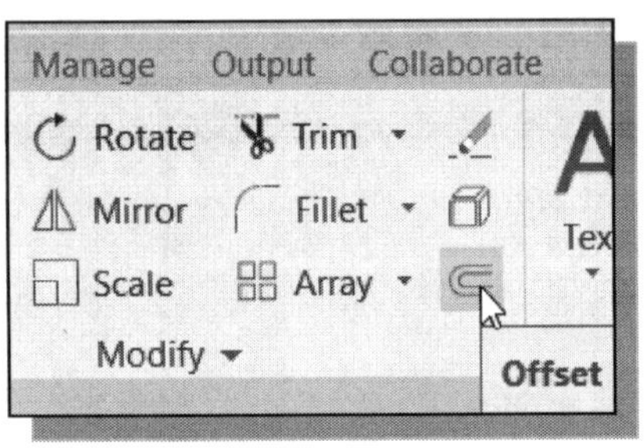

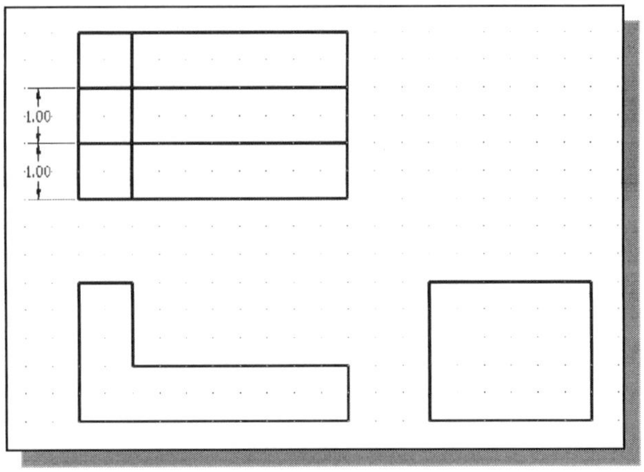

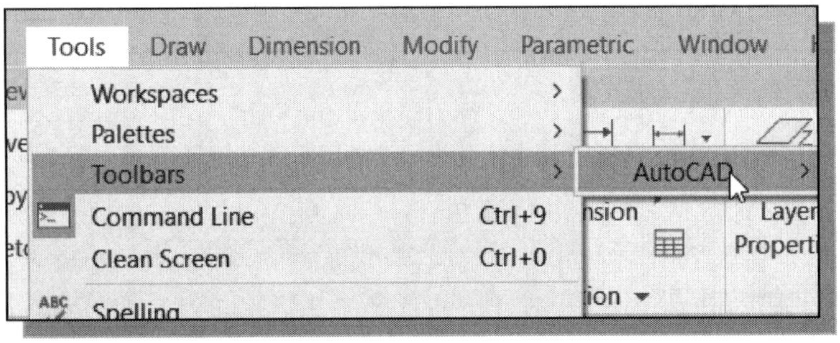

2. On your own, select **[Tools] → [Toolbars] → [Object Snap]** to display the *Object Snap* toolbar on the screen.

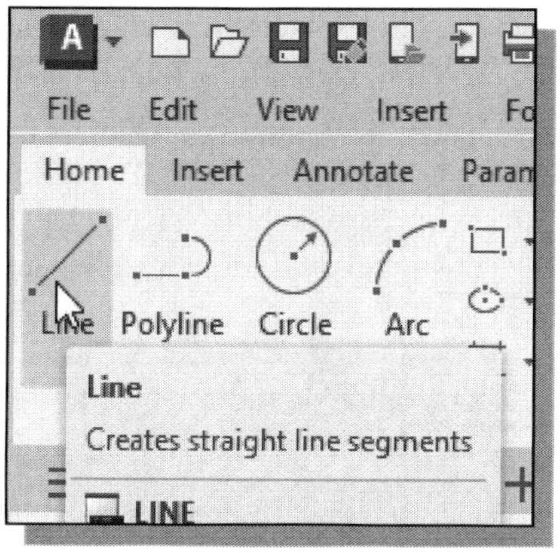

3. Select the **Line** command icon in the *Draw* toolbar. In the command prompt area, the message "*_line Specify first point:*" is displayed.

4. In the *Object Snap* toolbar, pick **Snap From**. In the command prompt area, the message "*_from Base point*" is displayed. AutoCAD now expects us to select a geometric entity on the screen.

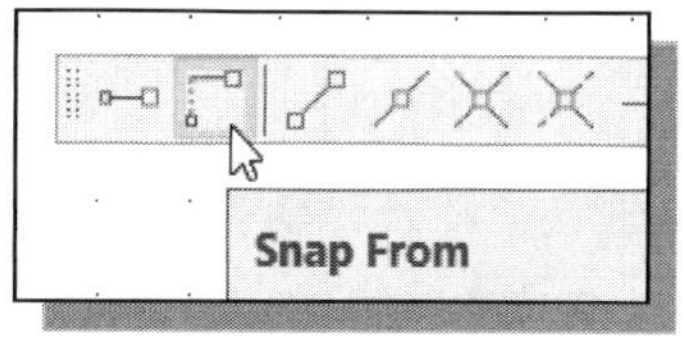

➢ The ***Single Point Object Snap*** overrides the ***Running Object Snap*** option.

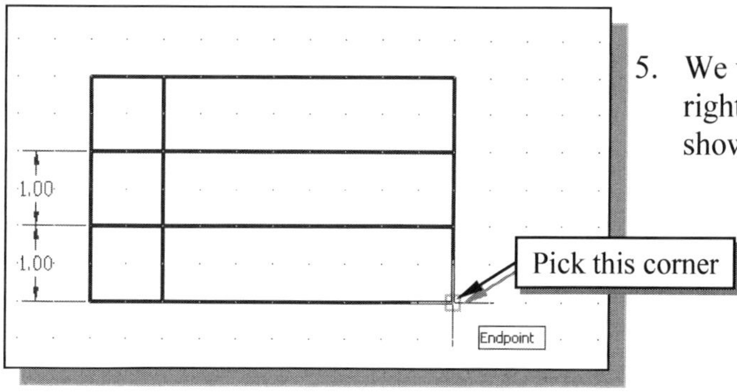

5. We will measure relative to the lower right corner. Pick the corner as shown.

6. In the command prompt area, enter ***@0,0.25*** **[ENTER]**.

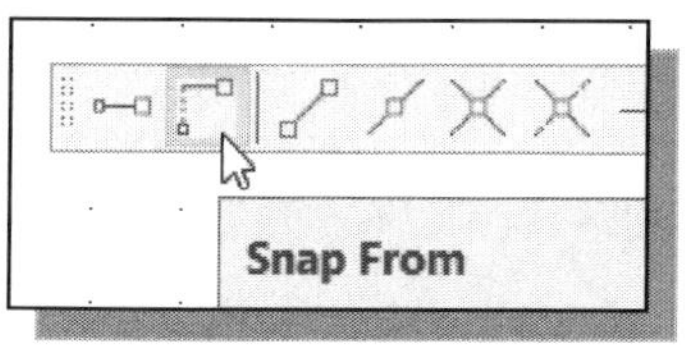

7. In the *Object Snap* toolbar, pick **Snap From**. Pick the lower right corner of the top view again.

8. In the command prompt area, enter ***@-1.75,0*** **[ENTER]**.

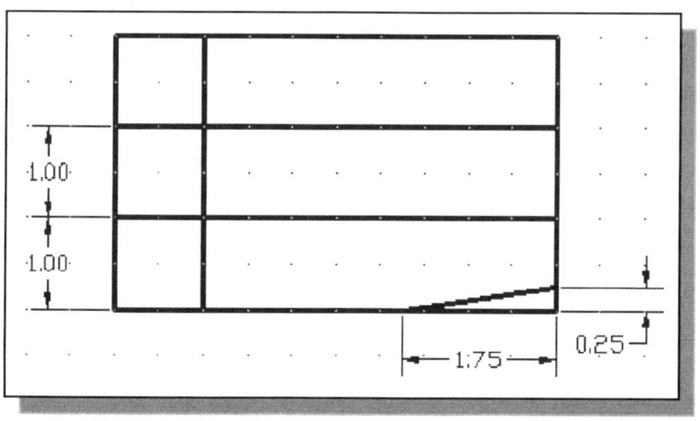

9. Inside the Drawing Area, right-click to activate the option menu and select **Enter** with the left-mouse-button to end the **Line** command.

10. Repeat the procedure and create the line on the top right corner as shown.

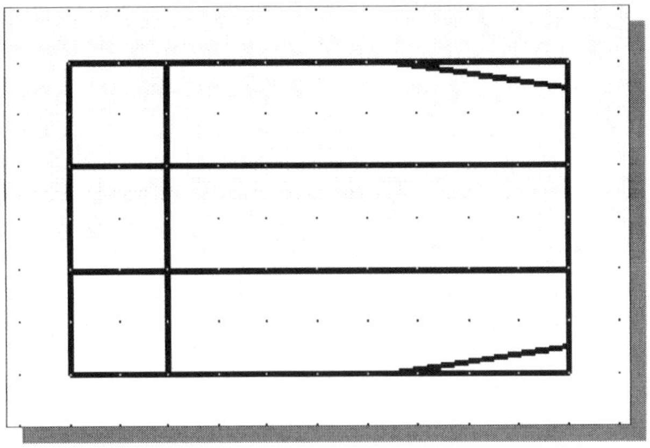

11. Using the *Snap From* option, create the circle (diameter ***1.0***) as shown.

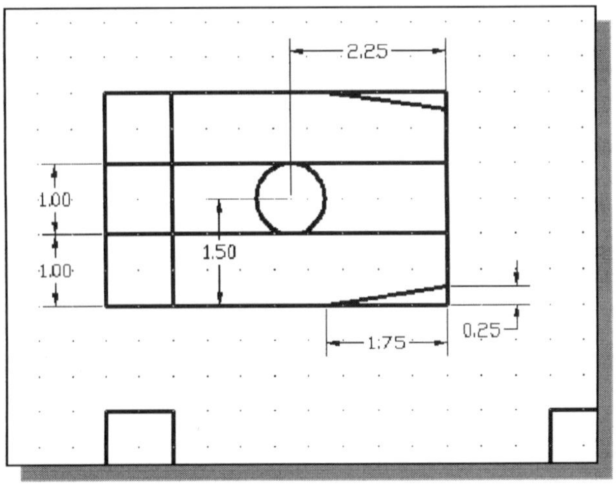

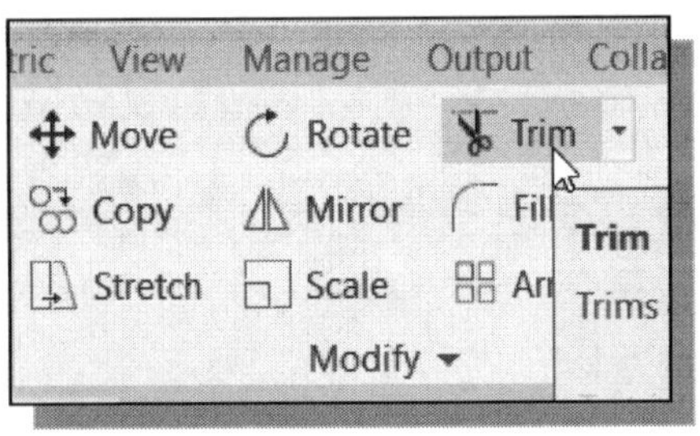

12. Select the **Trim** icon in the *Modify* toolbar.

13. In the command prompt area, click **cuTting edges** as shown.

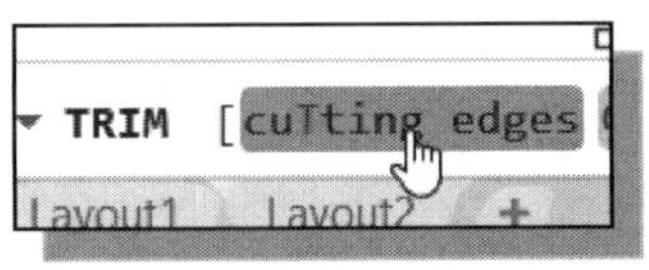

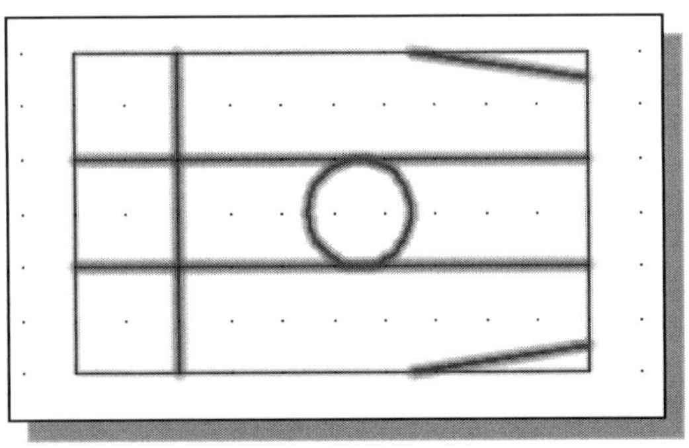

14. Pick the following objects as boundary edges: the circle and the lines that are near the circle.

15. Inside the *Drawing Area*, **right-click** to accept the selected objects.

16. Select the unwanted portions and modify the objects as shown.

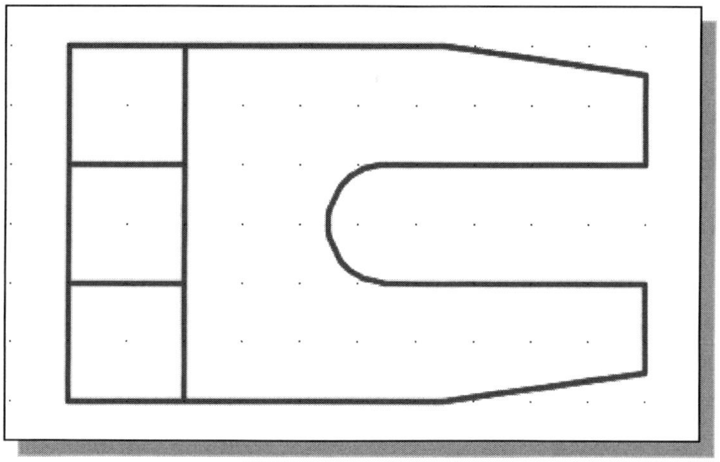

17. On your own, use the **Offset** and **Trim** commands and modify the top view as shown.

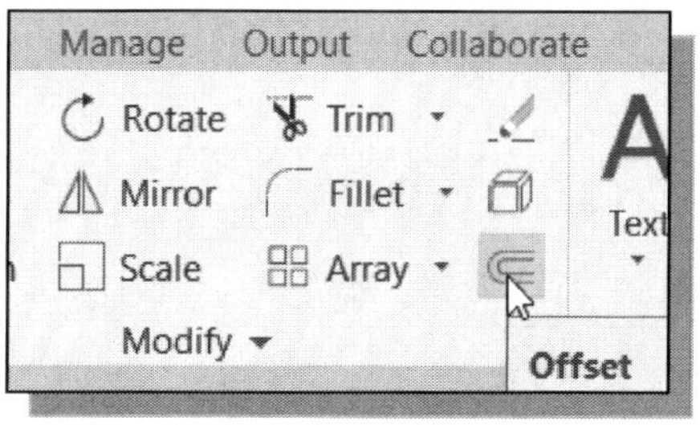

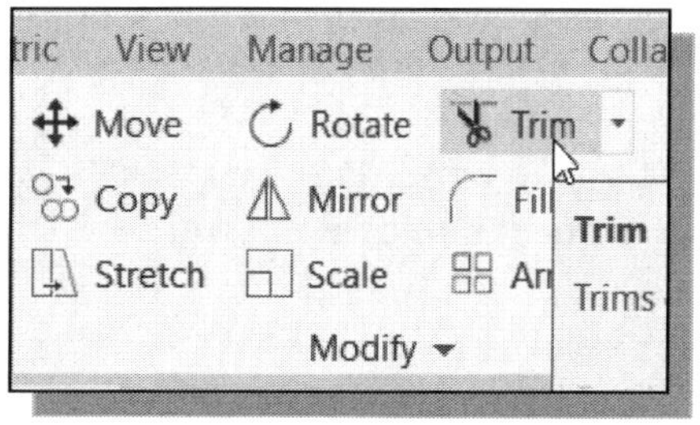

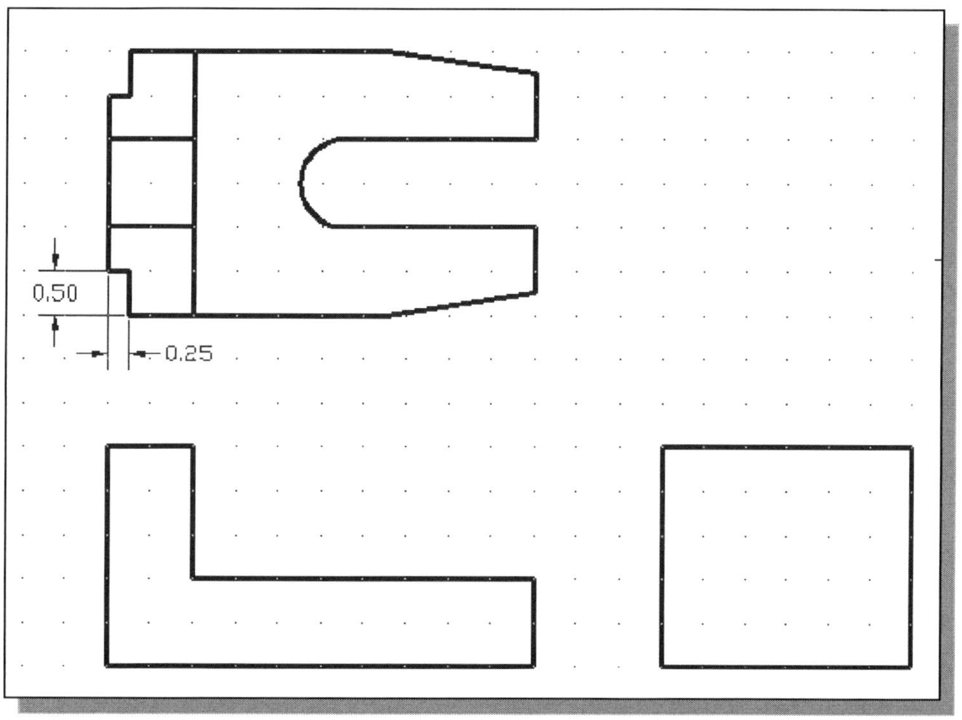

Drawing Using the Miter Line Method

The *45° miter line* method is a simple and straightforward procedure to transfer measurements in between the top view and the side view.

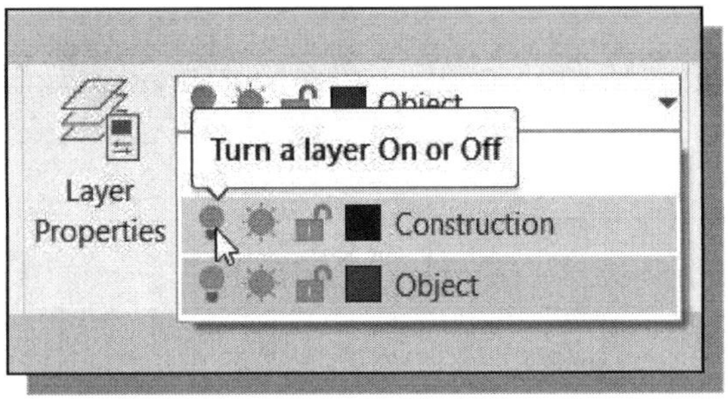

1. On the *Layers* toolbar panel, choose the ***Layer Control*** box by clicking once with the left-mouse-button.

2. Move the cursor over the **light-bulb** icon for layer ***Construction***. The tool tip "*Turn a layer On or Off*" appears.

3. **Left-click once** and notice the icon color is changed to a light color, representing the layer (layer *Construction*) is turned *ON*.

4. **Left-click once** over the name of the layer ***Construction*** to set it as the *Current Layer*.

5. Use the **Line** command and create the *miter line* by connecting the two intersections of the construction lines as shown.

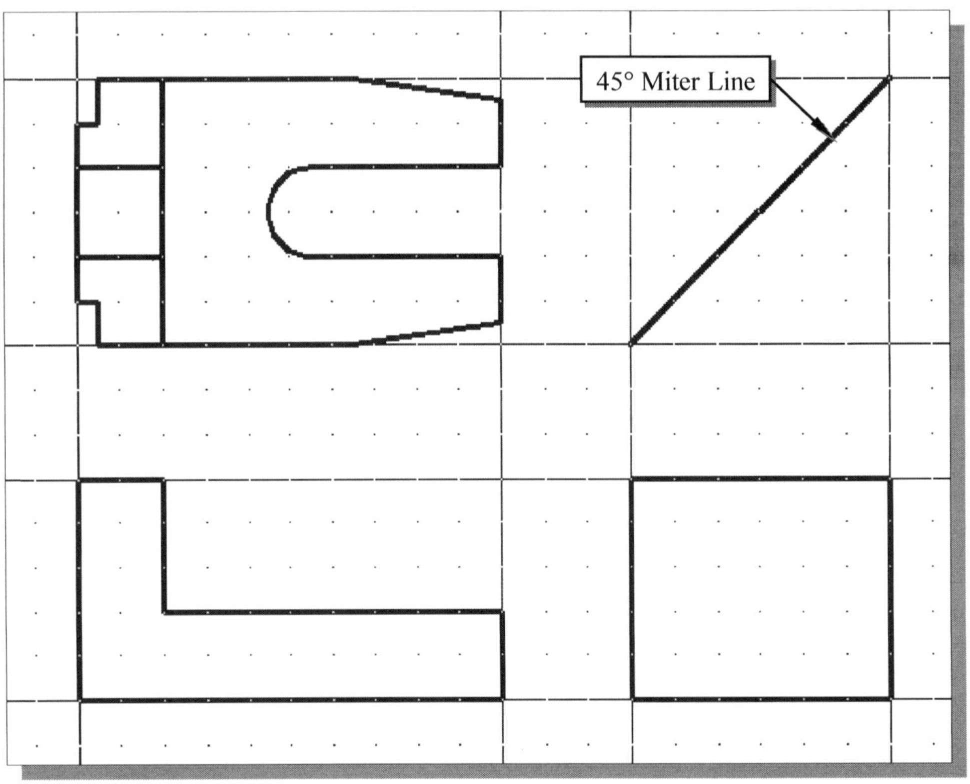

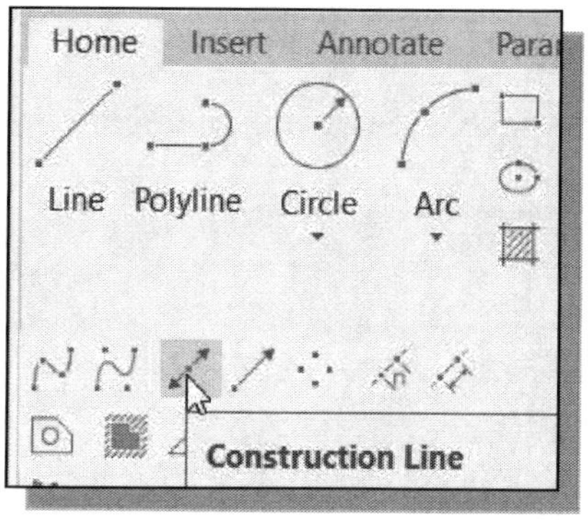

6. Select the **Construction Line** command in the *Draw* toolbar as shown.

7. In the *command prompt area*, select the **Horizontal** option as shown.

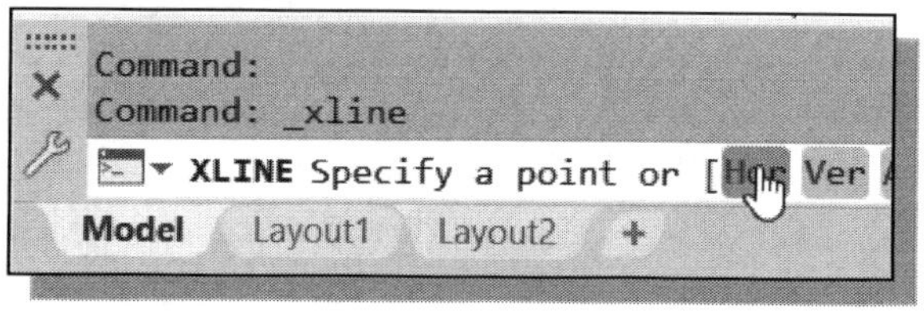

8. On your own, create horizontal projection lines through all the corners in the top view as shown.

9. Use the **Trim** command and trim the projection lines as shown in the figure below.

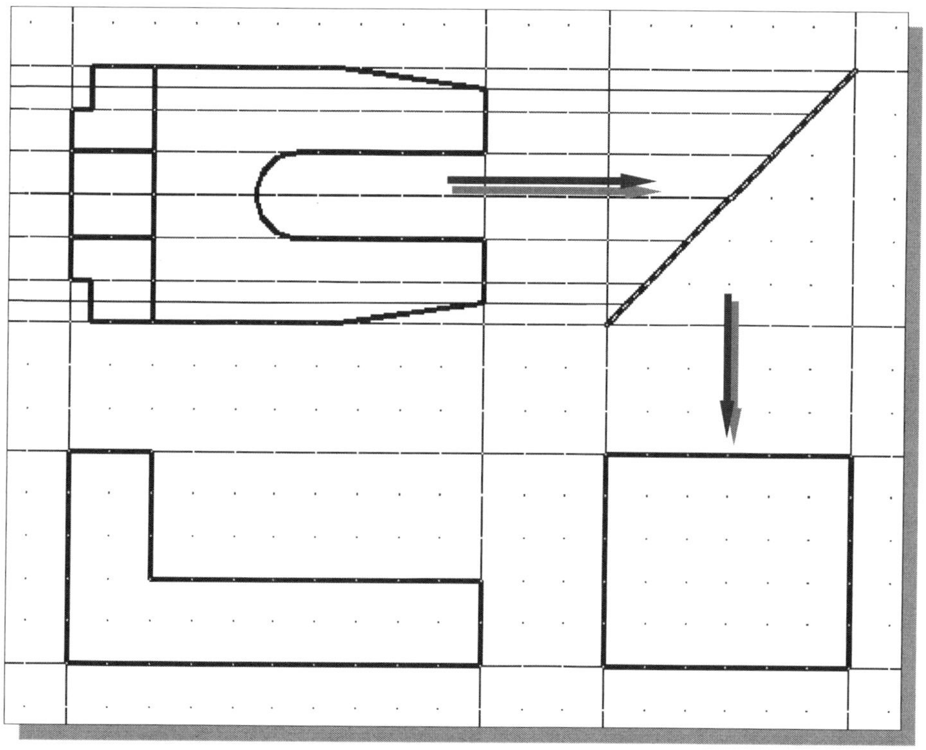

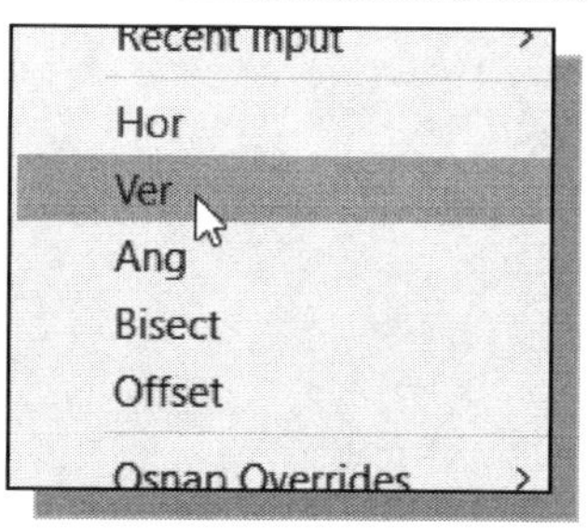

10. On your own, create additional Construction Lines (use the *vertical* option) through all the intersection points that are on the *miter line*.

More Layers Setup

1. Pick ***Layer Properties Manager*** in the *Layers* toolbar panel as shown in the figure below.

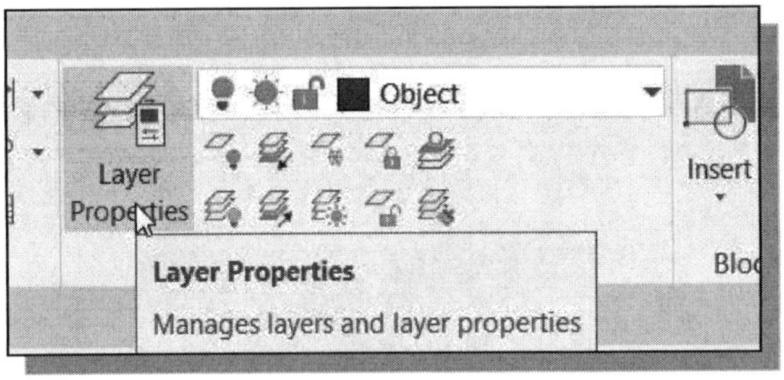

2. Click on the **New** icon to create new layers.

3. Create two **new layers** with the following settings:

Layer	***Color***	***Linetype***
Center	**Red**	**CENTER**
Hidden	**Cyan**	**HIDDEN**

- The default linetype is *Continuous.* To use other linetypes, click on the **Load** button in the *Select Linetype* dialog box and select the desired linetypes.

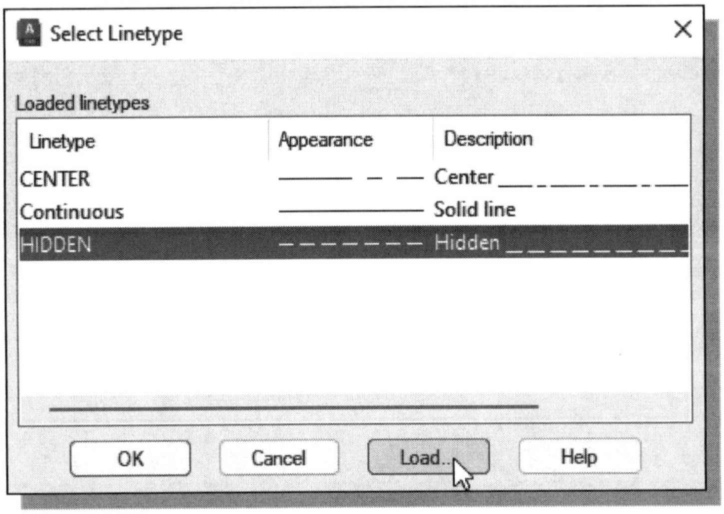

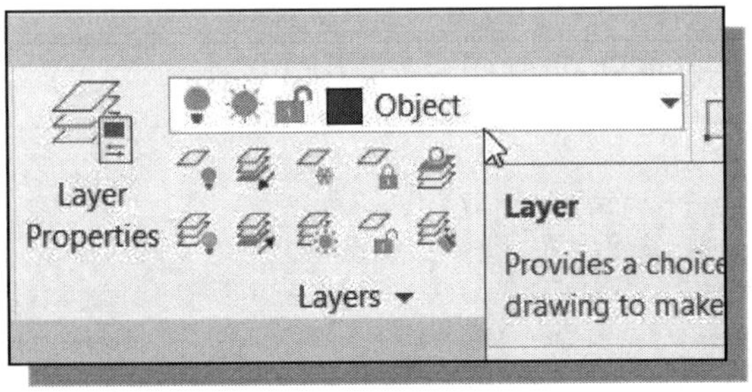

4. On your own, set the layer ***Object*** as the *Current Layer.*

Top View to Side View Projection

1. Using the *Running Object Snaps*, create the necessary **object-lines** in the side view.

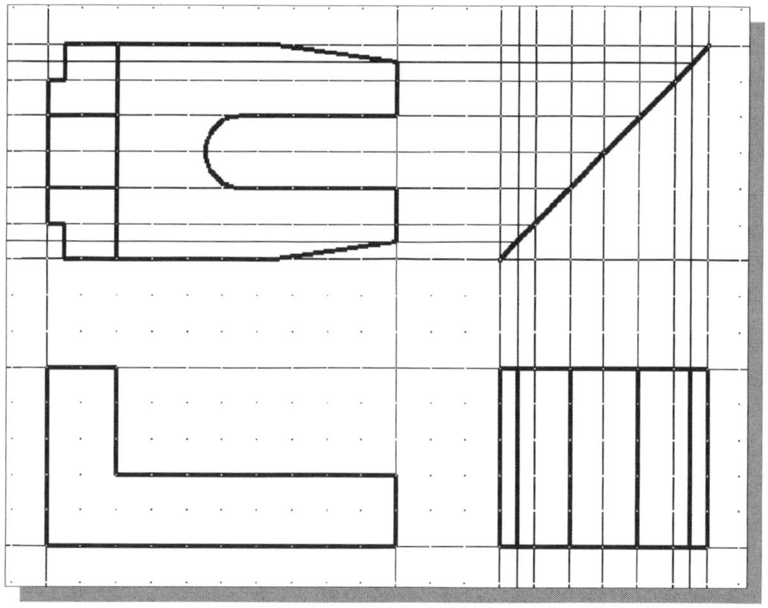

2. Set layer ***Hidden*** as the *Current Layer* and create the two necessary hidden lines in the side view.

3. Set layer ***Center*** as the *Current Layer* and create the necessary centerlines in the side view.

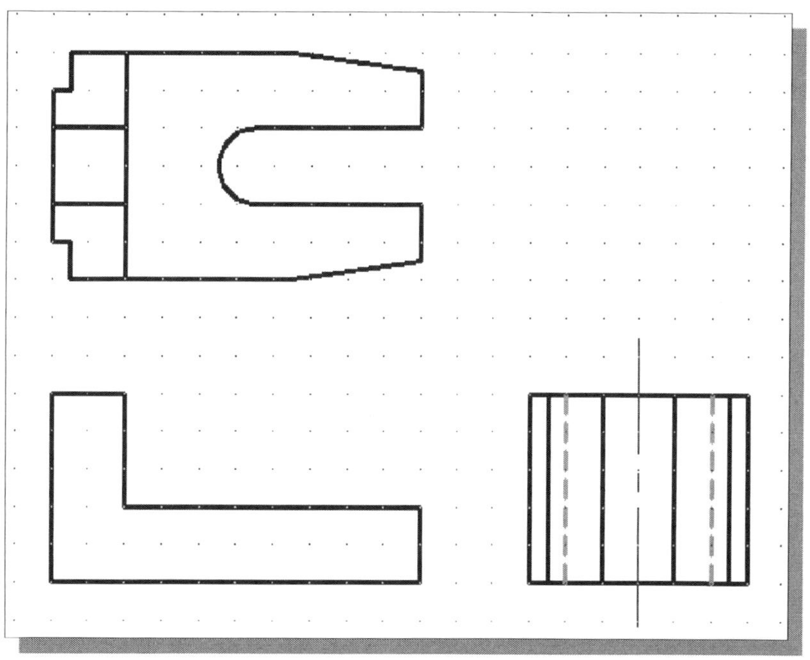

4. In the *Layer Control* box, turn ***OFF*** the ***construction lines***.

5. Set layer ***Object*** as the *Current Layer*.

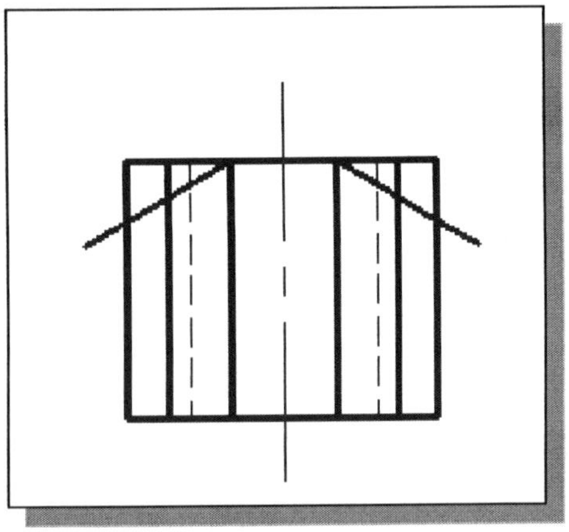

6. Use the **Line** command and create the two 30° inclined lines as shown.

   (Hint: Relative coordinate entries of ***@2.0<-30*** and ***@2.0<210***.)

7. Use the **Line** command and create a horizontal line in the side view as shown.

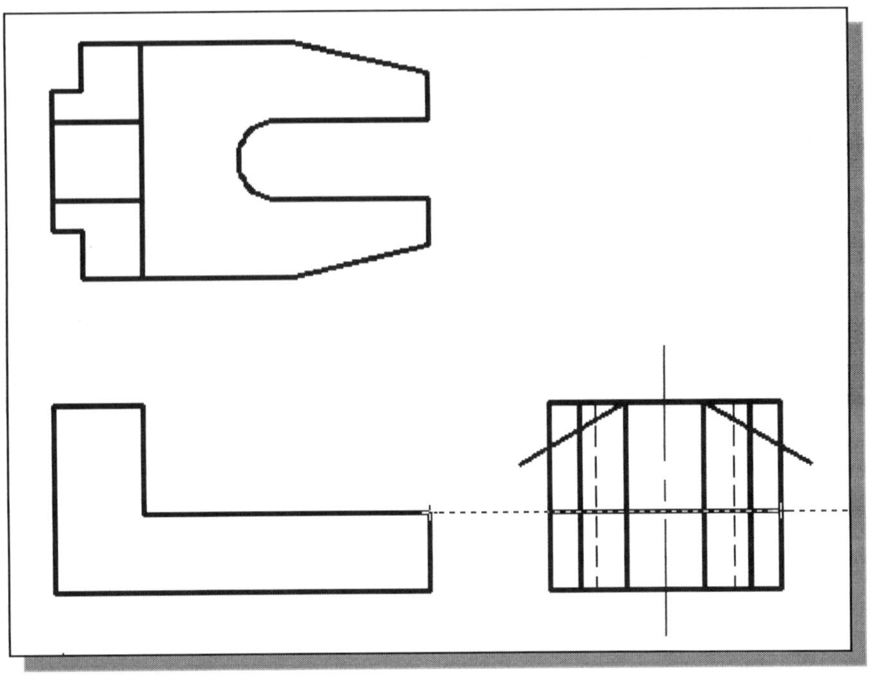

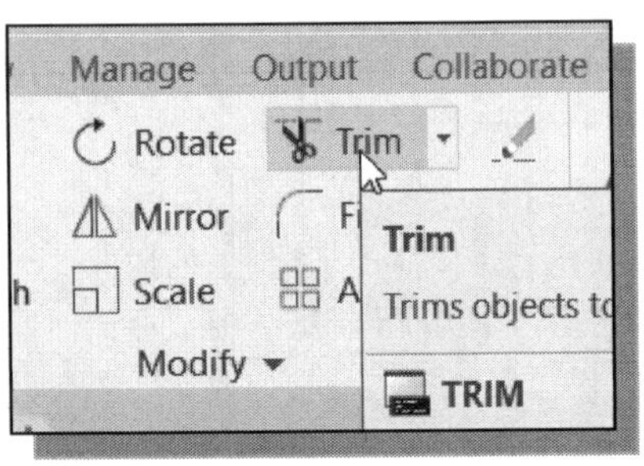

8. On your own, use the **Trim** command and remove the unwanted portions in the side view. Refer to the image shown on the next page if necessary.

Completing the Front View

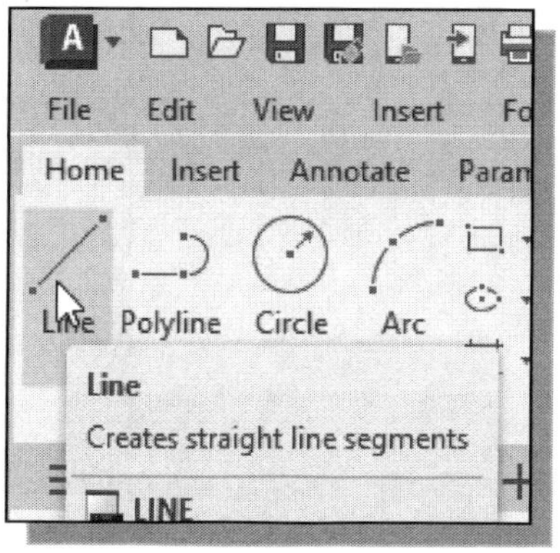

1. Select the **Line** command icon in the *Draw* toolbar. In the command prompt area, the message "*_line Specify first point:*" is displayed.

2. Move the cursor to the top left corner in the side view and the bottom left corner in the top view to activate the *Object Tracking* option to both corners.

3. Left-click once when the cursor is aligned to both corners as shown.

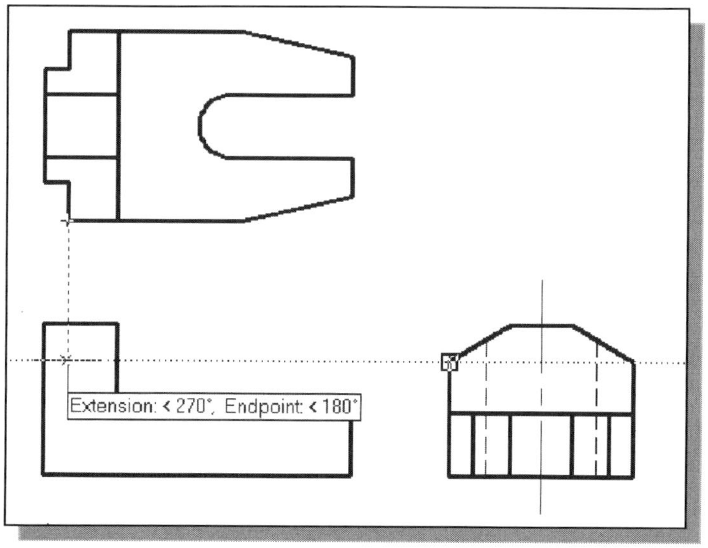

4. Create the **horizontal line** as shown.

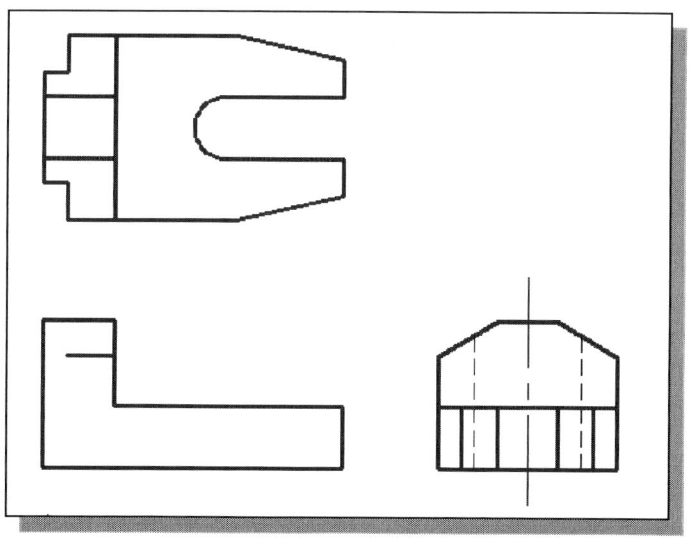

5. Repeat the procedure and create the lines in the front view as shown.

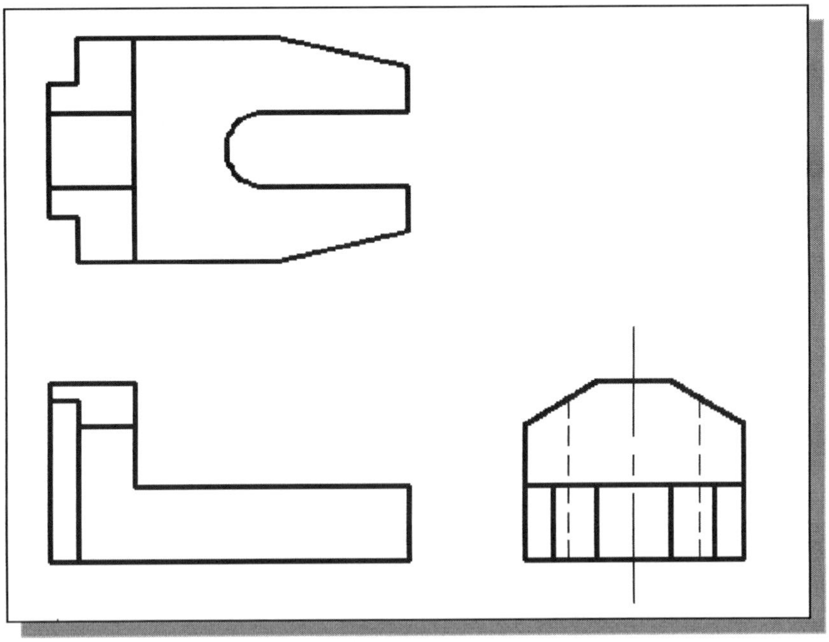

6. Add in any additional object lines that are necessary.

7. Set layer ***Hidden*** as the *Current Layer* and create the necessary hidden lines in the front view.

8. Set layer ***Center*** as the *Current Layer* and create the necessary centerlines in the top view and front view.

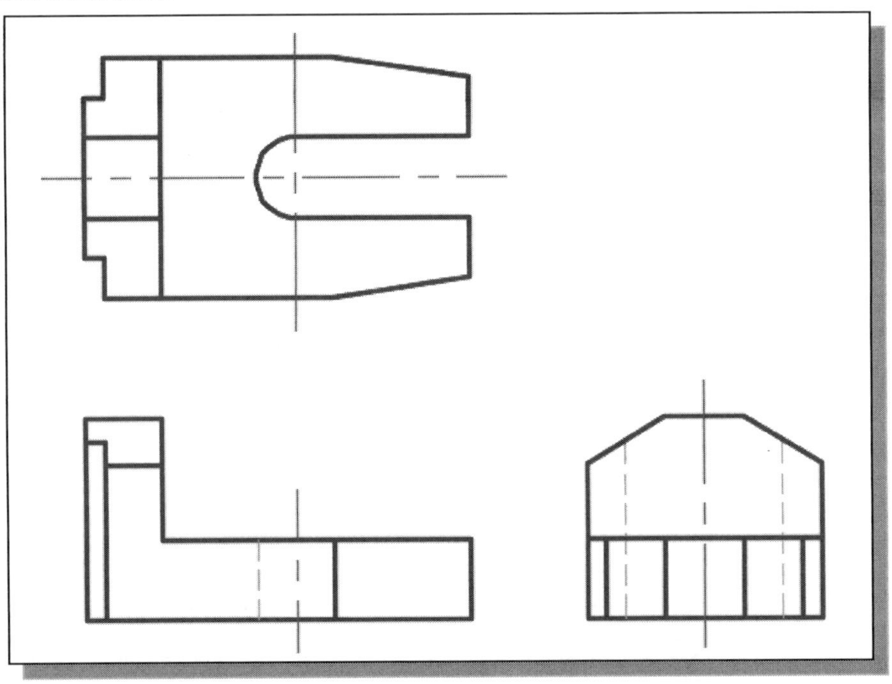

Object Information Using the List Command

AutoCAD provides several tools that will allow us to get information about constructed geometric objects. The **List** command can be used to show detailed information about geometric objects.

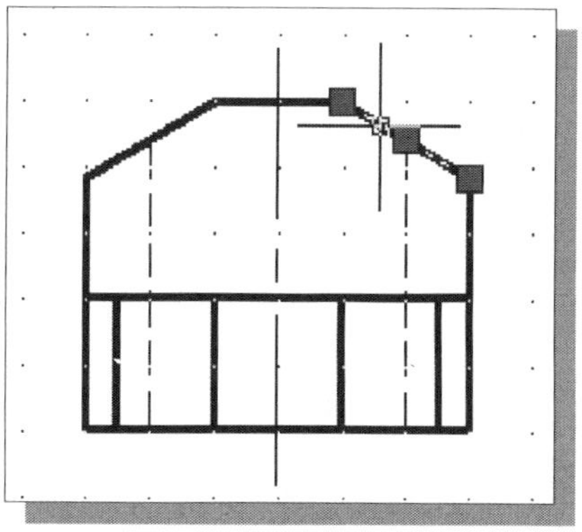

1. Move the cursor to the side view and select the inclined line on the right, as shown in the figure.

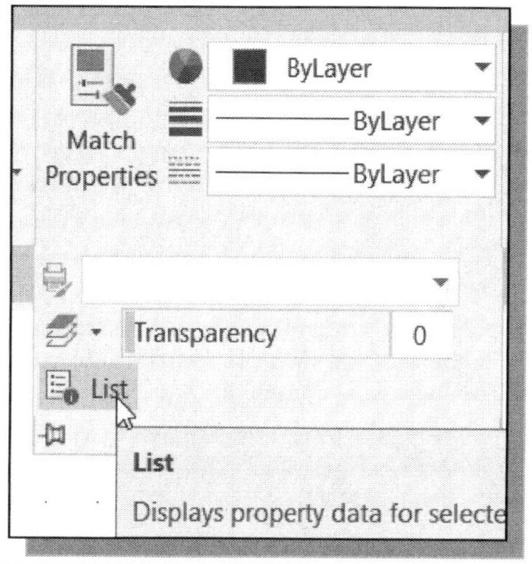

2. In the *Properties* toolbar, click on the **List** icon to activate the command.

- Note the information regarding the selected object is displayed in the *AutoCAD Text Window* as shown.

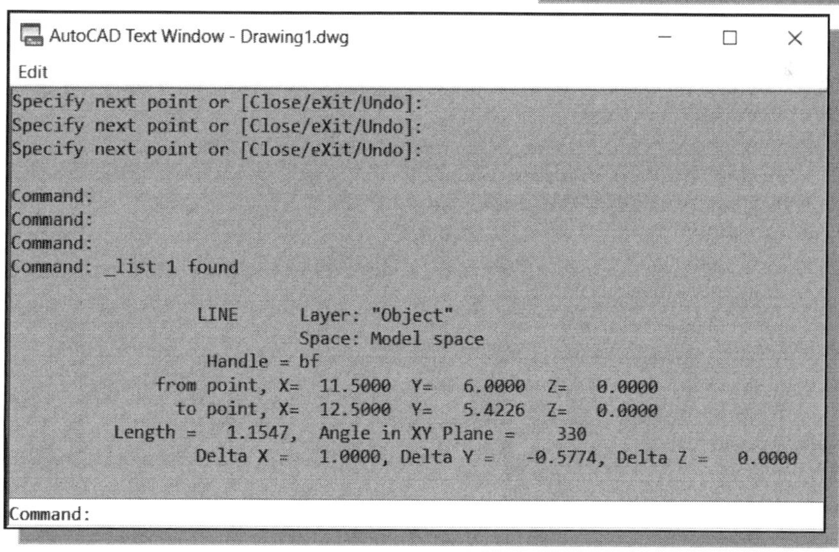

- Note the **List** command can be used to show detailed information about the selected line. The angle and length of the line, as well as the X, Y and Z components between the two endpoints are all listed in a separate window.

3. Press the [**F2**] key once to close the *AutoCAD Text Window*.

4. Press the [**Esc**] key once to deselect the selected line.

Object Information Using the Properties Command

AutoCAD also provides tools that allow us to display and change properties of constructed geometric objects. The **Properties** command not only provides the detailed information about geometric objects—modifications can also be done very quickly.

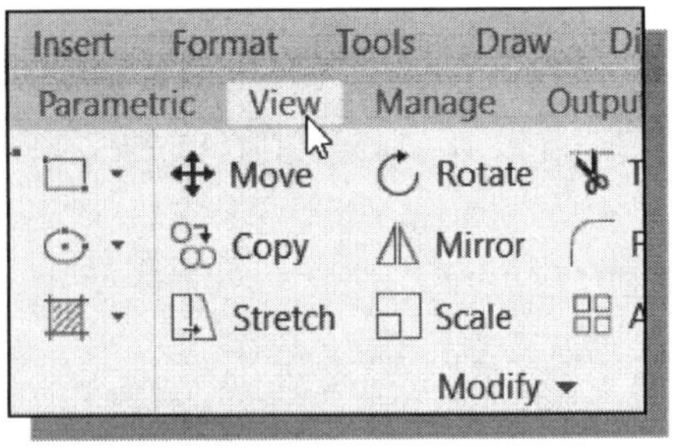

1. In the *Ribbon* tabs area, left-click once on the **View** tab as shown.

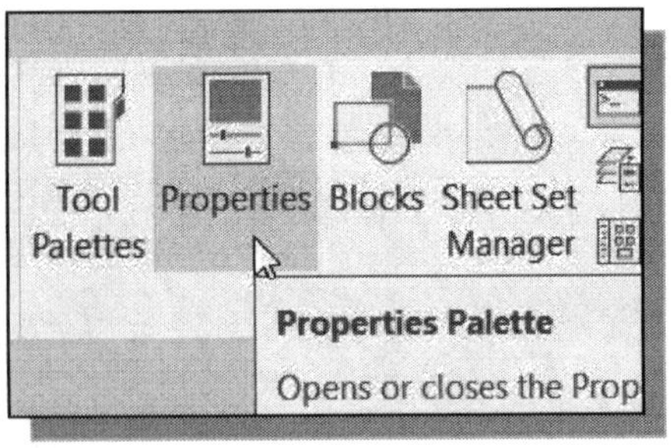

2. In the *Palettes* toolbar, click on the **Properties** icon to activate the command.

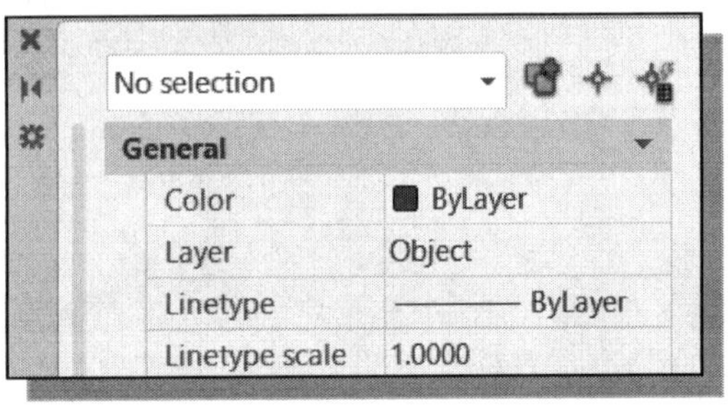

3. Note the *Properties* panel appears on the screen. The "*No selection*" on top of the panel indicates no object has been selected.

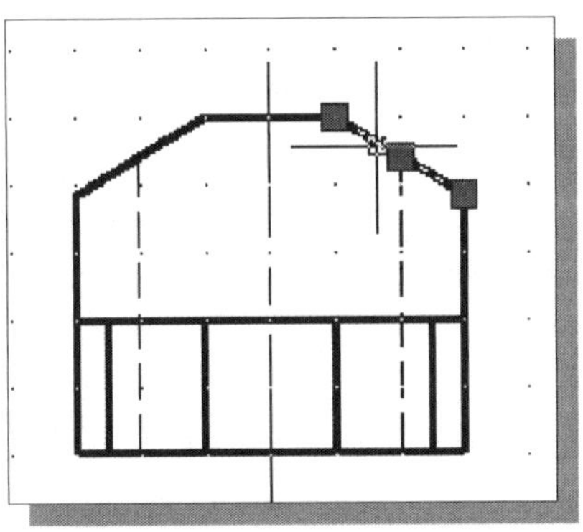

4. Move the cursor to the side view and select the inclined line on the right, as shown in the figure.

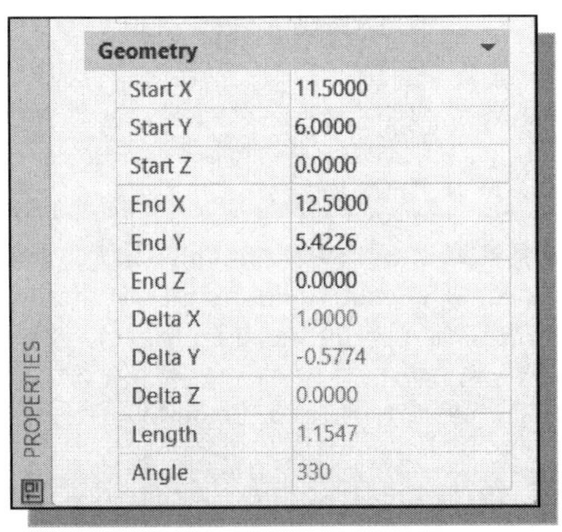

5. The geometry information is listed at the bottom section. Note the line length is *1.1547* and at the angle of *330* degrees.

Review Questions: (Time: 20 minutes)

1. Explain what an orthographic view is and why it is important to engineering graphics.

2. What does the *Running Object Snaps* option allow us to do?

3. Explain how a *miter line* can assist us in creating orthographic views.

4. Describe the AutoCAD *AutoSnap* and *AutoTrack* options.

5. List and describe two AutoCAD commands that can be used to get geometric information about constructed objects.

6. List and describe two options you could use to quickly create a 2-inch line attached to a 2-inch circle, as shown in the below figure.

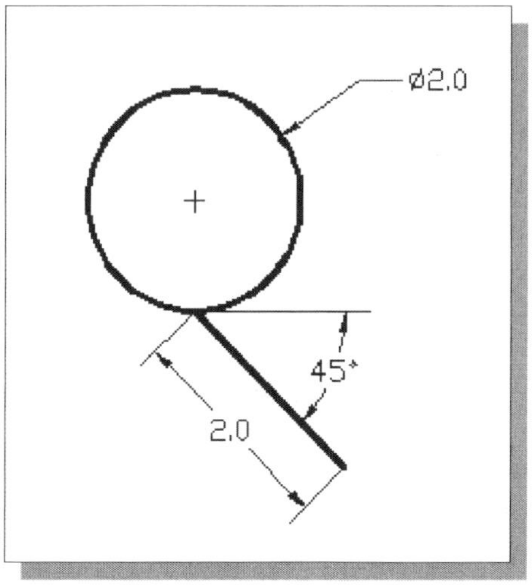

7. What are the length and angle of the inclined line, highlighted in the figure below, in the top view of the *Locator* design?

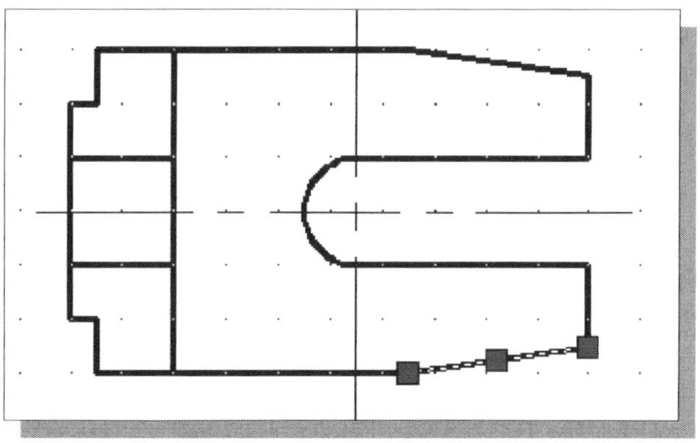

Exercises: (Time: 180 minutes)

(Unless otherwise specified, dimensions are in inches.)

1. Saddle Bracket

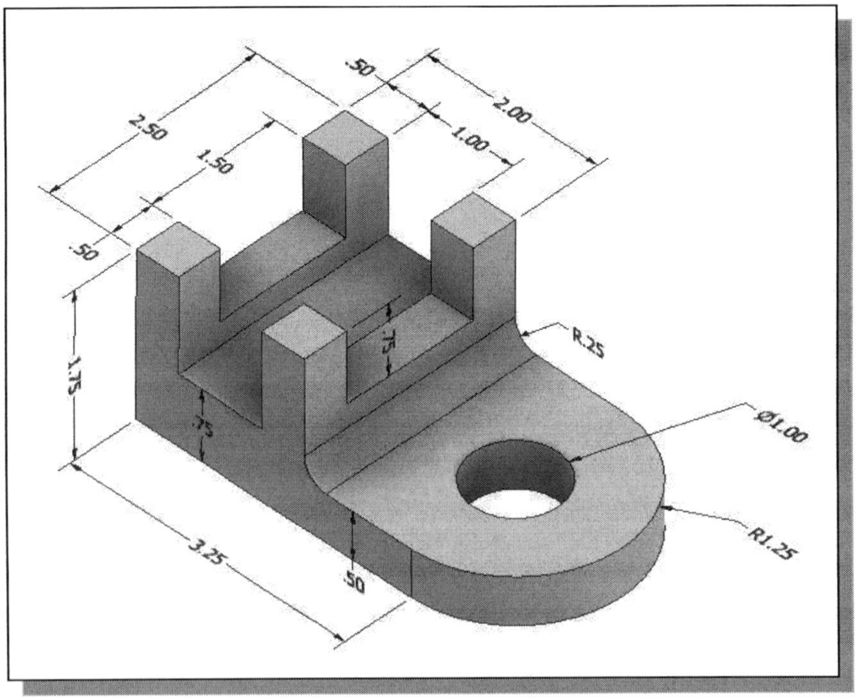

2. Anchor Base

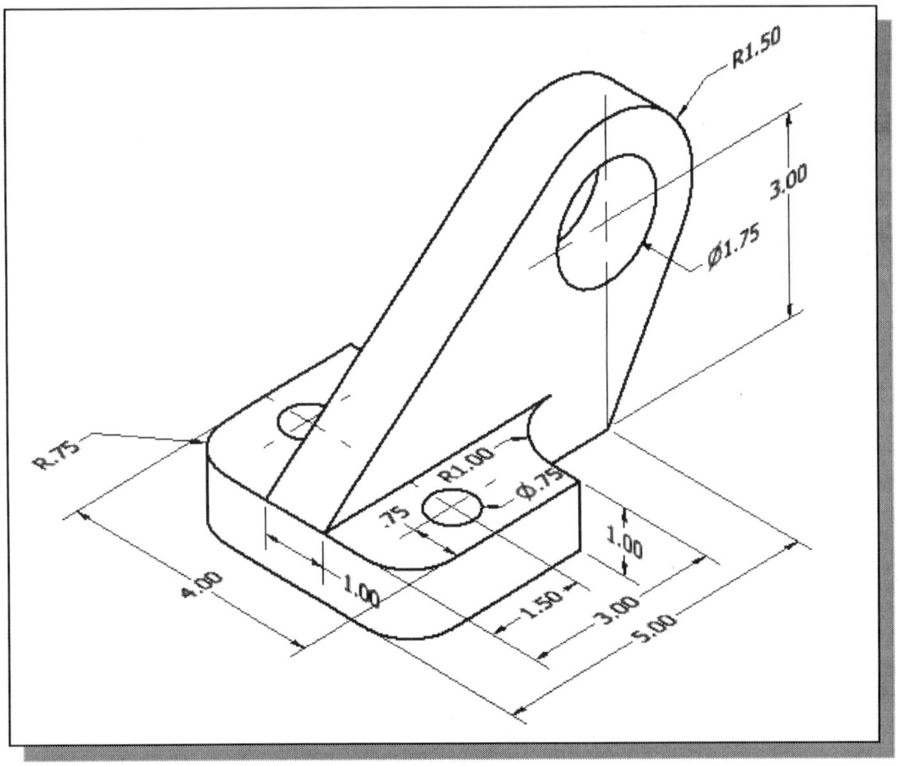

3. Bearing Base

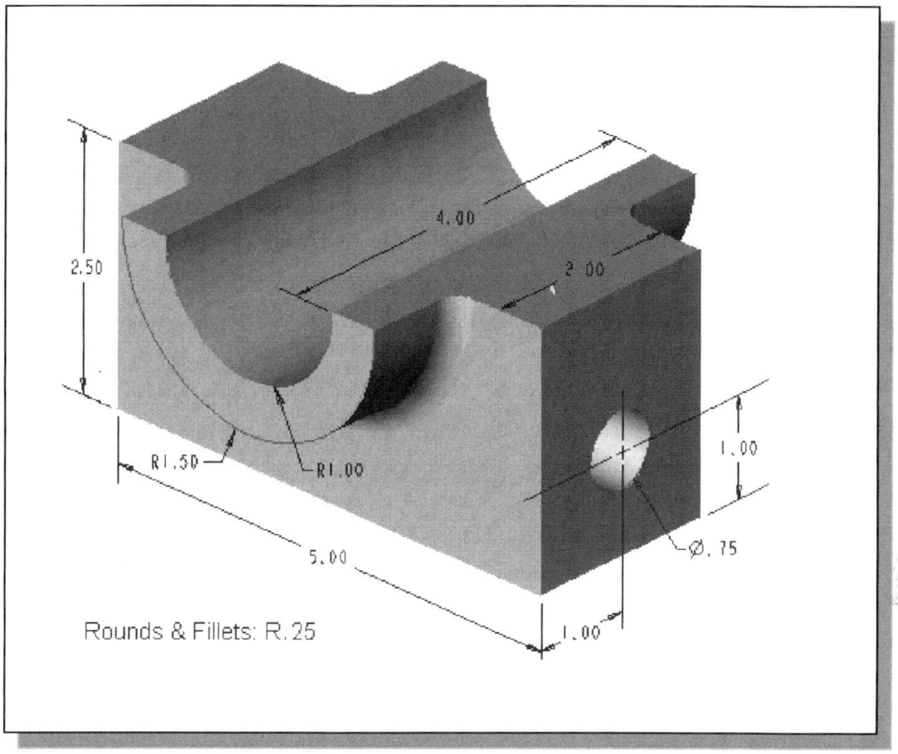

4. **Shaft Support** (Dimensions are in Millimeters. Note the two R40 arcs at the base share the same center.)

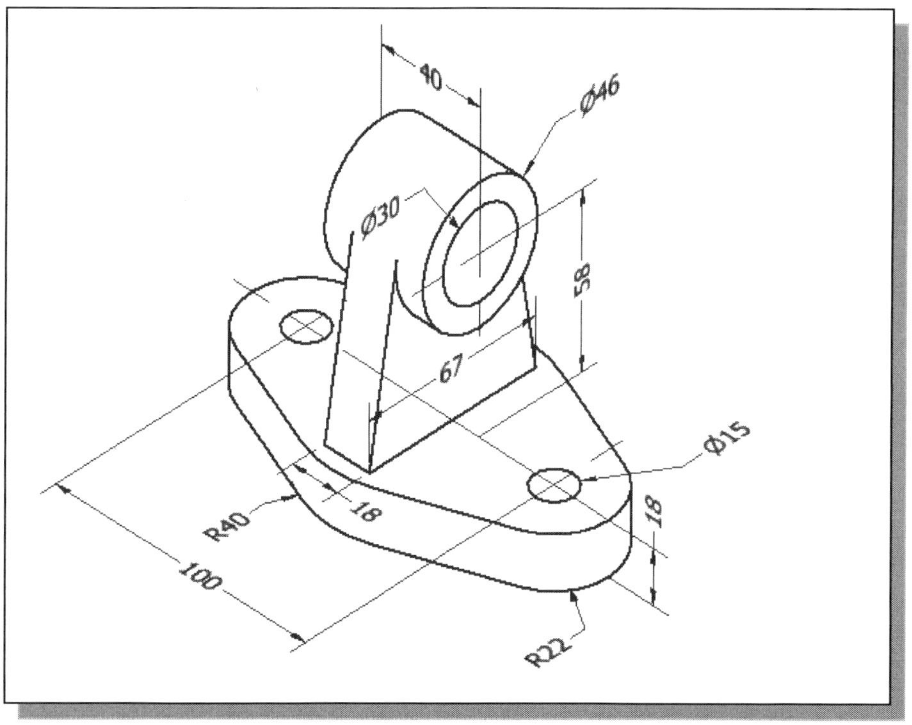

5. Connecting Rod

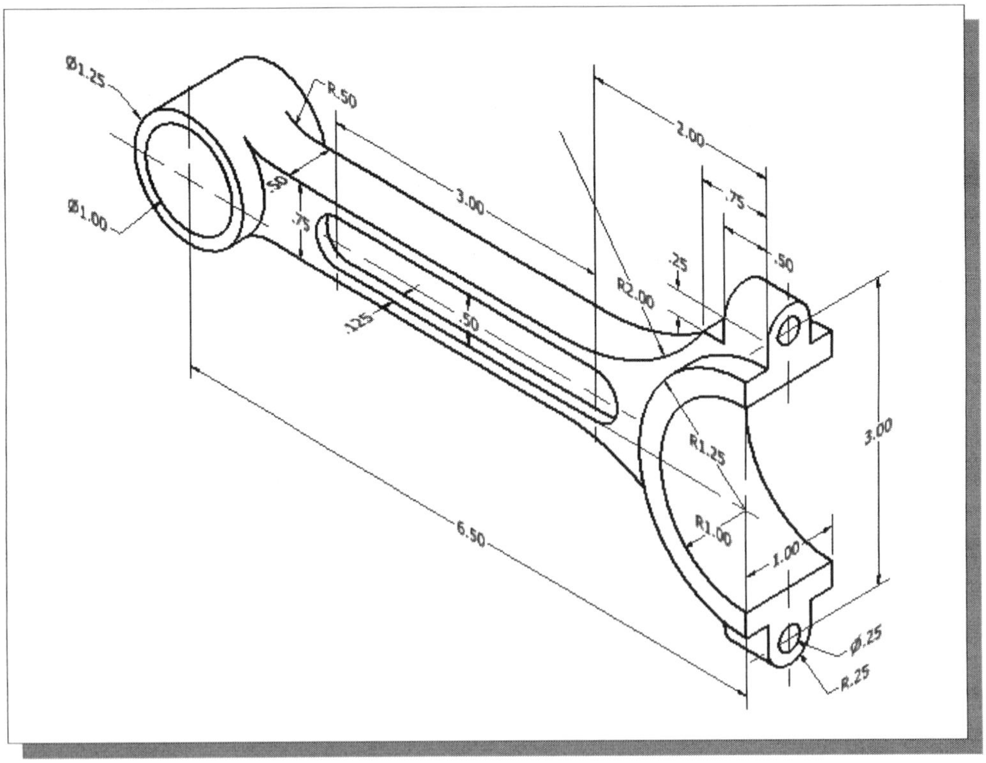

6. Tube Hanger

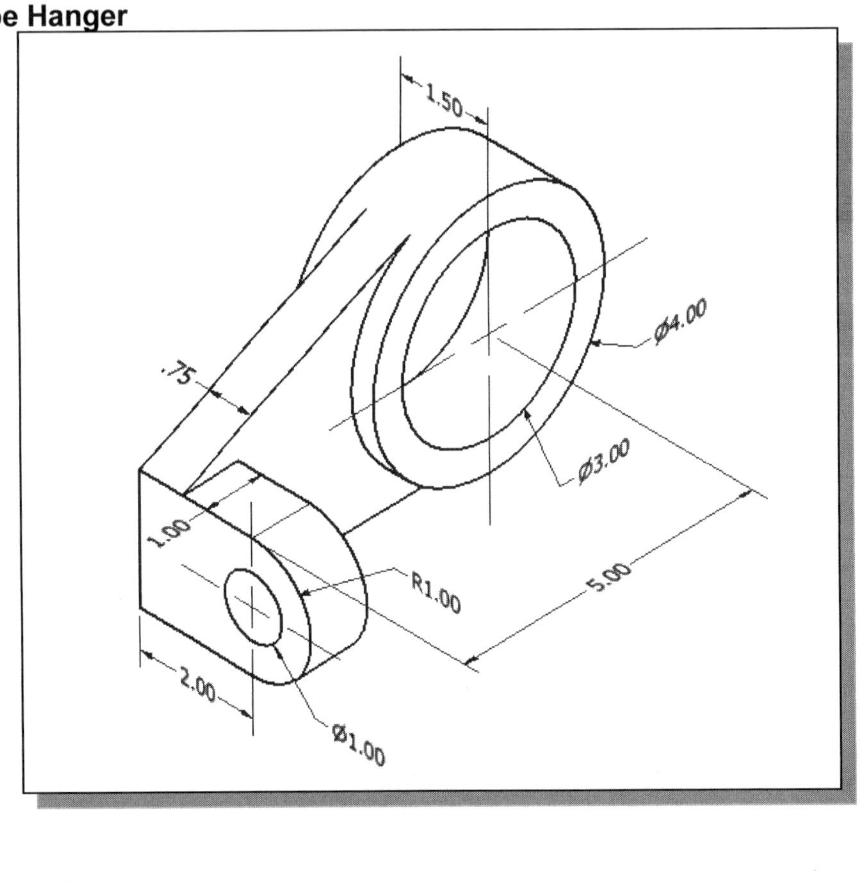

7. Tube Spacer

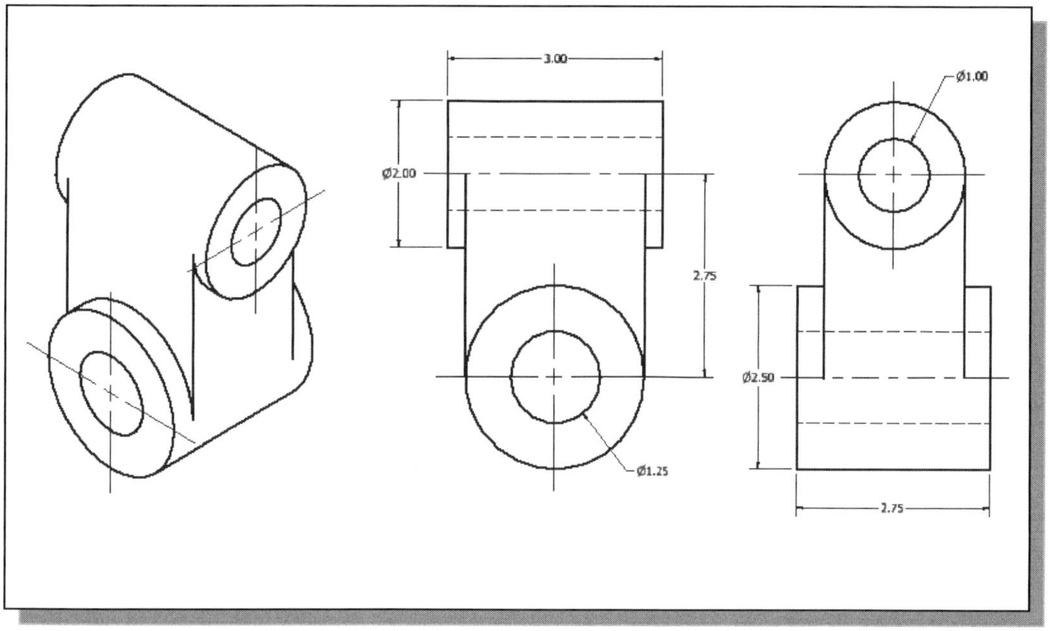

8. Slider (Dimensions are in Millimeters.)

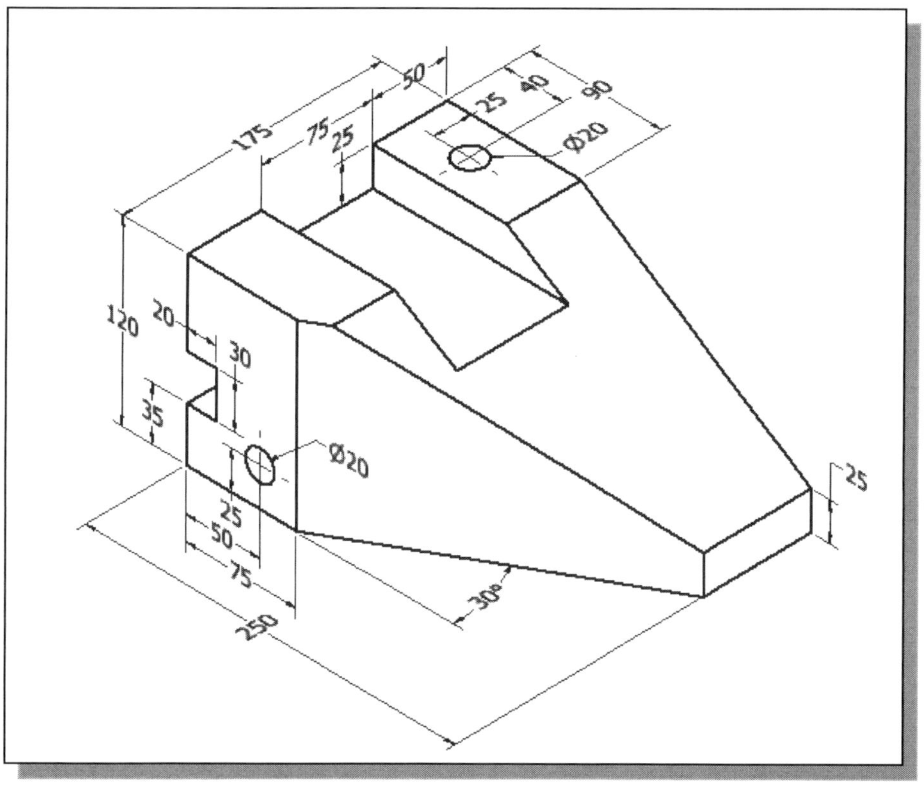

9. Rod Holder

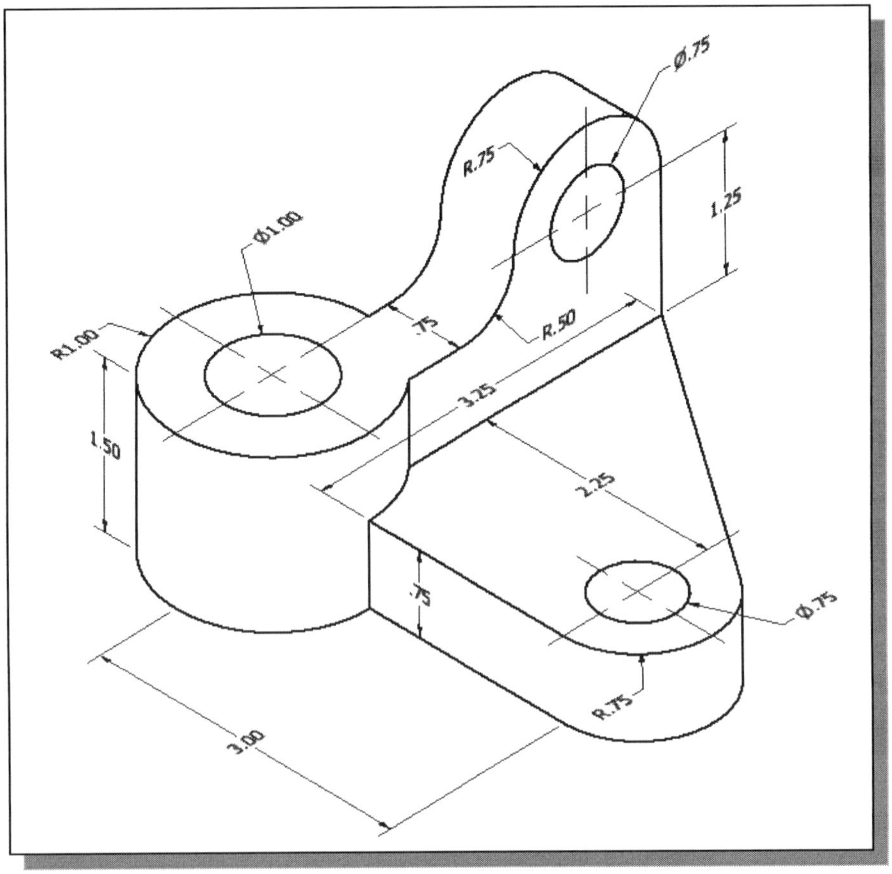

Chapter 5
Pictorials and Sketching

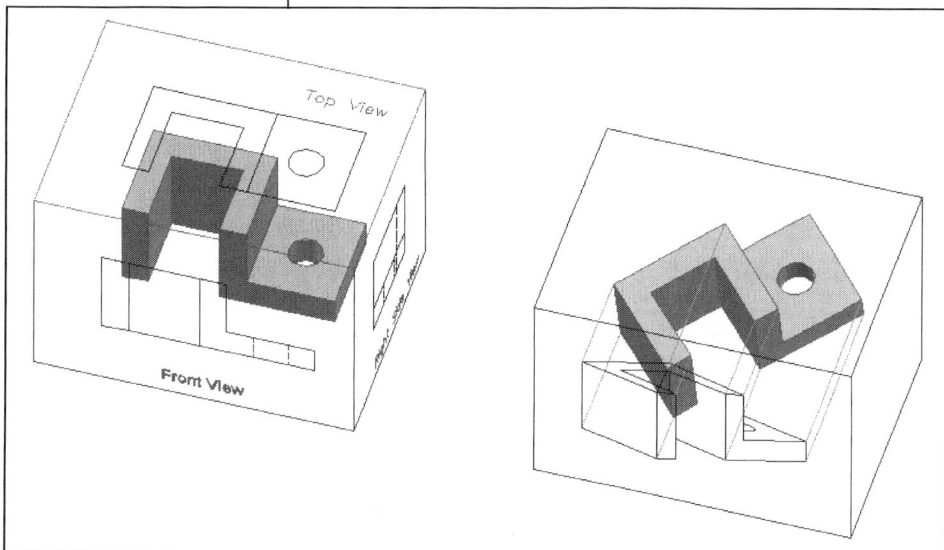

Learning Objectives

- Understand the Importance of Freehand Sketching
- Understand the Terminology Used in Pictorial Drawings
- Understand the Basics of the Following Projection Methods: Axonometric, Oblique and Perspective
- Be Able to Create Freehand 3D Pictorials

Engineering Drawings, Pictorials and Sketching

One of the best ways to communicate one's ideas is through the use of a picture or a drawing. This is especially true for engineers and designers. Without the ability to communicate well, engineers and designers will not be able to function in a team environment and therefore will have only limited value in the profession.

For many centuries, artists and engineers used drawings to express their ideas and inventions. The two figures below are drawings by Leonardo da Vinci (1452-1519) illustrating some of his engineering inventions.

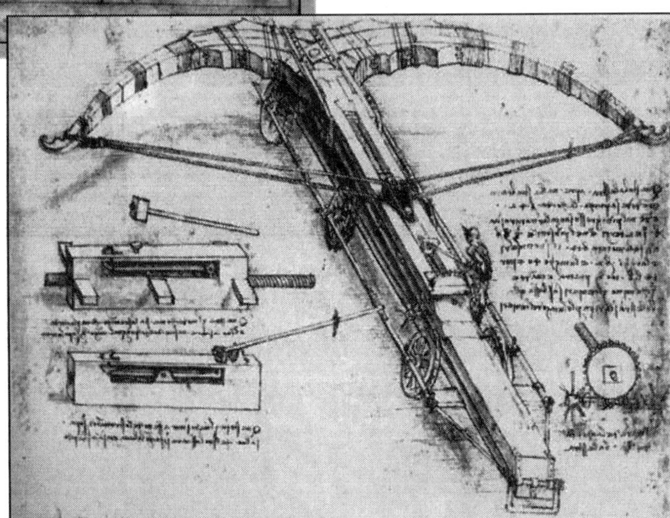

Engineering design is a process to create and transform ideas and concepts into a product definition that meets the desired objective. The engineering design process typically involves three stages: (1) Ideation/conceptual design stage: this is the beginning of an engineering design process, where basic ideas and concepts take shape. (2) Design development stage: the basic ideas are elaborated and further developed. During this stage, prototypes and testing are commonly used to ensure the developed design meets the desired objective. (3) Refine and finalize design stage: This stage of the design process is the last stage of the design process, where the finer details of the design are further refined. Detailed information of the finalized design is documented to assure the design is ready for production.

Two types of drawings are generally associated with the three stages of the engineering process: (1) Freehand Sketches and (2) Detailed Engineering Drawings.

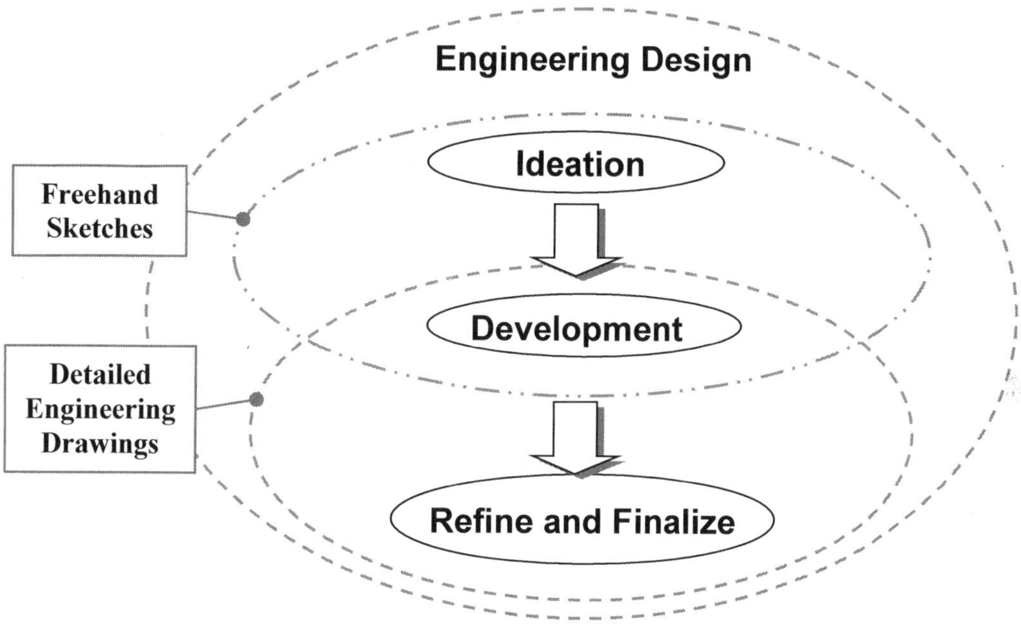

Freehand sketches are generally used in the beginning stages of a design process: (1) to quickly record designer's ideas and help formulate different possibilities, (2) to communicate the designer's basic ideas with others and (3) to develop and elaborate further the designer's ideas/concepts.

During the initial design stage, an engineer will generally picture the ideas in his/her head as three-dimensional images. The ability to think visually, specifically three-dimensional visualization, is one of the most essential skills for an engineer/designer. And freehand sketching is considered one of the most powerful methods to help develop visualization skills.

Detailed engineering drawings are generally created during the second and third stages of a design process. The detailed engineering drawings are used to help refine and finalize the design and also to document the finalized design for production. Engineering drawings typically require the use of drawing instruments, from compasses to computers, to bring precision to the drawings.

Freehand Sketches and Detailed Engineering Drawings are essential communication tools for engineers. By using the established conventions, such as perspective and isometric drawings, engineers/designers are able to quickly convey their design ideas to others. The ability to sketch ideas is absolutely essential to engineers.

The ability to sketch is helpful, not just to communicate with others, but also to work out details in ideas and to identify any potential problems. Freehand sketching requires only simple tools, a pencil and a piece of paper, and can be accomplished almost anywhere and anytime. Creating freehand sketches does not require any artistic ability. Detailed engineering drawing is employed only for those ideas deserving a permanent record.

Freehand sketches and engineering drawings are generally composed of similar information, but there is a tradeoff between time required to generate a sketch/drawing versus the level of design detail and accuracy. In industry, freehand sketching is used to quickly document rough ideas and identify general needs for improvement in a team environment.

Besides the 2D views, described in the previous chapter, there are three main divisions commonly used in freehand engineering sketches and detailed engineering drawings: (1) **Axonometric**, with its divisions into **isometric, dimetric** and **trimetric**; (2) **Oblique**; and (3) **Perspective**.

1. **Axonometric projection**: The word *Axonometric* means "to measure along axes." Axonometric projection is a special *orthographic projection* technique used to generate ***pictorials***. **Pictorials** show a 2D image of an object as viewed from a direction that reveals three directions of space. In the figure below, the adjuster model is rotated so that a *pictorial* is generated using *orthographic projection* (projection lines perpendicular to the projection plane) as described in Chapter 4. There are three types of axonometric projections: isometric projection, dimetric projection, and trimetric projection. Typically in an axonometric drawing, one axis is drawn vertically.

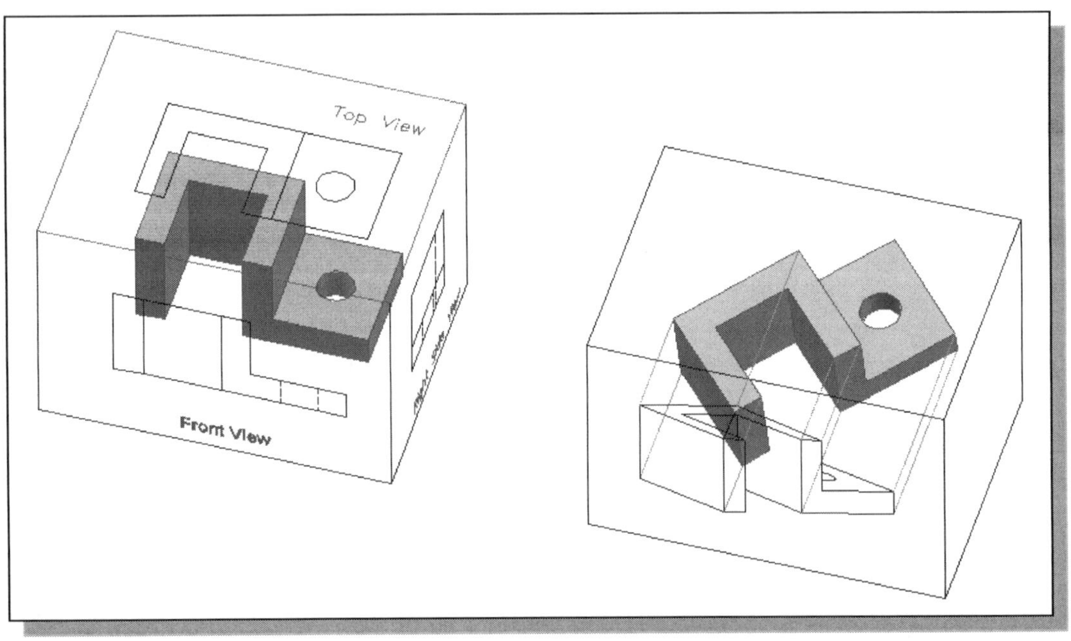

In **isometric projections**, the direction of viewing is such that the three axes of space appear equally foreshortened, and therefore the angles between the axes are equal. In **dimetric projections**, the directions of viewing are such that two of the three axes of space appear equally foreshortened. In **trimetric projections**, the direction of viewing is such that the three axes of space appear unequally foreshortened.

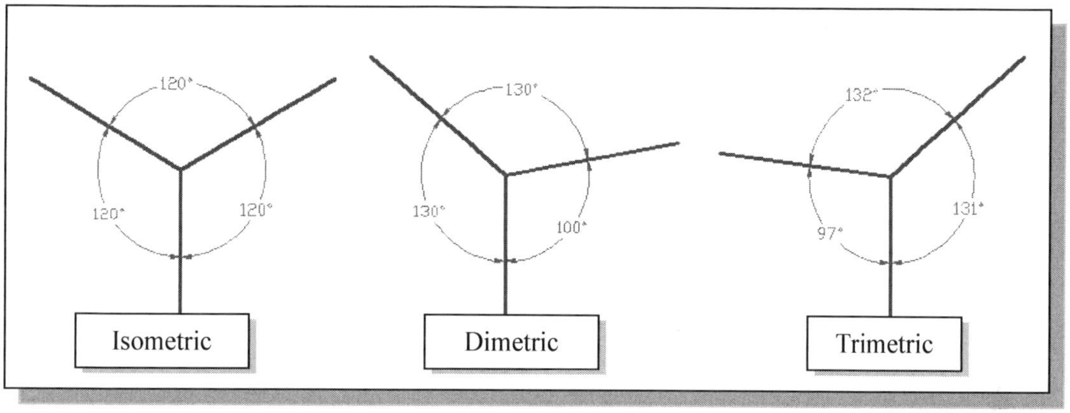

Isometric projection is perhaps the most widely used for pictorials in engineering graphics, mainly because isometric views are the most convenient to draw. Note that the different projection options described here are not particularly critical in freehand sketching as the emphasis is generally placed on the proportions of the design, not the precision measurements. The general procedure to constructing isometric views is illustrated in the following sections.

2. **Oblique Projection** represents a simple technique of keeping the front face of an object parallel to the projection plane and still reveals three directions of space. An **orthographic projection** is a parallel projection in which the projection lines are perpendicular to the plane of projection. An **oblique projection** is one in which the projection lines are other than perpendicular to the plane of projection.

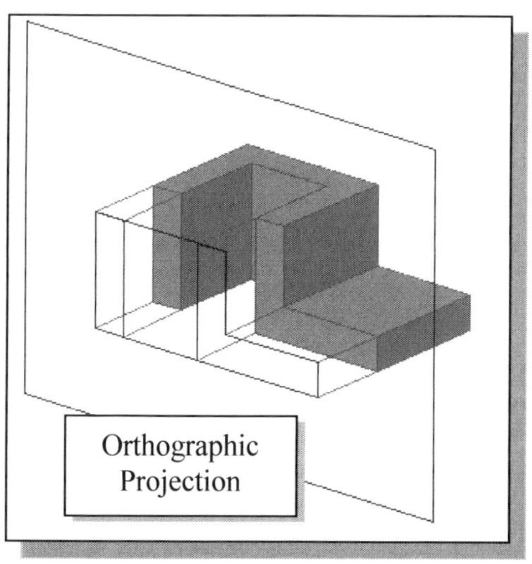

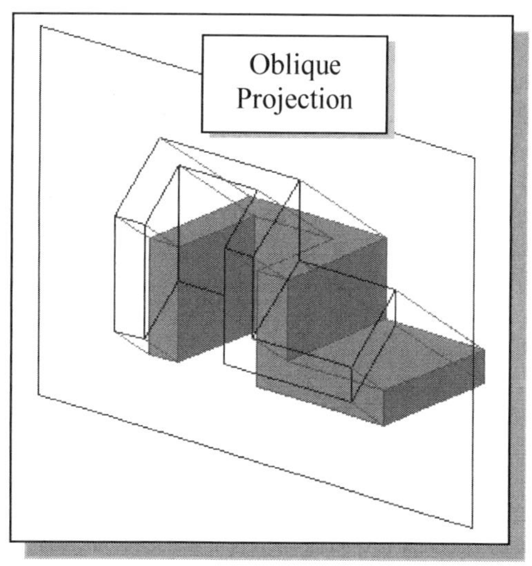

In an oblique drawing, geometry that is parallel to the frontal plane of projection is drawn true size and shape. This is the main advantage of the oblique drawing over the axonometric drawings. The three axes of the oblique sketch are drawn horizontal, vertical, and the third axis can be at any convenient angle (typically between 30 and 60 degrees). The proportional scale along the 3rd axis is typically a scale anywhere between ½ and 1. If the scale is ½, then it is a **Cabinet** oblique. If the scale is 1, then it is a **Cavalier** oblique.

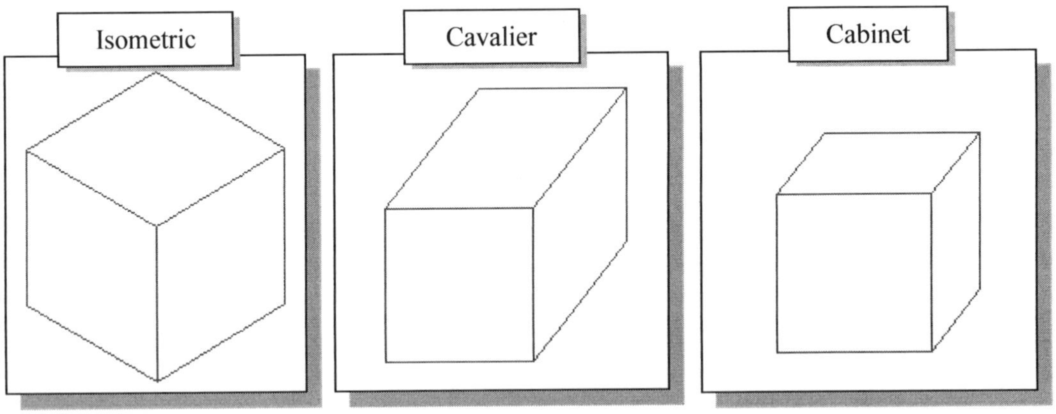

3. **Perspective Projection** adds realism to the three-dimensional pictorial representation; a perspective drawing represents an object as it appears to an observer: objects that are closer to the observer will appear larger to the observer. The key to the perspective projection is that parallel edges converge to a single point, known as the **vanishing point**. If there is just one vanishing point, then it is called a one-point perspective. If two sets of parallel edge lines converge to their respective vanishing points, then it is called a two-point perspective. There is also the case of a three-point perspective in which all three sets of parallel lines converge to their respective vanishing points.

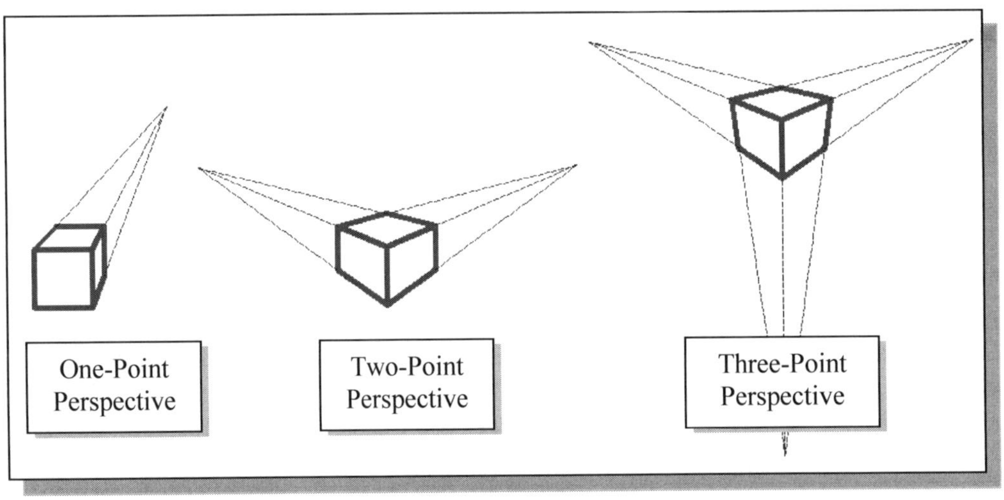

- Although there are specific techniques available to create precise pictorials with known dimensions, in the following sections, the basic concepts and procedures relating to freehand sketching are illustrated.

Isometric Sketching

Isometric drawings are generally done with one axis aligned to the vertical direction. A **regular isometric** is when the viewpoint is looking down on the top of the object, and a **reversed isometric** is when the viewpoint is looking up on the bottom of the object.

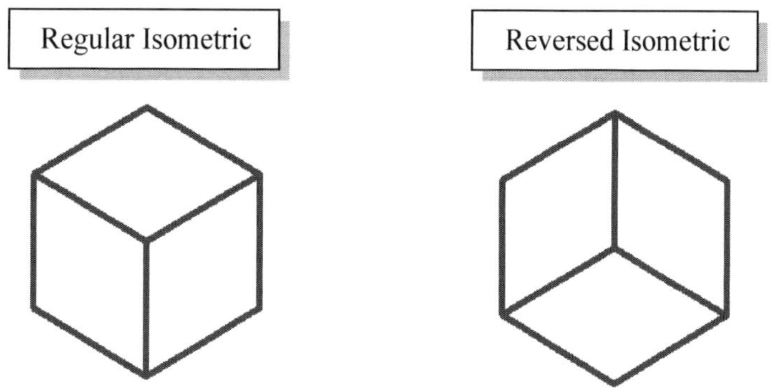

Two commonly used approaches in creating isometric sketches are (1) the **enclosing box** method and (2) the **adjacent surface** method. The enclosing box method begins with the construction of an isometric box showing the overall size of the object. The visible portions of the individual 2D-views are then constructed on the corresponding sides of the box. Adjustments of the locations of surfaces are then made, by moving the edges, to complete the isometric sketch.

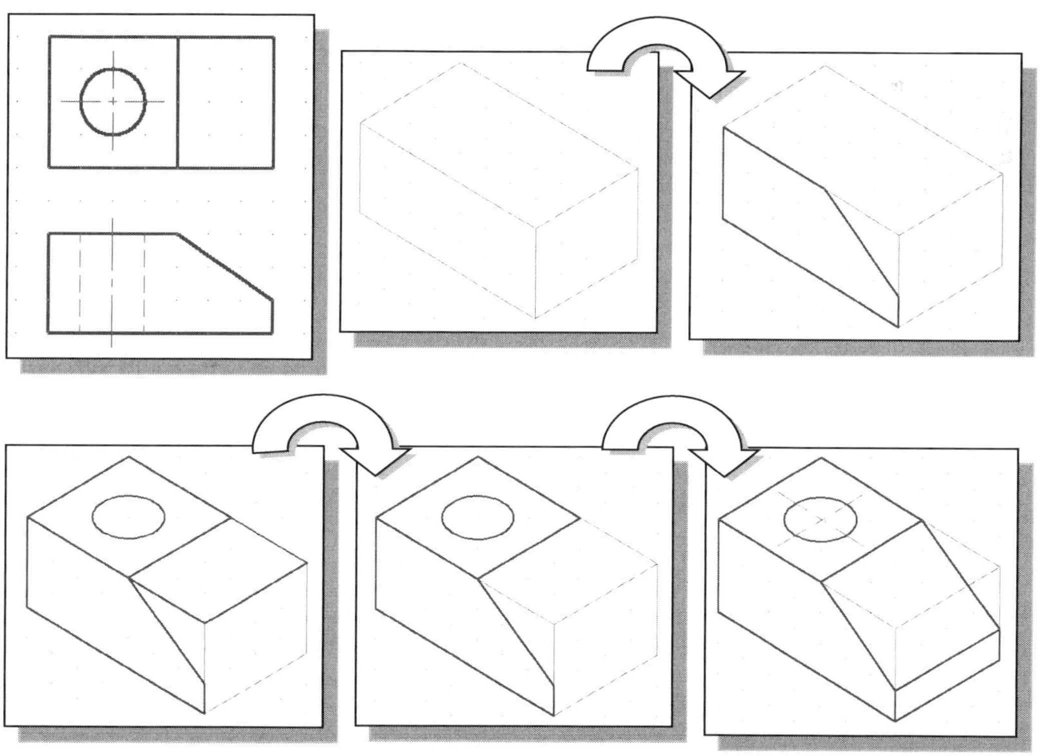

The adjacent surface method begins with one side of the isometric drawing, again with the visible portion of the corresponding 2D-view. The isometric sketch is completed by identifying and adding the adjacent surfaces.

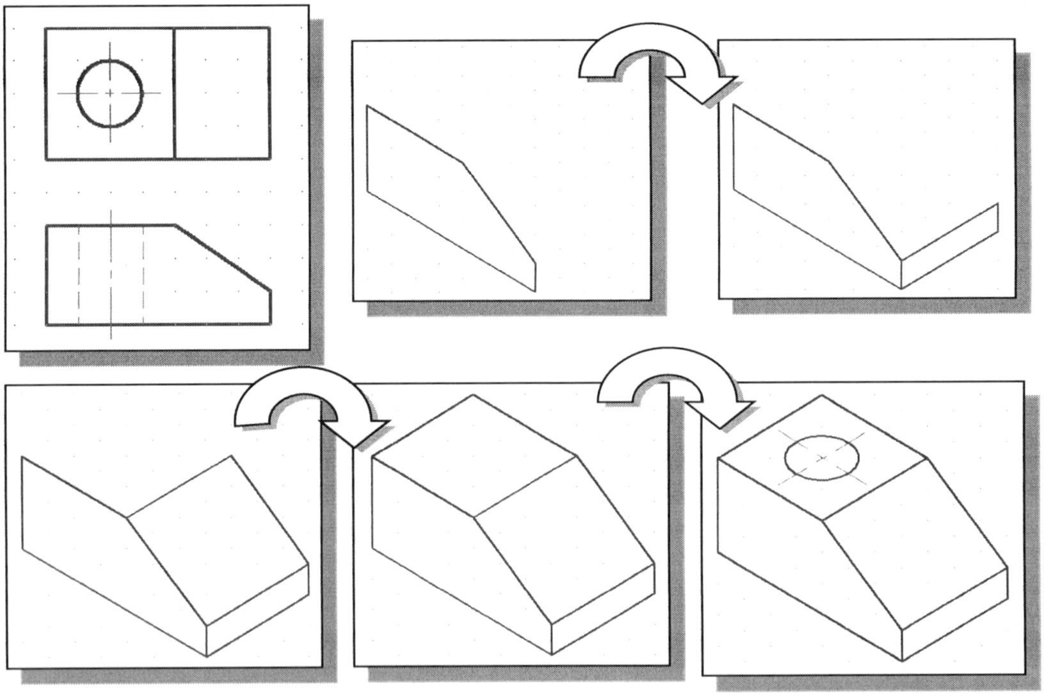

In an isometric drawing, cylindrical or circular shapes appear as ellipses. It can be confusing in drawing the ellipses in an isometric view; one simple rule to remember is the **major axis** of the ellipse is always **perpendicular** to the **center axis** of the cylinder as shown in the figures below.

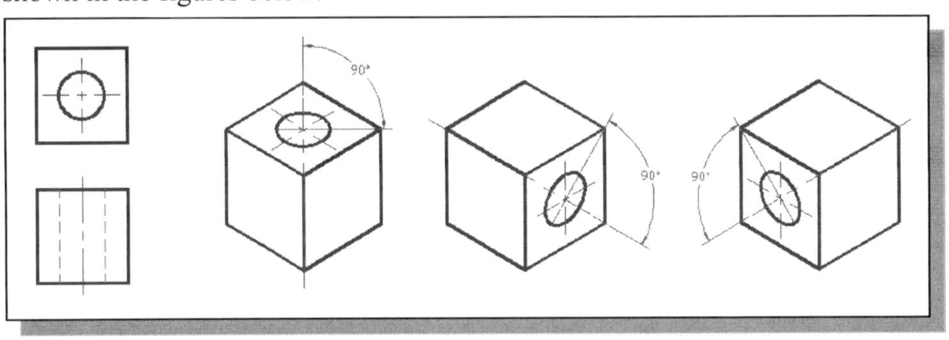

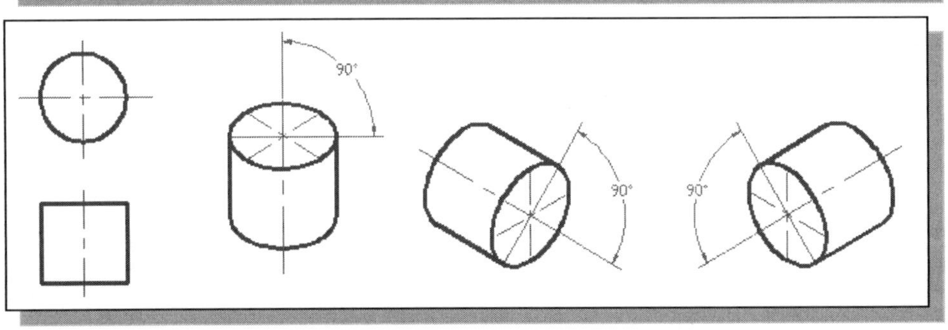

Chapter 5 - Isometric Sketching Exercise 1:

Given the Orthographic Top view and Front view, create the isometric view.

(Note that 3D Models of chapter examples and exercises are available at http://www.sdcpublications.com/downloads/978-1-63057-828-2.)

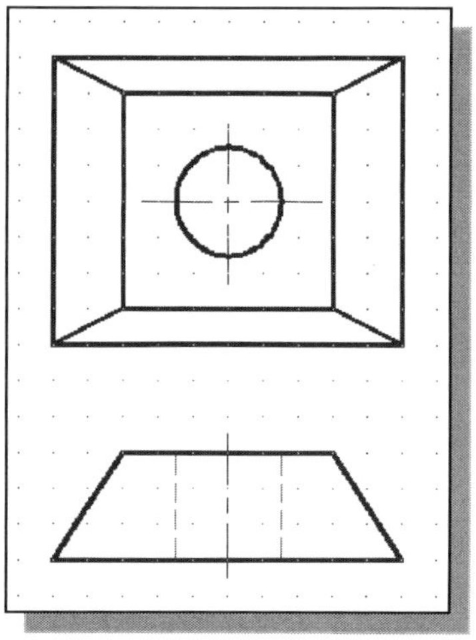

Name: ______________________ Date: ______________

Chapter 5 - Isometric Sketching Exercise 2:

Given the Orthographic Top view and Front view, create the isometric view.

(Note that 3D Models of chapter examples and exercises are available at http://www.sdcpublications.com/downloads/978-1-63057-828-2.)

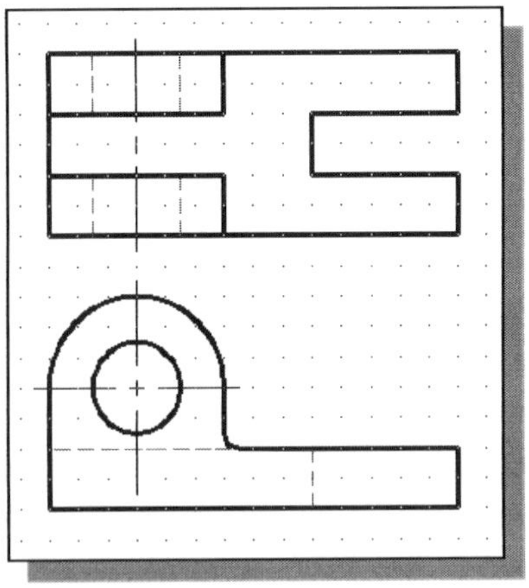

Name: ______________________ Date: ______________

Chapter 5 - Isometric Sketching Exercise 3:

Given the Orthographic Top view and Front view, create the isometric view.

(Note that 3D Models of chapter examples and exercises are available at http://www.sdcpublications.com/downloads/978-1-63057-828-2.)

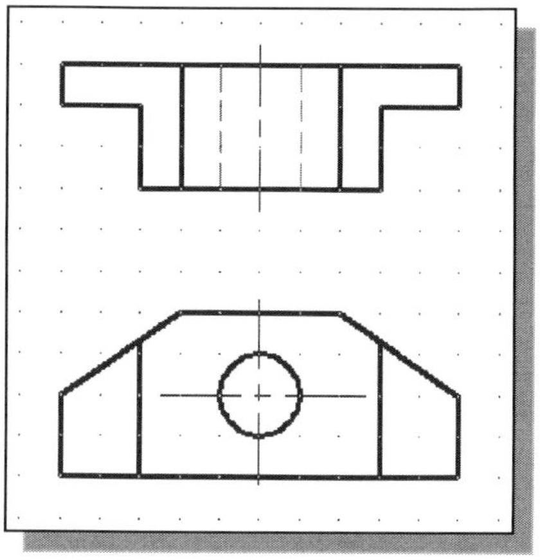

Name: ______________________________ Date: __________________

Chapter 5 - Isometric Sketching Exercise 4:

Given the Orthographic Top view and Front view, create the isometric view.

(Note that 3D Models of chapter examples and exercises are available at http://www.sdcpublications.com/downloads/978-1-63057-828-2.)

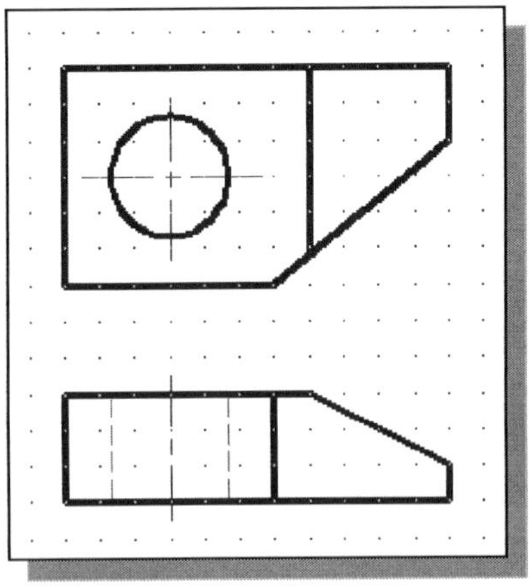

Name: ______________________ Date: ______________

Chapter 5 - Isometric Sketching Exercise 5:

Given the Orthographic Top view, Front view, and Side view create the isometric view.

(Note that 3D Models of chapter examples and exercises are available at http://www.sdcpublications.com/downloads/978-1-63057-828-2.)

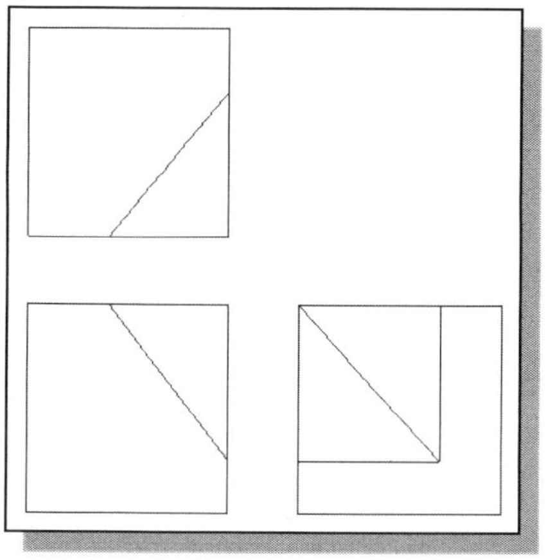

Name: ______________________ Date: ______________

Chapter 5 - Isometric Sketching Exercise 6:

Given the Orthographic Top view, Front view, and Side view create the isometric view.

(Note that 3D Models of chapter examples and exercises are available at http://www.sdcpublications.com/downloads/978-1-63057-828-2.)

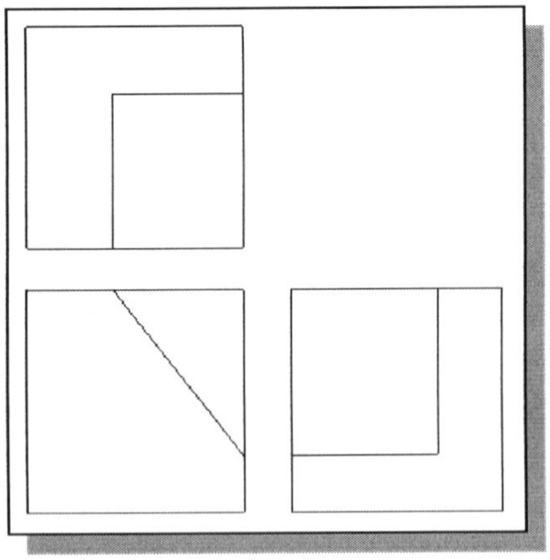

Name: ______________________________ Date: ____________________

Chapter 5 - Isometric Sketching Exercise 7:

Given the Orthographic Top view, Front view, and Side view create the isometric view.

(Note that 3D Models of chapter examples and exercises are available at http://www.sdcpublications.com/downloads/978-1-63057-828-2.)

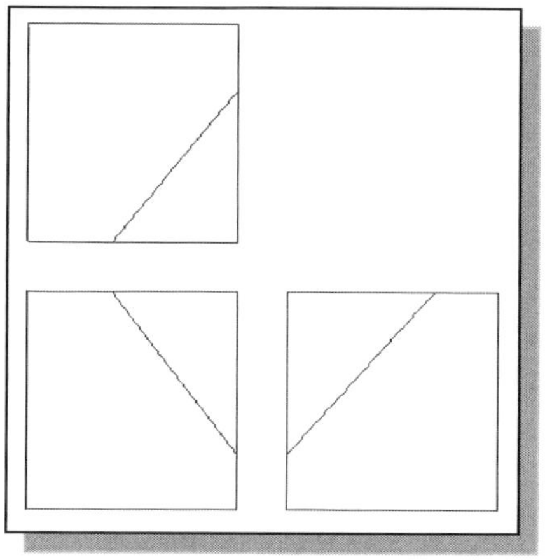

Name: ______________________________ Date: ____________________

Chapter 5 - Isometric Sketching Exercise 8:

Given the Orthographic Top view, Front view, and Side view create the isometric view.

(Note that 3D Models of chapter examples and exercises are available at http://www.sdcpublications.com/downloads/978-1-63057-828-2.)

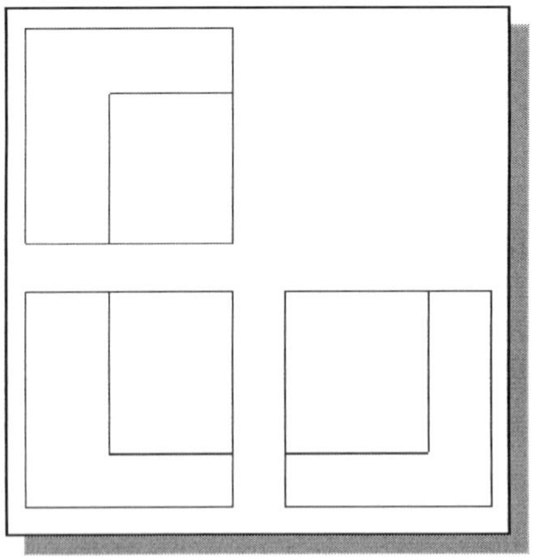

Name: ______________________ Date: ______________

Chapter 5 - Isometric Sketching Exercise 9:

Given the Orthographic Top view, Front view, and Side view create the isometric view.

(Note that 3D Models of chapter examples and exercises are available at http://www.sdcpublications.com/downloads/978-1-63057-828-2.)

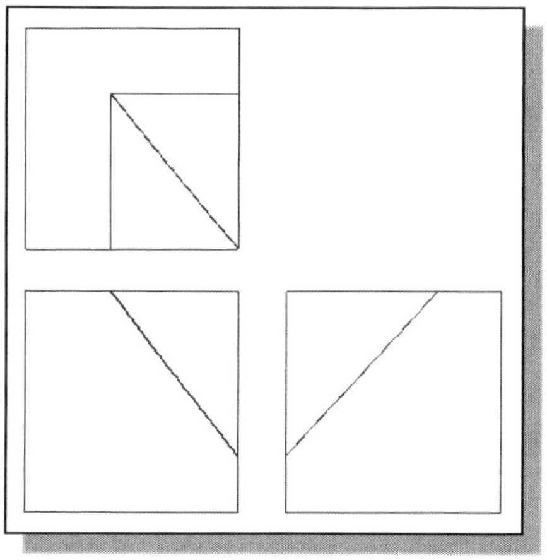

Name: ______________________ Date: ______________

Chapter 5 - Isometric Sketching Exercise 10:

Given the Orthographic Top view, Front view, and Side view create the isometric view.

(Note that 3D Models of chapter examples and exercises are available at http://www.sdcpublications.com/downloads/978-1-63057-828-2.)

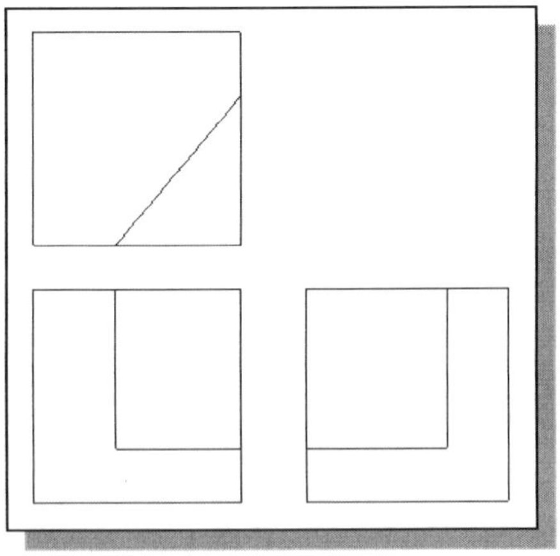

Name: ______________________ Date: ______________

Oblique Sketching

Keeping the geometry that is parallel to the frontal plane true size and shape is the main advantage of the oblique drawing over the axonometric drawings. Unlike isometric drawings, circular shapes that are paralleled to the frontal view will remain as circles in oblique drawings. Generally speaking, an oblique drawing can be created very quickly by using a 2D view as the starting point. For designs with most of the circular shapes in one direction, an oblique sketch is the ideal choice over the other pictorial methods.

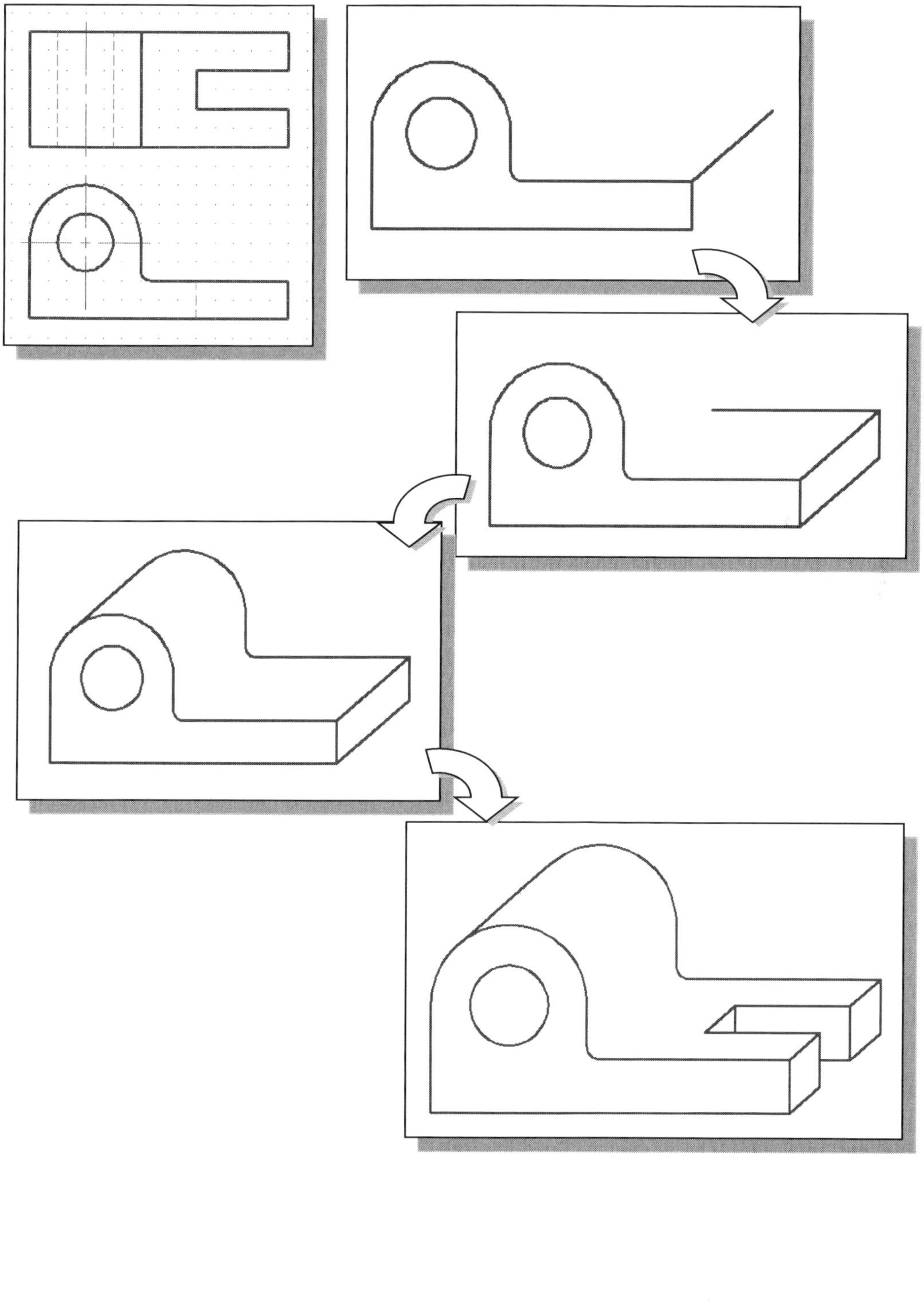

Chapter 5 - Oblique Sketching Exercise 1:

Given the Orthographic Top view and Front view, create the oblique view.

(Note that 3D Models of chapter examples and exercises are available at http://www.sdcpublications.com/downloads/978-1-63057-828-2.)

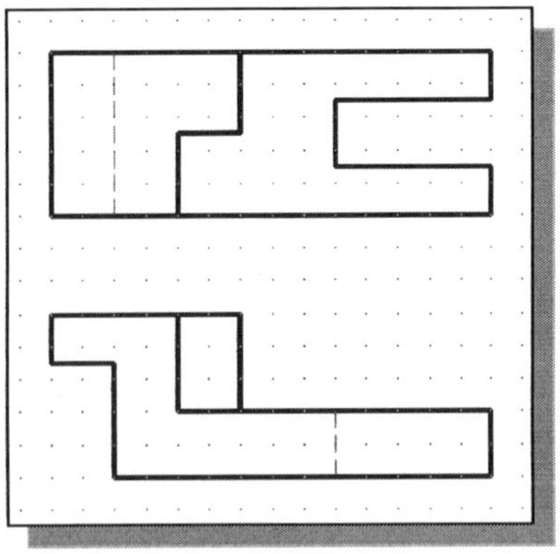

Name: ______________________ Date: ________________

Chapter 5 - Oblique Sketching Exercise 2:

Given the Orthographic Top view and Front view, create the oblique view.

(Note that 3D Models of chapter examples and exercises are available at http://www.sdcpublications.com/downloads/978-1-63057-828-2.)

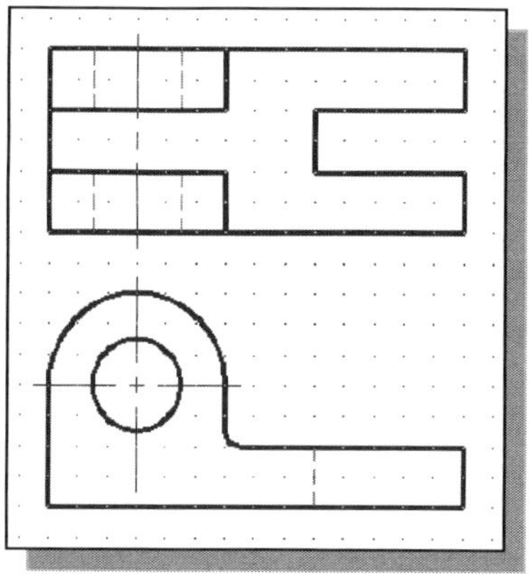

Name: ____________________ Date: ____________________

Chapter 5 - Oblique Sketching Exercise 3:

Given the Orthographic Top view and Front view, create the oblique view.

(Note that 3D Models of chapter examples and exercises are available at http://www.sdcpublications.com/downloads/978-1-63057-828-2.)

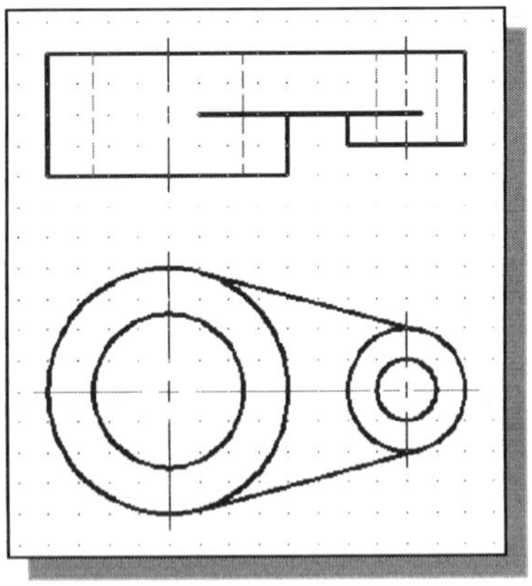

Name: ______________________ Date: ______________

Chapter 5 - Oblique Sketching Exercise 4:

Given the Orthographic Top view and Front view, create the oblique view.

(Note that 3D Models of chapter examples and exercises are available at http://www.sdcpublications.com/downloads/978-1-63057-828-2.)

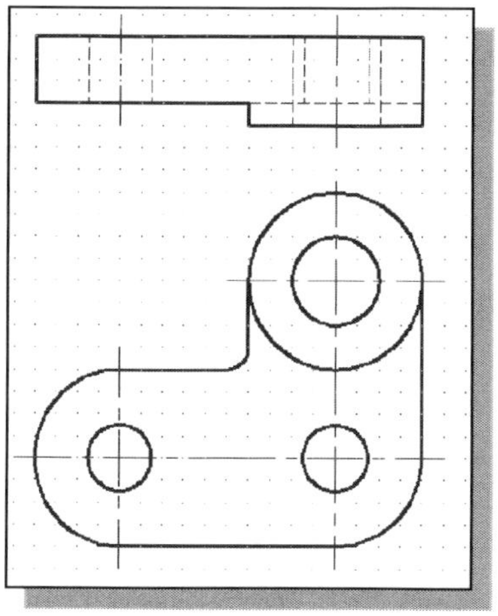

Name: ______________________ Date: ______________

Chapter 5 - Oblique Sketching Exercise 5:

Given the Orthographic Top view and Front view, create the oblique view.

(Note that 3D Models of chapter examples and exercises are available at http://www.sdcpublications.com/downloads/978-1-63057-828-2.)

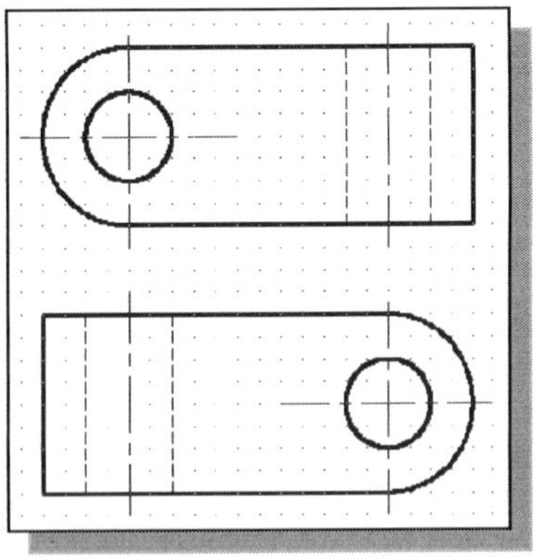

Name: ______________________ Date: ______________

Chapter 5 - Oblique Sketching Exercise 6:

Given the Orthographic Top view and Front view, create the oblique view.

(Note that 3D Models of chapter examples and exercises are available at http://www.sdcpublications.com/downloads/978-1-63057-828-2.)

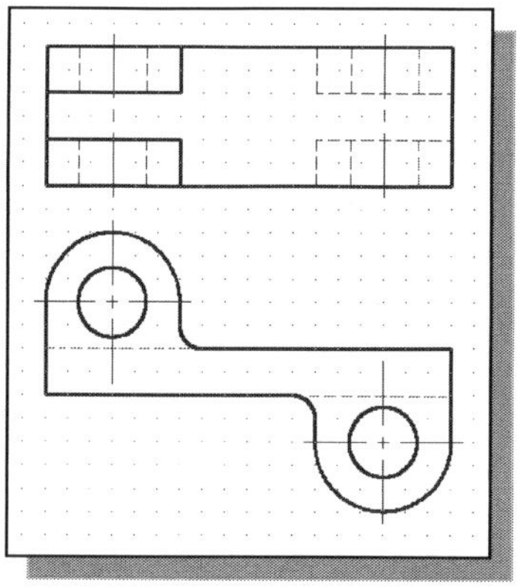

Name: ______________________ Date: ______________

Perspective Sketching

A perspective drawing represents an object as it appears to an observer; objects that are closer to the observer will appear larger to the observer. The key to the perspective projection is that parallel edges converge to a single point, known as the **vanishing point**. The vanishing point represents the position where projection lines converge.

The selection of the locations of the vanishing points, which is the first step in creating a perspective sketch, will affect the looks of the resulting images.

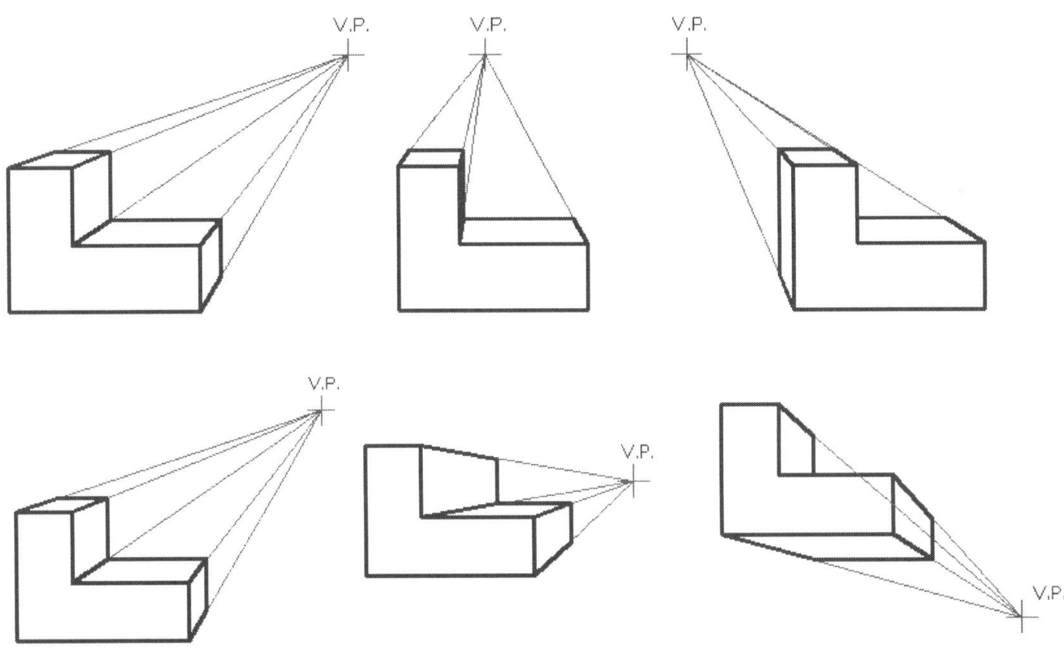

One-point Perspective

One-point perspective is commonly used because of its simplicity. The first step in creating a one-point perspective is to sketch the front face of the object just as in oblique sketching, followed by selecting the position for the vanishing point. For Mechanical designs, the vanishing point is usually placed above and to the right of the picture. The use of construction lines can be helpful in locating the edges of the object and to complete the sketch.

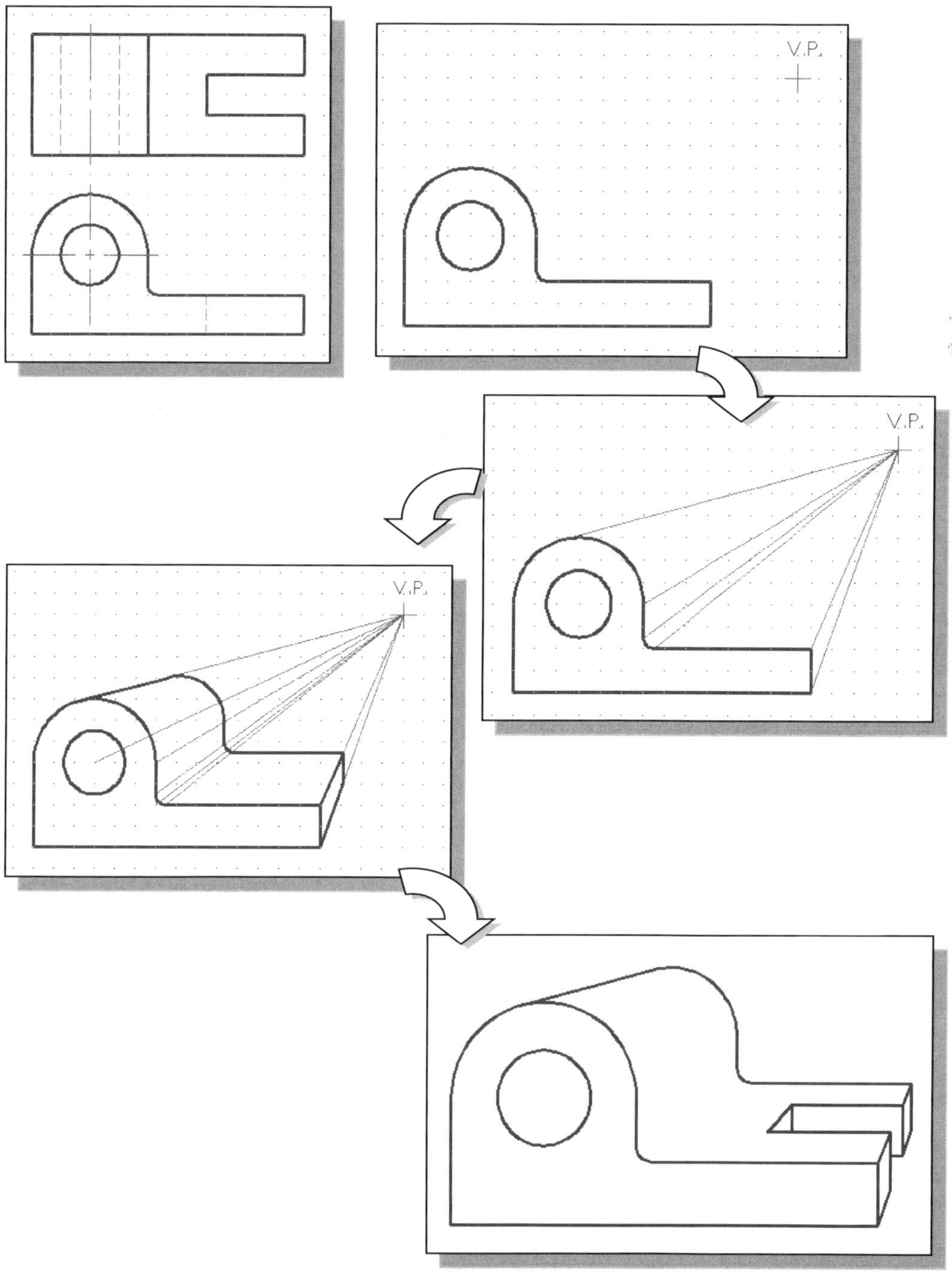

Two-point Perspective

Two-point perspective is perhaps the most popular of all perspective methods. The use of the two vanishing points gives very true to life images. The first step in creating a two-point perspective is to select the locations for the two vanishing points, followed by sketching an enclosing box to show the outline of the object. The use of construction lines can be very helpful in locating the edges of the object and to complete the sketch.

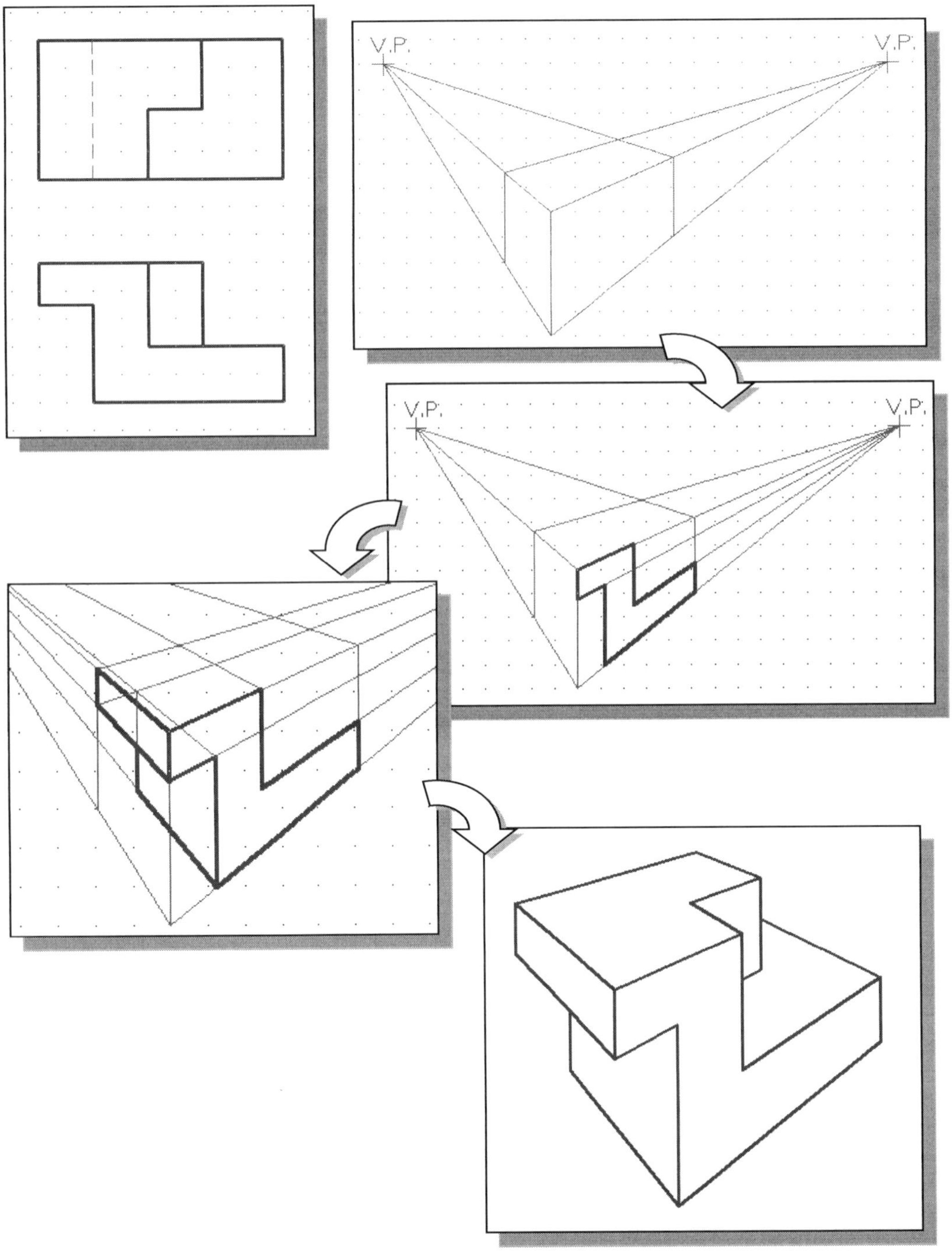

Chapter 5 - Perspective Sketching Exercise 1:

Given the Orthographic Top view and Front view, create one-point or two-point perspective views.

(Note that 3D Models of chapter examples and exercises are available at http://www.sdcpublications.com/downloads/978-1-63057-828-2.)

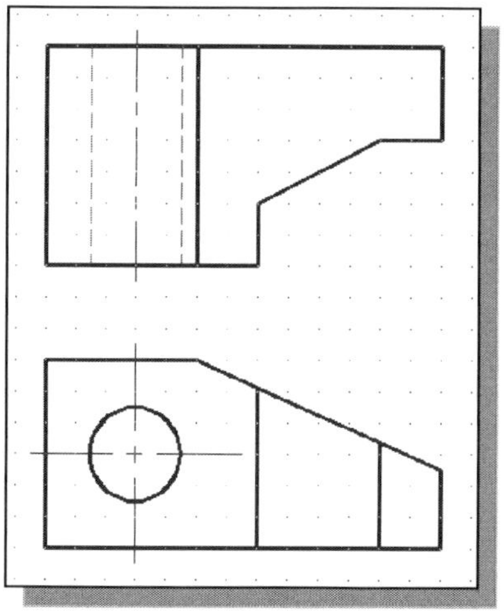

Name: ______________________ Date: ______________

Chapter 5 - Perspective Sketching Exercise 2:

Given the Orthographic Top view and Front view, create one-point or two-point perspective views.

(Note that 3D Models of chapter examples and exercises are available at http://www.sdcpublications.com/downloads/978-1-63057-828-2.)

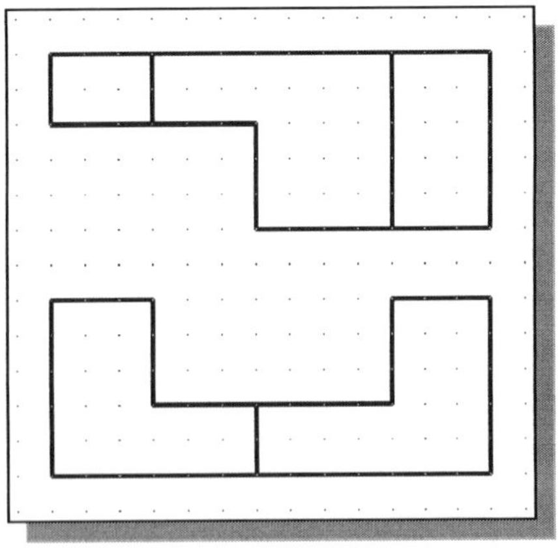

Name: ______________________ Date: ______________

Chapter 5 - Perspective Sketching Exercise 3:

Given the Orthographic Top view and Front view, create one-point or two-point perspective views.
(Note that 3D Models of chapter examples and exercises are available at http://www.sdcpublications.com/downloads/978-1-63057-828-2.)

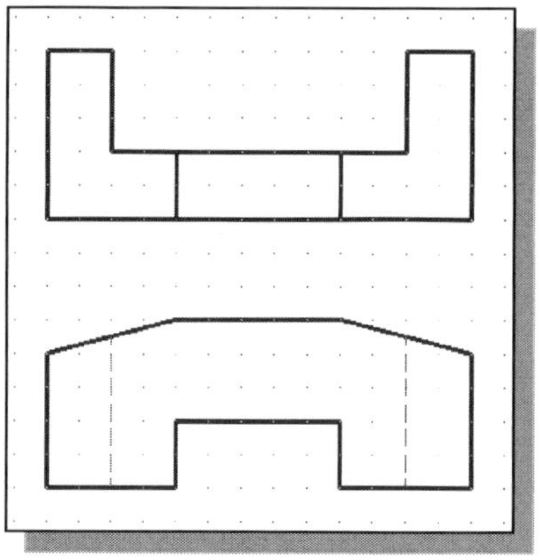

Name: ______________________ Date: ______________

Chapter 5 - Perspective Sketching Exercise 4:

Given the Orthographic Top view and Front view, create one-point or two-point perspective views.

(Note that 3D Models of chapter examples and exercises are available at http://www.sdcpublications.com/downloads/978-1-63057-828-2.)

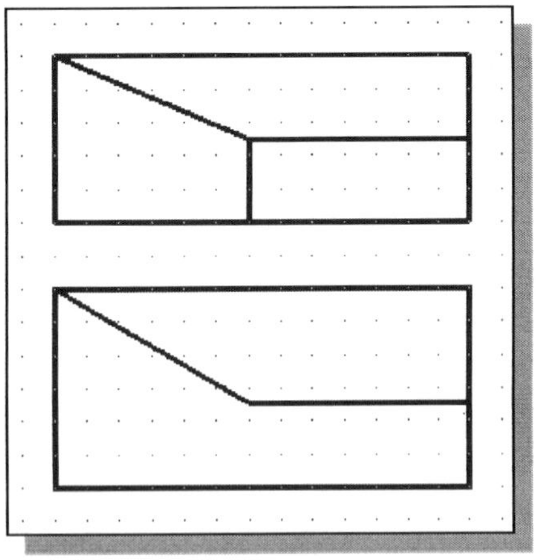

Name: ______________________ Date: ______________

Chapter 5 - Perspective Sketching Exercise 5:

Given the Orthographic Top view and Front view, create one-point or two-point perspective views.

(Note that 3D Models of chapter examples and exercises are available at http://www.sdcpublications.com/downloads/978-1-63057-828-2.)

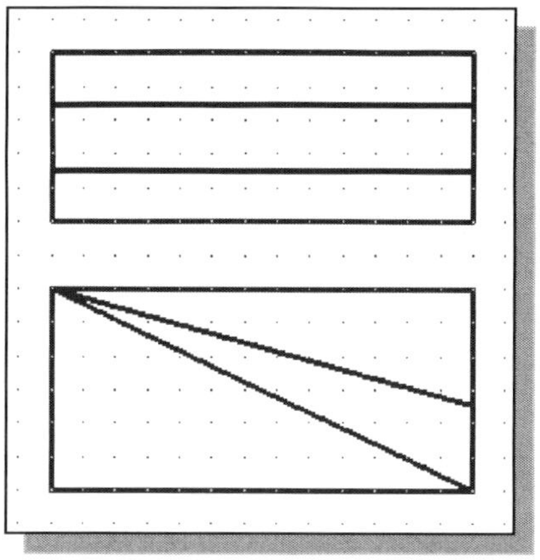

Name: ______________________ Date: ______________

Chapter 5 - Perspective Sketching Exercise 6:

Given the Orthographic Top view and Front view, create one-point or two-point perspective views.

(Note that 3D Models of chapter examples and exercises are available at http://www.sdcpublications.com/downloads/978-1-63057-828-2.)

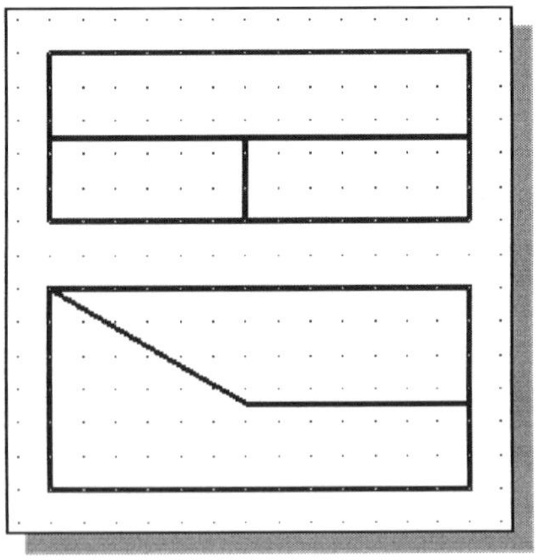

Name: ______________________ Date: ________________

Review Questions: (Time: 30 minutes)

1. What are the three types of *Axonometric projection*?
2. Describe the differences between an Isometric drawing and a *Trimetric* drawing.
3. What is the main advantage of *Oblique projection* over the isometric projection?
4. Describe the differences between a *one-point perspective* and a *two-point perspective*.
5. Which pictorial methods maintain true size and shape of geometry on the frontal plane?
6. What is a vanishing point in a *perspective drawing*?
7. What is a *Cabinet Oblique*?
8. What is the angle between the three axes in an isometric drawing?
9. In an *Axonometric* drawing, are the projection lines perpendicular to the projection plane?
10. A cylindrical feature, in a frontal plane, will remain a circle in which pictorial methods?
11. In an Oblique drawing, are the projection lines perpendicular to the projection plane?
12. Create freehand pictorial sketches of:
    - Your desk
    - Your computer
    - One corner of your room
    - The tallest building in your area

Exercises: (Time: 120 minutes)

Complete the missing views. (Create a pictorial sketch as an aid in reading the views.)

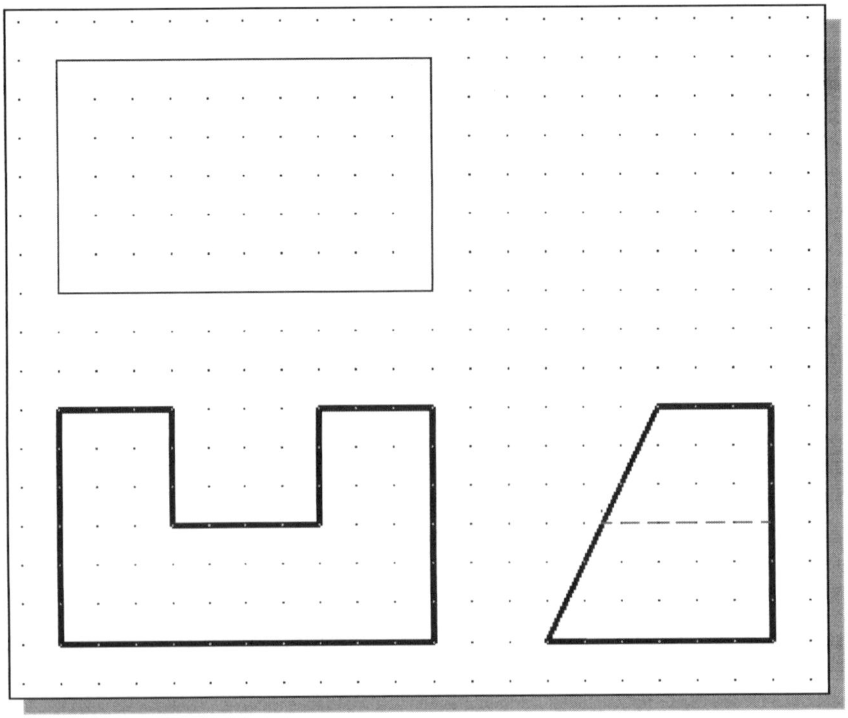

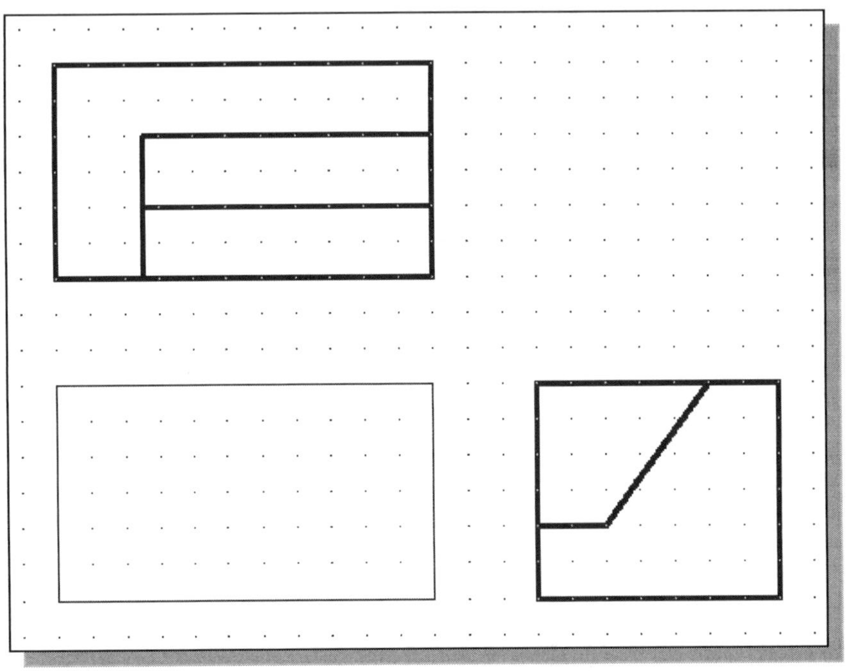

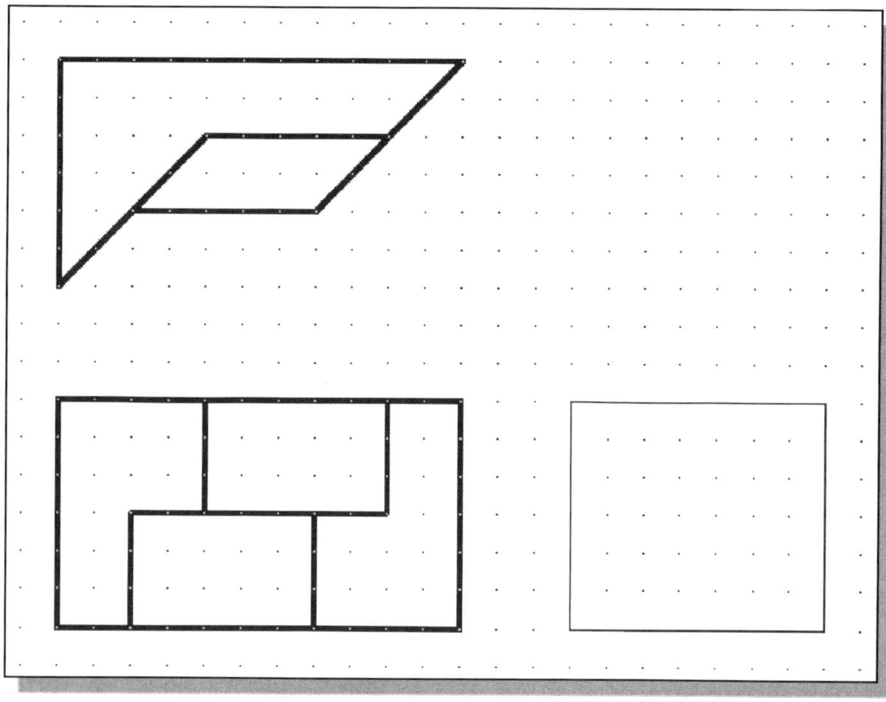

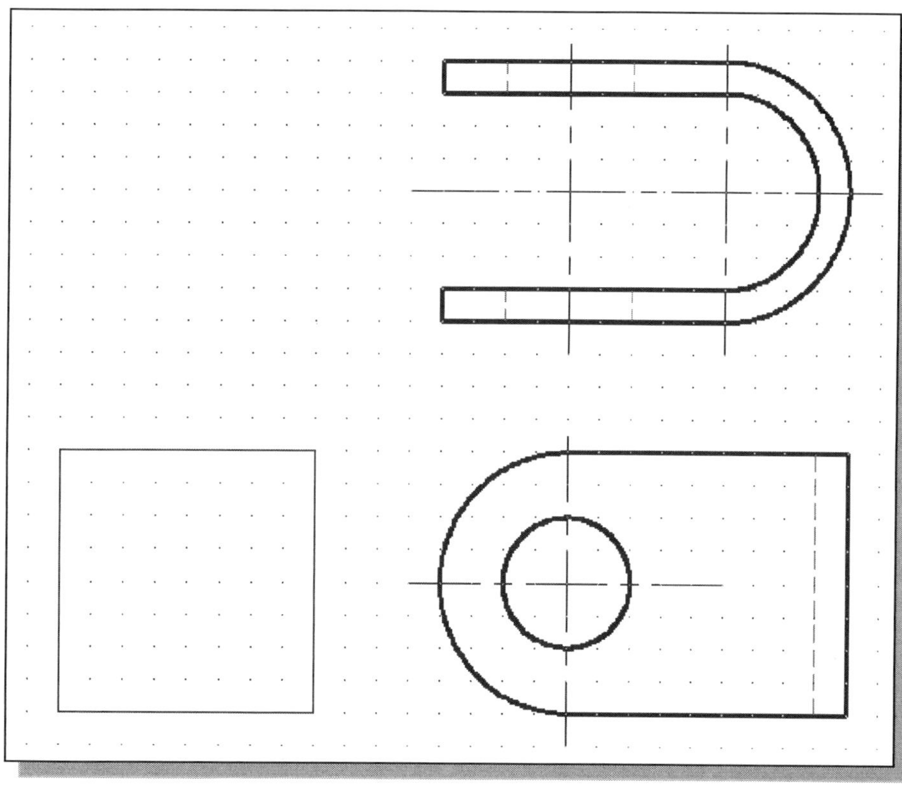

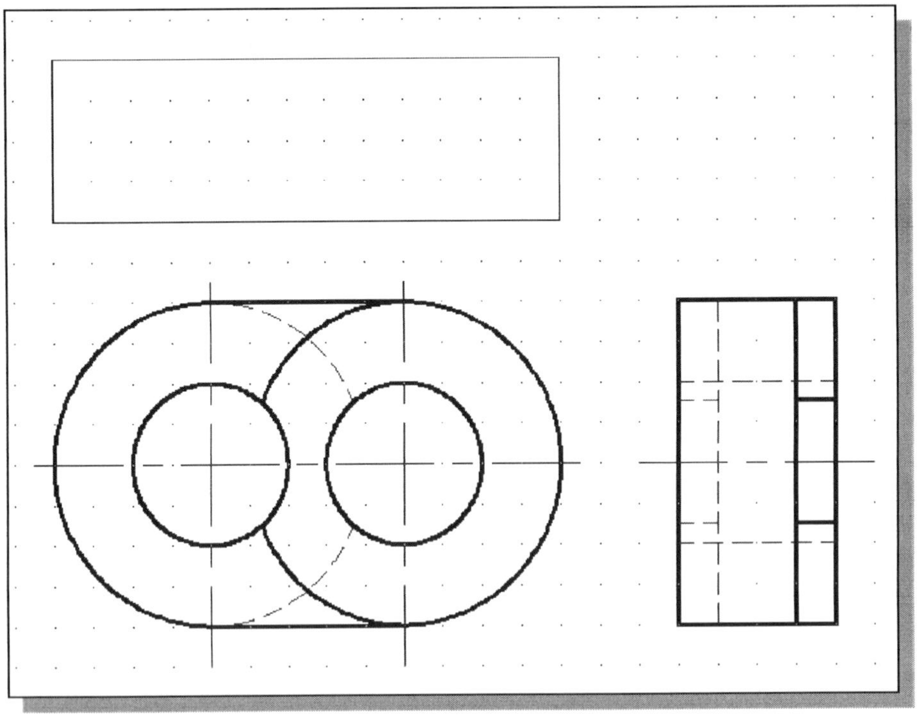

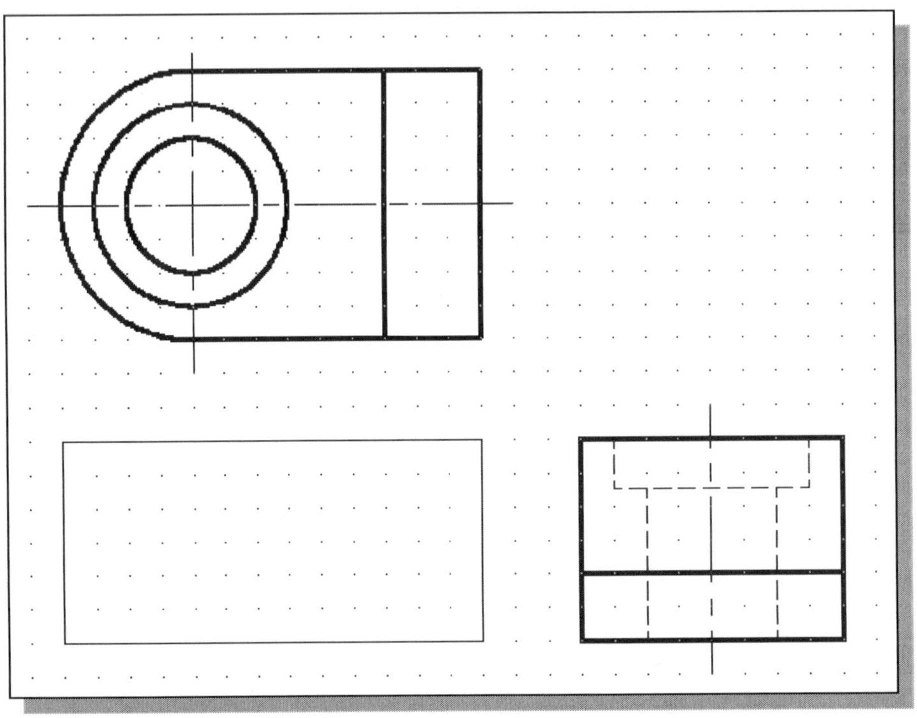

Chapter 6
AutoCAD 2D Isometric Drawings

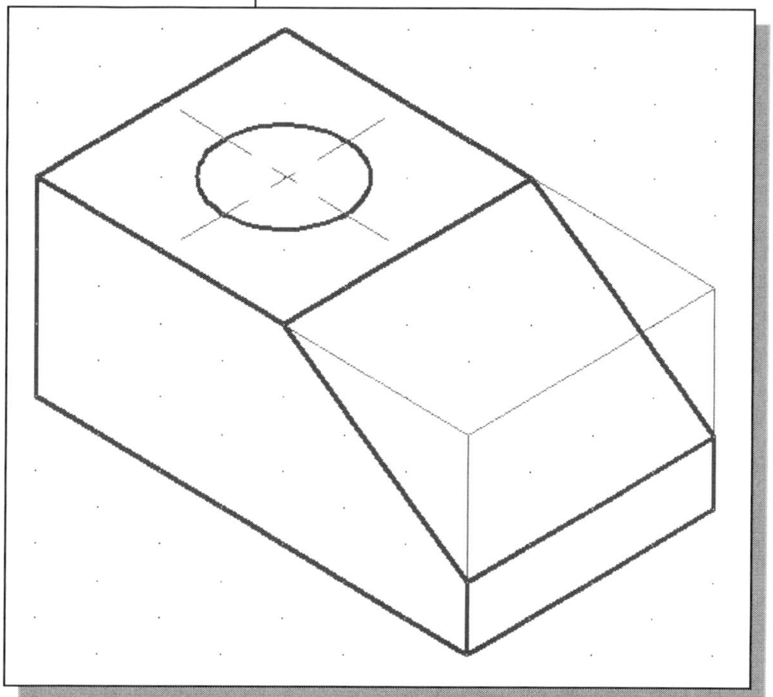

Learning Objectives

- ♦ Understand the Axonometric projections
- ♦ Use the AutoCAD 2D Isometric Drawing tools
- ♦ Understand and Use the AutoCAD Isoplane and Isodraft commands
- ♦ Create the AutoCAD Isocircles
- ♦ Use the Object Snap options
- ♦ Control Objects with the Parametric Geometry Constraint tools

AutoCAD Certified User Examination Objectives Coverage

This table shows the pages on which the objectives of the Certified User Examination are covered in Chapter 6.

Introduction

Although AutoCAD has full 3D solid modeling capabilities, it makes sense to use isometric drawing when all that is needed are some simple isometric views for design concepts and /or presentations. AutoCAD's 2D Isometric drawing is a simple 2D drawing to represent a 3D object. The isometric projection is a type of **axonometric projection**; the word *axonometric* means "to measure along axes." There are three types of axonometric projections: isometric projection, dimetric projection, and trimetric projection. Typically in an axonometric drawing, one axis is drawn vertically.

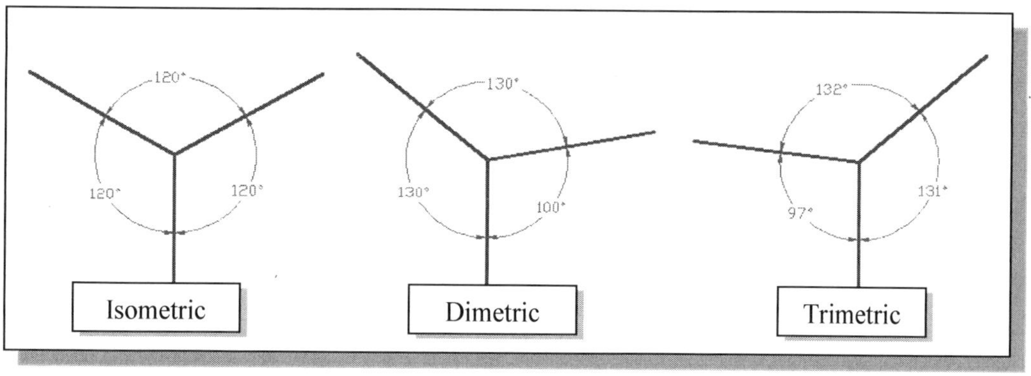

In **isometric projections**, the direction of viewing is such that the three axes of space appear equally foreshortened, and therefore the angles between the three axes are equal, while in **dimetric projections** and **trimetric projections** the directions of viewing are such that not all three axes of space appear equally foreshortened.

Isometric drawing is perhaps the most widely used for pictorials in engineering graphics, mainly because isometric views are the most convenient to draw. To create an isometric drawing, the visible portions of the individual 2D-views are constructed on the corresponding sides of the box. Adjustments of the locations of surfaces are then made, by moving the edges, to complete the isometric view.

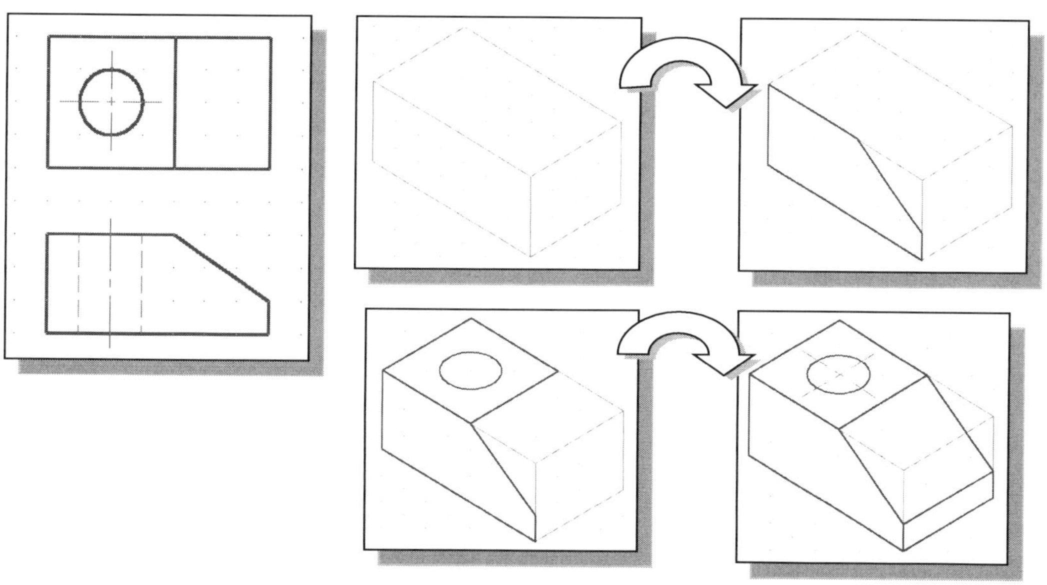

In an isometric drawing, cylindrical or circular shapes appear as ellipses. It can be confusing drawing the ellipses in an isometric view; one simple rule to remember is the **major axis** of the ellipse is always **perpendicular** to the **center axis** of the cylinder as shown in the figures below.

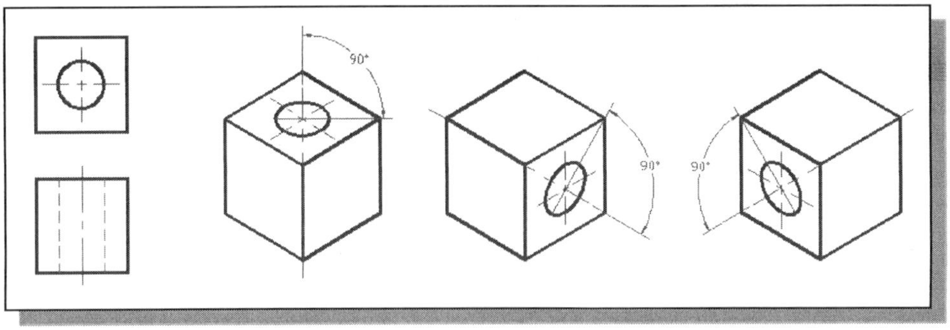

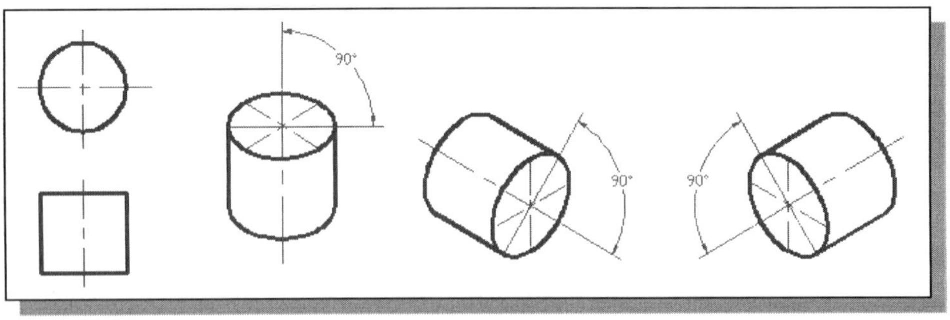

The general procedure to construct an AutoCAD 2D isometric drawing is illustrated in the following sections. Note that this is a fairly simple and effective way of representing a three-dimensional object in two-dimensional space.

The Angle Support Design

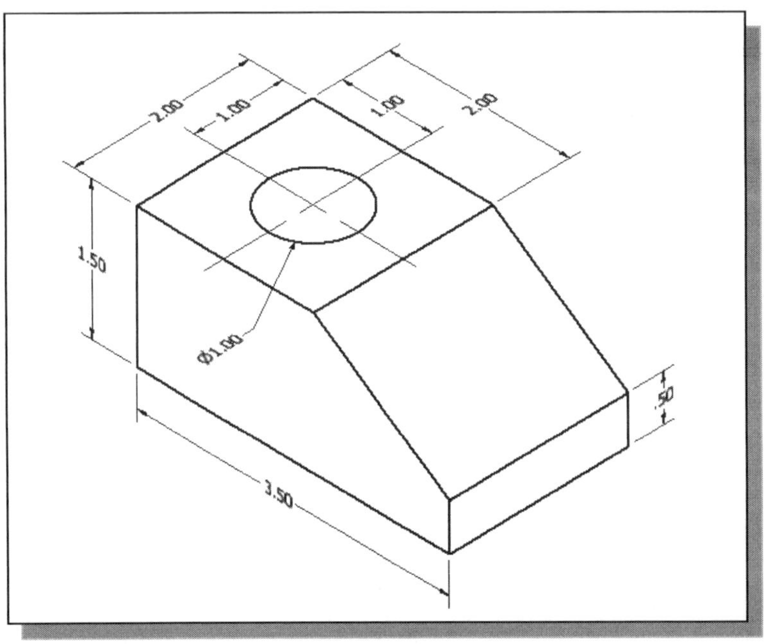

Starting Up AutoCAD 2026

1. Select the **AutoCAD 2026** option on the *Program* menu or select the **AutoCAD 2026** icon on the *Desktop*.

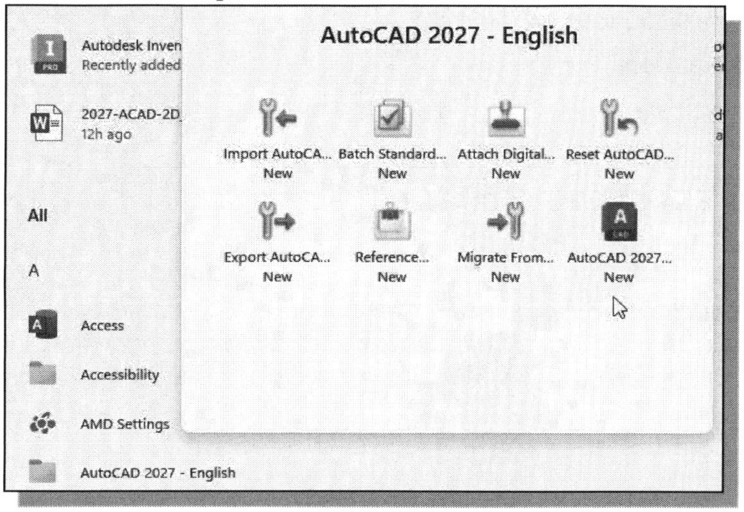

2. In the *Startup dialog box*, select **[Start from Scratch] → [Imperial (feet and inches)]** as shown.

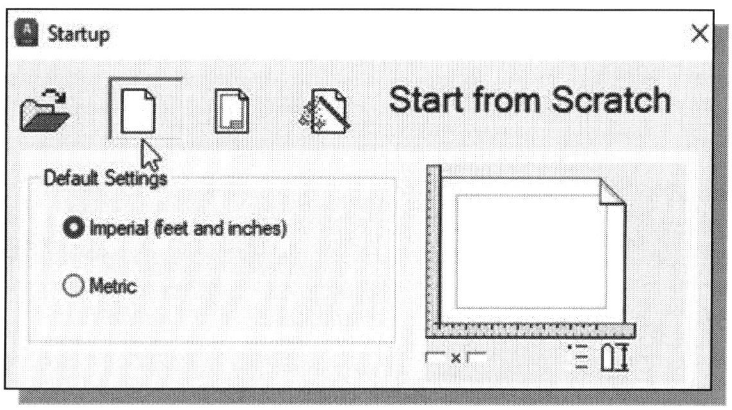

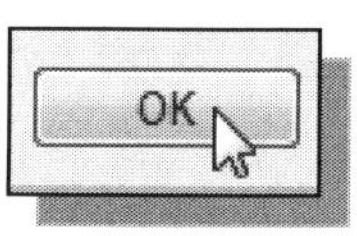

3. Click **OK** to accept the selection.

4. On your own, click on the down-arrow in the *Quick Access Bar* and select **Show Menu Bar** to display the **AutoCAD *Menu Bar***. The *Menu Bar* provides access to all AutoCAD commands.

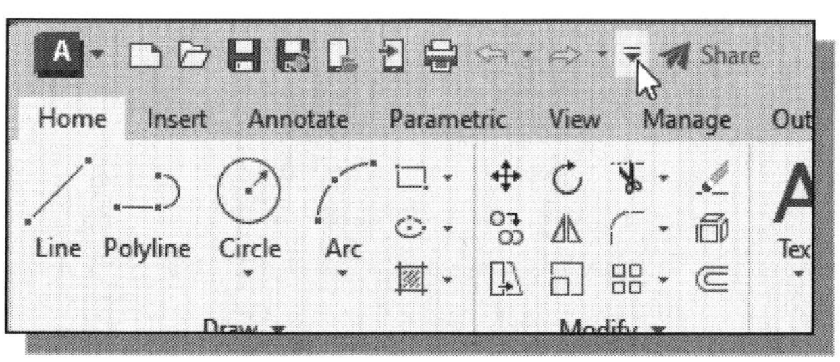

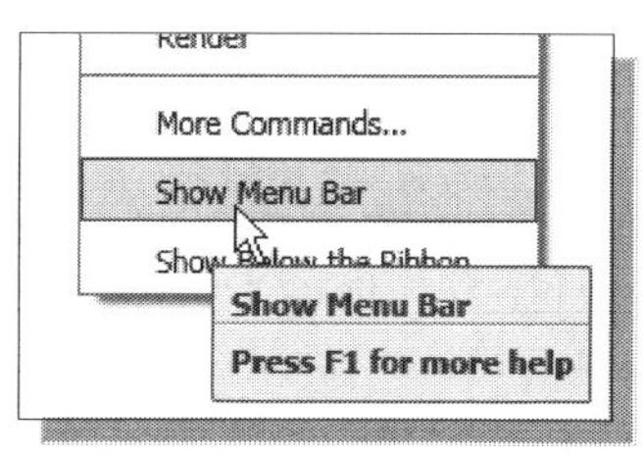

CAD Isoplane and Isodraft Commands

AutoCAD uses the Isoplane and Isodraft commands to control the alignment of the cursor to the three isometric axes. The following settings can be used when drawing 2D isometric representations of 3D models:

- Ortho directions
- Snap orientation
- Grid orientation and style
- Polar tracking angles
- Orientation of isometric circles

The isometric plane affects the cursor movement only when the snap style is set to *Isometric* in the *Drafting Settings* dialog box. When the *snap option* is set to *Isometric*, the *Ortho* mode will use the appropriate axis paired to 30, 90, and/or 150 degrees.

Left Plane

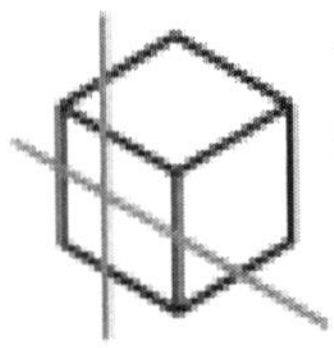

The cursor is aligned to the left-facing plane of the isometric axes.

Top Plane

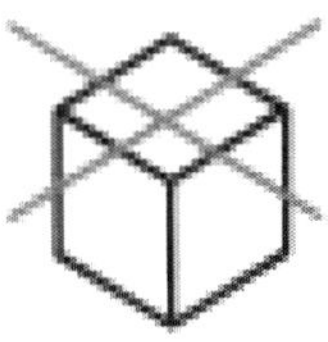

The cursor is aligned to the top-facing plane of the isometric axes.

Right Plane

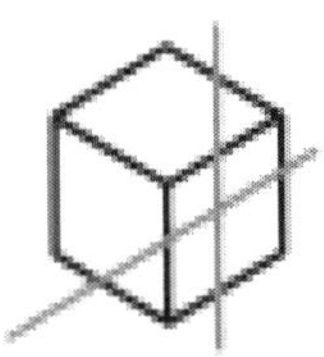

The cursor is aligned to the right-facing plane of the isometric axes.

➢ The three isometric planes can be selected by toggling the [**F5**] or [**Ctrl**+**E**] keys or using the **Isodraft** command.

The **Isodraft** command can be accessed through the icon in the *Status Bar* area. The primary advantage of *Isodraft* is that when it is toggled on, all the related settings are automatically set as well, so the cursor will be aligned to the isometric axes of the active *Isoplane*.

Layers Setup

1. Click **Layer Properties Manager** in the *Layers* toolbar.

❖ In AutoCAD, we always construct entities on a layer. It may be the default layer or a layer that we create. Each layer has associated properties such as the visibility setting, color, linetype, lineweight, and plot style.

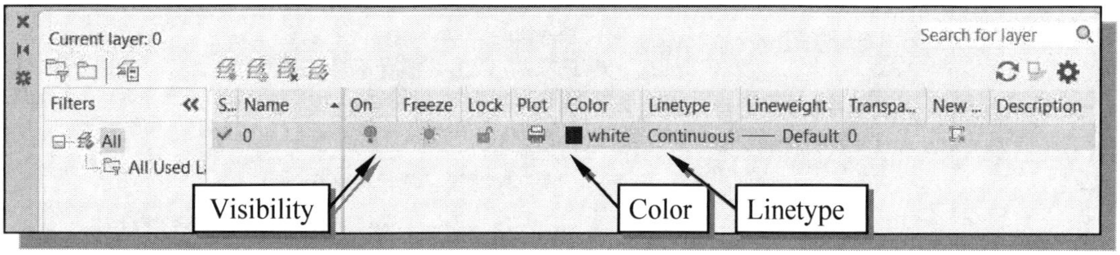

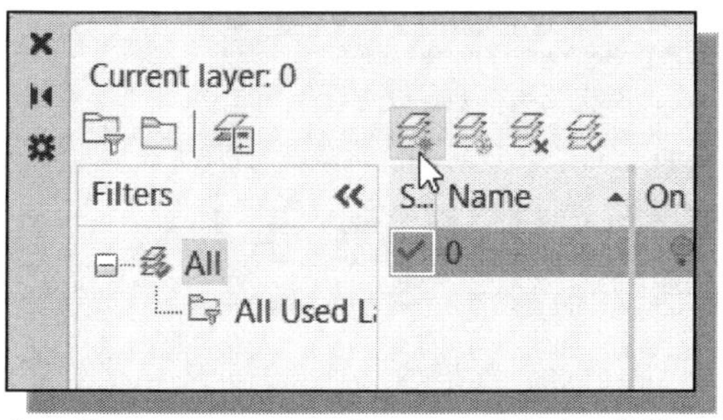

2. Click on the **New Layer** button. Notice a layer is automatically added to the list of layers.

3. Create **two new layers** with the following settings:

Layer	*Color*	*Linetype*	*Lineweight*
Construction	**Grey**	**Continuous**	**Default**
Object	**Cyan**	**Continuous**	**0.30mm**

4. Highlight the layer ***Construction*** in the list of layers.

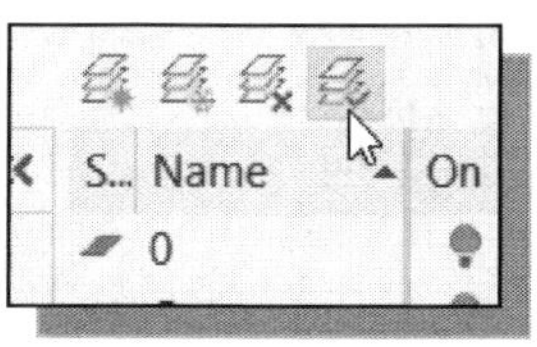

5. Click on the **Current** icon to set layer ***Construction*** as the *Current Layer*.

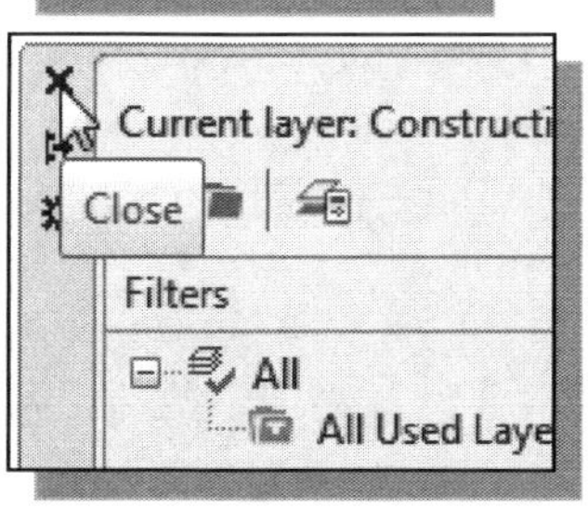

6. Click on the **Close** button to accept the settings and exit the *Layer Properties Manager* dialog box.

Create the Base Box of the Design

We will first use construction geometry to define the outer edges of the design.

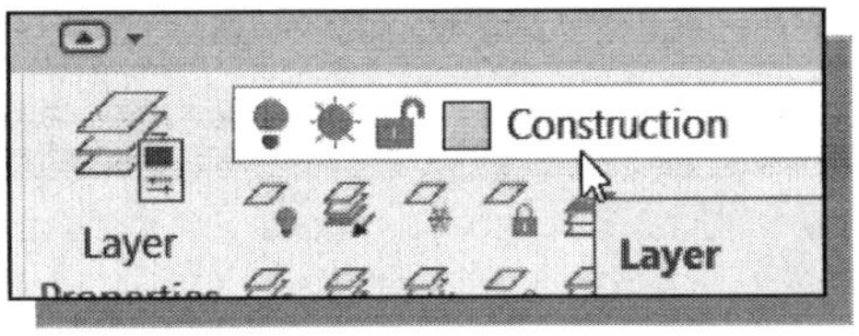

1. In the *Layer Control* box, confirm that layer *Construction* is set as the *Current Layer*.

2. Click on the *Customization* icon, and switch **on** the **Isometric Drafting** option as shown.

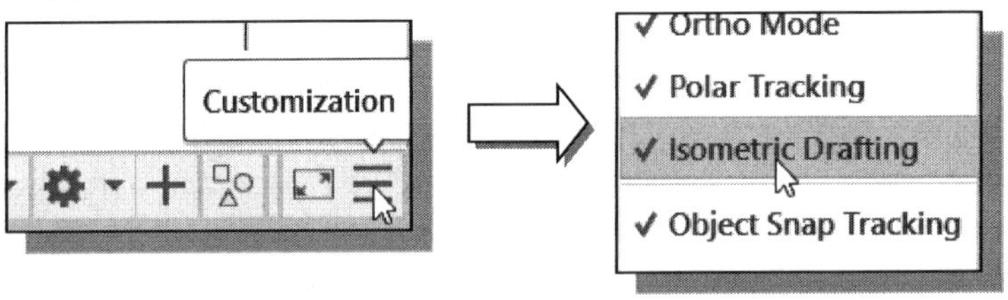

3. In the *Status Bar* area, reset the option buttons so that only the *GRID DISPLAY, Dynamic Input, Object Snap Tracking* and *Object Snap* options are switched ***ON.***

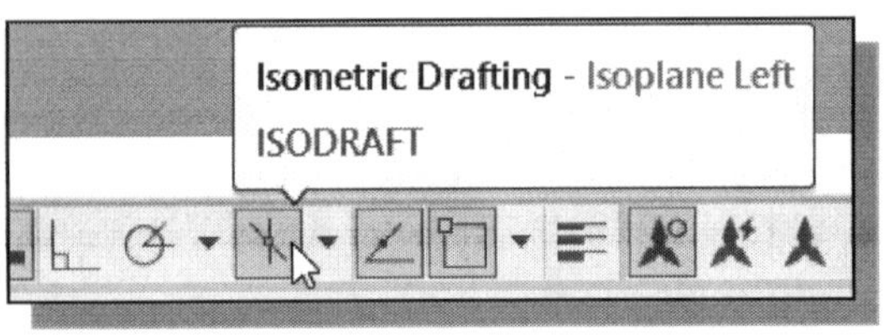

4. In the *Status Bar* area, click on the **Isodraft** icon to switch **on** the *Isoplane* option. Note the default isoplane is set to the *Left plane*.

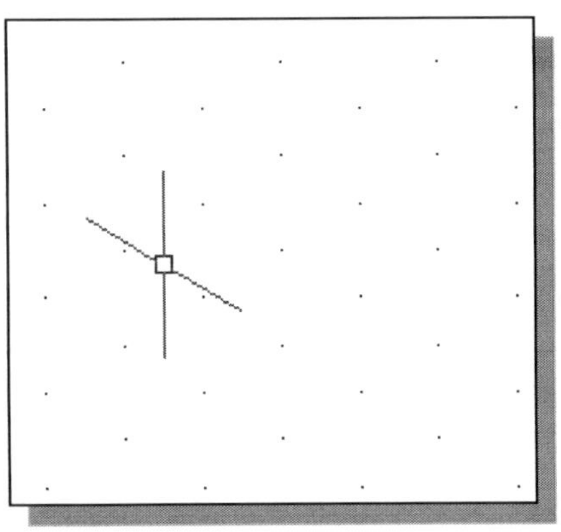

5. Inside the graphics area, notice the cursor is set to align to the **Left Isoplane**. The *Grid Display* is also aligned to the isoplane.

6. Hit the [**F5**] key or [**Ctrl+E**] once and notice the isoplane is now set to the *Top plane* as shown.

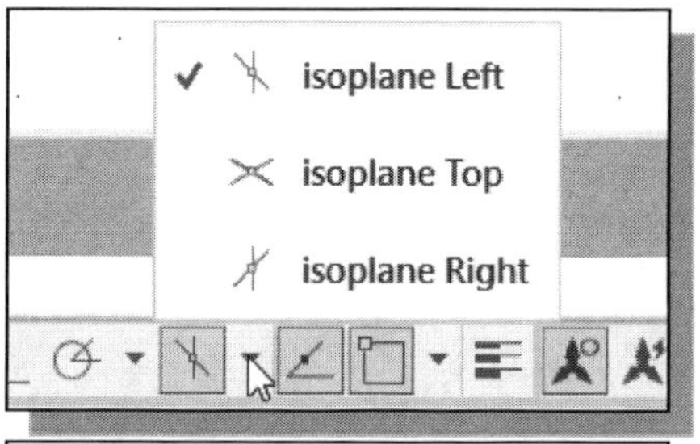

7. Hit the [**F5**] key or [**Ctrl+E**] twice and notice the isoplane is now set back to the *Left plane* as shown.

➢ Note that we can also click on the arrow next to the *Isodraft* icon to show and/or set the active *isoplane*.

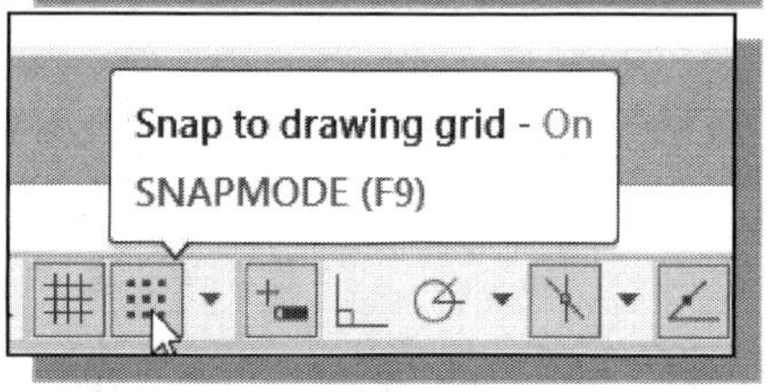

8. In the *Status Bar* area, click on the **Snap Mode** icon to switch **on** the *Snap to Grid* option.

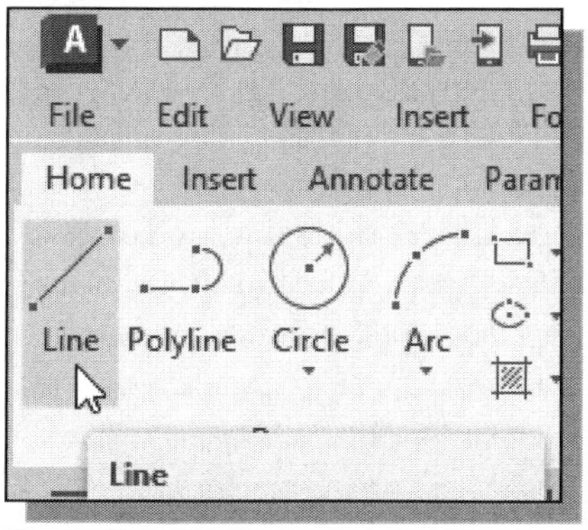

9. Activate the **Line** command in the *Draw* toolbar. Note that since the ***Snap*** mode is switched on, the cursor is aligned to the grid points in the directions of the left isoplane.

10. Place the first endpoint of the line near the center of the graphics area.

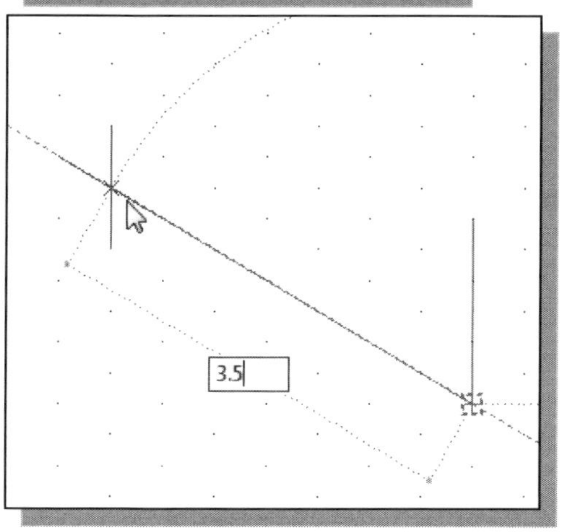

11. Move the cursor downward, and enter **1.5** as the distance to the second end point of the line sequence.

12. Move the cursor toward the left side, and align the cursor in the 150 degrees direction. Enter **3.5** as the distance to the third end point of the line sequence.

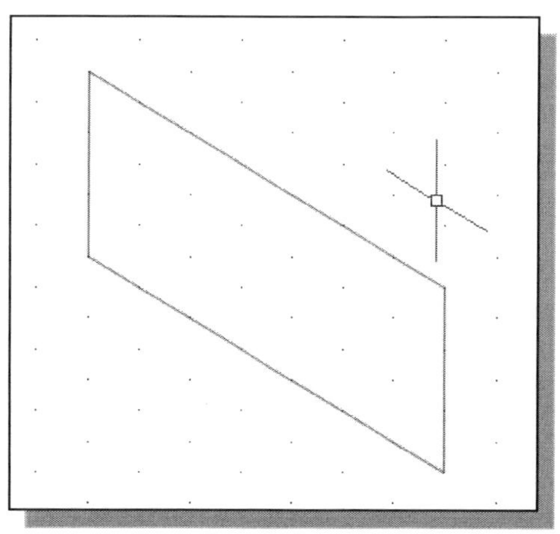

13. Repeat the above steps and create the front face of the isometric box for the *Angle Support design.*

14. Hit the [**Esc**] key once to end the line sequence.

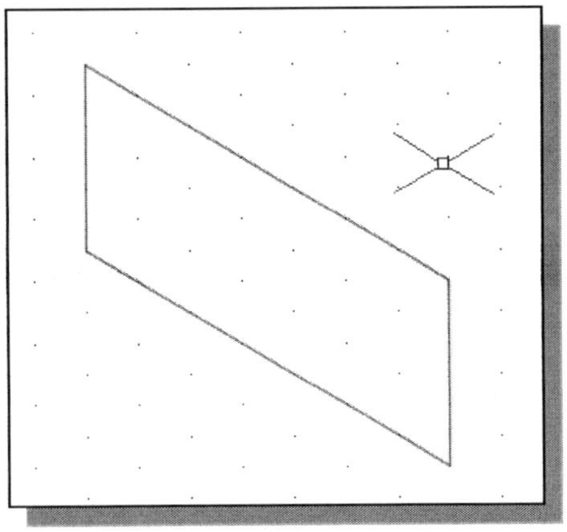

15. Hit the [**F5**] key or [**Ctrl+E**] once and notice the isoplane is now set back to the *Top plane* as shown.

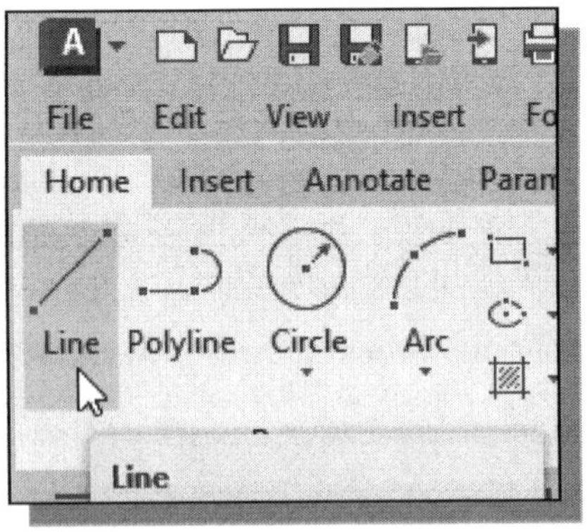

16. Activate the **Line** command in the *Draw* toolbar.

17. Snap to the **top left corner** of the polygon we just created.

18. Move the cursor toward the right side, and align the cursor in the 30 degrees direction. Enter **2.0** as the distance to the second end point of the line sequence.

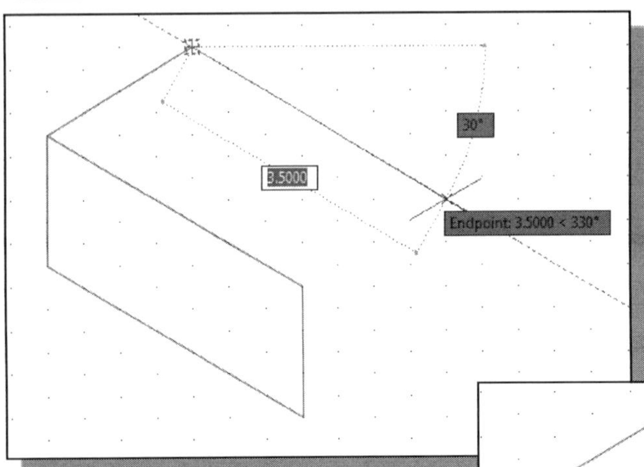

19. Move the cursor toward the right side, and align the cursor in the -30 degrees direction. Enter **3.5** as the distance to the third end point of the line sequence.

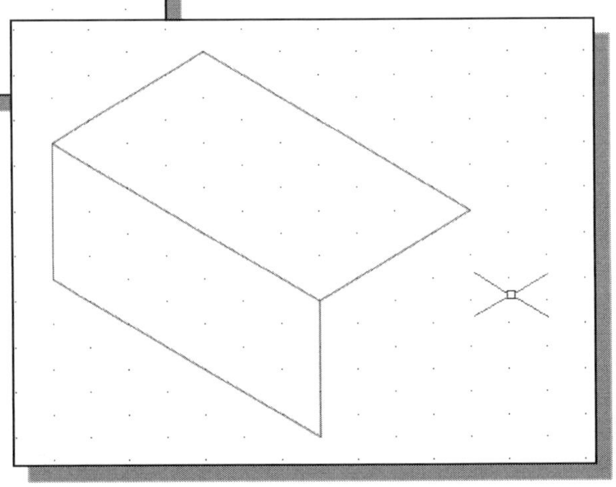

20. Snap to the **top right corner** of the front face of the isometric box to form the top face of the isometric box.

21. Hit the [**Esc**] key once to end the line sequence.

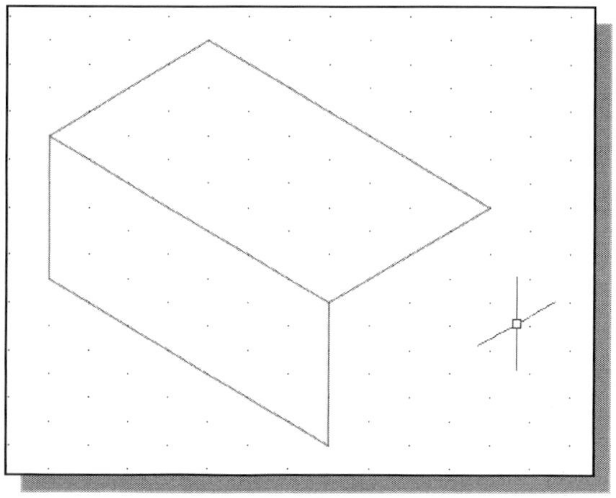

22. Hit the [**F5**] key or [**Ctrl+E**] once and notice the isoplane is now set back to the *Right plane* as shown.

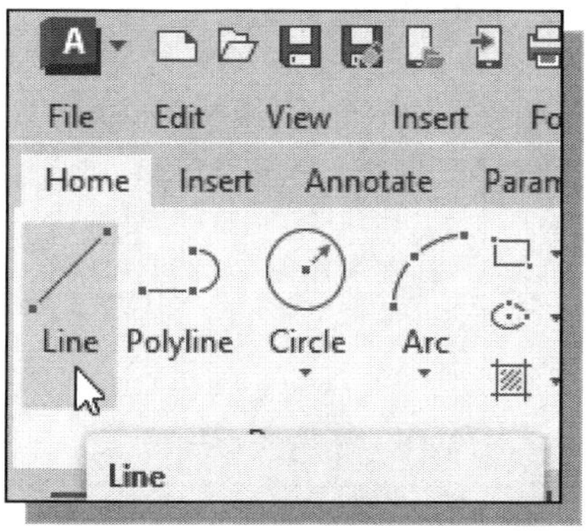

23. Activate the **Line** command in the *Draw* toolbar.

24. Move the cursor downward, and enter **1.5** as the distance to the second end point of the line sequence.

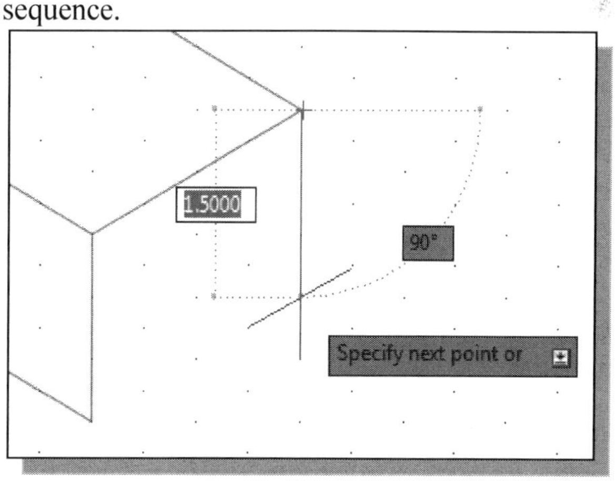

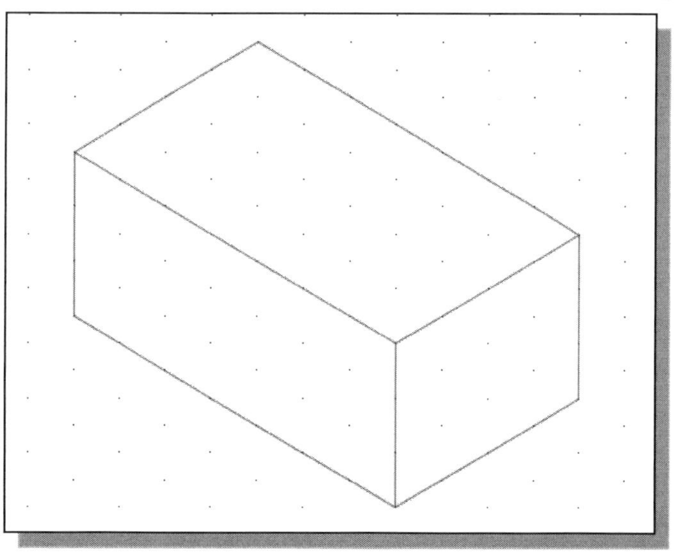

25. Snap to the **lower right corner** of the front face of the isometric box to form the right face of the isometric box.

- We will use the isometric box to help create the *Angle Support design.* Note that the entire process is done in two-dimensional space to represent a 3D design.

Create the Design inside the Base Box

We will now create the design using the base isometric box.

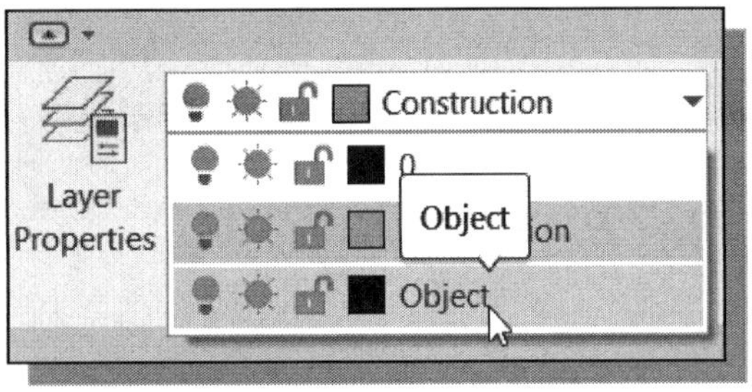

1. In the *Layer Control* box, set the layer *Object* as the *Current Layer*.

2. In the *Menu Bar* select **[Tools] → [Toolbars] → [AutoCAD] → [Object Snap]**.

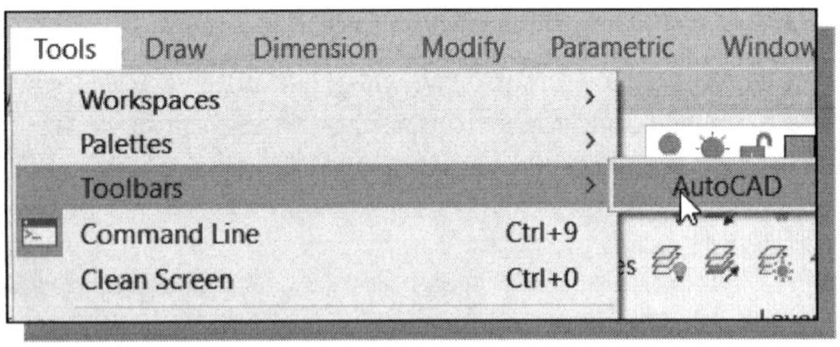

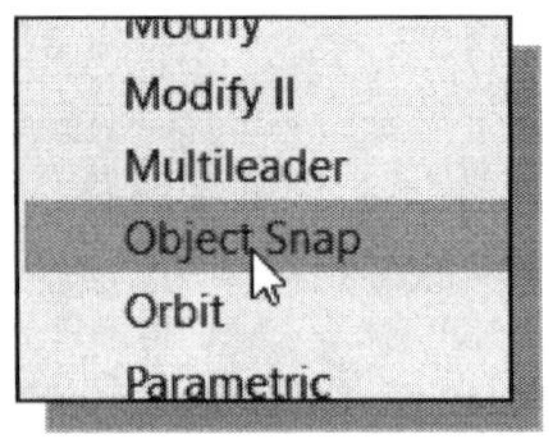

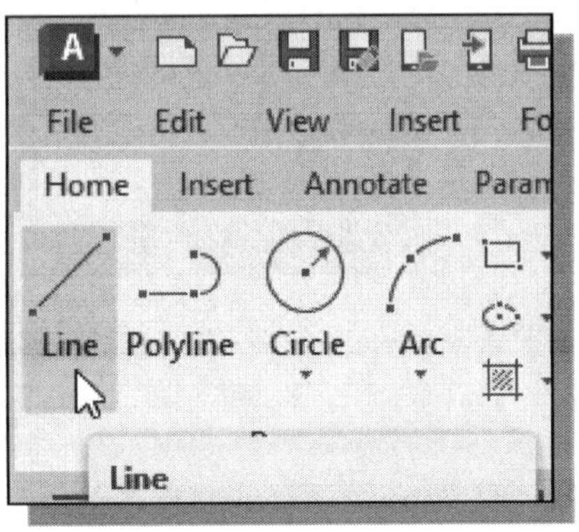

3. Activate the **Line** command in the *Draw* toolbar.

4. In the *command prompt* area, the message "*_line Specify first point:*" is displayed. Select **Snap From** in the *Object Snap* toolbar.

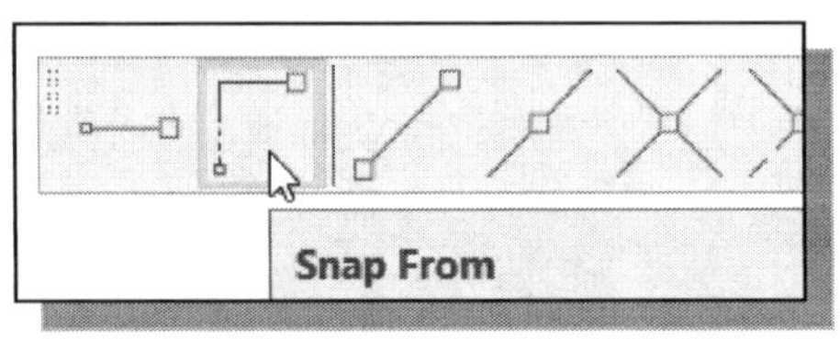

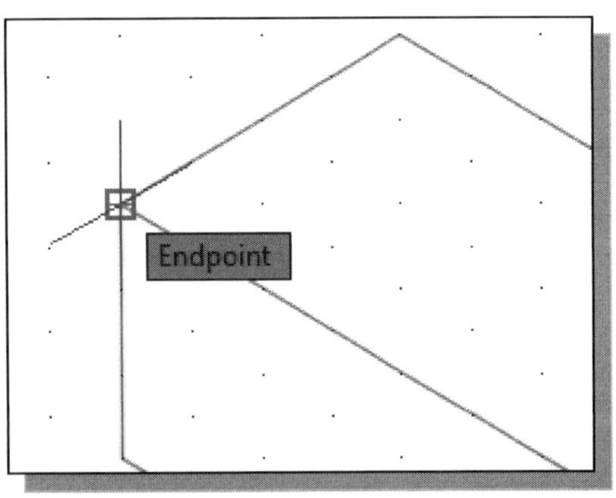

5. Select the **top left corner** of the base box as the reference point as shown.

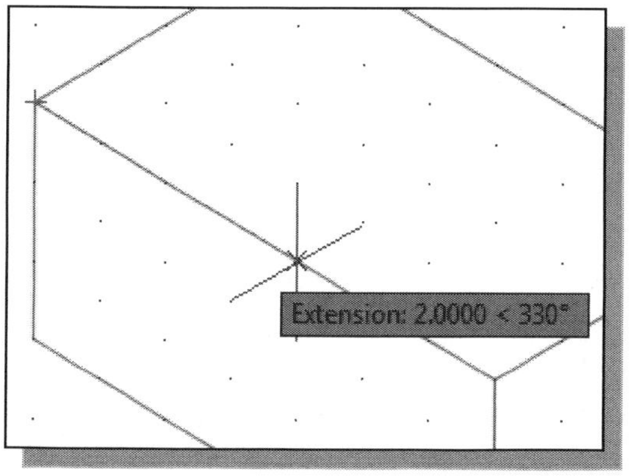

6. Move the cursor along the top edge of the front face and select the location at 2 units at 330 degrees (**2.0<330**) as shown.

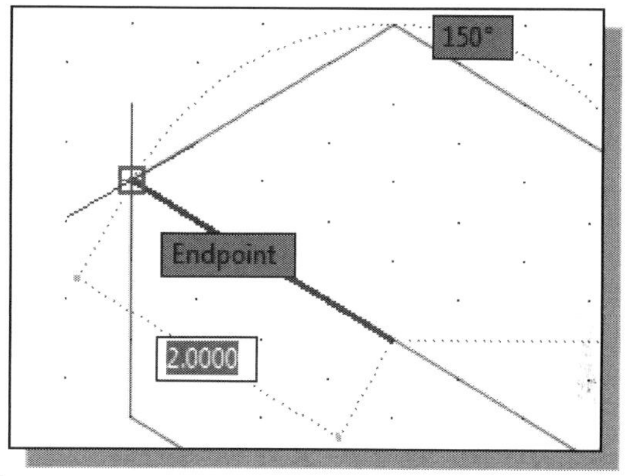

7. Snap to the **top left corner** of the base box as shown.

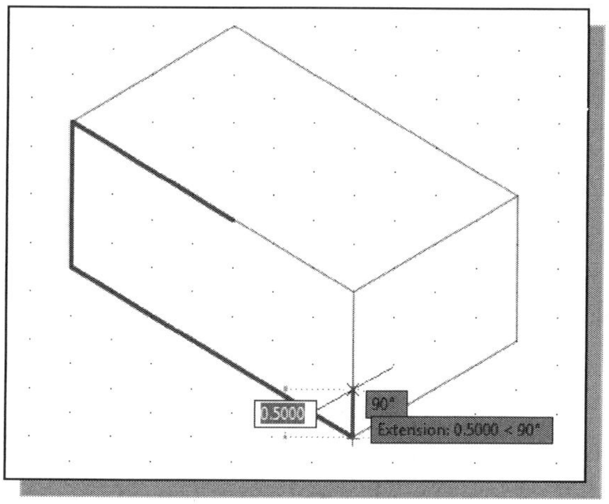

8. Follow along the front face of the base box and click on the three corners to create the three line segments as shown.

9. Move the cursor upward, and enter **0.5** as the distance to the next end point of the line sequence.

10. Right-click once to bring up the *option* list, and select **Close** to complete the front face of the design as shown.

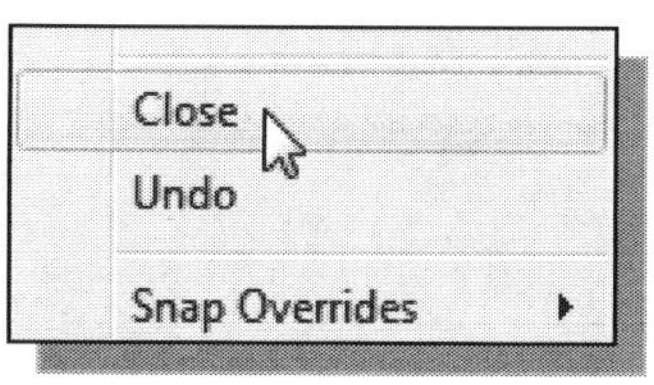

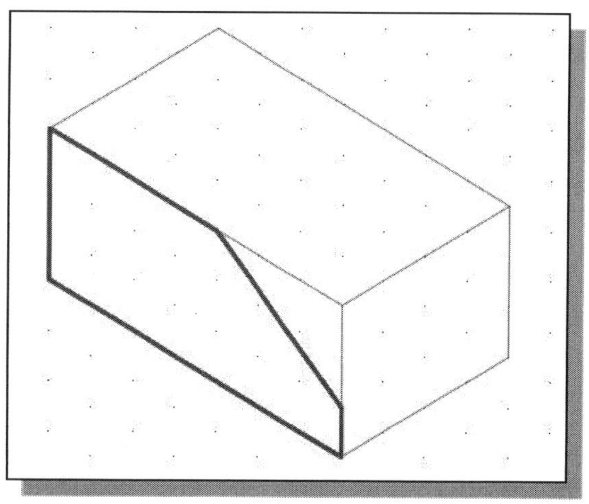

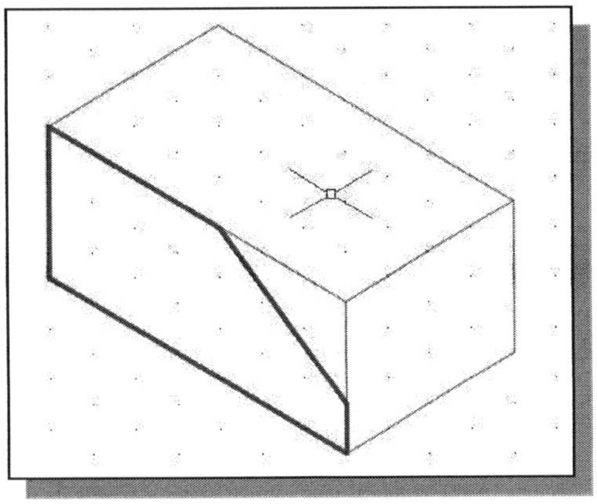

11. Hit the [**F5**] key or [**Ctrl+E**] once and notice the isoplane is now set to the *Top plane* as shown.

12. In the *Status Bar area*, switch on **Object Snap tracking** as shown.

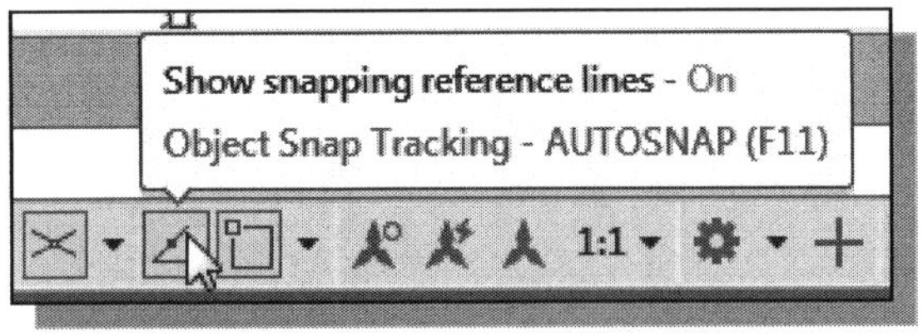

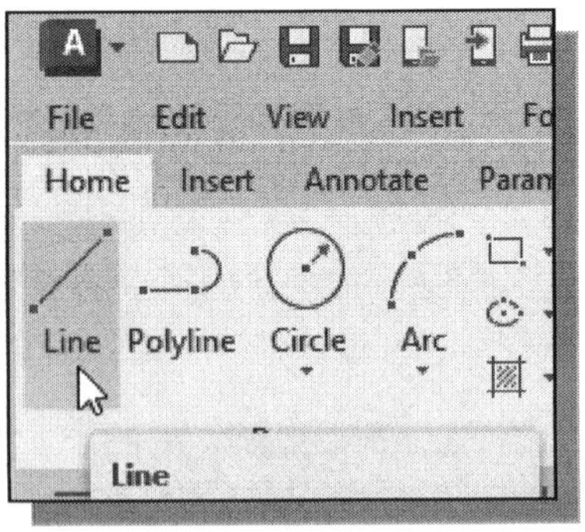

13. Activate the **Line** command in the *Draw* toolbar.

14. Snap to the **top left corner** of the base box and create the two line segment as shown. (Hint: Use the *AutoSnap* option to locate the corresponding corner.)

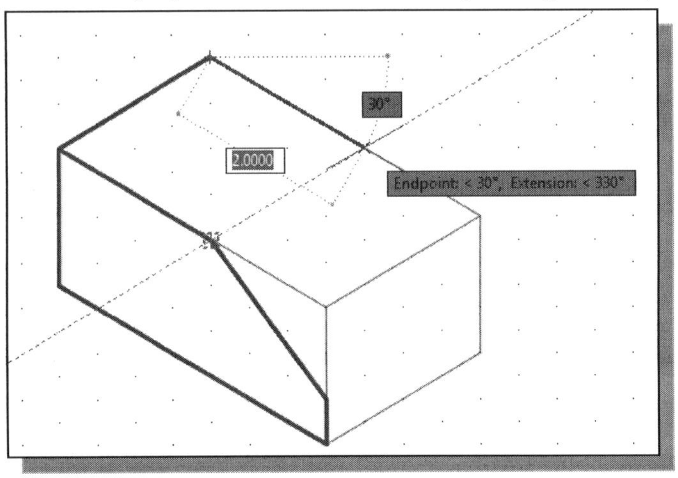

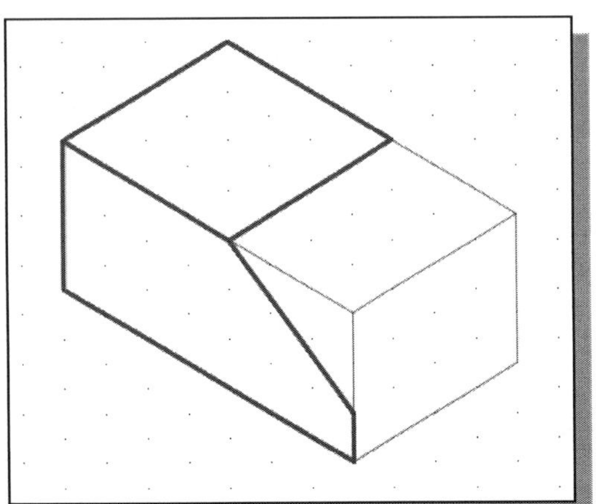

15. Complete the outlines of the top face of the design as shown.

16. Hit the [**Esc**] key once to end the line sequence.

Create the Isocircle on the top face

In an isometric drawing, cylindrical or circular shapes appear as ellipses. In AutoCAD, the current aligned isometric plane also determines the orientation of isometric circles created with the **Isocircle** option of the *ELLIPSE* command.

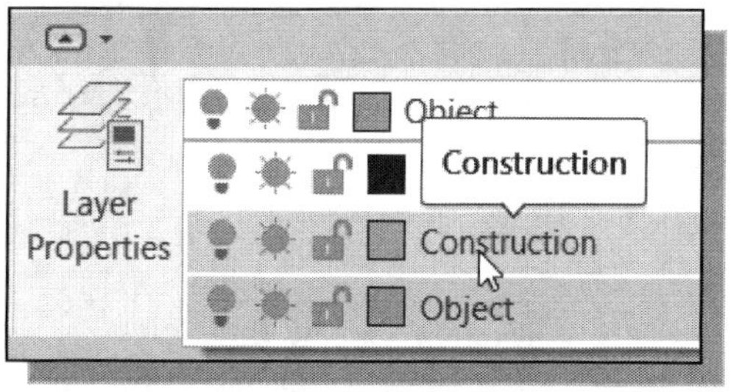

1. In the *Layer Control* box, set the layer *Construction* as the *Current Layer.*

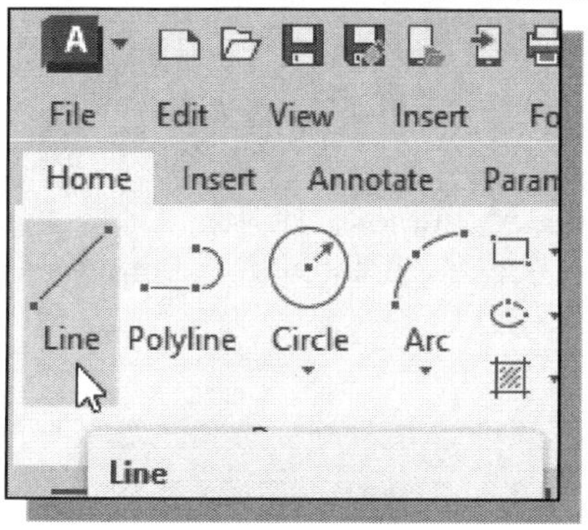

2. Activate the **Line** command in the *Draw* toolbar.

3. In the *command prompt* area, the message "*_line Specify first point:*" is displayed. Select **Midpoint** in the *Object Snap* toolbar.

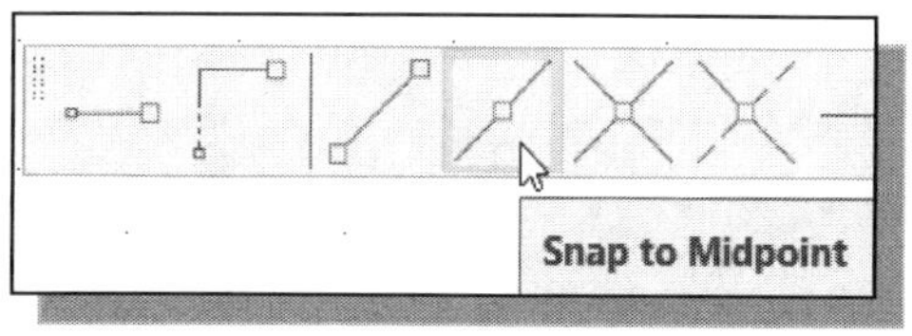

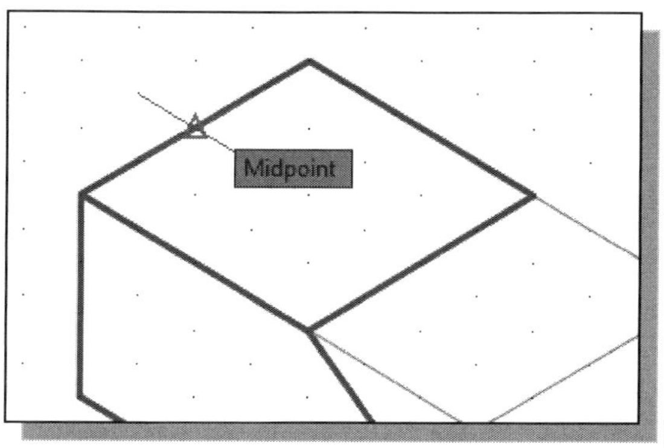

4. Select the midpoint of the top left edge of the top face of the design as shown.

5. Repeat the above step and create the two construction lines as shown. Note the intersection of the two lines identifies the center point of the circle.

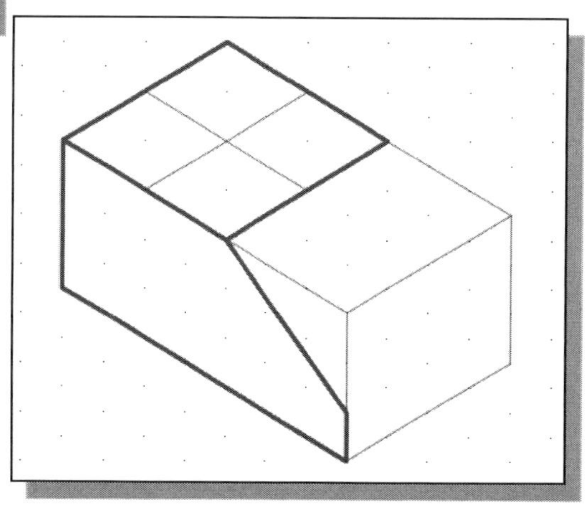

6. In the *Layer Control* box, set the layer *Object* as the *Current Layer*.

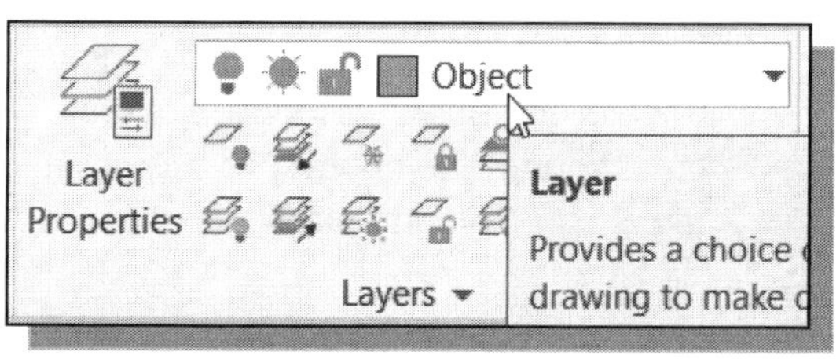

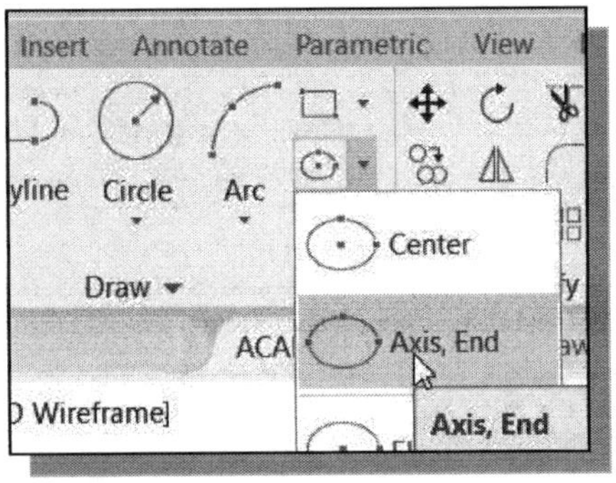

7. In the *Draw* toolbar, activate the **Axis, End Ellipse** command.

➤ In AutoCAD, the isometric circles are created with the **Isocircle** option of the *ELLIPSE* command (available with *Axis, End* or *Elliptical Arc* options.)

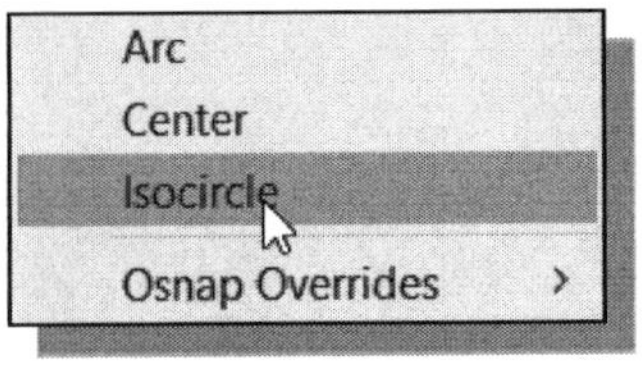

8. Right-click once to bring up the *option* list, and select **Isocircle** to create an isometric circle in an isometric view.

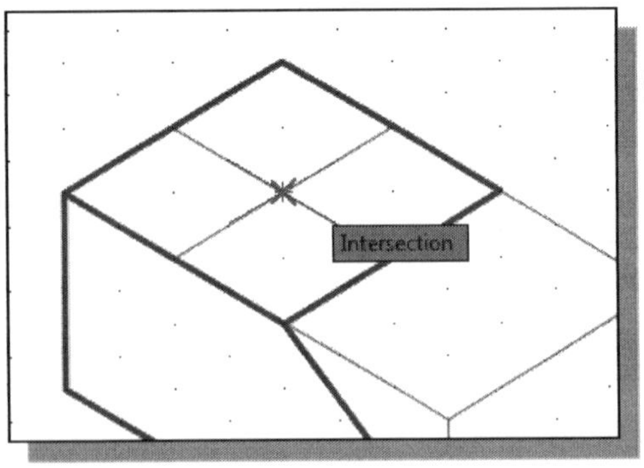

9. Select the intersection of the two construction lines we created in the previous section.

10. Enter **0.5** as the radius of the isocircle.

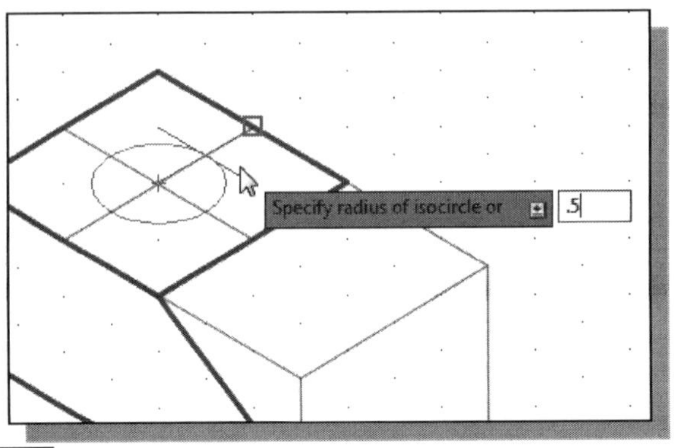

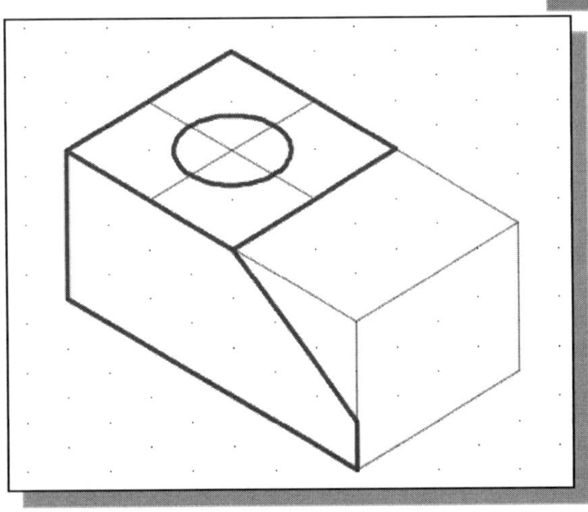

➤ In AutoCAD, the current aligned isometric top plane also determines the orientation of isometric circles created with the **Isocircle** option of the *ELLIPSE* command.

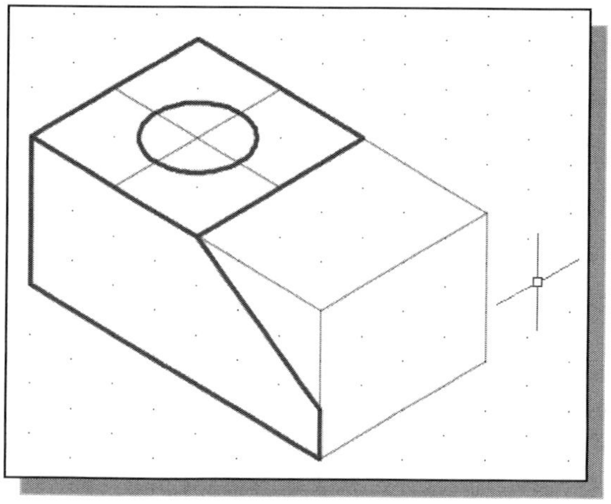

11. Hit the [**F5**] key or [**Ctrl+E**] once and notice the isoplane is now set to the *right plane* as shown.

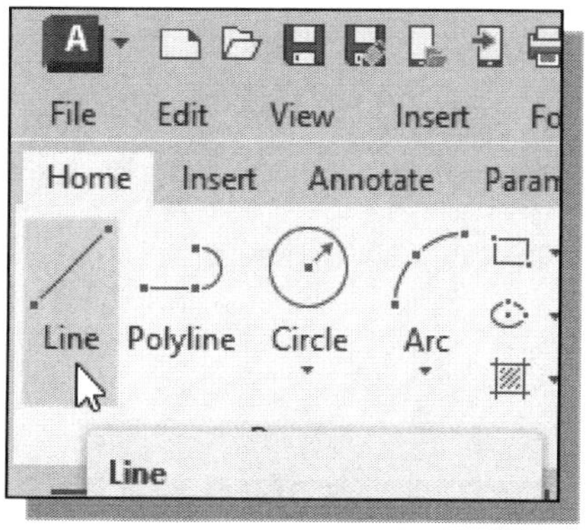

12. In the *Draw* toolbar, activate the **Line** command as shown.

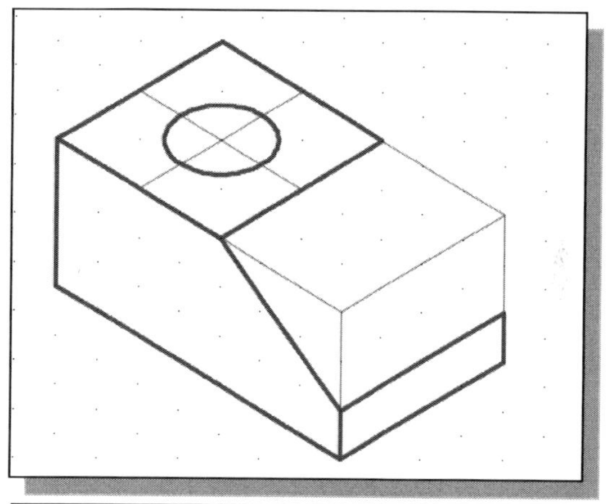

13. Snap to the **lower right corner** of the front face of the base box and create the two line segments as shown. (Hint: Use the *AutoSnap* option to locate the corresponding corner.)

14. On your own, complete the *Isometric drawing* as shown.

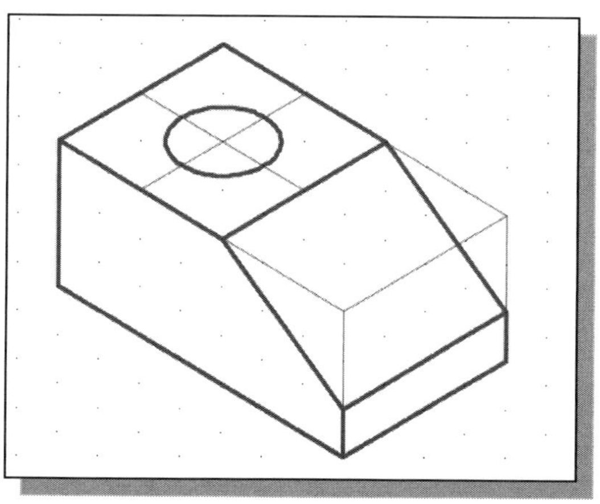

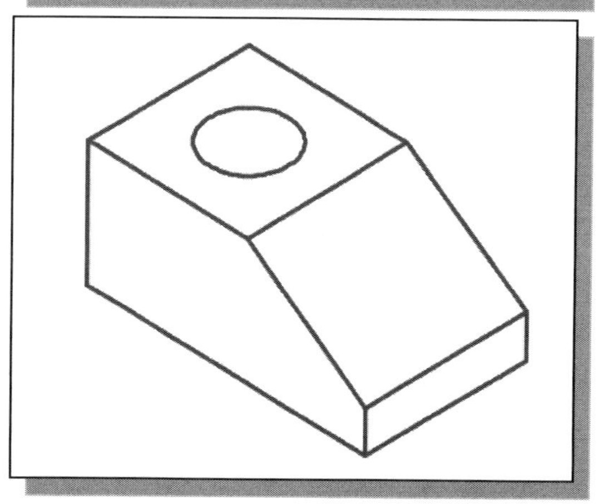

Using the Editing Tools in an Isometric drawing

In AutoCAD, the commonly used editing tools, such as **Move**, **Copy**, **Trim**, **Extend**, and **Erase**, can also be used to aid the construction of an isometric drawing. In the following section, the *Tube Anchor* design will be created using some of the AutoCAD editing tools.

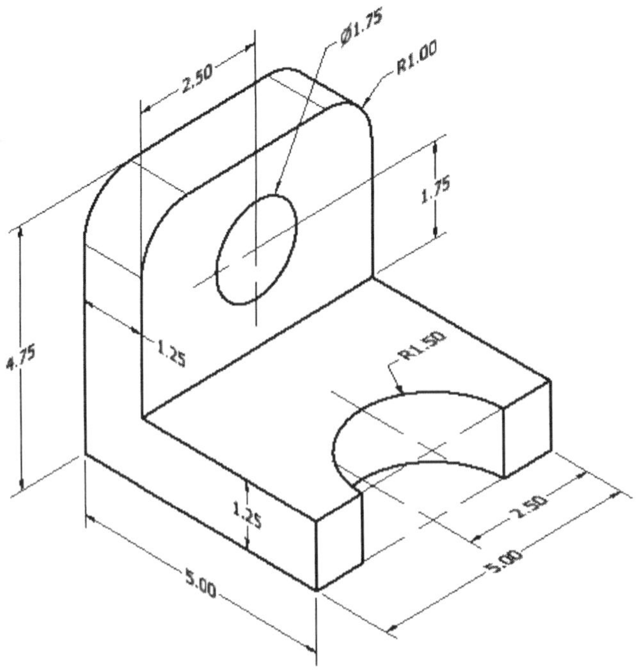

The Tube Anchor Design – Modeling Strategy

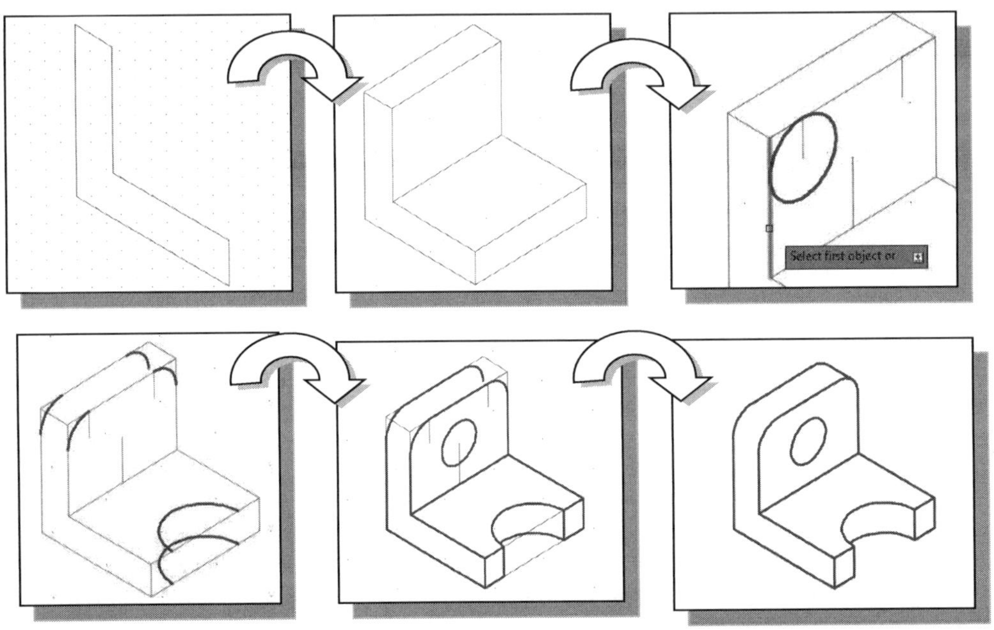

Start a New Drawing and Layers Setup

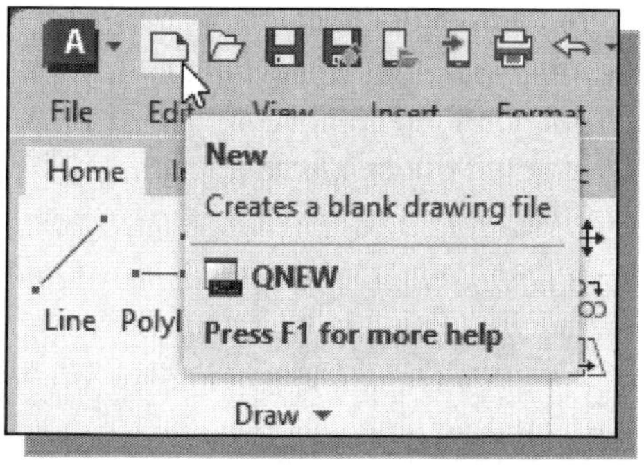

1. In the *Quick Access toolbar*, select **[New]**.
2. On your own, start a new **English Units** drawing.

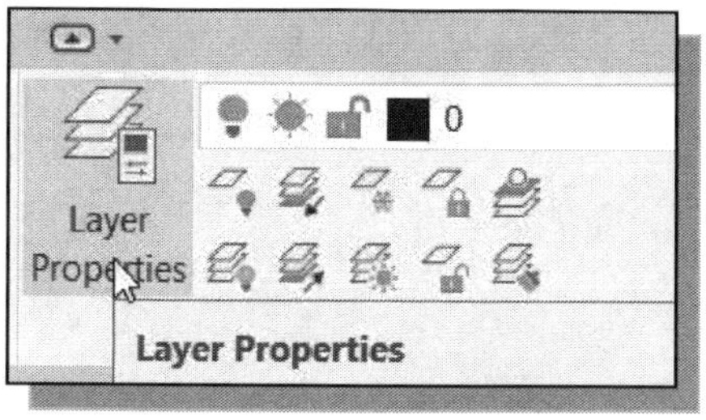

3. Click **Layer Properties Manager** in the *Layers* toolbar.

❖ In AutoCAD, we always construct entities on a layer. It may be the default layer or a layer that we create. Each layer has associated properties such as the visibility setting, color, linetype, lineweight, and plot style.

4. Click on the **New Layer** button. Notice a layer is automatically added to the list of layers.

5. Create **two new layers** with the following settings:

Layer	***Color***	***Linetype***	***Lineweight***
Construction	**Grey**	**Continuous**	**Default**
Object	**Cyan**	**Continuous**	**0.30mm**

6. Highlight the layer ***Construction*** in the list of layers.

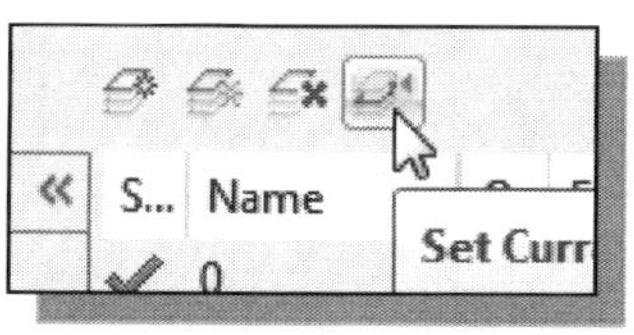

7. Click on the **Current** icon to set layer ***Construction*** as the *Current Layer*.

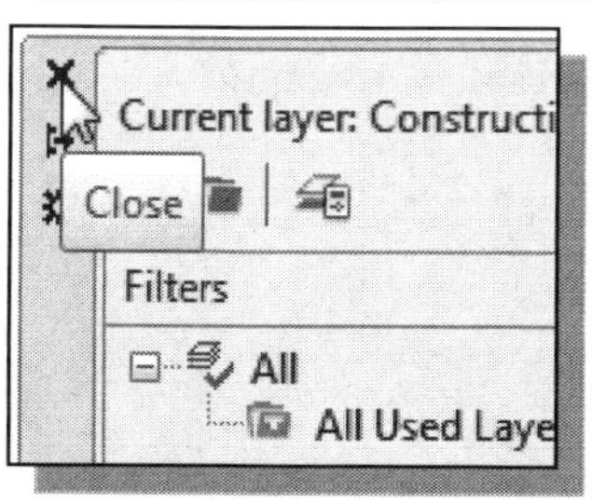

8. Click on the **Close** button to accept the settings and exit the *Layer Properties Manager* dialog box.

Create a Base Box of the Design

We will first use construction geometry to define the outer edges of the design.

1. In the *Status Bar* area, reset the option buttons so that only the *Grid Display, Dynamic Input, Ortho, Isodraft, Object Snap Tracking,* and *Object Snap* options are switched ***ON***.

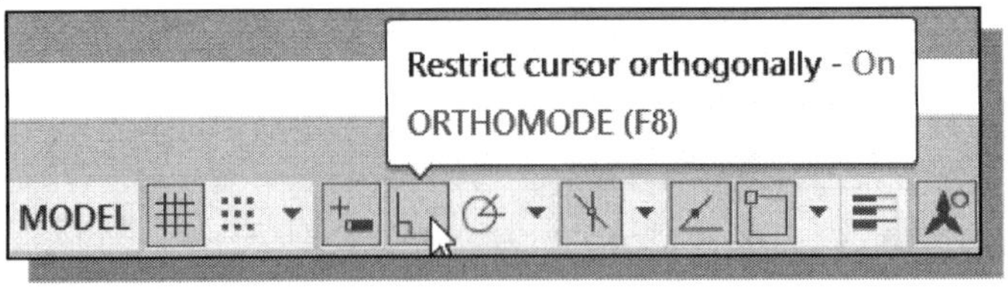

2. In the *Status Bar* area, set the *Isoplane* option to the *Left plane* as shown.

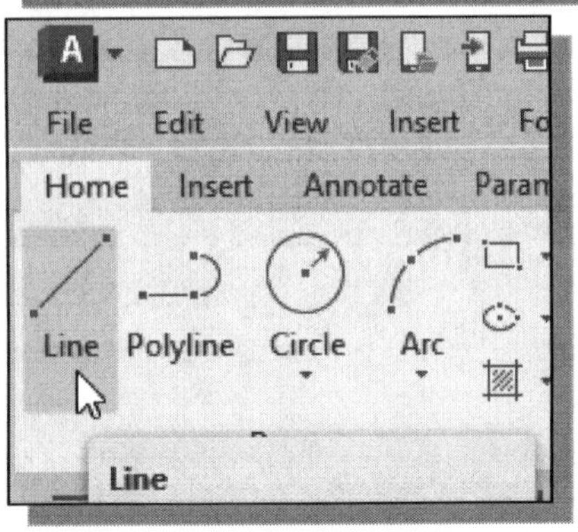

3. Activate the **Line** command in the *Draw* toolbar. Note that since the ***Ortho*** mode is switched on, the cursor is now aligned to the axes directions of the *left isoplane.*

4. Place the first endpoint of the line near the lower center of the graphics area.

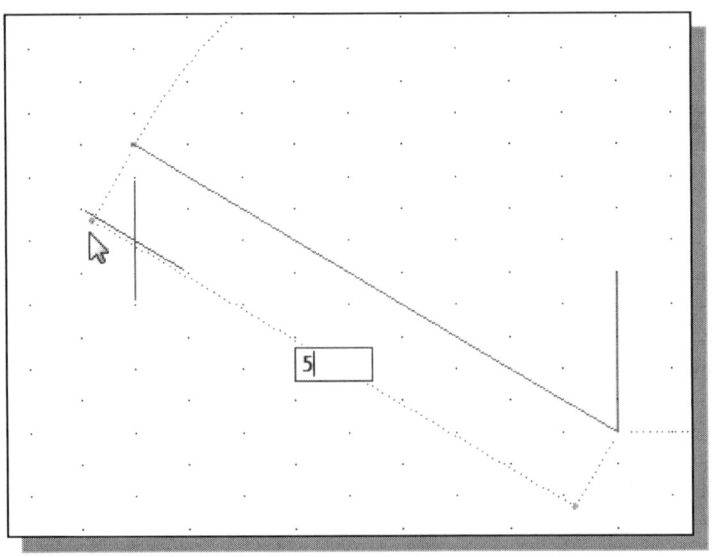

5. Move the cursor downward, and enter **1.25** as the distance to the second end point of the line sequence.

6. Move the cursor toward the left side, and align the cursor in the 150 degrees direction. Enter **5.0** as the distance to the third end point of the line sequence.

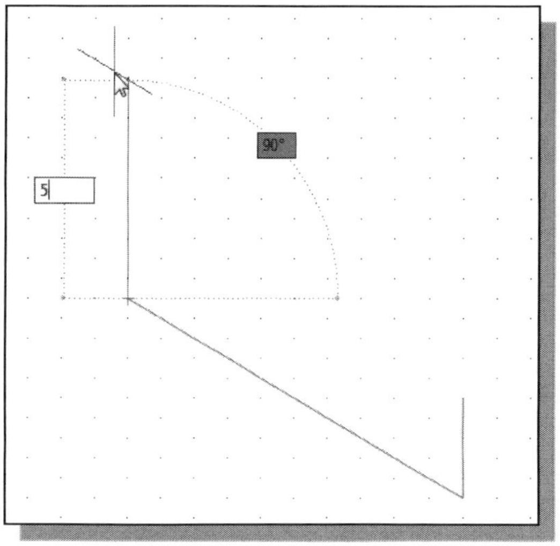

7. Move the cursor upward, and enter **5.0** as the distance to the next end point of the line sequence.

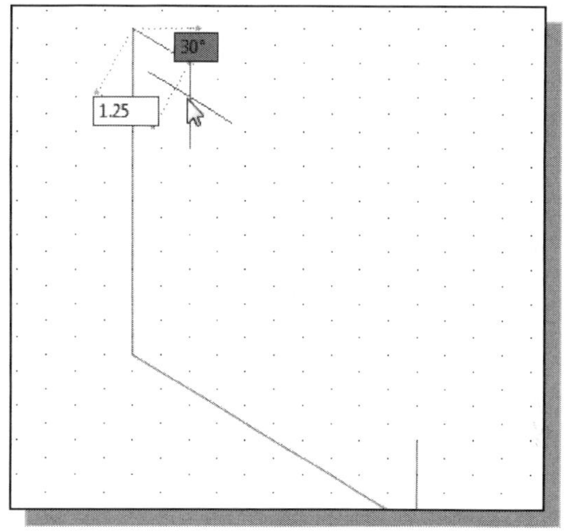

8. Move the cursor toward the left side, and align the cursor in the -30 degrees direction. Enter **1.25** as the distance to the next end point of the line sequence.

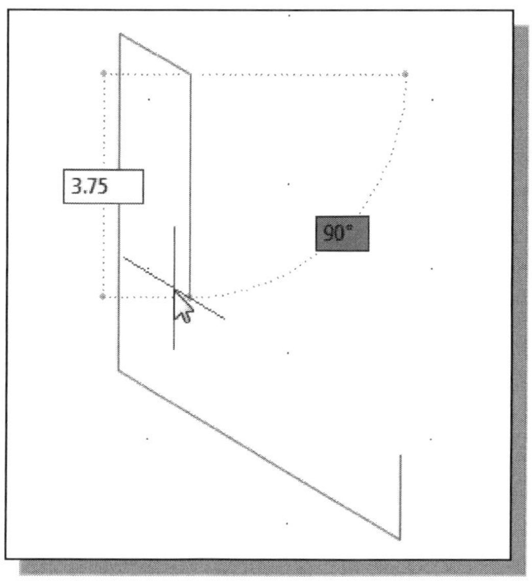

9. Move the cursor downward, and enter **3.75** as the distance to the second end point of the line sequence.

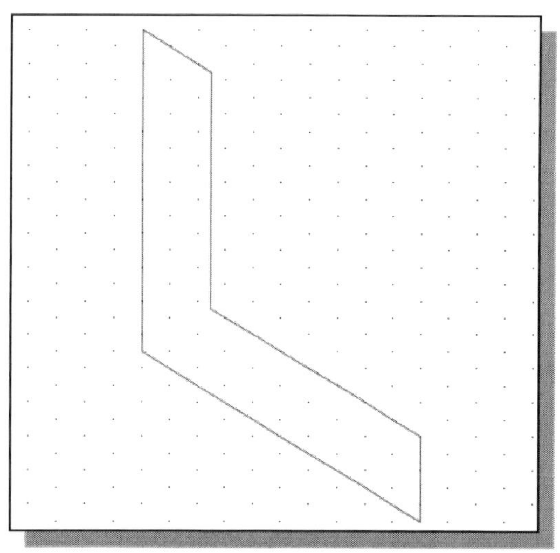

10. Right-click once to bring up the *option* list, and select **Close** to complete the front face of the design as shown.

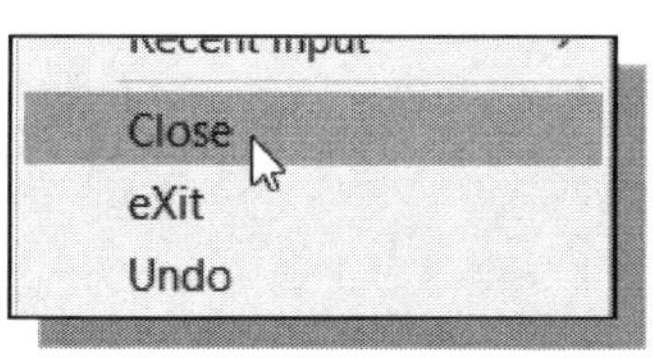

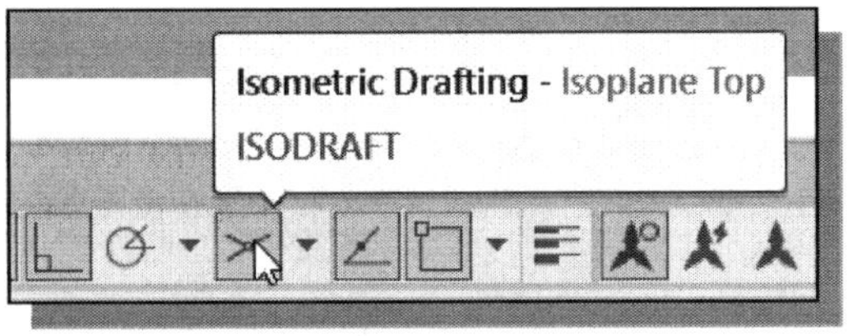

11. Hit the [**F5**] key or [**Ctrl+E**] once and notice the isoplane is now set to the *Top plane* as shown.

12. In the modify toolbar, activate the **Copy** command as shown.

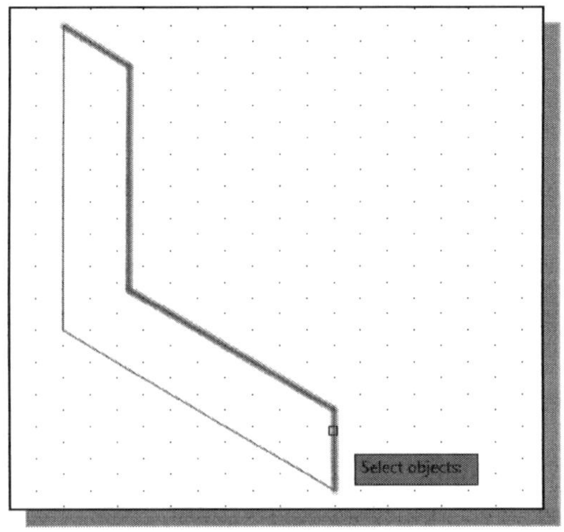

13. Select the four line segments as shown.

14. Right-click once to accept the selection and proceed with the **Copy** command.

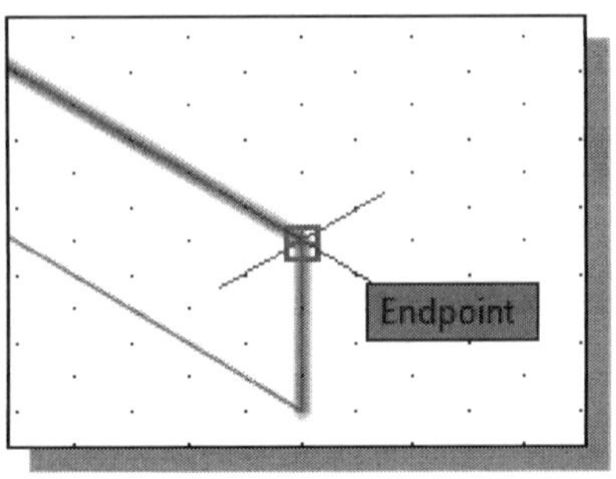

15. Select **one of the corners** as the copy reference point.

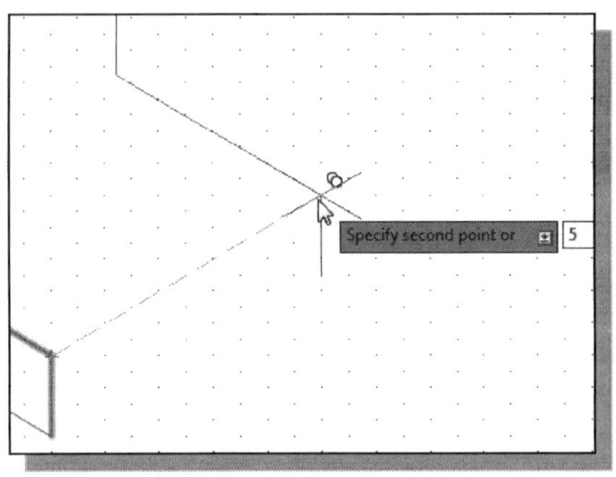

16. Move the cursor toward the right side and enter **5** as the distance to place the copy.

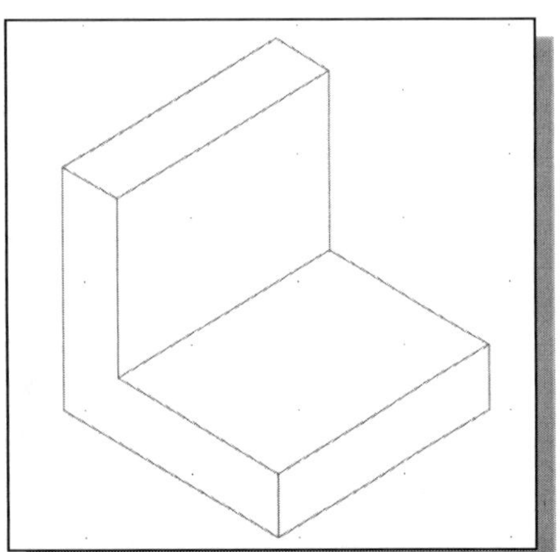

17. On your own, create additional lines to connect the corners of the front and back sides as shown.

Locate the Centers for the Isocircles

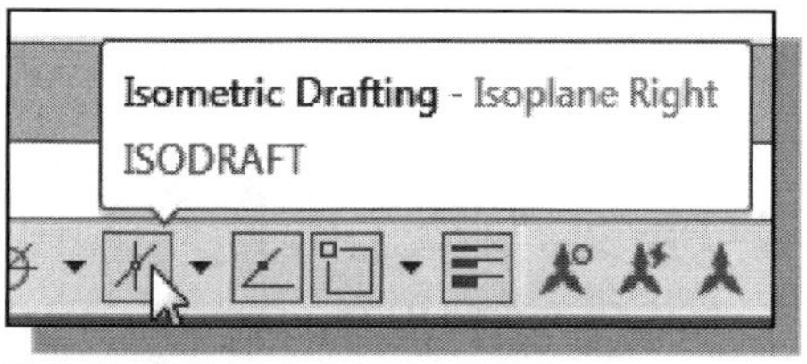

1. Hit the [**F5**] key or [**Ctrl+E**] once and notice the isoplane is now set to the *Right plane* as shown.

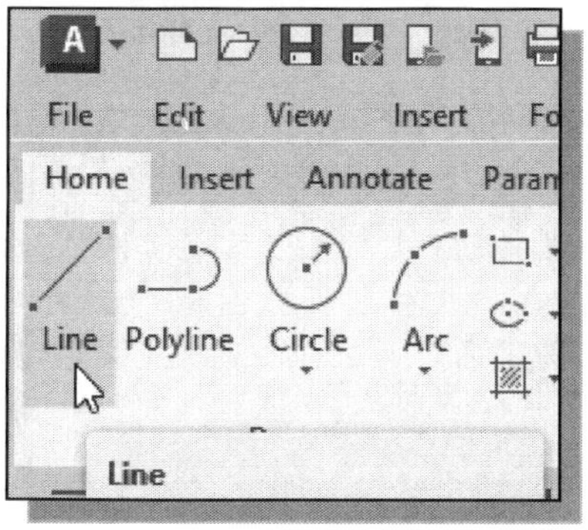

2. Activate the **Line** command in the *Draw* toolbar.

- We will first locate the center of the diameter 1.75 center circle of the design.

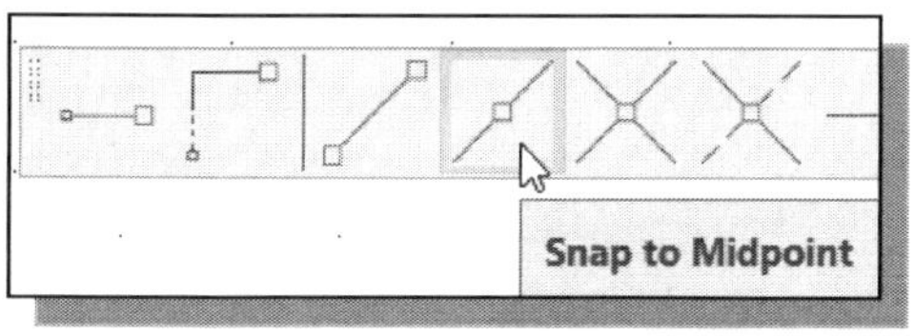

3. Activate the **Snap to Midpoint** option as shown.

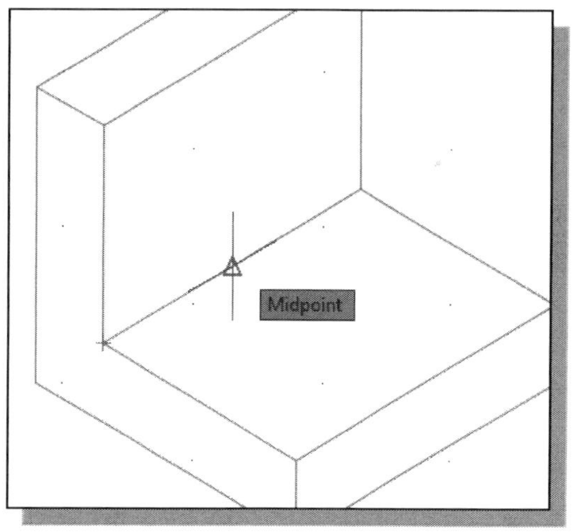

4. Select the bottom edge of the vertical section of the design as shown.

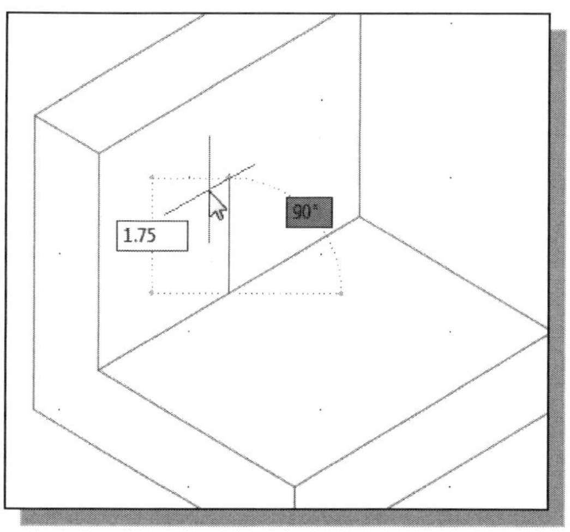

5. Move the cursor upward and enter **1.75** as the distance to the center point of the diameter 1.75 circle.

6. Hit the [**Esc**] key once to end the line command.

- We will also need to locate the center locations for the two rounded corners of the vertical section of the design.

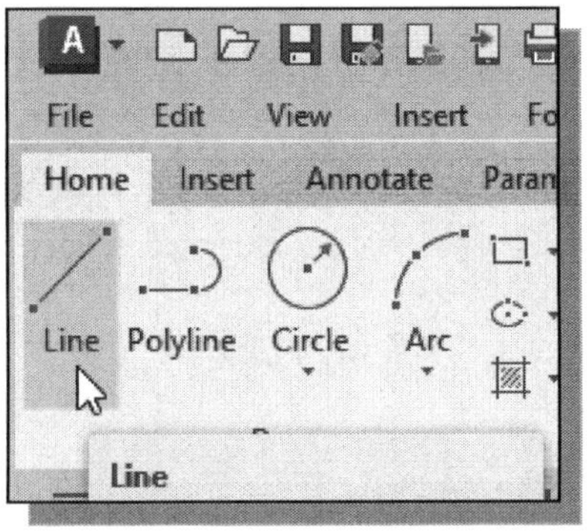

7. Activate the **Line** command in the *Draw* toolbar.

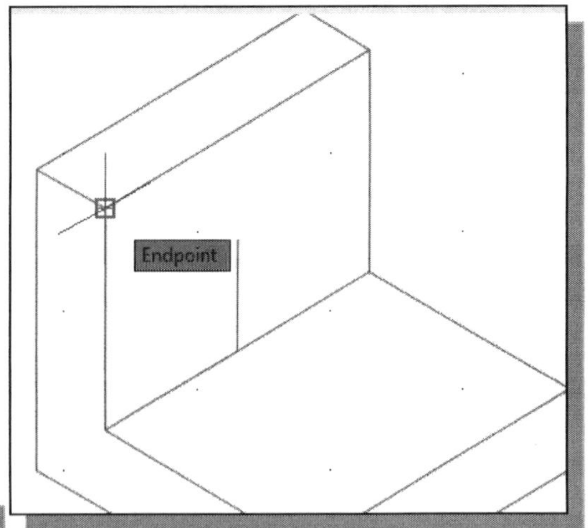

8. Snap to the upper left corner of the vertical section as shown.

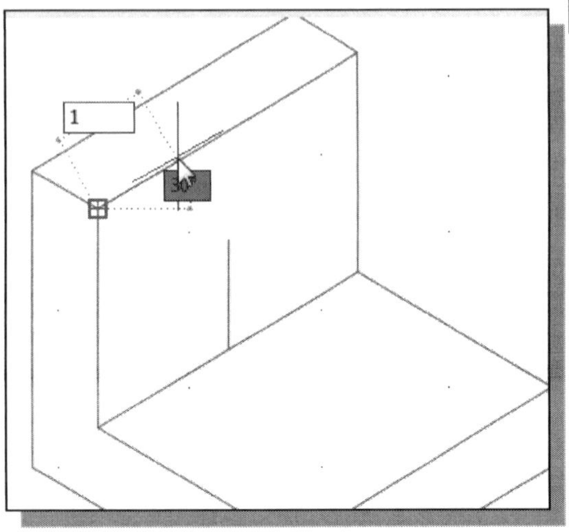

9. Move the cursor along the top edge and enter **1.0** as the distance as shown.

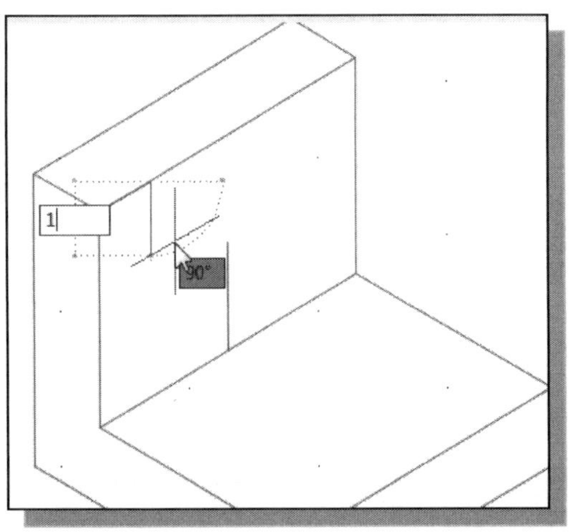

10. Move the cursor downward and enter **1.0** as the distance to locate the center point for the rounded corner as shown.

11. On your own, create two line segments to locate the center location of the rounded corner on **the other side**.

Create the Isocircles

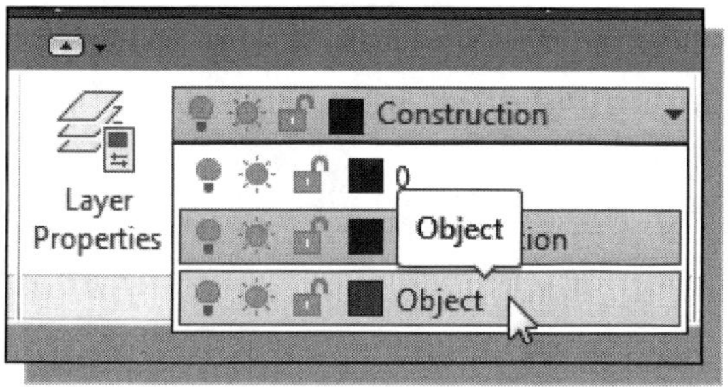

1. In the *Layer Control* box, set the layer *Object* as the *Current Layer*.

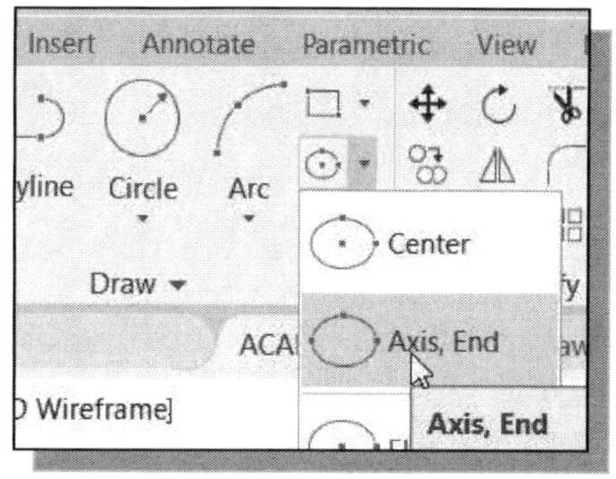

2. In the *Draw* toolbar, activate the **Axis, End Ellipse** command.

3. In the command prompt area, click Isocircle as shown.

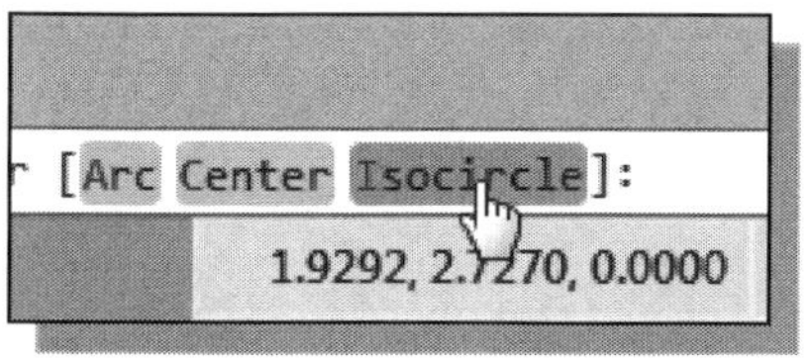

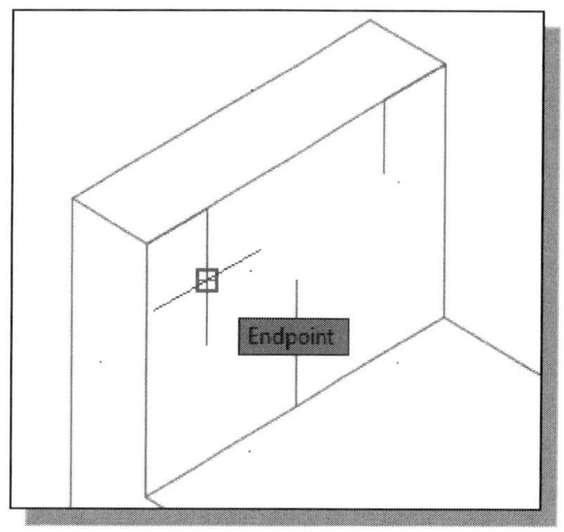

4. Snap to the bottom endpoint of the left line segment to place the center of the isocircle.

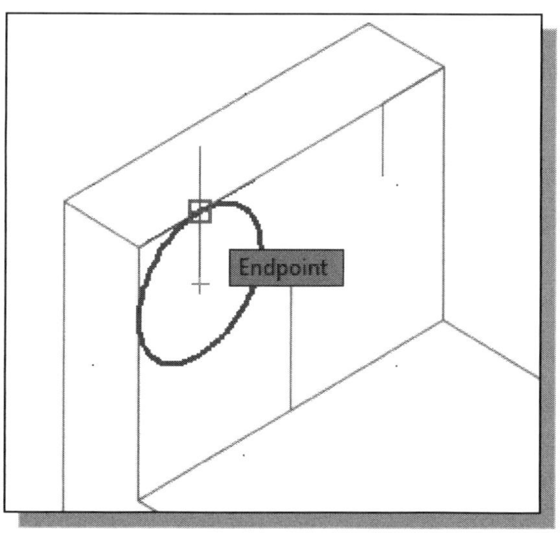

5. Snap to the top endpoint of the left line segment to create the isocircle representing the rounded corner.

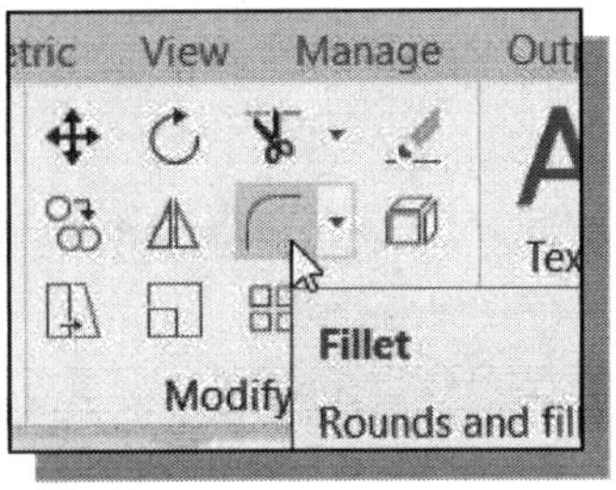

- Note that the *Fillet* command **does not** create the correct rounded corner in AutoCAD *Isometric views*; we will confirm this is the case.

6. In the *Modify* toolbar, activate the **Fillet** command.

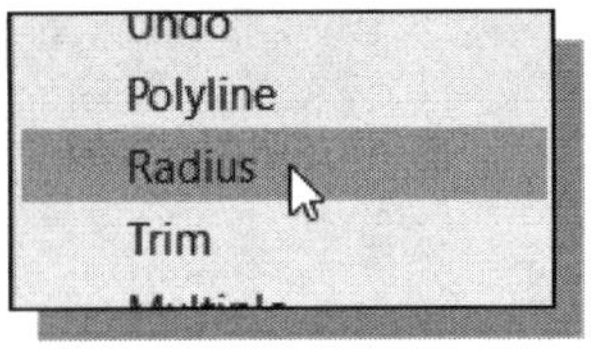

7. Right-click once to bring up the option list and select the **Radius** option.

8. Enter **1.0** as the radius of the fillet.

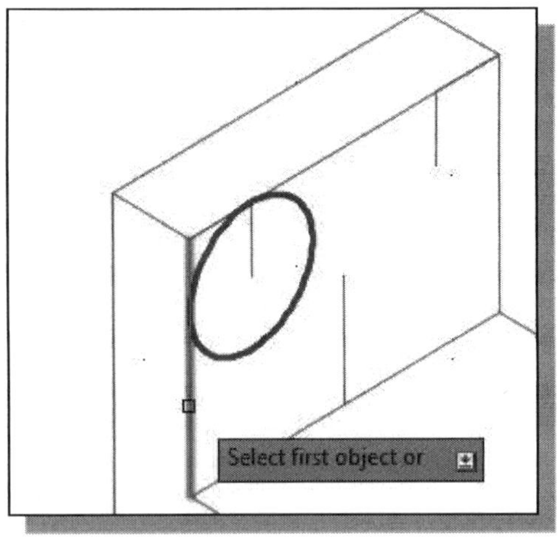

9. Select the left vertical edge as the first object as shown.

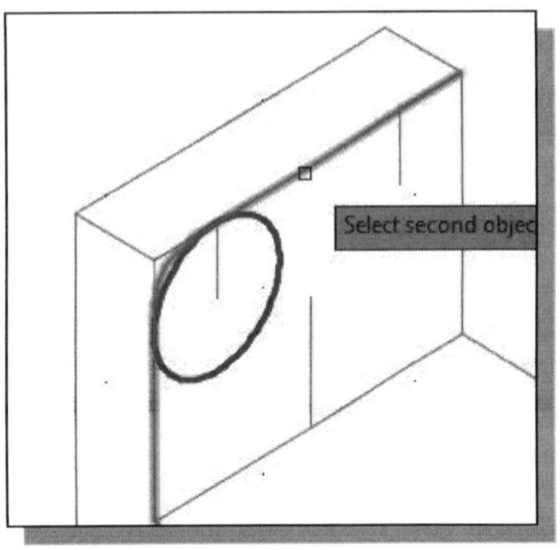

10. Select the top edge as the second object as shown.

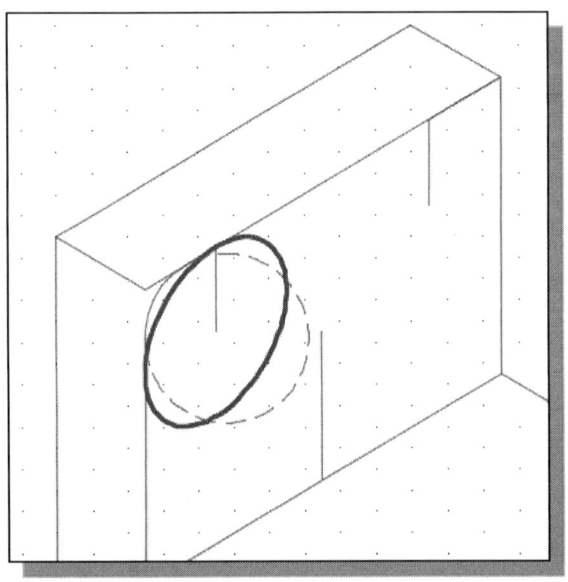

11. On your own, create a circle on top of the arc created with the fillet command to confirm the circle is aligned to the screen, not the isometric axes.

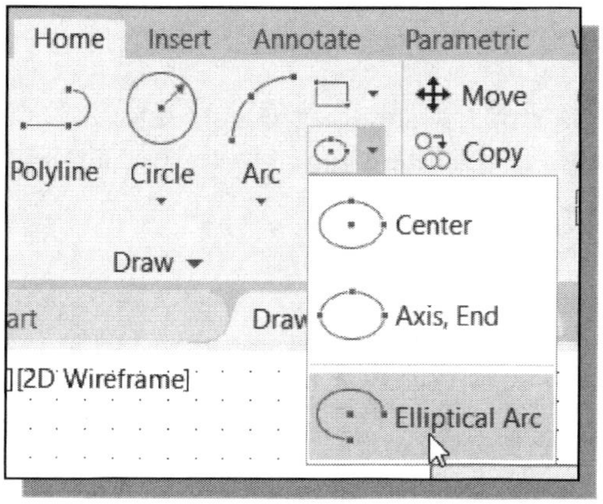

12. In the *Draw* toolbar, activate the **Elliptical Arc** command as shown.

13. In the command prompt area, click Isocircle as shown.

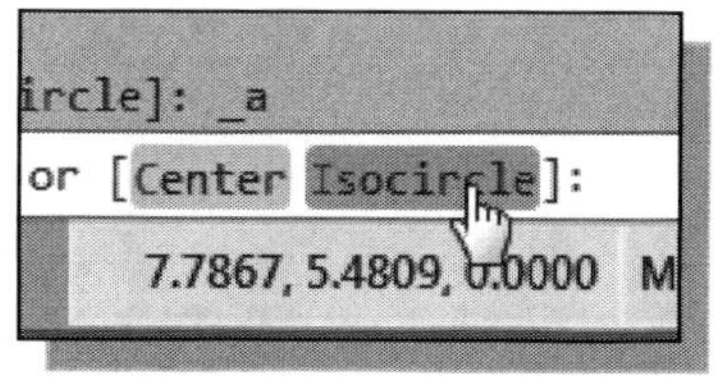

14. Snap to the bottom endpoint of the right line segment to place the center of the isocircle.

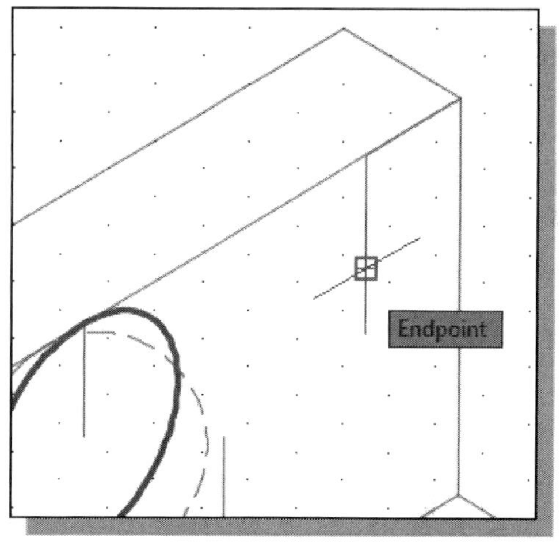

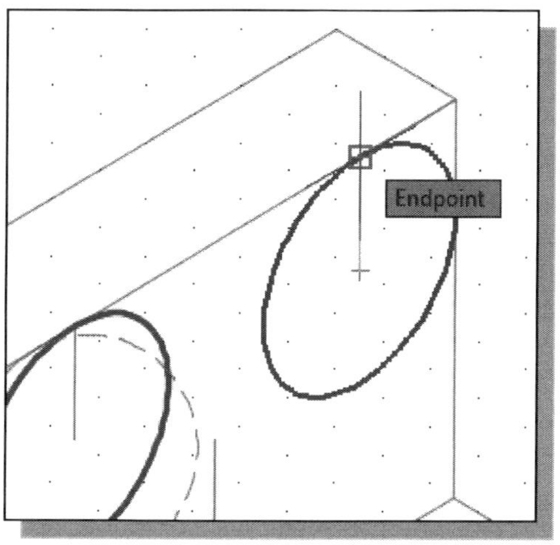

15. Snap to the top endpoint of the right line segment to accept the distance as radius.

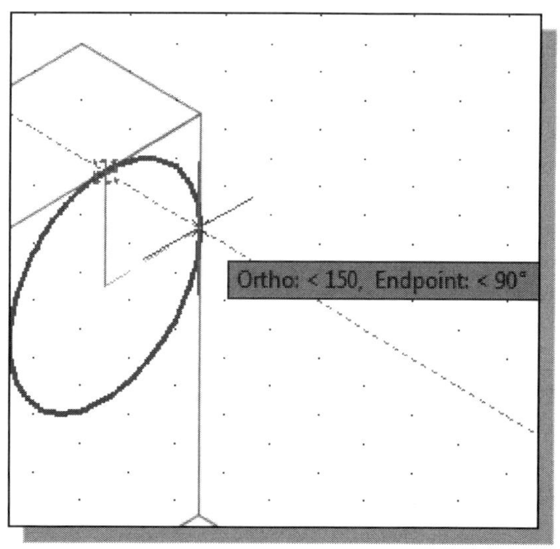

16. Select the **Endpoint angle** 90 degree location as the start angle of the arc.

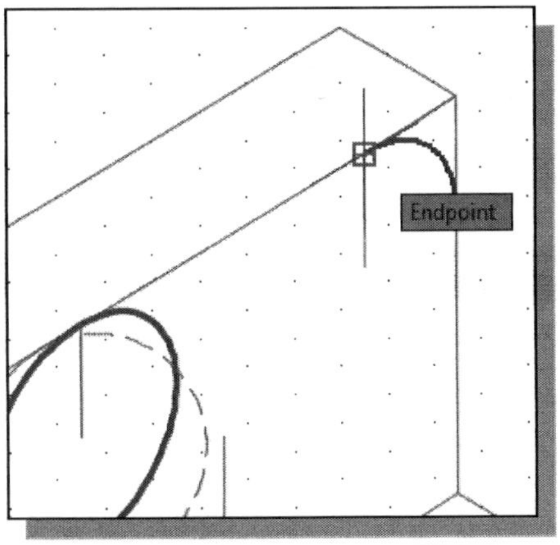

17. Snap to the top endpoint of the right line segment to accept the location as the end angle of the arc.

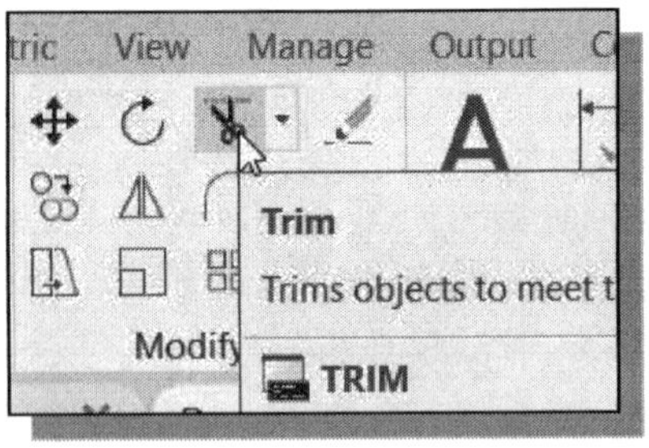

18. In the *Modify* toolbar, activate the **Trim** command as shown.

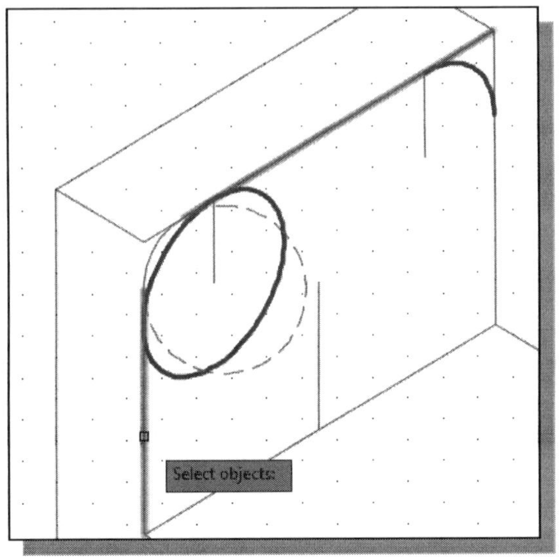

19. In the command prompt area, click **cuTting edges** as shown.

20. Select the top and the left edges as the trimming boundary as shown.

21. Click once with the right-mouse-button to accept the selection.

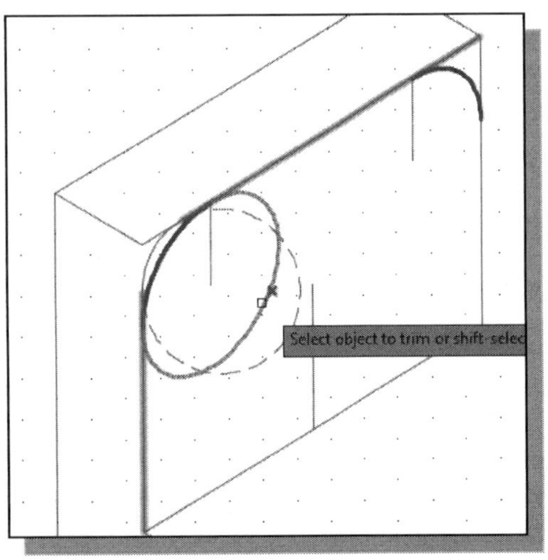

22. Click on the lower side of the isocircle to remove the lower portion as shown.

23. On your own, exit the trim command with the option list as shown.

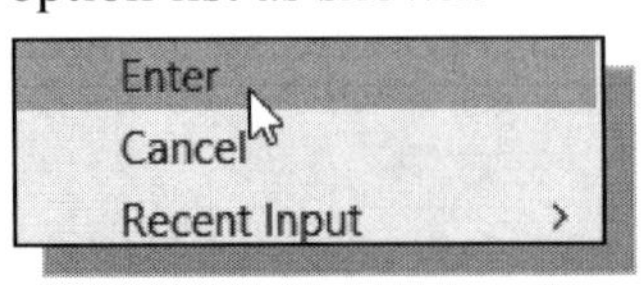

24. Hit the [**F5**] key or [**Ctrl+E**] twice and notice the isoplane is now set to the *top plane* as shown.

25. In the modify toolbar, activate the **Copy** command.

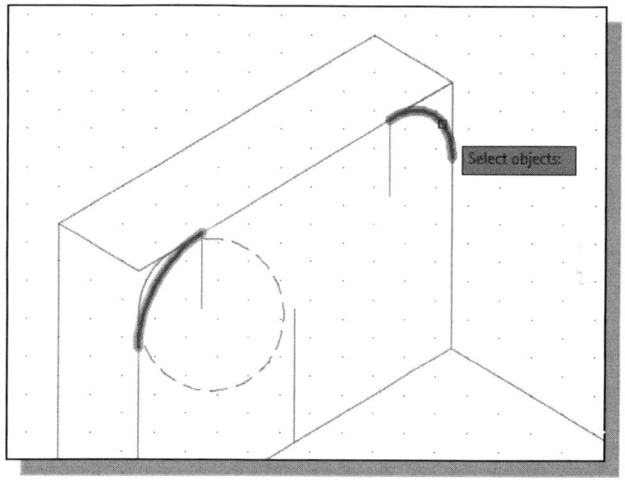

26. Select the two elliptical arcs as shown.

27. Right-mouse-click once to accept the selection and proceed with the **Copy** command.

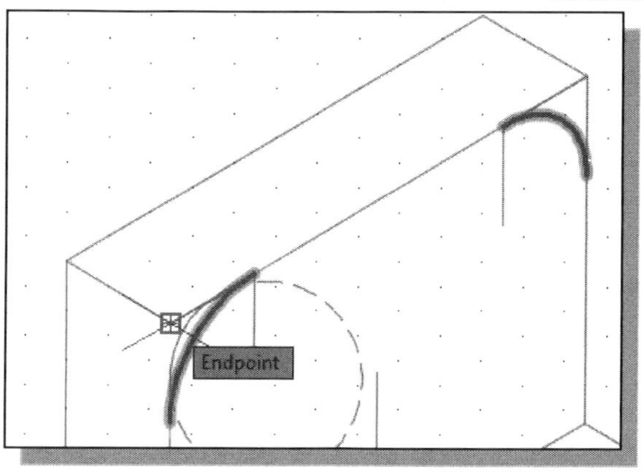

28. Select the **Front left corner** as the copy reference point.

29. Select the **back left corner** to place the two copies of arcs.

30. Hit the [**Esc**] key once to end the copy command.

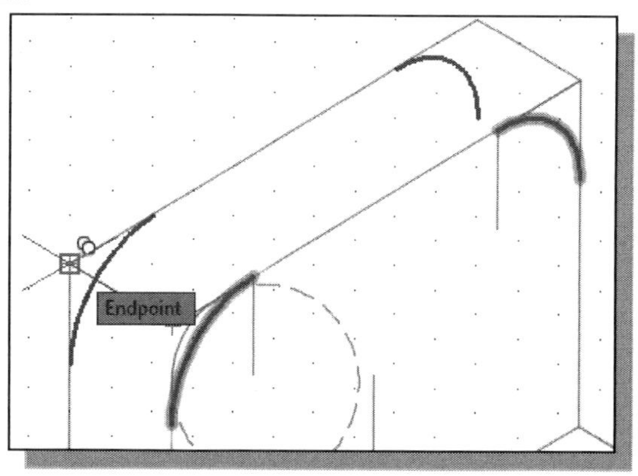

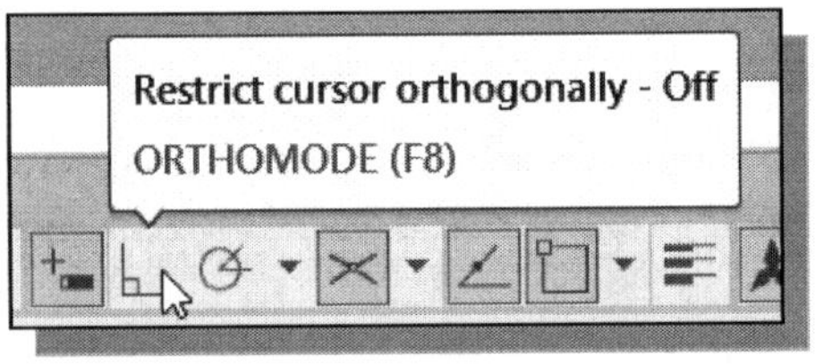

31. In the status bar area, turn off the **Ortho** mode as shown.

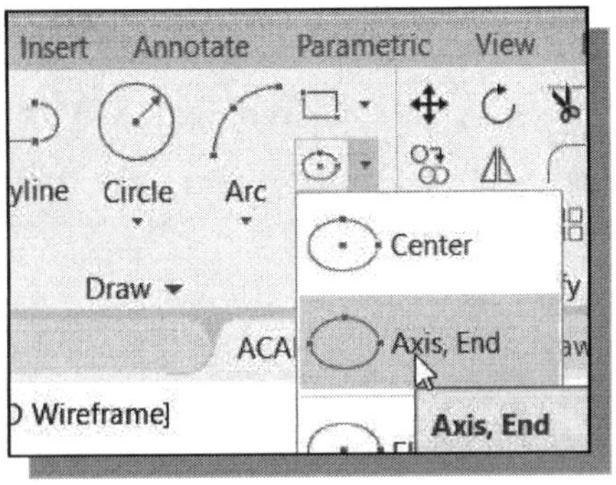

32. In the *Draw* toolbar, activate the **Axis, End Ellipse** command.

33. In the command prompt area, click Isocircle as shown.

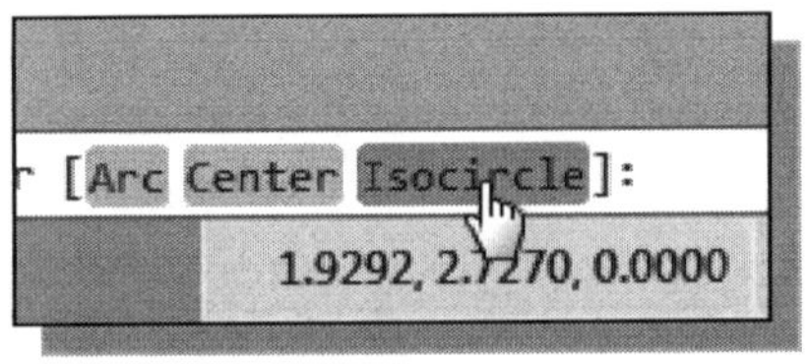

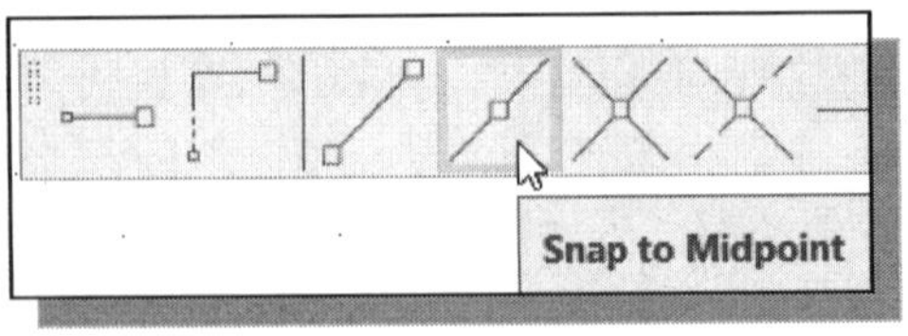

34. Activate the **Snap to Midpoint** option as shown.

35. Snap to the midpoint of the top edge of the horizontal section of the design to place the center of the isocircle.

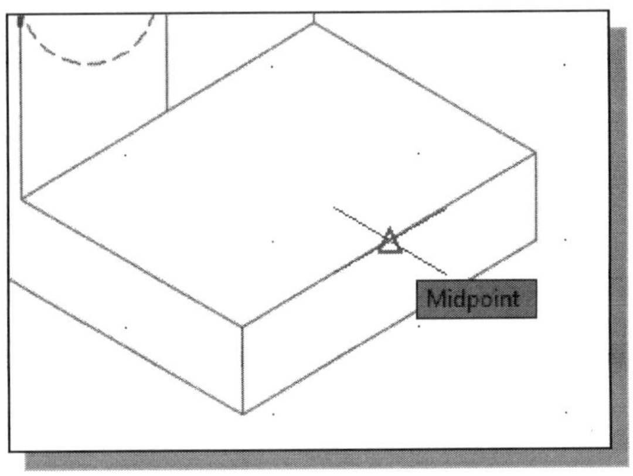

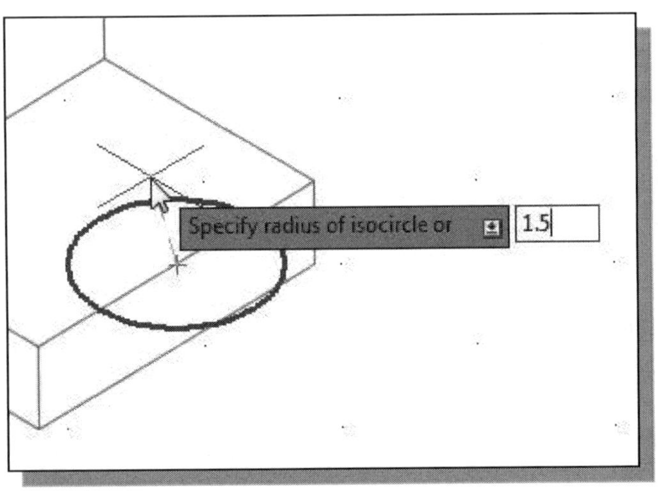

36. Enter **1.5** as the radius and create the isocircle.

37. On your own, use the **trim** and **copy** commands to create a copy of the elliptical arc to the bottom surface as shown.

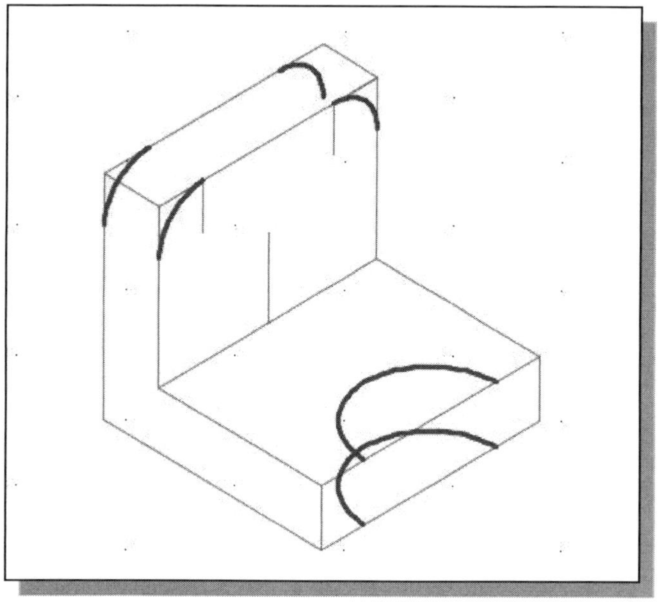

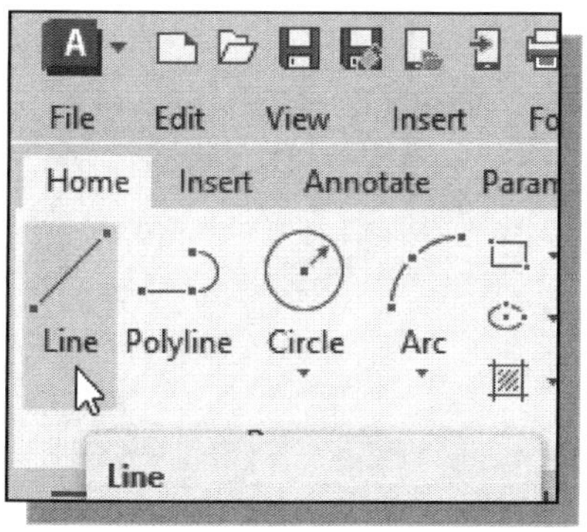

38. Activate the **Line** command in the *Draw* toolbar.

39. On your own, create the outline of the design by creating line segments connecting to the arcs as shown in the below figure.

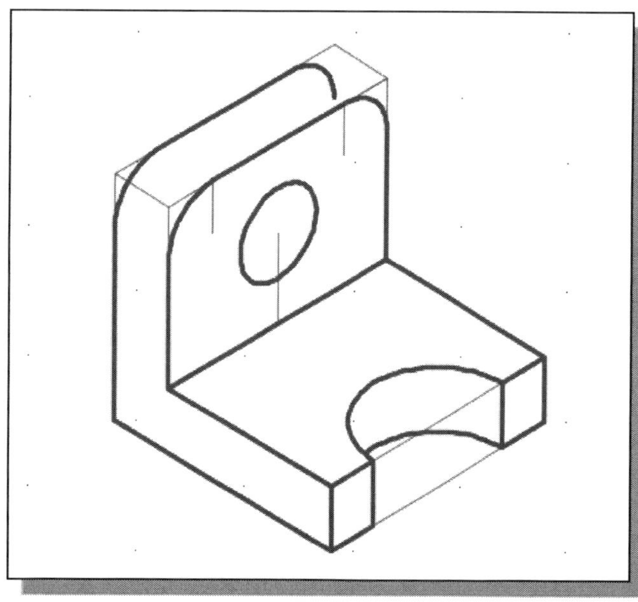

- Note that we need to identify the tangent edge for the top corner of the design.

Using the Parametric tools to complete the drawing

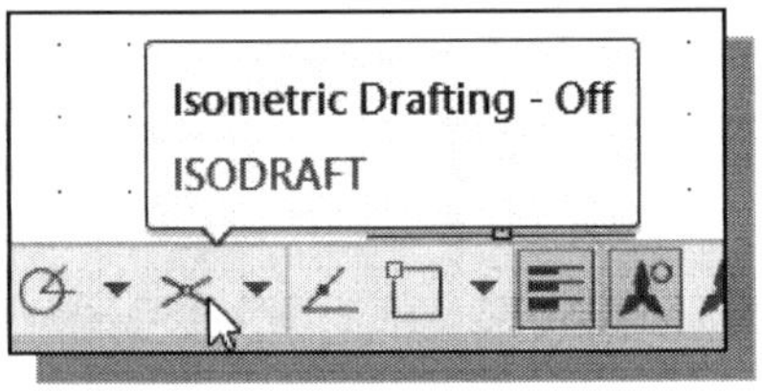

1. In the *Status Bar* area, turn off the *Isodraft*, *Object Snap Tracking* and *Object Snap* options as shown.

2. In the *modify toolbar*, activate the **Copy** command.

3. Select the **right edge** on the top face as shown.

4. Right-click once to accept the selection and proceed with the **Copy** command.

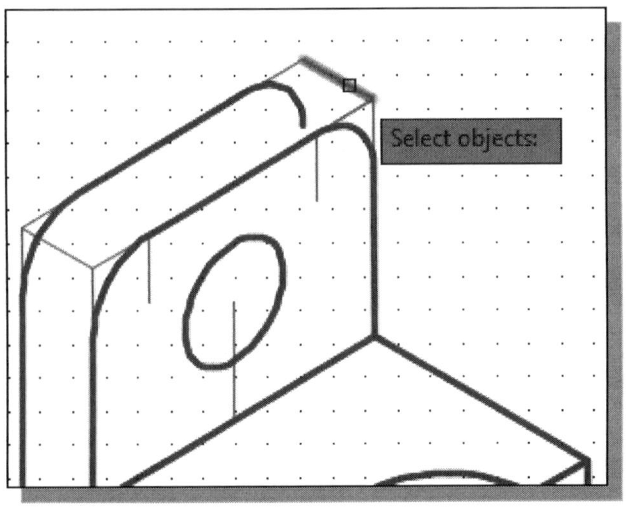

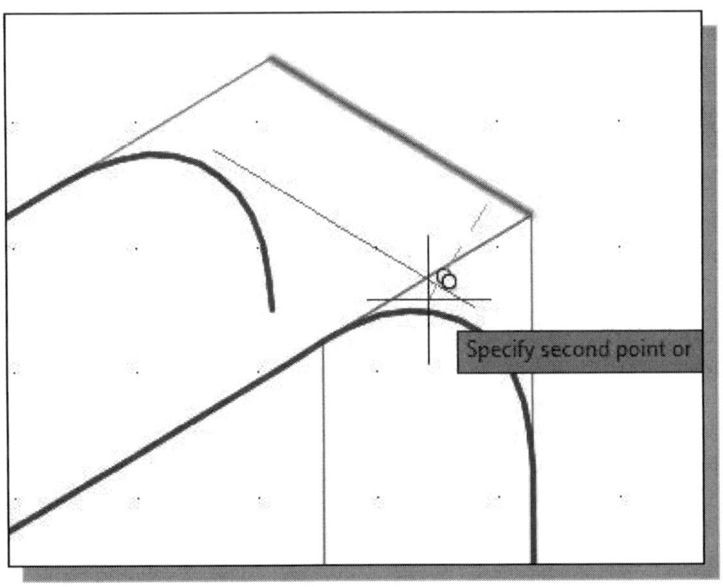

5. Select near the **right corner** as the copy reference point.

6. Place the line next to the two elliptical arcs; we will intentionally leave a gap.

7. Hit the [**Esc**] key once to exit the copy command.

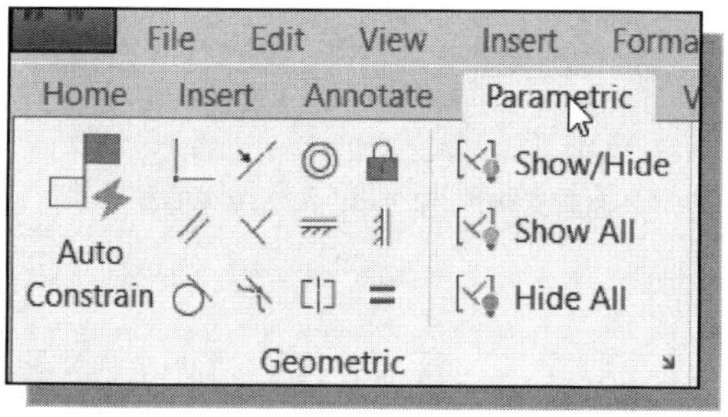

8. In the *Ribbon* toolbar, switch to the **Parametric toolbar** as shown.

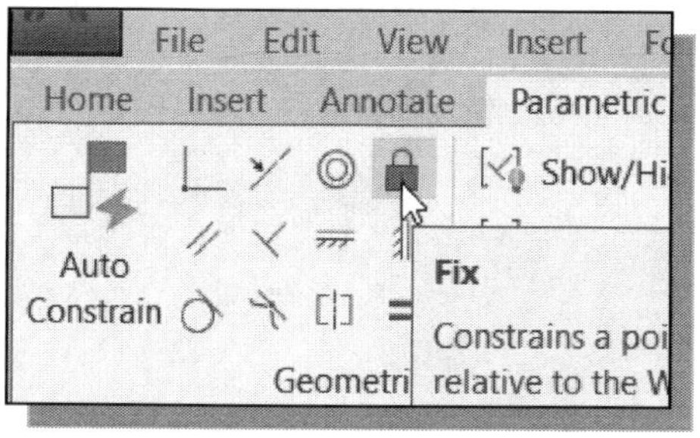

9. In the *Geometric* toolbar, activate the **Fix** constraint by clicking on the **Lock** icon as shown.

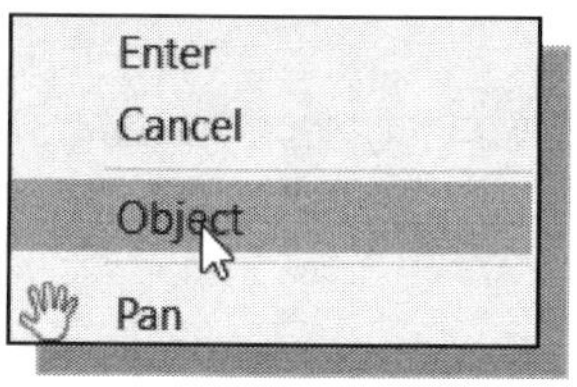

10. Right-click once to bring up the *option* list and select **Object** to apply the constraint to an object.

11. Select the arc on the left to apply the fix constraint.

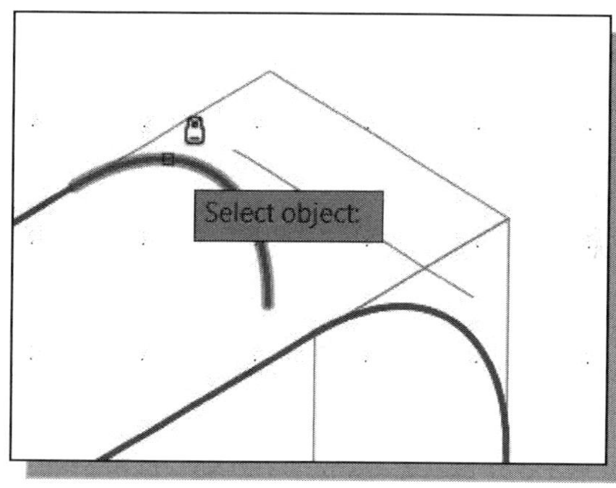

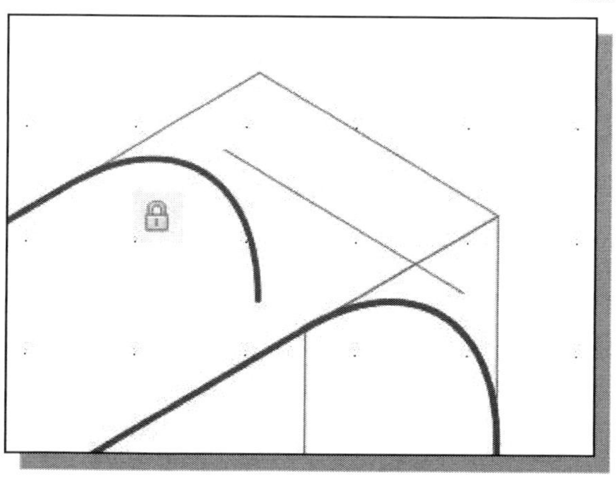

- The lock icon next to the arc indicates the object is fixed to its current location.

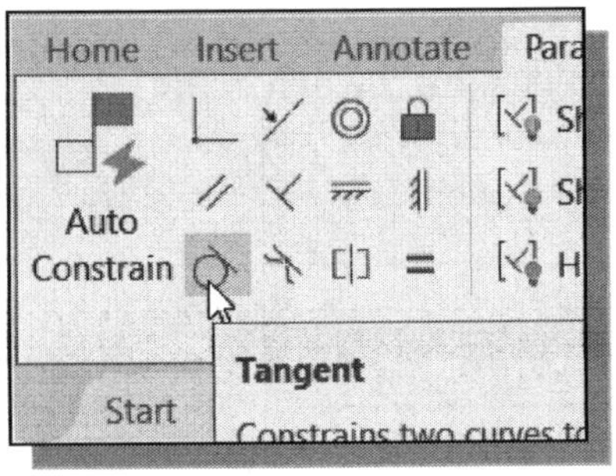

12. In the *Geometric* toolbar, activate the **Tangent** constraint by clicking on the icon as shown.

13. Select the inclined line as the first object to apply the tangent constraint.

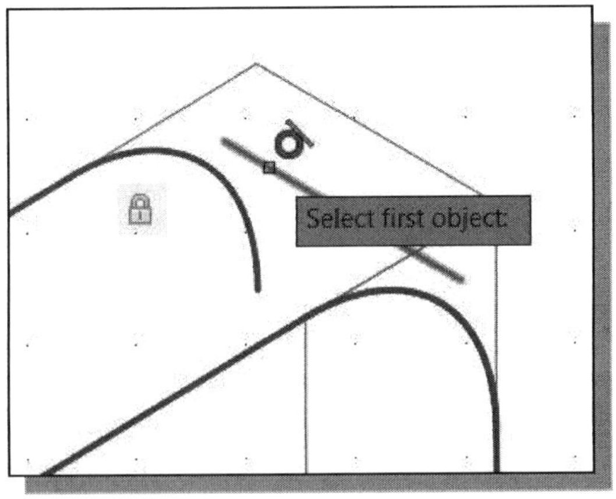

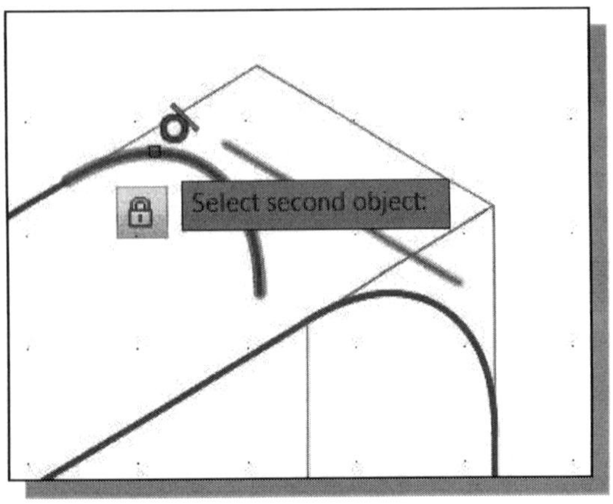

14. Select the **fixed arc** as the second object to apply the tangent constraint.

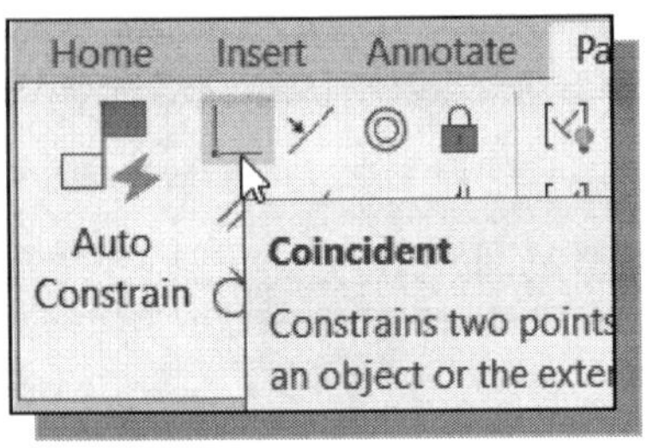

15. Click on the **Coincident** constraint as shown.

16. Click on the left end point of the line as shown.

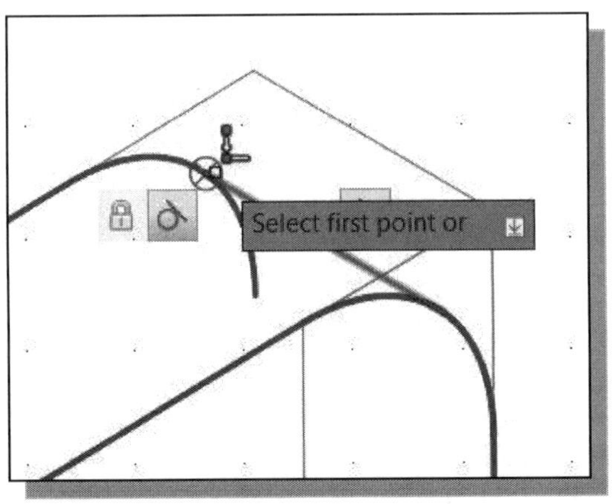

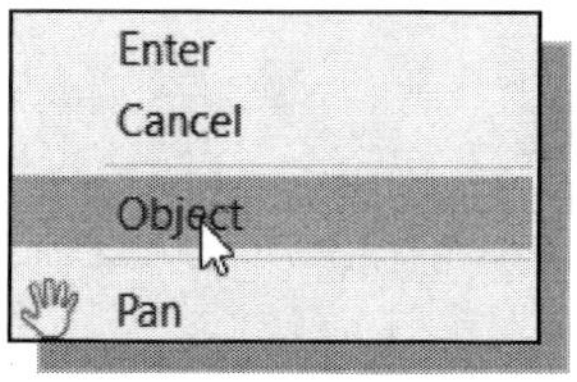

17. Right-click once to bring up the *option* list and select **Object** to apply the constraint to an object.

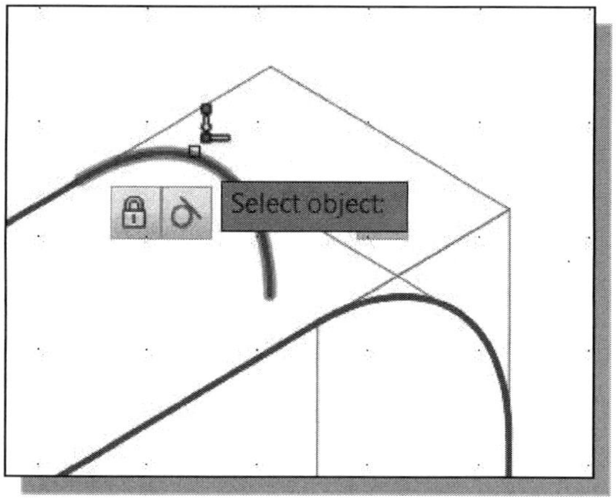

18. Select the fixed arc as the object to apply the constraint.

- Note the line is moved in place as the constraints are applied.

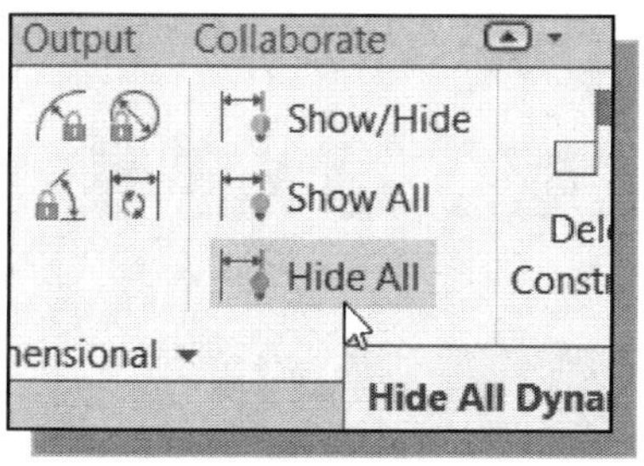

19. Click on the **Hide All** icon to remove all the constraints on the screen.

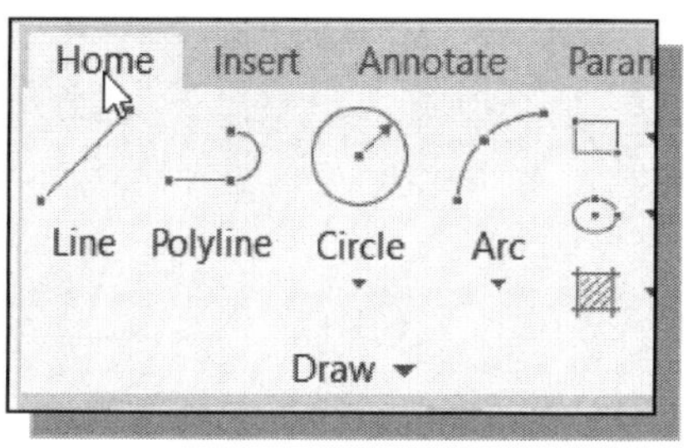

20. Click on the **Home** tab to switch back to the default 2D drawing toolbars.

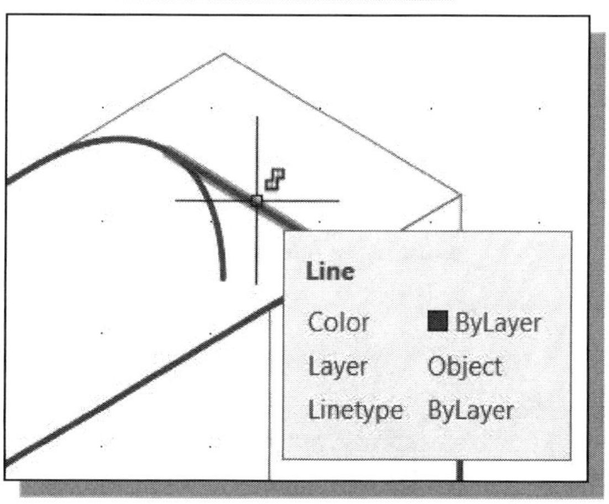

21. On your own, move the tangent line to the **Object layer**.

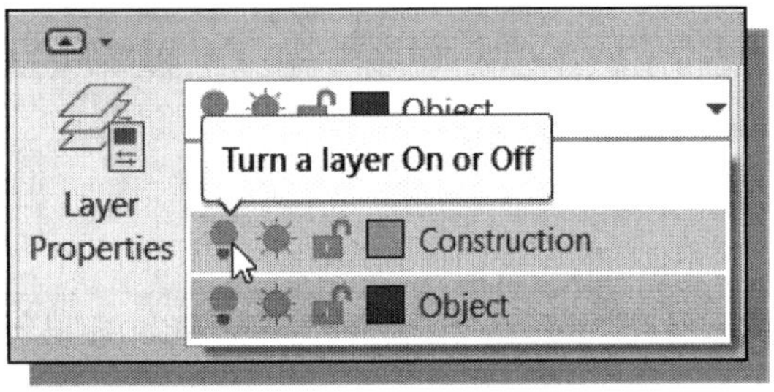

22. In the *Layer control* box, turn off the Construction layer as shown.

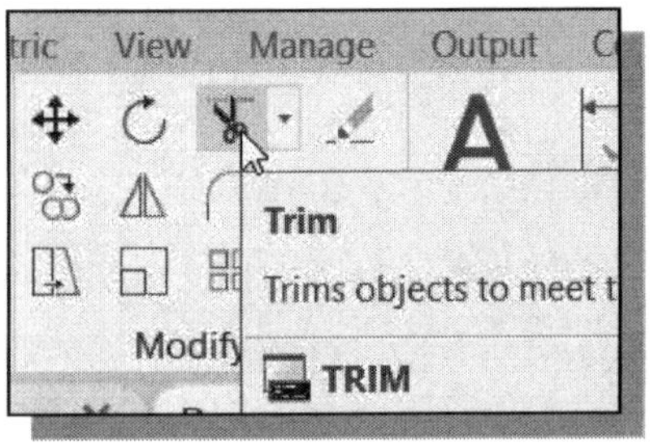

23. In the *Modify* toolbar, activate the **Trim** command as shown.

24. Trim the lower portion of the arc and complete the isometric drawing as shown.

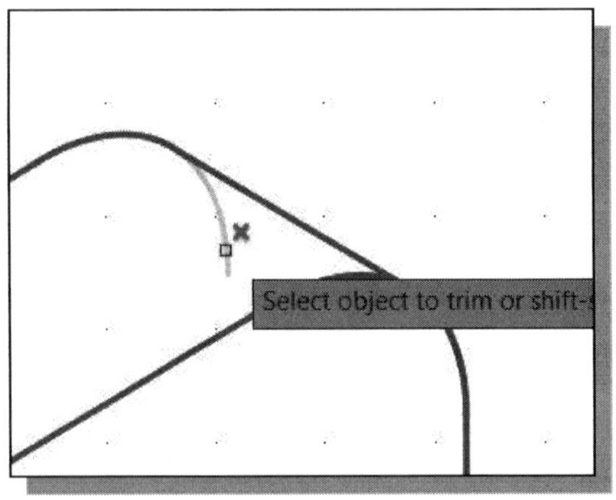

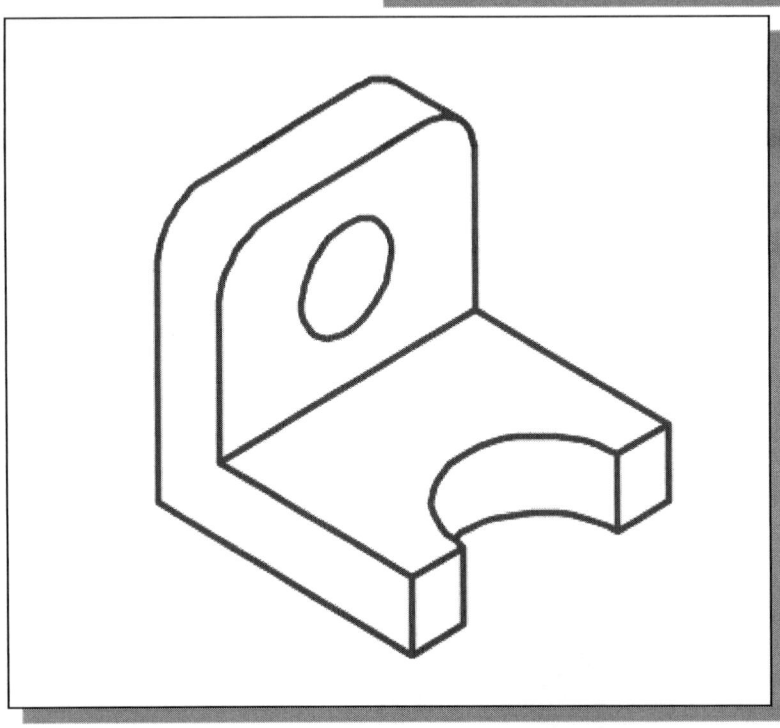

Review Questions:

1. What is the difference between *Isometric* and *Trimetric projections*?

2. In an isometric drawing, how do we determine the directions of the ellipses in representing cylindrical or circular shapes?

3. Describe some of the advantages and disadvantages of using the AutoCAD **2D Isometric** drawings over creating 3D models.

4. Can the Fillet command be used to create accurate rounded corners in AutoCAD 2D isometric drawings?

5. What are the axes' directions when the AutoCAD **Isoplane** is set to **Left plane**?

6. Identify the following commands:

(a)

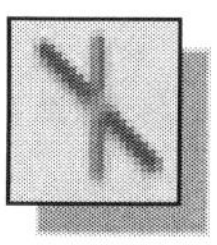

(b)

(c)

(d)

Exercises:

1. Dimensions are in inches. Thickness: Base 0.5 & Boss height 0.25
   The two holes, diameter 1.00, are through holes.

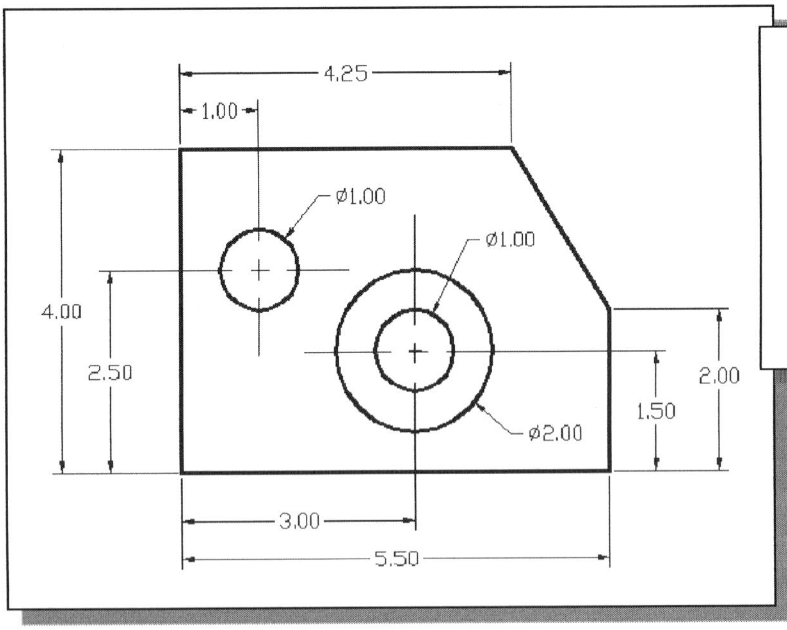

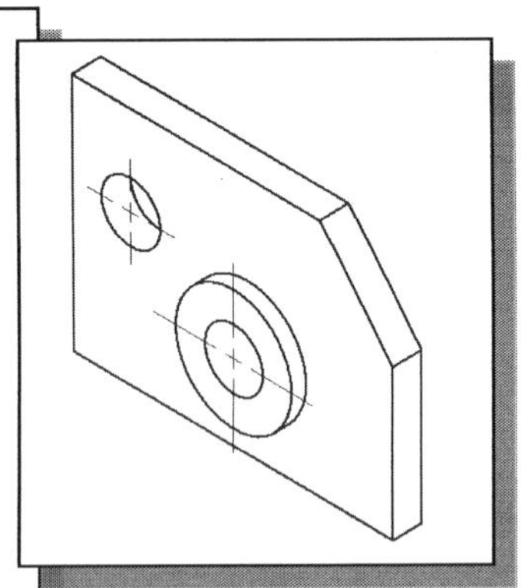

2. Dimensions are in inches.

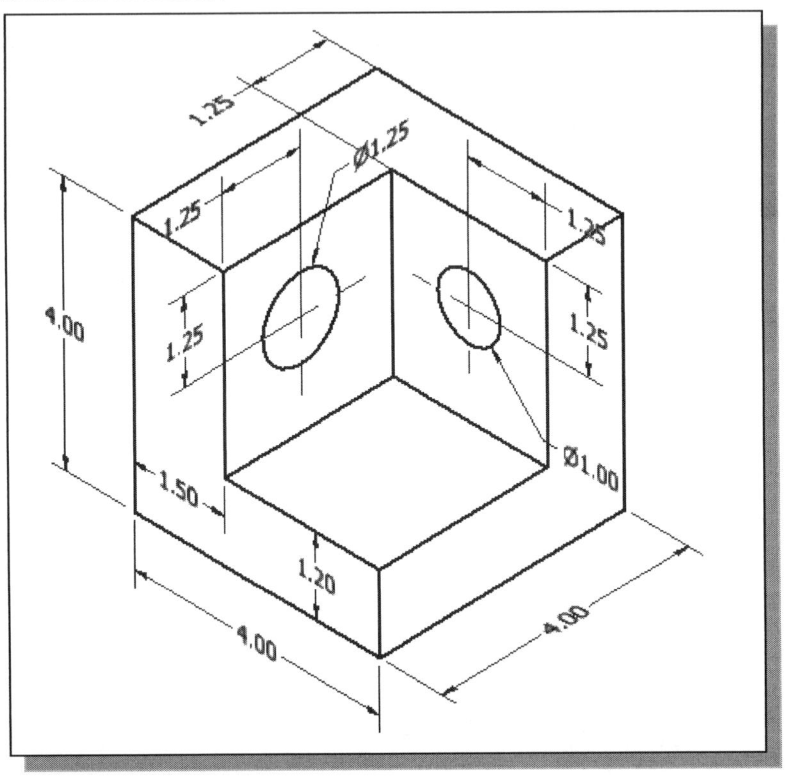

3. Dimensions are in inches.

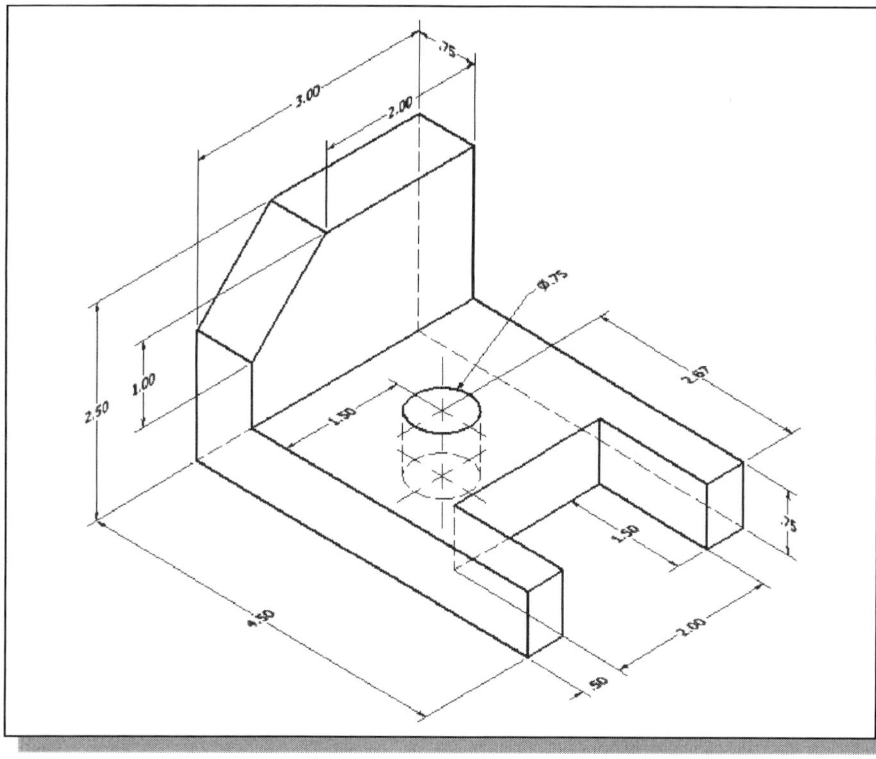

4. Dimensions are in inches.

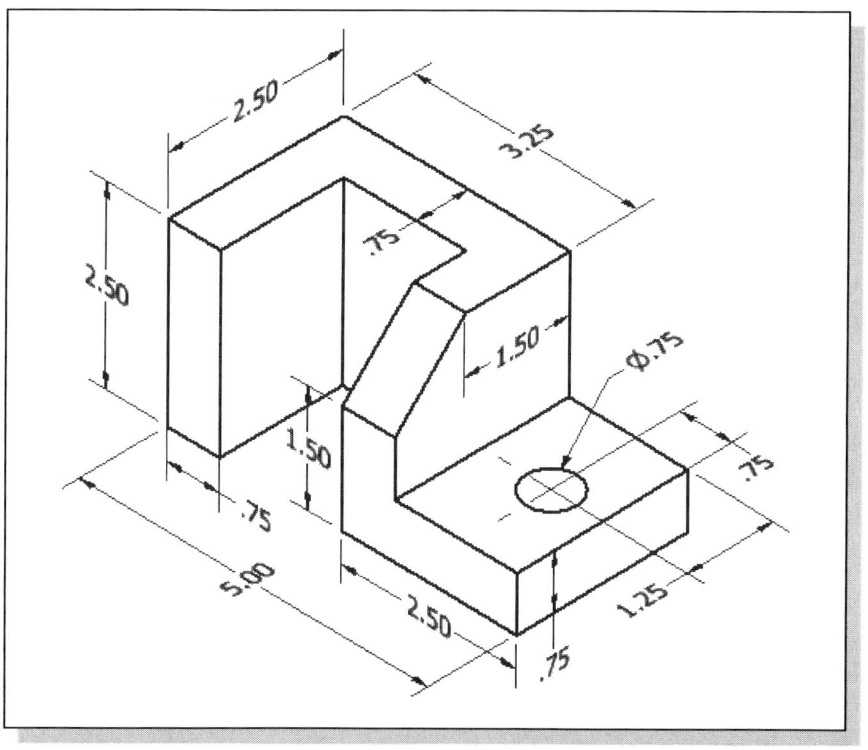

5. Dimensions are in inches.

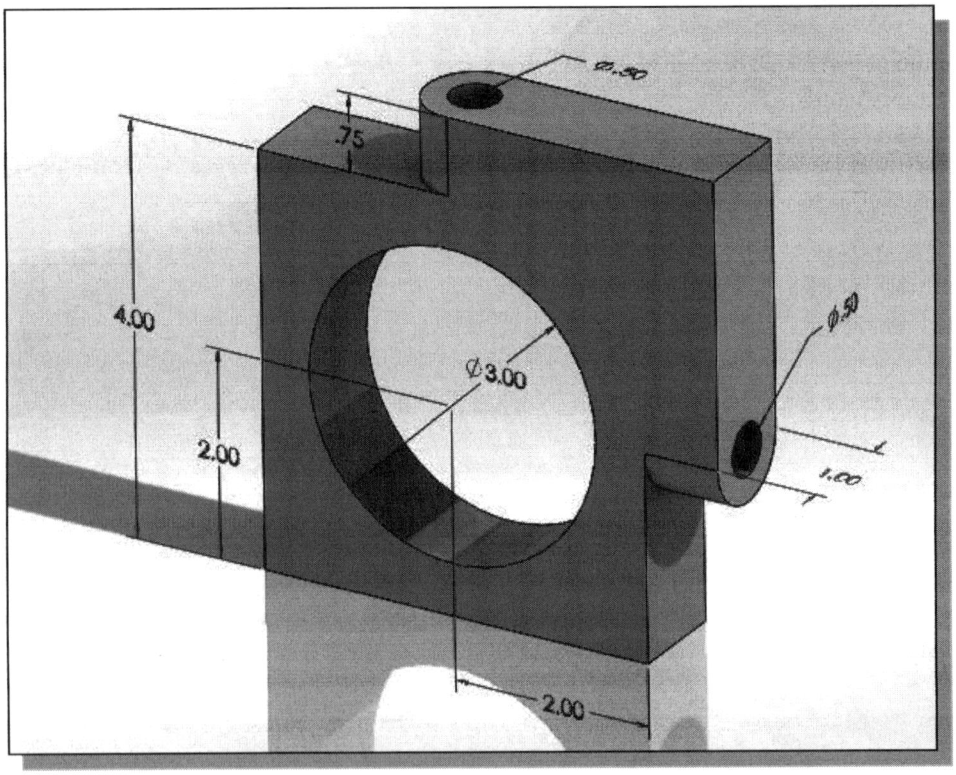

Chapter 7
Dimensioning and Notes

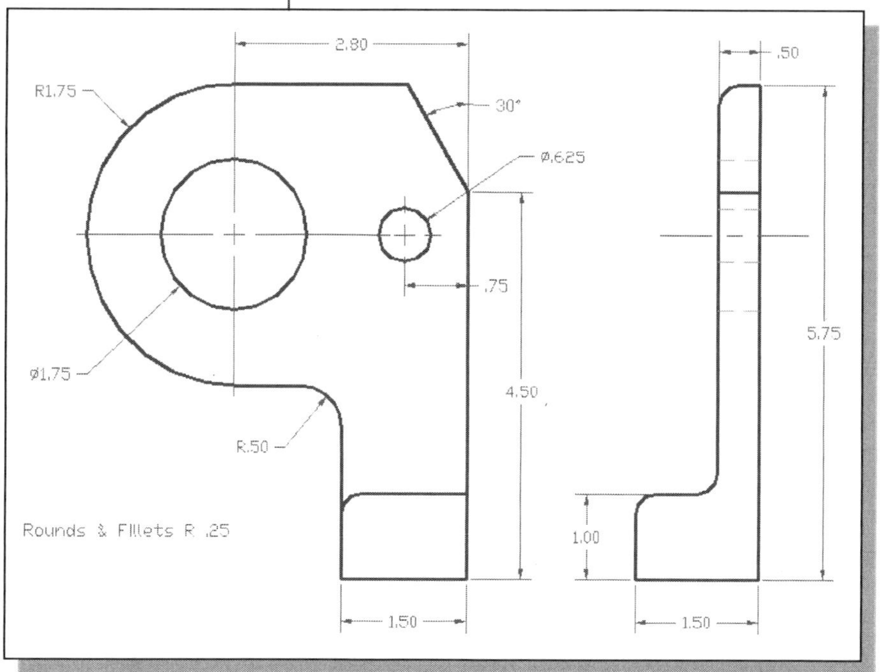

Learning Objectives

- **Understand Dimensioning Nomenclature and Basics**
- **Display and Use the Dimension Toolbar**
- **Use the AutoCAD Dimension Style Manager**
- **Create Center Marks**
- **Add Linear and Angular Dimensions**
- **Use the Single Line Text Command**
- **Create Special Characters in Notes**

AutoCAD Certified User Examination Objectives Coverage

Section 2: Creating Basic Drawings

Section 4: Drawing Organization and Inquiry Commands

Section 5: Altering Objects

Section 7: Annotating the Drawing

Section 8: Dimensioning

Section 10: Working with Reusable Content

Introduction

In engineering graphics, a detailed drawing is a drawing consisting of the necessary orthographic projections, complete with all the necessary dimensions, notes, and specifications needed to manufacture the design. The dimensions put on the drawing are not necessarily the same ones used to create the drawing but are those required for the proper functioning of the part, as well as those needed to manufacture the design. It is therefore important, prior to dimensioning the drawing, to study and understand the design's functional requirements; then consider the manufacturing processes that are to be performed by the pattern-maker, die-maker, machinist, etc., in determining the dimensions that best give the information. In engineering graphics, a **detailed drawing** is a drawing consisting of the necessary orthographic projections, complete with all the necessary dimensions, notes, and specifications needed to manufacture the design.

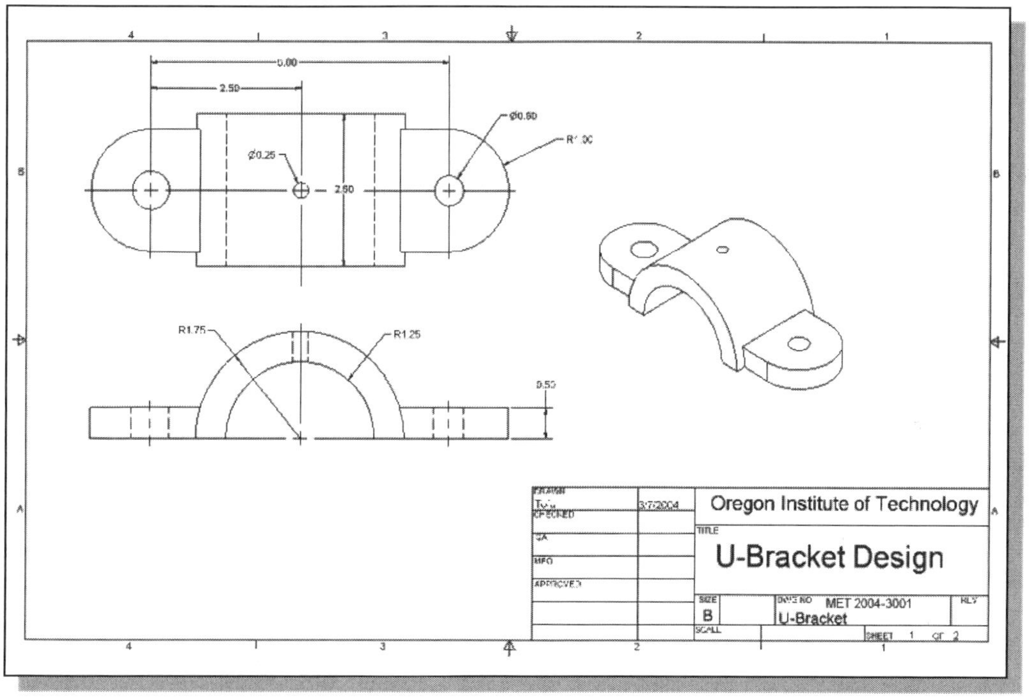

Considerable experience and judgment are required for accurate size and shape description. Dimensioning a design correctly requires conformance to many rules. For example, detail drawings should contain only those dimensions that are necessary to make the design. Dimensions for the same feature of the design should be given only once in the same drawing. Nothing should be left to chance or guesswork on a drawing. Drawings should be dimensioned to avoid any possibility of questions. Dimensions should be carefully positioned, preferably near the profile of the feature being dimensioned. The designer and the CAD operator should also be as familiar as possible with materials, methods of manufacturing and shop processes.

Dimensioning Standards and Basic Terminology

The first step to learning to dimension is a thorough knowledge of the terminology and elements required for dimensions and notes on engineering drawings. Various industrial standards exist for the different industrial sectors and countries; the appropriate standards must be used for the particular type of drawing that is being produced. Some commonly used standards include **ANSI** (American National Standard Institute), **BSI** (British Standards Association), **DIN** (Deutsches Institut fur Normüng), **ISO** (International Standardization Organization), and **JIS** (Japanese Industry Standards). In this text, the discussions of dimensioning techniques are based primarily on the standards of the *American National Standard Institute* (ANSI/ASME Y14.5); other commonsense practices are also illustrated.

In engineering graphics, two basic methods are used to give a description of a measurement on a drawing: **Dimensions** and **Notes**.

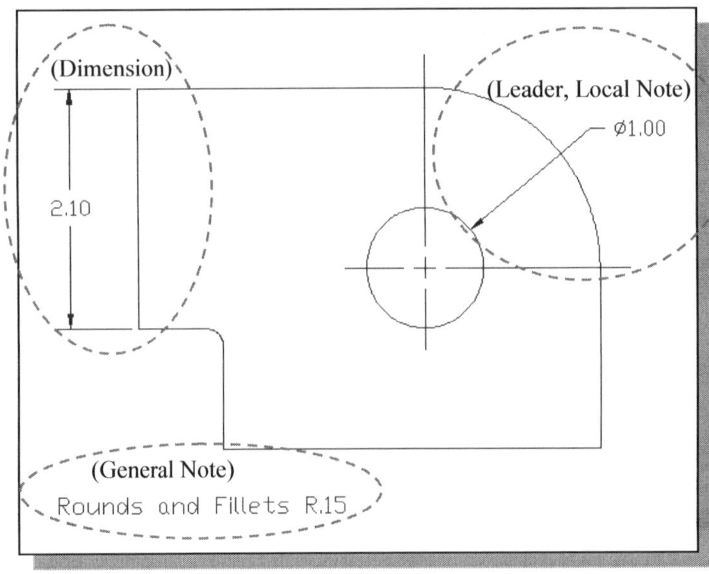

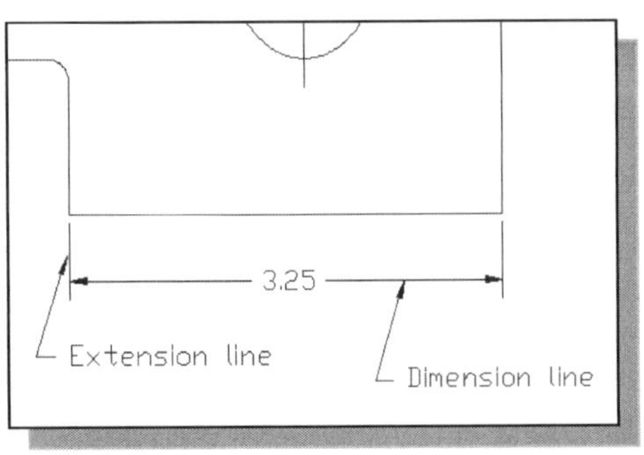

A dimension is used to give the measurement of an object or between two locations on a drawing. The **numerical value** gives the actual measurement, and the **dimension lines** and the **arrowheads** indicate the direction in which the measurement applies. **Extension lines** are used to indicate the locations where the dimension is associated.

Two types of notes are generally used in engineering drawings: **Local Notes** and **General Notes**. A *Local Note* is done with a leader and an arrowhead referring the statement of the note to the proper place on the drawing. A *General Note* refers to descriptions applying to the design as a whole and it is given without a leader.

Selection and Placement of Dimensions and Notes

One of the most important considerations to assure proper manufacturing and functionality of a design is the selection of dimensions to be given in the drawing. The selection should always be based upon the **functionality of the part**, as well as the **production requirements in the shop**. The method of manufacturing can affect the type of detailed dimensions and notes given in the drawing. It would be very beneficial to have a good knowledge of the different shop practices to give concise information on an engineering drawing.

After the dimensions and notes to be given have been selected, the next step is the actual placement of the dimensions and notes on the drawing. In reading a drawing, it is natural to look for the dimensions of a given feature wherever that feature appears most characteristic. One of the views of an object will usually describe the shape of some detailed feature better than with other views. Placing the dimensions in those views will promote clarity and ease of reading. This practice is known as the **Contour Rule**.

The two methods of positioning dimension texts on a dimension line are the **aligned** system and the **unidirectional** system. The *unidirectional* system is more widely used as it is easier to apply, and easier to read, the texts horizontally. The texts are oriented to be read from the **bottom** of the drawing with the *unidirectional* system. The *unidirectional* system originated in the automotive and aircraft industries and is also referred to as the "horizontal system."

For the *aligned* system, the texts are oriented to be aligned to the dimension line. The texts are oriented to be read from the **bottom or right side** of the drawing with the *aligned* system.

General Notes must be oriented horizontally and be read from the bottom of the drawing in both systems.

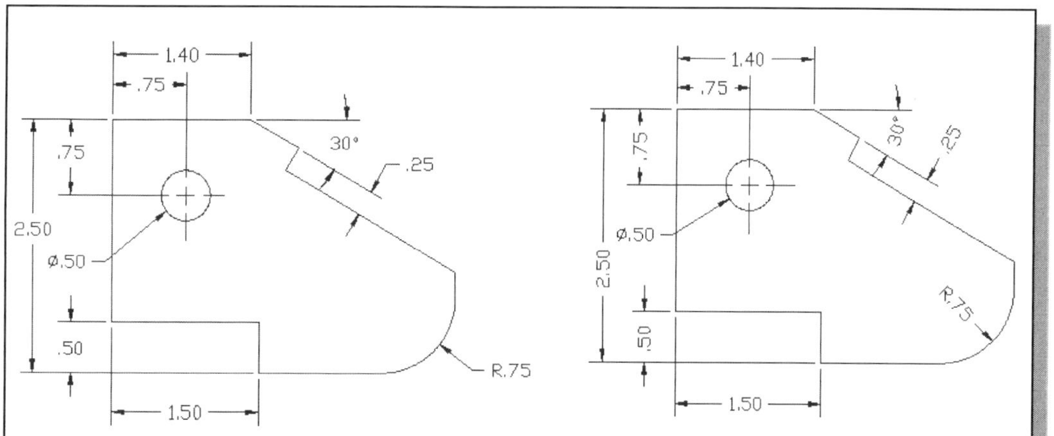

(a) Unidirectional System (b) Aligned System

The following rules need to be followed for clearness and legibility when applying dimensions or notes to a design:

1. Always dimension **features**, not the individual geometric entity. Consider the dimensions related to the **sizes** and **locations** of each feature.

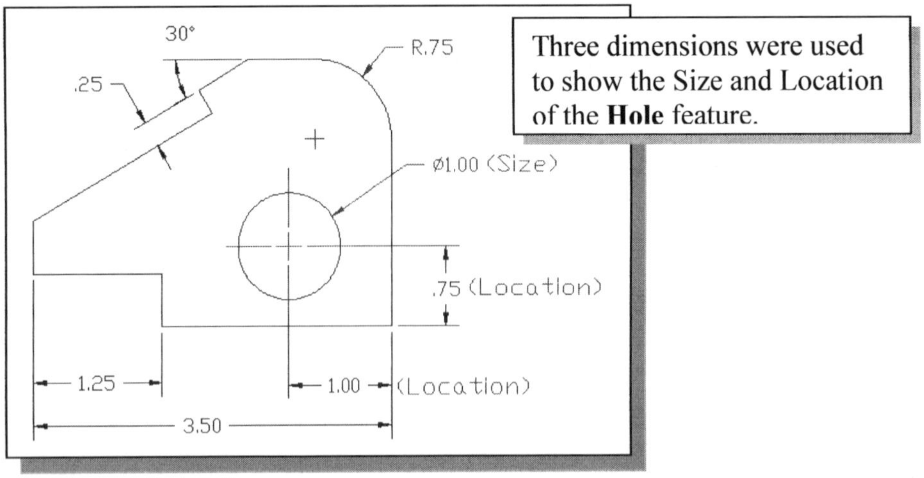

2. Choose the view that best describes the feature to place the associated dimensions; this is known as the **Contour Rule**.

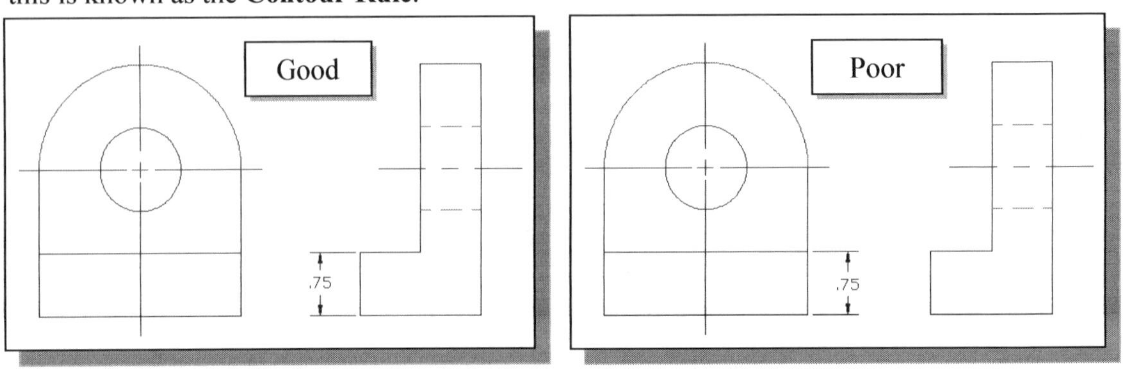

3. Place the dimensions next to the features being described; this is also known as the **Proximity Rule**.

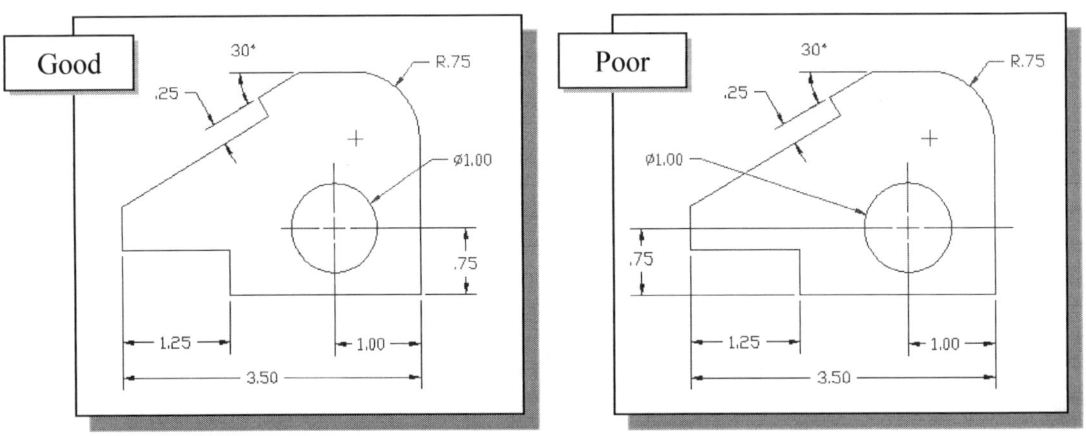

4. Dimensions should be placed outside the view if possible; only place dimensions on the inside if they add clarity, simplicity, and ease of reading.

5. Dimensions common to two views are generally placed in between the views.

6. Center lines may also be used as extension lines; therefore, there should be **no gap** in between an extension line and a center line.

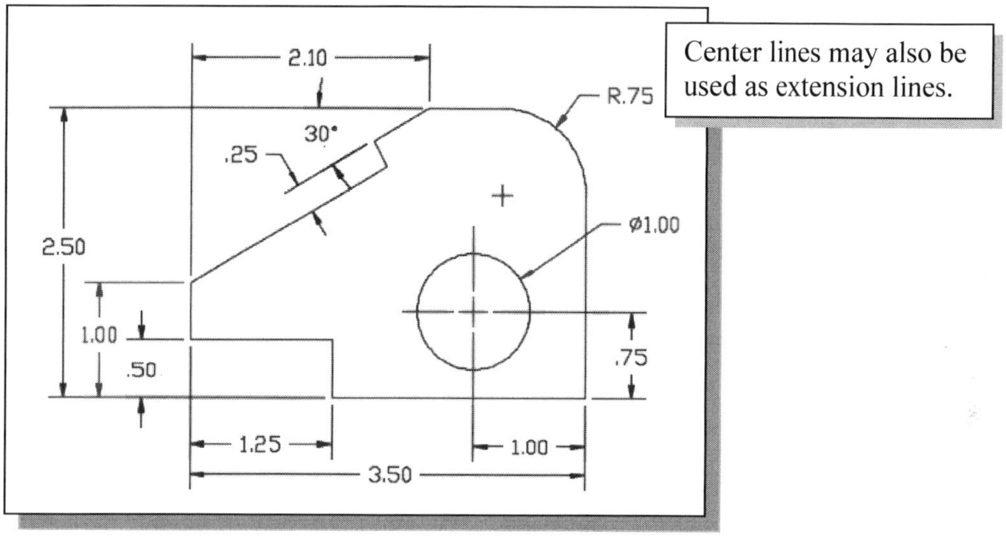

7. Dimensions should be applied to one view only. When dimensions are placed between views, the extension lines should be **drawn from one view**, not from both views.

8. Center lines are also used to indicate the **symmetry** of shapes and frequently eliminate the need for a positioning dimension. They should extend about 6 mm (0.25 in.) beyond the shape for which they indicate symmetry unless they are carried further to serve as extension lines. Center lines should not be continued between views.

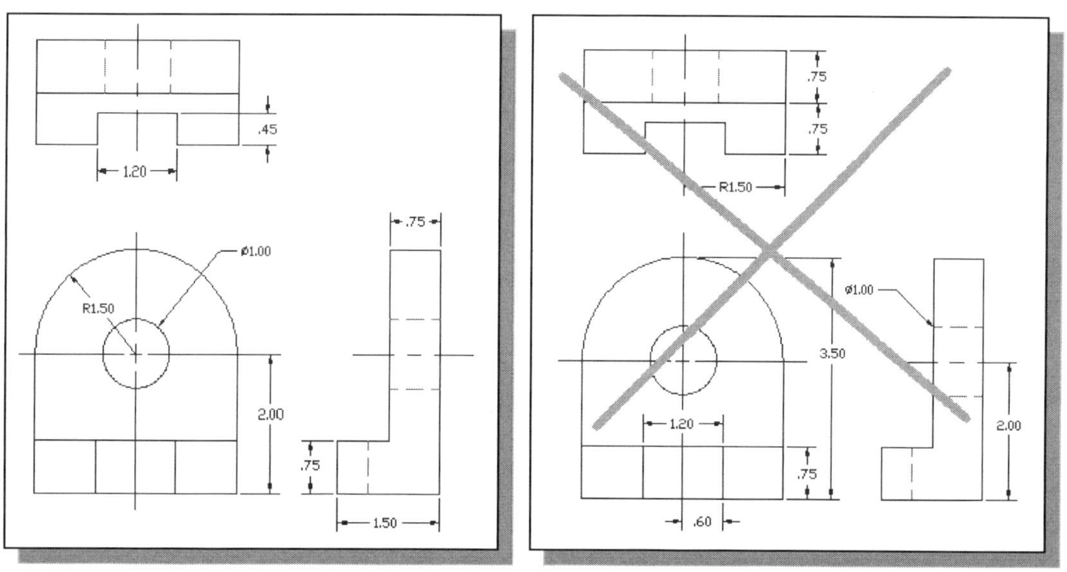

9. Dimensions should be placed only on the view that shows the measurement in its **true length**.

10. Always place a shorter dimension line inside a longer one to avoid crossing dimension lines with the extension lines of other dimensions. Thus, an overall dimension, the maximum size of part in a given direction, will be placed outside all other dimensions.

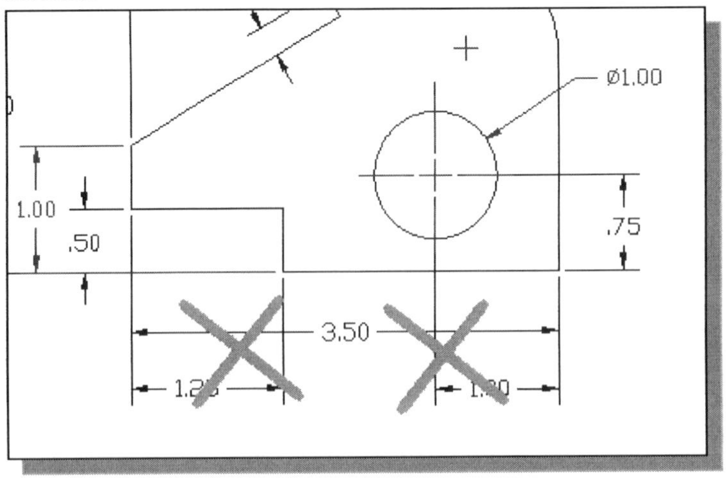

11. As a general rule, local notes (leaders) and general notes are created and placed after the regular dimensions.

12. Dimensions should never be crowded. If the space is small and crowded, an enlarged view or a partial view may be used.

13. Do not dimension to hidden lines; if necessary, create sectional views to convert the hidden features into visible features.

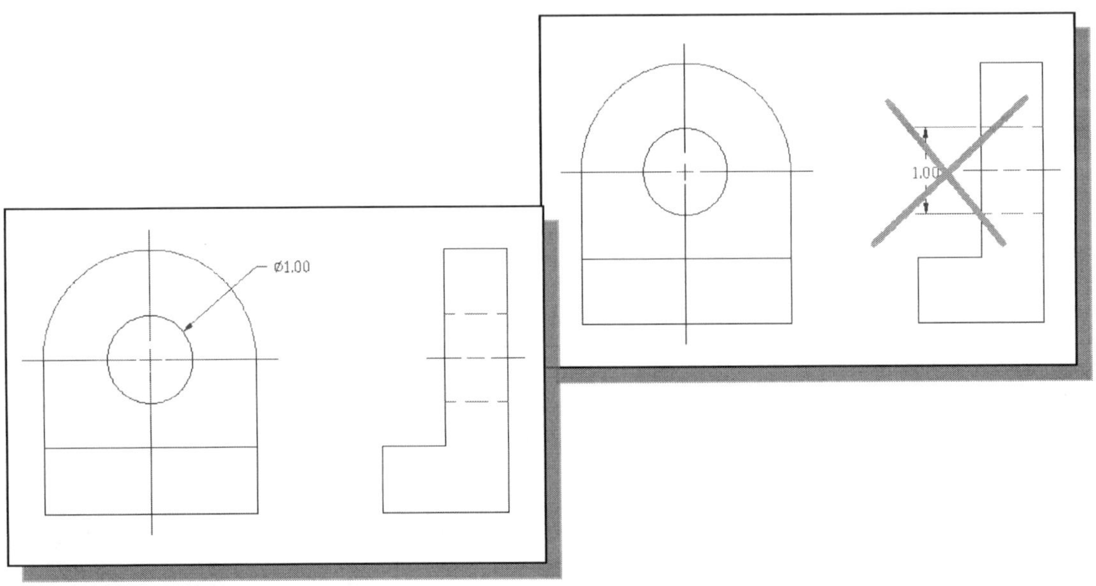

14. The spacing of dimension lines should be uniform throughout the drawing. Dimension lines should be spaced, in general, **10 mm** (0.4 inches) away from the outlines of the view. This applies to a single dimension or to the first dimension of several in a series. The space between subsequent dimension lines should be at least **6 mm** (0.25 inches) and uniformly spaced.

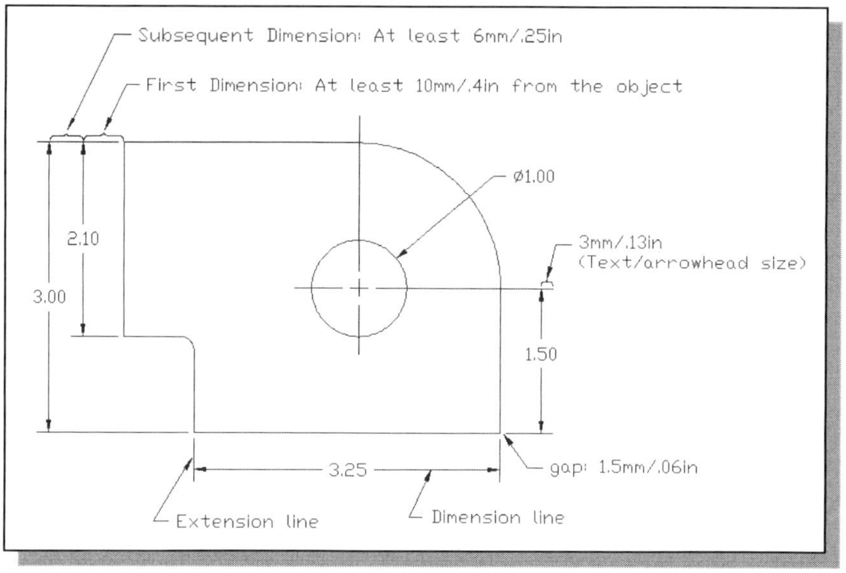

15. The **Overall Width**, **Height**, and **Depth** of the part should generally be shown in a drawing unless curved contours are present.

16. Never allow the crossing of dimension lines.

17. Dimension texts should be placed midway between the arrowheads, except when several parallel dimensions are present, where the texts should be staggered.

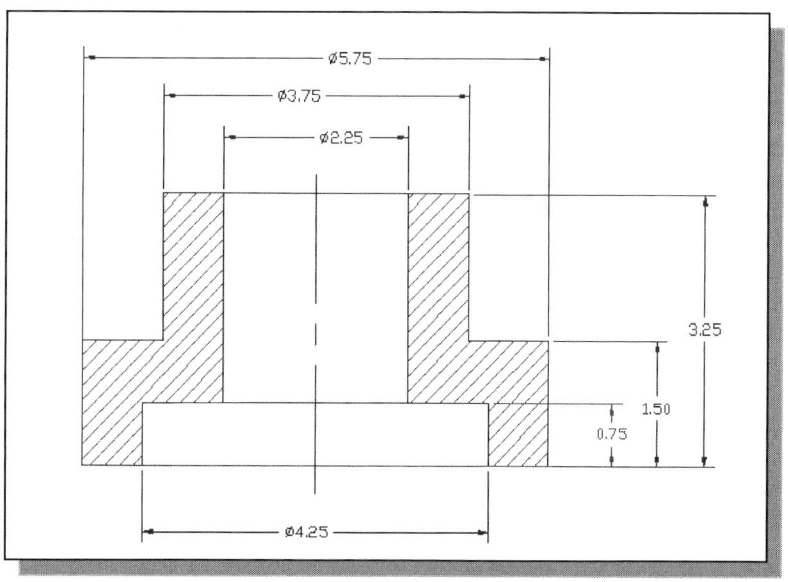

18. A leader should always be placed to allow its extension to pass through the **center** of all round features.

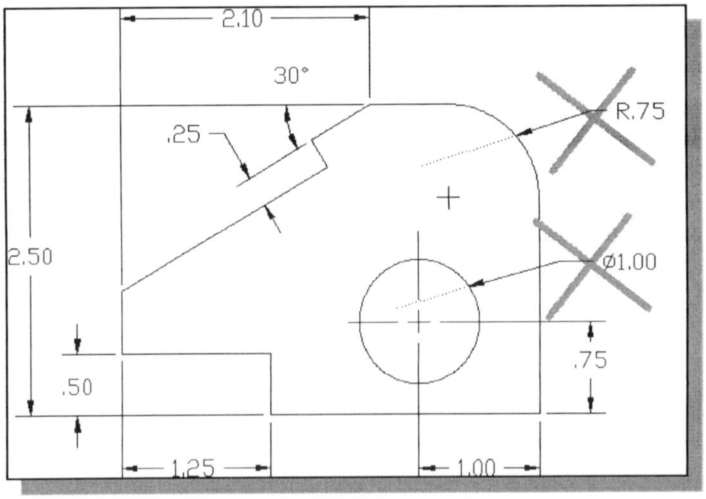

19. **Symbols** are preferred for features such as counter-bores, countersinks and spot faces; they should also be dimensioned using a leader. Each of these features has a special dimensioning symbol that can be used to show (a) Shape (b) Diameter and (c) Depth.

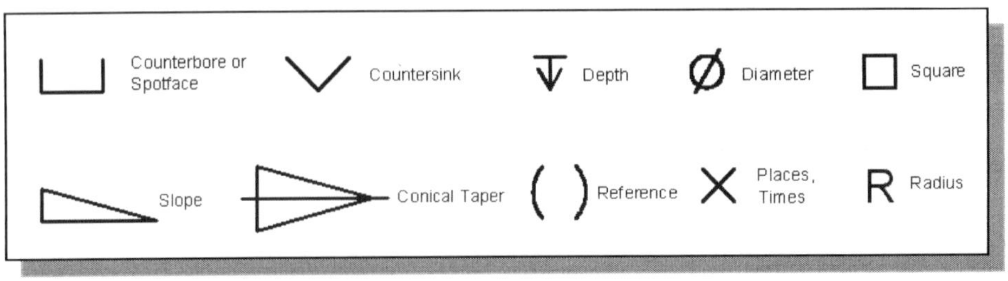

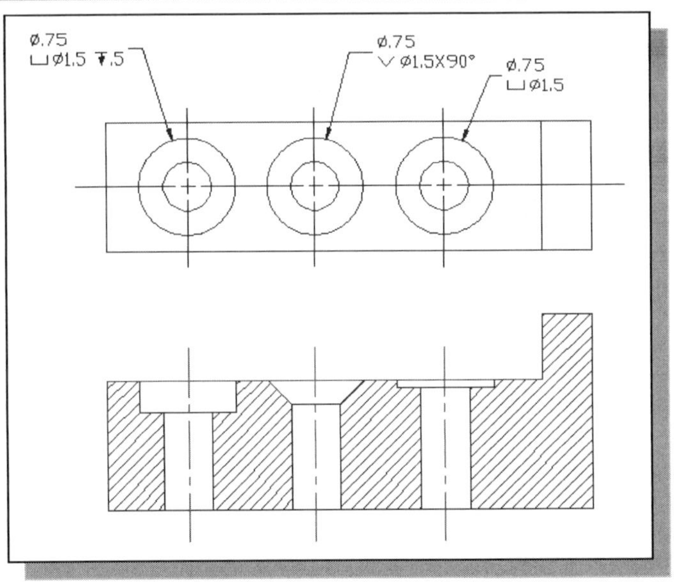

20. For leaders, avoid crossing leaders, avoid long leaders, avoid leaders in a horizontal or vertical direction, and avoid leaders parallel to adjacent dimension lines, extension lines, or section lines.

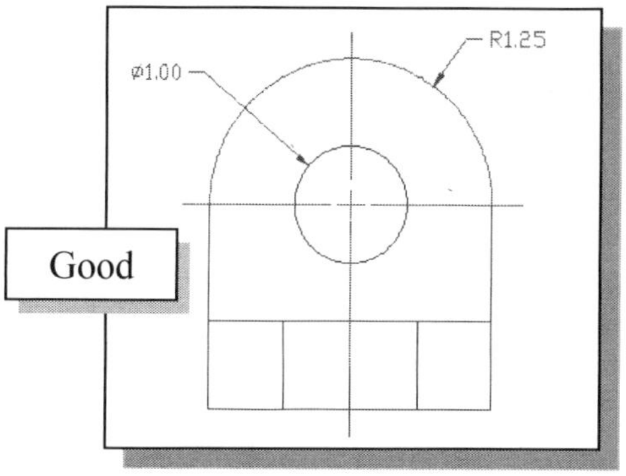

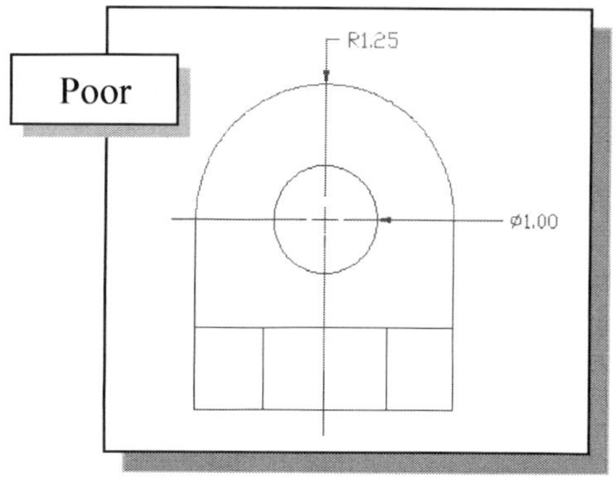

21. When dimensioning a circular feature, full cylinders (holes and bosses) must always be measured by their diameters. Arcs should always be shown by specifying a radius value. If a leader is used, the leader should meet the surface at an angle between 30° to 60° if possible.

22. Dual dimensions may be used, but they must be consistent and clearly noted. The dual-dimensioning can be shown by placing the alternate-units values below or next to the primary-units dimension, as shown in the figure.

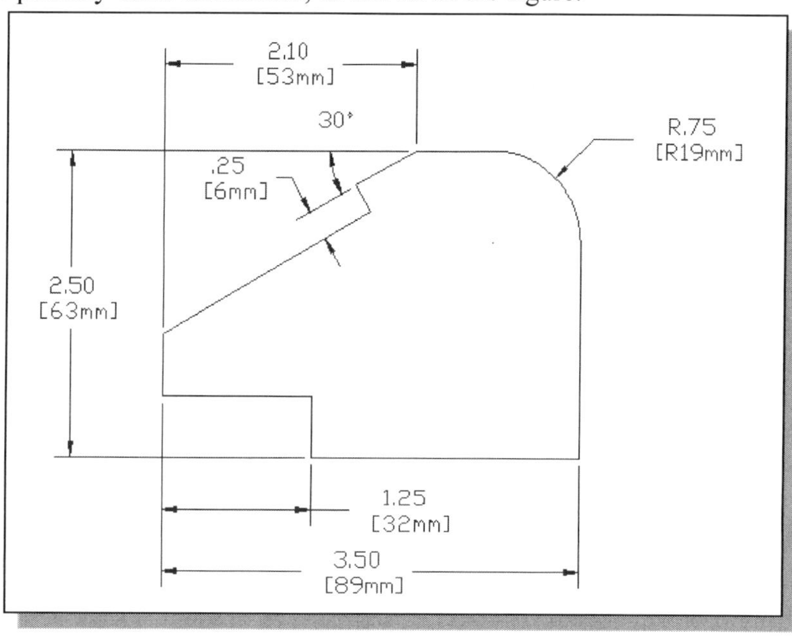

23. Never pass through a dimension text with any kind of line.

Metric Dimensioning versus English Dimensioning

In general, for Mechanical Engineering drawings, **Metric system** are given in **millimeters** and **English** system are given in **inches**.

- Millimeter (mm): common International System of Units (SI) unit of measure, generally **rounded to the nearest whole number**.
- Note on drawings: "UNLESS OTHERWISE SPECIFIED, ALL DIMENSIONS ARE IN MILLIMETERS"
- Omit the decimal point and trailing zeros when dimension is a whole number.
- Show a leading zero for values less than 1 unit.

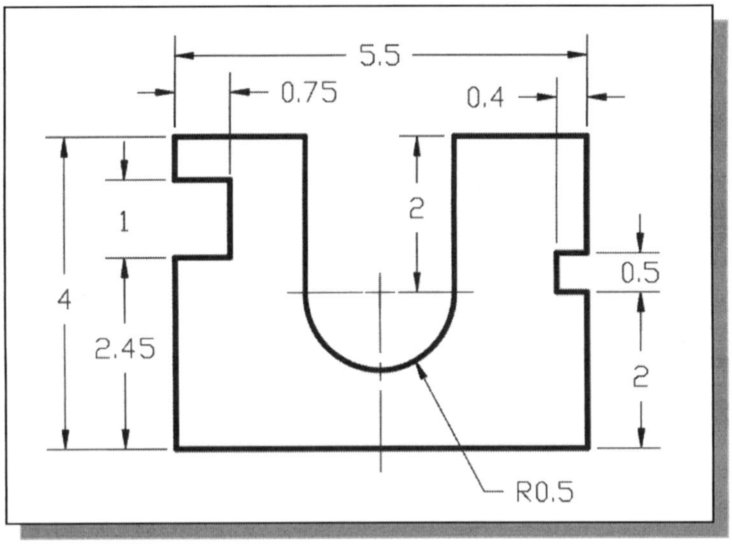

- Inch (IN): commonly used on US engineering drawings, and they are typically shown with **two decimal places**.
- Note on drawings: "UNLESS OTHERWISE SPECIFIED, ALL DIMENSIONS ARE IN INCHES"
- Omit the decimal point for values less than 1 unit; also show the trailing zeros after the decimal point.

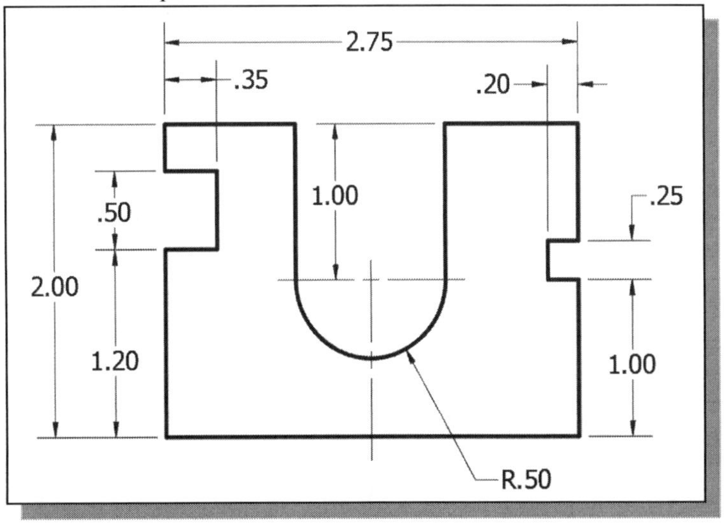

Machined Holes

In machining, a hole is a cylindrical feature that is cut from the work piece by a rotating cutting tool. The diameter of the machined hole will be the same as the cutting tool with matching the geometry. Non-cylindrical features, or pockets, can also be machined, but these features require end milling operations, not the typical hole-making operations. While all machined holes have the same basic form, they can still differ in many ways to best suit a given application.

A machined hole can be characterized by several different parameters or features which will determine the hole machining operation and tool that is required.

Diameter - Holes can be machined in a wide variety of diameters, determined by the selected tool. The cutting tools used for hole-making are available in standard sizes that can be as small as 0.0019 inches and as large as 3 inches. Several standards exist including fractional sizes, letter sizes, number sizes, and metric sizes. A custom tool can be created to machine a non-standard diameter, but it is generally more cost effective to use the standard sized tool.

Tolerance - In any machining operation, the precision of a cut can be affected by several factors, including the sharpness of the tool, any vibration of the tool, or the buildup of chips of material. The specified tolerance of a hole will determine the method of hole-making used, as some methods are suited for tight-tolerance holes. Refer to the next section and Chapter 9 for more details on tolerances.

Depth - A machined hole may extend to a point within the work piece, known as a blind hole, or it may extend completely through the work piece, known as a through hole. A blind hole may have a flat bottom but typically ends in a point due to the pointed end of the tool. When specifying the depth of a hole, one may reference the depth to the point or the depth to the end of the full diameter portion of the hole. The total depth of the hole is limited by the length of the cutting tool. For a through hole, the depth information is typically omitted in a drawing.

Recessed top - A common feature of machined holes is to recess the top of the hole into the work piece. This is typically done to accommodate the head of a fastener and allow it to sit flush with the work piece surface. Two types of recessed holes are typically used: a counterbore, which has a cylindrical recess, and a countersink, which has a cone-shaped recess.

Threads - Threaded holes are machined to accommodate a threaded fastener and are typically specified by their outer diameter and pitch. The pitch is a measure of the spacing between threads and may be expressed in the English standard, as the number of threads per inch (TPI), or in the metric standard, as the distance in between threads. For more details on threads, refer to Chapter 13 of this text.

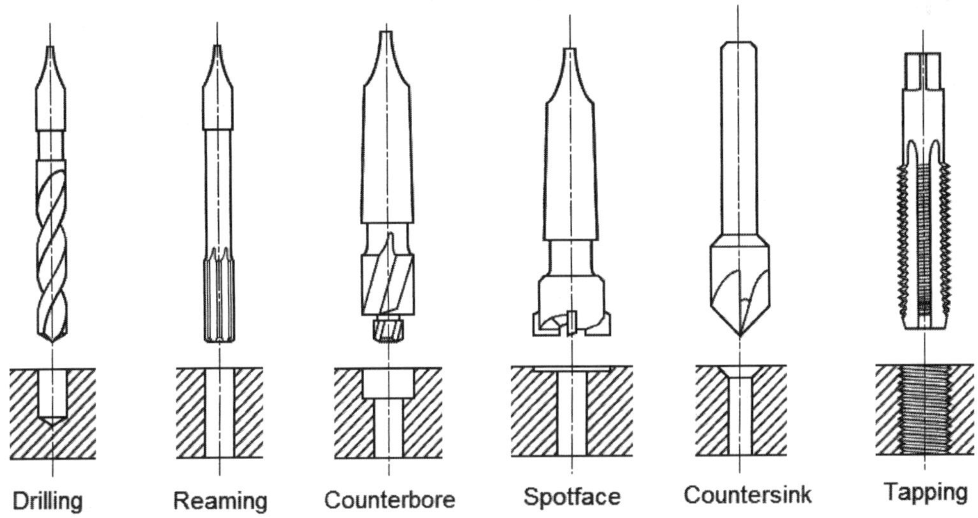

Drilling - A drill bit enters the work piece in the axial direction and cuts a blind hole or a through hole with a diameter equal to that of the tool. A drill bit is a multi-point tool and typically has a pointed end. A twist drill is the most commonly used, but other types of drill bits, such as center drill, spot drill, or tap drill can also be used to start a hole that will be completed by additional operation.

Reaming - A reamer enters the work piece in the axial direction and enlarges an existing hole to the diameter of the tool. A reamer is a multi-point tool that has many flutes, which may be straight or in a helix. Reaming removes a minimal amount of material and is often performed after drilling to obtain both a more accurate diameter and a smoother internal finish.

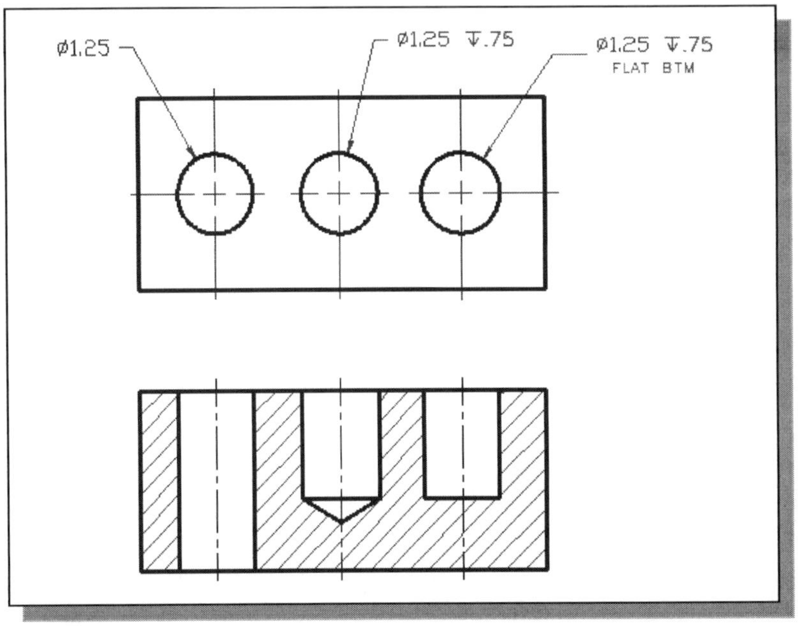

Counterbore - A counterbore tool enters the work piece axially and enlarges the top portion of an existing hole to the diameter of the tool. Counterboring is often performed after drilling to provide space for the head of a fastener, such as a bolt, to sit flush with the work piece surface. The counterboring tool has a pilot on the end to guide it straight into the existing hole. The depth of the counterbored portion is typically identified and dimensioned as a second operation on a drawing.

Spotface - A spotfaced hole is similar to a counterbored hole, but a spotfaced hole has a relatively shallow counterbored depth. The depth of the counterbored portion is left to the judgment of the machinist and thus, not dimensioned in the drawing. The smoothing is necessary in cast or forged surfaces to provide better contact between assembled pieces. For drawing purposes, the depth of the counterbored portion for a spotfaced hole is typically 1/16" or 2 mm.

Countersink - A countersink tool enters the work piece axially and enlarges the top portion of an existing hole to a cone-shaped opening. Countersinking is often performed after drilling to provide space for the head of a fastener, such as a screw, to sit flush with the work piece surface. Common included angles for a countersink include 60, 82, 90, 100, 118, and 120 degrees.

Tapping - A tap enters the work piece in the axial direction and cuts internal threads inside an existing hole. The existing hole is typically drilled with a drill size that will accommodate the desired tap. The tap is selected based on the major diameter and pitch of the threaded hole. Threads may be cut to a specified depth inside the hole (bottom tap) or the complete depth of a through hole (through tap).

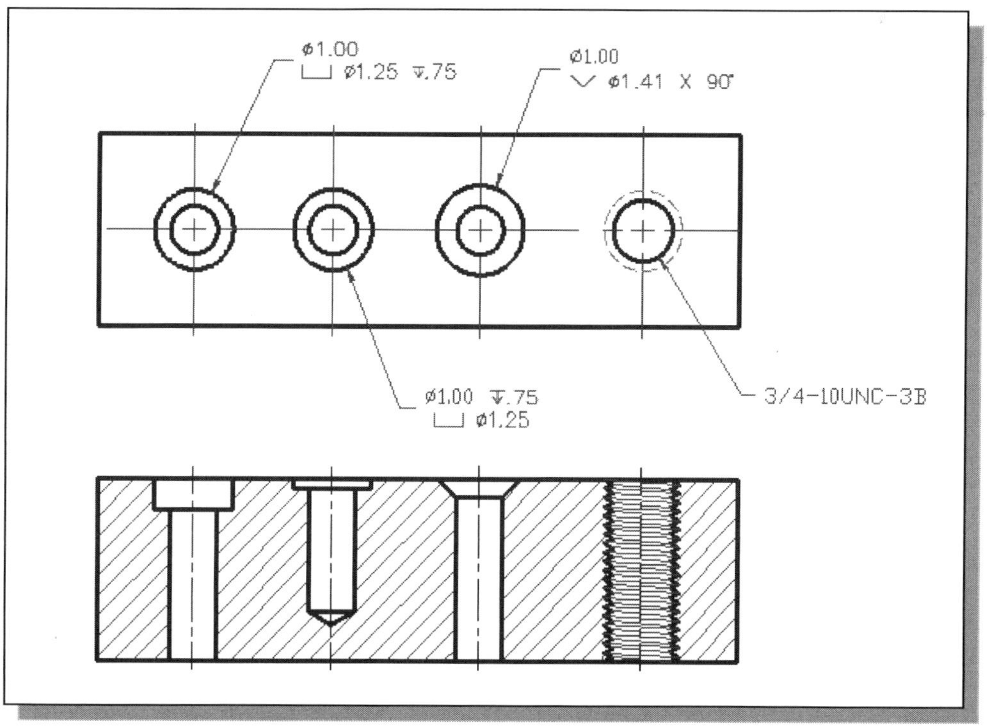

Baseline and Chain Dimensioning

Frequently the need arises to dimension a feature which involves a series of dimensions. Two methods should be considered for this type of situation: **Baseline dimensioning** and **Chain dimensioning**. The baseline dimensioning method creates dimensions by measuring from a common baseline. The chain dimensioning method creates a series or a chain of dimensions that are placed one after another. It is important to always consider the functionality and the manufacturing process of the specific features to be dimensioned. Note that both methods can be used for different features within the same drawing as shown in the below figure.

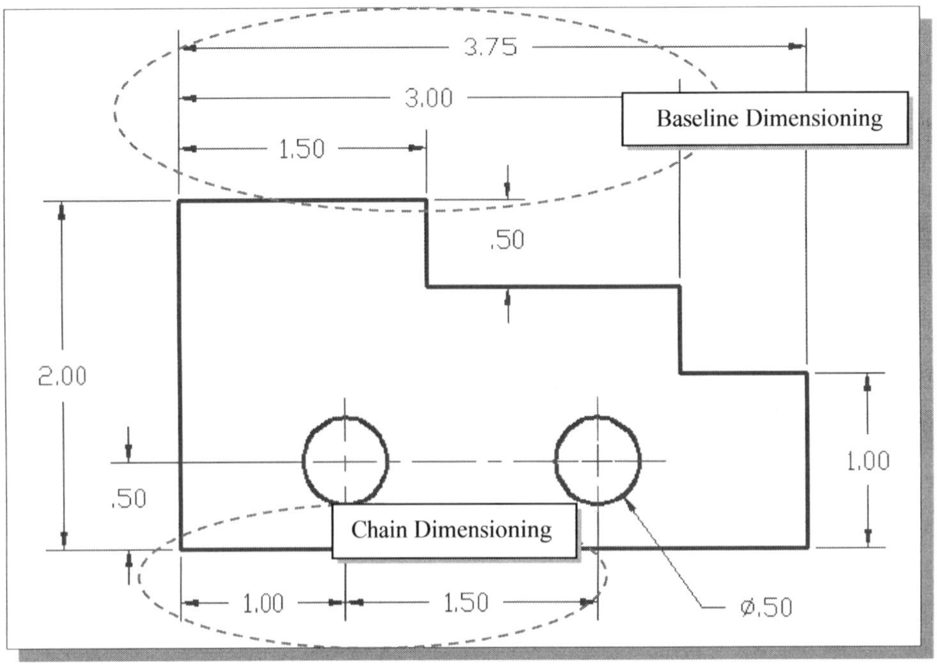

- **Baseline dimensioning:** used when the **location** of features must be controlled from a common reference point or plane.

- **Chain dimensioning:** Used when **tolerances** between adjacent features is more important than the overall tolerance of the feature—for example, dimensioning mating parts, hole patterns, slots, etc. Note that more in-depth discussions on tolerances are presented in the next section and also in the next chapter.

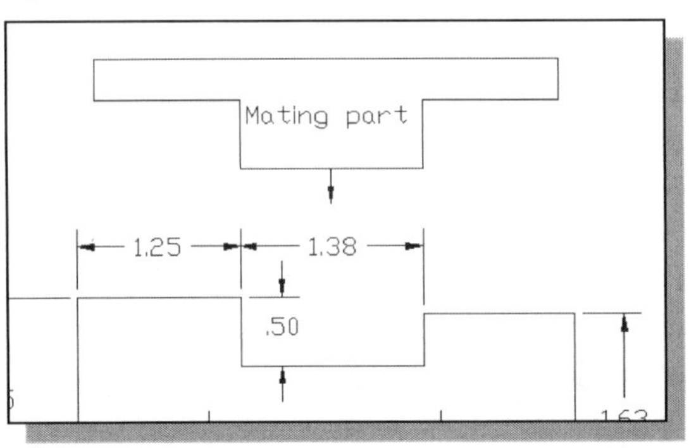

Dimensioning and Tolerance Accumulation

Drawings with dimensions and notes often serve as construction documents to ensure the proper functioning of a design. When dimensioning a drawing, it is therefore critical to consider the *precision* required for the part. *Precision* is the degree of accuracy required during manufacturing. Different machining methods will produce different degrees of precisions. However, one should realize it is nearly impossible to produce any dimension to an absolute, accurate measurement; some variation must be allowed in manufacturing. **Tolerance** is the allowable variation for any given size and provides a practical means to achieve the precision necessary in a design. With **tolerancing**, each dimension is allowed to vary within a specified zone. The general machining tolerances of some of the more commonly used manufacturing processes are listed in the figure below.

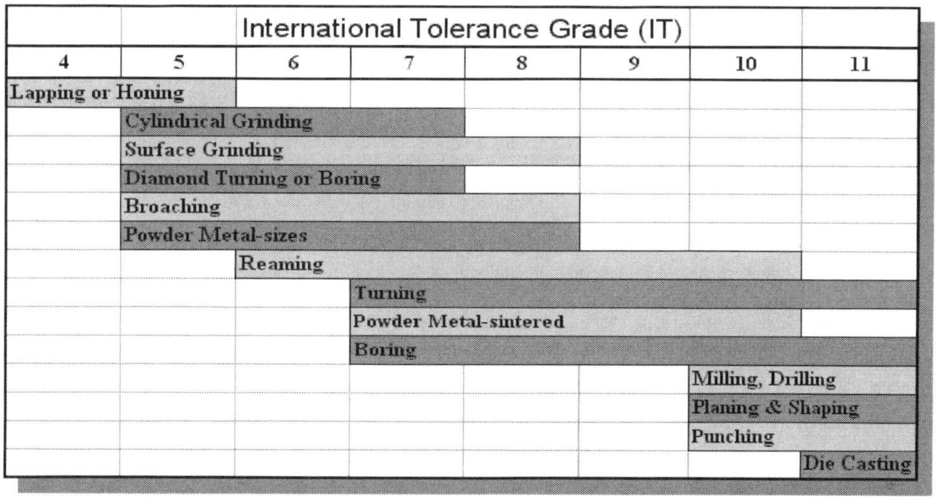

As it was discussed in the previous sections, the selections and placements of dimensions and notes can have a drastic effect on the manufacturing of the designs. Furthermore, a poorly dimensioned drawing can create problems that may invalidate the design intent and/or become very costly to the company. One of the undesirable results in poorly dimensioned drawings is **Tolerance Accumulation**. *Tolerance Accumulation* is the effect of cumulative tolerances caused by the relationship of tolerances associated with relating dimensions. As an example, let's examine the *tolerance accumulation* that can occur with two mating parts, as shown in the below figure, using a standard tolerance of ± 0.01 for all dimensions.

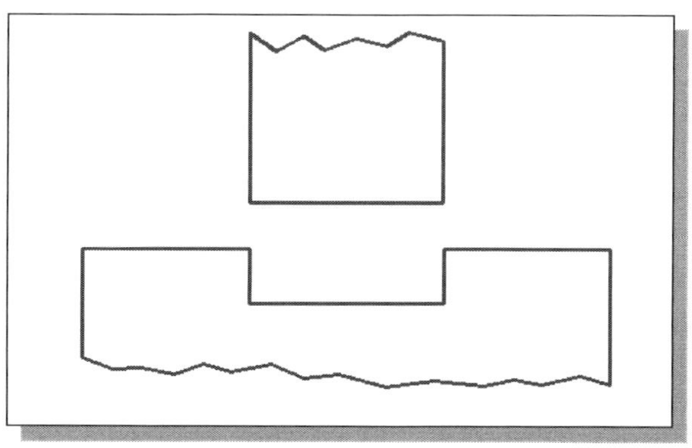

(1) Tolerance Accumulation - Baseline Dimensioning

Consider the use of the *Baseline dimensioning* approach, as described in the previous sections, to dimension the parts. At first glance, it may appear that the tolerance of the overall size is maintained and thus this approach is a better approach in dimensioning the parts!?

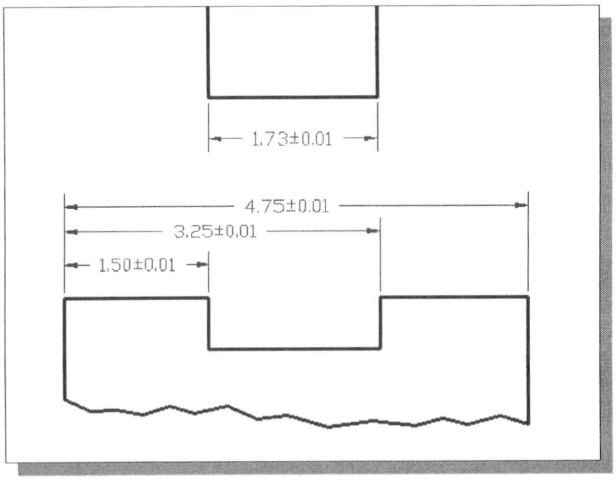

Now let's examine the size of the center slot, which is intended to fit the other part:

Upper limit of the slot size: 3.27-1.49= 1.77
Lower limit of the slot size: 3.24-1.51= 1.73

The tolerance of the center slot has a different range of tolerance than the standard ± 0.01. With this result, the two parts will not fit as well as the tolerance has been loosened.

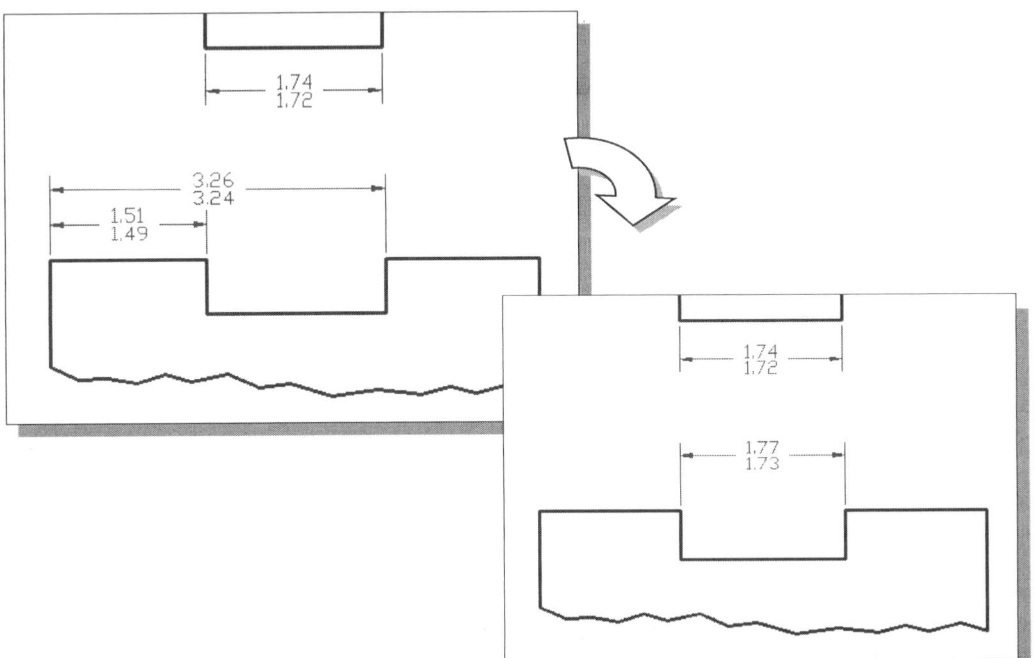

(2) Tolerance Accumulation - Chain Dimensioning

Now consider the use of the *chain dimensioning* approach, as described in the previous sections, to dimension the parts.

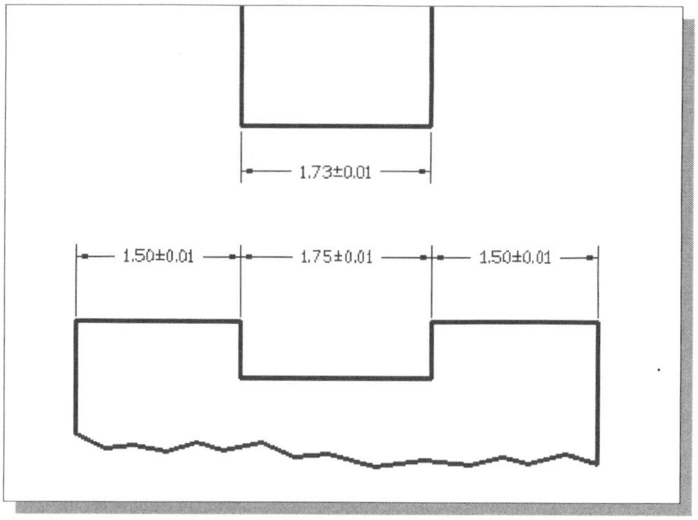

The *tolerance accumulation* occurred since the overall size is determined with the three dimensions that are chained together. Considering the upper and lower limits of the overall size of the bottom part:

Upper limit of the overall size: 1.51+1.76+1.51= 4.78
Lower limit of the overall size: 1.49+1.74+1.49= 4.72

With the chaining of the dimensions, the tolerance of the overall size has been changed, perhaps unintentionally, to a wider range.

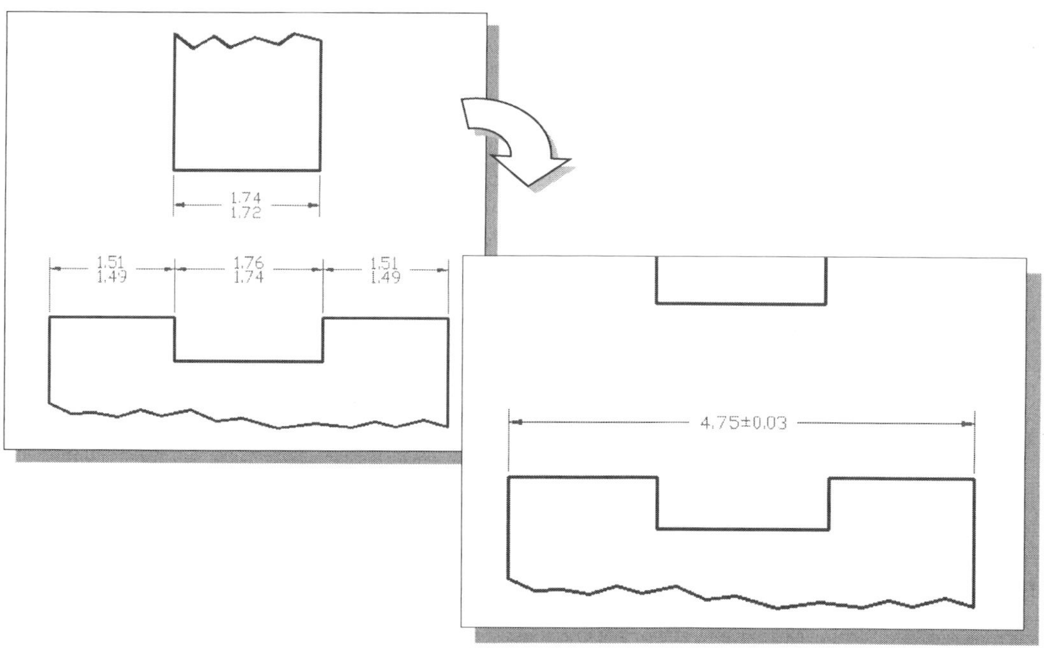

(3) Avoid Tolerance Accumulation – Dimensioning Features

The effect of the *tolerance accumulation* is usually undesirable. We could be using fairly precise and expensive manufacturing processes but resulting in lower quality products simply due to the poor selections and placements of dimensions.

To avoid *tolerance accumulation,* proper dimensioning of a drawing is critical. The first rule of dimensioning states that one should always dimension **features**, not an individual geometric entity. Always consider the dimensions related to the **sizes** and **locations** of each feature. One should also consider the associated **design intent** of the **feature**, the **functionality** of the design and the related **manufacturing processes**.

For our example, one should consider the center slot as a feature, where the other part will be fit into, and therefore the **size** and **location** of the feature should be placed as shown in the figure below.

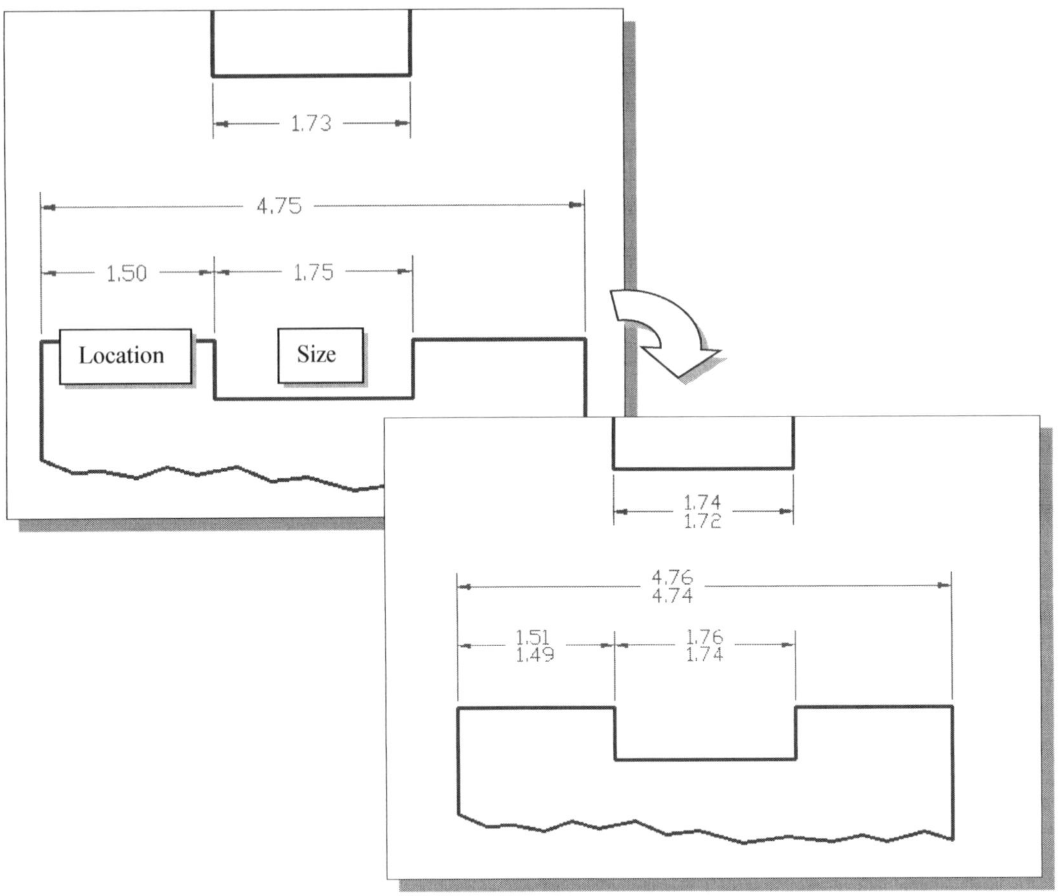

- More detailed discussions on tolerances are covered in the next chapter; however, the effects of *tolerance accumulation* should be avoided even during the initial selection and placement of dimensions. Note that there are also other options, generally covered under the topics of **Geometric Dimensioning and Tolerancing (GD&T)**, to assure the accuracy of designs through productions.

Dimensioning Tools in AutoCAD

Thus far, the use of **AutoCAD 2027** to define the ***shape*** of designs has been illustrated. For the rest of the chapter, the general procedures to convey the ***size*** definitions of designs using **AutoCAD 2027** are discussed. The *tools of size description* are known as *dimensions* and *notes*.

Considerable experience and judgment are required for accurate size description. As it was outlined in the previous sections, detail drawings should contain only those dimensions that are necessary to make the design. Dimensions for the same feature of the design should be given only once in the same drawing. Nothing should be left to chance or guesswork on a drawing. Drawings should be dimensioned to avoid any possibility of questions. Dimensions should be carefully positioned, preferably near the profile of the feature being dimensioned. The designer and the CAD operator should be as familiar as possible with materials, methods of manufacturing, and shop processes.

Traditionally, detailing a drawing is the biggest bottleneck of the design process; and when doing board drafting, dimensioning is one of the most time consuming and tedious tasks. Today, most CAD systems provide what is known as an **auto-dimensioning feature**, where the CAD system automatically creates the extension lines, dimensional lines, arrowheads, and dimension values. Most CAD systems also provide an **associative dimensioning feature** so that the system automatically updates the dimensions when the drawing is modified.

The P-Bracket Design

Starting Up AutoCAD 2027

1. Select the **AutoCAD 2027** option on the *Program* menu or select the **AutoCAD 2027** icon on the *Desktop*.

2. In the *Startup* window, select **Start from Scratch**, and select the **Imperial (feet and inches)** as the drawing units.

3. In the *Menu Bar*, select:

   [Tools] → [Drafting Settings]

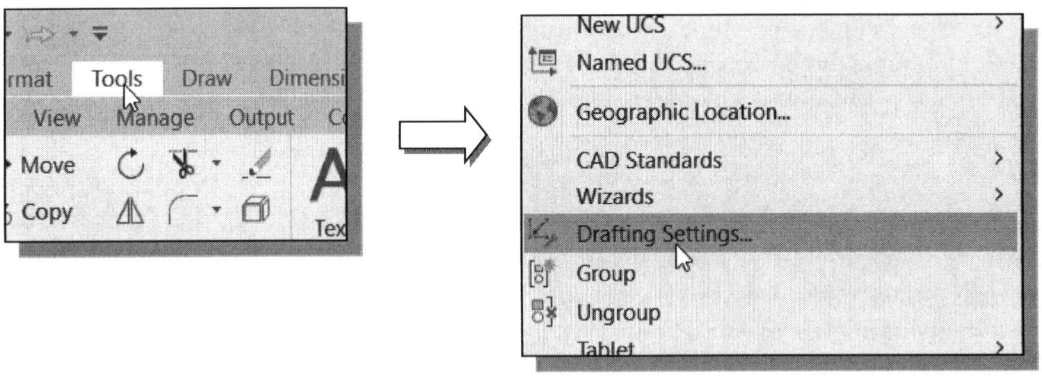

4. In the *Drafting Settings* dialog box, select the **SNAP and GRID** tab if it is not the page on top.

5. Change *Grid Spacing* to ***1.0*** for both X and Y directions.

6. Also adjust the *Snap Spacing* to ***0.5*** for both X and Y directions.

7. Pick **OK** to exit the *Drafting Settings* dialog box.

8. In the *Status Bar* area, reset the option buttons so that only *SNAP Mode* and *GRID Display* are switched ***ON***.

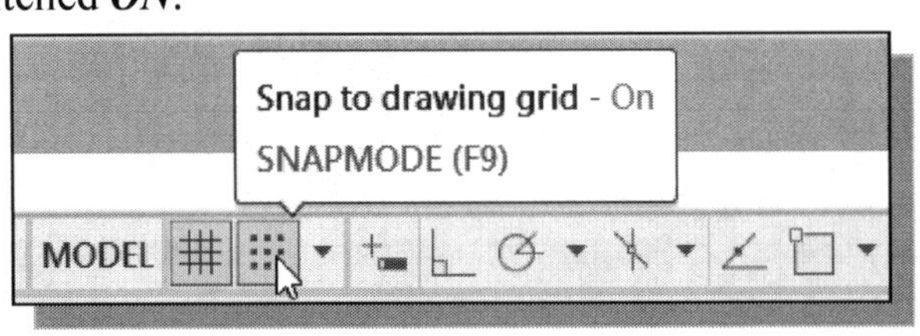

Layers Setup

1. Pick ***Layer Properties Manager*** in the *Object Properties* toolbar.

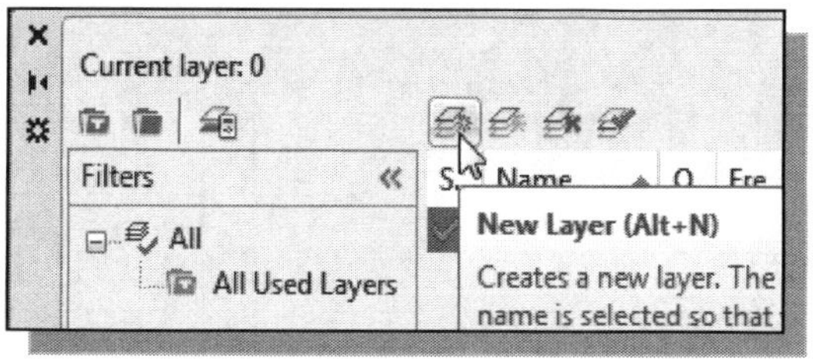

2. In the *Layer Properties Manager* dialog box, click on the **New** button (or the key combination [**Alt+N**]) to create a new layer.

3. Create **layers** with the following settings:

Layer	***Color***	***Linetype***	***Lineweight***
Construction	**Gray(9)**	**Continuous**	**Default**
Object_Lines	**Blue**	**Continuous**	**0.6mm**
Hidden_Lines	**Cyan**	**Hidden**	**0.3mm**
Center_Lines	**Red**	**Center**	**Default**
Dimensions	**Magenta**	**Continuous**	**Default**
Section_Lines	**White**	**Continuous**	**Default**
CuttingPlane_Lines	**Dark Gray(8)**	**Phantom**	**0.6mm**
Title_Block	**Green**	**Continuous**	**1.2mm**
Viewport	**White**	**Continuous**	**Default**

4. Highlight the layer ***Construction*** in the list of layers.

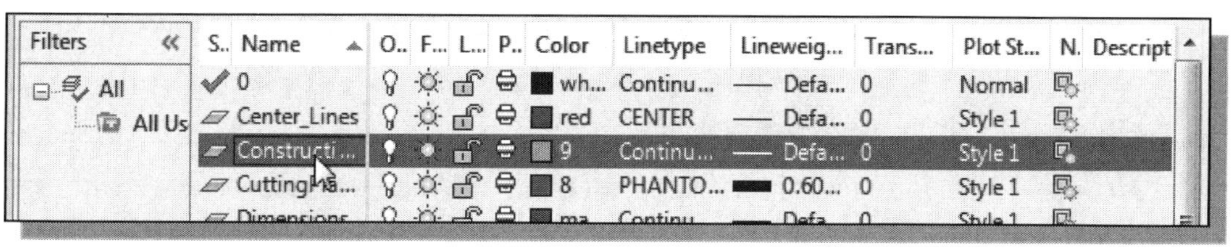

5. Click on the **Current** button to set layer ***Construction*** as the *Current Layer*.

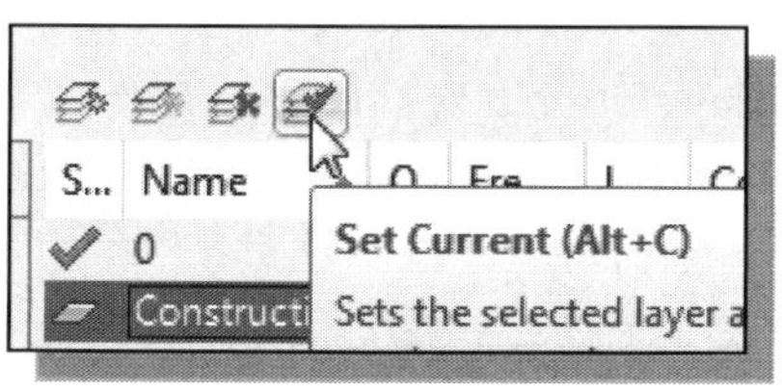

6. Click on the **Close** button to accept the settings and exit the *Layer Properties Manager* dialog box.

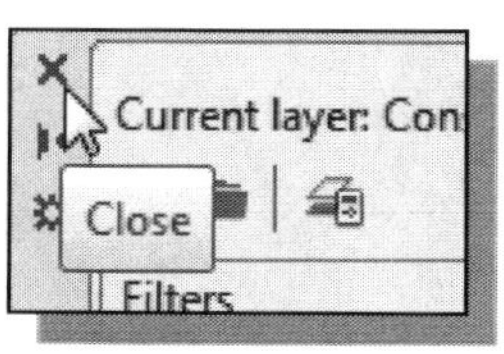

The P-Bracket Design

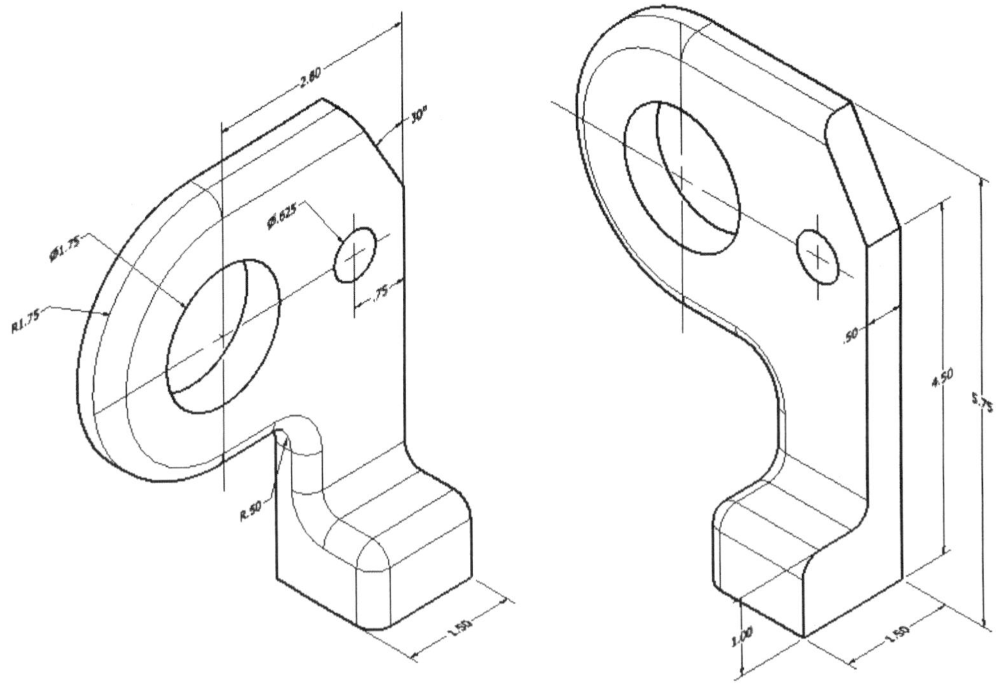

➤ Before going through the tutorial, make a rough sketch of a multiview drawing of the part. How many 2D views will be necessary to fully describe the part? Based on your knowledge of **AutoCAD 2027** so far, how would you arrange and construct these 2D views? Take a few minutes to consider these questions and do preliminary planning by sketching on a piece of paper.

LineWeight Display Control

The *LineWeight Display* control can be accessed through the Status bar area; we will first switch on the icon.

1. To show the icon for the AutoCAD LineWeight Display option, use the *Customization option* at the bottom right corner.

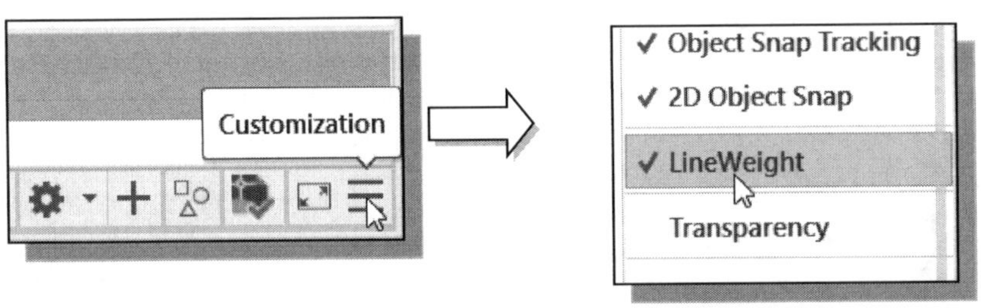

Drawing Construction Lines

We will place the construction lines on the *Construction* layer so that the layer can later be frozen or turned off.

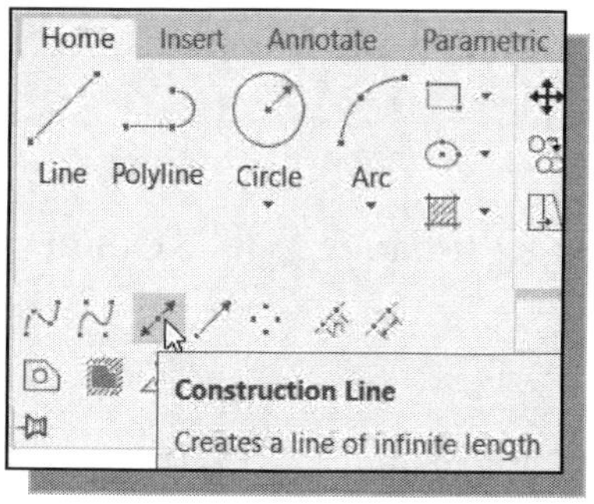

1. Select the **Construction Line** icon in the *Draw* toolbar. In the command prompt area, the message "*_xline Specify a point or [Hor/Ver/Ang/Bisect/Offset]:*" is displayed.

➢ To orient construction lines, we generally specify two points, although other orientation options are also available.

2. Place the first point at world coordinate (***3,2***) on the screen.

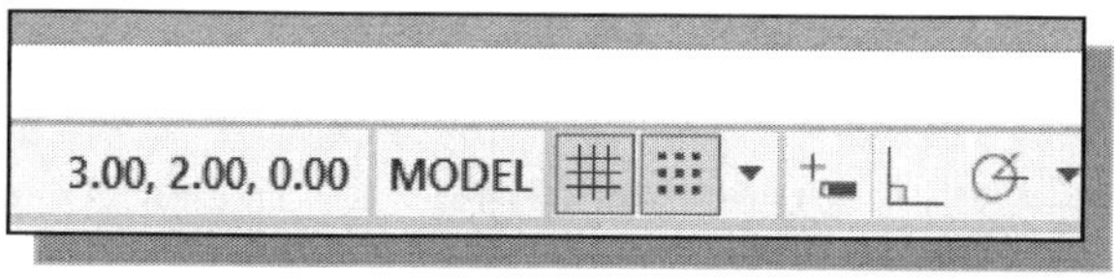

3. Pick a location above the last point to create a **vertical line**.

4. Move the cursor toward the right of the first point and pick a location to create a **horizontal line**.

5. In the *Status Bar* area, turn ***OFF*** the *SNAP* option.

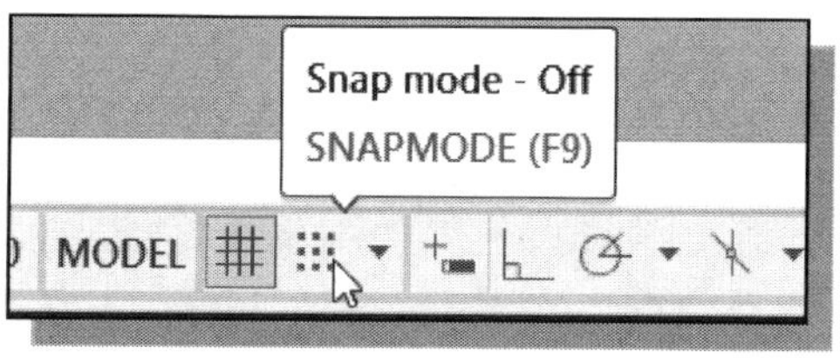

Using the Offset Command

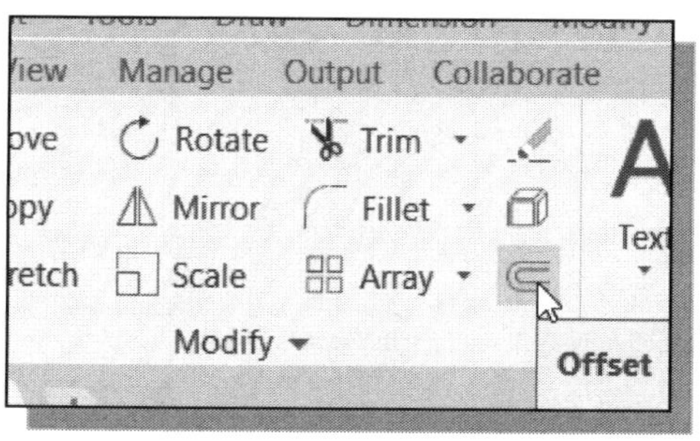

1. Select the **Offset** icon in the *Modify* toolbar. In the command prompt area, the message "*Specify offset distance or [Through]:*" is displayed.

2. In the command prompt area, enter ***2.80*** **[ENTER]**.

3. In the *command prompt area*, the message "*Select object to offset or <exit>:*" is displayed. Pick the **vertical line** on the screen.

4. AutoCAD next asks us to identify the direction of the offset. Pick a location that is to the **right** of the vertical line.

5. Inside the *graphics window*, right-click twice to **end** the Offset command.

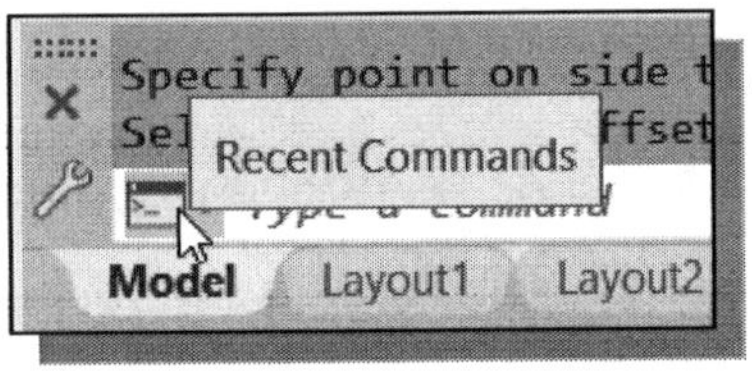

6. In the *command prompt* area, click on the small icon to access the list of recent commands.

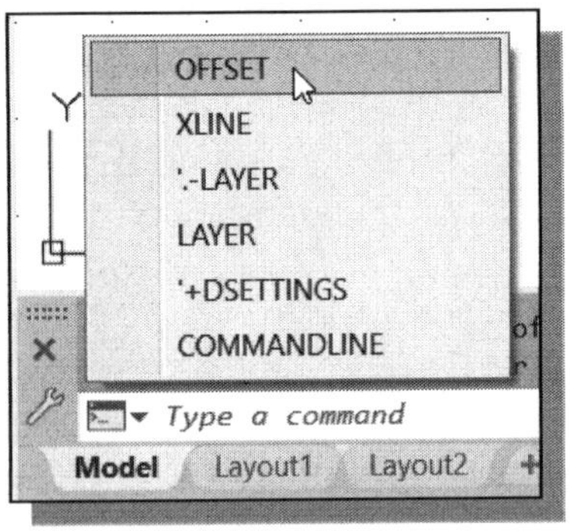

7. Select **Offset** in the pop-up list, to repeat the Offset command.

8. In *the command prompt* area, enter ***5.75*** **[ENTER]**.

9. In the *command prompt* area, the message "*Select object to offset or <exit>:*" is displayed. Pick the **horizontal line** on the screen.

10. AutoCAD next asks us to identify the direction of the offset. Pick a location that is **above** the horizontal line.

11. Inside the *graphics window*, **right-click** once to end the Offset command.

12. Repeat the **Offset** command and create the lines as shown.

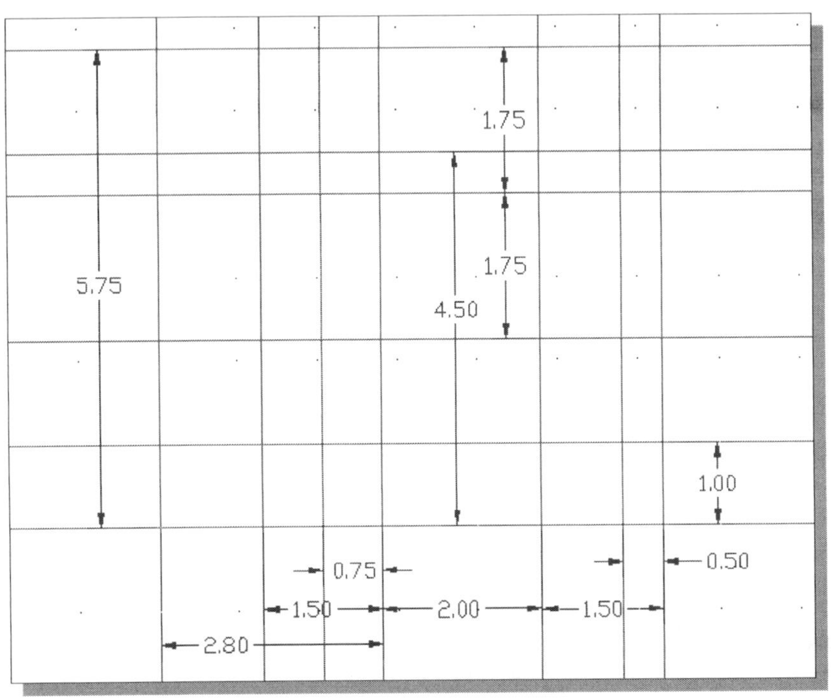

Set Layer Object_Lines as the Current Layer

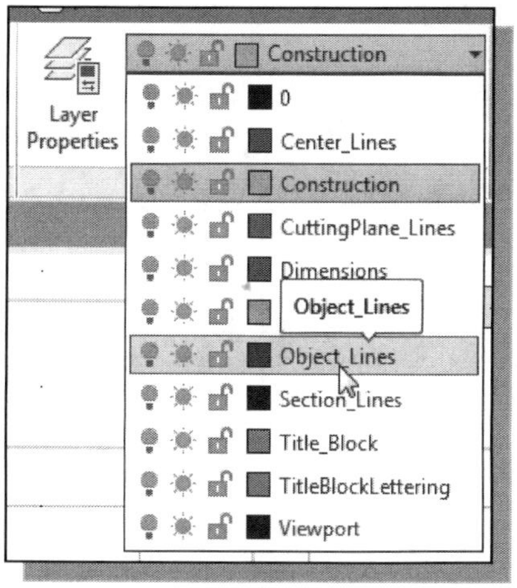

1. On the *Object Properties* toolbar, choose the ***Layer Control*** box with the left-mouse-button.

2. Move the cursor over the name of layer ***Object_Lines*** and the tool tip "*Object_Lines*" appears.

3. **Left-click once** and layer *Object_Lines* is set as the *Current Layer*.

4. In the *Status Bar* area, turn ***ON*** the *Object SNAP, Object TRACKing*, and *Line Weight Display* options.

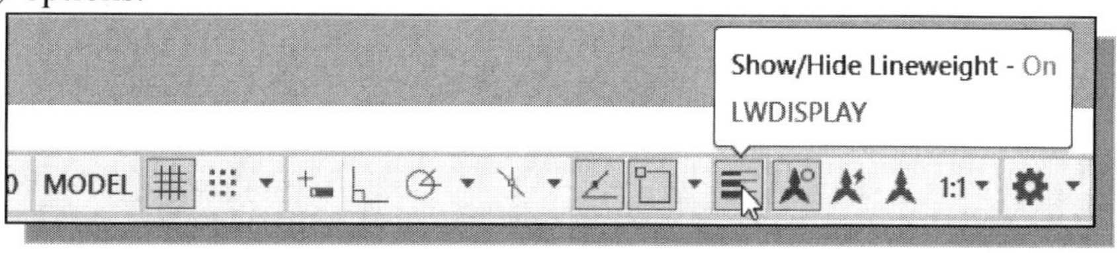

Creating Object Lines

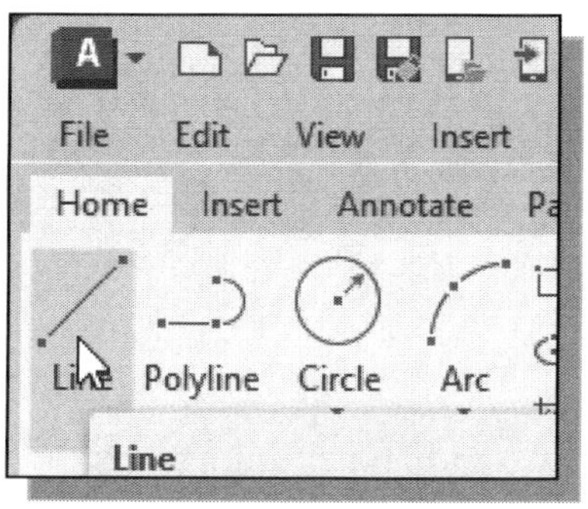

1. Select the **Line** command icon in the *Draw* toolbar. In the command prompt area, the message "*_line Specify first point:*" is displayed.

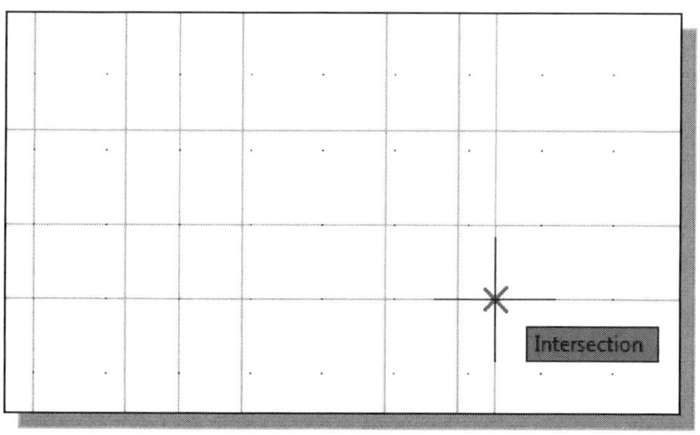

2. Move the cursor to the intersection of the construction lines at the lower right corner of the current sketch, and notice the visual aid automatically displayed at the intersection.

3. Create the object lines as shown below. (Hint: Use the *relative coordinate entry method* and the **Trim** command to construct the **30° line**.)

4. Use the Arc and Circle commands to complete the object lines as shown.

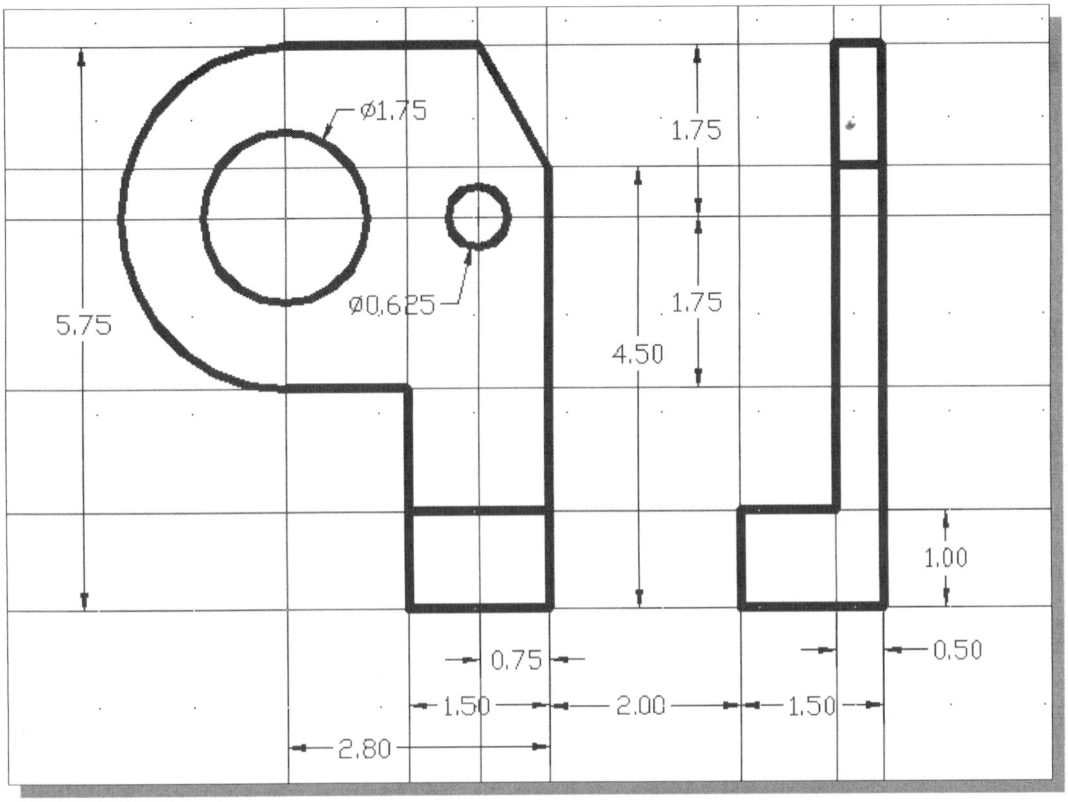

Creating Hidden Lines

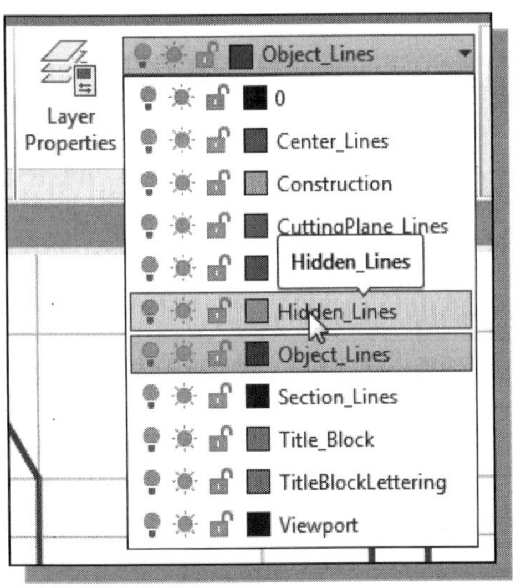

1. On the *Object Properties* toolbar, choose the *Layer Control* box with the left-mouse-button.

2. Move the cursor over the name of layer ***Hidden_Lines***, **left-click once**, and set layer *Hidden_Lines* as the *Current Layer*.

3. On your own, create the five hidden lines in the side view as shown on the next page.

Creating Center Lines

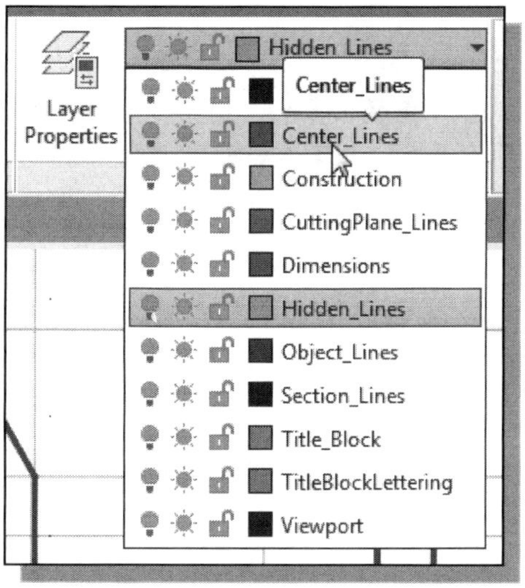

1. On the *Object Properties* toolbar, choose the *Layer Control* box to display the *Layer control list.*

2. Move the cursor over the name of layer ***Center_Lines***, and **left-click once** to set the layer as the *Current Layer.*

3. On your own, create the center line in the side view as shown in the below figure. (The center lines in the front-view will be added using the *Center Mark* option.)

Turn Off the Construction Lines

1. On the *Object Properties* toolbar, choose the *Layer Control* box with the left-mouse-button.

2. Move the cursor over the lightbulb icon for layer *Construction_Lines*, **left-click once**, and notice the icon color is changed to a gray tone color, representing the layer (layer *Construction_Lines*) is turned *OFF.*

3. Move the cursor over the name of layer ***Object_Lines***, **left-click once**, and set layer *Object_Lines* as the *Current Layer.*

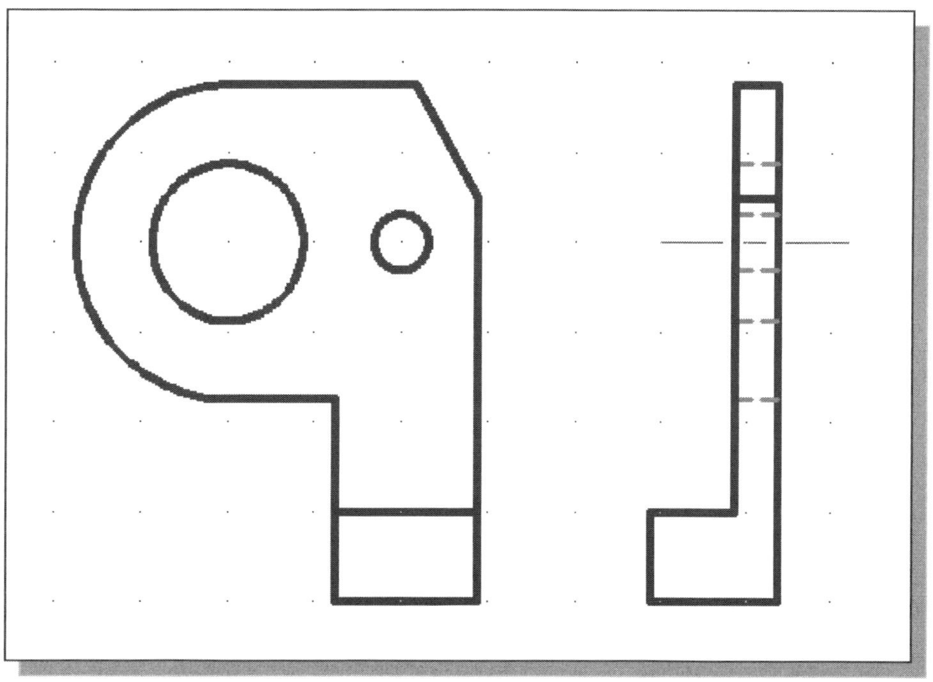

Using the Fillet Command

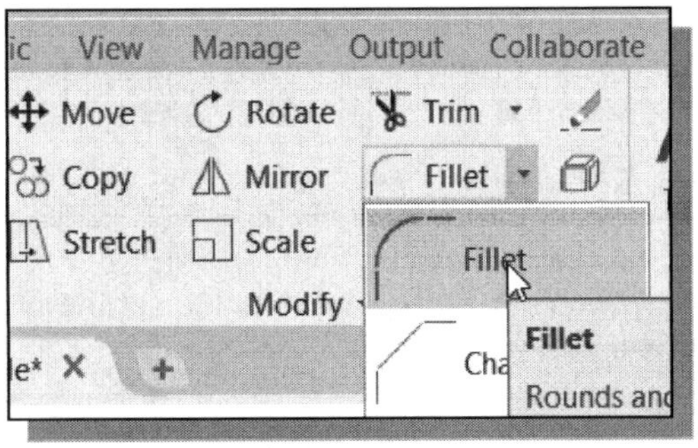

1. Select the **Fillet** command icon in the *Modify* toolbar. In the command prompt area, the message "*Select first object or [Polyline/Radius/Trim]:*" is displayed.

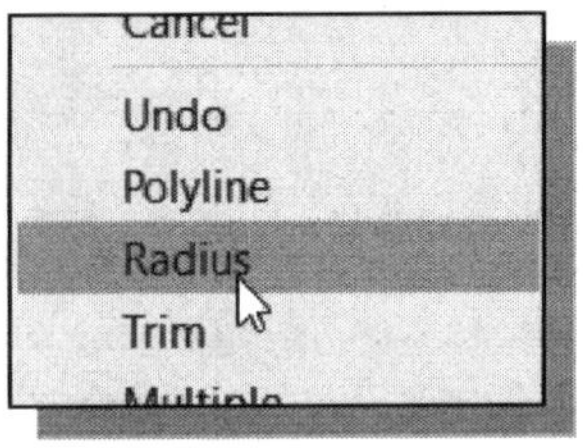

2. Inside the *graphics window*, right-click to activate the *option menu* and select the **Radius** option with the left-mouse-button to specify the radius of the fillet.

3. In the *command prompt* area, the message "*Specify fillet radius:*" is displayed. *Specify fillet radius:* **0.5 [ENTER]**.

4. Pick the **bottom horizontal line** of the front view as the first object to fillet.

5. Pick the **adjacent vertical line** connected to the arc to create a rounded corner as shown.

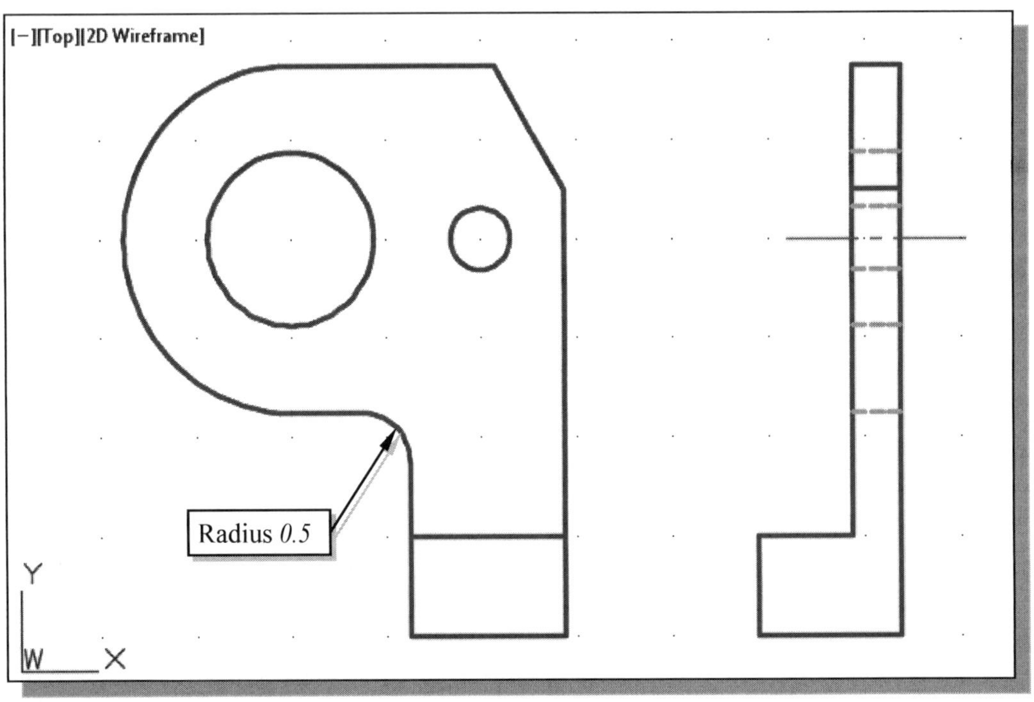

6. Repeat the **Fillet** command and create the four rounded corners (radius ***0.25***) as shown.

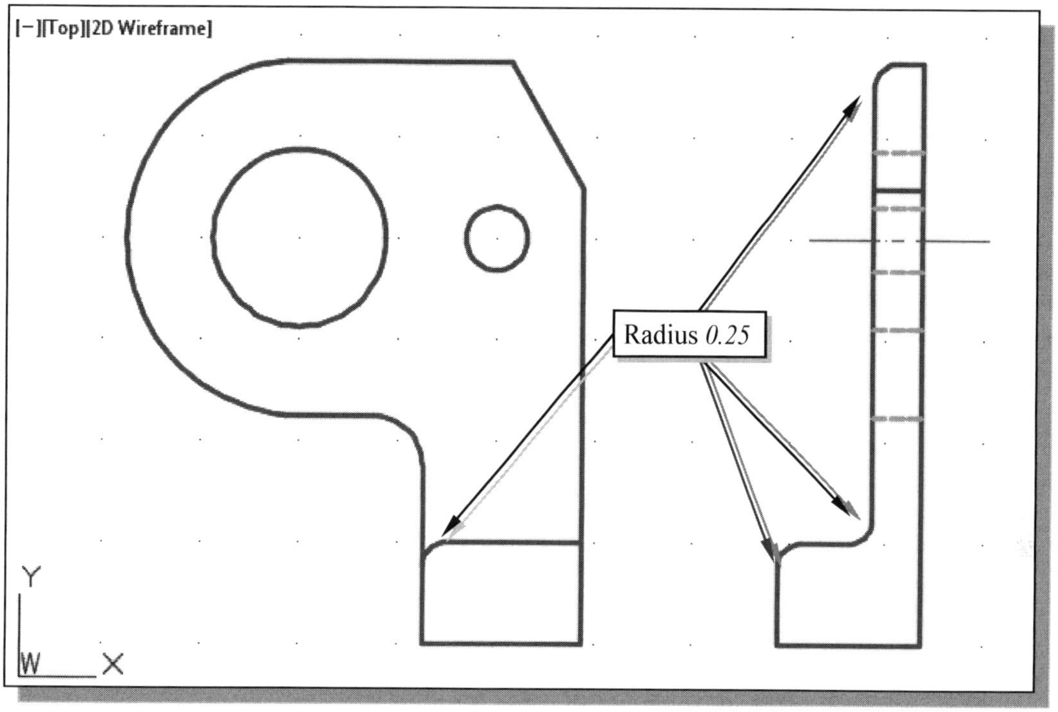

Saving the Completed CAD Design

1. In the *Menu Bar*, select: **[File] → [Save As]**.

2. In the *Save Drawing As* dialog box, select the folder in which you want to store the CAD file and enter ***Bracket*** in the *File name* box.

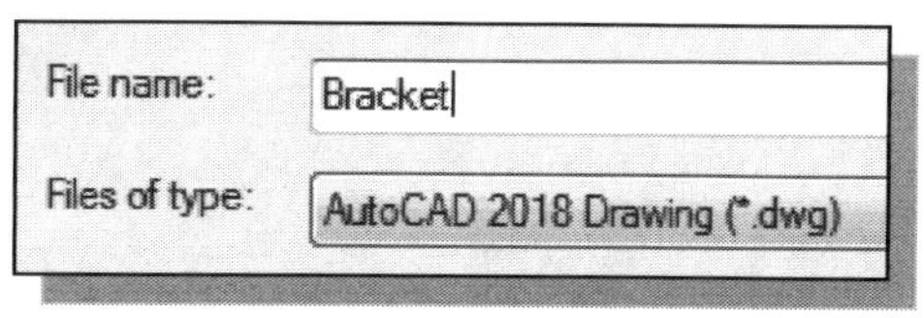

3. Click **Save** in the *Save Drawing As* dialog box to accept the selections and save the file.

Accessing the Dimensioning Commands

The user interface in AutoCAD has gone through several renovations since it was first released back in 1982. The purpose of the renovations is to make commands more accessible. For example, the dimensioning commands can be accessed through several options:

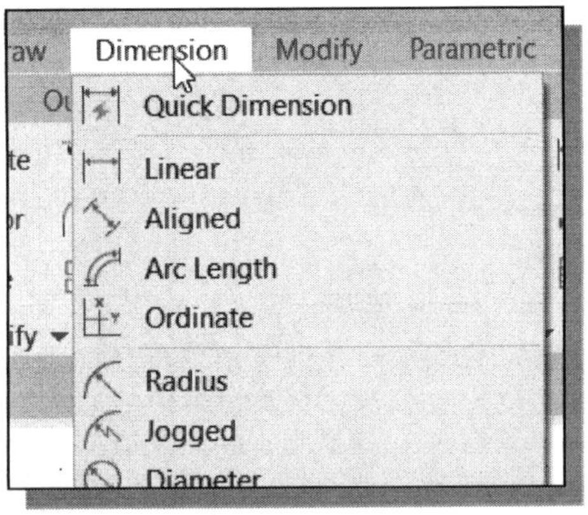

➢ The ***Menu Bar***: The majority of AutoCAD commands can be found in the *Menu Bar*. Specific task related commands are listed under the sub-items of the pull-down list. The commands listed under the *Menu Bar* are more complete, but it might take several clicks to reach the desired command.

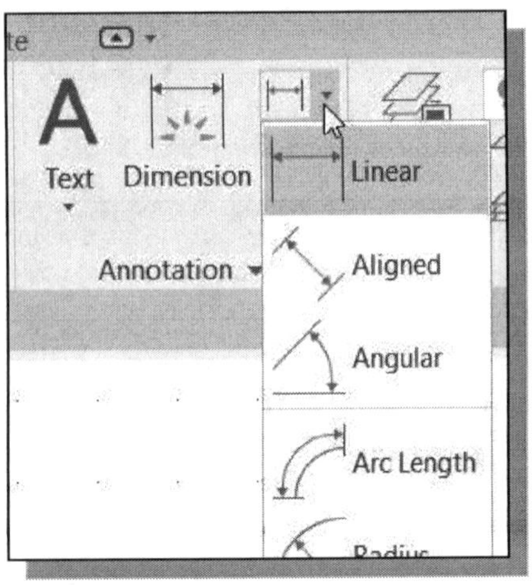

➢ The ***Ribbon* toolbar panels**: The more commonly used dimensioning commands are available in the *Annotation* toolbar as shown.

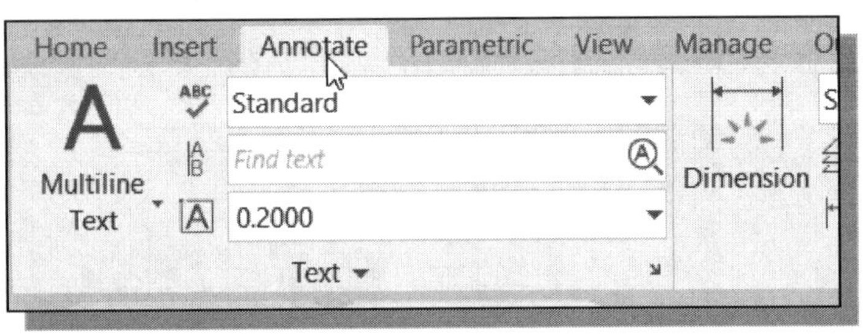

➢ The ***Dimensions* toolbar** under the **Annotate tab**: A more complete set of dimensioning commands.

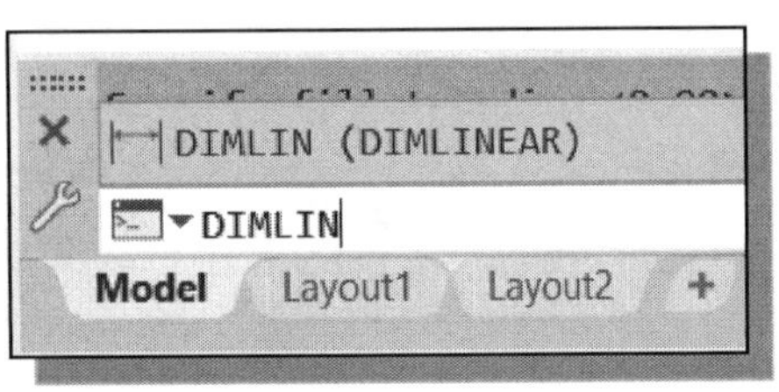

➢ The ***command prompt***: We can also type the command at the command prompt area. This option is always available, with or without displaying the toolbars.

The Dimension Toolbar

The *Dimension* toolbar offers the most flexible option to access the different dimensioning commands. The toolbar contains a more complete list than the *Ribbon* toolbars and this toolbar can be repositioned anywhere on the screen.

1. Move the cursor to the *Menu Bar* area and select:
   [Tools] → [Toolbars] → [AutoCAD] → [Dimension]

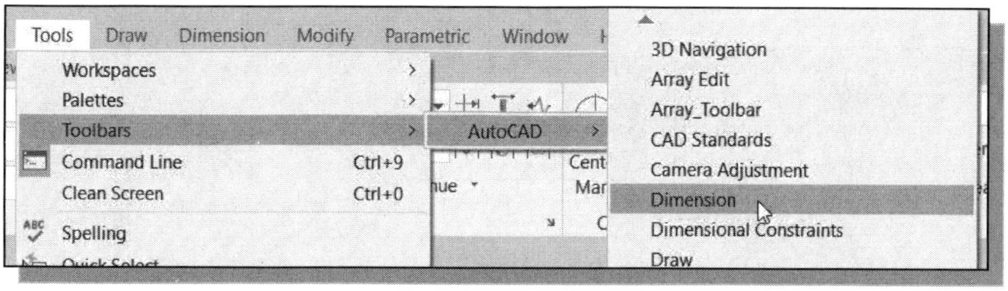

2. Move the cursor over the icons in the *Dimension* toolbar and read the brief description of each icon.

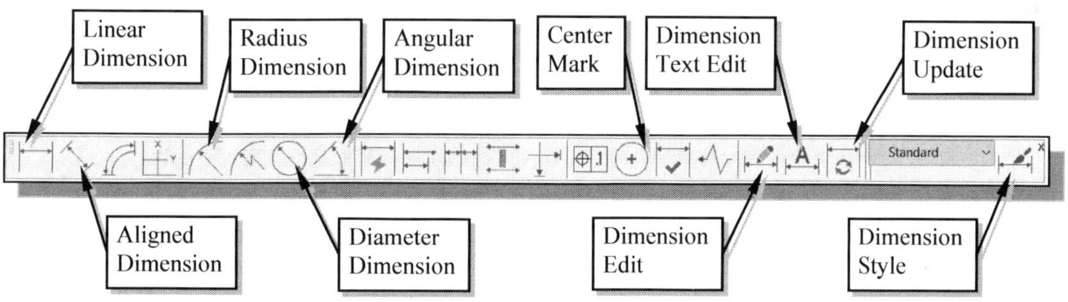

Using Dimension Style Manager

The appearance of the dimensions is controlled by *dimension variables*, which we can set using the *Dimension Style Manager* dialog box.

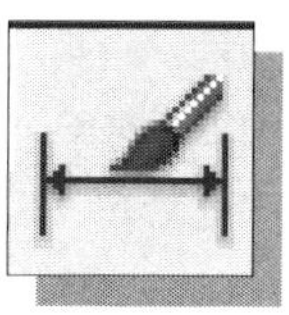

1. In the *Dimension* toolbar, pick **Dimension Style**. The *Dimension Style Manager* dialog box appears on the screen.

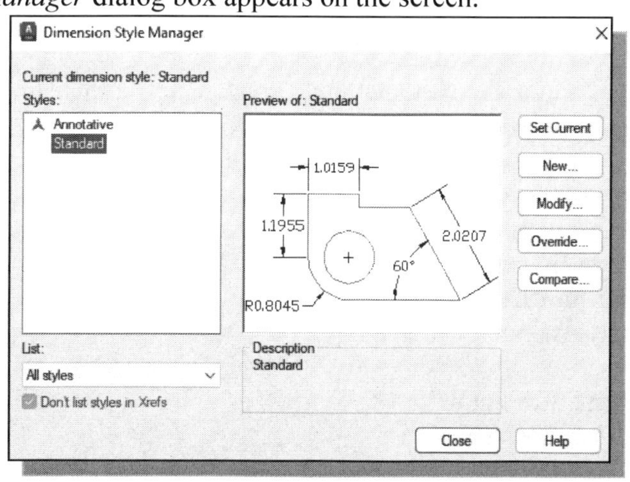

Dimensions Nomenclature and Basics

As it was stated in *Chapter 1*, the rule for creating CAD designs and drawings is that they should be created **full size** using real-world units. The importance of this practice is evident when we begin applying dimensions to the geometry. The features that we specify for dimensioning are measured and displayed automatically.

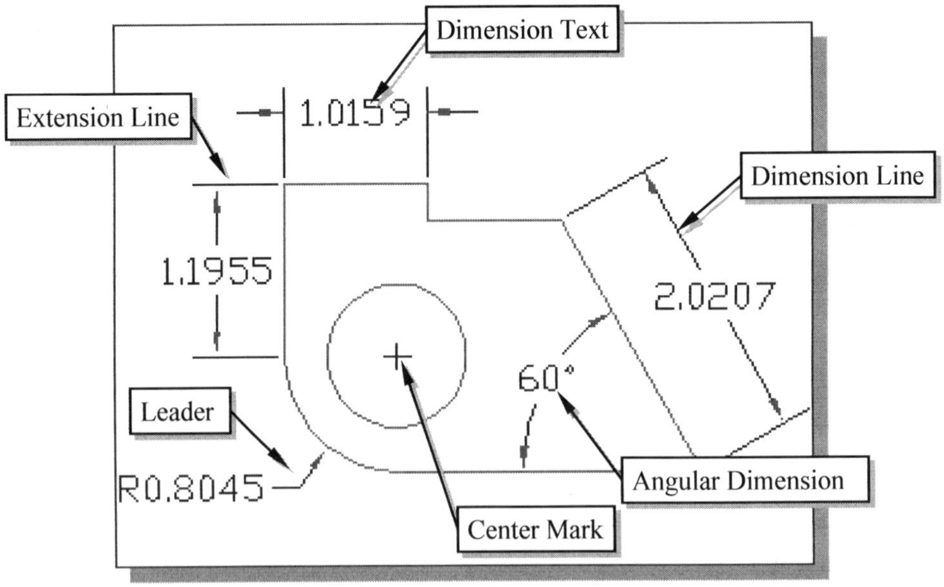

Selecting and placing dimensions can be confusing at times. The two main things to consider are (1) the function of the part and (2) the manufacturing operations. Detail drawings should contain only those dimensions that are necessary to make the design. Dimensions for the same feature of the design should be given only once in the same drawing. Nothing should be left to chance or guesswork on a drawing. Drawings should be dimensioned to avoid any possibility of questions. Dimensions should be carefully positioned, preferably near the profile of the feature being dimensioned.

Notice in the *Dimension Style Manager* dialog box, the AutoCAD default style name is *Standard*. We can create our own dimension style to fit the specific type of design we are working on, such as mechanical or architectual.

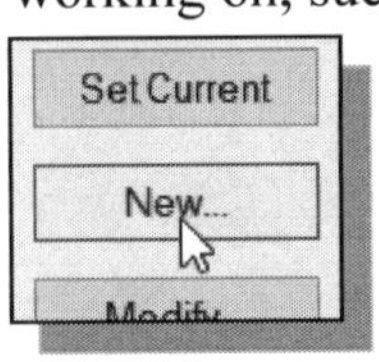

1. Click on the **New** button to create a new dimension style.

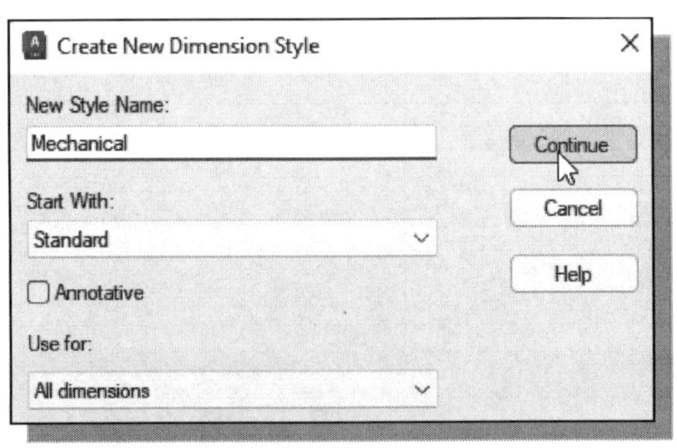

2. In the *Create New Dimension Style* dialog box, enter ***Mechanical*** as the dimension style name.

3. Click on the **Continue** button to proceed.

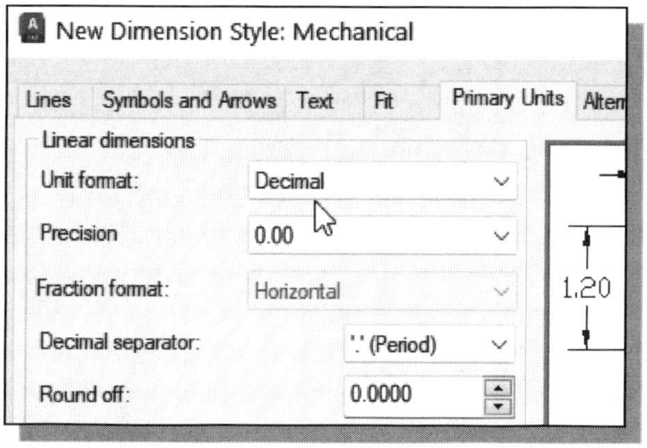

4. Click on the **Primary Units** tab.

5. Select ***Decimal*** as the *Unit format* and precision to **two digits after the decimal point** under the Primary Units tab. Also **suppress** the **leading zeros.**

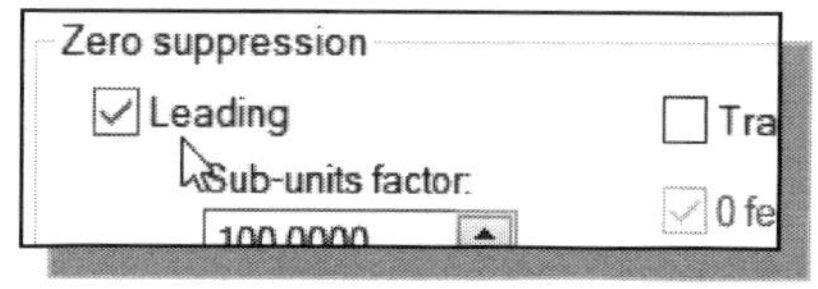

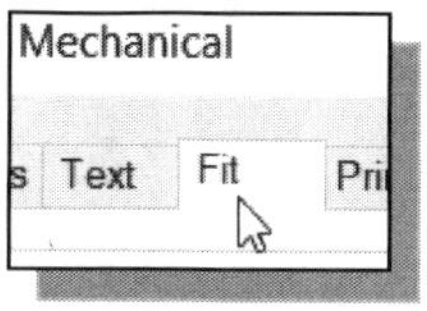

6. Select the **Fit** tab and notice the two options under *Scale for Dimension Features.*

❖ We can manually adjust the dimension scale factor or let AutoCAD automatically adjust the scale factor. For example, our current drawing will fit on A-size paper, and therefore we will use the scale factor of 1; this will assure the height of text size will be 1/8 of an inch on plotted drawing. If we change the Dimension Scale to 2.0 then the plotted text size will be ¼ of an inch on plotted drawing. In chapter 8, we will go over the procedure on using the AutoCAD layout mode, which allows us to plot the same design with different drawing sizes.

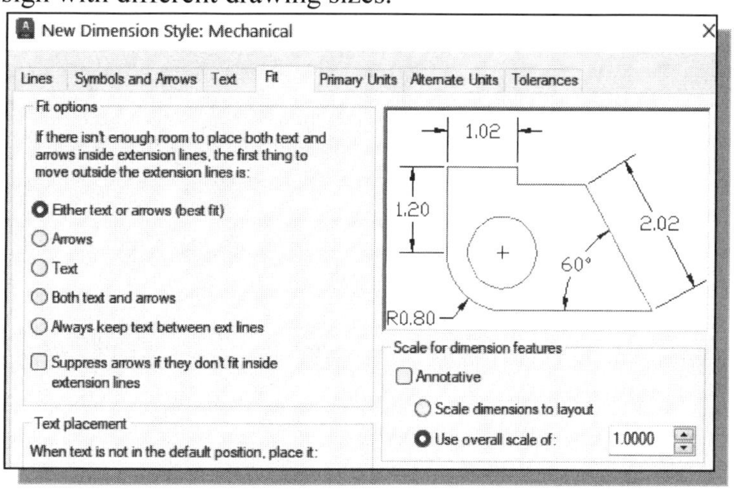

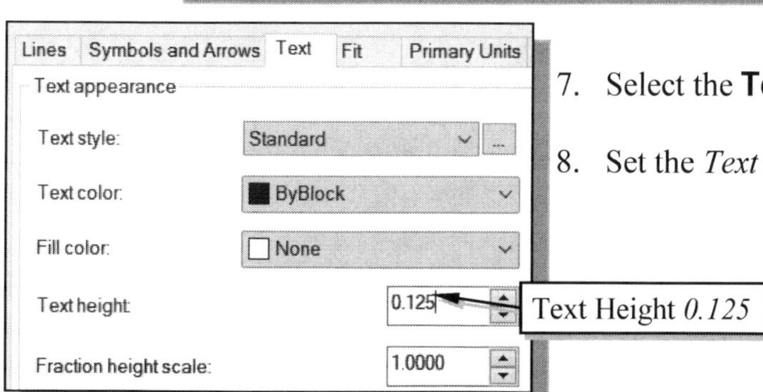

7. Select the **Text** tab.

8. Set the *Text Height* to ***0.125***.

9. Select the **Lines** tab and set *Extend beyond dim lines* to ***0.125***.

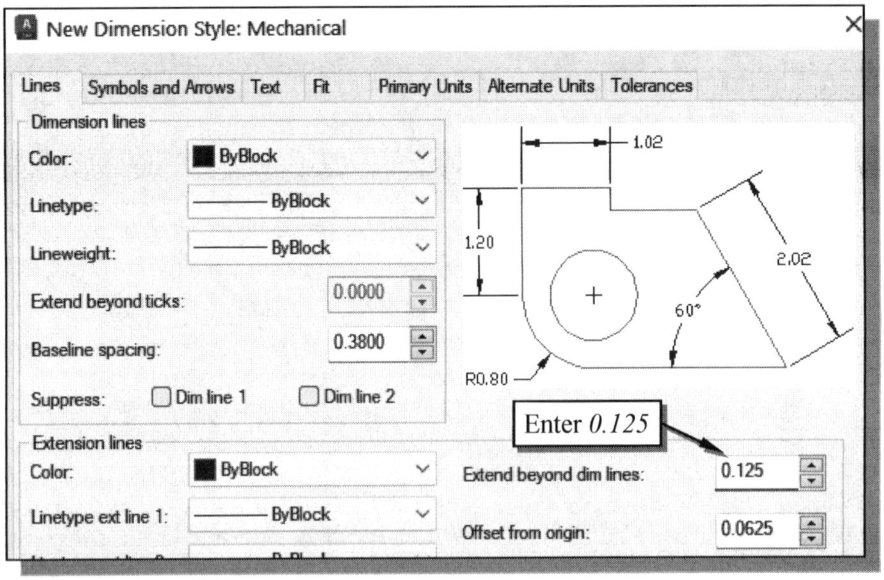

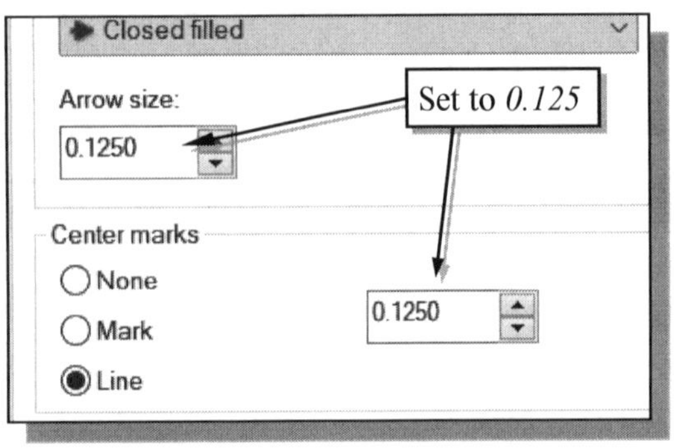

10. Select the **Symbols and Arrows** tab and set *Arrow size* and *Center marks* to ***0.125***. Also set the *Center marks* type to **Line**.

❖ Notice the different options available on this page, options that let us turn off one or both extension lines, dimension lines, and arrowheads.

➤ The **Center Mark** option is used to control the appearance of center marks and centerlines for diameter and radial dimensions.

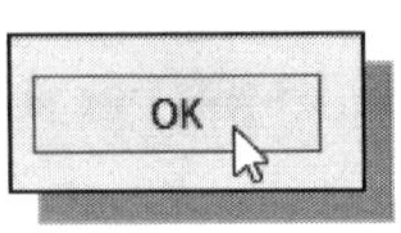

11. Click on the **OK** button to accept the settings and close the dialog box.

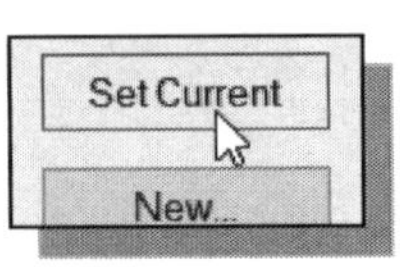

12. Pick the **Set Current** button to make the *Mechanical* dimension style the current dimension style.

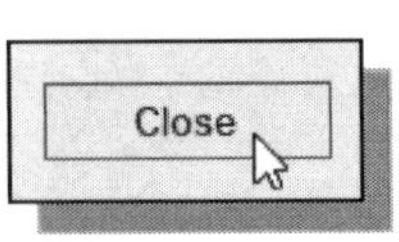

13. Click on the **Close** button to accept the settings and close the *Dimension Style Manager* dialog box.

➤ The **Dimension Style Manager** allows us to easily control the appearance of the dimensions in the drawing.

Using the Center Mark Command

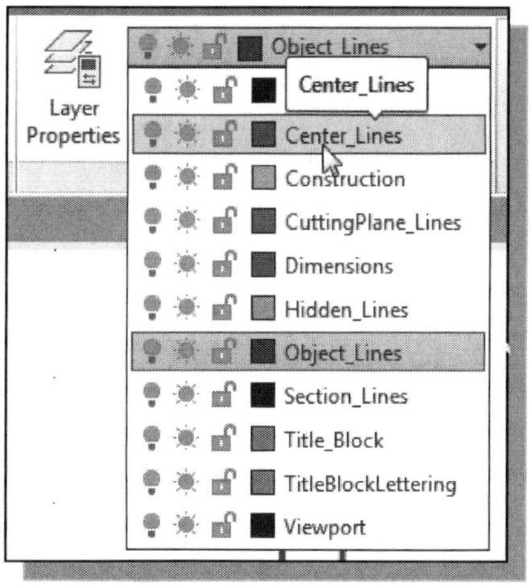

1. On the *Object Properties* toolbar, choose the ***Layer Control*** box with the left-mouse-button.

2. Move the cursor over the name of layer ***Center_Lines***, **left-click once**, and set layer *Center_lines* as the *Current Layer.*

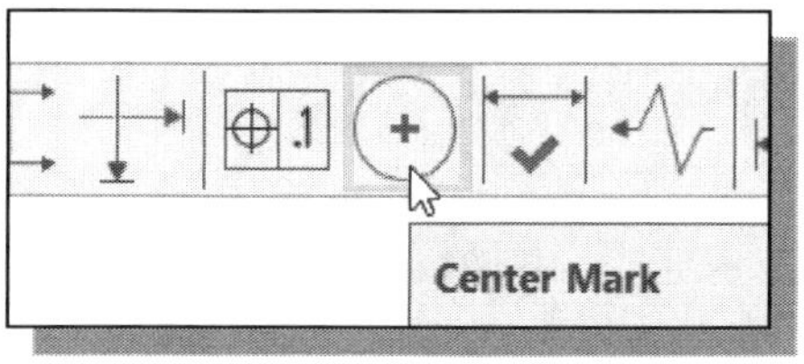

3. In the *Dimension* toolbar, click on the **Center Mark** icon.

4. Pick the **radius 1.75 arc** in the front view and notice AutoCAD automatically places two centerlines through the center of the arc.

5. Repeat the **Center Mark** command and pick the **small circle** to place the centerlines as shown.

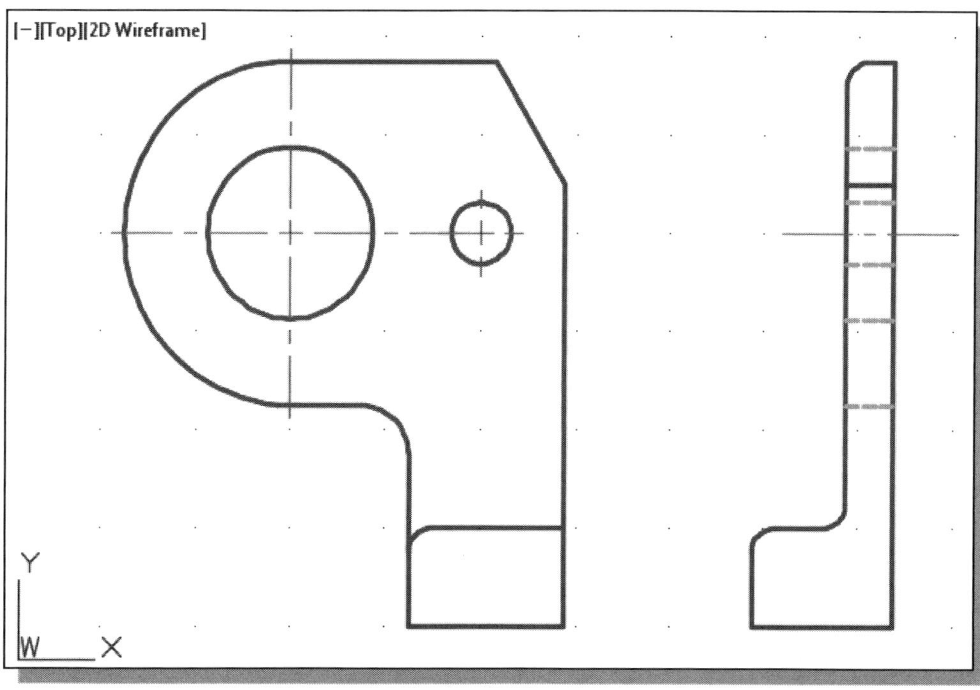

Adding Linear Dimensions

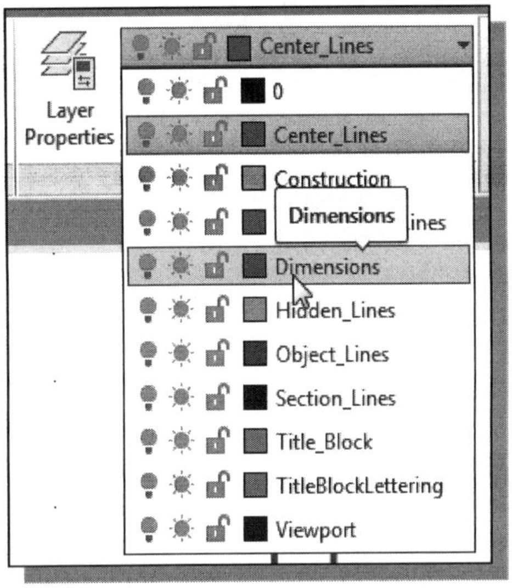

1. On the *Object Properties* toolbar, choose the ***Layer Control*** box with the left-mouse-button.

2. Move the cursor over the name of layer ***Dimensions***, **left-click once**, and set layer *Dimensions* as the *Current Layer.*

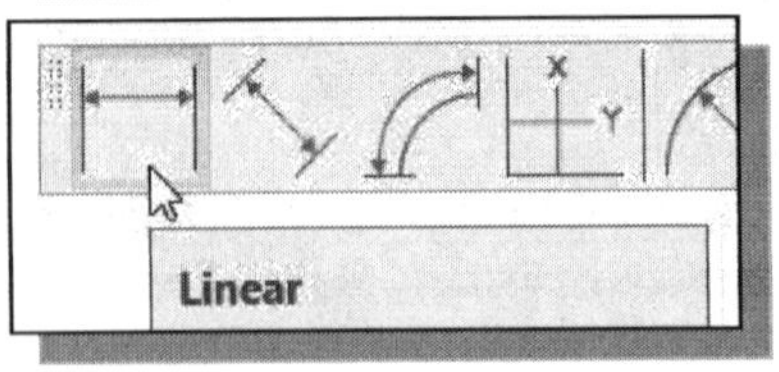

3. In the *Dimension* toolbar, click on the **Linear Dimension** icon.

➢ The **Linear Dimension** command measures and annotates a feature with a horizontal or vertical dimension.

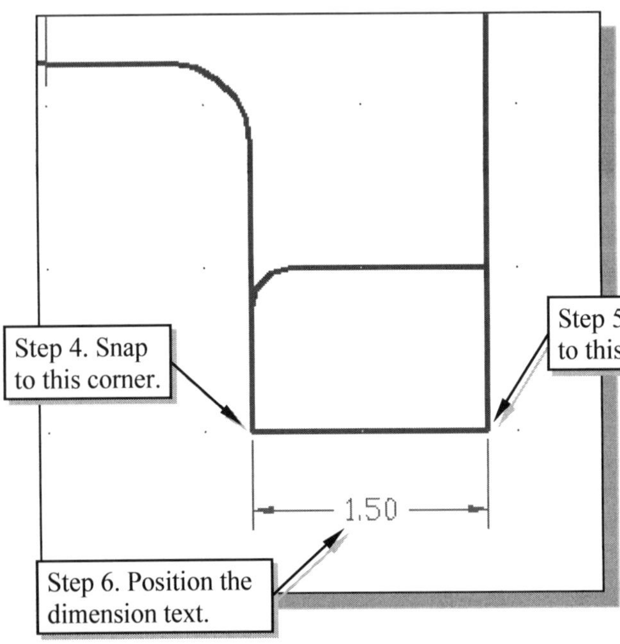

4. Pick the **lower left corner** of the front view of the part.

5. Pick the **lower right corner** of the front view of the part.

6. Pick a point that is about 0.5 inch below the bottom horizontal line of the front view to place the dimension text.

❖ Adding dimensions is very easy with AutoCAD's auto-dimensioning and associative-dimensioning features.

Adding Linear Dimensions using the Object option

In AutoCAD 2027, we can create horizontal, vertical, aligned, and radial dimensions with the DIM command. The type of dimension depends on the object that you select and the direction that you drag the dimension line.

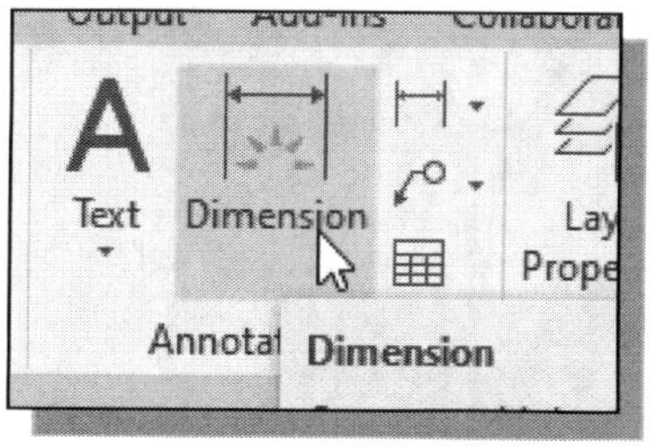

1. In the *Annotation* toolbar, click on the **Dimension** icon.

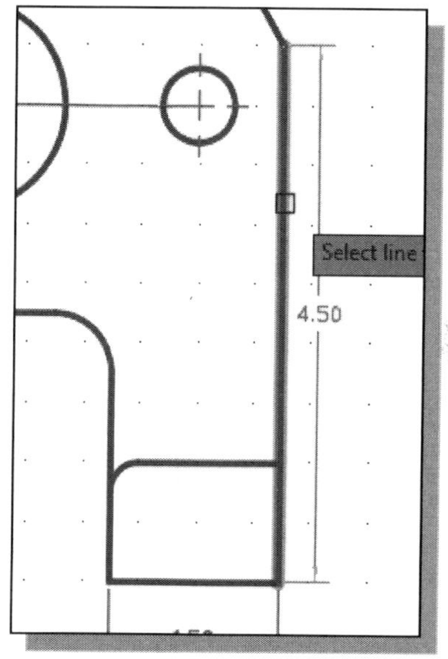

2. Move the cursor on top of the right vertical line in the front view and notice the associated length dimension is displayed next to the line.

3. Left-mouse-click once to accept the displayed dimension.

4. Move the cursor to the right and place the dimension as shown.

5. On your own, repeat the above steps and add the two dimensions in the side view as shown.

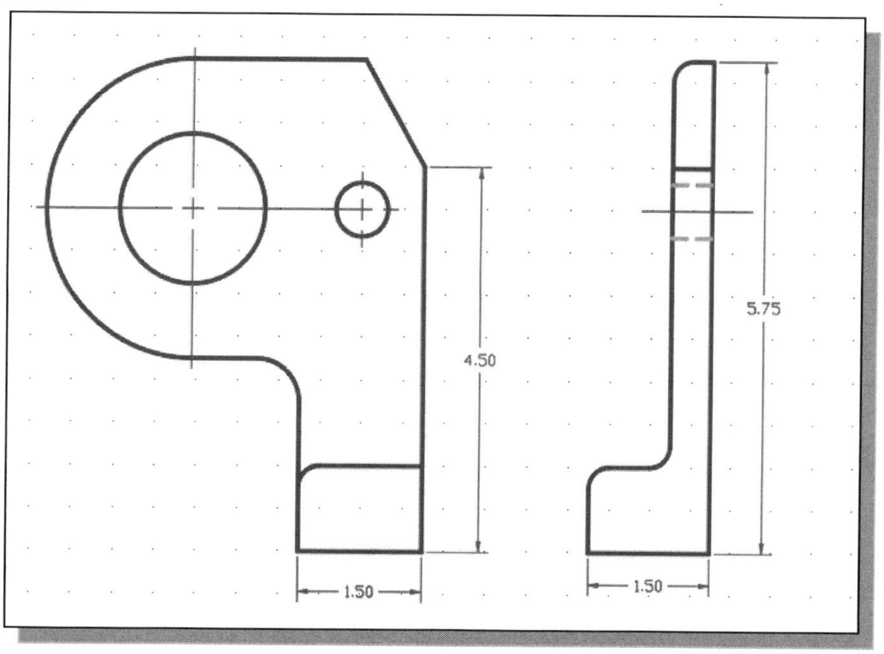

6. Select the right vertical line in the front view, then select the adjacent inclined line to display the related **angular dimension** as shown.

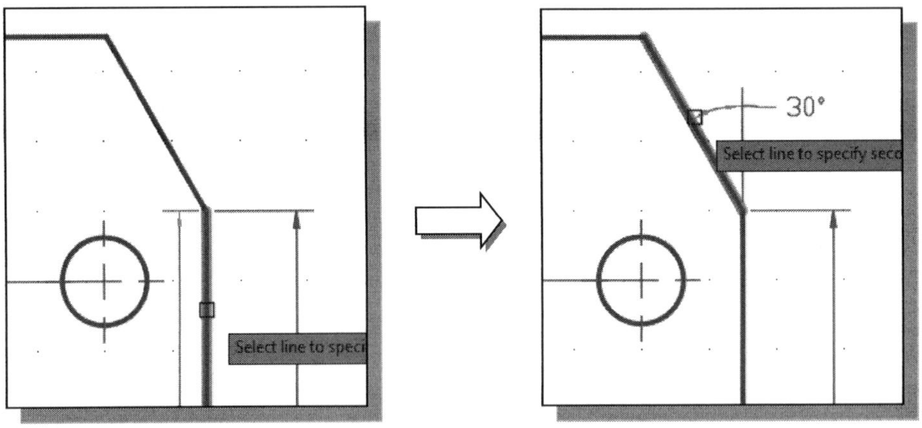

7. Left-mouse-click once to accept the displayed dimension.

8. On your own, move the cursor around and AutoCAD will show the different quadrant angle. Create the angular dimension as shown in the above figure.

9. Repeat the **Linear Dimension** or **Dimension** command and add the necessary linear dimensions as shown.

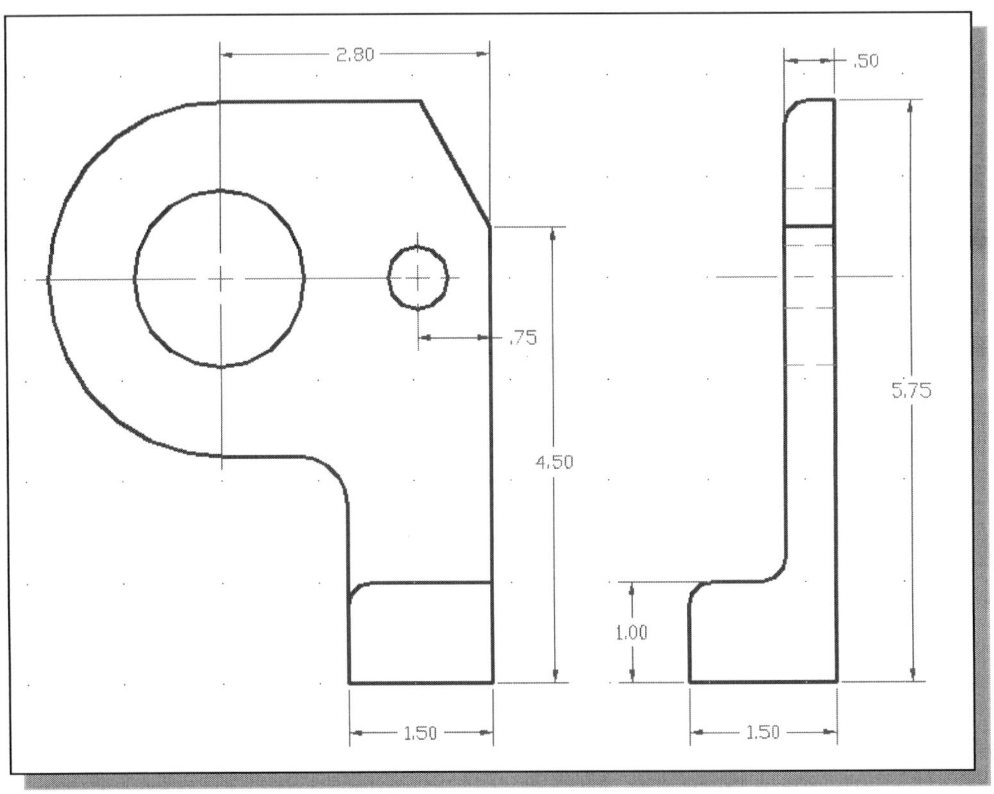

Adding Radius and Diameter Dimensions

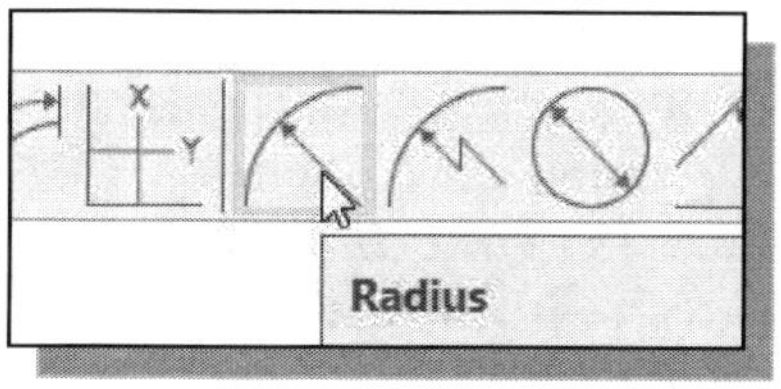

1. In the *Dimension* toolbar, click on the **Radius Dimension** icon.

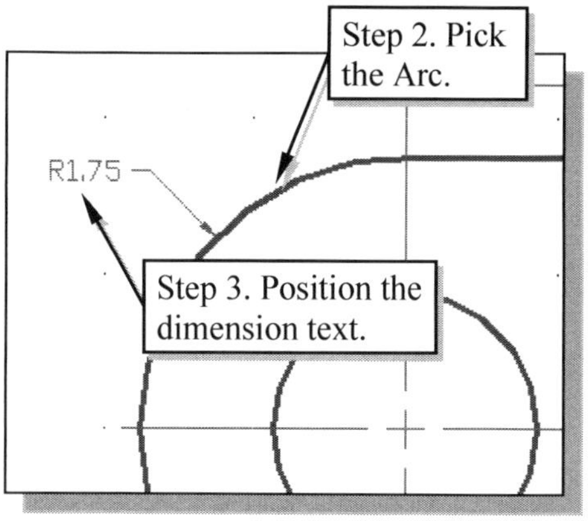

2. Pick the **large arc** in the front view.

3. Pick a point toward the left of the arc to place the dimension text.

4. Use the Radius Dimension and Diameter Dimension commands to add the necessary dimensions as shown.

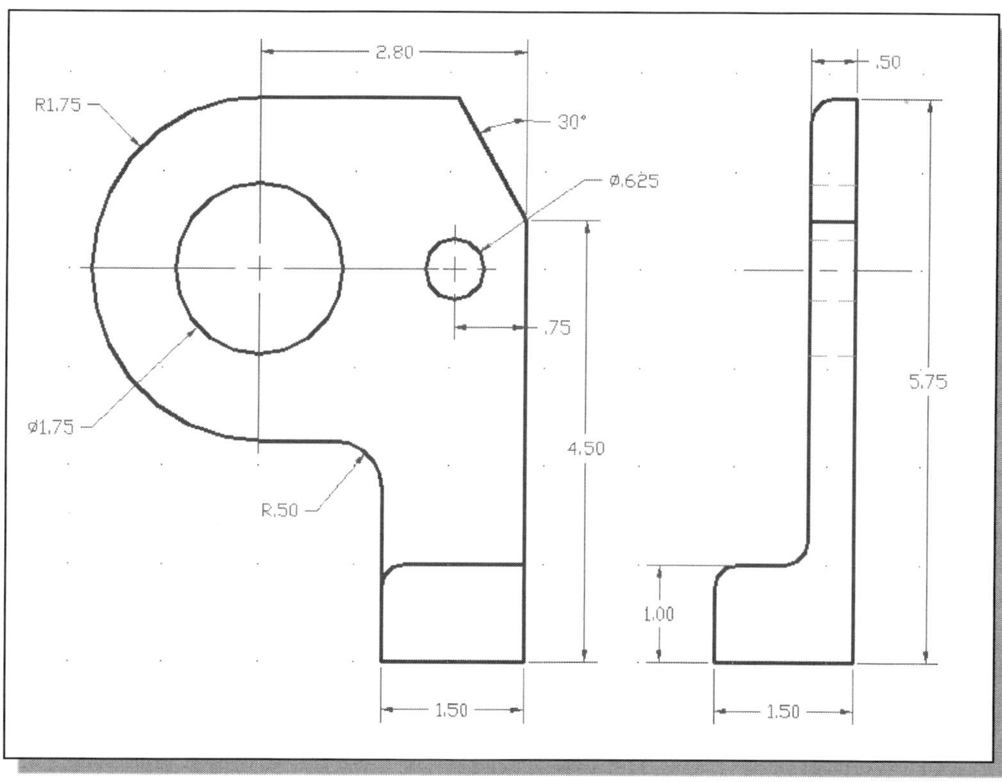

Using the Multiline Text Command

AutoCAD provides two options to create notes. For simple entries, we can use the **Single Line Text** command. For longer entries with internal formatting, we can use the **Multiline Text** command. The procedures for both of these commands are self-explanatory. The **Single Line Text** command, also known as the **Text** command, can be used to enter several lines of text that can be rotated and resized. The text we are typing is displayed on the screen. Each line of text is treated as a separate object in AutoCAD. To end a line and begin another, press the **[ENTER]** key after entering characters. To end the Text command, press the **[ENTER]** key without entering any characters.

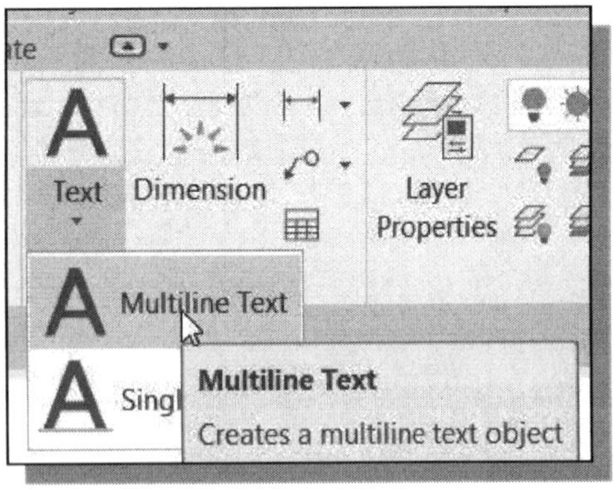

1. In the *Ribbon* toolbar panel, select:

   [Multiline Text]

2. In the *command prompt* area, the message "*Specify start point of text or [Justify/Style]:*" is displayed. Pick a location near the world coordinate ***(1,1.5)***.

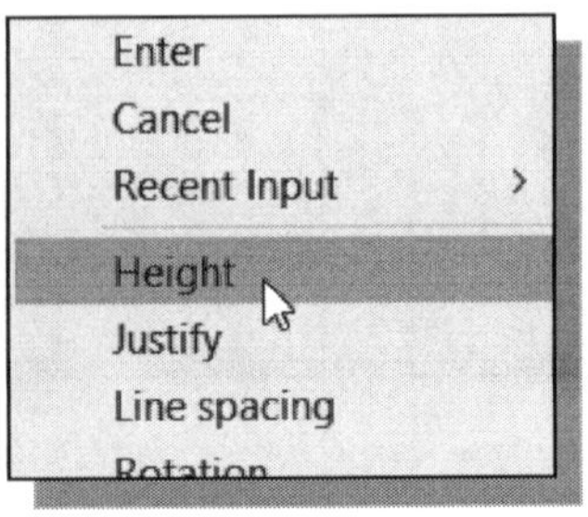

3. Right-click once to bring up the option list and choose **Height**. In the command prompt area, the message "*Specify Height:*" is displayed. Enter ***0.125*** as the text height.

4. Click a position toward the right and create a rectangle representing roughly the area for the notes.

5. In the command prompt area, the message "*Enter Text:*" is displayed. Enter: ***Rounds & Fillets R .25*** **[ENTER]**.

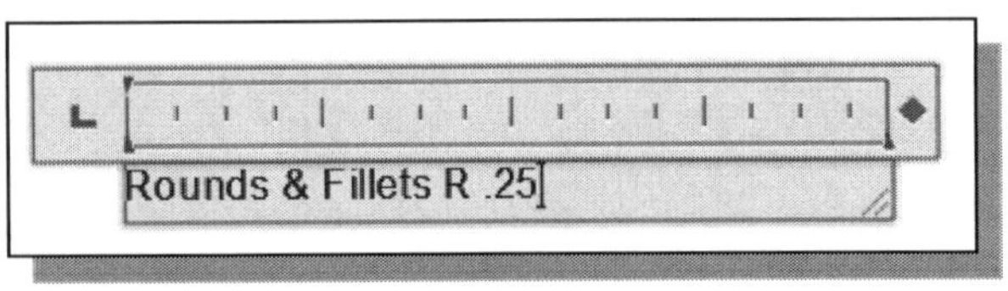

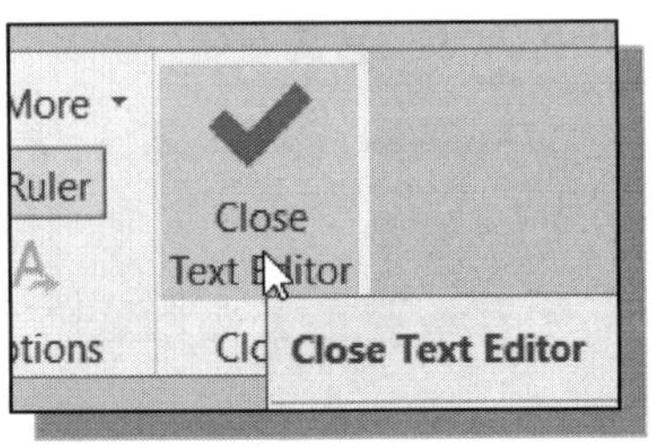

6. Note in the *Ribbon toolbar* area, the different command options are available to adjust the multiline text entered. Click **[Close Text Editor]** once to end the command.

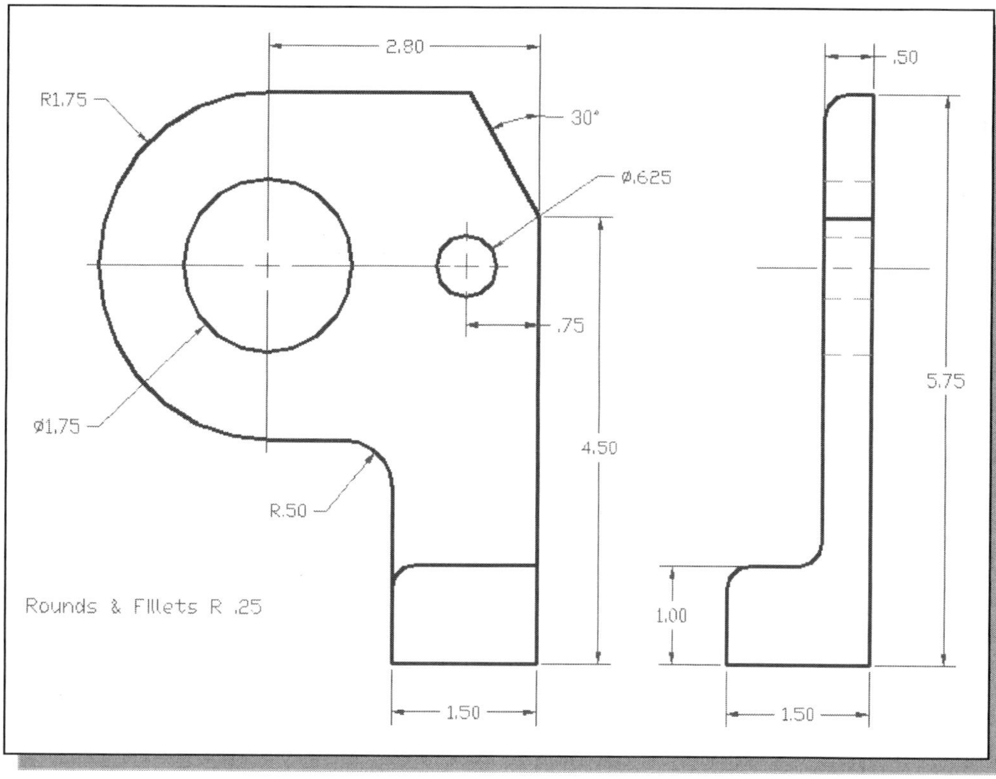

Adding Special Characters

We can add special text characters to the dimensioning text and notes. We can type in special characters during any text command and when entering the dimension text. The most common special characters have been given letters to make them easy to remember.

Code	***Character***	***Symbol***
%%C	Diameter symbol	∅
%%D	Degree symbol	°
%%P	Plus/Minus sign	±

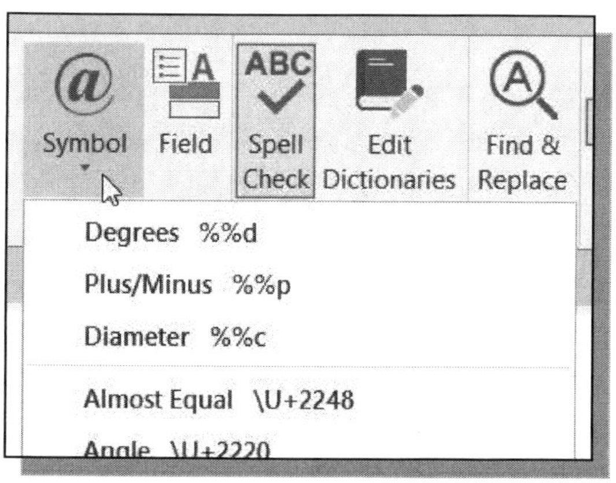

➢ On your own, create notes containing some of the special characters listed.

➢ Note the complete list of special characters can be accessed through the [Multiline Text] → [Symbol] dashboard.

Saving the Design

➢ In the *Quick Access Toolbar* area, select the **Save** icon.

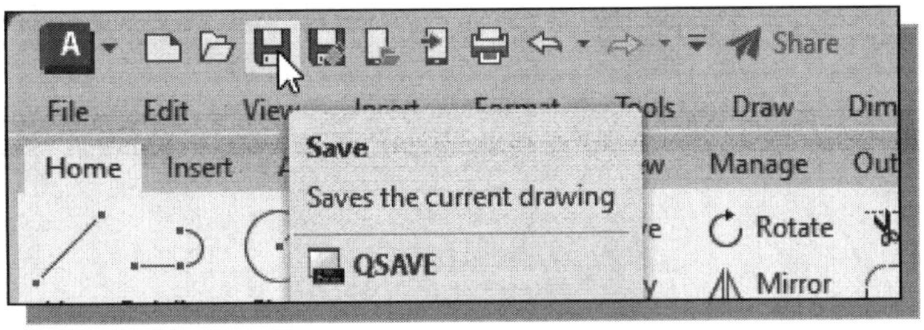

A Special Note on Layers Containing Dimensions

AutoCAD creates several hidden **BLOCKS** when we create associative dimensions and we will take a more in depth look at *blocks* in *Chapter 13*. AutoCAD treats **blocks** as a special type of object called a *named object*. Each kind of *named object* has a *symbol table* or a *dictionary*, and each table or dictionary can store multiple *named objects*. For example, if we create five dimension styles, our drawing's dimension style *symbol table* will have five dimension style records. In general, we do not work with *symbol tables* or *dictionaries* directly.

When we create dimensions in AutoCAD, most of the hidden blocks are placed in the same layer where the dimension was first defined. Some of the definitions are placed in the *DEFPOINTS* layer. When moving dimensions from one layer to another, AutoCAD does not move these definitions. When deleting layers, we cannot delete the current layer, *layer 0*, xref-dependent layers, or a layer that contains visible and/or invisible objects. Layers referenced by block definitions, along with the *DEFPOINTS* layer, cannot be deleted even if they do not contain visible objects.

To delete layers with hidden blocks, first use the **Purge** command **[Application → Drawing Utilities → Purge → Blocks]** to remove the invisible blocks. (We will have to remove all visible objects prior to using this command.) The empty layer can now be *deleted* or *purged*.

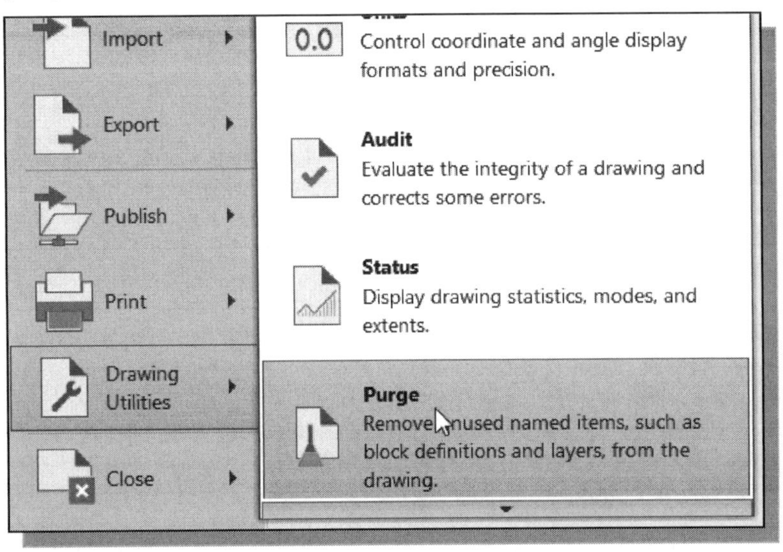

Review Questions: (Time: 25 minutes)

1. Why are dimensions and notes important to a technical drawing?

2. List and describe some of the general-dimensioning practices.

3. What is the effect of *Tolerance Accumulation*? How do we avoid it?

4. Describe the procedure in setting up a new *Dimension Style.*

5. What is the special way to create a diameter symbol when entering a dimension text?

6. What is the text code to create the **Diameter** symbol (Ø) in AutoCAD?

7. Which command can be used to delete layers with hidden blocks? Can we delete *Layer 0*?

8. Which quick-key is used to display and hide the *AutoCAD Text Window*?

9. What are the length and angle of the inclined line, highlighted in the figure below, in the front view of the *P-Bracket* design?

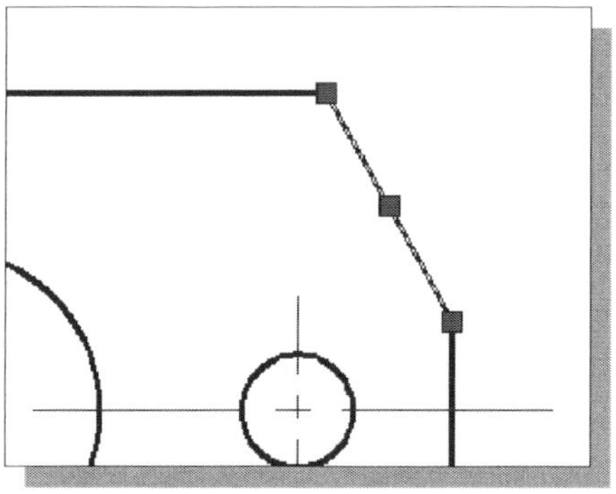

10. Construct the following drawing and measure the angle α.

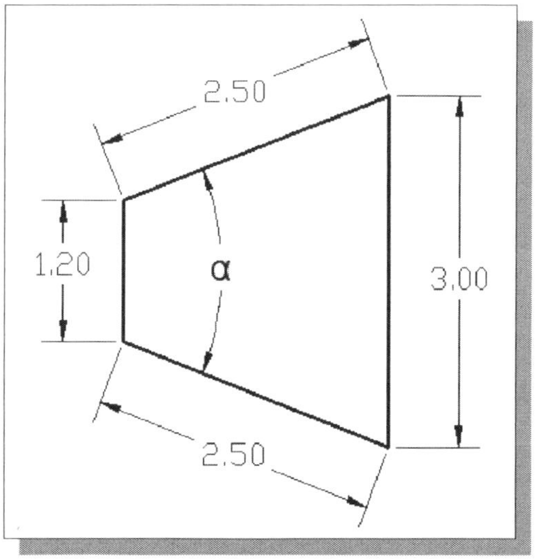

Exercises: (Time: 150 minutes)

1. **Shaft Guide** (Dimensions are in inches.)

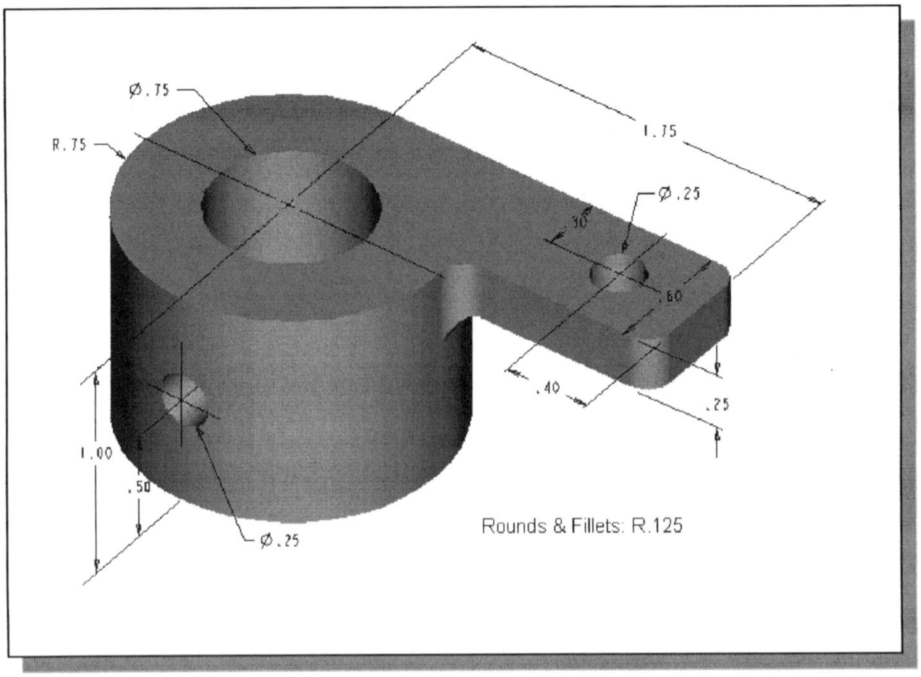

2. **Fixture Cap** (Dimensions are in millimeters.)

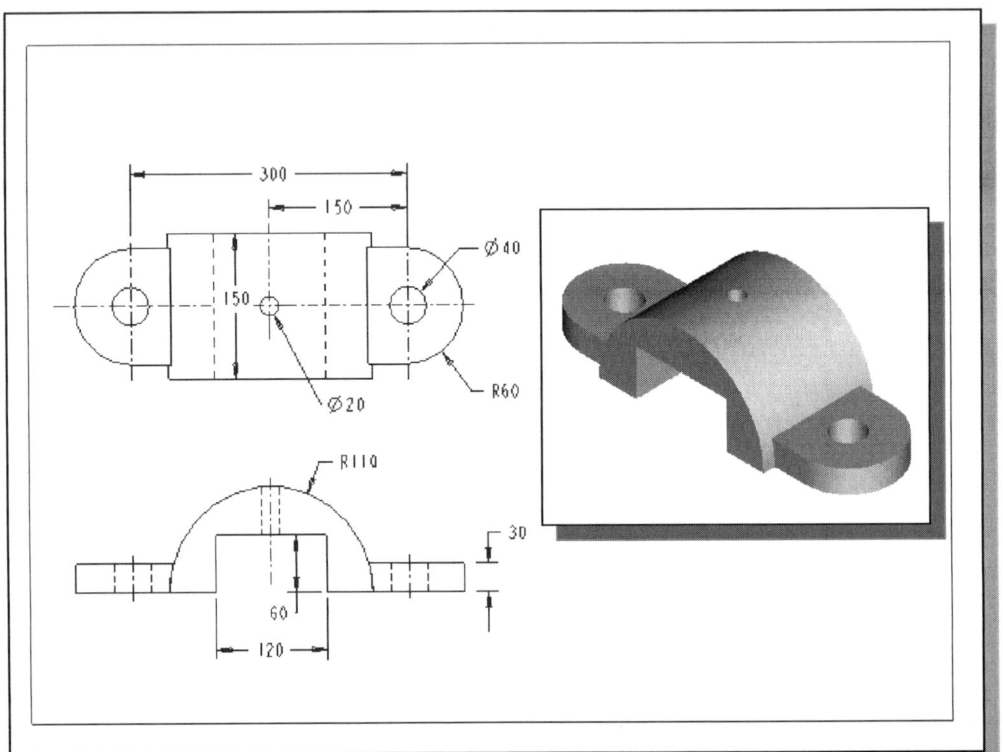

3. Cylinder Support (Dimensions are in inches.)

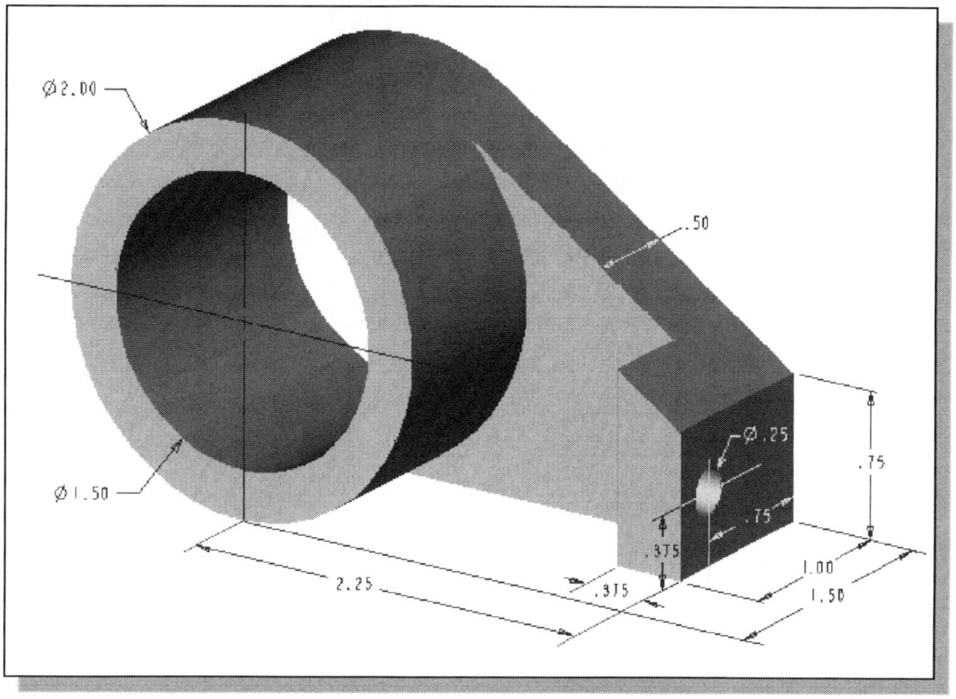

4. Swivel Base (Dimensions are in inches. Rounds: R 0.25)

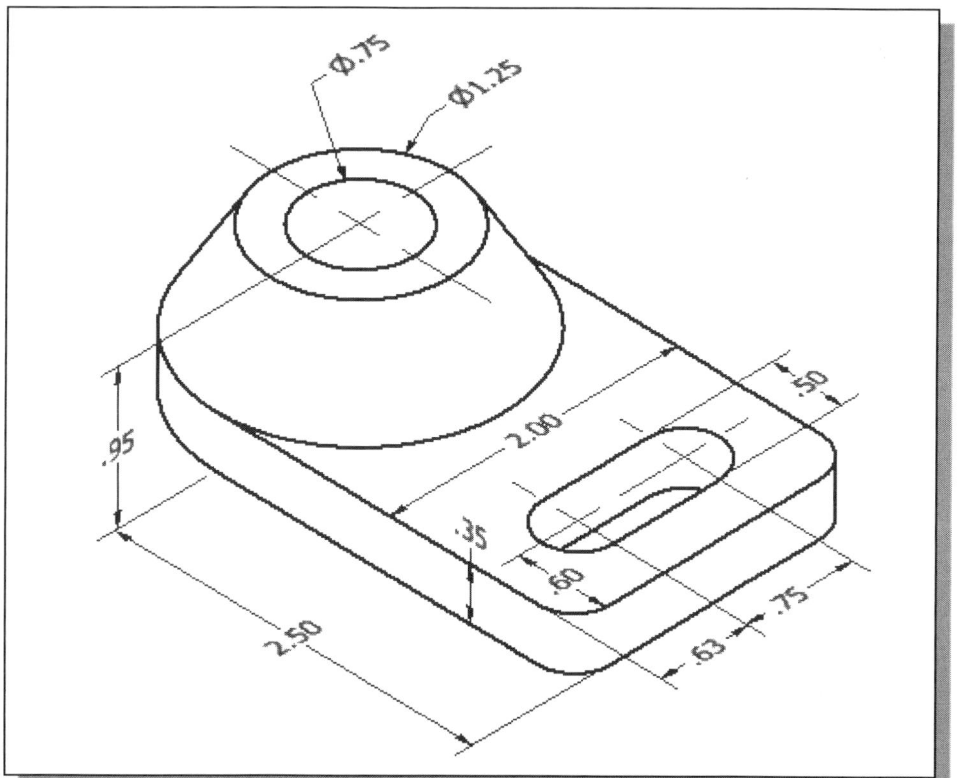

5. Pivot Holder (Dimensions are in inches.)

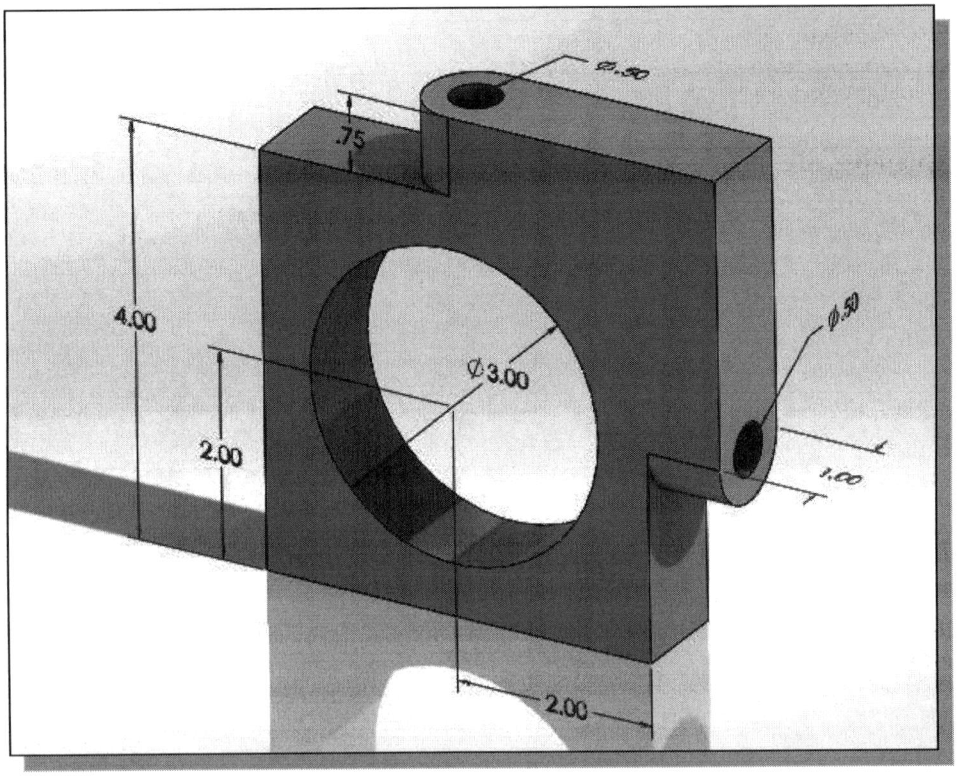

6. Shaft Guide (Dimensions are in inches.)

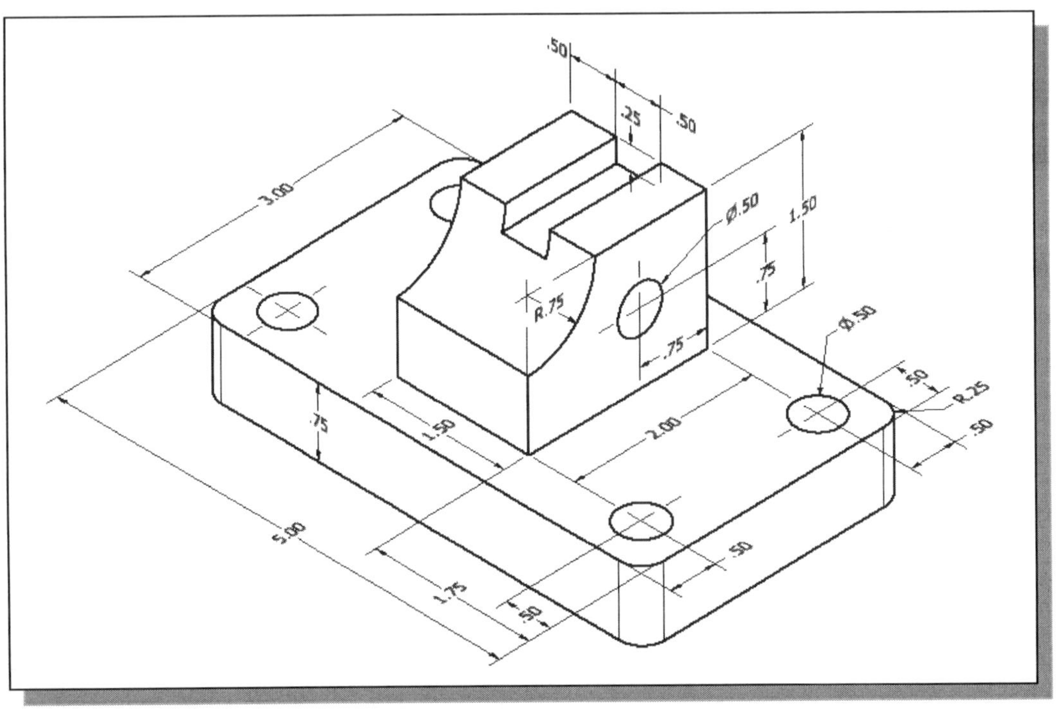

7. Indexing Stop (Dimensions are in millimeters.)

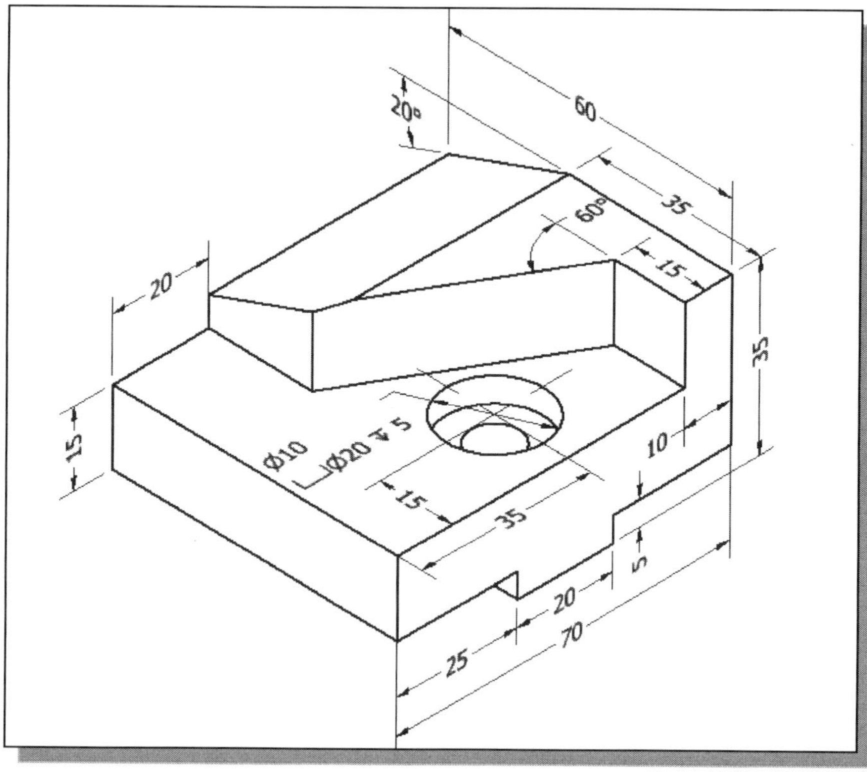

8. Tube Hanger (Dimensions are in inches.)

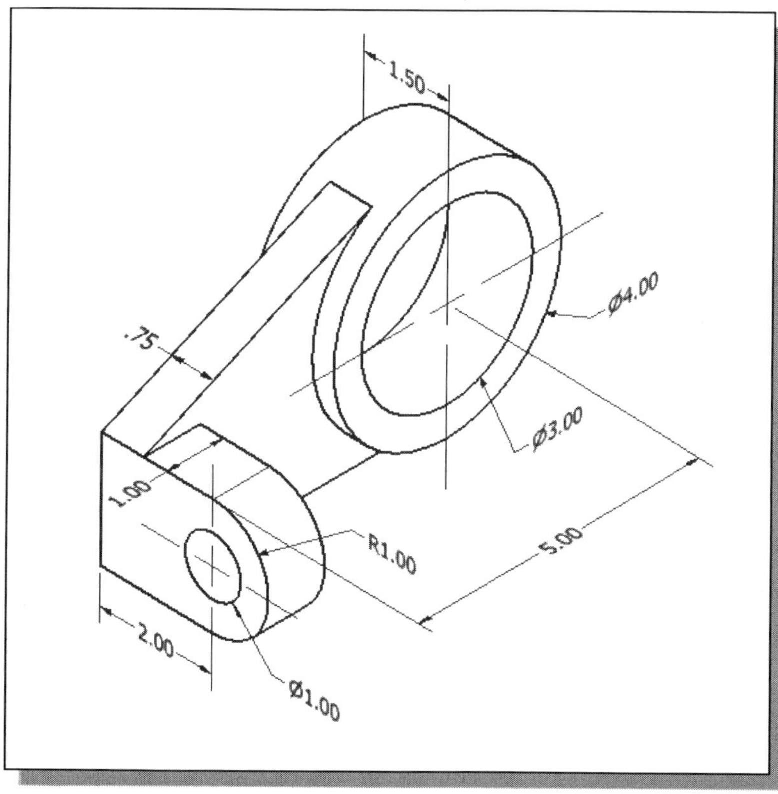

Notes:

Chapter 8
Tolerancing and Fits

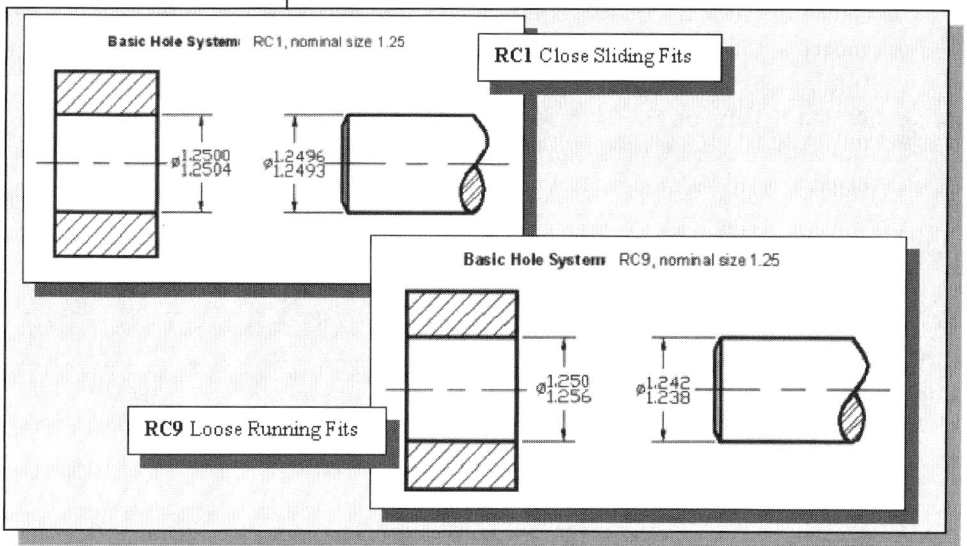

Learning Objectives

- Understand Tolerancing Nomenclature
- The Tolerancing Designation Method
- Understand the Basics of ANSI Standard Fits
- Use of the ISO Metric Standard Fits
- Use the Open Files AutoCAD Option
- Set up the Tolerancing Option in AutoCAD

Precision and Tolerance

In the manufacturing of any product, quality and cost are always the two primary considerations. Drawings with dimensions and notes often serve as construction documents and legal contracts to ensure the proper functioning of a design. When dimensioning a drawing, it is therefore critical to consider the *precision* required for the part. *Precision* is the degree of accuracy required during manufacturing. However, it is impossible to produce any dimension to an absolute, accurate measurement; some variation must be allowed in manufacturing. Specifying higher precision on a drawing may ensure better quality of a product but doing so may also raise the costs of the product. And requiring unnecessary high precision of a design, resulting in high production costs, may cause the inability of the design to compete with similar products in the market. As an example, consider a design that contains cast parts. A cast part usually has two types of surfaces: mating surfaces and non-mating surfaces. The mating surfaces, as they will interact with other parts, are typically machined to a proper smoothness and require higher precision on all corresponding dimensions. The non-mating surfaces are usually left in the original rough-cast form as they have no important relationship with the other parts. The dimensions on a drawing must clearly indicate which surfaces are to be finished and provide the degree of precision needed for the finishing.

The method of specifying the degree of precision is called **Tolerancing**. **Tolerance** is the allowable variation for any given size and provides a practical means to achieve the precision necessary in a design. Tolerancing also ensures interchangeability in manufacturing; parts can be made by different companies in different locations and still maintain the proper functioning of the design. With tolerancing, each dimension is allowed to vary within a specified zone. By assigning as large a tolerance as possible, without interfering with the functionality of a design, the production costs can be reduced. The smaller the tolerance zone specified, the more expensive it is to manufacture.

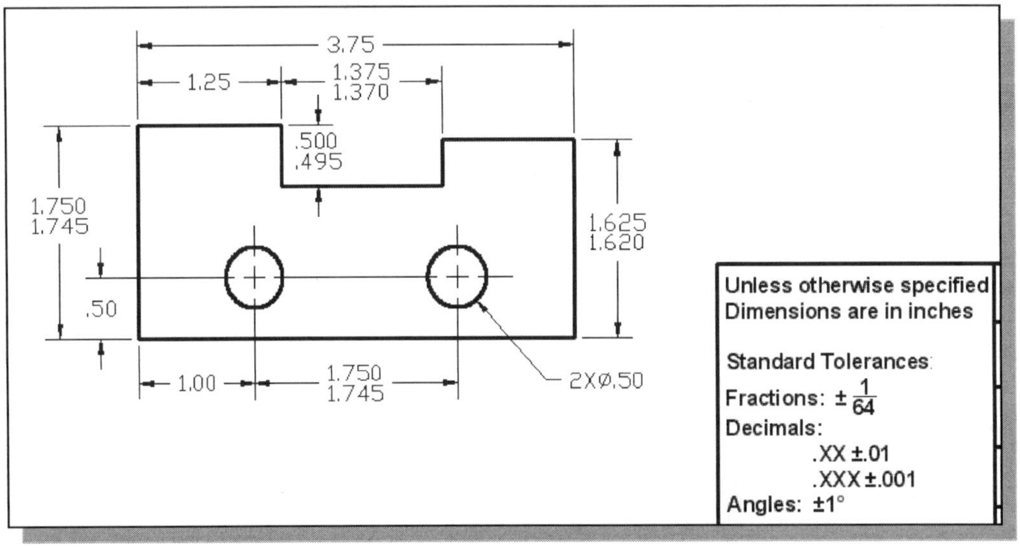

Methods of Specifying Tolerances – English System

Three methods are commonly used in specifying tolerances: **Limits**, **Unilateral tolerances** and **Bilateral tolerances**. Note that the unilateral and bilateral methods employ the use of a **Base Dimension** in specifying the variation range.

- Limits – Specifies the range of size that a part may be.
  This is the preferred method as approved by ANSI/ASME Y14.5M; the maximum and minimum limits of size and locations are specified. The maximum value is placed above the minimum value. In single-line form, a dash is used to separate the two values.

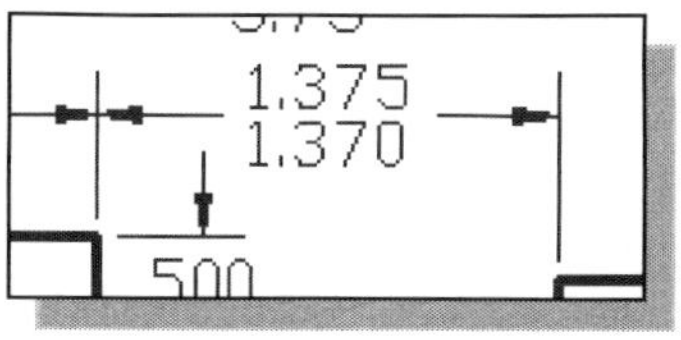

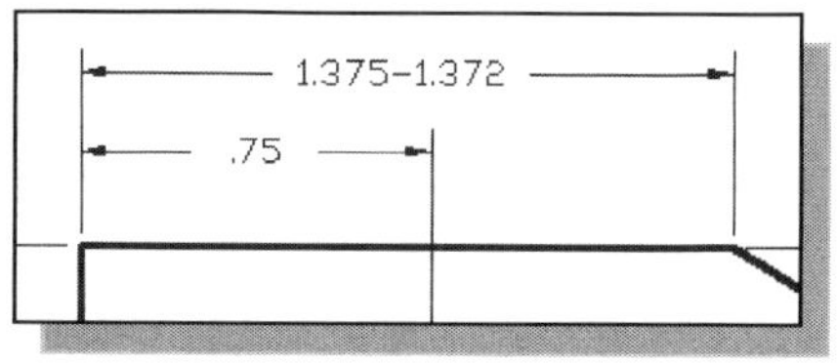

- Bilateral – Variation of size is in both directions.
  This method uses a basic size and is followed by a plus-and-minus expression of tolerance. The bilateral tolerances method allows variations in both directions from the basic size. If an equal variation in both directions is desired, the combined plus-and minus symbol is used with a single value.

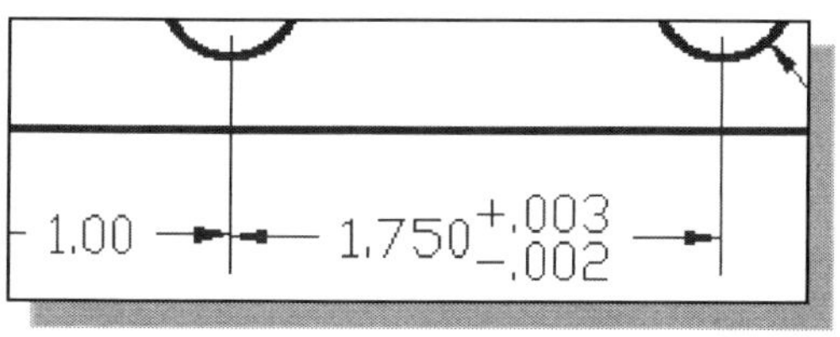

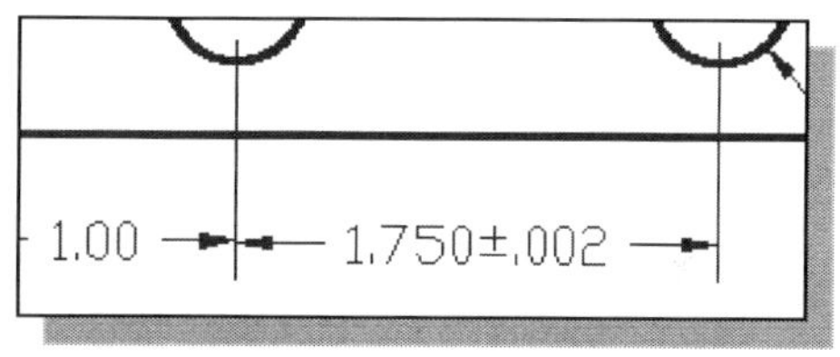

- Unilateral – Variation of size is in only one direction.
  This method uses a basic size and is followed by a plus-or-minus expression of tolerance. The unilateral tolerances method allows variations only in one direction from the basic size.

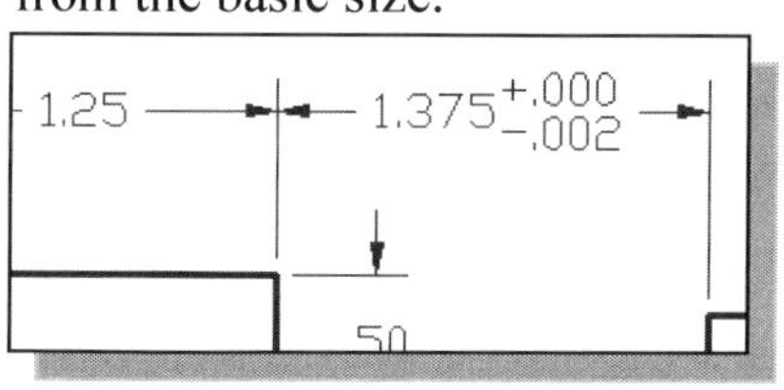

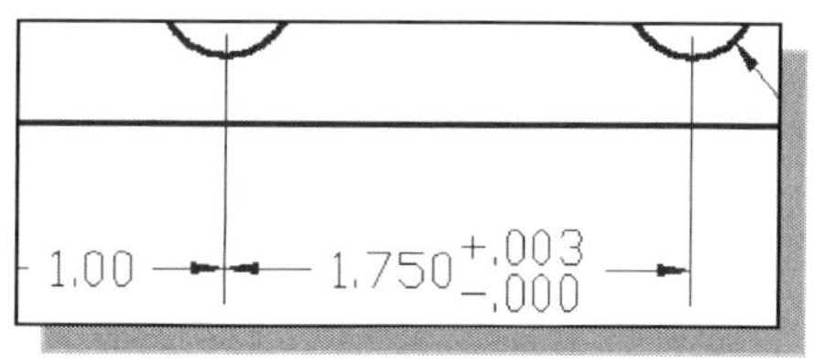

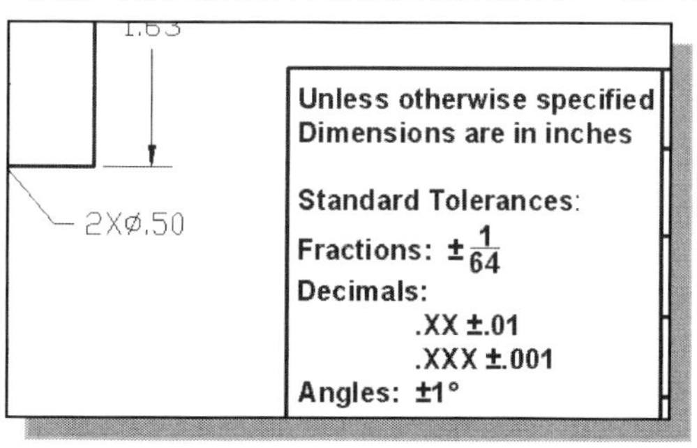

- General tolerances – General tolerances are typically covered in the title block; the general tolerances are applied to the dimensions in which tolerances are not given.

Nomenclature

The terms used in tolerancing and dimensioning should be clearly understood before more detailed discussion. The following are definitions as defined in the ANSI/ASME Y 14.5M standard.

- **Nominal size** is the designation used for the purpose of general identification.
- **Basic size, or basic dimension,** is the theoretical size from which limits of size are derived. It is the size from which limits are determined for the size or location of a feature in a design.
- **Actual size** is the measured size of the manufactured part.
- **Fit** is the general term used to signify the range of tightness in the design of mating parts.
- **Allowance** is the minimum clearance space or maximum interference intended between two mating parts under the maximum material condition.
- **Tolerance** is the total permissible variation of a size. The tolerance is the difference between the limits of size.
- **Maximum Material Condition** (MMC) is the size of the part when it consists of the most material.
- **Least Material Condition** (LMC) is the size of the part when it consists of the least material.

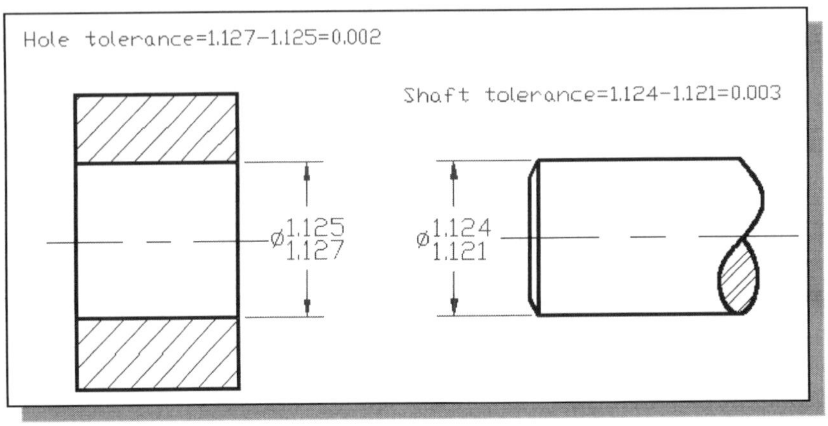

In the figure above, the tightest fit between the two parts will be when the largest shaft is fit inside the smallest hole. The allowance between the two parts can be calculated as:

Allowance = (MMC Hole)-(MMC Shaft) =1.125-1.124 = 0.001

The loosest fit between the above two parts will be when the smallest shaft is fit inside the largest hole. The maximum clearance between the two parts can be calculated as:

Max. Clearance = (LMC Hole)-(LMC Shaft) =1.128-1.121 = 0.006

➢ Note that the above dimensions will assure there is always a space between the two mating parts.

Example 8.1

The size limits of two mating parts are as shown in the below figure. Determine the following items, as described on the previous page: nominal size, tolerance of the shaft, tolerance of the hole, allowance and maximum clearance between the parts.

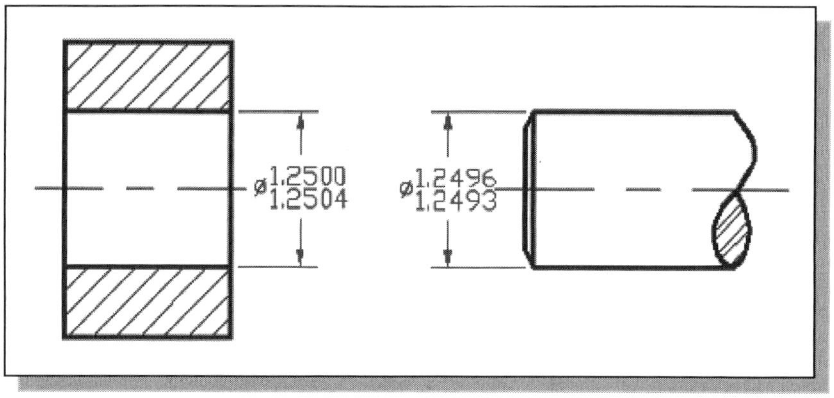

Solution:

Nominal size = 1.25

Tolerance of the shaft = Max. Shaft - Min. Shaft
= 1.2496-1.2493 = 0.0003

Tolerance of the hole = Max. Hole - Min. Hole
= 1.2504-1.2500 = 0.0004

Allowance = Min. Hole (MMC Hole) - Max. Shaft (MMC Shaft)
= 1.2500-1.2496 = 0.0004

Max. Clearance = Max. Hole (LMC Hole) - Min. Shaft (LMC Shaft)
=1.2504-1.2493 = 0.0011

Exercise: Given the size limits of two mating parts, determine the following items: nominal size, tolerance of the shaft, tolerance of the hole, allowance and maximum clearance between the parts.

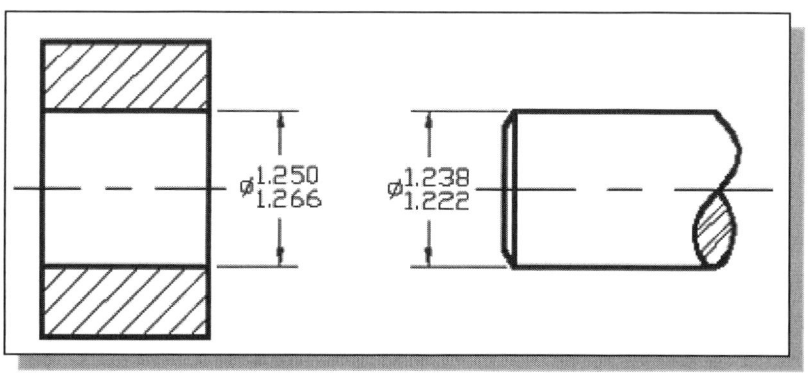

Fits between Mating Parts

Fit is the general term used to signify the range of tightness in the design of mating parts. In ANSI/ASME Y 14.5M, four general types of fits are designated for mating parts.

- **Clearance Fit:** A clearance fit is the condition in which the internal part is smaller than the external part and always leaves a space or clearance between the parts.

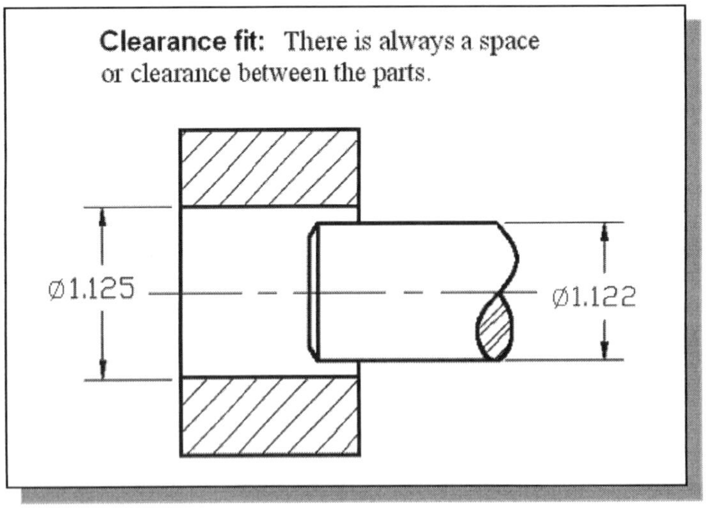

- **Interference Fit:** An interference fit is the condition in which the internal part is larger than the external part and there is always interference between the parts.

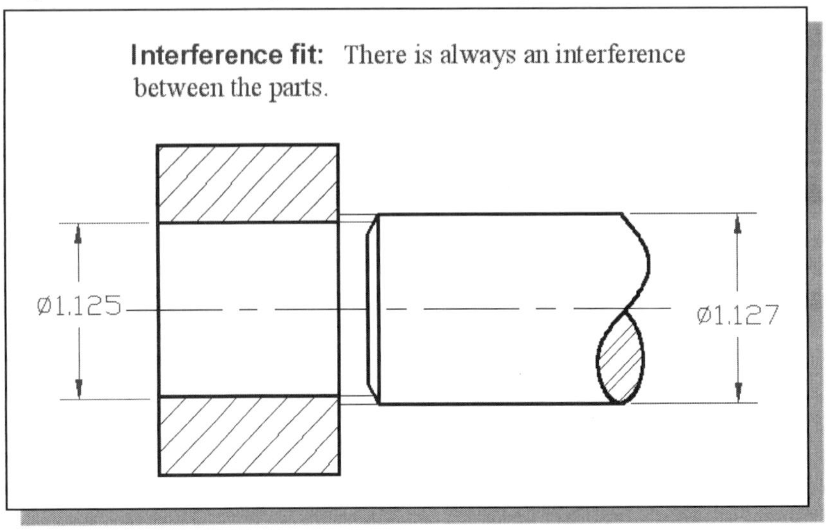

- **Transition Fit:** A transition fit is the condition in which there is either a *clearance* or *interference* between the parts.

- **Line Fit:** A line fit is the condition in which the limits of size are such that a clearance or surface contact may result between the mating parts.

Selective Assembly

By specifying the proper allowances and tolerances, mating parts can be completely interchangeable. But sometimes the fit desired may require very small allowances and tolerances, and the production cost may become very high. In such cases, either manual or computer-controlled selective assembly is often used. The manufactured parts are then graded as small, medium and large based on the actual sizes. In this way, very satisfactory fits may be achieved at much lower cost than manufacturing all parts to very accurate dimensions. Interference and transition fits often require the use of selective assembly to get the desirable interference or clearance.

Basic Hole and Basic Shaft Systems

In manufacturing, standard tools (such as reamers and drills) are often used to produce holes. In the **basic hole system**, the **minimum size of the hole** is taken as a base, and an allowance is assigned to derive the necessary size limits for both parts. The hole can often be made with a standard size tool and the shaft can easily be machined to any size desired.

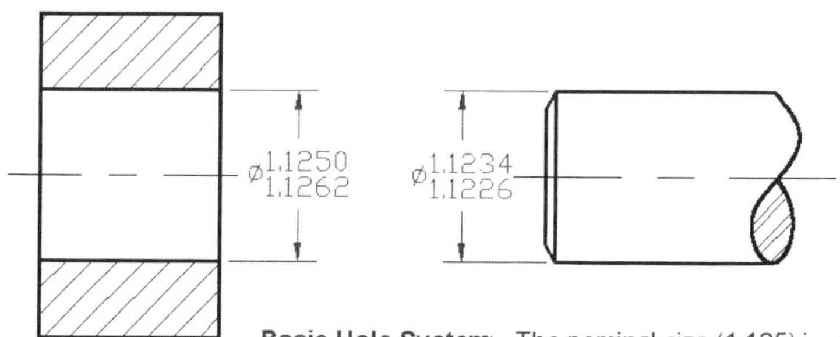

Basic Hole System: The nominal size (1.125) is assigned as the Minimum hole size.

On the other hand, in some branches of manufacturing industry, where it is necessary to manufacture the shafts using standard sizes, the **basic shaft system** is often used. This system should only be used when there is a special need for it; for example, if a shaft is to be assembled with several other parts using different fits. In the **basic shaft system**, the **maximum shaft** is taken as the basic size, and all size limits are derived from this basic size.

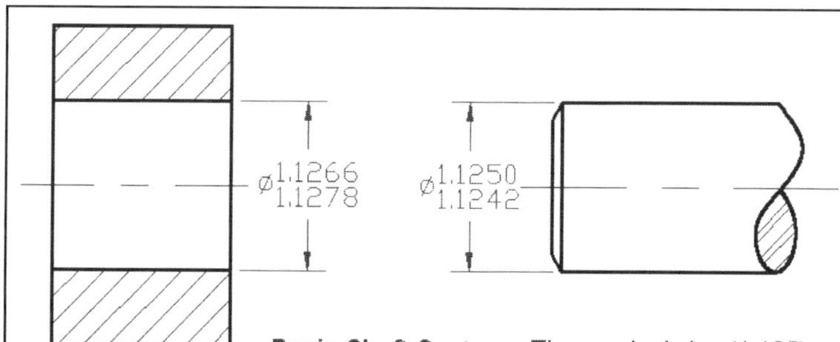

Basic Shaft System: The nominal size (1.125) is assigned as the Maximum Shaft size.

American National Standard Limits and Fits – Inches

The standard fits designated by the American National Standards Institute are as follows:

- **RC** Running or Sliding Clearance Fits (See appendix A for the complete table.)
- **LC** Locational Clearance Fits
- **LT** Transition Clearance or Interference Fits
- **LN** Locational Interference Fits
- **FN** Force or Shrink Fits

These letter symbols are used in conjunction with numbers for the class of fit. For example, **RC5** represents a class 5 Running or Sliding Clearance Fits. The limits of size for both of the mating parts are given in the standard.

1. **Running or Sliding Clearance Fits:** RC1 through RC9
   These fits provide limits of size for mating parts that require sliding and running performance, with suitable lubrication allowance.
   RC1, **close sliding fits,** are for mating parts to be assembled without much play in between.
   RC2, **sliding fits,** are for mating parts that need to move and turn easily but not run freely.
   RC3, **precision running fits,** are for precision work running at low speed and light journal pressure. This class provides the closest running fits.
   RC4, **close running fits,** are for moderate running speed and journal pressure in accurate machinery.
   RC5, RC6 and RC7, **medium running fits,** are for running at higher speed and/or higher journal pressure.
   RC8 and RC9, **loose running fits,** are for general purpose running condition where wide commercial tolerances are sufficient—typically used for standard stock parts.

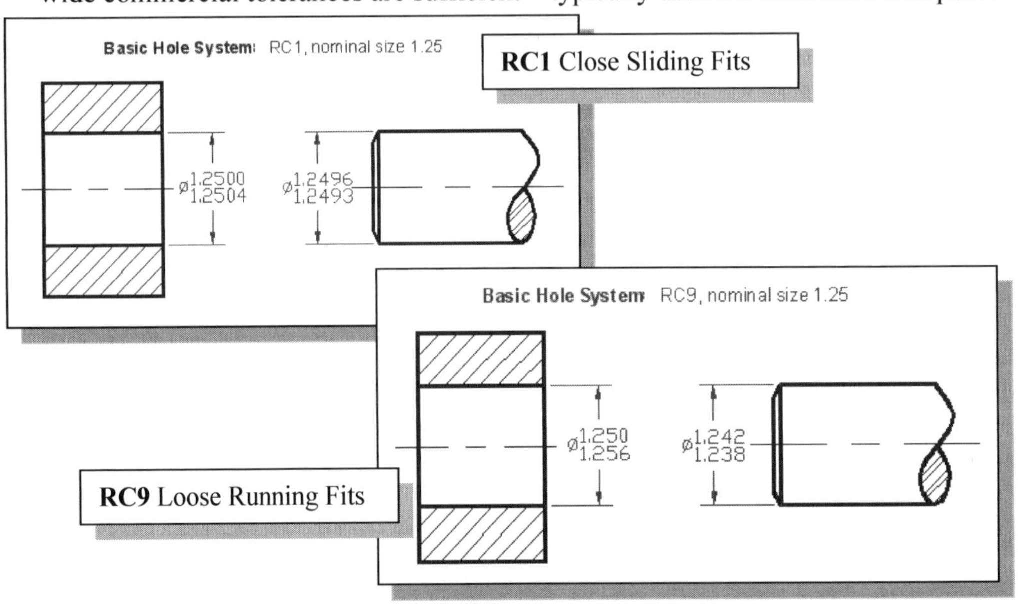

2. **Locational Clearance Fits:** LC1 through LC11
These fits provide limits of size for mating parts that are normally stationary and can be freely assembled and disassembled. They run from snug fits for parts requiring accuracy location, through the medium clearance fits for parts (such as spigots), to the looser fastener fits where freedom of assembly is of prime importance.

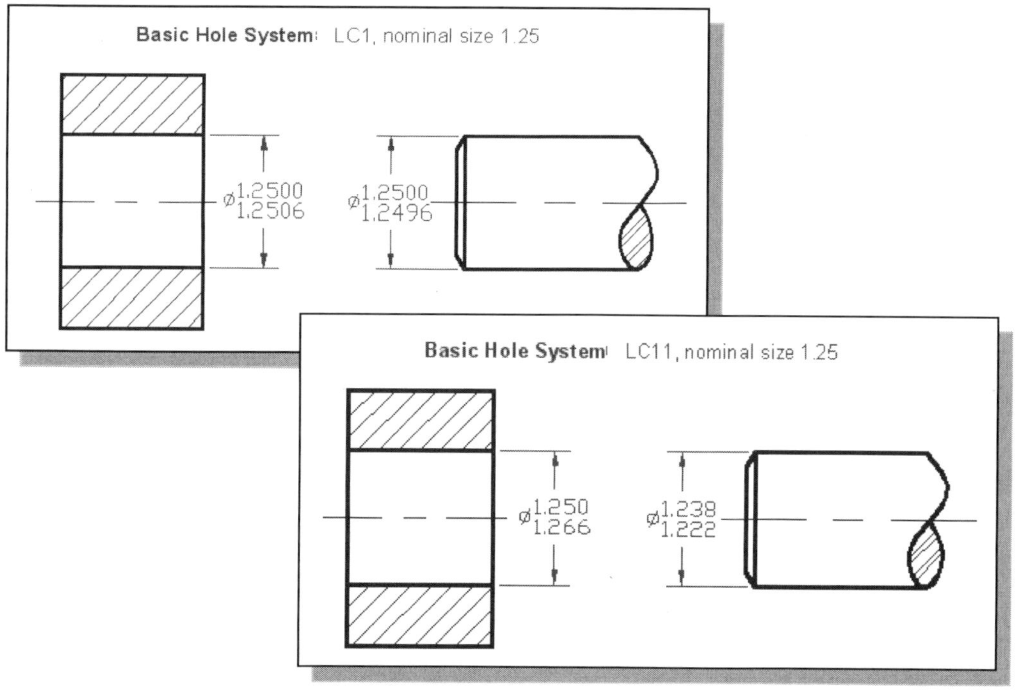

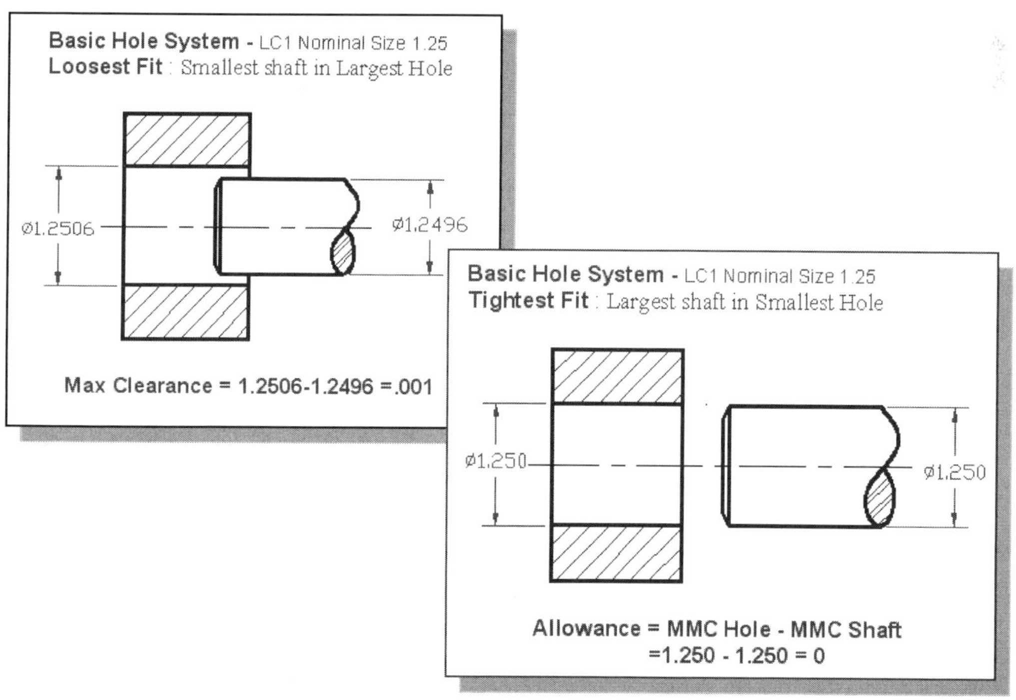

3. **Transition Clearance or Interference Fits:** LT1 through LT6
   These fits provide limits of size for mating parts requiring accuracy location but either a small amount of clearance or interference is permissible.

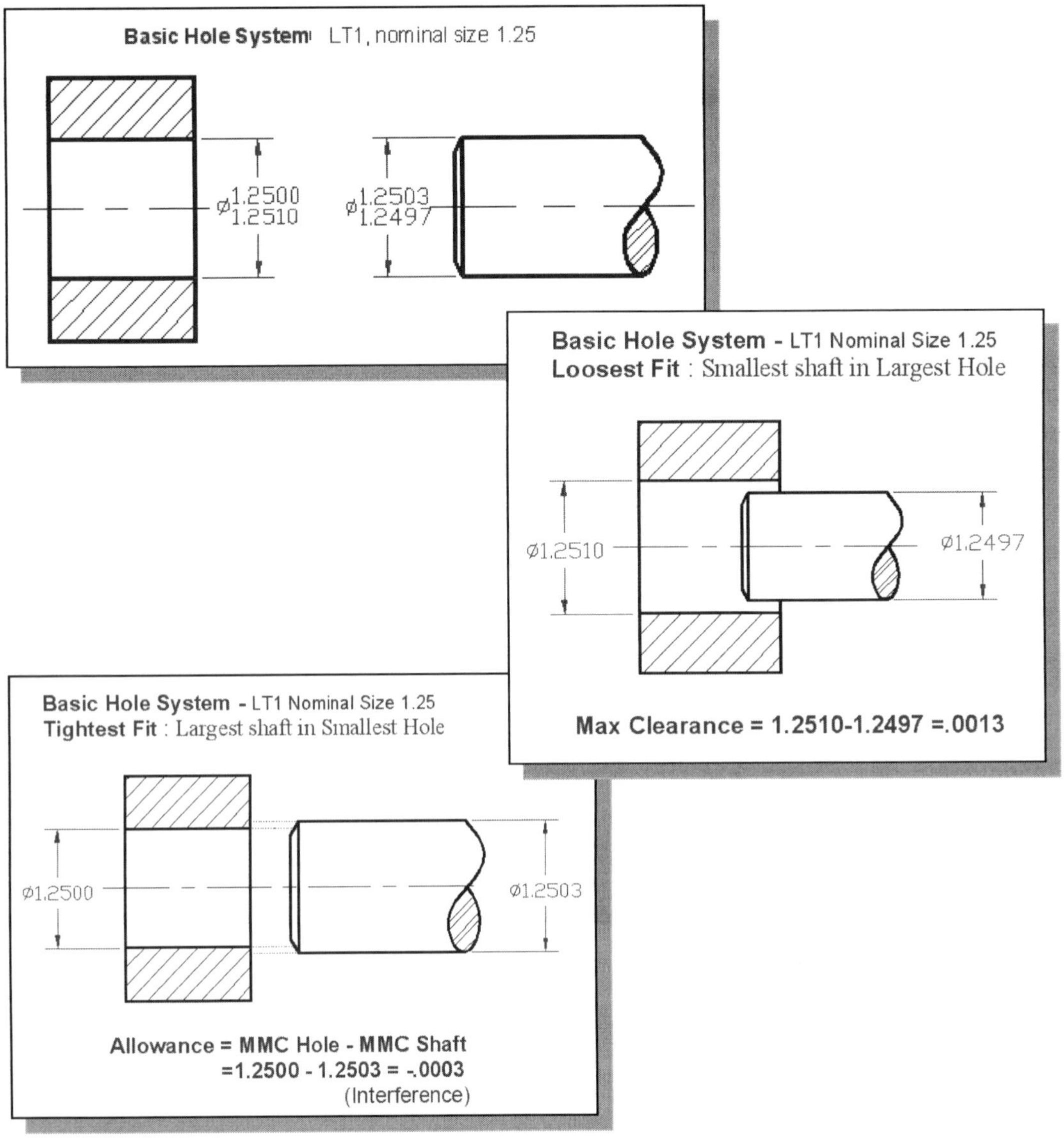

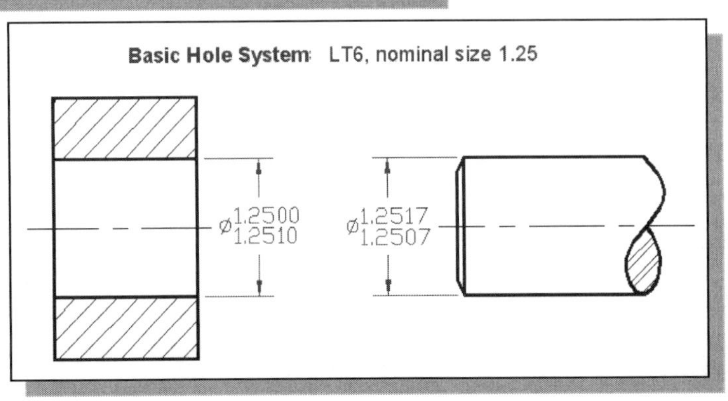

4. **Locational Interference Fits:** LN1 through LN3
These fits provide limits of size for mating parts requiring accuracy location and for parts needing rigidity and alignment. Such fits are not for parts that transmit frictional loads from one part to another by the tightness of the fit.

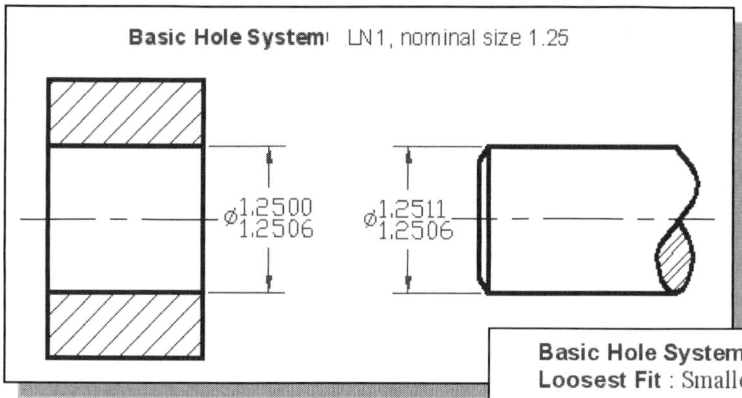

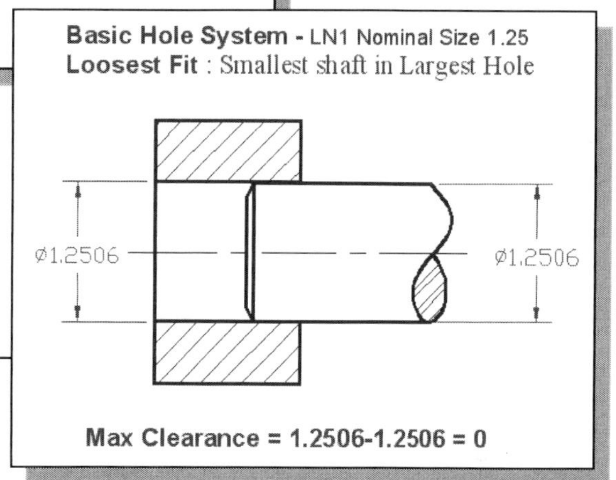

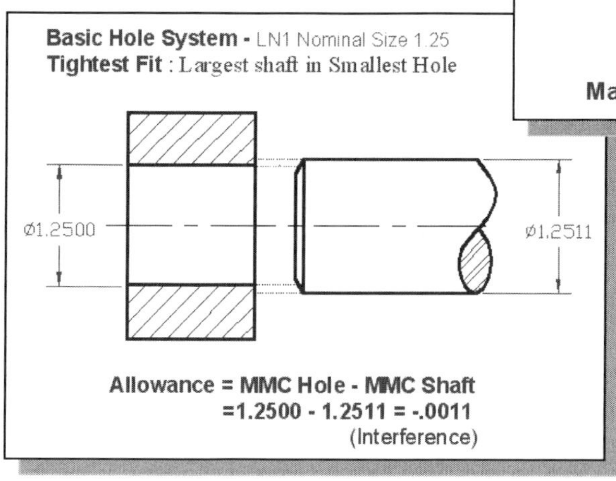

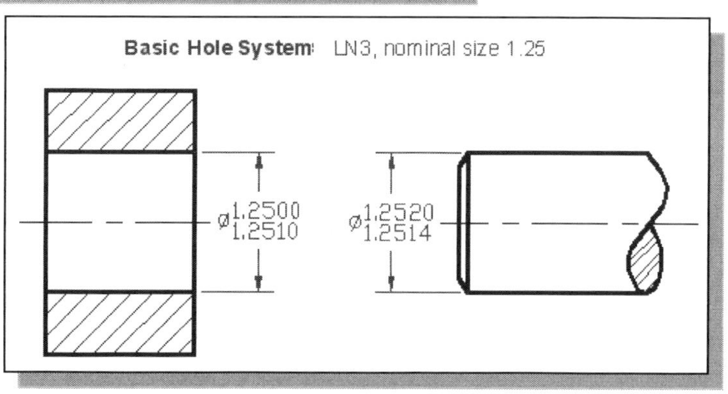

5. **Force or Shrink Fits:** FN1 through FN5
   These fits provide limits of size for mating parts requiring constant bore pressure in between the parts. The interference amount varies almost directly with the size of parts.
   FN1, **light drive fits,** are for mating parts requiring light assembly pressures, and produce more or less permanent assemblies. They are suitable for thin sections or long fits, or in cast-iron external members.
   FN2, **medium drive fits,** are suitable for ordinary steel parts or for shrink fits in light sections.
   FN3, **heavy drive fits,** are suitable for ordinary steel parts or for shrink fits in medium sections.
   FN4, **force fits,** are for parts that can be highly stressed or for shrink fits where heavy pressing forces are impractical.

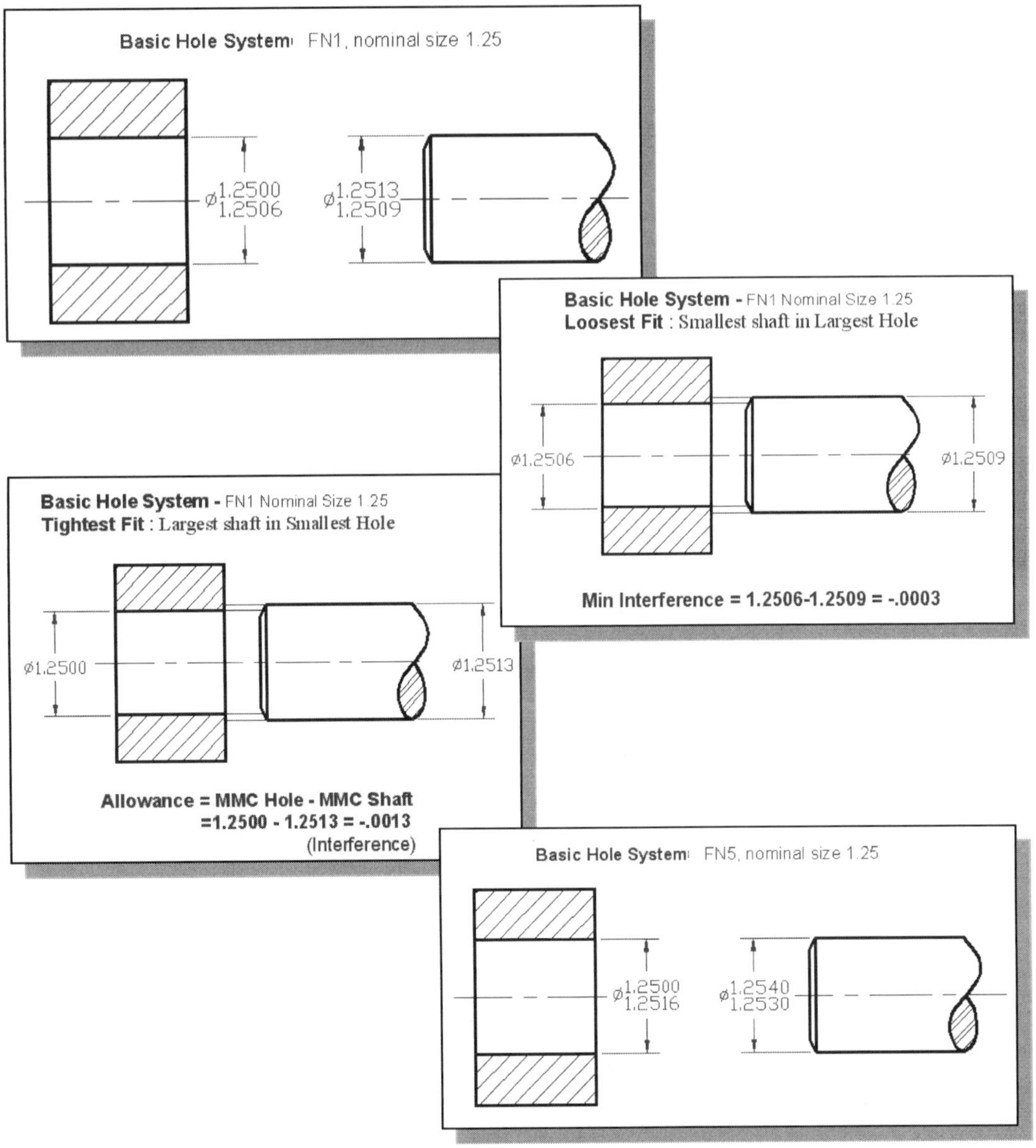

Example 8.2 Basic Hole System

A design requires the use of two mating parts with a nominal size of **0.75** inches. The shaft is to run with moderate speed but with a fairly heavy journal pressure. The fit class chosen is **Basic Hole System RC6**. Determine the size limits of the two mating parts.

From Appendix A, the RC6 fit for 0.75 inch nominal size:

Nominal size Range	**Limits of Clearance**	**RC6 Standard Limits – Basic Hole**	
		Hole	**Shaft**
0.71 - 1.19	**1.6** **4.8**	**+2.0** **-0.0**	**-1.6** **-2.8**

Using the *Basic Hole System*, the *BASIC* size 0.75 is designated as the minimum hole size. And the maximum hole size is 0.75+0.002 = 0.752 inches.

The maximum shaft size is 0.75-0.0016 = 0.7484 inches
The minimum shaft size is 0.75-0.0028 = 0.7472 inches

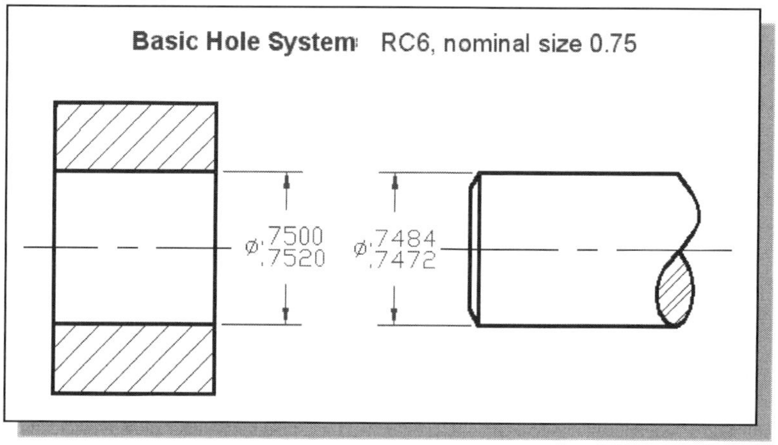

➢ Note the important tolerances and allowance can also be obtained from the table:

Tolerance of the shaft = Max. Shaft – Min. Shaft = 0.7484 – 0.7472 = 0.0012
This can also be calculated from the table above = 2.8 – 2.6 = **1.2 (thousandths)**

Tolerance of the hole = Max. Hole – Min. Hole = 1.2520 – 1.2500 = 0.002
This can also be calculated from the table above = 2.0 – 0.0 = **2.0 (thousandths)**

Allowance = Min. Hole (MMC Hole) – Max. Shaft (MMC Shaft)
= 0.7500 – 0.7484 = 0.0016
This is listed as the minimum clearance in the table above: **+1.6 (thousandths)**

Max. Clearance = Max. Hole (LMC Hole) – Min. Shaft (LMC Shaft)
= 0.7520 – 0.7472 = 0.0048
This is listed as the maximum clearance in the table above: **+4.8 (thousandths)**

Example 8.3 Basic Hole System

A design requires the use of two mating parts with a nominal size of **1.25** inches. The shaft and hub are to be fastened permanently using a drive fit. The fit class chosen is **Basic Hole System FN4**. Determine the size limits of the two mating parts.

From ANSI/ASME B4.1 Standard, the FN4 fit for 1.25 inches nominal size:

Nominal size Range	Limits of Interference	FN4 Standard Limits – Basic Hole	
		Hole	Shaft
1.19 - 1.97	1.5 3.1	+1.0 -0.0	+3.1 +2.5

Using the *Basic Hole System*, the *BASIC* size 1.25 is designated as the minimum hole size. And the maximum hole size is 1.25+0.001 = 1.251 inches.

The maximum shaft size is 1.25+0.0031 = 1.2531 inches
The minimum shaft size is 1.25+0.0025 = 1.2525 inches

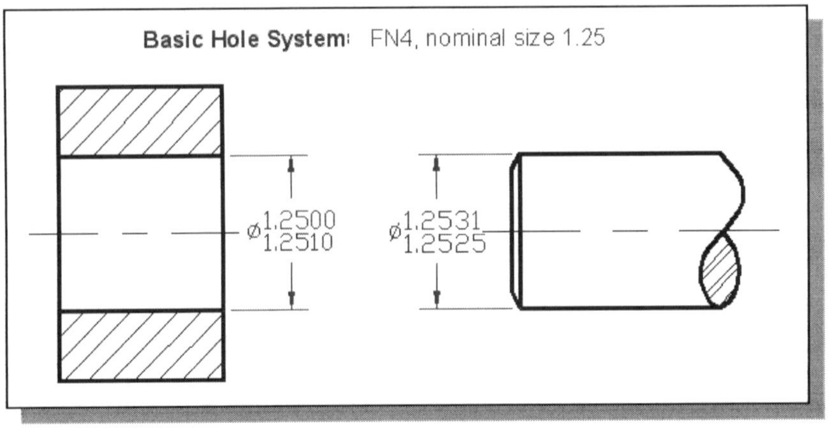

➢ Note the important tolerances and allowance can also be obtained from the table:

Tolerance of the shaft = Max. Shaft – Min. Shaft = 1.2531 – 1.2525 = 0.0006
This can also be calculated from the table above = **3.1 – 2.5 = 0.6 (thousandths)**

Tolerance of the hole = Max. Hole – Min. Hole = 1.2510 – 1.2500 = 0.001
This can also be calculated from the table above = **1.0 – 0.0 = 1.0 (thousandths)**

Allowance = Min. Hole (MMC Hole) – Max. Shaft (MMC Shaft)
= 1.2500 – 1.2531 = -0.0031
This is listed as the maximum interference in the table above: **3.1 (thousandths)**

Min. interference = Max. Hole (LMC Hole) – Min. Shaft (LMC Shaft)
= 1.2510 – 1.2525 = -0.0015
This is listed as the minimum interference in the table above: **1.5 (thousandths)**

Example 8.4 Basic Shaft System

Use the **Basic Shaft System** from example 8.2. A design requires the use of two mating parts with a nominal size of **0.75** inches. The shaft is to run with moderate speed but with a fairly heavy journal pressure. The fit class chosen is **Basic Shaft System RC6**. Determine the size limits of the two mating parts.

From Appendix A, the Basic Hole System RC6 fit for 0.75 inch nominal size:

Nominal size Range	**Limits of Clearance**	**RC6 Standard Limits – Basic Hole**	
		Hole	**Shaft**
0.71 - 1.19	**1.6** **4.8**	**+2.0** **-0.0**	**-1.6** **-2.8**

Using the Basic Shaft System, the BASIC size 0.75 is designated as the MMC of the shaft, the maximum shaft size. The conversion of limits to the Basic shaft System is performed by adding 1.6 (thousandths) to the four size limits as shown:

Nominal size Range	**Limits of Clearance**	**RC6 Standard Limits – Basic Shaft**	
		Hole	**Shaft**
0.71 - 1.19	**1.6** **4.8**	**+3.6** **+1.6**	**-0.0** **-1.2**

Therefore, the maximum shaft size is 0.75.
The minimum shaft size is 0.75-0.0012 = 0.7488 inches.
The maximum hole size is 0.75+0.0036 = 0.7536 inches.
The minimum hole size is 0.75+0.0016 = 0.7516 inches.

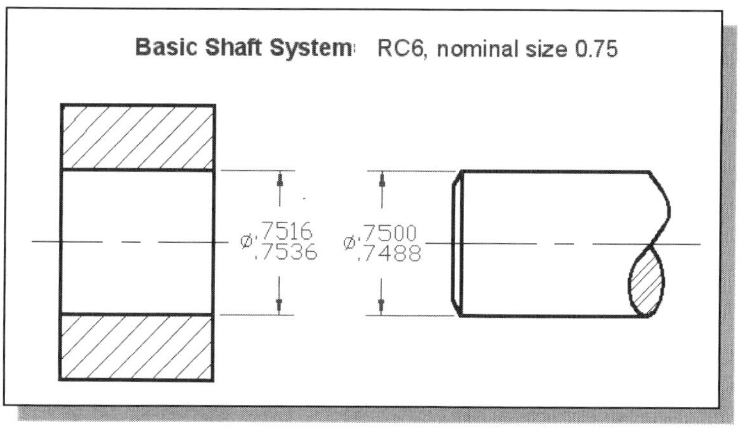

➢ Note that all the tolerances and allowance are maintained in the conversion.

Allowance = Min. Hole – Max. Shaft = 0.7517 – 0.7500 = 0.0016
This is listed as the minimum clearance in the table above: **1.6 (thousandths)**

Max. Clearance = Max. Hole – Min. Shaft = 0.7537 – 0.7488 = 0.0048
This is listed as the maximum clearance in the table above: **4.8 (thousandths)**

Example 8.5 Basic Shaft System

Use the **Basic Shaft System** from example 8.3. A design requires the use of two mating parts with a nominal size of **1.25** inches. The shaft and hub are to be fastened permanently using a drive fit. The fit class chosen is **Basic Shaft System FN4**. Determine the size limits of the two mating parts.

From ANSI/ASME B4.1 Standard, the FN4 fit for 1.25 inches nominal size:

Nominal size Range	Limits of Interference	FN4 Standard Limits – Basic Hole	
		Hole	Shaft
1.19 - 1.97	1.5 3.1	+1.0 -0.0	+3.1 +2.5

With the *Basic Shaft System*, the *BASIC* size 1.25 is designated as the MMC of the shaft, the maximum shaft size. The conversion of limits to the Basic shaft System is performed by subtracting 3.1 (thousandths) to the four size limits as shown:

Nominal size Range	Limits of Interference	FN4 Standard Limits – Basic Shaft	
		Hole	Shaft
1.19 - 1.97	1.5 3.1	-2.1 -3.1	-0.0 -0.6

Therefore, the maximum shaft size is 1.25.
The minimum shaft size is 1.25-0.0006 = 1.2494 inches.
The maximum hole size is 1.25-0.0021 = 1.2479 inches.
The minimum hole size is 1.25-0.0031 = 1.2469 inches.

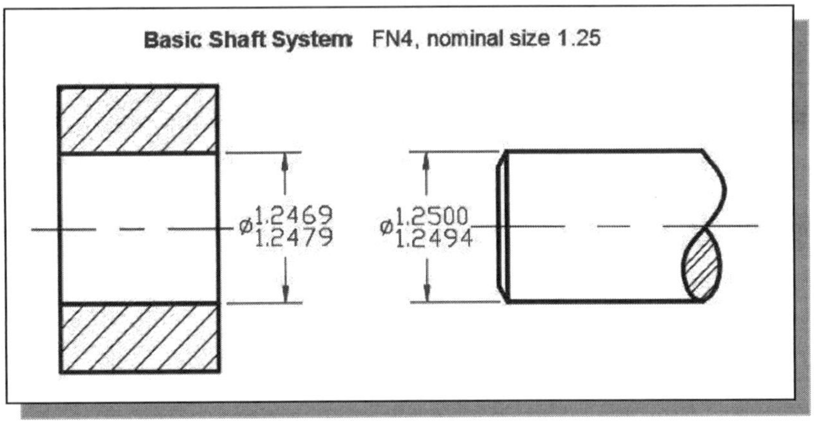

➢ Note that all the tolerances and allowance are maintained in the conversion.

Allowance = Min. Hole – Max. Shaft = 1.2469 – 1.2500 = -0.0031
This is listed as the maximum interference in the table above: **3.1 (thousandths)**

Min. Interference = Max. Hole – Min. Shaft = 1.2479 – 1.2494 = -0.0015
This is listed as the minimum interference in the table above: **1.5 (thousandths)**

Tolerancing – Metric System

The concepts described in previous sections on the English tolerancing system are also applicable to the Metric System. The commonly used system of preferred metric tolerancing and fits is outlined by the International Organization for Standardization (ISO). The system is specified for holes and shafts, but it is also adaptable to fits between features of parallel surfaces.

- **Basic size** is the theoretical size from which limits or deviations of size are derived.
- **Deviation** is the difference between the basic size and the hole or shaft size. This is equivalent to the word "Tolerance" in the English system.
- **Upper Deviation** is the difference between the basic size and the permitted maximum size. This is equivalent to "Maximum Tolerance" in the English system.
- **Lower Deviation** is the difference between the basic size and the permitted minimum size. This is equivalent to "Minimum Tolerance" in the English system.
- **Fundamental Deviation** is the deviation closest to the basic size. This is equivalent to "Minimum Allowance" in the English system.
- **Tolerance** is the difference between the permissible variations of a size. The tolerance is the difference between the limits of size.
- **International tolerance grade (IT)** is a set of tolerances that varies according to the basic size and provides a uniform level of accuracy within the grade. There are 18 IT grades- IT01, IT0, and IT1 through IT16.
    - ❖ IT01 through IT7 is typically used for measuring tools; IT5 through IT11 are used for Fits and IT12 through IT16 for large manufacturing tolerances.
    - ❖ The following is a list of IT grade related to machining processes:

<table>
<tr><th colspan="8">International Tolerance Grade (IT)</th></tr>
<tr><th>4</th><th>5</th><th>6</th><th>7</th><th>8</th><th>9</th><th>10</th><th>11</th></tr>
<tr><td colspan="2">Lapping or Honing</td><td></td><td></td><td></td><td></td><td></td><td></td></tr>
<tr><td></td><td colspan="3">Cylindrical Grinding</td><td></td><td></td><td></td><td></td></tr>
<tr><td></td><td colspan="4">Surface Grinding</td><td></td><td></td><td></td></tr>
<tr><td></td><td colspan="3">Diamond Turning or Boring</td><td></td><td></td><td></td><td></td></tr>
<tr><td></td><td colspan="4">Broaching</td><td></td><td></td><td></td></tr>
<tr><td></td><td colspan="4">Powder Metal-sizes</td><td></td><td></td><td></td></tr>
<tr><td></td><td></td><td colspan="5">Reaming</td><td></td></tr>
<tr><td></td><td></td><td></td><td colspan="5">Turning</td></tr>
<tr><td></td><td></td><td></td><td colspan="4">Powder Metal-sintered</td><td></td></tr>
<tr><td></td><td></td><td></td><td colspan="5">Boring</td></tr>
<tr><td></td><td></td><td></td><td></td><td></td><td></td><td colspan="2">Milling, Drilling</td></tr>
<tr><td></td><td></td><td></td><td></td><td></td><td></td><td colspan="2">Planing & Shaping</td></tr>
<tr><td></td><td></td><td></td><td></td><td></td><td></td><td colspan="2">Punching</td></tr>
<tr><td></td><td></td><td></td><td></td><td></td><td></td><td></td><td>Die Casting</td></tr>
</table>

Metric Tolerances and Fits Designation

Metric tolerances and fits are specified by using the fundamental deviation symbol along with the IT grade number. An uppercase **H** is used for the fundamental deviation for the hole tolerance using the **Hole Basis system**, where a lowercase **h** is used to specify the use of the **Shaft Basis System**.

1. **Hole: 30H8**

   Basic size = 30 mm
   Hole size is based on hole basis system using IT8 for tolerance.

2. **Shaft: 30f7**

   Basic size = 30 mm
   Shaft size is based on hole basis system using IT7 for tolerance.

3. **Fit: 30H8/f7**

   Basic size = 30 mm
   Hole basis system with IT8 hole tolerance and IT7 for shaft tolerance.

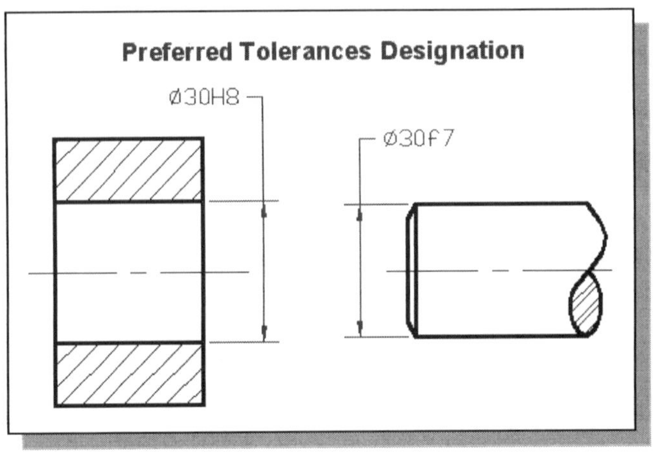

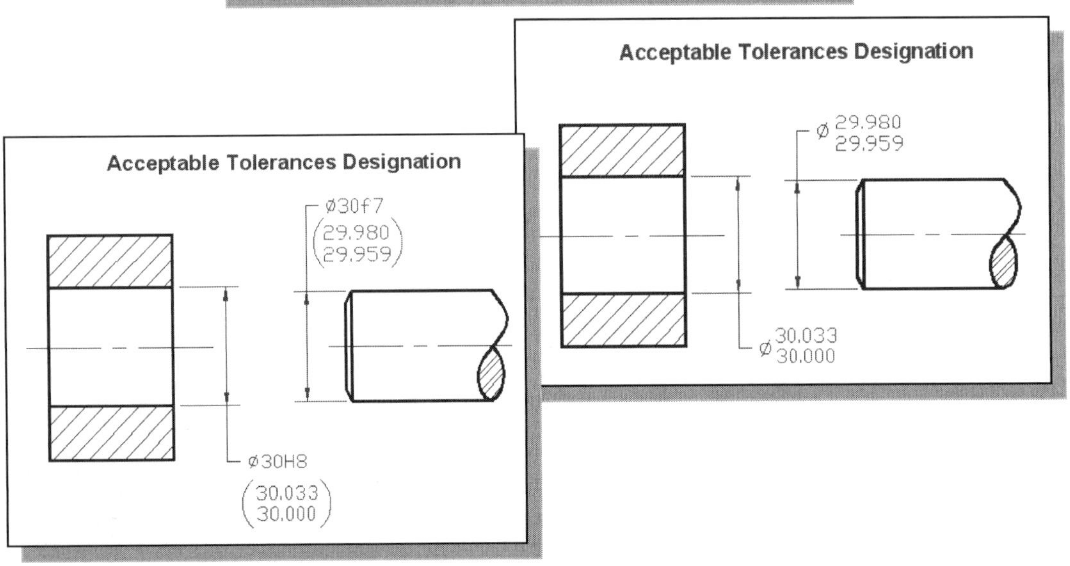

Preferred ISO Metric Fits

The symbols for either the hole-basis or shaft-basis preferred fits are given in the table below. These are the preferred fits; select the fits from the table whenever possible. See **Appendix B** for the complete *ISO Metric Fits* tables.

- The **Hole-Basis** system is a system in which the basic size is the minimum size of the hole. The *hole-basis* system is the preferred method; the fundamental deviation is specified by the uppercase **H**.

- The **Shaft-Basis** system is a system in which the basic size is the maximum size of the shaft. The fundamental deviation of the *shaft-basis* system is specified by the lowercase **h**.

ISO Preferred Metric Fits

	Hole Basis	Shaft Basis	Description
Clearance Fits	H11/c11	C11/h11	***Loose running*** fit for wide commercial tolerance or allowances.
Clearance Fits	H9/d9	D9/h9	***Free running*** fit not for use when accuracy is essential but good for large temperature variation, high running speed, or heavy journal pressure.
Clearance Fits	H8/f7	F8/h7	***Close running*** fit for running on accurate machines running at moderate speeds and journal pressure.
Clearance Fits	H7/g6	G7/h6	***Sliding*** fit not intended to run freely but to move and turn freely and locate accurately.
Transition Fits	H7/h6	H7/h6	***Locational clearance*** fit provides snug fit for locating stationary parts but can be freely assembled and disassembled.
Transition Fits	H7/k6	K7/h6	***Locational transition*** fit for accurate location, a compromise between clearance and interference.
Transition Fits	H7/n6	N7/h6	***Locational transition*** fit for accurate location where interference is permissible.
Transition Fits	H7/p6	P7/h6	***Locational interference*** fit for parts requiring rigidity and alignment with prime accuracy but without special bore pressure.
Interference Fits	H7/s6	S7/h6	***Medium drive*** fit for ordinary steel parts or shrink fits on light sections, the tightest fit usable with cast iron.
Interference Fits	H7/u6	U7/h6	***Force*** fit suitable for parts which can be highly stressed or for shrink fits where the heavy pressing forces required are impractical.

Example 8.6 Metric Hole Basis System

A design requires the use of two mating parts with a nominal size of **25** millimeters. The shaft and hub are to be fastened permanently using a drive fit. The fit class chosen is **Hole-Basis System H7/s6**. Determine the size limits of the two mating parts.

From Appendix B, the H7/s6 fit for 25 millimeters size:

Basic size	H7/s6 Medium Drive –Hole Basis		
	Hole H7	Shaft s6	Fit
25	25.021 25.000	25.048 25.035	-0.014 -0.048

Using the *Hole Basis System*, the *BASIC* size 25 is designated as the minimum hole size. And the maximum hole size is 25.021 millimeters.
The maximum shaft size is 25.048 millimeters.
The minimum shaft size is 25.035 millimeters.

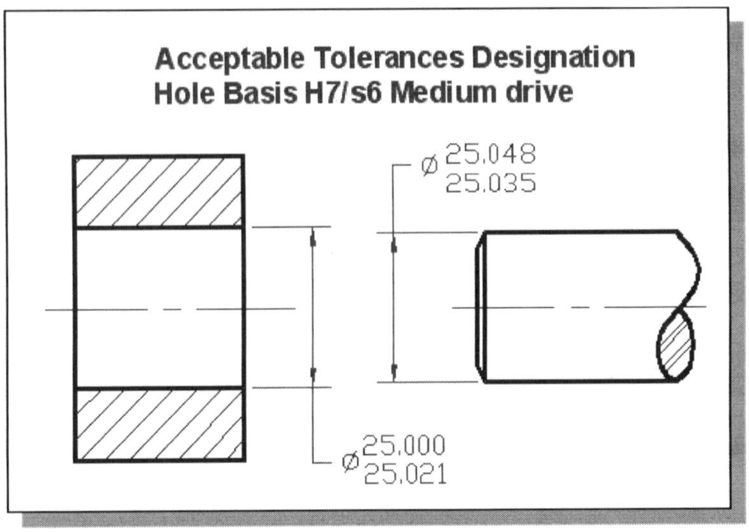

Tolerance of the shaft = Max. Shaft – Min. Shaft = 25.048 – 25.035 = 0.013

Tolerance of the hole = Max. Hole – Min. Hole = 25.021 – 25.000 = 0.021

Allowance = Min. Hole (MMC Hole) – Max. Shaft (MMC Shaft)
= 25.000 – 25.048 = -0.0048
This is listed as the maximum interference in the table above: **-0.048**

Min. interference = Max. Hole (LMC Hole) – Min. Shaft (LMC Shaft)
= 25.021 – 25.035 = -0.0014
This is listed as the minimum interference in the table above: **-0.0014**

Example 8.7 Shaft Basis System

A design requires the use of two mating parts with a nominal size of **25** millimeters. The shaft is to run with moderate speed but with a fairly heavy journal pressure. The fit class chosen is **Shaft Basis System F8/h7**. Determine the size limits of the two mating parts.

From Appendix B, the Shaft Basis System F8/h7 fit for 25 millimeters size:

Basic size	F8/h7 Medium Drive –Shaft Basis		
	Hole F8	Shaft h7	Fit
25	25.053 25.020	25.000 24.979	0.074 0.020

Therefore, the maximum shaft size is 25.
The minimum shaft size is 24.979.
The maximum hole size is 25.053.
The minimum hole size is 25.020.

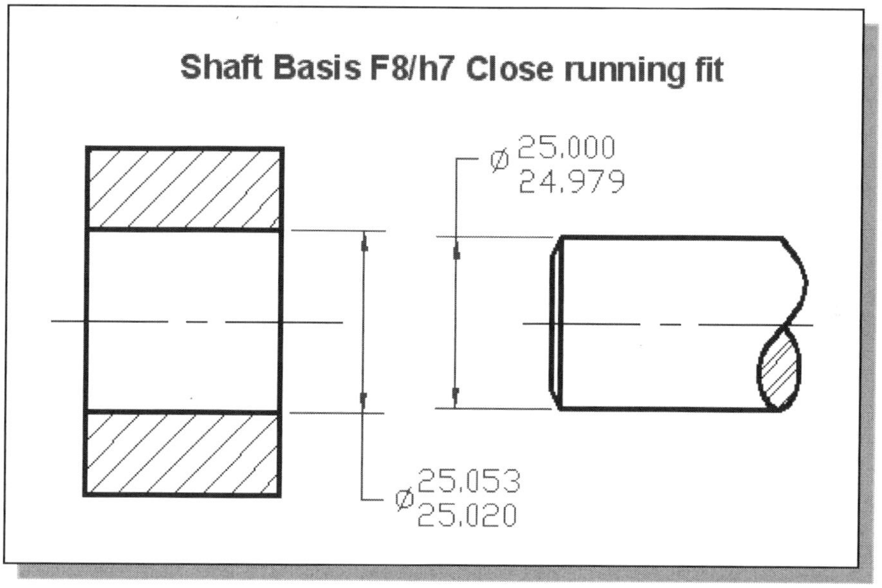

Tolerance of the shaft = Max. Shaft – Min. Shaft = 25.000 – 24.979 = 0.021

Tolerance of the hole = Max. Hole – Min. Hole = 25.053 – 25.020 = 0.023

Allowance = Min. Hole – Max. Shaft = 25.020 – 25.000 = 0.020
This is listed as the minimum clearance in the table above: **0.020**

Max. Clearance = Max. Hole – Min. Shaft = 25.053 – 24.979 = 0.074
This is listed as the maximum clearance in the table above: **0.074**

Updating the Bracket Drawing

1. Select the **AutoCAD 2027** option on the *Program* menu or select the **AutoCAD 2027** icon on the *Desktop*.

2. In the AutoCAD *Startup* dialog box, select **Open a Drawing** with a single click of the left-mouse-button.

3. In the *File* list section, pick ***Bracket.dwg***, the drawing from the last chapter, as the drawing to be loaded. (If the file is not listed in the *File* list, use the **Browse** button to locate the file.)

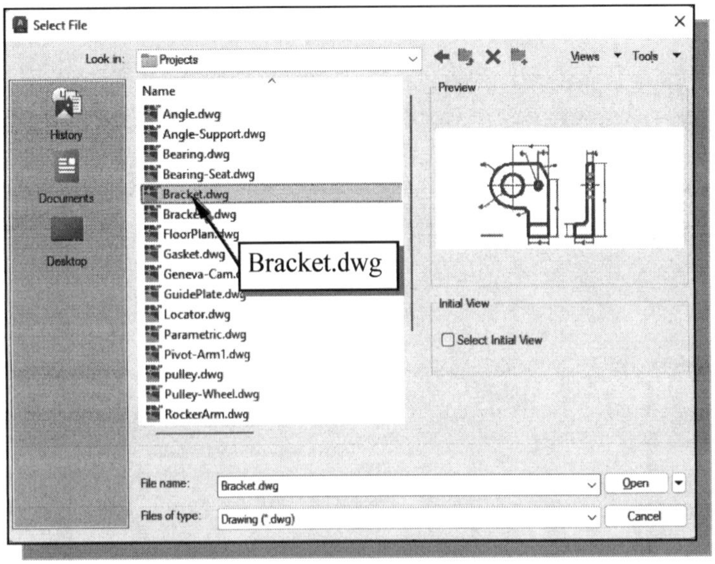

4. Click on the **OK** button to open the selected file.

The Dimension Style Manager

1. Move the cursor to the *Menu Bar* area and select:
   [Tools]→[Toolbars]→[AutoCAD]→[Dimension]

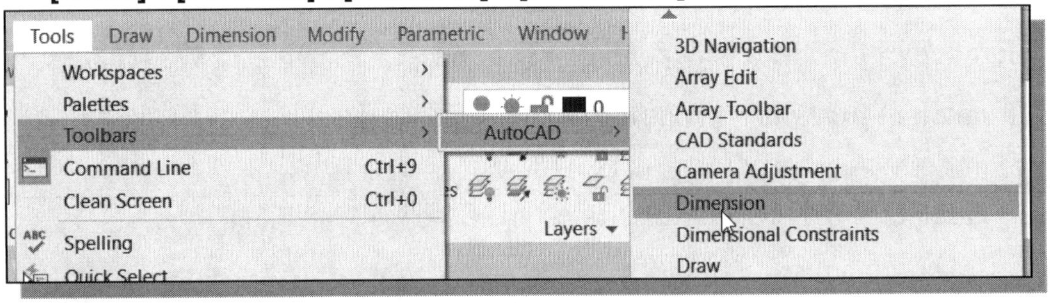

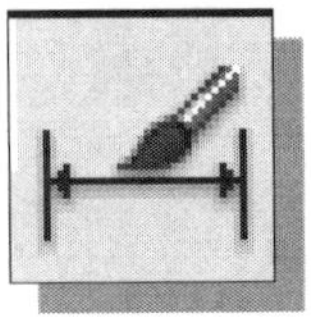

2. In the *Dimension* toolbar, pick **Dimension Style**. The *Dimension Style Manager* dialog box appears on the screen.

Tolerances Settings in the Dimension Style Manager

1. Confirm the **Mechanical** *Dimension Style* is the *current* style, and select **Modify** as shown.

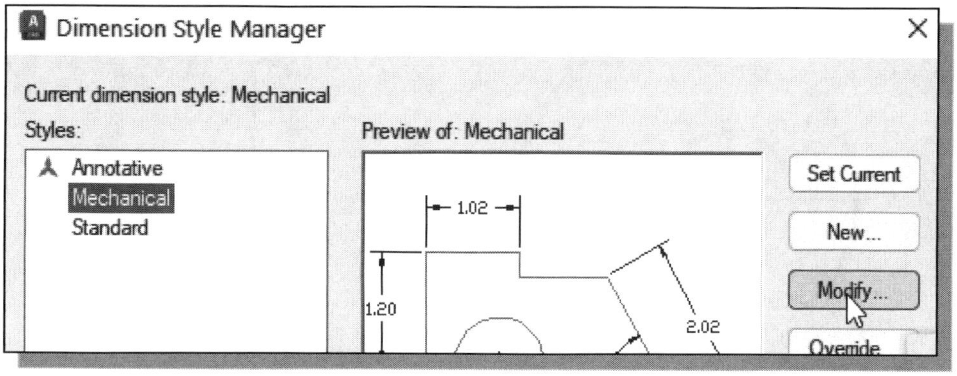

2. Click on the **Tolerances** tab and set the *Tolerance format* to **Limits** as shown in the figure below.

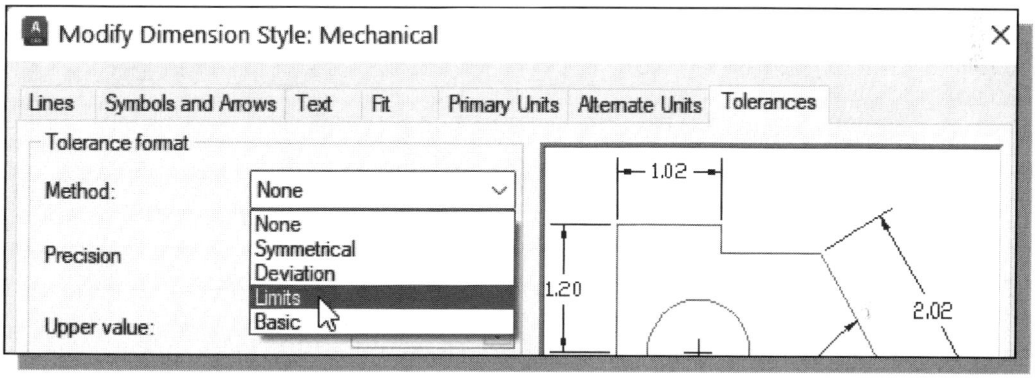

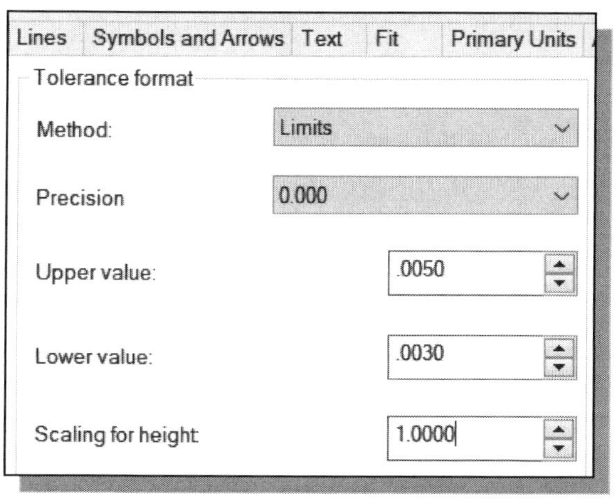

3. Set the *Precision* to **three digits** after the decimal point as shown.

4. Enter ***0.005*** for the *upper value* as shown.

5. Enter ***0.003*** for the *Lower value* as shown.

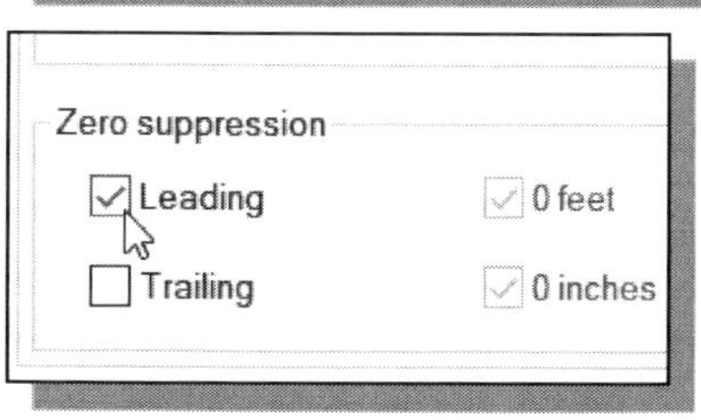

6. In the *Zero suppression* option area, turn on the **Leading Zero Suppression** as shown.

7. Click on the **OK** button to accept the settings.

8. Click on the **Close** button to accept the settings and exit the *Dimension Style* manager.

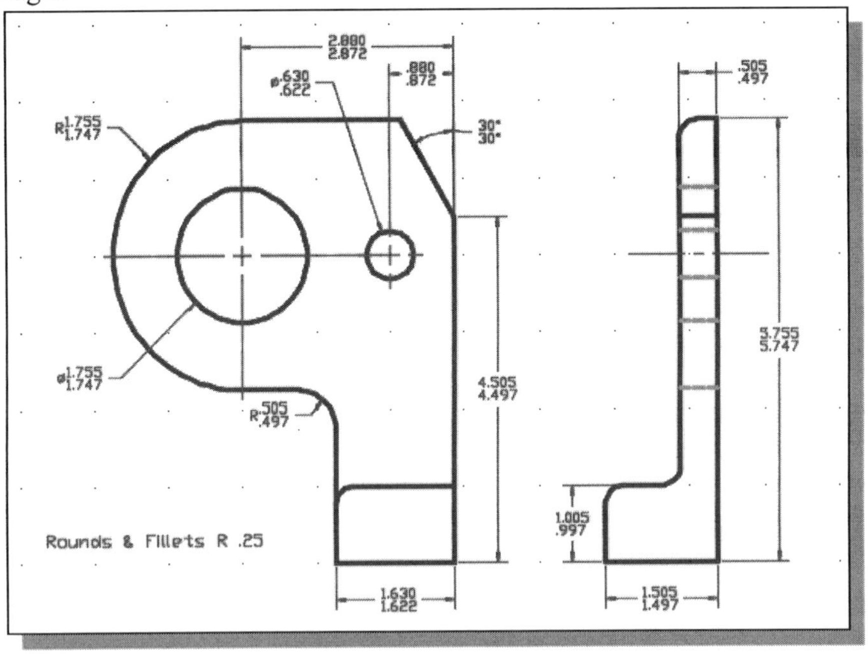

- Note that the tolerances settings affected all of the dimensions, the actual dimension values were used as the base dimensions and the limits are calculated using the upper and lower values we entered in the *Dimension Style Manager*.

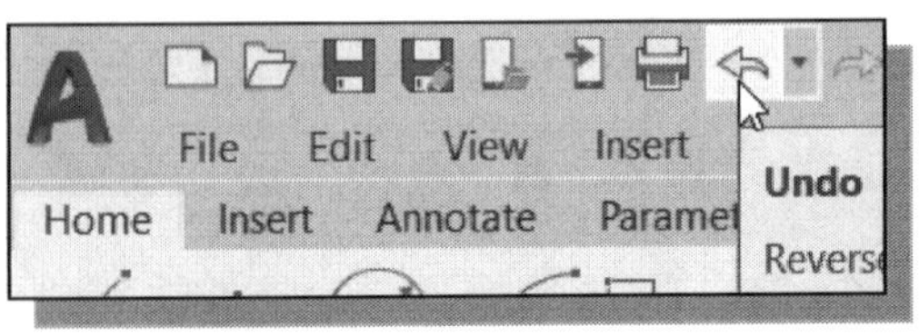

9. Click on the **Undo** button to remove the tolerances settings we made.

Determining the Tolerances Required

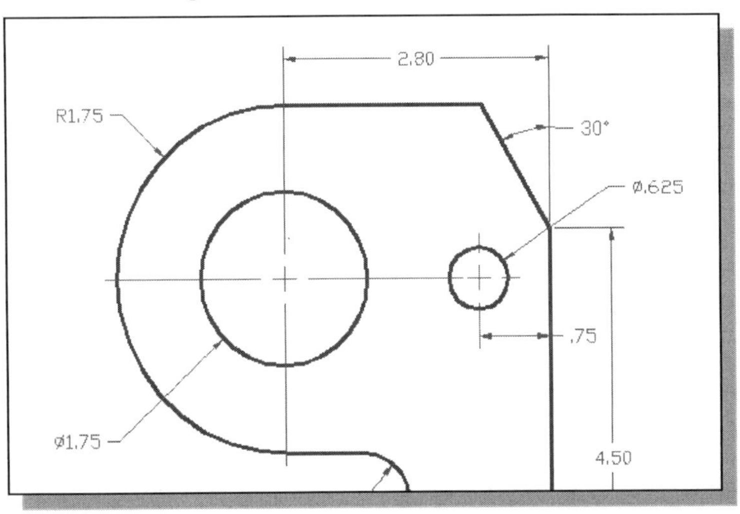

The *Bracket* design requires two sets of tolerances: (1) the nominal size of a **1.75** inch hole and (2) the nominal size of a **0.625** inch hole.

(1) The Nominal size of 1.75

A shaft is to run with moderate speed but with a fairly heavy journal pressure through the larger hole. The fit class chosen is **Basic Hole System RC6**. We will first determine the size limits of the two mating parts.

From Appendix A, the RC6 fit for 1.75 inch nominal size:

Nominal size Range	Limits of Clearance	RC6 Standard Limits – Basic Hole	
		Hole	Shaft
1.19 - 1.97	**2.0** **6.1**	**+2.5** **-0.0**	**-2.0** **-3.6**

Using the *Basic Hole System*, the *BASIC* size 1.75 is designated as the minimum hole size.

The maximum hole size is 1.75+0.0025 = 1.7525 inches.
The minimum hole size is 1.75-0.00= 1.7500 inches.

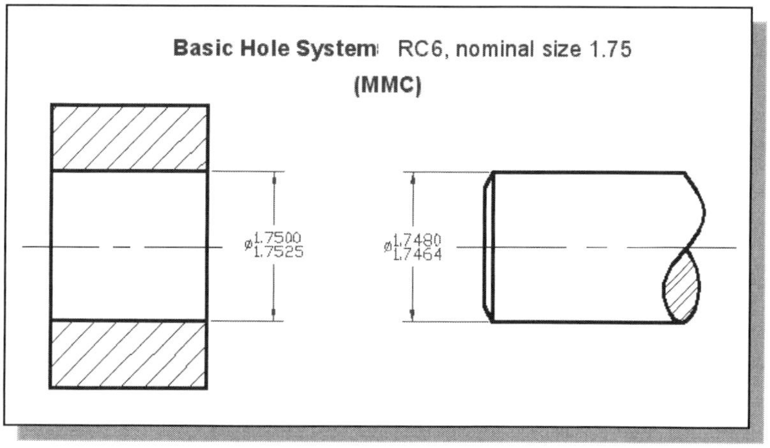

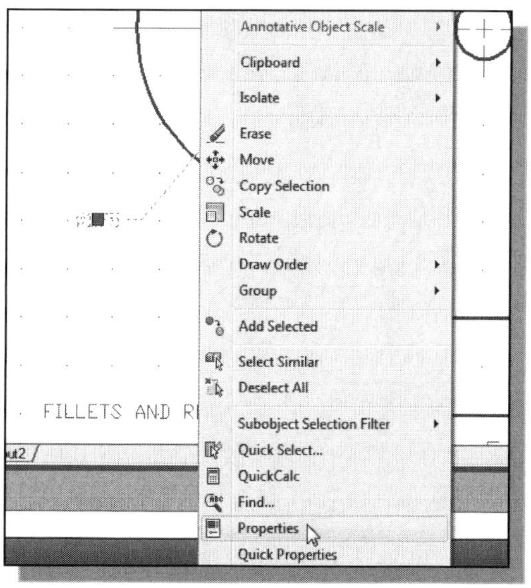

1. Pre-select the diameter **1.75** dimension as shown.

2. **Right-click** to bring up the option menu and select **properties** as shown.

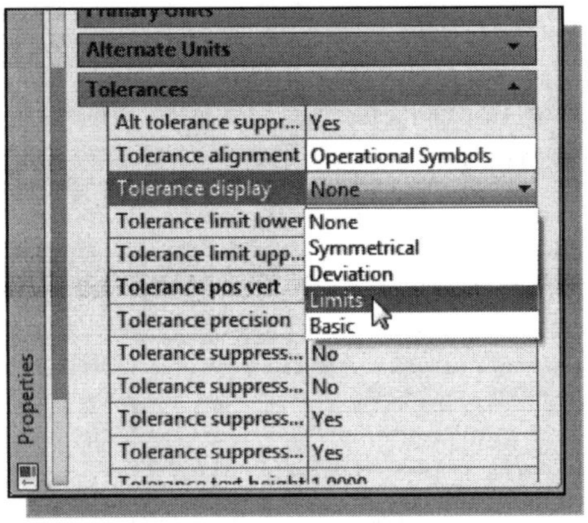

3. Set the *Tolerances display* option to **Limits** as shown.

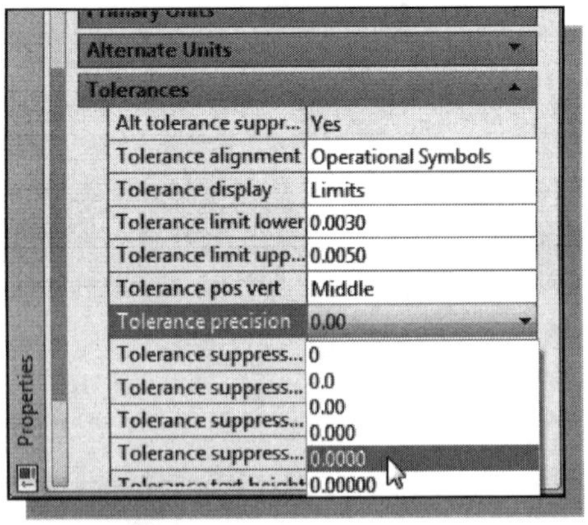

4. Set the *Tolerance precision* option to four digits after the decimal point as shown.

- Note that AutoCAD's tolerances setting will place the larger number on top.

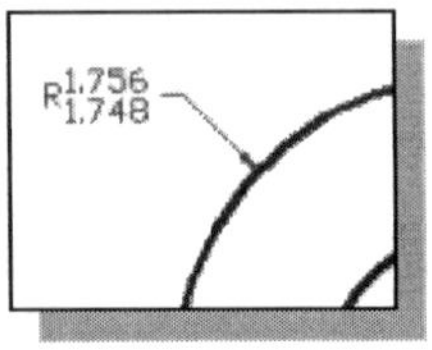

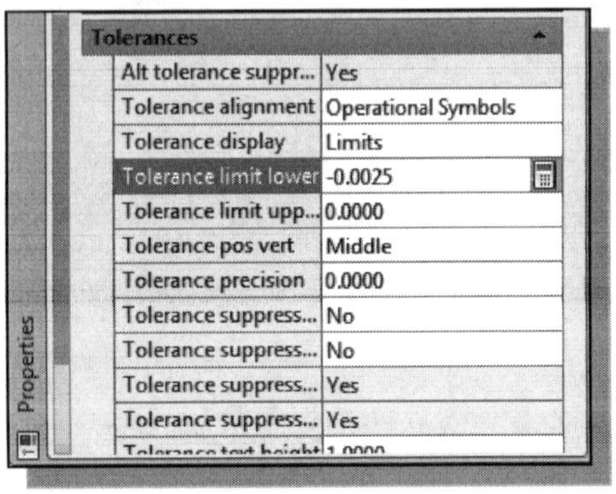

- In order to display the minimum hole size on top, we will **reverse** the tolerance values in the option boxes.

5. Enter ***-0.0025*** in the *Tolerance lower limit* box as shown.

6. Enter ***0.0000*** in the *Tolerance upper limit* box as shown.

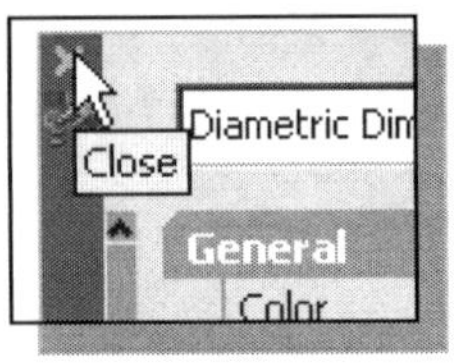

7. Exit the properties palette by clicking on the upper left [X] as shown. The toleranced dimension is as shown.

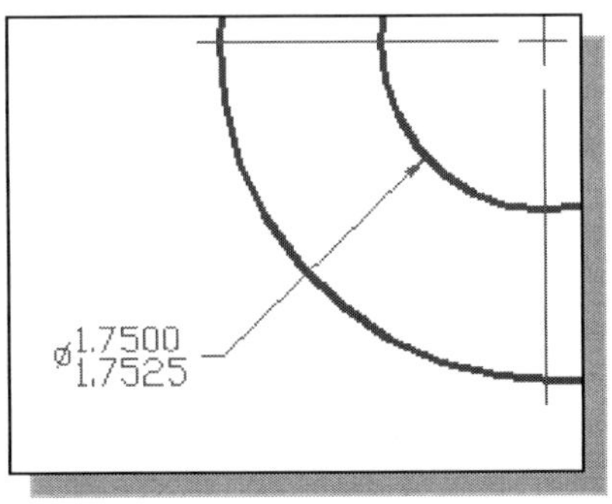

(2) The Nominal size of 0.625

A pin is to be placed through the diameter 0.625 hole. The fit class chosen is **Basic Hole System RC2**. We will first determine the size limits of the two mating parts.

From Appendix A, the RC2 fit for 0.625 inch nominal size:

Nominal size Range	Limits of Clearance	RC2 Standard Limits – Basic Hole	
		Hole	Shaft
0.40 - 0.71	0.25 0.95	+0.4 -0.0	-0.25 -0.55

Using the *Basic Hole System*, the *BASIC* size 0.625 is designated as the minimum hole size.

The maximum hole size is 0.625+0.0004 = 0.6254 inches.
The minimum hole size is 0.625-0.00= 0.62500 inches.

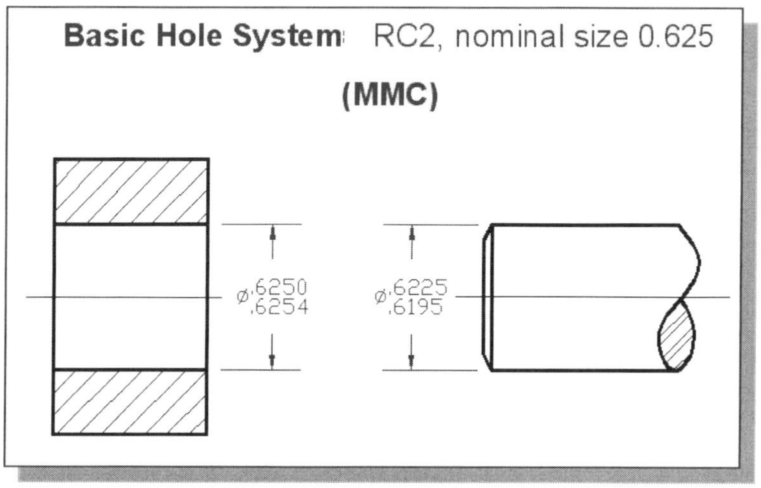

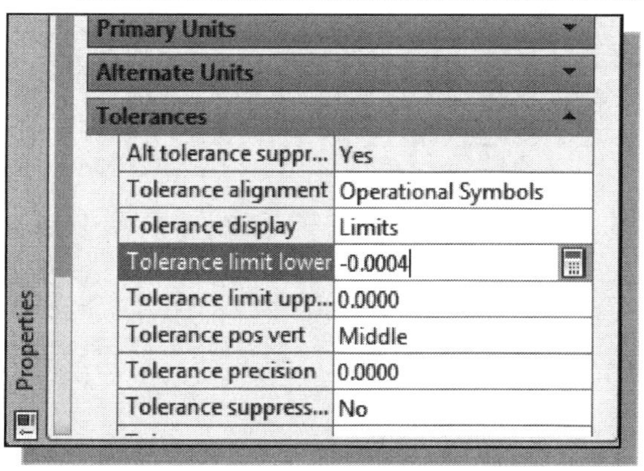

➤ On your own, set the tolerances using the above values.

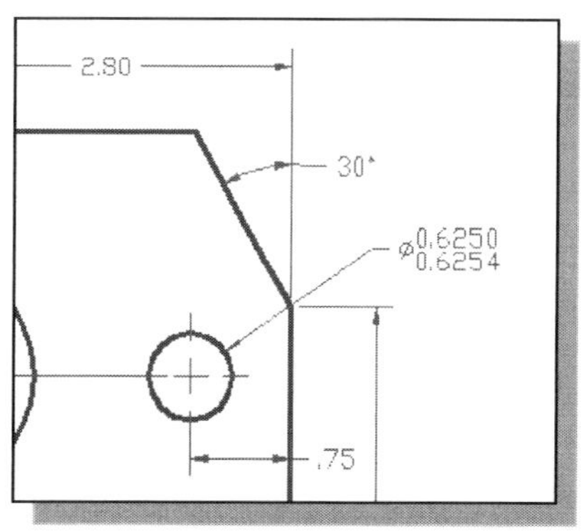

Review Questions: (Time: 45 minutes)

1. Why are **Tolerances** important to a technical drawing?

2. Using the **Basic Shaft system**, calculate the size limits of a nominal size of 1.5 inches.

   Use the following FN4 fit table for 1.5 inches nominal size: (numbers are in thousandth of an inch).

Nominal size Range	Limits of Interference	FN4 Standard Limits – Basic Hole	
		Hole	Shaft
1.19 - 1.97	1.5 3.1	+1.0 -0.0	+3.1 +2.5

3. Using the **Shaft Basis D9/h9** fits, calculate the size limits of a nominal size of 30 mm.

4. What is the procedure to set tolerances in AutoCAD?

5. Explain the following terms:

   (a) Limits

   (b) MMC

   (c) Tolerances

   (d) Basic Hole System

   (e) Basic Shaft System

6. Given the dimensions as shown in the below figure, determine the tolerances of the two parts, and the allowance between the parts.

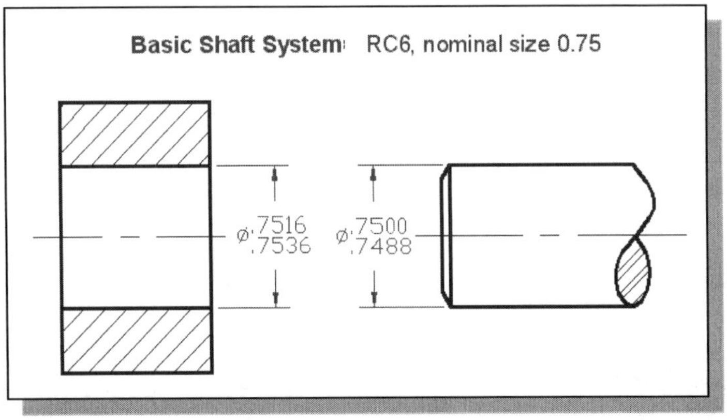

Exercises: (Time: 45 minutes)

(Create the drawings with the following Tolerances.)

1. **Shaft Guide** (Dimensions are in inches.)
Fits: Diameter 0.25, Basic Hole system RC1, Diameter 0.75, Basic Hole system RC6

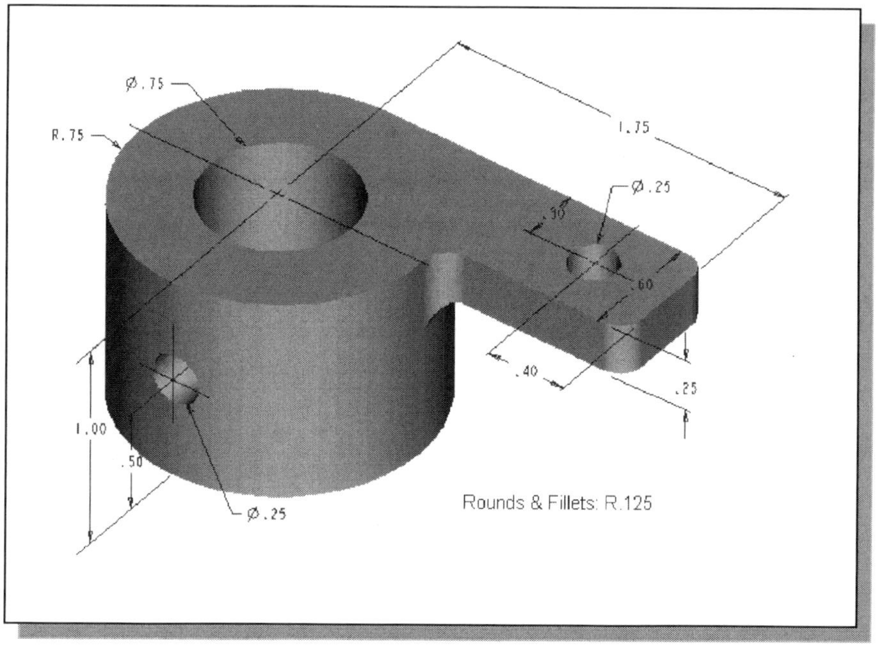

2. **Pivot Lock** (Dimensions are in inches.)
Fits: Diameter 0.5, Basic Hole system RC2, Diameter 1.00, Basic Hole system RC5

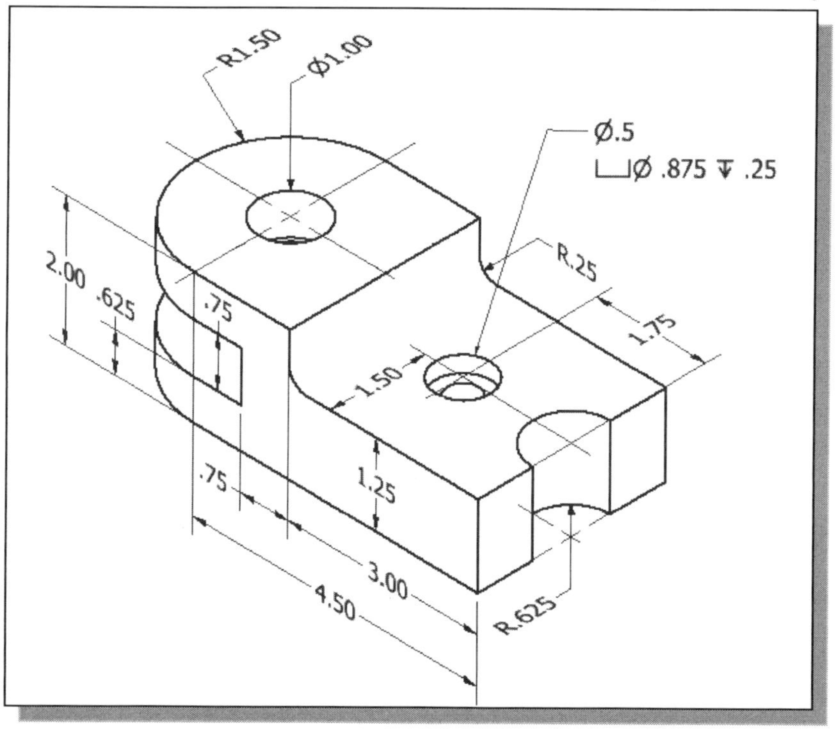

3. **Fixture Cap** (Dimensions are in millimeters.)
Fits: Diameter 40, H7/g6

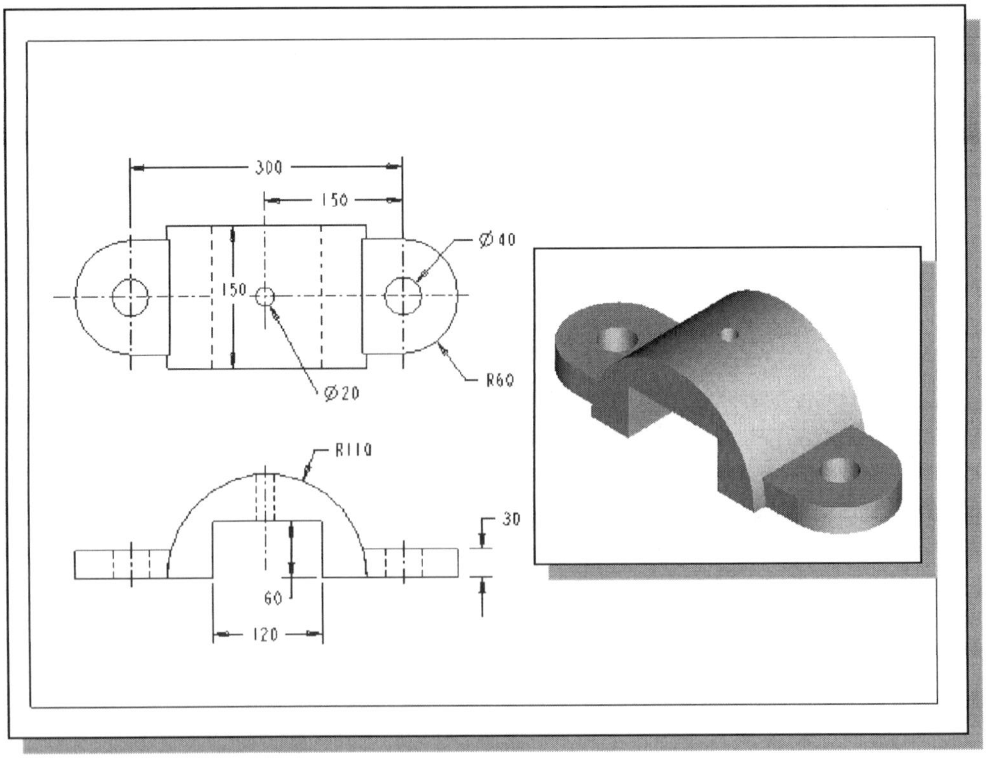

4. **Cylinder Support** (Dimensions are in inches.)
Fits: Diameter 1.50, Basic Hole system RC8.
Right side 0.375 vertical section, Basic Hole system RC4

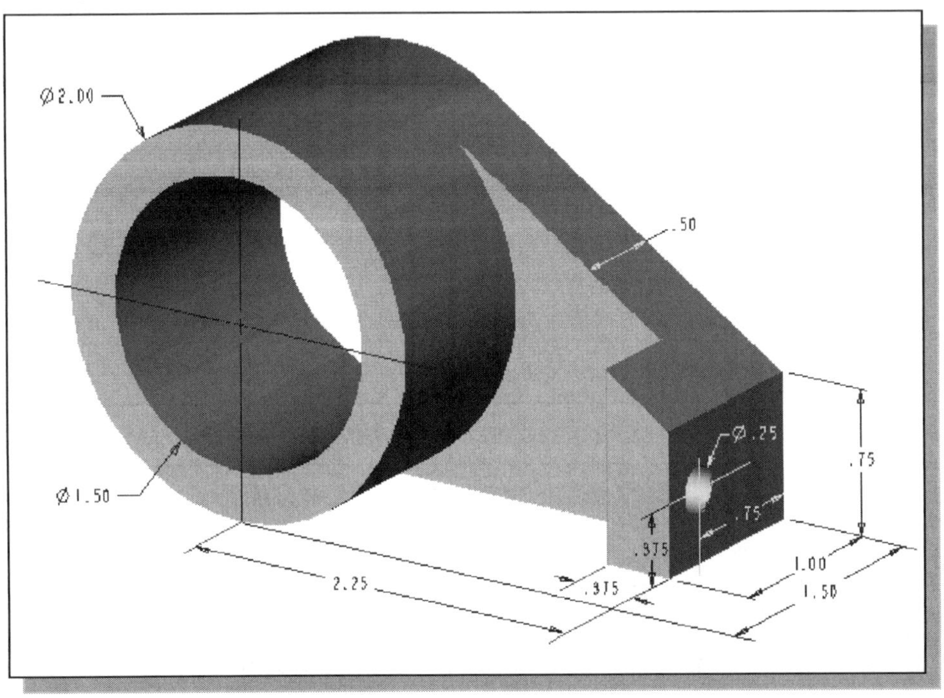

5. **Angle Lock** (Dimensions are in inches.)
Fits: Diameter 1.00 boss, Basic Shaft system RC5.
Diameter 0.75 Hole, Basic Shaft system RC5.

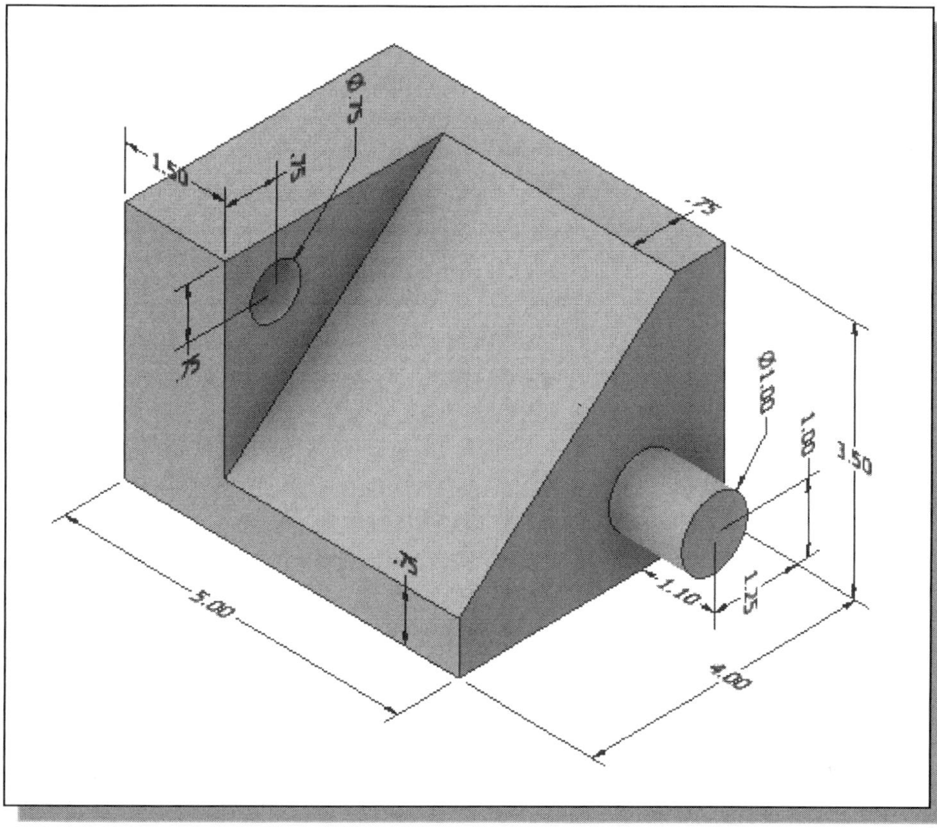

Notes:

Chapter 9
Symmetrical Features in Designs

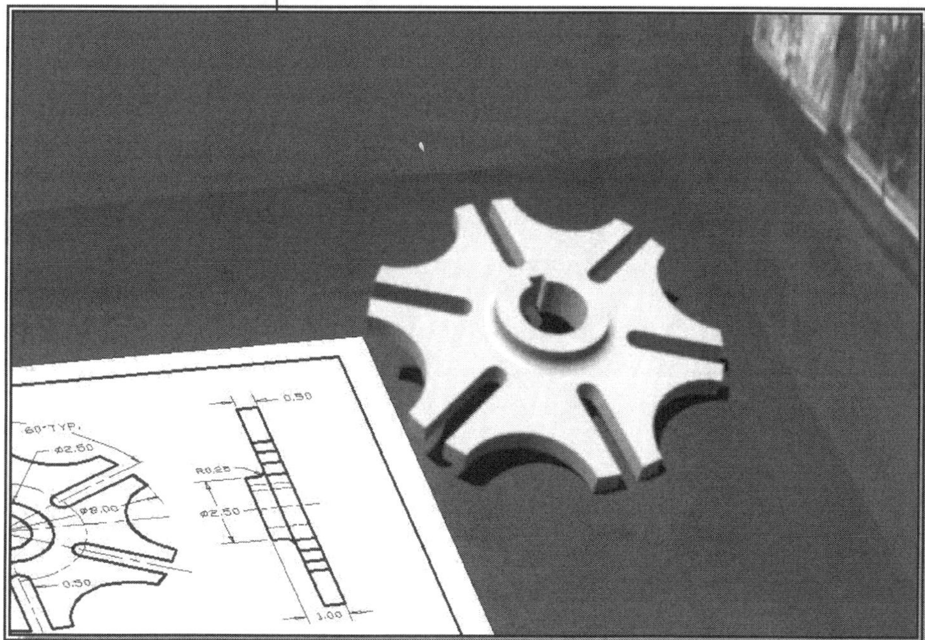

Learning Objectives

- Set up the AutoCAD Plot Style Option
- Create a Template File
- Use the Mirror Command
- Create Multiple Copies of Objects
- Set Up Layouts in Paper Space
- Create Viewports in Paper Space
- Use the Properties Command
- Adjust the Text Scale for Plotting

AutoCAD Certified User Examination Objectives Coverage

Introduction

One of the main advantages of using CAD systems is that we can easily reuse information that is already in the system. For example, many of the system settings, such as setting up layers, colors, linetypes and grids, are typically performed in all AutoCAD files. In **AutoCAD 2027**, we can set up **template files** to eliminate these repetitive steps and make our work much more efficient. Using template files also helps us maintain consistent design and drafting standards. In this chapter, we will illustrate the procedure to set up template files that can contain specific plotting settings, system units, environment settings and other drafting standard settings.

We can also reuse any of the geometry information that is already in the system. For example, we can easily create multiple identical copies of geometry with the **Array** command, or create mirror images of objects using the **Mirror** command. In this chapter, we will examine the use of these more advanced construction features and techniques in **AutoCAD 2027**.

Also in this chapter, we will demonstrate the printing/plotting procedure to create a hard copy of our design. **AutoCAD 2027** provides plotting features that are very easy to use. The **AutoCAD 2027** plotting features include WYSIWYG (What You See Is What You Get) layouts, onscreen lineweights, plot style tables, device-accurate paper sizes, and creating custom paper sizes.

The GenevaCam Design

Starting Up AutoCAD 2027

1. Select the **AutoCAD 2027** option on the *Program* menu or select the **AutoCAD 2027** icon on the *Desktop*.

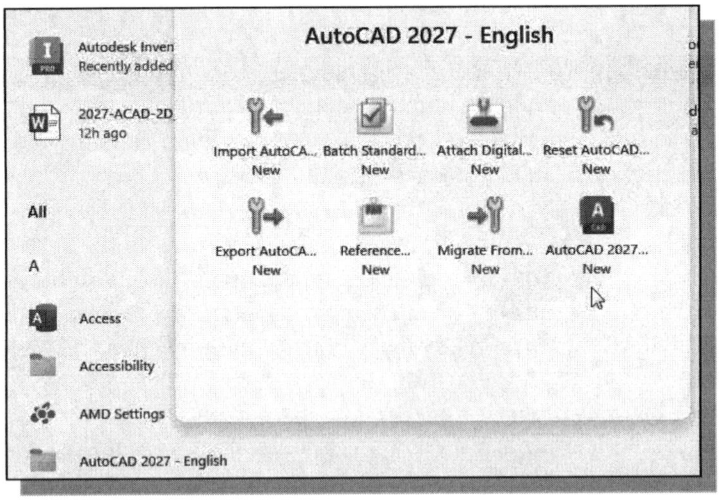

2. In the *Startup* window, select **Start from Scratch**, as shown in the figure below.

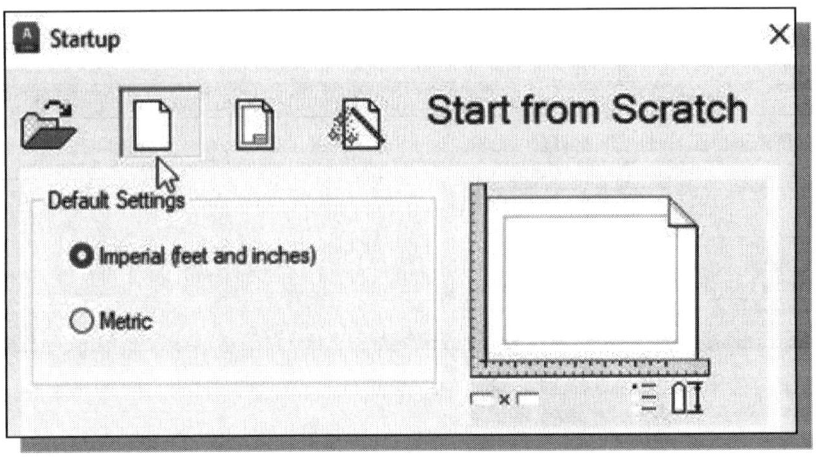

3. In the *Default Settings* section, pick **Imperial (feet and inches)** as the drawing units.

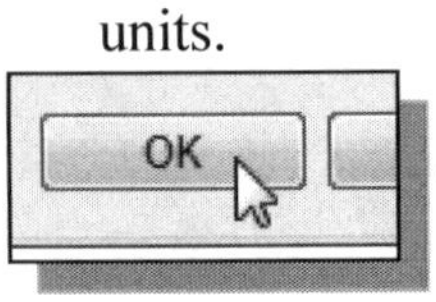

4. Pick **OK** in the startup dialog box to accept the selected settings.

❖ Note the units setting of *Drawing1* is set to the *English units* system. One of the important rules for creating CAD designs and drawings is that they should be created **full size**. The importance of this practice is evident when we are ready to create hard copies of the design, or transfer the designs electronically to manufacturing equipment, such as a CNC machine. Internally, CAD systems do not distinguish whether the one unit of measurement is one inch or one millimeter. **AutoCAD 2027** provides several options to control the units settings.

Setting up the Plot Style Mode

Using **AutoCAD 2027** *plot styles* and *plot style tables* allows us to control the way drawings look at plot time. We can reassign object properties, such as color, linetype, and lineweight, and plot the same drawing differently. The default **AutoCAD 2027** *Plot Style Mode* is set to use the *Color-Dependent plot style*, which controls the plotting of objects based on the object colors and is the *traditional* method of adjusting the plotted hardcopy in AutoCAD. The other plot method in **AutoCAD** is to use the *Named plot style table* that works independently of color. In this chapter, we will learn to plot with the new AutoCAD *Named plot style*, which provides a very flexible and fast way to control the plotting of our designs.

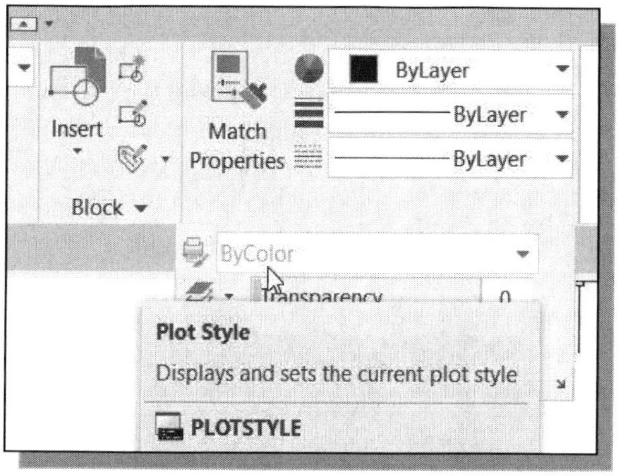

- Notice the *Plot Style* box, the first box in the *Object Properties* toolbar, displays the setting of ***ByColor*** and is grayed out. This indicates the plot style is set to the default *Color-Dependent* plot style, and therefore the object color is used to control plotting of the drawing.

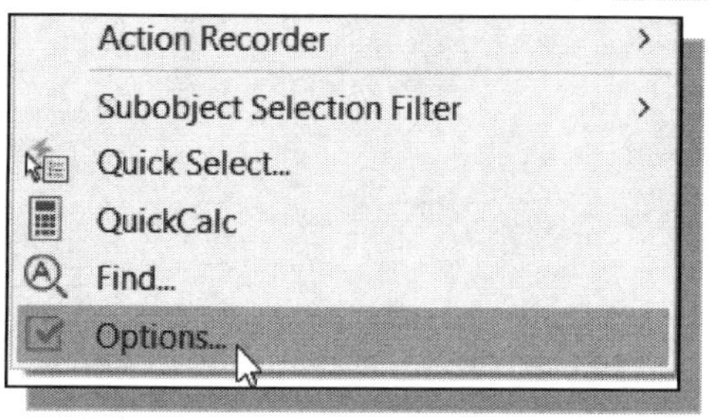

1. Inside the graphics area, **right-click** to bring up the option menu.

2. Select **Options** as shown in the figure.

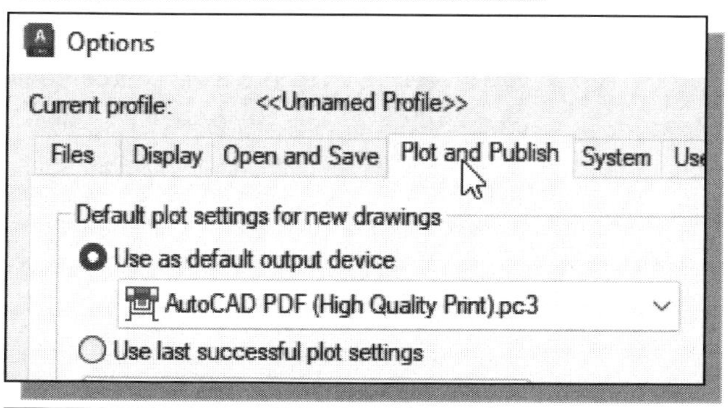

3. In the *Options* dialog box, select the **Plot and Publish** tab if it is not the active tab on top.

4. Click on the **Plot Style Table Settings** button as shown.

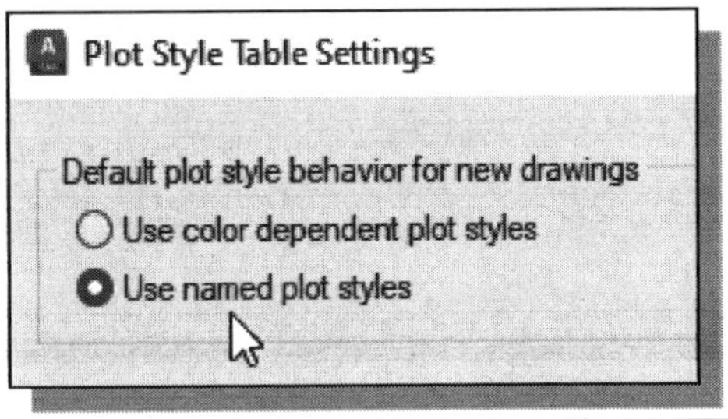

5. Switch *ON* the **Use named plot styles** as shown.

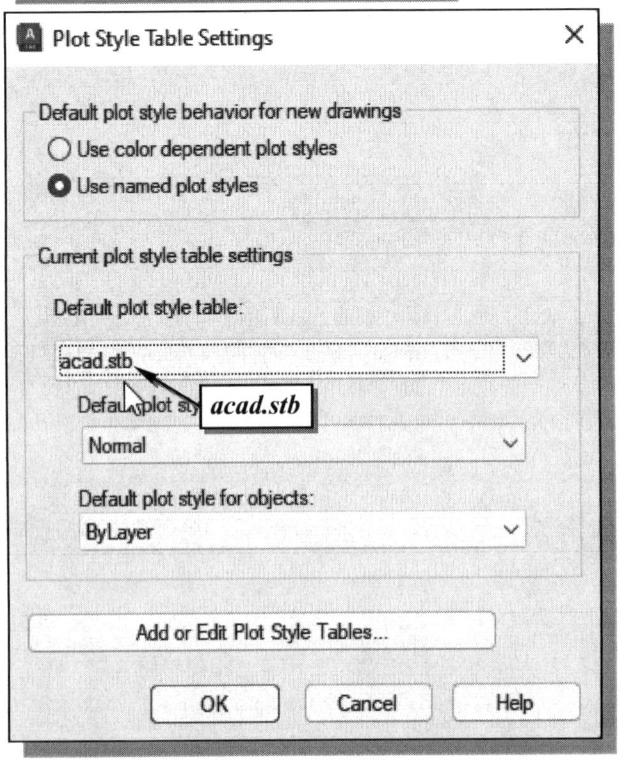

6. In the *Default plot style table*, select ***acad.stb*** from the list of plot style tables.

7. Click on the **OK** button to accept the modified plot style table settings.

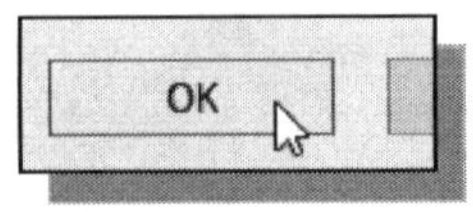

8. Pick **OK** to accept the selected settings and close the ***Options*** dialog box.

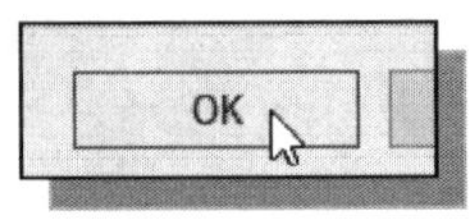

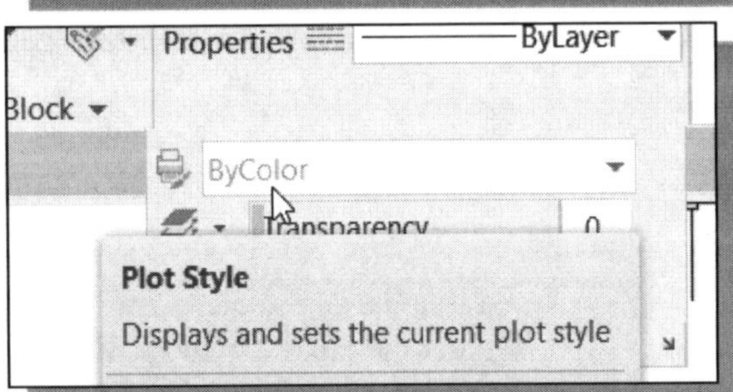

❖ Note the *Plot Style* box in the *Object Properties* toolbar is still grayed out. This is because the plotting settings are stored in each file as it is created. We will close this file and start a new file to have the new settings take effect.

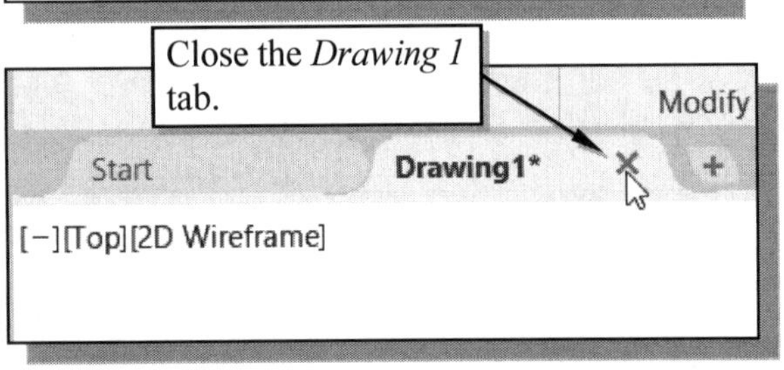

9. Click on the **[X]** button of the *Drawing 1* tab, to close the file.

10. In the AutoCAD *Warning* dialog box, select **NO** to close the file without saving.

Starting a New File

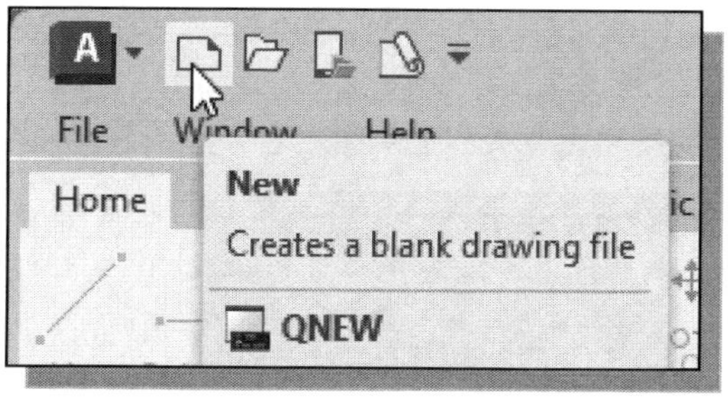

1. Click the **New** icon in the *Quick Access* toolbar.

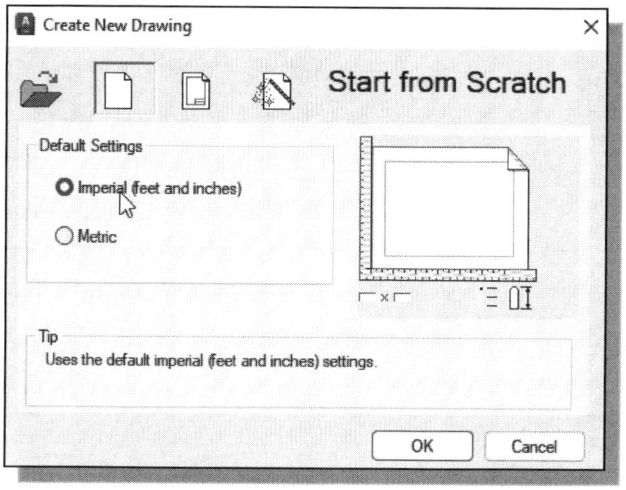

2. In the AutoCAD *Create New Drawing* dialog box, select the **Start from Scratch** option as shown.

3. Pick **Imperial (Feet and Inches)** as the drawing units.

4. Pick **OK** in the startup dialog box to accept the selected settings.

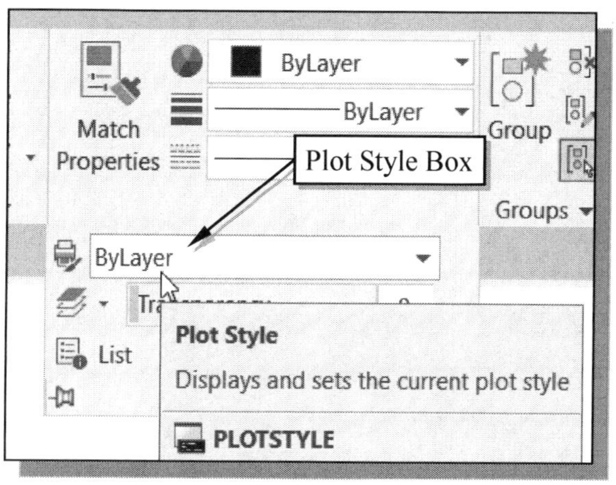

❖ Notice the *Plot Style* box in the *Object Properties* toolbar now displays the setting of *ByLayer* and is no longer grayed out. This indicates we are now using the *Named plot style*, with different options available to control plotting of the design.

➢ We will demonstrate the use of the ***Named plot style*** to create a hardcopy of the *Geneva Cam* design. The steps described in the above sections are required to set up the settings for the named plot style to be used in new drawings, and it should be done prior to creating the design. We can also convert an existing drawing to use named plot styles; it will require installing the ***AutoCAD Migration*** application and using the **Convertpstyles** command to perform the conversion. Note that after the conversion, any color-dependent plot style tables attached to layouts in the drawing are removed.

Grid and Snap Intervals Setup

1. In the *Menu Bar*, select:

   [Tools] → [Drafting Settings]

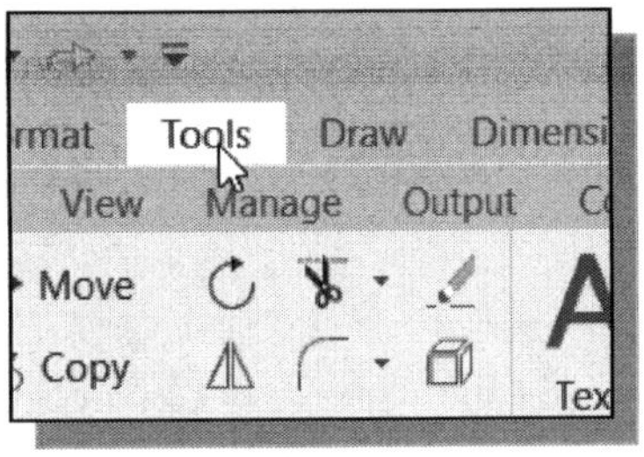

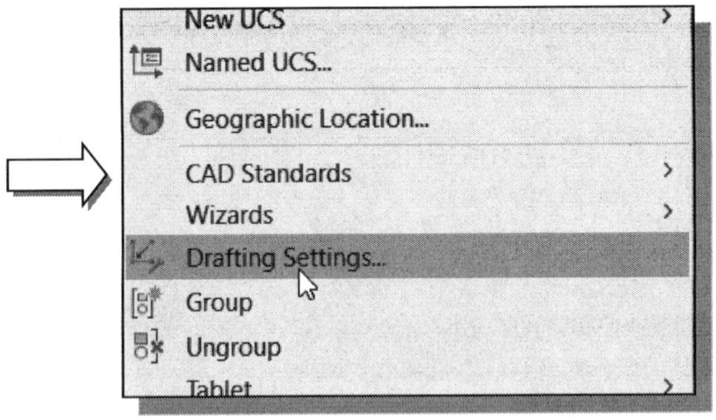

2. In the *Drafting Settings* dialog box, select the **SNAP and GRID** tab if it is not the page on top.

3. Change *Grid Spacing* to ***1.0*** for both X and Y directions.

4. Also adjust the *Snap Spacing* to ***0.5*** for both X and Y directions.

5. Pick **OK** to exit the *Drafting Settings* dialog box.

6. In the *Status Bar* area, reset the option buttons so that only *SNAP Mode* and *GRID Display* are switched ***ON***.

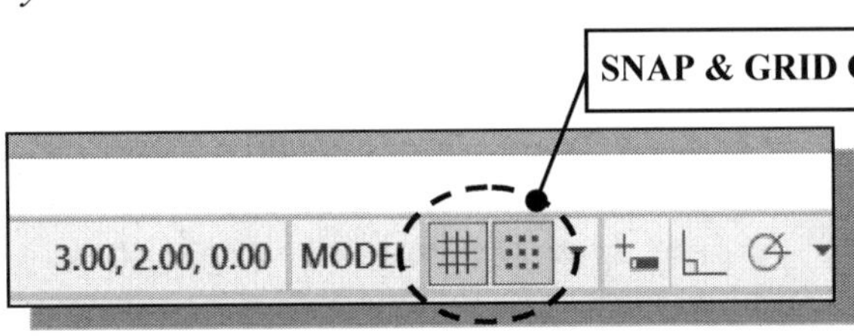

Layers Setup

1. Pick ***Layer Properties Manager*** in the *Object Properties* toolbar.

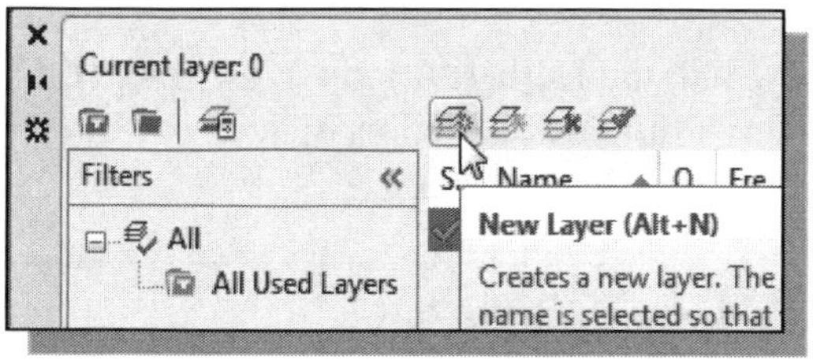

2. In the *Layer Properties Manager* dialog box, click on the **New** button (or the key combination [**Alt+N**]) to create a new layer.

3. Create **layers** with the following settings:

Layer	***Color***	***Linetype***	***Lineweight***	***PlotStyle***
Center_Lines	**Red**	**Center**	**Default**	**Normal**
Construction	**Gray**	**Continuous**	**Default**	**Normal**
CuttingPlane_Lines	**Dark Gray**	**Phantom**	**0.6mm**	**Normal**
Dimensions	**Magenta**	**Continuous**	**Default**	**Normal**
Hidden_Lines	**Cyan**	**Hidden**	**0.3mm**	**Normal**
Object_Lines	**Blue**	**Continuous**	**0.6mm**	**Normal**
Section_Lines	**White**	**Continuous**	**Default**	**Normal**
Title_Block	**Green**	**Continuous**	**1.2mm**	**Normal**
TitleBlockLettering	**Blue**	**Continuous**	**Default**	**Normal**
Viewport	**White**	**Continuous**	**Default**	**Normal**

➢ Using the ***Normal*** *PlotStyle* enables plotting of ***lineweights*** defined in the specific layer**.** Note that the **Lineweight** settings are set for proper printing of different linetypes and some may appear thicker on screen.

4. Highlight the layer ***Construction*** in the list of layers.

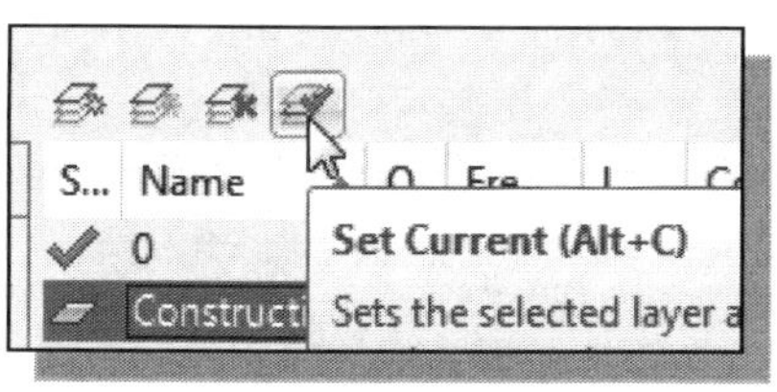

5. Click on the **Current** button to set layer ***Construction*** as the *Current Layer*.

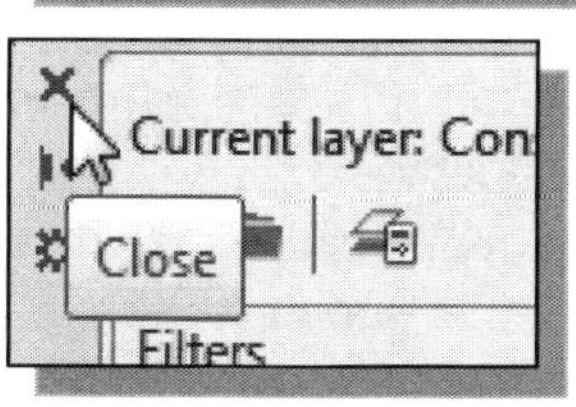

6. Click on the **Close** button to accept the settings and exit the *Layer Properties Manager* dialog box.

Adding Borders and Title Block in the Layout

AutoCAD 2027 allows us to create plots to any exact scale on the paper. Until now, we have been working in ***model space*** to create our design in **full size**. When we are ready to plot, we can arrange our design on a two-dimensional sheet of paper so that the plotted hardcopy is exactly what we wanted. This two-dimensional sheet of paper is known as the ***paper space*** in AutoCAD. We can place borders and title blocks on *paper space*, the objects that are less critical to our design.

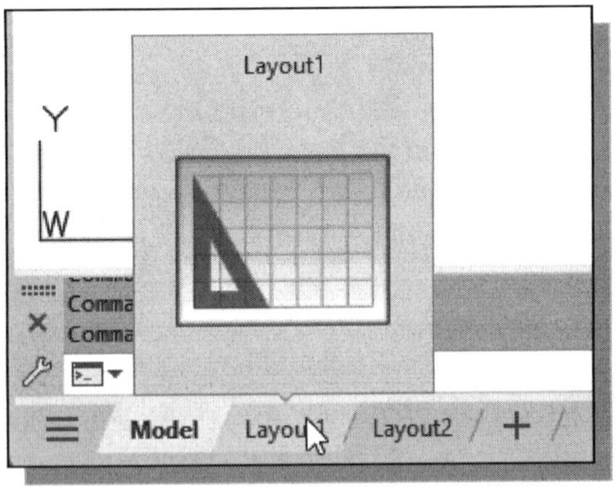

1. Click the **Layout1** icon to switch to the two-dimensional paper space.

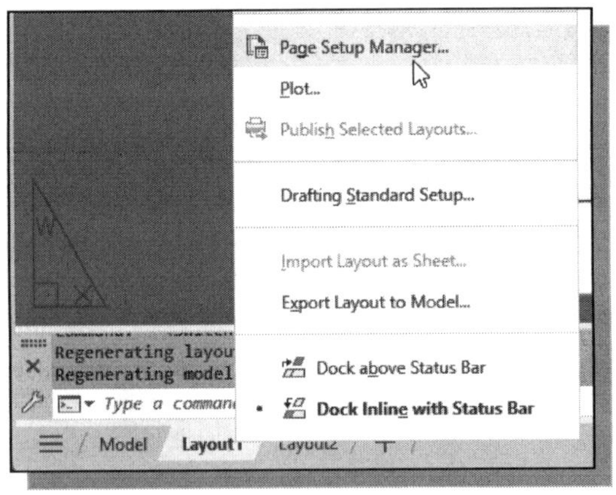

2. To adjust any *page setup* options, right-click once on the tab and select **Page Setup Manager**.

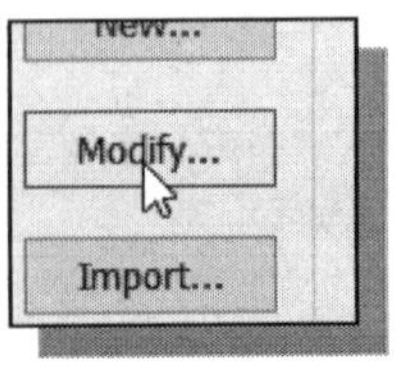

3. Choose the default layout in the *Page Setup Manager* and click **Modify**.

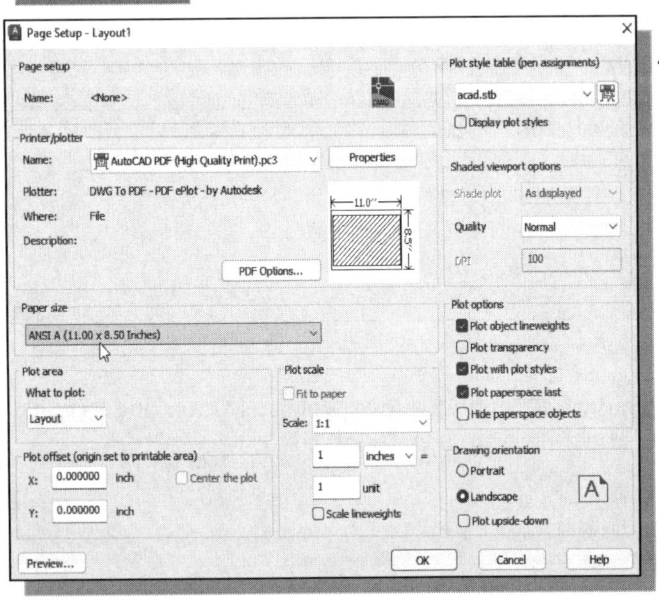

4. In the *Page Setup* dialog box, select a plotter or printer that is available to plot/print your design. Consult with your instructor or technical support personnel if you have difficulty identifying the hardware.

❖ Here we will set up the plotting for an A-size plot on a LaserJet printer. You can also select A4 paper size if your plotter supports the metric size papers.

➢ Also notice the *Printable area* listed in the *Paper size and paper units* section is typically smaller than the actual paper size, which is due to the limitations of the hardware.

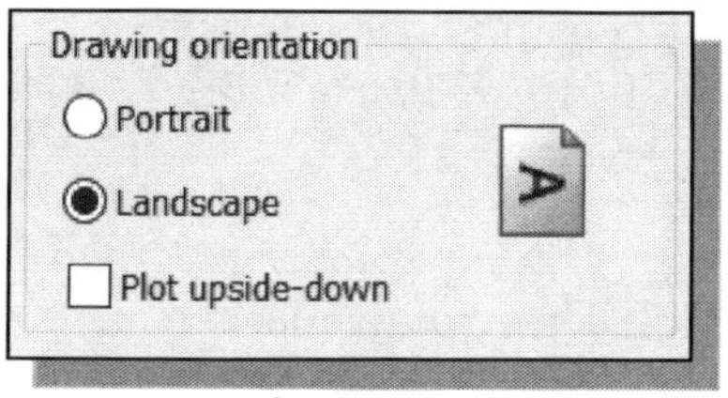

5. Set the *Paper size* to **Letter** or equivalent (8.5″ by 11″) and the *Drawing orientation* is set to **Landscape**.

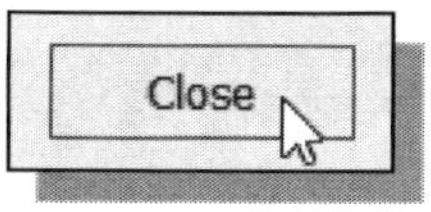

6. Click on the **OK** button and **Close** button to accept the settings and exit the *2027 Setup* dialog boxes.

❖ In the Drawing Area, a rectangular outline on a gray background indicates the paper size. The dashed lines displayed within the paper indicate the *printable area*.

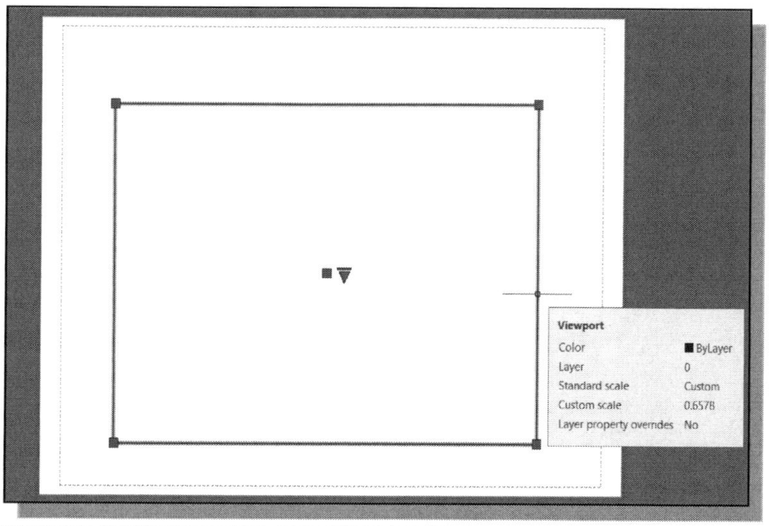

7. Select the rectangular viewport inside the dashed lines.

8. Hit the [**Delete**] key once to remove it.

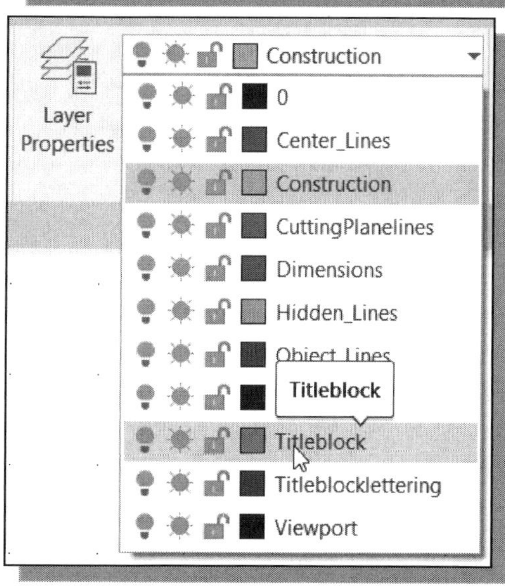

9. In the *Object Properties* toolbar area, select the ***Layer Control*** box and set layer ***Title_Block*** as the *Current Layer*.

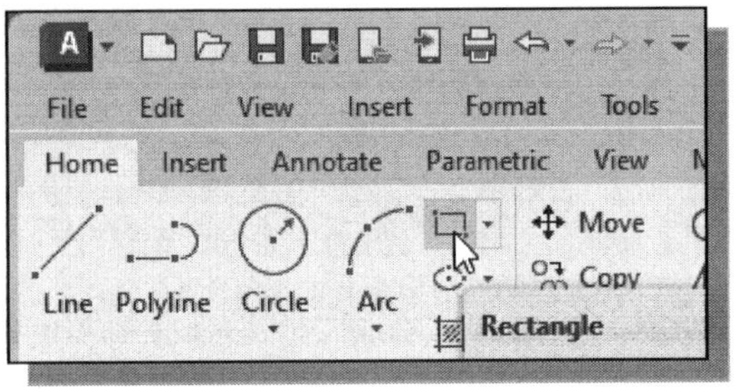

10. Select the **Rectangle** icon in the *Draw* toolbar. In the command prompt area, the message "*Specify first corner point or [Chamfer/Elevation/Fillet/Thickness/Width]:*" is displayed.

11. Pick a location that is on the inside and near the lower left corner of the dashed rectangle.

12. In the command prompt area, use the *relative coordinate entry method* and create a 10.25″ × 7.75″ rectangle.

13. Complete the title block as shown.

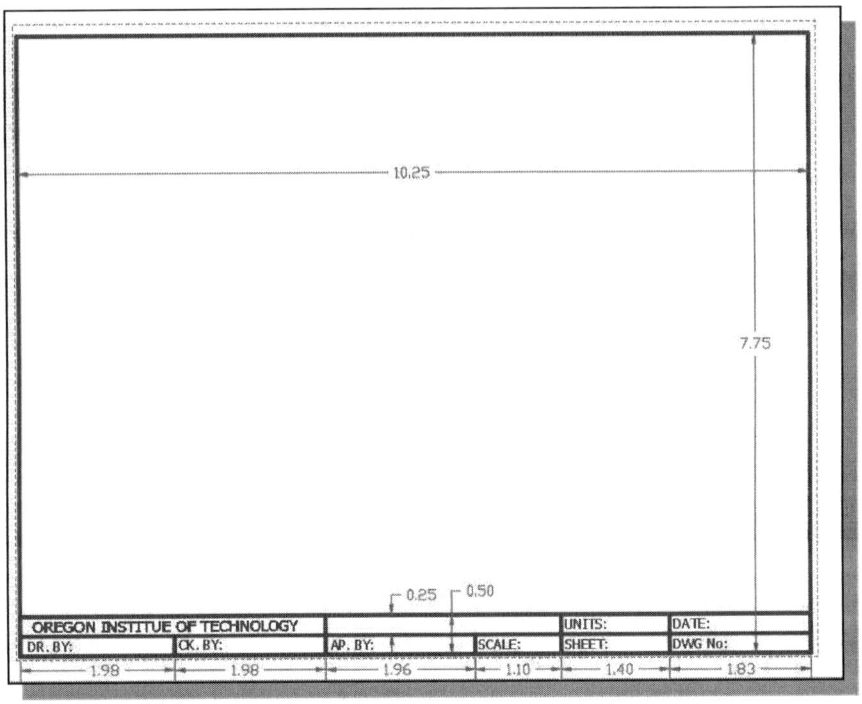

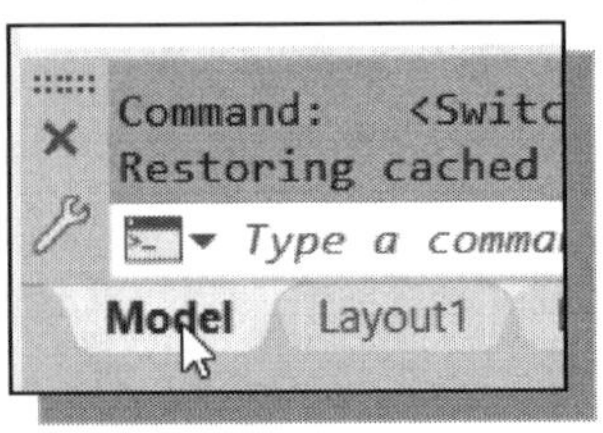

14. Click the **Model** tab to switch back to *model space*.

➤ Notice the title block we created is shown only in *paper space*.

15. On your own, select the ***Layer Control*** box and set layer *Construction Lines* as the *Current Layer*.

16. On your own, switch ***ON*** the following options in the status toolbar: ***SNAP***, ***GRID***, ***Object Snap***, and ***Object Snap Tracking*** and ***Line Weight Display***.

Create a Template File

The heart of any CAD system is the ability to reuse information that is already in the system. In the preceding sections, we spent a lot of time setting up system variables, such as layers, colors, linetypes and plotting settings. We will make a **template file** containing all of the settings and the title block we have created so far.

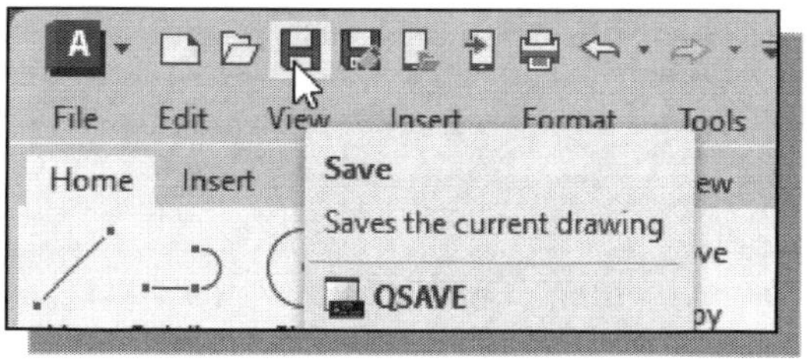

1. In the *Quick Access* toolbar, click the **Save** icon.

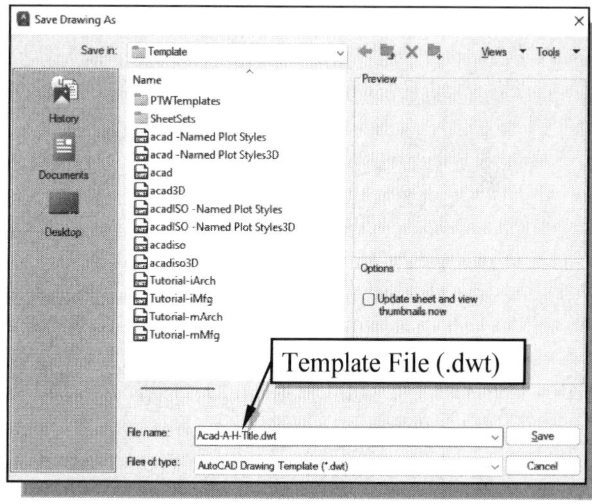

2. In the *Save Drawing As* dialog box, save to the default **AutoCAD template** folder (or select the folder in which you want to store the *template file).* Enter ***Acad-A-H-Title*** in the *File name* box.

3. Pick **Save** in the *Save Drawing As* dialog box to close the dialog box.

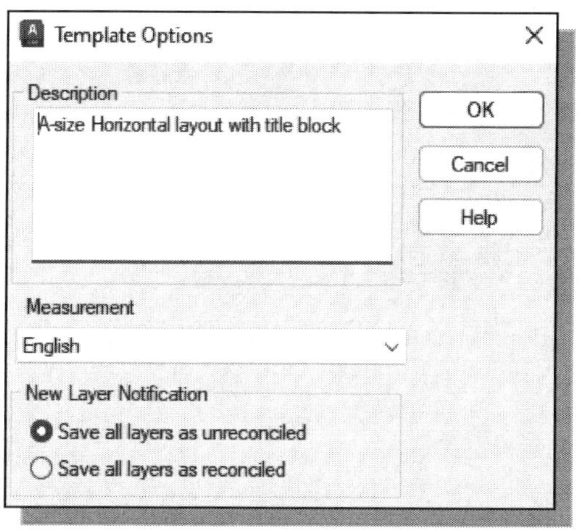

4. In the *Template Description* dialog box, enter ***A-size Horizontal layout with title block*** in the *Description* box.

5. Pick **OK** to close the dialog box and save the template file.

➢ The only difference between an AutoCAD template file and a regular AutoCAD drawing file is the filename extension, (.dwt) versus (.dwg). We can convert any AutoCAD drawing into an AutoCAD template file by simply changing the filename extension to *.dwt*. It is recommended that you keep a second copy of any template files on a separate disk as a backup.

Exit AutoCAD 2027

To demonstrate the effects of using a template file, we will exit and restart **AutoCAD 2027**.

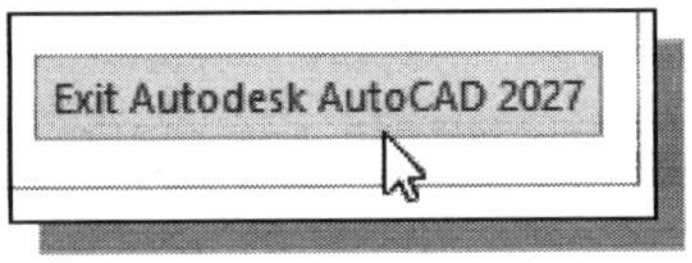

- Click on the *Application Bar* and select **Exit AutoCAD** from the pull-down menu as shown.

Starting Up AutoCAD 2027

1. Select the **AutoCAD 2027** option on the *Program* menu or select the **AutoCAD 2027** icon on the *Desktop*.

2. In the AutoCAD *Startup* dialog box, select the **Use a Template** option.

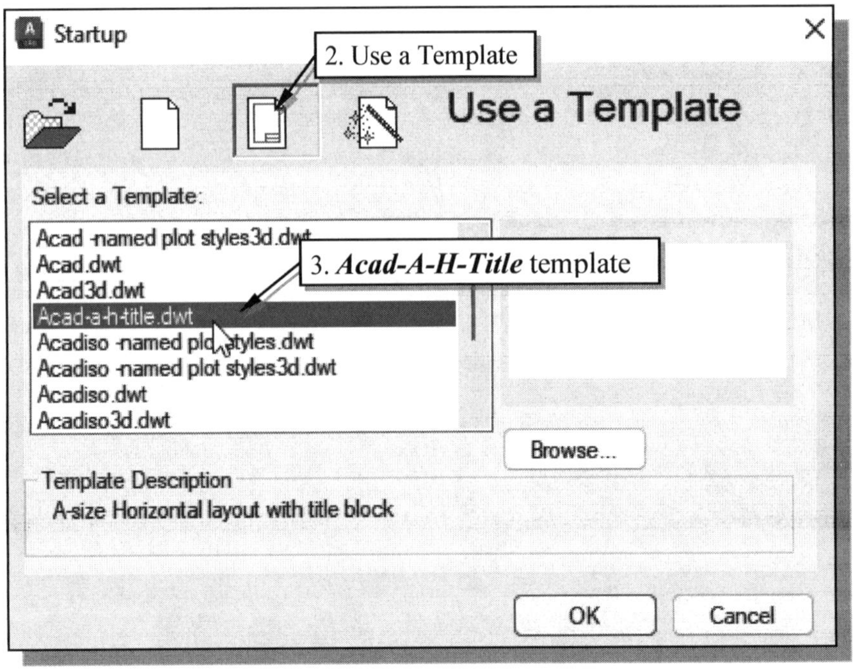

3. Select the ***Acad-A-H-Title*** template file from the list of template files. If the template file is not listed, click on the **Browse** button to locate it and proceed to open a new drawing file.

4. Pick **Layer Properties Manager** in the *Object Properties* toolbar.

5. Examine the layer property settings in the *Layer Properties Manager* dialog box.

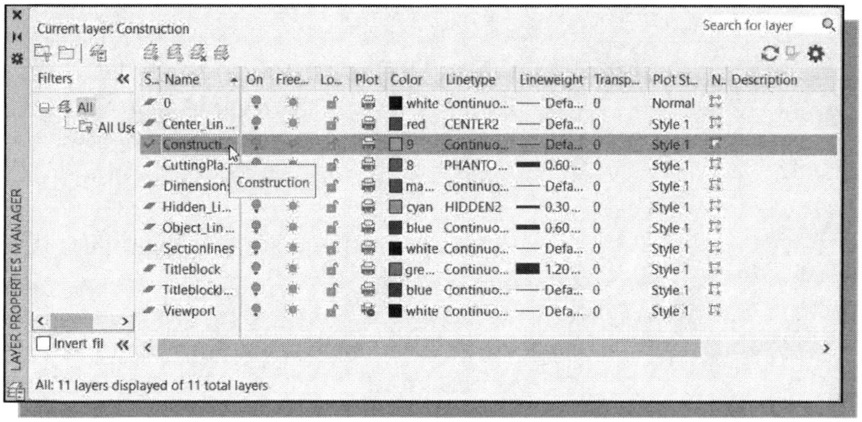

6. Confirm layer ***Construction*** is set as the *Current Layer*.

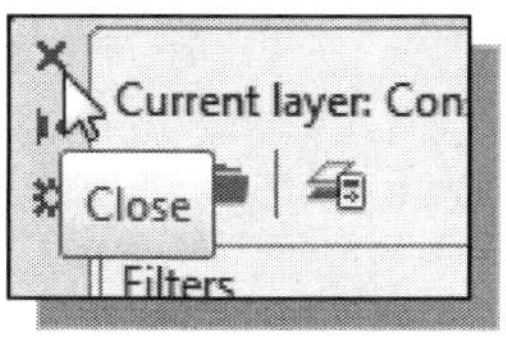

7. Click on the **Close** button to exit the *Layer Properties Manager* dialog box.

The Geneva Cam Drawing

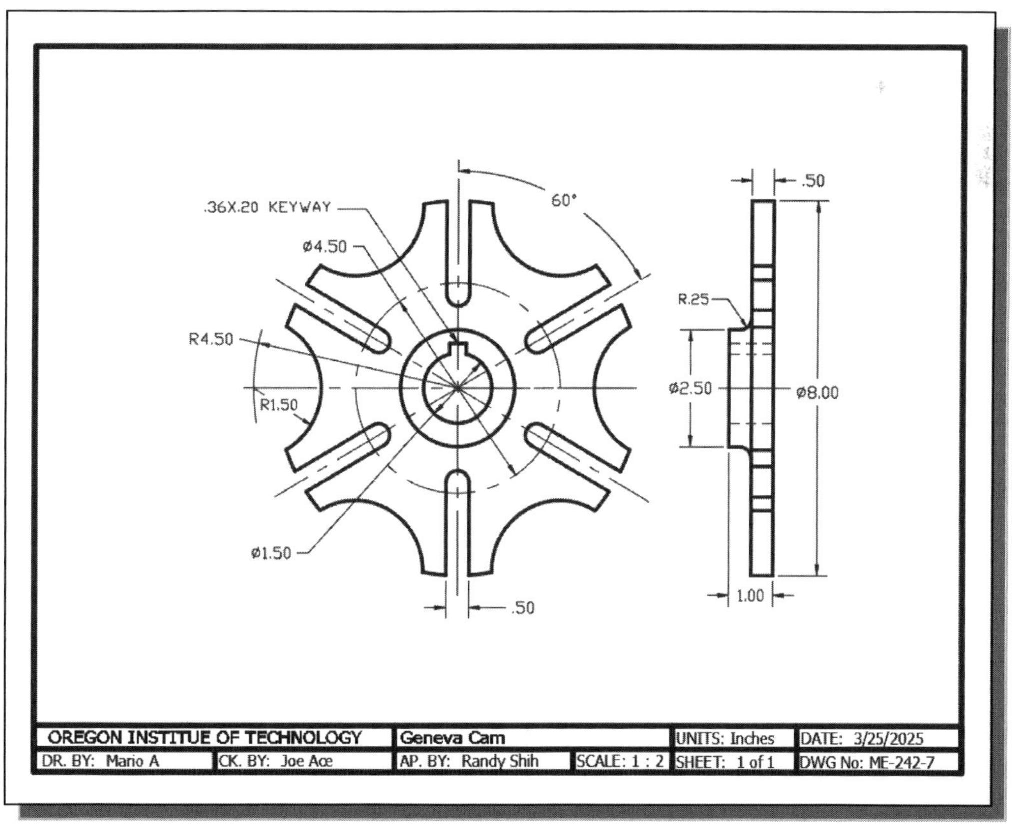

Drawing Construction Lines

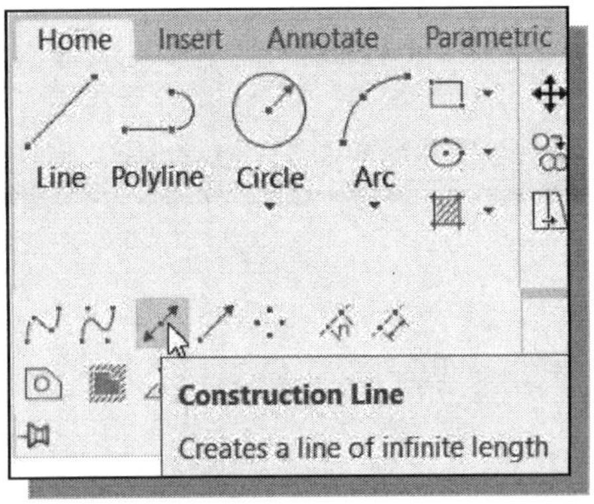

1. Select the **Construction Line** icon in the *Draw* toolbar. In the command prompt area, the message "*_xline Specify a point or [Hor/Ver/Ang/Bisect/Offset]:*" is displayed.

2. Place the first point at world coordinate **(5,4.5)** on the screen.

3. Pick a location above the last point to create a **vertical line**.

4. Move the cursor toward the right of the first point, and then pick a location to create a **horizontal line**.

5. Next, to create a construction line that is rotated 30 degrees from horizontal, enter ***@2<30*** **[ENTER]**.

6. Inside the *Drawing Area*, **right-click** to end the Construction Line command.

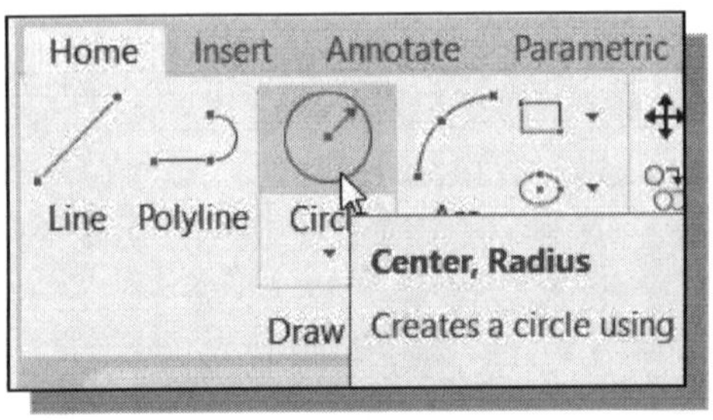

7. Select the **Circle** icon in the *Draw* toolbar. In the command prompt area, the message "*CIRCLE Specify center point for circle or [3P/2P/Ttr]:*" is displayed.

8. Pick the intersection of the lines as the center point of the circle.

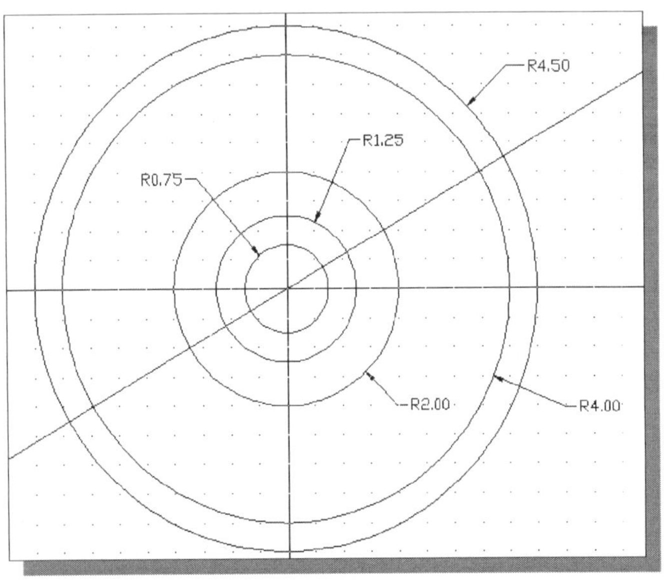

9. In the *command prompt area*, the message "*Specify radius of circle or [Diameter]:*" is displayed. Enter ***0.75*** **[ENTER]**.

10. Repeat the Circle command and create four additional circles of radii ***1.25***, ***2.0***, ***4.0*** and ***4.5*** as shown.

Creating Object Lines

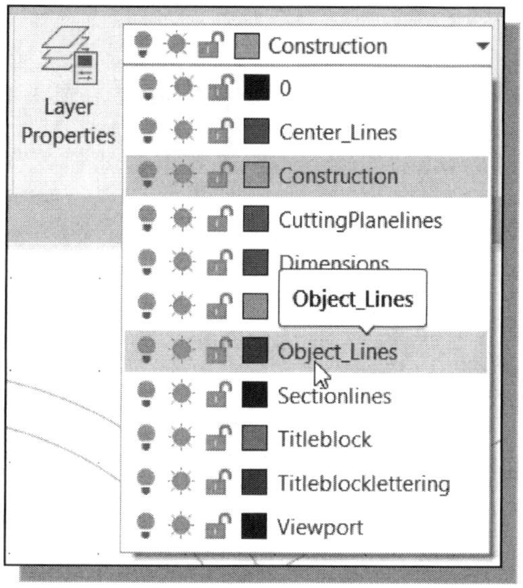

1. On the *Object Properties* toolbar, choose the ***Layer Control*** box with the left-mouse-button.

2. Move the cursor over the name of layer ***Object_Lines***; the tool tip "*Object_Lines*" appears.

3. **Left-click once** and layer *Object_Lines* is set as the *Current Layer.*

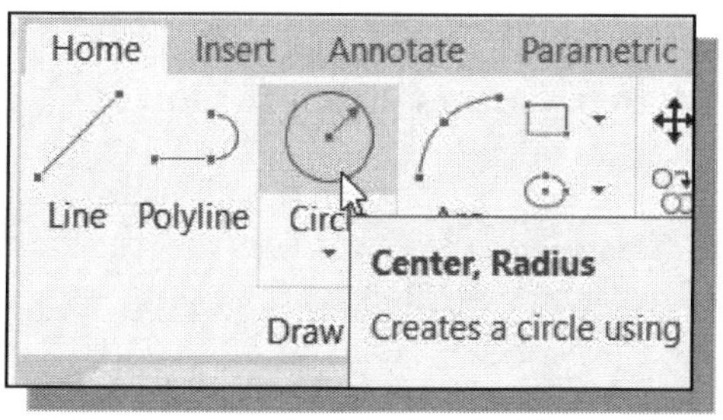

4. Select the **Circle** icon in the *Draw* toolbar. In the command prompt area, the message "*CIRCLE Specify center point for circle or [3P/2P/Ttr]:*" is displayed.

5. Move the cursor to the center of the circles, then left-click once to select the intersection as the center of the new circle.

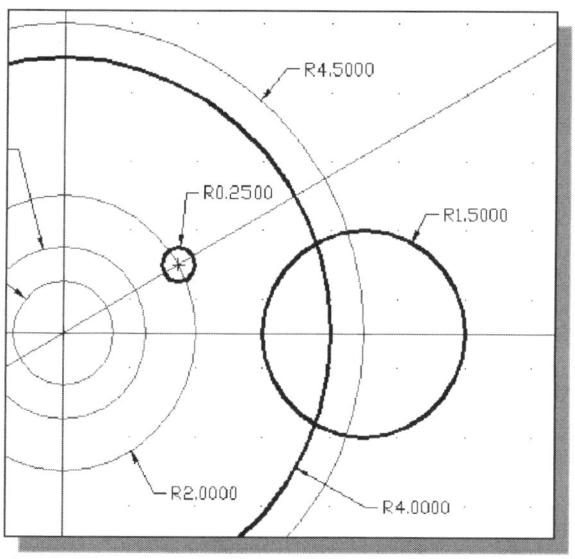

6. In the *command prompt area*, the message "*Specify radius of circle or [Diameter]:*" is displayed. Pick the **right intersection** of the *horizontal line* and the *radius 4.0 circle*.

7. Repeat the **Circle** command and pick the **right intersection** of the *horizontal line* and the *radius 4.5 circle* as the center point of the circle.

8. In the *command prompt area*, the message "*Specify radius of circle or [Diameter]:*" is displayed. Enter ***1.5*** **[ENTER]**.

9. Repeat the **Circle** command and create a circle of radius ***0.25*** centered at the intersection of the inclined line and the radius *2.0* circle as shown.

Using the Offset Command

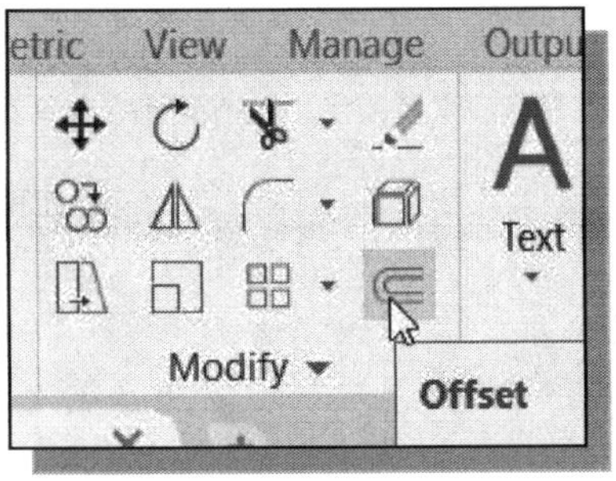

1. Select the **Offset** icon in the *Modify* toolbar. In the command prompt area, the message "*Specify offset distance or [Through]:*" is displayed.

2. In the command prompt area, enter ***0.25*** **[ENTER]**.

3. In the *command prompt area*, the message "*Select object to offset or <exit>:*" is displayed. Pick the **inclined line** on the screen.

4. AutoCAD next asks us to identify the direction of the offset. Pick a location that is **below** the inclined line.

5. Inside the *Drawing Area*, **right-click** and pick **Enter** to end the **Offset** command.

❖ Notice that the new line created by the **Offset** command is placed on the same layer as the line we selected to offset. Which layer is current does not matter; the offset object will always be on the same layer as the original object.

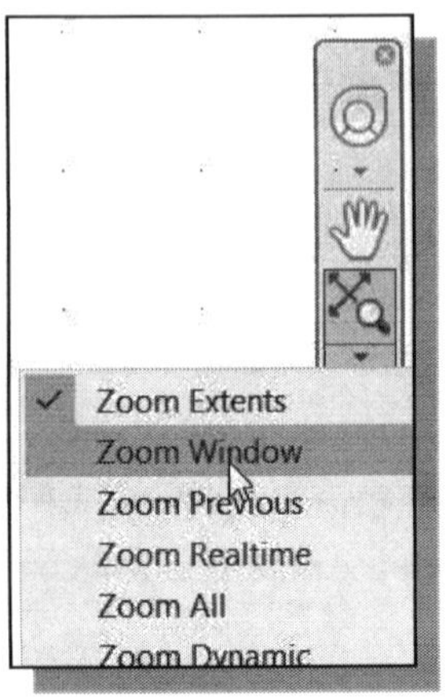

6. Use the **Zoom Window** command and zoom-in on the 30 degrees region as shown.

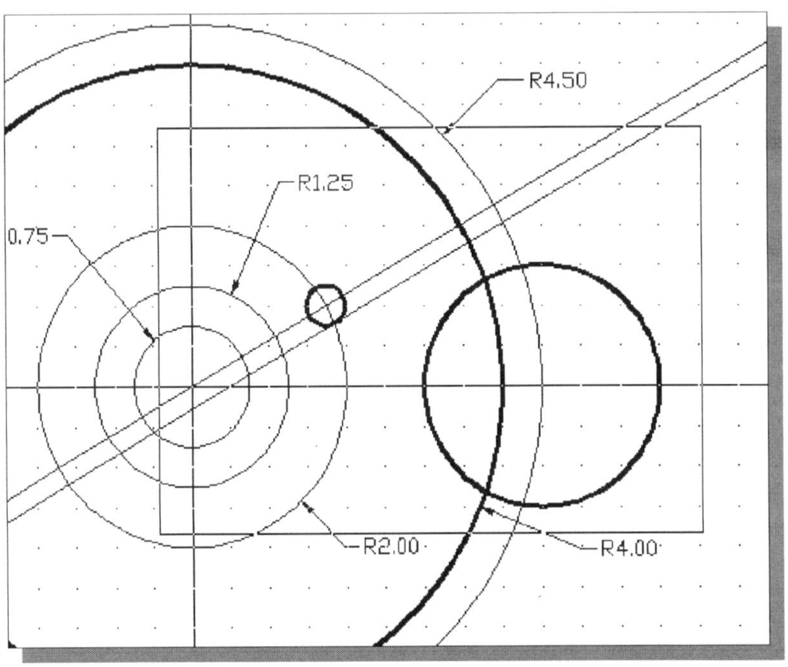

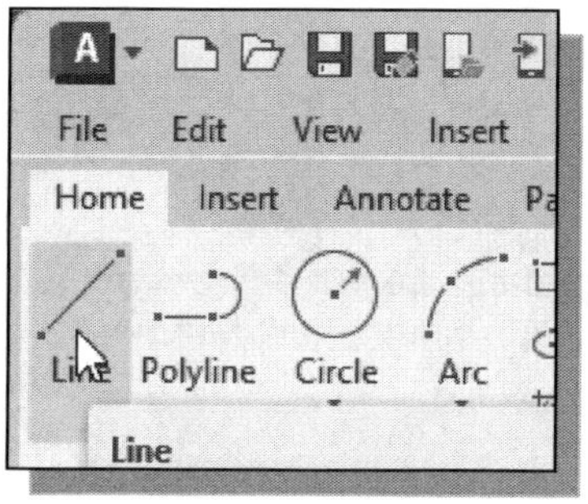

7. Select the **Line** command icon in the *Draw* toolbar. In the command prompt area, the message "*_line Specify first point:*" is displayed.

8. Move the cursor to the **intersection** of the *small circle* and the lower *inclined line* and notice the visual aid that automatically displays at the intersection. **Left-click** once to select the point.

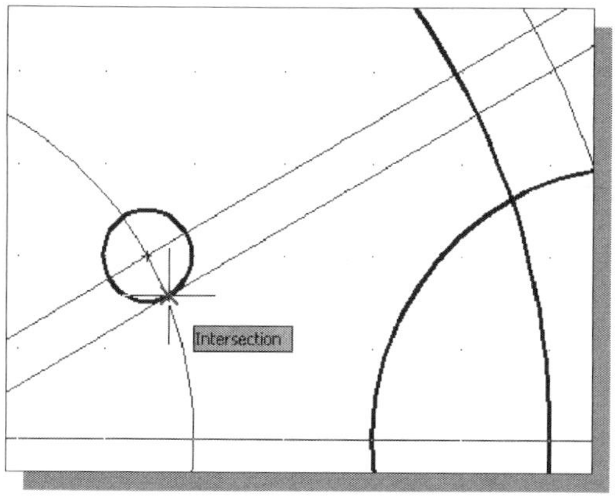

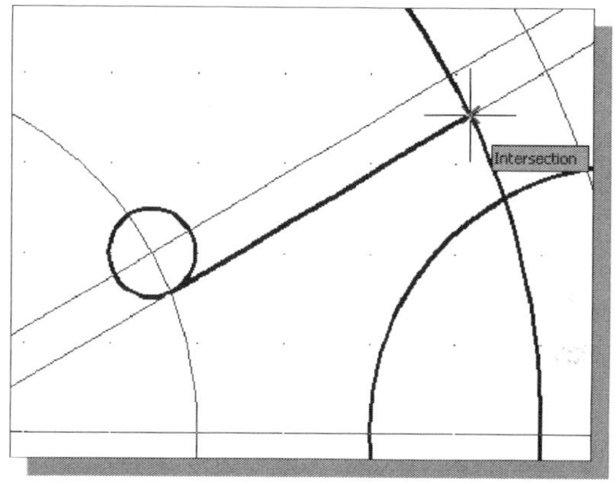

9. Pick the next **intersection point**, toward the right side, along the inclined line.

➢ On your own, use the **Trim** and **Erase** commands to remove the unwanted portions of the objects until your drawing contains only the objects shown below.

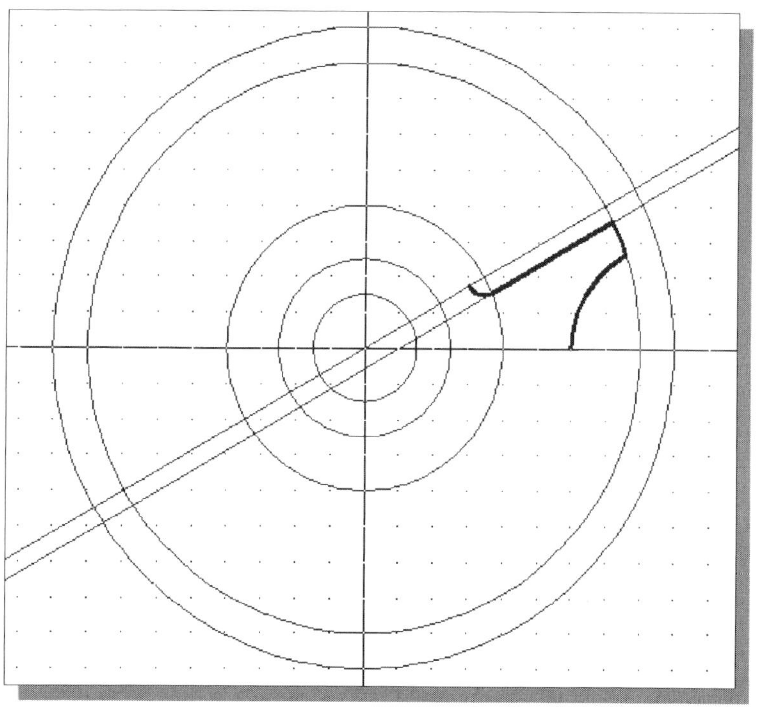

Using the Mirror Command

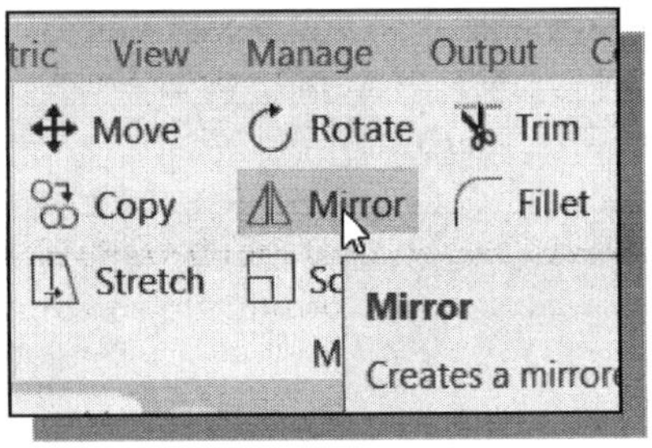

1. Select the **Mirror** command icon in the *Modify* toolbar. In the command prompt area, the message "*Select objects:*" is displayed.

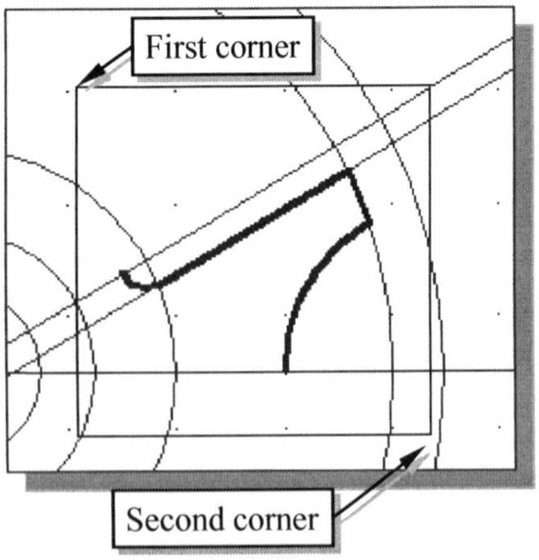

2. Create a *selection window,* with two single clicks of the left mouse button, by selecting the two corners as shown.

➢ Note that in **AutoCAD 2027**, creating the selection window from **left to right** will select only objects entirely within the selection area. Going from **right to left** (crossing selection) selects objects within and objects crossing the selection area. Objects must be at least partially visible to be selected.

3. Inside the *Drawing Area*, **right-click** to accept the selection and continue with the Mirror command.

4. In the *command prompt area*, the message "*Specify the first point of the mirror line:*" is displayed. Pick any **intersection point along the horizontal line** on the screen.

5. In the *command prompt area*, the message "*Specify the second point:*" is displayed. Pick any other intersection point along the **horizontal line** on the screen.

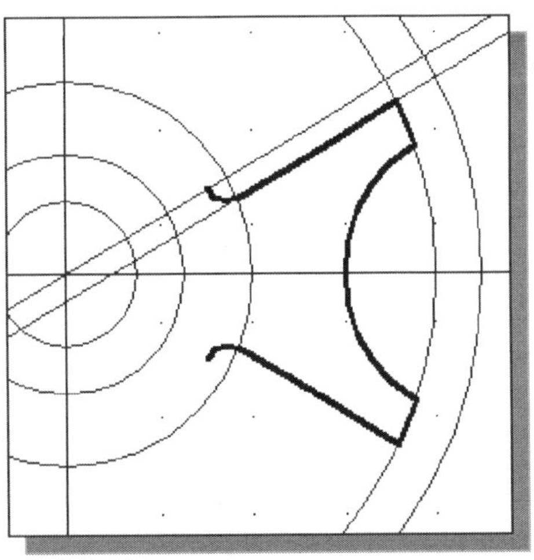

6. In the *command prompt area*, the message "*Delete source objects? [Yes/No] <N>:*" is displayed. Inside the *Drawing Area*, **right-click** and select **Enter** to retain the original objects.

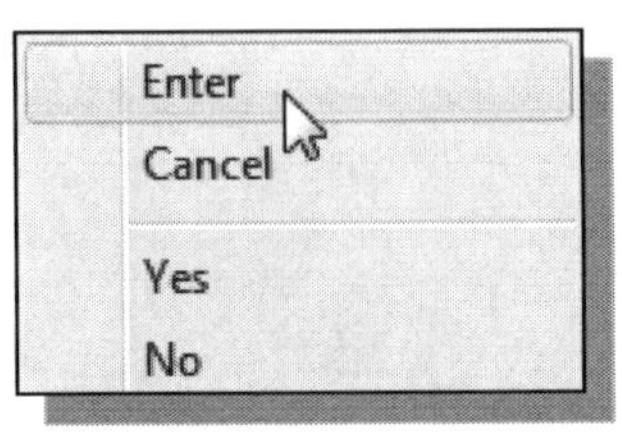

Using the Array Command

We can make multiple copies of objects in polar, rectangular or path arrays (patterns). For polar arrays, we control the number of copies of the object and whether the copies are rotated. For rectangular arrays, we control the number of rows and columns and the distance between them.

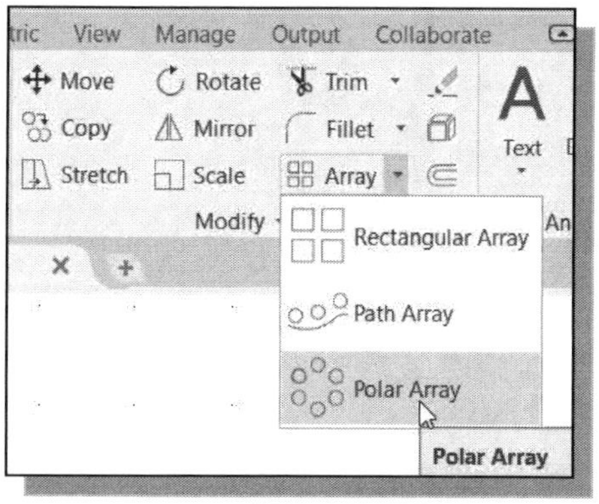

1. Select the **Polar Array** command icon in the *Modify* toolbar. In the command prompt area, the message "*Select objects:*" is displayed.

- Note the three different Array commands available in AutoCAD.

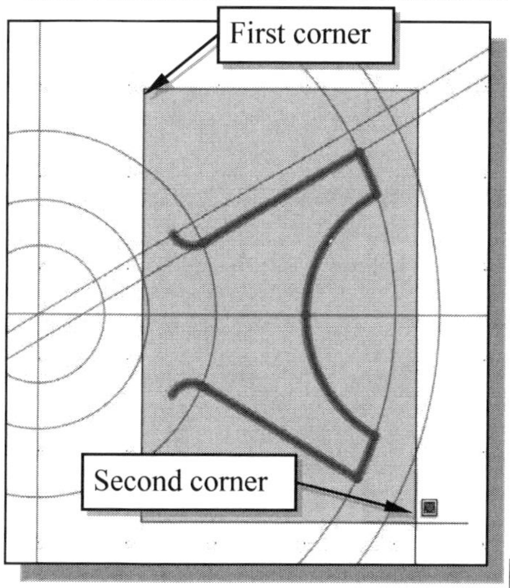

2. Using two single clicks of the left mouse button to create a ***selection* window**, enclose the objects we mirrored and the mirrored copies as shown.

3. In the command prompt area, the message "*Select Objects:*" is displayed. Inside the Drawing Area, **right-click** to end the selection.

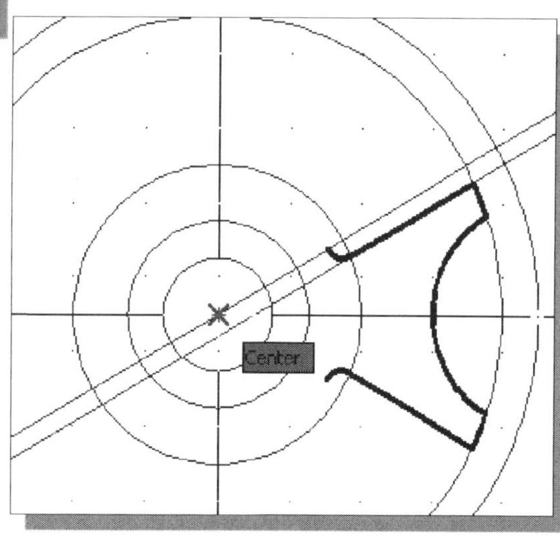

4. In the command prompt area, the message "*Specify the center point of array:*" is displayed. Pick the **Center point location** of the design as shown.

5. In the *Item* toolbar area, set the total number of ***Items*** as **6** as shown.

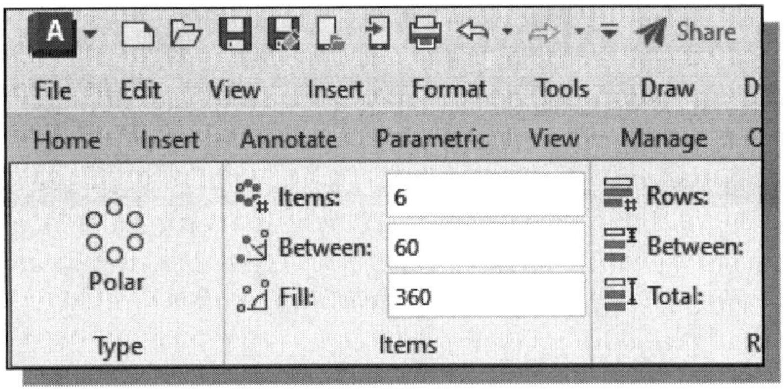

6. Set the angle to ***Fill*** to **360** as shown.

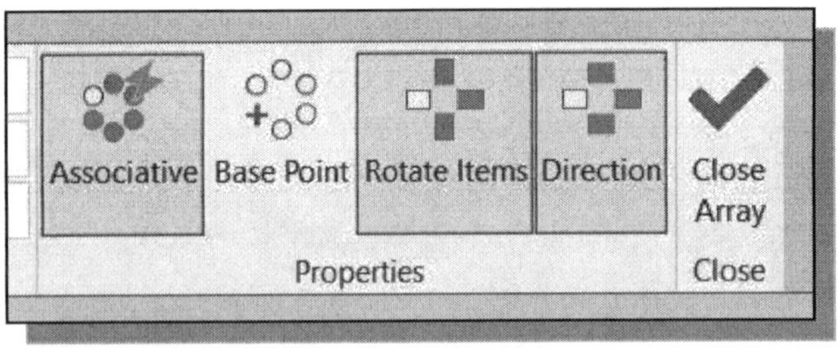

7. On your own, confirm the array ***Properties*** options are as shown.

8. Click **Close Array** to accept the settings and create the array as shown.

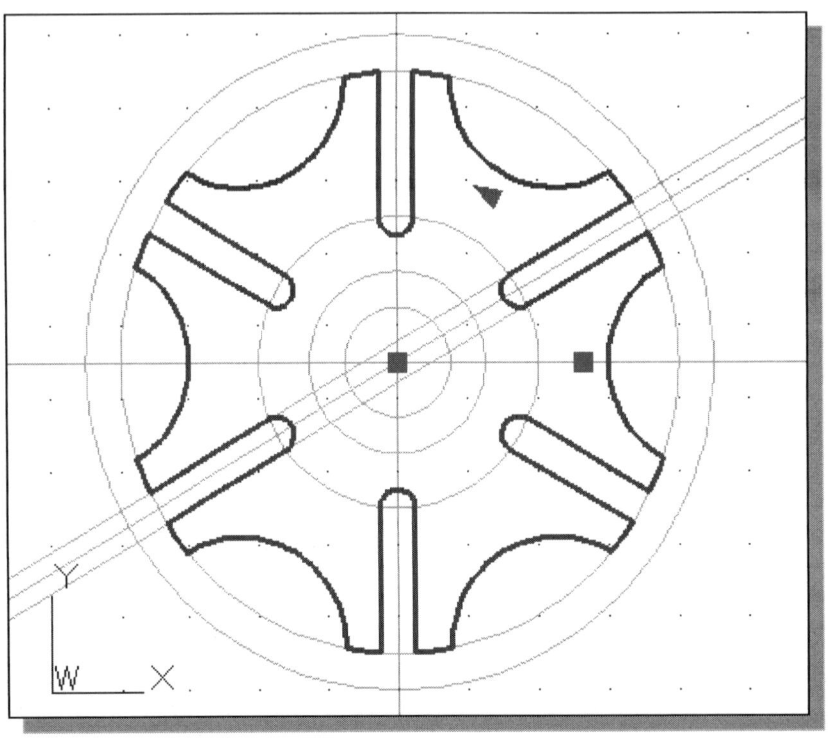

9. On your own, construct the **two inner circles** and the ***0.36 × 0.20*** keyway. (Hint: First create parallel lines at 0.95 and 0.18 distance of the horizontal and vertical construction lines.)

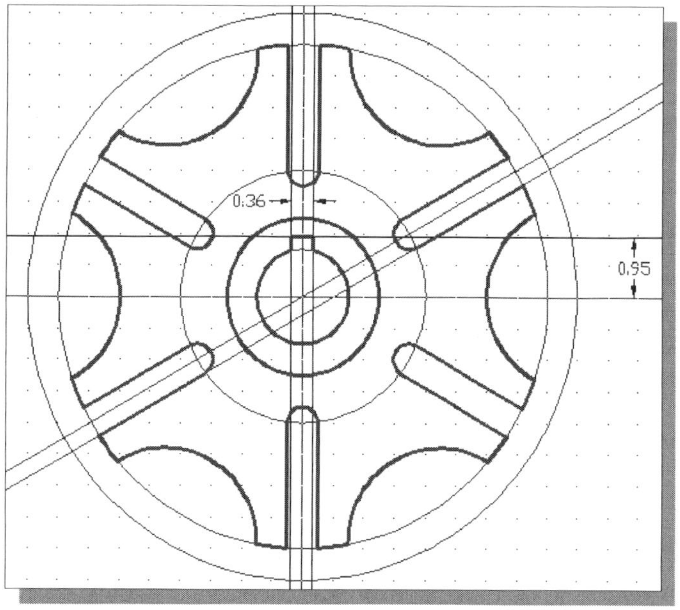

➢ On your own, complete the two views with dimensions. (In the *Dimension Style Manager*, set options under the **Fit** tab to control the appearance of radius and diameter dimensions.)

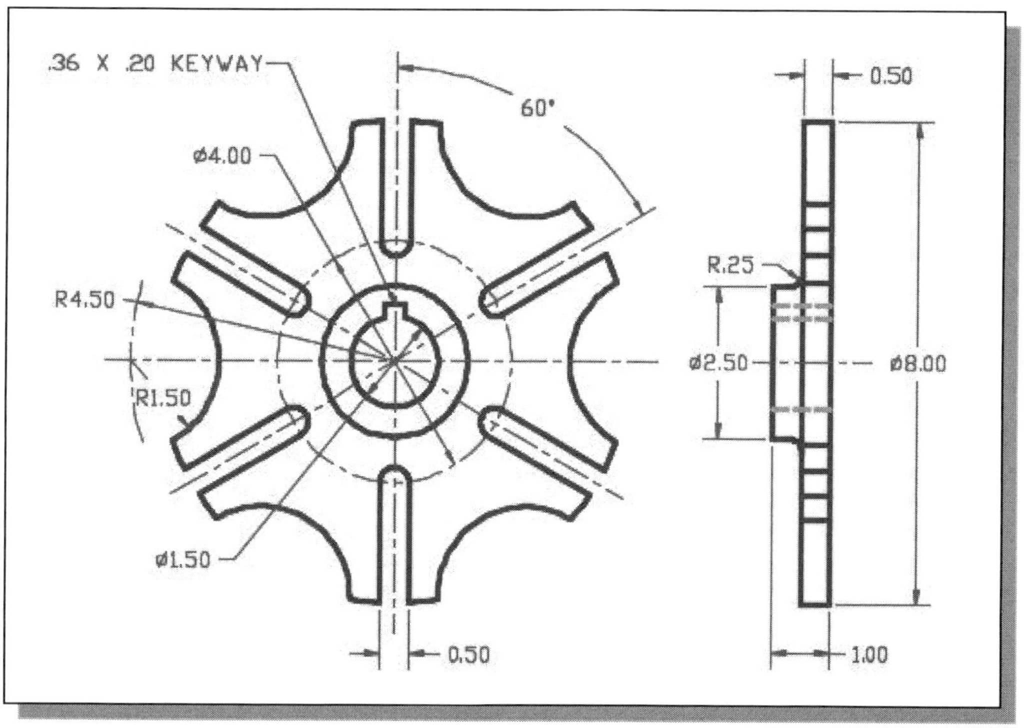

Creating a Viewport Inside the Title Block

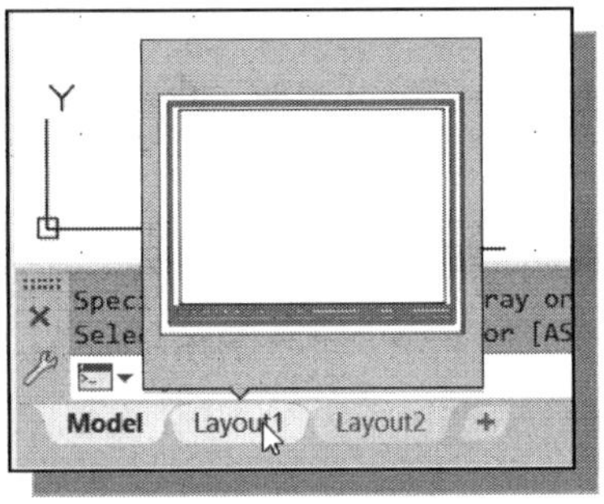

1. Click the **Layout1** tab to switch to the two-dimensional paper space containing the title block.

2. If a view is displayed inside the title block, use the **Erase** command and delete the view by selecting any edge of the **viewport**.

3. Set the ***Viewport*** layer as the *Current Layer*.

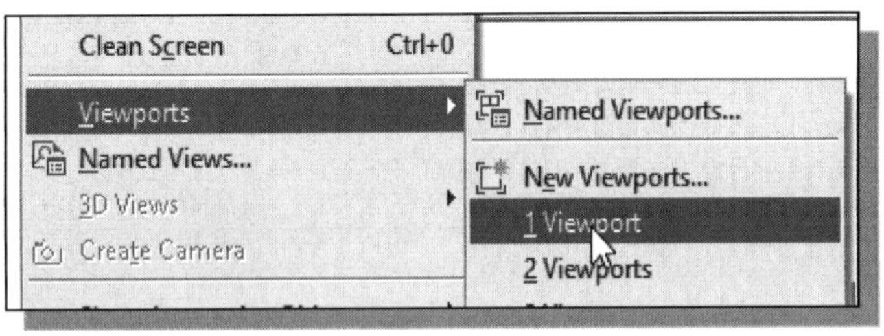

4. In the *Pull-down menu*, select **[View] → [Viewports] →[1 Viewport]**

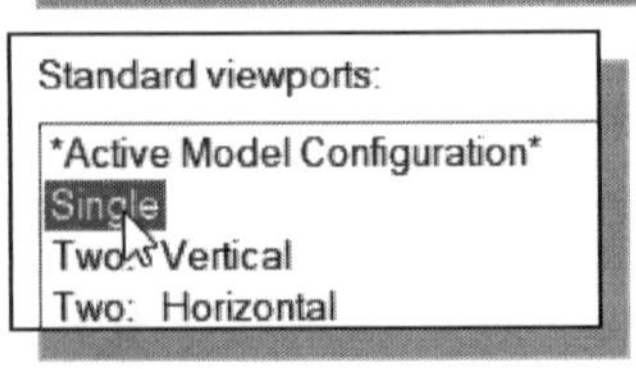

5. Select **Single** in the *Standard viewports* list.

6. Click **OK** to proceed with the creation of the new viewport.

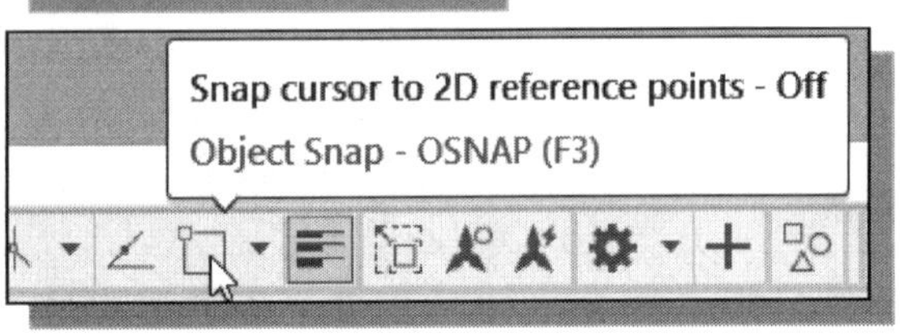

7. In the *Status Bar* area, turn ***OFF*** the *OSNAP* option.

8. Create a viewport inside the title block area as shown.

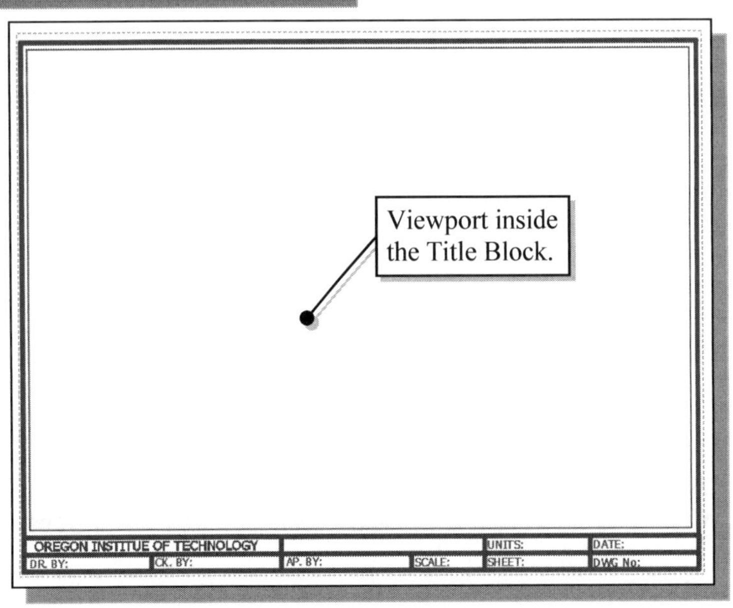

Viewport Properties

1. Pre-select the **viewport** by left-clicking once on any edge of the viewport.

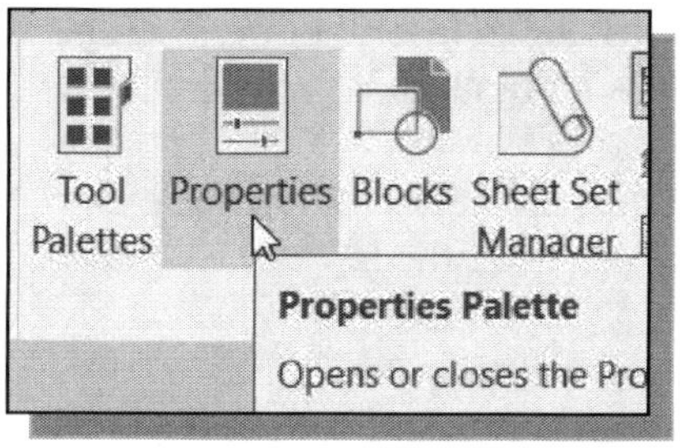

2. Switch to the **View** tab in the *Ribbon toolbars*, and select the **Properties Palette** icon.

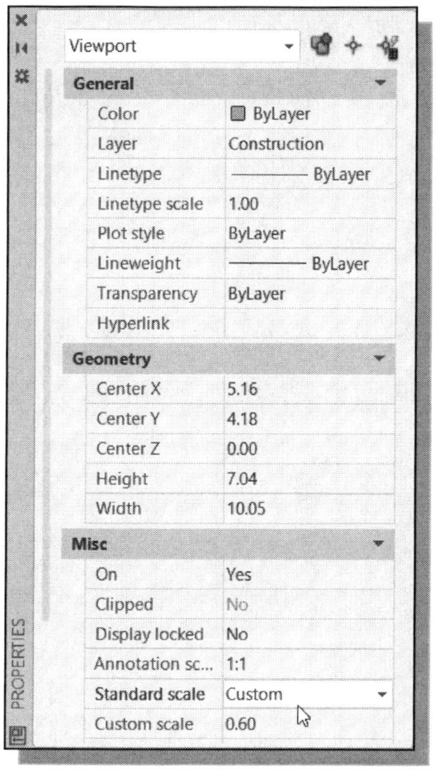

3. In the *Properties* dialog box, scroll down to the bottom of the list. Notice the current scale is set to *Custom*, *0.60*. (The number on your screen might be different.)

4. **Left-click** the *Standard scale* box and notice an arrowhead appears.

5. Click on the **arrowhead button** and a list of standard scales is displayed. Use the scroll bar to look at the list.

6. Set the ***Custom scale*** to **0.5** as shown. This will set the plotting scale factor to half scale.

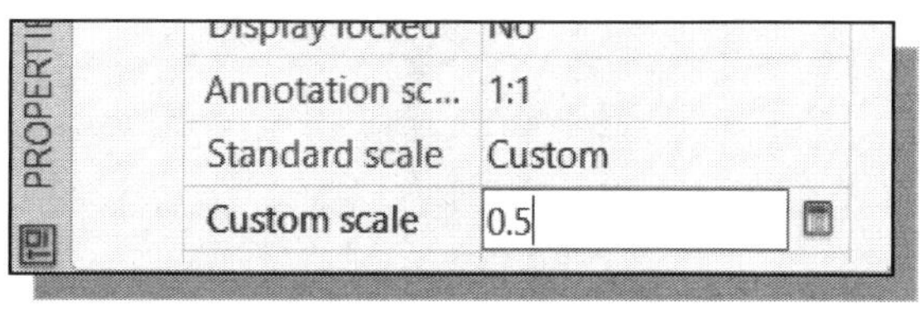

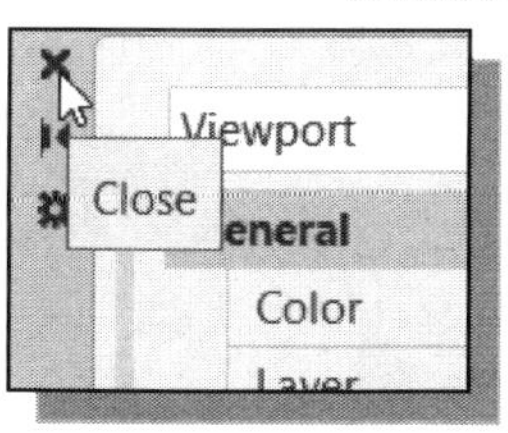

7. Click on the **[X]** button to exit the *Properties* dialog box.

Hide the Viewport Borders

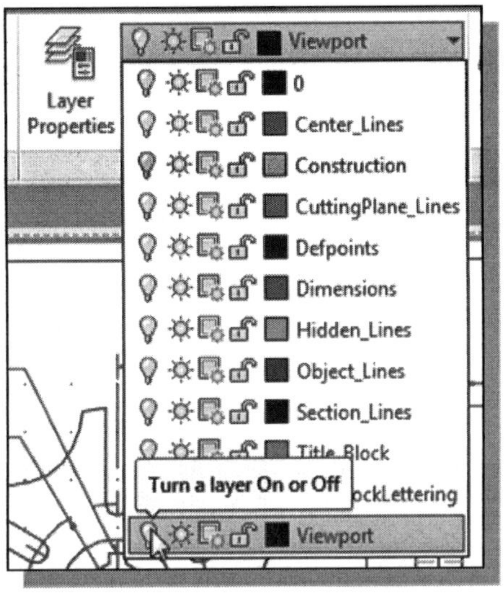

- ❖ We will **turn off** the *viewport borders* so that the lines will not be plotted.

1. With the viewport pre-selected, choose the ***Layer Control*** box with the left-mouse-button.

2. Move the cursor over the name of layer ***Viewport***, **left-click once**, and move the viewport to layer *Viewport.*

3. Turn ***OFF*** layer *Viewport* in the *Layer Control* box.

Adjusting the Dimension Scale

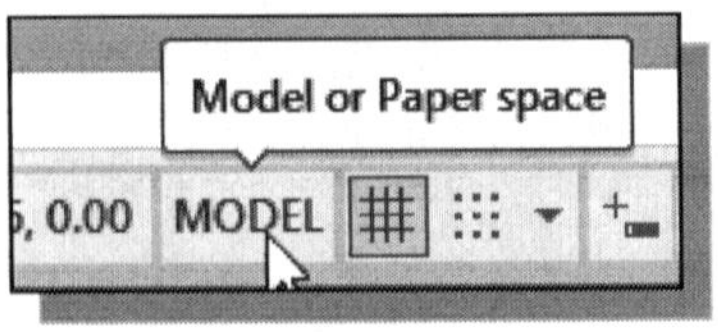

1. Activate the **Model space** in the status toolbar as shown.

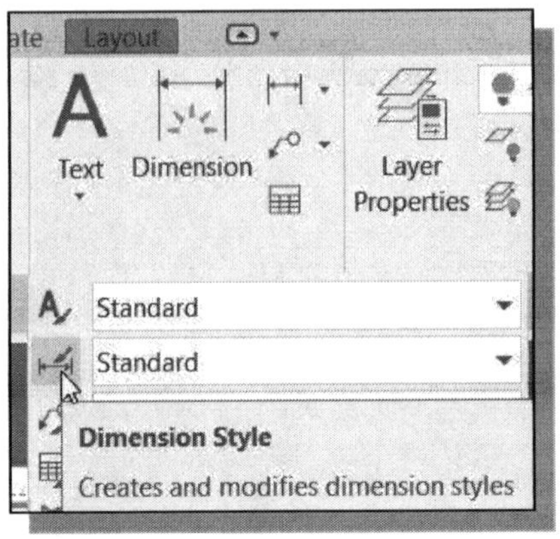

2. Move the cursor to the *Annotation* toolbar area and **left-click** the **down arrow** to display a list of toolbar menu groups.

3. Click on the **Dimension Style** icon.

4. In the *Dimension Style Manager* dialog box, select **Modify**.

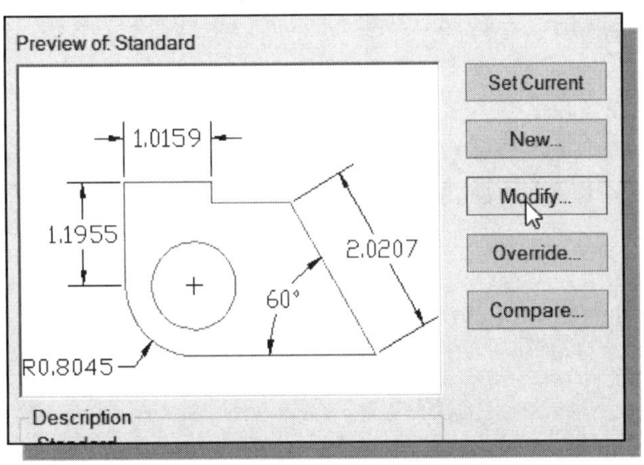

5. Under the **Fit** tab, choose the ***Text*** option in the *Fit options* section and set the overall scale for the dimension features to **2.0** as shown. (Why 2.0? What is the scale of the viewport in Layout1?)

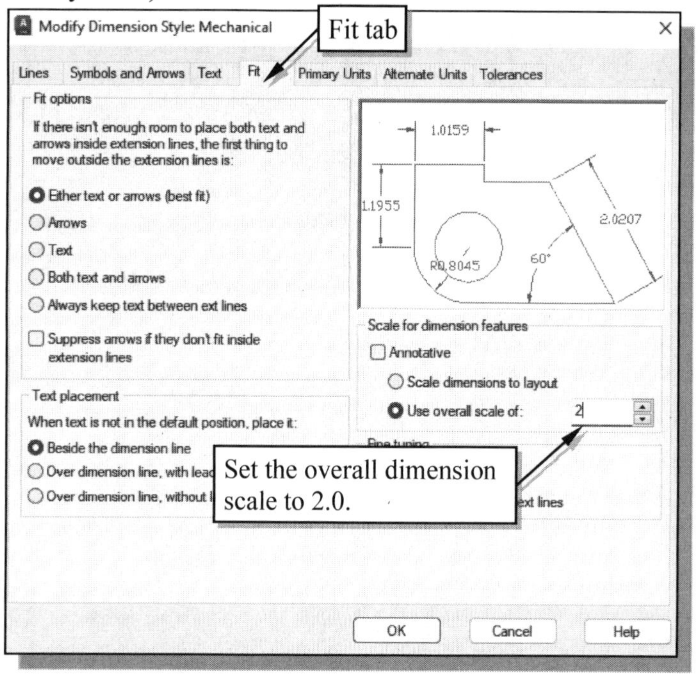

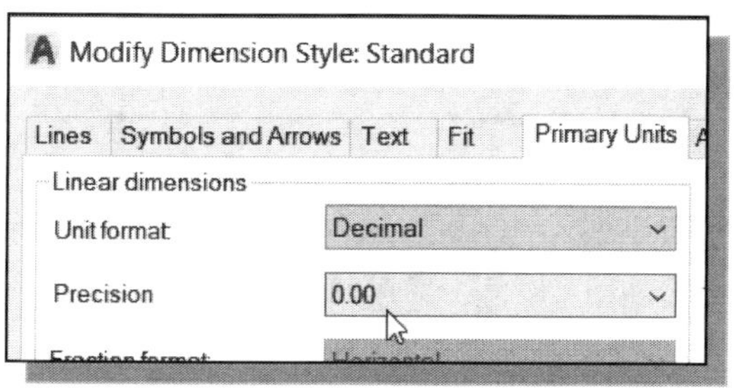

6. Click on the **Primary Units** tab, and set the Precision to two digits after the decimal point.

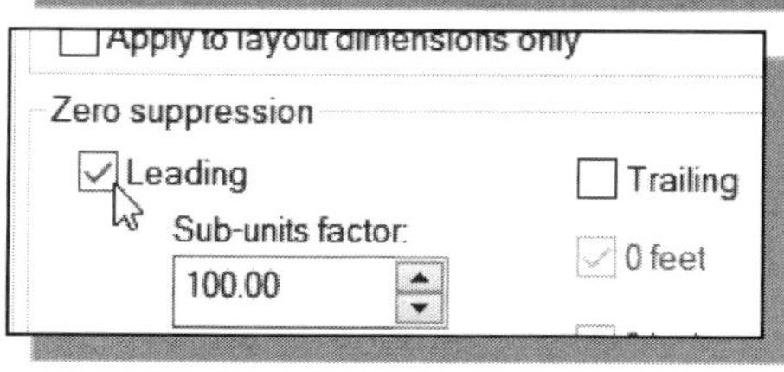

7. Set the *Zero suppression* of linear dimension to **Leading** as shown.

8. Click on the **OK** button to close the *Modify Dimension Style* dialog box.

9. Click on the **Close** button to close the *Dimension Style Manager* dialog box.

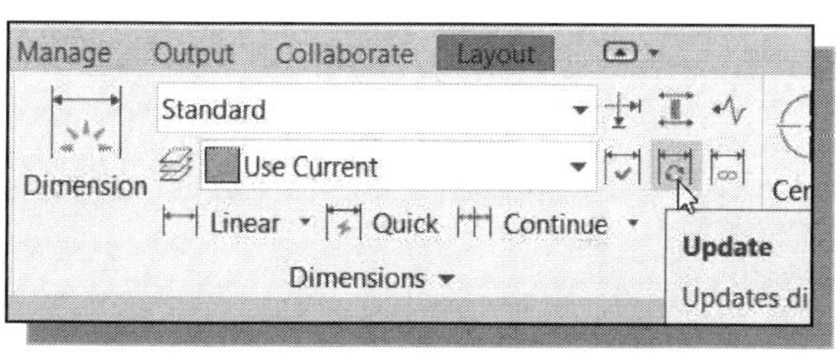

- Note the **Dimension Update** option, located under the **Annotate** tab, is available to apply the current dimension style to specific dimensions.

Plot/Print the Drawing – Color or Grey Scale Prints

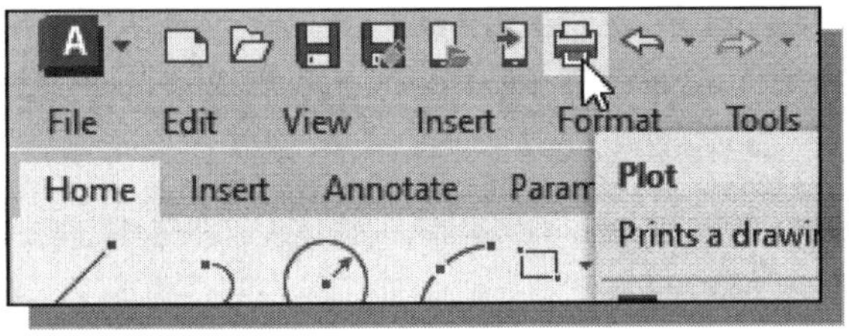

1. In the *Standard* toolbar, select the **Plot** icon.

2. Confirm the proper ***plot device*** is selected.

3. In the *Plot area* section, confirm it is set to ***Layout***.

4. In the *Plot scale* section, confirm it is set to ***1:1***. Our *paper space* is set to the correct paper size.

5. On your own, confirm all of the settings are appropriate for the selected printer/plotter.

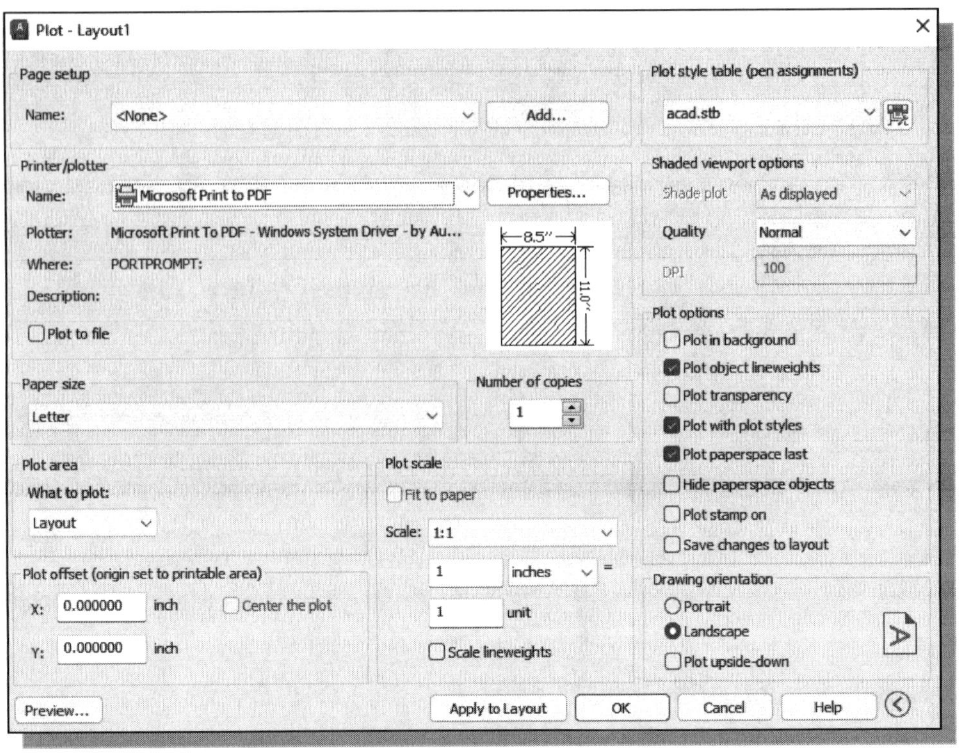

❖ Note the **Preview** option is also available.

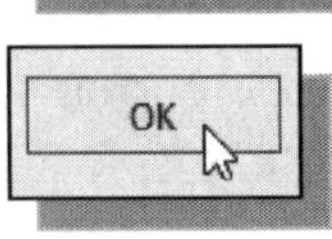

6. Click on the **OK** button to proceed with plotting the drawing.

- Note the current layout is set to print in color or grey scale; for black and white prints refer to the settings on page 10-24.

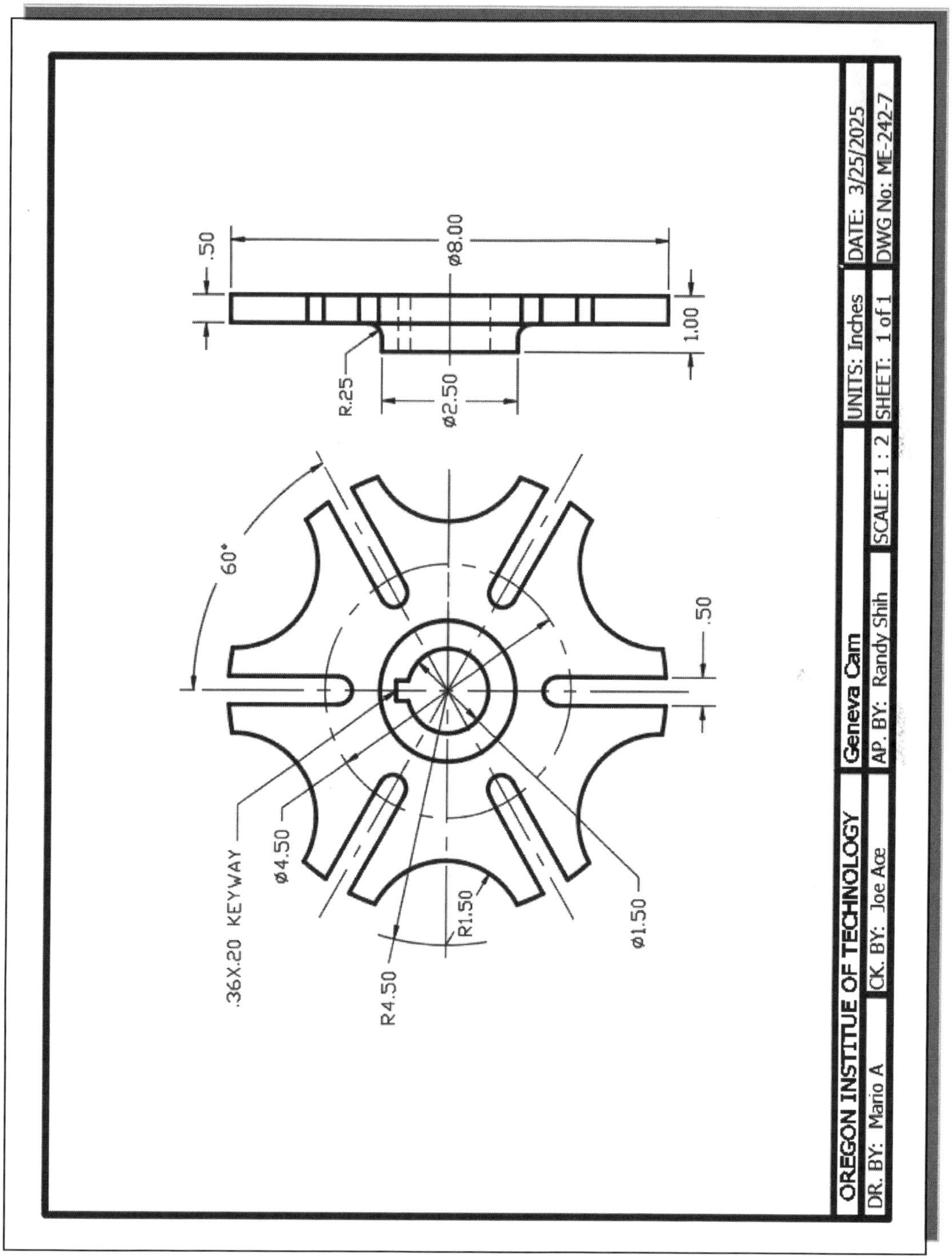

Create a B size Layout of the Design

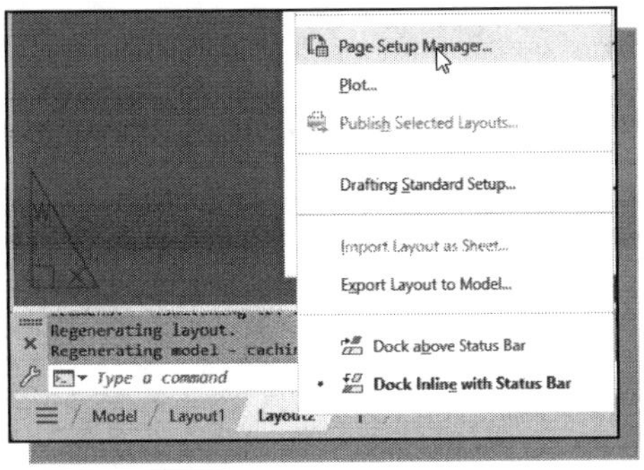

1. Click the **Layout2** tab to switch to the two-dimensional paper space containing the title block.

2. To adjust any *Page Setup* options, right-click once on the tab and select **Page Setup Manager**.

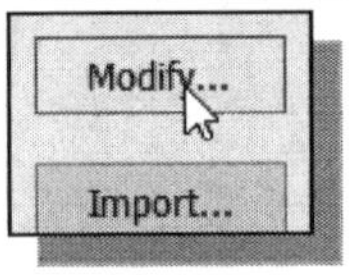

3. Choose the default layout, Layout2, in the *Page Setup Manager* and click **Modify**.

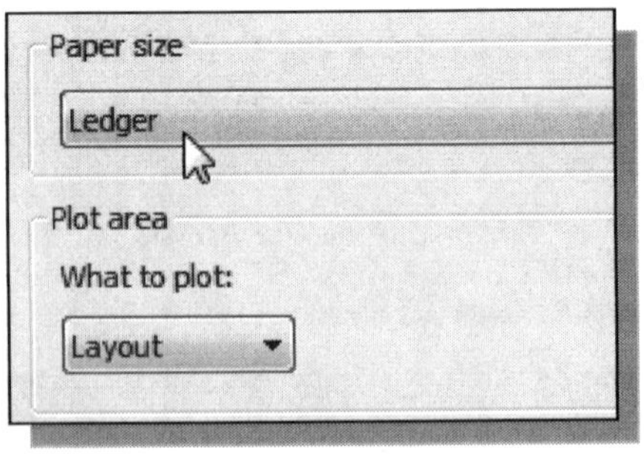

4. Set the *Paper size* to **Ledger** or equivalent (11″ by 17″) and confirm the *Drawing orientation* is set to **Landscape**.

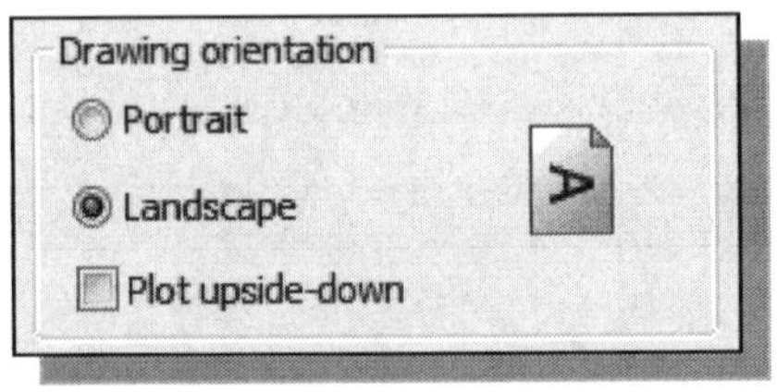

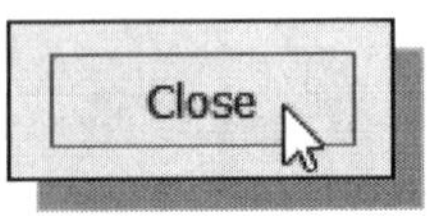

5. Click on the **OK** button and **Close** button to accept the settings and exit the *Page Setup* dialog boxes.

6. On your own, adjust the viewport to fit inside the *11X17* Page as shown. (See page 8-25 on how to set up and adjust a viewport in paper space.)

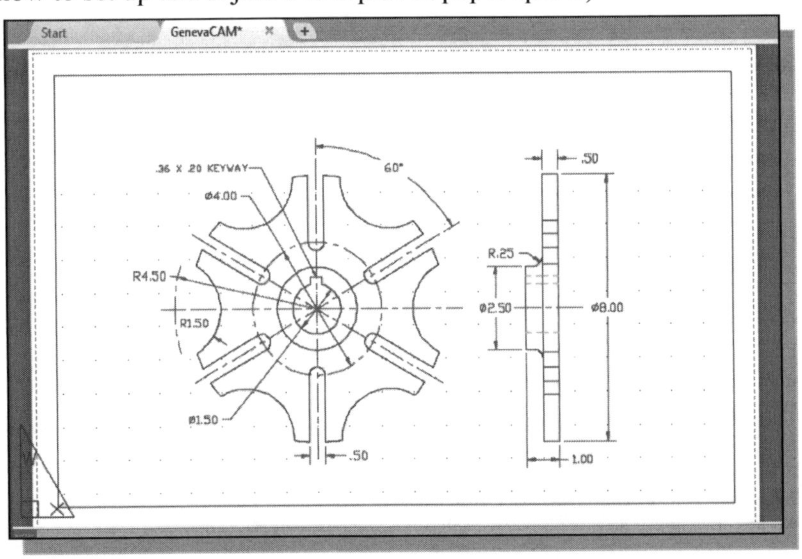

7. Switch to the **Model Space** by clicking on the status tool bar as shown.

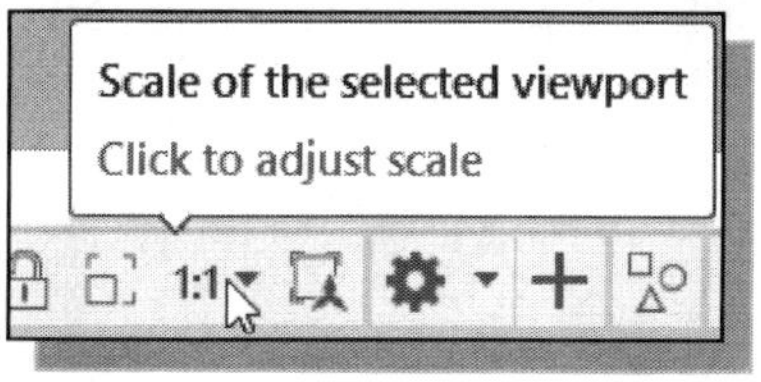

8. In the bottom of the main window, notice the scale of the current viewport is displayed as shown.

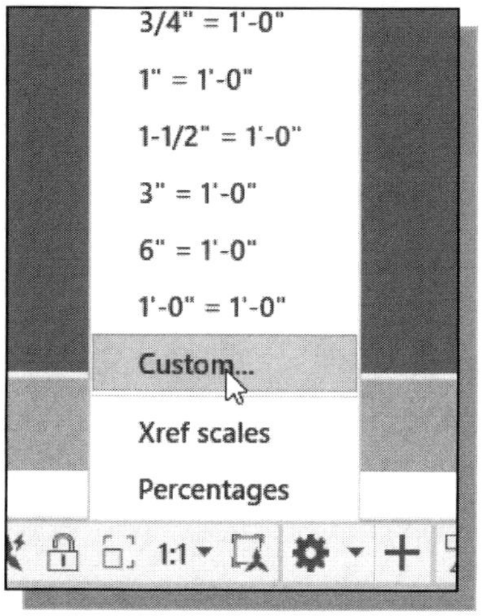

9. Click on the scale of the viewport to display a list of commonly used scales. Note the default *English scale format* is set to architectural style, for example 6" = 1' is really 1/2 scale.

10. Click on **Custom** to bring up the *Edit Drawing Scale* dialog box.

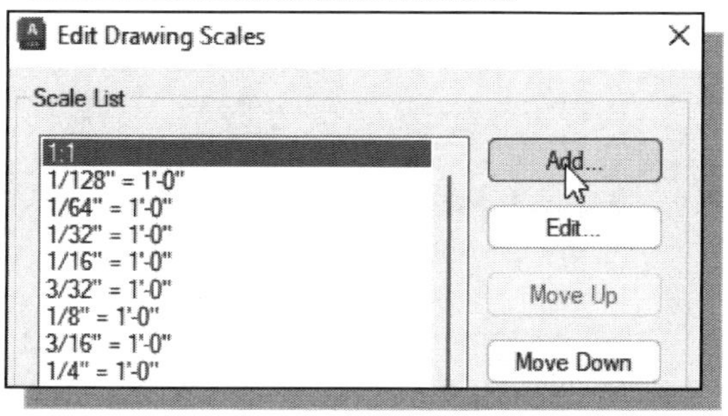

11. In the *Edit Drawing Scale* dialog box, note that we can add more scales to the list and/or edit any of the scales in the list.

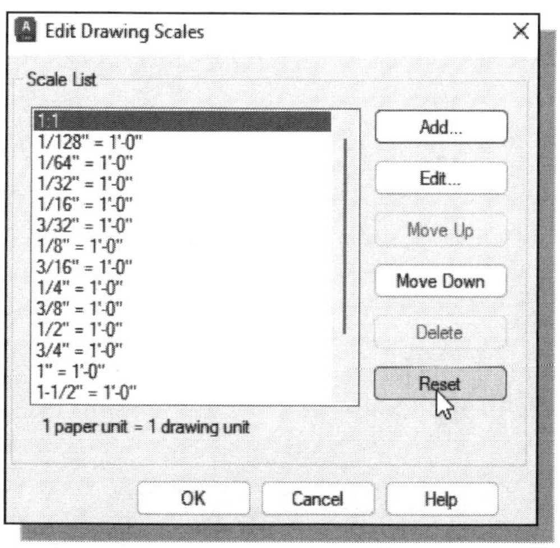

12. Instead of using the architectural scales, we will reset the list to include the basic engineering format. Click **Reset** to enter the reset scale list mode.

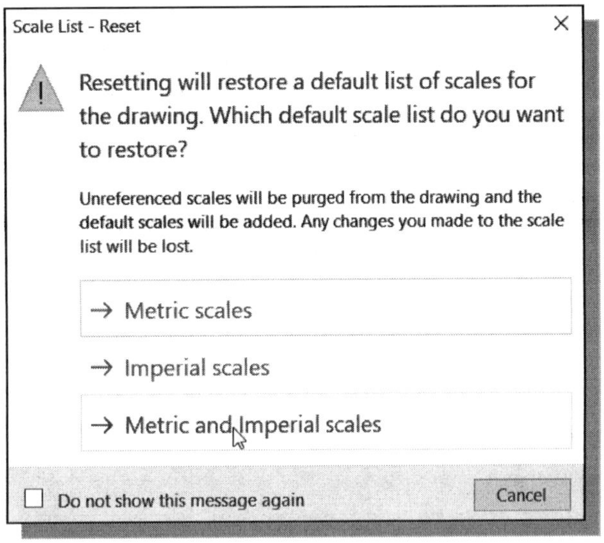

13. In the *Scale List –Reset* dialog box, click on **Metric and Imperial scales** to include both types in the *Scale Display List*.

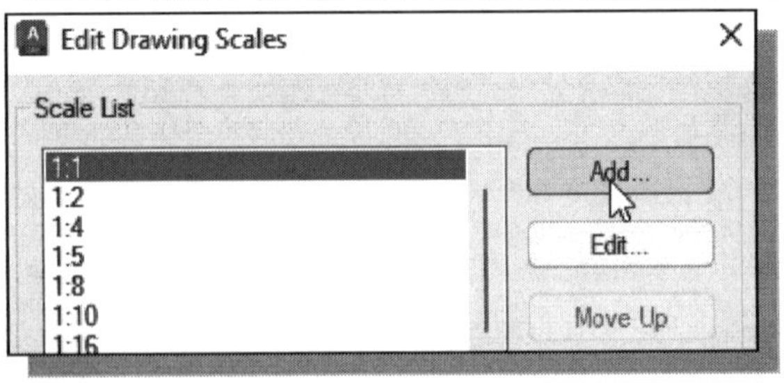

14. In the *Edit Drawing Scales* dialog box, click **ADD** to include a new drawing scale.

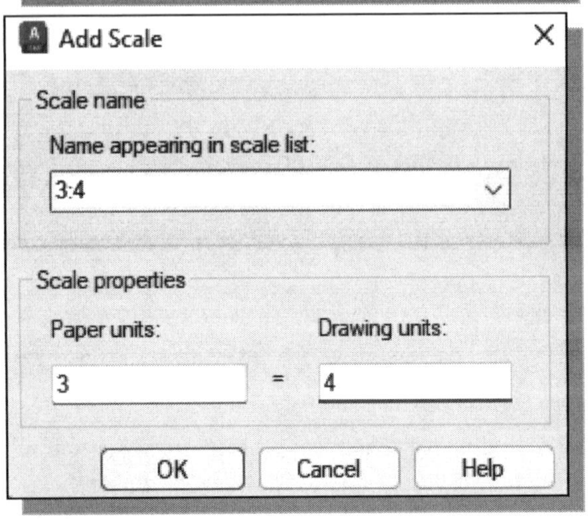

15. Enter **3:4** as the new *Scale name*.

16. Enter **3** as the *Paper units* and **4** as the *Drawing units* as shown.

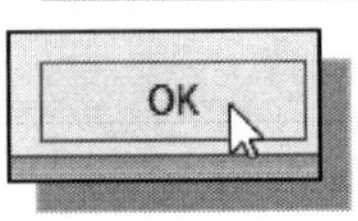

17. Click **OK** to proceed with the creation of the new *Drawing Scale*.

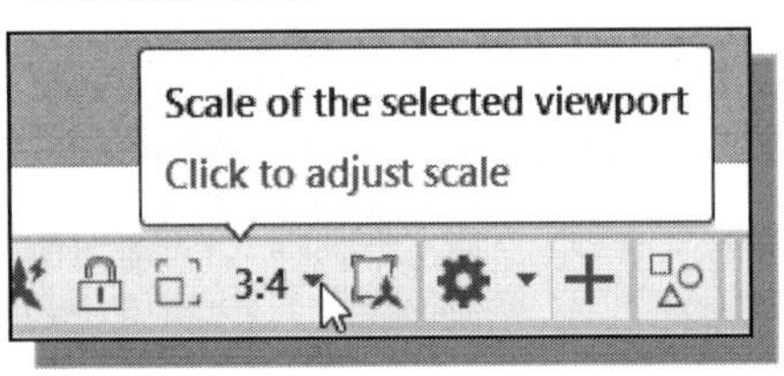

18. In the bottom of the main window, notice the new scale is applied to the current viewport as shown.

19. Switch back to the *Paper Space* by clicking on the **Model Icon** in the status toolbar.

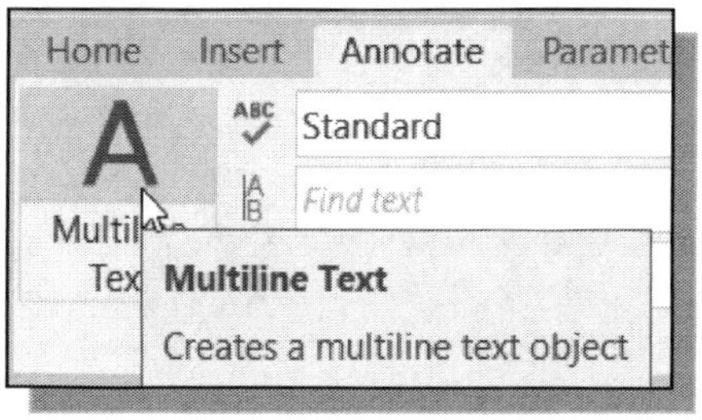

20. On your own, add some text near the bottom of the current layout; set the text height to 0.125.

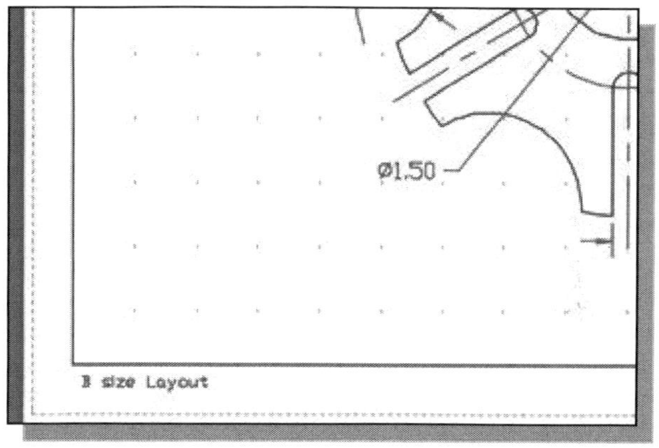

- The text height of the drawing dimensions seems much larger than 1/8 of an inch. What happened?

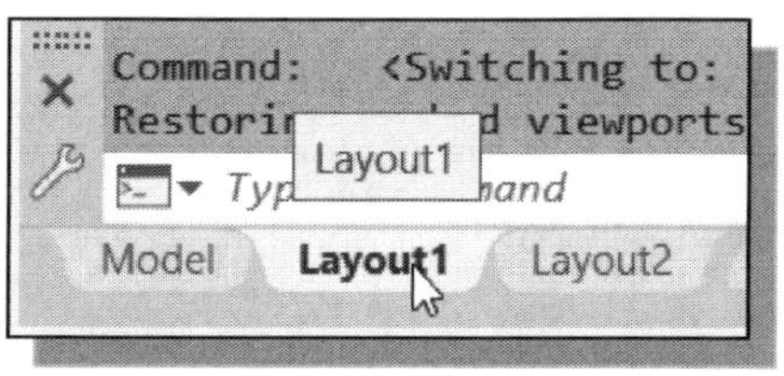

21. Click the **Layout1** tab to switch to the A size layout we created.

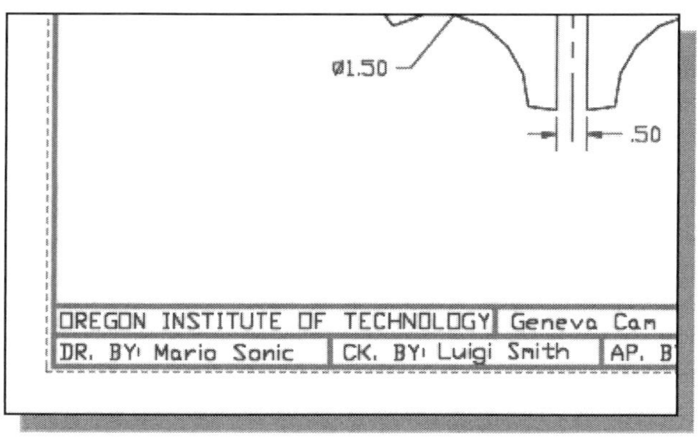

- Note the text height of the drawing dimensions matches the 1/8 of an inch text height in the title block.

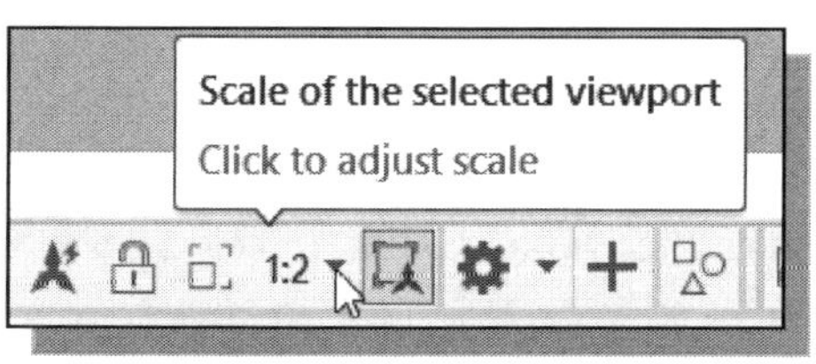

22. On your own, switch to the *Model Space* by clicking on the **Model Icon** in the status toolbar, and notice the scale of the selected viewport in ***Layout1*** is set to **1/2** scale.

- The text height of the drawing dimensions was set based on the viewport scale in Layout1; refer to page 8-25 and page 8-27 on the set up of the two scales.

Adjust the Dimension Scale for the B size Print

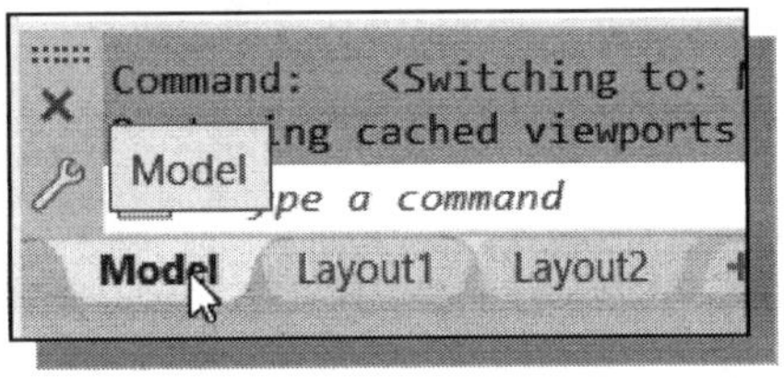

1. Click the **Model** tab to switch back to *Model Space*.

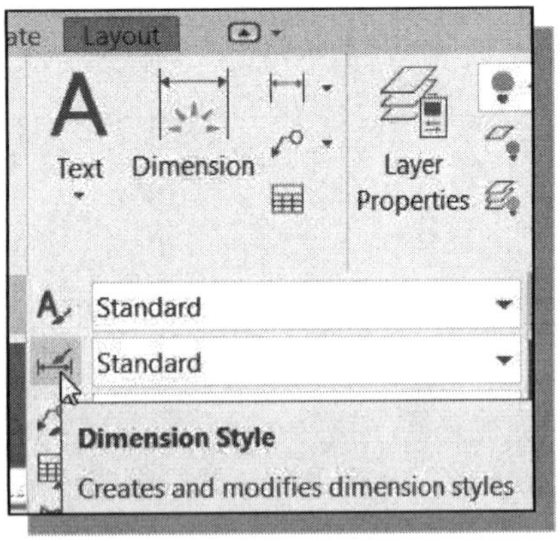

2. Move the cursor to the *Annotation* toolbar area and **left-click** the **down arrow** to display a list of toolbar menu groups.

3. Click on the **Dimension Style** icon.

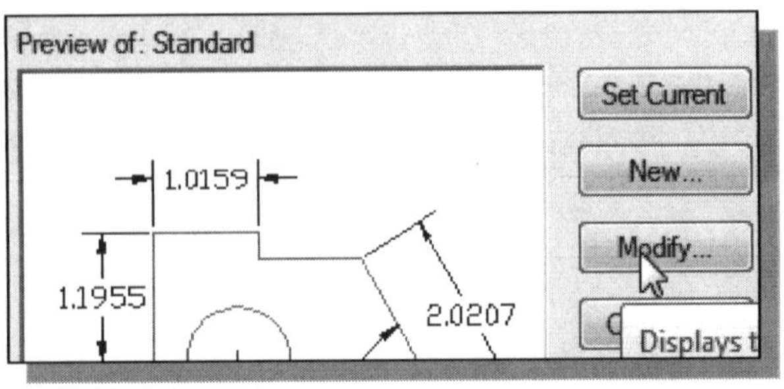

4. In the *Dimension Style Manager* dialog box, select **Modify**.

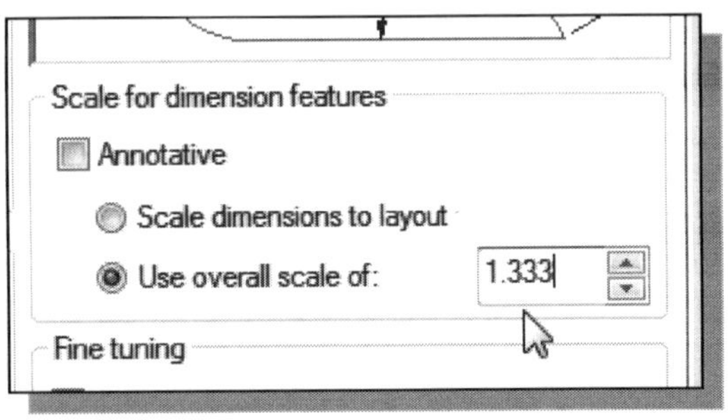

5. Under the **Fit** tab, choose the ***Text*** option in the *Fit options* section and set the overall scale for the dimension features to **1.333** as shown.

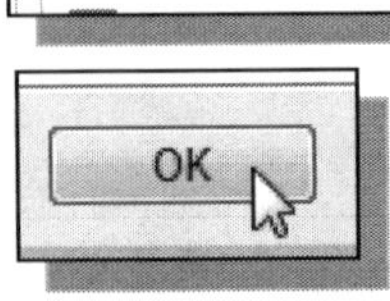

6. Click on the **OK** button to close the *Modify Dimension Style* dialog box.

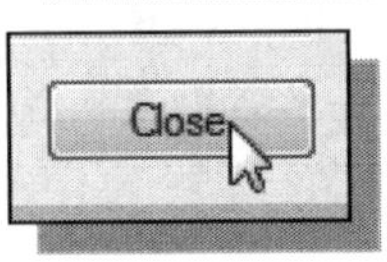

7. Click on the **Close** button to close the *Dimension Style Manager* dialog box.

- Note the text height of the drawing dimensions has been adjusted to the scale of **4/3**; this number came from the inverse of the viewport scale of **3/4**.

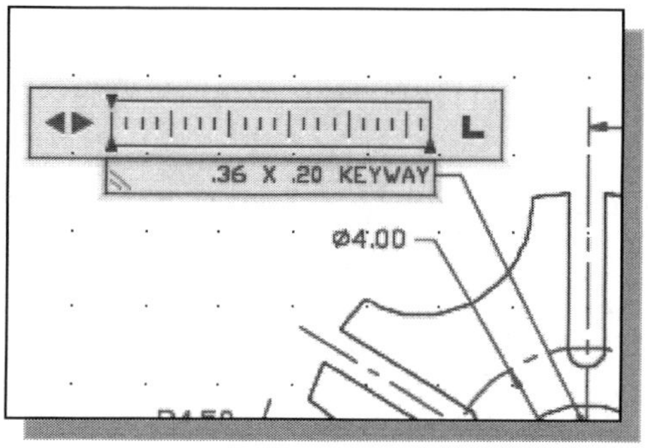

8. Double click on the local note for the keyway to enter the **Text Editor** mode as shown.

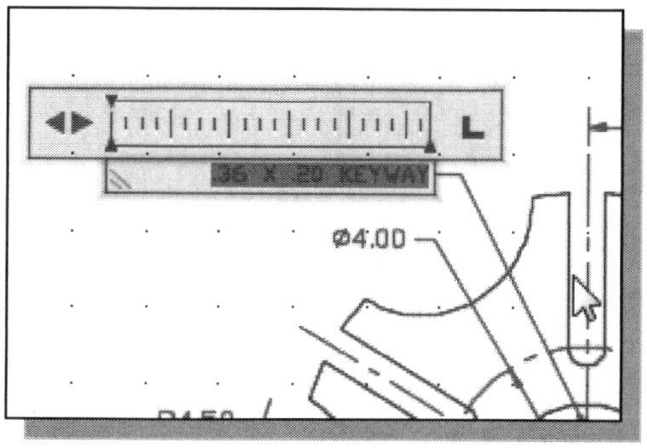

9. Select all of the text in the *Text Edit* box as shown.

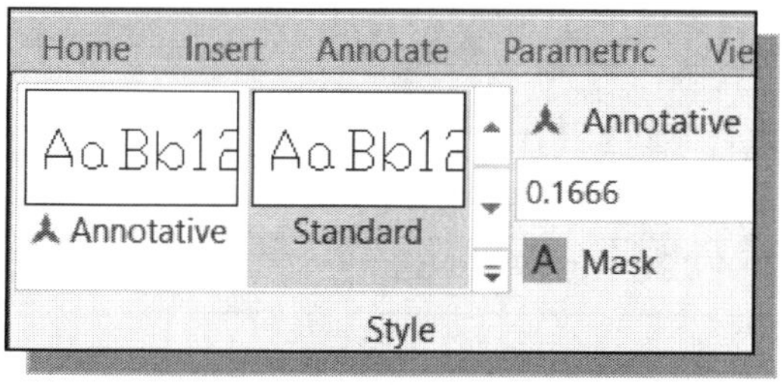

10. On your own, adjust the text height to **0.166** as shown. (Hit the **Enter** key once to make the change.)

- Note the text height is adjusted based on the viewport scale **0.125 X 1.333 = 0.1666**.

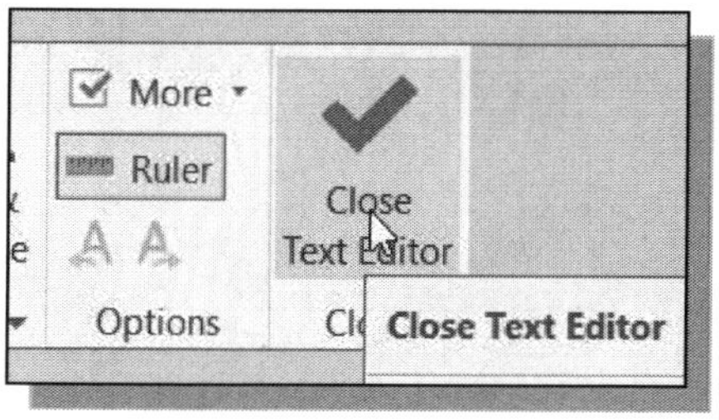

11. Click **Close Text Editor** to accept the adjustment and exit the Text Editor.

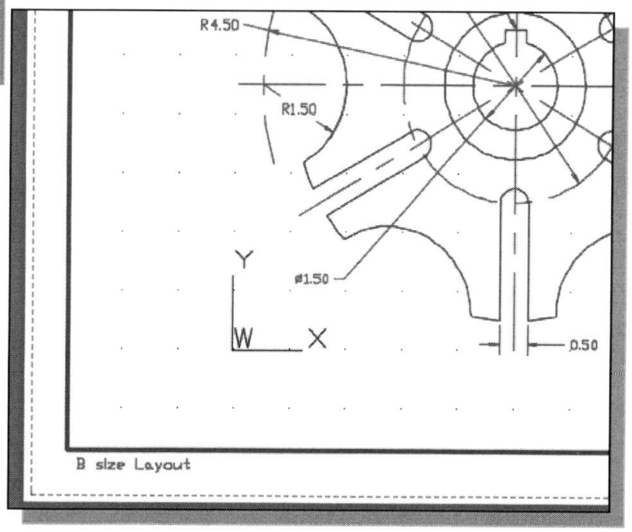

12. On your own, print a copy of the B size layout and confirm the text height is 1/8 of an inch.

Additional Title Blocks

Drawing Paper and Border Sizes

The standard drawing paper sizes are as shown in the below tables. The edges of the title block border are generally 0.5 ~ 1 inches or 10~20 mm from the edges of the paper.

American National Standard	Suggested Border Size
A – 8.5″ X 11.0″	A – 7.75″ X 10.25″
B – 11.0″ X 17.0″	B – 10.0″ X 16.0″
C – 17.0″ X 22.0″	C – 16.0″ X 21.0″
D – 22.0″ X 34.0″	D – 21.0″ X 33.0″
E – 34.0″ X 44.0″	E – 33.0″ X 43.0″

International Standard	Suggested Border Size
A4 – 210 mm X 297 mm	A4 – 190 mm X 276 mm
A3 – 297 mm X 420 mm	A3 – 275 mm X 400 mm
A2 – 420 mm X 594 mm	A2 – 400 mm X 574 mm
A1 – 594 mm X 841 mm	A1 – 574 mm X 820 mm
A0 – 841 mm X 1189 mm	A0 – 820 mm X 1168 mm

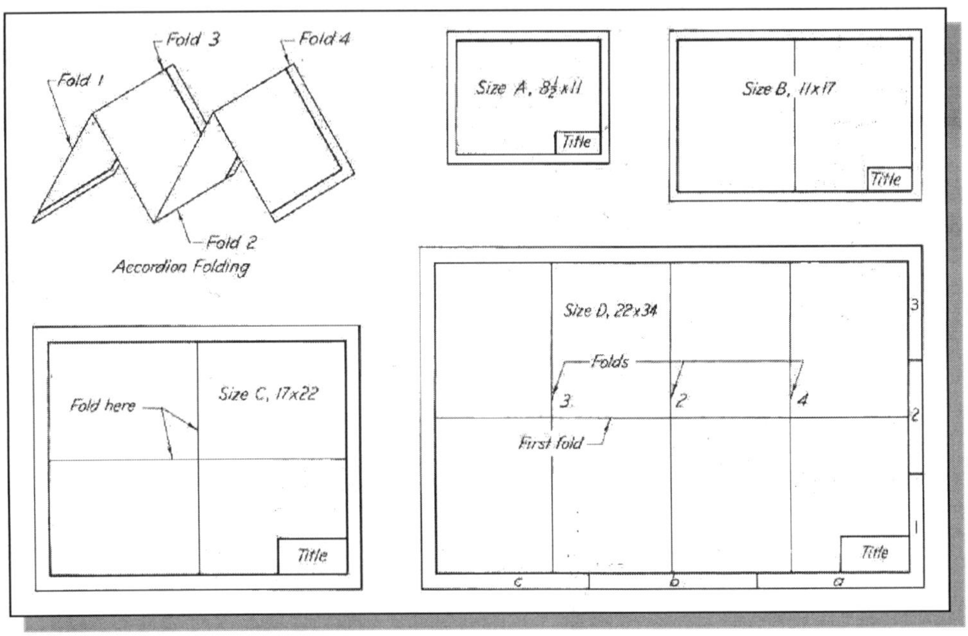

- **English Title Block** (For A size paper, main units are in inches)

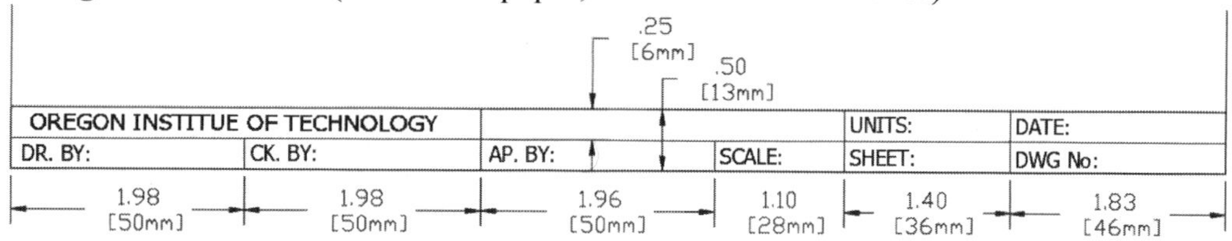

- **Metric Title Block** (For A4 size paper, main units are in mm.)

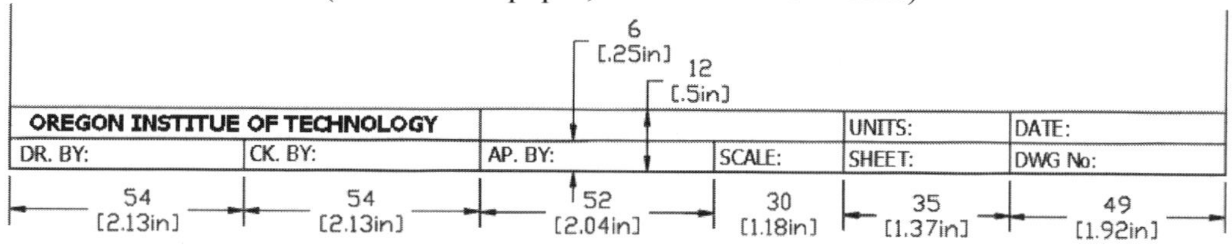

- **English Title Block** (For B size or larger paper, dimensions are in inches.)

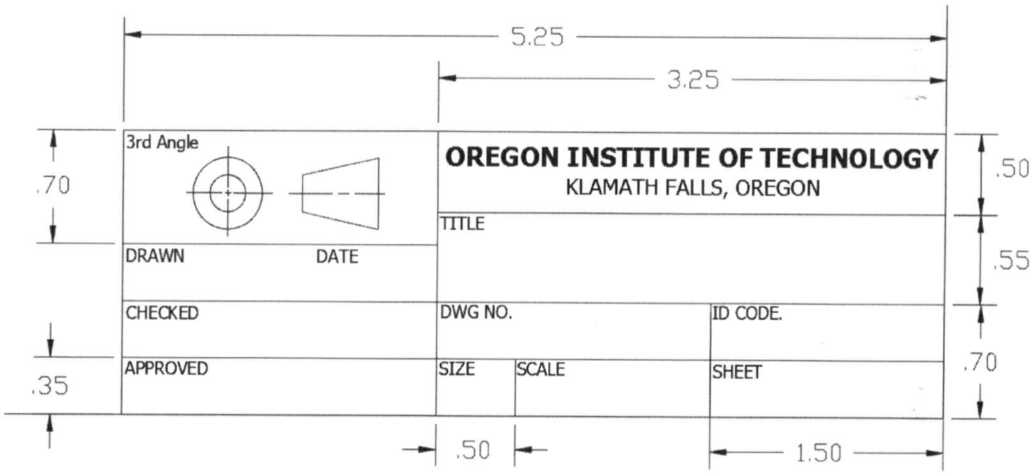

- **Metric Title Block** (For A3 size or larger paper, dimensions are in mm.)

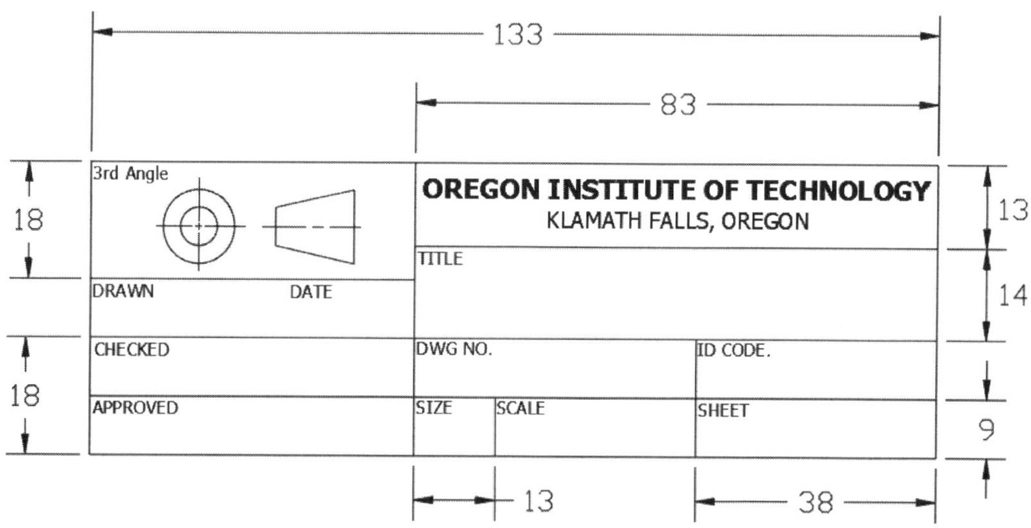

Review Questions: (Time: 25 minutes)

1. List and describe three advantages of using *template files*.
2. Describe the items that were included in the *Acad-A-H-Title* template file.
3. List and describe two methods of creating copies of existing objects in **AutoCAD 2027**.
4. Describe the procedure in determining the scale factor for plotting an **AutoCAD 2027** layout.
5. What is the difference between the AutoCAD *Model Space* and the *Paper Space*?
6. Why should we use the AutoCAD *Paper Space*?
7. What does the *ORTHO* option allow us to do?
8. Which AutoCAD command allows us to view and change properties of constructed geometric objects?
9. What is the difference between an AutoCAD drawing file (.dwg) and an AutoCAD template file (.dwt)?
10. What does the **Divide** command allow us to do?
11. Similar to the **Trim** command, the **Break** command can also be used to remove a portion of an object. Create 3 arbitrary lines as shown and remove the middle portion of the line, defined by the two intersecting lines, using the Break command.

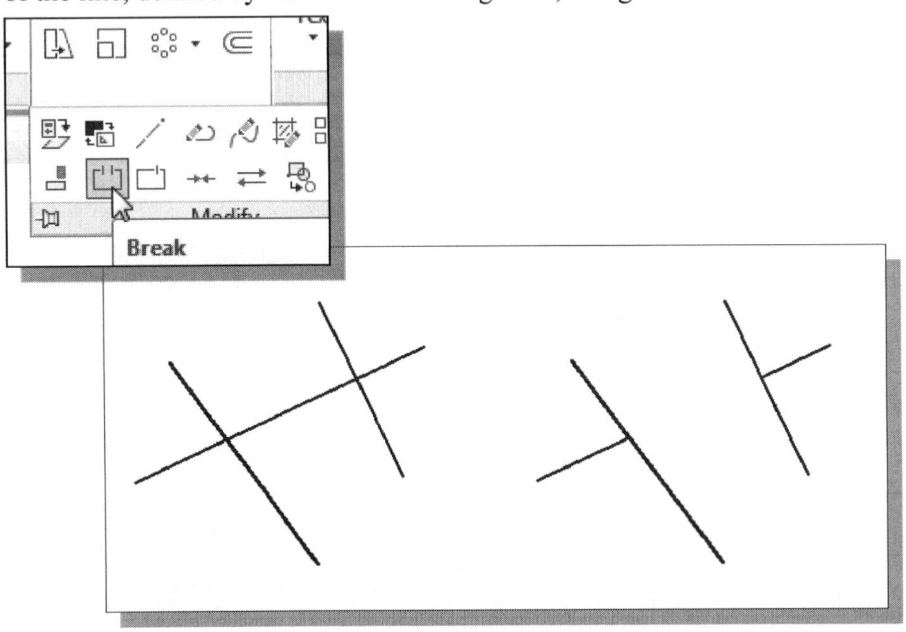

Exercises: (Time: 200 minutes)

(Unless otherwise specified, dimensions are in inches.)

1. Ratchet Plate (Thickness: 0.125 inch)

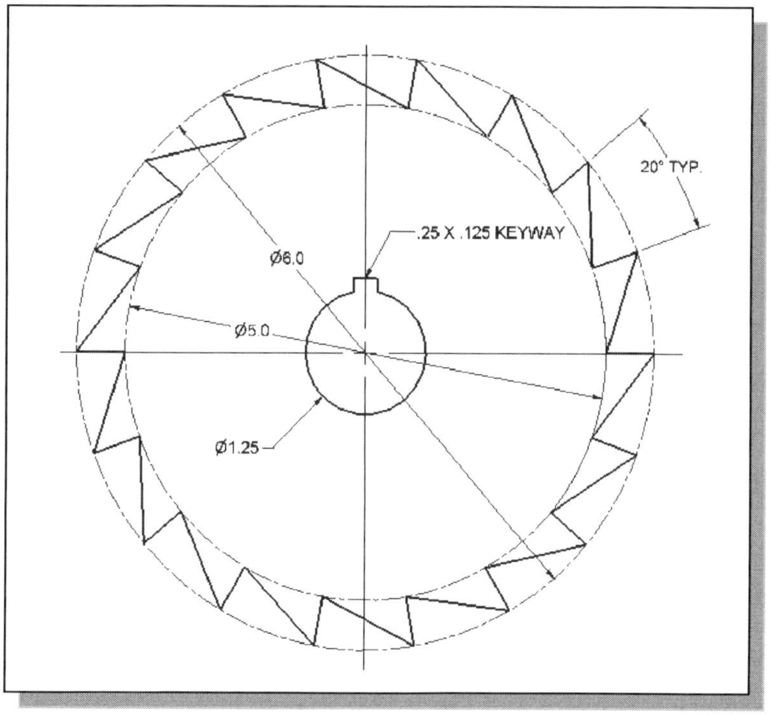

2. Switch Base

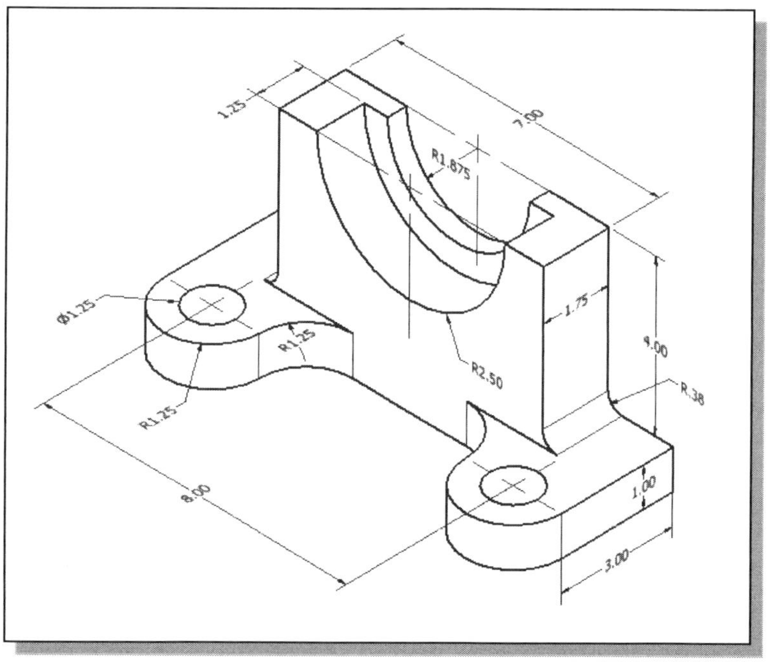

3. Auxiliary Support

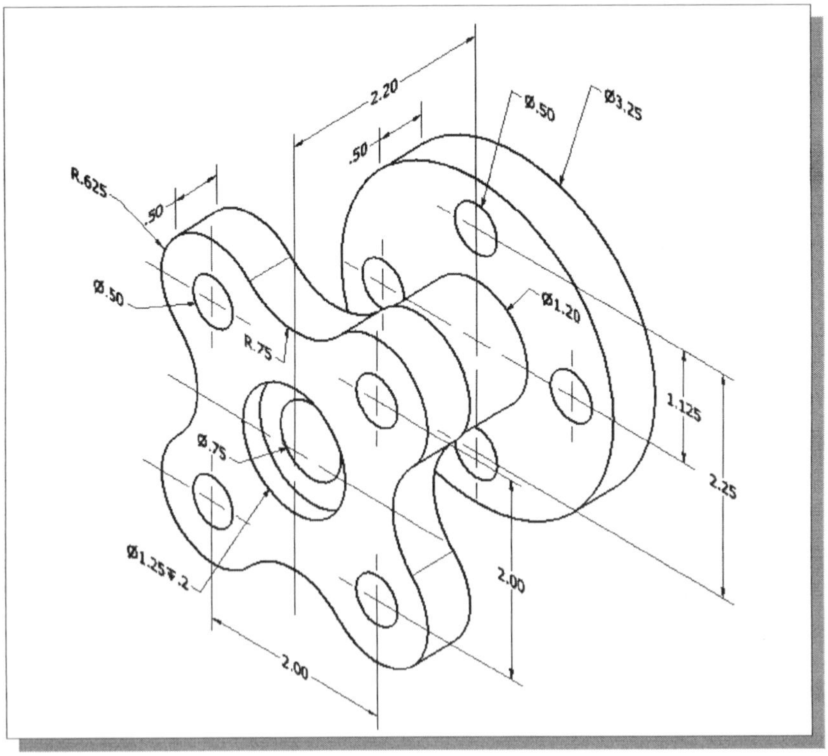

4. Indexing Guide

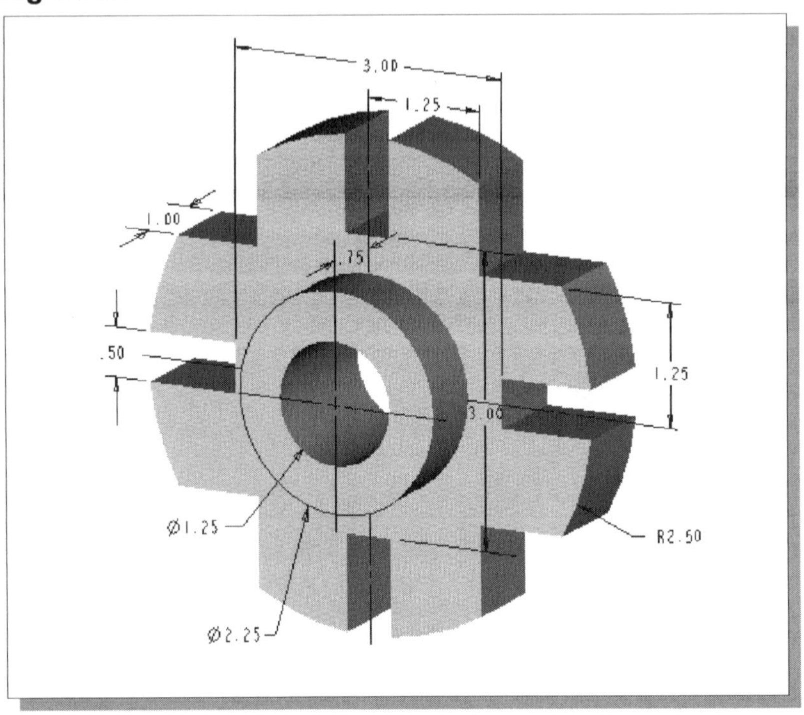

5. Coupling Base

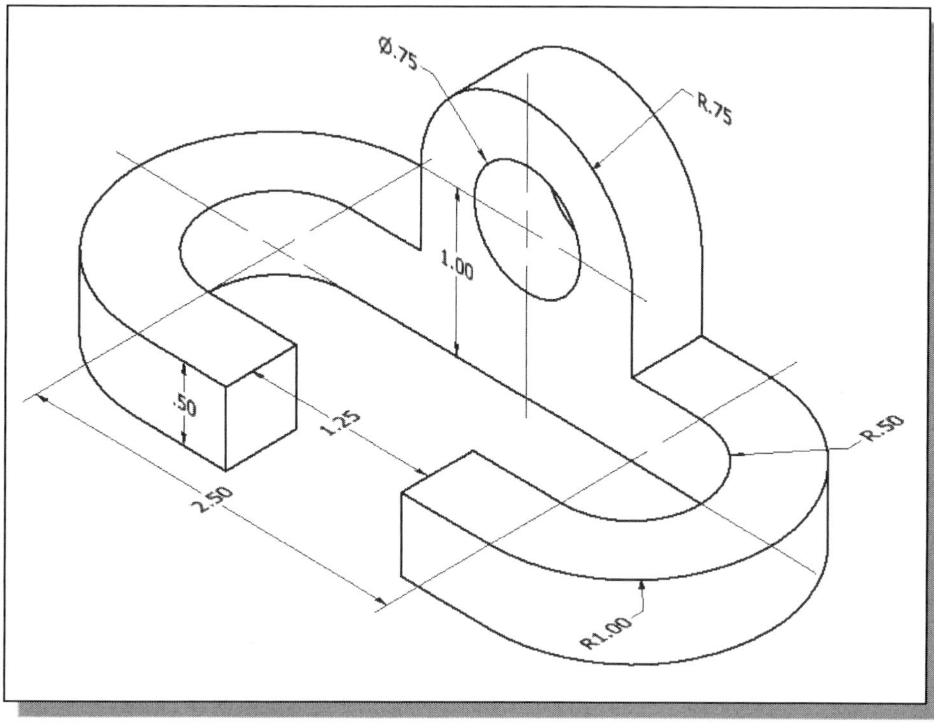

6. Anchor Base

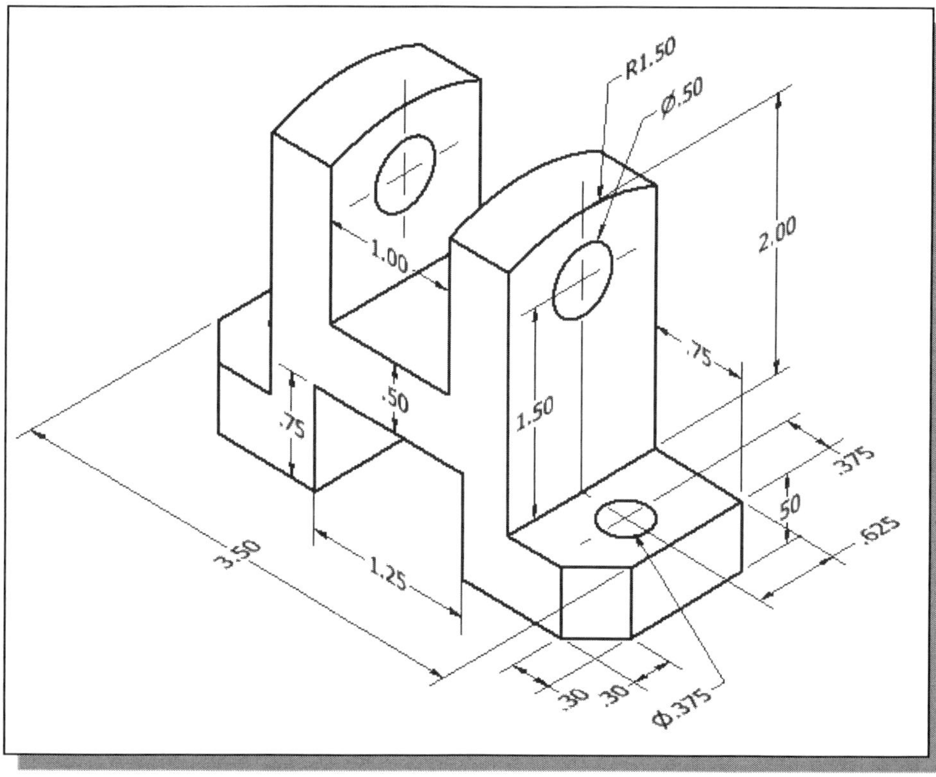

7. Intake Flange

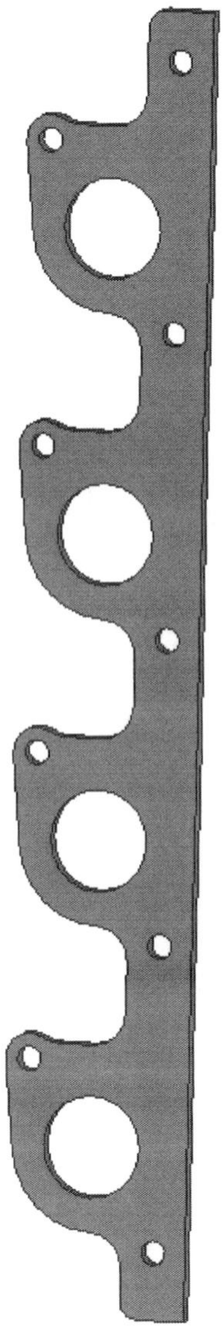

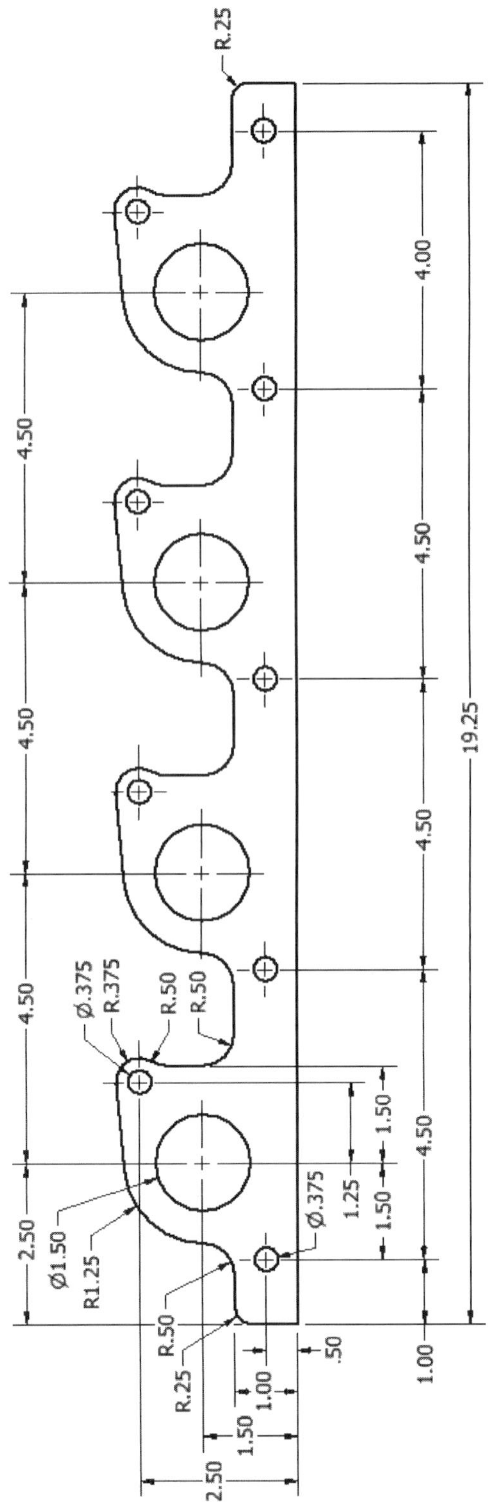

Chapter 10
Auxiliary Views

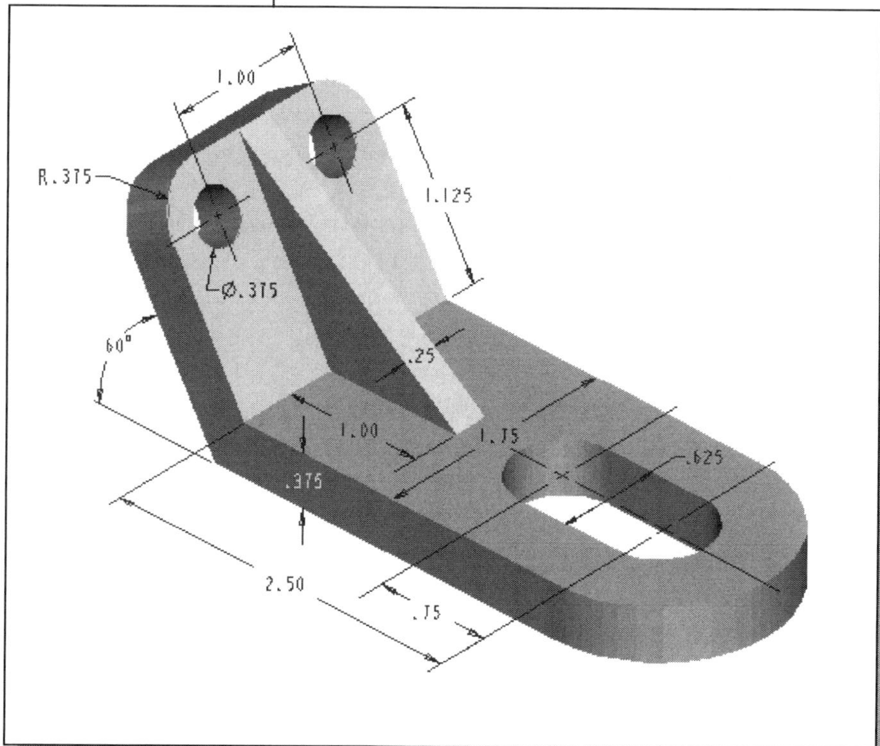

Learning Objectives

- ♦ Understand the Principles of Creating Auxiliary Views
- ♦ Use 2D Projection Method to Draw Auxiliary Views
- ♦ Create Rectangles
- ♦ Use the Basic Grips Editing Commands
- ♦ Set up and use the Polar Tracking Option
- ♦ Create Multiple Viewports in Paper Space

AutoCAD Certified User Examination Objectives Coverage

Section 2: Creating Basic Drawings

Section 3: Manipulating Objects

Section 4: Drawing Organization and Inquiry Commands

Section 5: Altering Objects

Section 12: Plotting Your Drawings

Introduction

An important rule concerning multiview drawings is to draw enough views to accurately describe the design. This usually requires two or three of the regular views, such as a front view, a top view and/or a side view.

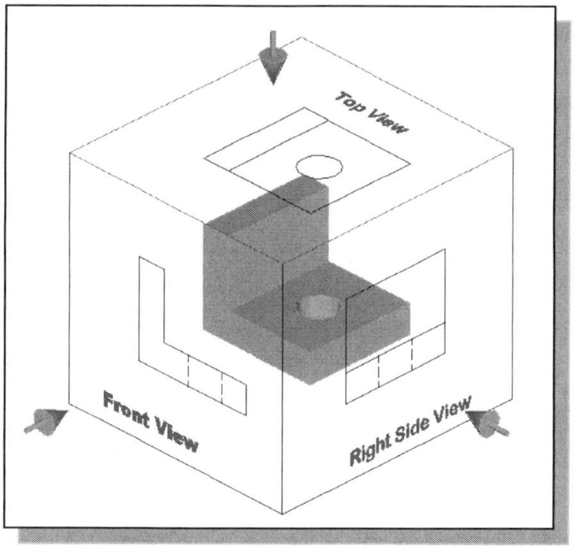

In the left figure, the L-shaped object is placed with the surfaces parallel to the principal planes of projection. The top, front and right side views show the true shape of the different surfaces of the object. Note especially that planes of projection are parallel to the top, front and right side of the object.

Based on the principle of orthographic projection, it is clear that a plane surface is shown in true shape when the direction of view is perpendicular to the surface.

Many designs have features located on inclined surfaces that are not parallel to the regular planes of projection. To truly describe the feature, the true shape of the feature must be shown using an **auxiliary view**. An *auxiliary view* has a line of sight that is perpendicular to the inclined surface, as viewed looking directly at the inclined surface. An *auxiliary view* is a supplementary view that can be constructed from any of the regular views. A primary *auxiliary view* is projected onto a plane that is perpendicular to one of the principal planes of projection and is inclined to the other two. A secondary *auxiliary view* is projected onto a plane that is inclined to all three principal planes of projection. In the figures below, the use of the standard views does not show the true shape of the upper feature of the design; the use of an auxiliary view provided the true shape of the feature and also eliminated the need of front and right side views.

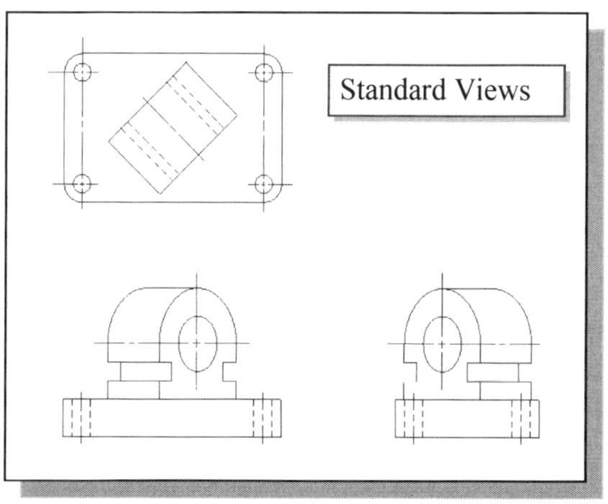

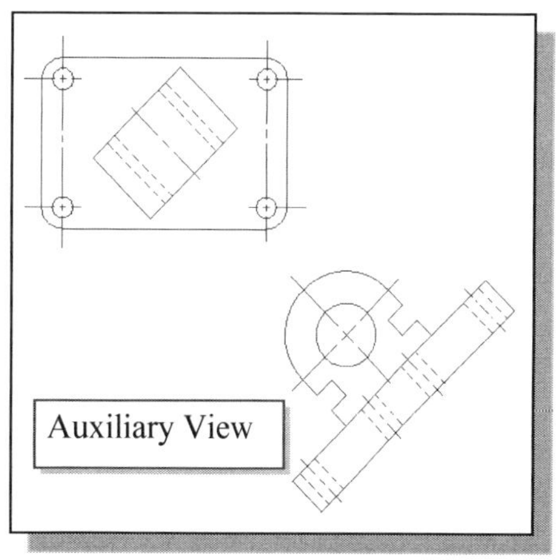

Normal View of an Inclined Surface

No matter what the position of a surface may be, the fundamentals of projecting a normal view of the surface remain the same: **The projection plane is placed parallel to the surface to be projected. The line of sight is set to be perpendicular to the projection plane and therefore perpendicular to the surface to be projected.** This type of view is known as **normal view**. In geometry, the word "*normal*" means "*perpendicular.*"

In the figure below, the design has an inclined face that is inclined to the horizontal and profile planes and **perpendicular to the frontal plane**.

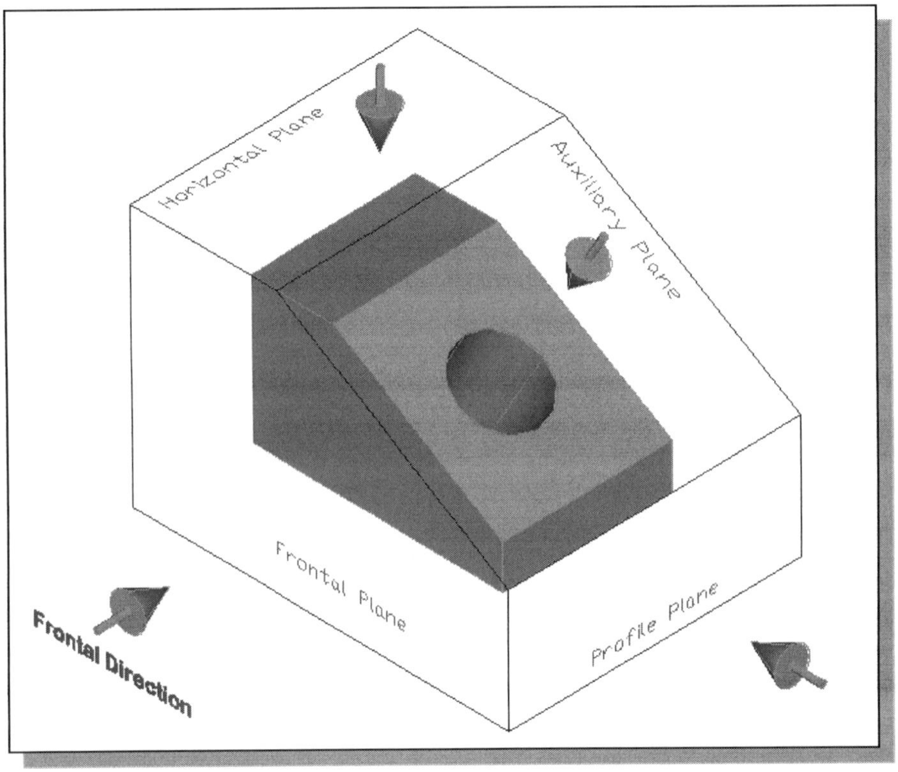

The principal views (Top, Front and Right side views) do not show the **true size and shape** of the inclined surface. Note the inclined surface does appear as an edge in the front view. To show the true size and shape of the inclined surface, a *normal* view is needed.

To get the normal view of the inclined surface, a projection is made perpendicular to the surface. This projection is made from the view where the surface shows as an edge, in this case, the front view. The perpendicularity between the surface and the line of sight is seen in true relationship in the 2D views. These types of extra normal views are known as **auxiliary views** to distinguish them from the principal views. However, since an auxiliary is made for the purpose of showing the true shape of a surface, the terms *normal view* and *edge view* are also used to describe the relations of the views.

An auxiliary is constructed following the rules of orthographic projection. An auxiliary view is aligned to the associated views, in this case, the front view. The line of sight is perpendicular to the edge view of the surface, as shown in the below figures.

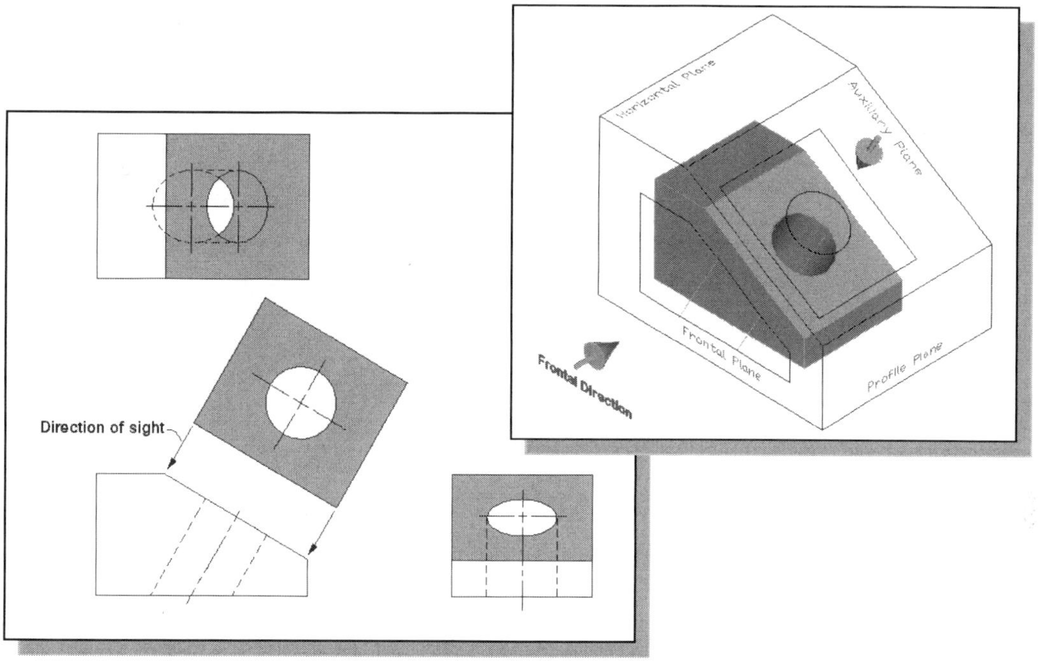

The orientation of the inclined surface may be different, but the direction of the normal view remains the same as shown in the below figures.

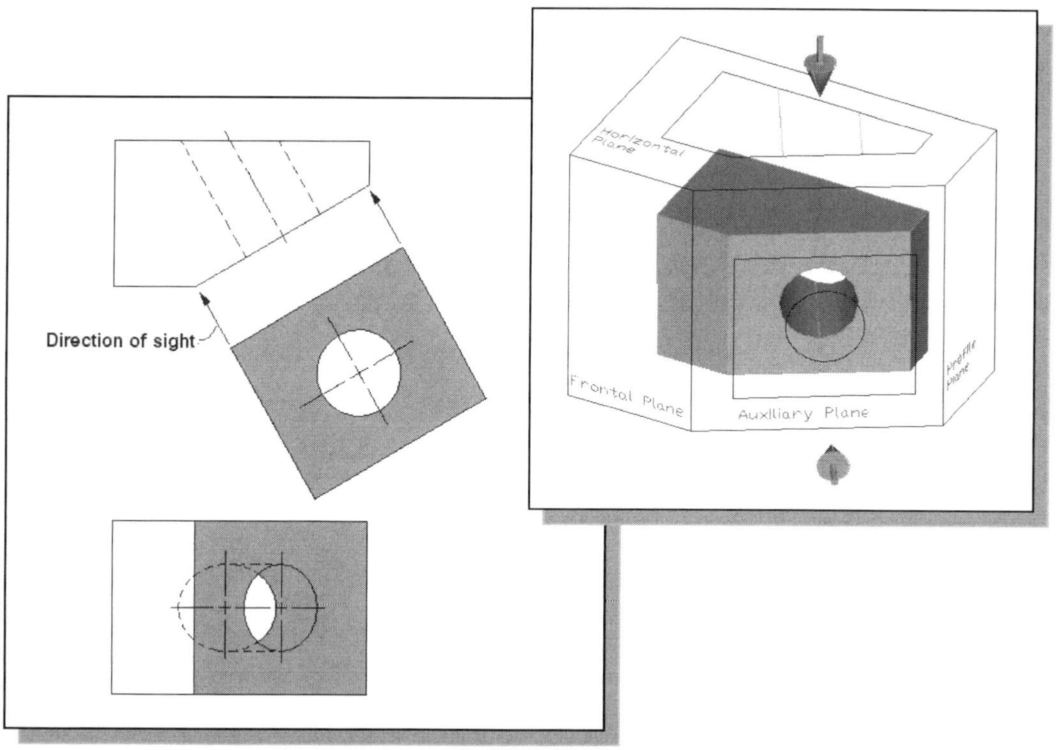

Construction Method I – Folding Line Method

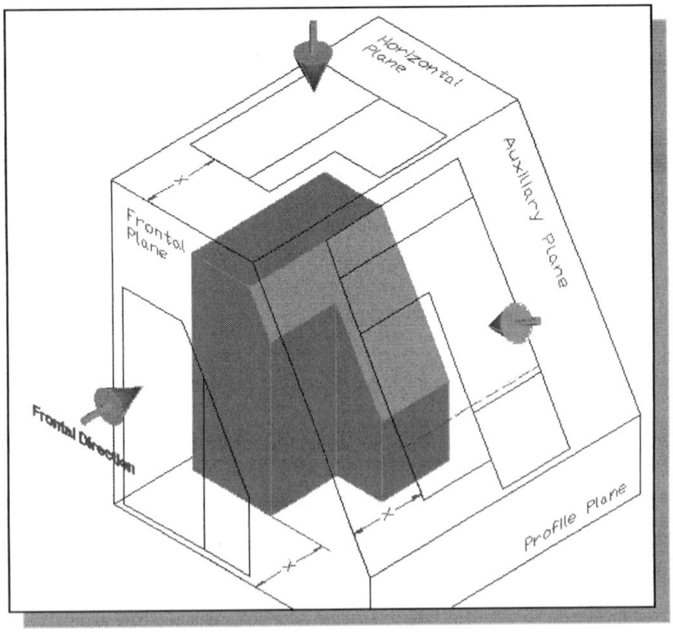

Two methods are commonly used to construct auxiliary views: the **folding-line** method and the **reference plane** method. The folding-line method uses the concept of placing the object inside a glass-box; the distances of the object to the different projection planes are used as measurements to construct the necessary views, including the auxiliary views.

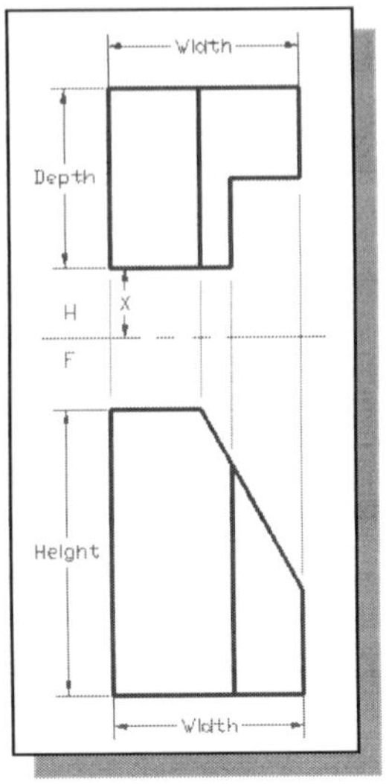

The following steps outline the general procedure to create an auxiliary view:

1. Construct the necessary principal views, in this case, the front and top views.

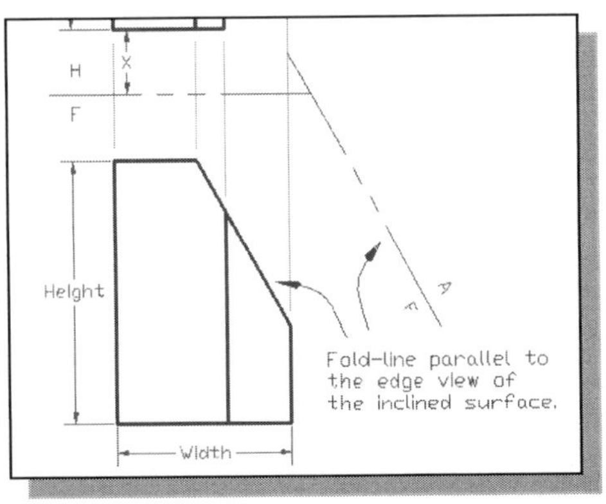

2. Construct a folding line parallel to the edge view of the inclined surface.

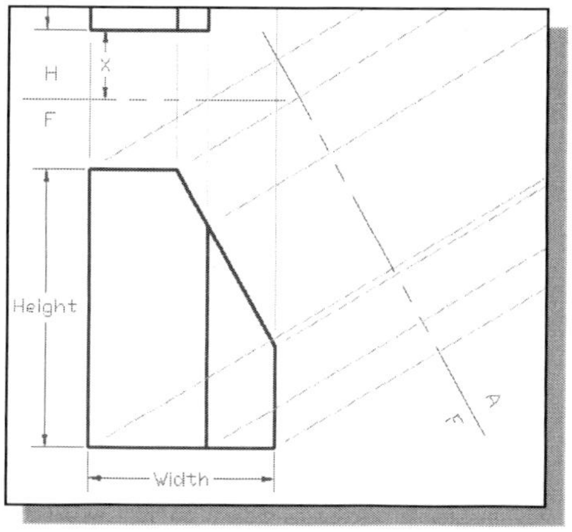

3. Construct the projection lines perpendicular to the edge view of the inclined surface and also perpendicular to the folding line.

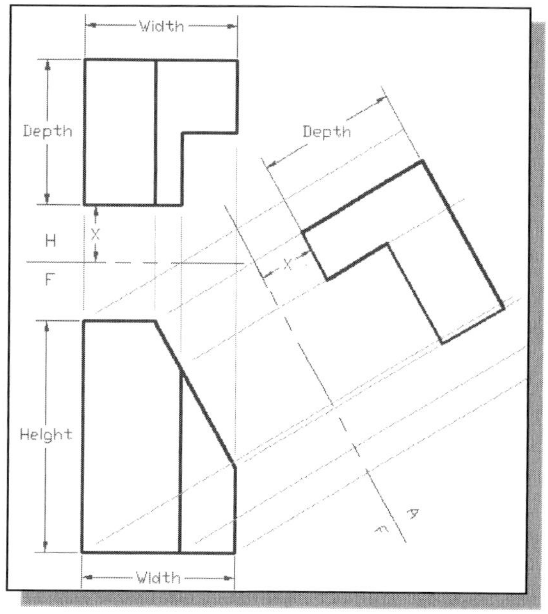

4. Use the corresponding distances, X, and the depth of the object from the principal views to construct the inclined surface.

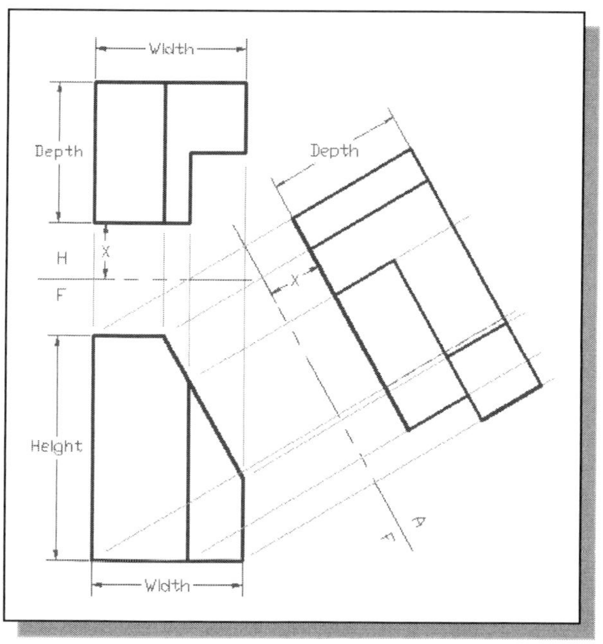

5. Complete the auxiliary view by following the principles of orthographic projection.

Construction Method II – Reference Plane Method

The **Reference plane method** uses the concept of placing a reference plane aligned with a surface of the object that is perpendicular to the inclined surface. The reference plane is, typically, a flat surface or a plane which runs through the center of the object. The distances of the individual corner to the reference plane are then used as measurements to construct the auxiliary view.

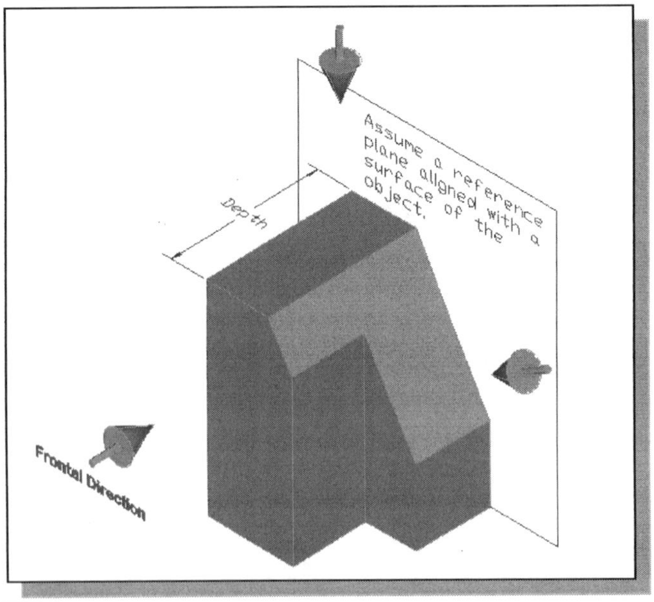

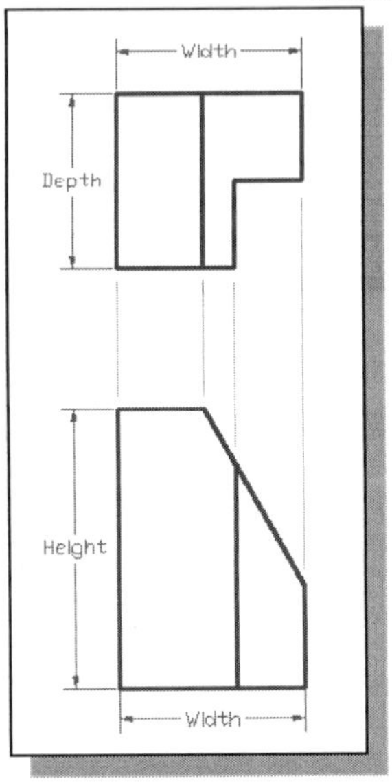

- The following steps outline the general procedure to create an auxiliary view:

1. Construct the necessary principal views, in this case, the front and top views.

2. Construct a reference plane line aligned to a flat face and perpendicular to the inclined surface of the object, in this case, the back face of the object.

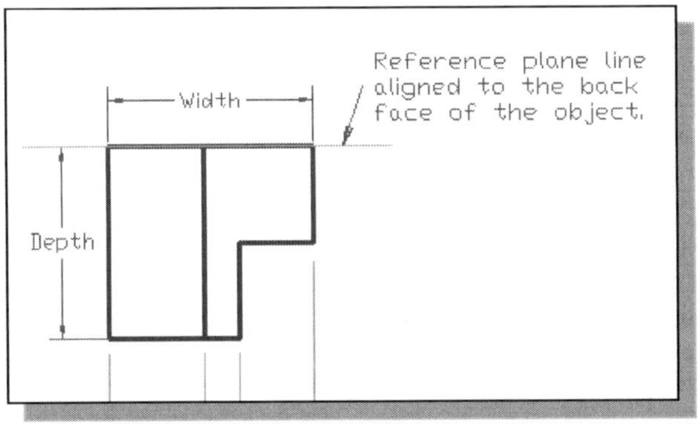

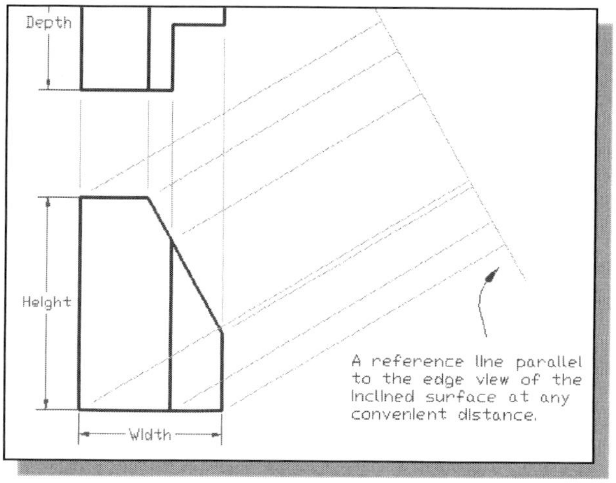

3. Construct a reference line parallel to the edge view of the inclined surface and construct the projection lines perpendicular to the edge view of the inclined surface.

4. Using the corresponding distances, such as the depth of the object, construct the inclined surface.

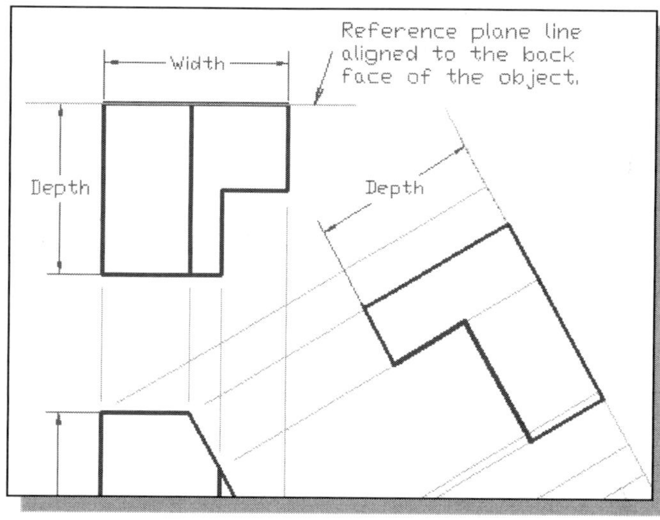

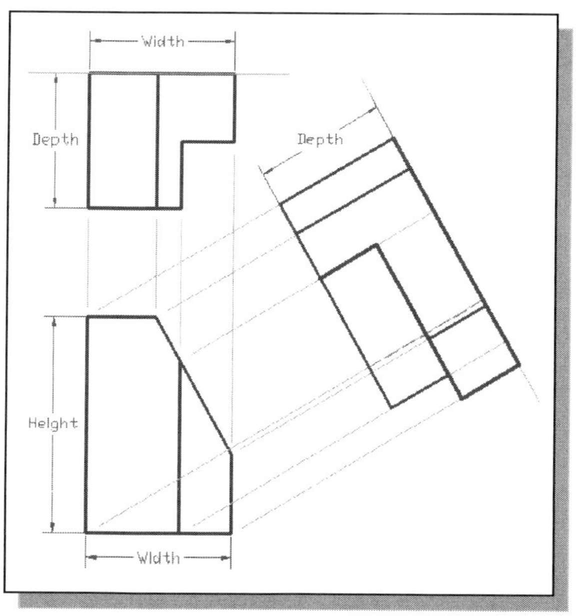

5. Complete the auxiliary view by following the principles of orthographic projection.

Partial Views

The primary purpose of using auxiliary views is to provide detailed descriptions of features that are on inclined surfaces. The use of an auxiliary view often makes it possible to omit one or more standard views. But it may not be necessary to draw complete auxiliary views, as the completeness of detail may be time consuming to construct and add nothing to the clearness of the drawing.

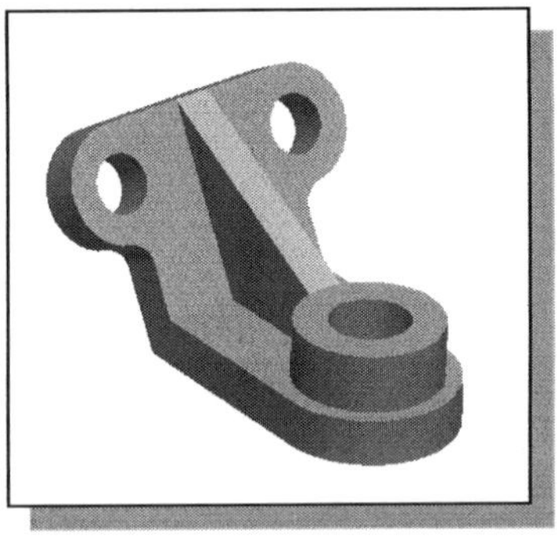

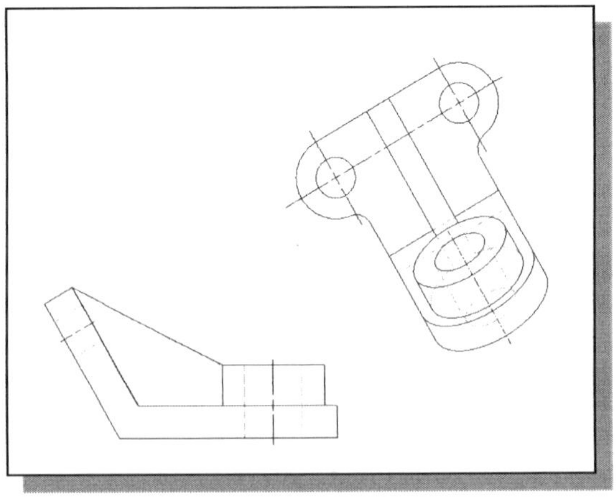

In these cases, partial views are often sufficient, and the resulting drawings are much simplified and easier to read.

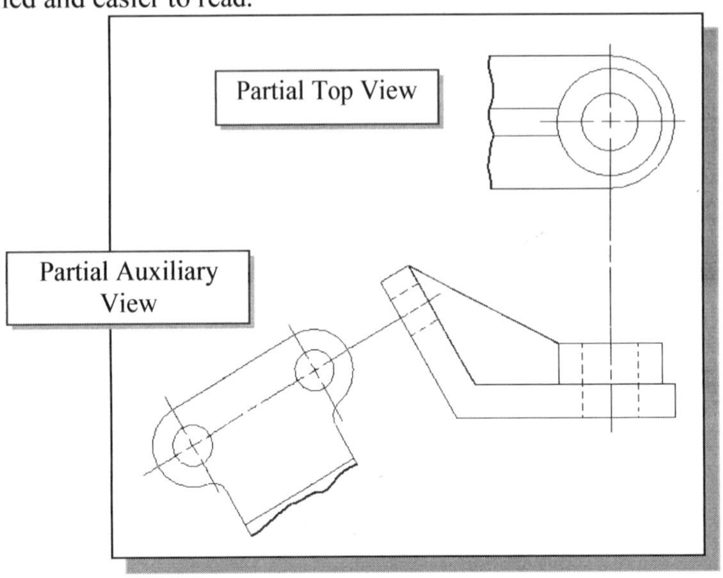

- To clarify the relationship of partial auxiliary views and the standard views, a center line or a few projection lines should be used. This is especially important when the partial views are small.

- In practice, hidden lines are generally omitted in auxiliary views, unless they provide clearness to the drawings.

Creating Auxiliary Views in AutoCAD

In the following sections, the general CAD techniques of constructing auxiliary views are demonstrated. Besides using the methods described in the previous sections, we will also examine the use of the very powerful AutoCAD *GRIPS* feature.

In **AutoCAD 2027**, a ***GRIP*** is a small square displayed on a pre-selected object. Grips are key control locations such as the endpoints and midpoints of lines and arcs. Different types of objects display different numbers of grips. Using grips, we can *stretch*, *move*, *mirror*, *scale*, *rotate*, and *copy* objects without entering commands or clicking toolbars. Grips reduce the keystrokes and object selection required in performing common editing commands.

To edit with grips, we select the objects before issuing any commands. To remove a specific object from a selection set that displays grips, we hold down the **[SHIFT]** key as we select the object. To exit the *grips mode* and return to the *command prompt*, press the **[ESC]** key.

The V-Block Design

The V-Block Design

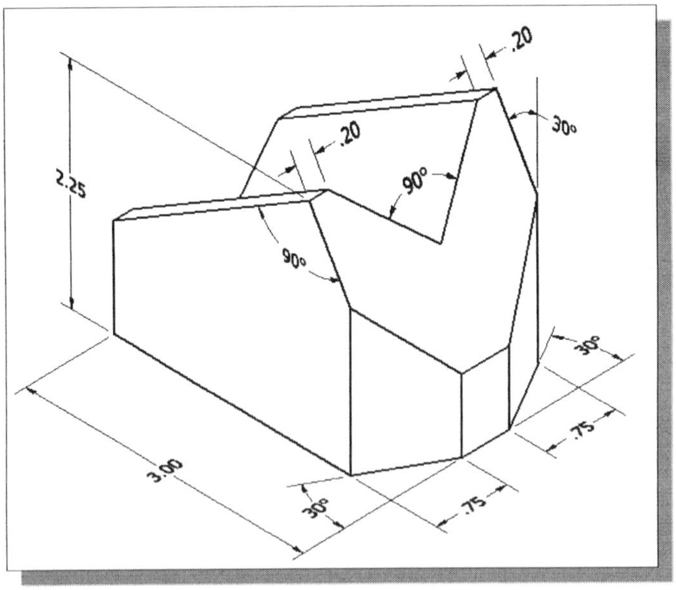

➤ Before going through the tutorial, make a rough sketch of a multiview drawing of the part. How many 2D views will be necessary to fully describe the part? Based on your knowledge of **AutoCAD® 2027** so far, how would you arrange and construct these 2D views? Take a few minutes to consider these questions and do preliminary planning by sketching on a piece of paper. You are also encouraged to construct the orthographic views on your own prior to going through the tutorial.

Starting Up AutoCAD 2027

1. Select the **AutoCAD 2027** option on the *Program* menu or select the **AutoCAD 2027** icon on the *Desktop*.

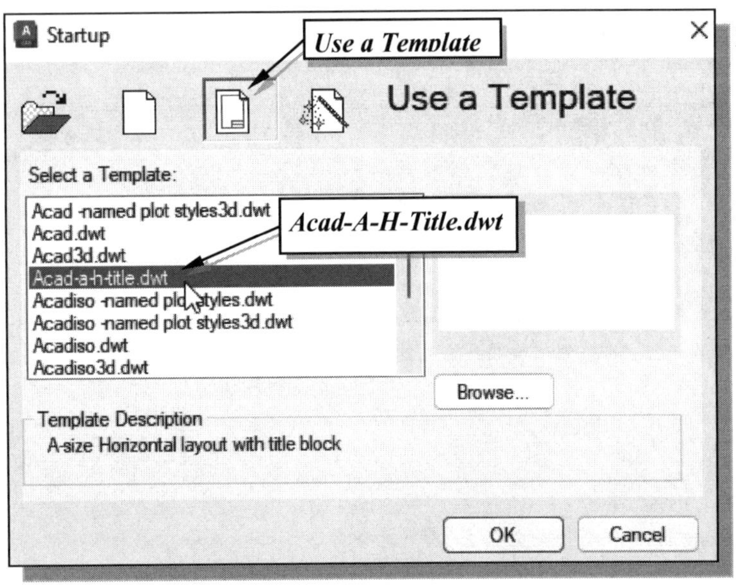

2. In the AutoCAD 2027 *Startup* dialog box, select the **Template** option.

3. Select the ***Acad-A-H-Title*** template file from the list of template files. If the template file is not listed, click on the **Browse** button to locate and proceed to open a new drawing file.

Setting up the Principal Views

1. In the *Layer Control* box, set layer ***Construction*** as the *Current Layer* if it is not the default layer.

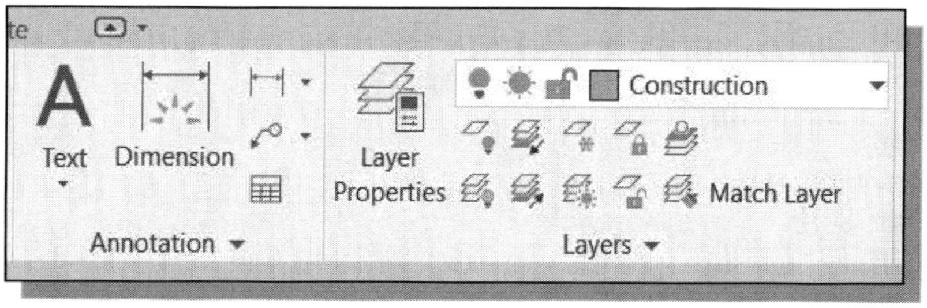

2. In the *Status Bar* area, switch ***ON*** the following options in the status toolbar: ***GRID Display***, ***Dynamic Input***, ***Object Snap Tracking***, ***Object Snap*** *and* ***Line Weight Display***.

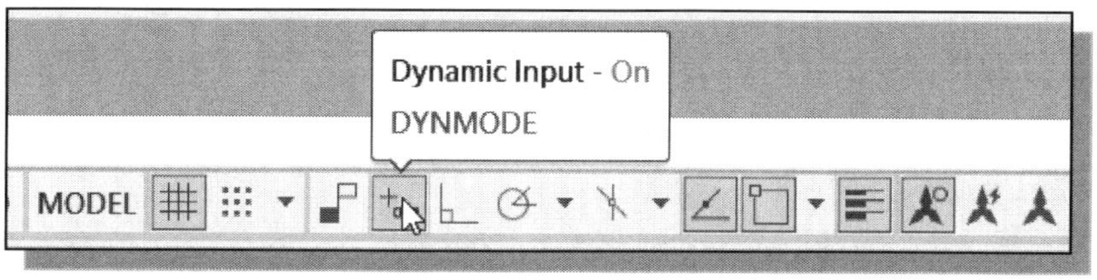

- We will first create construction geometry for the front view.

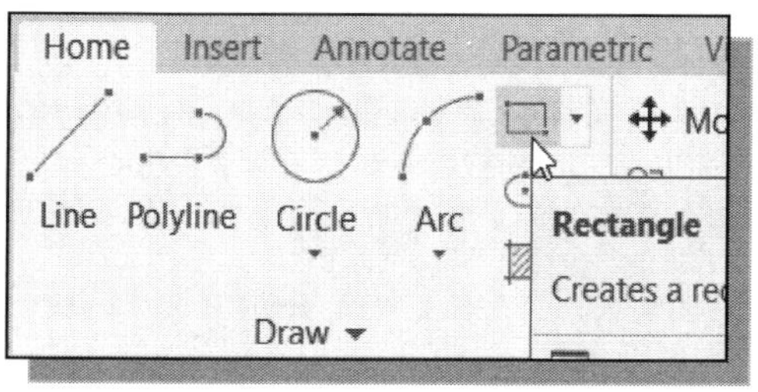

3. Select the **Rectangle** icon in the *Draw* toolbar. In the command prompt area, the message "*Specify first corner point or [Chamfer/Elevation/Fillet/Thickness/Width]:*" is displayed.

4. Place the first corner point of the rectangle near the lower left corner of the screen. Do not be overly concerned about the actual coordinates of the location; the CAD drawing space is a very flexible virtual space.

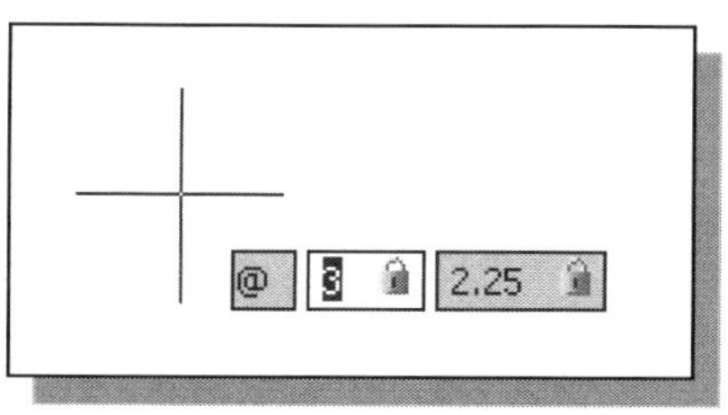

5. Create a 3″ × 2.25″ rectangle. Using the *Dynamic Input* option, enter ***@3,2.25*** **[ENTER]**.

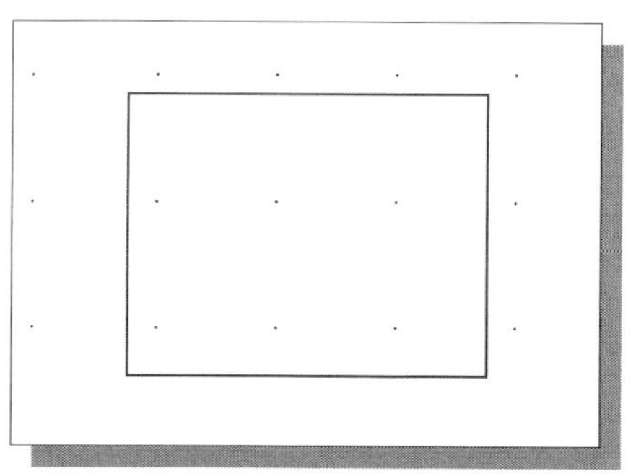

❖ The **Rectangle** command creates rectangles as *polyline* features, which means all segments of a rectangle are created as a single object.

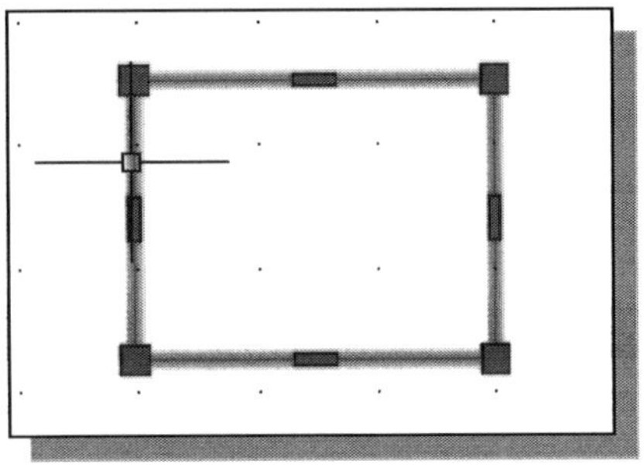

6. Next, we will use the *GRIPS* editing tools to make a copy of the rectangle. Pick any edge of the rectangle we just created. Notice that small squares appear at different locations on the rectangle.

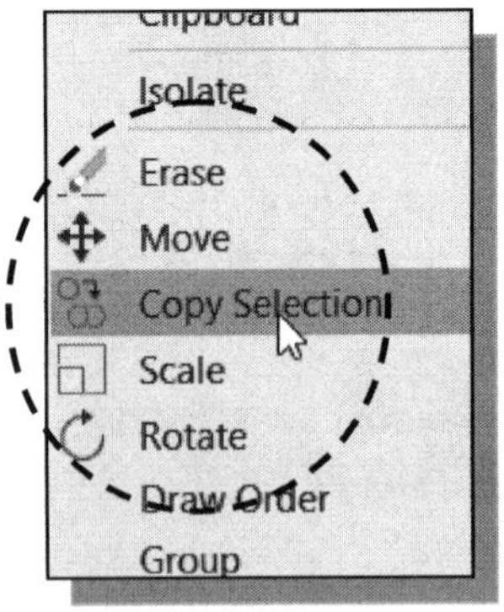

7. Inside the Drawing Area, **right-click** to bring up the **pop-up option menu**.

❖ In the center section of the pop-up menu, the set of GRIPS editing commands includes **Erase**, **Move**, **Copy Selection**, **Scale**, and **Rotate**.

8. In the pop-up menu, select the **Copy Selection** option.

9. In the command prompt area, the message "*Specify base point or displacement, or [Multiple]:*" is displayed. Pick the **lower right corner** as the base point. A copy of the rectangle is attached to the cursor at the base point.

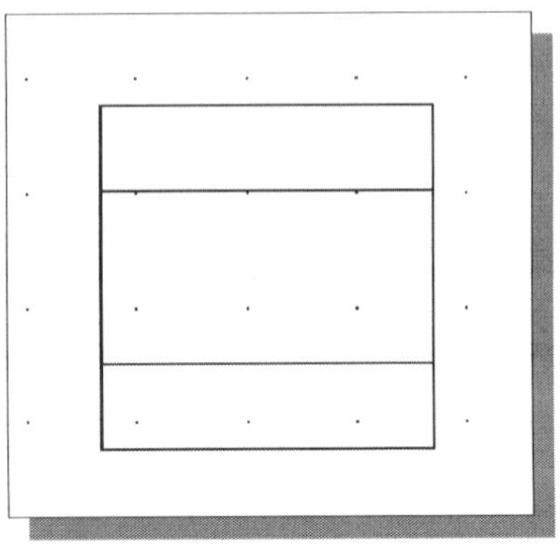

10. In the command prompt area, the message "*Specify second point of displacement, or <use first point as displacement>:*" is displayed. Enter ***@0,0.75*** **[ENTER]**.

❖ This will position the second rectangle at the location for the vertical 30-degree angle.

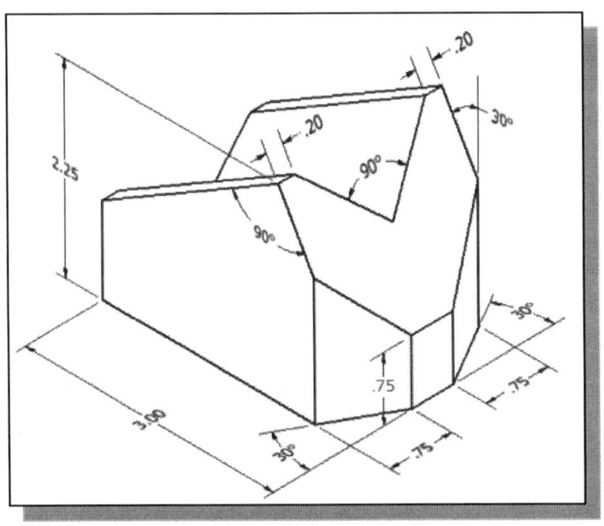

11. Inside the Drawing Area, **right-click** once to bring up the option menu and choose **Enter** to exit the **Copy** option.

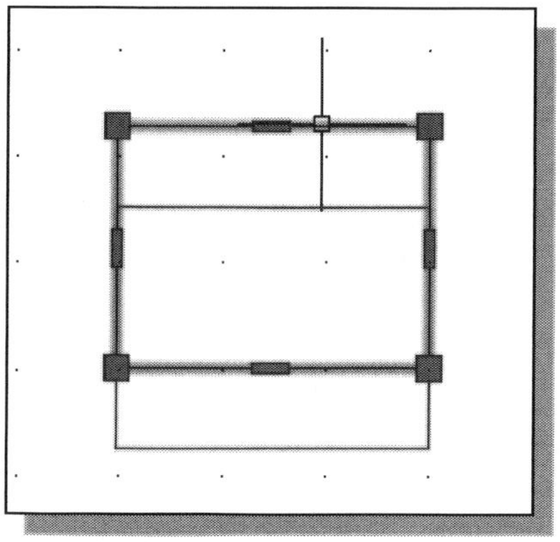

12. **Pre-select** the **copy** by picking the top horizontal line on the screen. The second rectangle, the copy we just created, is selected.

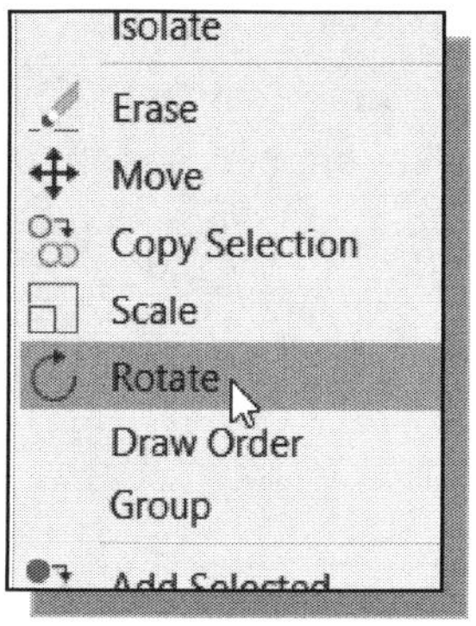

13. Inside the Drawing Area, **right-click** to bring up the pop-up option menu and select the **Rotate** option.

14. In the command prompt area, the message "*Specify base point:*" is displayed. Pick the **lower right corner** of the **selected rectangle** as the base point.

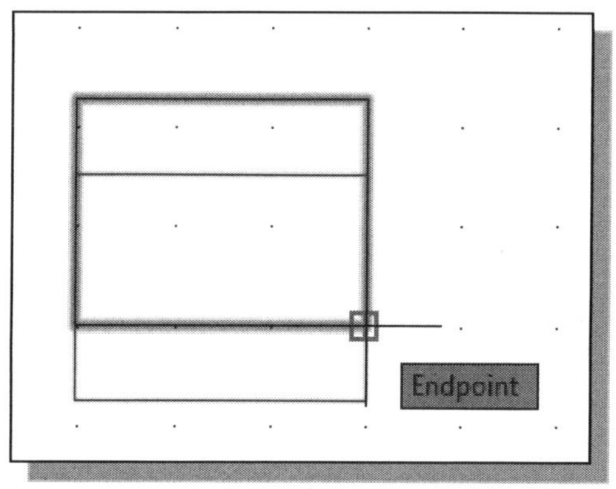

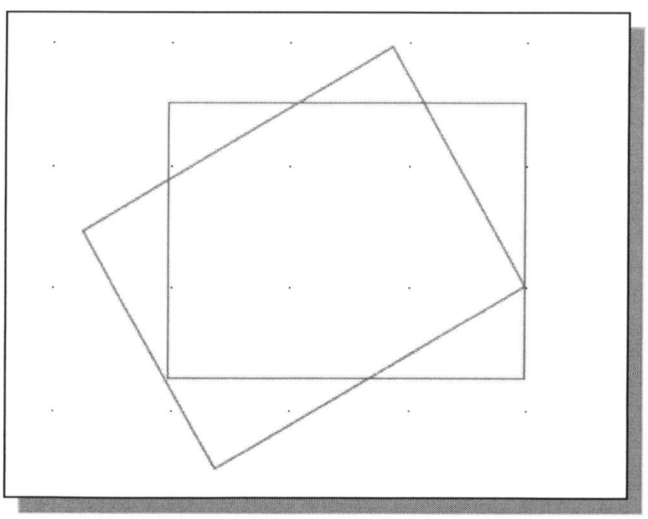

15. In the command prompt area, the message "*Specify the rotation angle or [Reference]:*" is displayed. Enter: ***30*** **[ENTER]**.

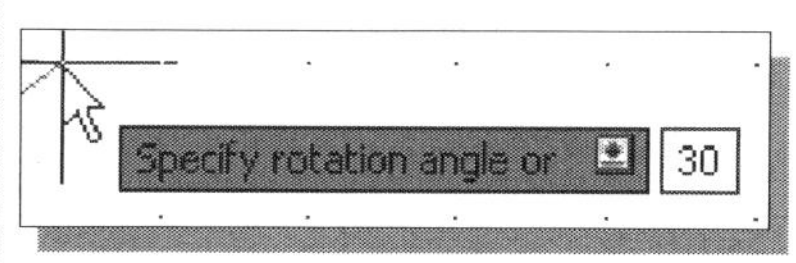

Setting up the Top View

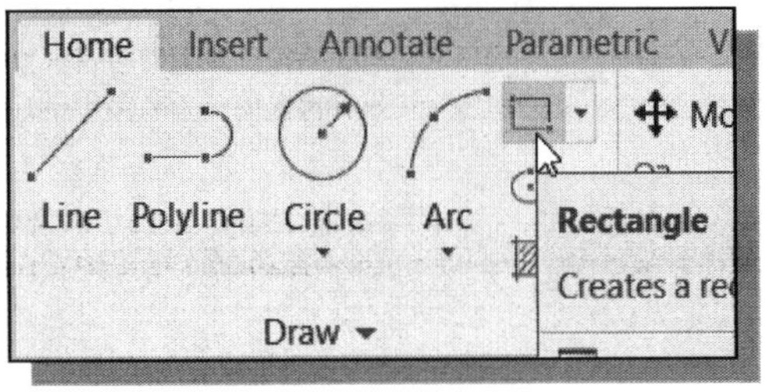

1. Select the **Rectangle** icon in the *Draw* toolbar. In the *command prompt area*, the message "*Specify first corner point or [Chamfer/Elevation/Fillet/Thickness/Width]:*" is displayed.

2. Move the cursor over the top left corner of the first rectangle we created. This will activate the ***object tracking*** alignment feature to the corner.

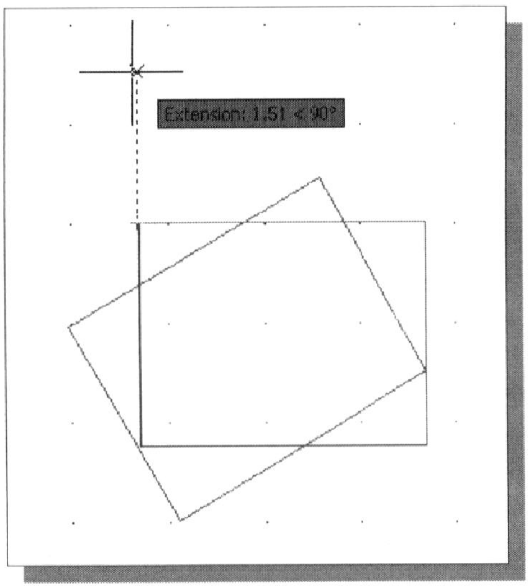

3. Move the cursor upward to a location that is about 1.5″ away from the reference point. (Read the *OTRACK* display on the screen.) Left-click once to place the first corner-point of the rectangle.

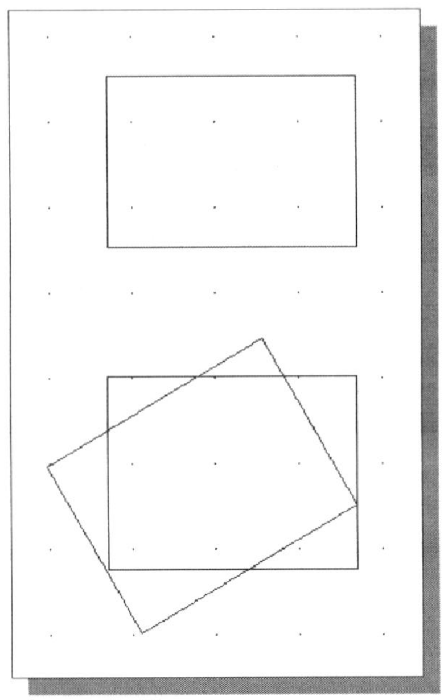

4. We will create a 3″ × 2″ rectangle. Enter **@3,2 [ENTER]**.

- We have created the outline of the top view of the *V-block* design.

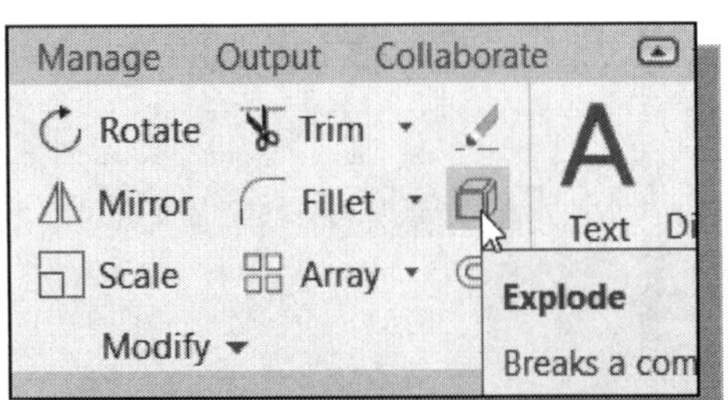

5. Pre-select the **rectangle** we just created by left-clicking any edge of the rectangle.

6. Select the **Explode** icon in the *Modify* toolbar.

- The top rectangle now consists of four separate line segments.

Using the Offset Command

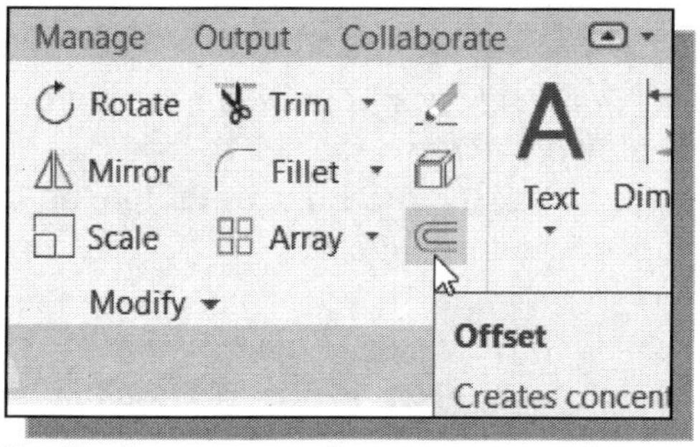

1. Click the **Offset** icon in the *Modify* toolbar. In the command prompt area, the message "*Specify offset distance or [Through]:*" is displayed.

2. In the command prompt area, enter ***0.2*** **[ENTER]**.

3. In the *command prompt area*, the message "*Select object to offset or <exit>:*" is displayed. Pick the **top horizontal line** of the top view on the screen.

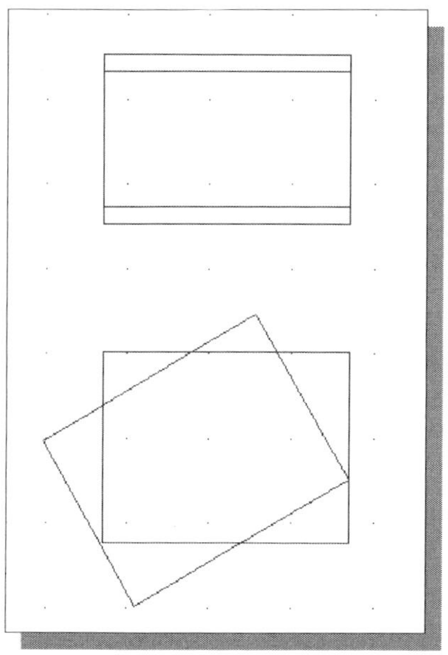

4. AutoCAD next asks us to identify the direction of the offset. Pick a location that is **below** the selected line.

5. In the command prompt area, the message "*Select object to offset or <exit>:*" is displayed. Pick the **bottom horizontal line** of the top view on the screen.

6. AutoCAD next asks us to identify the direction of the offset. Pick a location that is **above** the selected line.

7. Inside the *Drawing Area*, **right-click** and select **Enter** to end the **Offset** command.

8. Inside the Drawing Area, right-click to bring up the pop-up option menu and select the **Repeat Offset** option.

- Notice in the pop-up menu, none of the GRIPS editing commands are displayed; the GRIPS editing commands are displayed only if objects are pre-selected.

9. In the command prompt area, the message "*Specify offset distance or [Through]:*" is displayed. Enter ***0.75*** **[ENTER]**.

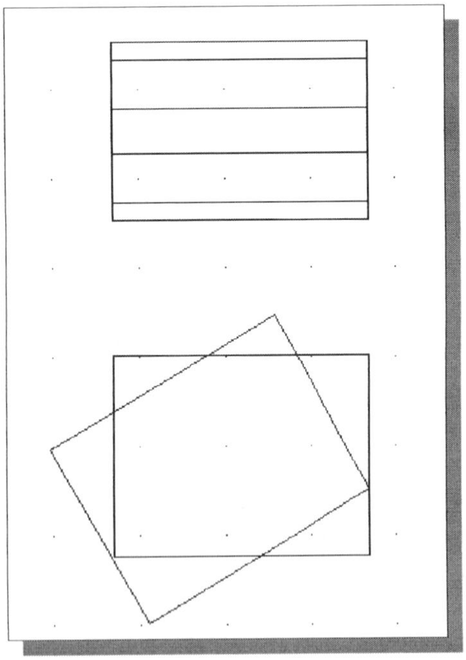

10. In the *command prompt area*, the message "*Select object to offset or <exit>:*" is displayed. Pick the **top horizontal line** of the top view on the screen.

11. AutoCAD next asks us to identify the direction of the offset. Pick a location that is **below** the selected line.

12. In the *command prompt area*, the message "*Select object to offset or <exit>:*" is displayed. Pick the **bottom horizontal line** of the top view on the screen.

13. AutoCAD next asks us to identify the direction of the offset. Pick a location that is **above** the selected line.

14. Inside the *Drawing Area*, **right-click** and choose **Enter** to end the **Offset** command.

- The four parallel lines will be used to construct the top v-cut feature and the two 0.75″ × 30° cut features at the base of the *V-block* in the top view.

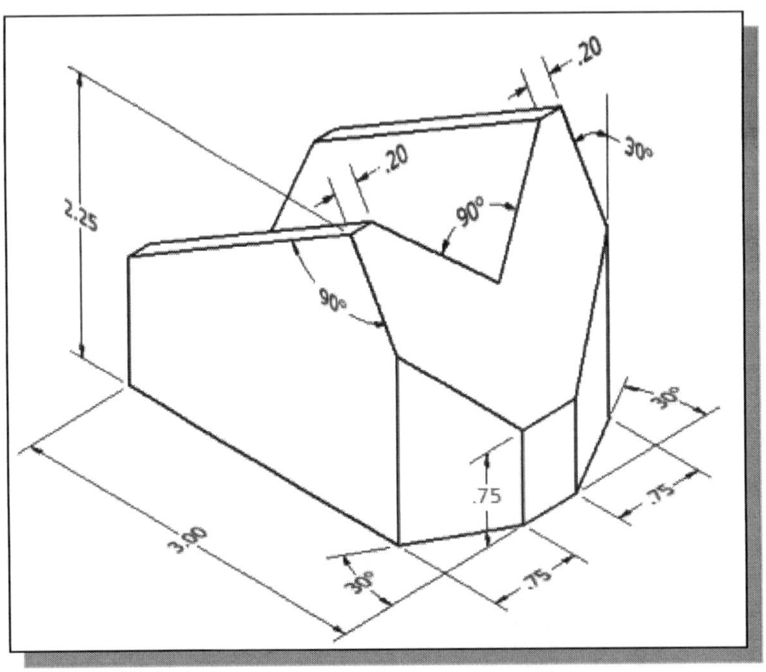

Creating Object Lines in the Front View

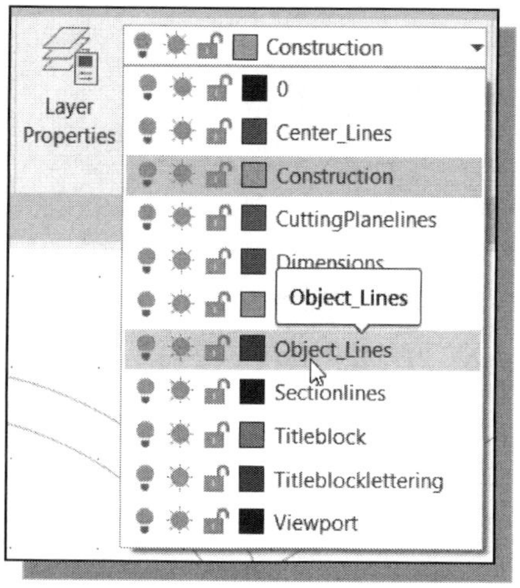

1. On the *Object Properties* toolbar, choose the **Layer Control** box with the left-mouse-button.

2. Move the cursor over the name of layer **Object_Lines**; the tool tip "*Object_Lines*" appears.

3. **Left-click once** and layer *Object_Lines* is set as the *Current Layer*.

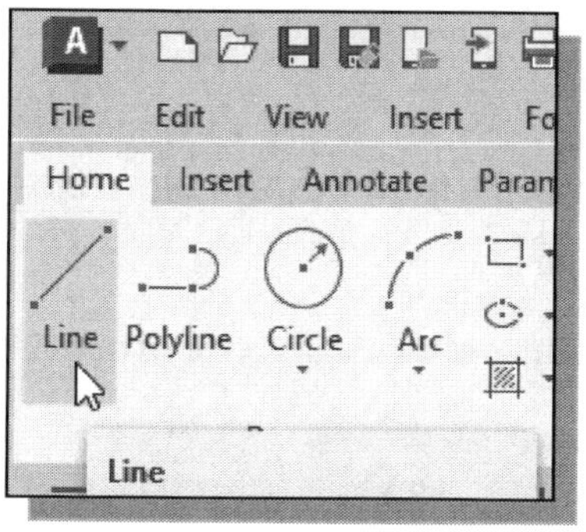

4. Select the **Line** command icon in the *Draw* toolbar. In the command prompt area, the message "*_line Specify first point:*" is displayed.

5. Pick the **lower left corner** of the bottom horizontal line in the front view as the starting point of the line segments.

6. Pick the **lower right corner** of the bottom horizontal line in the front view as the second point.

7. Select the **third** and **fourth** points as shown in the figure below.

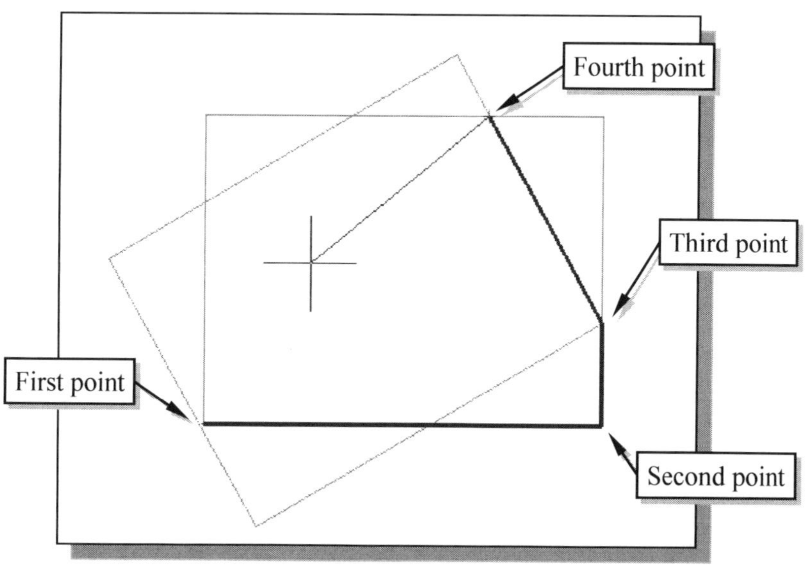

Setting the Polar Tracking Option

1. In the *Status Bar* area, turn ***ON*** the *Polar Tracking* option.

- Note that the *Polar Tracking* option is one of the *AutoCAD AutoTrack*™ features. The *AutoTrack* features include two tracking options: polar tracking and object snap tracking. When the *Polar Tracking* option is turned on, alignment markers are displayed to help us create objects at precise positions and angles. A quick way to change the settings of the *AutoTrack* feature is to use the option menu.

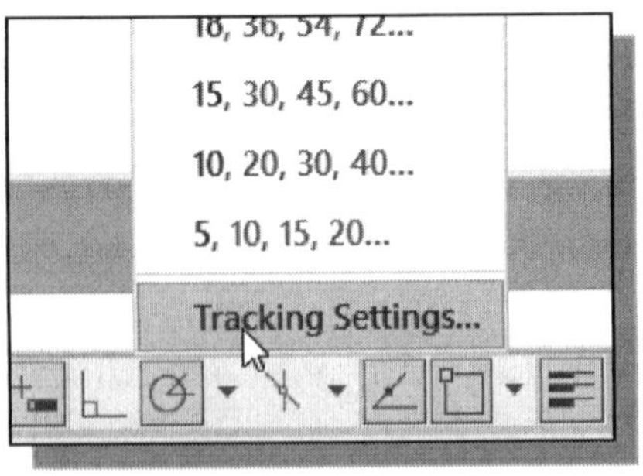

2. Move the cursor on top of the *Polar Tracking* option in the *Status Bar* area.
3. Click once with the **right-mouse-button** to bring up the option menu.
4. Select **Settings** in the option menu as shown in the figure.
5. In the *Drafting Settings* dialog box, set the *Increment angle* to ***30*** as shown in the figure below.

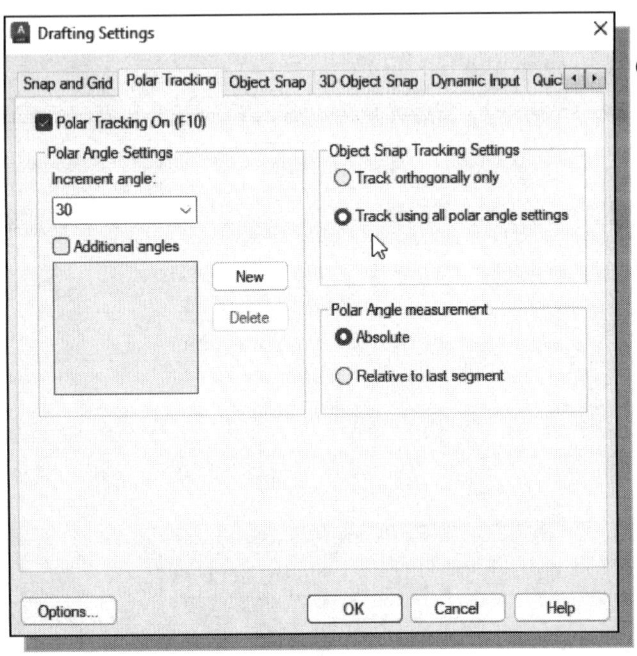

6. Under the *Object Snap Tracking Settings* option, turn ***ON*** the **Track using all polar angle settings** option as shown in the figure.
7. Click **OK** to accept the modified settings.

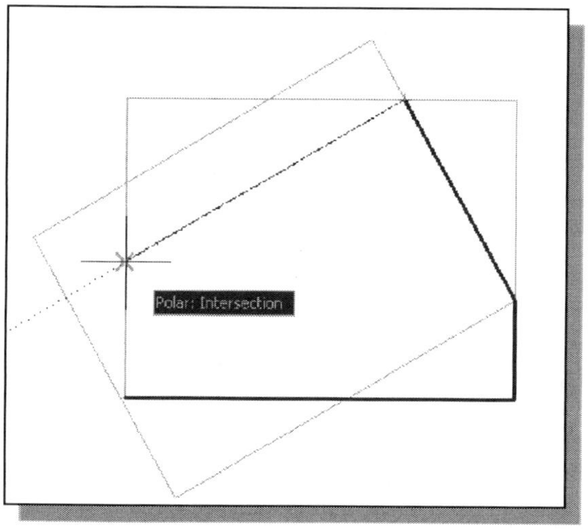

8. Move the cursor near the left vertical line as shown and notice that *AutoCAD AutoTrack* automatically snaps the cursor to the intersection point and displays the alignment marker as shown.

➢ In the following steps, we will illustrate the use of different *POLAR* settings to achieve the same result.

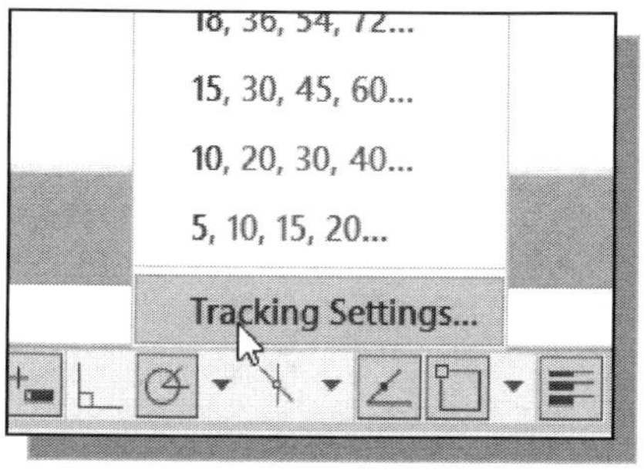

9. Click once with the right-mouse-button on the *POLAR* option in the *Status Bar* area to bring up the option menu.

10. Select **Settings** in the option menu as shown in the figure.

11. In the *Drafting Settings* dialog box, set the *Increment angle* to ***90*** as shown in the figure below.

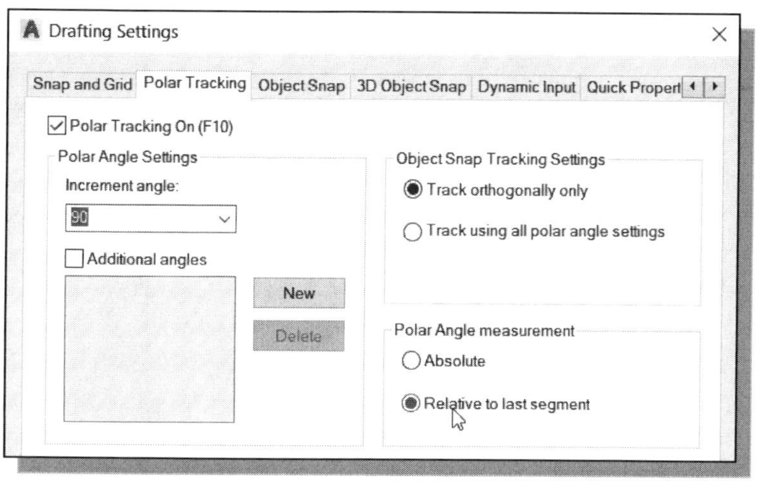

12. Under the *Object Snap Tracking Settings* option, turn *ON* the **Track orthogonally only** option as shown in the figure.

13. Under the *Object Snap Tracking Settings* option, turn *ON* the **Relative to last segment** option as shown in the figure above.

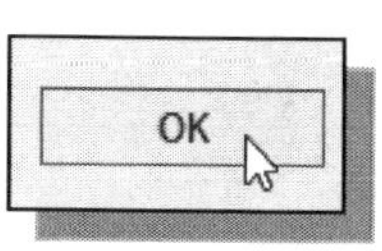

14. Click **OK** to accept the modified settings.

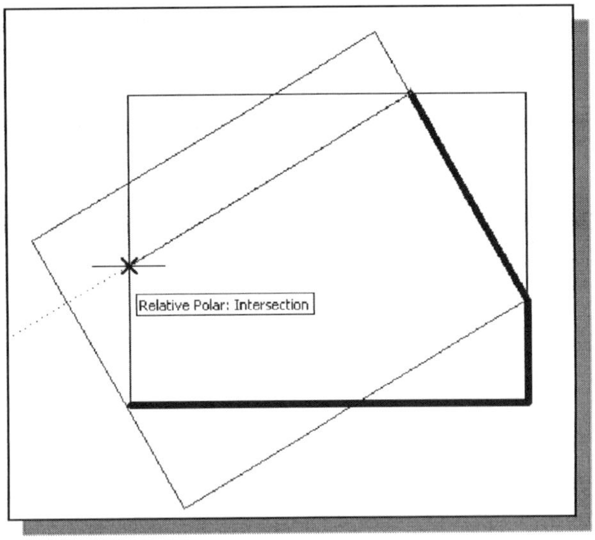

15. Move the cursor near the left vertical line and notice the *AutoTrack* feature automatically snaps the cursor to the intersection point and displays the alignment marker as shown.

- On your own, experiment with changing the settings to achieve the same *SNAP/POLAR* results.

16. **Left-click** at the *intersection point* as shown.

17. Click the **Close** option in the *command prompt area.* AutoCAD will create a line connecting the last point to the first point of the line sequence.

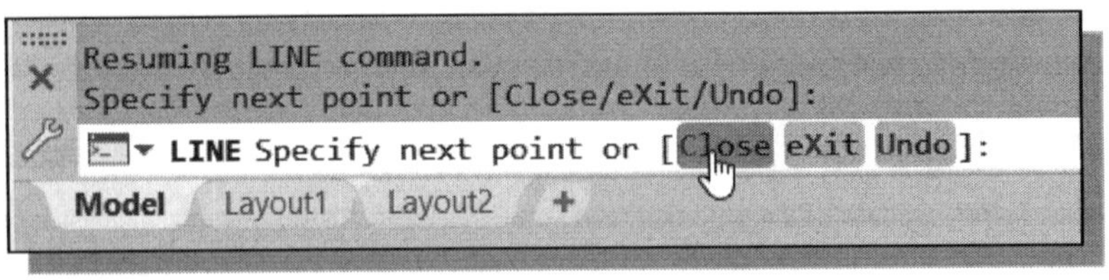

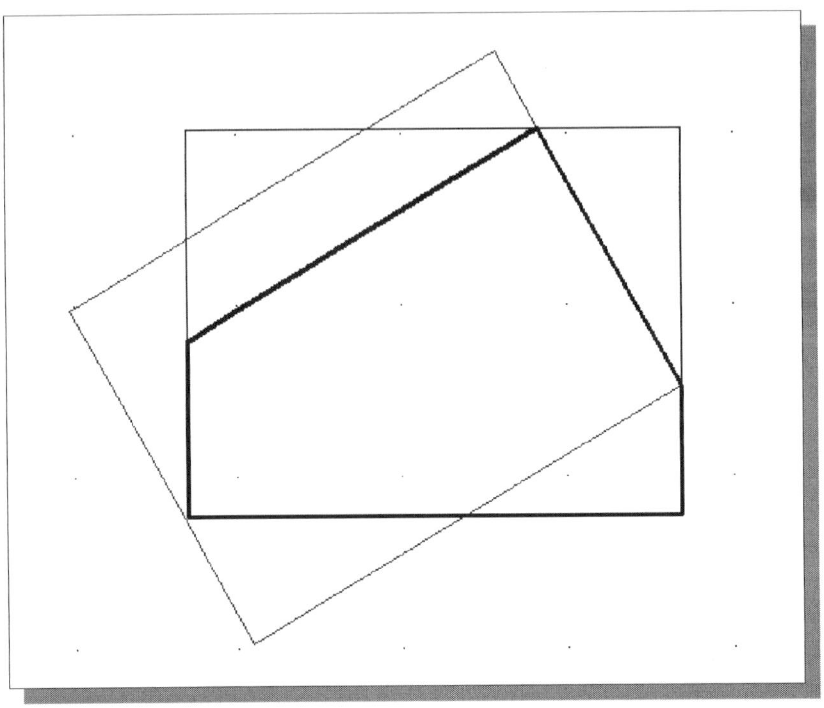

Setting up an Auxiliary View

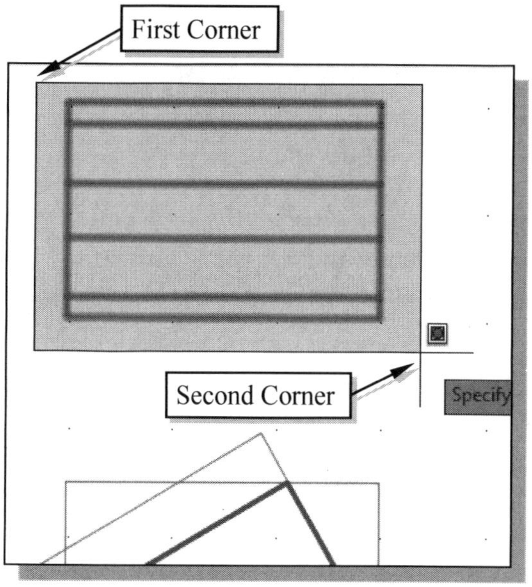

1. **Pre-select** all objects in the top view, by using two single clicks of the left mouse button, enclosing the objects inside a selection window.

2. Inside the *Drawing Area*, right-click to bring up the pop-up option menu and select the **Copy Selection** option.

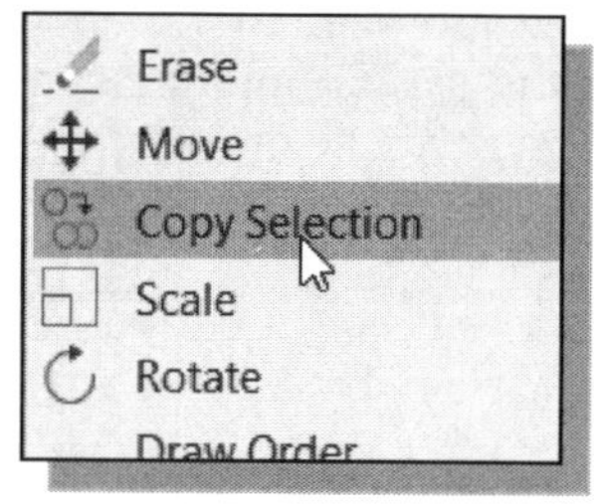

3. In the command prompt area, the message "*Specify base point or displacement, or [Multiple]:*" is displayed. Pick the **lower left corner** of the top view as the base point.

4. Using the *AutoTrack* feature, place the copy of the top-view by aligning it to the inclined object line we just created. **Left-click** once to position the copy about 2″ away from the top corner of the front-view.

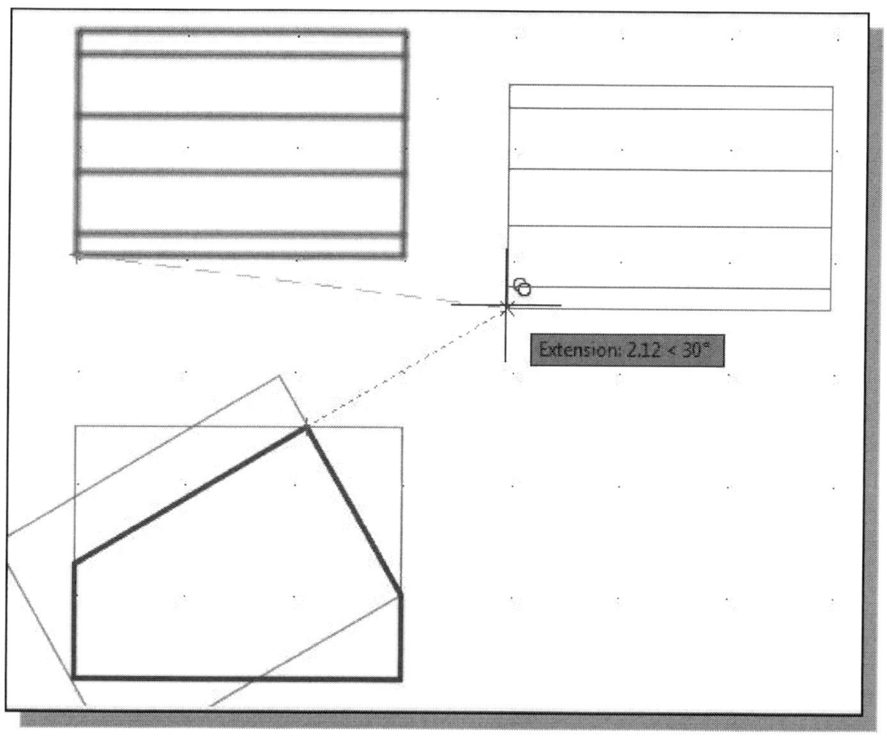

Aligning the Auxiliary View to the Front View

1. **Pre-select** all objects in the *auxiliary view* by enclosing the objects inside a selection window.

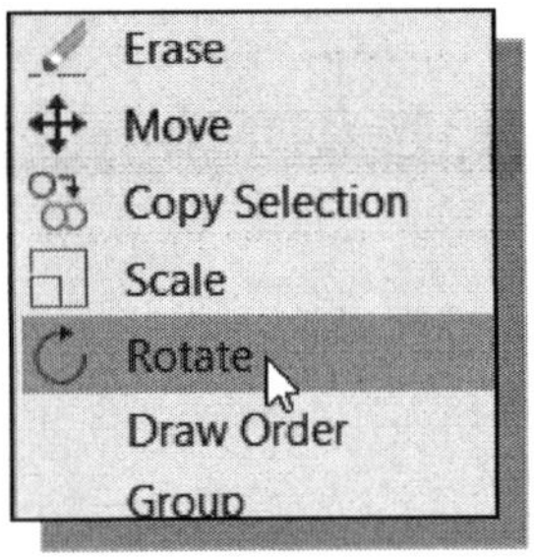

2. Inside the Drawing Area, right-click to bring up the pop-up option menu and select the **Rotate** option.

3. In the command prompt area, the message "*Specify base point:*" is displayed. Pick the **bottom left corner** of the auxiliary view as the base point.

4. In the command prompt area, the message "*Specify the rotation angle or [Reference]:*" is displayed. Enter ***-60*** **[ENTER]**.

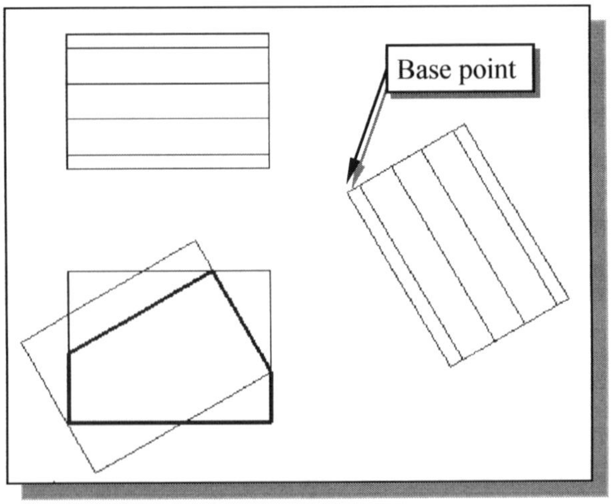

Creating the V-cut in the Auxiliary View

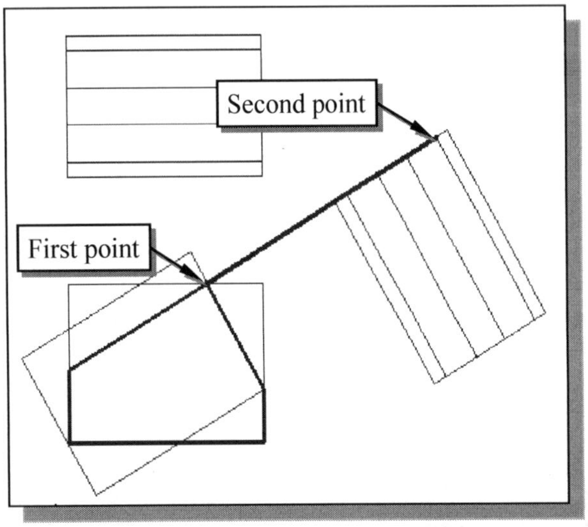

1. Select the **Line** icon in the *Draw* toolbar. In the command prompt area, the message "*_line Specify first point:*" is displayed.

2. Pick the **top corner** of the inclined object line in the front view as the starting point of the line segments.

3. Pick the **second top end point** in the auxiliary view as the second point.

4. Inside the *Drawing Area*, right-click and select **Enter** to end the Line command.

5. Pre-select the line we just created.

6. Inside the Drawing Area, right-click to bring up the pop-up option menu and select the **Rotate** option.

7. In the command prompt area, the message "*Specify base point:*" is displayed. Pick the top right endpoint of the line as the base point.

8. In the command prompt area, the message "*Specify the rotation angle or [Reference]:*" is displayed. Enter ***45*** **[ENTER]**.

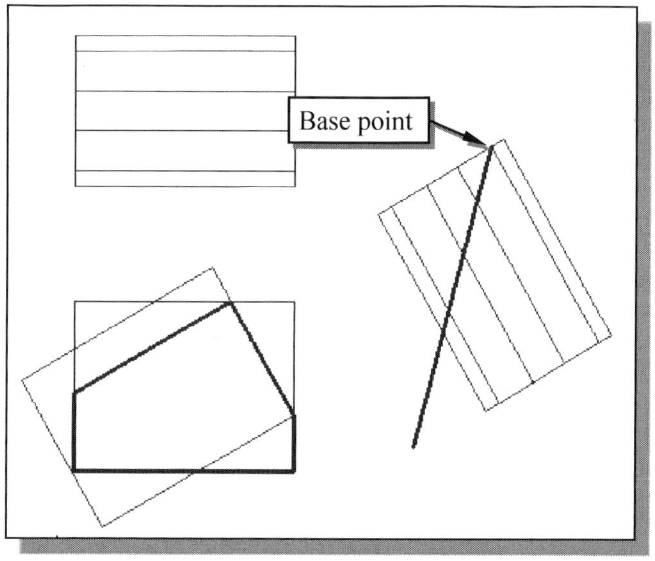

9. On your own, repeat the above steps and create the other line as shown.

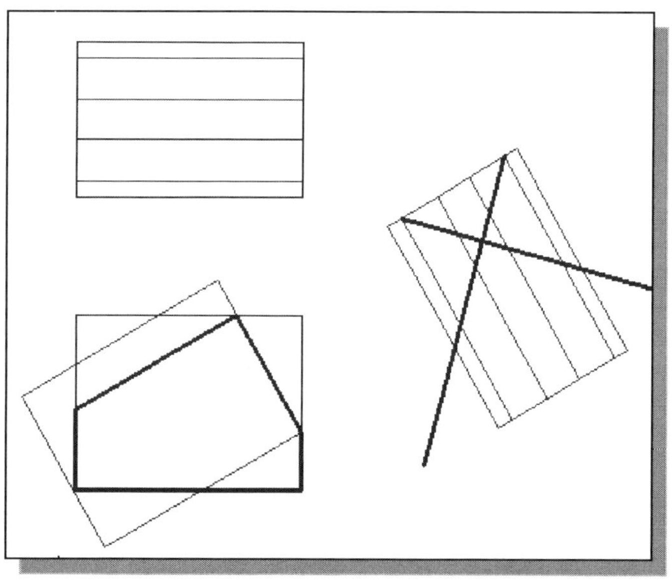

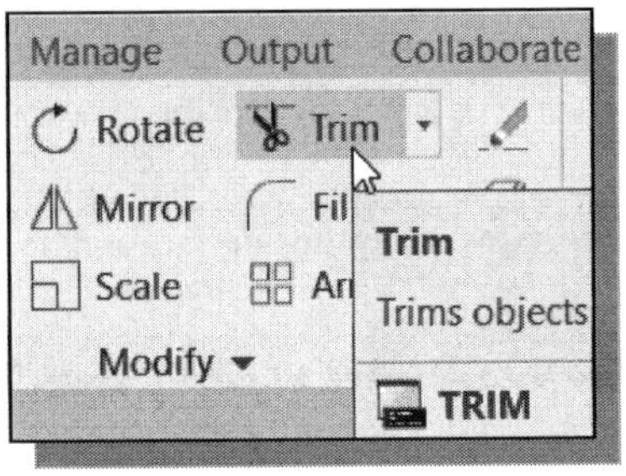

10. Select the **Trim** command icon in the *Modify* toolbar.

11. In the command prompt area, click **cuTting edges** as shown.

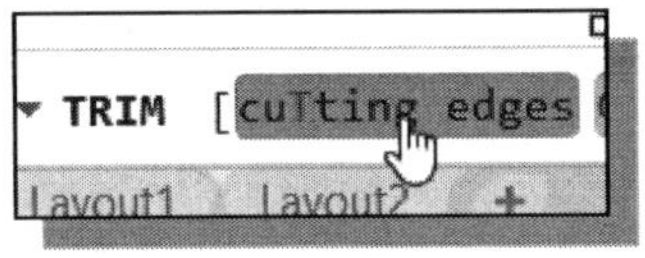

12. Pick the two inclined lines we just created in the auxiliary view as the *boundary edges*.

13. Inside the *Drawing Area*, **right-click** to proceed with the Trim command. The message "*Select object to trim or [Project/Edge/Undo]:*" is displayed in the command prompt area.

14. Pick the two lower endpoints of the two inclined lines to remove the unwanted portions.

15. Inside the Drawing Area, right-click to activate the option menu and select **Enter** with the left-mouse-button to end the Trim command.

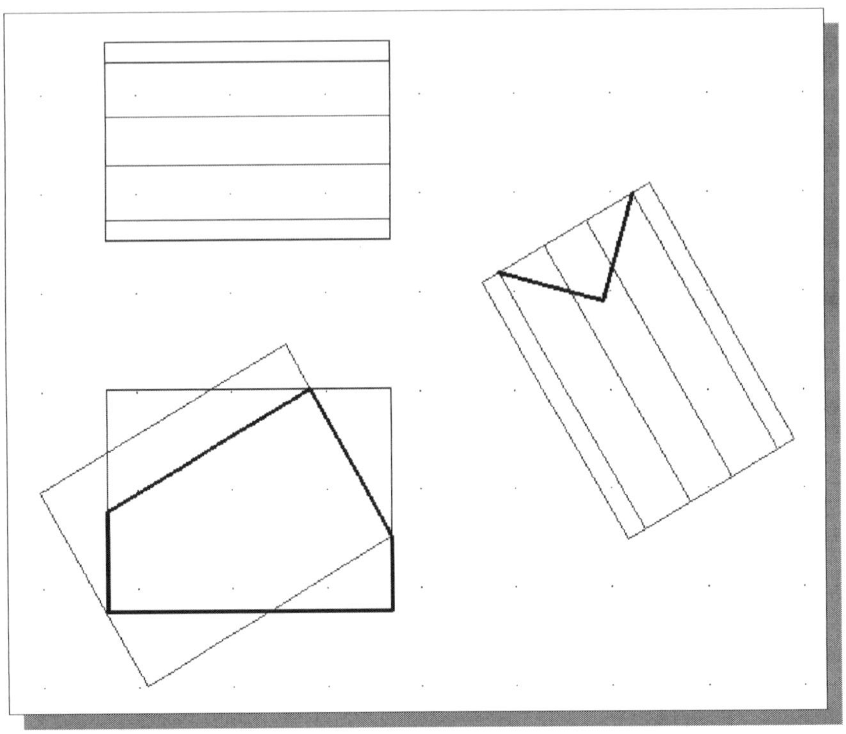

➢ The V-cut is shown at its true size and shape only in the auxiliary view. It is therefore necessary to create the V-cut in the auxiliary view. Now that we have constructed the feature in the auxiliary view, we can use projection lines to transfer the feature to the front view and top view.

Creating the V-cut in the Front View and Top View

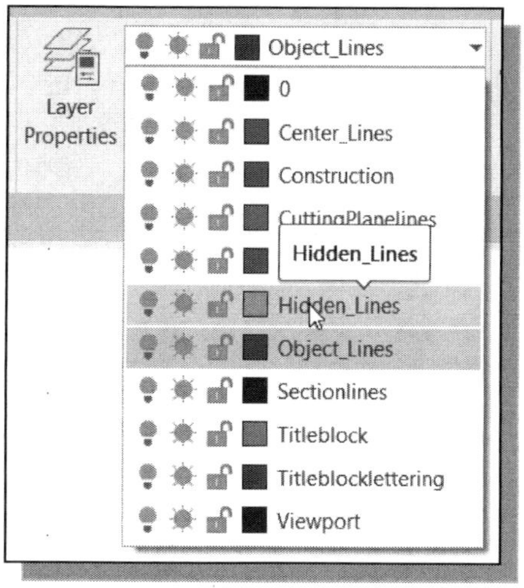

1. On the *Object Properties* toolbar, choose the *Layer Control* box with the left-mouse-button.

2. Move the cursor over the name of layer ***Hidden_Lines***; the tool tip *"Hidden_Lines"* appears.

3. **Left-click once** and layer *Hidden_Lines* is set as the *Current Layer.*

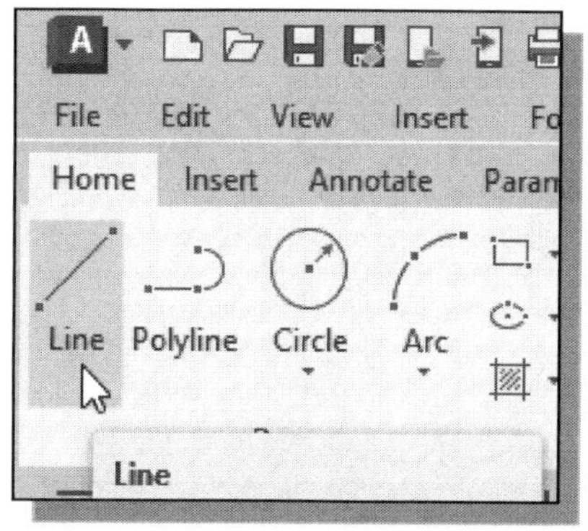

4. Select the **Line** command icon in the *Draw* toolbar. In the command prompt area, the message "*_line Specify first point:*" is displayed.

5. Pick the **vertex** of the V-cut in the *auxiliary view* as the first point of the line.

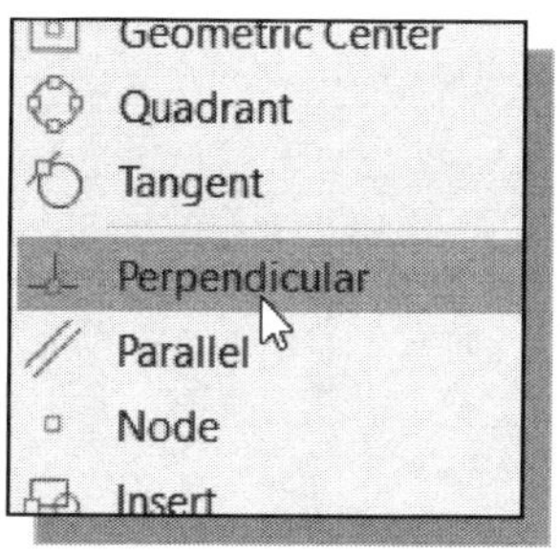

6. Inside the *Drawing Area*, hold down the **[SHIFT]** key and **right-click** once to bring up the *Object Snap* shortcut menu.

7. Select the **Perpendicular** option in the pop-up window.

8. Move the cursor to the front view on the inclined edge and notice the perpendicular symbol appears at different locations. Select the intersection point on the inclined line as shown.

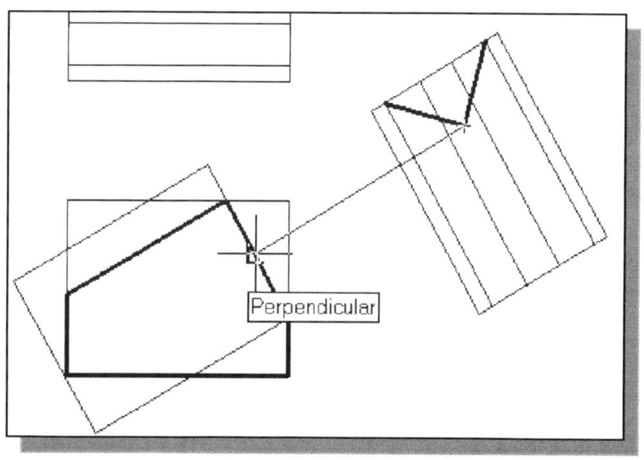

9. Inside the *Drawing Area*, right-click to activate the option menu and select **Enter** with the left-mouse-button to end the Line command.

10. On your own, use the **Trim** and **Extend** commands to adjust the hidden lines in the front view.

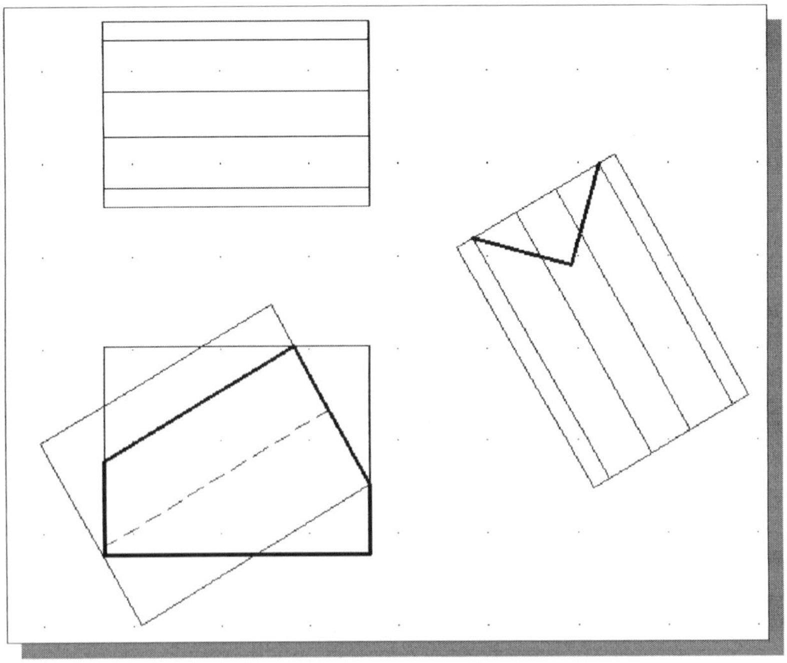

➢ On your own, first create the three construction lines and then construct the V-cut feature in the top-view. Use the Trim and Extend commands to assist the construction.

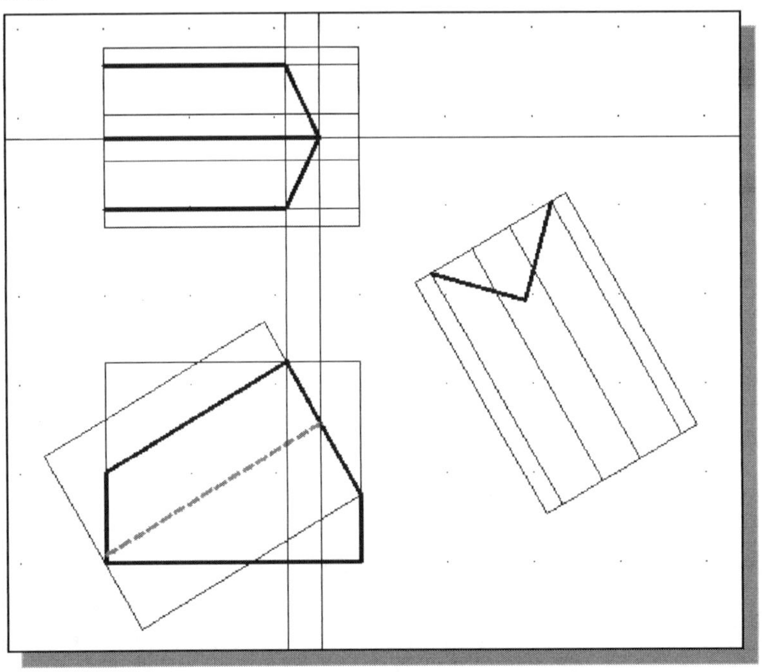

Setting the Polar Tracking Option

1. Move the cursor to the *Status Bar* area, over the ***Polar Tracking*** option button.

2. **Left-click once** on the **triangle icon** to bring up a pop-up option menu.

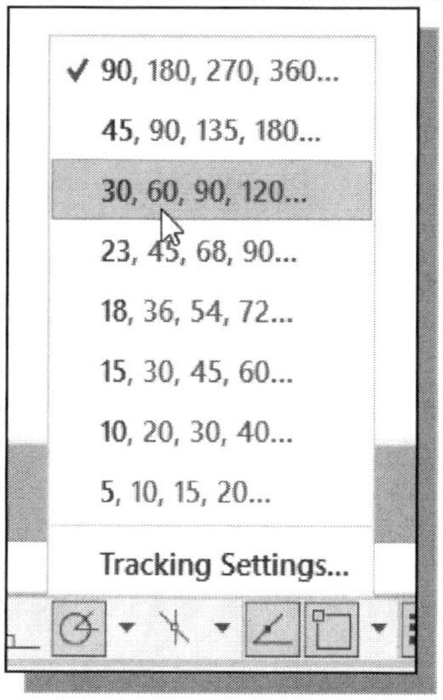

3. Select the **30, 60, 90, 120...** option by clicking once with the left-mouse-button. This is the shortcut to set the angles for the *Polar Tracking Angle Setting.*

➢ Notice the other settings that are available. We will use the absolute polar angle measurement for this example.

Completing the Top View

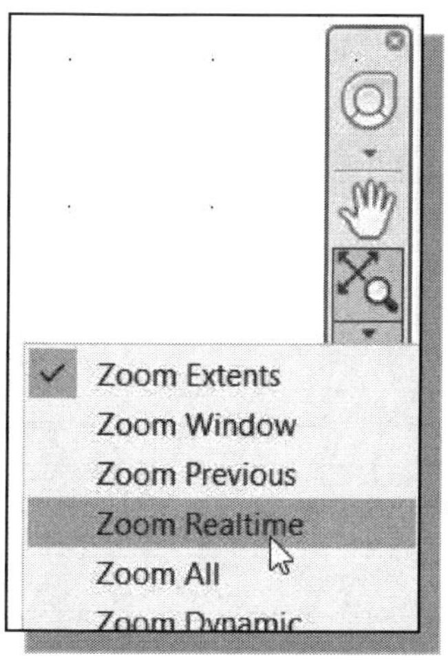

1. Click on the **Zoom Realtime** icon in the *View display* toolbar area.

2. Move the cursor near the center of the *Drawing Area.*

3. **Push and hold down the left-mouse-button**, then move upward to enlarge the current display scale factor. (Press the **[Esc]** key to exit the command.)

4. On your own, use the **Pan Realtime** option to reposition the display so that we can work on the top view of the *V-block.*

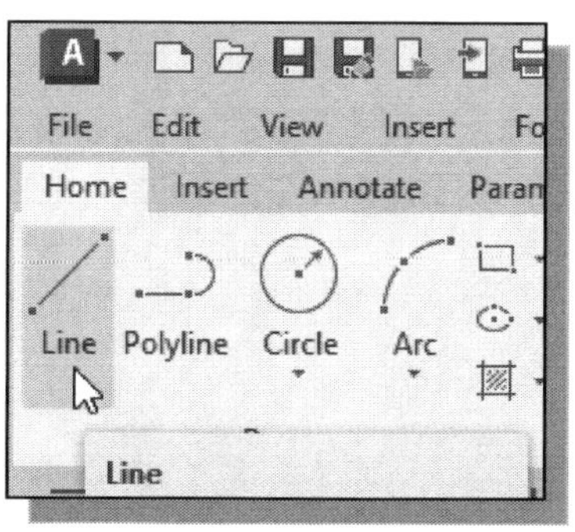

5. Select the **Line** icon in the *Draw* toolbar.

6. In the command prompt area, the message "*_line Specify first point:*" is displayed. Pick the **right endpoint** of the third horizontal line (from the top) in the top view as the starting point of the line segments.

7. Move the cursor toward the top horizontal line and observe the *AutoTracking* markers over different locations.

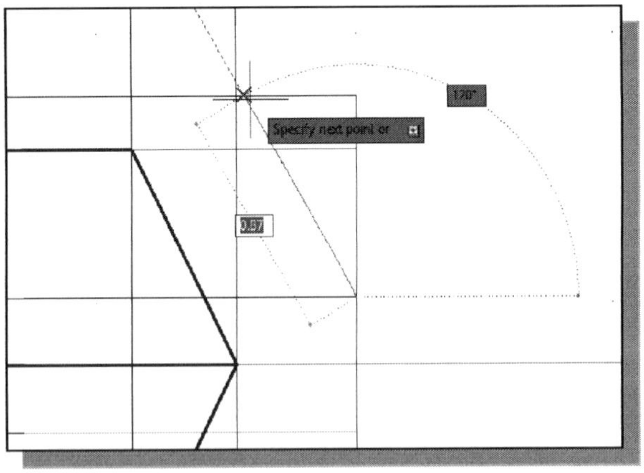

8. **Left-click** at the intersection of the polar tracking and the top horizontal line as shown. Do not select the intersection between the top horizontal line and the vertical line. (Use the Zoom Realtime command to zoom-in further, if necessary.)

9. Inside the *Drawing Area*, right-click and select **Enter** to end the Line command.

10. Repeat the above steps and create the other inclined line in the top view.

➢ On your own, complete the top view by adding all the necessary object lines in the top view. Use the Trim and Extend commands to assist the construction.

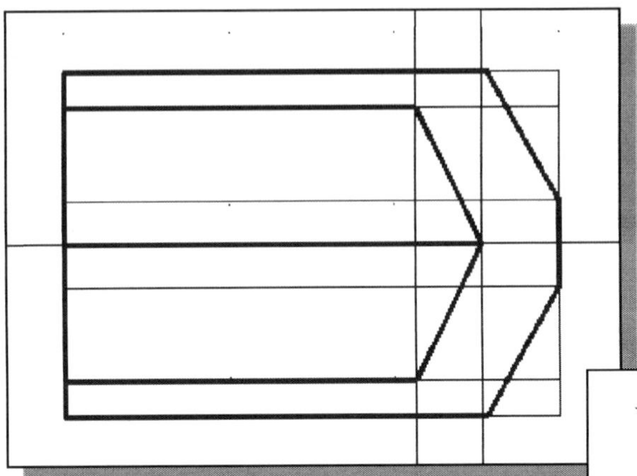

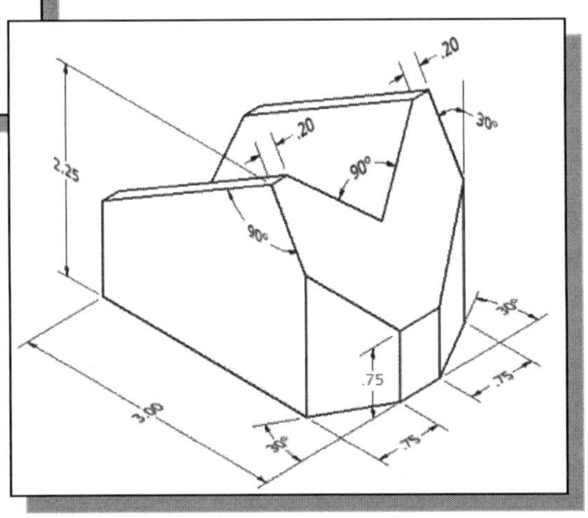

- Notice that the two 30° cut features are shown as **true size and shape** only in the top view and therefore it is necessary for us to construct the features in the top view.

➢ On your own, create the **vertical construction line** through the corner of the 30° cut as shown.

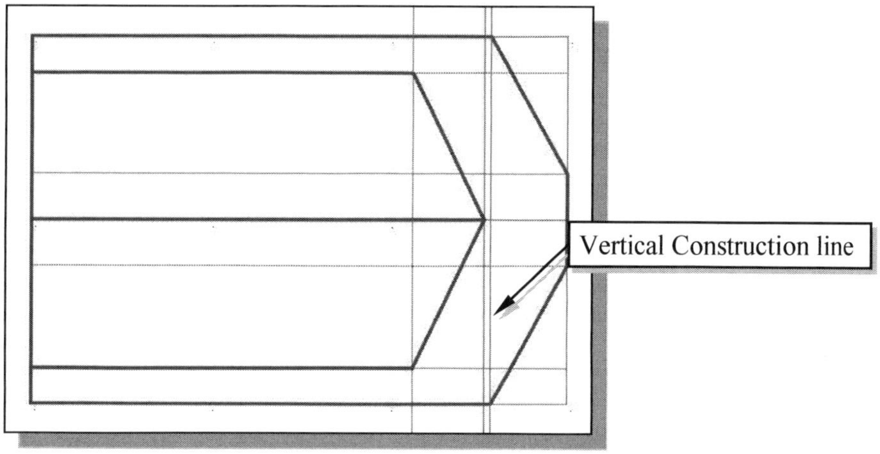

11. Complete the front view by adding the object line along the construction line as shown.

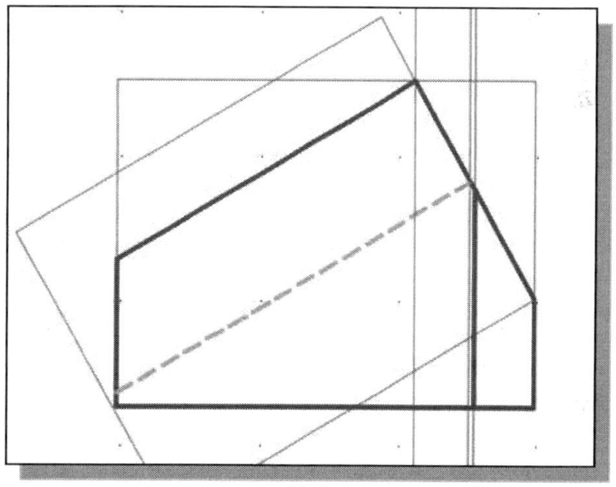

➢ On your own, complete the views by adding all the necessary object lines in the views.

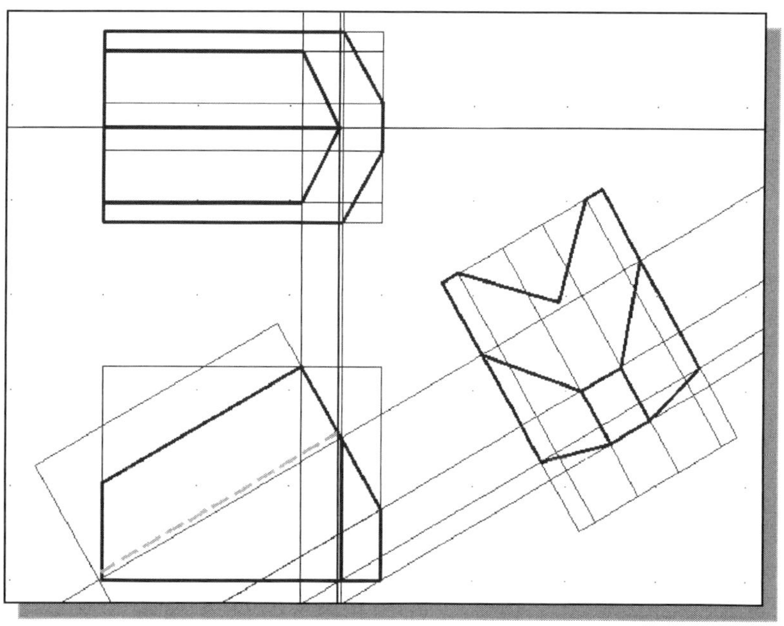

➢ Complete the drawing by adding the proper dimensions.

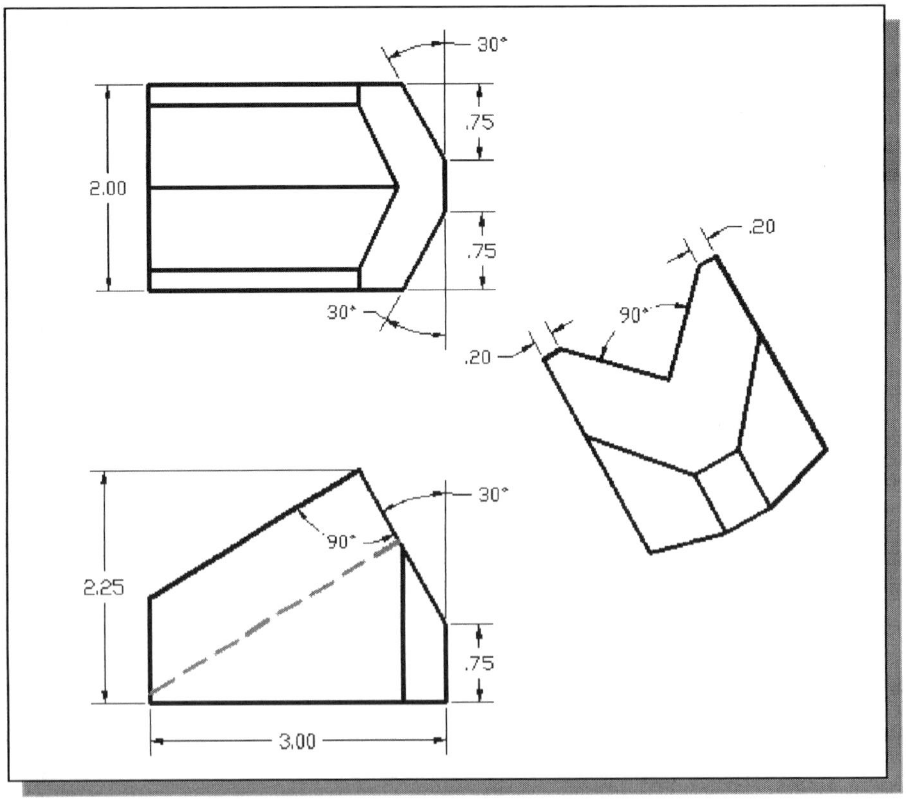

Edit the Plot Style Table - Black and White Prints

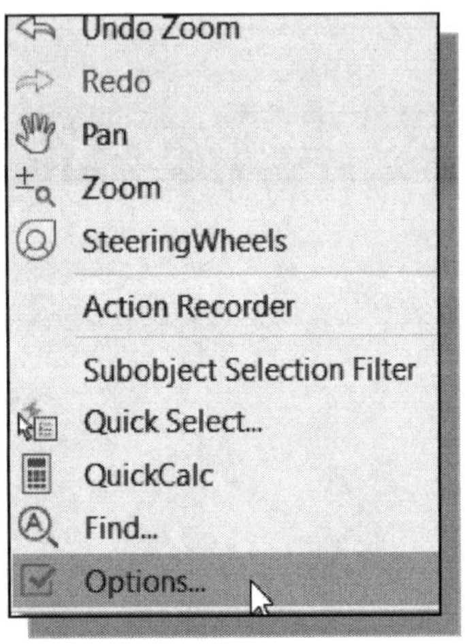

1. Inside the *Drawing Area*, right-click and select **Options** in the pop-up menu.

2. In the *Options* dialog box, select the **Plot and Publish** tab.

3. Click on the **Plot Style Table Settings** button as shown.

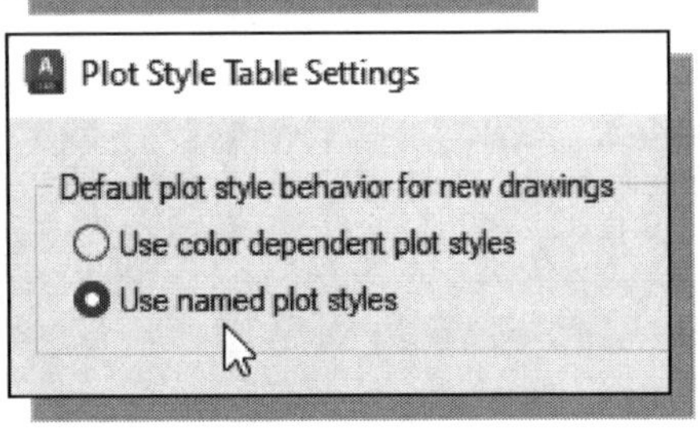

4. In the *Plot Style Table Settings* dialog box, switch ***ON*** the ***Use named plot styles*** option as shown.

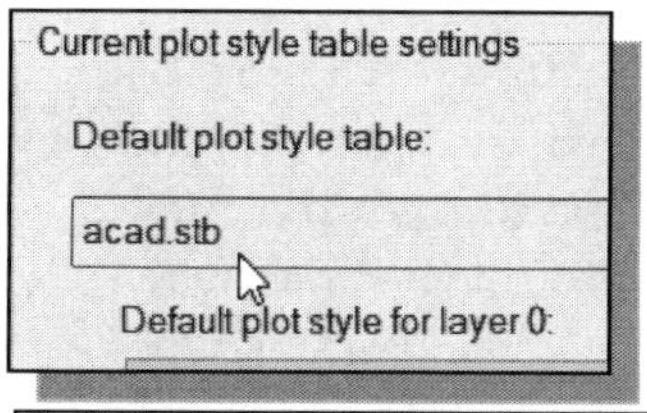

5. Choose the *acad.stb* as the default plot style table as shown.

6. In the *Options* dialog box, click on the **Add or Edit Plot Style Tables** button.

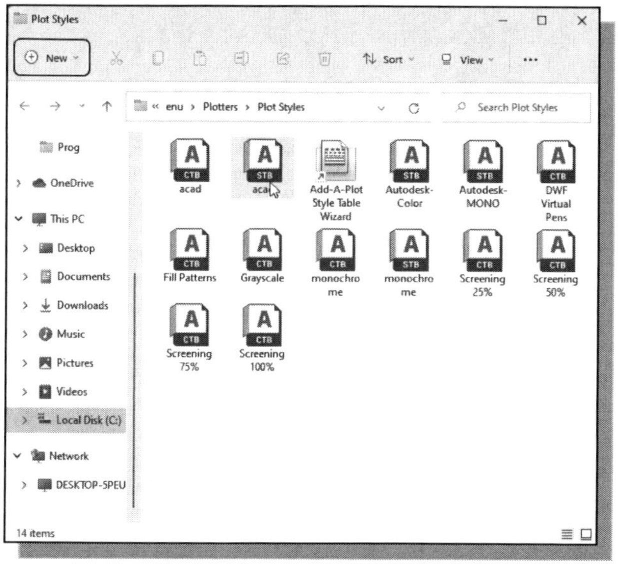

7. The *Plot Styles* folder appears on the screen.

8. Double-click the **acad.stb** icon with the left-mouse-button to open the plot style file.

9. In the *Plot Style Table Editor*, select the **Table View** tab.

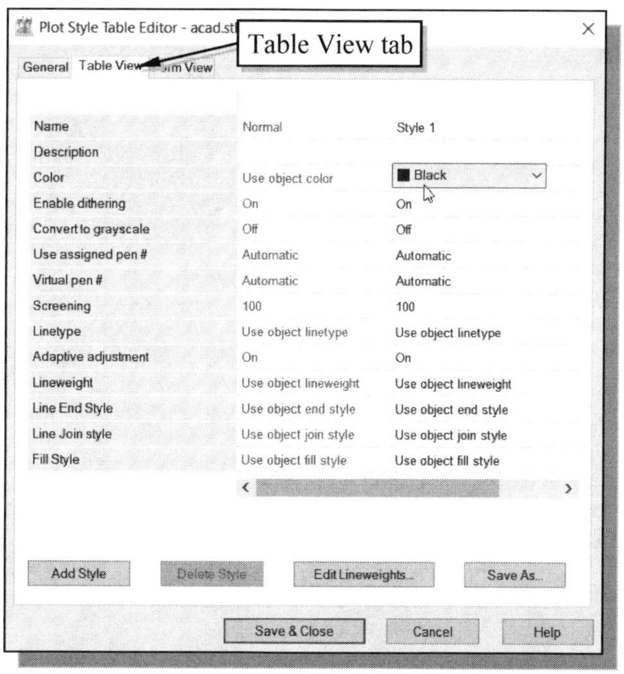

- The *Plot Style Table Editor* displays the plot styles that are in the current plot style table. The **Table View** and **Form View** tabs provide two methods to modify the existing plot style settings. Both tabs list all of the plot styles in the plot style table and their settings. In general, the **Table View** tab is more convenient if there are only a small number of plot styles. We can modify plot style color, screening, linetype, lineweight, and other settings. The first plot style in a named plot style table is *Normal* and represents an object's default properties (no plot style applied). We cannot modify or delete the *Normal* style.

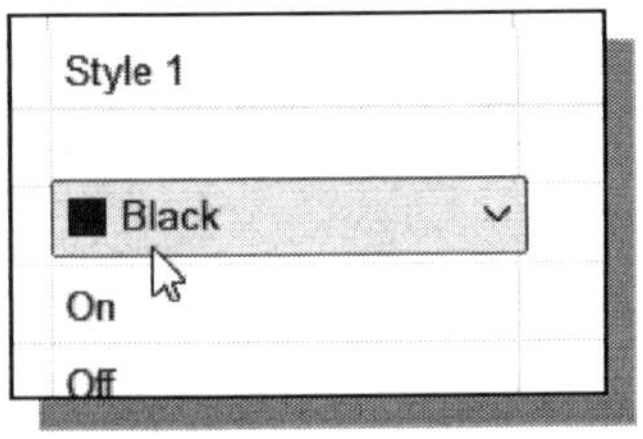

10. Change the *Color* setting for *Style 1* to **Black** so that all layers using this plot style will print using black.

11. Pick the **Save & Close** button to accept the settings and exit the *Plot Style Table Editor*.

12. On your own, adjust and confirm the *Plot Style* of the associated layers to use **Style 1** as shown.

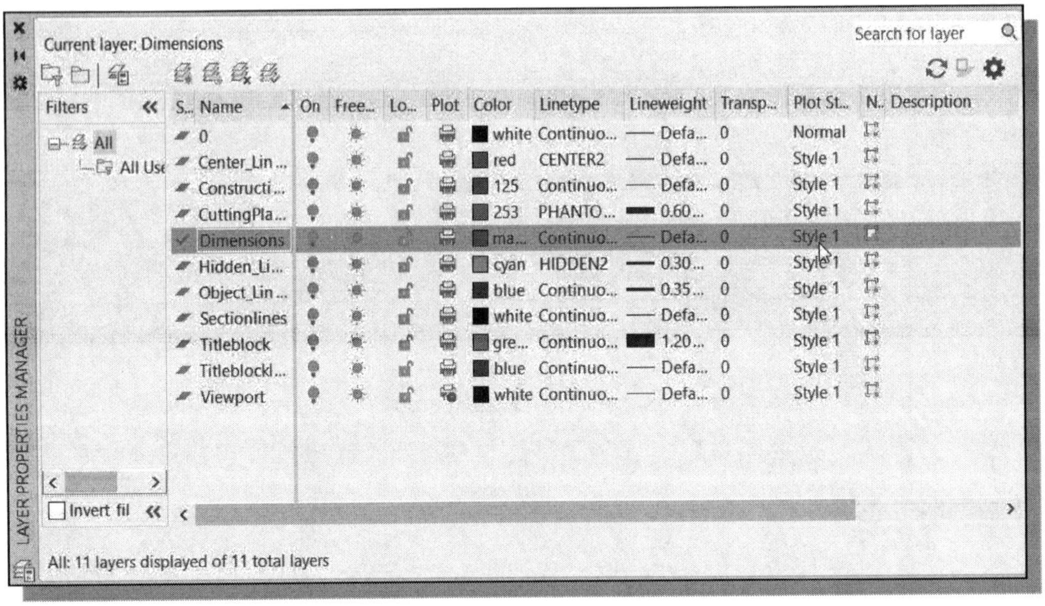

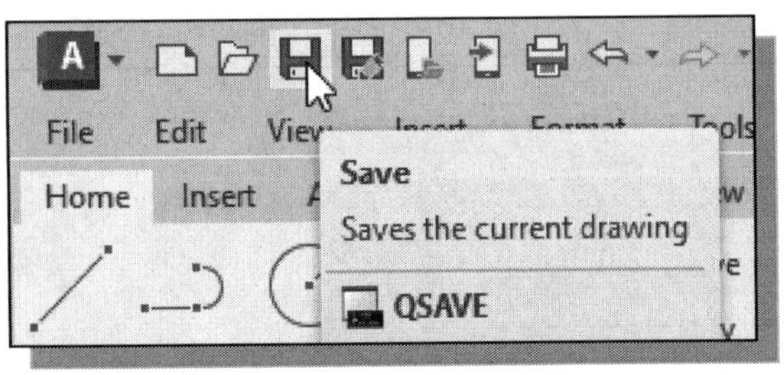

13. Use the **Save button** and save the *V-Block design*.

14. On your own, print out a copy of the *V-block* drawing using the modified plot style table.

Start a new drawing for a Metric Template File

In chapter 8, the procedure to create a template file was illustrated; in this section we will also create a metric template.

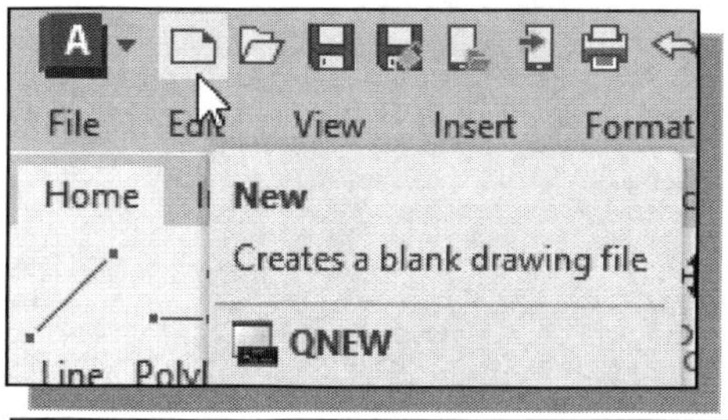

1. In the *Quick Access* toolbar, click the **New** icon.

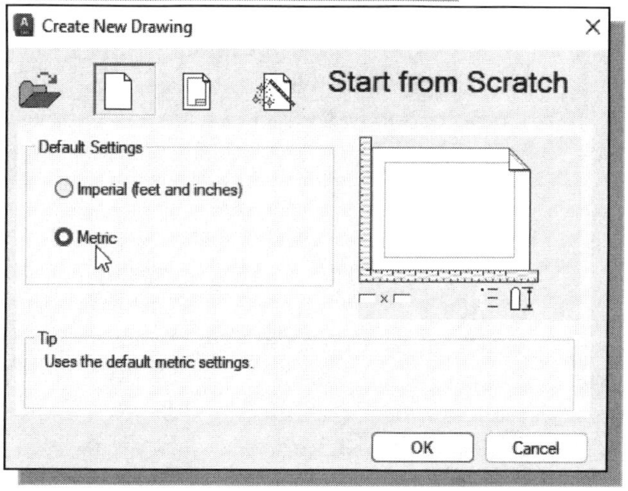

2. In the *Startup* dialog box, select the **Start from Scratch** option with a single click of the left-mouse-button.

3. In the ***Default Settings*** section, pick **Metric** as the drawing units.

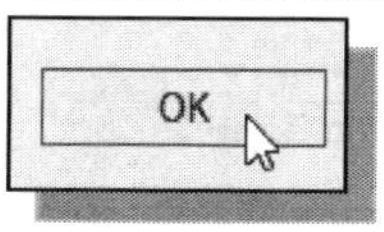

4. Click **OK** to accept the setting and start a new metric drawing.

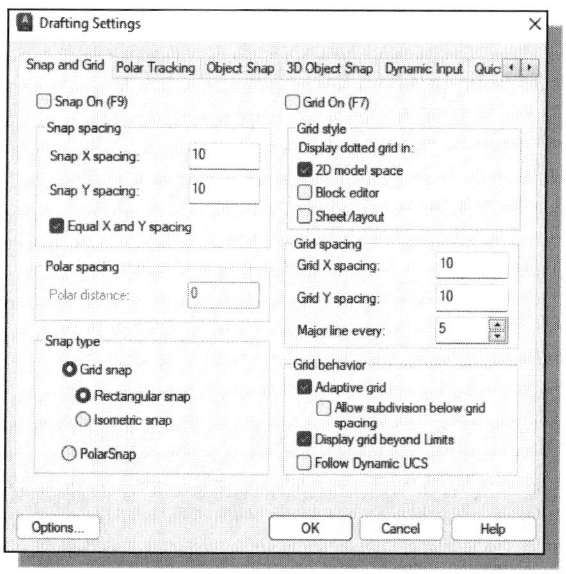

5. On your own, set up the *grid* and *snap spacing* to **10 mm** as shown.

6. Click **OK** to accept the modified settings.

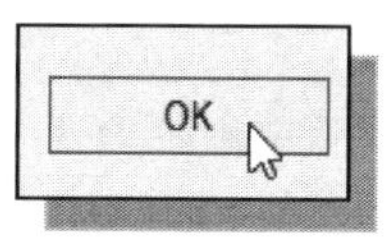

Layers Setup

1. Pick ***Layer Properties Manager*** in the *Object Properties* toolbar.

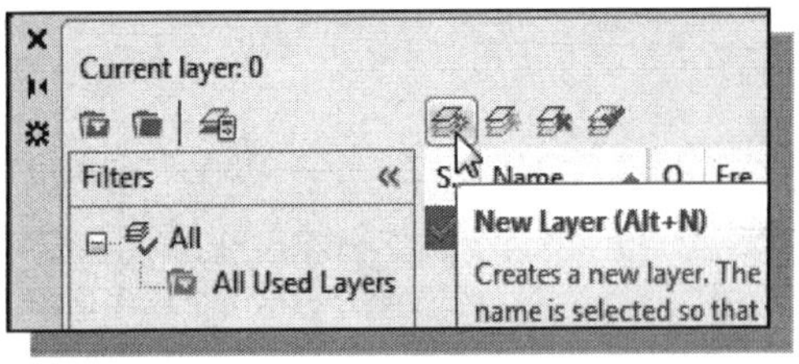

2. In the *Layer Properties Manager* dialog box, click on the **New** button (or the key combination [**Alt+N**]) to create a new layer.

3. Create **layers** with the following settings:

Layer	***Color***	***Linetype***	***Lineweight***	***PlotStyle***
Center_Lines	**Red**	**Center**	**Default**	**Style 1**
Construction	**Gray**	**Continuous**	**Default**	**Style 1**
CuttingPlane_Lines	**Dark Gray**	**Phantom**	**0.6mm**	**Style 1**
Dimensions	**Magenta**	**Continuous**	**Default**	**Style 1**
Hidden_Lines	**Cyan**	**Hidden**	**0.3mm**	**Style 1**
Object_Lines	**Blue**	**Continuous**	**0.6mm**	**Style 1**
Section_Lines	**White**	**Continuous**	**Default**	**Style 1**
Title_Block	**Green**	**Continuous**	**1.2mm**	**Style 1**
TitleBlockLettering	**Blue**	**Continuous**	**Default**	**Style 1**
Viewport	**White**	**Continuous**	**Default**	**Style 1**

➢ Using the ***Normal** PlotStyle* enables plotting of ***lineweights*** defined in the specific layer**.** Note that the **Lineweight** settings are set for proper printing of different linetypes and some may appear thicker on screen.

4. Highlight the layer ***Construction*** in the list of layers.

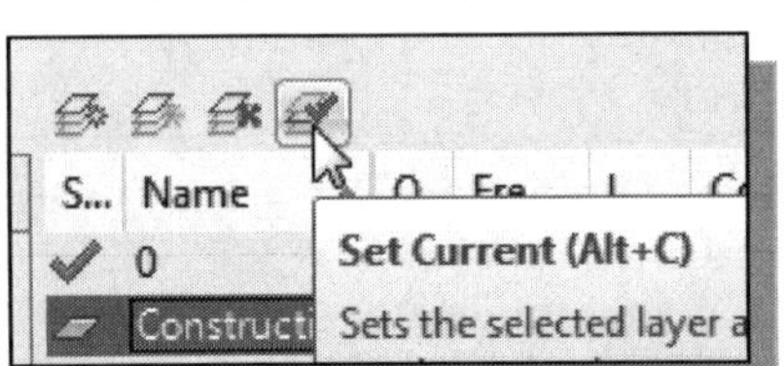

5. Click on the **Current** button to set layer ***Construction*** as the *Current Layer*.

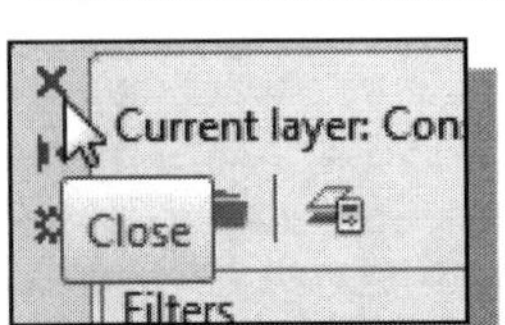

6. Click on the **Close** button to accept the settings and exit the *Layer Properties Manager* dialog box.

Set up the Metric Borders and Title Block by Copy & Paste

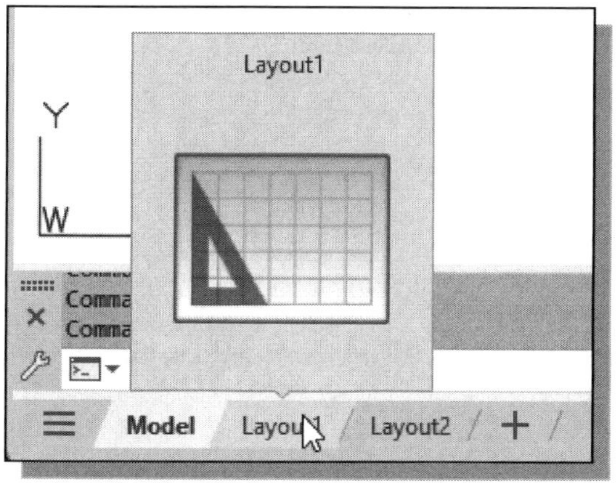

1. Click the **Layout1** icon to switch to the two-dimensional paper space.

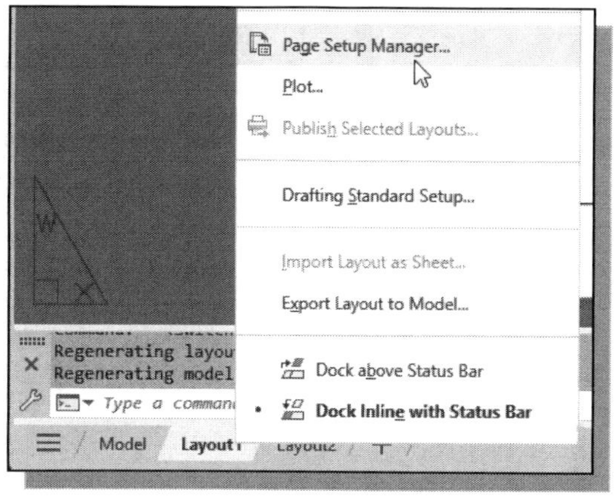

2. Right-click once on the tab and select **Page Setup Manager**.

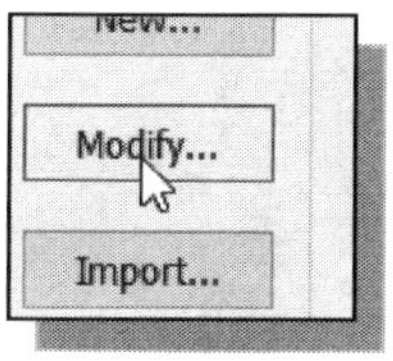

3. Choose the default layout in the *Page Setup Manager* and click **Modify**.

4. In the *Page Setup* dialog box, select a plotter/printer that is available to plot/print your design. Here we will set up the plotting for an **A-size plot** on a **LaserJet printer**. You can also use A4 paper size if your plotter supports the metric size papers.

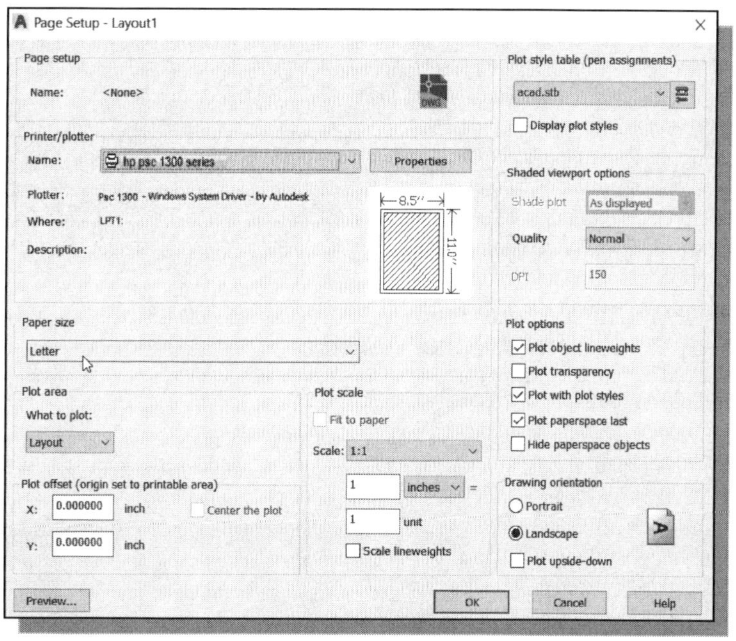

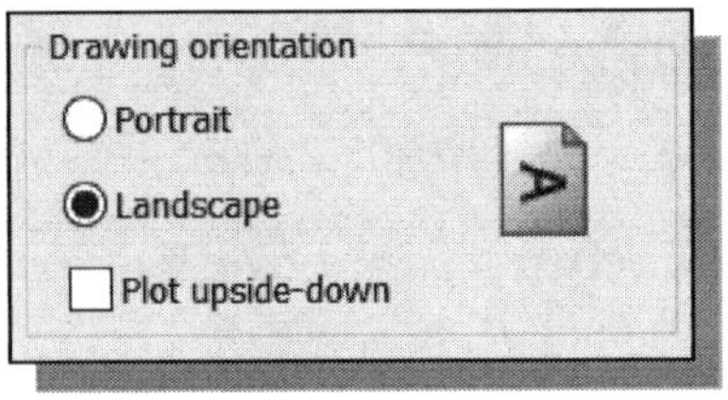

5. Set the *Paper size* to **Letter** and the *Drawing orientation* is set to **Landscape**.

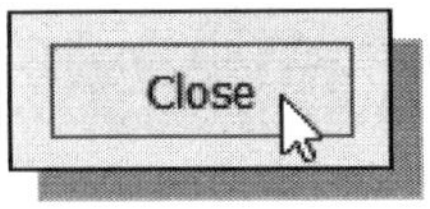

6. Click on the **OK** button and **Close** button to accept the settings and exit the *Page Setup* dialog boxes.

7. On your own, **switch** to the **Layout1** of the *V-Block drawing*. We will use the previously created borders and title block.

8. Pre-select only the borders and title block using a selection window as shown. (Hint: first delete the viewport.)

9. Inside the drawing area, **right-click** once to bring up the option list and select [**Clipboard**] → [**Copy with Base Point**] as shown.

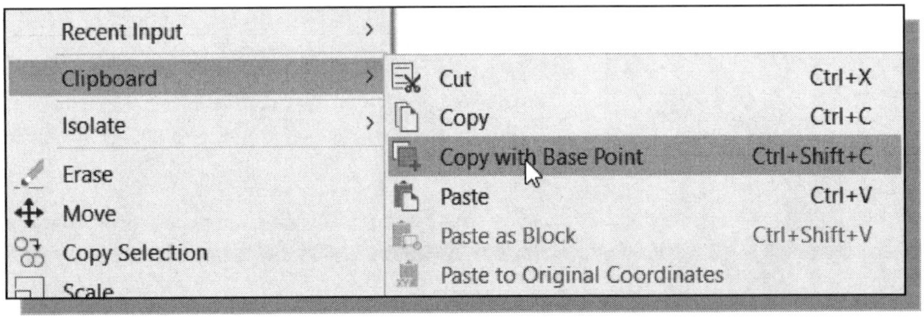

10. Zoom in and select the **lower left corner** of the borders as the base point.

11. On your own, switch back to the blank **Layout1** of the *new drawing.*

12. Inside the drawing area, right-click once to bring up the option list and select [**Clipboard**] → [**Paste**] as shown.

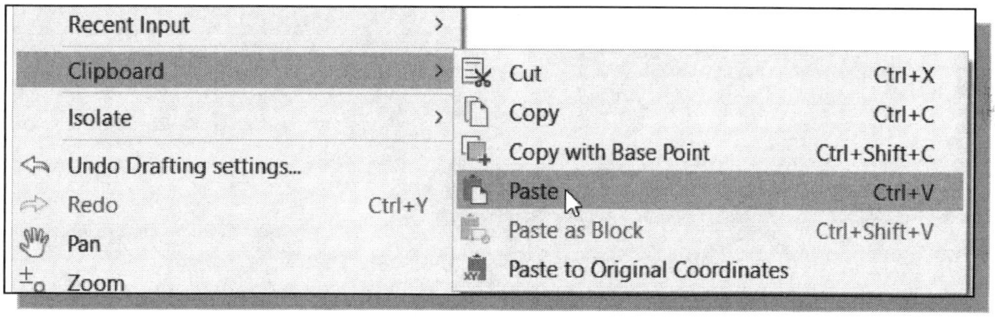

13. On your own, place the borders and the title block near the lower left corner of the dashed box as shown. Note the borders and the title block appeared to be fairly small; this is due to the difference in units.

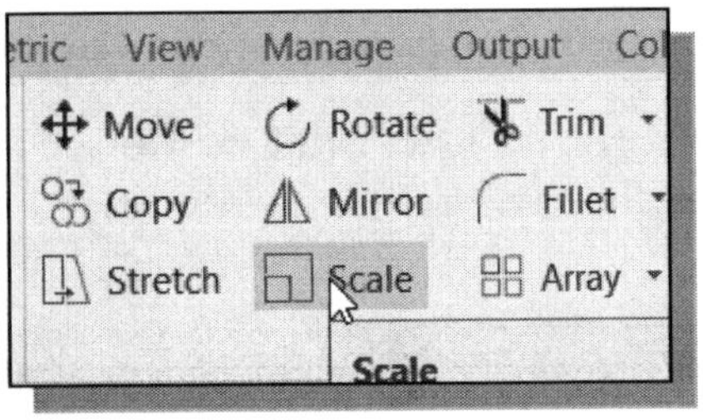

14. In the *Modify* toolbar, click the **Scale** icon to activate the command.

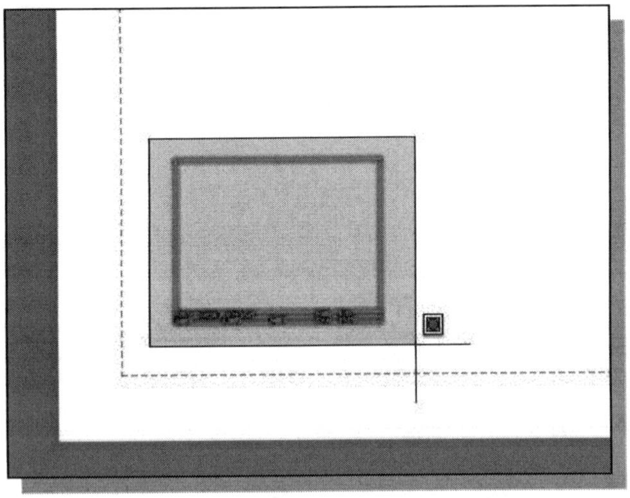

15. Select only the borders and title block using a ***selection window*** as shown.

16. Inside the drawing area, **right-click** once to accept the selection.

17. Select the **lower left corner** of the borders as the base point.

18. In the *command prompt* area, enter **25.4** as the scale factor.

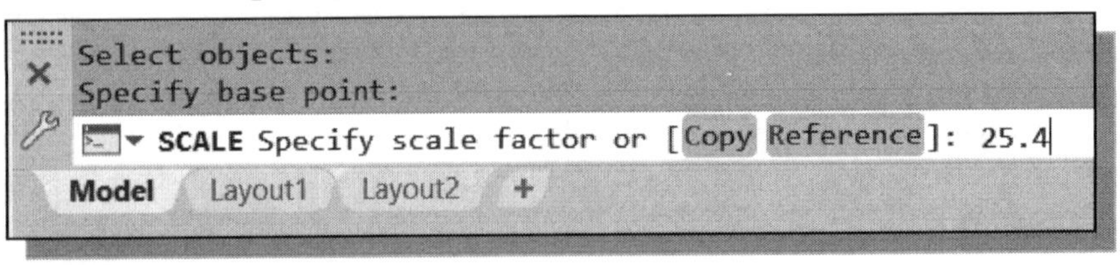

19. On your own, reposition the *borders and title block*, and add a viewport inside the borders as shown.

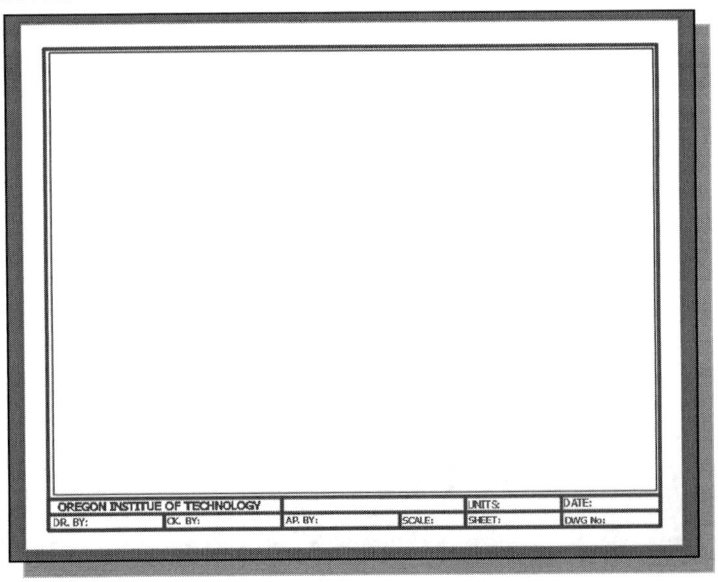

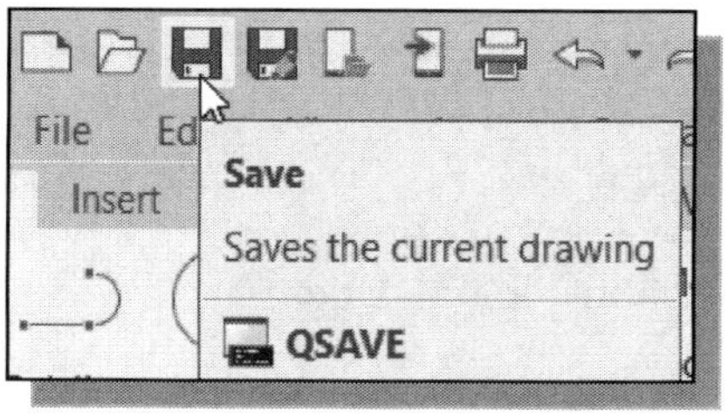

20. In the *Quick Access* toolbar, click the **Save** icon.

21. In the *Save Drawing As* dialog box, save to the default template folder (or select the folder in which you want to store the *template file).* Enter ***Acad-mm-A-H-Title*** in the *File name* box.

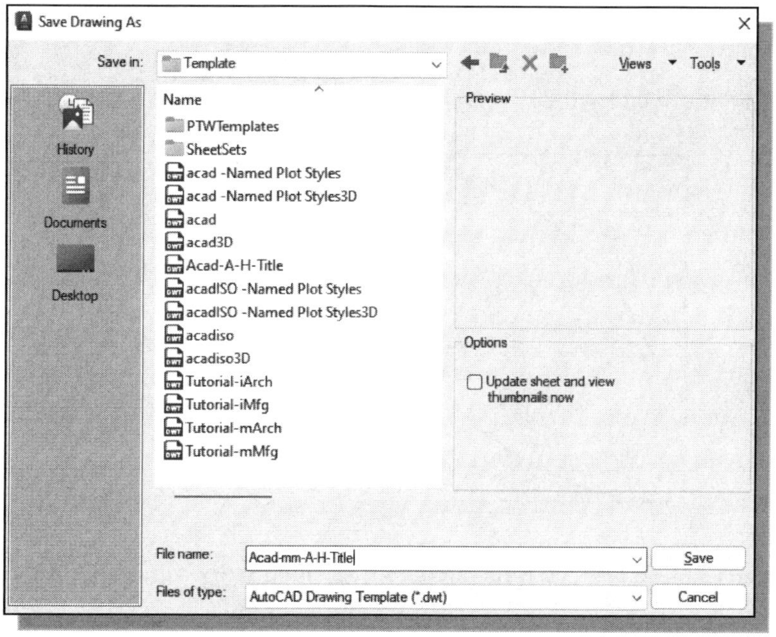

22. Pick **Save** in the *Save Drawing As* dialog box to close the dialog box.

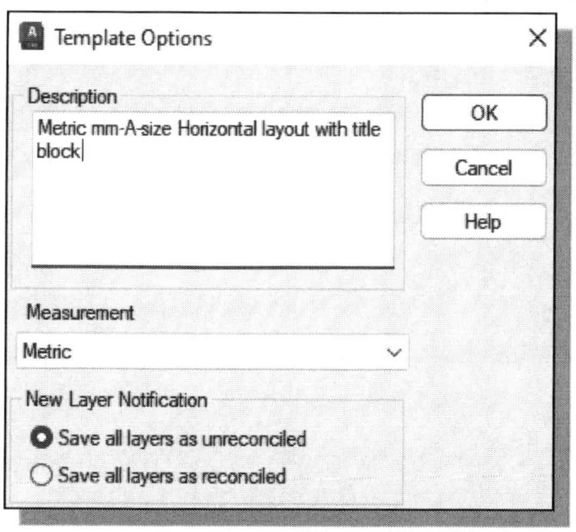

23. In the *Template Description* dialog box, enter ***mm-A-size Horizontal layout with title block*** in the *Description* box.

24. Pick **OK** to close the dialog box and save the template file.

➢ It is recommended that you keep a second copy of any template files on a separate disk as a backup.

Review Questions: (Time: 25 minutes)

1. What is an auxiliary view and why would it be important?

2. When is a line viewed as a point? How can a line be shown in true length?

3. What is a GRIP? What are the advantages of using the GRIPS?

4. List three GRIPS editing commands you have used in the tutorial.

5. What does the *Polar Tracking* option allow us to do?

6. Find the area A defined by the two arcs, as described in the figure below.

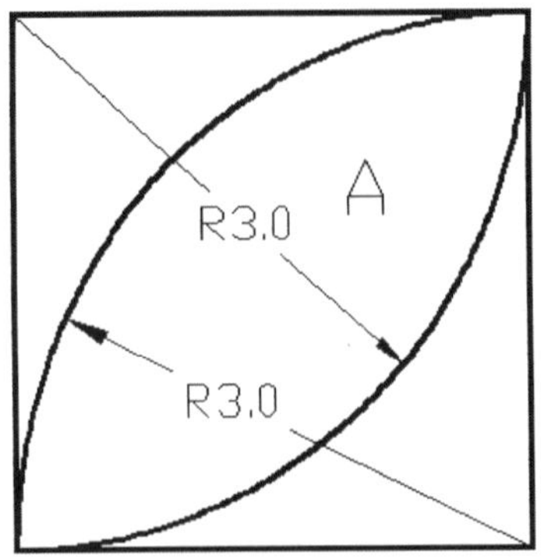

7. Find the area A defined by the three arcs, as described in the figure below.

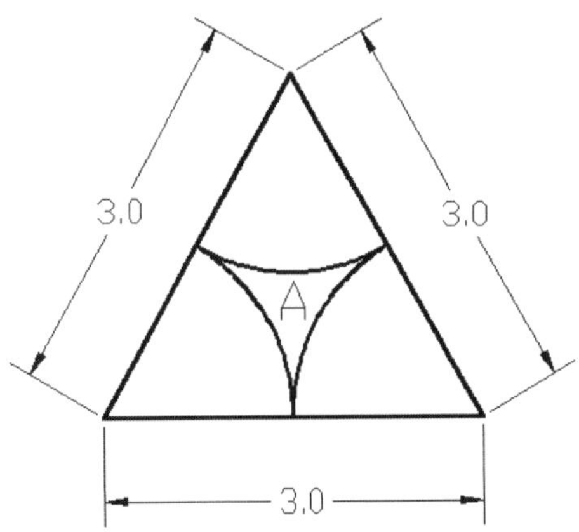

Exercises: (Time: 240 minutes)

1. **Angle Base** (Dimensions are in inches. Note the overall height of the part is 2.5)

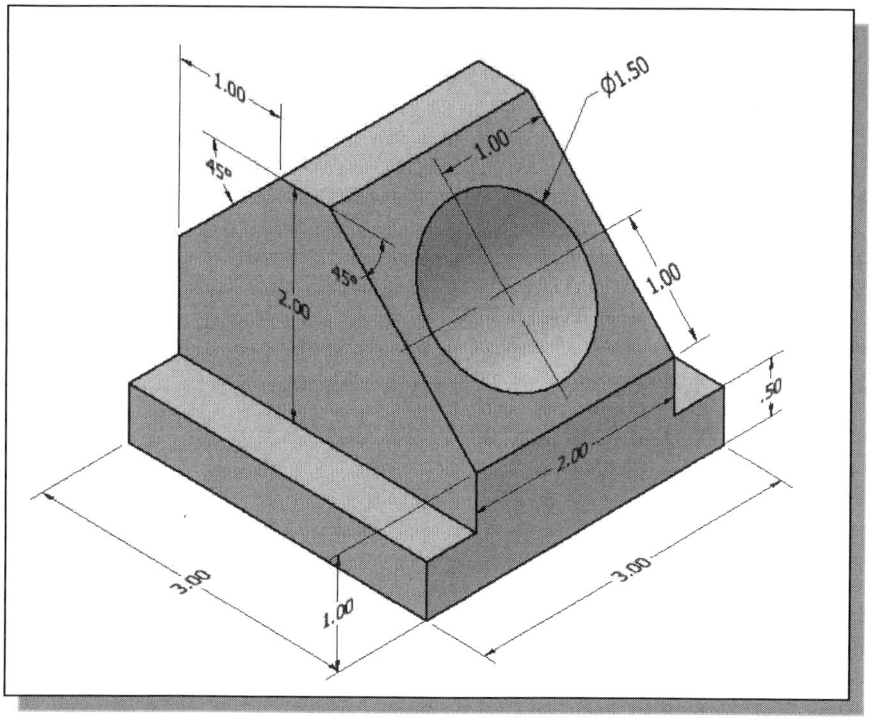

2. **Indexing Guide** (Dimensions are in inches.)

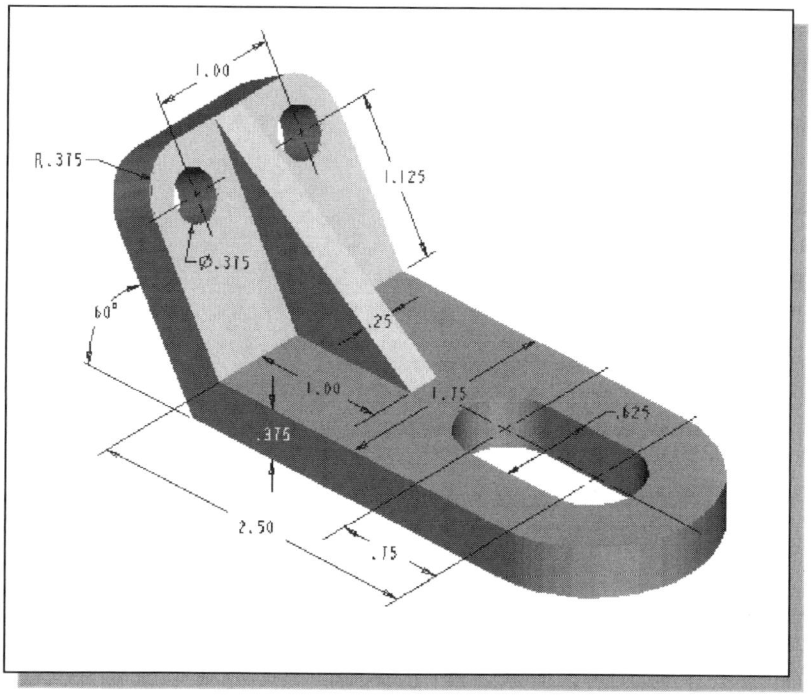

3. **Spindle Base** (Dimensions are in millimeters.)

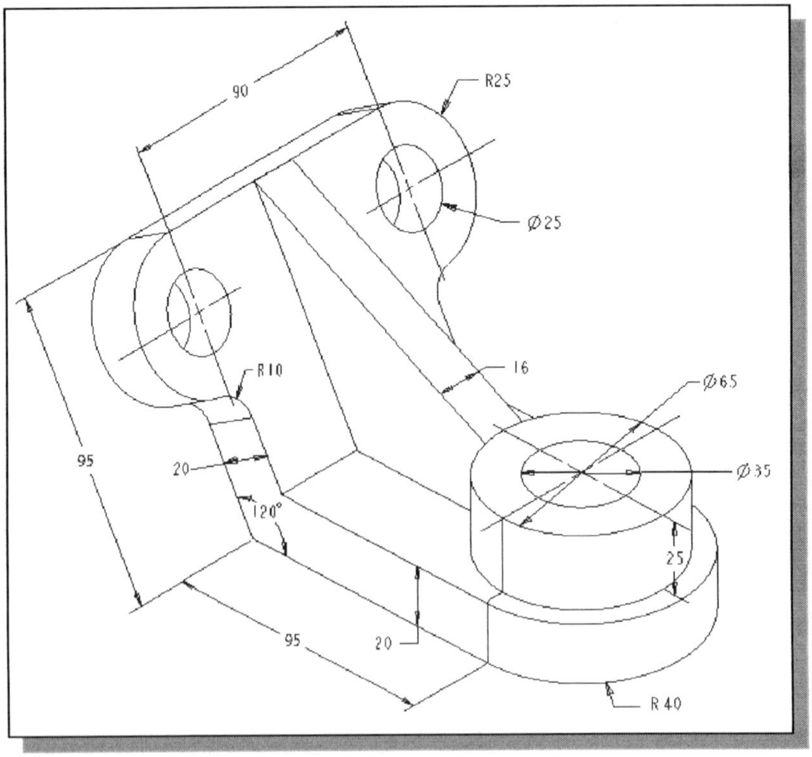

4. **Transition Support** (Dimensions are in inches.)

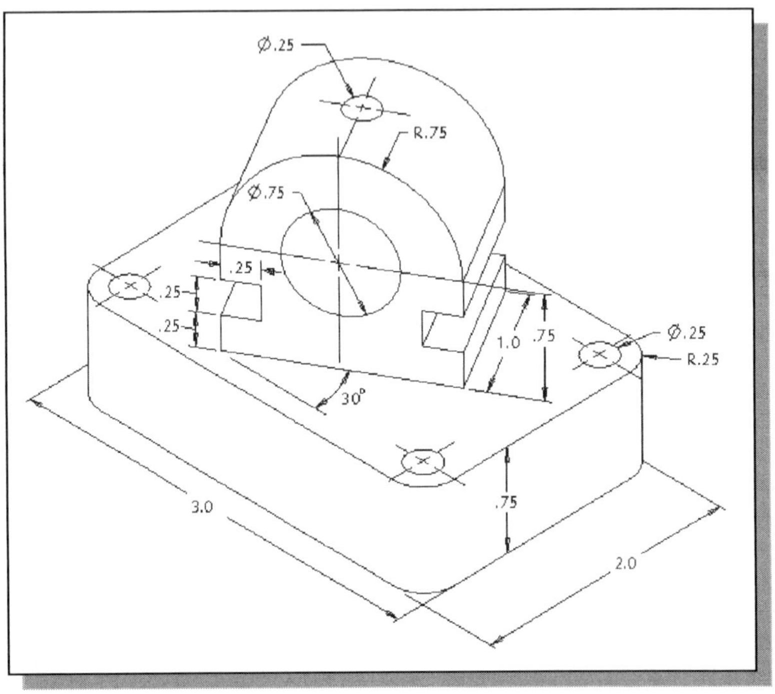

5. **Support Hanger** (Dimensions are in inches.)

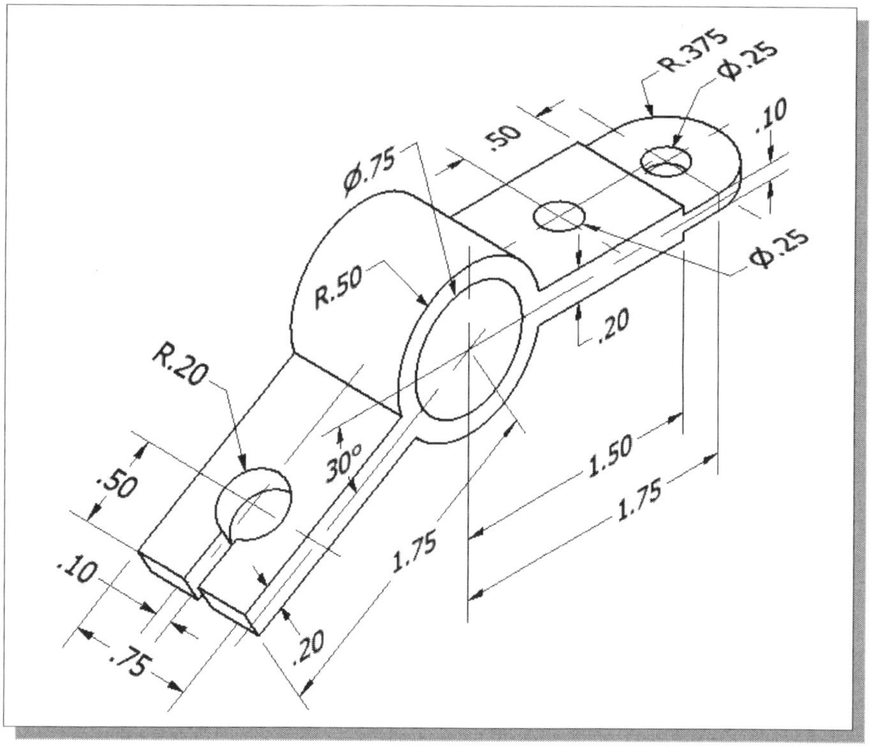

6. **Automatic Stop** (Dimensions are in inches.)

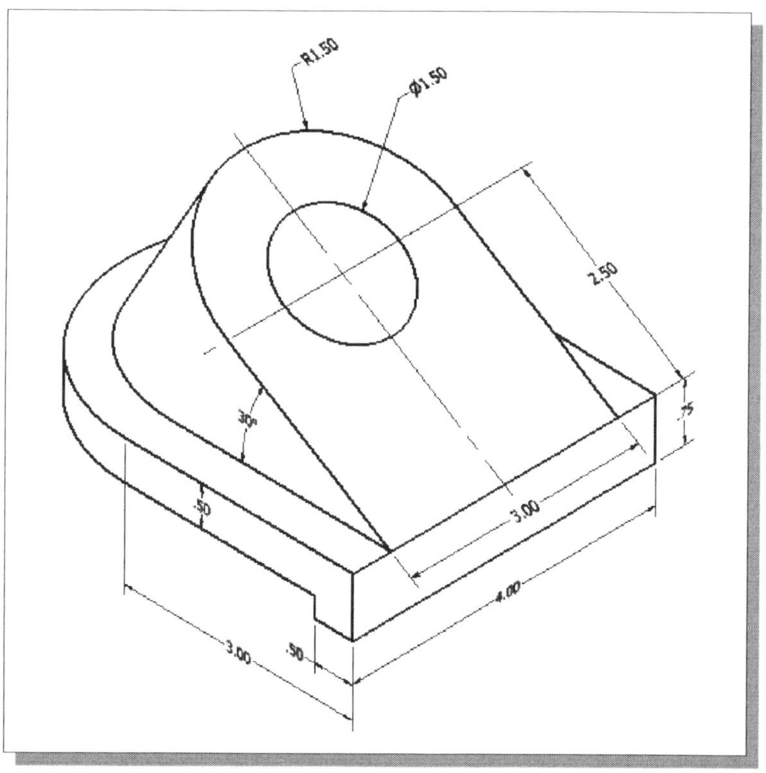

7. Angle V-Block (Dimensions are in inches.)

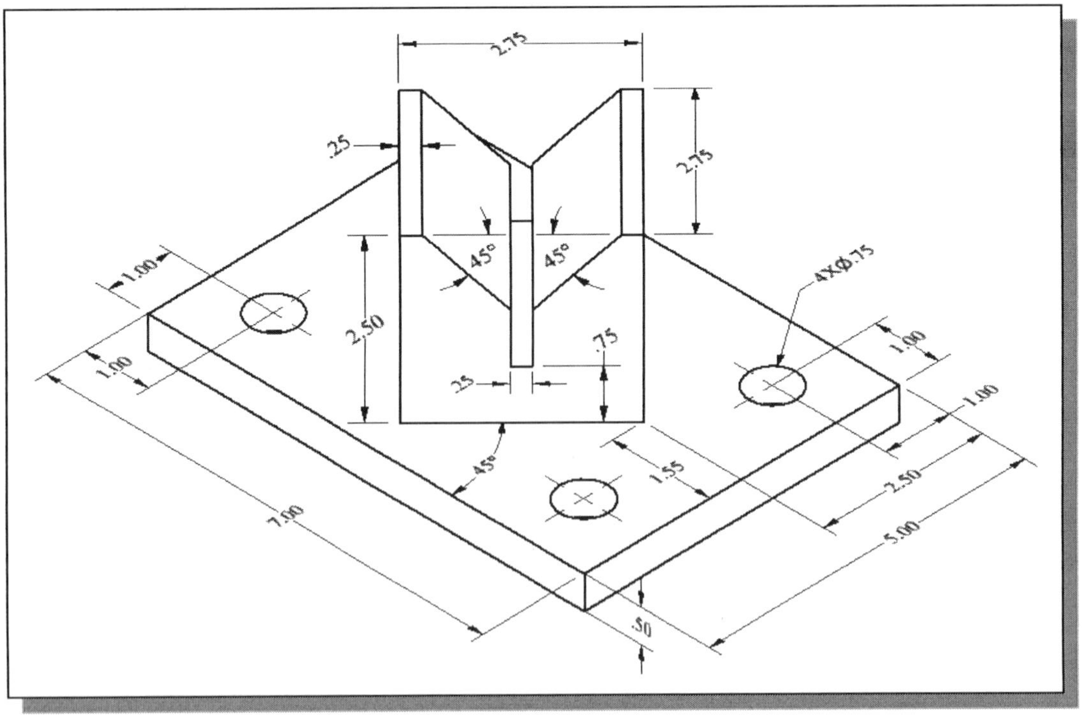

Chapter 11
Section Views

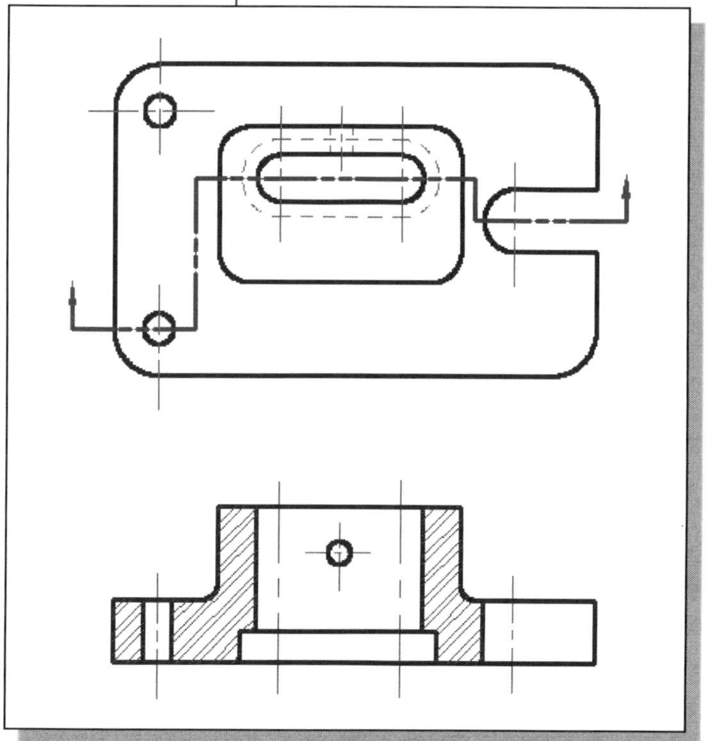

Learning Objectives

- ♦ Understand the Basic Principles of Section Views
- ♦ Use the Proper Types of Section Views
- ♦ Use CAD Methods to Create Section Views
- ♦ Use the Object Snap Shortcut Options
- ♦ Change the Linetype Scale Property
- ♦ Stretch and Move Objects with Grips
- ♦ Use the Hatch Command

AutoCAD Certified User Examination Objectives Coverage

Section 2: Creating Basic Drawings

Section 3: Manipulating Objects

Section 4: Drawing Organization and Inquiry Commands

Section 5: Altering Objects

Section 8: Dimensioning

Section 9: Hatching Objects

Section 10: Working with Reusable Content

Introduction

In the previous chapters, we have explored the basic CAD methods of creating orthographic views. By carefully selecting a limited number of views, the external features of most complicated designs can be fully described. However, we are frequently confronted with the necessity of showing the interiors of parts, or when parts are assembled, that cannot be shown clearly by means of hidden lines.

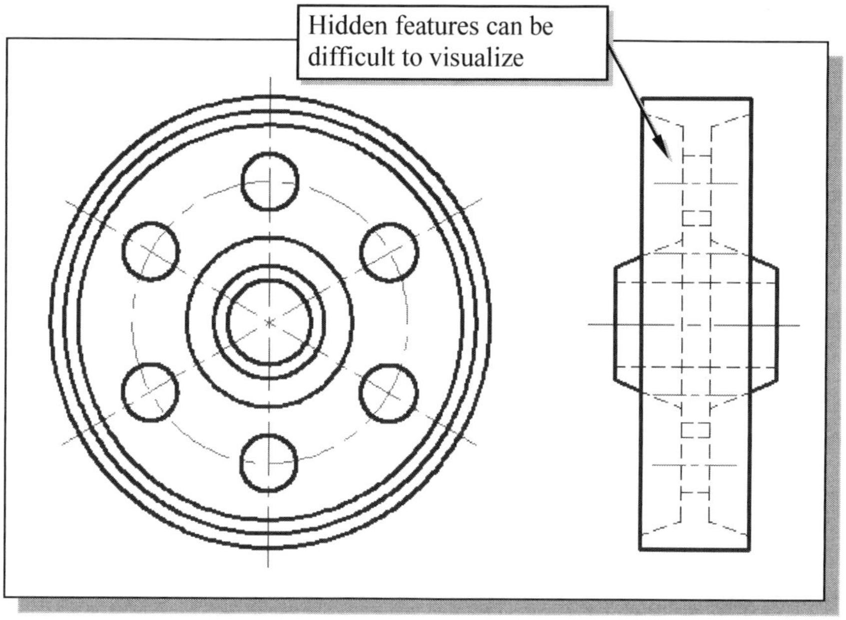

In cases of this kind, to aid in describing the object, one or more views are drawn to show the object as if a portion of the object had been cut away to reveal the interior.

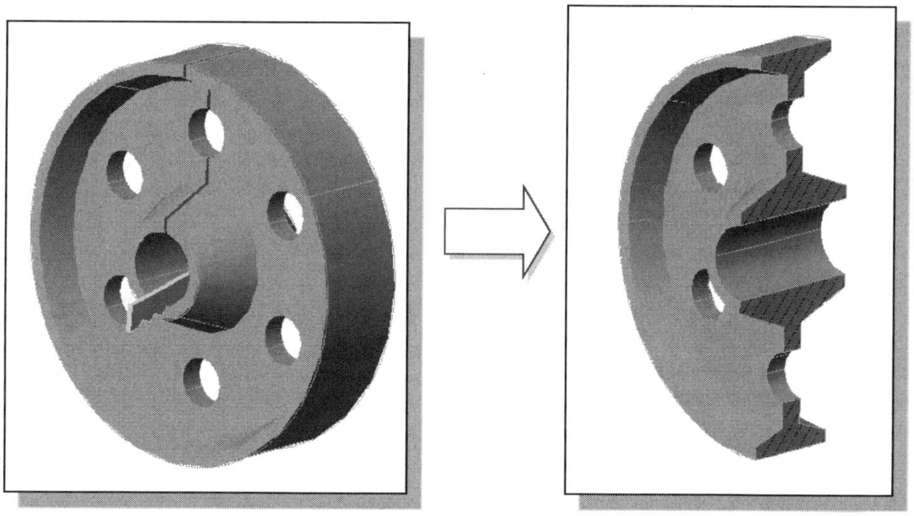

This type of convention is called a **section**, which is defined as an imaginary cut made through an object to expose the interior of a part. This kind of cutaway view is known as a **section view**.

In a *section view*, the place from which the section is taken must be identifiable on the drawing. If the place from which the section is taken is obvious, as it is for the below figure, no further description is needed.

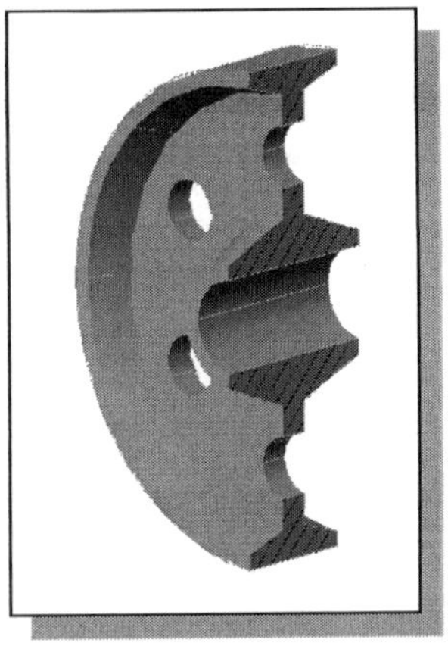

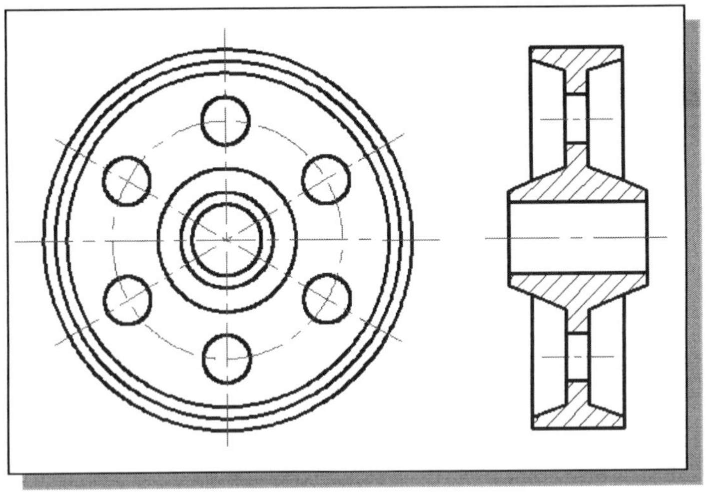

If the place from which the section is taken is not obvious, as it is for the below figure, a **cutting plane** is needed to identify the section. Two arrows are also used to indicate the viewing direction. A *cutting plane line* is drawn with the *phantom* or *hidden* line.

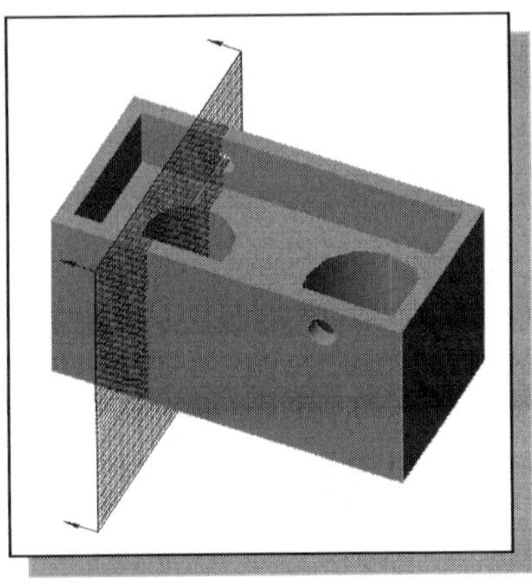

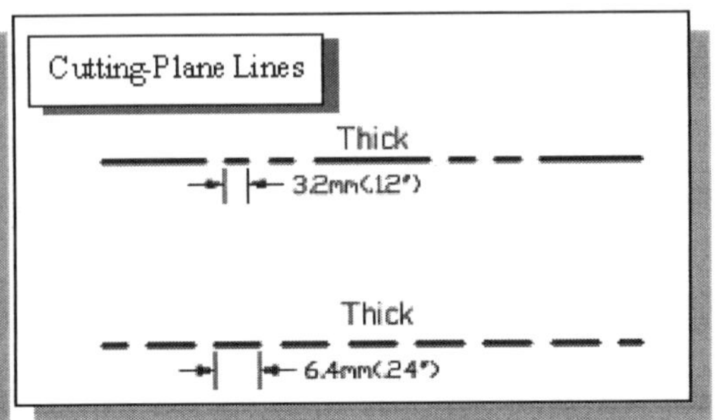

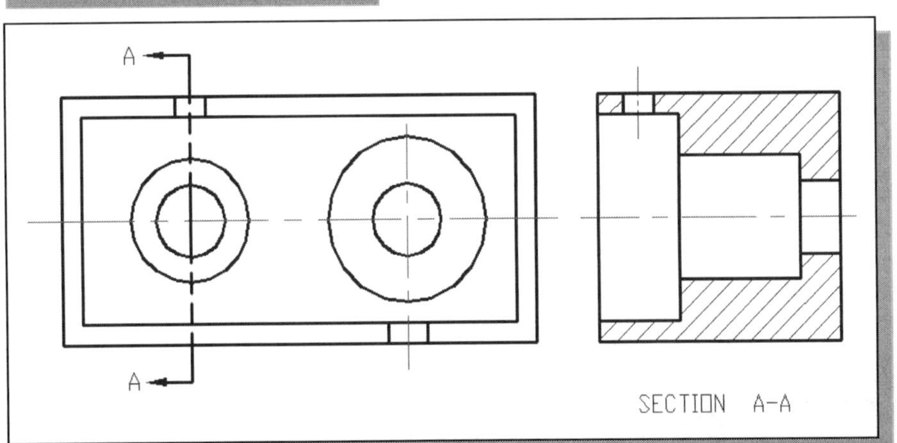

General Rules of Section Views

Section views are used to make a part drawing more understandable, showing the internal details of the part. Since the sectioned drawing is showing the internal features there is generally no need to show hidden lines.

A section view still follows the general rules of any view in a multiview drawing. Cutting planes may be labeled at their endpoints to clarify the association of the cut and the section views, especially when multiple cutting plane lines are used. When using multiple cutting planes, each sectioned drawing is drawn as if the other cutting plane lines do not exist. The cutting plane line takes precedence over center lines and, remember, cutting plane lines may be omitted when their location is obvious.

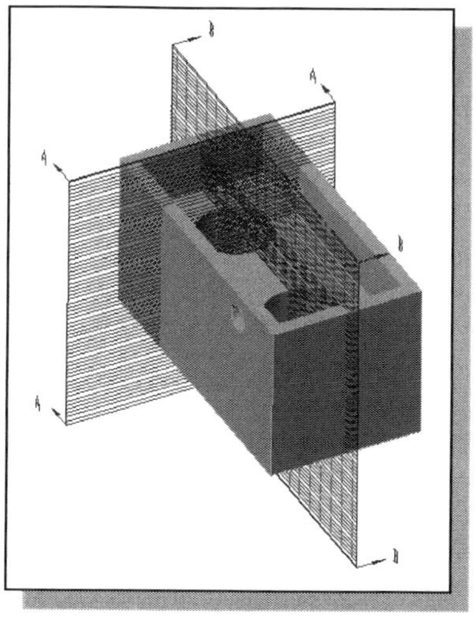

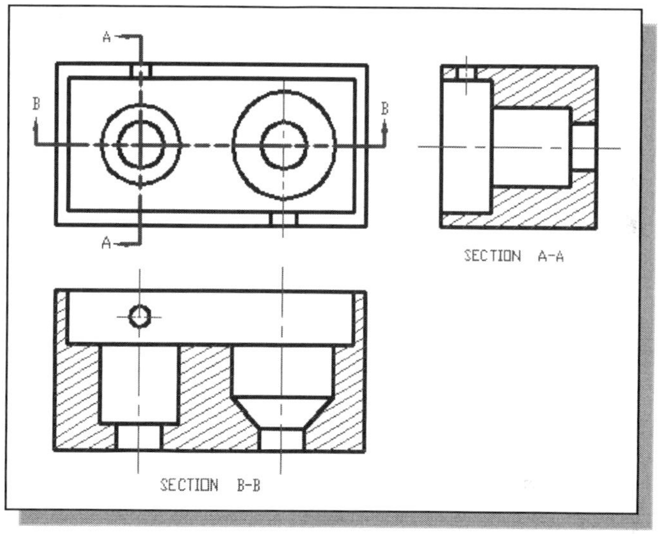

Section lines or **cross-hatch lines** are drawn where the cutting plane passes through the object. This is done as if a saw was used to cut the part and then section lines are used to represent the cutting marks left by the saw blade. Different materials are represented by the use of different section line types. The line type for iron may be used as the general section line type for any material.

Cast iron, Malleable iron and general use for all materials

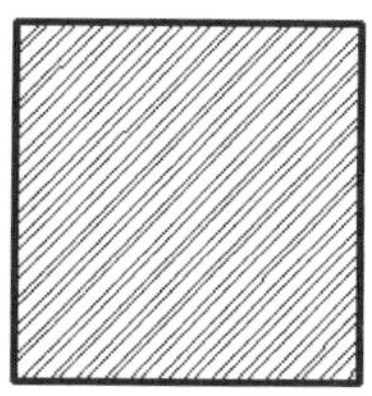

Steel

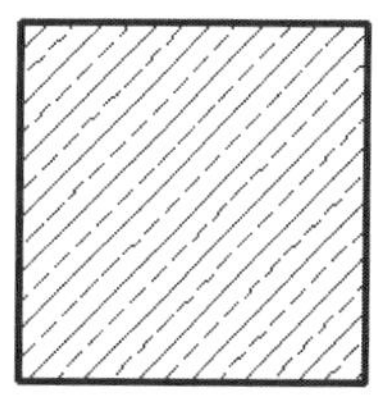

Bronze, Brass and composition Materials

Magnesium, aluminum and aluminum alloys

Section lines should not be parallel or perpendicular to object lines. Section lines are generally drawn at 45°, 30° or 60°, unless there are conflicts with other rules. Section lines should be oriented at different angles for different parts.

Section Drawing Types

- **Full Section:** The cutting plane passes completely through the part as a single flat plane.

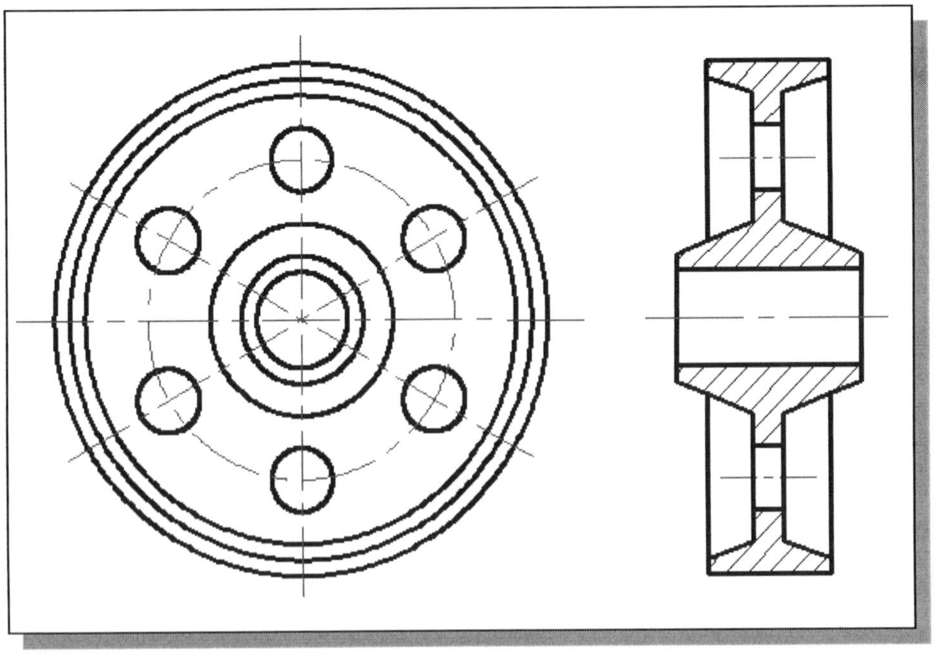

- **Half Section:** The cutting plane only passes halfway through the part and the other half is drawn as usual. Hidden lines are generally not shown on either half of the part to avoid confusion. Half section is mostly used on cylindrical parts, and a center line is used to separate the two halves.

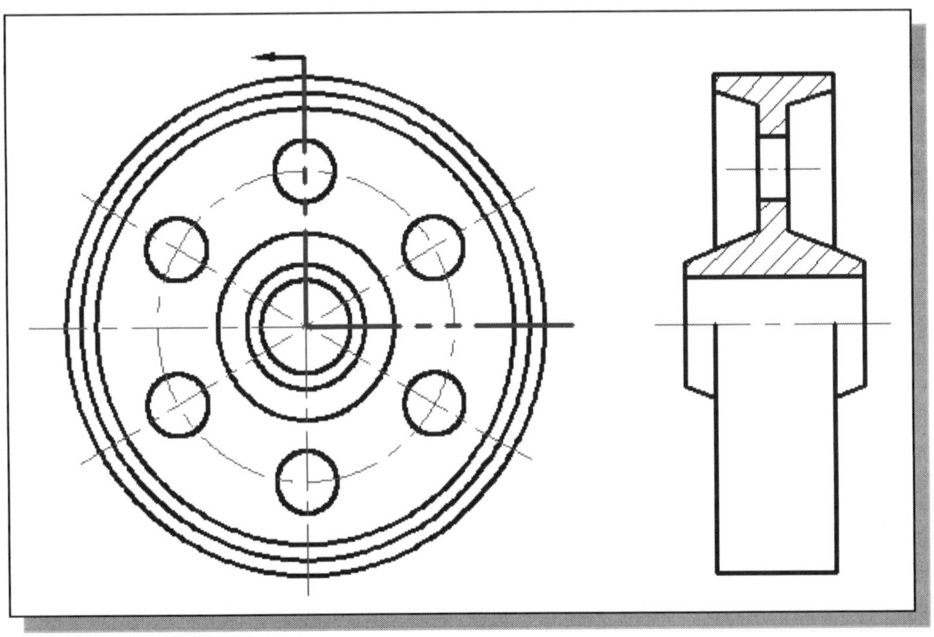

- **Offset Section:** It is often difficult to interpret a multiview drawing when there are multiple features on the object. An **offset section** allows the cutting plane to pass through several places by "**offsetting**" or **bending** the cutting plane. The offsets or bends in the cutting plane are all 90° and are *not* shown in the section view.

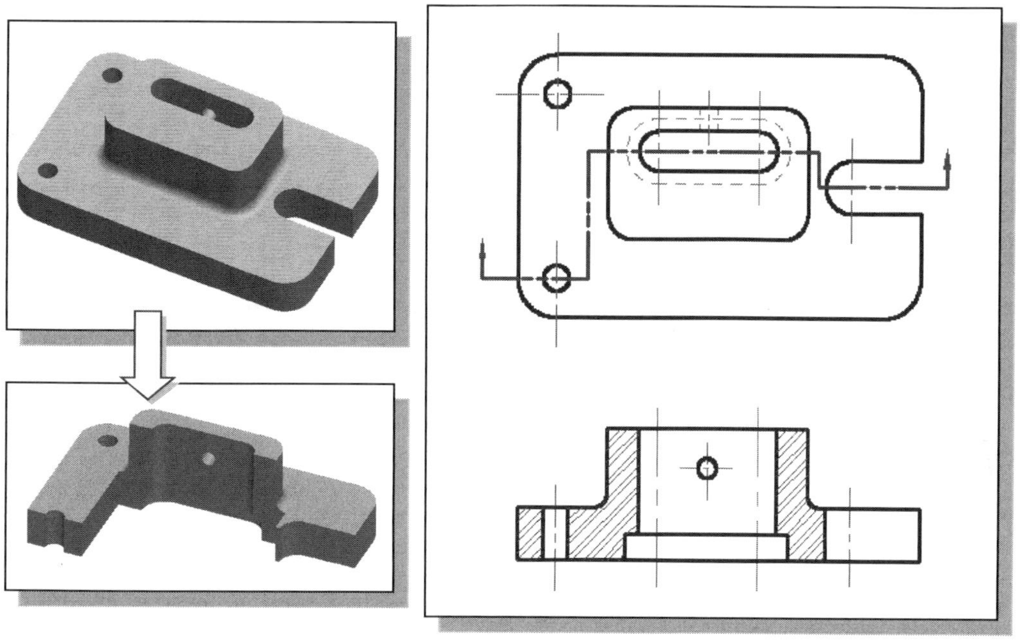

- **Broken-Out Section:** It is quite often that a full section is not necessary, but only a partial section is needed to show the interior details of a part. In a **broken-out section**, only a portion of the view is sectioned and a jagged break-line is used to divide the sectioned and un-sectioned portion of the view.

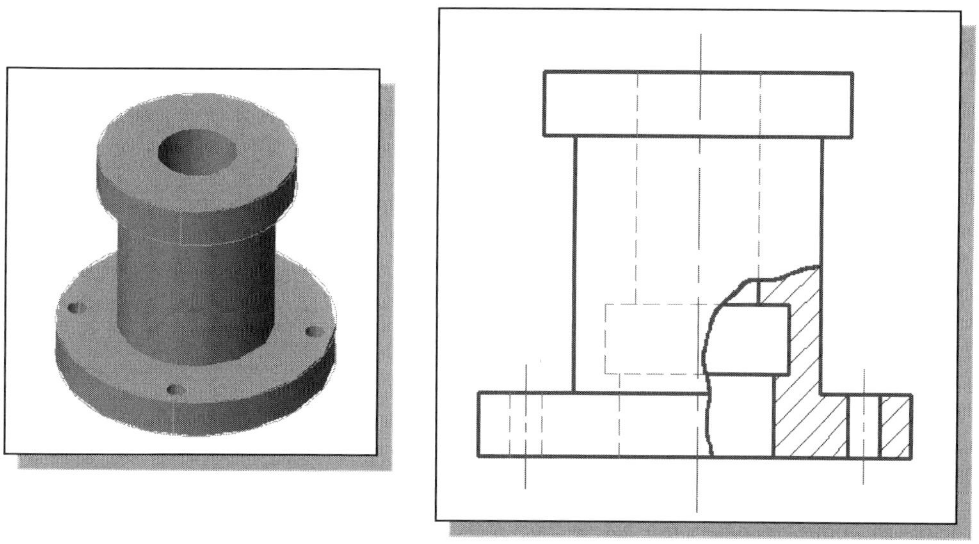

- **Aligned Section:** To include certain angled features in a section view, the cutting plane may be bent to pass through those features to their true radial position.

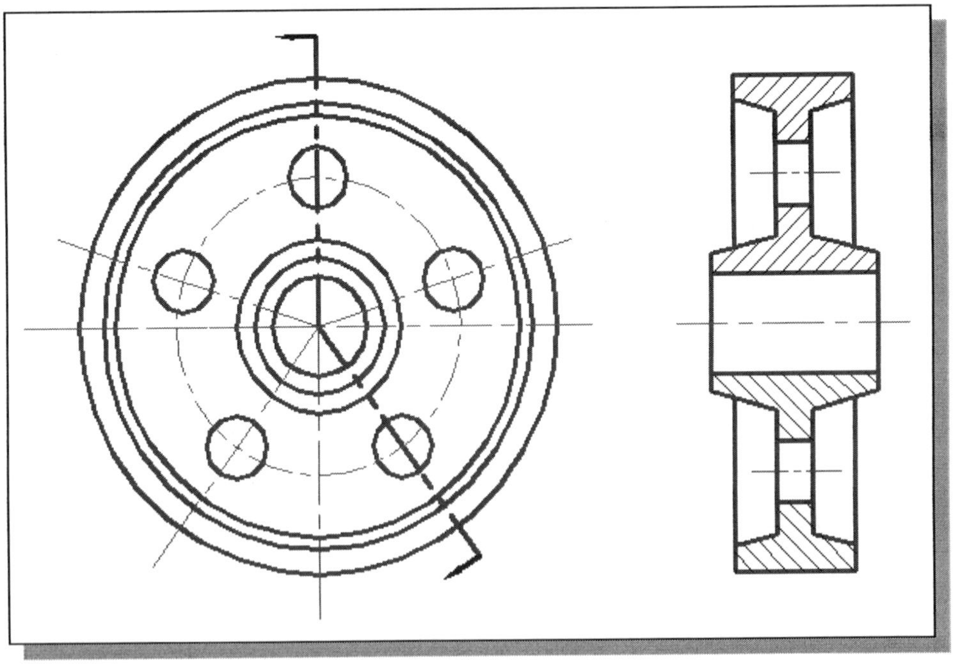

- **Half Views:** When space is limited, a symmetrical part can be shown as a half view.

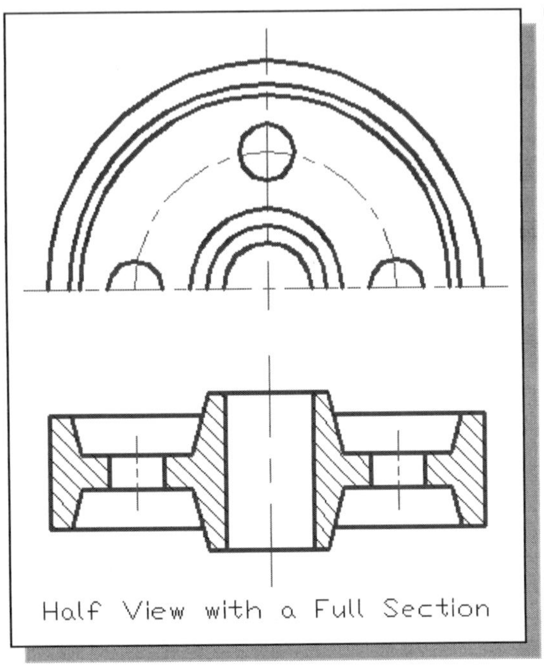

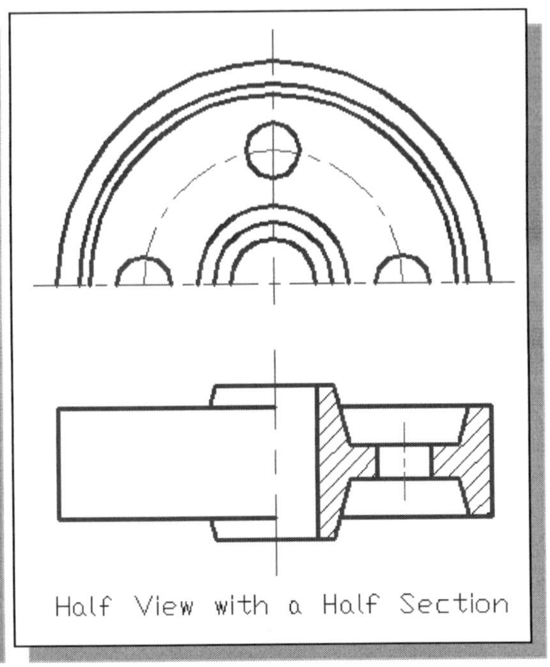

- **Thin Sections:** For thin parts, typically parts that are less than 3mm thickness such as sheet metal parts and gaskets, section lines are ineffective and therefore should be omitted. Thin sections are generally shown in solid black without section lines.

- **Revolved Section:** A cross section of the part is revolved 90° and superimposed on the drawing.

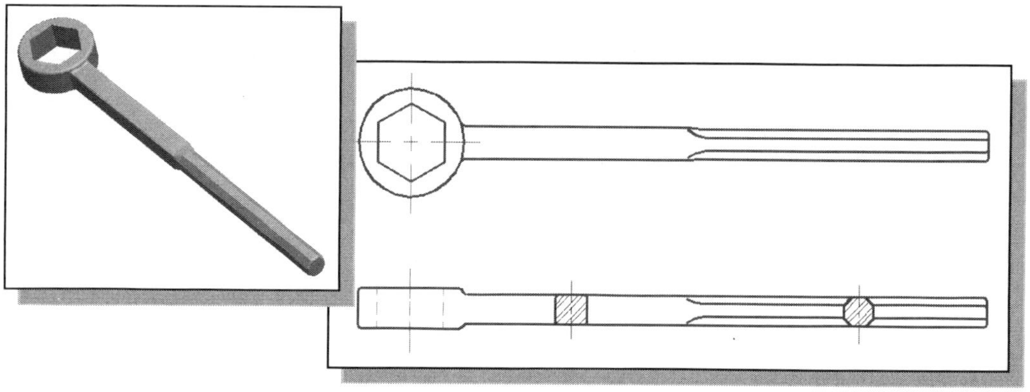

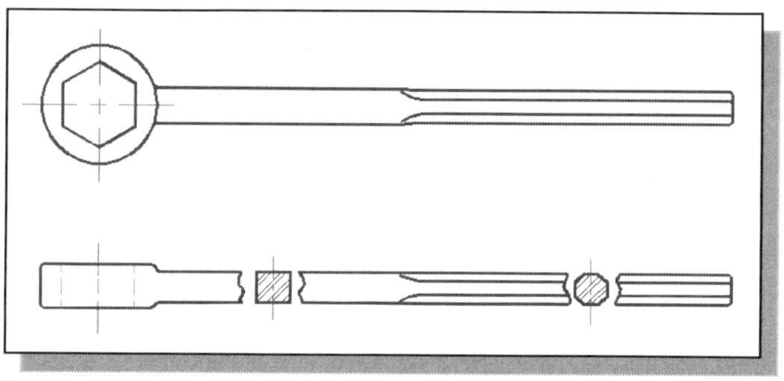

- The object lines adjacent to a revolved section may be broken out with short break lines. The true shape of a revolved section is retained regardless of the object lines in the view.

- **Removed Section:** Similar to the revolved section except that the sectioned drawing is not superimposed on the drawing but placed adjacent to it. The removed section may also be drawn at a different scale. Very useful for detailing small parts or features.

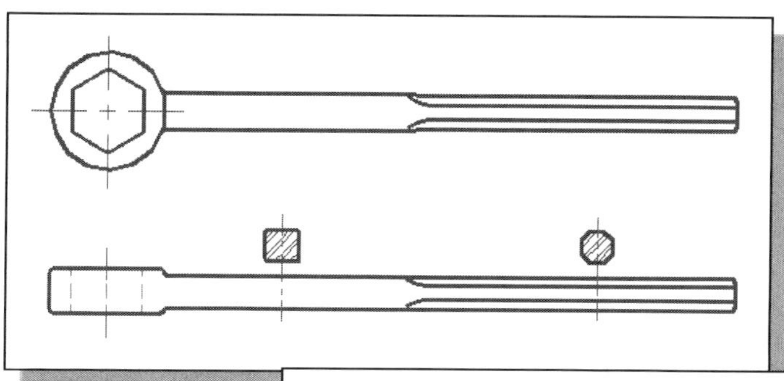

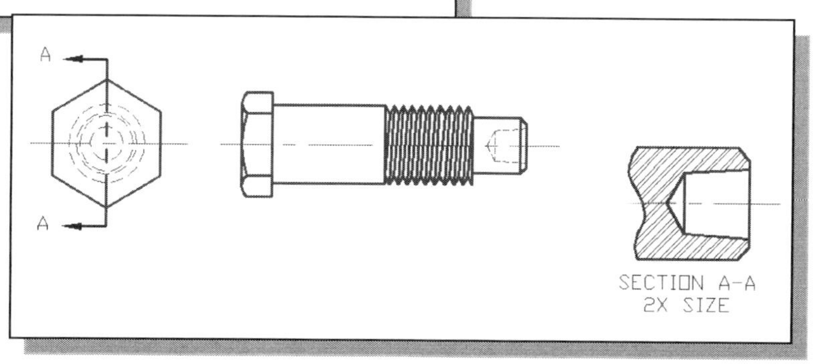

- **Conventional Breaks:** In making the details of parts that are long and with a uniform cross section, it is rarely necessary to draw its whole length. Using the Conventional Breaks to shorten such an object will allow the part to be drawn with a larger scale. S-Breaks are preferred for cylindrical objects and jagged lines are used to break non-circular objects.

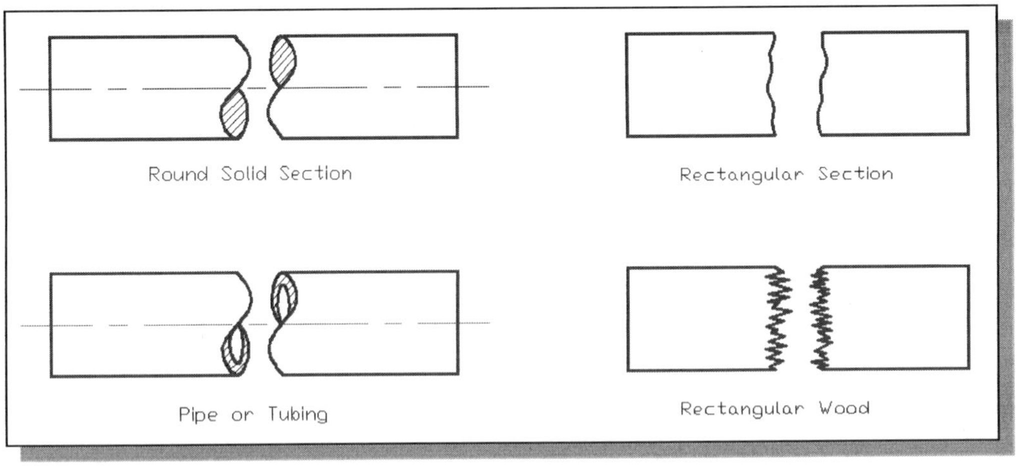

- **Ribs and Webs in Sections:** To avoid a misleading effect of thickness and solidity, ribs, webs, spokes, gear teeth and other similar parts are drawn without crosshatching when the cutting plane passes through them lengthwise. Ribs are sectioned if the cutting plane passes through them at other orientations.

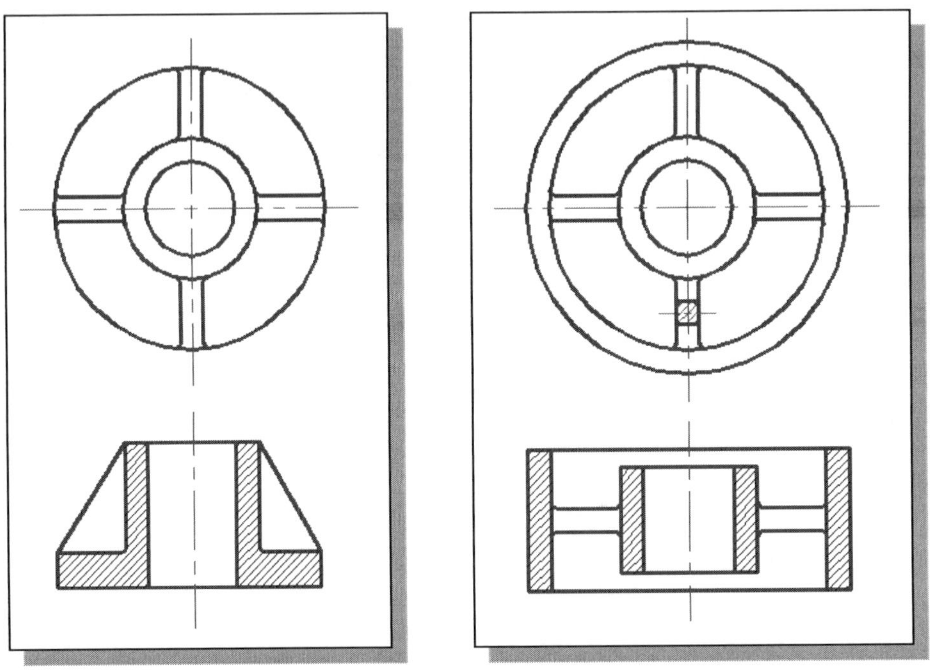

- **Parts Not Sectioned:** Many machine elements, such as fasteners, pins, bearings and shafts, have no internal features, and are generally more easily recognized by their exterior views. Do not section these parts.

Section Views in AutoCAD

In the following sections, we will demonstrate the procedure to construct a section view using **AutoCAD 2027**.

With a CAD system, once the geometric construction has been completed, the geometric properties of entities can be easily modified. For example, objects can be moved from one layer to another, and colors can be adjusted in a matter of seconds. In the following tutorial, the standard views of the bearing design are first constructed, and then by modifying the geometric properties of entities, a section view is generated.

In a section view, section lines, or crosshatch lines, are added to indicate the surfaces that are cut by the imaginary cutting plane. The type of section line used to represent a surface varies according to the type of material. AutoCAD's **Hatch** command can be used to fill a pattern inside an area. We define a boundary that consists of an object or objects that completely enclose the area. **AutoCAD 2027** comes with a solid fill and more than 50 industry-standard hatch patterns that we can use to differentiate the components of objects or represent object materials.

The Bearing Design

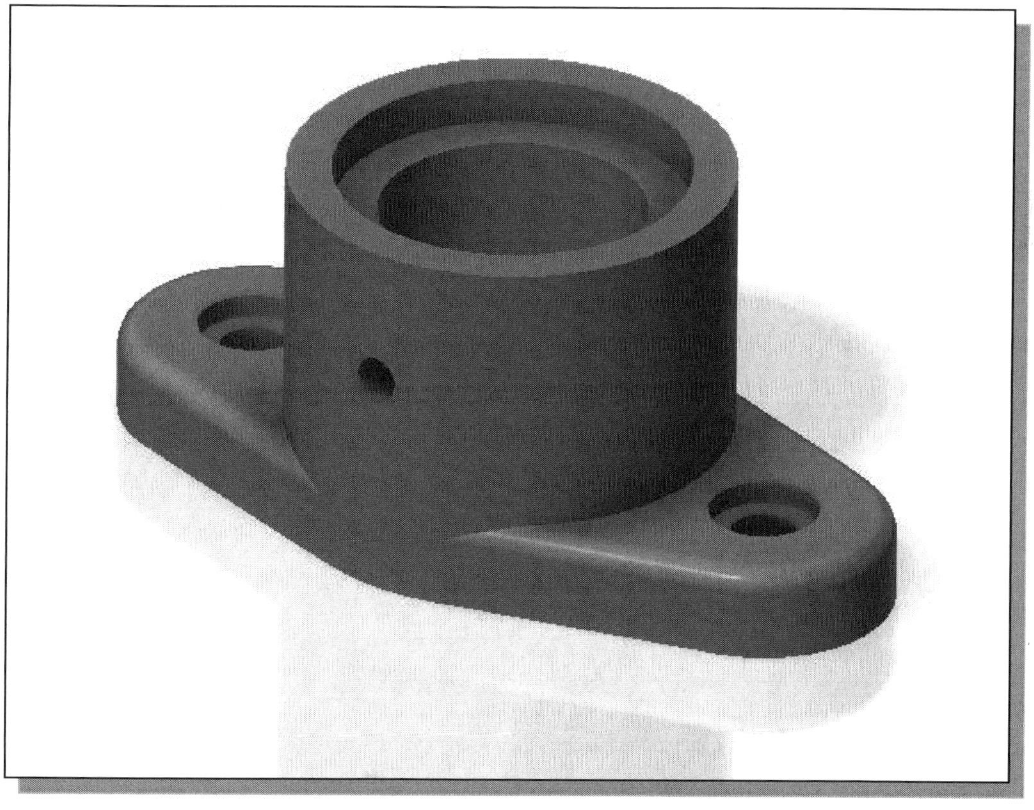

Starting Up AutoCAD 2027

1. Select the **AutoCAD 2027** option on the *Program* menu or select the **AutoCAD 2027** icon on the *Desktop*.

2. In the AutoCAD *Startup* dialog box, select the **Template** option.

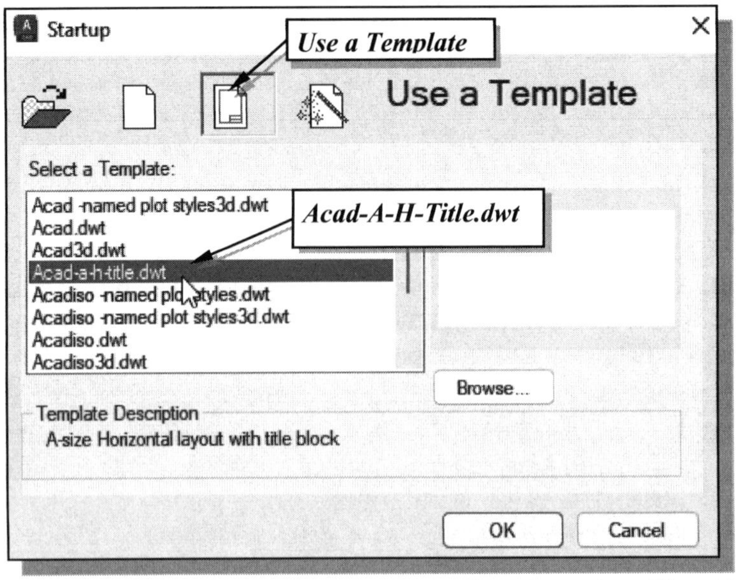

3. Select the ***Acad-A-H-Title*** template file from the list of template files. If the template file is not listed, click on the **Browse** button to locate and proceed to open a new drawing file.

4. Pick ***Layer Properties Manager*** in the *Object Properties* toolbar.

5. Examine the layer property settings in the *Layer Properties Manager* dialog box. (On your own, update the *Plot Style* to **Style 1** in the template.)

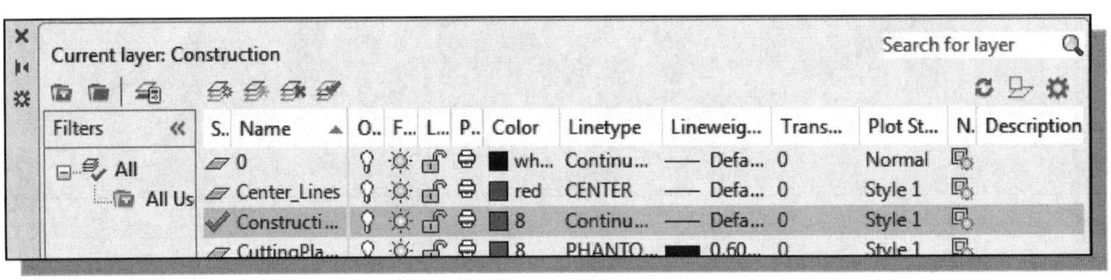

6. On your own, set layer ***Construction*** as the *Current Layer*, if necessary.

7. Click on the **Close** button to exit the *Layer Properties Manager* dialog box.

The Bearing Design

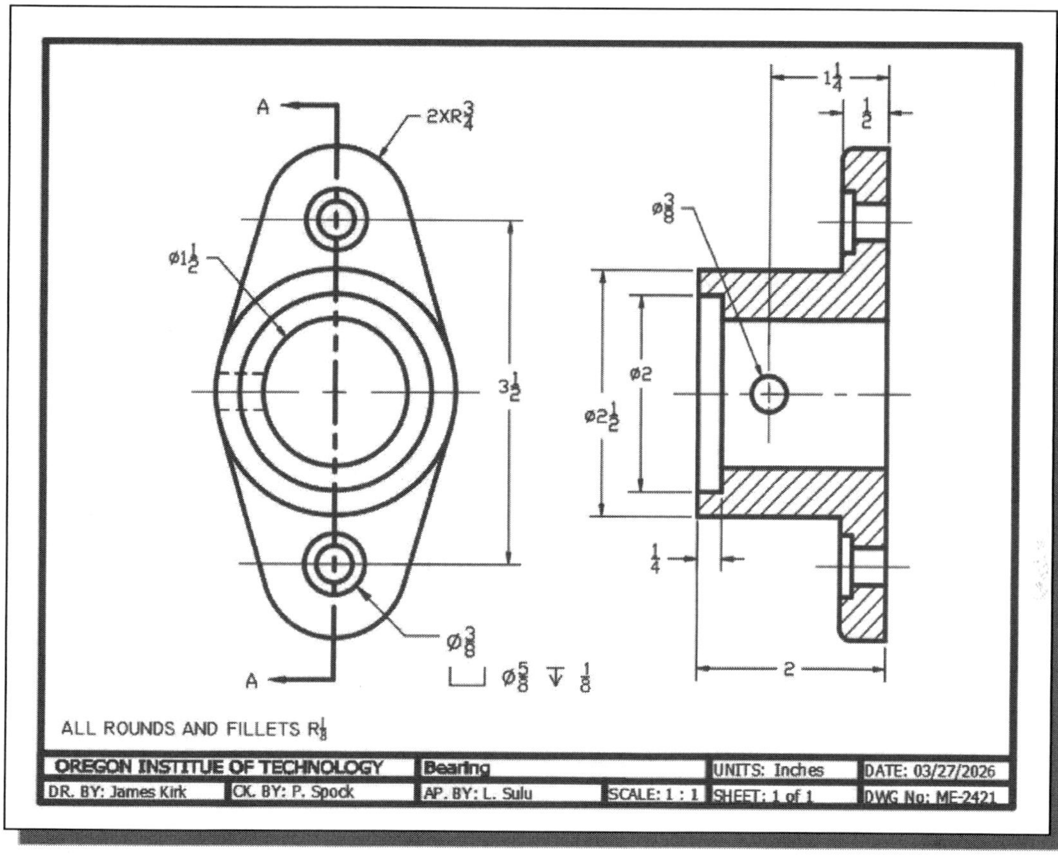

Setting up the Principal Views

1. In the *Status Bar* area, reset the options and turn ***ON*** the ***Dynamic Input, Polar Tracking, Object Snap, Object Tracking,*** and ***Line Weight Display*** options.

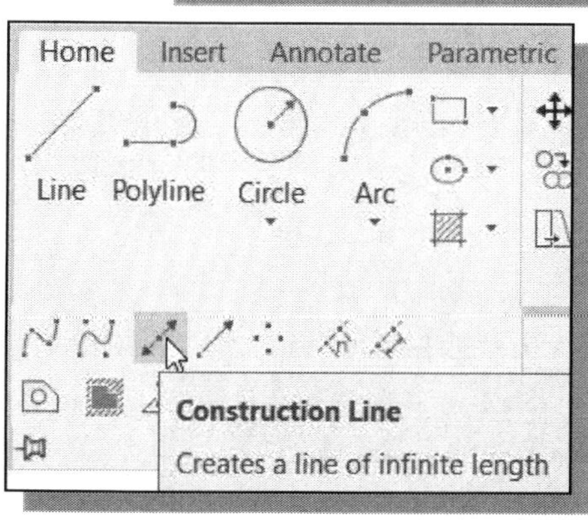

- We will first create construction lines for the front view.

2. Click the **Construction Line** icon in the *Draw* toolbar to activate the Construction Line command.

3. In the *command prompt area*, the message "*_xline Specify a point or [Hor/Ver/Ang/Bisect/Offset]:*" is displayed. On your own, create a vertical line and a horizontal line, near the left side of the screen, as shown in the figure below. These lines will be used as the references for the circular features of the design.

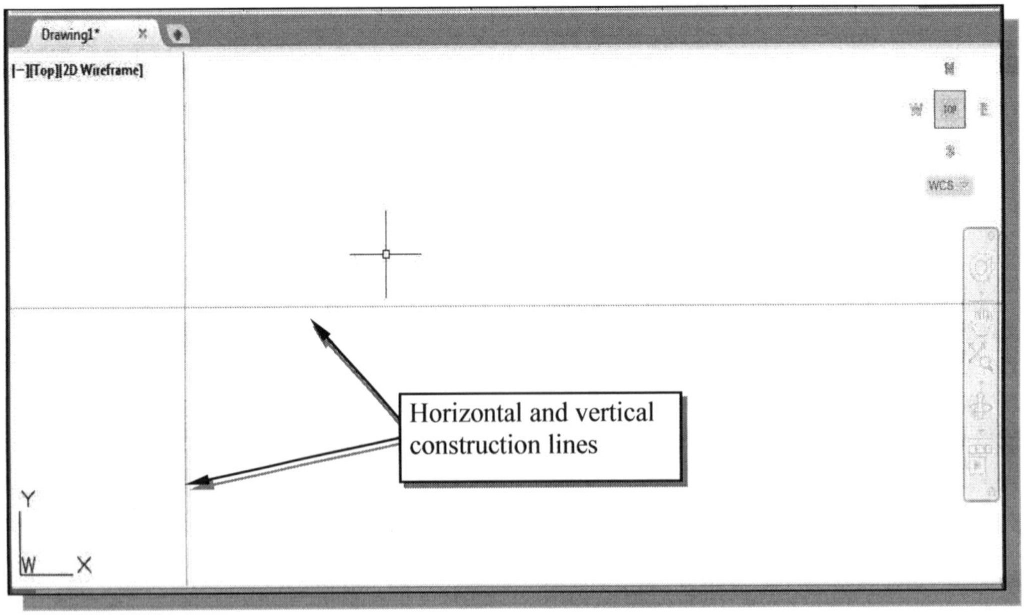

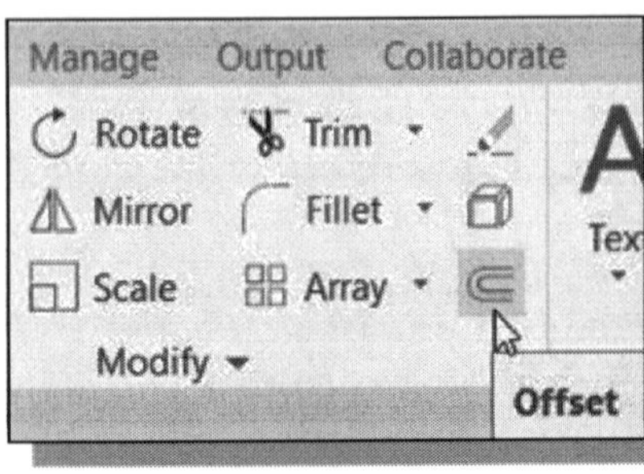

4. Click on the **Offset** icon in the *Modify* toolbar. In the command prompt area, the message "*Specify offset distance or [Through]:*" is displayed.

5. In the command prompt area, enter ***1.75*** **[ENTER]**.

6. In the command prompt area, the message "*Select object to offset or <exit>:*" is displayed. Pick the **horizontal line** on the screen.

7. AutoCAD next expects us to identify the direction of the offset. Pick a location that is **above** the selected line.

8. We will also create a line that is below the original horizontal line at 1.75. Pick the original **horizontal line** on the screen.

9. Pick a location that is **below** the selected line.

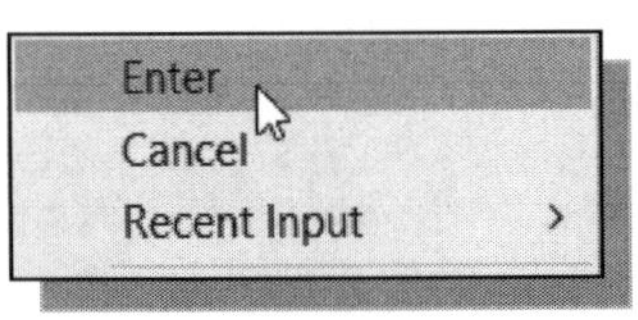

10. Inside the *Drawing Area*, **right-click** and select **Enter** to end the **Offset** command.

Creating Object Lines in the Front View

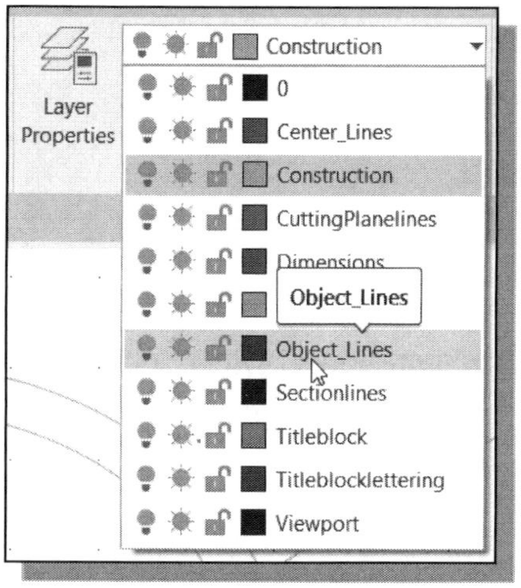

1. On the *Object Properties* toolbar, choose the ***Layer Control*** box with the left-mouse-button.

2. Move the cursor over the name of layer ***Object_Lines***; the tool tip "*Object_Lines*" appears.

3. **Left-click once** and layer *Object_Lines* is set as the *Current Layer*.

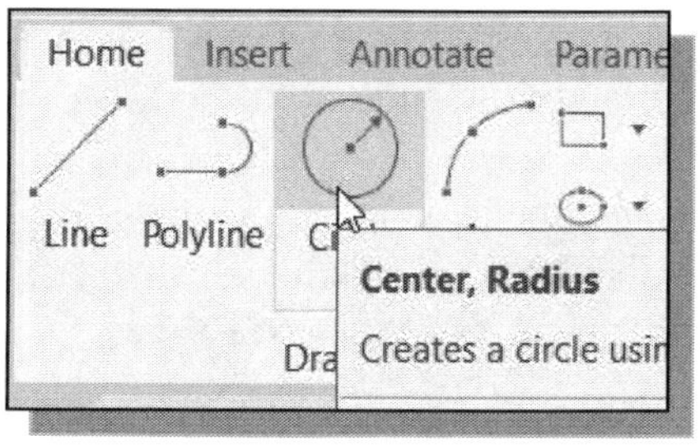

4. Click on the **Circle** icon in the *Draw* toolbar. In the command prompt area, the message "*Specify center point for circle or [3P/2P/Ttr (tan tan radius)]:*" is displayed.

5. Pick the center intersection point as the center of the circle.

6. In the command prompt area, the message "*Specify radius of circle or [Diameter]:*" is displayed. Enter ***1.25*** **[ENTER]**.

7. Repeat the **Circle** command and create the two **diameter *1.5*** circles as shown.

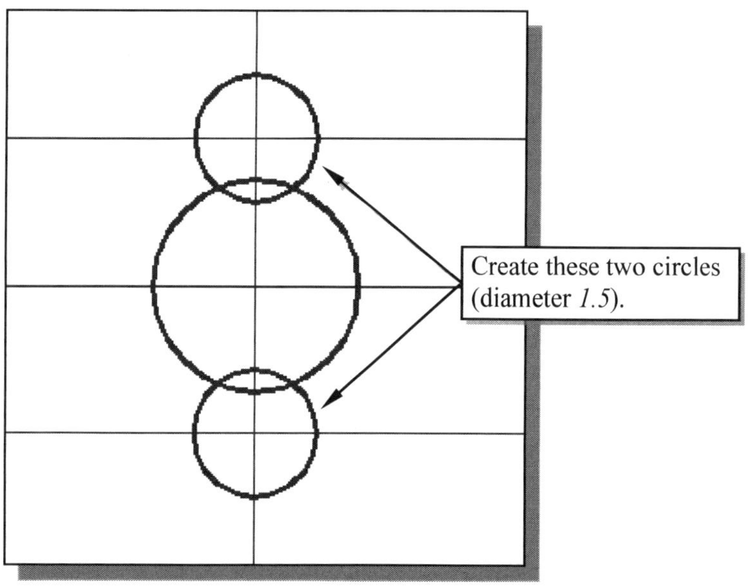

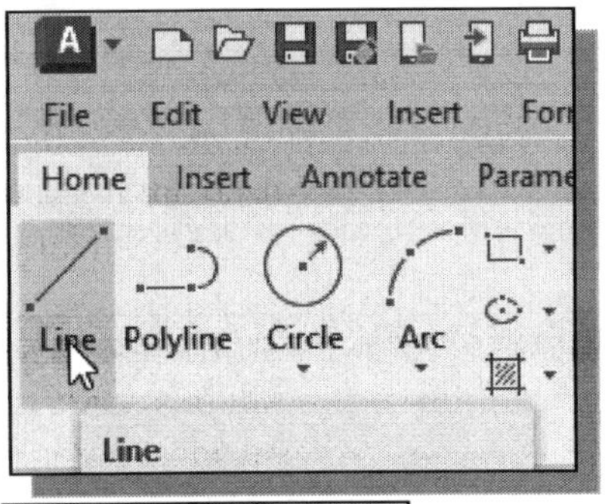

8. Select the **Line** command icon in the *Draw* toolbar. In the command prompt area, the message "*_line Specify first point:*" is displayed.

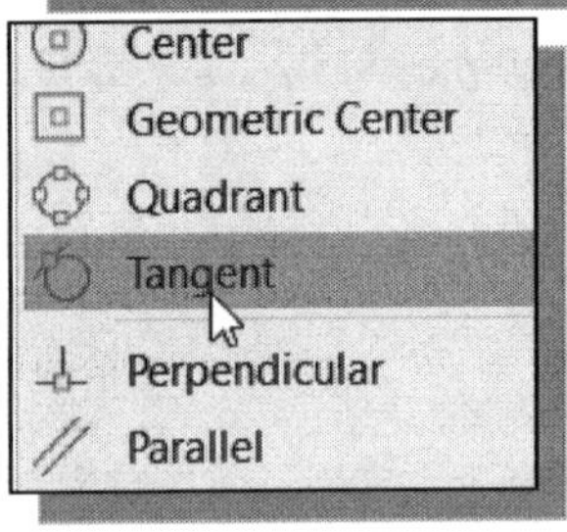

9. Inside the *Drawing Area*, hold down the **[SHIFT]** key and **right-click** once to bring up the *Object Snap* shortcut menu.

10. Select the **Tangent** option in the pop-up window. Move the cursor near the circles and notice the *Tangent* marker appears at different locations.

11. Pick the top circle by clicking on the upper right section of the circle.

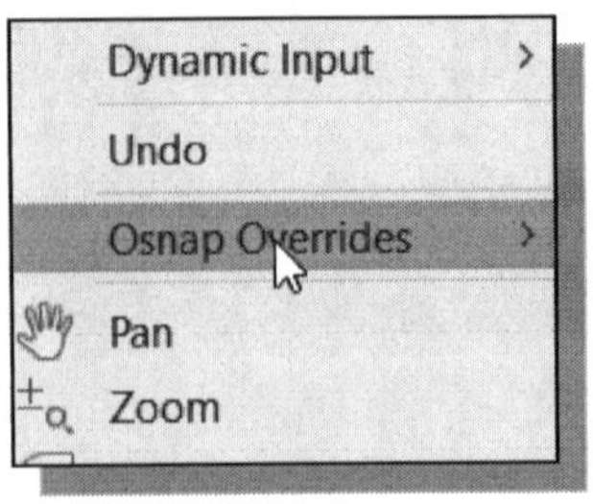

12. In the *command prompt area*, the message "*Specify the next point or [Undo]:*" is displayed. Inside the *Drawing Area*, **right-click** once and select **Snap Overrides**.

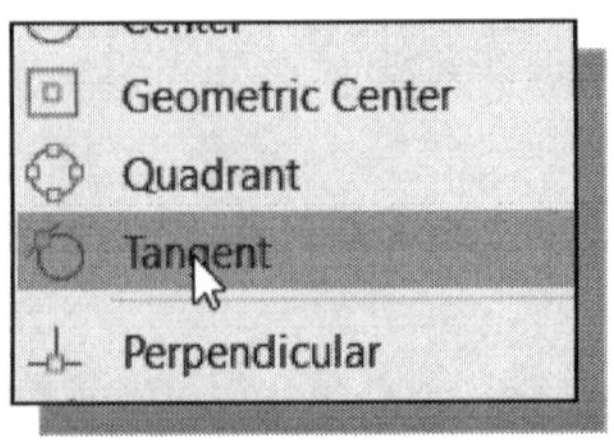

13. Select the **Tangent** option in the pop-up menu.

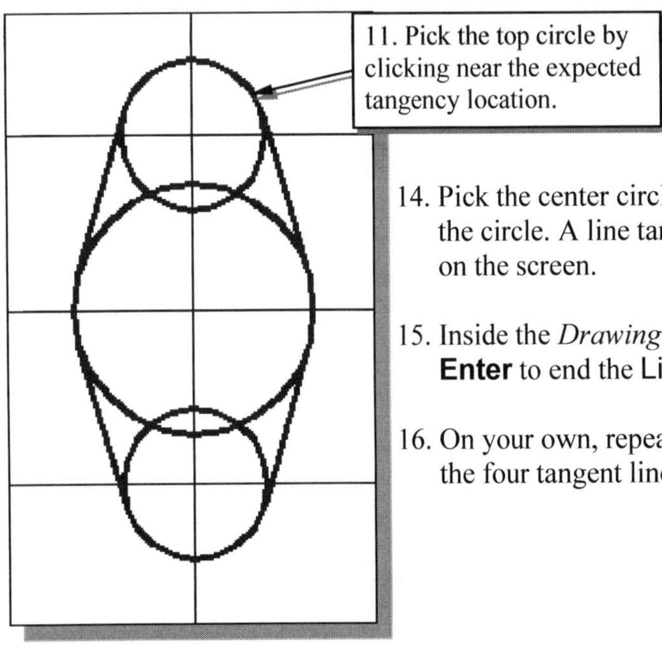

14. Pick the center circle by clicking on the right side of the circle. A line tangent to the two circles appears on the screen.

15. Inside the *Drawing Area*, right-click and select **Enter** to end the **Line** command.

16. On your own, repeat the **Line** command and create the four tangent lines as shown.

Editing the Circles

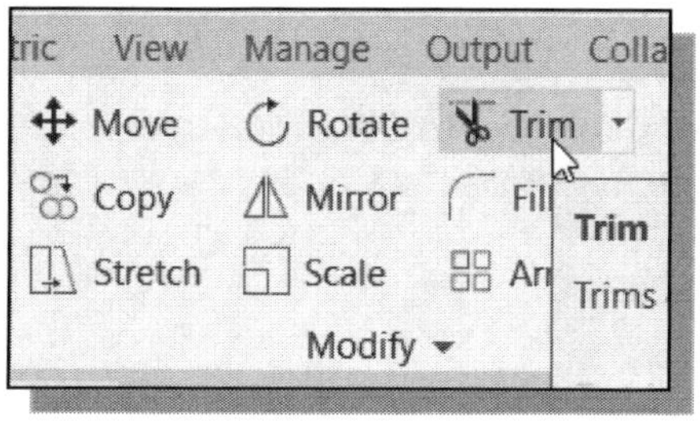

1. Select the **Trim** icon in the *Modify* toolbar. In the command prompt area, the message "*Select boundary edges... Select objects:*" is displayed.

2. Pick the four lines we just created as the *boundary edges*.

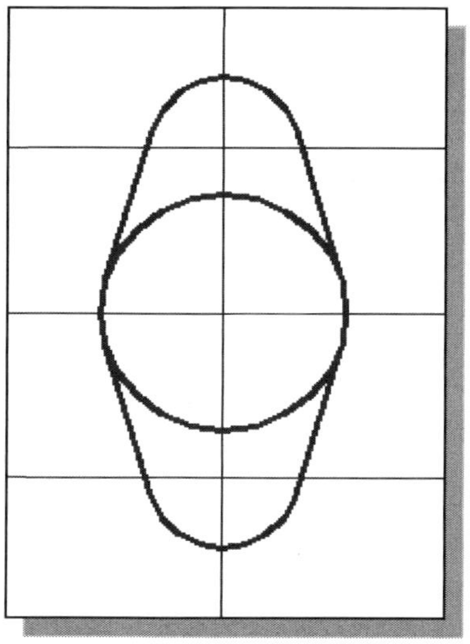

3. Inside the Drawing Area, **right-click** to proceed with the Trim command. The message "*Select object to trim or [Project/Edge/Undo]:*" is displayed in the command prompt area.

4. Trim the unwanted portions of the top and bottom circles and complete the outline of the front view as shown.

5. Inside the Drawing Area, right-click to activate the option menu and select **Enter** with the left-mouse-button to end the Trim command.

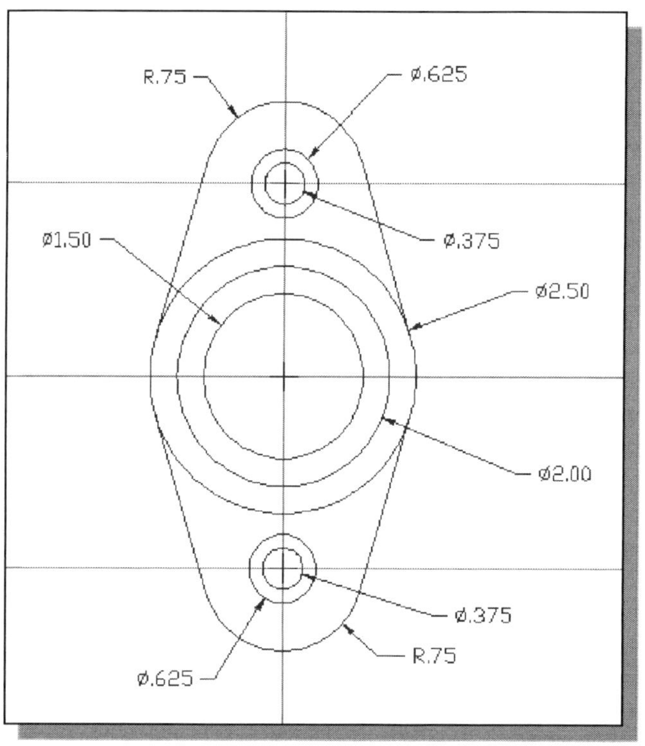

- On your own, create the additional circles as shown.

Setting up the Side View

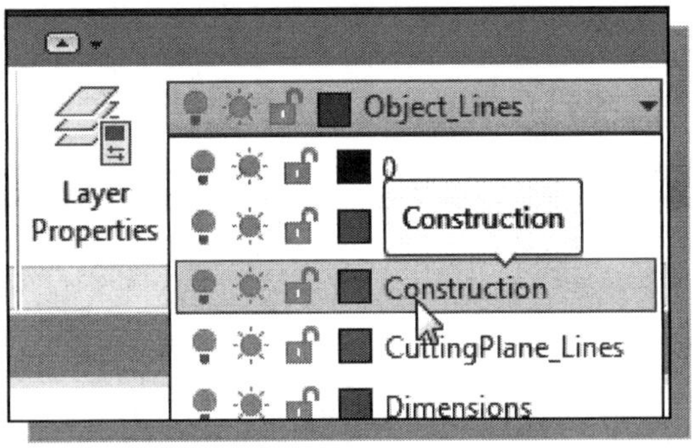

1. In the *Layer Control* box, set layer **Construction** as the *Current Layer*.

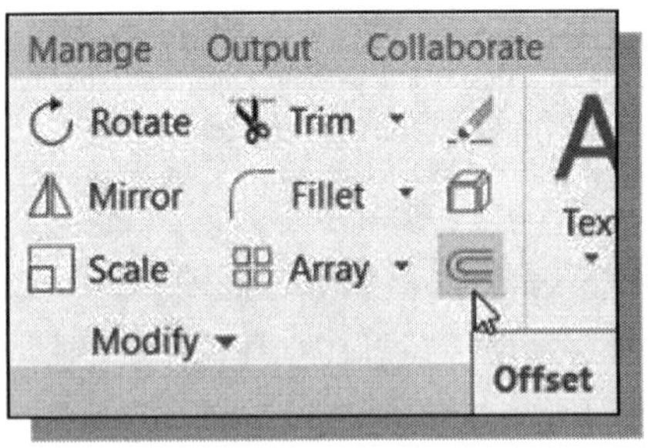

2. Select the **Offset** icon in the *Modify* toolbar. In the command prompt area, the message "*Specify offset distance or [Through]:*" is displayed.

3. In the command prompt area, enter ***5.0*** **[ENTER]**.

4. In the *command prompt area*, the message "*Select object to offset or <exit>:*" is displayed. Pick the **vertical line** on the screen.

5. AutoCAD next expects us to identify the direction of the offset. Pick a location that is toward the right side of the selected line.

6. Inside the *Drawing Area*, right-click to end the Offset command.

7. On your own, repeat the Offset command and create two additional lines parallel to the line we just created as shown (distances of ***0.5*** and ***2.0***).

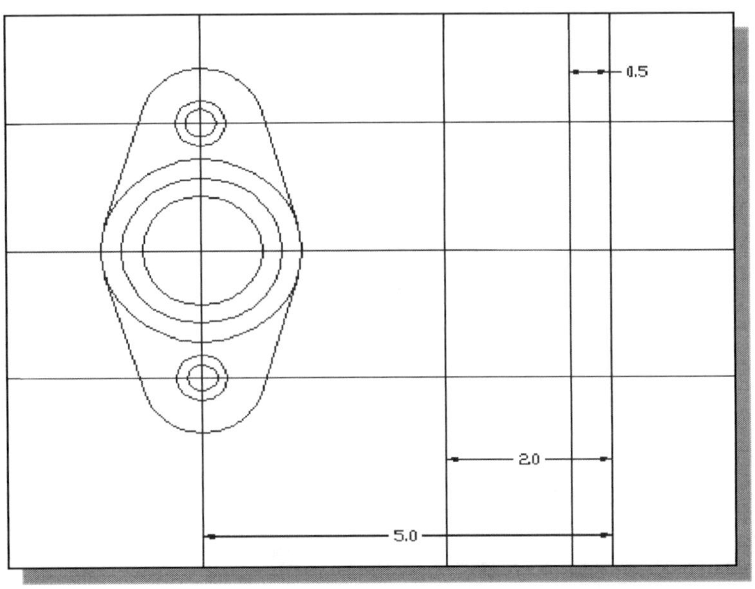

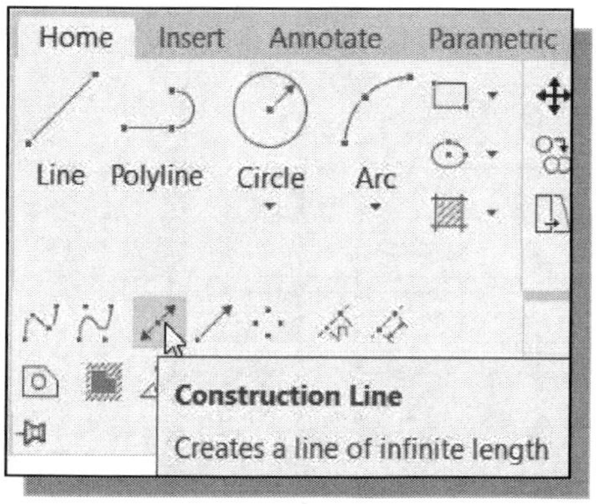

8. Select the **Construction Line** icon in the *Draw* toolbar. In the command prompt area, the message "*_xline Specify a point or [Hor/Ver/Ang/Bisect/Offset]:*" is displayed.

9. Select the **Hor** (horizontal) option in the command prompt area.

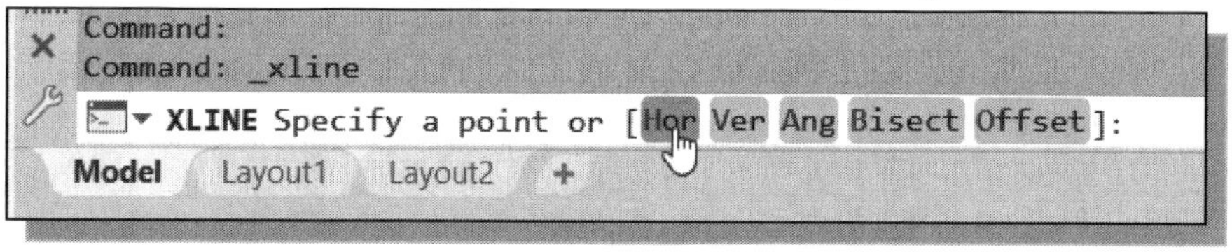

➢ The **Horizontal** option enables us to create a horizontal line by specifying one point in the Drawing Area.

10. Create **projection lines** by clicking at the intersections between the vertical line and the circles (and arcs) in the front-view.

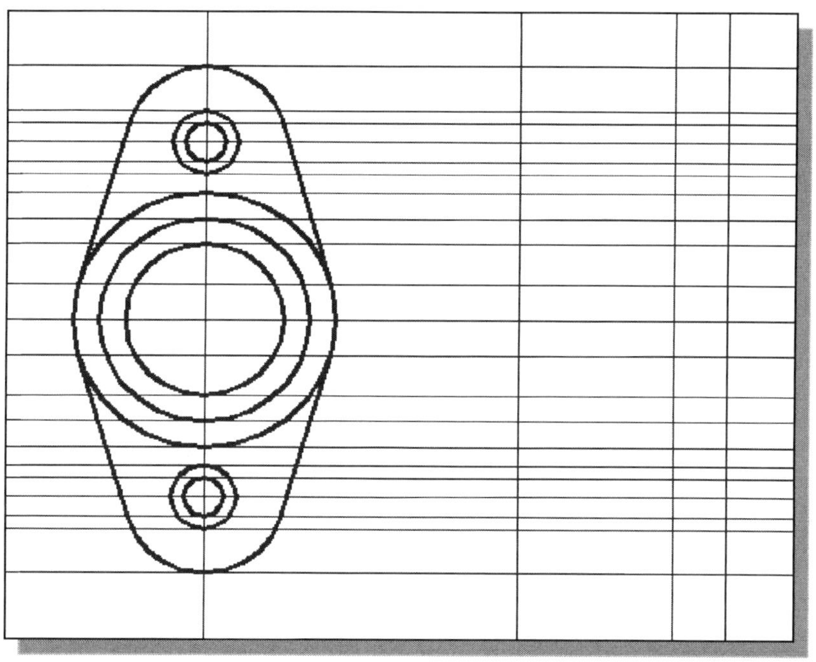

11. Also create two horizontal projection lines that pass through the two tangency-points on the ∅2.5 circle.

12. Inside the *Drawing Area*, right-click to end the Construction Line command.

➢ On your own, create object lines to show the outline of the side view.

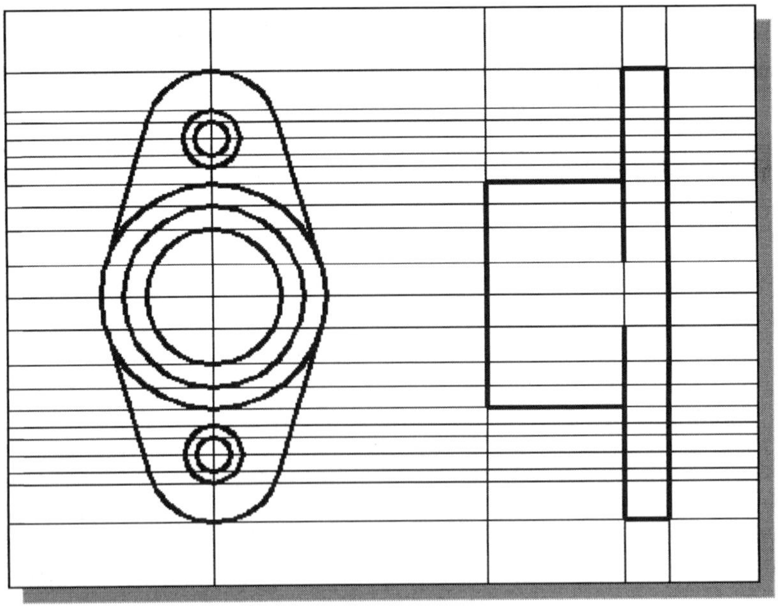

Adding Hidden Lines in the Side View

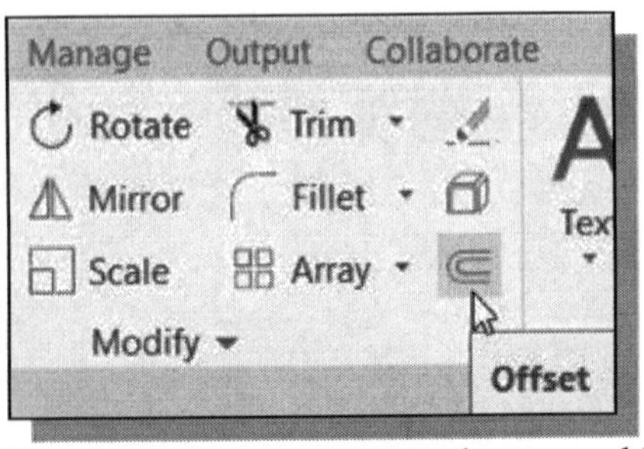

1. Click the **Offset** icon in the *Modify* toolbar. In the command prompt area, the message "*Specify offset distance or [Through]:*" is displayed.

2. On your own, create the two additional vertical lines for the counterbore features as shown.

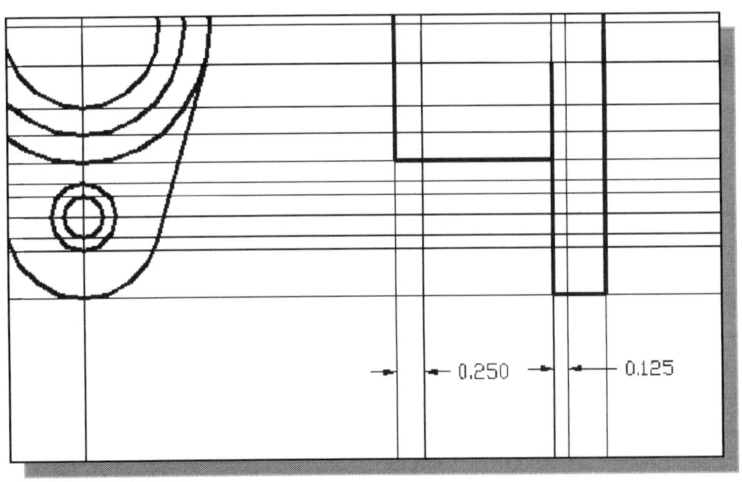

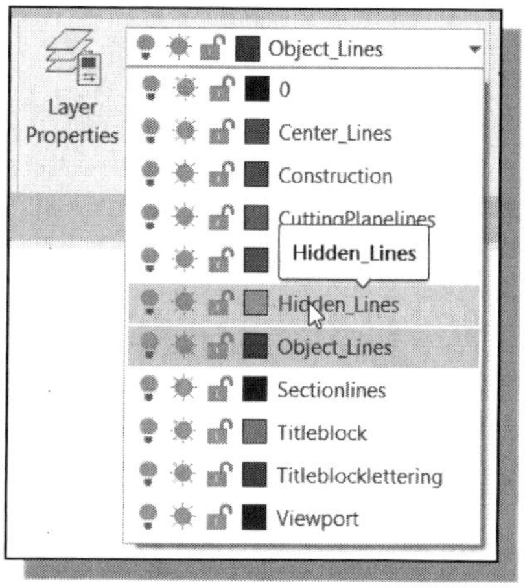

3. Set layer ***Hidden_Lines*** as the *Current Layer* in the *Layer Control* box.

4. Use the **Line** command and create the hidden lines as shown.

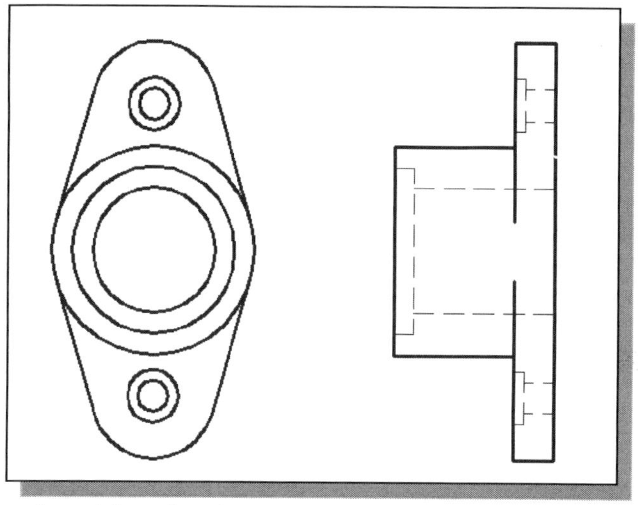

➢ On your own, complete the views by adding the side-drill, the centerlines, and the rounded corners as shown in the figure below.

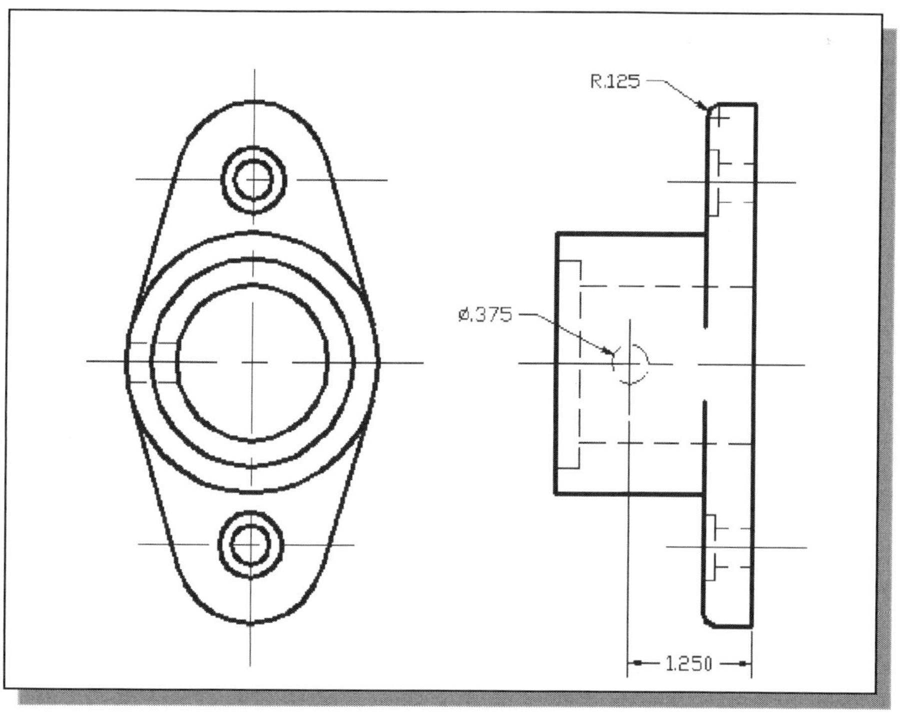

Changing the Linetype Scale Property

Looking at the side-drill feature and the centerlines we just created, not all of the lengths of the dash-dot linetypes appeared properly on the screen. The appearances of the dash-dot linetypes can be adjusted by modifying the ***Linetype Scale*** setting, which can be found under the *Object Property* option.

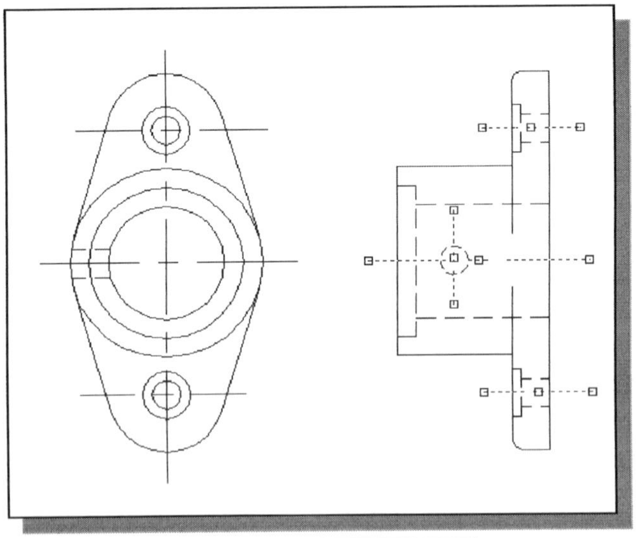

1. **Pre-select** the objects in the side view as shown (four lines and one circle).

2. Click once with the right-mouse-button to bring up the option list, and select the **Properties** option.

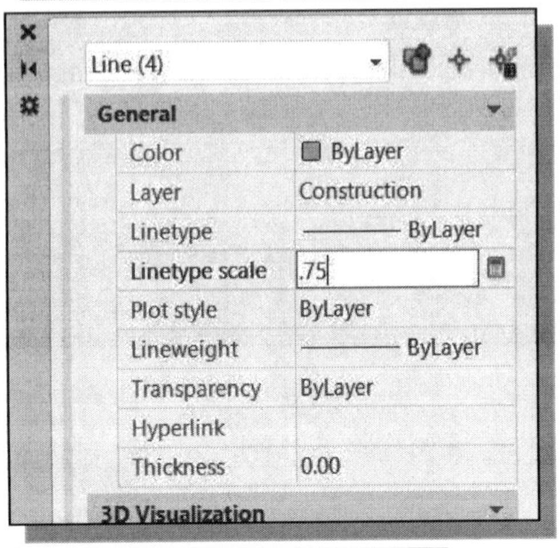

3. In the *Properties* dialog box, notice the default *Linetype scale* is 1.00.

4. Left-click on ***Linetype scale*** in the list and enter a new value: ***0.75*** **[ENTER]**.

5. Click on the **[X]** button to exit the *Properties* dialog box.

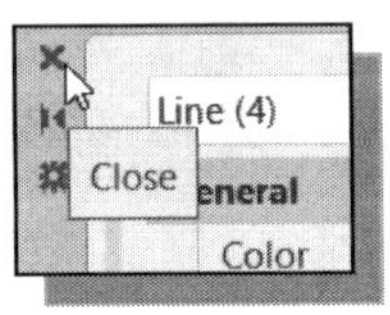

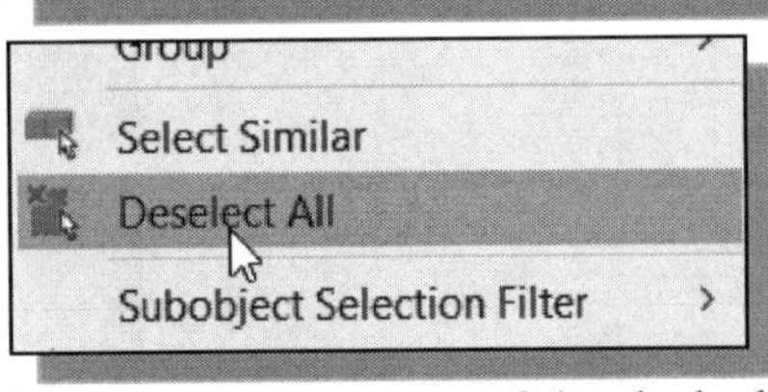

6. Inside the *Drawing Area*, **right-click** and choose **Deselect All**.

➢ The appearances of the dash-dot linetypes of the selected objects are adjusted to three-quarters the size of the other objects. Keep in mind that the dash-dot linetypes may appear differently on paper, depending on the type of printer/plotter being used. You may want to do more adjustments after examining a printed/plotted copy of the drawing. It is also more common to adjust the *Linetype Scale* for all objects of the same linetype to maintain a consistent presentation of the drawing.

Stretching and Moving Objects with Grips

We can usually *stretch* an object by moving selected grips to new locations. Some grips will not stretch the object but will move the object. This is true of grips on text objects, blocks, midpoints of lines, centers of circles, centers of ellipses, and point objects.

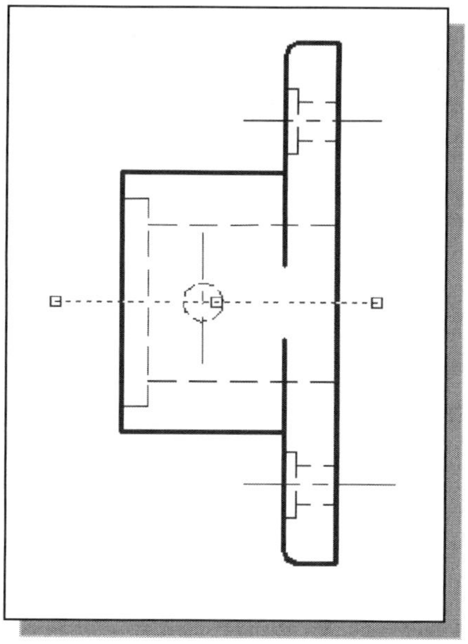

1. **Pre-select** the horizontal centerline that goes through the center of the part as shown.

2. Select the **right grip** by left-clicking once on the grip. Notice the grip is highlighted.

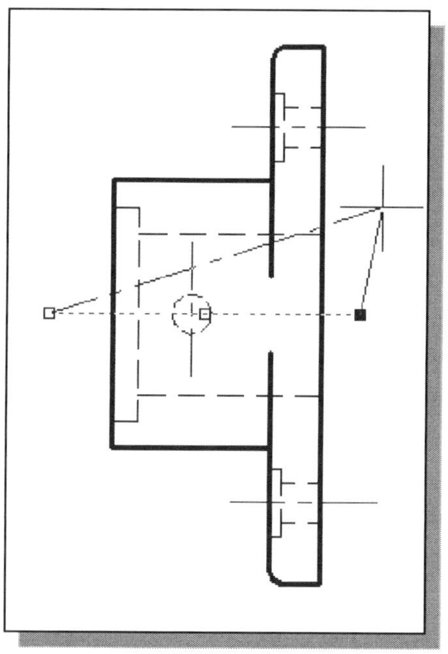

3. Move the cursor inside the Drawing Area and notice the center line is being stretched; the base point is attached to the cursor.

4. Pick a location on the screen to stretch the centerline.

5. Click on the **Undo** icon in the *Standard* toolbar area to undo the stretch we just did.

➢ On your own, experiment with moving the center grip of the centerline.

Drawing a Cutting Plane Line

Most section views require a *cutting plane line* to indicate the location on which the object is sectioned.

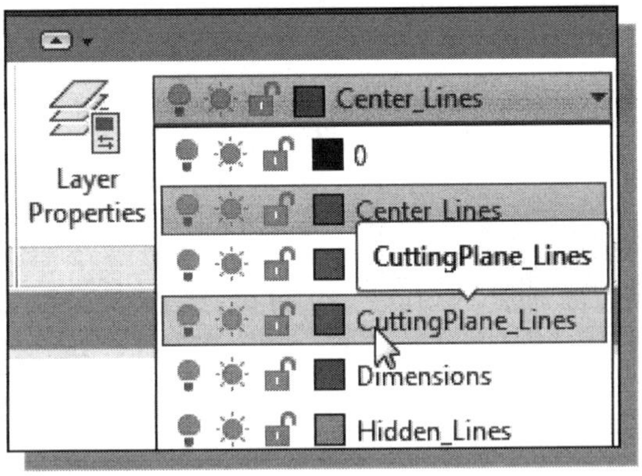

1. In the *Layer Control* box, turn ***OFF*** the *Construction* layer and set layer ***CuttingPlane_Lines*** as the *Current Layer*.

2. Use the **Line** command and create the vertical cutting plane line aligned to the vertical centerline of the front view.

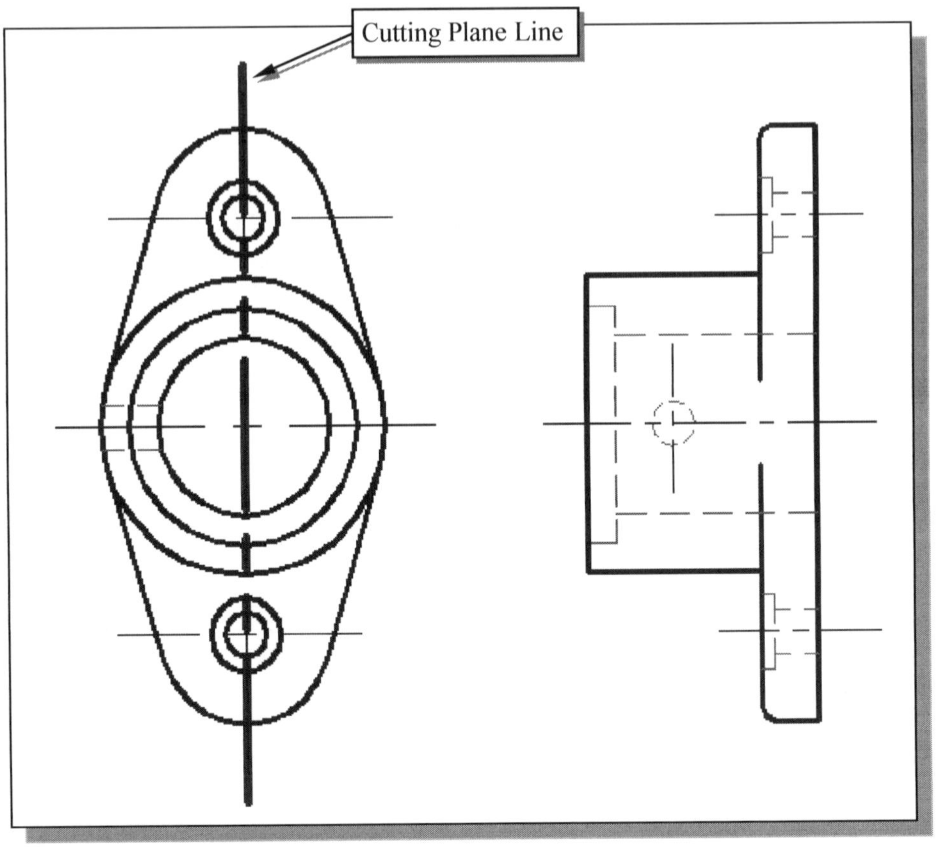

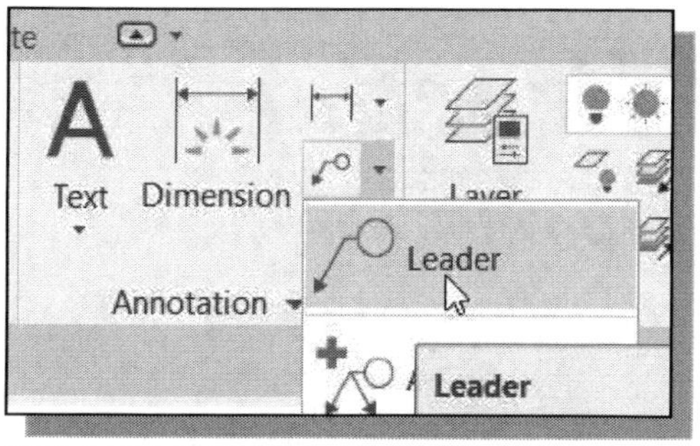

3. In the *Annotation toolbar*, select **Leader** as shown.

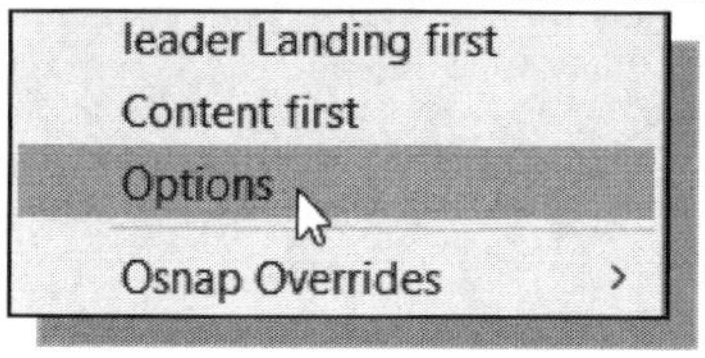

4. Inside the *Drawing Area*, **right-click** to bring up the *option menu* and select **Options** as shown.

5. Select **leader lAnding** and then **No** as shown.

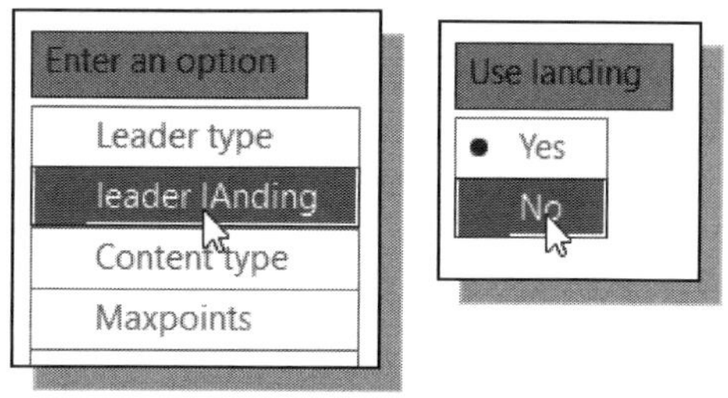

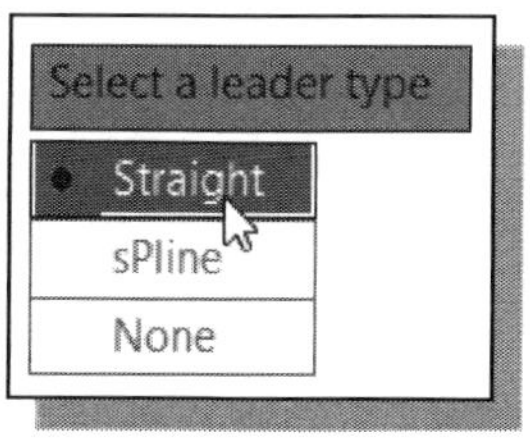

6. On your own, confirm the *leader type* is set to **Straight**.

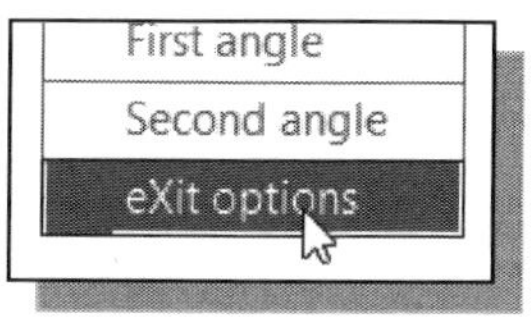

7. Select **eXit options** to end the setting options.

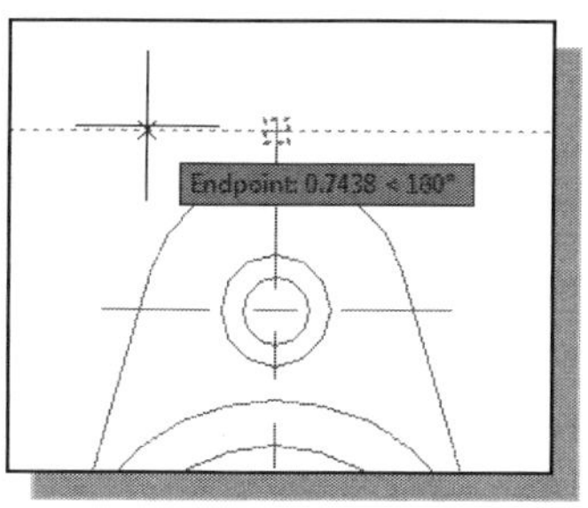

8. Use the object tracking option and set the endpoint of the leader about 0.75 to the left to set the starting point of the leader of the cutting plane line.

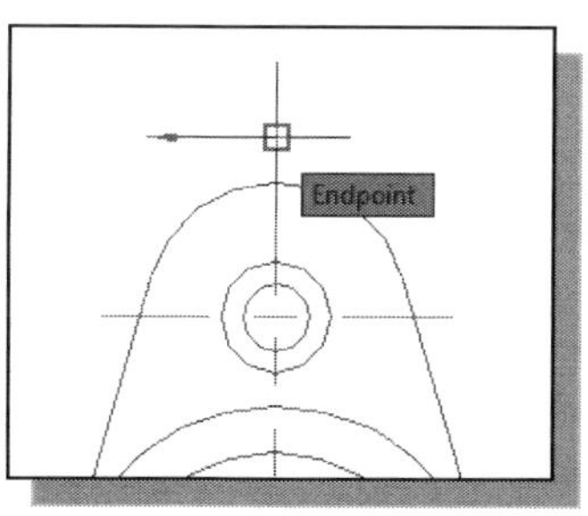

9. Pick the top endpoint of the cutting plane line to create a horizontal leader as shown.

Principles and Practice

An Integrated Approach to Engineering Graphics and AutoCAD 2027

Randy H. Shih
Oregon Institute of Technology

SDC PUBLICATIONS

SDC Publications
P.O. Box 1334
Mission, KS 66222
913-262-2664
www.SDCpublications.com
Publisher: Stephen Schroff

ISBN-13: 978-1-63057-828-2
ISBN-10: 1-63057-828-2

Printed and bound in the United States of America.

Preface

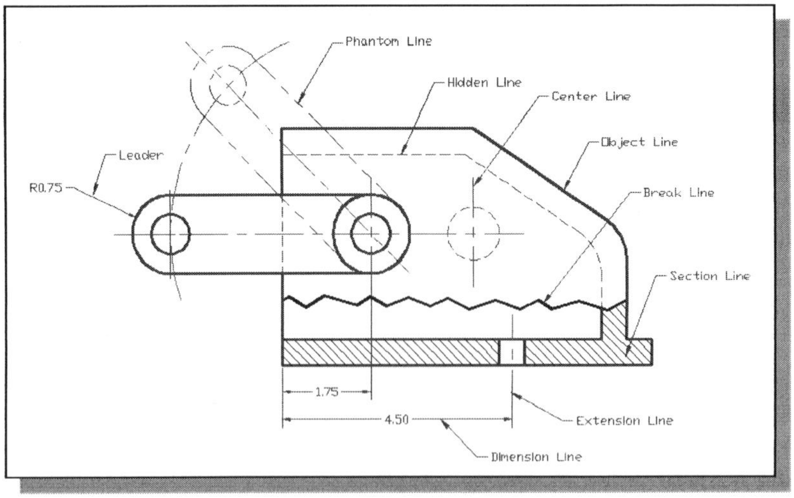

The primary goal of *Principles and Practice: An Integrated Approach to Engineering Graphics and AutoCAD 2027* is to introduce the aspects of Engineering Graphics with the use of a modern Computer Aided Design package – AutoCAD 2027. This text is intended to be used as a training guide for students and professionals. The chapters in this text proceed in a pedagogical fashion to guide you from constructing basic shapes to making complete sets of engineering drawings. This text takes a hands-on, exercise-intensive approach to all the important concepts of Engineering Graphics, as well as in-depth discussions of 2D CAD techniques. This textbook contains a series of twelve chapters, with detailed step-by-step tutorial style lessons, designed to introduce beginning CAD users to the graphic language used in all branches of technical industry. The CAD techniques and concepts discussed in this text are also designed to serve as the foundation to the more advanced parametric feature-based CAD packages such as Autodesk® Inventor. This book does not attempt to cover all of AutoCAD® 2027's features, only to provide an introduction to the software. It is intended to help you establish a good basis for exploring and growing in the exciting field of Computer Aided Engineering.

Acknowledgments

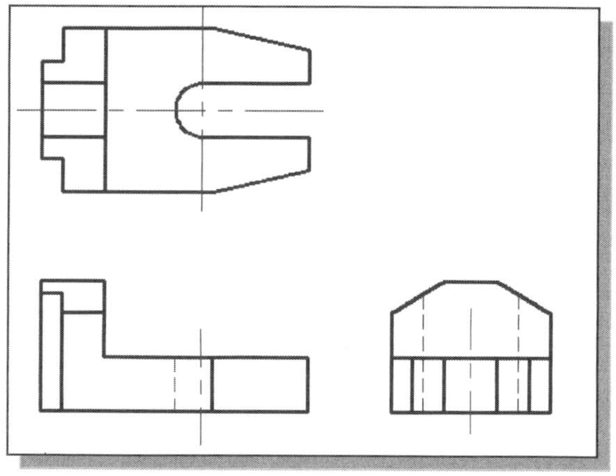

This book would not have been possible without a great deal of support. First, special thanks to two great teachers, Prof. George R. Schade of University of Nebraska-Lincoln and Mr. Denwu Lee from Taiwan, who taught me the fundamentals, the intrigue and the sheer fun of Computer Aided Engineering.

The effort and support of the editorial and production staff of SDC Publications is gratefully acknowledged. I would especially like to thank Stephen Schroff for his support of this project.

I am grateful that the Department of Mechanical Engineering and Manufacturing Engineering Technology at Oregon Institute of Technology has provided me with an excellent environment in which to pursue my interests in teaching and research. I would especially like to thank Emeritus Professor Charles Hermach for helpful comments and encouragement.

Finally, truly unbounded thanks are due to my wife Hsiu-Ling and our daughter Casandra for their understanding and encouragement throughout this project.

Randy H. Shih
Klamath Falls, Oregon
Spring, 2026

Table of Contents

Chapter 2
Geometric Constructions

Chapter 3
Object Properties and Organization

Chapter 4
Orthographic Projection and Multiview Constructions

Chapter 5
Pictorials and Sketching

Chapter 6
AutoCAD 2D Isometric Drawings

Chapter 7
Dimensioning and Notes

Chapter 8

Tolerancing and Fits

Chapter 9
Symmetrical Features in Designs

Chapter 10
Auxiliary Views

Chapter 11
Section Views

Chapter 12
Threads and Fasteners

Chapter 13
Working Drawings

Appendix

Index

Notes on using this book to prepare for the AutoCAD Certified User Examination

This edition of the text can also be used as a preparation guide for the AutoCAD Certified User examination. The book's content has been expanded to include the majority of the topics covered in the examination. The reference tables beginning on the next page and located at the beginning of each chapter show the textbook's coverage of the Certified User Examination performance tasks. Students taking the certification exam can use the reference tables as both a check list for topics that they need to understand and as a way of finding particular topics. The tables are provided as a reference only. It is important for the user to work through the book chapters in sequential order, as each chapter builds on the skills learned in previous chapters.

PLEASE NOTE:
Every effort has been made to cover the exam objectives included in the AutoCAD Certified User Examination. However, the format and topics covered by the examination are constantly changing, so students planning to take the Certified User Examination are advised to visit the Autodesk website and obtain information regarding the format and details about the AutoCAD Certified User Examination.

AutoCAD Certified User Examination Overview

The AutoCAD Certified User examination includes 12 sections. The following tables show where the performance tasks for each section are covered in this book.

This Reference Guide is provided to give you a checklist of performance tasks covered on the Certified User examination and to show you on which page(s) specific tasks are covered.

Section 1: Draw with Accuracy

Objectives: Describe and set the workspace.

Certification Examination Performance Task	Covered in this book on Chapter – Page
Precision	1-21
Drawing Limits	1-21
Zoom All	1-22
Status Bar	1-25
GRID Display	1-29
PAN Realtime	1-35
Drafting Settings	2-35
Drawing Limits	2-36
UCS Icon	2-36
Use a Wizard	3-4
Zoom Realtime	3-22
Layer Visibility	3-27

Section 2: Draw Objects

Objectives: Create and edit geometry using the *Dynamic Input* interface.
Use running *Object Snaps* and object snap overrides to select *Snap* points in the drawing.
Use *Polar Tracking* and *PolarSnap* efficiently and effectively.
Use *Object Tracking* to position geometry.
Use the *Units* command to set drawing units.

Certification Examination Performance Task	Covered in this book on Chapter – Page
Format	1-20
Units Setup	1-20
LINE Command	1-24
Coordinates	1-24
Interactive Input Method	1-25
SNAP Option	1-27
World Space	1-30
User Coordinate System	1-30
World Coordinate System	1-31
UCS Icon Display	1-31
Coordinate Systems	1-32

Section 3: Modify Objects

Objectives: Use several different *Selecting Objects* methods to select objects.
Select Objects for grip editing and identify the type of editing that can be done using grips.
Move objects in the drawing using *Object Snaps*, *Coordinate* entry, and *Object Snap Tracking* for precise placement.
Use the *Copy* command to copy objects in the drawing.
Use the *Rotate* command to rotate objects in the drawing.
Use the *Mirror* command to mirror objects in the drawing.
Use the *Array* command to pattern objects in the drawing.

Certification Examination Performance Task	Covered in this book on Chapter – Page
ERASE Command	1-28
Selection Window	1-29
Move Command	2-19
Rotate Command	2-23
Transfer of an Angle	2-23
Copy Command	2-23
Dividing a Given Line into Equal Parts	2-26
Point, Divide	2-26
Trim Command	2-44
Open Tee, Multiline	3-17
Multiline Edit	3-17
Moving Objects to a Different Layer	3-28
Trim	4-33
Mirror Command	9-20
Array Command	9-21
Grips Editing	10-14
Copy Selections, Grips	10-14
Rotate, Grips	10-15
Quick Select	11-27
Deselect All	11-22
Copy	13-18
Paste	13-18
Quick Select	13-19
Paste as Block	13-22
Copy with Base Point	13-25

Section 4: Organize Objects

Objectives: Use *Layer tools.*
Describe the use and effect of the *ByLayer* property.
Use the Match Properties command to apply the *Properties* from a source object to destination objects.
Use the inquiry commands (Distance, Radius, Angle, Area, List, and ID) to obtain geometric information from the drawing.

Certification Examination Performance Task — **Covered in this book on Chapter – Page**

Section 5: Altering Objects

Objectives: Use the *Offset* command to create parallel and offset geometry.
Use the *Fillet* command to create radius geometry connecting two objects.
Use the *Join* command to combine multiple objects into a single object.

Certification Examination Performance Task — **Covered in this book on Chapter – Page**

Section 6: Working with Layouts

Objectives: Create a new layout.
Create and manipulate *Viewports*.

Certification Examination Performance Task	Covered in this book on Chapter – Page
Layout Mode	9-10
Viewports	9-24

Section 7: Annotating the Drawing

Objectives: Use the *Multiline Text* command to create and format paragraphs of text.
Create and use *Text Styles*.

Certification Examination Performance Task	Covered in this book on Chapter – Page
Single Line Text	7-42
Special Characters	7-43

Section 8: Dimensioning

Objectives: Create different types of *Dimensions* on linear objects.
Create and modify *Dimension Styles* to control the appearance of dimensions.
Create and edit *Multileaders*.

Certification Examination Performance Task	Covered in this book on Chapter – Page
Fractional Dimension	7-30
Overall Dimension Scale	7-30
Dimensions Toolbar	7-33
Dimension Style	7-33
Linear Dimension	7-33
Angular Dimension	7-34
Center Mark	7-36
Radius Dimension	7-40
Dimension Style	9-26
Scale Dimension to Layout	9-26
Dimension Update	9-27
MULTILEADER	11-25
Multileader Style	13-26
Multileader	13-27
Add Leader	13-28

Section 9: Hatching Objects

Objectives: Create *Hatch* patterns and fills.

Certification Examination Performance Task	Covered in this book on Chapter – Page
Hatch	11-29

Section 10: Working with Reusable Content

Objectives: Use the *Block* command to create a block definition.
Use the *Insert* command to insert a block reference in a drawing.

Certification Examination Performance Task	Covered in this book on Chapter – Page
Purge Blocks	7-43
Template File	9-13
Use a Template	11-12
Make Block	13-14
Insert Block	13-16
Paste as Block	13-22

Section 11: Creating Additional Drawing Objects

Objectives: Work with *polylines*.
Edit *polylines*.

Certification Examination Performance Task	Covered in this book on Chapter – Page
Polylines	2-44
Table Style	13-31
Table Command	13-32

Section 12: Plotting

Objectives: Create and modify page setup.

Certification Examination Performance Task	Covered in this book on Chapter – Page
Plot Style Table Settings	9-5
Plot Style	9-7
Plot Command	9-27
Plot Style Table Settings	10-32

The AutoCAD Certified User Examination is a performance-based exam. The examination is comprised of approximately 30 questions to be completed in 50 minutes. The test items will require you to use the AutoCAD software to perform specific tasks and then answer questions about the tasks. Performance-based testing is defined as ***testing by doing***. This means you actually perform the given task then answer the questions regarding the task. Performance-based testing is widely accepted as a better way of ensuring the users have the skills needed, rather than just recalling information.

For detailed information, visit **http://www.autodesk.com/certification**.

Tips on Taking the AutoCAD Certified User Examination

1. **Study**: The first step to maximize your potential on an exam is to sufficiently prepare for it. You need to be familiar with the AutoCAD package, and this can only be achieved by doing drawings and exploring the different commands available. The AutoCAD Certified User exam is designed to measure your familiarity with the AutoCAD software. You must be able to perform the given task and answer the exam questions correctly and quickly.
2. **Make Notes**: Take notes of what you learn either while attending classroom sessions or going through study material. Use these notes as a review guide before taking the actual test.
3. **Time Management**: Manage the time you spend on each question. Always remember you do not need to score 100% to pass the exam. Also keep in mind that some questions are weighed more heavily and may take more time to answer.
4. **Be Cautious**: Devote some time to ponder and think of the correct answer. Ensure that you interpret all the options correctly before selecting from available choices.
5. **Use Common Sense**: If you are unable to get the correct answer and unable to eliminate all distracters, then you need to select the best answer from the remaining selections. This may be a task of selecting the best answer from amongst several correct answers, or it may be selecting the least incorrect answer from amongst several poor answers.
6. **Take Your Time**: The examination has a time limit. If you encounter a question you cannot answer in a reasonable amount of time, use the Save As feature to save a copy of the data file, and mark the question for review. When you review the question, open your copy of the data file and complete the performance task. After you verify that you have entered the answer correctly, unmark the question so it no longer appears as marked for review.
7. **Don't Act in Haste**: Don't go into panic mode while taking a test. Always read the question carefully before you look out for choices in hand. Use the ***Review*** screen to ensure you have reviewed all the questions you may have marked for review. When you are confident that you have answered all questions, end the examination to submit your answers for scoring. You will receive a score report once you have submitted your answers.
8. **Relax before the exam**: In order to avoid last-minute stress, make sure that you arrive 10 to 15 minutes early and relax before taking the exam.

Every effort has been made to cover the exam objectives included in the *AutoCAD Certified User Examination*. However, the format and topics covered by the examination are constantly changing; students planning to take the *Certified User Examination* are advised to visit the Autodesk website and obtain information regarding the format and details about the examination.

Chapter 1
Introduction and AutoCAD Fundamentals

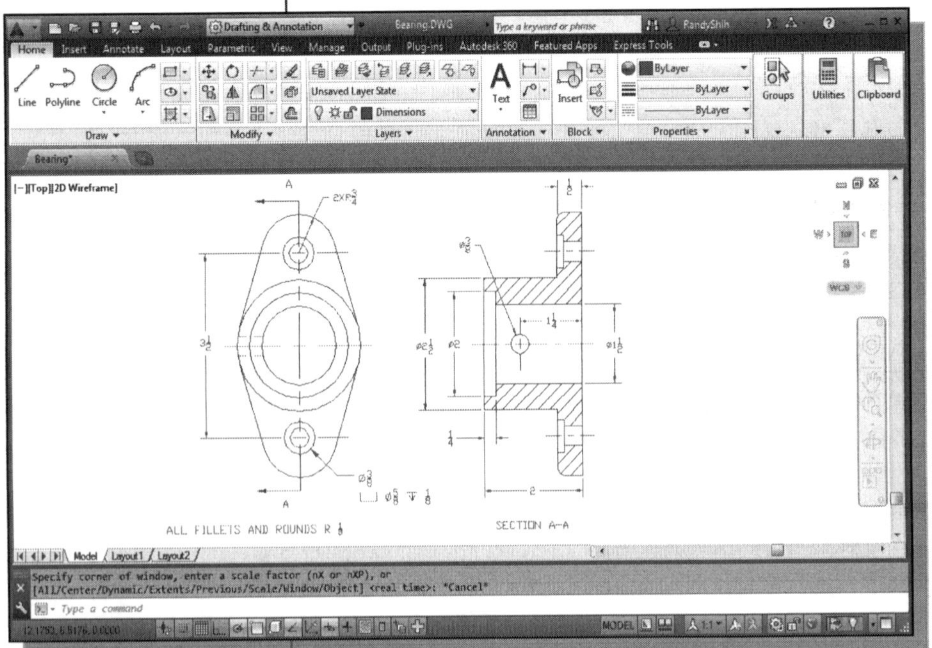

Learning Objectives

- The History and Importance of Engineering Graphics
- Be Familiar with the AutoCAD Toolbars
- Use the AutoCAD Visual Reference Commands
- Draw Using the Line and Circle Commands
- Use the Erase Command
- Define Positions Using the Basic Entry Methods
- Create and Save an AutoCAD Drawing

AutoCAD Certified User Examination Objectives Coverage

Section 1: Introduction to AutoCAD

Section 2: Creating Basic Drawings

Section 3: Manipulating Objects

Introduction

Engineering Graphics, also known as **Technical Drawing**, is the technique of creating accurate representations of designs, an *engineering drawing*, for construction and manufacturing. An **engineering drawing** is a type of drawing that is technical in nature, used to fully and clearly define requirements for engineered items, and is usually created in accordance with standardized conventions for layout, nomenclature, interpretation, appearance, size, etc. A skilled practitioner of the art of engineering drawing is known as a *draftsman* or *draftsperson.*

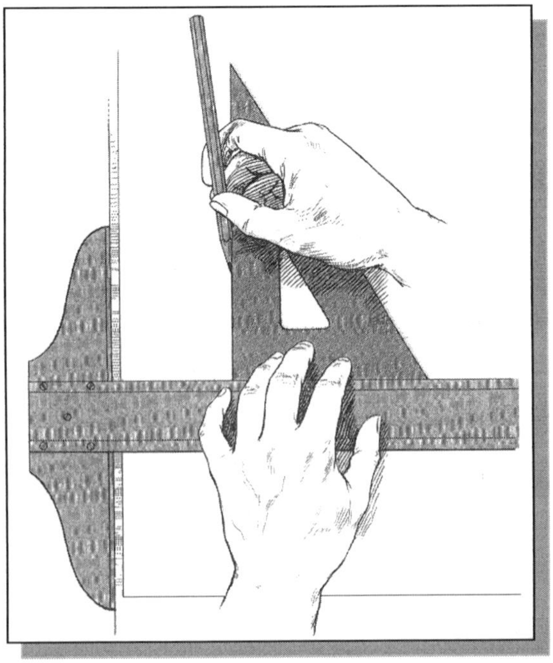

The basic mechanics of drafting is to use a pencil and draw on a piece of paper. For engineering drawings, papers are generally placed on a drafting table and additional tools are used. A T-square is one of the standard tools commonly used with a drafting table.

A T-square is also known as a *sliding straightedge*; parallel lines can be drawn simply by moving the T-square and running a pencil along the T-square's straightedge. The t-square is more typically used as a tool to hold other tools such as triangles. For example, one or more triangles can be placed on the T-square and lines can be drawn at the chosen angle on the paper.

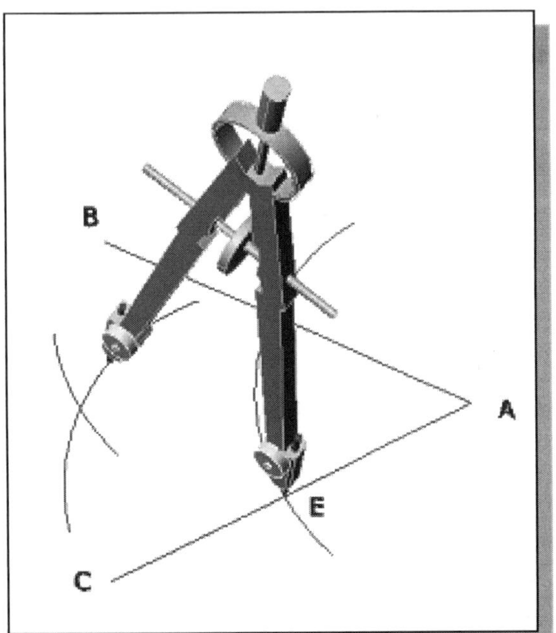

In addition to the triangles, other tools are used to draw curves and circles. Primary among these is the compass, used for drawing simple arcs and circles, and the French curve, typically a piece of plastic with a complex curve on it. A spline is a rubber coated articulated metal that can be manually bent to almost any curve.

This basic drafting system requires an accurate table and constant attention to the positioning of the tools. A common error was to allow the triangles to push the top of the t-square down slightly, thereby throwing off all angles. And in general drafting was a time-consuming process.

A solution to these problems was the introduction of the "**drafting machine**," which is a device that allowed the draftsperson to have an accurate right angle at any point on the page quite quickly. These machines often included the ability to change the angle, thereby removing the need for the triangles as well.

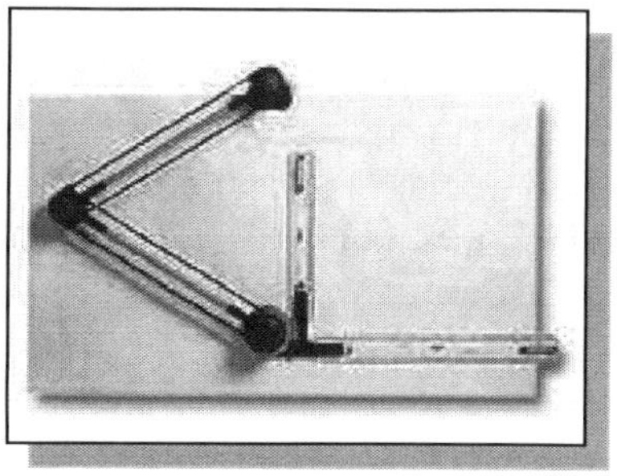

In addition to the mechanics of drawing the lines onto a piece of paper, drafting requires an understanding of geometry and the professional skills of the specific designer. At one time, drafting was a sought-after job, considered one of the more demanding and highly skilled of the trades. Today the mechanics of the drafting task have been largely automated, and greatly accelerated, through the use of **computer aided design** (CAD) systems. Proficiency in using CAD systems has also become one of the more important requirements for engineers and designers.

Drawing in CAD Systems

Computer Aided Design (CAD) is the process of doing designs with the aid of computers. This includes the generation of computer models, analysis of design data, and the creation of drawings. **AutoCAD 2027** is a computer-aided-design (CAD) software developed by *Autodesk Inc*. The **AutoCAD 2027** software is a tool that can be used for design and drafting activities. The two-dimensional and three-dimensional models created in **AutoCAD 2027** can be transferred to other computer programs for further analysis and testing. The computer models can also be used in manufacturing equipment such as machining centers, lathes, mills, or rapid prototyping machines to manufacture the product.

The rapid changes in the field of **computer aided engineering** (CAE) have brought exciting advances in industry. Recent advances have made the long-sought goal of reducing design time, producing prototypes faster, and achieving higher product quality closer to a reality.

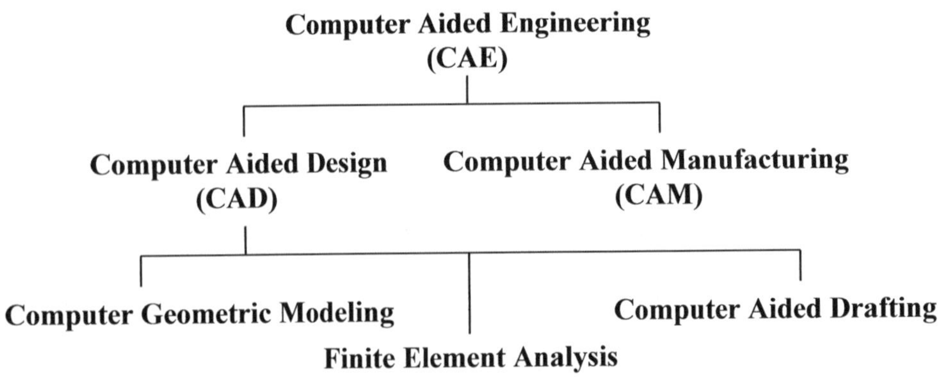

Development of Computer Geometric Modeling

Computer Aided Design is a relatively new technology, and its rapid expansion in the last fifty years is truly amazing. Computer modeling technology advanced along with the development of computer hardware. The first-generation CAD programs, developed in the 1950s, were mostly non-interactive; CAD users were required to create program codes to generate the desired two-dimensional (2D) geometric shapes. Initially, the development of CAD technology occurred mostly in academic research facilities. The Massachusetts Institute of Technology, Carnegie-Mellon University, and Cambridge University were the lead pioneers at that time. The interest in CAD technology spread quickly and several major industry companies, such as General Motors, Lockheed, McDonnell, IBM, and Ford Motor Co., participated in the development of interactive CAD programs in the 1960s. Usage of CAD systems was primarily in the automotive industry, aerospace industry, and government agencies that developed their own programs for their specific needs. The 1960s also marked the beginning of the development of finite element analysis methods for computer stress analysis and computer aided manufacturing for generating machine tool paths.

The 1970s are generally viewed as the years of the most significant progress in the development of computer hardware, namely the invention and development of **microprocessors**. With the improvement in computing power, new types of 3D CAD programs that were user-friendly and interactive became reality. CAD technology quickly expanded from very simple **computer aided drafting** to very complex **computer aided design**. The use of 2D and 3D wireframe modelers was accepted as the leading-edge technology that could increase productivity in industry. The developments of surface modeling and solid modeling technology were taking shape by the late 1970s, but the high cost of computer hardware and programming slowed the development of such technology. During this time period, the available CAD systems all required extremely expensive room-sized mainframe computers.

In the 1980s, improvements in computer hardware brought the power of mainframes to the desktop at less cost and with more accessibility to the general public. By the mid-1980s, CAD technology had become the main focus of a variety of manufacturing industries and was very competitive with traditional design/drafting methods. It was during this period of time that 3D solid modeling technology had major advancements, which boosted the usage of CAE technology in industry.

In the 1990s, CAD programs evolved into powerful design/manufacturing/management tools. CAD technology has come a long way, and during these years of development, modeling schemes progressed from two-dimensional (2D) wireframe to three-dimensional (3D) wireframe, to surface modeling, to solid modeling and, finally, to feature-based parametric solid modeling.

The first-generation CAD packages were simply 2D **computer aided drafting** programs, basically the electronic equivalents of the drafting board. For typical models, the use of this type of program would require that several to many views of the objects be created individually as they would be on the drafting board. The 3D designs remained in the designer's mind, not in the computer database. The mental translation of 3D objects to 2D views is required throughout the use of the packages. Although such systems have some advantages over traditional board drafting, they are still tedious and labor intensive. The need for the development of 3D modelers came quite naturally, given the limitations of the 2D drafting packages.

The development of the 3D wireframe modeler was a major leap in the area of computer modeling. The computer database in the 3D wireframe modeler contains the locations of all the points in space coordinates and it is sufficient to create just one model rather than multiple models. This single 3D model can then be viewed from any direction as needed. The 3D wireframe modelers require the least computer power and achieve reasonably good representation of 3D models. But because surface definition is not part of a wireframe model, all wireframe images have the inherent problem of ambiguity.

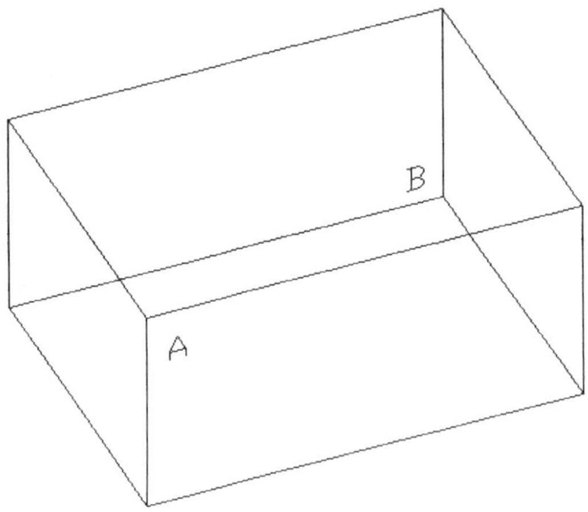

Wireframe Ambiguity: Which corner is in front, A or B?

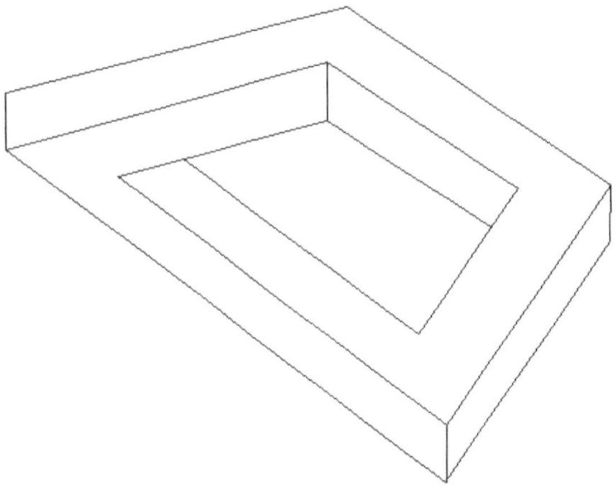

A non-realizable object: Wireframe models contain no surface definitions.

Surface modeling is the logical development in computer geometry modeling to follow the 3D wireframe modeling scheme by organizing and grouping edges that define polygonal surfaces. Surface modeling describes the part's surfaces but not its interiors. Designers are still required to interactively examine surface models to ensure that the various surfaces on a model are contiguous throughout. Many of the concepts used in 3D wireframe and surface modelers are incorporated in the solid modeling scheme, but it is solid modeling that offers the most advantages as a design tool.

In the solid modeling presentation scheme, the solid definitions include nodes, edges, and surfaces, and it is a complete and unambiguous mathematical representation of a precisely enclosed and filled volume. Unlike the surface modeling method, solid modelers start with a solid or use topology rules to guarantee that all of the surfaces are stitched together properly. Two predominant methods for representing solid models are **constructive solid geometry** (CSG) representation and **boundary representation** (B-rep).

The CSG representation method can be defined as the combination of 3D solid primitives. What constitutes a "primitive" varies somewhat with the software but typically includes a rectangular prism, a cylinder, a cone, a wedge, and a sphere. Most solid modelers allow the user to define additional primitives, which can be very complex.

In the B-rep representation method, objects are represented in terms of their spatial boundaries. This method defines the points, edges, and surfaces of a volume, and/or issues commands that sweep or rotate a defined face into a third dimension to form a solid. The object is then made up of the unions of these surfaces that completely and precisely enclose a volume.

By the 1990s, a new paradigm called *concurrent engineering* had emerged. With concurrent engineering, designers, design engineers, analysts, manufacturing engineers, and management engineers all work closely right from the initial stages of the design. In this way, all aspects of the design can be evaluated, and any potential problems can be identified right from the start and throughout the design process. Using the principles of concurrent engineering, a new type of computer modeling technique appeared. The technique is known as the *feature-based parametric modeling technique*. The key advantage of the *feature-based parametric modeling technique* is its capability to produce very flexible designs. Changes can be made easily, and design alternatives can be evaluated with minimum effort. Various software packages offer different approaches to feature-based parametric modeling, yet the end result is a flexible design defined by its design variables and parametric features.

In this text, we will concentrate on creating designs using two-dimensional geometric construction techniques. The fundamental concepts and use of different **AutoCAD 2027** commands are presented using step-by-step tutorials. We will begin with creating simple geometric entities and then move toward creating detailed working drawings and assembly drawings. The techniques presented in this text will also serve as the foundation for entering the world of three-dimensional solid modeling using packages such as **AutoCAD Mechanical Desktop, AutoCAD Architecture** and **Autodesk Inventor**.

Why use AutoCAD 2027?

AutoCAD was first introduced to the public in late 1982 and was one of the first CAD software products that were available for personal computers. Since 1984, **AutoCAD** has established a reputation for being the most widely used PC-based CAD software around the world. By 2019, it was estimated that there were over 6 million **AutoCAD** users in more than 150 countries worldwide. **AutoCAD 2027** is the forty-first release, with many added features and enhancements, of the original **AutoCAD** software produced by *Autodesk Inc.*

CAD provides us with a wide range of benefits; in most cases, the result of using CAD is increased accuracy and productivity. First of all, the computer offers much higher accuracy than the traditional methods of drafting and design. Traditionally, drafting and detailing are the most expensive cost elements in a project and the biggest bottleneck.

With CAD systems, such as **AutoCAD 2027,** the tedious drafting and detailing tasks are simplified through the use of many of the CAD geometric construction tools, such as *grids*, *snap*, *trim,* and *auto-dimensioning*. Dimensions and notes are always legible in CAD drawings, and in most cases, CAD systems can produce higher quality prints compared to traditional hand drawings.

CAD also offers much-needed flexibility in design and drafting. A CAD model generated on a computer consists of numeric data that describe the geometry of the object. This allows the designers and clients to see something tangible and to interpret the ramifications of the design. In many cases, it is also possible to simulate operating conditions on the computer and observe the results. Any kind of geometric shape stored in the database can be easily duplicated. For large and complex designs and drawings, particularly those involving similar shapes and repetitive operations, CAD approaches are very efficient and effective. Because computer designs and models can be altered easily, a multitude of design options can be examined and presented to a client before any construction or manufacturing actually takes place. Making changes to a CAD model is generally much faster than making changes to a traditional hand drawing. Only the affected components of the design need to be modified, and the drawings can be plotted again. In addition, the greatest benefit is that, once the CAD model is created, it can be used over and over again. The CAD models can also be transferred into manufacturing equipment such as machining centers, lathes, mills, or rapid prototyping machines to manufacture the product directly.

CAD, however, does not replace every design activity. CAD may help, but it does not replace the designer's experience with geometry and graphical conventions and standards for the specific field. CAD is a powerful tool, but the use of this tool does not guarantee correct results; the designer is still responsible for using good design practice and applying good judgment. CAD will supplement these skills to ensure that the best design is obtained.

CAD designs and drawings are stored in binary form, usually as CAD files, to magnetic devices such as diskettes and hard disks. The information stored in CAD files usually requires much less physical space in comparison to traditional hand drawings. However, the information stored inside the computer is not indestructible. On the contrary, the electronic format of information is very fragile and sensitive to the environment. Heat or cold can damage the information stored on magnetic storage devices. A power failure while you are creating a design could wipe out the many hours you spent working in front of the computer monitor. It is a good habit to save your work periodically, just in case something might go wrong while you are working on your design. In general, one should save one's work onto a storage device at an interval of every 15 to 20 minutes. You should also save your work before you make any major modifications to the design. It is also a good habit to periodically make backup copies of your work and put them in a safe place.

Getting Started with AutoCAD 2027

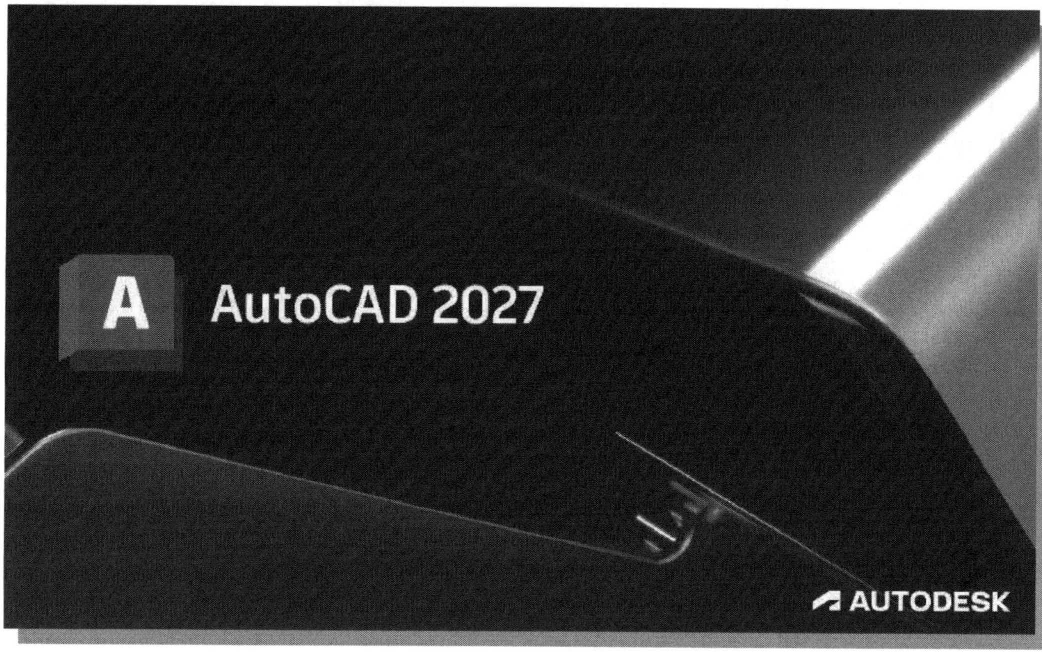

How to start **AutoCAD 2027** depends on the type of workstation and the particular software configuration you are using. With most *Windows* systems, you may select the **AutoCAD 2027** option on the *Start* menu or select the **AutoCAD 2027** icon on the *Desktop*. Consult with your instructor or technical support personnel if you have difficulty starting the software.

The program takes a while to load, so be patient. Eventually the **AutoCAD 2027** main *drawing screen* will appear on the screen. Click **New Drawing** as shown in the below figure. The tutorials in this text are based on the assumption that you are using **AutoCAD 2027**'s default settings. If your system has been customized, some of the settings may not work with the step-by-step instructions in the tutorials. Contact your instructor and technical support to restore the default software configuration.

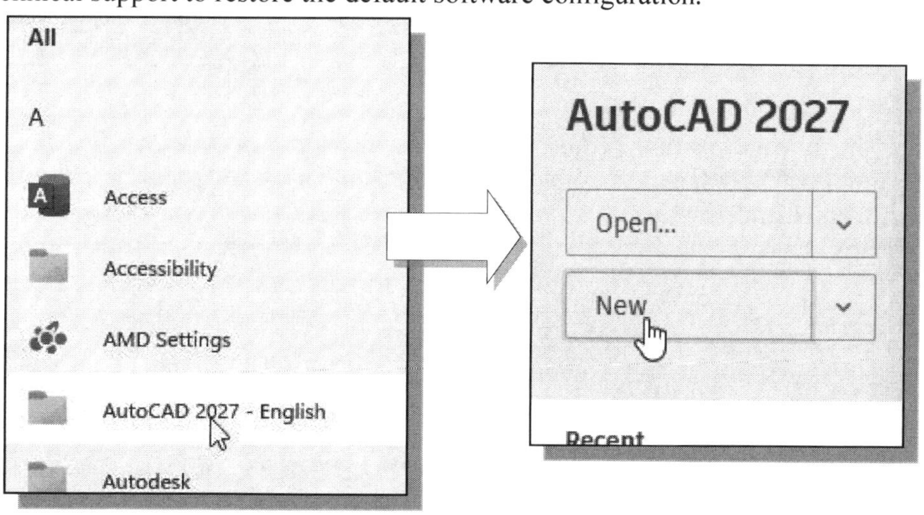

AutoCAD 2027 Screen Layout

The default **AutoCAD 2027** *drawing screen* contains the *pull-down* menus, the *Standard* toolbar, the *InfoCenter Help system,* the *scrollbars,* the *command prompt area*, the *Status Bar*, and the *Ribbon Tabs* and *Panels* that contain several *control panels* such as the *Draw and Modify* panel and the *Annotation* panel. You may resize the **AutoCAD 2027** drawing window by clicking and dragging at the edges of the window, or relocate the window by clicking and dragging at the window title area.

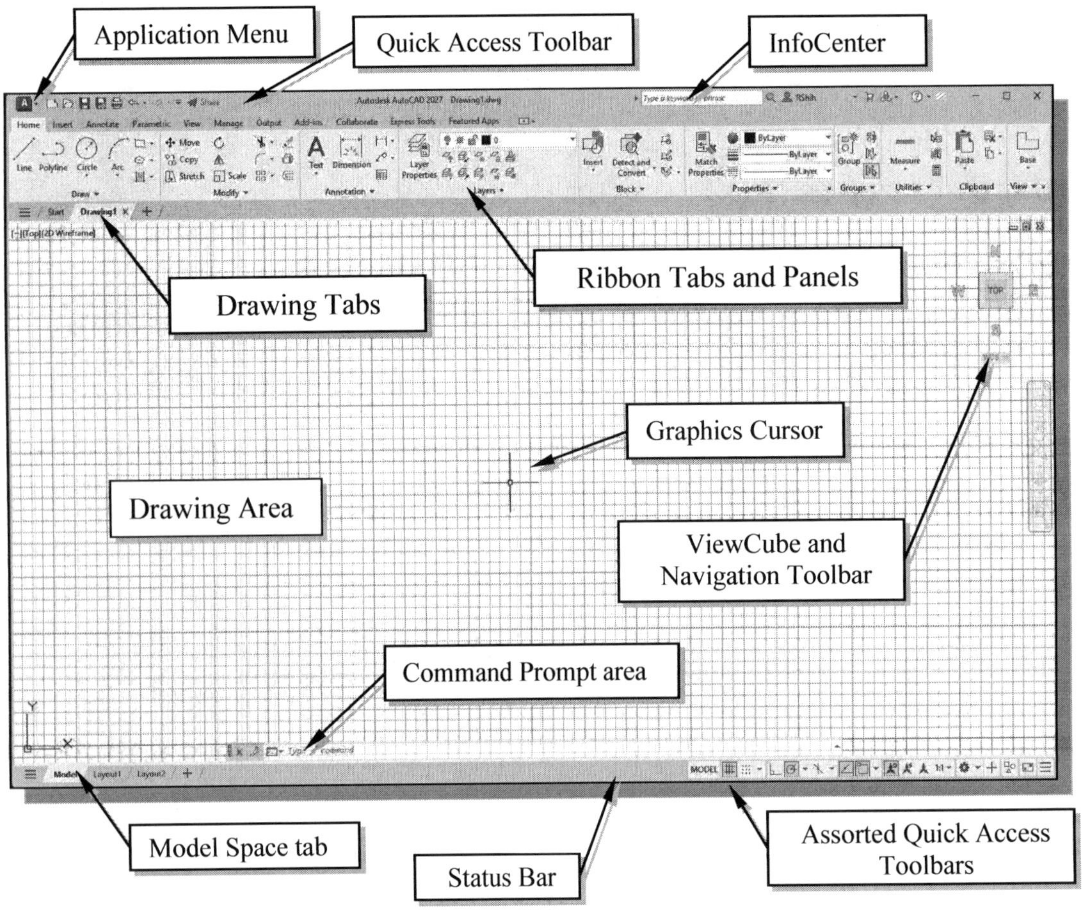

- Click on the down-arrow in the *Quick Access* bar and select **Show Menu Bar** to display the **AutoCAD *Menu*** bar. Note that the menu bar provides access to all of the AutoCAD commands.

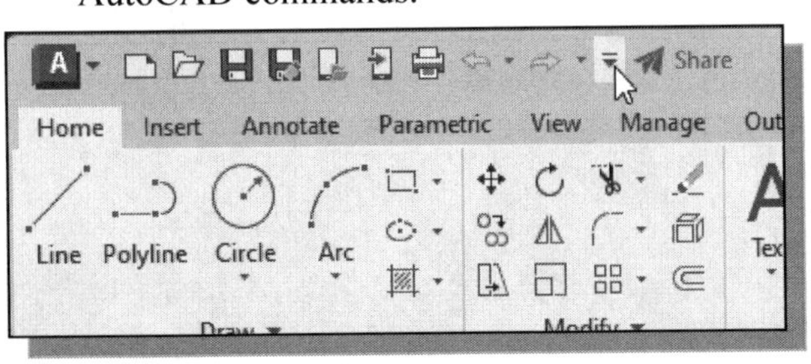

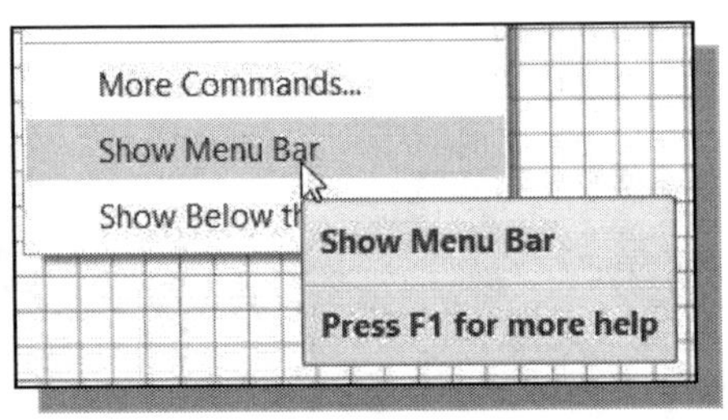

- **Application Menu**

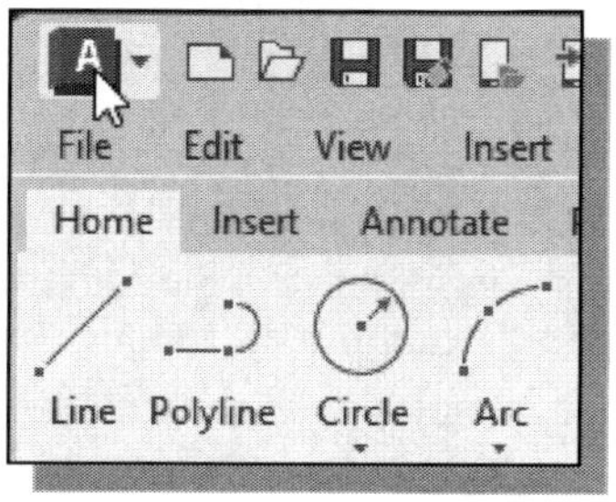

The *Application Menu* at the top of the main window contains commonly used file operations.

- **Quick Access Toolbar**

  The *Quick Access* toolbar at the top of the *AutoCAD* window allows us quick access to frequently used commands, such as Qnew, Open, Save and also the Undo command. Note that we can customize the quick access toolbar by adding and removing sets of options or individual commands.

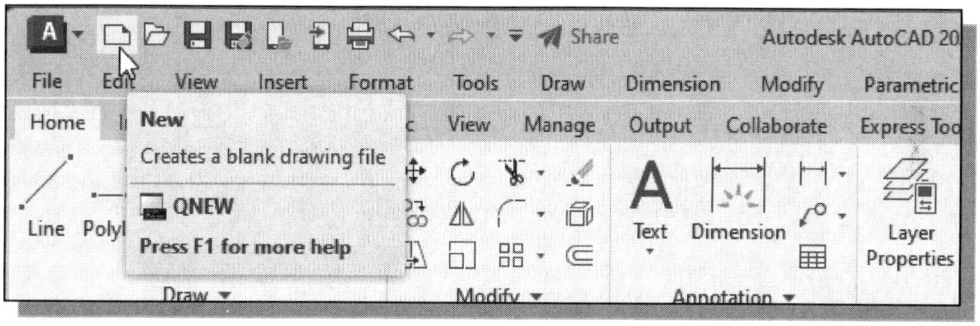

- **AutoCAD Menu Bar**

  The *Menu* bar is the pull-down menu where all operations of AutoCAD can be accessed.

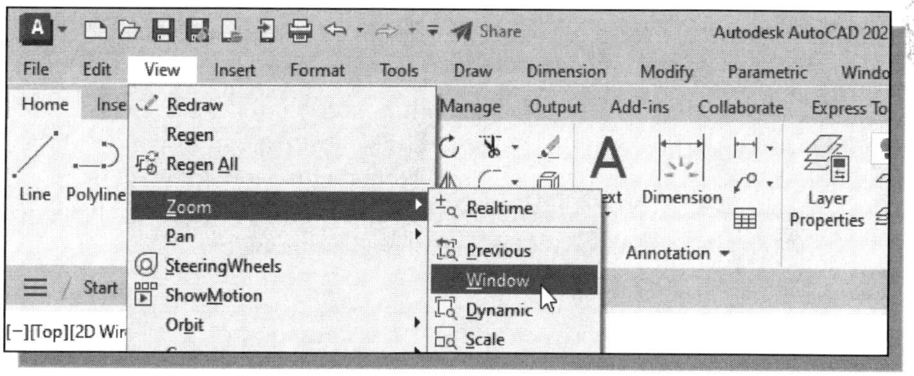

- **Layout tabs**

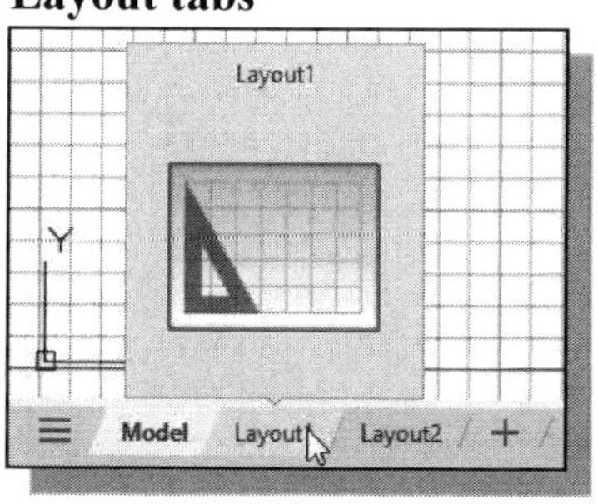

The Model/Layout tabs allow us to switch/create between different **model space** and **paper space**.

- **Drawing Area**
  The *Drawing Area* is the area where models and drawings are displayed.

- **Graphics Cursor or Crosshairs**

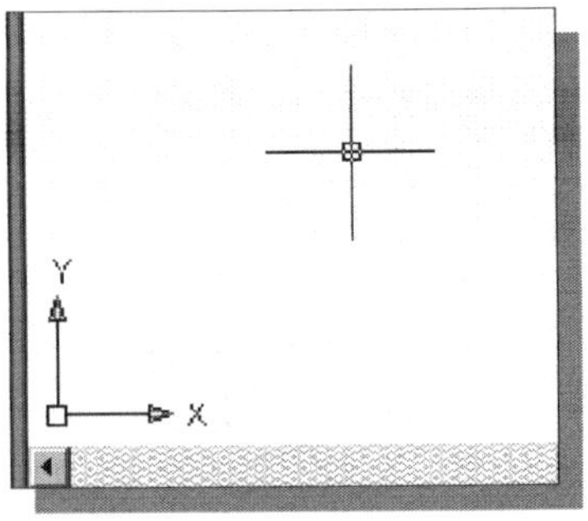

The *graphics cursor*, or *crosshairs*, shows the location of the pointing device in the Drawing Area. The coordinates of the cursor are displayed at the bottom of the screen layout. The cursor's appearance depends on the selected command or option.

- **Command Prompt Area**

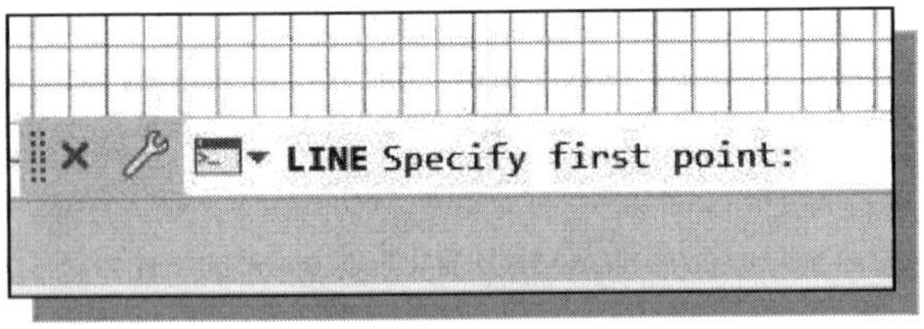

The *Command Prompt Area* provides status information for an operation and it is also the area for data input. Note that the *Command Prompt* can be docked below the drawing area as shown.

- **Cursor Coordinates**

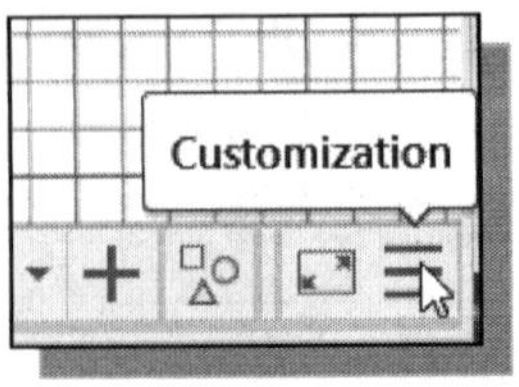

To switch on the **AutoCAD Coordinates Display**, use the *Customization option* at the bottom right corner.

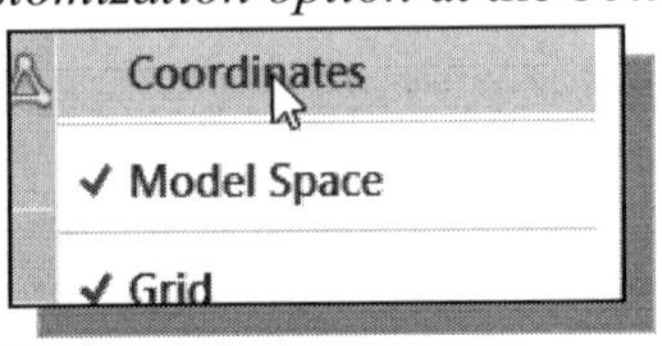

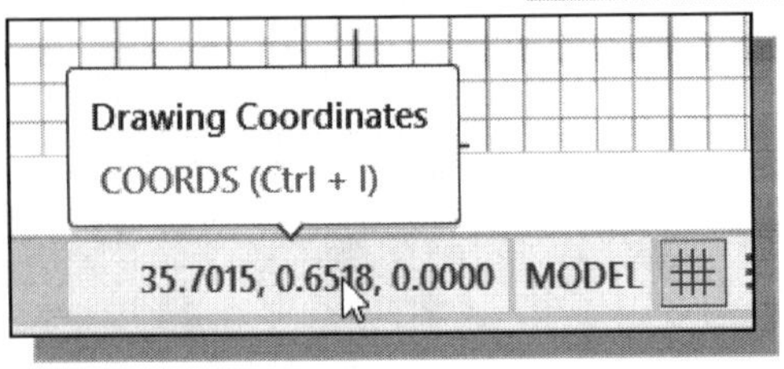

The bottom section of the screen layout displays the coordinate information of the cursor. Note that the quick-key option, [Ctrl+I], can be used to toggle the behavior of the displayed coordinates.

- **Status Toolbar**
  Next to the cursor coordinate display is the *Status* toolbar, showing the status of many commonly used display and construction options.

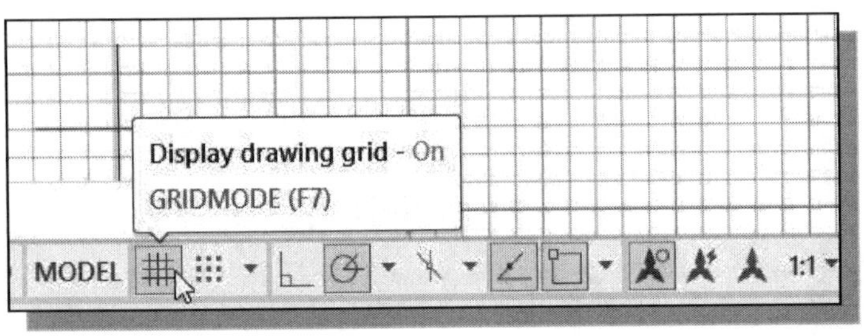

- **Ribbon Tabs and Panels**
  The top section of the screen layout contains customizable icon panels, which contain groups of buttons that allow us to pick commands quickly, without searching through a menu structure. These panels allow us to quickly access the commonly used commands available in AutoCAD.

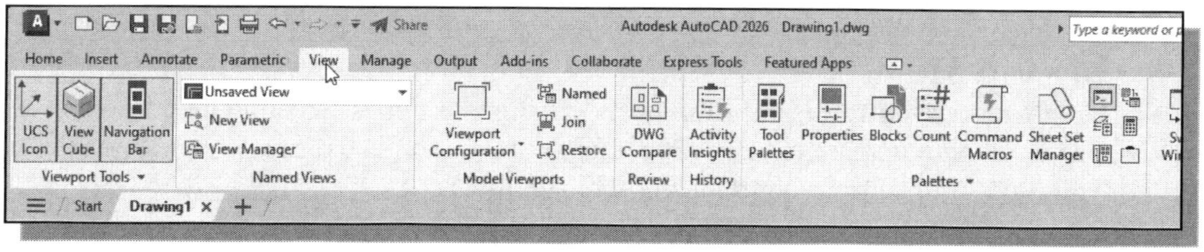

- **Draw and Modify Toolbar Panels**
  The *Draw* and *Modify* toolbar panels are the two main panels for creating drawings; the toolbars contain icons for basic draw and modify commands.

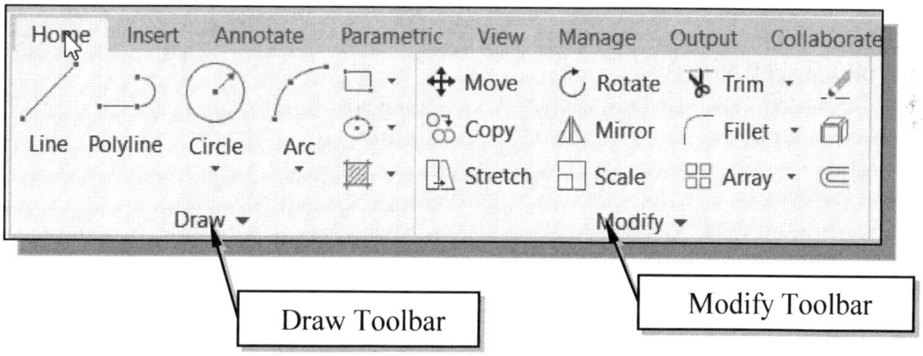

- **Layers Control Toolbar Panel**

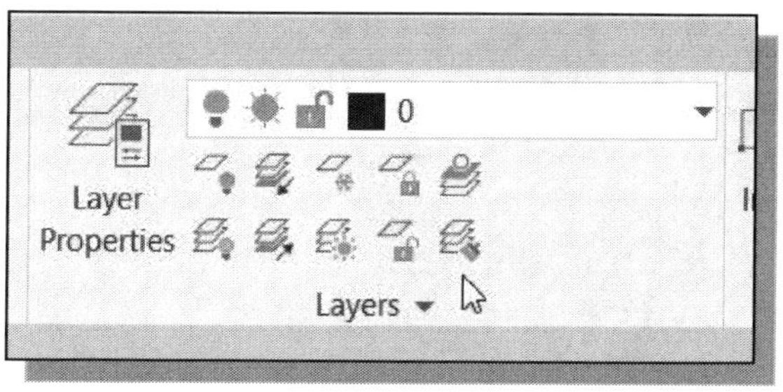

The *Layers Control* toolbar panel contains tools to help manipulate the properties of graphical objects.

- **Viewport/View/Display Controls**

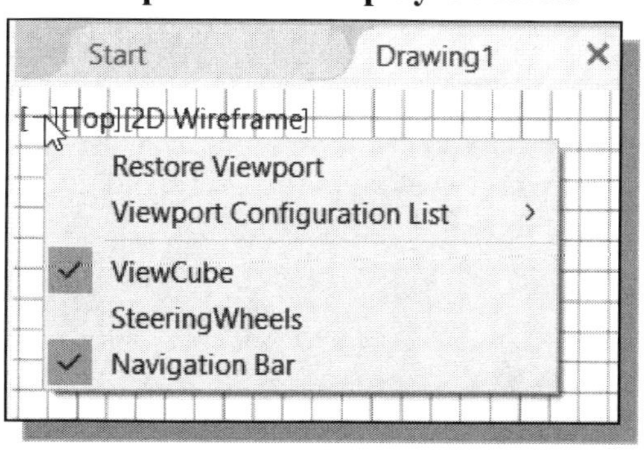

The *Viewport/View/Display controls panel* is located at the upper left corner of the graphics area and it can be used to quickly access viewing related commands, such as Viewport and Display style.

Mouse Buttons

AutoCAD 2027 utilizes the mouse buttons extensively. In learning **AutoCAD 2027**'s interactive environment, it is important to understand the basic functions of the mouse buttons. It is highly recommended that you use a mouse or a tablet with **AutoCAD 2027** since the package uses the buttons for various functions.

- **Left mouse button**
  The **left-mouse-button** is used for most operations, such as selecting menus and icons or picking graphic entities. One click of the button is used to select icons, menus and form entries and to pick graphic items.

- **Right mouse button**
  The **right-mouse-button** is used to bring up additional available options. The software also utilizes the **right-mouse-button** the same as the **ENTER** key and is often used to accept the default setting to a prompt or to end a process.

- **Middle mouse button/wheel**
  The middle mouse button/wheel can be used to Pan (hold down the wheel button and drag the mouse) or Zoom (rotate the wheel) real time.

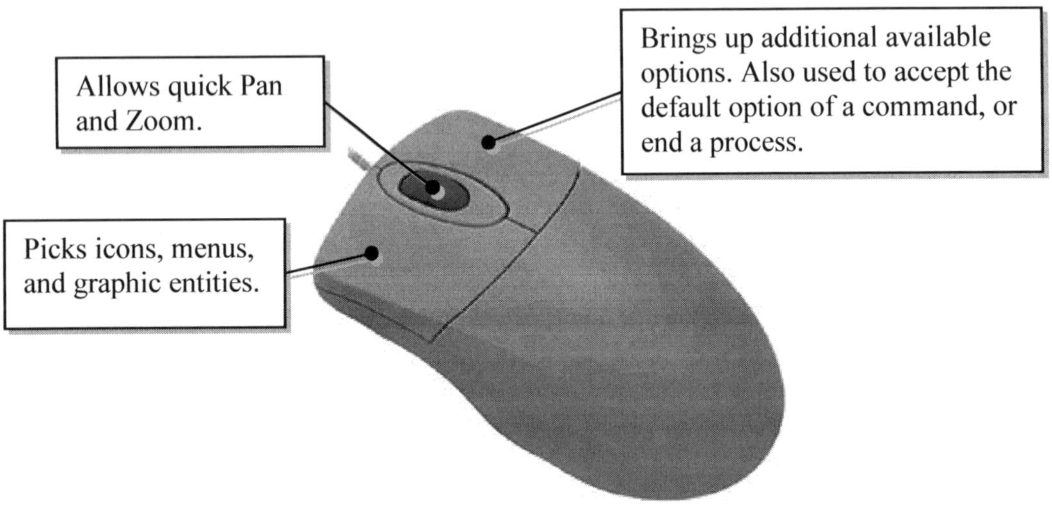

[Esc] – Canceling commands

The [**Esc**] key is used to cancel a command in **AutoCAD 2027**. The [**Esc**] key is located near the top-left corner of the keyboard. Sometimes, it may be necessary to press the [**Esc**] key twice to cancel a command; it depends on where we are in the command sequence. For some commands, the [**Esc**] key is used to exit the command.

Online Help

Several types of online help are available at any time during an **AutoCAD 2027** session. The **AutoCAD 2027** software provides many online help options:

- **Autodesk Exchange**:
  Autodesk Exchange is a central portal in AutoCAD 2027; AutoCAD Exchange provides a user interface for Help, learning aids, tips and tricks, videos, and downloadable apps. By default, *Autodesk Exchange* is displayed at **startup**. This allows access to a dynamic selection of tools from the *Autodesk community*; note that an internet connection is required to use this option.

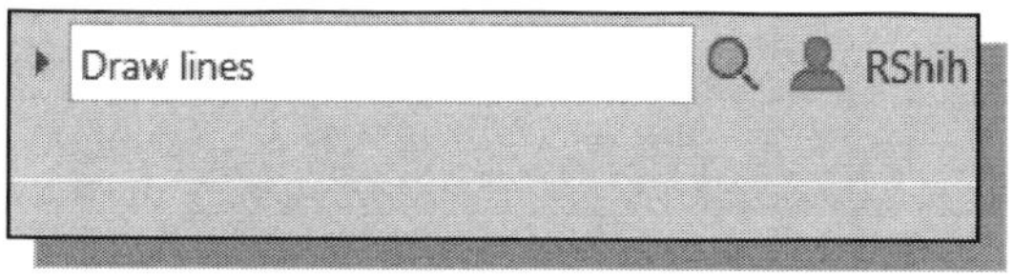

- To use *Autodesk Exchange*, simply type a question in the *input box* to search through the Autodesk's *Help* system as shown.

- A list of the search results appears in the *Autodesk Help* window, and we can also determine the level and type of searches of the associated information.

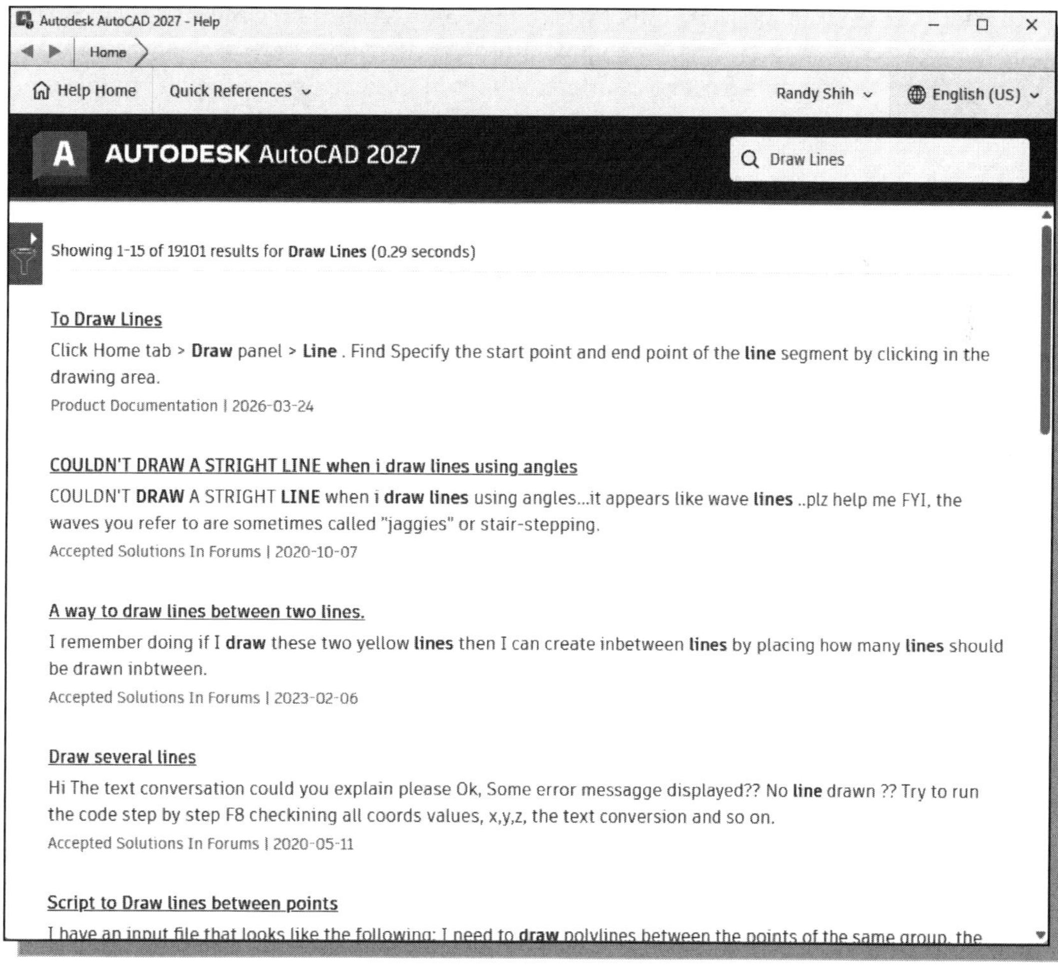

Leaving AutoCAD 2027

To leave **AutoCAD 2027**, use the left-mouse-button and click the **Application Menu** button at the top left corner of the **AutoCAD 2027** screen window, then choose **Exit AutoCAD** from the pull-down menu or type ***QUIT*** in the command prompt area.

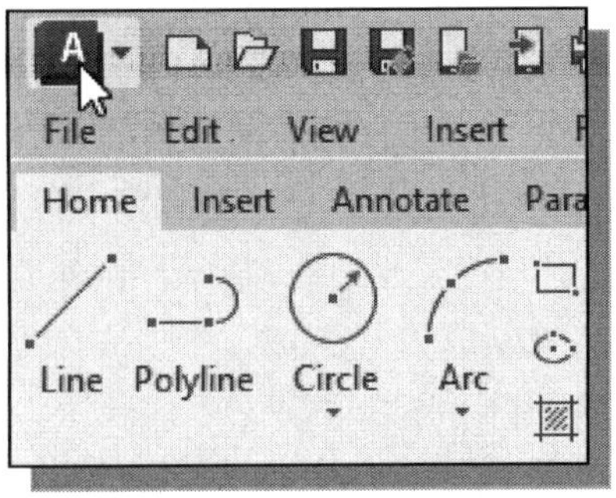

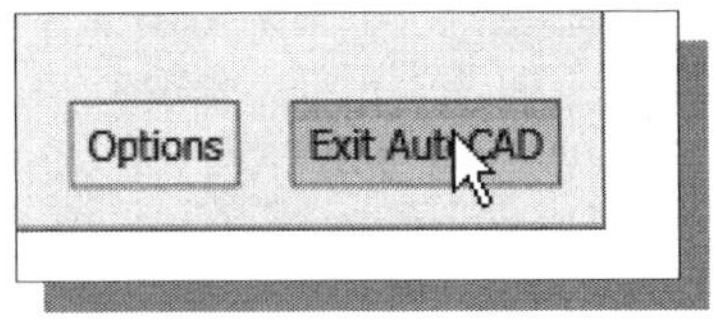

Creating a CAD File Folder

It is a good practice to create a separate folder to store your CAD files. You should not save your CAD files in the same folder where the **AutoCAD 2027** application is located. It is much easier to organize and back up your project files if they are in a separate folder. Making folders within this folder for different types of projects will help you organize your CAD files even further.

➢ To create a new folder in the *Microsoft Windows* environment:

1. On the *desktop* or under the *My Documents* folder in which you want to create a new folder.

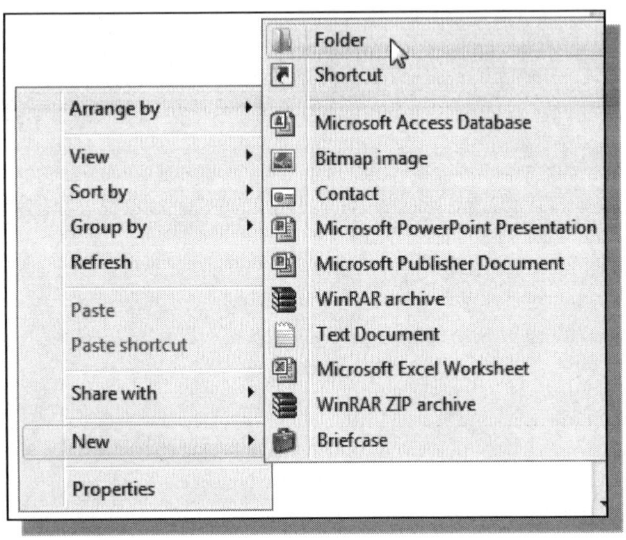

2. Right-mouse-click once to bring up the option menu, then select New→ Folder.

3. Type a name for the new folder, and then press **ENTER**.

Drawing in AutoCAD

Learning to use a CAD system is similar to learning a new language. It is necessary to begin with the basic alphabet and learn how to use it correctly and effectively through practice. This will require learning some new concepts and skills as well as learning a different vocabulary. All CAD systems create designs using basic geometric entities. Many of the constructions used in technical designs are based upon two-dimensional planar geometry. The method and number of operations that are required to accomplish the constructions are different from one system to another.

In order to become effective in using a CAD system, we must learn to create geometric entities quickly and accurately. In learning to use a CAD system, **lines** and **circles** are the first two, and perhaps the most important two, geometric entities that one should master the skills of creating and modifying. Straight lines and circles are used in almost all technical designs. In examining the different types of planar geometric entities, the importance of lines and circles becomes obvious. Triangles and polygons are planar figures bounded by straight lines. And Ellipses and Splines can be constructed by connecting arcs with different radii. As one gains some experience in creating lines and circles, similar procedures can be applied to create other geometric entities. In this chapter, the different ways of creating lines and circles in **AutoCAD 2027** are examined.

Starting Up AutoCAD 2027

1. Select the **AutoCAD 2027** option on the *Program* menu or select the **AutoCAD 2027** icon on the *Desktop*. Click **Start Drawing** to start a new drawing.

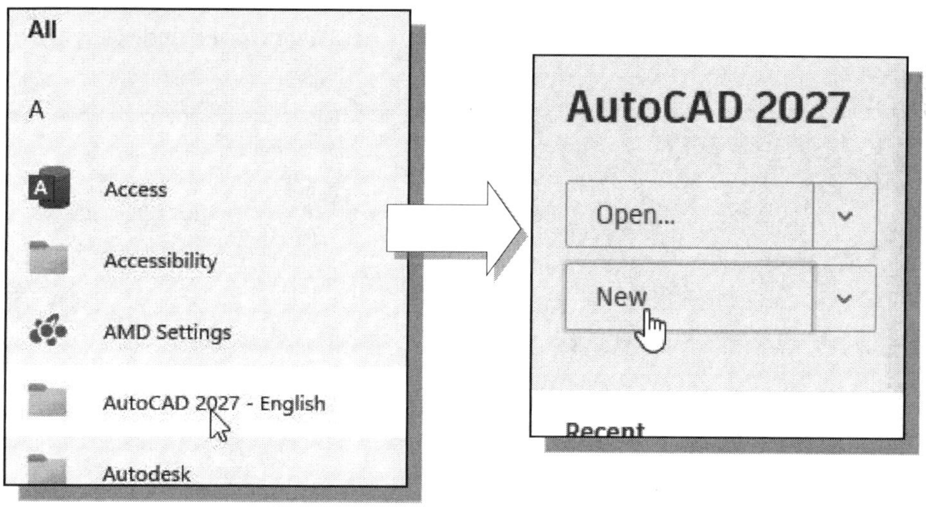

❖ Once the program is loaded into memory, the **AutoCAD 2027** main drawing screen will appear on the screen.

➢ Note that AutoCAD automatically assigns generic names, *Drawing 1*, as new drawings are created. In our example, AutoCAD opened the graphics window using the default system units and assigned the drawing name *Drawing1*.

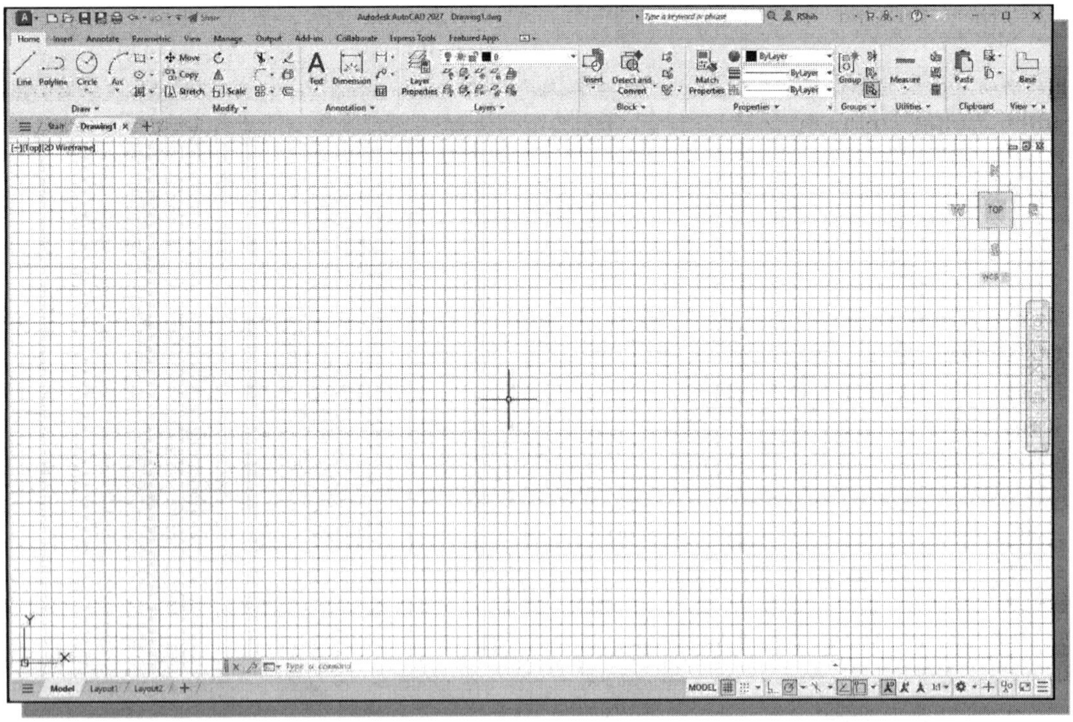

2. If necessary, click on the down-arrow in the *Quick Access* bar and select **Show Menu Bar** to display the **AutoCAD *Menu Bar***. The *Menu Bar* provides access to all AutoCAD commands.

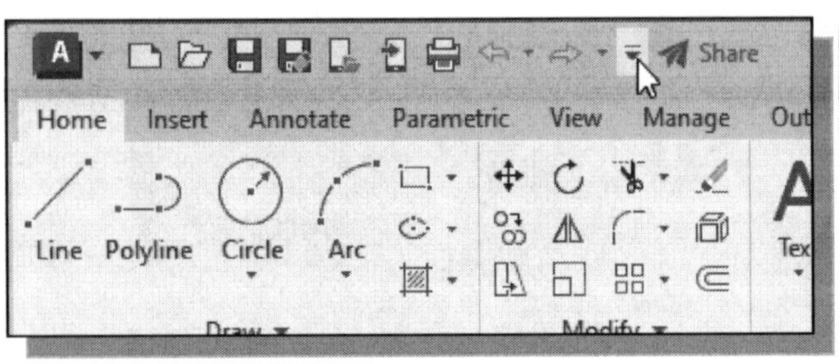

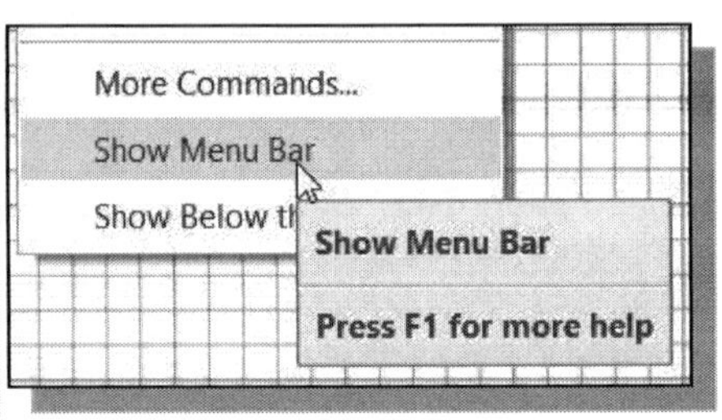

3. To switch on the **AutoCAD Coordinates Display**, use the *Customization option* at the bottom right corner.

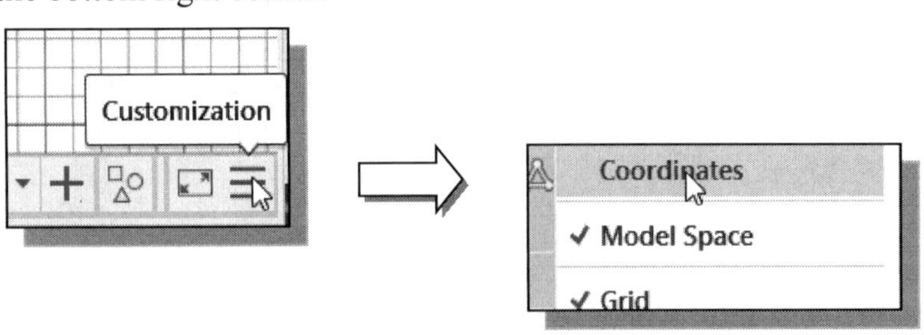

Drawing Units Setup

Every object we construct in a CAD system is measured in **units**. We should determine the system of units within the CAD system before creating the first geometric entities.

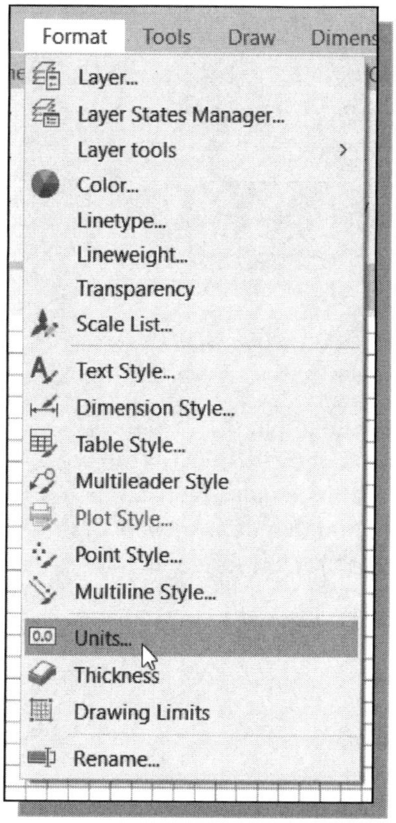

1. In the *Menu Bar* select:
   [Format] → [Units]

- The AutoCAD *Menu Bar* contains multiple pull-down menus where all of the AutoCAD commands can be accessed. Note that many of the menu items listed in the pull-down menus can also be accessed through the *Quick Access* toolbar and/or *Ribbon* panels.

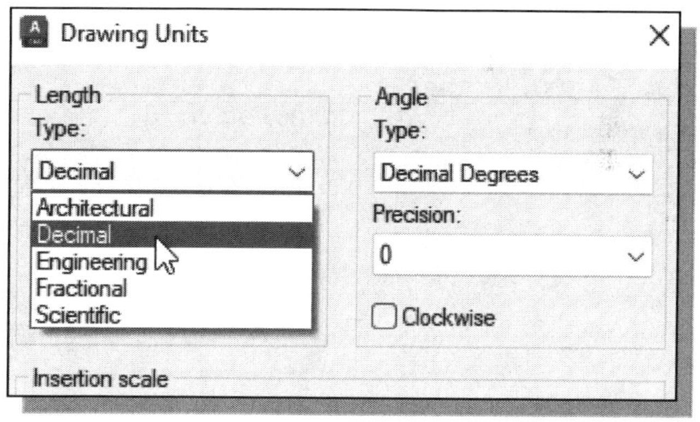

2. Click on the *Length Type* option to display the different types of length units available. Confirm the *Length Type* is set to **Decimal**.

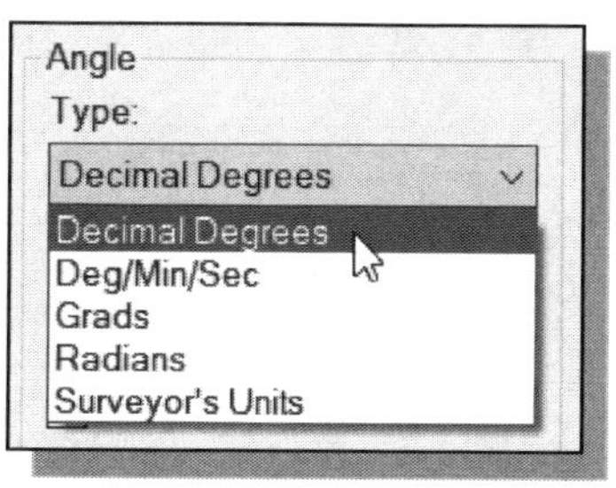

3. On your own, examine the other settings that are available.

- Also note the Insertion Scale section will show the default measurement system, such as the *English* units, inches.

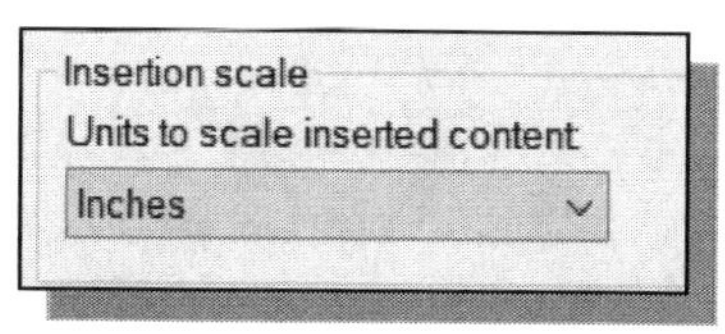

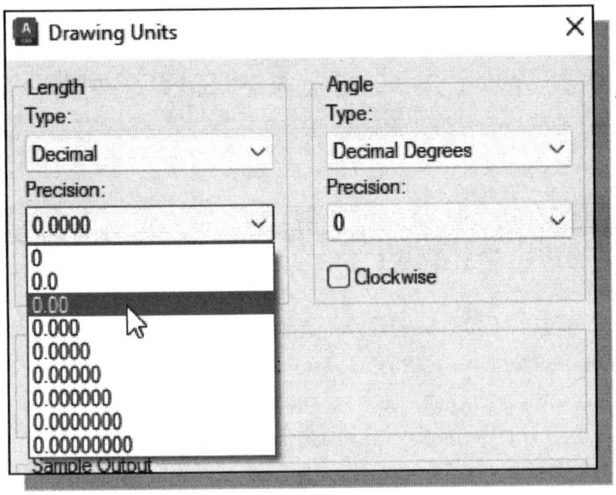

4. Set the *Precision* to **two digits** after the decimal point as shown in the above figure.

5. Pick **OK** to exit the *Drawing Units* dialog box.

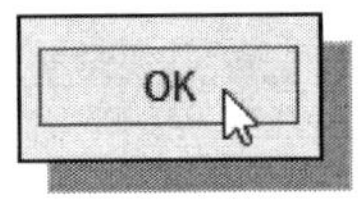

Drawing Area Setup

Next, we will set up the **Drawing Limits** by entering a command in the command prompt area. Setting the Drawing Limits controls the extents of the display of the *grid*. It also serves as a visual reference that marks the working area. It can also be used to prevent construction outside the grid limits and as a plot option that defines an area to be plotted and/or printed. Note that this setting does not limit the region for geometry construction.

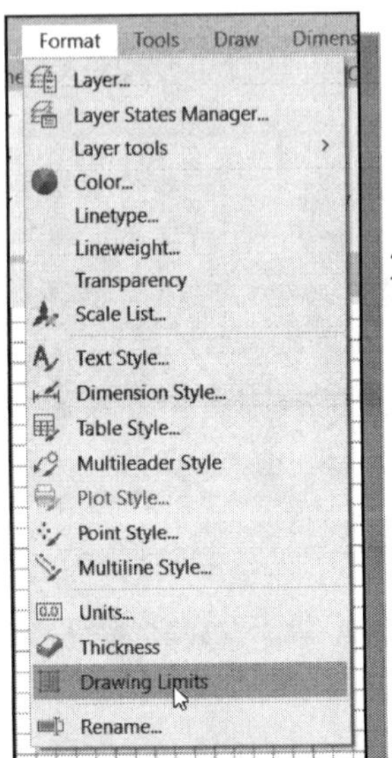

1. In the *Menu Bar* select:
   [Format] → [Drawing Limits]

2. In the command prompt area, the message "*Reset Model Space Limits: Specify lower left corner or [On/Off] <0.00,0.00>:*" is displayed. Press the **ENTER** key once to accept the default coordinates <**0.00,0.00**>.

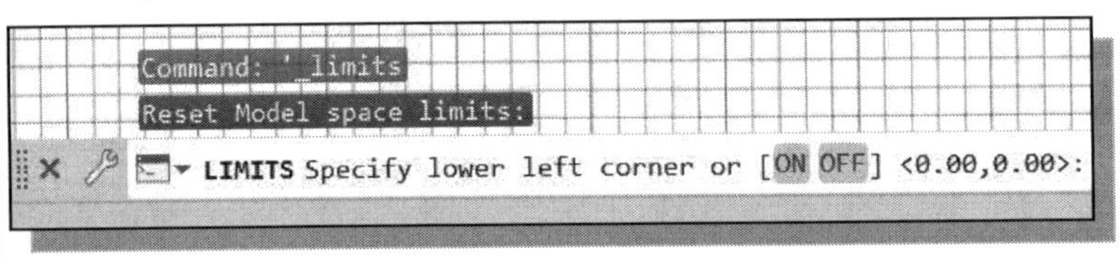

3. In the command prompt area, the message "*Specify upper right corner <12.00,9.00>:*" is displayed. Press the **ENTER** key again to accept the default coordinates <**12.00,9.00**>.

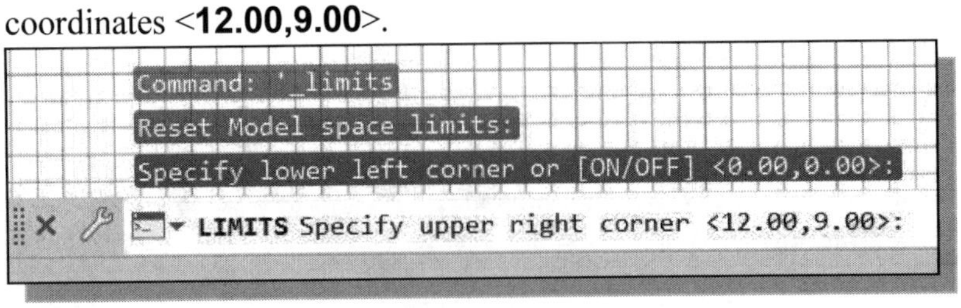

4. On your own, move the graphics cursor near the upper-right corner inside the drawing area and note that the drawing area is unchanged. (The **Drawing Limits** command is used to set the drawing area, but the display will not be adjusted until a display command is used.)

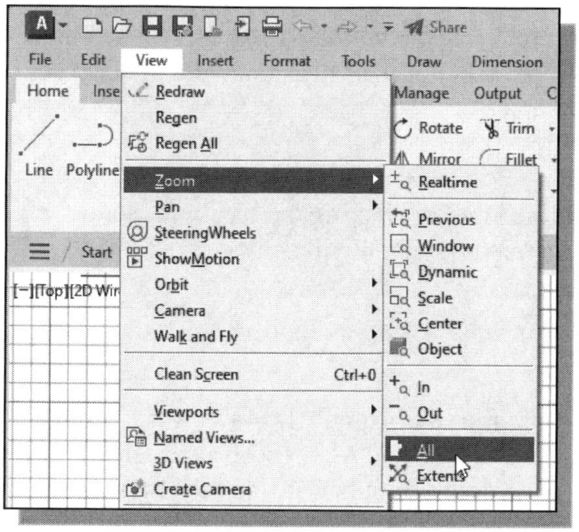

5. Inside the *Menu Bar* area select: **[View] → [Zoom] → [All]**

❖ The **Zoom All** command will adjust the display so that all objects in the drawing are displayed to be as large as possible. If no objects are constructed, the **Drawing Limits** are used to adjust the current viewport.

6. Move the graphics cursor near the upper-right corner inside the drawing area and note that the display area is updated.

7. Hit the function key [**F7**] once to turn **off** the display of the *Grid* lines.

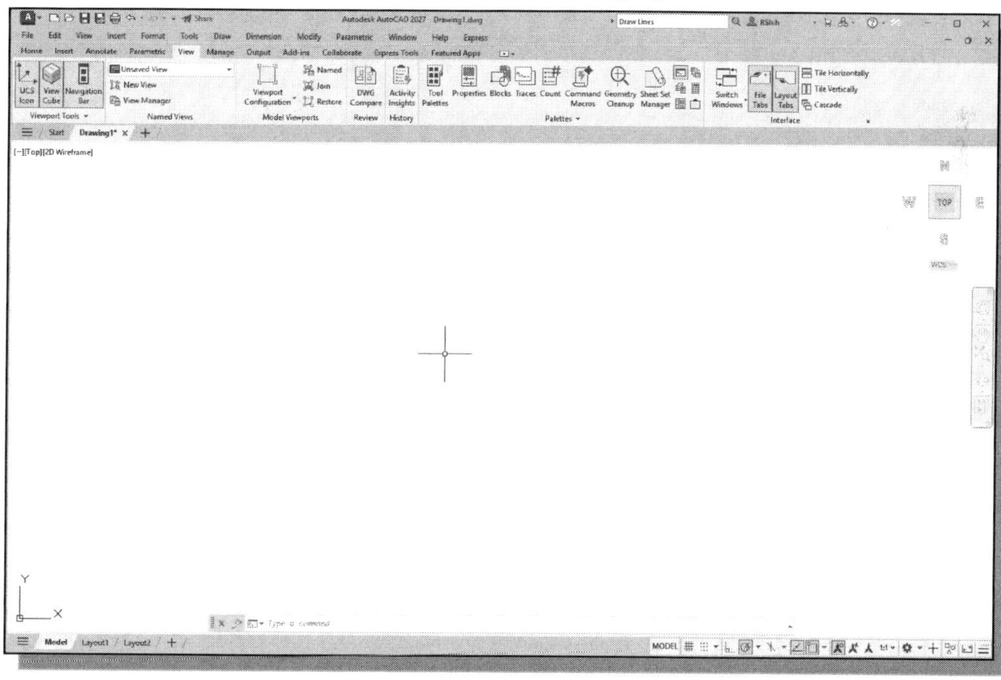

- Note that function key [**F7**] is a quick key, which can be used to quickly toggle on/off the grid display. Also, note the *command prompt area* can be positioned to dock below the drawing area or float inside the drawing area as shown.

Drawing Lines with the Line Command

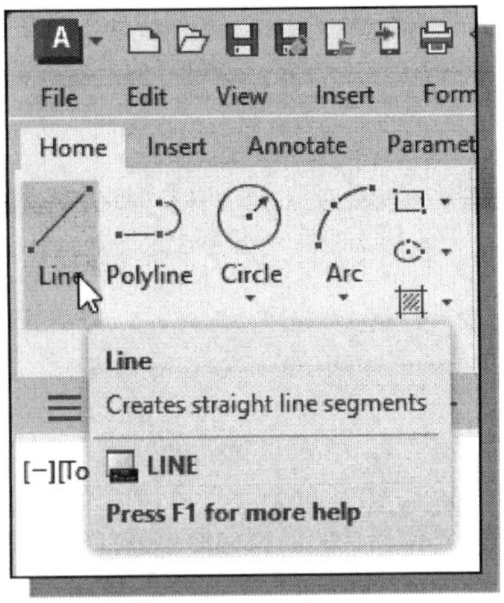

1. Move the graphics cursor to the first icon in the *Draw* panel. This icon is the **Line** icon. Note that a brief description of the Line command appears next to the cursor.

2. Select the icon by clicking once with the **left-mouse-button**, which will activate the Line command.

3. In the command prompt area, near the bottom of the AutoCAD drawing screen, the message "**Line** *Specify first point:*" is displayed. AutoCAD expects us to identify the starting location of a straight line. Move the graphics cursor inside the graphics window and watch the display of the coordinates of the graphics cursor at the bottom of the AutoCAD drawing screen. The three numbers represent the location of the cursor in the X, Y, and Z directions. We can treat the graphics window as if it was a piece of paper, and we are using the graphics cursor as if it was a pencil with which to draw.

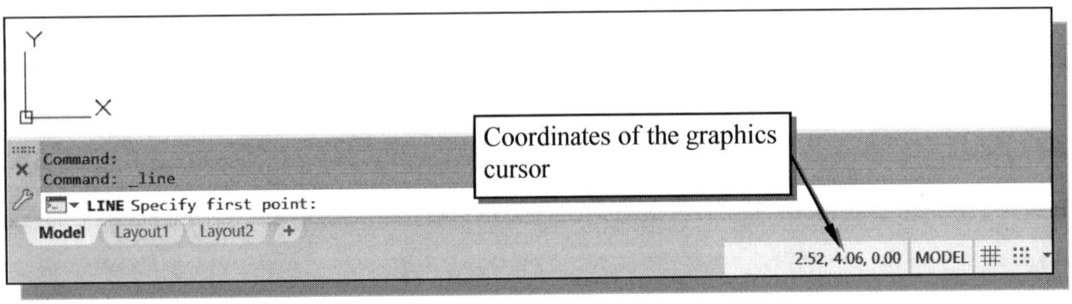

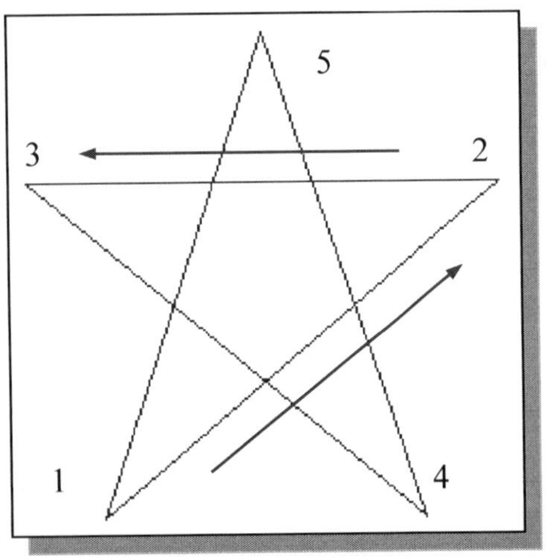

❖ We will create a freehand sketch of a five-point star using the Line command. Do not be overly concerned with the actual size or accuracy of your freehand sketch. This exercise is to give you a feel for the **AutoCAD 2027** user interface.

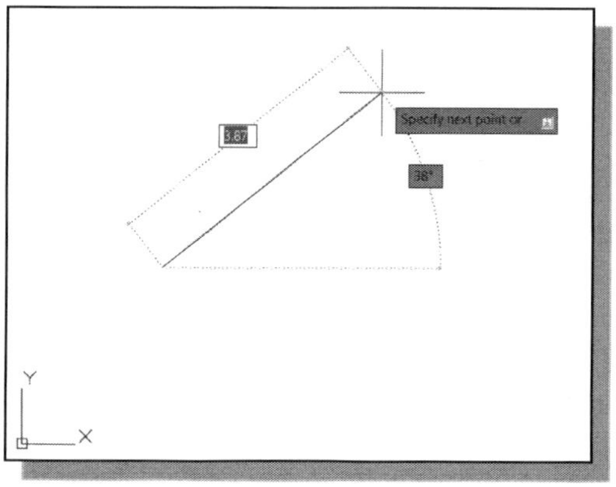

4. We will start at a location about one-third from the bottom of the graphics window. Left-click once to position the starting point of our first line. This will be *point 1* of our sketch. Next, move the cursor upward and toward the right side of *point 1*. Notice the rubber-band line that follows the graphics cursor in the graphics window. Left-click again (*point 2*) and we have created the first line of our sketch.

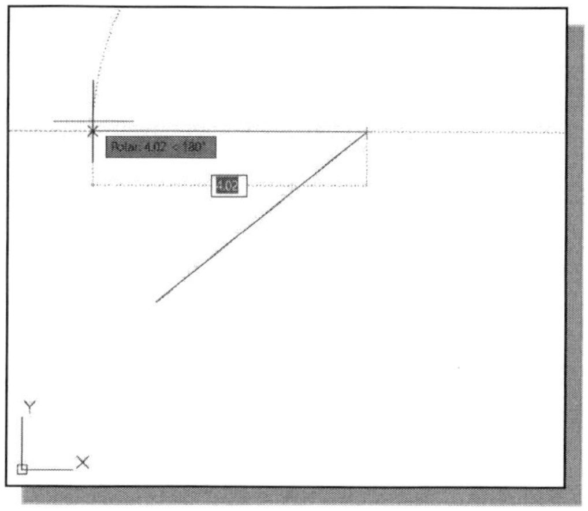

5. Move the cursor to the left of *point 2* and create a horizontal line about the same length as the first line on the screen.

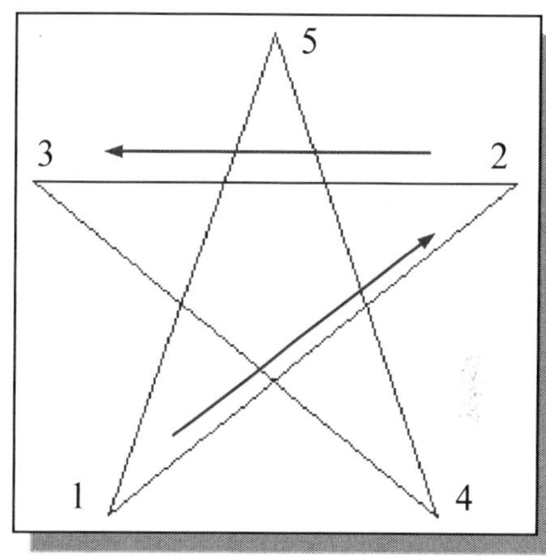

6. Repeat the above steps and complete the freehand sketch by adding three more lines (from *point 3* to *point 4*, *point 4* to *point 5*, and then connect to *point 5* back to *point 1*).

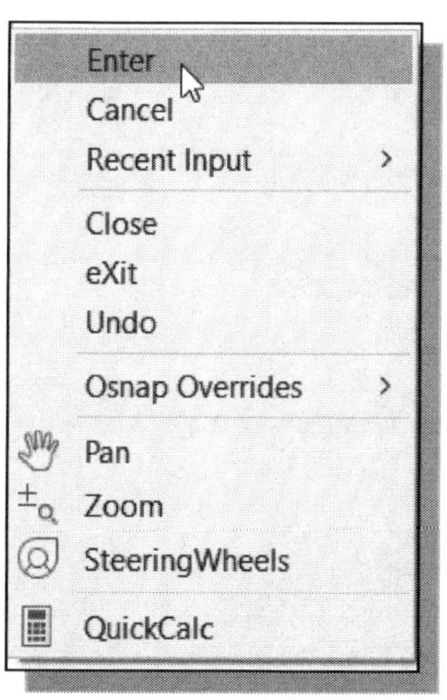

7. Notice that the **Line** command remains activated even after we connected the last segment of the line to the starting point *(point 1)* of our sketch. Inside the graphics window, **click once** with the **right-mouse-button** and a pop-up menu appears on the screen.

8. Select **Enter** with the left-mouse-button to end the **Line** command. (This is equivalent to hitting the [**ENTER**] key on the keyboard.)

9. Move the cursor near *point 2* and *point 3*, and estimate the length of the horizontal line by watching the displayed coordinates for each point.

Visual Reference

The method we just used to create the freehand sketch is known as the **interactive method**, where we use the cursor to specify locations on the screen. This method is perhaps the fastest way to specify locations on the screen. However, it is rather difficult to try to create a line of a specific length by watching the displayed coordinates. It would be helpful to know what one inch or one meter looks like on the screen while we are creating entities. **AutoCAD 2027** provides us with many tools to aid the construction of our designs. For example, the ***GRID*** and ***SNAP MODE*** options can be used to get a visual reference as to the size of objects and learn to restrict the movement of the cursor to a set increment on the screen.

The ***GRID*** and ***SNAP MODE*** options can be turned *ON* or *OFF* through the *Status Bar*. The *Status Bar* area is located at the bottom left of the AutoCAD drawing screen, next to the cursor coordinates.

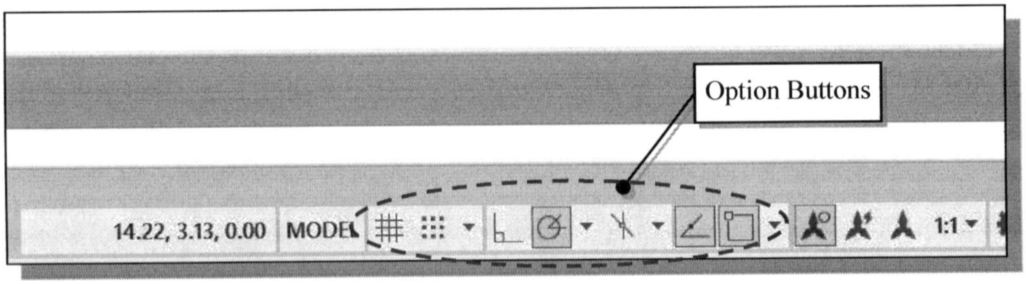

The second button in the *Status Bar* is the *SNAP MODE* option and the third button is the *GRID DISPLAY* option. Note that the buttons in the *Status Bar* area serve two functions: (1) the status of the specific option, and (2) as toggle switches that can be used to turn these special options *ON* and *OFF*. When the corresponding button is *highlighted*, the specific option is turned *ON*. Using the buttons is a quick and easy way to make changes to these *drawing aid* options. The buttons in the *Status Bar* can also be switched on and off in the middle of another command.

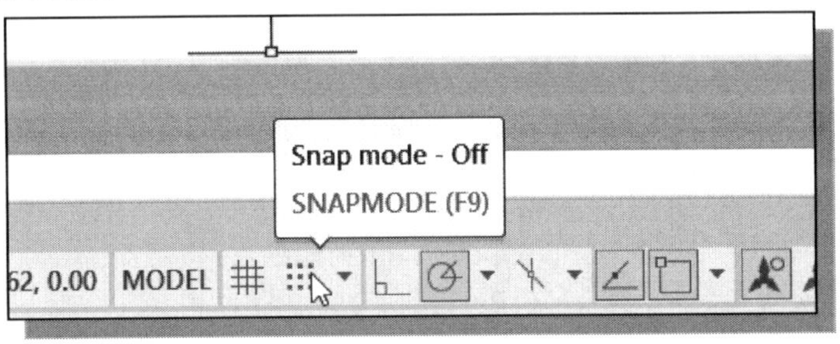

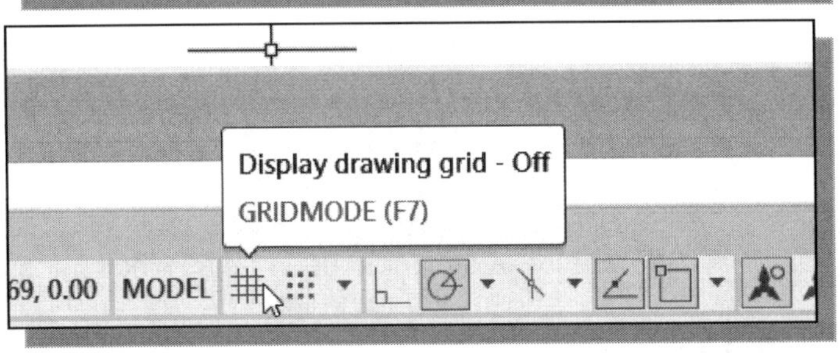

GRID ON

1. Left-click the ***GRID*** button in the *Status Bar* to turn ***ON*** the *GRID DISPLAY* option. (Notice in the command prompt area, the message *"<Grid on>"* is also displayed.)

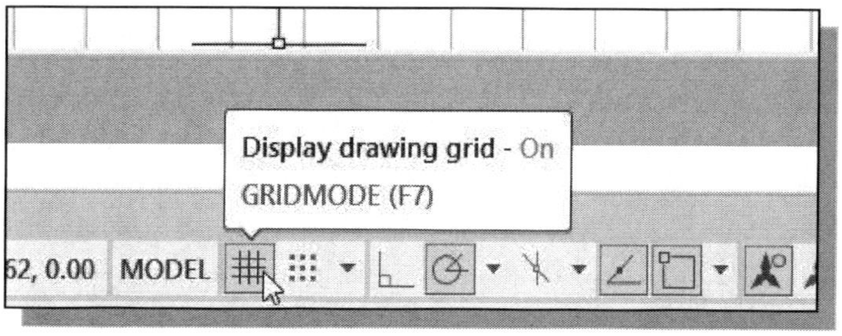

2. Move the cursor inside the graphics window, and estimate the distance in between the grid lines by watching the coordinates displayed at the bottom of the screen.

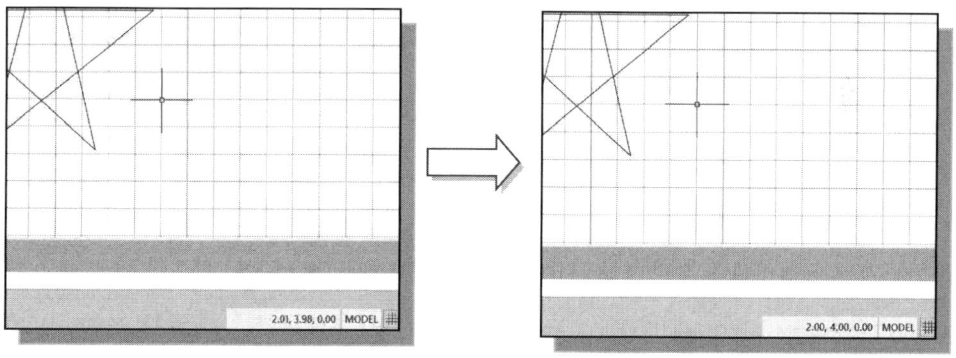

➢ The *GRID* option creates a pattern of lines that extends over an area on the screen. Using the grid is similar to placing a sheet of grid paper under a drawing. The grid helps you align objects and visualize the distance between them. The grid is not displayed in the plotted drawing. The default grid spacing, which means the distance in between two lines on the screen, is 0.5 inches. We can see that the sketched horizontal line in the sketch is about 4 inches long.

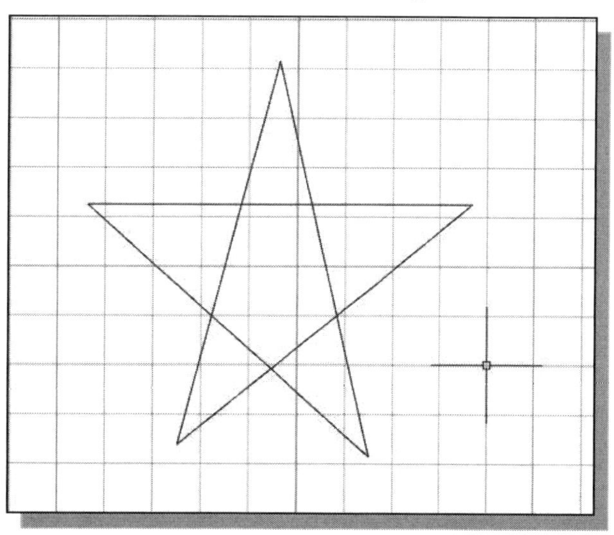

APPENDIX E – FASTENERS (INCH SERIES) Continued

DIMENSIONS OF SLOTTED FLAT COUNTERSUNK HEAD CAP SCREWS

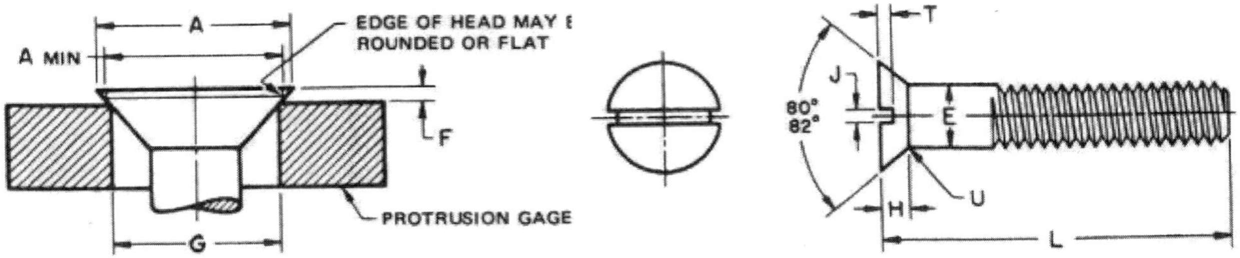

		E		A		H[2]	J		T		U	F[3]		G[3]
Nominal Size[1] or Basic Screw Diameter		Body Diameter		Head Diameter		Head Height	Slot Width		Slot Depth		Fillet Radius	Protrusion Above Gaging Diameter		Gaging Diameter
		Max	Min	Max, Edge Sharp	Min, Edge Rounded or Flat	Ref	Max	Min	Max	Min	Max	Max	Min	
1/4	0.2500	0.2500	0.2450	0.500	0.452	0.140	0.075	0.064	0.068	0.045	0.100	0.046	0.030	0.424
5/16	0.3125	0.3125	0.3070	0.625	0.567	0.177	0.084	0.072	0.086	0.057	0.125	0.053	0.035	0.538
3/8	0.3750	0.3750	0.3690	0.750	0.682	0.210	0.094	0.081	0.103	0.068	0.150	0.060	0.040	0.651
7/16	0.4375	0.4375	0.4310	0.812	0.736	0.210	0.094	0.081	0.103	0.068	0.175	0.065	0.044	0.703
1/2	0.5000	0.5000	0.4930	0.875	0.791	0.210	0.106	0.091	0.103	0.068	0.200	0.071	0.049	0.756
9/16	0.5625	0.5625	0.5550	1.000	0.906	0.244	0.118	0.102	0.120	0.080	0.225	0.078	0.054	0.869
5/8	0.6250	0.6250	0.6170	1.125	1.020	0.281	0.133	0.116	0.137	0.091	0.250	0.085	0.058	0.982
3/4	0.7500	0.7500	0.7420	1.375	1.251	0.352	0.149	0.131	0.171	0.115	0.300	0.099	0.068	1.208
7/8	0.8750	0.8750	0.8660	1.625	1.480	0.423	0.167	0.147	0.206	0.138	0.350	0.113	0.077	1.435
1	1.0000	1.0000	0.9900	1.875	1.711	0.494	0.188	0.166	0.240	0.162	0.400	0.127	0.087	1.661
1 1/8	1.1250	1.1250	1.1140	2.062	1.880	0.529	0.196	0.178	0.257	0.173	0.450	0.141	0.096	1.826
1 1/4	1.2500	1.2500	1.2390	2.312	2.110	0.600	0.211	0.193	0.291	0.197	0.500	0.155	0.105	2.052
1 3/8	1.3750	1.3750	1.3630	2.562	2.340	0.665	0.226	0.208	0.326	0.220	0.550	0.169	0.115	2.279
1 1/2	1.5000	1.5000	1.4880	2.812	2.570	0.742	0.258	0.240	0.360	0.244	0.600	0.183	0.124	2.505

[1] Where specifying nominal size in decimals, zeros preceding decimal and in the fourth decimal place shall be omitted.

[2] Tabulated values determined from formula for maximum **H**.

[3] No tolerance for gaging diameter is given.

Reprinted from The American Society of Mechanical Engineers-ANSI 318.6.2-R1993.

APPENDIX E – FASTENERS (INCH SERIES) Continued

DIMENSIONS OF SLOTTED ROUND HEAD CAP SCREWS

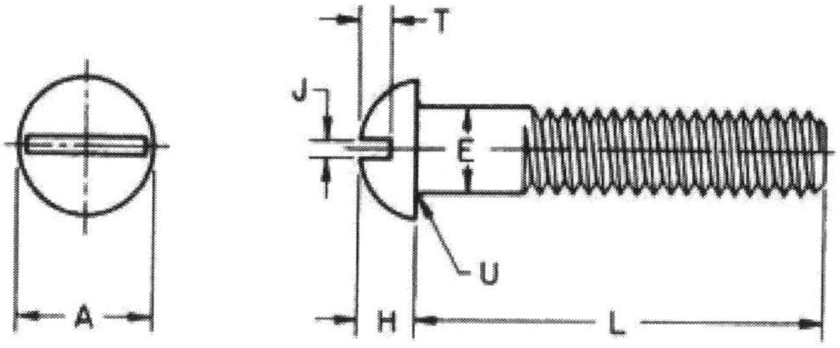

Nominal Size' or Basic Screw Diameter		E Body Diameter		A Head Diameter		H Head Height		J Slot Width		T Slot Depth		U Fillet Radius	
		Max	Min	Max	Min	Max	Min	Max	Min	Max	Min	Max	Min
1/4	0.2500	0.2500	0.2450	0.437	0.418	0.191	0.175	0.075	0.064	0.117	0.097	0.031	0.016
5/16	0.3125	0.3125	0.3070	0.562	0.540	0.245	0.226	0.084	0.072	0.151	0.126	0.031	0.016
3/8	0.3750	0.3750	0.3690	0.625	0.603	0.273	0.252	0.094	0.081	0.168	0.138	0.031	0.016
7/16	0.4375	0.4375	0.4310	0.750	0.725	0.328	0.302	0.094	0.081	0.202	0.167	0.047	0.016
1/2	0.5000	0.5000	0.4930	0.812	0.786	0.354	0.327	0.106	0.091	0.218	0.178	0.047	0.016
9/16	0.5625	0.5625	0.5550	0.937	0.909	0.409	0.378	0.118	0.102	0.252	0.207	0.047	0.016
5/8	0.6250	0.6250	0.6170	1.000	0.970	0.437	0.405	0.133	0.116	0.270	0.220	0.062	0.031
3/4	0.7500	0.7500	0.7420	1,250	1.215	0.546	0.507	0.149	0.131	0.338	0.278	0.062	0.031

'Where specifying nominal size in decimals, zeros preceding decimal and in the fourth decimal place shall be omitted.

DIMENSIONS OF SLOTTED FILLISTER HEAD CAP SCREWS

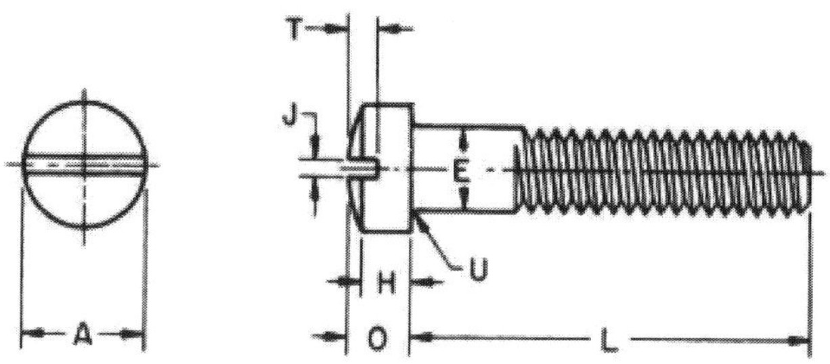

Nominal Size' or Basic Screw Diameter		E Body Diameter		A Head Diameter		H Head Side Height		O Total Head Height		J Slot Width		T Slot Depth		U Fillet Radius	
		Max	Min	Max	Min	Max	Min	Max	Min	Max	Min	Max	Min	Max	Min
1/4	0.2500	0.2500	0.2450	0.375	0.363	0.172	0.157	0.216	0.194	0.075	0.064	0.097	0.077	0.031	0.016
5/16	0.3125	0.3125	0.3070	0.437	0.424	0.203	0.186	0.253	0.230	0.084	0.072	0.115	0.090	0.031	0.016
3/8	0.3750	0.3750	0.3690	0.562	0,547	0.250	0.229	0.314	0.284	0.094	0.081	0.142	0.112	0.031	0.016
7/16	0.4375	0.4375	0.4310	0.625	0.608	0.297	0.274	0.368	0.336	0.094	0.081	0.168	0.133	0.047	0.016
1/2	0.5000	0.5000	0.4930	0.750	0.731	0.328	0.301	0.413	0.376	0.106	0.091	0.193	0.153	0.047	0.016
9/16	0.5625	0.5625	0.5550	0.812	0.792	0.375	0.346	0.467	0.427	0.118	0.102	0.213	0.168	0.047	0.016
5/8	0.6250	0.6250	0.6170	0.875	0.853	0.422	0.391	0.521	0.478	0.133	0.116	0.239	0.189	0.062	0.031
3/4	0.7500	0.7500	0.7420	1.000	0.976	0.500	0.466	0.612	0.566	0.149	0.131	0.283	0.223	0.062	0.031
7/8	0.8750	0.8750	0.8660	1.125	1.098	0.594	0.556	0.720	0.668	0.167	0.147	0.334	0.264	0.062	0.031
1	1.0000	1.0000	0.9900	1.312	1.282	0.656	0.612	0.803	0.743	0.188	0.166	0.371	0.291	0.062	0.031

APPENDIX E – FASTENERS (INCH SERIES) Continued

DIMENSIONS OF SLOTTED FLAT COUNTERSUNK HEAD MACHINE SCREWS

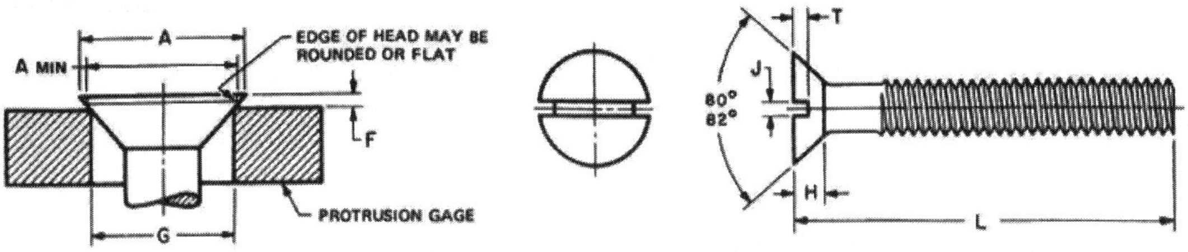

Nominal Size[1] or Basic Screw Diameter		L[2] These Lengths or Shorter are Undercut	A Head Diameter Max. Edge Sharp	A Head Diameter Min, Edge Rounded or Flat	H[3] Head Height Ref	J Slot Width Max	J Slot Width Min	T Slot Depth Max	T Slot Depth Min	F[4] Protrusion Above Gaging Diameter Max	F[4] Protrusion Above Gaging Diameter Min	G[4] Gaging Diameter
0000	0.0210	-	0.043	0.037	0.011	0.008	0.004	0.007	0.003	*	*	*
000	0.0340	-	0.064	0.058	0.016	0.011	0.007	0.009	0.005	*	*	*
00	0.0470	-	0.093	0.085	0.028	0.017	0.010	0.014	0.009	*	*	*
0	0.0600	1/8	0.119	0.099	0.035	0.023	0.016	0.015	0.010	0.026	0.016	0.078
1	0.0730	1/8	0.146	0.123	0.043	0.026	0.019	0.019	0.012	0.028	0.016	0.101
2	0.0860	1/8	0.172	0.147	0.051	0.031	0.023	0.023	0.015	0.029	0.017	0.124
3	0.0990	1/8	0.199	0.171	0.059	0.035	0.027	0.027	0.017	0.031	0.018	0.148
4	0.1120	3/16	0.225	0.195	0.067	0.039	0.031	0.030	0.020	0.032	0.019	0.172
5	0.1250	3/16	0.252	0.220	0.075	0.043	0.035	0.034	0.022	0.034	0.020	0.196
6	0.1380	3/16	0.279	0.244	0.083	0.048	0.039	0.038	0.024	0.036	0.021	0.220
8	0.1640	1/4	0.332	0.292	0.100	0.054	0.045	0.045	0.029	0.039	0.023	0.267
10	0.1900	5/16	0.385	0.340	0.116	0.060	0.050	0.053	0.034	0.042	0.025	0.313
12	0.2160	3/8	0.438	0.389	0.132	0.067	0.056	0.060	0.039	0.045	0.027	0.362
1/4	0.2500	7/16	0.507	0.452	0.153	0.075	0.064	0.070	0.046	0.050	0.029	0.424
5/16	0.3125	1/2	0.635	0.568	0.191	0.084	0.072	0.088	0.058	0.057	0.034	0.539
3/8	0.3750	9/16	0.762	0.685	0.230	0.094	0.081	0.106	0.070	0.065	0.039	0.653
7/16	0.4375	5/8	0.812	0.723	0.223	0.094	0.081	0.103	0.066	0.073	0.044	0.690
1/2	0.5000	3/4	0.875	0.775	0.223	0.106	0.091	0.103	0.065	0.081	0.049	0.739
9/16	0.5625	-	1.000	0.889	0.260	0.118	0.102	0.120	0.077	0.089	0.053	0.851
5/8	0.6250	-	1.125	1.002	0.298	0.133	0.116	0.137	0.088	0.097	0.058	0.962
3/4	0.7500	-	1.375	1.230	0.372	0.149	0.131	0.171	0.111	0.112	0.067	1.186

[1] Where specifying nominal size in decimals, zeros preceding decimal and in the fourth decimal place shall be omitted.
[2] Screws of these lengths and shorter shall have undercut heads as shown in Table 5.
[3] Tabulated values determined from formula for maximum H, Appendix V.
[4] No tolerance for gaging diameter is given.
* Not practical to gage.

APPENDIX E – FASTENERS (INCH SERIES) Continued

DIMENSIONS OF HEX NUTS AND HEX JAM NUTS

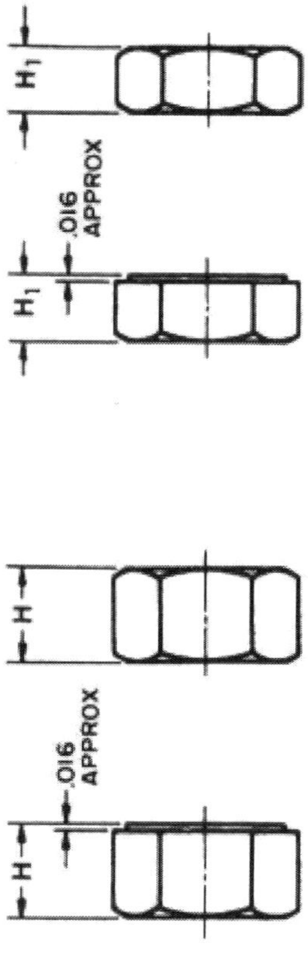

Nominal Size or Basic Major Dia of Thread		F Width Across Flats			G Width Across Corners		H Thickness Hex Nuts			H1 Thickness Hex Jam Nuts			Hex Nuts Specified Proof Load: Up to 150,000 psi	Hex Nuts Specified Proof Load: 150,000 psi and Greater	Jam Nuts All Strength Levels
		Basic	Max	Min	Max	Min	Basic	Max	Min	Basic	Max	Min	Runou of Bearing Face, FIR Max		
1/4	0.2500	7/16	0.438	0.428	0.505	0.488	7/32	0.226	0.212	5/32	0.163	0.150	0.015	0.010	0.015
5/16	0.3125	1/2	0.500	0.489	0.577	0.557	17/64	0.273	0.258	3/16	0.195	0.180	0.016	0.011	0.016
3/8	0.3750	9/16	0.562	0.551	0.650	0.628	21/64	0.337	0.320	7/32	0.227	0.210	0.017	0.012	0.017
7/16	0.4375	11/16	0.688	0.675	0.794	0.768	3/8	0.385	0.365	1/4	0.260	0.240	0.018	0.013	0.018
1/2	0.5000	3/4	0.750	0.736	0.866	0.840	7/16	0.448	0.427	5/16	0.323	0.302	0.019	0.014	0.019
9/16	0.5625	7/8	0.875	0.861	1.010	0.982	31/64	0.496	0.473	5/16	0.324	0.301	0.020	0.015	0.020
5/8	0.6250	15/16	0.938	0.922	1.083	1.051	35/64	0.559	0.535	3/8	0.387	0.363	0.021	0.016	0.021
3/4	0.7500	1 1/8	1.125	1.088	1.299	1.240	41/64	0.665	0.617	27/64	0.446	0.398	0.023	0.018	0.023
7/8	0.8750	1 5/16	1.312	1.269	1.516	1.447	3/4	0.776	0.724	31/64	0.510	0.458	0.025	0.020	0.025
1	1.0000	1 1/2	1.500	1.450	1.732	1.653	55/64	0.887	0.831	35/64	0.575	0.519	0.027	0.022	0.027
1 1/8	1.1250	1 11/16	1.688	1.631	1.949	1.859	31/32	0.999	0.939	39/64	0.639	0.579	0.030	0.025	0.030
1 1/4	1.2500	1 7/8	1.875	1.812	2.165	2.066	1 1/16	1.094	1.030	23/32	0.751	0.687	0.033	0.028	0.033
1 3/8	1.3750	2 1/16	2.062	1.994	2.382	2.273	1 11/64	1.206	1.138	25/32	0.815	0.747	0.036	0.031	0.036
1 1/2	1.5000	2 1/4	2.250	2.175	2.598	2.480	1 9/32	1.317	1.245	27/32	0.880	0.808	0.039	0.034	0.039

APPENDIX E – FASTENERS (INCH SERIES) Continued

Drill and Counterbore Sizes for Socket Head Cap Screws

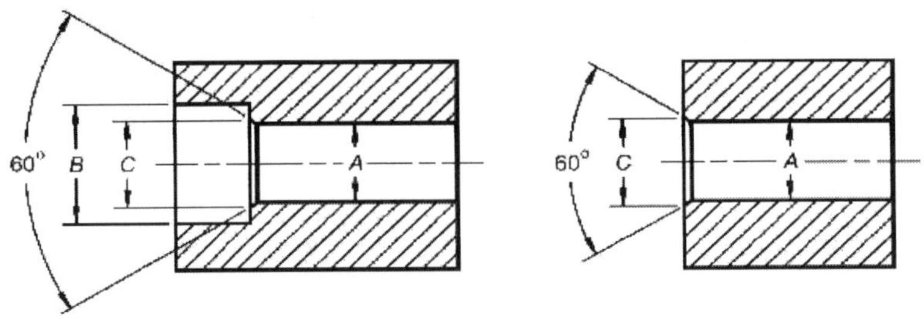

Nominal Size of Screw (D)	Nominal Drill Size (A)		Counterbore Diameter (B)	Countersink (C)
	Close Fit	Normal Fit		
#0 (0.0600)	(#51) 0.067	(#49) 0.073	1/8	0.074
#1 (0.0730)	(#46) 0.081	(#43) 0.089	5/32	0.087
#2 (0.0860)	3/32	(#36) 0.106	3/16	0.102
#3 (0.0990)	(#36) 0.106	(#31) 0.120	7/32	0.115
#4 (0.1120)	1/8	(#29) 0.136	7/32	0.130
#5 (0.1250)	9/64	(#23) 0.154	1/4	0.145
#6 (0.1380)	(#23) 0.154	(#18) 0.170	9/32	0.158
#8 (0.1640)	(#15) 0.180	(#10) 0.194	5/16	0.188
#10 (0.1900)	(#5) 0.206	(#2) 0.221	3/8	0.218
1/4	17/64	9/32	7/16	0.278
5/16	21/64	11/32	17/32	0.346
3/8	25/64	13/32	5/8	0.415
7/16	29/64	15/32	23/32	0.483
1/2	33/64	17/32	13/16	0.552
5/8	41/64	21/32	1	0.689
3/4	49/64	25/32	1 3/16	0.828
7/8	57/64	29/32	1 3/8	0.963
1	1 1/64	1 1/32	1 5/8	1.100
1 1/4	1 9/32	1 5/16	2	1.370
1 1/2	1 17/32	1 9/16	2 3/8	1.640
1 3/4	1 25/32	1 13/16	2 3/4	1.910
2	2 1/32	2 1/16	3 1/8	2.180

(1) Countersink. It is considered good practice to countersink or break the edges of holes that are smaller than F (max.) in parts having a hardness which approaches, equals, or exceeds the screw hardness. The countersink or corner relief, however, should not be larger than is necessary to ensure that the fillet on the screw is cleared. Normally, the diameter of countersink does not have to exceed F (max.). Countersinks or corner reliefs in excess of this diameter reduce the effective bearing area and introduce the possibility of imbedment or brinnelling or flaring of the heads of the screws.

(2) Close Fit. The close fit is normally limited to holes for those lengths of screws that are threaded to the head in assemblies where only one screw is to be used or where two or more screws are to be used and the mating holes are to be produced either at assembly or by matched and coordinated tooling.

(3) Normal Fit. The normal fit is intended for screws of relatively long length or for assemblies involving two or more screws where the mating holes are to be produced by conventional tolerancing methods. It provides for the maximum allowable eccentricity of the longest standard screws and for certain variations in the parts to be fastened, such as deviations in hole straightness, angularity between the axis of the tapped hole and that of the hole for the shank, differences in center distances of the mating holes, etc.

APPENDIX E – FASTENERS (INCH SERIES) Continued

Preferred Sizes of Type A Plain Washers

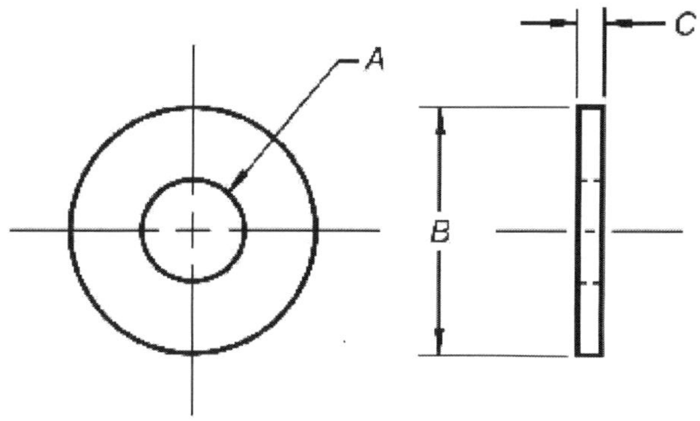

Nominal Washer Size*	Inside Diameter (A) Basic	Outside Diameter (B) Basic	Thickness (C)	Nominal Washer Size*	Inside Diameter (A) Basic	Outside Diameter (B) Basic	Thickness (C)
	0.078	0.188	0.020	1 N	1.062	2.000	0.134
	0.094	0.250	0.020	1 W	1.062	2.500	0.165
	0.125	0.312	0.032	1 1/8 N	1.250	2.250	0.134
#6 (0.138)	0.156	0.375	0.049	1 1/8 W	1.250	2.750	0.165
#8 (0.164)	0.188	0.438	0.049	1 1/4 N	1.375	2.500	0.165
#10 (0.190)	0.219	0.500	0.049	1 1/4 W	1.375	3.000	0.165
3/16	0.250	0.562	0.049	1 3/8 N	1.500	2.750	0.165
#12 (0.216)	0.250	0.562	0.065	1 3/8 W	1.500	3.250	0.180
1/4 N	0.281	0.625	0.065	1 1/2 N	1.625	3.000	0.165
1/4 W	0.312	0.734	0.065	1 1/2 W	1.625	3.500	0.180
5/16 N	0.344	0.688	0.065	1 5/8	1.750	3.750	0.180
5/16 W	0.375	0.875	0.083	1 3/4	1.875	4.000	0.180
3/8 N	0.406	0.812	0.065	1 7/8	2.000	4.250	0.180
3/8 W	0.438	1.000	0.083	2	2.125	4.500	0.180
7/16 N	0.469	0.922	0.065	2 1/4	2.375	4.750	0.220
7/16 W	0.500	1.250	0.083	2 1/2	2.625	5.000	0.238
1/2 N	0.531	1.062	0.095	2 3/4	2.875	5.250	0.259
1/2 W	0.562	1.375	0.109	3	3.125	5.500	0.284
9/16 N	0.594	1.156	0.095				
9/16 W	0.625	1.469	0.109				
5/8 N	0.656	1.312	0.095				
5/8 W	0.688	1.750	0.134				
3/4 N	0.812	1.469	0.134				
3/4 W	0.812	2.000	0.148				
7/8 N	0.938	1.750	0.134				
7/8 W	0.938	2.250	0.165				

*Nominal washer sizes are intended for use with comparable nominal screw or bolt sizes.

APPENDIX E – FASTENERS (INCH SERIES) Continued

Regular Helical Spring-Lock Washers

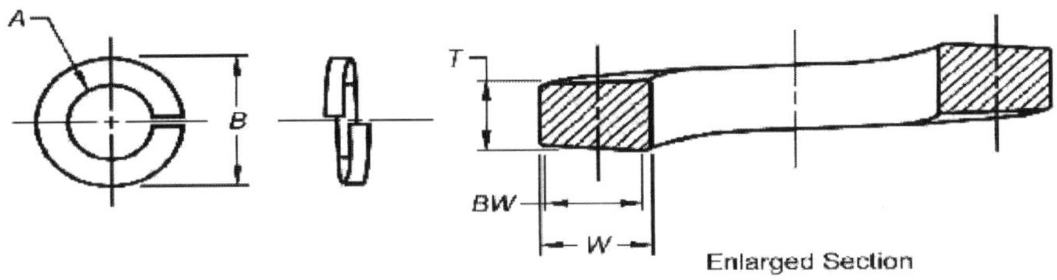

Nominal Washer Size	Min. Inside Diameter (A)	Max. Outside Diameter (B)	Mean Section Thickness (T)	Min. Section Width (W)	Min. Bearing Width (BW)
#2 (0.086)	0.088	0.172	0.020	0.035	0.024
#3 (0.099)	0.101	0.195	0.025	0.040	0.028
#4 (0.112)	0.114	0.209	0.025	0.040	0.028
#5 (0.125)	0.127	0.236	0.031	0.047	0.033
#6 (.0138)	0.141	0.250	0.031	0.047	0.033
#8 (0.164)	0.167	0.293	0.040	0.055	0.038
#10 (0.190)	0.193	0.334	0.047	0.062	0.043
#12 (0.216)	0.220	0.377	0.056	0.070	0.049
1/4	0.252	0.487	0.062	0.109	0.076
5/16	0.314	0.583	0.078	0.125	0.087
3/8	0.377	0.680	0.094	0.141	0.099
7/16	0.440	0.776	0.109	0.156	0.109
1/2	0.502	0.869	0.125	0.171	0.120
9/16	0.564	0.965	0.141	0.188	0.132
5/8	0.628	1.073	0.156	0.203	0.142
11/16	0.691	1.170	0.172	0.219	0.153
3/4	0.753	1.265	0.188	0.234	0.164
13/16	0.816	1.363	0.203	0.250	0.175
7/8	0.787	1.459	0.219	0.266	0.186
15/16	0.941	1.556	0.234	0.281	0.197
1	1.003	1.656	0.250	0.297	0.208
1 1/16	1.066	1.751	0.266	0.312	0.218
1 1/8	1.129	1.847	0.281	0.328	0.230
1 3/16	1.192	1.943	0.297	0.344	0.241
1 1/4	1.254	2.036	0.312	0.359	0.251
1 5/16	1.317	2.133	0.328	0.375	0.262
1 3/8	1.379	2.219	0.344	0.391	0.274
1 7/16	1.442	2.324	0.359	0.406	0.284
1 1/2	1.504	2.419	0.375	0.422	0.295
1 5/8	1.633	2.553	0.389	0.424	0.297
1 3/4	1.758	2.679	0.389	0.424	0.297
1 7/8	1.883	2.811	0.422	0.427	0.299
2	2.008	2.936	0.422	0.427	0.299
2 1/4	2.262	3.221	0.440	0.442	0.309
2 1/2	2.512	3.471	0.440	0.422	0.309
2 3/4	2.762	3.824	0.458	0.491	0.344
3	3.012	4.074	0.458	0.491	0.344

ASME B18.21.1 -1999 Standard. Reprinted by permission of the ASME.

APPENDIX F – METRIC FASTENERS

Metric Hex Bolts

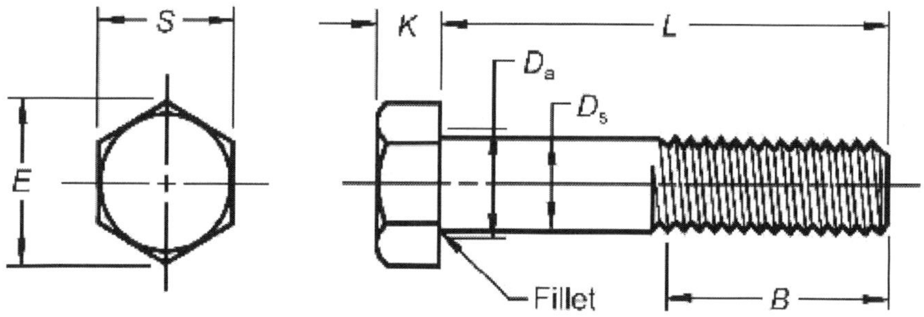

D	Ds	S	E	K	Da	Thread Length (B)		
Nominal Bolt Diameter And Thread Pitch	Max. Body Dia.	Max. Width Across Flats	Max. Width Across Corners	Max. Head Height	Fillet Transition Diameter	Bolt Lengths ≤ 125	Bolt Lengths > 125 and ≤ 200	Bolt Lengths >200
M5 x 0.8	5.48	8.00	9.24	3.88	5.7	16	22	35
M6 x 1	6.19	10.00	11.55	4.38	6.8	18	24	37
M8 x 1.25	8.58	13.00	15.01	5.68	9.2	22	28	41
M10 x 1.5	10.58	16.00	18.48	6.85	11.2	26	32	45
M12 x 1.75	12.70	18.00	20.78	7.95	13.7	30	36	49
M14 x 2	14.70	21.00	24.25	9.25	15.7	34	40	53
M16 x 2	16.70	24.00	27.71	10.75	17.7	38	44	57
M20 x 2.5	20.84	30.00	34.64	13.40	22.4	46	52	65
M24 x 3	24.84	36.00	41.57	15.90	26.4	54	60	73
M30 x 3.5	30.84	46.00	53.12	19.75	33.4	66	72	85
M36 x 4	37.00	55.00	63.51	23.55	39.4	78	84	97
M42 x 4.5	43.00	65.00	75.06	27.05	45.4	90	96	109
M48 x 5	49.00	75.00	86.60	31.07	52.0	102	108	121
M56 x 5.5	57.00	85.00	98.15	36.20	62.0		124	137
M64 x 6	65.52	95.00	109.70	41.32	70.0		140	153
M72 x 6	73.84	105.00	121.24	46.45	78.0		156	169
M80 x 6	82.16	115.00	132.79	51.58	86.0		172	185
M90 x 6	92.48	130.00	150.11	57.74	96.0		192	205
M100 x 6	102.80	145.00	167.43	63.90	107.0		212	225

ASME B18.3 - 2003 Standard. Reprinted from the standard listed by permission of the American Society of Mechanical Engineers.

APPENDIX F – METRIC FASTENERS (Continued)

Metric Hex Nuts

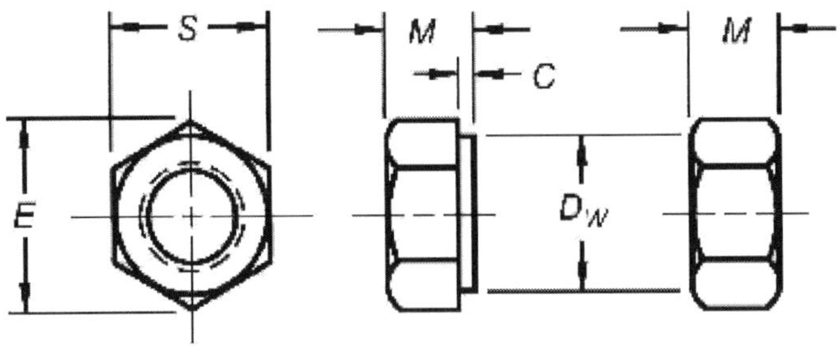

D	S	E	M	DW	C
Nominal Bolt Diameter and Thread Pitch	Max. Width Across Flats	Max. Width Across Corners	Max. Thickness	Min. Bearing Face Diameter	Max. Washer Face Thickness
M1.6 x 0.35	3.20	3.70	1.30	2.3	
M2 x 0.4	4.00	4.62	1.60	3.1	
M2.5 x 0.45	5.00	5.77	2.00	4.1	
M3 x 0.5	5.50	6.35	2.40	4.6	
M3.5 x 0.6	6.00	6.93	2.80	5.1	
M4 x 0.7	7.00	8.08	3.20	6.0	
M5 x 0.8	8.00	9.24	4.70	7.0	
M6 x 1	10.00	11.55	5.20	8.9	
M8 x 1.25	13.00	15.01	6.80	11.6	
M10 x 1.5	15.00	17.32	9.10	13.6	
M10 x 1.5	16.00	18.45	8.40	14.6	
M12 x 1.75	18.00	20.78	10.80	16.6	
M14 x 2	21.00	24.25	12.80	19.4	
M16 x 2	24.00	27.71	14.80	22.4	
M20 x 2.5	30.00	34.64	18.00	27.9	0.8
M24 x 3	36.00	41.57	21.50	32.5	0.8
M30 x 3.5	46.00	53.12	25.60	42.5	0.8
M36 x 4	55.00	63.51	31.00	50.8	0.8

ASME B18.2.4.1M - 2002 Standard. Reprinted from the standard listed by permission of the American Society of Mechanical Engineers.

APPENDIX F – METRIC FASTENERS (Continued)

Metric Socket Head Cap Screws

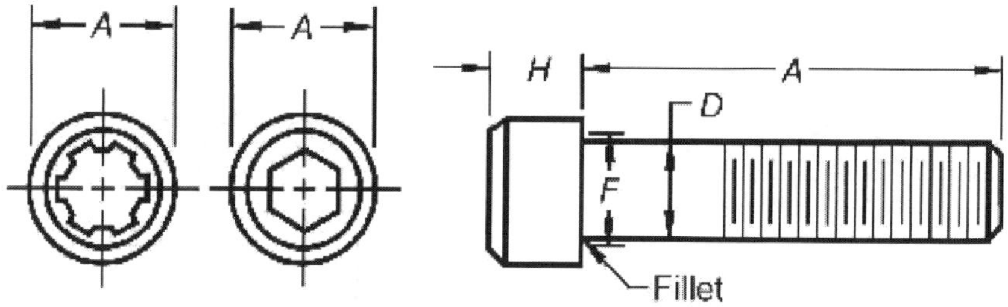

Screw Size (D)	Head Diameter (A)	Head Height (H)
1.6 through 2.5	See Table	
3 through 8	Max. A = 1.5 D + 1	Max. H = D
> 10	Max. A = 1.5 D	

Screw Size (D)	1.6	2	2.5
Max. Head Diameter (A)	3.00	3.80	4.50

ASME/ANSI B18.3.1M - 1986 (R2002) Standard. Reprinted from the standard listed by permission of the American Society of Mechanical Engineers.

Metric Countersunk Socket Head Cap Screws

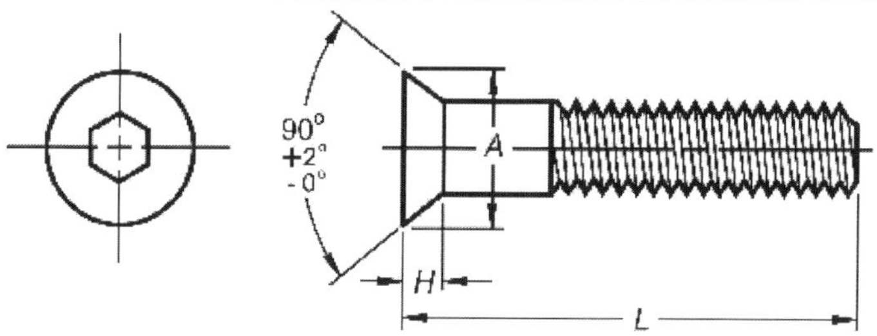

Basic Screw Diameter and Thread Pitch	Head Diameter (A) Theor. Sharp	Head Height (H)
M3 x 0.5	6.72	1.86
M4 x 0.7	8.96	2.48
M5 x 0.8	11.20	3.10
M6 x 1	13.44	3.72
M8 x 1.25	17.92	4.96
M10 x 1.5	22.40	6.20
M12 x 1.75	26.88	7.44
M14 x 2	30.24	8.12
M16 x 2	33.60	8.80
M20 x 2.5	40.32	10.16

ASME/ANSI B18.3.5M - 1986 (R2002) Standard. Reprinted from the standard listed by permission of the American Society of Mechanical Engineers.

APPENDIX F – METRIC FASTENERS (Continued)

Drill and Counterbore Sizes for Socket Head Cap Screws

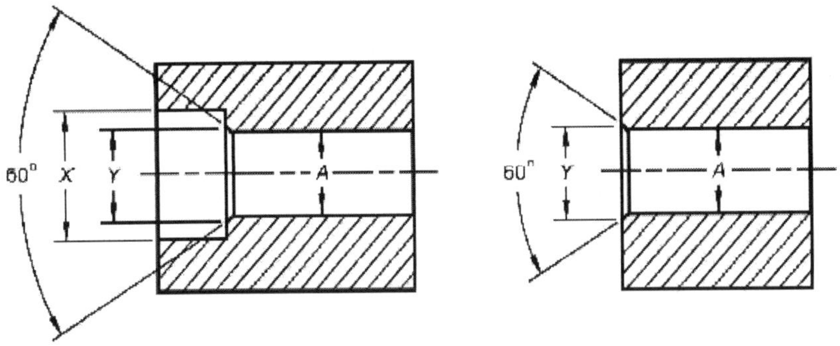

Nominal Size or Basic Screw Diameter	A		X	Y
	Nominal Drill Size		Counterbore Diameter	Countersink Diameter
	Close Fit	Normal Fit		
M1.6	1.80	1.95	3.50	2.0
M2	2.20	2.40	4.40	2.6
M2.5	2.70	3.00	5.40	3.1
M3	3.40	3.70	6.50	3.6
M4	4.40	4.80	8.25	4.7
M5	5.40	5.80	9.75	5.7
M6	6.40	6.80	11.25	6.8
M8	8.40	8.80	14.25	9.2
M10	10.50	10.80	17.25	11.2
M12	12.50	12.80	19.25	14.2
M14	14.50	14.75	22.25	16.2
M16	16.50	16.75	25.50	18.2
M20	20.50	20.75	31.50	22.4
M24	24.50	24.75	37.50	26.4
M30	30.75	31.75	47.50	33.4
M36	37.00	37.50	56.50	39.4
M42	43.00	44.00	66.00	45.6
M48	49.00	50.00	75.00	52.6

ASME/ANSI B18.3.1M - 1986 (R2002) Standard. Reprinted from the standard listed by permission of the American Society of Mechanical Engineers.

APPENDIX F – METRIC FASTENERS (Continued)

Drill and Countersink Sizes for Flat Countersunk Head Cap Screws

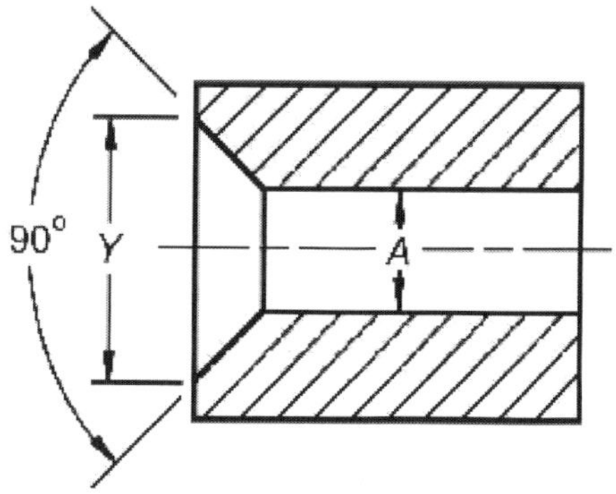

D	A	Y
Nominal Screw Size	Nominal Hole Diameter	Min. Countersink Diameter
M3	3.5	6.72
M4	4.6	8.96
M5	6.0	11.20
M6	7.0	13.44
M8	9.0	17.92
M10	11.5	22.40
M12	13.5	26.88
M14	16.0	30.24
M16	18.0	33.60
M20	22.4	40.32

ASME/ANSI B18.3.5M - 1986 (R2002) Standard. Reprinted from the standard listed by permission of the American Society of Mechanical Engineers.

APPENDIX G – FASTENERS

BOLT AND SCREW CLEARANCE HOLES

(1) Inch Clearance Holes

Nominal Screw Size	Fit Classes		
	Normal	Close	Loose
	Nominal Drill Size		
#0 (0.06)	#48 (0.0760)	#51 (0.0670)	3/32
#1 (0.073)	#43 (0.0890)	#46 (0.0810)	#37 (0.1040)
#2 (0.086)	#38 (0.1015)	3/32	#32 (0.1160)
#3 (0.099)	#32 (0.1160)	#36 (0.1065)	#30 (0.1285)
#4 (0.112)	#30 (0.1285)	#31 (0.1200)	#27 (0.1440)
#5 (0.125)	5/32	9/64	11/64
#6 (0.138)	#18 (0.1695)	#23 (0.1540)	#13 (0.1850)
#8 (0.164)	#9 (0.1960)	#15 (0.1800)	#3 (0.2130)
#10 (0.190)	#2 (0.2210)	#5 (0.2055)	B (0.238)
1/4	9/32	17/64	19/64
5/16	11/32	21/64	23/64
3/8	13/32	25/64	27/64
7/16	15/32	29/64	31/64
1/2	9/16	17/32	39/64
5/8	11/16	21/32	47/64
3/4	13/16	25/32	29/32
7/8	15/16	29/32	1 1/32
1	1 3/32	1 1/32	1 5/32
1 1/8	1 7/32	1 5/32	1 5/16
1 1/4	1 11/32	1 9/32	1 7/16
1 3/8	1 1/2	1 7/16	1 39/64
1 1/2	1 5/8	1 9/16	1 47/64

ASME B18.2.8 - 1999 Standard. Reprinted from the standard listed by permission of the American Society of Mechanical Engineers.

APPENDIX G – FASTENERS

BOLT AND SCREW CLEARANCE HOLES (Continued)

(2) Metric Clearance Holes

Nominal Screw Size	Fit Classes		
	Normal	Close	Loose
	Nominal Drill Size		
M1.6	1.8	1.7	2
M2	2.4	2.2	2.6
M2.5	2.9	2.7	3.1
M3	3.4	3.2	3.6
M4	4.5	4.3	4.8
M5	5.5	5.3	5.8
M6	6.6	6.4	7
M8	9	8.4	10
M10	11	10.5	12
M12	13.5	13	14.5
M14	15.5	15	16.5
M16	17.5	17	18.5
M20	22	21	24
M24	26	25	28
M30	33	31	35
M36	39	37	42
M42	45	43	48
M48	52	50	56
M56	62	58	66
M64	70	66	74
M72	78	74	82
M80	86	82	91
M90	96	93	101
M100	107	104	112

ASME B18.2.8 - 1999 Standard. Reprinted from the standard listed by permission of the American Society of Mechanical Engineers.

APPENDIX H – REFERENCES

- ASME B1.1 - 2003: Unified Inch Screw Threads (UN and UNR Thread Form)
- ASME B1.13M - 2001: Metric Screw Threads: M Profile
- USAS/ASME B4.1 - 1967 (R2004): Preferred Limits and Fits for Cylindrical Parts
- ANSI B4.2 - 1978 (R2004): Preferred Metric Limits and Fits
- ASME B18.2.1 - 1996: Square and Hex Bolts and Screws (Inch Series)
- ASME/ANSI B18.2.2 - 1987 (R1993): Hex Nuts and Jam Hex Nuts (Inch Series)
- ANSI B18.2.3.5M - 1979 (R2001): Metric Hex Bolts
- ASME B18.2.4.1M - 2002: Metric Hex Nuts, Style 1
- ASME B18.2.8 - 1999: Clearance Holes for Bolts, Screws, and Studs
- ASME B18.3 - 2003: Socket Cap, Shoulder, and Set Screws, Hex and Spline Keys (Inch Series)
- ASME/ANSI B18.3.1M - 1986 (R2002): Socket Head Cap Screws (Metric Series)
- ASME/ANSI B18.3.5M - 1986 (R2002): Hexagon Socket Flat Countersunk Head Cap Screws (Metric Series)
- ASME 18.6.2 - 1998: Slotted Head Cap Screws, Square Head Set Screws, and Slotted Headless Set Screws (Inch Series)
- ASME B18.21.1 - 1999: Lock Washers (Inch Series)
- ANSI B18.22.1 - 1965 (R2003): Plain Washers
- ASME Y14.2M - 1992 (R2003): Line Conventions and Lettering
- ASME Y14.3 - 2003: Multiview and Sectional view Drawings
- ASME Y14.4M - 1989 (R1999): Pictorial Drawings
- ASME Y14.5M - 1994: Dimensioning and Tolerancing
- ASME Y14.6 - 2001: Screw Thread Representation
- ASME Y14.100 - 2000: Engineering Drawing Practices

INDEX

J

K

L

M

N

O

P

U

V

W

Z

Review Questions: (Time: 25 minutes)

1. What is an *assembly drawing*? What are the basic differences between an assembly drawing and a detail drawing?

2. What is a *block*? List some of the advantages of using blocks in AutoCAD.

3. What are the differences between "*Copying and pasting with the Windows Clipboard*" and "*Copying with GRIPS*"?

4. Which command allows us to separate a block into its component objects?

5. Describe the differences between *PASTE* and *PASTE AS A BLOCK*.

6. Which command did we use to set the style of leaders?

7. Which command did we use to set up the style of *Parts_List* for the *Shaft Support* assembly?

8. Which *multileader type* did we use to set up the balloon callouts for the *Shaft Support* assembly?

9. Construct the drawing shown and measure the length **L**. Show the length with three digits after the decimal point. (Units: inches.)

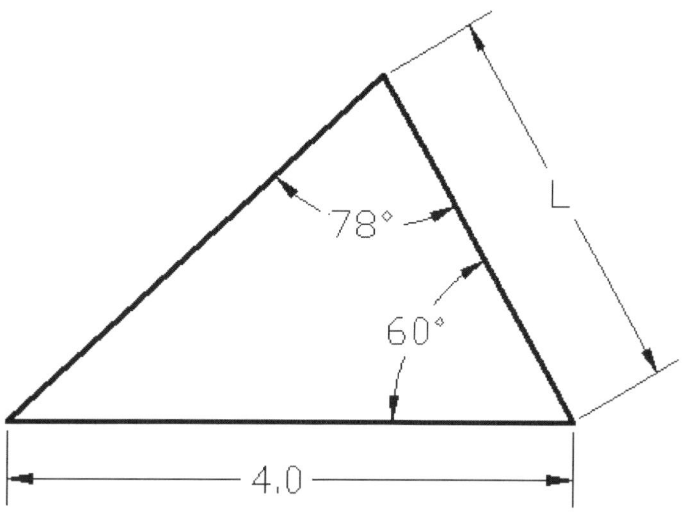

Exercises: (Time: 300 minutes)

1. **Wheel Assembly** (Create a set of detail and assembly drawings. All dimensions are in mm.)

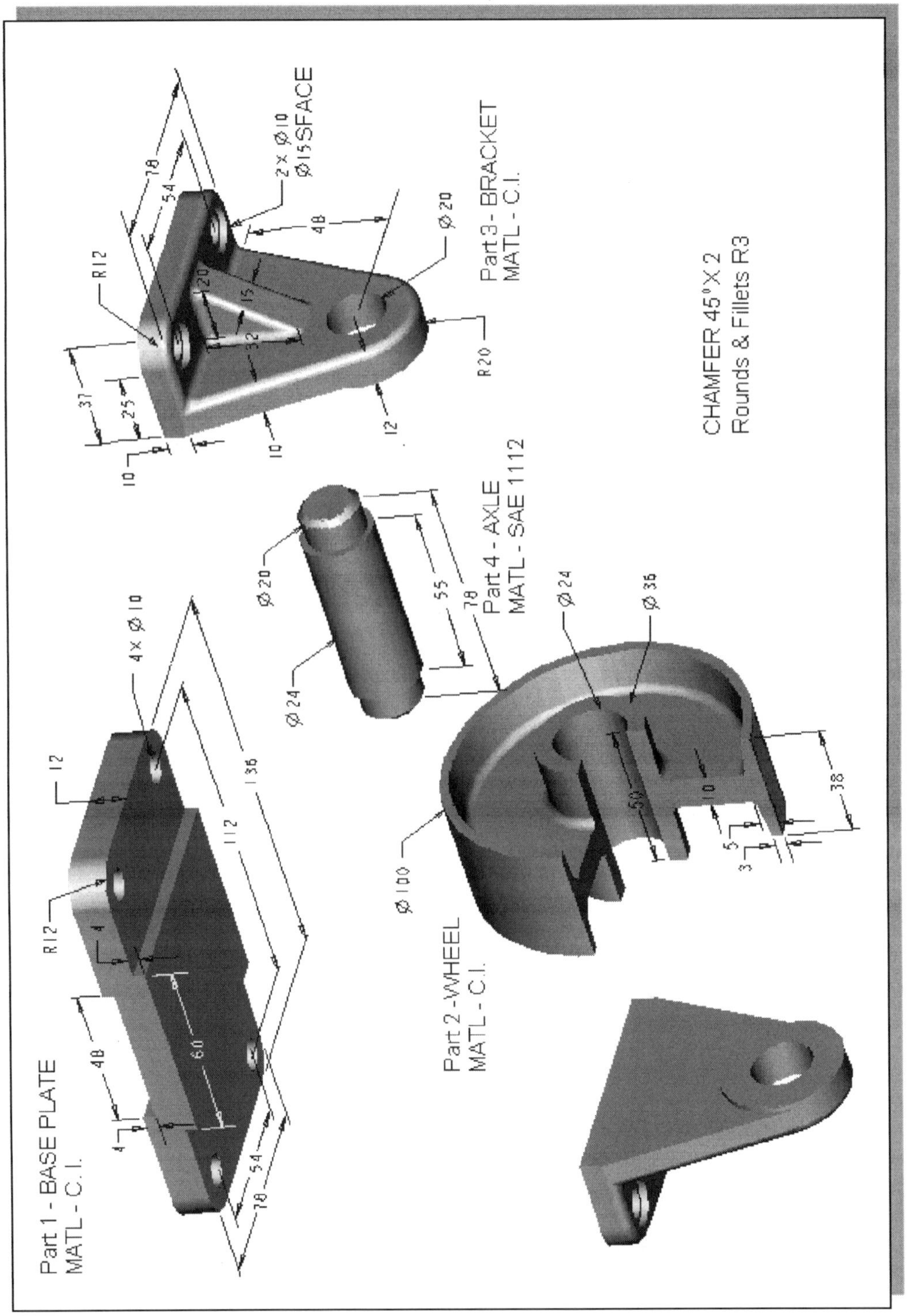

2. **Leveling Device: placed at the feet of high precision machineries.** (Create a set of detail and assembly drawings. All dimensions are in mm.)

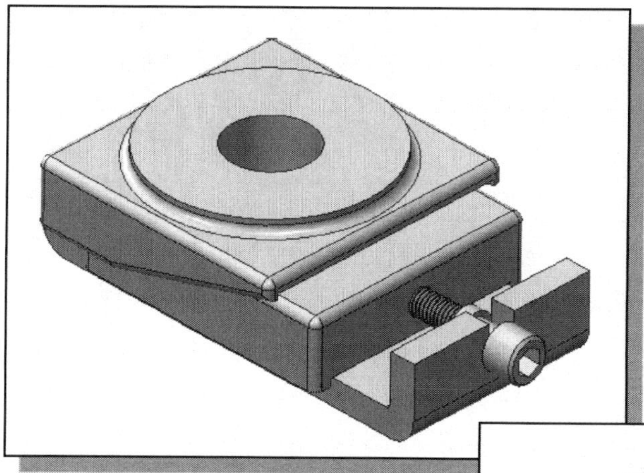

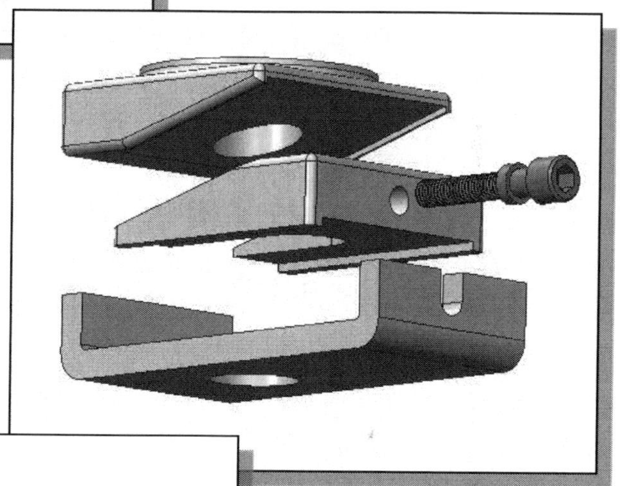

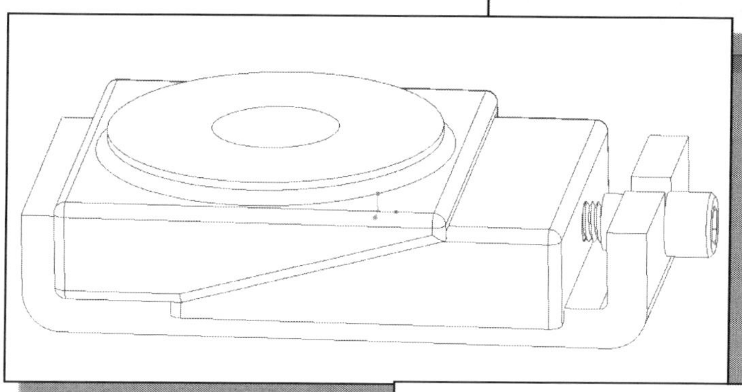

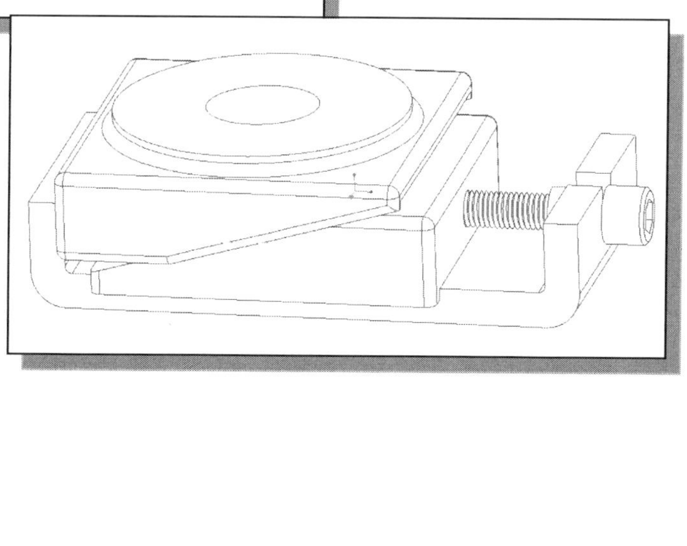

(a) **Base Plate**

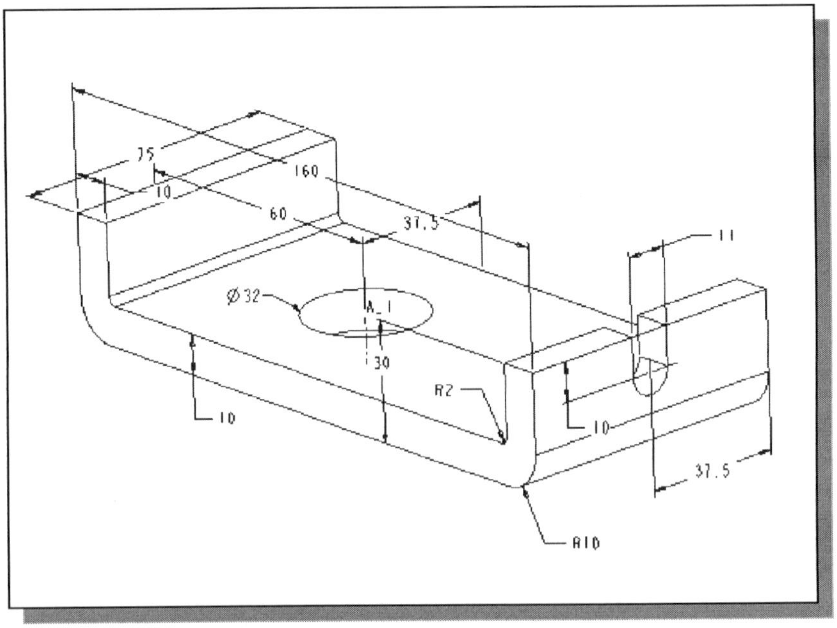

(b) **Sliding Block** (Rounds & Fillets: R3)

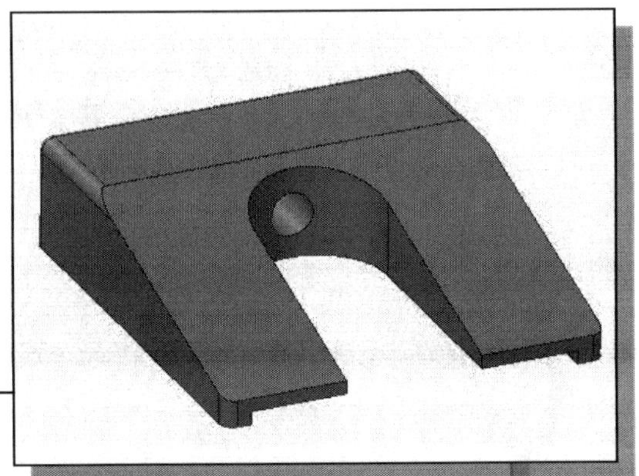

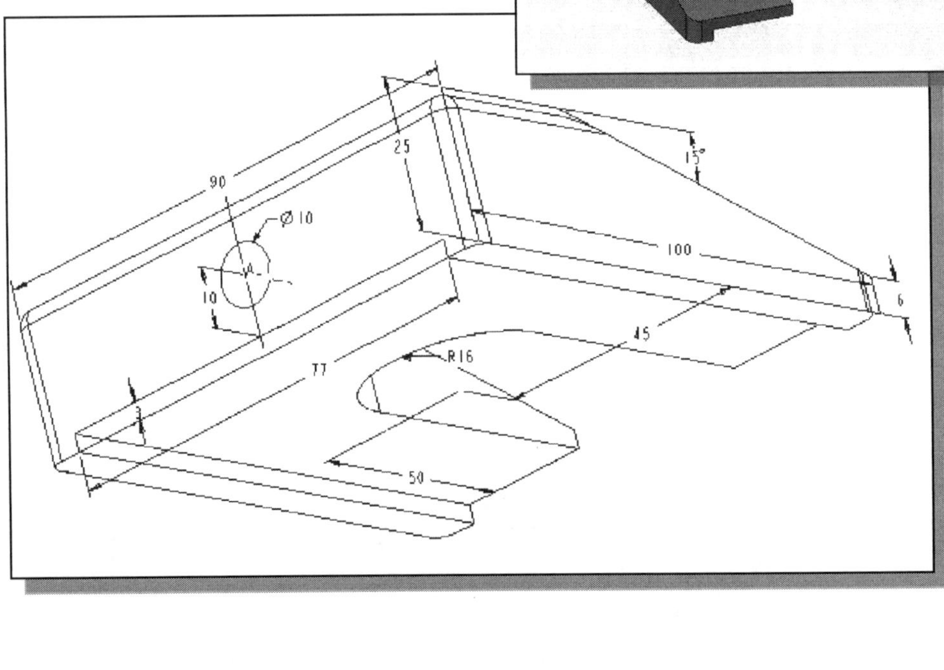

(c) **Lifting Block** (Rounds & Fillets: R3)

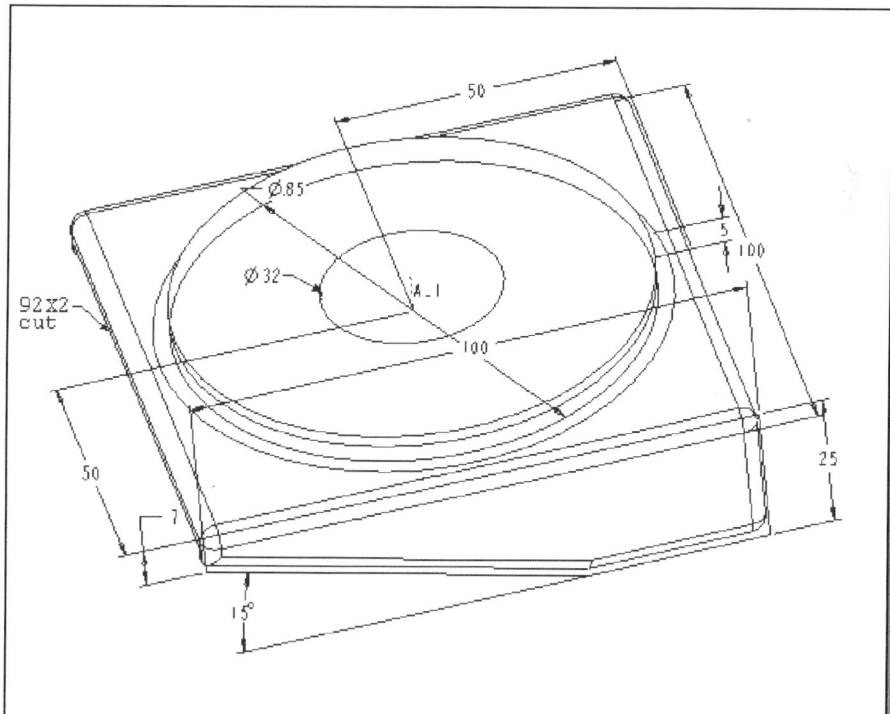

(d) **Adjusting Screw** (M10 X 1.5)

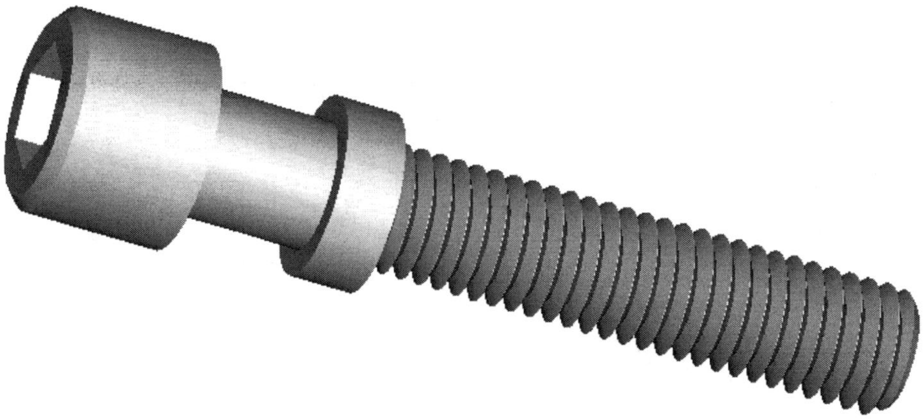

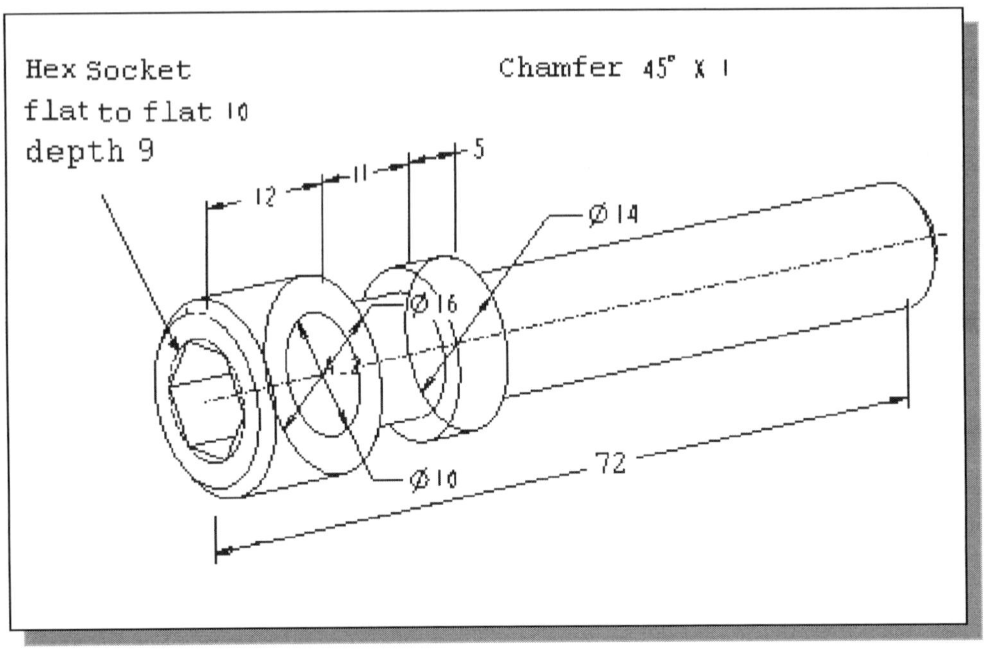

3. **Vise Assembly** (Create a set of detail and assembly drawings. All dimensions are in inches.)

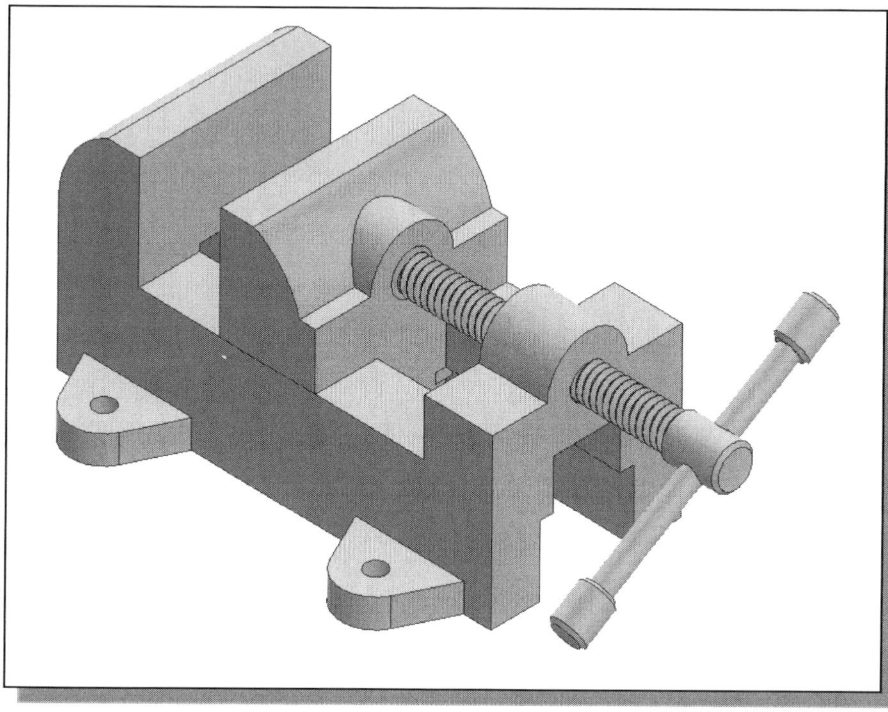

(a) **Base:** The 1.5 inch wide and 1.25 inch wide slots are cut through the entire base. Material: Gray Cast Iron. Threads: 5/8"-8-UNC-3B

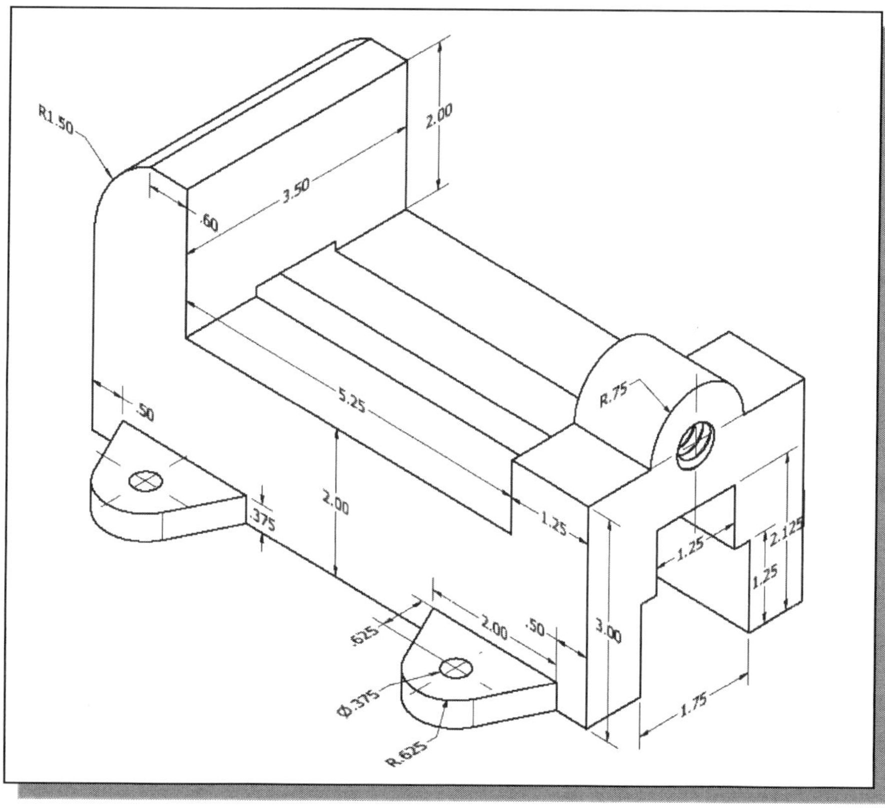

(b) **Jaw:** The shoulder of the jaw rests on the flat surface of the base and the jaw opening is set to 1.5 inches. Material: Gray Cast Iron.

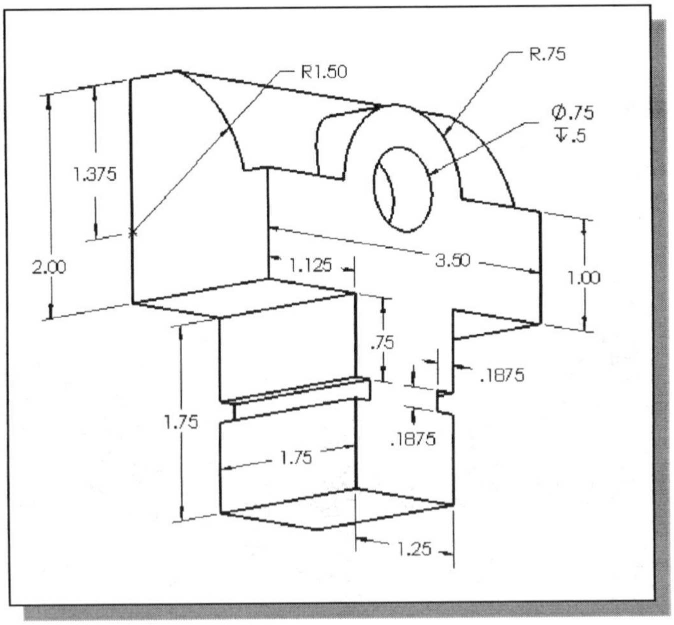

(c) **Key:** 0.1875 inch H x 0.3 inch W x 1.75 inch L. The keys fit into the slots on the jaw with the edge faces flush as shown in the sub-assembly to the right. Material: Alloy Steel.

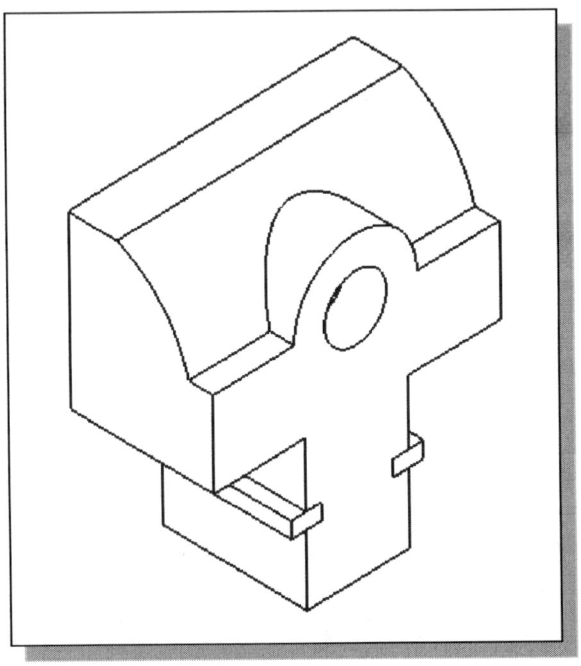

(d) **Screw:** 5/8"-8-UNC-3A There is one chamfered edge (0.0625 inch x 45°). The flat ∅ 0.75" edge of the screw is flush with the corresponding recessed ∅ 0.75 face on the jaw. Material: Alloy Steel.

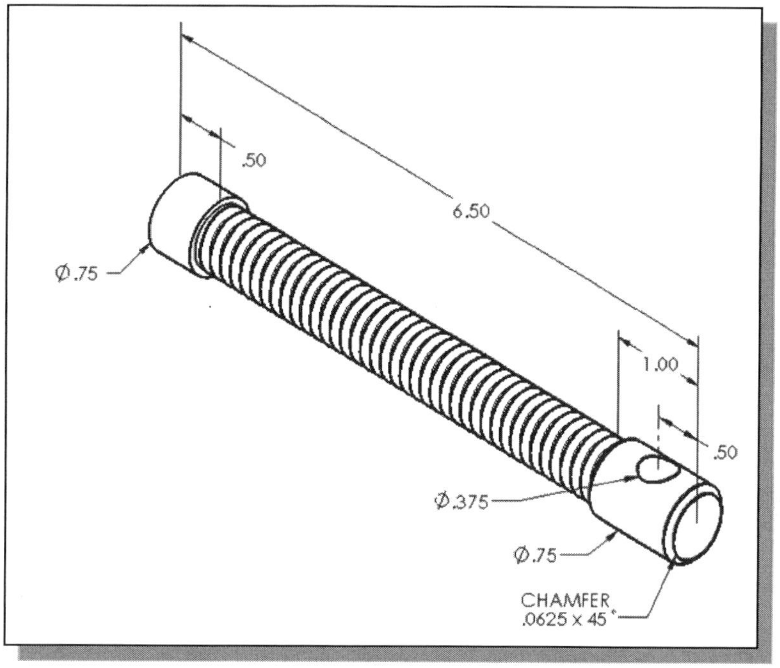

(e) **Handle Rod:** ∅ 0.375" x 5.0" L. The handle rod passes through the hole in the screw and is rotated to an angle of 30° with the horizontal as shown in the assembly view. The flat ∅ 0.375" edges of the handle rod are flush with the corresponding recessed ∅ 0.735 faces on the handle knobs. Material: Alloy Steel.

(f) **Handle Knob:** There are two chamfered edges (0.0625 inch x 45°). The handle knobs are attached to each end of the handle rod. The resulting overall length of the handle with knobs is 5.50". The handle is aligned with the screw so that the outer edge of the upper knob is 2.0" from the central axis of the screw. Material: Alloy Steel.

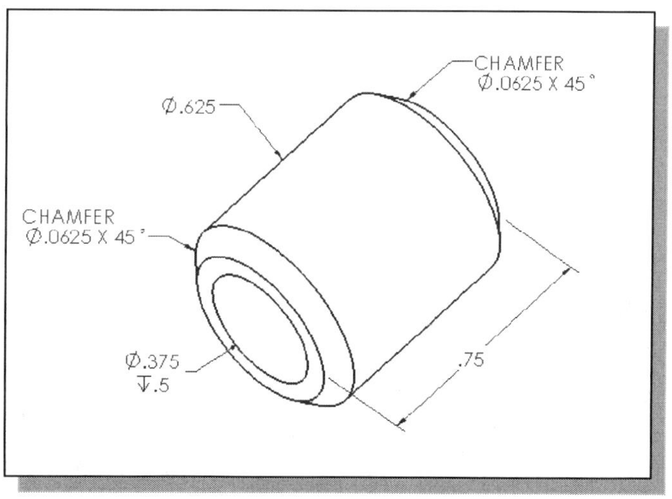

Notes:

APPENDIX A

Running and Sliding Fits – American National Standard (Inches)

Basic Hole System, Limits are in thousandths of an inch.
Limits for hole and shaft are applied to the basic size to obtain the limits of sizes for the parts.

Nominal Size Range, Inches	Class RC1			Class RC2			Class RC3			Class RC4		
Over To	Limits of Clearance	Standard Limits Hole H5	Standard Limits Shaft g4	Limits of Clearance	Standard Limits Hole H6	Standard Limits Shaft g5	Limits of Clearance	Standard Limits Hole H7	Standard Limits Shaft f6	Limits of Clearance	Standard Limits Hole H8	Standard Limits Shaft f7
0 – 0.12	0.1 0.45	+0.2 +0	-0.1 -0.25	0.1 0.55	+0.25 0	-0.1 -0.3	0.3 0.95	+0.4 0	-0.3 -0.55	0.3 1.3	+0.6 0	-0.3 -0.7
0.12 – 0.24	0.15 0.5	+0.2 0	-0.15 -0.3	0.15 0.65	+0.3 0	-0.15 -0.35	0.4 1.12	+0.5 0	-0.4 -0.7	0.4 1.6	+0.7 0	-0.4 -0.9
0.24 – 0.40	0.2 0.6	+0.25 0	-0.2 -0.35	0.2 0.85	+0.4 0	-0.2 -0.45	0.5 1.5	+0.6 0	-0.5 -0.9	0.5 2.0	+0.9 0	-0.5 -1.1
0.40 – 0.71	0.25 0.75	+0.3 +0	-0.25 -0.45	0.25 0.95	+0.4 0	-0.25 -0.55	0.6 1.7	+0.7 0	-0.6 -1.0	0.6 2.3	+1.0 0	-0.6 -1.3
0.71 – 1.19	0.3 0.95	+0.4 0	-0.3 -0.55	0.3 1.2	+0.5 0	-0.3 -0.7	0.8 2.1	+0.8 0	-0.8 -1.3	0.8 2.8	+1.2 0	-0.8 -1.6
1.19 – 1.97	0.4 1.1	+0.4 0	-0.4 -0.7	0.4 1.4	+0.6 0	-0.4 -0.8	1.0 2.6	+1.0 0	-1.0 -1.6	1.0 3.6	+1.6 0	-1.0 -2.0
1.97 – 3.15	0.4 1.2	+0.5 0	-0.4 -0.7	0.4 1.6	+0.7 0	-0.4 -0.9	1.2 3.1	+1.2 0	-1.2 -1.9	1.2 4.2	+1.8 0	-1.2 -2.4
3.15 – 4.73	0.5 1.5	+0.6 0	-0.5 -0.9	0.5 2.0	+0.9 0	-0.5 -1.1	1.4 3.7	+1.4 0	-1.4 -2.3	1.4 5.0	+2.2 0	-1.4 -2.8
4.73 – 7.09	0.6 1.8	+0.7 0	-0.6 -1.1	0.6 2.3	+1.0 0	-0.6 -1.3	1.6 4.2	+1.6 0	-1.6 -2.6	1.6 5.7	+2.5 0	-1.6 -3.2
7.09 – 9.85	0.6 2.0	+0.8 0	-0.6 -1.2	0.6 2.6	+1.2 0	-0.6 -1.4	2.0 5.0	+1.8 0	-2.0 -3.2	2.0 6.6	+2.8 0	-2.0 -3.8
9.85 – 12.41	0.8 2.3	+0.9 0	-0.8 -1.4	0.8 2.9	+1.2 0	-0.7 -1.6	2.5 5.7	+2.0 0	-2.5 -3.7	2.5 7.5	+3.0 0	-2.5 -4.5
12.41– 15.75	1.0 2.7	+1.0 0	-1.0 -1.7	1.0 3.4	+1.4 0	-0.7 -1.7	3.0 6.6	+2.2 0	-3.0 -4.4	3.0 8.7	+3.5 0	-3.0 -5.2
15.75– 19.69	1.2 3.0	+1.0 0	-1.2 -2.0	0.8 3.4	+1.6 0	-0.8 -1.8	4.0 8.1	+2.5 0	-4.0 -5.6	4.0 10.5	+4.0 0	-4.0 -6.5

USAS/ASME B4.1 – 1967 (R2004) Standard. For larger diameters, see the standard. ASME/ANSI B18.3.5M – 1986 (R2002) Standard. Reprinted from the standard listed by permission of the American Society of Mechanical Engineers.

APPENDIX A (Running and Sliding Fits Continued)

Running and Sliding Fits – American National Standard (Inches)

Basic Hole System, Limits are in thousandths of an inch.
Limits for hole and shaft are applied to the basic size to obtain the limits of sizes for the parts.

Nominal size Range, Inches	Class RC5			Class RC6			Class RC7			Class RC8			Class RC9		
Over To	Limits of Clearance	Standard Limits Hole H8	Standard Limits Shaft e7	Limits of Clearance	Standard Limits Hole H9	Standard Limits Shaft e8	Limits of Clearance	Standard Limits Hole H9	Standard Limits Shaft d8	Limits of Clearance	Standard Limits Hole H10	Standard Limits Shaft c9	Limits of Clearance	Standard Limits Hole H11	Standard Limits Shaft
0 – 0.12	0.6 1.6	+0.6 0	-0.6 -1 .0	0.6 2.2	+1.0 0	+0.6 -1.2	1.0 2.6	+1.0 0	-1.0 -1.6	2.5 5.1	+1.6 0	-2.5 -3.5	4.0 8.1	+2.5 0	-4.0 -5.6
0.12 – 0.24	0.8 2.0	+0.7 0	-0.8 -1.3	0.8 2.7	+1.2 0	-0.8 -1.5	1.2 3.1	+1.2 0	-1.2 -1.9	2.8 5.8	+1.8 0	-2.8 -4.0	4.5 9.0	+3.0 0	-4.5 -6.0
0.24 – 0.40	1.0 2.5	+0.9 0	-1.0 -1.6	1.0 3.3	+1.4 0	-1.0 -1.9	1.6 3.9	+1.4 0	-1.6 -2.5	3.0 6.6	+2.2 0	-3.0 -4.4	5.0 10.7	+3.5 0	-5.0 -7.2
0.40 – 0.71	1.2 2.9	+1.0 0	-1.2 -1.9	1.2 3.8	+1.6 0	-1.2 -2.2	2.0 4.6	+1.6 0	-2.0 -3.0	3.5 7.9	+2.8 0	-3.5 -5.1	6.0 12.8	+4.0 0	-6.0 -8.8
0.71 – 1.19	1.6 3.6	+1.2 0	-1.6 -2.4	1.6 4.8	+2.0 0	-1.6 -2.8	2.5 5.7	+2.0 0	-2.5 -3.7	4.5 10.0	+3.5 0	-4.5 -6.5	7.0 15.5	+5.0 0	-7.0 -10.5
1.19 – 1.97	2.0 4.6	+1.6 0	-2.0 -3.0	2.0 6.1	+2.5 0	-2.0 -3.6	3.0 7.1	+2.5 0	-3.0 -4.6	5.0 11.5	+4.0 0	-5.0 -7.5	8.0 18.0	+6.0 0	-8.0 12.0
1.97 – 3.15	2.5 5.5	+1.8 0	-2.5 -3.7	2.5 7.3	+3.0 0	-2.5 -4.3	4.0 8.8	+3.0 0	-4.0 -5.8	6.0 13.5	+4.5 0	-6.0 -9.0	9.0 20.5	+7.0 0	-9.0 -13.5
3.15 – 4.73	3.0 6.6	+2.2 0	-3.0 -4.4	3.0 8.7	+3.5 0	-3.0 -5.2	5.0 10.7	+3.5 0	-5.0 -7.2	7.0 15.5	+5.0 0	-7.0 -10.5	10.0 24.0	+9.0 0	-10.0 -15.0
4.73 – 7.09	3.5 7.6	+2.5 0	-3.5 -5.1	3.5 10.0	+4.0 0	-3.5 -6.0	6.0 12.5	+4.0 0	-6.0 -8.5	8.0 18.0	+6.0 0	-8.0 -12.0	12.0 28.0	+10.0 0	-12.0 -18.0
7.09 – 9.85	4.0 8.6	+2.8 0	-4.0 -5.8	4.0 11.3	+4.5 0	-4.0 -6.8	7.0 14.3	+4.5 0	-7.0 -9.8	10.0 21.5	+7.0 0	-10.0 -14.5	15.0 34.0	+12.0 0	-15.0 -22.0
9.85–12.41	5.0 10.0	+3.0 0	-5.0 -7.0	5.0 13.0	+5.0 0	-5.0 -8.0	8.0 16.0	+5.0 0	-8.0 -11	12.0 25.0	+8.0 0	-12.0 -17.0	18.0 38.0	+12.0 0	-18.0 -26.0
12.41– 15.75	6.0 11.7	+3.5 0	-6.0 -8.2	6.0 15.5	+6.0 0	-6.0 -9.5	10.0 19.5	+6.0 0	-10 -13.5	14.0 29.0	+9.0 0	-14.0 -20.0	22.0 45.0	+14.0 0	-22.0 -31.0
15.75– 19.69	8.0 14.5	+4.0 0	-8.0 -10.5	8.0 18.0	+6.0 0	-8.0 -12.0	12.0 22.0	+6.0 0	-12.0 -16.0	16.0 32.0	+10.0 0	-16.0 -22.0	25.0 51.0	+16.0 0	-25.0 -35.0

USAS/ASME B4.1 – 1967 (R2004) Standard. For larger diameters, see the standard. ASME/ANSI B18.3.5M – 1986 (R2002) Standard. Reprinted from the standard listed by permission of the American Society of Mechanical Engineers.

Locational clearance fits – American National Standard (Inches)

Basic Hole System, Limits are in thousandths of an inch.
Limits for hole and shaft are applied to the basic size to obtain the limits of sizes for the parts.

Nominal Size Range Inches	Class LC1		Class LC2		Class LC3		Class LC4	
	Standard Limits		Standard Limits		Standard Limits		Standard Limits	
Over To	Hole	Shaft	Hole	Shaft	Hole	Shaft	Hole	Shaft
0 - 0.12	+0.25	0	+0.4	0	+0.6	0	+1.6	0
	0	-0.2	0	-0.25	0	-0.4	0	-1.0
0.12 - 0.24	+0.3	0	+0.5	0	+0.7	0	+1.8	0
	0	-0.2	0	-0.3	0	-0.5	0	-1.2
0.24- 0.40	+0.4	0	+0.6	0	+0.9	0	+2.2	0
	0	-0.25	0	-0.4	0	-0.6	0	-1,4
0,40- 0.71	+0.4	0	+0.7	0	+1,0	0	+2.6	0
	0	-0.3	0	-0.4	0	-0.7	0	-1.6
0.71 - 1.10	+0.5	0	+0 .8	0	+1.2	0	+3.5	0
	0	-0.4	0	-0.5	0	-0.8	0	-2.0
1.19- 1.97	+0.6	0	+1 0	0	+1.6	0	+4.0	0
	0	-0.4	0	-0.6	0	-1.0	0	-2.5
1.97- 3.15	+0.7	0	+1.2	0	+1.8	0	+4.5	0
	0	-0.5	o	-0.7	0	-1.2	0	-3.0
3.15- 4.73	+0.9	0	+1.4	0	+2.2	0	+5.0	0
	0	-0.6	0	-0.9	0	-1.4	0	-3.5
4.73- 7.09	+1.0	0	+1.6	0	+2.5	0	+6.0	0
	0	-0.7	0	-1.0	0	-1.6	0	-4.0
7.09- 9.85	+1.2	0	+1.8	0	+2.8	0	+7.0	0
	0	-0.8	0	-1.2	0	-1.8	0	-4.5
9.85 - 12.41	+1.2	0	+2.0	0	+3.0	0	+8.0	0
	0	-0.9	0	-1.2	0	-2.0	0	-5.0
12.41 - 15.75	+1.4	0	+2.2	0	+3.5	0	+9.0	0
	0	-1.0	0	-1.4	0	-2.2	0	-6.0
15.75 - 19.69	+1.6	0	+2.5	0	+4.0	0	+10.0	0
	0	-1.0	0	-1.6	0	-2.5	0	-6.0

USAS/ASME B4.1 – 1967 (R2004) Standard. For larger diameters, see the standard. ASME/ANSI B18.3.5M – 1986 (R2002) Standard. Reprinted from the standard listed by permission of the American Society of Mechanical Engineers.

APPENDIX A (Locational clearance fits Continued)

Locational clearance fits – American National Standard (Inches)

Basic Hole System, Limits are in thousandths of an inch. Limits for hole and shaft are applied to the basic size to obtain the limits of sizes for the parts.

Nominal Size Range Inches		Class LC5		Class LC6		Class LC7		Class LC8	
		Standard Limits		Standard Limits		Standard Limits		Standard Limits	
Over	To	Hole	Shaft	Hole	Shaft	Hole	Shaft	Hole	Shaft
0	- 0.12	+0.4 0	-0.1 -0.35	+1.0 0	-0.3 -0.9	+1.6 0	-0.8 -1.6	+1.6 0	-1.0 -2.0
0.12	- 0.24	+0.5 0	-0.15 -0.45	+1.2 0	-0.4 -1.1	+1.8 0	-0.8 -2.0	+1.8 0	-1.2 -2.4
0.24	- 0.40	+0.6 0	-0.2 -0.6	+1.4 0	-0.5 -1.4	+2.2 0	-1.0 -2.4	+2.2 0	-1.6 -3.0
0.40	- 0.71	+0.7 0	-0.25 -0.65	+1.6 0	-0.6 -1.6	+2.8 0	-1.2 -2.8	+2.8 0	-2.0 -3.6
0.71	- 1.19	+0.8 0	-0.3 -0.8	+2.0 0	-0.8 -2.0	+3.5 0	-1.6 -3.6	-3.5 0	-2.5 -4.5
1.19	- 1.97	+1.0 0	-0.4 -1.0	+2.5 0	-1.0 -2.6	+4.0 0	-2.0 -4.5	+4.0 0	-3.0 -5.5
1.97	- 3.15	+1.2 0	-0.4 -1 1	+3.0 0	-1.2 -3.0	+4.5 0	-2.5 -5.5	+4.5 0	-4.0 -7.0
3.15	- 4.73	+1.4 0	-0.5 -1.4	+3.5 0	-1.4 -3.6	+5.0 0	-3.0 -6.5	+5.0 0	-5.0 -8.5
4.73	- 7.09	+1.6 0	-0.6 -1.6	+4.0 0	-1 .6 -4.1	+6.0 0	-3.5 -7.5	+6.0 0	-6.0 -10.0
7.09	- 9.85	+1.6 0	-0.6 -1.8	+4.5 0	-2.0 -4.8	+7.0 0	-4.0 -8.5	+7.0 0	-7.0 -11.5
9.85	- 12.41	+2.0 0	-0.7 -1.9	+5.0 0	-2.2 -5.2	+8.0 0	-4.5 -9.5	+8.0 0	-7.0 -12.0
12 41	- 15.75	+2.2 0	-0.7 -2.1	+6.0 0	-2.5 -6.0	+9.0 0	-5.0 -11.0	+9.0 0	-8.0 -14.0
15.75	- 19.69	+2.5 0	-0.8 -2.4	+6.0 0	-2.8 -6.8	+10.0 0	-5.0 -11.0	+10.0 0	-9.0 -15.0

USAS/ASME B4.1 – 1967 (R2004) Standard. For larger diameters, see the standard. ASME/ANSI B18.3.5M – 1986 (R2002) Standard. Reprinted from the standard listed by permission of the American Society of Mechanical Engineers.

APPENDIX A (Locational clearance fits Continued)

Locational clearance fits – American National Standard (Inches)

Basic Hole System, Limits are in thousandths of an inch. Limits for hole and shaft are applied to the basic size to obtain the limits of sizes for the parts.

Nominal Size Range Inches	Class LC9		Class LC10		Class LC11	
	Standard Limits		Standard Limits		Standard Limits	
Over To	Hole	Shaft	Hole	Shaft	Hole	Shaft
0 - 0.12	+2.5 0	-2.5 -4.1	+4.0 0	-4.0 -8.0	+6.0 0	-5.0 -11.0
0.12- 0.24	+3.0 0	-3.0 -5.2	+5.0 0	-4.5 -9.5	+7.0 0	-6.0 -13.0
0.25- 0.40	+3.5 0	-3.5 -6.3	+6.0 0	-5.0 -11.0	+9.0 0	-7.0 -16.0
0.40- 0.71	+4.0 0	-4.5 -8.0	+7.0 0	-6.0 -13.0	+10.0 0	-8.0 -18.0
0.71 - 1.19	+5.0 0	-5.0 -9.0	+8.0 0	-7.0 -15.0	+12.0 0	-10.0 -22.0
1.19- 1.97	+6.0 0	-6.0 -10.5	+10.0 0	-8.0 -18.0	+16.0 0	-12.0 -28.0
1.97- 3.15	+7.0 0	-7.0 -12.0	+12.0 0	-10.0 -22.0	+18.0 0	-14.0 -32.0
3.15- 4.73	+9.0 0	-8.0 -14.0	+14.0 0	-11.0 -25.0	+22.0 0	-16.0 -38.0
4.73- 7.09	+10.0 0	-10.0 -17.0	+16.0 0	-12.0 -28.0	+25.0 0	-18.0 -43.0
7.09- 9.85	+12.0 0	-12.0 -20.0	+18.0 0	-16.0 -34.0	+25.0 0	-22.0 -50.0
9.85 - 12.41	+12.0 0	-0.7 -1.9	+20.0 0	-20.0 -40.0	+30.0 0	-28.0 -58.0
12 41 - 15.75	+14.0 0	-14.0 -23.0	+22.0 0	-22.0 -44.0	+35.0 0	-30.0 -65.0
15.75 - 19.69	+16.0 0	--16.0 --26.0	+25.0 0	-25.0 -50.0	+40.0 0	-35.0 -75.0

USAS/ASME B4.1 – 1967 (R2004) Standard. For larger diameters, see the standard. ASME/ANSI B18.3.5M – 1986 (R2002) Standard. Reprinted from the standard listed by permission of the American Society of Mechanical Engineers.

APPENDIX A

Force and Shrink fits – American National Standard (Inches) - Partial List

Basic Hole System, Limits are in thousandths of an inch.
Limits for hole and shaft are applied to the basic size to obtain the limits of sizes for the parts.

❖ Values shown below are in thousandths of an inch

Nominal Size Range, Inches		Class FN 1			Class FN 2			Class FN 3			Class FN 4			Class FN 5		
		Interference Limits	Standard Limits		Interference Limits	Standard Limits		Interference Limits	Standard Limits		Interference Limits	Standard Limits		Interference Limits	Standard Limits	
Over	To		Hole	Shaft		Hole	Shaft		Hole	Shaft		Hole	Shaft		Hole	Shaft
			H6			H7	s6		H7	t6		H7	u6		H8	x7
0	0.12	+0.05	+0.25	+0.5	+0.2	+0.4	+0.85				+0.3	+0.4	+0.95	+0.3	+0.6	+1.3
		+0.5	0	+0.3	+0.85	0	+0.6				+0.95	0	+0.7	+1.3	0	+0.9
0.12	0.24	+0.1	+0.3	+0.6	+0.2	+0.5	+1.0				+0.4	+0.5	+1.2	+0.5	+0.7	+1.7
		+0.6	0	+0.4	+1.0	0	+0.7				+1.2	0	+0.9	+1.7	0	+1.2
0.24	0.4	+0.1	+0.4	+0.75	+0.4	+0.6	+1.4				+0.6	+0.6	+1.6	+0.5	+0.9	+2.0
		+0.75	0	+0.5	+1.4	0	+1.0				+1.6	0	+1.2	+2.0	0	+1.4
0.40	0.56	+0.1	+0.4	+0.8	+0.5	+0.7	+1.6				+0.7	+0.7	+1.8	+0.6	+1.0	+2.3
		+0.8	0	+0.5	+1.6	0	+1.2				+1.8	0	+1.4	+2.3	0	+1.6
0.56	0.71	+0.2	+0.4	+0.9	+0.5	+0.7	+1.6				+0.7	+0.7	+1.8	+0.8	+1.0	+2.5
		+0.9	0	+0.6	+1.6	0	+1.2				+1.8	0	+1.4	+2.5	0	+1.8
0.71	0.95	+0.2	+0.5	+1.1	+0.6	+0.8	+1.9				+0.8	+0.8	+2.1	+1.0	+1.2	+3.0
		+1.1	0	+0.7	+1.9	0	+1.4				+2.1	0	+1.6	+3.0	0	+2.2
0.95	1.19	+0.3	+0.5	+1.2	+0.6	+0.8	+1.9	+0.8	+0.8	+2.1	+1.0	+0.8	+2.3	+1.3	+1.2	+3.3
		+1.2	0	+0.8	+1.9	0	+1.4	+2.1	0	+1.6	+2.3	0	+1.8	+3.3	0	+2.5
1.19	1.58	+0.3	+0.6	+1.3	+0.8	+1.0	+2.4	+1.0	+1.0	+2.6	+1.5	+1.0	+3.1	+1.4	+1.6	+4.0
		+1.3	0	+0.9	+2.4	0	+1.8	+2.6	0	+2.0	+3.1	0	+2.5	+4.0	0	+3.0
1.58	1.97	+0.4	+0.6	+1.4	+0.8	+1.0	+2.4	+1.2	+1.0	+2.8	+1.8	+1.0	+3.4	+2.4	+1.6	+5.0
		+1.4	0	+1.0	+2.4	0	+1.8	+2.8	0	+2.2	+3.4	0	+2.8	+5.0	0	+4.0
1.97	2.56	+0.6	+0.7	+1.8	+0.8	+1.2	+2.7	+1.3	+1.2	+3.2	+2.3	+1.2	+4.2	+3.2	+1.8	+6.2
		+1.8	0	+1.3	+2.7	0	+2.0	+3.2	0	+2.5	+4.2	0	+3.5	+6.2	0	+5.0
2.56	3.15	+0.7	+0.7	+1.9	+1.0	+1.2	+2.9	+1.8	+1.2	+3.7	+2.8	+1.2	+4.7	+4.2	+1.8	+7.2
		+1.9	0	+1.4	+2.9	0	+2.2	+3.7	0	+3.0	+4.7	0	+4.0	+7.2	0	+6.0
3.15	3.94	+0.9	+0.9	+2.4	+1.4	+1.4	+3.7	+2.1	+1.4	+4.4	+3.6	+1.4	+5.9	+4.8	+2.2	+8.4
		+2.4	0	+1.8	+3.7	0	+2.8	+4.4	0	+3.5	+5.9	0	+5.0	+8.4	0	+7.0
3.94	4.73	+1.1	+0.9	+2.6	+1.6	+1.4	+3.9	+2.6	+1.4	+4.9	+4.6	+1.4	+6.9	+5.8	+2.2	+9.4
		+2.6	0	+2.0	+3.9	0	+3.0	+4.9	0	+4.0	+6.9	0	+6.0	+9.4	0	+8.0

USAS/ASME B4.1 – 1967 (R2004) Standard. For larger diameters, see the standard. ASME/ANSI B18.3.5M – 1986 (R2002) Standard.

APPENDIX B – METRIC LIMITS AND FITS

Hole Basis Clearance Fits

Preferred **Hole Basis Clearance Fits**. Dimensions in mm.

Basic Size	Loose Running		Free Running		Close Running		Sliding		Locational Clearance	
	Hole H11	Shaft c11	Hole H9	Shaft d9	Hole H8	Shaft f7	Hole H7	Shaft g6	Hole H7	Shaft h6
1 max	1.060	0.940	1.025	0.980	1.014	0.994	1.010	0.998	1.010	1.000
min	1.000	0.880	1.000	0.955	1.000	0.984	1.000	0.992	1.000	0.994
1.2 max	1.260	0.940	1.225	1.180	1.214	1.194	1.210	1.198	1.210	1.200
min	1.200	0.880	1.200	1.155	1.200	1.184	1.200	1.192	1.200	1.194
1.6 max	1.660	1.540	1.625	1.580	1.614	1.594	1.610	1.598	1.610	1.600
min	1.600	1.480	1.600	1.555	1.600	1.584	1.600	1.592	1.600	1.594
2 max	2.060	1.940	2.025	1.980	2.014	1.994	2.010	1.998	2.010	2.000
min	2.000	1.880	2.000	1.955	2.000	1.984	2.000	1.992	2.000	1.994
2.5 max	2.560	2.440	2.525	2.480	2.514	2.494	2.510	2.498	2.510	2.500
min	2.500	2.380	2.500	2.455	2.500	2.484	2.500	2.492	2.500	2.494
3 max	3.060	2.940	3.025	2.980	3.014	2.994	3.010	2.998	3.010	3.000
min	3.000	2.880	3.000	2.955	3.000	2.984	3.000	2.992	3.000	2.994
4 max	4.075	3.930	4.030	3.970	4.018	3.990	4.012	3.996	4.012	4.000
min	4.000	3.855	4.000	3.940	4.000	3.987	4.000	3.988	4.000	3.992
5 max	5.075	4.930	5.030	4.970	5.018	4.990	5.012	4.998	5.012	5.000
min	5.000	4.855	5.000	4.940	5.000	4.978	5.000	4.988	5.000	4.992
6 max	6.075	5.930	6.030	5.970	6.018	5.990	6.012	5.996	6.012	6.000
min	6.000	5.855	6.000	5.940	6.000	5.978	6.000	5.988	6.000	5.992
8 max	8.090	7.920	8.036	7.960	8.022	7.987	8.015	7.995	8.015	8.000
min	8.000	7.830	8.000	7.924	8.000	7.972	8.000	7.986	8.000	7.991
10 max	10.090	9.920	10.036	9.960	10.022	9.987	10.015	9.995	10.015	10.000
min	10.000	9.830	10.000	9.924	10.000	9.972	10.000	9.986	10.000	9.991
12 max	12.110	11.905	12.043	11.950	12.027	11.984	12.018	11.994	12.018	12.000
min	12.000	11.795	12.000	11.907	12.000	11.966	12.000	11.983	12.000	11.989
16 max	16.110	15.905	16.043	15.950	16.027	15.984	16.018	15.994	16.018	16.000
min	16.000	15.795	16.000	15.907	16.000	15.966	16.000	15.983	16.000	15.989
20 max	20.130	19.890	20.052	19.935	20.033	19.980	20.021	19.993	20.021	20.000
min	20.000	19.760	20.000	19.883	20.000	19.959	20.000	19.980	20.000	19.987
25 max	25.130	24.890	25.052	24.935	25.033	24.980	24.993	25.021	25.021	25.000
min	25.000	24.760	25.000	24.883	25.000	24.959	24.980	25.000	25.000	24.987
30 max	30.130	29.890	30.052	29.935	30.033	29.980	30.021	29.993	30.021	30.000
min	30.000	29.760	30.000	29.883	30.000	29.959	30.000	29.980	30.000	29.987
40 max	40.160	39.880	40.062	39.920	40.039	39.975	40.025	39.991	40.025	40.000
min	40.000	39.720	40.000	39.858	40.000	39.950	40.000	39.975	40.000	39.984

APPENDIX B – METRIC LIMITS AND FITS (Continued)

Hole Basis Transition and Interference Fits

Preferred **Hole Basis Clearance Fits**. Dimensions in mm.

Basic Size	Locational Transition		Locational Transition		Locational Transition		Medium Drive		Force	
	Hole H7	Shaft k6	Hole H7	Shaft n6	Hole H7	Shaft p6	Hole H7	Shaft s6	Hole H7	Shaft u6
1 max	1.010	1.006	1.010	1.010	1.010	1.012	1.010	1.020	1.010	1.024
min	1.000	1.000	1.000	1.004	1.000	1.006	1.000	1.014	1.000	1.018
1.2 max	1.210	1.206	1.210	1.210	1.210	1.212	1.210	1.220	1.210	1.224
min	1.200	1.200	1.200	1.204	1.200	1.206	1.200	1.214	1.200	1.218
1.6 max	1.610	1.606	1.610	1.610	1.610	1.612	1.610	1.620	1.610	1.624
min	1.600	1.600	1.600	1.604	1.600	1.606	1.600	1.614	1.600	1.618
2 max	2.010	2.006	2.010	2.020	2.010	2.012	2.010	2.020	2.010	2.024
min	2.000	2.000	2.000	2.004	2.000	2.006	2.000	1.014	2.000	2.018
2.5 max	2.510	2.510	2.510	2.510	2.510	2.512	2.510	2.520	2.510	2.524
min	2.500	2.500	2.500	2.504	2.500	2.506	2.500	2.514	2.500	2.518
3 max	3.010	3.010	3.010	3.010	3.010	3.012	3.010	3.020	3.010	3.024
min	3.000	3.000	3.000	3.004	3.000	3.006	3.000	3.014	3.000	3.018
4 max	4.012	4.012	4.012	4.016	4.012	4.020	4.012	4.027	4.012	4.031
min	4.000	4.000	4.000	4.008	4.000	4.012	4.000	4.019	4.000	4.023
5 max	5.012	5.009	5.012	5.016	5.012	5.020	5.012	5.027	5.012	5.031
min	5.000	5.001	5.000	5.008	5.000	5.012	5.000	5.019	5.000	5.023
6 max	6.012	6.009	6.012	6.016	6.012	6.020	6.012	6.027	6.012	6.031
min	6.000	6.001	6.000	6.008	6.000	6.012	6.000	6.019	6.000	6.023
8 max	8.015	8.010	8.015	8.019	8.015	8.024	8.015	8.032	8.015	8.037
min	8.000	8.001	8.000	8.010	8.000	8.015	8.000	8.023	8.000	8.028
10 max	10.015	10.010	10.015	10.019	10.015	10.024	10.015	10.032	10.015	10.037
min	10.000	10.001	10.000	10.010	10.000	10.015	10.000	10.023	10.000	10.028
12 max	12.018	12.012	12.018	12.023	12.018	12.029	12.018	12.039	12.018	12.044
min	12.000	12.001	12.000	12.012	12.000	12.018	12.000	12.028	12.000	12.033
16 max	16.018	16.012	16.018	16.023	16.018	16.029	16.018	16.039	16.018	16.044
min	16.000	16.001	16.000	16.012	16.000	16.018	16.000	16.028	16.000	16.033
20 max	20.021	20.015	20.021	20.028	20.021	20.035	20.021	20.048	20.021	20.054
min	20.000	20.002	20.000	20.015	20.000	20.022	20.000	20.035	20.000	20.041
25 max	25.021	25.015	25.021	25.028	25.021	25.035	25.021	25.048	25.021	25.061
min	25.000	25.002	25.000	25.015	25.000	25.022	25.000	25.035	25.000	25.048
30 max	30.021	30.015	30.021	30.028	30.021	30.035	30.021	30.048	30.021	30.061
min	30.000	30.002	30.000	30.015	30.000	30.022	30.000	30.035	30.000	30.048
40 max	40.025	40.018	40.025	40.033	40.025	40.042	40.025	40.059	40.025	40.076
min	40.000	40.002	40.000	40.017	40.000	40.026	40.000	40.043	40.000	40.060

APPENDIX B – METRIC LIMITS AND FITS (Continued)

Shaft Basis Clearance Fits

Preferred **Shaft Basis Clearance Fits**. Dimensions in mm.

Basic Size	Loose Running		Free Running		Close Running		Sliding		Locational Clearance	
	Hole C11	Shaft h11	Hole D9	Shaft h9	Hole F8	Shaft h7	Hole G7	Shaft h6	Hole H7	Shaft h6
1 max	1.120	1.000	1.045	1.000	1.020	1.000	1.012	1.000	1.010	1.000
min	1.060	0.940	1.020	0.975	1.006	0.990	1.002	0.994	1.000	0.994
1.2 max	1.320	1.200	1.245	1.200	1.220	1.200	1.212	1.200	1.210	1.200
min	1.260	1.140	1.220	1.175	1.206	1.190	1.202	1.194	1.200	1.194
1.6 max	1.720	1.600	1.645	1.600	1.620	1.600	1.612	1.600	1.610	1.600
min	1.660	1.540	1.620	1.575	1.606	1.590	1.602	1.594	1.600	1.594
2 max	2.120	2.000	2.045	2.000	2.020	2.000	2.012	2.000	2.010	2.000
min	2.060	1.940	2.020	1.975	2.006	1.990	2.002	1.994	2.000	1.994
2.5 max	2.620	2.500	2.545	2.500	2.520	2.500	2.512	2.500	2.510	2.500
min	2.560	2.440	2.520	2.475	2.506	2.490	2.502	2.494	2.500	2.494
3 max	3.120	3.000	3.045	3.000	3.020	3.000	3.012	3.000	3.010	3.000
min	3.060	2.940	3.020	2.975	3.006	2.990	3.002	2.994	3.000	2.994
4 max	4.145	4.000	4.060	4.000	4.028	4.000	4.016	4.000	4.012	4.000
min	4.070	3.925	4.030	3.970	4.010	3.988	4.004	3.992	4.000	3.992
5 max	5.145	5.000	5.060	5.000	5.028	5.000	5.016	5.000	5.012	5.000
min	5.070	4.925	5.030	4.970	5.010	4.988	5.004	4.992	5.000	4.992
6 max	6.145	6.000	6.060	6.000	6.028	6.000	6.016	6.000	6.012	6.000
min	6.070	5.925	6.030	5.970	6.010	5.988	6.004	5.992	6.000	5.992
8 max	8.170	8.000	8.076	8.000	8.035	8.000	8.020	8.000	8.015	8.000
min	8.080	7.910	8.040	7.964	8.013	7.985	8.005	7.991	8.000	7.991
10 max	10.170	10.000	10.076	10.000	10.035	10.000	10.020	10.000	10.015	10.000
min	10.080	9.910	10.040	9.964	10.013	9.985	10.005	9.991	10.000	9.991
12 max	12.205	12.000	12.093	12.000	12.043	12.000	12.024	12.000	12.018	12.000
min	12.095	11.890	12.050	11.957	12.016	11.982	12.006	11.989	12.000	11.989
16 max	16.205	16.000	16.093	16.000	16.043	16.000	16.024	16.000	16.018	16.000
min	16.095	15.890	16.050	15.957	16.016	15.982	16.006	15.989	16.000	15.989
20 max	20.240	20.000	20.117	20.000	20.053	20.000	20.028	20.000	20.021	20.000
min	20.110	19.870	20.065	19.948	20.020	19.979	20.007	19.987	20.000	19.987
25 max	25.240	25.000	25.117	25.000	25.053	25.000	25.028	25.000	25.021	25.000
min	25.110	24.870	25.065	24.948	25.020	24.979	25.007	24.987	25.000	24.987
30 max	30.240	30.000	30.117	30.000	30.053	30.000	30.028	30.000	30.021	30.000
min	30.110	29.870	30.065	29.948	30.020	29.979	30.007	29.987	30.000	29.987
40 max	40.280	40.000	40.142	40.000	40.064	40.000	40.034	40.000	40.025	40.000
min	40.120	39.840	40.080	39.938	40.025	39.975	40.009	39.984	40.000	39.984

ANSI B4.2 – 1978 (R2004) Standard. ASME/ANSI B18.3.5M – 1986 (R2002) Standard.

APPENDIX B - METRIC LIMITS AND FITS (Continued)

Shaft Basis Transition and Interference Fits

Preferred **Shaft Basis Transition and Interference Fits.** Dimensions in mm.

Basic Size	Locational Transition		Locational Transition		Locational Interference		Medium Drive		Force	
	Hole K7	Shaft h6	Hole N7	Shaft h6	Hole P7	Shaft h6	Hole S7	Shaft h6	Hole U7	Shaft h6
1 max	1.000	1.000	0.996	1.000	0.994	1.000	0.986	1.000	0.982	1.000
min	0.990	0.994	0.986	0.994	0.984	0.994	0.976	0.994	0.972	0.994
1.2 max	1.200	1.200	1.196	1.200	1.194	1.200	1.186	1.200	1.182	1.200
min	1.190	1.194	1.186	1.194	1.184	1.194	1.176	1.194	1.172	1.194
1.6 max	1.600	1.600	1.596	1.600	1.594	1.600	1.586	1.600	1.582	1.600
min	1.590	1.594	1.586	1.594	1.584	1.594	1.576	1.594	1.572	1.594
2 max	2.000	2.000	1.996	2.000	1.994	2.000	1.986	2.000	1.982	2.000
min	1.990	1.994	1.986	1.994	1.984	1.994	1.976	1.994	1.972	1.994
2.5 max	2.500	2.500	2.496	2.500	2.494	2.500	2.486	2.500	2.482	2.500
min	2.490	2.494	2.486	2.494	2.484	2.494	2.476	2.494	2.472	2.494
3 max	3.000	3.000	2.996	3.000	2.994	3.000	2.986	3.000	2.982	3.000
min	2.990	2.994	2.986	2.994	2.984	2.994	2.976	2.994	2.972	2.994
4 max	4.003	4.000	3.996	4.000	3.992	4.000	3.985	4.000	3.981	4.000
min	3.991	5.992	3.984	5.992	3.980	5.992	3.973	5.992	3.969	5.992
5 max	5.003	5.000	4.996	5.000	4.992	5.000	4.985	5.000	4.981	5.000
min	4.991	4.992	4.984	4.992	4.980	4.992	4.973	4.992	4.969	4.992
6 max	6.003	6.000	5.996	6.000	5.992	6.000	5.985	6.000	5.981	6.000
min	5.991	5.992	5.984	5.992	5.980	5.992	5.973	5.992	5.969	5.992
8 max	8.005	8.000	7.996	8.000	7.991	8.000	7.983	8.000	7.978	8.000
min	7.990	7.991	7.981	7.991	7.976	7.991	7.968	7.991	7.963	7.991
10 max	10.005	10.000	9.996	10.000	9.991	10.000	9.983	10.000	9.978	10.000
min	9.990	9.991	9.981	9.991	9.976	9.991	9.968	9.991	9.963	9.991
12 max	12.006	12.000	11.995	12.000	11.989	12.000	11.979	12.000	11.974	12.000
min	11.988	11.989	11.977	11.989	11.971	11.989	11.961	11.989	11.956	11.989
16 max	16.006	16.000	15.995	16.000	15.989	16.000	15.979	16.000	15.974	16.000
min	15.988	15.989	15.977	15.989	15.971	15.989	15.961	15.989	15.956	15.989
20 max	20.006	20.000	19.993	20.000	19.986	20.000	19.973	20.000	19.967	20.000
min	19.985	19.987	19.972	19.987	19.965	19.987	19.952	19.987	19.946	19.987
25 max	25.006	25.000	24.993	25.000	24.986	25.000	24.973	25.000	24.960	25.000
min	24.985	24.987	24.972	24.987	24.965	24.987	24.952	24.987	24.939	24.987
30 max	30.006	30.000	29.993	30.000	29.986	30.000	29.973	30.000	29.960	30.000
min	29.985	29.987	29.972	29.987	29.965	29.987	29.952	29.987	29.939	29.987
40 max	40.007	40.000	39.992	40.000	39.983	40.000	39.966	40.000	39.949	40.000
min	39.982	39.984	39.967	39.984	39.958	39.984	39.941	39.984	39.924	39.984

APPENDIX C – UNIFIED NATIONAL THREAD FORM

(External Threads) Approximate Minor diameter = D – 1.0825P P = Pitch

Nominal Size, in.	Basic Major Diameter (D)	Coarse UNC		Fine UNF		Extra Fine UNEF	
		Thds. Per in.	Tap Drill Dia.	Thds. Per in.	Tap Drill Dia.	Thds. Per in.	Tap Drill Dia.
#0	0.060	...	...	80	3/64	...	...
#1	0.0730	64	0.0595	72	0.0595	...	...
#2	0.0860	56	0.0700	64	0.0700	...	...
#3	0.0990	48	0.0785	56	0.0820	...	...
#4	0.1120	40	0.0890	48	0.0935	...	...
#5	0.1250	40	0.1015	44	0.1040	...	...
#6	0.1380	32	0.1065	40	0.1130	...	...
#8	0.1640	32	0.1360	36	0.1360	...	...
#10	0.1900	24	0.1495	32	0.1590	...	...
#12	0.2160	24	0.1770	28	0.1820	32	0.1850
1/4	0.2500	20	0.2010	28	0.2130	32	7/32
5/16	0.3125	18	0.257	24	0.272	32	9/32
3/8	0.3750	16	5/16	24	0.332	32	11/32
7/16	0.4375	14	0.368	20	25/64	28	13/32
1/2	0.5000	13	27/64	20	29/64	28	15/32
9/16	0.5625	12	31/64	18	33/64	24	33/64
5/8	0.6250	11	17/32	18	37/64	24	37/64
11/16	0.675	...	...	...	...	24	41/64
3/4	0.7500	10	21/32	16	11/16	20	45/64
13/16	0.8125	...	...	...	...	20	49/64
7/8	0.8750	9	49/64	14	13/16	20	53/64
15/16	0.9375	...	...	...	...	20	57/64
1	1.0000	8	7/8	12	59/64	20	61/64
1 1/8	1.1250	7	63/64	12	1 3/64	18	1 5/64
1 1/4	1.2500	7	1 7/64	12	1 11/64	18	1 3/16
1 3/8	1.3750	6	1 7/32	12	1 19/64	18	1 5/16
1 1/2	1.5000	6	1 11/32	12	1 27/64	18	1 7/16
1 5/8	1.6250	...	...	...	...	18	1 9/16
1 3/4	1.7500	5	1 9/16	...	...	...	...
1 7/8	1.8750	...	...	...	...	...	...
2	2.0000	4 1/2	1 25/32	...	...	...	...
2 1/4	2.2500	4 1/2	2 1/32	...	...	...	...
2 1/2	2.5000	4	2 1/4	...	...	...	...
2 3/4	2.7500	4	2 1/2	...	...	...	...

ASME B1.1 – 2003 Standard. Reprinted from the standard listed by permission of the American Society of Mechanical Engineers.

APPENDIX D – METRIC THREAD FORM

(External Threads) Approximate Minor diameter = D – 1.2075P P = Pitch
Preferred sizes for commercial threads and fasteners are shown in boldface type.

Coarse (general purpose)		Fine	
Nominal Size & Thread Pitch	**Tap Drill Diameter, mm**	**Nominal Size & Thread Pitch**	**Tap Drill Diameter, mm**
M1.6 x 0.35	1.25	---	---
M1.8 x 0.35	1.45	---	---
M2 x 0.4	1.6	---	---
M2.2 x 0.45	1.75	---	---
M2.5 x 0.45	2.05	---	---
M3 x 0.5	2.5	---	---
M3.5 x 0.6	2.9	---	---
M4 x 0.7	3.3	---	---
M4.5 x 0.75	3.75	---	---
M5 x 0.8	4.2	---	---
M6 x 1	5.0	---	---
M7 x 1	6.0	---	---
M8 x 1.25	6.8	**M8 x 1**	7.0
M9 x 1.25	7.75	---	---
M10 x 1.5	8.5	**M10 x 1.25**	8.75
M11 x 1.5	9.50	---	---
M12 x 1.75	10.30	**M12 x 1.25**	10.5
M14 x 2	12.00	**M14 x 1.5**	12.5
M16 x 2	14.00	**M16 x 1.5**	14.5
M18 x 2.5	15.50	**M18 x 1.5**	16.5
M20 x 2.5	17.5	**M20 x 1.5**	18.5
M22 x 2.5*	19.5	**M22 x 1.5**	20.5
M24 x 3	21.0	**M24 x 2**	22.0
M27 x 3*	24.0	**M27 x 2**	25.0
M30 x 3.5	26.5	**M30 x 2**	28.0
M33 x 3.5	29.5	M33 x 2	31.0
M36 x 4	32.0	**M36 x 2**	33.0
M39 x 4	35.0	M39 x 2	36.0
M42 x 4.5	37.5	**M42 x 2**	39.0
M45 x 4.5	40.5	M45 x 1.5	42.0
M48 x 5	43.0	**M48 x 2**	45.0
M52 x 5	47.0	M52 x 2	49.0
M56 x 5.5	50.5	**M56 x 2**	52.0
M60 x 5.5	54.5	M60 x 1.5	56.0
M64 x 6	58.0	**M64 x 2**	60.0
M68 x 6	62.0	M68 x 2	64.0
M72 x 6	66.0	**M72 x 2**	68.0
M80 x 6	74.0	**M80 x 2**	76.0
M90 x 6	84.0	**M90 x 2**	86.0
M100 x 6	94.0	**M100 x 2**	96.0

*Only for high strength structural steel fasteners

ASME B1.13M – 2001 Standard. Reprinted from the standard listed by permission of the American Society of Mechanical Engineers. All rights reserved.

APPENDIX E – FASTENERS (INCH SERIES)

Dimensions of Hex Cap Screws (Finished Hex Bolts)

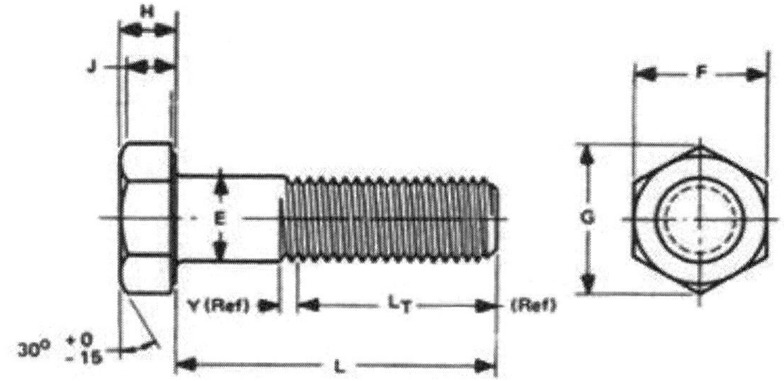

Nominal Site or Basic Product Dia		E Body Dia		F Width Across Flats			G Width Across Corners		H Height			J Wrenching Height	L_T Thread Length For Screw Lengths 6 in. and Shorter	L_T Thread Length For Screw Lengths Over 6 in.	Y Transition Thread Length	Runout of Bearing Surface FIM
		Max	Min	Basic	Max	Min	Max	Min	Basic	Max	Min	Min	Basic	Basic	Max	Max
1/4	0.2500	0.2500	0.2450	7/16	0.438	0.428	0.505	0.488	5/32	0.163	0.150	0.106	0.750	1.000	0.250	0.010
5/16	0.3125	0.3125	0.3065	1/2	0.500	0.489	0.577	0.557	13/64	0.211	0.195	0.140	0.875	1.125	0.278	0.011
3/8	0.3750	0.3750	0.3690	9/16	0.562	0.551	0.650	0.628	15/64	0.243	0.226	0.160	1.000	1.250	0.312	0.012
7/16	0.4375	0.4375	0.4305	5/8	0.625	0.612	0.722	0.698	9/32	0.291	0.272	0.195	1.125	1.375	0.357	0.013
1/2	0.5000	0.5000	0.4930	3/4	0.750	0.736	0.866	0.840	5/16	0.323	0.302	0.215	1.250	1.500	0.385	0.014
9/16	0.5625	0.5625	0.5545	13/16	0.812	0.798	0.938	0.910	23/64	0.371	0.348	0.250	1.375	1.625	0.417	0.015
5/8	0.6250	0.6250	0.6170	15/16	0.938	0.922	1.083	1.051	25/64	0.403	0.378	0.269	1.500	1.750	0.455	0.017
3/4	0.7500	0.7500	0.7410	1 1/8	1.125	1.100	1.299	1.254	15/32	0.483	0.455	0.324	1.750	2.000	0.500	0.020
7/8	0.8750	0.8750	0.8660	1 5/16	1.312	1.285	1.516	1.465	35/64	0.563	0.531	0.378	2.000	2.250	0.556	0.023
1	1.0000	1.0000	0.9900	1 1/2	1.500	1.469	1.732	1.675	39/64	0.627	0.591	0.416	2.250	2.500	0.625	0.026
1 1/8	1.1250	1.1250	1.1140	1 11/16	1.688	1.631	1.949	1.859	11/16	0.718	0.658	0.461	2.500	2.750	0.714	0.029
1 1/4	1.2500	1.2500	1.2390	1 7/8	1.875	1.812	2.165	2.066	25/32	0.813	0.749	0.530	2.750	3.000	0.714	0.033
1 3/8	1.3750	1.3750	1.3630	2 1/16	2.062	1.994	2.382	2.273	27/32	0.878	0.810	0.569	3.000	3.250	0.833	0.036
1 1,/2	1.5000	1.5000	1.4880	2 1/4	2.230	2.175	2.598	2.480	1 5/16	0.974	0.902	0.640	3.250	3.500	0.833	0.039
1 3/4	1.7500	1.7500	1.7380	2 5/8	2.625	2.538	3.031	2.893	1 3/32	1.134	1.054	0.748	3.750	4.000	1.000	0.046
2	2.0000	2.0000	1.9880	3	3.000	2.900	3.464	3.306	1 7/32	1.263	1.175	0.825	4.250	4.500	1.111	0.052
2 1/4	2.2500	2.2500	2.2380	3 3/8	3.375	3.262	3.897	3.719	1 3/8	1.423	1.327	0.933	4.750	5.000	1.111	0.059
2 1/2	2.5000	2.5000	2.4880	3 3/4	3.750	3.625	4.330	4.133	1 17/32	1.583	1.479	1.042	5.250	5.500	1.250	0.065
2 3/4	2.7500	2.7500	2.7380	4 1/8	4.125	3.988	4.763	4.546	1 11/16	1.744	1.632	1.151	5.750	6.000	1.250	0.072
3	3.0000	3.0000	2.9880	4 1/2	4.500	4.350	5.196	4.959	1 7/8	1.935	1.815	1.290	6.250	6.500	1.250	0.079

ASME B18.3 - R1993 Standard. Reprinted from the standard listed by permission of the American Society of Mechanical Engineers.

APPENDIX E – FASTENERS (INCH SERIES) Continued

DIMENSIONS OF HEXAGON AND SPLINE SOCKET HEAD CAP SCREWS (1960 SERIES)

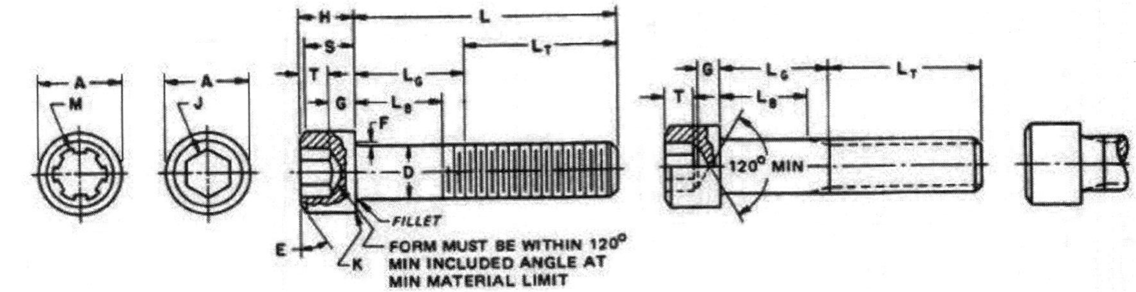

Nominal Size or Basic Screw Diameter		D Body Diameter		A Head Diameter		H Head Height		S Head Side Height	M Spline Socket Size	J Hexagon Socket Size	T Key Engagement	G Wall Thick-ness	K Chamfer or Radius
		Max	Min	Max	Min	Max	Min	Min	Nom	Nom	Min	Min	Max
0	0.0600	0.0600	0.0568	0.096	0.091	0.060	0.057	0.054	0.060	0.050	0.025	0.020	0.003
1	0.0730	0.0730	0.0695	0.118	0.112	0.073	0.070	0.066	0.072	1/16 0.062	0.031	0.025	0.003
2	0.0860	0.0860	0.0822	0.140	0.134	0.086	0.083	0.077	0.096	5/64 0.078	0.038	0.029	0.003
3	0.0990	0.0990	0.0949	0.161	0.154	0.099	0.095	0.089	0.096	5/64 0.078	0.044	0.034	0.003
4	0.1120	0.1120	0.1075	0.183	0.176	0.112	0.108	0.101	0.111	3/32 0.094	0.051	0.038	0.005
5	0.1250	0.1250	0.1202	0.205	0.198	0.125	0.121	0.112	0.111	3/32 0.094	0.057	0.043	0.005
6	0.1380	0.1380	0.1329	0.226	0.218	0.138	0.134	0.124	0.133	7/64 0.109	0.064	0.047	0.005
8	0.1640	0.1640	0.1585	0.270	0.262	0.164	0.159	0.148	0.168	9/64 0.141	0.077	0.056	0.005
10	0.1900	0.1900	0.1840	0.312	0.303	0.190	0.185	0.171	0.183	5/32 0.156	0.090	0.065	0.005
1/4	0.2500	0.2500	0.2435	0.375	0.365	0.250	0.244	0.225	0.216	3/16 0.188	0.120	0.095	0.008
5/16	0.3125	0.3125	0.3053	0.469	0.457	0.312	0.306	0.281	0.291	1/4 0.250	0.151	0.119	0.008
3/8	0.3750	0.3750	0.3678	0.562	0.550	0.375	0.368	0.337	0.372	5/16 0.312	0.182	0.143	0.008
7/16	0.4375	0.4375	0.4294	0.656	0.642	0.438	0.430	0.394	0.454	3/8 0.375	0.213	0.166	0.010
1/2	0.5000	0.5000	0.4919	0.750	0.735	0.500	0.492	0.450	0.454	3/8 0.375	0.245	0.190	0.010
5/8	0.6250	0.6250	0.6163	0.938	0.921	0.625	0.616	0.562	0.595	1/2 0.500	0.307	0.238	0.010
3/4	0.7500	0.7500	0.7406	1.125	1.107	0.750	0.740	0.675	0.620	5/8 0.625	0.370	0.285	0.010
7/8	0.8750	0.8750	0.8647	1.312	1.293	0.875	0.864	0.787	0.698	3/4 0.750	0.432	0.333	0.015
1	1.0000	1.0000	0.9886	1.500	1.479	1.000	0.988	0.900	0.790	3/4 0.750	0.495	0.380	0.015
1 1/8	1.1250	1.1250	1.1086	1.688	1.665	1.125	1.111	1.012	...	7/8 0.875	0.557	0.428	0.015
1 1/4	1.2500	1.2500	1.2336	1.875	1.852	1.250	1.236	1.125	...	7/8 0.875	0.620	0.475	0.015
1 3/8	1.3750	1.3750	1.3568	2.062	2.038	1.375	1.360	1.237	...	1 1.000	0.682	0.523	0.015
1 1/2	1.5000	1.5000	1.4818	2.250	2.224	1.500	1.485	1.350		1 1.000	0.745	0.570	0.015
1 3/4	1.7500	1.7500	1.7295	2.625	2.597	1.750	1.734	1.575	...	1 1/4 1.250	0.870	0.665	0.015
2	2.0000	2.0000	1.9780	3.000	2.970	2.000	1.983	1.800		1 1/2 1.500	0.995	0.760	0.015
2 1/4	2.2500	2.2500	2.2280	3.375	3.344	2.250	2.232	2.025	...	1 3/4 1.750	1.120	0.855	0.031
2 1/2	2.5000	2.5000	2.4762	3.750	3.717	2.500	2.481	2.250	...	1 3/4 1.750	1.245	0.950	0.031
2 3/4	2.7500	2.7500	2.7262	4.125	4.090	2.750	2.730	2.475		2 2.000	1.370	1.045	0.031
3	3.0000	3.0000	2.9762	4.500	4.464	3.000	2.979	2.700	...	2 1/4 2.250	1.495	1.140	0.031
3 1/4	3.2500	3.2500	3.2262	4.875	4.837	3.250	3.228	2.925		2 1/4 2.250	1.620	1.235	0.031
3 1/2	3.5000	3.5000	3.4762	5.250	5.211	3.500	3.478	3.150	..	2 3/4 2.750	1.745	1.330	0.031
3 3/4	3.7500	3.7500	3.7262	5.625	5.584	3.750	3.727	3.375	...	2 3/4 2.750	1.870	1.425	0.031
4	4.0000	4.0000	3.9762	6.000	5.958	4.000	3.976	3.600		3 3.000	1.995	1.520	0.031

ASME B18.3 - R1993 Standard. Reprinted from the standard listed by permission of the American Society of Mechanical Engineers.

APPENDIX E – FASTENERS (INCH SERIES) Continued

DIMENSIONS OF HEXAGON AND SPLINE SOCKET FLAT COUNTERSUNK HEAD CAP SCREWS

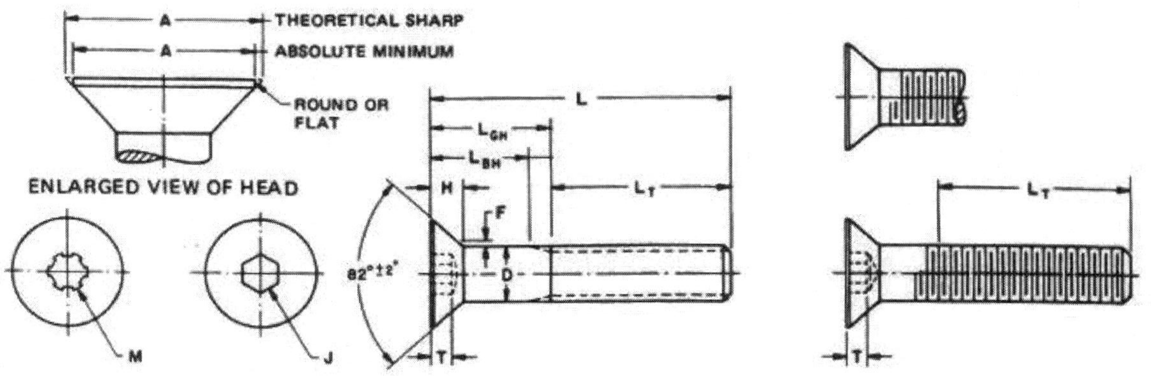

Nominal Size or Basic Screw Diameter		D Body Diameter Max	D Body Diameter Min	A Head Diameter Theoretical Sharp Max	A Head Diameter Abs. Min	H Heat Reference	H Height Flushness Tolerance	M Spline Socket Size	J Hexagon Socket Size Nom	T Key Engagement Min	F Fillet Extension Above D Max Max
0	0.0600	0.0600	0.0568	0.138	0.117	0.044	0.006	0.048	0.035	0.025	0.006
1	0.0730	0.0730	0.0695	0.168	0.143	0.054	0.007	0.060	0.050	0.031	0.008
2	0.0860	0.0860	0.0822	0.197	0.168	0.064	0.008	0.060	0.050	0.038	0.010
3	0.0990	0.0990	0.0949	0.226	0.193	0.073	0.010	0.072	1/16 0.062	0.044	0.010
4	0.1120	0.1120	0.1075	0.255	0.218	0.083	0.011	0.072	1/16 0.062	0.055	0.012
5	0.1250	0.1250	0.1202	0.281	0.240	0.090	0.012	0.096	5/64 0.078	0.061	0.014
6	0.1380	0.1380	0.1329	0.307	0.263	0.097	0.013	0.096	5/64 0.078	0.066	0.015
8	0.1640	0.1640	0.1585	0.359	0.311	0.112	0.014	0.111	3/32 0.094	0.076	0.015
10	0.1900	0.1900	0.1840	0.411	0.359	0.127	0.015	0.145	1/8 0.125	0.087	0.015
1/4	0.2500	0.2500	0.2435	0.531	0.480	0.161	0.016	0.183	5/32 0.156	0.111	0.015
5/16	0.3125	0.3125	0.3053	0.656	0.600	0.198	0.017	0.216	3/16 0.188	0.135	0.015
3/8	0.3750	0.3750	0.3678	0.781	0.720	0.234	0.018	0.251	7/32 0.219	0.159	0.015
7/16	0.4375	0.4375	0.4294	0.844	0.781	0.234	0.018	0.291	1/4 0.250	0.159	0.015
1/2	0.5000	0.5000	0.4919	0.938	0.872	0.251	0.018	0.372	5/16 0.312	0.172	0.015
5/8	0.6250	0.6250	0.6163	1.188	1.112	0.324	0.022	0.454	3/8 0.375	0.220	0.015
3/4	0.7500	0.7500	0.7406	1.438	1.355	0.396	0.024	0.454	1/2 0.500	0.220	0.015
7/8	0.8750	0.8750	0.8647	1.688	1.604	0.468	0.025	...	9/16 0.562	0.248	0.015
1	1.0000	1.0000	0.9886	1.938	1.841	0.540	0.028	...	5/8 0.625	0.297	0.015
1 1/8	1.1250	1.1250	1.1086	2.188	2.079	0.611	0.031	...	3/4 0.750	0.325	0.031
1 1/4	1.2500	1.2500	1.2336	2.438	2.316	0.683	0.035	...	7/8 0.875	0.358	0.031
1 3/8	1.3750	1.3750	1.3568	2.688	2.553	0.755	0.038		7/8 0.875	0.402	0.031
1 1/2	1.5000	1.5000	1.4818	2.938	2.791	0.827	0.042		1 1.000	0.435	0.031

ASME B18.3 - R1993 Standard. Reprinted from the standard listed by permission of the American Society of Mechanical Engineers.

APPENDIX E – FASTENERS (INCH SERIES) Continued

DIMENSIONS OF SLOTTED FLAT COUNTERSUNK HEAD CAP SCREWS

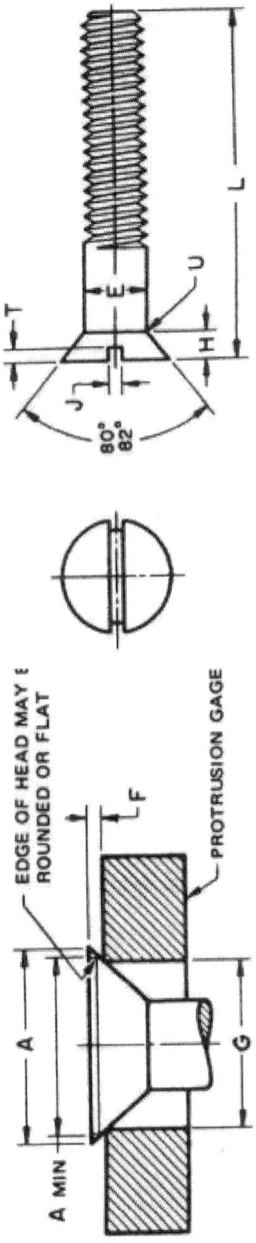

Nominal Size[1] or Basic Screw Diameter		E Body Diameter		A Head Diameter		H[2] Head Height	J Slot Width		T Slot Depth		U Fillet Radius	F[3] Protrusion Above Gaging Diameter		G[3] Gaging Diameter
		Max	Min	Max, Edge Sharp	Min, Edge Rounded or Flat	Ref	Max	Min	Max	Min	Max	Max	Min	
1/4	0.2500	0.2500	0.2450	0.500	0.452	0.140	0.075	0.064	0.068	0.045	0.100	0.046	0.030	0.424
5/16	0.3125	0.3125	0.3070	0.625	0.567	0.177	0.084	0.072	0.086	0.057	0.125	0.053	0.035	0.538
3/8	0.3750	0.3750	0.3690	0.750	0.682	0.210	0.094	0.081	0.103	0.068	0.150	0.060	0.040	0.651
7/16	0.4375	0.4375	0.4310	0.812	0.736	0.210	0.094	0.081	0.103	0.068	0.175	0.065	0.044	0.703
1/2	0.5000	0.5000	0.4930	0.875	0.791	0.210	0.106	0.091	0.103	0.068	0.200	0.071	0.049	0.756
9/16	0.5625	0.5625	0.5550	1.000	0.906	0.244	0.118	0.102	0.120	0.080	0.225	0.078	0.054	0.869
5/8	0.6250	0.6250	0.6170	1.125	1.020	0.281	0.133	0.116	0.137	0.091	0.250	0.085	0.058	0.982
3/4	0.7500	0.7500	0.7420	1.375	1.251	0.352	0.149	0.131	0.171	0.115	0.300	0.099	0.068	1.208
7/8	0.8750	0.8750	0.8660	1.625	1.480	0.423	0.167	0.147	0.206	0.138	0.350	0.113	0.077	1.435
1	1.0000	1.0000	0.9900	1.875	1.711	0.494	0.188	0.166	0.240	0.162	0.400	0.127	0.087	1.661
1 1/8	1.1250	1.1250	1.1140	2.062	1.880	0.529	0.196	0.178	0.257	0.173	0.450	0.141	0.096	1.826
1 1/4	1.2500	1.2500	1.2390	2.312	2.110	0.600	0.211	0.193	0.291	0.197	0.500	0.155	0.105	2.052
1 3/8	1.3750	1.3750	1.3630	2.562	2.340	0.665	0.226	0.208	0.326	0.220	0.550	0.169	0.115	2.279
1 1/2	1.5000	1.5000	1.4880	2.812	2.570	0.742	0.258	0.240	0.360	0.244	0.600	0.183	0.124	2.505

[1] Where specifying nominal size in decimals, zeros preceding decimal and in the fourth decimal place shall be omitted.

[2] Tabulated values determined from formula for maximum **H**.

[3] No tolerance for gaging diameter is given.

Reprinted from The American Society of Mechanical Engineers-ANSI 318.6.2-R1993.

APPENDIX E – FASTENERS (INCH SERIES) Continued

DIMENSIONS OF SLOTTED ROUND HEAD CAP SCREWS

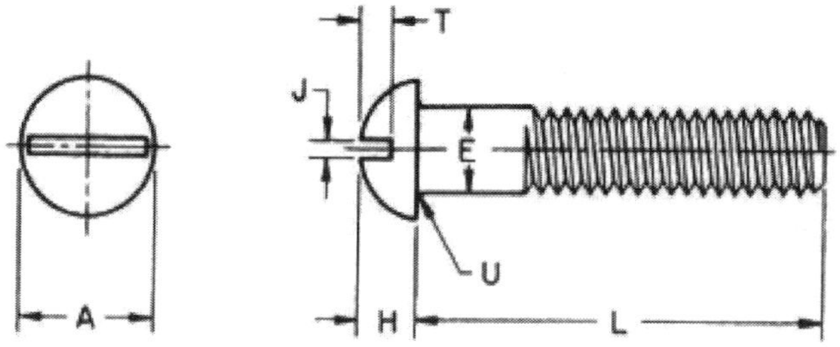

Nominal Size' or Basic Screw Diameter		E Body Diameter		A Head Diameter		H Head Height		J Slot Width		T Slot Depth		U Fillet Radius	
		Max	Min	Max	Min	Max	Min	Max	Min	Max	Min	Max	Min
1/4	0.2500	0.2500	0.2450	0.437	0.418	0.191	0.175	0.075	0.064	0.117	0.097	0.031	0.016
5/16	0.3125	0.3125	0.3070	0.562	0.540	0.245	0.226	0.084	0.072	0.151	0.126	0.031	0.016
3/8	0.3750	0.3750	0.3690	0.625	0.603	0.273	0.252	0.094	0.081	0.168	0.138	0.031	0.016
7/16	0.4375	0.4375	0.4310	0.750	0.725	0.328	0.302	0.094	0.081	0.202	0.167	0.047	0.016
1/2	0.5000	0.5000	0.4930	0.812	0.786	0.354	0.327	0.106	0.091	0.218	0.178	0.047	0.016
9/16	0.5625	0.5625	0.5550	0.937	0.909	0.409	0.378	0.118	0.102	0.252	0.207	0.047	0.016
5/8	0.6250	0.6250	0.6170	1.000	0.970	0.437	0.405	0.133	0.116	0.270	0.220	0.062	0.031
3/4	0.7500	0.7500	0.7420	1,250	1.215	0.546	0.507	0.149	0.131	0.338	0.278	0.062	0.031

'Where specifying nominal size in decimals, zeros preceding decimal and in the fourth decimal place shall be omitted.

DIMENSIONS OF SLOTTED FILLISTER HEAD CAP SCREWS

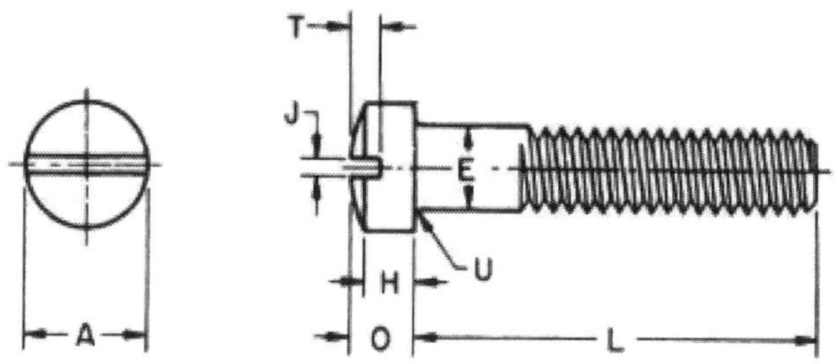

Nominal Size' or Basic Screw Diameter		E Body Diameter		A Head Diameter		H Head Side Height		O Total Head Height		J Slot Width		T Slot Depth		U Fillet Radius	
		Max	Min	Max	Min	Max	Min	Max	Min	Max	Min	Max	Min	Max	Min
1/4	0.2500	0.2500	0.2450	0.375	0.363	0.172	0.157	0.216	0.194	0.075	0.064	0.097	0.077	0.031	0.016
5/16	0.3125	0.3125	0.3070	0.437	0.424	0.203	0.186	0.253	0.230	0.084	0.072	0.115	0.090	0.031	0.016
3/8	0.3750	0.3750	0.3690	0.562	0,547	0.250	0.229	0.314	0.284	0.094	0.081	0.142	0.112	0.031	0.016
7/16	0.4375	0.4375	0.4310	0.625	0.608	0.297	0.274	0.368	0.336	0.094	0.081	0.168	0.133	0.047	0.016
1/2	0.5000	0.5000	0.4930	0.750	0.731	0.328	0.301	0.413	0.376	0.106	0.091	0.193	0.153	0.047	0.016
9/16	0.5625	0.5625	0.5550	0.812	0.792	0.375	0.346	0.467	0.427	0.118	0.102	0.213	0.168	0.047	0.016
5/8	0.6250	0.6250	0.6170	0.875	0.853	0.422	0.391	0.521	0.478	0.133	0.116	0.239	0.189	0.062	0.031
3/4	0.7500	0.7500	0.7420	1.000	0.976	0.500	0.466	0.612	0.566	0.149	0.131	0.283	0.223	0.062	0.031
7/8	0.8750	0.8750	0.8660	1.125	1.098	0.594	0.556	0.720	0.668	0.167	0.147	0.334	0.264	0.062	0.031
1	1.0000	1.0000	0.9900	1.312	1.282	0.656	0.612	0.803	0.743	0.188	0.166	0.371	0.291	0.062	0.031

APPENDIX E – FASTENERS (INCH SERIES) Continued

DIMENSIONS OF SLOTTED FLAT COUNTERSUNK HEAD MACHINE SCREWS

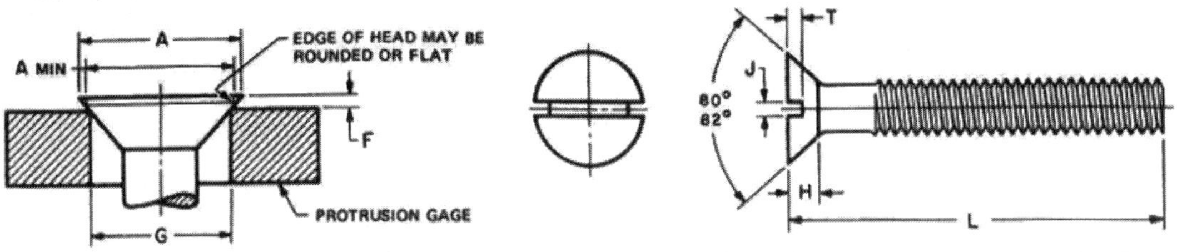

Nominal Size[1] or Basic Screw Diameter		L[2] These Lengths or Shorter are Undercut	A Head Diameter Max. Edge Sharp	A Head Diameter Min, Edge Rounded or Flat	H[3] Head Height Ref	J Slot Width Max	J Slot Width Min	T Slot Depth Max	T Slot Depth Min	F[4] Protrusion Above Gaging Diameter Max	F[4] Protrusion Above Gaging Diameter Min	G[4] Gaging Diameter
0000	0.0210	-	0.043	0.037	0.011	0.008	0.004	0.007	0.003	*	*	*
000	0.0340	-	0.064	0.058	0.016	0.011	0.007	0.009	0.005	*	*	*
00	0.0470	-	0.093	0.085	0.028	0.017	0.010	0.014	0.009	*	*	*
0	0.0600	1/8	0.119	0.099	0.035	0.023	0.016	0.015	0.010	0.026	0.016	0.078
1	0.0730	1/8	0.146	0.123	0.043	0.026	0.019	0.019	0.012	0.028	0.016	0.101
2	0.0860	1/8	0.172	0.147	0.051	0.031	0.023	0.023	0.015	0.029	0.017	0.124
3	0.0990	1/8	0.199	0.171	0.059	0.035	0.027	0.027	0.017	0.031	0.018	0.148
4	0.1120	3/16	0.225	0.195	0.067	0.039	0.031	0.030	0.020	0.032	0.019	0.172
5	0.1250	3/16	0.252	0.220	0.075	0.043	0.035	0.034	0.022	0.034	0.020	0.196
6	0.1380	3/16	0.279	0.244	0.083	0.048	0.039	0.038	0.024	0.036	0.021	0.220
8	0.1640	1/4	0.332	0.292	0.100	0.054	0.045	0.045	0.029	0.039	0.023	0.267
10	0.1900	5/16	0.385	0.340	0.116	0.060	0.050	0.053	0.034	0.042	0.025	0.313
12	0.2160	3/8	0.438	0.389	0.132	0.067	0.056	0.060	0.039	0.045	0.027	0.362
1/4	0.2500	7/16	0.507	0.452	0.153	0.075	0.064	0.070	0.046	0.050	0.029	0.424
5/16	0.3125	1/2	0.635	0.568	0.191	0.084	0.072	0.088	0.058	0.057	0.034	0.539
3/8	0.3750	9/16	0.762	0.685	0.230	0.094	0.081	0.106	0.070	0.065	0.039	0.653
7/16	0.4375	5/8	0.812	0.723	0.223	0.094	0.081	0.103	0.066	0.073	0.044	0.690
1/2	0.5000	3/4	0.875	0.775	0.223	0.106	0.091	0.103	0.065	0.081	0.049	0.739
9/16	0.5625	-	1.000	0.889	0.260	0.118	0.102	0.120	0.077	0.089	0.053	0.851
5/8	0.6250	-	1.125	1.002	0.298	0.133	0.116	0.137	0.088	0.097	0.058	0.962
3/4	0.7500	-	1.375	1.230	0.372	0.149	0.131	0.171	0.111	0.112	0.067	1.186

[1] Where specifying nominal size in decimals, zeros preceding decimal and in the fourth decimal place shall be omitted.

[2] Screws of these lengths and shorter shall have undercut heads as shown in Table 5.

[3] Tabulated values determined from formula for maximum H, Appendix V.

[4] No tolerance for gaging diameter is given.

* Not practical to gage.

APPENDIX E – FASTENERS (INCH SERIES) Continued

DIMENSIONS OF HEX NUTS AND HEX JAM NUTS

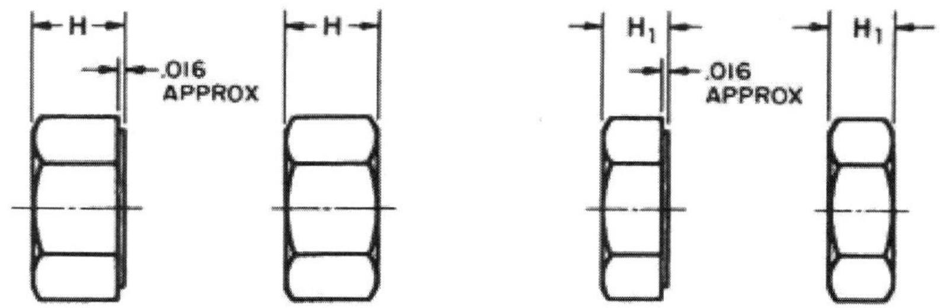

Nominal Size or Basic Major Dia of Thread		F Width Across Flats			G Width Across Corners		H Thickness Hex Nuts			H_1 Thickness Hex Jam Nuts			Hex Nuts Specified Proof Load: Up to 150,000 psi	Hex Nuts Specified Proof Load: 150,000 psi and Greater	Jam Nuts All Strength Levels
		Basic	Max	Min	Max	Min	Basic	Max	Min	Basic	Max	Min	Runou of Bearing Face, FIR Max		
1/4	0.2500	7/16	0.438	0.428	0.505	0.488	7/32	0.226	0.212	5/32	0.163	0.150	0.015	0.010	0.015
5/16	0.3125	1/2	0.500	0.489	0.577	0.557	17/64	0.273	0.258	3/16	0.195	0.180	0.016	0.011	0.016
3/8	0.3750	9/16	0.562	0.551	0.650	0.628	21/64	0.337	0.320	7/32	0.227	0.210	0.017	0.012	0.017
7/16	0.4375	11/16	0.688	0.675	0.794	0.768	3/8	0.385	0.365	1/4	0.260	0.240	0.018	0.013	0.018
1/2	0.5000	3/4	0.750	0.736	0.866	0.840	7/16	0.448	0.427	5/16	0.323	0.302	0.019	0.014	0.019
9/16	0.5625	7/8	0.875	0.861	1.010	0.982	31/64	0.496	0.473	5/16	0.324	0.301	0.020	0.015	0.020
5/8	0.6250	15/16	0.938	0.922	1.083	1.051	35/64	0.559	0.535	3/8	0.387	0.363	0.021	0.016	0.021
3/4	0.7500	1 1/8	1.125	1.088	1.299	1.240	41/64	0.665	0.617	27/64	0.446	0.398	0.023	0.018	0.023
7/8	0.8750	1 5/16	1.312	1.269	1.516	1.447	3/4	0.776	0.724	31/64	0.510	0.458	0.025	0.020	0.025
1	1.0000	1 1/2	1.500	1.450	1.732	1.653	55/64	0.887	0.831	35/64	0.575	0.519	0.027	0.022	0.027
1 1/8	1.1250	1 11/16	1.688	1.631	1.949	1.859	31/32	0.999	0.939	39/64	0.639	0.579	0.030	0.025	0.030
1 1/4	1.2500	1 7/8	1.875	1.812	2.165	2.066	1 1/16	1.094	1.030	23/32	0.751	0.687	0.033	0.028	0.033
1 3/8	1.3750	2 1/16	2.062	1.994	2.382	2.273	1 11/64	1.206	1.138	25/32	0.815	0.747	0.036	0.031	0.036
1 1/2	1.5000	2 1/4	2.250	2.175	2.598	2.480	1 9/32	1.317	1.245	27/32	0.880	0.808	0.039	0.034	0.039

APPENDIX E – FASTENERS (INCH SERIES) Continued

Drill and Counterbore Sizes for Socket Head Cap Screws

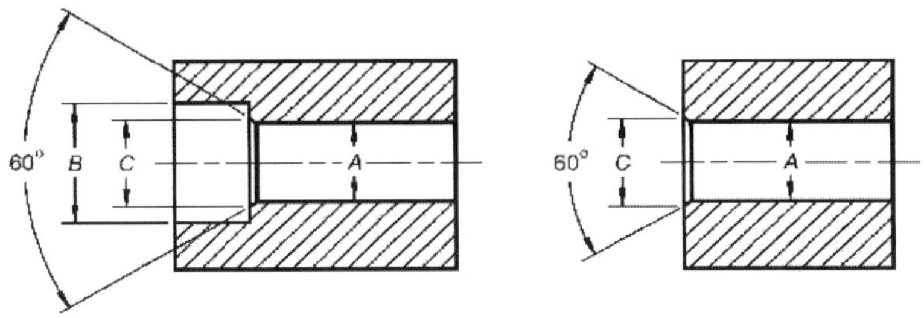

Nominal Size of Screw (D)	Nominal Drill Size (A) Close Fit	Nominal Drill Size (A) Normal Fit	Counterbore Diameter (B)	Countersink (C)
#0 (0.0600)	(#51) 0.067	(#49) 0.073	1/8	0.074
#1 (0.0730)	(#46) 0.081	(#43) 0.089	5/32	0.087
#2 (0.0860)	3/32	(#36) 0.106	3/16	0.102
#3 (0.0990)	(#36) 0.106	(#31) 0.120	7/32	0.115
#4 (0.1120)	1/8	(#29) 0.136	7/32	0.130
#5 (0.1250)	9/64	(#23) 0.154	1/4	0.145
#6 (0.1380)	(#23) 0.154	(#18) 0.170	9/32	0.158
#8 (0.1640)	(#15) 0.180	(#10) 0.194	5/16	0.188
#10 (0.1900)	(#5) 0.206	(#2) 0.221	3/8	0.218
1/4	17/64	9/32	7/16	0.278
5/16	21/64	11/32	17/32	0.346
3/8	25/64	13/32	5/8	0.415
7/16	29/64	15/32	23/32	0.483
1/2	33/64	17/32	13/16	0.552
5/8	41/64	21/32	1	0.689
3/4	49/64	25/32	1 3/16	0.828
7/8	57/64	29/32	1 3/8	0.963
1	1 1/64	1 1/32	1 5/8	1.100
1 1/4	1 9/32	1 5/16	2	1.370
1 1/2	1 17/32	1 9/16	2 3/8	1.640
1 3/4	1 25/32	1 13/16	2 3/4	1.910
2	2 1/32	2 1/16	3 1/8	2.180

(1) Countersink. It is considered good practice to countersink or break the edges of holes that are smaller than F (max.) in parts having a hardness which approaches, equals, or exceeds the screw hardness. The countersink or corner relief, however, should not be larger than is necessary to ensure that the fillet on the screw is cleared. Normally, the diameter of countersink does not have to exceed F (max.). Countersinks or corner reliefs in excess of this diameter reduce the effective bearing area and introduce the possibility of imbedment or brinnelling or flaring of the heads of the screws.

(2) Close Fit. The close fit is normally limited to holes for those lengths of screws that are threaded to the head in assemblies where only one screw is to be used or where two or more screws are to be used and the mating holes are to be produced either at assembly or by matched and coordinated tooling.

(3) Normal Fit. The normal fit is intended for screws of relatively long length or for assemblies involving two or more screws where the mating holes are to be produced by conventional tolerancing methods. It provides for the maximum allowable eccentricity of the longest standard screws and for certain variations in the parts to be fastened, such as deviations in hole straightness, angularity between the axis of the tapped hole and that of the hole for the shank, differences in center distances of the mating holes, etc.

APPENDIX E – FASTENERS (INCH SERIES) Continued

Preferred Sizes of Type A Plain Washers

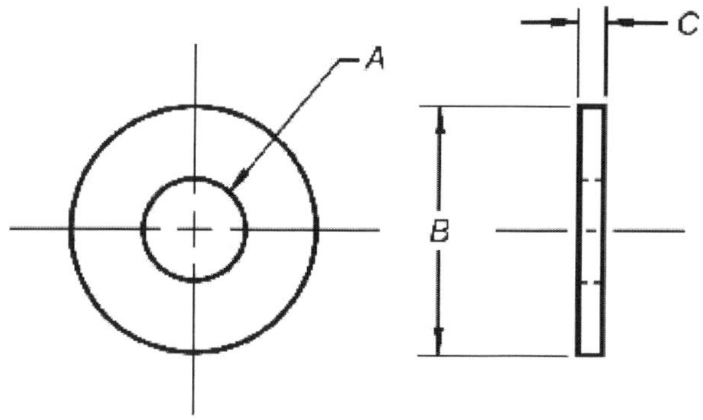

Nominal Washer Size*	Inside Diameter (A) Basic	Outside Diameter (B) Basic	Thickness (C)	Nominal Washer Size*	Inside Diameter (A) Basic	Outside Diameter (B) Basic	Thickness (C)
	0.078	0.188	0.020	1 N	1.062	2.000	0.134
	0.094	0.250	0.020	1 W	1.062	2.500	0.165
	0.125	0.312	0.032	1 1/8 N	1.250	2.250	0.134
#6 (0.138)	0.156	0.375	0.049	1 1/8 W	1.250	2.750	0.165
#8 (0.164)	0.188	0.438	0.049	1 1/4 N	1.375	2.500	0.165
#10 (0.190)	0.219	0.500	0.049	1 1/4 W	1.375	3.000	0.165
3/16	0.250	0.562	0.049	1 3/8 N	1.500	2.750	0.165
#12 (0.216)	0.250	0.562	0.065	1 3/8 W	1.500	3.250	0.180
1/4 N	0.281	0.625	0.065	1 1/2 N	1.625	3.000	0.165
1/4 W	0.312	0.734	0.065	1 1/2 W	1.625	3.500	0.180
5/16 N	0.344	0.688	0.065	1 5/8	1.750	3.750	0.180
5/16 W	0.375	0.875	0.083	1 3/4	1.875	4.000	0.180
3/8 N	0.406	0.812	0.065	1 7/8	2.000	4.250	0.180
3/8 W	0.438	1.000	0.083	2	2.125	4.500	0.180
7/16 N	0.469	0.922	0.065	2 1/4	2.375	4.750	0.220
7/16 W	0.500	1.250	0.083	2 1/2	2.625	5.000	0.238
1/2 N	0.531	1.062	0.095	2 3/4	2.875	5.250	0.259
1/2 W	0.562	1.375	0.109	3	3.125	5.500	0.284
9/16 N	0.594	1.156	0.095				
9/16 W	0.625	1.469	0.109				
5/8 N	0.656	1.312	0.095				
5/8 W	0.688	1.750	0.134				
3/4 N	0.812	1.469	0.134				
3/4 W	0.812	2.000	0.148				
7/8 N	0.938	1.750	0.134				
7/8 W	0.938	2.250	0.165				

*Nominal washer sizes are intended for use with comparable nominal screw or bolt sizes.
ANSI B18.22.1 - 1965 (R2003) Standard. Reprinted from the standard listed by permission of the American Society of Mechanical Engineers.

APPENDIX E – FASTENERS (INCH SERIES) Continued

Regular Helical Spring-Lock Washers

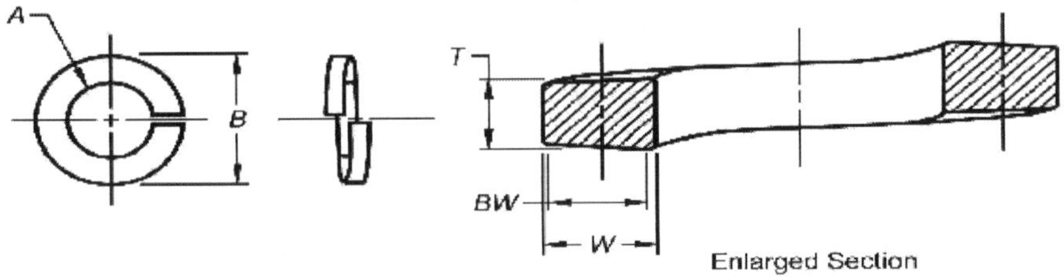

Nominal Washer Size	Min. Inside Diameter (A)	Max. Outside Diameter (B)	Mean Section Thickness (T)	Min. Section Width (W)	Min. Bearing Width (BW)
#2 (0.086)	0.088	0.172	0.020	0.035	0.024
#3 (0.099)	0.101	0.195	0.025	0.040	0.028
#4 (0.112)	0.114	0.209	0.025	0.040	0.028
#5 (0.125)	0.127	0.236	0.031	0.047	0.033
#6 (.0138)	0.141	0.250	0.031	0.047	0.033
#8 (0.164)	0.167	0.293	0.040	0.055	0.038
#10 (0.190)	0.193	0.334	0.047	0.062	0.043
#12 (0.216)	0.220	0.377	0.056	0.070	0.049
1/4	0.252	0.487	0.062	0.109	0.076
5/16	0.314	0.583	0.078	0.125	0.087
3/8	0.377	0.680	0.094	0.141	0.099
7/16	0.440	0.776	0.109	0.156	0.109
1/2	0.502	0.869	0.125	0.171	0.120
9/16	0.564	0.965	0.141	0.188	0.132
5/8	0.628	1.073	0.156	0.203	0.142
11/16	0.691	1.170	0.172	0.219	0.153
3/4	0.753	1.265	0.188	0.234	0.164
13/16	0.816	1.363	0.203	0.250	0.175
7/8	0.787	1.459	0.219	0.266	0.186
15/16	0.941	1.556	0.234	0.281	0.197
1	1.003	1.656	0.250	0.297	0.208
1 1/16	1.066	1.751	0.266	0.312	0.218
1 1/8	1.129	1.847	0.281	0.328	0.230
1 3/16	1.192	1.943	0.297	0.344	0.241
1 1/4	1.254	2.036	0.312	0.359	0.251
1 5/16	1.317	2.133	0.328	0.375	0.262
1 3/8	1.379	2.219	0.344	0.391	0.274
1 7/16	1.442	2.324	0.359	0.406	0.284
1 1/2	1.504	2.419	0.375	0.422	0.295
1 5/8	1.633	2.553	0.389	0.424	0.297
1 3/4	1.758	2.679	0.389	0.424	0.297
1 7/8	1.883	2.811	0.422	0.427	0.299
2	2.008	2.936	0.422	0.427	0.299
2 1/4	2.262	3.221	0.440	0.442	0.309
2 1/2	2.512	3.471	0.440	0.422	0.309
2 3/4	2.762	3.824	0.458	0.491	0.344
3	3.012	4.074	0.458	0.491	0.344

APPENDIX F – METRIC FASTENERS

Metric Hex Bolts

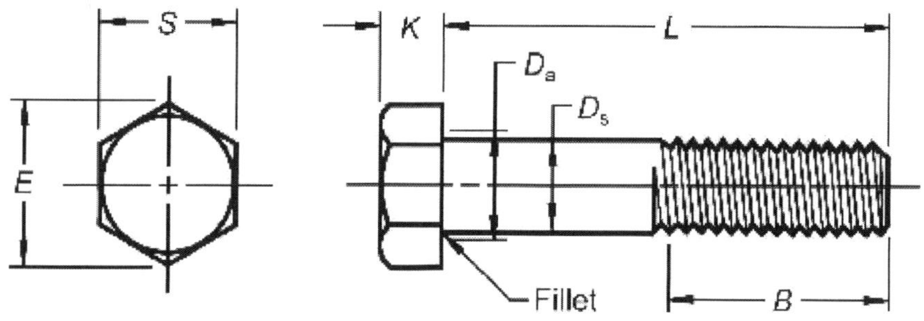

D	Ds	S	E	K	Da	Thread Length (B)		
Nominal Bolt Diameter And Thread Pitch	Max. Body Dia.	Max. Width Across Flats	Max. Width Across Corners	Max. Head Height	Fillet Transition Diameter	Bolt Lengths ≤ 125	Bolt Lengths > 125 and ≤ 200	Bolt Lengths >200
M5 x 0.8	5.48	8.00	9.24	3.88	5.7	16	22	35
M6 x 1	6.19	10.00	11.55	4.38	6.8	18	24	37
M8 x 1.25	8.58	13.00	15.01	5.68	9.2	22	28	41
M10 x 1.5	10.58	16.00	18.48	6.85	11.2	26	32	45
M12 x 1.75	12.70	18.00	20.78	7.95	13.7	30	36	49
M14 x 2	14.70	21.00	24.25	9.25	15.7	34	40	53
M16 x 2	16.70	24.00	27.71	10.75	17.7	38	44	57
M20 x 2.5	20.84	30.00	34.64	13.40	22.4	46	52	65
M24 x 3	24.84	36.00	41.57	15.90	26.4	54	60	73
M30 x 3.5	30.84	46.00	53.12	19.75	33.4	66	72	85
M36 x 4	37.00	55.00	63.51	23.55	39.4	78	84	97
M42 x 4.5	43.00	65.00	75.06	27.05	45.4	90	96	109
M48 x 5	49.00	75.00	86.60	31.07	52.0	102	108	121
M56 x 5.5	57.00	85.00	98.15	36.20	62.0		124	137
M64 x 6	65.52	95.00	109.70	41.32	70.0		140	153
M72 x 6	73.84	105.00	121.24	46.45	78.0		156	169
M80 x 6	82.16	115.00	132.79	51.58	86.0		172	185
M90 x 6	92.48	130.00	150.11	57.74	96.0		192	205
M100 x 6	102.80	145.00	167.43	63.90	107.0		212	225

ASME B18.3 - 2003 Standard. Reprinted from the standard listed by permission of the American Society of Mechanical Engineers.

APPENDIX F – METRIC FASTENERS (Continued)

Metric Hex Nuts

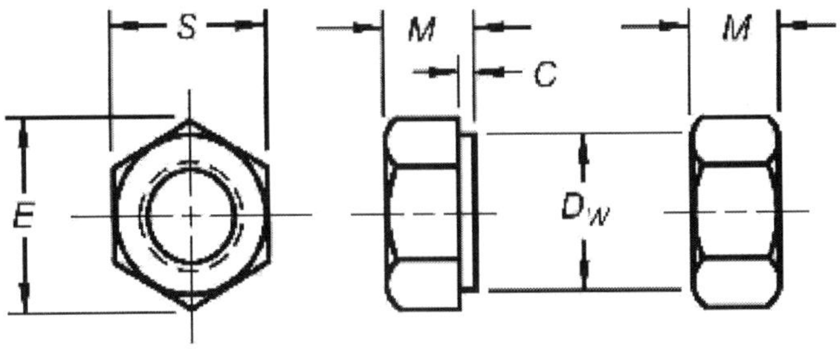

D	S	E	M	DW	C
Nominal Bolt Diameter and Thread Pitch	Max. Width Across Flats	Max. Width Across Corners	Max. Thickness	Min. Bearing Face Diameter	Max. Washer Face Thickness
M1.6 x 0.35	3.20	3.70	1.30	2.3	
M2 x 0.4	4.00	4.62	1.60	3.1	
M2.5 x 0.45	5.00	5.77	2.00	4.1	
M3 x 0.5	5.50	6.35	2.40	4.6	
M3.5 x 0.6	6.00	6.93	2.80	5.1	
M4 x 0.7	7.00	8.08	3.20	6.0	
M5 x 0.8	8.00	9.24	4.70	7.0	
M6 x 1	10.00	11.55	5.20	8.9	
M8 x 1.25	13.00	15.01	6.80	11.6	
M10 x 1.5	15.00	17.32	9.10	13.6	
M10 x 1.5	16.00	18.45	8.40	14.6	
M12 x 1.75	18.00	20.78	10.80	16.6	
M14 x 2	21.00	24.25	12.80	19.4	
M16 x 2	24.00	27.71	14.80	22.4	
M20 x 2.5	30.00	34.64	18.00	27.9	0.8
M24 x 3	36.00	41.57	21.50	32.5	0.8
M30 x 3.5	46.00	53.12	25.60	42.5	0.8
M36 x 4	55.00	63.51	31.00	50.8	0.8

ASME B18.2.4.1M - 2002 Standard. Reprinted from the standard listed by permission of the American Society of Mechanical Engineers.

APPENDIX F – METRIC FASTENERS (Continued)

Metric Socket Head Cap Screws

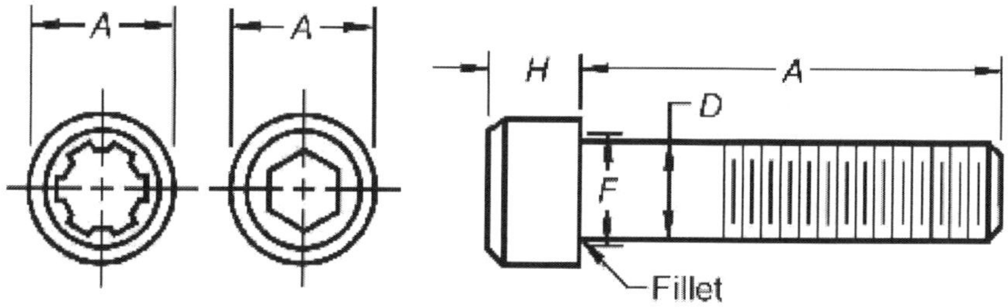

Screw Size (D)	Head Diameter (A)	Head Height (H)
1.6 through 2.5	See Table	
3 through 8	Max. A = 1.5 D + 1	Max. H = D
> 10	Max. A = 1.5 D	

Screw Size (D)	1.6	2	2.5
Max. Head Diameter (A)	3.00	3.80	4.50

ASME/ANSI B18.3.1M - 1986 (R2002) Standard. Reprinted from the standard listed by permission of the American Society of Mechanical Engineers.

Metric Countersunk Socket Head Cap Screws

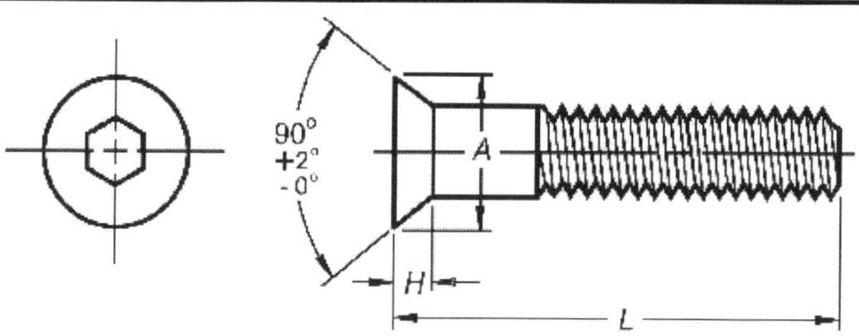

Basic Screw Diameter and Thread Pitch	Head Diameter (A) Theor. Sharp	Head Height (H)
M3 x 0.5	6.72	1.86
M4 x 0.7	8.96	2.48
M5 x 0.8	11.20	3.10
M6 x 1	13.44	3.72
M8 x 1.25	17.92	4.96
M10 x 1.5	22.40	6.20
M12 x 1.75	26.88	7.44
M14 x 2	30.24	8.12
M16 x 2	33.60	8.80
M20 x 2.5	40.32	10.16

ASME/ANSI B18.3.5M - 1986 (R2002) Standard. Reprinted from the standard listed by permission of the American Society of Mechanical Engineers.

APPENDIX F – METRIC FASTENERS (Continued)

Drill and Counterbore Sizes for Socket Head Cap Screws

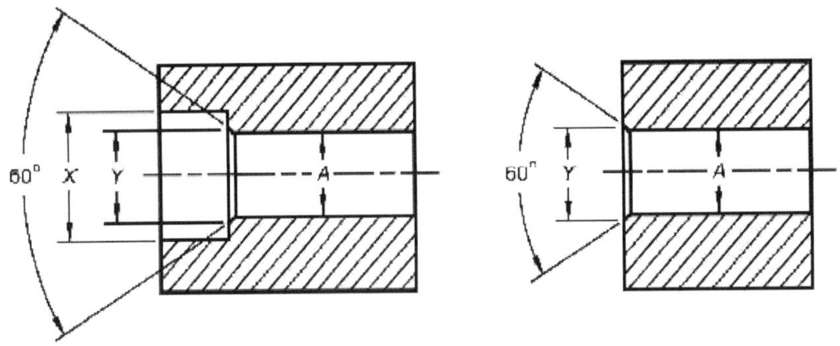

Nominal Size or Basic Screw Diameter	A		X	Y
	Nominal Drill Size		Counterbore Diameter	Countersink Diameter
	Close Fit	Normal Fit		
M1.6	1.80	1.95	3.50	2.0
M2	2.20	2.40	4.40	2.6
M2.5	2.70	3.00	5.40	3.1
M3	3.40	3.70	6.50	3.6
M4	4.40	4.80	8.25	4.7
M5	5.40	5.80	9.75	5.7
M6	6.40	6.80	11.25	6.8
M8	8.40	8.80	14.25	9.2
M10	10.50	10.80	17.25	11.2
M12	12.50	12.80	19.25	14.2
M14	14.50	14.75	22.25	16.2
M16	16.50	16.75	25.50	18.2
M20	20.50	20.75	31.50	22.4
M24	24.50	24.75	37.50	26.4
M30	30.75	31.75	47.50	33.4
M36	37.00	37.50	56.50	39.4
M42	43.00	44.00	66.00	45.6
M48	49.00	50.00	75.00	52.6

ASME/ANSI B18.3.1M - 1986 (R2002) Standard. Reprinted from the standard listed by permission of the American Society of Mechanical Engineers.

APPENDIX F – METRIC FASTENERS (Continued)

Drill and Countersink Sizes for Flat Countersunk Head Cap Screws

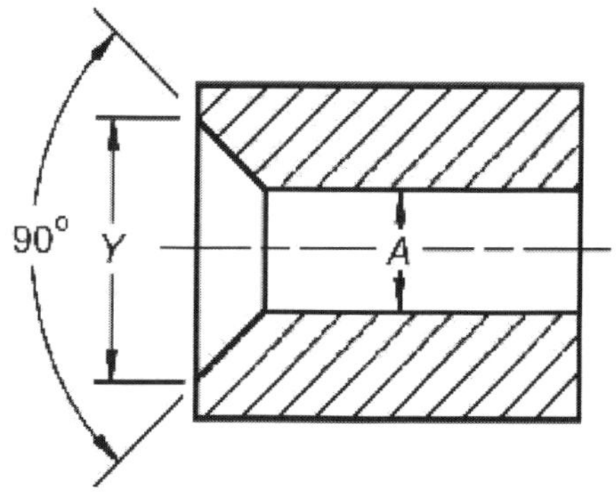

D	A	Y
Nominal Screw Size	Nominal Hole Diameter	Min. Countersink Diameter
M3	3.5	6.72
M4	4.6	8.96
M5	6.0	11.20
M6	7.0	13.44
M8	9.0	17.92
M10	11.5	22.40
M12	13.5	26.88
M14	16.0	30.24
M16	18.0	33.60
M20	22.4	40.32

ASME/ANSI B18.3.5M - 1986 (R2002) Standard. Reprinted from the standard listed by permission of the American Society of Mechanical Engineers.

APPENDIX G – FASTENERS

BOLT AND SCREW CLEARANCE HOLES

(1) Inch Clearance Holes

Nominal Screw Size	Fit Classes		
	Normal	Close	Loose
	Nominal Drill Size		
#0 (0.06)	#48 (0.0760)	#51 (0.0670)	3/32
#1 (0.073)	#43 (0.0890)	#46 (0.0810)	#37 (0.1040)
#2 (0.086)	#38 (0.1015)	3/32	#32 (0.1160)
#3 (0.099)	#32 (0.1160)	#36 (0.1065)	#30 (0.1285)
#4 (0.112)	#30 (0.1285)	#31 (0.1200)	#27 (0.1440)
#5 (0.125)	5/32	9/64	11/64
#6 (0.138)	#18 (0.1695)	#23 (0.1540)	#13 (0.1850)
#8 (0.164)	#9 (0.1960)	#15 (0.1800)	#3 (0.2130)
#10 (0.190)	#2 (0.2210)	#5 (0.2055)	B (0.238)
1/4	9/32	17/64	19/64
5/16	11/32	21/64	23/64
3/8	13/32	25/64	27/64
7/16	15/32	29/64	31/64
1/2	9/16	17/32	39/64
5/8	11/16	21/32	47/64
3/4	13/16	25/32	29/32
7/8	15/16	29/32	1 1/32
1	1 3/32	1 1/32	1 5/32
1 1/8	1 7/32	1 5/32	1 5/16
1 1/4	1 11/32	1 9/32	1 7/16
1 3/8	1 1/2	1 7/16	1 39/64
1 1/2	1 5/8	1 9/16	1 47/64

ASME B18.2.8 - 1999 Standard. Reprinted from the standard listed by permission of the American Society of Mechanical Engineers.

APPENDIX G – FASTENERS

BOLT AND SCREW CLEARANCE HOLES (Continued)

(2) Metric Clearance Holes

Nominal Screw Size	Fit Classes		
	Normal	Close	Loose
	Nominal Drill Size		
M1.6	1.8	1.7	2
M2	2.4	2.2	2.6
M2.5	2.9	2.7	3.1
M3	3.4	3.2	3.6
M4	4.5	4.3	4.8
M5	5.5	5.3	5.8
M6	6.6	6.4	7
M8	9	8.4	10
M10	11	10.5	12
M12	13.5	13	14.5
M14	15.5	15	16.5
M16	17.5	17	18.5
M20	22	21	24
M24	26	25	28
M30	33	31	35
M36	39	37	42
M42	45	43	48
M48	52	50	56
M56	62	58	66
M64	70	66	74
M72	78	74	82
M80	86	82	91
M90	96	93	101
M100	107	104	112

APPENDIX H – REFERENCES

- ASME B1.1 - 2003: Unified Inch Screw Threads (UN and UNR Thread Form)
- ASME B1.13M - 2001: Metric Screw Threads: M Profile
- USAS/ASME B4.1 - 1967 (R2004): Preferred Limits and Fits for Cylindrical Parts
- ANSI B4.2 - 1978 (R2004): Preferred Metric Limits and Fits
- ASME B18.2.1 - 1996: Square and Hex Bolts and Screws (Inch Series)
- ASME/ANSI B18.2.2 - 1987 (R1993): Hex Nuts and Jam Hex Nuts (Inch Series)
- ANSI B18.2.3.5M - 1979 (R2001): Metric Hex Bolts
- ASME B18.2.4.1M - 2002: Metric Hex Nuts, Style 1
- ASME B18.2.8 - 1999: Clearance Holes for Bolts, Screws, and Studs
- ASME B18.3 - 2003: Socket Cap, Shoulder, and Set Screws, Hex and Spline Keys (Inch Series)
- ASME/ANSI B18.3.1M - 1986 (R2002): Socket Head Cap Screws (Metric Series)
- ASME/ANSI B18.3.5M - 1986 (R2002): Hexagon Socket Flat Countersunk Head Cap Screws (Metric Series)
- ASME 18.6.2 - 1998: Slotted Head Cap Screws, Square Head Set Screws, and Slotted Headless Set Screws (Inch Series)
- ASME B18.21.1 - 1999: Lock Washers (Inch Series)
- ANSI B18.22.1 - 1965 (R2003): Plain Washers
- ASME Y14.2M - 1992 (R2003): Line Conventions and Lettering
- ASME Y14.3 - 2003: Multiview and Sectional view Drawings
- ASME Y14.4M - 1989 (R1999): Pictorial Drawings
- ASME Y14.5M - 1994: Dimensioning and Tolerancing
- ASME Y14.6 - 2001: Screw Thread Representation
- ASME Y14.100 - 2000: Engineering Drawing Practices

INDEX

J

K

L

M

N

O

P